REVISED EDITION

Sunset
Western Garden Book

BY THE EDITORIAL STAFFS OF
SUNSET BOOKS & SUNSET MAGAZINE

UNDER THE DIRECTION OF

Walter L. Doty
Director, Editorial Research
Sunset Magazine

Paul C. Johnson
Editor
Sunset Books

LANE BOOK COMPANY   MENLO PARK, CALIFORNIA

The following sections of this book have been revised so as to incorporate the latest and most accurate information: Soil; Pests and Diseases (principally the chart of insecticides); Weed Killers; Composting; Lawns; Container Gardening; Roses; Succulents. Minor changes were made in several other chapters.

PHOTOGRAPHS

Julius Shulman: page 6 (left). Alfred A. Monner: page 6 (right). Hal Rumel: page 7 (left). Ernest Braun: pages 7 (right), 39, 209 (right). Herman J. Willis: page 41 (left). E. S. Ross: page 41 (right). Childress & Halberstadt: page 26. Clyde Childress: pages 81, 112 (top left). Oregon State Colleges: pages 112 (top right), 113 (bottom left). Bob Cox: pages 102, 112 (bottom center), 115. Aplin-Dudley Studios: page 119. William C. Aplin: page 125. Mason Weymouth: page 169. John Robinson: pages 197 (top left and bottom right), 209 (left), 276, 358. Ron Partridge: page 197 (top right). Charles Pearson: page 217.

All rights reserved throughout the world. This book, or parts thereof, may not be reproduced in any form without permission of the publishers

Library of Congress Catalog Card Number 61-5495

Title No. 385

Second Edition

Fourth Printing September 1962

Copyright 1954, 1961

LANE BOOK COMPANY, MENLO PARK, CALIFORNIA

By the publishers of *Sunset* Books and *Sunset,* The Magazine of Western Living

LITHOGRAPHED IN U. S. A.

ACKNOWLEDGMENTS

To the hundreds of Western garden scientists, growers, nurserymen, specialists, and expert dirt gardeners who helped us with this book . . .

We wish we could add each of your names as co-authors in recognition of the work you have done. But this book can have no authors in the accepted sense of the word because it has thousands of authors.

This book acknowledges the first period of the coming of age of Western gardening. Comparatively speaking, Western gardening is very young. We point with genuine awe at 50 to 70-year-old Western gardens while the gardeners in England and Europe and Asia are working in 300 and 500-year-old gardens.

Yet in one man's lifetime we have gathered from all over the world a greater variety of plants than have ever been cultivated in any other one section of the world. Westerners are gardening in more than a dozen different subclimates. In many of these subclimates the plantings of collected material are less than 10 years old, some are in their 30th or 40th year, a few are 90 years old.

How will each plant grow in each subclimate? We will know **right** answers in another hundred years.

But we garden today.

Our plan for this book said that we would collect observations from every corner of the West and check them, correct them, and put them in their true perspective.

You who helped us will find yourself scattered here and there through many pages. Sometimes you are just one of a roundtable of 12 to 20 around one shrub or one tree. You, the botanist; you, the veteran nurseryman; you, the pomologist; you of the experiment stations; you, the county agent; you, the grower and collector of native plants; all of you are here. So are you, the geneticists, you of the city parks, you of soils and irrigation, you, the landscape architects.

This is your book. It is not a finished book, not yet, but it is a truly Western garden book, and your efforts have made it.

This is your own good contribution to better gardening in the West. And every Westerner devoted to gardening should be grateful to you.

TABLE OF CONTENTS

Introduction
    Western Gardening—Challenge and Opportunity 6

How To Grow Plants

How Plants Grow 8
Western Garden Climates 14
Garden Care
    SOIL 26
    WATERING 33
    PESTS AND DISEASES 40
    PEST CONTROL CHART 50
    PRUNING 55
    GENERAL MAINTENANCE 61

Garden Engineering 75
Starting Plants 81
    SEEDS IN FLATS 82
    TRANSPLANTING 88
    SEEDS IN OPEN 90
    VEGETATIVE PROPAGATION 93
    COLDFRAMES 99

Lawns 102

How To Use Plants

Gardener's Language 115
Container Gardening 119
Annuals 125
    PLANTING CALENDAR 127
    ENCYCLOPEDIA 128

Perennials 138
    ENCYCLOPEDIA 142
    CHRYSANTHEMUMS 164
    PRIMROSES 166

How To Use Plants (Continued)

Bulbs ... 169
- ENCYCLOPEDIA ... 170
- TUBEROUS BEGONIAS ... 181
- DAFFODILS ... 183
- DAHLIAS ... 186
- IRIS ... 188
- LILIES ... 192
- TULIPS ... 195

Vines ... 197
- ENCYCLOPEDIA ... 199

Ground Covers ... 209
- ENCYCLOPEDIA ... 211

Shrubs ... 217
- ENCYCLOPEDIA ... 221
- CAMELLIAS ... 253
- FUCHSIAS ... 255
- RHODODENDRONS ... 257
- AZALEAS ... 261
- ROSES ... 264

Flowering Fruits ... 272
Trees ... 276
- ENCYCLOPEDIA ... 281

Western Specialties

Natives ... 306
- ENCYCLOPEDIA ... 310

Pines ... 320
Bamboo ... 323
Palms ... 326
Succulents ... 327
Miniatures ... 329

Home Food Garden

Vegetables ... 331
Small Fruits ... 336
Deciduous Fruit Trees ... 343
Evergreen Fruit Trees ... 351
Herbs ... 355

Indoor Gardening ... 358

Zone Calendars ... 366

Index ... 378

Western Gardening –

The Western garden is in many places:

...it is on a hilltop above Santa Ana, looking down on an orange tree checkerboard;

...you find it on a creek in Walla Walla, looking across miles of wheat up into the Blue Mountains;

...it's hidden behind a row of eucalyptus that stands high to lift the wind from the floor of the Salinas Valley;

...and then it's a hidden courtyard alongside a hundred courtyards in an old fig orchard in the San Joaquin;

...it could be a stone's throw from the quiet salt water of Hood Canal and a skip and a jump from the swirling race of the Columbia;

...or it's perched on a canyon's edge in the Wasatch Mountains and dug into the hills of Hollywood.

It catches the spray of waves that were born in the Gulf of Alaska; it meets a surf that began as a storm deep in the Southern Hemisphere.

Wherever he is, the Western gardener seems to be working with a very special mixture of the earth's elements. Delivered to him are soil, water, sunlight, air moisture, wind, and heat in a special pattern, never exactly duplicated anywhere else in the world. In no other one place in the world is there concentrated as great a variety of plants.

And in that pattern is his opportunity and challenge. He can find plants that should grow there and do grow there more enthusiastically than in any other place in the world; he can also bring in some less likely plants that surprise him by growing in his particular Western garden. He can work with the soil and sun he finds there and, with little effort, have a thriving and beautiful garden; or he can change the soil and control the sun and play the host to plants from everywhere.

The gardeners who have accepted the challenge

Challenge and Opportunity

are converting the West into a strange and wonderful world. Californians think of Australia's eucalyptus as native Californians. They are sure that the oleander must have always grown in California's interior valleys.

In such a land, is there a choice between opportunity and challenge? Most gardeners in the West never know which they want most. Is it an opportunity or a challenge to grow camellias? Is the orange, lemon, lime, or grapefruit a natural for your garden or are you asking it to make too great an adjustment?

Will you specialize in ferns, azaleas, rhododendrons, primroses, ginger, irises, cacti, tuberous begonias, fuchsias, guavas, alpines, subtropicals, miniatures? To each garden in the West one or more of them are naturals.

Native to the land you live in are flowers and shrubs and trees that have never been brought into cultivation. Do they belong in your garden?

The West challenges in another way. Gardeners are building gardens to live in as well as look at. Shrubs and trees have become building materials for wind screens and fences and overhead canopies. Vines absorb the Western sun and cool house walls.

The Westerner living many months of the year in his garden begins to see the design and structure of plants as well as their color and leaves. With shrubs and trees and vines, he designs an outdoor living room with the blue sky as his ceiling, the many subtle shades of evergreen foliage as walls, grass or low growing plants as carpets.

Throughout Western gardening, regardless of type or kind, there runs the common thread of opportunity to discover. So very little is known about the plants that will grow here. So much is yet to be discovered.

The opportunity and challenge of this book is to see what we can discover together.

How Plants Grow

No man who has poked a kernel of corn into the ground can help but watch with wonder and disbelief the consequence of this simple act.

The vigorous shoots seem to boil out of the ground and the sturdy cane mounts swiftly until it is soon as tall as the gardener himself. Then, in a few weeks, the plant matures its seeds and declines into a dry, rustling death.

The gardener who witnesses this miracle—who has seen a seed grow into a plant as large as a man in three short months—cannot help but wonder how it happened. How did those thick stalks grow from the seedling? How did this plant get all the food it needed from his erratic watering? What laws of physics drew the life-giving fluids up the stalks? And what made the ears taste so sweet?

The gardener also sees in this plant's life the story of every other growing thing in his garden, from the petunias he takes for granted to the 100-year oak that seems more permanent than the house it shades.

To satisfy curiosity about how a plant grows does more than make a good conversationalist out of a gardener—it makes him a smarter gardener. For in many subtle ways, the gardener is chained to these same processes. Just as surely as the peach tree brings forth fruit, so does it bring forth the gardener when it reaches certain stages in its annual cycle. When it shuts down for the winter, the gardener works it over with pruning shears and dormant spray; when buds are about to open in spring, he mixes up his sprays again; in summer, when the leaves give off more water than the roots take in, the gardener sees the signs and irrigates; when the fruit is ripe, he harvests it and cleans the deadfalls off the ground; after the leaves have fallen, he gathers them up for composting; and when the weeds announce the coming of spring, he discs them under.

By knowing more about what goes on inside his plants, the gardener can serve them more intelligently, can avoid unnecessary work, or get his licks in early.

SEEDS

All garden plants—except ferns and mosses—start from seeds.

Seeds range from golfball size (buckeye) down to tiny granules, smaller than the periods on this page. Regardless of size, each seed carries within its protective casing a minute plantlet (embryo) and a supply of food to start it on its way.

The reservoir of food that each seed contains is familiar to everyone. It is this seed-food that we eat in grains of wheat, kernels of rice or corn, peas, beans, nuts. When this food is first formed it is rich in sugar; but as it ages, it turns to starch. (This is why garden-fresh peas and corn always taste sweeter than those that are left too long in the vegetable plot.) In many seeds, some sugar is converted into proteins or fats (oils). Some seeds contain all three foods—starch, proteins, fats.

The embryo plant within the seed contains all its essential parts; root, stem, leaves. Most plants have two seed leaves; some, such as corn, iris, or lily, have only one; some have more than two—some pines have as many as eighteen. You see this tiny plant in large seeds like lima beans and peanuts. Next time you eat a peanut, shuck off the shell and split the nut apart. You will see at one end a small projection that locks the two halves

HOW PLANTS GROW 9

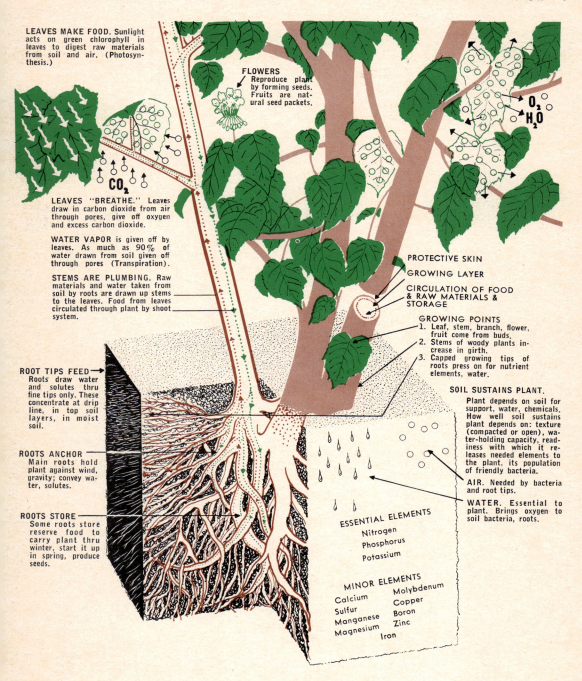

LEAVES MAKE FOOD. Sunlight acts on green chlorophyll in leaves to digest raw materials from soil and air. (Photosynthesis.)

FLOWERS Reproduce plant by forming seeds. Fruits are natural seed packets.

LEAVES "BREATHE." Leaves draw in carbon dioxide from air through pores, give off oxygen and excess carbon dioxide.

WATER VAPOR is given off by leaves. As much as 90% of water drawn from soil given off through pores (Transpiration).

STEMS ARE PLUMBING. Raw materials and water taken from soil by roots are drawn up stems to the leaves. Food from leaves circulated through plant by shoot system.

PROTECTIVE SKIN

GROWING LAYER

CIRCULATION OF FOOD & RAW MATERIALS & STORAGE

GROWING POINTS
1. Leaf, stem, branch, flower, fruit come from buds.
2. Stems of woody plants increase in girth.
3. Capped growing tips of roots press on for nutrient elements, water.

ROOT TIPS FEED Roots draw water and solutes thru fine tips only. These concentrate at drip line, in top soil layers, in moist soil.

ROOTS ANCHOR Main roots hold plant against wind, gravity; convey water, solutes.

ROOTS STORE Some roots store reserve food to carry plant thru winter, start it up in spring, produce seeds.

SOIL SUSTAINS PLANT. Plant depends on soil for support, water, chemicals. How well soil sustains plant depends on: texture (compacted or open), water-holding capacity, readiness with which it releases needed elements to the plant, its population of friendly bacteria.

AIR. Needed by bacteria and root tips.

WATER. Essential to plant. Brings oxygen to soil bacteria, roots.

ESSENTIAL ELEMENTS
Nitrogen
Phosphorus
Potassium

MINOR ELEMENTS
Calcium   Molybdenum
Sulfur   Copper
Manganese Boron
Magnesium Zinc
           Iron

WHAT MAKES PLANTS GROW?

On the left is a young tree (False linden) growing contentedly in a redwood plant box. Just what is happening inside this plant? What keeps it going from day to day?

As indicated above, there is a great deal going on inside the plant. Typical of all flowering plants, it makes full use of sun, air, soil, water, and an assortment of chemical elements to live and grow. It draws raw materials from the air and the soil and converts them to food in its leaves, then circulates nourishment back to the growing areas. It draws water from the soil and expels some of it through its leaves. It stores food in stem and root to carry it through its slow-down season.

The partnership of leaves and roots is so close that any damage to one affects the other. Thus, root pruning reduces foliage; branch pruning retards roots.

Be it noted that a plant gives off oxygen and takes in carbon dioxide, to the benefit of all animals, who take in oxygen and breathe out carbon dioxide.

The plant's primary objective is to reproduce itself. To this end, all of its energies lead to the ultimate development of seeds.

together. This is the embryo plant. The two halves of the seed that you eat are its fat seed leaves.

The ability of the seed to carry its own food explains one simple gardening fact: the seed contains enough food to start off in life; therefore, it doesn't require fertilizer or enriched soil to help it on its way. Indeed, seeds will sprout in a medium without any nutrient, such as water, damp blotters, expanded mica, sand, or peat moss.

SEED GERMINATION

When the seed is placed in the soil, it needs only moisture and warmth to trigger the germination process.

Some seeds begin to germinate almost as soon as they are planted. Others take weeks, months, even years. The long-enduring types go through further internal change in the soil before sprouting; some, such as nuts, have a tough outer shell that must split in order to release the sprouts.

Some seeds will not germinate unless subjected to freezing temperatures, some need the searing heat of fire, some will not germinate until they have passed through the intestinal tract of a bird.

When the seed germinates, its casing opens, and a rootlet starts downward; a sprout, carrying the seed leaves, heads for the surface. Seed leaves often remain in the shell—as with acorns.

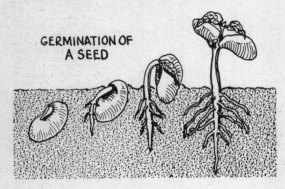

GERMINATION OF A SEED

ROOT

The single root begins to branch out in the soil with tender, white rootlets which follow moisture. These rootlets draw in chemical substances needed for plant life, and also draw water to carry these substances to the different parts of the plant. The roots do not seek out water—they follow it. That is, they grow only in moist ground and don't penetrate dry ground to reach water. This explains why it is necessary to water thoroughly in order to fully moisten the subsoil and provide roots with ample area in which to grow.

As they grow, the roots take on special functions. They anchor the plant and supply it with water (which contains food from the soil) and minerals. As they grow, they develop a firm outer covering similar to bark, but the delicate feeder tips remain white and hairlike. The tips grow outward or downward seeking water. With many plants, they form a ring near the surface around the plant at the drip line, where they are assured of some moisture dropping off the foliage from condensed dew and watering. The knowing gardener is aware of their presence in this area; he avoids deep cultivating in their zone and soaks the ground where roots are feeding.

Some plants have only one main root, known as a tap root. It will send out short feeder roots, but it will not develop a complex system like other plants do. A probing tap root is a highly tenacious means for anchoring a plant—as any gardener can testify who has attempted to uproot an oak tree —or a dandelion.

ROOT HAIRS IN LOAM SHOWING SAND PARTICLES

Roots draw in their water and soluble food only through their tips. Here, fine root hairs—really extensions of individual cells—absorb soluble materials from the soil. These microscopic whiskers live only a few days, and the root tip is continually pressing on for new sources of food. These microscopic hairs are very delicate and if exposed to sunlight or open air, they quickly shrivel and die. This is why the gardener is cautioned to transplant swiftly and without exposing the roots any more than necessary. It is the loss of these hairs that causes wilting in a new transplant. Until the plant grows a new set, it cannot draw food from the soil.

STEM

The stem breaks the surface of the soil, and after it reaches a certain height, opens its seed leaves. At the tip of the stem, between the two leaves, is a bud or growing tip. This continues to grow until the stem reaches a certain point; then side buds appear, and these develop into the first true leaves.

In this way, most plants grow. A growing bud, also called a "terminal bud" because it is found at the end of branches, carries the plant upward. Side buds, known as "lateral buds" because of their position along the side of the stem, develop into leaves. As the plant grows, some of the lateral buds also develop into branches.

If a terminal bud is removed or damaged, the side buds take over the growth of the branch; and if the side buds are removed, energy is temporarily directed to the growth of the terminal bud. This is the simple situation behind the gardener's art of "pinching": by nipping terminal or lateral buds, he can shape a plant by channeling growth into the direction he wishes; also, he can produce larger flowers by diverting more energy to selected buds.

Functions of Stems

The main function of the stem is to transmit water and minerals from the soil to the growing points (buds, leaves, flowers). This plumbing system operates with great efficiency. In the course of a summer's day, a large shrub will draw several gallons of water from the soil and expel it through its leaves. During a hot summer, a tree will transport several tons of water from the soil to the leaves. A spirelike redwood will lift this water 20 stories.

Another primary function of the stem is to support the above-ground structure of the plant. Woody stems of shrubs, trees, and many perennials are quite rigid because of the sturdy structure of the cell wall due to the abundance of cellulose, lignin, and similar substances. Stems of some plants are incapable of holding up the plant's weight without assistance. So it is that vines depend on adhesive discs, root-like holdfasts, and tendrils; some have a twining habit; others gain the strength of a heavy stem by intertwining several lighter ones. Some plants are notoriously weak-stemmed—notably carnation and chrysanthemum—and need staking.

Third function of the stem is to store food to tide the plant through dormancy, start growth in spring, or to bring forth seeds. Some plants store it in the pith, some in a milky latex (poinsettia), some in sap, some in bulbs. When food moves through the plant, it is usually in a sugary form; when it is stored, it changes to a starch. When it is ready to move again in spring for the plant's use, it changes back to sugar. The annual harvesting of maple sugar takes advantage of this process.

Some plants store food in underground stems called "tubers" or "rhizomes." A familiar example of a food-laden tuber is the potato. Examples of rhizomes are familiar to every gardener who has planted irises and callas, for the so-called "bulb" is a rhizome, packed with food for the following seasons. The ability of rhizomes to store food accounts for the difficulty most gardeners have in wiping out certain weeds and Bermuda grass. Each time the above-ground foliage is chopped off, the food stored in the rhizome permits the plant to send up another shoot. In time, the gardener will be able to force the rhizome to give up if he persistently removes top growth.

Rhizomes have a further peculiarity common to most stems: if cut apart and inserted in soil, the pieces will take root. This is a boon to the gardener who is dividing irises, but a nuisance to him when he is chopping rhizomatous weeds or trying to uproot Bermuda grass; for when he chops or discs these, he merely propagates them by stem cuttings.

Parts of the Stem

The stem of woody or herbaceous (herb-like) plants are made up of many identifiable parts, some of them of concern to the gardener.

Around the outside is a corky skin that protects growing tissues beneath it and seals the stem against water loss. The efficiency of this covering as a waterseal can be judged from the manner in which this same material holds the moisture trapped inside the potato, which is a form of stem. Cork used to stopper bottles and form gaskets is taken from the thick bark of a species of oak that grows in California.

The bark is not wholly impervious, however, because it often contains breathing pores like those in the leaves, for admitting gases needed in assimilation of food and for releasing water vapor. These are sometimes visible—for instance, the little dashes on the bark of birch contain the breathing pores for that tree.

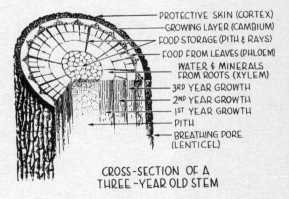

CROSS-SECTION OF A THREE-YEAR OLD STEM

Well protected by the outer skin is an inner growing layer called the "cambium." Here all increase in girth occurs and the growing cells of the plant concentrate. When the cambium is injured or cut, the plant becomes handicapped or killed. The gardener quickly discovers this when he cinches a plant-tie too tightly and girdles the plant or stem. Some insects also kill or injure plants by gnawing their way around the outside. Bears have been known to kill young redwood trees by stripping bark and eating the nutritious cambium and phloem beneath.

Within the core of the stem are bundles of cells that carry fluids from the roots and food from the leaves. Some of these store food.

LEAVES

As soon as the true leaves open to the sun, the plant gets down to work as a complete organism. Sunlight strikes the leaves, and through the action of green matter in them known as chlorophyll, carbon dioxide from the air and water from the soil are converted to food. This explains why seedlings are not transplanted when their first leaves appear—they are not yet established. This also explains why the plant needs richer soil after true leaves appear: these true leaves have put the roots to work drawing nutrients from the soil.

The top side of most leaves does the work of converting carbon dioxide and soil water to food (glucose). Leaves vary in size, shape, and intensity of green color according to the plant's need for sunlight. This is why large-leafed plants are usually at home in shade, where their large area of chlorophyll draws the utmost from the reduced supply of sunlight. At the other extreme, desert plants usually have small, grayish leaves that are adapted to the merciless exposure to the sun.

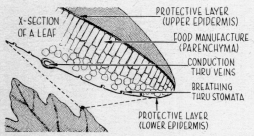

On the bottom surface are hundreds of minute breathing pores. Each opening is ringed with a pair of bean-shaped cells that open and close to release excess water vapor and oxygen and to admit carbon dioxide, a substance that is essential to the plant's manufacturing processes. At night, these openings expel the extra carbon dioxide that has not been used during the daylight hours.

The pores close when the weather is dry, open when it is moist. In this way, they keep the plant from losing more water than it is taking in through the roots. In desert areas, for instance, leaves of native plants shut off release of water vapor during the searing daytime to keep from exhausting the limited moisture in the soil and dehydrating themselves to a swift death.

Because a plant depends on the action of these breathing pores, the undersurface of the leaf is usually fashioned so it will not be choked with excess surface moisture or dust. Most leaves are covered with a waxy substance—the same material that gives polish to apples—but the underside is often waxier than the top. If you dip one in water and take it out, you will notice that the top side will be covered with a film of water, but the bottom will be dry in patches. In this manner, plants keep from absorbing more moisture from dew and rain than they can use. This explains why a spreader or a wetting agent is often added to water sprays to make insecticides adhere to the leaf surface.

FLOWERS

It may surprise some gardeners to know that every plant in the garden—with a few exceptions—produces flowers each year. Everyone is familiar with the showy display of the rose, sweet pea, geranium, and flowering shrubs and trees; but some may easily have missed the inconspicuous spring display of other garden plants. Some plants show their blooms so modestly that they seem to be dusted over for a few days or afflicted with leaf blight. Common vegetables, if left in the ground too long, develop flowers that few people see outside the seed-growing acres. The carrot, if left in the ground a year, produces flat clusters of yellow, or pale pink flowers; the beet produces green flowers; and lettuce, small blue, yellow, or white blossoms.

The flower is primarily a means for reproducing the plant. It contains within itself male and female organs that produce the seed. The male part, known as the stamen, produces pollen; the female, known as the pistil, produces ovules. When the pollen is brought into contact with the stigma (tip of the pistil), a chain reaction starts which converts the ovule into a fertile seed.

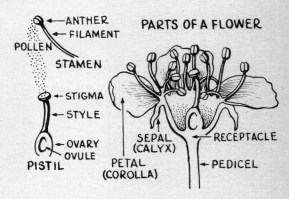

Some species have separate male and female flowers on the same plant; others have the male and female flowers on separate plants that must be paired to produce fruit.

Flowers are efficiently contrived to make sure that pollen and stigma meet. Most plants depend upon winged insects to transfer pollen to the stigma. The hungry insects brush against the pollen when they visit the flower to enjoy the nectar or the pollen itself. The bright colors and scents that charm the gardener also charm the insects. Some plants that are most fragrant in the evening—nicotiana, evening primrose stock—depend upon night-flying insects for pollination and draw them with their odor and their light, highly visible flowers.

Not only are the flowers colored and scented to advertise their presence, they are also designed to attract and accomodate only certain insects, and their parts are so formed that these particular favorites alone can reach the store of nectar and in so doing carry pollen to the stigma. Nectar in the buttercup, for instance, can only be reached by an insect with a tongue exactly $\frac{1}{8}$ inch long. No others need apply. So it is that no casual passerby can wrench open the jaws of the snapdragon; only husky insects, like the honey bee, can gain entrance.

HOW PLANTS GROW

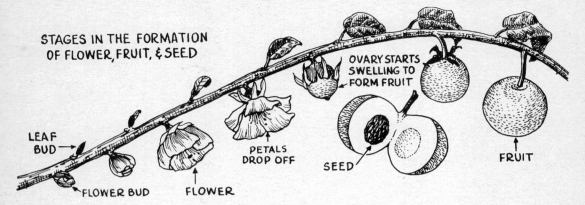

STAGES IN THE FORMATION OF FLOWER, FRUIT, & SEED

Some plants, of course, do not depend upon insects but rely upon the wind to distribute the pollen. For example, the blossoms that form the tassel on a corn stalk drop their pollen onto the silks, each thread of which is connected with an individual kernel by a long-distance stigma.

As they are formed to attract only those insects that will do them the most good, they are also protected against crawlers that might be attracted to the sweets, but would wander around without brushing pollen against the stigma. Some plants excrete a sticky substance that discourages crawlers from climbing up from the ground; others rely on a hairy surface to act as a barbed-wire barrier. However, they are not completely protected, and pests like the ubiquitous aphis get to the stores anyhow. As a final protection against extinction, most plants produce an over-supply of pollen.

The shape of flowers may vary considerably. They are borne on single stems, in clusters, on individual branchlets. Some are large enough to serve as doll costumes; some are tiny miniatures, no larger than the head of a pin. Some are simple in form, others contain a hundred flowers in a single head: for example, the yellow center of the Shasta daisy, if you examine it under a glass, will be seen to consist of hundreds of complete flowers.

If left to themselves, flowers turn to fruit and to seed. This process draws upon the plant's full resources, for production of seed is an exhausting phenomenon—indeed some plants will bloom themselves to death if forced in a mild climate. If the gardener keeps picking flowers before they start to turn, he will keep the plant from spending itself and will prolong the season of bloom. Some annuals can be husbanded over more than their appointed year if they are conscientiously picked during the blooming season.

FRUIT

If a plant produces flowers, chances are that it also produces fruit. Seldom is it edible; in fact, it is usually difficult to recognize it as fruit.

Technically, fruit is the container in which the seed is formed. When the flower has been fertilized, the seeds start forming within the ovary, and the blossom begins to change into a fruit. The ovary swells and grows until it becomes the skin and flesh of the apple, apricot, cherry, or peach; nut, berry, or gourd.

A single apple tree may bear several hundred apples, and each apple will have several seeds. Thus, in a season, a tree may cast several thousand seeds, yet only a fraction of them will ever grow. If the tree had to rely on the seeds that fell about its roots, it might not produce enough young trees to keep the species alive. It therefore uses every means it can to get its seeds planted. It bears a great many more seeds than will ever germinate. It relies on wind and animals to spread its seeds.

As flowers attract insects to help them become fertilized, so do the fruits take advantage of larger helpers—birds, squirrels, deer, man—to help scatter their seeds. Birds are drawn by the color and the sweet meat of orchard fruits, and as they consume the fruit they scatter the pits or seeds. Squirrels carry nuts and fruits and bury them in the ground where some will germinate. Some fruits are armed with burs that stick to the fur of passing animals. A few, notably the witch hazel, explode and shoot out their seeds. Some broadcast their seeds upon the wind.

As a protection against premature harvesting, fruit is bitter to the taste before the seed ripens, and birds and animals leave it alone. But when the seed is matured, the fruit becomes sweet and its color changes to catch the flying eye.

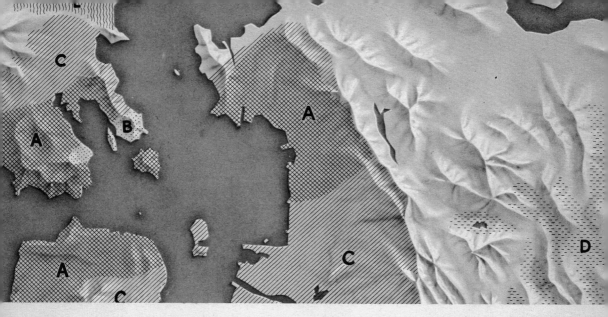

Western Garden Climates

This chapter is keyed in some way into every other chapter in this book. It deals with the basic forces that make Western gardening an exclusively Western problem—the myriads of different garden climates in *Sunset's* corner of the world, the seven Western states and Hawaii.

Here in the West, climate doesn't merely change from north to south. It changes from west to east abruptly and erratically. And within every change from west to east and north to south there are changes up and down.

The wrinkled profile of the West creates climates without regard to latitude and longitude. The ocean's softening influences meet a barrier and within a few miles of a fog-cooled belt of land we find the hot desert's trademarks. Climb 20 miles from the floor of a valley that counts 250 frost-free days a year and you move into a climate that can expect frost every month the year around.

How then can climates be classified? How can anyone say what will grow in any region of the West?

We have done it this way. We have defined 13 subclimates and have given them the location on the map where they are most frequently to be found. Then the adaptation of each shrub, tree, and vine to these 13 subclimates is noted.

To follow a plant through its listing of zones is like taking a garden tour of 13 Western gardens scattered through that many Western subclimates to find out how that plant will compare in performance and grow for you.

You don't have to set up a weather bureau to use this system. You do have to use your weather sense and compare your special climate to the common one listed for your area or another one that would apply better.

Gardeners know more about garden climates than they realize. Garden climates are measured by plant growth response rather than weather bureaus. You know the difference in response you get in different sections of your garden and the differences in the areas you have traveled through.

How gardeners learn about climates

Gardening, every step of it, is timed to climate. No one has ever become a successful gardener without becoming intimately familiar with the climatic factors with which he works. The process of learning gardening is a day-by-day process of becoming sensitive to plants and their response to the forces that make up climate.

No man can have a *green thumb* unless he also has an *eye for the weather*. And in all probability he will not be aware that he has either. A successful

ABOVE. Plant climates vary by the yard. In this portion of the San Francisco Bay Area you see located 5 distinct subclimates. The dominant influences throughout most of the area are the even tempered ocean air and low light intensities from fog which produce climate A. The fog pattern is not uniform. Consistent breaks in it where the ocean influence is direct create "banana" belts—climate B. Where fog cover thins out and ocean air is slightly less dominant we find climate C, which is intermediate between climates A and B. As elevations form barriers to the ocean air and fog cover, climates increase in summer warmth and winter cold. Some approach the climate of the interior valleys—climate D; others the transitional climate of the coastal valleys—climate E.

gardener automatically moves in accordance with the forces of climate. Fertilizing, cultivating, pruning, planting, and watering are things to do so that the forces of sunlight and temperatures can go to work for him. To carry out the chores of gardening without knowledge of the garden's climate is like following the recipe for a cake without knowing how to turn on the oven or what the oven will do after it is turned on.

Western gardeners have learned about the climates of the West without paying much attention to weather bureau statistics. The plants they have worked with have been their climate-recording instruments.

Every gardener who moves into a new climate goes through the same guessing game that all gardeners before him have gone through. If he's an optimist he looks at the plants around him, sniffs the air, asks how long this weather has been going on, and starts looking for plants that are not grown there. It was just such gardeners who planted wine grapes in the foothills of California's Sonoma and Napa valleys, oranges in the Oroville area of Northern California, apples in Washington's Wenatchee and Yakima valleys, rhododendrons in Seattle, blueberries in Puyallup Valley, filberts around Portland.

And it was just such optimists that discovered where many of our Western plants wouldn't grow. We have them to thank for records of frost damage.

If the cautious gardener moves into a new climate, he too looks at the plants around him. The older shrubs and trees in the park interest him. The trees and shrubs in the oldest cemetery are safe bets and they'll probably stand a lot of neglect. Talks with the local nurserymen round out the picture of the plants of his new climate.

But in the minds of both there is always a nagging suspicion that everything hasn't been told about the climate he's in.

Every gardener in the West is well aware that the factor of hardiness alone, which is the basis of most garden climate maps of the United States, is no guide of plant performance in most Western areas.

Plant growth response is influenced by many climatic factors.

WINTER CHILLING—LACK OF WINTER COLD

The lack of winter cold is a limiting factor with many deciduous shrubs, trees, and perennials. All deciduous trees have their own chilling requirements. Each needs a certain number of hours below 45° before the buds are ready to break dormancy. This is the mechanism in deciduous trees and plants that prevents the buds from opening in the middle of winter when a short warm spell comes along. After the buds have had their quota of cold hours they are ready to open only when their requirement for spring warmth is met.

Many fruit trees and deciduous shrubs fail to get sufficient winter cold in the warm winter sections of California. The result is that buds open weeks late in a staggering half-hearted fashion, many of the buds dropping just before blossoming time.

Throughout the lists of deciduous shrubs, trees, and fruit trees, mention is made of high chilling requirements for plants that demand it.

Lack of winter cold adversely affects many deciduous plants by keeping them in active growth too long. Many deciduous plants require a definite cycle of growth followed by a winter food storage period. Long-blooming season and continued vegetative growth into the winter shortens the life span of many perennials in warm-winter areas.

SUMMER TEMPERATURES

Each plant has its need for high summer temperatures and a limit of tolerance to extremes in temperatures. Warm-weather annuals, such as zinnias, make a poor showing in the coolest summer sections of the Northwest. Many shrubs have need for high summer temperatures and do poorly along the coast even where the total heat accumulated over a long growing season is high. Best known examples of high temperature plants in California are the oleander, crape myrtle, and the gardenia.

Plants subject to sunburn and sunscald cannot be used in the 100° summer-temperature areas.

It is important to remember that the duration of temperature extremes is very important. An occasional extremely warm day is not as damaging as a succession of days at a somewhat lower temperature.

DAY AND NIGHT TEMPERATURES

Growers of flowers and vegetables learned by experience that every plant has two temperature regulators—not only day temperatures but night temperatures too. In some plants night temperatures seem to be the critical growth factor. It has been proved, for example, that almost regardless of day temperatures, the tomato will not set buds until temperatures reach 45°. The effect of night temperatures on growth of all plants in the warm day winters of Southern California is another example of its critical effect. Regardless of a succession of day temperatures as high as spring temperatures in a colder climate, all winter annuals practically stand still when night temperatures fall below 45°.

Of what value is the fact that night temperatures are important in plant growth? You don't know what the plant wants in degrees; you don't know the night temperature in your garden; and what can you do to change it if you did know?

One use is this: you are continually called on to diagnose the behavior of plants. Each season you check growth as it develops to see that it is proceeding as it should. If it isn't you must find the reason. When all the usual reasons are checked remember that night temperatures also control

16 WESTERN GARDEN CLIMATES

plant growth. In fact if you are doing a bad job guessing the best planting date for vegetables or if annuals just sit around after you have planted them out, you might be smart to read or listen to the weather report and key your plantings to the "lows" reported.

ACCUMULATED HEAT—LIGHT INTENSITIES

You can't be around a garden very long without observing that each process in a plant's growth has its own temperature and light requirements. Most plants will put out leaf growth with less sunlight than required to set buds. Many sun loving plants will grow in the shade but they will not flower there.

Many fruiting plants will grow in colder weather than is required for fruit production. Melons will grow and form fruit in cool summer climates but the fruits of the vines will probably be small and without flavor. Vines of the European type grapes will grow in the coolest seashore exposures but the grapes produced will not be sweet.

All citrus will grow wherever winter temperatures allow them to live, but each citrus variety has its own requirements of total heat for making the kind of fruit you can eat and enjoy.

In the chapters on grapes and citrus you can see how knowledge of the total heat requirements of varieties and types of fruit can help in choosing plants for your garden.

Heat accumulations are expressed in degree days.

A base temperature is selected based on the plant's growth response. The grape is measured from a 50° base while the citrus is measured from 55°. Every degree the average temperature of the day is above the base figure is counted as a degree day. Thus if the average temperature for the month were 60° and the month were 30 days long, the degree days would be 300 or 150 depending upon whether you were using 50° or 55° as the base.

The degree days used in the descriptions of the 13 typical climates are figured on the basis of 50° and for the period of April through October.

YOUR GARDEN CLIMATE

With full knowledge that climates change by the yard and cannot be mapped accurately, we have divided the 7 Western states into 13 climate zones and located them roughly.

The climates defined for each zone are found within the geographic limits of each zone but not in every part of it.

These climates are offered for purpose of comparison. As a gardener observing the climate in your own garden and in those you drive past on your daily rounds, you have a good idea how your climate compares with that of your neighborhood.

You know whether your location is more or less sunny; whether you get frosts earlier or later; whether the last cold spell damaged your plants more or less than it did the plants in a garden a block away.

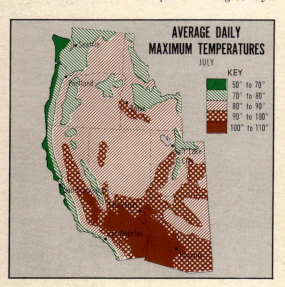

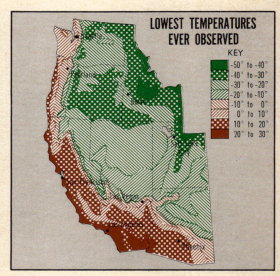

These three maps give the weather bureau's picture of the big climates of the West. No one of them completely defines plant climates. The lowest winter temperatures constitute the most potent factor in plant selection. Low temperatures, however, are modified by their duration. So days between frosts must be considered with it. But what happens in the growing season is dependent upon the third factor—average maximum summer temperatures. By putting together these three maps you can see the weather bureau's picture of the West's subclimates. How garden plants define these subclimates is defined in the following pages.

Many factors make the complex we call "climate," and climate is only a part of a plant's total environment. But given the same soil, water, and food, plant behavior differs according to air temperatures, temperature patterns —day versus night, summer versus winter, humidity, light intensities, total heat accumulations, wind, day length.

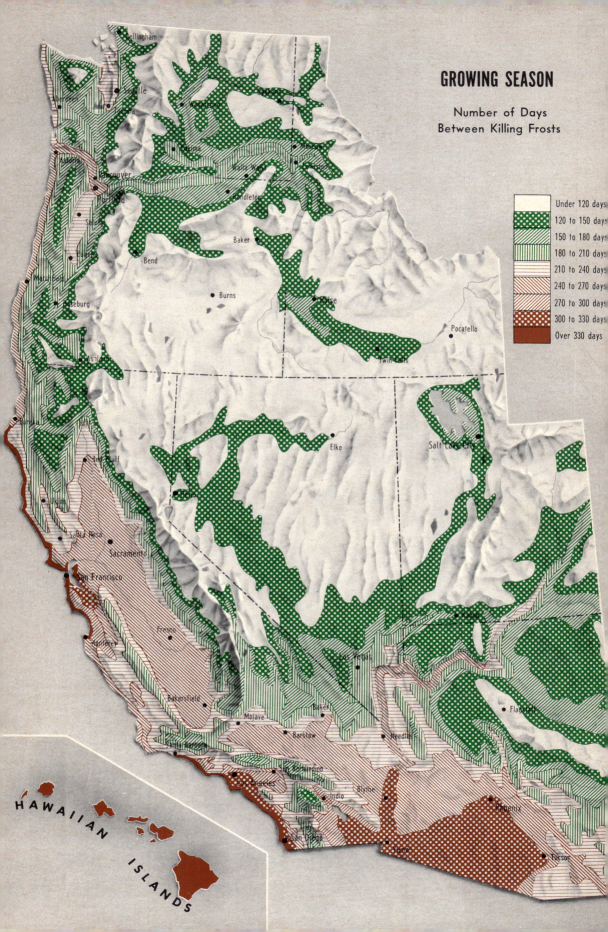

18 WESTERN GARDEN CLIMATES

As your climate differs from the usual pattern of your neighborhood, so will your garden climate differ from the one described for your zone.

If there are sharp changes within your area you may have to handicap your climate a plus or minus or a complete zone. Consider your climate in relation to the neighboring zones as well as your own.

In specifying zones for each plant, the adaptability of the plant to this average climate was considered.

The extremely local variations within a climate zone, and within a garden, are generally caused by the orientation of garden site and the drainage of cold air.

Here is a simplified illustration of localized variations.

Climate No. 1. The valley floor may be 10° colder on the days of frost than either the north or south hillsides.

Climate No. 2. The growing season will be shorter on the north slope. Total amount of heat received from the sun will be lower. Growth will start later in the spring.

Climate No. 3. If the difference between success and failure is a few degrees each day of winter warmth, the south side of the hill could support a crop that would fail on the north slope.

If within climate No. 3 you would build a solid fence or a tight windbreak half way up the slope the climate along the upperside of the fence or windbreak would again be altered.

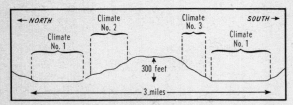

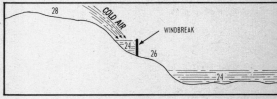

Frost temperatures above the windbreak would be almost as low as those on the valley floor.

ZONE 1

INTERMOUNTAIN

Several subclimates have been grouped into this one climate, not because the differences among them are small, but for the reason that even if 5 subclimates were defined, individual gardeners would still have to make comparisons. No map can fully chart the area. Changes in climate occur by the 100 feet of elevation. A pinpoint on the map, representing a place wherein the elevation changes from 2,300 to 5,300 feet, may contain three different climates.

Such favored areas as Boise and Salt Lake City have growing season in the 170-180 day range with summer temperatures reaching averages of 90°. High elevations will cut the number of growing days to less than 100 and drop maximum temperatures 1° for about every 225 feet of elevation. Summer light intensities are high and the air is dry.

Usual winter lows vary from 10° above zero to 40° below. However, even the warmest areas are likely to get a minus 10°-20° freeze every few years. In zoning plants for the area, we have considered the extremes. Experimental-minded gardeners will go beyond our recommendations and choose some plant materials from those recommended for zones 2 and 3.

Many different meanings are given the word "hardy." To a gardener a perfectly hardy plant is one that not only lives through the winter but blooms or bears fruit or does whatever it is supposed to do in the seasons that follow. A plant is considered hardy by some gardeners if it is injured but once in a generation and recovers with no more damage than the loss of one season's flowers or fruit. Some plants are considered hardy even when cut back by frost each winter, if spring and summer recovery is rapid.

The intermountain area can be divided into 4 or 5 subclimates according to winter lows. But you can't draw lines on a map close enough together to show how one place differs from another.

In a favorable climate the Japanese maple and Japanese cherry are perfectly hardy. A few miles distant, at a higher elevation, both need protection, and at a still higher elevation, neither should be planted. *Cercis canadensis* and *Cornus florida* are of value in the favorable areas and of no value in the coldest areas.

Some areas within the intermountain zone are fortunate in that a snow cover can be depended upon. Wherever a snow cover can be anticipated, quite a number of low growing broad-leafed evergreens can be planted with considerable success.

In this group we find *Daphne cneorum*, helianthemum, *Erica carnea* varieties, and *Berberis buxifolia nana*. Other broad-leafed evergreens which are fairly dependable in this zone would include the following: *Euonymus fortunei radicans*, *Vinca major*, *Vinca minor*, *Yucca filamentosa*. All can be seen around Redmond, Bend, and Klamath Falls.

Of course other factors than low temperatures and high temperatures affect plant growth here. Growing season heat accumulations vary from 2,900 in Salt Lake City, through 2,400 in Boise to 1,600-1,800 in Moscow, Idaho, and Spokane, Washington, areas.

ZONE 2

COLUMBIA BASIN

This subclimate is set apart by relatively mild winters and a long growing season of 200 days. Last frost date in late April; first frost in late October. High light intensities persist throughout the spring and summer growing season and July and August temperatures average 88°. Total heat accumulations April through October average 3,000 degree days.

The one limiting factor to the widest selections in evergreen plant material is the occasional big freeze with below zero temperatures.

The above pattern is found with slight variation in Yakima, Kennewick, and Walla Walla, Washington; in Pendleton and The Dalles, Oregon; and in Lewiston, Idaho.

The Wenatchee and Ellensburg areas depart from the pattern with lower winter temperatures, shorter growing season, and lower summer heat accumulations.

Much planting is based on the usual lows of 10°-15° above zero. An unlimited selection of American-type grapes is possible and fruit trees of every type are planted (see chapter on home food garden for varieties). All summer annuals and warm-weather vegetables give their top performance. Many ornamentals not ordinarily considered winter hardy in cold winters are planted: Flowering dogwood, *Magnolia soulangeana* and its hybrids, the full list of flowering cherries, evergreen boxwood, and most of the conifers.

Because hardy evergreens grow fast in this climate, large eastern nurseries operate growing grounds here.

The hardy evergreen azaleas should find increasing acceptance in this area.

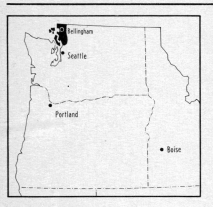

ZONE 3

COOL PUGET

The weather bureau would have difficulty locating this climate, but all gardeners who have it, know it. It is typified by the Bellingham area but is found again in locations farther south. These climates are characterized by more frequent extreme low winter temperatures than waterside Tacoma or Seattle. In the year Tacoma drops to 9°, Bellingham will hit 0°. Growing season varies between 110 and 210 days with an average of 180 days as compared to 240-250 days in the warmest spots in the Tacoma-Seattle area. A cumulative heat total of 1,250 in April-October indicates the coolness of the summer months.

The effect of the low summer heat totals is illustrated in grape variety selection. Of the many American varieties grown in zone 5, only the Island Belle is sure to ripen here.

Gardeners in these subclimates cannot expect to get results with plants that are of borderline tenderness in the Northwest area. Choisya should be planted with the expectation of getting bloom every other year at the most. Plantings of *Pittosporum tobira* and raphiolepis should be regarded as purely experimental. Nandina will live but it won't look too happy. All warm weather plants must be given the hottest spot in the garden.

There's no better weather sequence anywhere for perennials and bulbs.

All delicate flowers give optimum performance here.

20 WESTERN GARDEN CLIMATES

ZONE 4

PUGET SOUND

Mild has been the word for the Puget Sound climate with the exception of the year of the big freeze. Lows of −10° have been experienced following 30 years with no temperatures lower than 0°. However, most gardening is done on the plus 0° basis. Growing season stretches into 250 days immediately above the water and drops to 162 days in valleys a mile or two inland. Local frost pockets are frequent throughout the area. Summer heat totals are low at about 1,800. Inland valleys will carry a higher total of heat—2,200 to 2,400. The difference between valley and waterside is enough to put more sugar in the valley-grown blueberry.

Peaches are not sure of enough heat each year and varieties should be selected to fit the climate.

Rhododendrons must be chosen for extra hardiness when buying for places not directly affected by water or not favorably located on a slope.

This subclimate should not be expected to produce outstanding warm-weather annuals. However, the slow and easy march of spring into a cool summer is just what many of the perennials want.

The broad-leafed evergreens seem to be at their cleanest, shiniest best in these subclimates.

Low light intensities and low summer temperatures must be considered in selecting grapes, fruit trees, and vegetable varieties. See chapters on each.

Optimistic gardeners in zones 4 and 5, situated on south- or west-facing slopes with good cold-air drainage in winter, enjoy many plants that have no business growing in those zones. Here are some of the surprises: *Callistemon rigidus*, growing slowly but growing after a 15° winter. *Eucalyptus camaldulensis (E. rostrata)* and *E. viminalis* as small 4-year-old trees. *Gunnera manicata*, with special winter protection of the crowns. *Osmanthus fragrans*, growing as small shrubs grouped with kalmia and pieris. *Phyllostachys bambusoides* to 30 feet; *P. aurea* to 18 feet; *P. sulphurea* to 18 feet; *P. henryi* to 25 feet. The California native, *Carpenteria californica*, as a lush 3-foot specimen. Lack of summer warmth slows down the growing rate of the silk tree (*Albizzia julibrissin*) and the ginkgo.

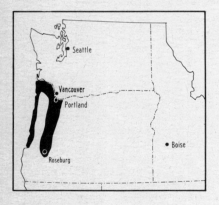

ZONE 5

WILLAMETTE

Garden climates here are blessed with the same long spring season that typifies the Puget Sound climate but midsummer temperatures are 5° to 8° warmer. The growing season averages well above 200 days. Portland has experienced years of more than 300 days between frosts.

The heat accumulations total 2,000 degree days as compared to 1,600 for the Puget Sound climate. This difference is reflected in the type of fruit and vegetables that can be grown. The Elberta peach, for example, ripens satisfactorily in this climate but fails to mature satisfactorily in zone 4.

Arbutus unedo, reluctant to bloom or fruit in the Puget Sound climate, performs beautifully here.

Average lows are not significantly higher than those of zone 4 and the big freeze allowed measurements of plant behavior at −10°. Such extreme lows are rare enough to be overlooked in much of the planting. Rhododendrons, for example, that are known to be tender to such extremes continue to be planted, and should be. The long mild-tempered growing season makes this climate along with the Puget Sound climate favored ones for large scale commercial growing of ornamental evergreens, conifers, roses, lilies, iris, daffodils, pansies, primroses, rhododendrons, and azaleas.

This balance of climatic forces seems to be near perfect for many of the evergreen aristocrats of the garden. Pieris, skimmia, osmanthus, holly, and the like attain the exact balance between lushness and restraint that the shrubs require to look their best. If the climate were much colder they would look stunted; if it were much warmer they would appear rank.

Portland and Vancouver, Washington, are representative of this climate called Willamette. As with all climates local cold-air drainage conditions will make differences of as much as 10° in winter lows and as many as 20 days in length of growing season. In coastal strip areas the extremes will be less pronounced.

WESTERN GARDEN CLIMATES

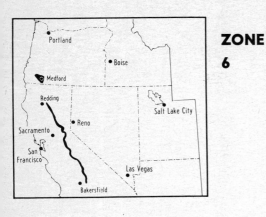

ZONE 6

SISKIYOU-SIERRA FOOTHILL

The valley of the Rogue, the Grants Pass, Medford and Ashland areas of southern Oregon, presents a climate picture that is repeated many times in Oregon and northern California. Ashland, at 1,970 feet elevation, and Placerville, California, at 1,925 feet elevation, have almost identical climates. Both have an average growing season of 182 days. You'll find the same climate again at elevations of 2,200 to 2,700 feet in Butte County, California. In this climate, high but not extreme, midsummer averages of 86°-90° allow growing of fruits that need more heat than offered by the Willamette climate and less than the Central Valley climate. Winter low temperatures average 30° to 36° but lows of 6° to 10° rule out many plants in the low valleys. Gardeners in these climates enjoy rather sharply defined season without being penalized by severe winter cold. Deciduous plants, flowering shrubs, flowering cherries, peonies and lilacs that give a fair-to-middling performance along the coast, because of the warm winters, thrive here.

In several locations, climates are favorable to the fig and the olive. European grapes are on the borderline of hardiness in most gardens. Some gardeners grow them by covering the canes with soil each winter. The American type grapes produce well without protection.

High light intensities compensate for shorter growing season; and vegetable crops that require 150 days from seed to harvest in the Willamette climate will mature here in 100 days.

ZONE 7

CENTRAL VALLEY

High summer heat accumulations, high light intensities, more than 95 per cent of possible sunshine in midsummer, long growing seasons averaging around 270 days characterize this climate.

Winter temperatures of 16° are not uncommon and limit the use of many subtropicals found in the more temperate coastal valleys.

Slight elevations above the valley floor and fortunate cold-air drainage result in thermal belts that raise winter temperatures sufficiently to admit citrus. The Oroville-Orland section in the north and the Porterville-Lindsay section in the south end of the valley are commercial citrus districts.

The march of temperatures through the year call for sharp timing in planting many flowers. The February-March-April-May period is as pleasant a spring gardening season as anyone could ask for.

In those months the climate of the coastal valleys and the central valleys is almost identical.

All cool weather annuals that will complete their life cycle in that period are worthwhile. However, spring comes to an abrupt end in June. By mid-June maximum temperatures reach an average of 90°-93° and by the end of June they crowd 100°. These extremes hold on through July, August, and mid-September. Heat accumulations average above 4,000 degree days as compared to 2,700 in the coastal valleys.

Several notable ornamentals give their top performance in this climate. Most used examples are oleander, crape myrtle, gardenia, and nandina.

Gardeners have introduced many plants into this climate by modifying it in various ways. A long list of plants that are almost indicators of cool summer climates are grown here—begonias, fuchsias, and azaleas are outstanding examples. Enough shade to protect the flowers and to avoid high soil temperatures is the first step in climate modification. The most successful adjustments are those that maintain fairly high light intensities but cut direct sun.

Fresno has lower humidity than Phoenix, Arizona in July, August, September. This low humidity offers a mixed blessing to the Central Valley. There is little trouble from mildew but you must protect the cool summer zone plants from hot dry winds.

ZONE 8A

LOW DESERT

Typical of this climate are sustained high temperatures in summer, a 300 day growing season, and winter minimums that occasionally drop to near 20°. The lows are affected greatly by variable elevations. There are gardens in Palm Springs that have remained above 26°. A low of 5° at Blythe has been recorded. Throughout the Coachella and Imperial valleys and Salt River Valley of Arizona temperatures occasionally approach the 20° mark and rule out many subtropicals as far as winter hardiness is concerned. The *average* minimums however are above 35°. Examples: January minimums in Phoenix, 38°, Calexico 38°, Imperial 37°. The cold extremes are usually of short duration.

Extreme high temperatures in both day and night through June, July, and August make up the most potent limiting factor in the choice of garden shrubs, trees, and vines. A high of 125° has been recorded at Indio. However, more and more plants are being found that can take it and they are so noted in the chapters on plant material.

Gardeners here generally divide themselves into two classes: those who encourage the desert and its plants to come to their door; those who hold off the desert with flower color and the green of growing things.

The growing season for many of the cool weather annuals and vegetables begins in October, coasts through the short winter and takes up again in February, and ends in June. See chapter on annuals.

Heat accumulation totals, April-October above 50°, reach 6,500 degree days as compared to 4,500 in the high desert.

ZONE 8B

HIGH DESERT

In relation to their total areas there are not many weather bureau stations or people on the desert plateaus. In setting up this climate we thought of gardens in the foothills neighboring low deserts as well as those on the desert plateaus.

Typical of this climate is an occasional winter low of 10° as compared to the low desert minimums of 20°-24°. Winter is long enough and cold enough to build up enough cold units to allow the planting of deciduous fruit such as apples, cherries, and standard varieties of peaches that can't be grown in warm winter sections. The winters are cold enough for deciduous shrubs and even peonies and lilacs.

The high desert annual curve of low and high average is illustrated here. To show how this pattern is repeated at similar elevations in Southern California and Arizona we have plotted the temperatures for the following on one chart; Benson, Bowie, Douglas, and Thatcher in Arizona, and Barstow in California.

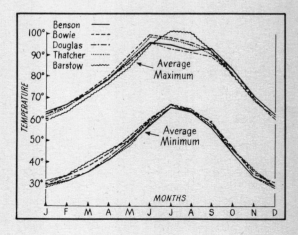

Days between frosts, 225. Difference between day and night temperatures is from 35°-40° as compared to a difference of 25° in the low desert areas.

Much the same pattern as above is repeated in Victorville, Palmdale, and Lancaster, California.

WESTERN GARDEN CLIMATES 23

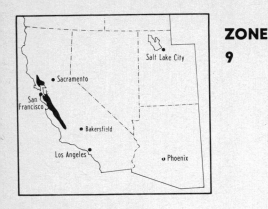

ZONE 9

COASTAL VALLEYS

This climate varies in two ways: local elevations and exposures within one valley; the influence of the ocean air on the valley. Characteristic of these valleys is a middle ground between the direct coastal climate and the interior valley climate.

Santa Rosa, Healdsburg, St. Helena have midsummer averages ranging from 81° to 90°. In the same areas winter lows of 15° to 19° can be expected. Growing season averages from 200 to 260.

In Menlo Park, Palo Alto, and San Jose midsummer temperatures average 77° to 83°. Low winter temperatures of 22° to 24° are experienced now and then. Growing season varies from 270 to 330 days.

To the south, Gilroy and King City pick up higher summer temperatures and lower winter extremes. Heat accumulations range from 2,600 to 3,000 degree days.

To the east, Livermore and Walnut Creek areas, influenced less by the ocean, enjoy higher summer temperatures. Heat accumulations in Walnut Creek are the highest for the area bringing it into the Thompson Seedless climate. Here, lower winter temperatures rule out many of the subtropicals planted in the Santa Clara Valley.

In favored locations this climate allows the experimenter the time of his life. With any provision for protection against occasional winter lows everything except the near tropical seem to be worth trying. Citrus, hardy varieties of avocado, banana, lantana, hibiscus, bougainvillea, and other subtropicals are planted and enjoyed. Serious damage every 10 years or so is only a temporary detriment

It's a middle ground for many plants that do well in climates to the north and poorly in southern climates. The flowering cherries which lack this chilling requirement in warm winter sections to the south are creditable performers here. Cool weather perennials and deciduous flowering shrubs are satisfactory in this climate.

The winters are cold enough for medium chilling requirement and at the same time warm enough to allow several annuals to coast through. September planting for winter bloom of snapdragons and stock is the usual practice.

ZONE 10

BAY AREA-NORTH-COASTAL

Defined geographically, this climate can be seen as a narrow line extending down the coast from Crescent City in the north to Carmel in the south. It works its way inland for a few miles here and there, notably into the Bay of San Francisco.

The Mendocino Coast compares more closely to San Francisco than Santa Cruz. Maximum temperature for June through September ranges from 65° to 68° in Scotia-Fort Bragg and San Francisco. Santa Cruz is warmer—74° to 76°. Winter averages coming down the Coast are Crescent City 39°, Scotia-Fort Bragg 42°, San Francisco 45°, and Santa Cruz 39°. The low extremes range from 29° in San Francisco to 20° in Santa Cruz.

Percentage of possible sunshine in San Francisco is 65 per cent for the year, 69 per cent for the summer. Growing season for San Francisco is 350 days, Berkeley 350, Oakland 349, Monterey 305.

Very few of the subtropicals planted in the most favorable spots of Southern California will be damaged by winter cold in the Bay Area but many find the absence of summer warmth just as fatal to life.

In the fog belt, hibiscus isn't killed by frost but just refuses to grow, becomes weaker, and damps off.

The climate is a perfect one for fuchsias, rhododendrons, evergreen azaleas, ferns, begonias, and pelargoniums. Many rhododendrons, too tender for the Northwest, find this climate to their liking.

The slightest break in the fog cover pattern will boost summer heat enough to admit many of the subtropical vines and shrubs. The "banana belts" of Sausalito, Belvedere, and Berkeley are results of consistent open areas in the fog overhead.

Heat accumulation figures are in the 2,100 to 2,300-degree-day range.

24 WESTERN GARDEN CLIMATES

The sequence in which they are delivered is not as favorable to warm weather crops as the same totals wherein one or two months reach a higher peak.

ZONE 11

SOUTHERN CALIFORNIA INTERIOR VALLEYS

Limiting the selection of plant material for this climate are the following factors: colder and longer winters, warmer and longer summers than in zone 12.

This is the climate of Riverside, San Bernardino, Redlands, and Pomona.

Midsummer maximum temperatures average 93°-96° or 20° higher than coastal temperatures and 10° higher on the average than those of the coastal valleys.

Summer extremes hit 116°-118°.

Plants growing in zone 13 which do not appear to have a high heat requirement are candidates for trials in all the warm spots of this subclimate.

Night temperatures throughout the year are 2°-4° cooler than in zone 12. Minimums drop lower—to 18°.

Frosts occur over a longer period of time and number of days between frosts is shortened from 300 days in zone 12 to 240-260 days in zone 11. However, daytime winter temperatures are high and re-radiation of daytime stored heat from the soil at night lessens frost damage.

In winter, extreme daily swings from 80° daytime temperatures to 20° at dawn have occurred.

With plant protection that holds temperatures 2°-3° above general lows, the selection of subtropicals is widened tremendously.

Heat accumulations roll up to 4,000 degree days or better on the 50° base in April-October. The yearly total on the 55° base is above 3,000 degree days. Such heat is delivered in a sequence that makes possible the growing of Navel oranges. The pomegranate and persimmon find this heat to their liking and the pecan comes over from the low desert.

Spring temperatures end abruptly in June and cool weather annuals, perennials, and bulbs should be of the earliest blooming types. High summer temperatures do not limit hot weather annuals.

Continued summer heat in September makes early planting of winter blooming annuals difficult and fall planting is not the general practice.

ZONE 12

SOUTHERN INNER COASTAL

Perhaps both zone 12 and zone 11 should be called transition zones. All of the interior valleys of Southern California are transitions from the climate of the seacoast to the climate of the desert.

We place in zone 12 those gardens that are influenced in part by the ocean. Summer temperatures are 10°-12° higher than the coast but average less than 90°. Average winter minimum is near 40° and the extreme lows stay close to 20°.

Contrasted to zone 13 it is 10°-12° warmer in midsummer and compared to zone 11 it is 10°-12° cooler.

Number of days in the year between frost dates is more than 300 as compared to 250-270 days in zone 11.

Santa Ana, Pasadena, Sierra Madre, and portions of Los Angeles are typical of this climate. No map can go into the detail needed to locate this climate geographically. Locations in the San Fernando Valley with summer heat in the 92°-93° range belong in zone 11 in that season but the gardens there with more than 300 days without frost almost make the limits of the zone 13. Each garden will vary enough because of local geography measured in feet to make this climate classification a matter of individual observation.

The limiting factors in relation to subtropicals are the near 20° lows and the spells of dry wind.

Subtropicals adapted to zone 13 only, are continuously taken over the line into it. Where cold air drainage is favorable the plants live; where temperatures are as reported by the weather bureaus, the imports are periodically wiped out.

The frost figure of 20° is not as serious a limit as the same figure in zones 9 or 11 where prolonged low temperatures of the same figure can be expected. Sharp frosts of 20° for a night or two are less damaging than 22° for a week.

Every attention to plant location pays off handsomely. Frost protection of young plants is worth the trouble because the hardiness of maturity is enough to allow the plant to grow without protection.

Humidities are not constant. They are relatively high when the influence of the ocean is felt; very low when the desert is in control. Generally lower humidities over the year give the climate a plus factor in growing roses, crape myrtle, and other mildew susceptibles.

Total heat accumulation from April-September averages around 3,500 degree days which is 500 higher than the coastal areas and 500 or more lower than the interior valleys.

While the avocado thrives in many areas of zones 12 and 13, its fruiting habits frequently are disappointing. This response often can be attributed to excessively cool or hot breezes which may prevail during the blooming and fruit setting season. The Fuerte variety is especially sensitive to cool winds at this period. Other varieties such as Hass, Clifton, and others are less affected by these environmental conditions, hence generally bear satisfactorily under more varied conditions. Choice of variety, therefore, is of prime importance if one wishes maximum fruit production.

ZONE 13

SOUTHERN CALIFORNIA COASTAL

This is the subtropical subclimate of the West. Traveling or sailing down the Pacific Coast you practically cross a line approximately at Point Conception where the influence of the northern ocean ceases and the waves and the air of the southern oceans take over.

In the pattern of temperatures over the year this climate is intermediate between that of San Francisco and the truly tropical temperature pattern of Hawaii

Whether it should be called subtropical or not is open to argument. It is a marginal climate for the true tropicals such as papayas, monsteras, and bananas. It is also marginal for those semi-tropicals that need warm nights. It is optimum for the subtropicals that grow well in cool nights and cool winters.

It's a mild climate all year. Summer maximum temperatures average 73° in San Diego, 76° in Santa Barbara. January minimum temperatures average 46° and, 43° for the same cities. San Diego may go along for 12 to 15 years without a frost; Santa Barbara for 1 or 2. San Diego has 365 frostless days; Santa Barbara 335. Lows in the 23°-26° range may occur at intervals of 8-12 years or two years in a row.

Plant damage by frost varies by the plant and the condition of the plant but all that are hardy only to this zone show tolerances almost by degree. The difference between 22° and 26° may mean the difference between life and death to many plants. The difference between making use of re-radiation of solar heat by the soil at night or the difference in a clear or overcast night sky, is often the difference between damage or no damage even with the same low night temperature. (See section on frost.)

The effect of slight difference in low temperatures makes selection of planting site very important for the subtropical. On a hillside there is often a difference of 8°-10° due to good or bad air drainage. Protection of roof overhangs, walls that absorb and re-radiate heat, tree canopies should be utilized wherever possible. South and west facing slopes are most favorable for subtropical plants.

The extent of the influence of the ocean is not uniform. If often plays back into the hills but in many cases cannot be depended upon since a reversal of wind may pour hot or cold air of the desert into the draws and canyons of the hillside.

The mild winters of this climate limit the introduction of plants of high chilling requirements such as flowering cherry, mountain ash, hawthorne, and other deciduous flowering or fruiting deciduous plant material. Because of the unusually long growing season, many perennials which are accustomed to at least a 4-month winter rest, bloom themselves into a short life or simply refuse to behave normally.

The mild summer builds up respectable heat totals—around 3,000 degree days—but totals for even the warmest months are not high enough for many of the hot-summer plants.

Light intensities and heat totals differ markedly due to local fog patterns.

Garden Care

SOIL

Soil can limit growth and the fun of gardening in many ways. If soil is too sandy, it needs more frequent fertilization, because watering leaches out some of the nutrients. If soil is heavy clay, it is hard to work, slow to warm up in the spring, and easily waterlogged in the rainy season. If it is too alkaline, as is often the case in sections where rainfall is light, you will have trouble with acid-loving plants such as rhododendrons, azaleas, and camellias.

If you plan to grow a great variety of plants and want full production every month in the year, you will probably find a soil improvement program necessary. Even if you do not wish to go to the trouble of improving your soil, you should know enough about it to choose plants and organize your planting dates so as to make full use of it.

GOOD SOIL STRUCTURE

Sandy loam and medium loam are the best garden soils. Their value comes not only from their nice balance between sand and clay, but also from the decayed vegetable matter they often contain. Decayed vegetable matter is one kind of humus. You will meet this magic ingredient under many names, all meaning the same thing in the end: decayed vegetable matter, organic matter, compost material, leaf mold, well-rotted manure, and so on. Humus is decomposed organic (animal or vegetable) material as opposed to sand and clay, which are inorganic (mineral).

WHAT MAKES SOIL

Soil is a mass of mineral particles mixed with living and dead organic matter. All interact and are interdependent to a degree.

The size of the preponderant mineral particles and the balance of the different sizes determine the texture of your soil. Clay or adobe is a mass of many small—almost microscopic—particles. You can't see them. When you rub wet clay between your fingers, you make a smooth, glossy smear. Clay dries either as a compact mass or in crumbs, each of which represents billions of clay particles. Beach sand lies at the other extreme, its particles being the giant boulders of some soil's make-up. Silt particle size is in the middle. Mineral particles, whatever their size, do two things. They determine a soil's texture. They also determine how rich or weak a soil may be in nutrients. The smaller a particle is, the better job it does of attracting and holding the minute electrically charged nutrient ions in the soil.

The soil's organic matter—living and dead roots, decayed leaves, manure, and the like—also serve two ways. The organic material separates the soil's mineral particles. The amount of organic matter also helps "tilth," or workability of a soil. Since plants store nutrients in their tissues, dead plant matter contains some nutrients which eventually become available to growing plants. After organic matter breaks down to its final stage, the very small humus particles hold and release nutrient ions just as small mineral soil particles do.

Bacteria and other microorganisms act on both the organic and the inorganic material in the soil. The result is a release of elements needed for plant growth in forms that are available to the plant.

SOIL NUTRIENTS

In addition to light, air, water, and root room, a growing plant requires a group of 16 essential elements or "nutrients."

Plants need many of the nutrients only in tiny amounts. Most nutrients probably are already in your soil in ample quantity. Big exceptions are nitrogen, phosphorus, and occasionally potassium. They may be present in adequate total amount, but only a fraction of the total is normally in a chemical form that the plant can use directly.

In an unfertilized soil, a plant's main supply of nitrogen comes from decomposing organic matter. The nitrogen in this organic matter is not directly available to the plant. Microorganisms must convert it into amino acids, then ammonia, then nitrites, and finally the nitrate form that plants find most usable. This process goes on rapidly in soil only if the soil is warm and moist and there is ample vegetative matter for microorganisms to work on, and ample nitrogen to meet needs of microorganisms in breaking down the material. If you wait for the natural supply of nitrogen to become available, your plants will probably not get their full nitrogen ration. (Total nitrogen in most Western soils is so low that even if it all became available it wouldn't suffice for long.) Yellow leaves are one indication that plants may be nitrogen-starved.

With phosphorus, the limiting factor is the rate at which the soil's supply is readily available to the plant, and not the absolute amount in the soil. Most soils contain at least moderate amounts of phosphorus. Fertilizer containing phosphates supplements the immediate supply.

Most of a plant's natural potassium (or potash) supply is in mineral form—solid particles that become soluble very slowly. Again, most soils contain plenty of such potassium, but it becomes available so slowly that supplementary feedings of potassium are often advisable. You thus supplement the readily available supply, rather than replenish an exhausted supply.

SOIL PROBLEMS

A garden soil without a few shortcomings is rare indeed. Here in the West, the soil deficiencies in one garden are usually different from those in the garden on the next block, and they are almost always different from those in the next county. Still, except for some areas which have deep-seated problems, the main things most of our Western soils need in order to grow good plants are: 1) nitrogen, and possibly phosphorus, and 2) water.

How can you evaluate your soil? And once you've determined its weaknesses, what can you do about it? A careful soil analysis by a commercial laboratory can be helpful sometimes, but your own direct observation—especially over a rather

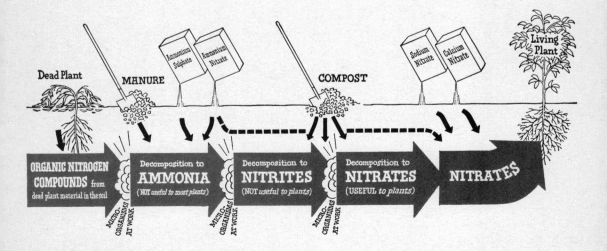

long period of time—will probably serve you best.

You can make your own analysis in these ways:

Test the soil yourself, using one of the reliable soil testing kits offered for sale to home gardeners at a moderate cost.

Learn the general characteristics of your soil. Sandy, loamy, clay, or adobe? Low or high in humus content? How deep is it, and what is the nature of the subsoil? In a few seasons, you learn these characteristics simply from routine digging and spading.

Incidentally, never dig in your garden unless the soil crumbles when you hit it with the back of a spade or shovel. If you cultivate wet soil, you compact it and drive out essential oxygen, thereby upsetting the structure of the soil.

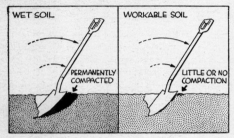

Nutrient Deficiency

You can supplement your soil's nutrient supply in several ways. Since most soils, left to themselves, yield the three major elements—nitrogen, phosphorus, and potassium—very slowly, most gardeners may want to stay on the safe side by using a commercial fertilizer which supplies them all. Nearly all Western soils have a need for nitrogen. Some soils need phosphorus; these are mostly in the higher rainfall areas. Even fewer soils need potassium, but again, like phosphorus, they are mainly in the higher rainfall areas.

Complete chemical fertilizers contain all three elements. Ratios vary, but most formulations sold in garden stores do a good job in the local areas. If you follow label directions, you can hardly go wrong. Applications are almost sure to improve your soil and make greener foliage, more flowers, better growth. Some soils are so amply supplied with nutrients that they can go almost indefinitely without feedings of this type. But they are few and far between.

Also sold in packages are special formulations of nitrogen or phosphorus compounds that make these single nutrients available to plants. Most commonly used in the West to supply nitrogen is ammonium sulphate.

Phosphorus comes as ordinary superphosphate, as treble (or concentrated) superphosphate, and as ammonium phosphate. All are good sources of phosphorus for plants.

Commercial organic fertilizers include blood, bone, seed, or fish meals and activated sewage sludge. All of these products have the advantage of working from a label that tells you exactly how much of the material to apply to a given area. Follow label directions carefully because overdoses may set plant growth back.

Manure is the age-old plant food. It contains all the essential elements, but varies greatly in quality depending on the original animal diet and how the manure was gathered and stored. Manures from the Southwest generally contain an appreciable amount of soluble salts, 3 to 4% being quite common. Because of this, manures that originate in semi-arid to arid regions should not be placed in direct contact with plant roots. Preferably, such manures should be leached before using, to wash out any excess salt. Not much nitrogen would be lost by such leaching since most of the nitrogen in manure, if it is not composted, is in organic form.

Compost is artificial manure from vegetable matter digested by microörganisms, rather than animals. Nutrients released by composting come from all parts of a plant, especially the leaves. Well-handled compost makes an excellent supplier of organic matter and soil lightener.

Leaf mold. Of the five correctors of nutrient deficiency, leaf mold is probably the weakest in nutrient supply. It is usually a nature-made compost; and if you go back to the logic that says a compost is only as rich as the material from which it was made, you will see that leaf mold—usually formed from plant debris in forests and hillsides where soil is scanty—would itself tend to be scanty in nutrient content.

Humus Deficiency

How do you know if your soil is deficient in organic matter? In dry soil regions that make up so much of the West, you can usually assume that the uncultivated soil is deficient in organic matter (humus). This is because rainfall is too low to grow an abundance of organic matter (that's the case in the arid parts of the Southwest), and because summer temperatures are so high that organic matter breaks down rapidly.

Microörganisms need nitrogen in their process of consuming organic matter. The amount they need depends on the amount of carbon in the organic matter.

Normal soils, left to their own devices, keep a more or less constant carbon-nitrogen ratio of 10 units of carbon to one of nitrogen. If you apply an organic material with a higher ratio (such as straw, which is mostly carbon and has a carbon-nitrogen ratio of 40), the microörganisms must use soil nitrogen in order to break down the organic matter. This robs plants of their nitrogen, and it will remain in short supply until the ratio has leveled itself off once again.

You can build up the humus supply in your soil with any of these materials:

Organic fertilizers supply humus as well as nutrients, but furnishing nutrients is their main

SPREAD 3-INCH LAYER OF HUMUS MATERIAL ON GROUND

WORK IT IN TO A DEPTH OF 9 OR 10 INCHES

function. The bulk or fiber will break down to become humus.

Manure is not high in nitrogen, but it ordinarily contains enough to supply the microörganisms so the soil is not robbed during decomposition of the organic matter.

Compost rates high as a soil humus supplier. Most of the leveling off of the carbon-nitrogen ratio is done while the raw material is composting in the pile or box.

Leaf mold may be in any of several conditions. Ideally, it is well decomposed, black or dark matter produced from rotting leaves. In such a form, it does a good job of putting usable organic matter into the soil. However, if it is in the form of rough dry leaves, you'd better apply nitrogen with it, since the carbon-nitrogen ratio may be high. Figure on nitrogen at about 1 per cent the weight of the leaves. Five pounds of ammonium sulfate would furnish 1 pound of nitrogen, enough for 100 pounds of dry leaves.

Sawdust and ground bark are high in carbon when you put them on the soil, so nitrogen is definitely needed. Used without nitrogen, these products would draw heavily on soil nitrogen in the breakdown process. Put on a little more nitrogen than you would on dry leaves.

Peat moss may contain a little nitrogen and other nutrients, but their quantity is usually insignificant. The benefits are strictly physical. Peat moss doesn't deplete soil nitrogen like sawdust and dry leaves do. As a mulch, peat is easy to use (soak and knead it first), and it makes garden beds look good. If used in quantity, it turns sandy soils into water-holding soils.

Soil Too Heavy

Clay and adobe soil that's sticky when soaked, and brick-like and cracked when dry, is probably the West's most universal garden headache. Every gardener who has such a soil rightfully thinks that his "black adobe" or "red clay" is the worst in the country, for this kind of soil is frustrating and difficult to work.

Clay or adobe looks heavy and feels at certain stages like the toughest kind of soil imaginable. Yet the whole cause of the trouble is the minute size of its particles, much too small to see.

If the contrary texture of clay or adobe isn't too bothersome, you can take some satisfaction in knowing that this kind of soil is often the very richest in nutrients. Clay particles have a way of attaching plant food elements to themselves and making them continually available to plants. However, those gardeners who want to make their rich clay into friable soil they can run their hands through must turn to soil conditioners.

Five of the organic materials mentioned earlier are also soil conditioners—manure, compost, leaf mold, sawdust or ground bark, and peat moss.

Pumice, perlite, and *vermiculite* are all porous, granular minerals that physically hold apart the clay particles and prevent them from running together again as a sticky mass when water soaks them. After an irrigation or rain, a soil which has had these conditioner particles mixed into it will dry into a more open textured mass than it would otherwise. You can work it with a fork.

Other benefits of mixing in these particles: They are completely inert in nature and will not break down. They are full of air spaces and give the soil a certain amount of aeration that it wouldn't otherwise get (this is especially true of pumice). Unlike heavy sand particles, these larger and lighter mineral granules stay in the upper soil to give a long-time effect.

Alkalinity

(A mathematical symbol called *pH* is used to indicate acidity or alkalinity: *pH* 7 means neutral reaction; *pH* below 7 means an acid reaction; *pH* above 7 an alkaline one. A soil of *pH* 5 is decidedly acid; one of *pH* 9, decidedly alkaline.)

Alkalinity, although it rates as the most common soil condition in the West, is not as serious a problem as is sometimes believed. Most plant species grow quite normally under moderately alkaline soil conditions (*pH* levels up to about 8). This is fortunate, for many of our Western soils are alkaline due to their containing relatively large amounts of lime (calcium carbonate), and these soils are extremely difficult to neutralize. To do so requires that enough acid (often very large amounts) be added to react with *all* of the

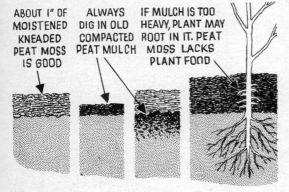

ABOUT 1" OF MOISTENED KNEADED PEAT MOSS IS GOOD

ALWAYS DIG IN OLD COMPACTED PEAT MULCH

IF MULCH IS TOO HEAVY, PLANT MAY ROOT IN IT. PEAT MOSS LACKS PLANT FOOD lime present. Otherwise, any reduction in pH accomplished is very temporary.

Alkaline soil can be made worse or better by the type of water you use. Usually, a hard water (containing calcium or magnesium) is ideal for leaching out the salts that make a soil alkaline. Softened water (high in sodium) can increase a soil's alkalinity, or actually build up alkaline salts in a soil that was previously close to neutral in reaction.

True hard water, as it comes from its source, carries quantities of calcium, magnesium, and other salts in solution. It is this compound that makes soap produce curds instead of lather. To make such water more usable in washing, the water company —or maybe your own water-softener—puts it through a process in which sodium is exchanged for calcium. The sodium makes the water more usable around the house but not in the garden.

Acid-loving plants do not forage well for iron in alkaline soils and commonly develop chlorosis, a symptom of iron deficiency. This is generally the main problem gardeners have with alkaline soils. To get around this problem, either replace the soil around acid loving plants with U. C. Mix (which is naturally acid) or apply iron chelate to the soil (chelates are discussed on page 31).

Excess Sodium

Excess sodium is the culprit that makes soil *extremely* impermeable and requires a chemical amendment, plus leaching, to correct.

Gypsum, calcium chloride, calcium polysulfide (lime sulfur), sulfur, sulfuric acid, ferric sulfate, and aluminum sulfate are effective remedies for a high-sodium condition.

Excess Acidity

In the West this general rule holds up pretty well: Expect to find acid to neutral soils in areas of heavy rainfall (30 inches or more), and expect to find alkaline to neutral soils in semi-arid and arid areas (20 inches of rainfall or less).

Another rule-of-thumb: Sandy soils are more likely to be acid than are clay soils. These rules are wide open to exceptions, of course, especially in ocean beach areas. There's nothing especially wrong with a mildly acid soil, but when the acidity becomes fairly intense (below pH 5) soil conditions become unfavorable for the growth of most plants.

County agents, nurserymen, experienced local gardeners, or laboratory tests can determine the acidity of your soil.

Liming materials will neutralize an acid-reacting soil. Many fertilizers will increase acidity of soil (all ammonium-containing fertilizers do). Lime decreases soil acidity by direct chemical reaction with the soil; all acid soils are low in calcium (lime). Some rather acid peat soils, when properly fertilized but still acid, become very productive. The reaction, or pH, of a soil is merely one factor that affects growth. Never rely on it alone as a guide to understanding soil conditions.

Salinity

An excess of salt in soil is a very widespread problem in the West. It can prevent germination, or, if plants are already growing, it stunts them and in advanced cases burns the foliage and finally kills them. Ornamentals in general rank at the top of the list of salt-sensitive plants.

Soil salinity is caused by an accumulation of salts that are in water, fertilizers, and chemical amendments. Symptoms of salinity are: stunting, burning of leaf margins, and a white deposit of salt on the surface of the soil. The only sure way to diagnose the problem, though, is to have your soil tested.

Periodic and thorough leaching will correct a salinity problem by flushing the salt down below the root zone; no chemical amendment is needed.

Soil Too Shallow

You may have noticed as you spade in your garden that your soil changes when you dig down a few inches. Most soils have distinct layers or strata of different kinds of materials, one on top of the other. A few test borings with a post-hole auger can tell much about a soil's profile.

If your soil changes to a layer of hardpan or more impervious material within the top 18 inches, you are in for a certain amount of travail. Roots won't be able to grow as deep as they should. Water won't drain or percolate down as fast as it might. Sometimes, if you can bore through that tough layer a foot or so, you may find another layer that is soft and permeable. If you do, you are in luck again. Thereafter, every time you set out a plant that roots deeply or one that requires good drainage, get out the auger and drill through the tough layer. Then refill the hole to the level of the bottom of the root ball with a sandy or loamy mix, or with gravel. Water thoroughly before planting. Building contractors have a careless but expedient way of pushing excavated soil from a building site all over the lot. This soil may be unfit for planting and growing things. Make it a rule to dig out this subsoil for each planting hole. Dig down to the original native topsoil and replace with as much good soil as is necessary to fill beneath and around the root ball of the plant. If the situation is extreme, remove all of the overlying subsoil right at the beginning, and replace it with good topsoil. You can also mix in plenty of humus, or use soil conditioners.

The gardener who finds beneath his topsoil a layer of solid rock or other hardpan that *does not* have a pervious layer beneath it or will not even take a test auger, is unfortunate. This gardener is left with a limited choice. He can truck in loads of added topsoil, switch to raised bed gardening, blast a drain system, lay a tile pipeline on top of the impermeable layer, or concentrate on container gardening.

Chlorosis

When an insufficient amount of iron is available to a plant, the formation of chlorophyll is impaired and the leaves of the plant show evidence of *chlorosis*. If the deficiency is mild, flecks of yellow show up between the veins of the leaf; if the deficiency is severe, the entire leaf except the veins turns yellow.

Iron deficiency in the plant is only occasionally the result of deficient amounts of iron in the soil. Such a deficiency is more frequently the result of an excess of some other substance rendering the iron unavailable. In most cases iron is made unavailable by excess of lime; in some instances, manganese. When a soil has a high lime content the addition of iron to the soil is of only temporary value because of the iron-fixing power of such soils.

Gardeners in areas where the soil lime content is high are generally further plagued by alkaline water which gradually changes even special soil mixes to the point where they fix, or bind, the iron.

Some plants are more efficient than others in fighting for iron. The plants that suffer at the slightest deficiency are the acid-loving plants—gardenias, azaleas, camellias, rhododendrons.

Soils which contain relatively large amounts of lime are extremely difficult to neutralize. Enough acids (often very large amounts) must be added to react with *all* of the lime present. Otherwise, any reduction in pH accomplished is very temporary due to the buffering action of the lime.

For gardenias, azaleas, camellias, and rhododendrons, spraying iron sulfate on the leaves (½ oz. dissolved in a gallon of water) shows fairly immediate results. First spray should bring out small green spots in the leaves in less than a week. Spray at 10-day intervals until leaves are green. The earlier in the season the spraying is done the more effective it will be. Late afternoon is the best time to spray.

As we touched upon in a previous paragraph, the general disadvantage of all methods used in past years is that results have been very temporary. Treated soil reverts to an unbalanced state. Acidifiers build up concentrations of unwanted substances. The logical way out, since the plants require iron in such minute amounts, is to find a way to render iron resistant to the fixing power of the soil.

The substance called *chelating agents* (pronounced kee-lating) will turn in just such a performance. It renders soil iron available to plants generally without regard to the soil's pH.

The chelates are highly complex substances. EDTA, one of the first tested, is formally known as ethylene diamine-tetracetic acid. Other ones have even more formidable names. Chelates have the important ability to hold iron, zinc, copper, and manganese—all minor elements essential to plant growth—in soluble form available to plants.

Every plant tested has shown response to applications of one of the chelates: new green leaves, new vigor, new life. These, among other chlorotic plants, have been tested: liquidambar, camellia, azalea, gardenia, leptospermum, bauhinia, *Magnolia grandiflora*, avocado, citrus, rose, abelia, ochna, macadamia, and hydrangea.

Response is usually evident 2 or 3 weeks after very small amounts of the material are dusted on the soil and watered in. Applications have lasted 60 days or more (in the case of one of the chelating compounds); and newer chelates may have even longer lasting effects.

The one big hazard involved in using chelating compounds is danger of an overdose, which can cause severe and even fatal burning. Most chelates contain about 12 per cent iron. Dosage in this concentration for a gallon-can plant runs up to ¼ teaspoonful at the very most. Azaleas, especially, are highly sensitive to overdoses, and considerably milder applications are recommended. Follow manufacturer's label directions carefully.

U. C. MIX: THE NEW ARTIFICIAL SOIL

In 1950, soil scientists at the University of California, striving to develop an economical program for growing disease-free plants in containers, completed a set of formulas for an artificial soil known as U. C. Mix. Today, the Mix (and the U. C. System that goes with it) offers nurserymen and home gardeners a plant growing medium that can be controlled in a way that no known combination of the best loam, leaf mold, peat moss, and compost can be controlled.

The basis for the U. C. basic mixture is a combination of fine sand, peat moss (or redwood sawdust, ground bark), and fertilizer, blended in varying proportions to meet the needs of different classes of plants and types of containers. The fine sand is technically "minus 30 and plus 270"—meaning that the grains pass a 30-mesh screen but not a 270 mesh. The peat, sawdust, or ground bark supplies the organic portion. Unlike manures, leaf molds, and composts, they are of uniform and known quality. Furthermore, it is also of known low fertility, thus leaving the supply of nutrients almost wholly to the fertilizer formulas designed to go with the Mix.

Many Advantages

Better aeration. You can't have vigorous top growth without vigorous root growth. And you can't have root growth without aeration—a constant supply of oxygen and a constant removal of carbon dioxide. Probably the most important advantage of the U. C. Mix over most garden soils is in its improved aeration. It can't be waterlogged; even after watering, it remains well aerated. Because the Mix is highly permeable and drains quickly, the amount of soil air, or oxygen, is at all times higher than in heavy soils that drain slowly.

Better water availability. The fine sand mix delivers all of its contained water to the root system with equal ease. There is no increase in tension until the Mix is almost completely dry. It changes from wet to dry all of a sudden—there is no warning period as there is with a clay soil. U. C. Mix needs water about as often as sandy loam, much more often than a clay soil, much less often than a mixture of common coarse sand and peat moss.

Easy to leach. Build-up of harmful salts in the soil can easily be avoided by periodic leaching with water. This flush-out process is ideally suited to the Mix with its near-perfect drainage characteristics. To leach salts from a container, simply water double the requirement of the container. How often you leach will depend on the quality of your water—in areas where garden water contains an excessive amount of salts, leaching should be frequent and heavy.

Uses for the Home Gardener

Use of the U. C. Mix is not recommended for every gardener. It is not for the hit-or-miss gardener. It calls for a regular system of watering and fertilizing. However, if you are a garden hobby specialist, or a gardener who likes to know exactly what he is doing and exactly what plant performance to expect, then the Mix will give you fascinating and wholly worthwhile results.

The Mix was developed for container gardening, and it is in this field that the home gardener can avail himself of its many benefits. The big-volume use of the U. C. Mix is in raised bed gardening. If drainage or other soil problems make gardening difficult, a concentration of plantings above ground in raised beds with new soil is often cheaper in the long run than fighting difficult garden soil.

Filling a raised bed 3 by 30 feet to a 12-inch depth will take 90 cubic feet or a little more than 3 yards. In bulk quantities the U. C. Mix costs from $10 to $15 a yard. The initial expense is high, but you lick the drainage and soil problems once and for all.

The cost in small quantities is much more, but a few cubic feet of Mix will fill enough pots, boxes, and tubs to provide your patio with a truly impressive portable garden.

Four Basic Mixes

Blends vary, depending on how the Mix is to be used. Here are four effective formulations:

1. For the majority of plants—annuals, perennials, roses, citrus, conifers, ferns, African violets.
Rooting medium: 50% fine sand, 50% peat moss
Fertilizer (per yard of mix):
    2½ lbs. hoof and horn or blood meal
    8 oz. potassium sulfate
    2½ lbs. single superphosphate
    7½ lbs. dolomite lime
    2½ lbs. calcium carbonate lime

2. Useful for cacti, succulents, and other drought-resistant plants.
Rooting medium: 75% fine sand, 25% peat moss
Fertilizer (per yard of mix):
    2½ lbs. hoof and horn or blood meal
    10 oz. potassium sulfate
    2½ lbs. single superphosphate
    4½ lbs. dolomite lime
    1¼ lbs. calcium carbonate lime
    1¼ lbs. gypsum

3. Suitable for indoor and outdoor planting beds where drainage is poor or restricted. Recommended for azaleas, camellias, rhododendrons, and other acid-tolerant plants.
Rooting medium: 25% fine sand, 75% peat moss
Fertilizer (per yard of mix):
    2½ lbs. hoof and horn or blood meal
    8 oz. potassium sulfate
    2½ lbs. single superphosphate
    5 lbs. dolomite lime
    4 lbs. calcium carbonate lime

4. Very lightweight mix. Suitable for azaleas, rhododendrons, camellias.
Rooting medium: 100% peat moss
Fertilizer (per yard of mix):
    2½ lbs. hoof and horn or blood meal
    8 oz. potassium sulfate
    2½ lbs. single superphosphate
    2½ lbs. dolomite lime
    4 lbs. calcium carbonate lime

If You Use Ground Bark or Sawdust

Ground bark and sawdust use up nitrogen as they break down. So, when ground bark or redwood sawdust is used in place of peat moss, increase the hoof and horn or blood meal. Use 4¼ pounds per yard with Mix containing 25 per cent bark or sawdust; use 5 pounds with Mix containing 50 per cent bark or sawdust; use 6½ pounds with Mix containing 75 per cent bark or sawdust; use 7½ pounds with Mix containing 100 per cent bark or sawdust. (Some bark products are pre-treated by composting and nitrogen addition. Use these with same fertilizers as recommended for peat moss.)

Follow-up Fertilizings

Here are the proportions:
    6 lbs. hoof and horn or blood meal
    1 lb. ammonium nitrate
    1 lb. treble superphosphate
    1 lb. sulfate of potash
    6 lbs. gypsum

Apply once monthly through the growing season at the rate of two heaping teaspoons to each gallon can or six-inch pot. Use in proportion for larger containers. In borders and raised beds, apply three pounds per 100 square feet.

Garden Care

WATERING

There is more garden abuse committed in the name of watering than in any other garden operation.

The worst offenders seem to appear when they can do the most harm—when summer days are the hottest. These misguided gardeners like to hold the hose and walk about the garden feeling and smelling the coolness they bring to the plants.

If you follow behind these nervous waterers you will probably find water standing on the surface of the soil, but dry soil below the top inch.

Even when this daily sprinkle is stretched out in time, and water penetrates the first few inches, the garden is in trouble. Roots of plants establish themselves in the first couple of inches of soil and are at the mercy of the broiling action of the sun if neglected for even one day.

A contrast to the light sprinkler is the daily soaker. He is almost as dangerous. He fills the soil with water, drives out the air, and suffocates his plants, because they cannot live without air.

The successful gardener follows a happy medium. He knows when and how to sprinkle, and when to soak the soil to capacity. He follows one simple, two-edged rule: WATER THOROUGHLY—AND INFREQUENTLY.

Behind this simple law are a number of factors that all add up to sensible irrigation.

WATER THOROUGHLY

One of the basic and little-understood facts about watering is this: *A little water wets only a little soil; you can't half-water soil.*

Water moves down through the soil by progressively satisfying the water-holding capacity of every soil particle. When every particle in the first inch of soil has its clinging film of water, additional water becomes "free" water. It's free to move down to soil particles below.

You can't "dampen" soil to any depth by watering it lightly. You can have a damp soil only by wetting it thoroughly, then allowing it to become partially dried out.

When you read that a plant should be kept "on the dry side," remember that you can't keep a plant on the dry side by giving it a little water. The only way not to overwater is to stretch the interval between watering.

Don't assume that water spreads out horizontally underground. There is very little lateral movement of water in soil. Keep this in mind in building basins or ditches. A basin around the trunk of a tree will tend to keep the roots in a very small area. Water in a ditch six inches or more from a row of vegetables will not water the entire root zone. Soak every square inch of soil.

SHALLOW WATERING CREATES SHALLOW ROOT SYSTEM

Roots develop where there are water, soil, air, and nutrients. If all are present in an area of deep soil, the root system will be as deep as the plant can make it (some plants such as camellias are nat-

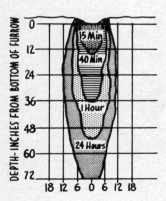

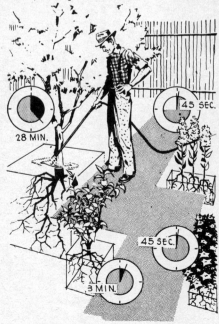

ABOVE. No matter how long you let water run, there is very little lateral spread in a well drained loam soil. Good reason for covering all soil surface with water.

RIGHT. If you could see the plant roots and could watch the water percolate downward, you would be able to meet the water needs of each plant perfectly.

urally shallow rooted). If only the top foot of soil is kept watered, the roots of all plants will develop as best they can in that top layer.

The depth to which plants will exhaust the available moisture in the soil will probably astonish the average gardener. As shown in the diagram below, roots will reach down from 2 to 10 feet. Experiments conducted by the University of California at Davis have shown that even lawn grasses—popularly classed as short rooted—will run roots from 10 to 36 inches in deep soil if properly irrigated.

The majority of garden plants can work on water in the 2-foot and deeper level. Yet the watering program of most gardeners is likely to be based on a root depth of one foot or less.

HOW MUCH WATER TO APPLY

Granting that you wish to give your plants deep watering, your next question is probably: How much water does it take to irrigate down to the 2-foot level?

The answer to this depends principally upon the type of soil in your garden, because each soil type has its own water-holding capacity. Some soils absorb water rapidly, some slowly; some hold it for short periods, others for long stretches.

Sandy soils are made up of particles many times larger than clay soil particles. Loamy soils are in between the two, with a mixture of sizes. The smaller the particles of soil, the more water it takes to cover them.

The difference in size between the sand particle and the clay particle accounts for their difference in water-holding capacity. Tests show that it takes ¾ inch of rain to wet sand to a depth of 1 foot, and 2½ inches of rain to wet clay to the same depth.

It takes twice as much paint to cover the surfaces of the small blocks as to cover the large block. The same principle applies to water requirements of various soils made up of different sized soil particles.

Thus, if you have a 100-square-foot garden bed that you wish to soak to 2 feet, you would need to apply 125 gallons to a sandy soil, 190 gallons to loam, and 330 gallons to clay. If you were applying the water from a garden hose under normal volume (about 5 gallons per minute), you would need about 25 minutes to soak the sandy bed, 38 minutes for the loamy soil, and an hour and 5 minutes for the clay soil. Actually, it might take longer for the clay, because it absorbs water more slowly than the other two.

This does not mean that the water bill will be greater for the fine soil which takes up great quantities of water than for the sandy soil which is thoroughly wet in a much shorter time. The sandy soil will need to be watered more than twice as often as the clay.

HOW LONG TO RUN THE SPRINKLERS

If you are using a sprinkler to apply the water—as on a lawn—you can easily compute the amount to apply and figure how long you should let the sprinkler run.

Start with the fact that 1 inch of rain will penetrate 12 inches in sandy soil, about 7 inches in loam, and 4 to 5 inches in clay. Thus, if a lawn is to be watered to 12 inches, it would need 1 inch of rain if planted in sandy soil and $2\frac{1}{2}$ inches if in clay.

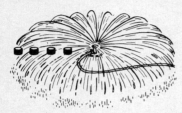

Next question in the formula is how much "rain" your sprinkler produces. This is determined simply with a novel procedure. Place a number of coffee cans spaced at regular intervals in a line running out from the sprinkler. Turn on the spray and note the time it takes to fill the cans to 1 inch. (This experiment may also provide you with revealing information about the efficiency of your sprinkler. Usually, the cans nearest the sprinkler will fill first.)

When you know how long it takes your sprinkler to rain an inch, you can then multiply this interval by the number of inches required and then determine just how long you should leave the sprinkler turned on.

Ordinarily, conscientious watering by clock and calendar should guarantee adequate irrigation for your garden. Weather conditions, however, are likely to upset such a schedule.

The loss of water through the leaves by transpiration is influenced by sunlight, temperature, humidity, and movement of air. Under the influence of a hot, dry wind, the rate of transpiration is so rapid that shallow-rooted plants sometimes cannot carry water fast enough to prevent wilting.

Thus, in periods of cool, humid weather, less frequent watering may be required than in intervals of hot, dry weather.

There is one watering test that can be applied safely to all types of soils and climates. This guide is provided by testing the soil before you water. If you cannot easily insert a trowel, spade, or sharpened stick more than 3 or 4 inches into the soil, watering is necessary.

AVOID THE RUN-OFF PROBLEM

If subsoil is dry despite adequate amounts of water, you may have a run-off problem. On a heavy soil, the penetration of water can be so slow that more than 50 per cent of the water is lost by run-off if there is the slightest slope. In other words, you could easily sprinkle on 6 inches of water and get only 3 inches into the soil.

There are several ways to overcome this condition. You can have the soil aerated. On some soils, spiking will work wonders; but on a heavy clay soil, you are likely to compact the soil around the holes you drive and lose all the benefit of spiking. The spiking tools that remove a core of earth do

36 WATERING Garden Care

not have this fault; but some clay soils are so tough you cannot use this type of tool. (See chapter on lawns.)

You can aerate the soil and add gypsum (up to 10 pounds per 100 square feet) to improve water penetration. A bottled lime-sulfur spray product is available which acts on alkaline soils as liquid gypsum.

Most gardeners find it necessary to adjust sprinkler delivery to match the water absorption of the soil. Many sprinklers on the market put on more water per minute than the very heavy soils will absorb, and they have to be operated at reduced pressure. As soon as water from your lawn sprinkler starts running down the gutter, you can be assured that your soil has taken all it is going to absorb for the time being.

Another way to lick heavy soil run-off is to operate the sprinklers until run-off starts, and then shut them off for a half-hour interval. Turn them on again until run-off starts and then shut off. Continue this on-and-off sequence until water seeps to desired level.

"FREE" WATER IS DANGEROUS

The danger of overwatering comes from the build-up of free water in the soil. When water fills the interspaces, the supply of oxygen is shut off and the plant begins to drown.

Water can be poured through sand almost continuously without harming the roots, because oxygen fills the interspaces of the sand immediately as the water drains away.

Any reduction in oxygen supply below the requirements of the roots for respiration has a direct effect on growth. Nutrient absorption and rate of elongation of the roots are greatly reduced. When the soil is low in oxygen, the wrong kind of bacteria thrive and the right kind die. Roots also become more susceptible to attack from fungus, bacteria, and salts. Many fungus diseases—sour-sap, crown rot, root rot—take their toll in low-oxygen soils.

Plants vary greatly in their ability to resist these diseases. For example, if you planted a mixed orchard on poorly drained clay, the peaches and nectarines would die quickly, cherries would struggle a little longer, avocados would not last long, plums might show no distress, and apples and pears would survive to a ripe old age.

ALTERNATE WET-DRY IS BENEFICIAL

Agriculturists make use of information that can often help the home gardener. For instance, when you give your soil a deep soaking you are wetting each layer of soil, as the water drains through it, to a condition the agriculturist calls *field capacity*. (That is, the soil holds all the water possible against the pull of gravity.)

At this point each soil particle has its own fat film of water, and the air space in the soil is at its lowest percentage.

In the days following, the plant roots and evaporation draw water from the films, and more space is gained for entrance of soil-air and oxygen.

The agricultural experiment stations recommend that the interval between irrigations be based on the time lapse required to deplete the soil moisture from field capacity to approximately the wilting point of the plant.

A long series of experiments indicate that at all stages of soil drying, from field capacity down nearly to the wilting point, the plant has enough water for satisfactory growth.

Experiments with some plants show that the rate of leaf growth can be increased by applying water well in advance of wilting point, but this more frequent irrigation does not increase the dry weight of the plant material produced.

From these experiments, you see that you should not keep your garden soil at field capacity.

Where roots are deep and soil is heavy, stretch the interval between watering.

WATER INFREQUENTLY

As explained above, *how much* water depends upon soil type and root depth of plants you are watering. *How often* is estimated by how long the supply of available water in the soil reservoir will last.

The rate of use is based on water use of the plant—transpiration of leaves plus that lost by evaporation from the soil.

The rate of use depends upon many things—light intensity, temperature, humidity, and wind. It is influenced by the amount of planting, and competition from the roots of other trees, shrubs, and grasses.

Although you will want to work out your own schedule after trial, tests, and weather observations, you can get a rough idea of the number of days between waterings from these University of California observations. Table is based on an average garden in full growth.

How Many Days Between Waterings?

	Sandy	Loam	Clay
Shallow-rooted	4-6	7-10	10-12
Medium-rooted	7-10	10-15	15-20
Deep-rooted	15-20	20-30	30 or more

The rate of use of water in the soil reservoir by lawns in the various climates of the West is estimated as follows:

Water use by lawn per week (in inches)

California:
- Dry desert areas 2.5
- San Joaquin Valley 2.1
- Sacramento Valley 1.8
- Inland coastal areas 1.5
- Coastal slopes 1.0

Oregon-Washington:
- Cool 1.0
- Moderate 1.4
- Hot 1.8

If the *use* of 1 inch per week is charted against root depth of grasses in lawns, you get this picture:

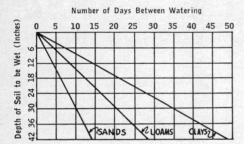

How to read chart: If you are watering a lawn where rate of use averages 1 inch per week and root depth is 12 inches and soil is loam, catch the 12-inch line and run across the chart to the loam diagonal where you read off approximately 7 days. If your soil is in the clay class, the chart says that for a 12-inch depth the interval could be 14 days. Since this figure is based on cool climates (1 inch used per week), the interval would be cut to 7 days in hot climates (2 inches per week).

If you are now watering every other day, you will insist that the chart is good theory "but they don't know my lawn."

It is very true that you can't change from an every-other-day interval to a twice-a-month interval in one jump. As a matter of fact, *the time to make the switch is right at the end of the rainy season.* Start right out watering very deep at your maximum interval, and stick with the schedule through spring, summer, and fall—or until the rains take over again. If water penetration and drainage are good, you can get subsoil moisture by increasing the length of each irrigation.

Garden Care WATERING

WAYS TO APPLY

Each type of soil has its own rate of water penetration and each plant its own water requirements. To suit different situations, you will use several methods of watering and a variety of equipment.

Some general rules apply: The more water outlets you scatter around the place, the better watering job you will do. Nothing discourages thorough waterings more than dragging long lengths of hose. Try for 25 feet of hose at four stations rather than 50 feet at two. The more automatic equipment you have, the more likely you are to keep the garden watered. Anyone planning trips that will take him away from home in the watering months will benefit from some sort of automatic plan. If the neighborhood boy who waters your garden is required only to turn valves on and off, your garden is less likely to suffer while you are away. But don't let the convenience of automatic watering get you in the habit of too little and too often.

If your soil is the type that forms a crust or if your ground slopes, the first step is to prepare the soil for watering. If necessary, build up dikes where the water will run off, and make miniature canals, ditches, basins, and dams where needed to direct or hold the flow of water. This job can be done with a hoe in a few minutes in a fairly level garden, but takes longer on a slope.

Next, go slow on the water. The best results come with a twice-over application. Cover the soil, let the basins, trenches, etc., fill about halfway on the first trip around. After that application has soaked in go over the garden again.

Half-throttle

Even though the force of the water is broken, the full volume of the open faucet is hard to handle. When a big volume flows on, a wide area is covered so quickly that you must move on before the soil has enough water for penetration. The safest procedure is a slow run-on.

Basins

Basins offer one of the most effective methods of watering large trees or shrubs. Surround each plant with a depression extending a few inches beyond the drip line and fill slowly with water until it no longer sinks in. Shrubs with roots close to the surface, such as azalea and rhododendron, should be surrounded with a ridge of soil but no surface soil should be scraped away to make the basin.

38 WATERING Garden Care

Basins around full-grown, deep-rooted trees should be at least 9 to 12 inches deep. It is a good idea to build a cone of dry soil around the trunk of citrus, walnut, and oak trees to prevent direct contact of irrigation water with the root crown.

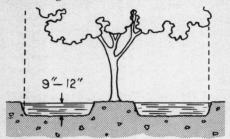

It is hardly possible to make tree basins too large in warmer areas when the trees are not surrounded by lawn. The worst conditions are usually found in parking strips where a 2- by 6-foot strip of soil or lawn is bounded on one side by a paved street and on the other by a cement sidewalk. You must water extra heavily here to compensate for limited irrigation surface—if you want to get the most from your trees.

Standpipe

In dry areas where water is scarce, many gardeners husband water by sinking perforated tin cans around a plant. This method saves by cutting down evaporation and wasted water from run-off. But don't expect a plant to concentrate its root system at one point; use a circle of cans.

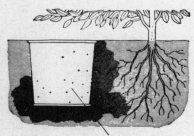

VERY SMALL HOLES IN OLD CAN OR PAIL

After soaking, place a mulch of peat moss or manure around each plant. Then soak the soil between the trees or shrubs so that the entire area is thoroughly watered.

Some gardeners sink drain tiles vertically around large shrubs and trees to get deep penetration without water loss. Sink the tiles vertically beside the plants and fill them with rocks or broken tile to prevent clogging by soil.

Soil Soakers

Tie a piece of burlap over the end of the hose. Place the covered end on the ground among plants and let the water seep out slowly. This is one of the best methods for watering delphiniums, zinnias, roses, squash and melons, snapdragons, hollyhocks, tomatoes, and dahlias, which may be attacked by mildew or rust if watered overhead; also, salpiglossis, chrysanthemums and other tall plants that tend to bend under weight of leaf water if not sprinkled overhead from infancy.

A modern version of the burlapped hose is the canvas attachment used for soaking plants, especially in rows. Both long and short soakers are available. A similar device, made of perforated plastic, is also very serviceable.

Water Wands

Among the best of devices for soil soaking are long-handled rods made of lightweight aluminum alloy with cylindrical or dome-shaped heads that release the water in an easy, steady gurgling flow. When heads are placed within an inch of the ground, the water can be turned on full force without washing away soil or disturbing roots. Long handles make it possible to reach across wide borders and up into hanging baskets.

(These instruments do not in themselves insure proper watering but they do give the impatient gardener a chance to get more water into the soil in less time than with the spray nozzle.)

Subsoil Irrigator

Another specialized watering device is a sharpened pipe which can be attached to the hose. When pushed into the ground around the plant, it carries water directly into the root zone. It is a miniature of the jetting tool described in the chapter on garden engineering.

Furrow Watering

The furrow takes the place of the basin when plants are grown in rows. It is easy to make by scooping out soil between the rows with a shovel. Furrows provide the best method for watering pole beans, berries, corn, tomatoes, and cut flowers, such as asters, zinnias, dahlias, and delphiniums that should be watered from below.

Wide, shallow furrows are preferable in most instances to deep ones as there is less danger of injuring surface roots when scooping out soil, or of uncovering them when a strong force of water is used. Because there is little lateral movement of water in the soil, the wide furrow assures saturation of a larger root area. Furrowing should, of course, be done before roots develop to a point where they might be injured by the gardener's stirring up the soil.

Uncovering of roots by a stream of water can be prevented by placing the end of the hose in a can, bucket, or jar, or on a board or piece of metal, folded burlap or canvas.

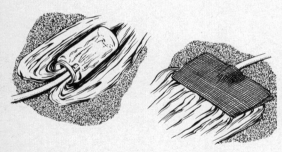

Multiple furrow-watering devices include wooden sluice-boxes with holes bored so as to center on the furrows; and sections of pipe joined together with T's from which water flows out into the furrows.

Wooden plugs can be used to plug up sluice-box holes and caps can cover the ends of pipes not needed in a watering operation.

If your garden is on a slope, check dams will be necessary or water will not soak deeply into the soil. Place a board or piece of metal across the furrow with the top edge on a level with the highest part of the ridge. Let it remain in place until a section has been filled; then move it on to the next section. Even simpler is the method of holding back water by placing a shovel or spade upright in the center of the furrow.

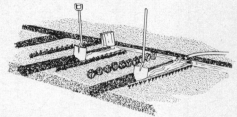

OVERHEAD WATERING

The best way to apply water evenly over a large area is to sprinkle overhead with a fine and mist-like spray so that penetration is gradual and run-off will be reduced to a minimum. If gently and slowly applied, it is the best way to get water on sloping ground.

One disadvantage of this method is that in sections where humidity is high, mildew, rust, and other diseases are encouraged. However, this drawback can be overcome if watering is done in the morning so that foliage is dry before nightfall.

A large group of plants, including fuchsias, hydrangeas, rhododendrons, azaleas, kalmias, camellias, ferns, and begonias prefer overhead sprinkling. Attacks by certain pests, such as thrips and red spider, are also discouraged by dousings with water. Plants also benefit from a rinsing that washes dust off leaves.

A few flowers bend under a load of overhead water. However, you'll find that many plants grow stronger stems if they get overhead water from the start. This is especially true of chrysanthemums.

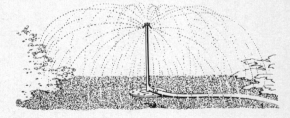

Pipe Sprays

A piece of pipe fitted out with small spray heads simplifies watering of long borders, rows of vegetables or cut flowers, and lawn panels. If you wish to make your own, use ¾-inch pipe, drill and thread holes at 2- to 3-foot intervals, and insert spray heads, which are available commercially. Cap one end and attach a hose-to-pipe coupling at other end.

If a short length of hose is permanently attached to the open end, and the garden hose is connected to this, rather than directly to the pipe, wear and tear on the garden hose is reduced when the pipe is being moved around. An 8- to 10-foot length is a good average for most gardens.

If the pipe is mounted on a frame with wheels at one end, it can be moved easily around the garden. This arrangement is convenient for watering higher borders. The pipe should be attached to the wooden frame loosely to permit turning of the pipe.

Perforated pipes of aluminum alloy, made in 5-foot lengths that can be fitted together to make a longer pipe, may be purchased in garden supply stores.

Mist Sprays

Hot climate gardeners appreciate the humidifying effect of fine overhead sprays which not only cool off plants but make the garden a more pleasant place in which to live during the summer.

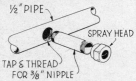

Rhododendron growers in dry climates find that a mist-spray head screwed to the top of a tall pipe offers the best solution for overhead sprinkling. Spray is fine and mist-like and is a good substitute for fog or light rain so beneficial to these plants.

The Sprinkling System

The garden sprinkling system presents both advantages and disadvantages. The greatest advantage is that if well installed, it can reach every section of the garden. It is easy to use. It washes off foliage and flowers. It is best of all on lawns.

Some of the disadvantages: the fixed position of the pipes prevents much changing of beds or borders. Taller plants close to upright sprinklers will be beaten down. Overhead watering packs the soil.

EVAPORATIVE SOIL COOLING

Using water to cool the soil surface is a simple gardening aid in high temperature areas. Soil surface temperature can climb to as high as 152° when the air temperature reaches 100°. Watering can reduce the soil surface temperature to less than 90°. Gardeners in hot summer sections can use this sprinkling-for-cooling every day as a supplement to their regular periodic heavy soakings or irrigations. But it is only a supplement—the daily sprinkling will add little water to the soil reservoir.

SOFTENED WATER

In many areas of the Southwest, the tap water is chemically treated to soften it. Unfortunately, the chemicals used sometimes affect plant growth. Since this becomes a problem in soil management, it is discussed in the soil chapter.

Garden Care
PESTS AND DISEASES

Your garden may be just a minute piece of this world's surface, but it can be a large and bountiful kingdom for many of the earth's smaller creatures. Some bugs fly over man-made boundaries. Others can work out their lifetime careers in a cupful of soil or in a single flower bed.

Their vigorous and undiminishing reproduction is appalling. You can expect pests as long as you keep a garden.

A victory over plant-damaging insects is merely a state of deadlock. You have to keep renewing the attack with controls that act as regular, seasonal checks to their development. You can keep pest damage at a minimum only if you spray or apply specific controls when they are needed (or as a preventive before they are needed), and if you keep your garden as clean as possible.

It helps if you garden in a way that discourages pests. Know the equipment and techniques with which controls can be applied most efficiently, but don't harm those garden creatures that are your friends.

PEST-CONTROL PROGRAM

Here are ten common-sense rules for a pest-control program. Half of them should save time and money in using sprays and dusts; half suggest other measures you can take to reduce the frequency of applications.

1. When you spray or dust do a thorough job.
2. Read the fine print on labels and packages.
3. Apply in the right weather at the right time of day.
4. Apply at the right time of growth.
5. Combine two or more jobs in one, whenever possible.
6. Frequently use just plain water as a spray.
7. Be a good garden janitor.
8. Catch, trap, squash, pick, burn, drown, and otherwise destroy bugs—without sprays.
9. Encourage the pest's enemies.

10. Keep plants in good normal health.

Here's how to check your performance against par for every rule.

1. Spray Thoroughly

Let's face it. Most gardeners do not do a really thorough job of spraying. To be truly effective, spray must be applied so it covers every leaf, both top and bottom, and every inch of stem, branch, and trunk.

If you use a hose-attachment sprayer, you will have to get the spray nozzle into the plant at several levels, from every side. Because most sprays can be dangerous to humans, it is wise to wear rubber gloves and a simple face shield. The kind of mask used by painters when they are spray painting is very satisfactory. Most large paint stores and large mail order houses carry them. The proper kind of mask will cover the eyes as well as the nose; the thin skin around the eyes—in addition to the eyeballs themselves—must be protected from toxic materials. It is a good idea to wear old clothes when spraying, including a shirt or jacket with full-length sleeves. When you are finished with the job, change to fresh clothing.

A tank sprayer or a motor-driven rig with a long extension nozzle makes it possible to get the spray into the center of the plant without touching the foliage. Even so, protection is advisable.

What type of spray application is most thorough? A spray or a finely atomized mist? The answer depends on the insects to be killed. If you are spraying for aphis or red spider, the very fine spray is as effective as a drenching. And, of course, the more atomized the spray solution, the less concentrate is used.

On the other hand if you are spraying for ants and earwigs along walks or around the foundation of the house, the finely atomized application would be wasted. In this case you should really drench all surfaces in order to build up a high concentration of poison and leave a residue when it dries. Too light an application is worthless and a waste of money.

Another job that should have heavy and thorough application is the winter clean-up. Here you are after insects of the hardy type—beetles in the bark of trees, twig borers, stem borers, scale. Sprays should be forced into the cracks and crevices of the bark. Any excess spray solution that runs down the bark and into the soil, will not benefit the insects, that's certain.

In winter-spraying nothing is lost if you get as much on the ground as you do on the plants. Ground spray cleans up fungus spores and some soil insects.

Thoroughness in control of juice-sucking insects means hitting every insect. Thoroughness in control of leaf-eating insects means hitting them or covering all leaf surfaces with poison. Thoroughness in control of bark and stem attackers means getting at them.

But don't expect the impossible. Remember that most sprays don't make insects drop dead on contact. An hour after you spray, you will see aphis wriggling around. Ants will continue their march over a treated trail. It takes some time for most sprays to act. Wait a day or so to pass judgment on a spray's effect. After the aphis are all dead, you can wash off their remains for the sake of appearance. However, if you find usual activity several days after you have sprayed, you'd better check your methods: coverage, mix measurements, thoroughness, etc.

2. Follow Directions on the Label

Have you a teaspoon and a tablespoon on the garden medicine shelf? Have you a gallon can? Some gardeners guess that the bottle top is a teaspoonful. Some guess and add a little for good measure.

Chewing insects gnaw away portions of leaf, stem, fruit, blooms. Insecticide residue on plant's surface destroys pest when it eats the poisoned plant tissue.

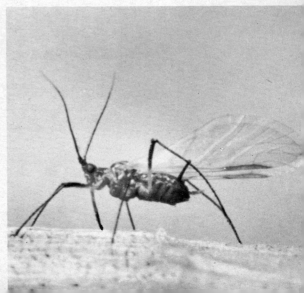

Sucking insects drain juices from plant, as shown by close-up of aphis with beak inserted. Insecticide must contact insect, because he draws food from beneath surface.

Increasing the concentration of spray solutions is not only wasteful but often dangerous to plants, people, and wildlife.

The very fine print will answer many questions that worry the gardener who sprays and dusts. If the preparation is injurious to certain plants, the label will name them. If the preparation should not be used on vegetables or fruits too close to harvest, the label will carry that caution.

Read the label for safety cautions. Several sprays require very special handling. Remember that all sprays should be kept out of reach of children.

As a rule, bodily contact with spray materials is not advisable, but if you get a little diluted spray of most common insecticides on your clothing, it won't do any harm. However, some sprays are definitely dangerous, especially in high concentrations. These are listed in the insect control chart on a following page. Whatever type of spray you use, wash it off your hands, and try not to get any on your face.

3. Apply in the Right Weather

Winter: Since you should have three or four days of clear weather after a dormant spray clean-up, it's wise to do the job before the rainy season begins in earnest. There is no need to wait until all the leaves have fallen before tackling the winter clean-up. Dormant spray is not harmful to leaves of deciduous material in the fall. In fact, cleaning up the leaves on trees and shrubs prevents some insects and diseases from spreading to the ground and to the compost pile.

Spring and Summer: Apply dusts in early morning when dew is present, so they will cling to foliage.

As a rule, it's a good idea to spray in the morning, too. There is less wind then and the dew helps to spread the spray.

Sulfur will not do its work when temperatures are low; but, if applied under low temperatures, it's ready to work when temperatures rise. Do not apply in extremely hot weather, because it may burn foliage.

4. Apply at Right Stage of Growth

You can spray a small plant more quickly and for less money than a larger plant. That simple sounding statement doesn't mean a thing to the gardener who wants to believe that his plants may go through the year without an attack.

However, spraying or dusting young tomato plants to ward off insects will prevent virus damage later on. You avoid the virus by killing the insects which might carry the virus.

To avoid the disfiguration of sprays or dusts on a pest-susceptible plant that is in bloom, apply the material when the plant is in the early bud stage.

Early-season application catches the adults with millions of potential offspring.

5. Do Two Jobs at One Time

Numerous multipurpose spray combinations are available. By combining insecticides and fungicides in one application, the gardener cuts his spraying time in half. From the same manufacturers, you can buy insecticides and fungicides in separate containers and mix them in solutions to control either insects or diseases.

Before mixing your own all-purpose spray, read the labels for warnings on mixtures. Some materials won't mix.

When mixing sprays add each concentrate separately to the water. Never mix the spray concentrate directly.

Take advantage of the spray materials that do an extensive job of killing. In the control chart on a following page, you can see how many insects can be controlled by just a few of these sprays.

6. Use a Blast of Plain Water as a Spray

Washing or syringing aphis and red spider from leaves and twigs is good garden practice, and a very satisfying procedure to the man with the hose. Unfortunately they, or their relatives, are back on the plant too soon.

Washing off a tree with water before applying the insecticides saves spray and makes what you use more effective. The excess of insects, dust and honeydew on a tree heavily infested with aphis, may inhibit the spray's effectiveness. In such cases, hose the tree with a fine but forceful water spray. Let it dry, and then spray on the insecticide. Spray the ground to take care of insects that were knocked off by water and not contacted with the spray.

This water-spray treatment is especially helpful when you are spraying a high climbing rose or tree and your equipment will not send the spray to the top of the plant. Spray the entire plant with a strong jet of water, and reach as much of the plant as you can with the insecticide spray. This method will give reasonable control of aphis, red spider, and leafhopper nymphs.

Dust-covered leaves are more susceptible to red spider than clean leaves. Keep trees and shrubs washed clean. Frequent washing of rose foliage may reduce the rose spray schedule. It is best to water-spray in the morning so that the roses will go into the evening with dry leaves.

7. Be a Good Garden Janitor

Most garden pests spend at least one life phase in the ground or in protected places, usually during the winter months. If you and your neighbors can keep your garden free of surface bug-havens— weeds, leaves, trash, lumber and other flat-bottom objects—you will eliminate breeding and hiding places of many pests. It's a wise practice to store flats, pots, lumber, and other miscellaneous supplies off the ground on racks or shelves. You can trap earwigs by taking advantage of their inclination to hide under boards. Lay short lengths of boards under plants where earwig damage has been noticed. Next day, lift the boards and spray or step on earwigs.

8. Catch, Trap, Burn, Drown

The gardener who feels that it's rather useless to kill a few insects by hand when he is going to have to spray anyway, often misses opportunities to stop an insect attack before it gets underway.

Here are some of the simple methods used by gardeners who don't like to spray any more often than is absolutely necessary: *borers*, cut and burn infested canes or branches; *earwigs*, catch and burn in rolled-up newspapers; *leaf miner*, destroy infested leaves—they contain the larvæ; *scale*, scrub off with a tooth brush dipped in summer oil; *slugs and snails*, hand pick (wear gloves if you are squeamish) at night with the aid of a flashlight and coffee can; *spittle bug*, hose off the froth and the nymph inside—sunlight or natural enemies will destroy the nymphs; *tent caterpillar*, burn the silken tents which hold young larvæ with a rag soaked in kerosene.

9. Encourage Their Enemies

Among the small creatures in the garden, count these as your friends: toads, lady bird beetles (feed on aphis); syrphid fly larvae (feed on aphis); honeybee; carabid beetles (iridescent, purplish black—scavenge and attack slugs and snails); lacewing flies (1¼ inch brown or green insects with iridescent wings—feed on aphis); and certain types of wasps that parasitize and eat caterpillars.

Western birds that feed almost exclusively on insects are towhees, bush-tits, song sparrows, wrens, thrushes, warblers, and blackbirds.

Certain insecticides — notably DDT — kill off friend and foe alike. Their use should be moderate, and you should hold off altogether if you see birds and predators cleaning out your pests.

10. Keep Plants in Normal Health

While it's true that healthy, succulent plants do not "throw off" or "resist" sucking insects, they can weather the attacks without being weakened to the point where they become susceptible to other pests and diseases. Also, a healthy plant will resist many organisms of low power.

PEST CONTROL CALENDAR

Controlling garden pests can be a year-long battle or a simple, easy task depending on how well you time spray or dust applications.

The actual calendar dates vary by your climate and by the weather. The cycle of growth sets your dates.

General Program

The simplest program calls for four applications:

Late winter. At the end of winter, after frost danger, when buds of deciduous plants are swelling, spray all deciduous shrubs and trees with a dormant spray. Favorite materials are lime-sulfur, oil, Bordeaux solution, or the mixture of these that the label suggests. At this time you control overwintering insects, insect eggs, plant diseases, scale, the first broods of aphis. Spray the surface of the soil for good measure.

Early spring. Time this spray with the unfolding of new leaves. Use an all-purpose spray with a wide range of kill. Be sure it includes a miticide. Cover every leaf in the garden. Perhaps the only insect you will see will be aphis, but you will be taking care of scale, red spider and other mites, and other insects. This preventive spray is the most important spray of the year as it stops the build-up of large populations of insects.

Late spring. Four weeks after the first spray, repeat the all-purpose spray application. This takes care of anything that escaped the first spray and all visitors.

Summer. Again use the all-purpose spray to protect against the leaf eaters—diabrotica, leaf hoppers, worms, and others.

Special Programs

In addition to a general program, several special programs must be followed.

Snails and slugs are controlled best by an early spring application of spray, dust, or bait. Time it when daffodils show color. As an extra precaution, give special attention to young transplants and seedlings. Several baits will also control cutworms.

Earwig activity begins in early summer. Use baits, sprays, or dusts.

Weevils require special soil treatment to kill grubs and beetles as they emerge. Follow label directions.

Soil insects such as wireworms are controlled by treating the soil before planting.

Roses. To grow perfect roses, you must follow a regular twice-a-month schedule. Several rose kits are available that contain controls for both insects and diseases. It is much better to prevent rather than try to cure.

Flowering fruit trees. Follow same program as specified for fruit trees. See page 344.

Lawn insects and diseases. See pages 110, 111, 113, and 114 of the chapter on lawns.

WHICH PEST IS WHICH?

In the following pages you will find a brief guide to the most notorious Western garden pests. This guide is designed to display the pests as they characteristically reveal themselves to the gardener. If they are large enough to be visible, they are pictured full size. If they are too small or too shy to be seen, the clues to their presence are shown in terms of tattered foliage or nibbled blossoms.

Not all of your garden's pests are included in this rogues' gallery—there are literally thousands known to exist—but the most troublesome should be found in the guide. If you do not find a particular specimen, show a damaged leaf or bloom or a captured insect to your nurseryman or county agent, or consult your public library's technical books on insect pests.

APHIS AND ANTS

Aphis are small, soft-bodied sucking insects; black, green, yellowish or pinkish in color. Some are winged, some wingless. Live in colonies. Suck sugars from plant juices, weaken plant, and excrete honeydew that attracts ants and encourages growth of fungus. Control: Spray regularly (every 2-3 weeks) in warm weather; in winter, use dormant spray to kill adults, eggs. ANTS tend aphis, protect them from enemies, carry them from plant to plant to secure honeydew. Control: Use ant cups, or brush or spray recommended insecticide on trails.

ROOT WEEVILS

Of many root-eating weevils, these two probably cause the most damage in the West. Adults feed on leaves and fruit; larvæ on roots. Grubs often sever main roots of host plants, girdle stem just below soil surface. STRAWBERRY ROOT WEEVIL favors strawberry, bush berries, grasses, deciduous shrubs and trees, young conifers. BLACK VINE WEEVIL attacks yew, many shrubs, perennials, vines. Night-feeder. Menace in greenhouse. Control: For both pests, apply baits or dusts in spring when weevils emerge from soil. Apply around base of plants 2 or 3 times.

DIABROTICA

This small beetle can do a lot of garden damage in a summer. Although known as the CUCUMBER BEETLE, its damage is not confined to cucumbers. It feeds on most vegetables and many flowering plants and shrubs. Severe infestations can defoliate plant. Larvæ feed on roots, adults on leaves, stems, flowers. Adults hibernate in winter in garden debris; in spring, deposit eggs in soil cracks; larvæ emerge as full-grown beetles in midsummer. Control with dust or spray indicated on chart. For heavy infestations, use dust as it deposits heavier residue.

EARWIG

By day, earwigs hide under rocks, boards, rubbish, and within flower and leaf clusters. Emerge at night to eat holes in leaves, flowers, vegetables (also cloth, paper). Breed in early summer; most active April-July. Control: Not easy to control because they sample many kinds of food but do not prefer any one of them. Baits give partial control; dusting ground in late spring is better. Can be trapped by placing rolled up paper or folded sacks near feeding area. Earwigs will retire to these for daytime, may be picked up and destroyed.

FULLERS ROSE BEETLE

This is a true weevil—non-flying beetle with a snout—that works only at night and whose presence can thus be guessed only by the damage he does. Chews notches in from the margins of leaves and also eats flowers and buds. Leaves black excrement behind. The larvæ feed on roots and, if abundant, can turn foliage yellow. Favors citrus and gardenia, but is also found on roses. Control: Shake pests off leaves into jar partly filled with insecticide; spray leaves and ground with recommended control.

Garden Care **PESTS AND DISEASES** 45

LAWN MOTH

Larvæ of LAWN MOTH or SOD WEBWORM feed on new grass blades, cause brown patches and stunted blades. First sign: 1-inch, tan moths hovering over lawn at dusk in spring-summer, dropping eggs into grass. Larvæ hatch in week; full-size, gray worms (2/3") hide in silken tubes near surface of soil. Similar pest, CUTWORM, burrows deeper, is twice as long. To verify infestation, mix 2 tsp. of 2% pyrethrin in 1 gallon water, and apply to square yard of lawn. Webworms will wriggle to surface. Control: Use recommended controls every 2-3 weeks in season.

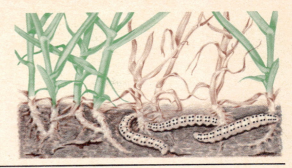

LEAFHOPPER

Small whitish or greenish, hopping insects that feed on leaves of grape, ivy, plum, apple, and some annuals and shrubs. Cause whitish stipling on the leaves, but their most serious damage is transmission of plant viruses, such as curly top (affect potatoes, tomatoes, beans, squash, cucumbers). They are also known to carry a petunia blight. Control: Dust or spray underside of leaves in spring-summer at the first signs of them and as often as they show up thereafter. See chart for specific controls.

MEALYBUG

White waxy sucking insects that develop in colonies at leaf and stem joints. Lay eggs in white, cottony masses. Young are crawlers like scale. Breeding increases during summer and fall. Adults over-winter. Excrete large amounts of honeydew that attracts ants, encourages black mold fungus. Control: Hose off leaves frequently. Control with recommended spray in summer-fall. Soil type, which attacks roots of lawn grasses, annuals, perennials, and shrubs, requires soil insecticide or control by repeated, light cultivation.

SCALE

Small insects, covered by protective shells, that attach themselves to stems and undersurfaces of leaves and suck out plant juice. Generally, they are able to move about in younger stages, but become stationary or nearly so in adulthood. An unarmored type, which attaches itself to woody plants, excretes honeydew, thereby attracting ants and causing fungus. Control: Prune and destroy localized infestations. Kill crawlers in summer with oil spray or contact insecticide; use winter-oil spray to smother over-wintering adults. Spray often.

WHITEFLIES

Whiteflies are tiny (1/16") sucking insects that live mostly on underside of leaves. When disturbed, they fly off like a white cloud. Eggs laid on underside of leaf. Growth through larval stage to adult is rapid in warm months. Stationary, scale-like nymphs do most of damage, sucking juices and excreting honeydew, thereby attracting ants and encouraging fungus growth. Leaves turn yellow and drop in severe infestations. Control: Contact insecticide, thoroughly applied to underside of foliage. Begin spraying early. Destroy heavily infested foliage.

PESTS AND DISEASES Garden Care

SLUGS AND SNAILS
If slimy trails and tattered foliage indicate snail and slug invasion, hunt down these pests and destroy them. In daytime, look under rocks, leaves, densely foliaged plants, boards, boxes, plant tubs, or any object that rests on the ground. At night, use a flashlight to find them at their work. Control: Hand means, if you are not squeamish; otherwise, frequently scatter poison baits (pellets last longer, go further) about favored plants, or dust plants with stomach poison (see chart). Bait seed beds to protect plantings.

GRASSHOPPERS
These pests feed on foliage of many plants, usually in late summer when fields next to gardens become dry. Most often found in warm, interior valleys. Eggs laid in soil, do not hatch until following spring. Young and adults attack plants. In severe infestations, large plants may be defoliated, tender bark stripped from trees and shrubs. Control: Spray or dust plants with recommended control, or spread bait in garden and surrounding area early in morning before it becomes hot. Repeat baiting every three days until damage stopped.

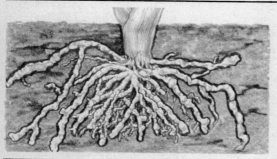

ROOT-KNOT NEMATODES
Microscopic worms that infest garden soils throughout West, attack roots of various plants, and form galls or root knots. With damaged root systems unable to supply enough water to their tops, infested plants wilt or die in hot weather. Most active in sandy soils. Inactive in cold weather, hence infested beds can be used for cold-weather crops. Control: No sure cure. Rotate use of soil so infested bed can be left fallow for 1 or 2 years; or plant resistant strain for two seasons, susceptible for one; or treat soil with fumigant.

CORN EARWORM
If kernels of corn are eaten away near silk, your corn patch is being visited by CORN EARWORMS. These caterpillars are larvæ of fawn-colored moth that lays eggs on silk at night. Although corn is its favorite, it attacks 30 other plants, including beans, cabbages, tomatoes, peaches. CONTROL: Apply as for CATERPILLAR. For corn, apply insecticide in oil on silk inside top of ear. Use eye dropper or small oil can. Don't apply oil before silks wilt, as it interferes with pollination. Or dust regularly when half of ears are partially out. Do not feed treated husks to livestock.

TENT CATERPILLARS
If you discover gauzy tents formed around crotches of tree branches, you will doubtless find them inhabited by tent caterpillars. These pests favor a wide selection of trees, some shrubs, a few vines. In late summer, moths deposit eggs in bunches, partially or completely surrounding small branches of host plant. Caterpillars develop in the egg but don't hatch until following spring. When leaves unfold, pests emerge and eat leaves and young fruit, and form their tents. Control: Remove and burn twigs with egg masses in winter, early spring, destroy tent colonies in summer. Dust or spray.

Garden Care **PESTS AND DISEASES** 47

BORERS

Larvæ of moths, beetles, sawflies, and wasps may burrow into stem or trunk of fruit trees, roses, and berry vines. Presence indicated by sawdust around holes in cane of rose or berry, and by sticky brown patches on bark of trees. Watch for signs on fruiting and flowering species of almond, apricot, cherry, peach, plum, and prune trees. Control: Spray canes or trunk to kill hatching larvæ. Once they have appeared under the bark, prune affected canes of vine or rose below infestation. Remove borers from bark of tree with knife; seal wound with copper compound.

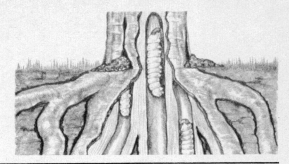

SPITTLE BUGS

The common spittle bug is easily recognized. It surrounds itself with a protective froth which is plainly visible on the plant. This is a sucking insect that attaches itself to stems and drains plant juices from its host. Commonly found on strawberry, currant, gooseberry. Control: A strong spray of water will usually remove this pest. If there are a great number of spittle bugs, dust the plant with a multipurpose garden dust.

SOWBUGS and PILLBUGS

Sowbugs are more of an annoyance than a menace in the garden. They feed more on decayed organic matter than they do on soft plants. If there is enough rough material in the beds for them to consume, they won't bother with roots of plants. They prefer to work in damp conditions; so if you let soil dry out before evening, they will be less active than if ground is damp at night. Both sowbugs and pillbugs breathe with gills. Pillbug rolls into ball when disturbed; sowbug does not. Control: Apply dust or bait to infested ground or to their hideouts under rocks, boards, etc.

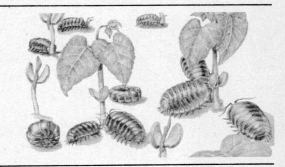

WIREWORMS

Waxy, yellow-colored, 1-inch worms that live in light soils and feed on many plants. They cut off roots, bore into tubers and bulbs, bore into plant stems, and attack germinating seed. The larva remains in soil from one to three years before developing into adult click beetle. Control: Because they live in the soil, they are difficult to arrest. Incorporating insecticidal dust into soil may give satisfactory control. Surest control is to prevent their taking over by treating soil in advance of or at time of planting. Fumigate soil with ethylene bromide.

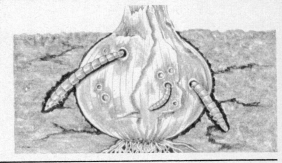

CATERPILLARS

Caterpillars may be found in many sizes and colors. Some are bristled, some smooth skinned. All represent one stage of the life cycle of butterflies and moths—egg, larva (caterpillar), pupa (cocoon), and adult (butterfly or moth). All eat irregular holes in leaves of vegetables and flowering plants; some eat vegetables and fruit. All are voracious and destructive. Moth larvæ shown: ARMYWORM or CUTWORM, HORNWORM, WOOLLY BEAR, LOOPER, CANKERWORM. Control: Hand pick or apply stomach poison recommended in chart. Use dusts on vegetables.

48 PESTS AND DISEASES Garden Care

SILVERED LEAF
If leaf is blotched with brown, reddish, or yellowish tones, examine its underside for evidence of RED SPIDER MITES. Look for silvery webbing and for tiny red, pink, yellow, or green pests, best seen through a hand glass. Found in summer on ornamentals, some perennials, shade and fruit trees; asparagus; bean and strawberry vines. Overuse of DDT-type insecticides destroys insects that feed on mites, encourages latter to multiply. Control: Hose off foliage frequently; spray underside of leaves with miticide (caution—some are lethal).

NIBBLED LEAF
If a leaf has great holes eaten out of it around the edge or on the inside, it is obviously being consumed by one of several chewing pests. Most of its visitors can be killed by a stomach poison or multipurpose insecticide. If holes are near ground level, bait for SLUGS, SNAILS; if higher in plant, apply controls for ROOT WEEVILS, CATERPILLAR, EARWIG, FULLERS ROSE BEETLE. Neat, circular holes in rose leaves are caused by LEAF CUTTER BEE that saws out circular discs for nest lining.

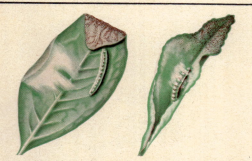

ROLLED LEAF
Opposite edges of leaves pinched together or tips rolled back and held in place with webbing; also, terminal leaf clusters distorted, with individual leaves stuck together. This is the work of the LEAF ROLLER or LEAF TIER, a small (⅜-¾") caterpillar that wraps leaves around itself for shelter and food during weeks of pupation in summer. Attracted to roses, fruit trees, broad-leafed shrubs, some vegetables. Control: hand pick and destroy; pinch leaves and kill hidden caterpillars inside; spray with standard controls recommended on chart.

POWDERED LEAF
Gray-white powdery patches on leaf, branch, and bud surfaces coupled with distorted growth indicate POWDERY MILDEW. Most likely to affect chrysanthemum, dahlia, phlox, rose, sweet pea, and zinnia. Control: Treat susceptible plants with fungicide in early spring to kill spores; at first signs of mildew, apply fungicide to arrest development. For some of the effective fungicides, see page 52. Use same controls for DOWNY MILDEW (yellowish blotches on top of leaf, gray fuzz beneath), sometimes found in too-humid greenhouses.

MINED LEAF
Brown or window-like blotches, or winding, serpentine tunnels found on leaves are sure sign of LEAF MINER. Found in leaves of vegetables, flowering plants, and ornamentals. Culprit is maggot of a fly that lays eggs on leaf surfaces. Upon hatching, larvæ enter leaf tissues and feed between the two surfaces. Once at work inside leaf, maggot is difficult to control because leaf protects it from insecticides. Control: Spray foliage to kill adults before they lay eggs; remove and burn infected leaves while maggots still in mines (visible against light).

Garden Care **PESTS AND DISEASES** 49

CURLED LEAF

Leaf that is tightly curled in from the edges owes distortion to insect or fungus attack. Clenching of leaf is caused by inner portion growing at normal rate while outer section is accelerated by infestation. In fruit trees—apricot, plum, peach—caused by fungus, PEACH LEAF CURL. Control: spray or brush fungicide on stems and trunk in winter to kill spores. On ornamentals, leaf curl may be caused by APHIS, LEAFROLLER (see control chart, p. 50); fuchsias may be affected by indoor pest CYCLAMEN MITE (treat same as APHIS) brought from nursery.

RIDDLED LEAF

If leaf is riddled with small holes, it is probably being visited by beetles, which favor almost all types of vegetation. Small shot-holes may indicate FLEA BEETLES; larger oval holes, DIABROTICA. Apply control to upper side of leaf (use dust for heavy infestation). Other possibilities: tiny holes plus black specks may be SCALE (use oil); small irregular holes may indicate small SLUGS or CATERPILLARS (spray undersides). Shot-holes may also be caused by fungus (use copper).

GALLED LEAVES

Leaves and blossoms covered with small, knot-like growths indicate infestation by MIDGE or GALL FLY. Commonly found on chrysanthemums, hence pest is often called CHRYSANTHEMUM MIDGE. In severe cases, plant will be twisted and distorted with galls. Pest lays eggs in plant tissues, larvæ form within galls. CONTROL: Remove affected parts; apply spray or dust. ROSE MIDGE attacks roses. Fly lays eggs in flower or leaf buds; maggots feed on them, cause them to blacken. Maggots fall to ground and pupate. CONTROL: Spray or dust plant and ground beneath it.

STREAKED BLOSSOMS, LEAVES

Blossoms that are streaked or have been eaten out inside are probably damaged by THRIPS, a nearly invisible ($1/25''$) winged insect. Thrips can also cause foliage to become distorted and deadened by rasping surface cells. Silvering of foliage sometimes resembles red-spider damage. Injure many plants, including gladioli, rose, chrysanthemum, and some trees and shrubs. CONTROL: Difficult to control because insects work only at night, hide in day. Use long-residue spray or dust on underside of foliage. To protect gladioli corms, fumigate with naphthalene flakes (3 wks. in closed container) or dust with DDT.

YELLOWED LEAF

If leaves turn yellow with veins still green or if leaves turn yellow in blotches, this is usually a sign of CHLOROSIS. This is neither a disease nor an infestation; it's a condition of nutritional deficiency. Many factors can make plant take on this unhealthy appearance, but most common is excess of lime in soil that prevents plant from absorbing sufficient iron. Common to: acid-tolerant plants, violet, agathea, rose, hibiscus, hydrangea, fuchsia, phlox, delphinium, hollyhock, foxglove, lemon and pear trees. CONTROL: See section on chlorosis in soil chapter.

PEST CONTROL CHART

GARDEN PESTS	Nicotine	Pyrethrum	Rotenone	Oil	DDT	DDD	Methoxychlor	Lindane	Chlordane	Dieldrin	Aldrin	Heptachlor	Malathion	Arsenates	Baits	Hand means	Miscellaneous
Ants					A			A	AAA	AAA	A	AA	A		A		
Aphis	AAA	A	A					AAA		A	A		AAA				
Borers					AA			A		A				A		A	
Bristly rose slug	A				AA	AA	AA	AA						AAA			
Cabbageworm			AA		AAA	AA	AA						A	AA			
Caterpillars			A		AAA	AA	AA	A	A		A		A	A		A	
Codling moth					AAA	AAA	AA	A						AA			Sevin—AAA
Cutworm					AAA			AA	AA	AAA	AA	AA	A	AA	AA		
Diabrotica		A	A		AAA			A	A	AAA	AA	AA	AA	A			
Earwig					A			AA	AAA	AA	AA	AA	AA		A	A	Sevin—AAA
Flea beetle			AA		AAA		A	AA	AA	AA	AAA	AA	A	A			
Fuller's rose beetle					AAA			AA	AAA						A		
Grasshopper								AA	AAA	AAA	AA	AA		AA	A		
Lawn moth		A			AAA		A	AA					AAA				
Leafhopper	AA	AA			AAA		A	AA		AAA	AA	AA	A				
Leaf miner	A				A		AA	A					AA	A			
Leaf roller		A			AAA	AAA	AA	A	AA	AAA	AA	AA	AA				
Mealybug	A			AA									AA				
Mites, red spider				AA													Aramite, Tedion, Kelthane } AAA
Oak moth					AAA												
Scale (hard and soft)				AA									AA	AAA			Malathion+Oil—AAA
Slugs/snails															AAA	A	Metaldehyde sprays and dusts—AA
Sowbugs/pillbugs					AA			AA	A	AAA	AA		A	AA	AAA		
Spittlebug	A				AAA		A	A	AA	AAA	A		AAA	AAA	AA	A	Flood/Wash—A
Tent caterpillar					AAA		AA	AAA	AAA	A	AA		AA				
Thrips	AAA	A	A		A			A	A	AA							
Weevil (root)				AA	A						AA						
Whitefly	A	A			AA			AA	AA	AAA	AAA	AA	AA				
White grubs										AAA	AA	AA					Malathion+Oil—AAA
Wireworm								AA	AAA	AAA	AA	AA					
PATIO PESTS																	
House fly		A			A		A	AA	A	A	A		A				Diazinon spray—A
Yellowjacket		A			AAA			AA	AAA	AAA	AA	AA	A				
Mosquito					AA			AA	AA			AA	A				

KEY:
AAA—Best control
AA—Good control
A—Some control

NOTE ON TOXICITY: All insecticides are potentially harmful to gardener if heavy concentration inhaled or contacts skin. Some are poisonous, but labels marked with poison symbol. Follow label warnings; avoid inhaling spray, dust; wash after using.

PEST CONTROL CHART

INSECTICIDE CHEMICALS

Following are the chemicals in common use in branded insecticides. The names listed are those in the formulas printed on each bottle or package. For indication of their relative effectiveness, see chart on opposite page.

Nicotine Sulfate
Organic insecticide, made from waste products of tobacco industry; a tried-and-true aphis killer. In the main, kills only soft-bodied insects. Has little effect on mature chewing insects, but if you use it the first of season and frequently, you'll get them in their early stages. Loses killing power quickly through exposure to air. **Nicotine is very poisonous when taken internally; can also be absorbed through the skin; wash hands thoroughly after using. Avoid excessive breathing of spray vapors.**

Pyrethrum
Organic insecticide used as contact spray or dust for quick knock-down; non-toxic to warm-blooded animals. Loses its killing power in a short time. Often combined with rotenone.

Rotenone
Organic insecticide (made from roots of a member of the legume [pea] family) has wider scope than either nicotine sulfate or pyrethrum; often combined with the latter. Has limited residual value; loses killing power in a few days, and so must be applied at frequent intervals.

Mineral Oil
Spray made from oil of very light lubricating type that has been highly refined and treated with special emulsifiers to mix readily with water. Principal control for insects protected from poisons by a waxy coating or by armor. Oil swathes these pests and smothers them; also kills larvae and eggs of flying and crawling pests such as whitefly. Of no value against mature, fast-moving insects; has no effect on chewing pests such as caterpillars. Sometimes lightweight oils are used in summer; slightly heavier grades for dormant spraying. With some brands, the same oil is used year-round but in greater dilution in summer than in winter. Use mineral oil by itself as an oil spray or in combination with other toxic agents to act as a spreader. Burns foliage if used in wrong dilution.

DDT
Well-known insecticide DDT is synthetic organic product, made up of elements chlorine, hydrogen, and carbon (dichloro-diphenyl-trichloroethane). Effectiveness due to contact and stomach poisoning. Kills a very wide variety of insects and leaves a residue that retains its killing power over a long period of time. Has two weaknesses: (1) it does not affect most aphis, scale insects, mites, and red-spiders; moreover, the latter two may actually increase as a result of its use because DDT kills off their natural enemies; (2) strains of certain insects, such as the housefly, have become resistant to it. There is still much to be learned about its long-range or cumulative poisoning effect on humans and animals; moreover it is definitely harmful to certain forms of wildlife, including birds and fish. **Do not use indiscriminately.**

DDD
Another member of the DDT family that differs very little from DDT as far as the home gardener is concerned. Manufacturers use it instead of DDT because its processing better suits their own methods and facilities and it is more specific on certain pests. Also shown on labels as dichloro-diphenyl-dichloroethane.

Methoxychlor
A chlorinated hydrocarbon and analog of DDT. It is particularly effective in the control of certain caterpillars, beetles, and miscellaneous garden insects. It acts largely by stomach poison and is usually included in products which are used as a residual spray on foliage which must be eaten by the insects that are to be controlled. It is considerably less toxic than DDT and is not effective on as wide a range of insects as DDT; however, it is more suitable to certain garden product formulations.

Lindane
Chlorinated hydrocarbon, distantly related to DDT. Contains chlorine, hydrogen, and carbon, in different chemical arrangement. Its action is similar to that of DDT, although its residual effects are not so prolonged. It will kill some insects more rapidly than DDT. Not effective on red spider or scale insects, but controls many other garden and household insects. Has a higher order of toxicity to humans than other chlorinated hydrocarbons, but does not accumulate in body tissues as do DDT and some others.

Chlordane
Another chlorinated hydrocarbon in the DDT family. Kills by contact and stomach action. Excellent control for ants, earwigs, lawn moths; effective on many chewing insects. Has staying properties that make it hold its killing power for long periods. In concentrated doses, likely to be toxic to pets and may sometimes temporarily retard growth of some grasses.

Dieldrin
A chlorinated hydrocarbon insecticide somewhat related to chlordane but of a considerably different nature with regard to its toxicity and general use. Dieldrin is primarily a soil pest insecticide for control of lawn moth, white grubs, cutworms, earwigs, ants, and other insects found in or on the soil. It is somewhat more toxic to humans than DDT and some of the other pesticides, and must be used with some additional caution. It combines effective initial action with long lasting residual action.

Aldrin
Related to dieldrin. Specific for certain soil insects such as wireworms, cutworms, and white grubs. It is used in certain products for soil application.

Heptachlor
Closely related to chlordane, dieldrin, and aldrin and—like them—is a chlorinated hydrocarbon that controls the same general type of pest. Its primary use is as a soil insecticide. Good residual action.

Malathion
Phosphate compound that serves as effective miticide and an efficient insecticide for a wide variety of pests; can be combined with other insecticides, but doesn't mix with fungicides. Loses its killing power after several days exposure. Has powerful odor. If used in high concentration, can be toxic to humans and animals.

Lead Arsenate
Inorganic chemical compound that effectively controls certain pests such as chewing insects. Limitations: Does not control sucking insects at all; if not used according to instructions, is likely to burn foliage of some plants; **is poisonous with long-lasting residue.** If used in the soil, it will remain active for many months.

Calcium Arsenate
Inorganic chemical compound, formerly used on truck crops, now mostly in baits. Has long residual life. Liberates arsenic more freely than does lead arsenate. Limitations: Likely to damage plant if too concentrated; more toxic to humans than lead arsenate because it is more soluble in water.

Poison Bait
Baits for control of certain pests commonly consist of a stomach poison, an attractant, and a binding agent, such as bran. Baits for slugs, snails, and cutworms contain two poisons: metaldehyde or meta acetaldehyde; calcium arsenate or fluorine. For slugs alone, baits contain metaldehyde as the sole poisoning agent. Sowbugs and pillbugs may be partially controlled with slug-snail bait. Grasshopper baits contain sodium fluosilicate or paris green. Some pests controlled by baits also succumb to garden dusts. Ant poisons—actually poison baits—are popular and effective.

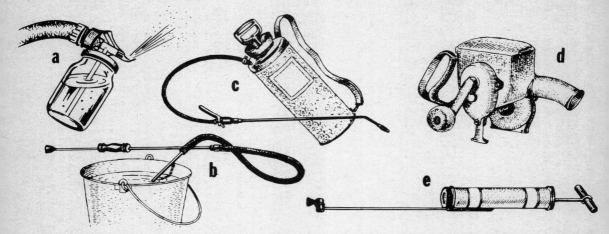

DEVICES FOR SPRAYS AND DUSTS: (a) Hose attachment for liquids or wettable powder. (b) Trombone sprayer for liquids or wettable powder. (c) Tank sprayer, available in many sizes and shapes; for use with liquids or wettable powder. (d) Rotary-type duster. (e) Plunger-type duster.

DISEASE-CONTROL PROGRAM

Not only do plants suffer from insect infestation, but, like all living things, they are also subject to diseases.

Vegetables and flowering plants can fall ill to a bewildering variety of ailments. This is because each plant has its own particular set of afflictions to which it alone succumbs, and few plant diseases affect more than one species. Fortunately for the gardener, a detailed understanding of these myriads of ailments is not necessary, because most plant diseases can usually be kept in check by following a few common-sense rules.

Types of Plant Diseases

Plant diseases fall into three types: virus, fungus, and bacterial infections.

Most serious of these are the rare virus infections—such as mosaic, spotted wilt, and curlytop—because they are incurable. They spread swiftly, but they can sometimes be arrested by removing and burning infected foliage as soon as it appears. Complete elimination of the insects that are known to transmit viruses—aphis, thrips, and leafhopper—will help prevent infection.

Bacterial diseases are likewise difficult to cure, but they are not too common in Western gardens. They are mostly seed-borne, and seeds raised and marketed in the West are largely free of harmful bacteria.

Diseases caused by fungus (microscopic plants that attach themselves as parasites to host plants) are well known to most gardeners. They include mildew, rust, leaf spot, and damping-off. Many of them can be prevented through dormant spraying, and most can be arrested if controls are applied at the first signs of spotting or grayish discoloration. Such symptoms usually appear on a warm day following a series of damp ones.

Control Practices

Here are ways to keep your garden disease-free:

1. Keep your garden free of litter, weeds, and fallen fruits and flowers. Where your plants have become diseased, pull them out and burn them. Do not add them to the compost pile.

2. Spray or dust at first appearance of insects that are known to carry viruses: leafhopper, aphis, thrips; and at the first appearance of those that excrete the honeydew that encourages development of fungus: aphis, mealy bug, and soft scale.

3. Whenever possible, buy varieties of seeds and plants that are offered in disease-resistant strains.

4. Rotate annual plantings as a general rule. If a bed becomes infected, plant a succession of different plants in that location for several years.

5. Keep plants healthy with proper feedings and watering so they can resist disease; but do not overfeed and cause them to become so succulent that they attract sucking insects.

6. Take care to set plants in exposures (sun or shade) that suit their needs, otherwise they may not be able to ward off disease. Do not set mildew-susceptible plants too close together; leave room for air to circulate among them. Do not plant them in cool, dense shade. Allow for change in the sun's path, for a bed that is sunny in July may be in full shade in November.

7. Prevent damping-off by treating seeds with fungicide and sterilizing seedbed. (See chapter on starting plants.)

8. To prevent fungus diseases, or to help bring them under control once they have started, spray or dust plants with chemicals. Among the many effective fungicides: sulfur, lime sulfur, Phaltan, dinitro capryl phenyl crotonate, captan, copper, karathane, and carbamates.

GOPHERS

The gopher is a garden trouble-maker that respects no man's gardening skill. In many sections of the West, gophers may show up at any time—even though you haven't seen one for years—and can damage the best tended of gardens. No single surefire method of control is recognized by any large segment of gardeners.

Gophers' Tunnel System

The gopher spends his entire life underground in search of food, working the year around in a system of self-made tunnels.

The main runways of the tunnel system usually run at a depth of at least 8 to 10 inches below the surface of the ground. In mining these runways, the gopher naturally must deposit surplus dirt somewhere. He does this in two ways. He uses dirt to fill old runways and he digs short, branch tunnels up to the ground surface, through which he pushes the loosened dirt in armfuls, forming the familiar mounds by which we recognize the gopher's presence.

The dirt is shoved out of the opening and distributed in a crescent-shaped pattern, so that, when the gopher is excavating, the mound extends only part way around the opening. The holes are not permanent external openings to the gopher's tunnel system. When he has stopped using a particular dumping ground, he plugs the opening from below.

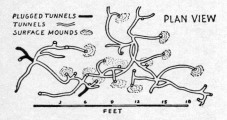

Viewed from above, the mound then will show a concentric rim, and commonly a slight depression, indicating the position of the branch tunnel.

How to trap a gopher

The easiest place to set a gopher trap would be down the branch tunnel below a surface mound. But, this particular lateral may never be used again. The gopher may refill it, trap and all, and move along. On the other hand, the gopher is pretty sure to keep open the main runway from which the branch was dug. It is there that you will get the best catch, setting two traps, one in each direction.

Gopher traps are not baited. They catch the animal when he passes through or over them. The Macabee gopher trap, in use for many years, is still considered the most successful trap. It is designed to spring when a gopher pushes against the flat trigger pan. The box type trap with a choker effect is also succesful, but it requires more digging to adjust it.

Insert the trap like this: If the mound is plugged, dig away the plug and the loose dirt in the branch tunnel with a long-handled spoon. Follow the branch down to the main run. They usually run at angles to the main runs and may be 6 to 12 inches long.

When the main run is located, enlarge the excavation so that traps can be inserted in the run. With a spoon, clean loose dirt out of each end of the tunnel, being careful not to disturb it any more than necessary.

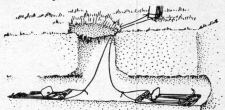

Fasten a long, soft wire or light chain to the trap and tie the other end to a stake outside the hole to prevent loss of the trap.

You can cover the hole or leave it uncovered. According to one theory, if light is let in, a curious gopher will come to see what is taking place. And, according to another, a gopher instinctively closes all open burrows to keep out natural enemies, and a trap placed in a lighted hole may be sprung by the dirt the gopher brings to plug the hole. If you cover it, use a large clod, a board, or a handful of grass.

How to poison a gopher

Poisoning, although less sure than trapping because you seldom find the dead gopher, is easier because it requires much less digging.

Farmers and some home gardeners have a regular method, called probing, for placing poisons. With a specially made probing tool, they probe

through the soil at various distances back from the opening of the lateral until they find the main run—signalled by a sudden drop of the probe as it breaks through the ceiling of the runway and hits the floor. Then they rotate the probe, or use the opposite thicker end, so that a hole may be made which is big enough to drop the poison through to the runway. This type of probe can be

54 PESTS AND DISEASES Garden Care

made at a metal working shop. The handle should be about 30 inches long.

Use commercially prepared poison baits, or pieces of root vegetables or dried prunes dusted with powdered strychnine.

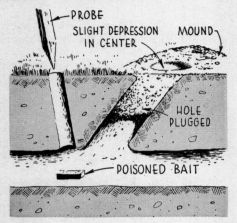

Methyl Bromide treatment

Methyl bromide is a gas which is packaged in liquefied form but which immediately volatilizes into an invisible, heavier-than-air gas when released. For home use, it is put up in sealed cans with a necessary patented dispenser. It kills within 15 minutes of application.

The gas is safe to handle when used as directed. True, it is a poison, but when used in the open air, there is only slight danger of fumes reaching the operator in concentration heavy enough to do him any harm. It is not inflammable. There is no danger of secondary poisoning to pets who might pick up the carcass of a gopher gassed with methyl bromide.

The danger in using methyl bromide is in possible damage to surrounding plants. If you are treating gophers on a lawn, be doubly sure not to squirt the gas on the surface; it will kill grass if it comes in direct contact with it.

Do not apply more than one shot to a hole because, under certain circumstances, overdosages can burn the roots of nearby plants and possibly kill them. It is not advisable to make an application within two feet of valuable growing plants.

Squirt the gas into fresh gopher holes. Ten cubic centimeters is all that is needed for one hole. Be sure to follow manufacturer's directions about how to use the dispenser. When you come to a plugged mound, probe around in it with the dispenser tube and squirt when you feel it drop into the gopher's tunnel. Close holes after inserting tube, but before dispensing gas, by pressing dirt in with heel.

MOLES

The mole's damage usually is limited to rumpling seed beds, disturbing plants, and making mounds on lawns. The mole never eats plants, but may eat sprouting seeds.

The mole spends most of its life looking for something to eat. In searching for food, he literally swims through the ground surface, making furrows which he is likely never to use again.

However, he has a deeper burrow system which he uses all the time. He disposes of dirt excavated from the deep burrow by pushing it straight up. The mound thus made is generally a volcano-like heap with no visible openings.

Moles usually are trapped in their surface runs, not in their deep burrows. There are three available traps which are recommended for trapping them—the choker type, the lateral-jawed type, and the spear type. In all cases, the trap is released by the upward pressure of the mole's body as he passes through a runway. In field tests, the lateral-jawed type has proven most efficient.

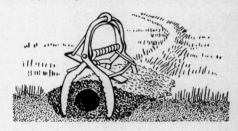

The big difficulty in trapping moles is to find a runway which is in use. You can step down on the soil of several runways, and if one is raised again soon, it should be a good one over which to set a trap. Straddle the runway with the trap, the trigger pan pressed against the earth at the top of the run.

There are several mole baits on the market, none of which is consistently effective. Moles' surface burrows are probed for dropping bait in the same way as are gophers' main runs.

Lye, paradichlorobenzene, or naphthalene flakes, placed in mole runways every 10 or 15 feet, have been found helpful in ridding the garden of moles. But in most cases this just sends the mole on into the neighbor's garden.

Methyl bromide gas is effective for moles if it is applied into the deep burrow which is found by probing the conical surface mound. Methyl bromide applied in surface runways is usually ineffective for two reasons: the mole seldom returns to his deep burrows through these channels, and the roofs of the surface runways are so thin that they allow all the gas to leak out before it reaches the mole.

Garden Care

PRUNING

A great day in gardening arrives when you can say to yourself: I am in control of the way plants grow in this garden. I can, with a little pruning now and then and a little pinching here and there, make a plant grow the way I want it to grow. With just the nails on my thumb and index finger I can direct plant growth mechanisms that are more intricate and more delicately balanced than anything man has ever invented.

You become a director of plant growth, and not just a pruner following arbitrary rules when you realize that every type of pruning is based upon one single, simple principle: Natural processes of plant growth are controlled by the flow of food to its various parts. You prune to divert food into the channels that will make the plant do what you want it to do.

Food manufactured by the leaves must move to the growing tips, to storage in the seeds, to reserve storage in bark of branches and trunk, and to the roots.

In this discussion of pruning we are bringing forth two concepts of pruning not fully developed in previous pruning literature.

(1) Leaves manufacture plant growth. The more leaves you allow to remain on the plant the faster and stronger growth the plant will make. Instead of trimming or pruning a plant right down to the basic form you want in a single operation, gradually remove growth that you don't want.

(2) A basic process that makes branches extend themselves in length is the production of hormones or auxins in certain terminal buds. These substances dictate flow of growth. By pinching and nipping, you can encourage or discourage flow of growth in any direction, and so reduce much of the usual winter pruning.

TIP PINCHING

Several mechanisms divert the manufactured food from one part of the plant to another. One of the most interesting and significant of these mechanisms—if you are to become a director of plant growth—is powered by the production of a hormone that controls flow of food to growing tips and buds.

Production of this hormone or *auxin* takes place in the extreme twig tip and youngest leaves of all branches. As long as a tip remains on the plant to produce auxin, food flows to it. If a tip is cut off or pinched out, diversion of food to that tip stops and most of its share of food becomes available to other growing tips and buds. Some of it is used by the buds just below the cut, and when those buds begin producing auxin one will take over and establish the flow of food to itself.

The growing tips are attractors of food to themselves. Or, looked at in a mechanical way, you could picture them as suction pumps at the ends of a distributing system of pipes. Picture a small tree as a network of various sized growing pipes through which food is flowing to all growing points. When you pinch the tip out, the valve partially closes and more food flows to other branches. The valve doesn't open again until other tips are formed and auxin is produced again.

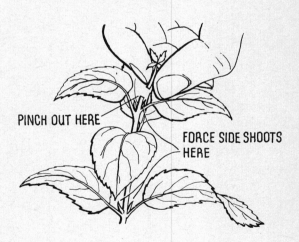

Whether you know it or not, you may have been putting this growth response to work in your gardening habits all along. When you pinch tips of side branches you speed up the growth of the central leader (main trunk); when you pinch out the tips of the leader and the main branches you speed up growth of side branches.

Watch how the two principles are followed in each of the following examples of pruning and shaping: (1) encouragement of food manufactured by maximum number of leaves possible; and (2) directing food diversion according to selection of buds. In every case some leaves are left to grow in areas where they aren't wanted until the leaf area of the new structure can take over the load.

56 PRUNING Garden Care

First, let's say that you want a tree against a wall that will give you this effect.

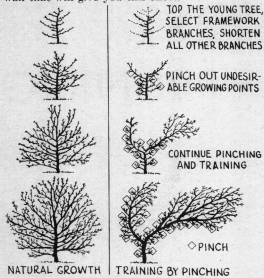

Starting with almost any tree that is not, by its nature, too rigidly upright or formal in growth you continually remove growing points that would take growth in the direction you don't want, and you allow the rest of the growing points to have their own way.

Espaliering uses the same principle of food control. You start with a two- or three-year-old tree.

1. Top the tree at desired height.
2. Cut back all branches on side against wall or fence.
3. Select the framework branches and the shoots that will become framework branches.
4. Shorten all other branches.
5. Allow enough leaf surface to remain to shade limbs and trunk and manufacture food.
6. Pinch out new growing points that you don't want as they form.

Pruning for Umbrella-shape

Here's another way to make use of the tip-produced auxins. Let's say you want an umbrella-shaped tree for the patio—a tree that you can walk under. And, let's assume that you choose a shade tree with a slow to moderate rate of growth. The fast growers, such as willow, poplar, Chinese elm, mulberry, and fig, are exceptions to the usual training rules. Under best growing conditions they are so vigorous that they will reach the height at which you want horizontal branches before you know it—regardless of what you do. You don't have to use any special care to maintain a full quota of foliage. With the moderate to slow growers, get the umbrella stage most efficiently this way:

1. Choose a type that naturally has a good share of horizontal branches—flowering dogwood, Washington thorn, silk tree, apple tree, almond, and the like.

2. First spring: Allow the tree to grow.

3. First midsummer: Select the upright shoot that is to be the trunk and pinch back any competitors around it; also pinch out tips of vigorous side branches. Repeat pinching wherever new growth takes over on the wrong place.

4. First winter: If the tree has formed strong overly-developed side branches, cut them back to a weak side shoot. Don't remove the summer-tipped lower branches.

5. Second summer: If main stem is 8 feet or more pinch out the tip. Tree should be tipped 1-1½ feet above the height you want the branches. Continue to pinch back tips of lower branches.

6. Second winter: Select framework of top branches and prune out other top branches. Shorten but do not remove side branches below the top.

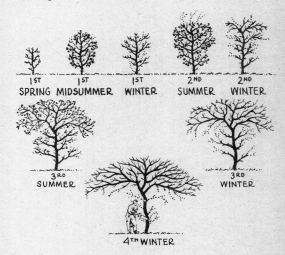

7. Third summer: Keep side branches tipped except those of the top frame that you selected in winter. Allow the top frame branches to develop as strong as they will.

8. Third winter: Supplement the second winter procedure.

9. Fourth winter: Top should have enough leaf surface to go it alone. Remove all side branches up to the point of branching.

SEED PRODUCTON CONTROL

Several well-known sets of instructions to the pruner take on significance when the pruner understands that the processes are really diverting food flow to fruit and seed production.

In many annuals for instance, seed production marks the end of the plant's growth. A petunia that is allowed to form seed pods will bloom itself out in a few weeks while a plant from which dead flowers are removed every day will continue to produce flowers for months.

Many low-growing perennials such as arabis, aubrieta, penstemon Blue Bedder, and the sun rose,

Garden Care PRUNING

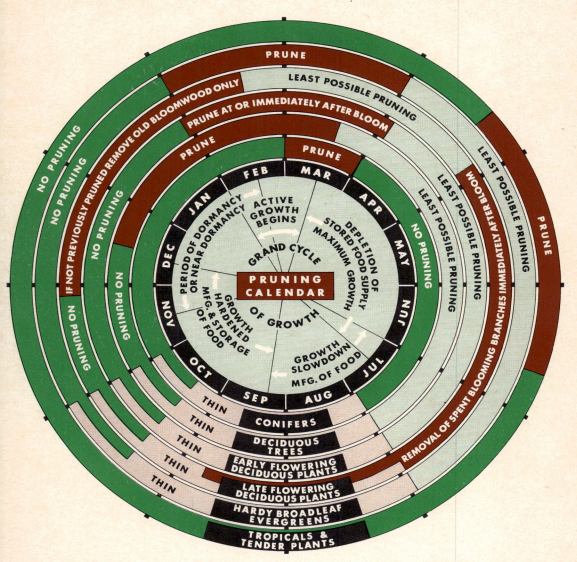

have the habit of blooming profusely in the spring and then diverting their energies to seed production. The shearing of such plants, cutting back enough growth to remove all seed heads, allows the plants to produce new growth, another set of buds, and scattered flowers through the summer.

DIVERSION OF STORED FOOD

A great number of pruning acts involve the diversion of stored food within the plant. To make use of this process you must know when and where the storage takes place in each plant you prune.

Every plant, evergreen and deciduous, has some reserve storage ready to take care of emergencies. However, with all deciduous plants seasonal food storage in branch, trunk, and root is a definite and distinct part of the grand cycle of growth. In dormant, leafless period, all the food that was manufactured by the leaves during the previous growing season except that lost in fruit, seed, and leaf fall has been stored.

In the first days of spring, growth begins at the expense of the stored material.

In April and May, for a considerable period the plant withdraws more materials from these storage tissues than it manufactures in the new growth.

In early summer to midsummer, the growth of new shoots slows down, leaves become mature. Total leaf surface is now capable of manufacturing enough food for new growth, and finally contributing to the renewal of new growth.

In late summer almost all manufactured foods go into storage—wood, bark, fruit, and seed. The only drains from total storage are those for slight top growth, normal respiration and root growth.

Pruning and pinching are keyed in with the cycle of growth in many ways.

58 PRUNING Garden Care

Pruning for renewal within the mature framework of shrub and tree is based upon diversion of stored food to productive parts by removal of unproductive portions of the plant.

A blackberry cane that has borne fruit is unproductive. You cut it to ground in order to give new canes their allotment of food that is stored in the roots. In this case we have 100% renewal every year.

Deciduous shrubs that grow out new stems from the ground should be renewed by removing old stems annually. How many to cut will generally depend on how many new ones are produced each year.

The new growth and the new buds may occur in approximately the same spot for several years, as with the fruiting spurs of cherry and apple trees. (See fruit tree pruning in chapter on home food garden.) Or the new growth with its new flower buds may take the form of long shoots, as with peaches, or with forsythia, or spirea, or any of the flowering shrubs with long stems and few laterals.

In spring-flowering shrubs the new shoots of the past spring carry the flower buds. The portion of the old shoots which have flowered are flowerless. An unpruned spring-flowering shrub would be a combination of new shoots from the ground and new shoots that elongated from old ones.

SPIREA REJUVENATION

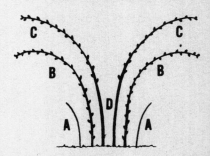

Generally the less vigorous a shrub is the more it needs renewal by selection of new wood. And generally the least efficient plants store more in roots than they do in stem and branch. The herbaceous perennial stores nothing above ground.

The woody perennial stores small amounts above ground. The perennial shrub stores still more above ground, and so on. The fast growing deciduous shrub holds the middle ground between the perennial and the tree.

To go back to the pipe system analogy, how much renewal a shrub needs depends upon the efficiency of its water system. When a shrub of many stems reaches its mature height many of its old stems show signs of what you might call water stress, and, as a result new developing leaves and flowers become smaller. Next the old stem dies and a new stem from near the crown takes over. When the plumbing system of the replacement stem becomes overtaxed, it becomes unproductive and finally dies.

If you renew inefficient stems before they show their age, the shrub will retain the vigor and fresh appearance of youth.

In each case you renew by directing the flow of stored food to the youthful stems.

RENEWAL AND BUD SELECTION

Renewal and bud selection go hand in hand. When and how you renew depends upon where and when the buds you want to grow are formed.

The blooms you see on early spring-flowering shrubs and trees are from flower buds that were formed the previous summer. All were formed on new growth.

Shoots (a) developed in the summer and formed no buds. Shoots (b) developed in previous spring and set buds along complete stem. Shoots (c) are growth from stems (d) that flowered the previous spring.

To follow the advice of pruning out all wood that has flowered you cut to the ground all stems but (a).

On a vigorous growing deciduous shrub that is pruned annually there will always be enough new shoots to carry the plant.

Summer-flowering deciduous shrubs and vines bloom from flower buds formed in the spring.

The plant enters the spring growing season with leaf buds that develop into stems that bear the flowering buds.

The rule of cutting out wood that has flowered is followed here either immediately after flowering in summer or in the dormant season.

Other spring and summer-flowering shrubs will develop more new wood from laterals and less from the base of the plant. Like this:

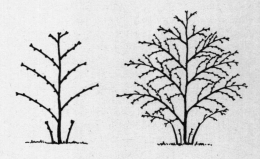

When such a plant has bloomed you cut out the wood that has borne flowers, just as in the case above, but you need to cut only to the laterals since new wood will form from them.

As such shrubs grow old the number of stems from the ground increases and proportion of the shrub that is without flower buds becomes greater.

Removing old stems to the ground removes the wood that has the least number of flowering buds on it and diverts the stored food in the roots to the new fresh growth.

Some shrubs are in their prime with 12-16 stems from 1 to 4 years old. To keep the shrub young and full of buds, remove 4 old stems and get 4 new ones each year.

A shrub that bears from new branches and forms no new stems must be renewed by either thinning out or cutting back or both. The need for such pruning is noted in the decline in size of flower and leaf.

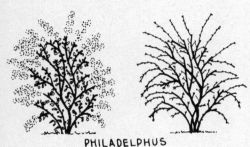
PHILADELPHUS

On other shrubs the entire top growth flowers on one year wood—the flowering peach must be cut back for complete renewal.

FLOWERING PEACH

Going back to the pipe system analogy again: The reason why cutting back deep will in most cases produce a more luxuriant growth than a light heading is explained by the differences of water systems. If you cut back to buds that are near the source of water, they will produce new efficient growth that will grow quickly to the height of the old stems.

Tall growth that is cut back lightly tends to develop more bushy growth and possibly more flowers but not the rush of new growth that a hard cutting-back produces.

If there is a reserve of food a deep cut will create a more vigorous and taller shrub.

LIGHT PRUNING

DEEP CUTTING

What you have here is a new set of water pipes, plus the push furnished by stored food, sending shoots higher than old cut-back shoots.

This deep cutting principle cannot be followed in warm winter climates with plants that refuse to go dormant. In such cases the food storage is not concentrated in the plants' lower parts and roots. If you remove the reserve in the stems there is no push to start the plant off on the grand cycle of growth. For example, see pruning section in chapter on roses.

PRUNING EVERGREENS

Evergreen shrubs and trees do not follow the same definite grand cycle of growth as the deciduous shrub or tree. There is no one-time mass movement of food out of the leaves into storage. The interchange between stored and manufactured food is constantly going on. The cycle of the evergreen, especially the evergreen fruit tree, is intermittent. It is seen in flushes of growth that appear almost any time. They usually occur with the increasing spring temperatures in April and May.

Pruning has the least effect on the processes of the tree if it is done just in advance of the flush of growth. Light pruning can be done at any time. Heavy pruning that is likely to produce new succulent growth should be done sufficiently in advance of frost date to allow the new growth to harden.

Pruning bearing oranges, lemons, and other citrus works out best in the home garden if it is done after the fruit is set. You can see how much of the crop you are cutting out.

Severe pruning of evergreen trees is measured by the amount of leaf surface that is removed rather than the size of the branch. It is less weakening to the tree to remove a single old branch with 100 leaves than to cut many small stems that carry a total of more than 100 leaves.

Prune according to type of growth. In handling subtropicals the above method is followed. With hardy evergreens, prune only to control form of the plant. Fast growers can be pruned more severely than slow growers. Occasional branches that outgrow the plant can be cut back or removed. As with all plants, tip pinching to direct growth saves heavier cutting later.

60 PRUNING Garden Care
PRUNING PRIMER
(Digested from "Sunset Pruning Handbook")

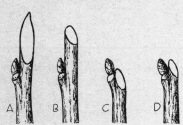

PRUNING CUTS, right and wrong. (A) Too slanting, exposes heartwood. (B) Much too long, causes die-back. (C) Too short, interferes with bud growth. (D) Ideal cut.

ANVIL-TYPE SHEARS are light, easy to use, have surprising capacity. Insert branch deep into jaws for best leverage. Never twist or turn while cutting; bruises branch, springs shears.

DROP-FORGED hook shears make a smooth, close cut, if kept clean, sharp (have sharpened by expert). Always hold thin cutting blade towards part of branch to be left on plant.

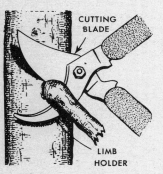

LOPPING SHEARS are used for branches up to 1 in.; compound-lopper will cut branches to 1½". Long handles give reach for pruning sucker growth, thorny shrubs, high branches.

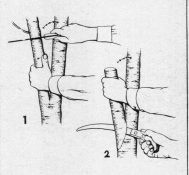

PRUNING SAW best for removing limbs. To prevent splitting, stripping bark, remove limb in 2 steps: (1) Cut off 6 in. above finish cut. (2) Remove stub with slanting cut. Dress wound.

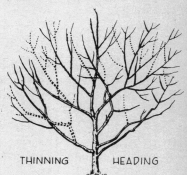

THINNING AND HEADING are two common pruning terms. "Thinning" is complete removal of branches to trunk or ground. "Heading" is cutting back branches to buds; always leaves stub.

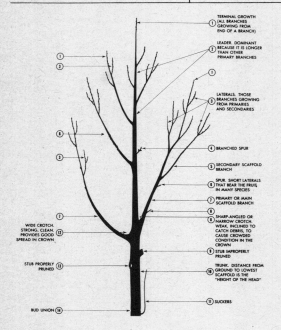

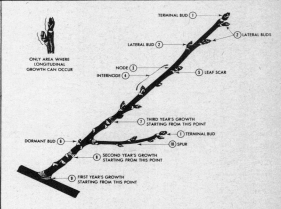

PRUNING TERMINOLOGY. Certain terms are used repeatedly in pruning directions. ABOVE are those applicable to buds. Branch grows from terminal bud (1); leaves, flowers, fruit from lateral buds (2). Leaves join stem at nodes (3); space between nodes called internode (4). Dormant buds (6) do not break at normal season. LEFT. Plant framework has leader (2) which dominates; primary, secondary scaffolds (5, 7) from which laterals (3) spurs (4) grow.

Garden Care

GENERAL MAINTENANCE

THE GARDENER'S YEAR
(For zone calendars, see page 366.)

Your garden is part of your life the year around. Many of the fundamentals of gardening lie in the knowledge of the month-by-month needs of your garden and in the proper steps to take during each period of the year. Each month differs slightly from the previous one and each has its characteristic gardening significance.

In back of the book is a guide divided into the months of the year and also into the thirteen Western climate zones where climate variations greatly affect gardening techniques.

In the zone guide, we haven't listed all plants that may be started in a given month or listed specific gardening procedures, since this information is contained in other chapters of the book. Nor is everything included that can or should be done in the garden. Not even a good-sized library could exhaust those possibilities. You will find information and suggestions here, however, and perhaps the inspiration for a comprehensive garden notebook of your own.

SPRING

With the arrival of spring, the speed of growth steps up day by day. The wealth nature has stored through the winter in trees, bulbs, and roots has not yet been spent. An early start on the routine garden jobs will pay rich dividends later, when spring really bursts out all over with its insistent demands. Now you should clean up, prune, prepare the ground, and look ahead to the planting.

In any location, spring tempts the gardener with a drawer full of seed packets. Seeds of summer annuals can be started in flats and set out when the weather and soil are ready. Plant summer bulbs; divide perennials; make cuttings. Nurseries will have tempting stocks of started annuals and perennials. Since the vegetable garden's abundant crops usually do not come in until midsummer, vegetables that ripen sooner in your climate are especially welcome and should be included in the schedule.

Spring is a good time to make and repair lawns and to clean up after winter storms. Invigorate lawns by perforating heavy soil and putting on a top dressing of peat and commercial fertilizer; or by feeding sandy soil with sifted compost and fertilizer. On thin spots, add grass seed to the top dressing. New lawns may be put in now when the warmth of spring and summer will speed the growth.

Throughout the garden, growth begins in earnest when the soil is warm. Begin your spring fertilizing program with this point in mind: the trick is to apply nitrogen at the exact time plants need it for leaf growth, not before. As lawns begin to green up, apply balanced fertilizer according to manufacturer's directions. Feed deciduous trees, shrubs, and roses when they begin to show new growth; azaleas, camellias, and rhododendrons before new growth begins. Give a light feeding to bulb beds to encourage more leaf production and to aid in development of bulbs for next year's bloom. See the chapter on lawns for a choice of year-around lawn feeding schedules.

The same warm days that bring out new growth in plants will stir pests into activity. Begin regular use of a multipurpose spray or dust. The earlier you start, the less troublesome are pests apt to be. Start spraying early for aphis even before you see the first one.

Spring pruning in the garden consists mainly of cutting back shrubs after the blooming is definitely over. If you cut or pick the flowers when they bloom, you will eliminate some of this pruning, but there will always be plenty of final trimming to do.

If you didn't cut back summer and fall-blooming shrubs to old wood after blooming ceased last year, do it now to force out new growth for the coming year's show. As soon as most of the hard frosts are past, you can safely prune fuchsias. Cut them back hard if you want them to bloom heavily this year.

When spring growth starts, it is easy to spot the dead wood that should be cut out of deciduous trees. Begin regular deep watering of your lawns and garden as soon as the heavy rains are over. Pay particular attention to newly planted annuals, and be sure that trees and shrubs set out during the past winter do not become dry.

62 MAINTENANCE Garden Care

Get after the weeds as soon as they become noticeable. If you must choose, remember that a sketchily planned garden well maintained is more attractive than a well-designed but untended one. Generally you can keep ahead of all weeds, if you hand-weed once every two weeks. It is work whenever you do it, but you can keep the upper hand if you start early and keep at it regularly. Don't overlook the maintenance jobs that take on added importance as your garden begins to flourish. Stake tall plants as they need it; tie up straying vines; pinch back new annuals to make them bushy and more flower-laden; thin seedlings; nip faded blossoms from plants.

SUMMER

Summer is, above all, a time to enjoy the garden and to delight in the rewards of creative effort. The planning, planting, sowing, and pruning that went into the garden during the cool months of the year show truly impressive results now. The work is far from finished, however, for maintenance is essential. In a matter of weeks, heat, dryness, and uncontrolled growth can make a shambles of the most inspired garden design.

No matter where you garden, watering is the principal garden task during the summer months. Make your watering count. When you water, soak the soil deep. Don't water too far in a sidewise direction from the root system of plants. Watering in the later afternoon or at night cuts down loss of moisture by evaporation. A summer mulch around shrubbery plantings, on flower beds, or in the vegetable garden will help to hold moisture in the soil and to keep surfaces looking neat and clean. Best of all, the mulch will help to keep down the weeds.

There are innumerable garden tasks that can be done while you are watering, the quick little jobs which pay off. First, you'll see the weeds. After water has soaked the ground, they are easy to pull. Keep an eye on the ground surface where you may find exposed roots to be covered with nearby loose soil or mulching material. Look under plants which form a mass of leaves at ground level. You may find some sow bugs to kill; snails and slugs will be around. Keep on the lookout for them and destroy them. Spot plants which need tying up.

It's a good idea to carry a pair of shears and a paper bag with you on your watering tour. Collect infected and pest-ridden leaves and growth as you go along. Cut off dead flowers as you come to them and drop them into the sack. Prune leggy growth and awkward shoots. If you see a few aphis-infested stems here and there on a bushy plant, nip them off below the infestation and drop these pickings in the bag. When the job is complete, destroy the sack and its contents.

Many plants need a midseason application of fertilizer. Pay particular attention to the shrubs that have already bloomed, for feeding now helps them to make strong new growth before winter and to develop next spring's bloom. Don't omit a midsummer feeding of lawns. Fertilize annuals and fast-growing shrubs. Look to the plant itself for clues on the amount to supply: rank, rapid growers need heavy feeding; slow growers, light. Heavy feeders are: lawns; roses; gardenias; leaf and cole vegetables; chrysanthemums; fast-growing annuals and perennials. Light feeders are: camellias; azaleas; slow-growing ornamental shrubs.

Pests become increasingly troublesome as the summer goes on. All-out control against them is important. Keep up a weekly prevention program with bait, spray, or dust.

Although the emphasis during the summer is on maintenance, there is still planting that can be done. Annuals can still be planted and sown for bloom next year. Vegetables started now will be ready to harvest in later summer and fall. There are bulbs to plant for fall and winter color.

If you would like to grow your own perennials from seed, the time to start them is summer or early fall. Sow in flats. Transplant the seedlings to a set of growing flats, and you will have young plants to set out by fall or early spring. Protect the flats from intense sun, heat, and dryness.

You can keep busy with all of these jobs, but you will undoubtedly have some lazy moments. Summer demands will taper off and there will still be some time left before the urgent requirements of fall take over your time. This is the ideal moment to take a quick inventory of your garden—to reappraise your spring planting in the hot light of summer.

The gardener usually plans his garden in late winter and early spring when the earth is moist, the lawns and leaves have the new look, and the planting fever is upon him. Too often he thinks of his garden only in terms of spring, failing to look ahead to the torrid mid-year when the bright color and cool greenness of a well-planned garden are more important than ever.

A midsummer inventory may reveal the need for some adjustments: more summer-blooming plants, or more fall-flowering subjects ready to take over when summer color passes. Consider the location of spring-planted shrubs. Does exposure suit them, or are they wilting under summer sun or growing spindly in shade that wasn't there when you planted them? Take note of bulbs that should be moved during dormancy next winter.

Consider maintenance. Is your garden getting out of hand? You may want to begin a gradual move from high maintenance material toward low maintenance shrubs and natives. Annuals may give way to perennials, perennials to flowering shrubs, lawn to ground cover and paving. Summer is a good time to take a long, close look at your garden with these points in mind. Note its shortcomings and take them under consideration when you plan future plantings.

Clean up orchards. Fallen fruit makes a winter haven for many larvæ, borers, worms, and fungus spores and is attractive also to field mice.

It's a good idea to dig ground now for beds that are to be planted next spring. After digging, place a mulch or layer of straw or leaves over the surface to prevent packing by rains. A topdressing on newly-cleaned garden beds in fall makes the garden look attractive and keeps the bed soft and loose for easy working next spring.

If you plan to do any potting or planting this winter, collect some soil before the rains start. Sift a good rich mixture of loam and compost. Add peat and sand if your soil is either excessively heavy or very sandy. Store the mixture in a dry place for use during the winter.

FALL

Fall is a period of transition in gardens everywhere. It is an ideal time for planting, for making new additions to the garden, and for the general clean-up work that will pay big dividends next spring. The activities which confront the gardener at this time of year can be grouped generally under two headings: preparation for winter, and advance planning for spring.

During the early part of the season, watering and summer upkeep will go on as usual. As the season progresses, the gardener will become occupied with fall planting. This is the time to fill the empty spaces with spring-flowering bulbs and perennials. Bulbs planted now will be certain to give rich rewards in the spring. Perennials will help to supply the ever-present need for permanent planting in the garden.

Try sowing some hardy annuals this fall. The plants may not look like much through the winter, but the roots will have grown well down in the soil by spring. The plants will be sturdier and bloom earlier than those sown in spring. Because the ground doesn't dry out as easily in fall as in summer, you don't have to cover the seed deeply at this time. Though some seeds may not germinate this fall, they will come up as soon as the soil warms a little in spring and still will be ahead of spring-sown seed.

You will probably find that some of your spring-blooming perennials are ready for division now. The general rule is to move and divide spring and summer-blooming plants in the fall, and fall-blooming ones in the spring. To supplement your overwintering supply of tender plants, make cuttings of their new shoots and grow them under protection during the winter.

Every week of the year, gardeners spend some of their time raking and cleaning. But when growth begins to reach the end of its annual cycle, garden clean-up becomes a major job and continues so until the last annual plant, fallen leaf, or dropped fruit is cleaned out. If you start removing the old material early and stay with the task all fall, it will be easier—and the garden will be healthier.

Clean out all dead or dying annual plants. Put healthy, pest-free material on the compost pile. Burn any infected or diseased plants, such as those affected with rust, and any woody plants which do not compost easily. You can compost weeds, but if they have gone to seed or are close to it, your finished compost will make more weeds when you use it as a topdressing.

Remove withered leaves and dead blossoms. Faded material of any kind is better out of the garden, both for trim looks and the general health of other plants. Give rose beds a thorough clean-up before bedding them down for the winter. Clip out dead wood, twiggy growth, and leaves or stems that are spotted or mildewed.

WINTER

Give the experienced gardener a cold windless winter day, a pair of sharp pruning shears, and a spray gun, and he is ready for one of the most soul-satisfying days that gardening can offer. It's a basic

MAINTENANCE Garden Care

day. Pruning prepares for the glory of spring. Spraying insures garden health for the coming year.

There is a lot of pruning to be done in gardens now while trees and shrubs are dormant. The first time you prune shrubs and fruit trees, half the battle is won when you overcome the fear of doing the wrong thing. You may make a few mistakes, but they seldom hurt the tree too much.

You can do certain pruning any time during the dormant season. The sooner you do it, the sooner your garden is ready for spring. Fruit trees, summer and fall-blooming deciduous shrubs, grapes and roses require regular winter pruning. Roses should be pruned at the end of the dormant season, since premature pruning can force frost-tender new growth.

Pests are now at their most lifeless stage, and with the leaves gone from fruit trees and other deciduous material, you have an excellent opportunity to cover them thoroughly with a strong dormant spray. Use dormant spray at maximum strength according to directions, but take care to keep it off evergreen material. If spray happens to hit evergreen plants, wash it off immediately. Be sure to get the job of dormant spraying done before new growth starts.

A top priority job for the winter months—when soil is in condition to be dug (not frozen or soggy wet)—is the planting of deciduous shrubs and trees, berries, and small fruits that you want to establish this year. Planted now, they have a chance to settle in their new locations before active growth comes on in the spring. The sooner you get them planted, the better. A short spell of warm weather will bring on the growth of fine, new roots. Some roots are usually damaged or destroyed in planting and the plants set back considerably until more develop.

Midwinter is also the best time of year to set out hardy evergreen shrubs so that the rains will give them the best possible start. In selecting trees, consider ultimate height, spread, and future root competition with nearby flower beds. Some evergreens, such as deodar cedars, are fast-growing and "hungry"; others are more modest in their growth and nutrient demands.

It is not easy to look at one's own garden objectively. However, this is a fine time to take that long, honest look. Every garden has at least one shrub or tree which should be removed. There's at least one corner where competition for growing space has reached the danger point.

This is an excellent time also to settle down and make a basic garden plan. Draw up a long-range program of development around which you can plan your activities for the coming year. Draw your plan to scale and keep it for permanent reference. With such a plan, you can pick random portions of your garden for current development and be sure that, upon completion, the individual units will fit harmoniously.

When you get the chance, do a little midwinter garden cleaning in order to keep up with the debris that gathers even at this time of the year. The effort will pay off in healthier plants when spring comes. You might spend a day spreading a load of manure around your shrubbery beds and spring-planting areas. Winter rains will leach the nutrients down into the soil to the root zone where you want them; and when the growing season starts, growth will be stronger and more lush.

HOW TO USE THE RIGHT TOOL

Whether much of the gardening you do is a pleasure or just sheer drudgery depends a great deal on using the right tool in the right way. Used incorrectly, for example, a hoe is a back-jarring instrument. When handled in the right manner, the aches and pains are taken out of hoeing, and the gardener is left with a feeling of satisfaction in a job carried through to a neat-looking finish.

How to Use a Hoe

Most gardeners find that they can work most efficiently with a hoe of medium size and of fairly light weight. A hoe with a large, heavy blade, which is likely to have a long, heavy handle, makes hoeing a tiresome operation. Also, because a large hoe usually has a thicker blade, it is more difficult to keep sharp.

Hoe forward, facing the section to be cleared. Hold the hoe so that the blade is at about a 30-degree angle; thus there will be a smooth, horizontal movement, not a chopping action which makes an uneven surface and jars the person holding the hoe.

Start by hoeing off 3 or 4 inches in from the front edge of the weed patch. After the hoe blade strikes the ground, pull the blade backward toward you, so that the ground is left clean and the cut weeds are deposited in a straight line. As you continue to work, pull back the weeds until there is a cleared section about 3 feet wide. You are then ready to start depositing weeds in another ridged pile across the weed patch. It will be easy to scoop up the debris from these parallel rows into a wheelbarrow or garden cart.

Spade vs. Shovel

The shovel was designed for the purpose of moving soil, and the spade for digging. Use them interchangeably, and you lose your efficiency.

The handle of a shovel is placed at such an angle that it is impossible to insert the blade into the soil in a vertical position without holding the handle far forward. Furthermore, the curved blade resists pressure when pushed down, does not cut in a straight line, and is uncomfortable to the foot.

On the other hand, the spade, being straight on all sides, slips down into the soil easily, is rightly built to support the foot, and may be inserted at a vertical angle. This results in a deeper, neater job of digging.

Garden Care MAINTENANCE

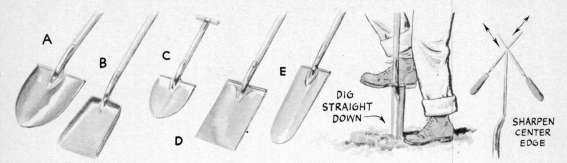

THE SHOVEL FAMILY. Shovel (A) is gardener's favorite tool for digging, mixing, and moving soil. Handles with curved shank easiest for mixing, moving soil; with straight shank, easiest for digging. The square-bladed shovel (B) useful for moving soil, mixing concrete, cleaning up around paved surfaces. Small trench spade (C) handy for close-quarter excavating. Standard spade (D) designed for digging trenches, pruning roots, spading soil. Favored by some gardeners over shovel for digging. Narrow spade (E) used for ditching, balling plants. HOW TO USE: To dig, drive blade straight down. Blade will work more easily in clay soil if kept clean, oiled, and rust-free. HOW TO SHARPEN: Use file to center cutting edge, but don't sharpen too thin.

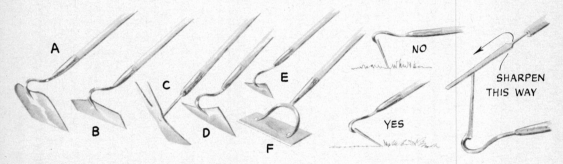

THE HOE FAMILY. A useful group of tools, designed for cultivating, furrowing, weeding. Standard hoe (A) obtainable with long and short handles, in heavy and light weights. Wide-bladed hoe (B) useful for light cultivation and for working under low plants. Good for cramped quarters. Two-pronged weeding hoe (C) is sturdily made for uprooting weeds with pronged side, breaking up dry soil with blade. Warren hoe (D) is designed for weeding, scraping, hilling. Used for making seed drills: when seeds planted, hoe is turned over and drawn down the furrow. Its "ears" draw dirt into furrow. Similar V-shaped hoe (E) is ideal for weeding or cultivating between plants. Scuffle hoe (F) has double-edged blade, is pushed along surface of ground to cut down weeds. Fine for weeding gravel paths. HOW TO USE HOES. Standard hoe should be swung with blade nearly parallel to ground. Chopping makes it dig in. TO SHARPEN, draw file across blade as shown above.

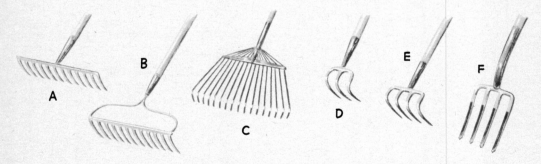

RAKES AND CULTIVATORS. Rakes are designed for breaking up spaded soil, smoothing seedbeds, renewing lawns. Level-headed rake (A) is sturdy and light, best for use in heavy clay soils. Bow rake (B) is springy and light, best for working lighter soils. Both types are obtainable in light weight forms. Grass rake (C), available in steel or bamboo, used for removing leaves. Bamboo cheap, short-lived, but gentle. Small, 3-pronged cultivator (D) is used for breaking up soil crust, light weeding and cultivating. Heavier type, known as potato hook (E), is useful for cultivating, but is heavy enough to stand-in for the spading fork. Used vigorously, it can prepare a planting bed in record time. Spading fork (F) is made for breaking up soil, uprooting rootstocks, etc. Penetrates deeper than spade, breaks up soil as it is turned over. Obtainable with straight or D-handles.

Many a good word may be put in for the shovel, however. Once you have learned to use it correctly —pushing it so that most of the effort is exerted from the hips down—you will count it among your favorite tools for furrows, for shifting soil from one level to another. If used instead of a hoe for skimming off weeds, it saves shoulders and back from many a jarring.

Care of Tools

Good care of your tools pays many dividends. Above all, it saves time and the cost of replacement. Keep a flat stick or a putty knife in your pocket at gardening time; scrape off masses of dirt from your tools as you work, and wipe them clean when finished. A file is useful for hoes and flat weeders.

One of the simplest and most effective methods of cleaning is to work the tool up and down in a bucket of oiled sand, and then wipe it off with a cloth. Or clean it first with kerosene, wipe off well to prevent rust, and apply a little oil or vaseline.

Pruning shears, lawn edgers, saws, and other small tools should have cutting edges sharpened and all parts cleaned and oiled at regular intervals.

The garden hose will give much longer service if treated with respect. Do not leave it lying in the hot sun when not in use. Avoid twisting, jerking, or pulling it around obstacles. Before storing it for the winter, drain out the water, coil in 3 or 4-foot circles, tie in several places, and hang in a dry, cool place.

A CANVAS AND A PLANK

A 5-foot square of canvas or burlap and a stout wooden plank are two of the professional gardener's handiest pieces of equipment. The home gardener can use them, too.

The square of canvas takes the place of a wheelbarrow to haul light trash, grass clippings, leaves, and prunings. It often holds more than a wheelbarrow, it's easy to rake onto, and the trash won't spill in transit.

When you want to move a balled shrub that is too heavy to lift onto a wheelbarrow, roll it on the square and drag it to the new spot without danger of breaking root ball or trunk.

Spread canvas on the grass when dirt or fertilizer has to be piled on the lawn.

The plank comes in as a ramp for a wheelbarrow, and lies on the lawn to prevent the wheelbarrow from cutting into soft or wet turf.

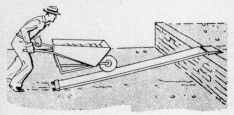

After digging a tree or shrub for transplanting, shove the plank as far as possible under the roots. Then use it as a lever to lift the plant out of the hole.

WEED KILLERS

In the chart on these pages are listed the weed control products that are available either at garden stores or at farm supply stores. In all cases, we made special note on how the chemical works: those that kill or knock down weeds by contact; those that kill weeds by intake through the leaves (translocate, systemic); those that kill weeds and seeds when absorbed in the soil.

Knowing how a chemical works is the very best guide on how to use it. If a tough weed is "killed" merely by contact (severe leaf burn), it may grow back again from its vigorous root system. But if the same weed is attacked by a chemical that it takes in through its leaves and moves down into its stems and roots, it may be killed forever.

Crabgrass can be taken out of a lawn with a contact chemical, one that moves through the leaves, or one that works on the seeds of crabgrass. No one chemical is better than others, but each has its best-time use because of the way it works, and you may prefer one to the other. For example, many chemicals that work on seeds don't discolor the grass, and that is important to many people.

Some chemicals act as a fumigant in soil to kill seeds. To be effective, the gas must move through *all* of the soil. Understandably, the method will not work in soil that is compacted or cloddy, nor in soil that is too wet (saturated).

APPLYING WEED KILLERS

Although a garden sprayer may be used to apply liquid weed killers, a sprinkling can does the job efficiently and is easier to clean. Clean all equipment thoroughly after applying weed killers. *Caution:* Set aside one sprayer for applying weed killers only. Do not use the same dispenser for insecticides, because traces of weed killer probably will remain in the equipment.

Apply weed killer on windless days to prevent it from being carried to nearby plants. Be careful about applying next to fences, because of possible damage to neighbors' plantings.

Below is a list of weed killers, with their uses, advantages, and limitations. The chemical names used may be found on the labels.

As new products are likely to appear on the market from time to time, check with your garden supply or nursery for latest information.

All of these weed killers are effective for their purpose. But they are tricky. And if used incorrectly or carelessly, they can be dangerous. Follow all precautions printed on labels.

WEED KILLERS USED IN ESTABLISHED LAWNS

Three types of chemicals are used in eliminating weeds in established lawns. The best known and most used are those that kill broad leafed weeds but do not harm grass—the 2,4-D and 2,4,5-T types. In the second group are the seed and seedling killers that prevent growth of crabgrass. Newest weed killers are the non-selective chemicals—dalapon, monuron—used in low dosages to kill specific weeds or weedy grasses.

Do not use a selective weed killer on a dichondra lawn, unless the label states that it may be used safely with dichondra (see *monuron*, below).

Chemical	Uses	Precautions and Remarks
2,4-D	Broad leafed weeds in established turf grass. Use only low dosages on bent grasses.	May be necessary to make more than one application. Selective. Translocated through leaves.
2,4,5-T	Broad leafed weeds in established turf grass. Oxalis and clover control. Also mouse-ear chickweed and speedwell in established turf.	May be necessary to make more than one application. Selective. Translocated through leaves.
2,4-D plus 2,4,5-T	Broad leafed weeds in established turf grass.	Necessary to spray regrowth for best results. Selective. Translocated through leaves.
2,4,5-TP	Broad leafed weeds in established turf grass. Especially useful for mouse-ear chickweed and oxalis.	May be necessary to make more than one application. Selective. Translocated through leaves.
Di-sodium methyl arsenate	Removes crabgrass from established turf grass. (Some good on Dallis grass.)	Lawn may show browning from overdosing. 3 applications 1 week apart will eradicate even old crabgrass plants and will kill or severely inhibit Dallis grass. Selective but kills by foliage contact.
PMA—Phenyl mercuric acetate	Removes crabgrass in turf. (Also good turf fungicide for brown patch, dollar spot, etc.)	More than one treatment will probably be necessary, since seed of crabgrass may continue to germinate throughout season. Selective but kills by foliage contact.
Lead arsenate	Crabgrass control in grass lawns.	Apply in winter or early spring. Irrigate. Selective. Kills germinating seedlings.
Chlordane for crabgrass	Crabgrass control in grass lawns. Will help control cutworms and sod webworms.	Application should be made in winter or early spring. Should be done before any germination of crabgrass occurs (in many areas, as early as February). Selective. Kills seeds as they germinate.
Monuron	In this product, a cut-down percentage of monuron is used to kill oxalis and annual bluegrass **in dichondra lawns only.**	Best to use every 6 months—spring and fall—to get successive generations. Light dosage of non-selective soil sterilant makes it selective. Inaccurate application or spillage can sterilize spots for long periods.
Dalapon	Kills Bermuda, Dallis, Johnson, and velvet grass, and other annual and perennial weedy grasses. Use as a spot killer of weedy grasses in lawn. Also used for spot treatment in dichondra, ivy.	Not highly selective. Do not use in root areas of established plants. Don't irrigate for 24 hours after application. Several applications may be necessary for best results. Spot treat areas as they start to show regrowth.

WEED KILLERS THAT KNOCK DOWN ALL VEGETATION

Chemicals in this group kill only the plants or portions of plants actually touched by the weed killer. Success depends on *thorough* coverage of all the weeds. Annual weeds are usually killed by one treatment. Perennial weeds usually require several treatments—sometimes as many as six or seven. Young weeds are most susceptible. Keep these materials off garden plants.

Chemical	Uses	Precautions and Remarks
Petroleum oils—	Destroys top growth of all vegetation. Can be used to kill seedling weeds in and around ornamental plantings. No build-up in soil (volatile).	Repeat treatment necessary on perennials. Also necessary on annuals as successive crops germinate. Annual bluegrass germinates throughout the winter. Use guard on spray nozzle to keep from wetting nearby ornamentals.

(Continued on next page.)

MAINTENANCE   Garden Care

Weed Killers that Knock Down All Vegetation (continued):

Fortified diesel or stove oils	Destroys top growth of all vegetation. Good for use on empty lots, roadsides, etc. Addition of extra chemicals makes the kill last longer.	Can eradicate Bermuda grass with repeated application. Not for use in small garden or where stain could be a problem.
Ammate	Annual vegetation, woody vegetation, poison oak. Knocks down quickly, but regrowth is likely.	Thoroughly wash all spray equipment after use to prevent corrosion. Quick knock-down of weeds is major advantage. Produces mild residual toxic effect in soil.
Amino triazole	Spot treatment, poison oak, perennial grasses, cattails, blackberries, other woody perennials. Substitute for diesel where no danger to ornamentals. To control annual weeds, use when weeds are in seedling stage. No odor or discoloring. Slow acting; be patient. Also available combined with Simazine, a soil sterilant.	Will kill or damage desirable grasses and ornamentals. Unlike 2,4-D, doesn't require use of separate sprayer. No residue. Effective up to time poison oak leaves change color. May be necessary to spray regrowth again, particularly with poison oak.

WEED KILLERS THAT PREVENT WEED GROWTH IN GARDEN PLANTINGS

These chemicals kill seeds as the seeds sprout, or kill the weeds after they are up—depending on the chemical and the use made of it. The chemicals must be carried into the soil by sprinkling or rainfall. Selectivity depends upon plant tolerance, location of chemical in the soil, and the weeds' special growth habits.

Preventive weed killers are for the gardener who wants to throw away both spade and hoe. All are used to prevent grass and weed growth in flower and shrub borders. Once this non-cultivation program is started, don't change to the spade-hoe-rake program. These chemicals will almost certainly cause trouble with roots of surrounding plants if spaded in. Do not use where you expect to sow seeds of plants later.

Chemical	Uses	Precautions and Remarks
Chloro IPC	Keeps down annual grass around woody and perennial plantings. Most effective on winter annual weeds and effective for only a short time. Not for use on lawns.	Cultivate, then sprinkle on soil, work lightly into surface. More effective on winter annual weeds.
Neburon	Controls annual weeds in some established perennial plantings. Good control for 3 to 4 months.	Used on irrigated rows of nursery fields, azaleas, canned and field planted nursery stock. Most effective in warm growing season. Do not use with annuals. Apply only to established turf.
EPTC	Kills seed of annual grasses and purslane. Controls nutgrass, Johnson grass, quack grass by stunting growth. Can be used around shrubs and trees.	If soil surface is wet, chemical must be mixed into soil within 2 hours of application.
Sesone	To kill weeds and weed seedlings in ground containing bulbs, perennials, strawberries, shrubs, trees.	Can be combined with IPC to increase range of weed kill.
Alanap 3, Alanap 20G	To kill weeds and weed seedlings in ground containing bulbs, perennials, shrubs, and trees.	Rainfall or sprinkler irrigation application is necessary to activate.

WEED KILLERS THAT STERILIZE THE SOIL

Use these chemicals where you want to prevent all plant growth for periods varying from months to years. The length of time the soil will remain sterile will depend largely on the chemical used, the amount supplied, rainfall, soil type, and composition.

Heed warnings against use near ornamentals. In the case of soil sterilants, there is a further danger of movement in the soil. These chemicals—like most weed killers—should not be used on sloping ground where surface drainage might carry them into the root areas of ornamentals.

Chemical	Uses	Precautions and Remarks
Chlorates	Prevents growth of all vegetation on non-planted areas.	**Fire hazard.** Keep off clothing. Sprayed vegetation flammable when dry.
Chlorates plus borates	Prevents growth of all vegetation on non-planted areas. Good under asphalt but not brick. Sterilizes for as long as several years.	Do not use where treated area may contain roots of desirable plants. Goes deep with rain to kill Johnson grass and Bermuda grass. Translocated throughout plants from roots.

Weed Killers that Sterilize the Soil (continued):

Diuron	Prevents growth of all vegetation on non-planted areas. Good annual weed control; not for deep rooted perennials.	Do not use where treated area may contain roots of desirable plants. Carefully follow directions on package label. Translocated throughout plants from roots.
Monuron	Prevents growth of all vegetation on non-planted areas. Good annual weed control; not for deep rooted perennials. Excellent for control of velvet grass.	Do not use where treated area may contain roots of desirable plants. Use where an area is to be free of vegetation for a long time. Translocated throughout plants from roots. Especially toxic to oaks.
Monuron plus chlorates and/or borates	Gives control of both annual weeds and most deep rooted perennials.	Do not use where treated area may contain roots of desirable plants. This is a good combination but fairly expensive. Translocated throughout plants from roots.
Sodium arsenate	Removes and prevents growth of all vegetation on non-planted areas.	**Poisonous.** Careless use killed 7 persons in California in the space of a year. Danger from residue in measuring container. Should not be used where treated area is used by children or pets. Once leached into the soil, it is not hazardous. Plan with care before you buy, use, or store arsenic in this form around the house.
Sodium TCA	Use to control Johnson, Dallis, Bermuda, or quack grass. Not a general sterilant.	Do not use where treated areas may contain roots of desirable plants. More than one application may be necessary.
Simazine	Prevents growth of vegetation. Use on non-planted areas. Excellent control for 6 months or more. Also available combined with amino triazole, a weed killer that kills all vegetation.	Primarily for annual weeds. Not good for Bermuda, Johnson grass. Do not use where treated areas may contain roots of desirable plants.

CHEMICALS FOR COMPLETE SOIL CLEAN-UP

These chemicals usually function as a vapor or gas, which diffuses through the soil. They have a relatively short life in the soil. The treated area can be replanted within a month or less. Success with soil fumigation depends on condition of soil and weed seeds in it. Irrigate deeply 10 days before treatment to get dormant seeds into growing condition.

Chemical	Uses	Precautions and Remarks
Carbon disulfide	Removes infestation of deep rooted perennial weeds. Also used to kill rodents. A specific control for oak root fungus.	**Flammable.** Best to have done by commercial pest control companies. Treated area should be rolled or packed immediately to seal vapors in soil. After fumigating, leave soil undisturbed for 2 weeks, then work the treated soil and wait 1 more week before planting in it.
Methyl bromide	Removes infestation of perennial weeds and kills many seeds in soil. Good control for Bermuda, nutgrass. Will not completely kill out seed of malva, bur clover, morning glory. Also controls soil diseases and nematodes.	**Poisonous.** Avoid inhalation or skin contact. Do not use where treated area may contain roots of desirable plants. Dianthus (carnations) are very susceptible to the bromine residue which remains in soil; do not treat soil where they are to be planted. Difficult to use on sloping ground because gas will "drain" to low point.
Vapam	A liquid material that removes all vegetation, kills many seeds, but not too effective on seed of malva, amaranthus (pigweed), morning glory. (Kills some seeds but not all.) Also controls some soil diseases, some nematodes.	Do not use where treated area may contain roots of desirable plants. **Avoid breathing fumes.** Do not get on shoes. Following application, wait 3 weeks before planting.
Mylone	A granular material that is carried by water into the soil to kill most weeds and weed seeds (possible exceptions: malva, nutgrass). Also controls some nematodes and some soil fungi.	Easy to apply. Do not apply under dripline of trees or shrubs. Apply evenly over soil with fertilizer spreader; in irregular areas apply by hand but wear gloves. Following application, wait 3 weeks before planting.
Cyanamid	Pre-treatment of areas to be planted to turf. Unlike the chemical above, it is not a fumigant but a temporary soil sterilant. Safer to use than most fumigants.	Allow 24 to 30 days before planting. Avoid deep cultivation after application. Supplies nitrogen.

70 MAINTENANCE Garden Care

FROST CONTROL

The assortment of winter weather on the Pacific Coast includes some marked differences from zone to zone—everything from frost-free weather to the complete freeze. Within the colder zones, the problem of plant protection and the methods used will depend on whether frosts or freezes predominate.

Here we are concerned with ways to trap stored solar heat as a frost preventive or to provide its equivalent with heat from heaters.

Heat Storage

The all-important phenomenon of heat which is stored during the day and radiated back at night gives the gardener many ways to protect plants.

During the day, the heat from the sun warms the soil and the bricks or concrete in walks, patios, and walls. How much heat is stored will depend upon the nature and depth of the material and the condition of the ground and its slope. A masonry wall will store more heat than a thin wooden one.

Radiation by night of stored heat in soil is often stopped by low clouds. Frost occurs most frequently on clear nights. On nights overcast with low clouds, the loss from the soil is balanced by incoming radiation from the atmosphere heated during the day.

Cold air, being heavy, moves downward, while warm air goes upward. Hillside gardens should be planted with this fact in view. Hardy, late-flowering, or late-bearing plants should be planted at the bottom of the slope, the less hardy at the top.

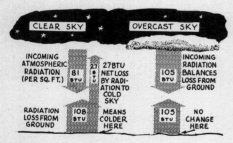

How to Trap Stored Heat

A canopy of trees, a porch roof, or a wide overhang will have nearly the same effect as an overcast sky.

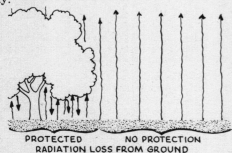

The principle of trapping heat from the soil explains why plant covers save plants from frost. The hotcap used as a protection for vegetables planted early does not work on the theory of keeping out the cold, but on the principle of conserving the warmth of the soil.

Its paraffin-treated cover allows the short waves of the sun to penetrate the soil during the day and slows up the loss by reradiation from the soil at night.

Use of plastic film

Two plastic films, polyethylene and polyvinyl chloride (vinyl for short), offer useful climate control possibilities. Strong and flexible, the films are impervious to water and most chemicals. They make good "slickers" for your planting beds and outdoor areas. As plant covers, they hold the heat and reduce temperature extremes. The sun penetrates the film during the day and heats both plant and soil; then the film holds in the heat at night. Plastic films deteriorate in sunlight within a year, so they work best as seasonal or emergency weather controls.

Both kinds of film are sold in rolls, and you have a fairly wide choice of widths. Polyethylene is slightly milky in appearance, less expensive than vinyl, and not as strong. When you need transparency and extra strength, choose vinyl.

One excellent way to use plastic film is to set up a temporary "greenhouse" under the eaves. To protect a planting bed next to a house, unroll enough film to reach from the eaves to the ground and cover the bed. On warm days you can leave the plastic rolled up. When cold is expected, drop the screen to trap the warmth and to prevent frost damage. After the danger of cold is past, you can take down and store the plastic. Used this way the film should last for several winters.

Plastic film also makes excellent individual covers for shrubs. For plants too large to be protected by inexpensive hotcaps, make a frame of bamboo, wood stakes, heavy wire, or coat hangers.

BAMBOO 6" INTO GROUND

Fashion them like an igloo or tepee (or pup-tent style if plants you want to protect are in rows), and cover with plastic. No part of the plant should touch the plastic, because the plant could freeze at the point of contact.

Use of Burlap

The burlap cover has been used with fair success on small trees for many years. It does not, however, work on the principle of keeping cold air out. The heat from the sun filters through the burlap and warms the soil around the plant during the day; and the burlap sides and ceiling slow up loss by radiation at night.

If the burlap is dropped directly on the leaves of the plant, the leaves touching the cover have no protection. They lose heat to the cold sky by radiation. This loss is not serious to a mature, densely-foliaged plant. The small percentage of its total leaf exposure affected is minor. However, a young plant with few leaves could easily suffer serious damage. Hence, the common practice of throwing an old sheet or what-have-you directly over a shrub on frosty nights may not give proper protection.

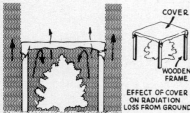
EFFECT OF COVER ON RADIATION LOSS FROM GROUND

A cover above a shrub is often just as effective as both top and side covers. Side covers, by shading soil around plant, lessen storage of heat from sun by day.

Use of Aluminum

An ideal method of conserving heat stored in the earth by day is to place a "ceiling" of aluminum sheet or foil over the plant at night.

The aluminum, being highly reflective, bounces back the rays radiating from the soil. Because aluminum is a poor emitter, as well as a good reflector, there is less heat loss by reradiation. Aluminum cover gives greatest protection, reflects and conserves heat from the soil. Remove during the day for the health of the plants.

Any Ceiling Helps

When plants "see" cold sky, they lose precious heat. The effectiveness of a "ceiling" is noted everywhere in freezes. Plants under eaves escape severe injury while those a foot away are burned.

South Wall Protection

A plant against a south wall of a house which has been warmed by the sun during the day will withstand lower air temperatures than a plant in the open.

Classic frost protection device: training tender vines on south wall, which absorbs heat during day, and radiates heat at night. However, a south exposure receives the early sun and if plants are frozen, damage from quick thawing may result.

Insulators

In all conservation efforts, it must be remembered that the soil must receive heat by day or there is nothing to conserve. Plant coverings that shut out the sun are of no value unless they are good insulators. Rare plants in tubs covered by heavy blankets night and day can be brought through a freezing spell. Plants covered by canvas both night

 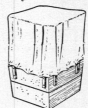

and day suffer damage, however, because canvas is a poor insulator. Canvas covering during the day cuts down on the amount of heat stored in the soil. Dry soil absorbs less heat. Soil when damp is a good conductor of heat; dry soil is a poor conductor. A long dry spell preceding a freeze cuts down the amount of heat absorbed by the soil. When this important night heat source is impaired, the cold air does full damage.

Orchard Heater in Home Garden

The orchardist protects trees against frost by supplementing the heat released from the ground with orchard heaters and by mixing cold and warm air with wind machines.

Orchard heaters have been improved to the point where heating can be carried out without smudge, smog, or smoke. The return-stack heater, developed by the University of California, returns inert stack gas to dilute the fuel vapor which then has time to burn completely.

The advantage of this heater, in addition to its cleanliness, is high radiant output. The heater is effective outdoors, over a 400-square-foot area or more, under calm air conditions. But the number of heaters cannot always be figured on a square foot basis. If your garden or small orchard is exposed on all sides, it would be necessary to have extra heaters around the borders.

The number of heaters necessary to heat a small enclosed garden, 40 by 50 feet in size, is a matter of experiment. Two principles must be kept in mind. Radiant heat source warms only objects which it can "see." Radiant heat travels like light —in straight lines. Also, if the number of heaters is such that the air is warmed to the point where it will create a chimney action, cold air will flow in a rate that will lessen the heating effect.

If plants are in containers and can be massed under a high tree or overhang of any sort, two heaters should give excellent protection.

Remember that part of the effective heat is radiant heat and therefore should "see" all the sensitive plants.

The home owner can use reflective material, such as aluminum, to direct and increase radiated heat. Of course, if the home gardener can improvise a ceiling that will bounce back rays from the heater, he will do a most effective job in frost protection. Heaters of any type placed in a lath-house-greenhouse or on a porch would be multiplied many times in effectiveness if a "ceiling" of aluminum could be placed over them at night. Heaters that furnish heat by convection are of questionable value unless the area to be heated is almost completely enclosed.

Warning on Frosted Plants!

Frosted plants reached by early morning sunshine are more apt to be lost than those not warmed until later. To effect a gradual thawing-out, sprinkle frosted plants with water before the sun reaches them. Also, place tender plants out of range of early winter sun.

Do not prune plants that have been nipped or blackened by severe frosts. Trimmed plants may appear neater, but pruning may cause even greater damage if a similar cold wave strikes later.

Wait to prune until after hard frosts are past and new leaf buds start breaking below the frozen portions of your plants. When that time comes, probably in late March or April, cut back to a green shoot below the dead wood. Some shrubs, such as *Eugenia myrtifolia*, may not show signs of life for as long as 3 or 4 months. But if there is life in the roots, growth will return, and you can expect normal-looking plants by the next year.

If your potted or movable plants freeze, take them in immediately before the sun has a chance to thaw them and place them in a shaded coldframe or lighted cellar where the air, although above freezing, is cold. There they may be allowed to thaw out as slowly as possible. Annuals which have become badly frozen can seldom be brought back to health, and therefore should be thrown away.

If plants of doubtful hardiness are left unprotected after their second year of frost injury, the probability is that they will lose their vigor and die. When possible, these should be wintered in a greenhouse or a coldframe to bolster their strength before facing the cold.

Mulching is another important winter protection for roses and many shrubs and hardy perennials. (See below.)

Frost warnings are printed in the weather forecast and farm sections of newspapers, and are released by radio. Local information about probable dates of frost may be obtained from your local branch of the U. S. Weather Bureau, or from agricultural colleges and experiment stations.

MULCHING

Mulching is nature's way of protecting plants from drying out. Wildflowers are mulched naturally by grasses and weeds in open meadows and by leaf mold on the floor of the forest.

In gardening, any loose material used to cover the soil for protection against drying out, crusting, rain damage, or extremes in temperatures is called a mulch.

The type of mulch you use will depend upon the plants you are working with, your soil, your climate, and the availability of suitable materials.

If you are growing plants which thrive on an acid soil—azaleas, camellias, rhododendrons—the preferred mulches are leaf mold, peat moss, compost of oak leaves. In addition to their help in maintaining an always moist soil, even in the top inches, required by these shallow-rooted plants, these mulches have an acid reaction.

Gardeners in sections where summer temperatures are high can save on work and water by applying 3-inch mulches of such material as manure, sawdust, straw, ground redwood bark, chopped hay, peat moss, leaves, or any similar material.

Such thick blanket mulches smother weed growth and lengthen the interval between waterings. If you are forced to be away from your garden from time to time during the dry season, a thick mulch is the best insurance against drying out.

All of the above mulches are composed of organic materials, and when mixed into the soil, decompose in time and thus increase the content of humus.

Experienced desert gardeners in the Pacific Southwest know that a mulch can often be the deciding factor in a plant's struggle for survival, for it keeps the soil damp and cool in summer,

Garden Care MAINTENANCE

insulates it against winter frosts, and keeps it from crusting. These mulches often depart from the ordinary. For example, we know a rose enthusiast in Kingman, Arizona, who uses a 3 to 4-inch mulch of crushed yucca fiber (from a local processing plant) around his plants. To this he adds a layer of coarse manure. Many rose fanciers in Phoenix report that a mulch of cottonseed hulls cuts down watering to once every 8 to 10 days, even during the hottest summer months. Cottonseed hulls are usually available in most cotton producing areas. In Tucson, we have seen grass clippings dried in the sun, then spread into the water basins around trees and shrubs.

When mulching a heavy clay soil, it is best to use a material that decomposes slowly, such as redwood bark or sawdust, or perhaps one of the inorganics, such as pumice or coal dust. When the last two are incorporated into the top layer of a clay soil—after serving as mulch—they stay put and permanently lighten the clay.

In light, sandy soils strawy manure and peat moss are most beneficial because they increase the water-holding capacity.

When working with clay soils, a mulch during the rainy season will save you a lot of work by preventing packing of the top inch of soil. A driving rain will pound the air out of the soil and leave a brick-like crust.

"Mulching" with Paper or Plastic

In this method, heavy building paper, tar paper, or similar paper is placed on the soil; use pegs or earth to hold it down. Holes are cut in the paper for the plants. Usefulness of the paper mulch depends on whether it solves the problems of the particular home garden. The principal advantages are: it gives effective control of weeds, smothering all varieties; and it prevents, to some extent, excessive drying out of the soil. Its disadvantages are: it provides a breeding place for insects; it brings a coolness to the soil which may be at times undesirable; and it creates difficulties in watering the soil under the paper. The paper mulch should be used only after all of these factors have been studied. If you have a rank weed growth or a kind of weed that is difficult to control, the paper mulch may solve your problem.

A black-pigmented polyethylene film, long used for certain agricultural purposes, is now also available in home and garden supply stores in 12, 18, and 40-inch widths. Small slits, at about 6-inch intervals, permit irrigation. Although the black film reflects some sunlight, it absorbs more of the sun's warmth than clear polyethylene film, and prevents re-radiation from the soil. It results in more and cleaner crops of fruits and vegetables that tend to rot when in contact with wet soil—strawberries, melons, unstaked tomatoes. Wherever summers are too cool for the full ripening of warm weather vegetables such as tomatoes and melons, the black plastic may make ripening possible by raising the soil temperature above normal. Like paper (see paragraph above) it makes an effective general weed killer. You can smother weeds with the plastic, and then cover it with peat moss, gravel, or a layer of soil to hide the black shiny material itself.

COMPOST

The compost pile, once considered to be an altogether necessary and worthwhile backyard fixture, is losing favor in many sections of the West. There are several reasons for this, but the basic and underlying explanation is that they simply are not compatible—particularly from a health standpoint—with the smaller lots which comprise so many of our modern neighborhoods. Unless handled with a high degree of know-how, a compost pile will breed flies—and bad smells.

A three-foot pile of grass clippings appears to be harmless. The grass on the surface turns brown and the pile, representing several weeks' mowings, looks like a suburban version of a haystack. But just stick a spade under the stack, turn it over, and see what's going on inside; it is not a pretty sight at all. Experiments have shown that as many as 3,000 house fly larvae (maggots) have been found in a *single pint* of decomposing grass.

If you own a large piece of property, in a region where compost piles seem to be an accepted part of most people's yards, you may wish to start one of your own. Below are some pointers that should help you to establish a compost pile that will be useful as well as inoffensive.

What Is Composting?

Composting is probably as old as gardening. In its simplest form, all it amounts to is piling up refuse, (grass clippings, leaves, certain kitchen material such as coffee grounds), covering it with soil, and leaving it to decompose. Months later, you spade it back into the garden, thus adding nitrogen and humus to the soil in much the same manner as manure.

Keep the debris in an enclosed bin where you can work with it easier. Some bins are shallow so low heat will enable earthworms to thrive in the compost mass. Others are tall, miniature silos, open at top and bottom. Some have solid masonry walls, and some are made of wire fencing. All a bin amounts to is a way of enclosing raw material while the microbes work on it.

The purpose of turning a compost pile is to put air into the center and to relocate material in the various phases of decomposition. The whole compost-making process can be carried out successfully only if there is a balance of moisture, air, and microbe action. In the center of the pile, high heat bacteria go to work on soft, easily rotted material. In the presence of moisture and air, they actually cook the material. Fungi, other essential

74 MAINTENANCE Garden Care

workers, come on the scene in about a week. They work out toward the cooler edges of the pile. Actinomycetes bacteria live in the medium warm parts of the pile and work with the fungi in breaking down the woody materials.

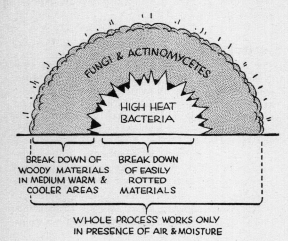

Every time you turn the compost pile, you rearrange the decaying material, bringing soft matter into the center of the pile and woody matter out toward the edges. If you are a weekend gardener, you will probably turn the pile once a week (try not to let more than two weeks go by). Don't forget to keep the pile moist at all times; without moisture, the decomposition process slows up and comes to a halt.

How Long Does Decomposition Take?

Most organic material should decompose thoroughly in 3 to 12 months. The rate of decomposition depends on moisture, type of material used, aeration (comes with turning the pile), fertilizer or manure, and air temperature (the process speeds up in warm weather).

Removal and Use of Compost

To remove compost, make a clean, vertical cut through the pile with a spade. The pile will remain intact, but the portion you remove will crumble. Sift the compost through a 1-inch wire screen or sieve. For a finer texture, use a ½-inch screen.

Use the coarse compost on flower beds and around shrubs. Use the fine compost for potting or seeding mixtures or as lawn dressings. It's a good idea to sift an extra box or two to save in covered bins for early spring potting.

Types of Compost Housing

Ingenious gardeners have erected many devices to house compost. Some are bins easily constructed of wood and wire; some are three-part units with removable front panels for easy access; others have circular wire mesh vents and a sprinkling system.

Look around your neighborhood and you'll probably find at least six completely different compost structures. If you understand the basic process of compost building, you can't go too far wrong in designing a compost factory for yourself.

For more information on composting, see the *Sunset* book, *Garden Work Centers*.

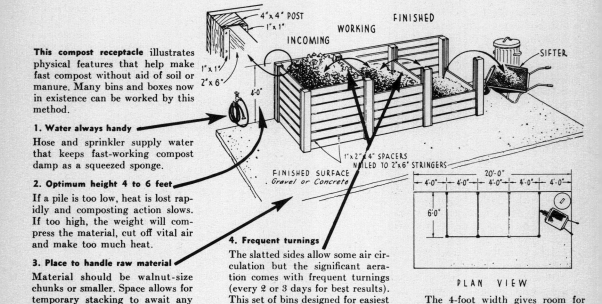

This compost receptacle illustrates physical features that help make fast compost without aid of soil or manure. Many bins and boxes now in existence can be worked by this method.

1. Water always handy
Hose and sprinkler supply water that keeps fast-working compost damp as a squeezed sponge.

2. Optimum height 4 to 6 feet
If a pile is too low, heat is lost rapidly and composting action slows. If too high, the weight will compress the material, cut off vital air and make too much heat.

3. Place to handle raw material
Material should be walnut-size chunks or smaller. Space allows for temporary stacking to await any necessary grinding, chopping.

4. Frequent turnings
The slatted sides allow some air circulation but the significant aeration comes with frequent turnings (every 2 or 3 days for best results). This set of bins designed for easiest possible access with manure fork.

The 4-foot width gives room for wheelbarrow and manure fork.

Garden Engineering

Garden engineering includes all the hard-headed planning and back-breaking work you have to do before you are ready to plant and watch things grow. It's like the foundation, insulation, plumbing and wiring in a house—necessary even though you don't see them in the completed house.

Magnificent stands of plants grow wild without any meddling by garden engineers. Actually, garden engineering is usually directed toward restoring the site to "natural" conditions, repairing the damage almost inevitably done by the building of a house—and all the other houses around it.

These improvements often involve hard labor, considerable cost, or both. However, every drain tile, length of pipe, concrete foundation, or piece of lumber that you install may repay you many times in convenience and enjoyment of gardening.

One practical piece of advice about garden engineering: When on your own, tackle only those jobs where failure is of no consequence. As an amateur engineer, you can do many things to insure proper garden conditions. But don't tamper with major alterations—changes in level, cuts, fills, and drainage—until you know what you are doing. If you have any doubts about your plans or ability, call in a landscape architect or contractor.

Houses have toppled down hillsides, hillsides have crashed into houses, friendly neighbors have become enemies . . . just because someone knew a bit—but not quite enough—about engineering.

WATER RUN-OFF

Probably 75 per cent of good garden development is in the field of hydraulics—handling water in motion. You create a problem in hydraulics when you put up a roof, and you add to it with each driveway, patio, walk, or any kind of hard surface that you install. You complicate the hydraulics on hillsides when you cut into a natural slope, create a fill by depositing the dirt somewhere, and even when you remove native vegetation.

When your neighborhood was still untouched by man, chances are that rain water was absorbed mostly by soil. Now, roofs and paved surfaces collect the water that would have been absorbed and concentrate it in small areas so that the soil can no longer absorb it. The result is run-off, erosion, and flooding.

One of your basic concerns, then, is how to collect this water and lead it away from the house foundation, from garden beds where it can drown plants, from low spots where it can make mud mires and from the face of steep banks.

Run-off water can be safely diverted in two ways: (1) tile lines or surface drainage; (2) sumps or dry wells. Most landscape architects favor surface and tile lines wherever possible.

Drainage Sumps

The primary fault with a sump (big, deep hole in the ground) or a dry well is that, however large it may be, it has a limited capacity. In addition, when rainfall is heavy and continuous, the soil around the sump may become saturated. Seepage then stops completely and the hole fills up.

Substrata in the soil may also make sumps impractical in many cases. Beneath the topsoil, there may be a deep layer of hard, impervious material. In extreme cases the hard layer may be very deep. The drilling of a hole 32 inches in diameter here would simply create a big tank, because there would be no seepage.

However, an experienced landscape architect will tell you of many jobs where sumps were the only way of getting rid of run-off water. In these cases the sumps had to be *made* to work—sometimes at considerable expense where holes needed to go very deep before they struck a layer of sand or permeable rock. A small pump installation has proved necessary to empty the sump in some situations.

Sumps for draining run-off water can be made by hand with a post-hole auger. You can drill as far as 14 feet or so if you thread a pipe extension into the auger. Refilled with gravel, such a hole should carry water away fast enough. You will probably need to drill several deep holes for adequate control.

In open surroundings, the best procedure is to bring in a power-driven auger rig mounted on a truck or jeep and drill to hit a stratum that drains well. As a test, drill a hole, run water into it and note whether it drains efficiently.

Drain Lines

When we recommend drain lines or surface drainage to take off excess water, we assume that you can lead water off to a street that has gutters and

76 GARDEN ENGINEERING

storm sewers, to a downhill drainage arrangement of some kind, or to a gully, ravine, creek, or ditch.

These drain lines work best when they are part of a garden's all-over grading. (*Grade* is the rate of rise or fall of a surface.) The best time to make a proper grade is before the garden goes in, or, in the case of an older, poorly graded garden, right at the start of the remodeling work.

On a flat lot, these are the principles of grading:

The grade must fall away from the house in all directions so that water will flow away from the foundations. The rate of the fall varies according to type of surface. On smooth paving you get adequate drainage with a fall of only one-eighth of an inch per running foot. A fall of one-fourth of an inch, or slightly more, to a foot is better for rough surfaces such as flagstone because they tend to catch water. On lawns, allow one-eighth of an inch or more fall per foot.

To grade a flat property where there are perhaps less than 2 feet of fall to work with, you must use stakes and transits and do an accurate surveying job to determine the high and low spots. A good bulldozer operator can blade the surface down to within a 2-inch tolerance of the staked-out grade.

At the low spots in the grading, the water goes to a catch basin and/or to an agricultural drain tile line leading out to the street.

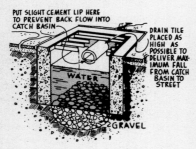

A catch basin is usually located at the lowest point of the property to be drained. It is a cement-lined square hole, with a layer of gravel in the bottom. Water flow is directed to it by a natural surface grade. Water is picked up at the catch basin and carried off the property through nonporous bell-joint pipes to an outlet. This kind of pipe, different from agricultural drain tile, is for transporting water only.

Bell-joints in this tile are usually mortared. If the fall is minimum ($\frac{1}{8}$ inch per foot or less) it is a good idea to install tees every 40 feet or so to allow you to clear out debris which tends to accu-

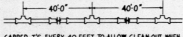

mulate where water flow is slow. Tees are capped. Y-joints are easier to get into.

Agricultural tile is like a dry well laid horizontally. It picks up water from saturated soil around it and moves it off. Best rate of fall is 1 to 2 inches in 8 feet. The tile simply fills with water by absorption, taking the course of least resistance.

There are several patented drain tiles with holes in the sides, but the commonest type is terra cotta "ag" tile, which comes in 1-foot lengths. Lay it on the bottom of the ditch, with rock over it, the joints set one-half inch apart. Lay a square of tar paper over the top side of the open joint, and put a couple of shovelfuls of crushed rock on top of it. If the surface is to be cultivated, cover the rock layer with at least 6 inches of soil.

TOPSOIL FILL

Transporting soil from one place to another within your garden, or bringing it in from the outside, is the answer to many landscaping problems. However, new soil sometimes complicates the garden's below-surface workings.

Here we consider bringing plant beds and lawns up to grade, making raised beds, and ways of avoiding certain troubles that may result from stacking soil on soil.

DIFFERENT LAYERS OF SOIL

When you put a layer of your garden's native soil on top of soil from the same garden, you don't change the natural arrangement very much—hardly enough to consider. It's the radical changes in soil strata—when you combine soils of quite different structures—that cause the serious drainage and rooting depth troubles. Any abrupt discontinuity in the soil profile may restrict the downward penetration of plant roots.

Regardless of what soils you combine, cultivate the native soil before adding new soil. If there are weeds or other plant growth on the old grade surface, and you bury it, you may form a matted layer of vegetation that will decay very slowly and possibly act as a seal against irrigation water. A considerable amount of vegetable matter would surely make earth above it settle when it finally decays.

The soil layer combination that leads to most troubles is a sandy soil laid on top of heavy clay, or colloidal soil. Water drains very fast through the sandy soil and stops when it reaches the clay. Clay takes water much more slowly than sandy or light soil (see chapter on watering). The backing up that results often makes a film of water through which roots won't pass at the junction of the two soils. As a result, roots stay within the sandy soil layer, foraging for all their nutrients and water there. If this soil is weak in nutrients, or if the soil is shallower than the roots would naturally go, the plants growing in it will continually need water and fertilizer, and they will exhaust them quickly in their limited root area.

When you put a layer of heavy clay soil over a sandy soil, you can count on trouble, too. A normal watering program that keeps the clay layer adequately moist isn't adequate for the sand. As a result the total rooting area is not capable of supplying water to plants.

Solution: Make an Intermediate Mixer Layer

There is a logical way to avoid the shortcomings of soil layering. Simply make an intermediate layer in which you mix the native soil and the introduced soil. A handy way to do this is to add enough new soil to bring the level of the bed or lawn area halfway up to the proposed grade. Mix it in thoroughly with the native soil below it, using a spade or a power tiller, and then fill with the imported soil up to the new level.

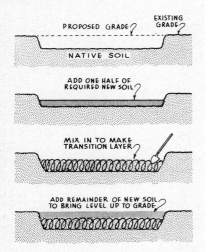

There are exceptions, of course. If you are adding only an inch of sandy soil to a lawn bed, the roots will go through it easily. The sandy soil will simply act as a germinating layer. But, even here, it's a good idea to loosen original soil first.

You should mix peat moss, pumice, or other water-retentive material, deeply into a very sandy soil, even before you make an intermediate mixed layer.

Where New Grading Goes Deep

When you add two to three feet, or more, of new soil to your native soil, the effect of the transition will be practically nil because few major feeding roots of garden plants go that deep.

There is one important factor you should consider when adding topsoil to a considerable depth. (It is something that a conscientious landscape architect will always take care of.) Before spreading the topsoil layer, grade the subsoil to get a steeper grade, particularly if you think drainage is going to be a problem. In applying topsoil over a very heavy or rocky subsoil, try for a fall in grade of perhaps one-half inch per foot, with one-fourth inch per foot fall on the topsoil grade. The water that gathers beneath the topsoil will drain off instead of making underground sumps.

THEORY OF THE RAISED BED

The characteristics of fill soil that make it a problem on a hillside can be used to advantage in the raised bed.

Remove a large amount of soil, tumble it up, and deposit it in a heap. Although it may soon crust up again and show the same physical characteristics that it always had, it actually doesn't settle down again into its original solid mass for many years. Meanwhile, water will penetrate it more quickly than it will penetrate solid, bare soil. This porosity is one of the factors that make trouble in untreated fills, but it works in your favor when you put soil into a raised bed. It is one way of creating the good drainage which is so often necessary for many plants.

Increasing drainage by way of raised beds has two beneficial results: (1) it allows all-important increase of oxygen in soil; and (2) allows a quicker warm-up of soil in spring, thereby advancing planting and growing seasons. Water-logged, heavy soil excludes air and remains cold, while porous soil without free water allows heat to penetrate.

Raised beds have a very definite place in some over-all drainage schemes. The one essential part of garden drainage, as outlined above, is taking water away from the house and foundations. Once this is done, you have protected your big investment. If the work and cost of draining water away from all the garden beds are too much for you, you can still have plants in the low spots by elevating planting beds above the rainy season water table.

In raised beds six inches deep or deeper, most plants will be out of harm's way should there be a garden flood, even if the true grade level is swamped. The composition of filled soil will insure good water conditions around the plants' feeder roots and root crowns, and the elevation will keep them above the flood level.

The esthetic values of raised beds are obvious. They give the garden a permanent design element —in third dimension—no matter what happens to leaves, flowers, and plant form. Since a raised bed has the third dimension, it is a garden structure the same as a fence, screen, or overhang. Its shape should fit into the over-all design of the garden.

In practical terms raised beds keep dogs and children out of plantings. Raised beds set in a pattern make alleys in which children can run, hide, and ride a tricycle. It is also easier to cultivate and tend plants in raised beds than those down at ground level.

HEADER BOARDS

Header boards have established their place in the Western garden. They make a neat demarcation between lawn and plants, they keep grass and weeds out of plant beds, and they hold water within the root area of shrubs and plants. They also make handsome edging and division strips in brick, concrete, or other garden paving.

Redwood and cedar are the most often used woods because they contain their own preservative. You can leave them alone, or treat them with any of the commercial preservatives. The difference in longevity won't be considerable.

For driveways and garden beds, two special mill finishes are sometimes available. Advantage is to save splitting and shredding of the sharper square

edge of standard board. Added milling costs are nominal.

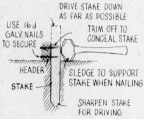

Above is one standard procedure for driving stakes and attaching the header board, in average soft soil. The stake should be driven level with the header board, then be bevelled off—a keyhole saw will help.

On header boards surrounding any planting area where you might use a power rotary tiller, try to place the stakes on the outside of the board so that they won't be disturbed by the machine blades.

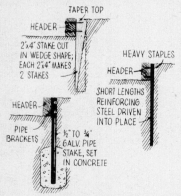

If you are working with firmly packed soil, you may want to try one of the suggestions above for stakes. They will drive into the ground more easily, stay put once they're there.

The galvanized pipe set in concrete is a special solution, applicable only where you want added strength in the stake and permanence in the header board.

If you have a slope, it's a simple matter to build a raised bed to give you a level planting surface. Omit the upper 2 by 4 if you prefer. A series of such beds would help to insure control of erosion on any problem slope.

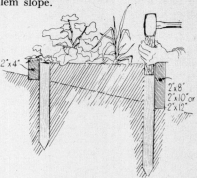

One alternate method of pounding any additional stakes after the board has been placed is shown above. Use a short piece of the stake material as a pounding block. You won't damage the top edge of the header. The stake will be below ground and still offer plenty of nailing surface.

For a foundation wall of rough concrete, consider raising a plant bed to within 2 inches of bottom of your siding. Plants will welcome the raised bed with its better drainage, but it will be an invitation to termites and damp rot in mudsills and framing.

Protect your house against both evils with a coating of roofing asphalt—or treat the concrete

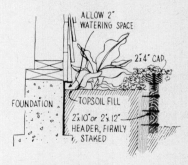

with a moisture sealer, then the bottom of the siding with a wood preservative. Where a termite preventive isn't used, plants in the bed will hide not only the concrete, but also any small termite tunnels, built from the soil level to wood framing or mudsills.

If your raised bed encounters air vents in the foundation wall, be sure to leave them clear. Block off the plant bed with a vent well made from small sections of header material or galvanized metal.

Curved Header Boards
There are few hard-and-fast rules for putting down a curved header board. It is possible to bend lumber from ½ to 2 inches thick. Your choice will depend upon how tight you need to bend the curve, and

GARDEN ENGINEERING

the quality of lumber you use.

Green lumber bends more easily than dry; thin boards bend more easily than thick. Small knots won't do any harm, but a big knot (especially one all the way across a board) will cause the board to break rather than bend.

You may have to experiment to find the size stock that will do the job. Width of most curved header boards is 4 inches, but thicknesses vary. For a radius of less than 10 feet, use lumber no more than ½ inch thick. For larger curves, use 1 or 2-inch stock.

Where the curve is made of just one thickness of lumber, splice all boards together before bending. Thus you work with a flexible whip of lumber which is as long as the circumference of the circle or the length of the curve.

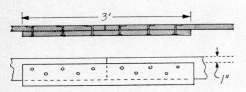

Some landscape architects use a number of ½-inch or 1-inch-thick boards laminated in place to a thickness of 3 or 4 inches. This adds strength. Also, a wider header is better scaled to the out-of-doors.

Anchor one end of the header against 2 stakes, as shown, or against the edge of a walk or patio. Then, bend into shape. You may have to stake the

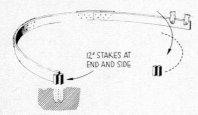

header temporarily on the inside, tacking it to the stakes, until the outside stakes are all in place. The important thing is that you first bend your header into the desired curve, *then* set the stakes around it.

CUTS AND FILLS

On a hillside place, the drainage problem is not so much how to get rid of run-off water as how to tame and direct its fast downhill flow.

The water runs down off the roofs, roads, paved surfaces, and thin soil from which vegetation has been removed. If water crosses land that has had its natural structure altered, it erodes and moves the soil, which is soft and unable to take water. Water has the same effect on loose soil concentrated in a pile or fill.

Because houses usually have to be built on flat surfaces, and because people like fairly flat areas for driving, walking, playing, and gardening, build-

ers and engineers slice into hills and make cuts and fills.

The cut and fill, being highly unnatural, is vulnerable to the elements in many ways. The two most vulnerable points are the bare cliff that remains after cutting and the filled-in area where the dirt from the cut was deposited.

The standard devices for protecting these two vulnerable points are: diversion ditches above the exposed surfaces to route water away from them; flumes or other devices to carry water over or under the surfaces where necessary; and revetment walls, diversion ditches, or catch basins (sometimes, sumps or dry wells), to take water away from the level surfaces as well as from the cuts and the fills.

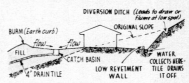

Naturally, all cuts and fills can't be handled in exactly the same manner as illustrated above. Below, we describe a number of modifications and developments of the cut-and-fill idea that landscape engineers have developed. You may find your situation described and illustrated here.

When you pour loose soil down a hillside or into a gully, some water will penetrate it and eventually reach the packed soil of the original grade. When water reaches this point during a heavy and prolonged storm, it begins to build up above the old grade, adding the weight of water to that of wet earth above it. This process goes on until the weight of the entire mass is sufficient to start it sliding.

As an experiment, fill a bucket with loose soil, then let water run in it until the bucket will take no more. Heft the bucket and see how much the combination of soil and water have increased the weight of the mass. Figure how many bucketfuls of soil there are in your fill and you will have a healthy respect for the potential power in a great mass of loose wet earth.

People who have lived through the lava-like menace of moving mud and silt need not be warned that the source of trouble is not always on the home owner's own property. Sources of all run-off water in the district should be suspect, whether they be 10 blocks or 10 miles away. Meanwhile, plan whatever protection you need right on your own place.

RETAINING WALLS

Some types of soil will never settle down, except behind strong retaining walls. Such barriers however are really a form of dam and should be properly engineered or constructed under supervision of experts. A good example of this thinking is the law in Los Angeles and many other cities that requires an engineer's approval on any retaining walls above 3 feet in height. This means any wall that is constructed to prevent material in an embankment or cut from sliding.

As an example of the "Hoover Dam" aspect of a well-made, large-size, fill-retaining wall, below are simplified details of a large, round, earth holding wall that was recently installed in a Western garden.

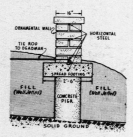

Below the 3-foot level, however, you can usually design and install your own retaining walls safely. The next illustration shows a type of low wall that amateurs can build by themselves with success.

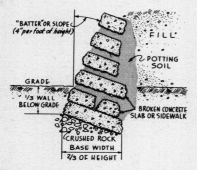

A fill should really be "constructed" like the wall of a house. Although you use only a single material, you should work to keep the structure stationary. Compacting with water is one way to bind the interior of the fill together.

A method called jetting does a thorough job of setting up fill soil to a good firm structure. The jetting tool, which you can make yourself, is a length of ¾ or 1-inch pipe, cut a few feet longer than the depth of the fill. It is attached to a garden hose by means of a coupling and T-connection. A valve controls the flow of the water at the tool end of the hose.

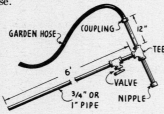

You poke the long pipe into the loose fill and turn the water on. Raise the jet in the hole as the lower levels become saturated. At the same time, work the pipe from side to side in order to flood as large an area as possible. When you see water coming up to the top of the fill, remove the jet and repeat the process in another hole 2 feet away. This may seem like a lot of work but the results are permanent. A good jetting job can make a fill compact enough so that you'll have to use a pick to get into it a few weeks later.

Where a slope rises steeply behind a retaining wall, it is best to cut it into steps. Place fill in horizontal layers not over 8 inches thick, tamping it fairly solid and using water sparingly as the fill progresses. (Beginning at the bottom of the hill, cut steps one or two at a time as the fill progresses.) End result will be *vertical* pressure on the horizontal steps, thus preventing fill pressure from acting along the angle of the slope with the possibility of overturning the retaining wall.

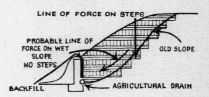

If it is necessary to carry water that gathers behind the fill's shoulder over the surface of the fill, do it with a trough, flume, or pipe. Where the water empties, make a splash apron to cut erosion from spillage. The splash should be on solid ground.

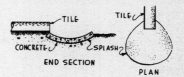

Catch basins and lead-off lines or agricultural drain tile lines in crushed rock ditches are used quite commonly at the base of a cut and at the rear of the level spot in order to drain off the water that gathers on this terrace.

A backfill, such as the one in the sketch near the top of this column, serves to take excess water from the fill soil. The backfill is of gravel or other porous material. Weep holes through the base of the retaining wall can also be made to deliver excess fill water to lead-off lines on the outside.

Diversion ditches at the top of the cut serve the same purposes as the curb or burm at the outer edge of the fill. They carry water around the exposed surface of the cut.

On a fill which has been properly constructed, planting is one means of keeping contours in shape. Root systems of plants are rugged and tenacious. Roots of initial plantings—fast growers such as grass or mustard—don't go very deep, but they start building reinforcement from the outside in. The grasses make a mulch into which you can start more deeply rooted plants, once grass is established. The foliage of any dense plant cover breaks up the force of raindrops. The litter and leaves that gather under the plants absorb the impact of rain and help the soil to resist the washing action of moving water.

Starting Plants

When a gardener sows seeds, sets out transplants, or tends a box of cuttings, he embarks on one of the most enjoyable phases of gardening. His is the pleasure of creating for the future—the adventure of challenging the unknown. In his mind, it is not a pellet that he drops into the furrow, nor a wobbly seedling that he sets in the planting hole, nor a cut stem that he sticks in sand—it is a fully grown plant, big and bright as the picture in the catalog or on the packet. And as the plant comes along, he feels a personal pride in its development—as though he had actually fashioned it himself.

When you propagate plants, you are really following all the methods that nature has set in motion for the generating, multiplying, and continuance of plant life. The wise gardener, therefore, duplicates natural conditions as closely as possible. For instance, it is natural for the petunia to drop seed on soft, moist, shady loam beneath the parent plant where it is covered and protected by a fallen leaf or wind-blown soil. In the same way, the gardener must carefully choose his soil and provide protection for the seed. Again, most plants are spendthrift in their seed production, so that no mishap will destroy the entire crop. For the same reason, the gardener sows more seeds than he expects to grow. Repeatedly throughout this book, you will notice that plant propagation and care are simply an imitation or modification of natural methods.

ANNUALS

Annuals may be started either from seed or from seedlings obtained from the nursery. Choice between the two methods is largely a matter of the gardener's convenience. If started from seed, some must be sown indoors in flats, some can be sown in the open. For discussion of the proper timing and recommendations for the method best suited to each plant, see the chapter on annuals.

PERENNIALS

Perennial seeds may be sown directly in the ground after the first frost in fall, or started in flats in the spring and the hardened plants set out in their permanent home in the fall.

Unlike annuals, perennials do not flower until a year or longer after the seeds are sown. Sometimes it takes as long as two or three years for the plants to mature. Most gardeners prefer to reduce their wait by choosing nursery-grown plants, but even these must have time to become established. As a rule, no matter how early in the spring they are set out, they will not flower until the next year. Fall-blooming perennials, however, may be purchased in gallon cans at nurseries in the spring and will sometimes bloom the same year they are set out.

OTHER PLANT MATERIALS

Directions for starting bulbs, shrubs, and trees are included in the chapters on these subjects.

Starting Plants
SEEDS IN FLATS

Many flower and vegetable seeds are hardy enough to be sown directly in open ground, in the location intended for them. But most plants—even the hardy ones—get off to a better start if sown in containers—such as flats or seed-pans—and seedlings are later transplanted to the open ground.

Starting plants this way has many advantages: it permits the gardener to get the jump on the seasons and to have his plants well established while the weather is still hostile; it speeds germination of seeds by providing artificial conditions that are more favorable than those outdoors; it lessens the danger of losing young plants to pests, birds, rain, or soil diseases; and it provides the gardener with a convenient method of tending to the needs of the germinating seeds.

Starting plants in this manner, however, requires a protected place in which to keep them, for the containers must be shielded from the elements by whatever means is most satisfactory under the natural weather prevailing when the seed is sown.

The following pages describe the principles in starting plants by this method.

1. SELECT A SUITABLE CONTAINER

You have a wide choice among containers suitable for seed starting. Almost any small wooden box, clay pot or tin can will do—if it is deep enough to allow seedlings to root and wide enough to prevent their becoming cramped.

Seed Flats

A wooden box large enough to be used for starting seeds is known as a "flat." The standard size used by nurserymen is 14½ by 23 inches by 3 inches deep. It is made of redwood or cedar, because these are rot-resistant woods. It can easily be built at home or one can be bought at the nursery, garden supply store, or lumberyard.

Although the standard flat is a very practical container, it is heavy to carry when filled with damp soil (40 lbs.). Some gardeners favor a half-flat—12 inches square or 12 by 18 inches—because it is easier to handle. It can also be dunked in a laundry tub, while the standard size cannot.

Smaller boxes than these are serviceable, too. Cigar boxes make good miniature flats, if provided with drainage holes. Cheese boxes will fit on a windowsill.

Clay Seed-Pans

Earthenware seed-pans (shallow pots) are preferred by some gardeners for sowing a small number of seeds or for sowing rock garden plants that will remain in their seedling container for a long time. Clay containers are more permanent, are easier to clean and store.

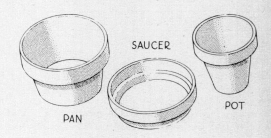

Seed-pans are shallow pots that range in size from 5 to 14 inches in diameter; 2½ to 7 inches in depth. A 10-inch pan is a good size. Pot saucers can also be used, providing the seedlings are removed from them soon after they germinate to prevent their roots from becoming cramped in the shallow container.

When only a few seeds are to be germinated, the ordinary 4-inch flower pot is entirely satisfactory.

Plant Bands

Another frequently used container for seed sowing is known as a "plant band." This is a small, square, bottomless box made of specially treated paper or

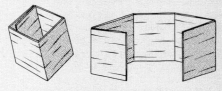

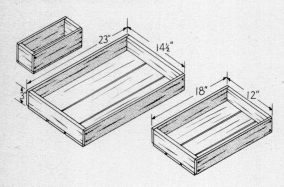

light wood veneer. Because of their shape, a quantity of these bands can be fitted into a flat (a standard flat holds 54 2½-inch bands). A plant started in a plant band can be set out in the garden without disturbing the roots. Sometimes the transplant is set into the garden with the band left in place and the band soon rots away. Usually the band is carefully peeled off and the cube of soil set into the ground. Plant bands are ideal containers for starting plants that are set back if their roots are disturbed, such as squash, cucumber, melon, tomato, morning glory, and poppy.

Practical substitutes for plant bands can be made from paper cups, cut-off milk cartons (pint), electric bulb cartons, or small clay pots.

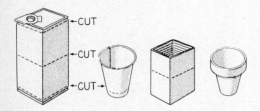

Seed Doll

Use of the seed doll—a cloth in which seeds are rolled—is a practical way of hastening the germination process, as well as lessening the dangers of rotting, soil crusting, drying out, and other hazards.

This is also a quick way of testing the condition of seeds left over from the previous year.

When planting in a seed doll, no allowance need be made for sprouting failures; only loss from insect damage need be considered in spacing the seeds.

Construction of a seed doll is simple. A long strip of heavy cotton or linen can be used. A dish towel, folded in the middle with the edges sewn up after the filler has been put in is satisfactory. The filler is sawdust, peat moss, or scraps of cloth. After filling the doll, moisten it thoroughly and lay

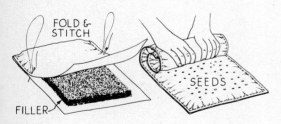

it out flat; spread out the seeds, and roll the doll up tightly. This gives the seeds constant moisture and warmth. Examine them often to see if they have germinated. When the seeds sprout, prick out to a transplanting flat (see below) or into a prepared seed row in the garden.

2. PREPARE CONTAINER FOR PLANTING

Before you fill your flat or seed-pan with seed compost, you should follow some preliminary steps to make sure that the container itself will not hinder the seed in germinating. Such interference might come from fungus spores or insect pests harbored in the container, or it might be due to inadequate drainage provisions that would encourage damping-off.

Damping-Off Disease

Damping-off is a complex, soil-borne disease that destroys seedlings when they first poke their leaves above ground. Once the seedlings sprout their true leaves, the danger is usually passed. It occurs when three conditions are present:

1. The damping-off fungi are present, either in the soil or with the seed.
2. The soil is kept too damp.
3. Not enough air reaches the surface of the seed-bed.

These conditions can be controlled by: (1) disinfecting seeds and/or sterilizing the soil, or by sowing in a naturally sterile medium, such as sand, expanded mica, or sphagnum moss (see SEED COMPOST below); (2) by carefully withholding water from the seed flat; and (3) by raising the covering occasionally to let air into the seed-bed. (See step 6 below.)

Damping-off disease also affects seeds sown in open ground and in coldframes. See discussion under these topics below.

Cleaning Containers

To clean clay pots or pans, place them in a tub and pour over them hot soapy water to which household bleach has been added; scrub with a stiff brush; rinse with plain water; and let dry thoroughly to evaporate bleach.

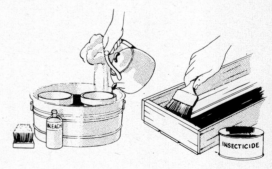

To clean flats, brush out old dirt and scrub with plain water and stiff brush. Set in full sun for two or three days. As an added precaution, you can brush an insecticide solution into the corners and joints.

If you have been having trouble with soil pests, such as nematode or wireworm, you may want to take stronger measures and fumigate the containers. Small flats, pots, or seed-pans may be placed in an air-tight drum with a fumigant. Flats may be stacked, covered with an air-tight canvas or plastic sheet, and fumigated with methyl bromide. (See chapter on pests and diseases.)

84 SEEDS IN FLATS   Starting Plants

Provide for Drainage

Although the starting compost is naturally porous and self-draining, the container in which it is put should allow water to pass through. This is particularly necessary if the seeds are slow and have to spend several weeks in the container.

Clay pans or pots should have a drain hole. The bottom boards of flats should be set slightly apart, and if they are not, several ¾-inch holes should be drilled through them. Wooden boxes with solid bottoms—e.g., cheese or cigar boxes—should likewise be drilled.

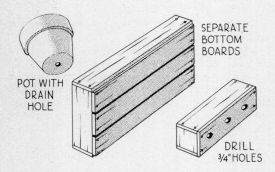

In addition, a ½-inch layer of drainage material should be spread over the bottom of the flat before the seed compost is added. Such a layer may consist of gravel, crushed brick (obtainable from roofing contractors), sphagnum moss, or broken pot shards. If the bottom slats on a flat are too far apart, cover with newspaper before putting in drainage material. Slash the paper in two or three places over the wood to let water pass.

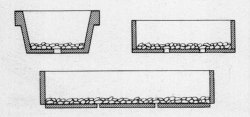

3. PREPARE THE SEED-BED

Many seeds can be successfully germinated in any sandy topsoil or any mixtures containing soil, if precautions are taken to supply the proper conditions of heat and moisture and to prevent the surface from crusting over. Generally, however, it pays to prepare a special mixture, tailored to the needs of germinating seeds.

Requirements for a good seed compost are simple: It should be free of weed seeds, fungus spores, and garden pests; and it should be sufficiently porous to allow the delicate rootlets to penetrate and to admit air and moisture.

Seed compost need not be particularly rich. The seed carries within itself all the food it needs for germination. It does not start to draw food from the soil until it grows its first set of true leaves, and shortly after that stage it is usually transplanted.

Seed Compost

Here's the recipe for a standard compost, suitable for a wide range of seeds:

1 part loam
1 part clean river sand
1 part leaf mold or peat moss

Work loam and leaf mold or peat through ¼ or ½-inch mesh screen before blending. Mix ingredients thoroughly.

For acid-tolerant plants, use:
1 part clean river sand
1 part sifted leaf mold or peat moss

For drought-resistant types, such as desert plants, sow in a straight river sand or a 50-50 mixture of sand and pumice.

For seeds that have a strong tendency to damp-off, use expanded mica, sand, or sphagnum moss. The latter should be worked through a ½-inch wire screen.

Sterilizing Soil

If you have reason to believe that the soil used in your seed compost may be harboring spores or pests, or if you simply like to be on the safe side, you can sterilize the seed mixture.

One method is to bake the mixture in an oven at 160° to 180° for 2 hours. Another is to saturate the soil with a solution of 1 part formalin to 5 or 6 parts water. When this treatment is used, the seeds should not be sown in the mixture until 24 to 48 hours afterward. Or the soil may be fumigated, as described in the chapter on pests and diseases.

Filling Flat or Pan

Sift the compost into the flat on top of the drainage layer described above. With fingers work it in well, especially around edges and in corners. Tap or

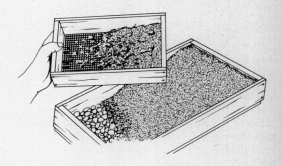

jostle the flat to settle the soil, then tamp it level and firm with a block, brick, float or the palm of your hand so it comes to about ½ inch below the top.

Use a flat-bottomed jar or drinking glass to firm compost in a circular container, such as a pot, pan, or tin can.

To provide a very smooth surface for tiny seeds, such as primulas or petunias, add an extra sifting of compost through a fine sieve, or sift expanded mica, sphagnum moss, or peat over the surface. Press down surface again so it's smooth and level.

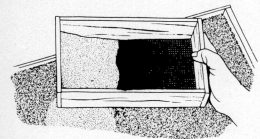

Watering
Soak the soil-filled flat thoroughly before sowing. If you wait until after the seeds are sown, you run the risk of washing them out of place.

Best method is to let the flat or pan soak water from below by placing in a basin partially filled with water. Place it so water is level with the surface of the soil. When the surface becomes damp, remove the container and let it drain for an hour before sowing.

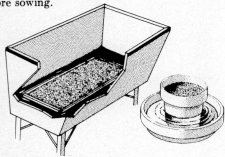

If you do not have a basin large enough to accommodate a seed-flat—and many gardeners do not—use a very fine sprinkler so that the level surface will not be disturbed, and apply enough water to saturate the soil completely. Allow excess moisture to drain off before sowing. Generally it will not be necessary to water again until after seeds have germinated.

Disinfect Seed
Seeds may be treated with a chemical disinfectant before sowing in order to prevent damping-off, seed rot, and other diseases. This step is not essential when you are sowing seeds in a sterile medium, such as peat, sand, sphagnum, or mica, or fumigated soil. However, some gardeners make seed treatment a regular practice.

Seed disinfectants should be used with due caution. If applied in excess, they sometimes cause stunting of seedlings or prevent germination. For an ordinary seed packet, use only as much disinfectant as can be held on the tip of a jackknife blade or a spoon handle. Drop powder into the seed packet through an open corner, shake together, then shake in a fine sieve to remove excess. Follow explicitly the directions that accompany the disinfectant.

Large seeds such as corn, peas, and beans can be treated in a jar with a lid. Shake seeds and powder together until seeds are thoroughly covered. Again, follow manufacturer's directions.

A jar is also a good means for inoculating legumes, such as beans and peas, with nitrogen-fixing bacteria available in powder form. These materials will often increase yield by encouraging development of the bacteria that store nitrogen in the nodules of leguminous plants. Often especially helpful to peas sown in ground in which they have never before been sown, as well as in soils that are lime-deficient or acid in reaction.

4. SOW THE SEEDS
The manner in which seeds are placed in the soil depends to a large degree on their size.

Fine Seeds
Some seeds are almost as fine as dust and should be broadcast over a smooth-surfaced seed-bed and pressed gently into the surface with a float. They are not covered with a mulch.

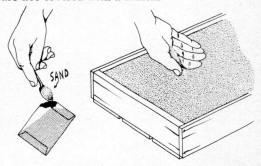

Sometimes, mixing fine sand with tiny seed will help in casting, for it will enable you to see where the seed falls.

86 SEEDS IN FLATS Starting Plants

Medium-Sized Seeds

Medium-sized seeds are often sown in miniature furrows called "drills."

To make drills, press a ruler or a straight-edged stick about 1/8 inch into the seed-bed. Space the rows about 2 inches apart. If you plan to work

with a quantity of seed-flats, you many find a gang drill, such as the one pictured, a convenience. With this device, drills for an entire flat can be made in one operation.

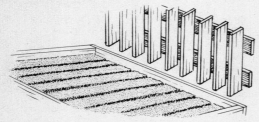

To sow seed, pour about a third of the contents of the seed packet into the palm of one hand, and with the thumb and forefinger of the other, scatter seed thinly but evenly down the drill. Keep them 1/4 to 1/2 inch apart and make sure that none touches each other. Plant more seeds than you need, because not all of them will germinate and those that do can be thinned to the most desirable plants.

If you are sowing several varieties in a single flat, identify the drills with wooden plant labels or green bamboo stakes, or write the name on the side of the flat. Also mark the planting date as a check against the anticipated germination time. When mixing different varieties in a single flat, it is wise to group plants together that have the same germination period so they will all come up at about the same time.

Large Seeds

Big seeds can be planted in deeper drills (1/4"), or broadcast over the surface of the seed-bed, poked in slightly with your finger, and then covered. Seeds for plants that do not transplant happily should be started in small pots, paper containers, or plant bands. This is a good way to start beans, peas, melons, cucumbers, and squash which can be transplanted only when the soil is not disturbed around their roots. Poke two or three seeds into the soil with your finger. When the seedlings appear, thin to the strongest individual plants.

Some seeds with very hard shells can be encouraged to sprout by soaking in warm water or nicking the shell with a sharp knife or file before sowing.

5. COVER THE SEEDS

Cover the seeds by sifting seed mixture through a fine sieve held above the seed-bed. Hold the sifter high enough so you can see where the soil falls.

Some gardeners prefer to cover with sand, sifted peat moss, sifted sphagnum, or expanded mica. It is possible that these sterile coverings might have some advantage in situations where damping-off may be expected; but a covering of the seed mixture itself is thoroughly satisfactory for most seed sowings.

Rough rule of thumb: cover large seeds to a depth equal to twice their width. As stated above do not cover fine seeds broadcast over the surface, merely press them gently into the soil with a flat, level piece of wood.

After covering, tamp down the surface gently but firmly with float, brick, or palm of your hand.

This simple step is important to make sure that seed and soil have total contact. This helps to insure a good percentage of germination.

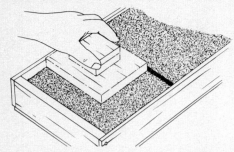

Next, cover with a pane of glass and a sheet of newspaper or use a doubled newspaper in place of both. Lift glass slightly on one side for ventilation. Place the flat in warm spot not reached by direct sunlight, such as a lathhouse, coldframe, the shade of a tree, or a basement. If set in the open, shade with burlap, plastic screen, or lath. As soon as the first seedlings appear, remove the covering and give the flat full light, but not direct sun.

6. CARE FOR GERMINATING SEEDS

Protect seedlings from temperature fluctuations. The less temperature change there is during the germination period, the quicker and more constant will be the germination and growth of seedling. Sharp changes of temperature or undue exposure may arrest or stop germination.

The moisture of the soil should be checked occasionally. Dry soil can stop germination; but overwatering can encourage damping-off. Generally, no watering will be needed until the seeds start germinating, unless, of course, the seed is very slow or the weather unusually warm. When watering is necessary, soak by immersion if possible.

If the seedflats are covered or are indoors, the seedling may suffer from lack of moving air. Petunia, poppy, and delphinium seeds may often be prevented from damping-off if they get sufficient air.

The first leaves that show are not true leaves but seed leaves (cotyledons). The seedlings should continue to get some protection until the first true leaves come; they are not ready for transplanting until one or two sets of true leaves are visible. Thin out seedlings as soon as their leaves begin to touch, to keep them from growing spindly. Remove weaklings and weeds.

7. PRICK OUT SEEDLINGS

The process of transplanting seedlings from the seed-flat to another flat is called "pricking out." This step gives the seedlings the chance to start development of root and leaf systems before the plants are left to fend for themselves in the garden.

Seedlings should be pricked out as soon as possible after they have two sets of leaves. Carefully remove the delicate plants so as not to injure them.

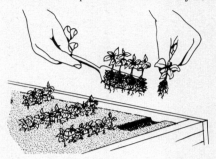

Use a sharp stick, handle of a spoon, tines of a table fork, or a knife blade to help get them out. Pry out a short section of the seed row, going deep enough to avoid breaking the seedling's roots. Gently break the seedling away from those clustered about it. If seedlings come up with their roots entangled, they can be separated by soaking the root ball in water.

Work rapidly and in shade, out of drying winds or drafts.

Transplant Flat

The flat to which pricked-out seedlings are to be transferred should be prepared for them in the same manner as the seed-flat described above. The standard-size flat will probably prove more convenient than the half size that many gardeners prefer for seed starting, because the transplants need more root room. The standard flat holds 4 to 6 dozen transplants, depending on the variety.

Compost for the transplant flat is slightly richer than the seed mixture. Here is the formula:
- 2 parts loam
- 1 part clean river sand
- 1 part sifted peat moss or leaf mold

Transplanting Seedlings

Punch holes in the seed-bed with a dibble—a stick with a pointed or rounded end. Poke the dibble down to the drainage layer, and space holes 2 inches apart each way.

SEEDS IN FLATS Starting Plants

Working quickly, insert the roots of the individual seedlings in the holes and firm them in with either the dibble or with forefinger and middle finger. If you use the dibble, insert it into the soil

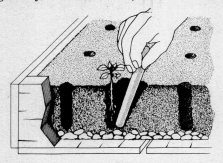

slightly to one side of the planting hole—at least ½ inch away from the roots—and press the soil against the roots. It is necessary to eliminate all air pockets, because the roots of small seedlings dry rapidly. If roots of a seedling are so lengthy

that they would have to be doubled over in the planting hole, cut them off with shears or sharp knife.

When the flat is filled, water it with a fine spray from a hand syringe to settle the soil around the roots and to freshen wilted stems and leaves.

If plants are particularly soft and subject to wilting, such as cineraria, cover the flat with a sheet of newspaper or another flat turned upside down. Keep it in the same location as the seed flat so there will be no pronounced change in temperature. Remove the covering when seedlings have stiffened up.

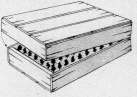

In about 4 or 5 weeks, the young plants will be ready to go out into the open ground. A week before planting, start hardening the plants by gradually increasing exposure to sun and air. Before finally setting in the garden, give them several days of full sunlight; and if they are going into a sunny position, hold back on the watering.

Starting Plants
TRANSPLANTING

Transplanting small plants from flat to the open garden is a simple, everyday garden task; yet, there are certain tricks in doing this that often make the difference between losing and holding plants.

1. CHOOSE RIGHT TIME OF DAY
Cloudy or foggy days are ideal for setting out plants, preferably in early morning. Next best time is the late afternoon, for the plants then have the night hours in which to recover from the initial shock of transplanting. This is especially helpful to zinnias, marigolds, petunias, and other plants with large leaf surfaces.

Do not let your plants get too large before you set them out. If they are allowed to remain in the flats too long, the root systems become intertwined and the plants suffer setback when the roots are severed.

2. BLOCK OUT FLAT
To avoid root disturbance in transplanting lift plants with as much soil as possible around the roots. Block out (cut in squares) the soil a day

ahead of planting. Use a wide putty or paint knife to keep root ball intact and to lessen the shock of moving. Water the plants several hours before setting them out.

When you are ready to remove plants from the flat, tip it on end and give it a sharp rap so the soil mass will slip slightly to one end. This will leave a free space at the other from which the blocked-out plants can be easily removed.

3. PREPARE PLANTING HOLES

Dig generous-sized planting holes, cutting the sides vertically with the trowel instead of sloping them inward. Work up the soil in the bottom to make a soft cushion for the roots to penetrate. If soil is on the dry side, run water into the hole slowly until the soil is soaked.

Set the holes far enough apart to allow ample root room. A 9 to 12-inch spacing is satisfactory for small to medium-sized plants; 18 to 24 inches gives plenty of scope to the larger ones. Remember that setting them too close together will start a competitive race among them for food, water, and sun. Planting distances are usually noted on the seed packet.

4. SET OUT PLANTS

Remove a blocked-out plant from the flat and place it gently in the hole. If the transplant is growing in plant bands or paper containers, remove them before setting the plant.

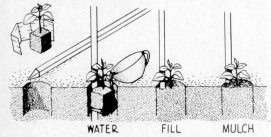

If the plants must be supported, place a stake beside each one at the time it is set out. Tomatoes, for example, should be staked early to avoid injuring the roots.

Place the plant in the hole—slightly lower than it was in the flat—fill in around it with well pulverized, slightly moist soil, and leave a shallow basin around the transplant. Water in thoroughly.

Next apply a mulch to conserve soil moisture. Use sawdust, peat moss, or rotted manure; or cover with a layer of dry soil.

5. SHIELD TRANSPLANTS FROM SUN, WIND

To prevent newly set out plants from wilting in warm weather, shade the transplants for a few days, or until tops stiffen and roots take hold. If

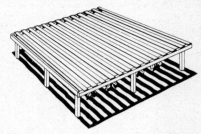

you wish to cover many plants, a lath screen is most efficient. Laths nailed to 1x2-inch ends make excellent shades and let through enough light for vigorous growth. A 4x4-foot panel covers 16 plants. The shade can be used later on a coldframe.

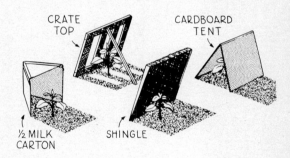

Wind is more damaging to plants than many gardeners realize. In the case of new plants, where the root system has not had time to establish itself, even a slight wind puts a strain on a plant. The air moving across the leaf surface increases the rate of transpiration beyond the ability of the roots to

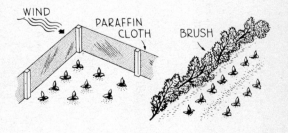

supply water. Even in well-established plants, you'll find that wind stunts growth and complicates watering. In transplanting, protection may be

90 TRANSPLANTING Starting Plants

afforded by attaching paraffin cloth, cello-glass, burlap, or muslin to stakes placed on the windward side. Bushy twigs or brush also can be used as temporary windbreakers, but they may also serve as a hiding place for marauding pests.

6. PROTECT FROM PESTS

It is a wise precaution to sprinkle snail and slug bait liberally around a bed of newly set plants; otherwise you are likely to discover some morning that your new plants have provided a community breakfast for these pests.

If plants are a variety that appeals to cutworms, surround each with a 3-inch disc of tar paper, slit so it can be slipped around the stem. Or, insert a cut-off milk carton or tin can a half inch into the soil to form a protective collar.

Birds can likewise consume tender new transplants. Best protection against them is to fashion a shield of wire screen or cheesecloth that completely denies them access to the plants. A simple method of covering row plantings is to form a tent

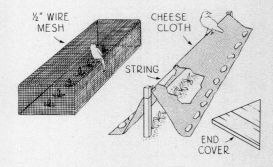

of cheesecloth or plastic screen by draping the material over a taut string attached to stakes. The walls of the tent can be held at ground level with rocks; and the ends should be closed with box ends, brush, or a triangle of wire screening.

Starting Plants
SEEDS IN OPEN

Many hardy annuals, such as larkspur, godetia, clarkia, candytuft, can be sown in the open ground and, given fair weather conditions, will develop into better plants in less time than if sown in a flat and transplanted. All plants with tap roots, sweet peas for example, will not stand transplanting unless handled without root disturbance, and they are better off if sown right in place in the garden.

Principal advantage of sowing seeds in place is the elimination of transplant setback. Main disadvantages are the length of time the ground is without bloom, the loss of unprotected seedlings, and the difficulty of spacing plants.

Many gardeners sow a good part of their cut-flower garden in the open ground in rows. Seeds of marigolds, zinnias, cornflowers, and other large-seeded plants take care of themselves in the open. Often, cut-flowers can be successfully interplanted with vegetables.

It is possible, of course, to give outdoor plantings almost as much protection as seeds in flats. The seed-bed itself can be provided with a special seed mixture; seeds can be planted in the same way as in a flat, and they can as easily be protected from hungry pests and the elements.

The simplest and most direct methods of sowing seeds are sowing them in furrows and broadcasting them in the open ground. Here are the principal steps:

1. PREPARE SEED-BED

To prepare a piece of ground for sowing, water thoroughly a few days ahead (unless it is moist from rains). Fork deeply, and rake to break up clods and to get a fine, smooth, level surface.

If you have a fairly large area over which you plan to broadcast seed, apply commercial fertilizer over the entire surface at a rate of 3-4 pounds per 100 square feet. For fast, even distribution, use a spreader. After spreading, chop the fertilizer in with a hoe or cultivator, and water in well.

When sowing seed of vegetables or flowers in rows, you can assure yourself of stronger, larger plants by applying commercial fertilizer in furrows 1 inch deeper than the seed and 2 inches on either side of the seed row. Use fertilizer at the rate of

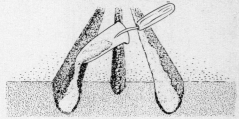

1 cup to 10 feet of row. By test, this method of placing fertilizer alongside the seed has proven more successful than scattering it with, beneath, or above the seed.

2. SOW BY A PLANTING PLAN

Experienced gardeners never sow seeds in the open until they know the movement of the sun and wind through the gardening area. Injury from wind can be lessened by planting vegetables or ornamental vines that are trellised so the prevailing winds blow the vines into the trellis and not away from it. Wherever winds are severe, windbreaks either of cloth, glass, or close plantings should be provided.

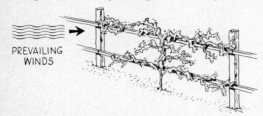

Row plantings should be oriented to take full advantage of the sun's path. Rows that run north-south receive sun on both sides, whereas rows that run east-west have one side in perpetual shade.

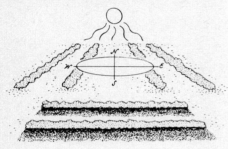

When planting in rows, follow exactly the seed packet instructions on the distance between rows. These calculations are based upon the root room required by the plants, rather than on their above-ground spread. A cabbage plant, for example, will take up 3 or 4 square feet of ground surface, but its roots will fill in a 6-foot circle and pentrate to a

depth of 5 feet. Failures in corn, melons, cucumbers, and head lettuce are often due to overcrowding. A single melon vine will yield as much fruit as two vines crowded into one planting hill.

Starting Plants **SEEDS IN OPEN** **91**

Some vegetables, such as sweet corn and melons, are planted in hills rather than rows. Planting in hills does not mean that the soil is hilled up. It is more accurately described as a group of 3 or 4 plants, the seed of which is sown in a circle from 12 to 15 inches in diameter. The seeds, generally 7 to 10 in number, are evenly spaced in the hill, and after the plants are up, all but the strongest are removed. This technique is described further in the chapter on vegetables.

Mark the planting rows with string stretched between two stakes. If you are laying out a large bed with a number of parallel rows, you may find it easier if you construct a row marker such as the one illustrated. With this tool, you merely lay out the first row with string and stakes and follow the line with the marker.

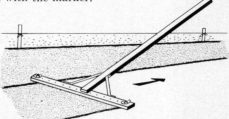

The V-shaped furrow can be made with the corner of a garden hoe, a Warren hoe, pointed stick, or a rake held at an angle.

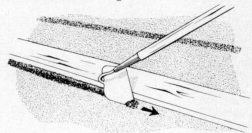

To avoid tramping soil, walk on a plank as you cut the furrows. You can also use the edge like a ruler to guide your hoe when you make the furrow.

3. SOW AND COVER SEEDS

To sow seeds, empty a small amount from the seed packet into your hand. For sowing flowers in borders or large beds, scatter them broadcast. Sow thickly and thin seedlings later. For row planting, drop the seeds into the furrows, following planting distances recommended on seed packet.

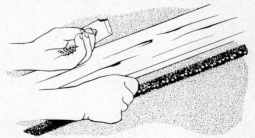

Backfill the furrow with the back of the rake or the hoe blade. Cover such seeds as carrot, lettuce with ½ inch of soil and larger seeds with an inch or

more. When planting in heavy soil, cover seeds lightly or with sifted soil so the tender shoots can easily penetrate to the surface.

After covering, tamp the soil firmly so there will be no air pockets left around the seed. Use the back of the rake or the hoe blade, bringing the tool down firmly over the top of the covered furrow. Another

method is to lay a plank over the furrow and walk back and forth over it. Such precautions are especially important in warm weather.

After tamping, water in thoroughly with watering can or a gentle spray from the hose. Too much

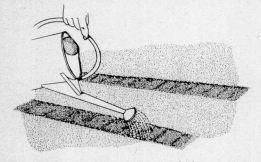

force unearths the seeds. It is a good idea to go over lightly once, then repeat.

As a final step, apply a thin mulch to prevent the soil from crusting, to keep the surface of the soil moist, and to protect seeds from being worked out by watering. Use peat moss, sawdust, sifted manure, pumice, or expanded mica. Or you can place strips of burlap over the furrows. The cloth will keep the soil moist, but it must be removed as soon as the seedlings germinate.

4. PROTECT SEED FROM PESTS

Seed rows require protection from birds and garden pests. A wire-screen tent, as described under transplanting, will keep birds at a desirable distance; and when the seedlings appear, a dusting of insecticide or planting of baits will keep slugs, snails, and cutworms away from the appetizing young plants.

5. CARE THROUGH GERMINATION

The seeds should not be allowed to dry out while they are germinating. On the other hand, they should not be drowned by over-enthusiastic watering. Check the soil frequently, particularly during hot weather, to make sure that it is moist. If it feels dry, sprinkle it gently with a fine spray or irrigate in furrows alongside the planting row.

When the seedlings appear, start thinning them out. Don't delay too long. Root systems will become interlaced and the removal of seedlings will injure the roots of the remaining plants and check their growth. Let them grow sufficiently so you can tell which ones will be the most vigorous, and remove the rest. Refer to the thinning recommendations on the seed packet to make sure that you don't thin too close together or too far apart.

While the seedlings are coming along, keep weeds down in the space between rows. In chopping out weeds, be extremely careful not to injure roots of seedlings.

Starting Plants

VEGETATIVE PROPAGATION

Sowing seed is not the only way of starting plants—in fact, some plants are more successfully started by another method, known as "vegetative propagation." This technique relies on a trait peculiar to most perennials and bulbs and many annuals: namely, if a piece of root, stem, or leaf is placed in a starting mixture, it will strike root and it may in time be planted in the garden.

This is a good way of starting perennials and shrubs, because it eliminates the long wait from seed. It also has one marked difference from propagating from seed: a new plant reproduced from a part of a parent plant will have the same characteristics as the parent while one grown from seed may not.

INCREASING PLANTS BY DIVISION

Dividing, or "separating," is a familiar routine in every garden in which perennials are grown. This is, simply, the process of producing one or more new plants by splitting apart a parent plant. All but tap-rooted perennials can be propagated in this manner, which is the easiest and most usual method of increasing stock.

However, dividing is more than a means to increasing your plantings; because most perennials need to be separated every 2 or 3 years for their own health. Their roots become intertwined into tight, thick clumps that function with less and less efficiency. If not divided periodically, the plants grow with reduced vigor and produce fewer or skimpier blooms.

Some perennials can be divided very easily, since they naturally come apart in divisions; but others must be forced with the help of a knife, spade, or spading fork. To a large degree, the ease with which the plants can be separated depends upon the type of root system.

When to Divide

The best time to divide most herbaceous perennials is in fall or spring. Those which bloom from early to late spring—arabis, aubrieta, primrose, iris, and violet, for example—can be divided directly after blooming if planted immediately and not allowed to dry out. Otherwise, wait until September.

Perennials which bloom in summer and fall, such as chrysanthemum, should be divided in spring. Plants which are liable to rot in cold wet winters, such as Transvaal daisy and delphinium, are best divided in spring.

It is a wise practice to go through your garden during the blooming period and check on times and quality of bloom. Tag plants while they are still flowering, so you can later identify the most desirable ones at dividing time when they are bare of bloom and leaf.

How to Divide

After plants have bloomed and the tops have died back, lift the overgrown clumps out of the bed, cut them apart to form new sections, and plant sections in freshly prepared beds.

When separating most perennials, divide into fairly small divisions, because they increase rapidly and soon become crowded. A general rule is to plant divisions 12 to 18 inches apart, depending on the ultimate size of the plant. Divisions of smaller plants such as *Campanula portenschlagiana* can be planted 12 inches apart; perennial asters 2 to 3 feet apart.

There are roughly three ways of dividing perennials, according to the nature of the plants. These are discussed below.

Plants with Fleshy Roots or Stems

Many perennials store food in their roots or stems to carry them through winter and to start their growth the following spring. Some store it in plump roots called "tubers" (dahlia, sweet potato), and some in a fattened stem called a "rhizome" or "rootstock" (iris, calla, daylily). Plants of this type are divided as follows:

1. Lift out the root mass with a spading fork.

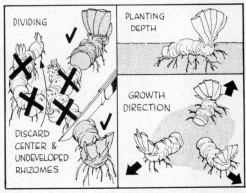

2. Cut apart with a sharp knife, spade, or axe. Cut the clump into segments, each piece having roots and stem, some with eyes (buds).

3. Replant in freshly prepared bed.

94 VEGETATIVE PROPAGATION Starting Plants

Many bulbs are divided in this same manner. However, in some climates, some bulbs require a removal from the garden during their dormant months. For details on this process, see the chapter on bulbs.

Plants with Multiple Crowns

Some perennials grow fresh shoots directly from the crown. As the season progresses, their crowns become jammed with shoots, the oldest in the center and the newest on the outside. Plants of this type (Michaelmas daisy, Shasta daisy, achillea) should be divided in this manner:

1. Dig out the root clump with a spading fork. Some plants make such a tight, tangled root clump that they are difficult to divide without taking stern measures. Here is a sure-fire method of breaking up the clumps: Insert two spading forks back to back in the center of the clump, pry the handles apart. Even the toughest will yield.

2. Carefully remove the fresh young shoots on the outside of the clump.

3. Replant the new shoots, and discard the old core.

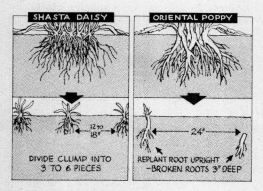

Plants with Runners or Rooting Stems

A few perennials propagate themselves by means of runners—prostrate shoots that root at the joints. Plants with this tendency include strawberry, violet, ivy, pachysandra.

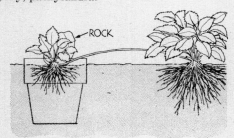

With some help from the gardener, runner types can be encouraged to multiply.

To divide strawberry plants, for example, cut the runner connecting the mother and daughter plants after the latter are well rooted. This permits the mother plant to direct energy into starting additional plantlets.

Plants with aerial runners can be propagated by pinning the tip of the runner to moist soil and letting it remain attached to the mother plant until rooted.

LAYERING

Layering is an easy and convenient method of increasing plants by rooting branches while they are still attached to the parent plant. Many herbaceous plants as well as shrubs can be propagated this way. Among them are dianthus, aubrieta, berberis, peony, daphne, rhododendron and azalea.

The method is simple. Bend down a branch, make a slit underneath, and insert a pebble to hold it open. This stimulates roots. Hold the layered stem in place with a peg, and cover with soil in which some sand and peat have been mixed. Support the upright shoot with a stake.

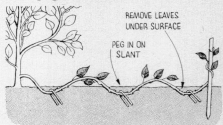

Layers of soft-wooded plants, such as dianthus, often root in 6-8 weeks. When they are rooted, sever with a sharp knife from the parent plant. Pot up or plant out in well prepared soil. Keep buds pinched off until a good root system is developed.

Hard-Wooded Shrubs

With certain hard-wooded shrubs, such as rhododendron and azalea, old branches are layered. They must be buried at least 4 inches deep, or to the point of the previous year's growth. Surround the layered portions with a mixture of sand and peat to help along rooting.

After completing the layering operation and the staking of the end of the branch, place a brick or stone as a weight over the layer. Not only will this hold the branch firmly in place, but it will help prevent drying out.

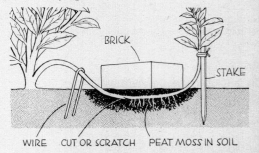

Most layers are rooted within 1 year. Often the layered plant is severed from the mother plant and allowed to remain in the ground until its root system is well established. Rhododendron layers usually take 2 or 3 years to form strong roots.

HOW TO PROPAGATE FROM CUTTINGS

Any Western gardener who is acquainted with the common geranium is likely to be familiar with the principles of starting plants from cuttings. Seemingly, almost any part of this accommodating plant will take root if it is cut off the parent and stuck into a pot filled with sand. Indeed, in some localities, pieces of geranium will root right in the garden if placed in soil.

Many other plants can be reproduced in this same or a similar manner. Few are as quick to take hold as the geranium—some take months to form roots—but a generous selection of plants may be propagated from cuttings.

As the name of the process implies, a new plant is grown from a part cut off a parent plant. Depending on the type of plant, the cutting may be taken from the stem, root, or leaf—and if given proper attention, it will sprout roots in time. When it has sprouted, it may be potted or placed in the garden, depending on the variety and the time of year.

Unlike seed sowing, this method of propagation utilizes a section of the parent plant, and consequently the gardener is almost certain that his cutting will reproduce the exact variety and quality of the original.

Another advantage of cuttings is economy. You can duplicate some of your expensive plants—such as rhododendrons, daphne, and camellias—and save the cost of buying additional ones, or you can secure a large quantity of plants at little or no cost. A few boxwood, privet, or laurel plants can furnish material for a sizeable hedge—or you can root prunings from the hedge next door. A hedge of still choicer plants—aucuba, elæagnus or viburnum, for example—might be out of the question costwise if you had to buy enough plants for the back or sides of a lot.

HOW TO MAKE STEM CUTTINGS

There are three types of stem cuttings: softwood, hardwood, and semi-hardwood (hardened green). Softwood cuttings are taken from plants whose stems are normally soft, such as geraniums or chrysanthemums, and from the immature, soft, growing tissue of other plants. Hardwood cuttings, taken from mature or dormant wood, require longer to root. In summer, when the wood is in a half-ripened state, semi-hardwood cuttings may be taken.

Softwood Cuttings

Softwood cuttings promise more success to the beginner, because they root more readily than hardwood. Chrysanthemums, for instance, sometimes root within three weeks; whereas deutzia, a hardwood cutting, occasionally takes as long as a year. Softwood cuttings strike root easily and are readily rooted under glass.

Time: Generally spring and early summer are the best time for softwood cuttings in the West. The best cuttings are made from non-flowering sideshoots of vigorous, healthy plants. If the stem snaps, it is ready for cutting; if it bends or crushes, it is too young or too old.

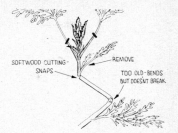

Making the cut: Cut the stem as follows:

1. Allow for a cutting 2-4 inches long. With a sharp knife make a clean cut, slanting at 45-degree angle, about ¼ inch below a node (growth bud).

2. Trim lower leaves from cutting with knife, razor, or other sharp tool, but retain 2 or 3 top leaves to provide food for the cutting until new roots have formed.

3. If leaves are large, trim sides of leaf to reduce transpiration. Do not cut off tips, because they store substances (auxins) important to growth.

Plants propagated by softwood cuttings:

Abutilon	Ivy
Arabis	Lantana
Aubrieta	Mesembryanthemum
Begonia	Penstemon
Cactus	Poinsettia
Chrysanthemum	Rehmannia
Dahlia	Salvia
Dianthus	Santolina
Felicia	Sedum
Fuchsia	Senecio
Gardenia	Streptosolen
Geranium	Tecoma
Heliotrope	Verbena
Iberis	Vinca

Semi-hardwood (Hardened Green) Cuttings

Broad-leafed and coniferous trees and shrubs may be propagated from stem cuttings of ripened or nearly-ripened wood taken between midsummer and fall. The tissue at the tips of the branches is then changing from a succulent to a woody condition.

Half-ripened wood cuttings should be neither too hard nor too soft. They should be flexible, yet firm enough so that when bent at an acute angle, the stem snaps off, leaving a bit of the outside bark attached.

Making the cut: Length of cutting varies with species. Follow same procedure used for softwood.

Heel cuttings: Certain coniferous evergreens do better if rooted with a heel. Heel cuttings are sideshoots removed from a branch with a small portion or "heel" of the parent branch attached to the base. Often the heel consists merely of the enlarged and

96 VEGETATIVE PROPAGATION Starting Plants

hardened section at the base of the sideshoot where it is attached to the main stem.

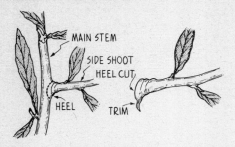

It is best to remove heel cuttings with a sharp knife, taking care not to tear the bark of the parent branch. The heel is then trimmed so that edges and surface of the cut are smooth.

Plants propagated by semi-hardwood cutting: Midsummer and fall.

Abelia	Jasmine
Arborvitæ	Lavender
Azalea	Lilac
Buddleja	Mahonia
Calycanthus	Myrtle
Celastrus	Osmanthus
Choisya	Pleroma
Cotoneaster	Plumbago
Daphne	Polygala
Escallonia	Pyracantha
Eugenia	Taxus
Forsythia	Thuja
Fuchsia	Veronica
Heather	Weigela
Hydrangea	Yew

Hardwood Cuttings

Although cuttings of half-ripened wood from both evergreen and deciduous plants root most readily in summer, there are strong arguments in favor of fall and winter propagation with fully-ripened wood, particularly in warmer climates. Late in the year, wood suited for cutting has hardened; and because the weather is cooler, cuttings wilt less easily. There is less growing heat, of course, and plant tissues are hardened, so you must expect hardwood cuttings to root more slowly than others.

Fall cuttings are usually taken from ripe wood of the past season's growth, occasionally from older wood. With evergreen and semi-deciduous plants, you may take branch tips or sections of stem farther down; with deciduous material it's best to discard the few inches at the top in favor of the thicker, lower sections. Deciduous cuttings may be stripped of all foliage, but evergreens must retain a few leaves at the top.

Making the cut: Cut the stem as follows:

1. Cutting should be 6-8 inches long and about the diameter of a pencil. Deciduous cuttings should contain at least two growth buds, one for rooting area and one for top shoot above the ground; try to select pieces with closely spaced nodes—the more nodes the better.

2. Most propagators make bottom cut about ¼ inch below node, but this practice is not vital because roots form at more than one point.

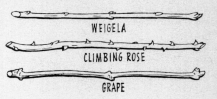

3. Make top cut of deciduous plant just above a node. Top cut should be straight and bottom cut slanted; this system is used to differentiate between top and bottom of cutting—if you attempt to root cutting upside-down, it won't grow.

4. Some evergreens root better if cut with a heel (a small portion of parent plant attached to base of cutting).

5. If evergreen leaves are too broad they may be trimmed. Avoid cutting off tips, for they contain growth substances (auxins) important to rooting.

Storing: Some experts take deciduous cuttings in early winter and store them until spring. This practice is essential where soil freezes in winter. Even in mild climates it is a good idea to store cuttings in a cool place until the time comes for normal growth to start. Storage duplicates natural winter dormancy. By spring, the end of a buried cutting will have formed a callus (knobby growth), and from this formation most of the roots will grow.

Tie cuttings in bundles, label them, and pack them in boxes filled with soil, sand, peat or sawdust. Store them in a cool, frost-free place. Keep stored cuttings dark and dry, or else some of them may be lost through premature sprouting.

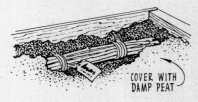

Plants propagated by hardwood cuttings: Fall and winter.

Actinidia	Philadelphus
Akebia	Pomegranate
Albizzia	Poplar
Ampelopsis	Privet
Chænomeles	Rose
Cornus	Salix (willow)
Deutzia	Spiræa
Elæagnus	Symphoricarpos
Forsythia	Syringa (lilac)
Hydrangea	Tamarix
Kolkwitzia	Weigela
Lagerstrœmia	Vitis (grape)
	Wisteria

The following, however, do not root satisfactorily from hardwood cuttings and are normally propagated from seed, grafting, or budding: fruit trees, most nut trees, maple, oak, eucalyptus, birch, linden, and beech trees.

SETTING OUT DECIDUOUS HARDWOOD CUTTINGS

In milder climates, deciduous hardwood cuttings can be placed directly in the ground out-of-doors. In sections where the ground freezes in winter, set them out in spring after the bottoms have callused.

ROOTING STEM CUTTINGS IN SAND

You may root a number of species in water, but most cuttings require sand or other rooting media. A flat or box at least 3 inches deep makes an ideal container for the medium, although a large pot may also be used.

Rooting Media

Builder's sand is the most popular and inexpensive rooting medium. Beach sand is unsatisfactory because it contains salt and is too fine to permit free drainage and thorough aeration. Be sure sand is clean of all foreign matter. For acid-loving plants many propagators add peat moss, the ratio depending upon the type of cutting.

There are certain special rooting media which offer advantages of light weight, porosity and moisture-holding capacity. Among these are perlite, pumice, and expanded mica (vermiculite). In watering expanded mica, use a very light hand.

How to Insert the Cutting

1. If you use a wooden box, cover cracks in bottom with sphagnum moss, or cover entire bottom with newspaper. Place medium in container; then firm and soak thoroughly. If you use a large amount of peat, press out excess moisture with hands. Cuttings can be set more firmly in damp medium, and need an even supply of moisture.

2. If box is used, make rows 2 inches apart with putty knife. If you use a pot, insert cuttings slightly inside the edge of the pot.

3. Dip end of cutting in water, then in hormone-fungicide mixture. Artificial hormones are organic chemicals that may be used to encourage cell growth. Plant hormones are sold in powder or liquid form: powder may be dusted on tips of cuttings. Be sure to follow directions on label carefully.

4. Set cuttings 1 inch apart in trenches with 2 or 3 nodes below surface. After trench is filled, place board or brick on medium so that edge touches row of plants. Tamp board heavily with hammer to

firm mixture around cuttings. Water. Label each group of cuttings, noting variety and date.

5. In cold or dry climates, a covering of glass or cello-glass over cuttings is desirable; cuttings thrive in close, humid atmosphere. In spring or early summer, leave covering slightly ajar to admit air. If late in year, keep top closed, except for brief period in morning when it is opened for watering and to admit air. Turn glass over at this time, or else wipe off moisture.

6. Keep medium constantly damp; but do not allow it to become water-logged, or cuttings will rot. Shade cuttings for several days. Some plants require bottom heat, and most are benefited by it. (See chapter on coldframes.)

POTTING ROOTED CUTTINGS

After cuttings have formed roots, shift them from the rooting box to a pot.

Many softwood cuttings root in 2-8 weeks, some may take longer. Hardwood cuttings may take as long as a year. Cuttings which are callused (i.e., have achieved a knobby growth at base) but are still unrooted may be dusted with rooting hormone again and set back in the medium.

Transferring to Pot

1. Remove cuttings from rooting bed with as much medium as possible adhering to roots.

2. Place in 2½-4 inch pot, depending on size of the root ball. Always use clean pots.

3. Fill pot with seed-sowing mixture of equal parts of loam, sand, and peat moss or leaf mold. Acid-tolerant plants may be potted in half sand, half leaf mold.

4. Place pots in sheltered spot with filtered shade, preferably with pots sunk to rims in damp peat, sand, or wood shavings to conserve moisture.

"Knocking Out"

When roots begin to show through the bottom of the pot, the plant is ready for "knocking out" and

98 VEGETATIVE PROPAGATION Starting Plants

either shifting (potting on) to a larger container or planting directly in the ground.

1. Place hand, palm down, on top of pot with plant stem between first and second fingers. Then turn pot and plant upside-down (steadying it with other hand).

2. Rap the rim of pot on the edge of bench or any solid wooden surface. Ball of soil will slide into one hand and pot will remain in the other. Be sure soil is moist when plant is knocked out. If very dry, the ball may fall apart; if too wet, the soil may puddle and later bake.

Planting in Ground
Prepare ground carefully before planting. Plant cuttings in a cushion of moist peat. In warm weather shade with laths or paper. Water regularly until established. (See text on transplanting in preceding chapter.)

ROOT CUTTINGS
Cuttings may be taken from the roots of any plant that produces suckers of sprouts from the roots. True root cuttings are made from roots which have only adventitious, not visible buds; the buds develop only after the cutting is planted. Plants which may be propagated from root cuttings include: *Anemone japonica*, Oriental poppy, trumpet creeper (campsis), wistaria, plumbago, blackberry, raspberry, and horse-radish.

Make root cuttings as follows:

1. Select roots 3/16 to 3/8 inch in diameter from vigorous plants. Cut roots into pieces 1-3 inches long. Fill a box or flat to within about 1 inch of the top with light, rich soil; place cuttings 2 inches apart in a horizontal position on top of soil. (Cuttings of horse-radish, usually set directly in the ground, should be placed in an upright position to prevent misshapen roots.)

2. Cover with about ½ inch of additional soil. Water thoroughly.

3. Cover with glass or paper and place in shade.

LEAF CUTTINGS
Under favorable conditions, even the leaves of certain plants will send out roots. Leaf cuttings are possible with fleshy-leafed plants such as rex begonia, cotyledon, and other succulents, because a considerable amount of food is stored in the leaves. African violet and gloxinia can also be propagated from leaf cuttings.

Sometimes the whole leaf is used to propagate roots, in which case the petiole, or leaf stalk, is inserted in sand. In other cases the leaf is shortened, or cut into triangular sections. In the latter circumstance, leave a section of the petiole in each

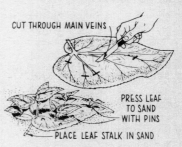

portion. Plant these pieces ½ inch deep in moist sand. Bottom heat helps to speed rooting. Rex begonia leaves will root if they are placed whole on top of moist sand, held down with toothpicks, kept moist, shaded and at constant temperature.

INCREASING PLANTS BY GRAFTING
Plants that will not grow from cuttings may often be multiplied by grafting. This is the process of bringing together the growing regions of two different plants to make them unite and grow as one.

In grafting, there are two basic materials to work with: a plant that is rooted, called the stock; and a piece cut from some part of another plant, such as a twig or root. This is called a scion or cion (child or descendant). The scion is grafted onto the stock.

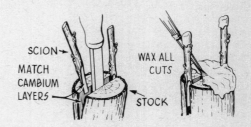

The stock and the scion do not blend into one plant; each keeps its individuality. But the bark and wood of both grow together so that the scion receives food and water from the stock. What actually takes place is that the layer of growing cells inside the bark of the scion (known as the cambium layer) is brought into direct contact with the growing cells of the stock. Thus, the two tissues knit to form a single growing unit.

In the West, grafting is usually done in the winter or early spring. In autumn the tree has not yet become fully dormant. For the best results, grafting should be done when the buds are dormant and just as the sap begins to flow in the spring.

There are many methods of grafting, some quite complicated. The two simplest—cleft and whip grafting—are discussed in the chapter on fruit trees.

BUDDING

In budding, a bud, rather than a scion, of one plant is inserted between the bark and the cambium of the stock plant. It is practiced mainly on plants whose bark slips (peels) readily, such as plum, cherry, peach, pear, apple, and rose.

Pick out a branch which has more than the usual number of buds—an indication that it is healthy. Use a budding knife to cut off the leaf, retaining a part of the leaf stalk.

For shield budding, cut downward, under the bark, cutting out the bud just below the leaf stalk in the form of a tiny shield.

Make a T-shaped cut in the bark of the stock. Take care to cut just through the bark and not into the wood. Gently pry back the bark at the top of the "T" to facilitate the insertion of the bud. Work quickly and handle the bud as little as possible so that it will not dry out; use a gentle downward pressure to insert it. Put the bark back in place over the bud.

The trick in inserting the bud is to see that it goes in flatly and snugly. Tie in place with raffia, leaving the bud itself uncovered.

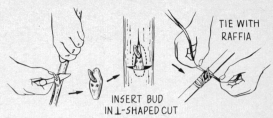

Budding is not always successful, but the results are quickly apparent, enabling one to try once more. If the bud withers, the union did not "take"; if it still looks fresh 10 days after the budding, the job succeeded. Although the best time to bud varies somewhat with different plants and in different climates, in general the months from June to September are favorable for most plants propagated by this method.

Starting Plants
COLDFRAMES

The true gardener finds a choice rose, a rare camellia or azalea, or an exotic philodendron infinitely more satisfying if he has managed to grow it from a cutting. And a dozen plate-sized tuberous begonias somehow seem more beautiful if he has produced them from a pinch of seed he could have lost under his thumbnail.

Propagation holds more of the mystery, the challenge, the trial-and-error, and the gratifying rewards in gardening than all the rest of its phases together. There's no beginning or end to its fascinations and discoveries. When you tackle your first "difficult" plant—set about growing it from seed or cutting in the special environment it requires—you're on your way as a real gardener.

To provide that environment, you must wrap up a special climate in a tight package and keep it insulated from the weather outside. The package can run from a steam-heated greenhouse down to a jelly glass, inverted over a cutting.

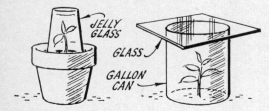

Far and away the cheapest, easiest, and most efficient way of packaging climate is the coldframe, which provides maximum area for propagation, minimum air space to be kept warm and humid, and efficient light control through its transparent top. Many a greenhouse propagation job can be done just as well in a simple coldframe; if you supply it with heat, the possibilities are almost limitless.

WHAT A COLDFRAME CAN DO

Properly used, a coldframe will more than pay its cost in a single season. You can use annuals with a free hand—in hundreds, rather than dozens—and at a cost in cents instead of dollars. One flat of rooted cuttings of choice shrubs makes the investment in heating cable and thermostat worthwhile.

Here are some of the things you can do with a coldframe:

Raise specialties such as begonias, gloxinias, and streptocarpus which have tiny seeds almost as fine as dust.

Grow new varieties of flowers and vegetables not often available in nurseries.

Make advance sowings of summer annuals and warm-weather vegetables.

Start seed of perennials in summer and, in mild winter climates, start annuals for winter color.

100 COLDFRAMES Starting Plants

Start cuttings of begonias, chrysanthemums, coleus, pelargoniums, impatiens, and tip cuttings of such annuals as fancy petunias which do not come true from seed. Also set in leaf cuttings of many succulents, Rex begonias, African violets. Root-hardened green cuttings of camellias, azaleas, rhododendrons, and other choice shrubs.

Grow salad greens and other small vegetables in the colder months. Force bloom of potted bulbs after roots have developed.

Use frames for reconditioning house plants needing a warm, moist atmosphere after a long period in a dry, heated house.

Protect small tender patio pot plants during midwinter.

Act as a summer boarding house for pot plants while you're off on vacation. (Sink pots in damp peat, wood shavings, or sawdust.) Turn it into a fumigation chamber (when empty) for sterilizing soil.

SIMPLE COLDFRAMES

A simple coldframe requires only 4 walls and a transparent roof. For example.

Cover a sturdy wooden box with a piece of glass or plastic screening, and put 3 inches of rooting medium (for cuttings) or soil mixture (for seeds) in the bottom. Be sure the box is not too deep; otherwise, sufficient light can't penetrate.

Knock the bottom out of a seed flat, tack on a piece of plastic screening, and invert it over a second flat containing seedbed or cuttings.

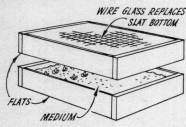

These devices are minimum size, portable coldframes you can put together in a few minutes. They may be moved indoors or out, depending on the weather. However, the job they can do for you is out of all proportion to their size. In a few square feet of coldframe space you can root enough cuttings to start an entire garden.

INTERMEDIATE SIZE COLDFRAME

An intermediate type of coldframe is basically just a box built to size, but its construction does require some carpentry.

Simplest version is a bottomless box made of 1 by 12-inch redwood, cedar, or treated fir, with 2 by 4's at the corners. If you use some form of overlapping siding instead of ordinary 1 by 12's you will have a tighter box and better heat and humidity retention. To avoid rot caused by constant dampness, use rot-resistant woods or other woods treated with a preservative.

Where rains are heavy, a sloping top is necessary to shed water, provide more glass area, and let in as much light as possible. Allow about an inch of slope per foot of width.

The top may be covered with glass or plastic screening, framed in $\frac{1}{2}$-inch battens. It should be hinged on one side. Plastic screening comes in 3 and 4-foot widths. It is not so durable as glass and tends to become cloudy and less efficient in transmitting light as it ages.

COMMERCIAL FRAME

If you build your box as a single or multiple of a 3 by 6-foot rectangle, the top can be standard nursery sash. A sash costs considerably more than plastic but it lasts much longer. Of course, it is also heavier to handle. The solidly built, glass-covered commercial frame simply takes these features and improves on them. Such frames are usually 6 feet wide and about 16 inches high at the rear, sloping down to 9 inches at the front. They are made of heavy 2 by 12-inch stock for sturdiness and battened on the outside to make them air-tight. Glass sash is set on slides and is weather-stripped with burlap so sashes can be shoved back for access, instead of lifted.

HEATED COLDFRAMES

The advanced coldframe calls for the addition of artificial heat, which adds to cost but doubles usefulness. With a heated frame, you can root cuttings which would otherwise be difficult to start, and you get a headstart on spring seed sowing.

Ancestor of the heated frame is, of course, the hotbed; and there's absolutely nothing wrong with the idea if fresh manures and raw organic material are easily obtainable. Place about 18 inches of material in a pit dug to fit the frame, and set the frame on top. By mixing fresh leaves and other raw vegetable waste with the manure, the bed will produce satisfactory heat for 10 or 12 weeks—longer than necessary for almost any single propagating task. Decaying material is covered with a piece of fine-mesh hardware cloth, then a 3-inch layer of gravel to make the floor of the frame. After setting up a hotbed, allow two weeks for initial heat to taper off before putting it into use.

You can use the same principle with the portable box frame and its derivatives by setting it on a binful of newly piled compost, or you can supply electric heat by placing a second box, containing a 10-watt light, underneath.

Soil Cable

Of all ways of heating a frame, by far the simplest and most convenient is electric soil cable, laid across the bottom of the frame in tight, hairpin turns. For safety be sure all connections are waterproof. With a cable and thermostat, you can produce temperatures ranging from 35° to 100°, guaranteeing at least minimum temperatures day and night, summer and winter. Furthermore, cable heats the ground, and it is bottom heat, not air heat, that does the trick. Operating costs are low, for the cable draws little wattage and generates a comparatively large amount of heat.

Both lead and plastic-covered cables are available. Whichever type you use, be sure to ground it to avoid danger of electric shock. Also, check with your building inspector to determine if a special permit or special wiring is required in your locality.

The length of soil cable required depends on the size of the area to be heated. For example, a 30-foot cable sold by one manufacturer draws 180 watts, serves a 1-sash frame 3 by 6 feet; a 60-foot length draws 400 watts and serves twice the frame area. Multiples of these two units should take any home gardener as far as he wants to go.

Assemblies including both thermostat and double plug outlet are available. The hermetically sealed thermostat is partly buried in the planting medium in order to control soil, rather than air temperature. It is connected with the switch box and feed wires at the end of the frame or cutting bed.

Airtight construction is important in a heated frame. Joints should be tight, cracks sealed or covered with battens, and the top made snug with weather-stripping or burlap. Banking up soil against outside walls is helpful during winter cold.

Level the ground in the bottom of the frame, and cover it with 2 to 4 inches of coarse river sand. Arrange the cable in evenly spaced loops (be sure loops do not overlap), and cover with a 1-inch layer of sand, and next with 1-inch mesh hardware cloth to protect the cable from damage by tools. If

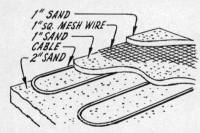

you expect to grow cuttings or seedlings in flats (by far the most usual method), place only 1 inch of sand over the hardware cloth. If you are growing them directly in the soil medium, place a 5 to 6-inch layer of sand or some other rooting medium over hardware cloth. In using electric cable, it's important to know the exact soil temperature. Aquarium supply houses sell inexpensive thermometers, made to float in aquaria, which can be plugged into the soil easily. Cheese thermometers and photographic thermometers can also be used. For germinating most seeds, a temperature of 70° is about right. For rooting the cuttings of most hardy plants, it should run from 65° to 70°; for propagating tropical foliage plants, about 87°

OPERATING A COLDFRAME

Aside from serving as a shelter from rain and wind, the coldframe controls three factors vital to plant growth: light, humidity, and temperature. The unheated frame merely modifies the temperature factor; the heated frame controls it. Getting the most out of a coldframe means providing, as nearly as possible, each of these vital factors at optimum levels.

Light

A gentle light is ideal for seedlings and cuttings. Direct sun is harmful, even worse than deep shade. Light coming through a cloth shade is about right—direct sun with the sting taken out of it.

Best plan is to locate the frame for maximum light, then modify light as needed with a shade or cover. Location is especially important when the sun's arc is low during winter. Most gardeners place frames in a southern exposure, with slanting tops facing south.

To make the most of light during winter, it's a good idea to paint the inside of the frame with white or aluminum paint, thus increasing reflection.

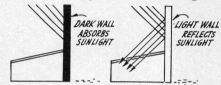

Humidity

The second factor is fully as vital as light. Optimum humidity for most propagation is 80 per cent, and a well made, tight frame should keep it there.

If the frame is airtight, little watering is needed. The soil should stay damp, but not soggy. A layer of sand or gravel on the bottom of the frame makes for good drainage and helps build up humidity. Even in warm climates, a weekly watering is usually sufficient for an unheated, tight frame. With the addition of heating cable, more frequent watering becomes necessary.

Heavy condensation on the glass roof may indicate too much moisture, easily corrected by raising the sash an inch or so for a few minutes in the morning.

Heat

The third factor varies in importance with the severity of the climate. In warm climates the coldframe functions primarily as a control over light and humidity, only secondarily as a collector of heat. A thin-walled, unheated frame can do an excellent job almost all year long, although the addition of artificial bottom heat is still vital in some types of propagating. In colder climates, however, collection and storage of heat are of prime importance.

In addition to its use as a propagating tool, the coldframe opens another important door: out-of-season gardening. For year-around, use the cool-climate coldframe should be built with thick walls of 2-inch stock, rather than 1-inch. Some northern gardeners use masonry walls of pumice block, which has high insulation values.

Lawns

There are about 1,500 different kinds of grasses growing in the United States. This figure includes pasture grasses, range grasses, and such wayward members of the grass family as bamboo, corn, and sugar cane. Only about forty types of grass have a place in lawns, but even this number gives you a multitude of choices.

Grass blades elongate from the lower end, so that when you mow off the tips, the leaves renew their length from the other end or new leaves come up from the base. This characteristic is what makes grasses unique and universally adapted to use for close-cropped ground cover. (For complete information on grasses and their use, see the *Sunset Lawn and Ground Cover Book.*)

There are two lawn variety lists on the following pages—one of cool-season grasses and one of warm-season subtropical grasses. Here in the West, the line between cool-season grass country (above the line) and warm-season grass country (below the line) goes roughly like this: Santa Cruz north to Redding, southeast to Barstow, California, northeast to Las Vegas, Nevada, east to Utah's Bryce Canyon country, south to Arizona's Mogollon Rim and east along the rim to New Mexico.

COOL-SEASON GRASSES

These are the cool-season grasses—the staple items for lawns north of the line described above.

Your main use for the list below will probably be to get a general idea of the lawn texture, color, and maintenance that can be expected from any particular seed mixture you might look at on the nursery or garden supply store shelves. For example, if you find a big percentage (over 35%) of a coarse grass such as meadow fescue, you will know that it probably will be a coarse-looking lawn. A good fine grass mix would be high in Kentucky bluegrass or its varieties and would contain no rye grass. If the ingredient list shows a big percentage of bents, you can figure that it will be a high-maintenance lawn—bents are very susceptible to summer diseases and they

ABOVE. Section of 3½-acre Sunset lawn in Menlo Park, California. Lawn is composed of 60 per cent Kentucky Blue Grass, 20 per cent Creeping Red Fescue, 10 per cent Astoria Bent, 10 per cent Merion Blue Grass.

need low mowing. Some single grass varieties are packaged and sold by themselves. They perform well enough as turf grasses to stand alone; other varieties are not considered necessary to supplement them.

Bent Grasses

Astoria. Fine leaves. Thick turf. Dull green to light green. Spreads by rooting at joints. Not very vigorous; gets summer diseases. Healthy growth in winter. Likes sun or part shade, not full shade.

Highland. Fine, upright leaves. Grayish-green. Tougher than Astoria. Strong growth September to June. Likes sun or part shade, not deep shade.

Penncross. Fine, flat, narrow leaves. Bluish green. Likes sun or part shade, not deep shade. Definitely best with low (½-inch) mow.

Seaside. Fine, flat, narrow leaves. Bluish green. Runners visible more than on Astoria. Quite susceptible to summer diseases. Slow but healthy growth September to June. Likes part shade, not deep shade. Definitely best with low (½-inch) mow.

Fine Fescues

All of these have fine, rolled leaves—like tiny soft needles. Along with Kentucky bluegrass, the fescues comprise the heaviest portion of most fine-leafed lawn mixtures. Fescues are supposedly less particular about soil conditions than either bluegrass or bent grass, blend well with bluegrass, should not be used alone because they get clumpy. Fescues are fairly drought-tolerant, grow best in cool areas.

Creeping Red. Fine texture. Dense turf. Texture mixes with bluegrasses. One of the varieties to look for in mixes for shady places. Cut at 1½-2 inches.

Illahee. Very fine texture. Bright green. Susceptible to summer diseases. Tends to grow in clumps. One of the varieties to look for in mixes for shady places. Cut at 1½-2 inches.

Rainier. Dainty, soft, and deep green. Not a strong hot-summer performer. One of the varieties to look for in mixes for shady places. Cut at 1½-2 inches.

Chewings. Dainty, soft, gray-green. Better than most where moisture and food are limited. Does not heal fast after injury. Yellows in winter cold. Cut at 1½-2 inches.

Blue Grasses

Kentucky Bluegrass is not a pure strain. A lawn of it contains many distinct types (distinct to a grass expert). Merion, Newport, Delta, and Park are special selections from Kentucky Blue.

Kentucky. Dense sod. Leaves are dark green, smooth, soft. Probably the best all-around lawn grass in the cool-season grass country. Slows in summer, grows fastest in cool season. Poor in shade. Cut not lower than 1½ inches.

Merion Kentucky. More prostrate grower and denser than ordinary Kentucky Bluegrass. Dark blue-green. More drought-resistant than Kentucky Blue. Susceptible to rust. Recommended mowing at ¾ or 1 inch.

Newport. About the same texture as Merion, but less susceptible to rust. Poor in shade. Cut not lower than 1½ inches.

Delta. Very similar to common Kentucky Bluegrass; no advantage over it. Finer, stiffer, more erect, but not as dense.

Park. Very similar to common Bluegrass, but high seedling vigor.

Poa Trivialis. Fine textured. Upright leaves. Apple-green color. No other grass grows as well in wet, shady spots. Can suffer in summer like bents.

Rye Grasses

Bunch grasses, so it can never make a really tight, self-knitting turf. Temporary ground cover in Southwest.

Perennial. Medium-coarse; waxy sheen on rather sparsely set leaves. Good in wide variety of climates. Bunchy growth habit; hard to mow in summer. Mow at 1½ inches.

Annual. Coarser than perennial rye. Used for quick cover and for winter grass on Bermuda lawns. Always contains some perennial rye which will survive in clumps. Most Annual Rye dies out in one year's time. Mow at 1½ inches.

Coarse Fescues

All of these very wide-bladed, clumping grasses are best for football fields and lawns that get very rough treatment. Must be seeded at 6-8 lbs. per 1,000 square feet for best results. Sow as pure stand. In mix, coarse fescues develop as large, coarse weeds in lawns. Sow at heavy rate and texture will be finer.

Meadow. Medium-coarse. Soft, pliant. Dark green. Quick-growing, permanent, tough. Mow at 1½ inches.

Alta or Kentucky 31. Coarser than Meadow. Very wear-resistant, drought-resistant, and long-lived. Tends to clump. Must be mowed regularly; if neglected, gets tough. Cut ¾ to 2 inches.

Redtop

Used primarily as temporary "nurse" grass. Less aggressive than rye grass in most climates. Component of mix for neglected, uncared for area that needs cover. Varies from coarse weedy clumps in spring to fine bent-grass type in late summer. Will grow in wet or dry soils, shade, or sun. Cut ¾ to 1 inch high.

Clover

Under good conditions it manufactures its own nitrogen so that a grass and clover lawn generally needs less feeding. Dark green, soft and lush.

Can be controlled to a degree by fertilizing. High phosphate fertilizers encourage clover. Nitrogen pushes grasses. Stains clothing badly. Gets lanky in deep shade. High mowing encourages it; low mowing discourages.

SUBTROPICAL GRASSES

These are the subtropical grasses, also called stoloniferous grasses because some of them spread rampantly by means of above-ground runners (stolons) and are frequently planted as sections of these stolons. In logical opposition to the term "cool-season grasses," these could be called "warm-season grasses." In most of the milder latitudes of the United States, these grasses grow vigorously in the warm season and go dormant (dead grass color) in the cool season.

You usually buy subtropical grasses in one of these ways: a bag of separated runners (sprigs); squares of sod, with the dirt washed off, that you tear into sprigs and plant; flats of grass from which you plant plugs; rolled-up sod, ready to install on a lawn bed that has been prepared more or less the same way as for seeding.

Several big turfgrass growers in the Pacific Southwest grow these grasses. Your nursery may sell some of the grasses, or your nurseryman can probably help you place an order with one of the growers.

Common Bermuda grass, U-3 Bermuda, and *Zoysia japonica* are the only subtropical grasses from which seed is grown, packaged, and sold. The U-3 Bermuda seed is not considered very reliable. It segregates into many different types, producing an uneven turf. Seed of *Zoysia japonica* is even less satisfactory and not generally offered.

All of the hybrid Bermuda grasses cover faster than zoysias from root-runners. All of the zoysias and hybrid Bermudas can substantially crowd out broad-leafed weeds.

Zoysia Grasses

When zoysias first came on the market they suffered from irresponsible advertising (no grass is perfect!). Zoysia is outstanding for its strong, dense turf, once established (no weeds, Bermuda, insects, or diseases). Its one big fault is dormancy in winter.

All zoysias are slow-growing and require 1 to 3 years for development of a solid turf. A single edging-board will contain them. Useful for shaded areas when the general lawn expanse is of hybrid Bermuda because they blend well with Bermuda in texture and color. Same general care. They are more durable when dormant than other warm-season grasses.

Z. japonica. Rather coarse, as tropical grasses go. Disease-resistant, drought-tolerant. Requires long time to develop solid cover (1 to 2 years). Poor winter color. Grows well in shade. Mow at 1½ inches.

Meyer. Blades broad at base, tapering to point at tips. Established turf looks much like top quality bluegrass lawn. Drought and weed-resistant, pest-free, wear-resistant. Easy to maintain. Soft to walk on in bare feet. Takes intense playground punishment. Winter color is brown. Grows fair in shade. Mow low, ½ inch.

Z. Matrella. Medium and fine texture. Slick, slightly bristly, dense. Easy to maintain. Wear-resistant. Turns straw color in winter. Grows in shade. Mow low, ½ inch.

Emerald (a hybrid of *Z. Matrella*). Very fine; wiriest of zoysias. Denser than Meyer. Darker green. More prickly than any other zoysia. Easy to maintain. Good wear-resistance. Dense, wiry blades make cutting difficult. Turns straw color in winter. Grows in shade. Mow low, ½ inch.

St. Augustine Grass

Coarse. Very wide blades. Dark green. Makes an attractive, rugged, serviceable lawn. Completely pest-free. Needs little feed or water. Coarse texture makes power mower a necessity. Turns brown in winter if it gets any frost. Grows in shade. Cut at 1½ inches.

Common Bermuda Grass

This is the original garden lawn Bermuda. Prettier if fertilized regularly, but because of bad seeding habits and invasive growth it is not a perfect lawn grass. Makes a comparatively pest-free and disease-free lawn if well tended. Coarser, has more seed spikes than hybrids (below). Brown or straw-colored all winter. Grow from sprigs or hulled seeds. Won't grow in shade. Mow as low as you can (½ inch if possible).

Hybrid Bermudas

These are the new hybrids—each considered an improvement on one count or another. All will crowd out Common Bermuda. Best adapted grasses for all areas of the Southwest. More difficult to overseed with "winter-grass" (bluegrass, red fescue, rye) than Common Bermuda. Winter green is assisted by fertilization in September and October and removal of thatch, which insulates the grass from the warm soil, by September 1.

U-3. Finer textured than Common, coarser than most other hybrids. Seed spikes just as obvious as on Common. Tough enough for athletic fields. Tends to build up instead of out. From seed, it is not always dependable—may revert to Common Bermuda. Browns off in winter. Won't grow in shade. Mow as low as you can (½ inch if possible).

Everglades #3. Fine textured and a bright, deep green. Soft feeling. Exceptionally nice color. Browns off in winter. Won't grow in shade. Mow low (½ inch if possible).

Tifgreen. Fine-textured; dense. Deep blue-green. Shows promise for desert areas. Made to order for putting green. Browns off in winter. Won't grow in shade. Mow low (½ inch if possible).

T-35-A. Fine-textured, dense, light green, upright leaf growth. Does not take traffic as well as other hybrids, nor is turf as dense. Browns off in winter. Won't grow in shade. Mow low (½ inch if possible).

Tiffine. One of the finest textures. Yellow-green color. Produces masses of seed heads during most of summer. Browns off in winter. Won't grow in shade. Mow low (½ inch if possible).

Sunturf. Along with Tiffine, it is the finest textured lawn grass we've seen. It's almost like Irish moss in texture. Browns off in winter. Won't grow in shade. Mow low (½ inch if possible).

Vereening. Fine-textured. Very drought-resistant. Good color. Browns off in winter. Won't grow in shade. Mow low (½ inch if possible).

HOW TO INSTALL A LAWN

Subtropical grasses definitely should be planted in spring (before July 1). The stolons need as many weeks of heat as they can get in order to become established and to spread well the first year.

Cool-season grasses, on the other hand, usually come up best from a sowing in early fall—September in the Northwest and east of the Sierra-Cascades, October in California. Fall sowing allows seedlings to grow to maturity before they must suffer the strain of heat and dryness. However, it is possible to sow cool-season grasses in spring. The grass will grow faster in spring than in fall, but you will have to give it much more attention, particularly watering.

Preparing the Soil

Break up and pulverize the soil with a spade or power tiller to an even depth of from 6 to 9 inches, if possible. Pick out rocks and debris that you find on the surface. You should remove large rocks and other buried objects because they interfere with water penetration.

Pull up or dig up by the roots all perennial weeds, and hoe off annual weeds. Do not turn them under, because it takes several months for them to decay. If you are in no hurry to seed, however, addition of this organic matter can improve the soil.

To find out exactly where your soil measures in the acid-alkaline scale, you can test it with a soil-testing kit, or send a soil sample to a testing laboratory for analysis.

To correct an undesirable condition:

1. If your soil is acid enough to limit growth (pH below 5.5), neutralize it by applying lime (agricultural lime) at the rate of 50 to 75 pounds per 1,000 square feet per application. The lime decreases the soil's acidity by direct chemical action. Apply on dry soil with a spreader. Prevent chemical from contacting roots of acid-loving shrubs.

Calcium nitrate, a nitrogen fertilizer, has the same effect as lime, although it requires more poundage for results (so much that you may find the cost prohibitive).

2. If you have an alkaline soil, you can use one of several products to reduce the alkalinity and at the same time improve soil structure. Actually, you should strive to lower pH only if it is above 8.3 or 8.4. Gypsum is the most widely used for this purpose. In areas where water companies soften the water supply, gypsum is the best way to prevent a "tight" soil. It has the advantage of practically limitless safe application. Spread as much as you wish on top of the soil (the usual recommendation is "like a light snow") and spade it in. About 35 to 50 pounds per 1,000 square feet will usually suffice.

If you are working on a soil that you feel is deficient in nutrients (such as scalped subsoil) you would be wise to dig into the future root area a source of phosphorus (10 pounds of superphosphate to 1,000 square feet). There isn't much sense in applying anything for a long-term nitrogen source. Nitrogen is always of a temporary, transient nature in the soil.

If your soil is a compacting type, this is the time to mix in a soil conditioner. Incorporate to the full cultivated depth whichever of these meets your needs:

1. Pumice or perlite—provides physical looseness to soil.

2. Peat moss (1 bale to 1,000 sq. ft.)—improves soil structure for many months.

3. Steer manure—enriches soil slightly, adds organic matter for physical looseness, but may also introduce diseases, salts, or weed seed.

4. Wood shaving, sawdust, ground fir bark, ground redwood bark—every year more of these soil-conditioning products come on the market. Happily, we now find by-products of logging, millwork, pulp production, mushroom-growing and other processes now coming to us in paper sacks as quite usable soil conditioners. Use these materials freely to loosen up a clayey soil or to add water-holding body to a sandy soil. But keep in mind that if the organic matter that you add to the soil is high in carbon, soil organisms that work to decompose it may have to take nitrogen from the soil. For that reason, you would probably do best to mix $1\frac{1}{8}$ pounds of ammonium sulfate or $1\frac{7}{8}$ pounds of ammonium nitrate per 100 square feet 1 inch deep of woody material (bark, sawdust, or shavings). Another way of expressing it is 1 pound of actual nitrogen to 100 pounds of woody material. This supplementary nitrogen will keep the carbon-nitrogen ratio in balance.

But if the soil is hopelessly poor, or if it is below grade and must be filled in, you will have to add

106 LAWNS

introduced soil. If the new soil differs much from your native soil, make a transitional layer in which native soil is blended with introduced soil.

Making the Lawn Bed Smooth

A lawn bed should be as smooth and flat as possible. However, it should have a slight pitch, even in flatland gardens. Figure on a fall of 6 to 12 inches in 100 feet so that water can run off once the root area has reached its saturation point. Only about one lawn in fifty requires drain tile to take off the excess.

Drag the cultivated soil until it is level, free of clods, and conforming to grade or desired pitch. You can make a good drag for first leveling by overlapping a series of planks so that the drag rides on the down-facing exposed edges.

A rectangle of flexible steel matting, 3 feet by 5 feet, makes a wonderful smoothing and leveling device.

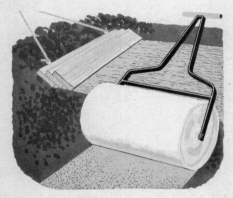

To firm the seedbed, go over the smoothed surface in two directions with a full roller. The heavy rolling process may develop some low spots. If it does, fill them in with another raking or dragging, and roll again.

Feeding the Seedbed

Get enough complete commercial fertilizer to cover the area according to label directions for new lawns.

It should go on the bed as evenly as possible. A good spreader will do the job perfectly.

This fertilizer is to supply the nutrients the grass plants will need as they begin to grow in your lawn. It won't, by any means, satisfy your lawn for a lifetime—probably not even for a full year. It is just a send-off boost.

Remember, we suggested digging a phosphate fertilizer into the soil before leveling. Phosphates do not move through soil very well (if at all) so your only chance to get a luxury supply of this important nutrient into the rooting area is before leveling and planting. Also, we suggested added nitrogen (most likely in the form of ammonium sulfate) if you use a woody material as a soil conditioner. If you did both of these things (dug in phosphates and mixed nitrogen with the woody soil conditioner), the immediate preplanting application of fertilizer on the surface could probably be skipped. But, on the other hand, it shouldn't do any harm at this stage and it might do some good, so include it if you feel generous.

Seeding a Prepared Lawn Bed

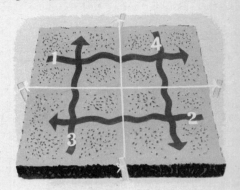

Fall sowing is preferred by most experienced lawn installers because the lower temperatures reduce danger of heat injury (most grasses prefer to grow at temperatures between 50° and 70°). Fall seeding should be done early enough to allow 6 weeks of growth before heavy frosts come and the soil gets cold. Grass sown too late in the fall may not germinate at all; or an early heavy rain might wash out the seedbed.

Grass sown in spring will get the benefit of months of heat, which if combined with ample water, will make for luxuriant growth. Main weakness of spring planting is the travail of pulling a new lawn through the heat of summer and through the season of most active weed growth.

Broadcast the seed on the prepared lawn bed while the air is quiet.

Here is a way to get the seed on uniformly: divide the amount of seed necessary for your area (per label direction on seed packages) into four equal portions, so you can make four approaches over the seedbed. Divide the seedbed in half by running a string down the middle. Broadcast one quarter portion down each half, spreading it evenly and uniformly within each marked area. Then run string across the middle of the lawn in the opposite direction and scatter the remaining two quarter portions on these two halves.

You can broadcast the seed uniformly with a mechanical seeder or do it with your hands (some masters say that if you have the "touch," this gives best coverage of all).

After the seed is broadcast, rake it in lightly to insure a thorough contact of seed with seedbed soil. Very lightly brush up the seeded surface with a wire rake—use light circular motions, straight motions, or whatever appears to disperse the seed most evenly for you. If you come across concentrated patches of seeds, in spite of your care, swirl them out lightly into the surrounding area to make an even coverage. At this stage, your heels may make an undesirable impression in the seedbed—try doing the cross-raking and mulching in flat-soled shoes, tennis shoes, or barefooted.

After seeding and cross-raking, put on a ⅛ to 3/16 inch layer of peat moss, screened sawdust that has been aged at least a year, or well-rotted and pulverized steer manure. Scatter the mulch on as evenly as possible. Don't toss it upward so that it falls in piles.

Many people find peat moss troublesome because of its reluctance to take up water. Some lawn builders scatter the dry peat over the seedbed and then wet it with hand sprinkling. If you make certain that the peat has become saturated, you can use this method successfully.

Most reliable method—and also the most tedious—is to pre-soak the peat before applying it.

Whatever the covering, roll it smooth with a light roller (empty) after you have applied it. If a peat moss covering is lumpy, chop up the lumps with the backside of a wire rake before rolling.

For initial watering, you will need adequate hose to get all the way around your lawn without dragging across it, and a hand sprinkler that throws out a thorough but gentle spray. You will also need up to half an hour a day for 20 to 30 days for watering. When days are warm and windy you may have to water 2 or 3 times a day to keep the surface continually wet. Keep the mulch dark with moisture until all the grasses are up. This may take up to three weeks if your seed mix includes slow-germinating varieties.

Where labor is being paid for, weeding is often skipped. Instead, a broad-leafed weed killer is applied to the lawn when it is from 6 to 8 weeks old, or after the second or third mowing.

Mow the lawn for the first time when the grass is about two inches high. One sensible recommendation says mow when the grass blades get tall enough to take on a noticeable curvature.

Sodding a Prepared Lawn Bed

Prepare soil as previously discussed. But instead of working toward a finished soil grade at the level of surrounding paving, the soil surface should be settled ¾ inch below grade.

Some lawn contractors say you get a much better take-off if you spread a layer of complete fertilizer (label-prescribed amount for new lawns) on the soil and lay the sod directly on it.

Unroll the sod on the prepared soil. Lay the strips parallel, with the strip ends staggered as in the bricklayers' running bond pattern. Press each successively laid strip snugly up against the one next to it.

After the sod strips are all laid in this fashion, roll the sod with a roller half full of water to smooth out rough spots and bond the sod with the soil.

Now all you have to do is water a little more carefully than usual for a few days.

Sprigging and Broadcasting Stolons On a Prepared Lawn Bed

This consists of tearing apart clumps of the grass stems to get pieces an inch or two long, each carrying a few tufts of leaves. Usually the stems are torn apart from nursery flats or from growing grass in nursery areas.

First, pre-soak the prepared planting bed so it will be slightly damp (not bone dry) when you plant the stolons or sprigs. When it is dry enough to work without sticking, make a series of parallel trenches 1 inch deep, 6 to 18 inches apart (the closer the spacing, the faster the complete coverage).

Plant individual stolons horizontally in trenches and press the soil together by putting pressure on a board laid beside the trench. Water the sprigged area soon after planting and keep it moist continually until the sprigs have rooted and begun to grow.

An easier way is to broadcast the stolons. This is not new, but it is coming into use more for Bermudas, zoysias, and bent grasses. After the lawn bed surface is prepared, scatter pieces of stems (stolons) by hand over the entire area. Approximately 3 to 5 bushels should cover 1,000 square feet.

Roll the entire planting with a half-filled lawn roller to firm the stolons against the soil surface.

After broadcasting and rolling, cover the stem pieces with some material that will hold moisture well during the rooting time. This might be a half-inch of screened, weed-free topsoil, peat moss, sawdust, or ground bark.

Except for topsoil, these materials should be thoroughly presoaked, as they are very difficult to wet through when applied dry. Straw and shredded newspaper have been used where cost had to be kept low. Roll again after applying the layer of cover material, to insure that it is in firm contact with the stolons.

Water immediately after the second rolling. Thereafter, water the mulched surface frequently (maybe several times a day in warm weather) so that it will not dry out at any time. Of all ways to start Bermuda and similar grasses, this one calls for most painstaking maintenance after planting.

Plugging a Prepared Lawn Bed

Cut and lift plugs of the new grass from flats with a special plugging tool (1½ inches in diameter and 3 inches long). Then plant the plugs in small holes made in the prepared lawn area with the same plugging tool. As an extra, put a teaspoon of complete fertilizer in each hole before planting. It will make the grass grow faster. Plugs are usually spaced 12 to 15 inches apart.

Growth from plugs may be fast, but somewhat slower than with sprigging. Plugging is most frequently used for planting hybrid Bermuda and dichondra.

LAWN WATERING

To sum up the advice in the chapter on watering: A little water wets only a little soil; you can't half-water soil. Each soil type has its own water-holding capacity—clay soil takes water slowly and gives it up slowly; sandy soil takes less water, faster, and dries out more quickly. Deep watering at long intervals will encourage roots to go down to their full depth (10 to more than 36 inches, depending on variety) and, hence, stay less dependent on you and your hose or sprinkler system. How much water to apply at one time depends on soil type and root depths of the grasses you are watering. How often to water depends on how long the supply of available water will last in your particular soil reservoir. You will find specific details, figures, and charts to bear out these rules in the water chapter.

A rule-of-thumb or two about watering: first sign that a lawn is beginning to wilt from need of water is loss of resilience in the blades. Grass that is ready for a watering will not spring up after you step on it. Next sign is a smokiness, a dull, dark-gray green color to the grass. Finally comes browning of individual plants and death. In cool climates, water in a lawn is lost by transpiration (leaf action) and evaporation at the rate of about one inch a week; in hot climates at about two inches a week. Figure how much water your sprinkler applies and water, when necessary, accordingly.

LAWN FEEDING

If your lawn grows and stays green without fertilizer or with just a single feeding each year, you can count yourself as lucky and as an exception among Western lawn growers. The usual feeding pattern that stands behind a green lawn goes like one of these: a label-recommended feeding with complete commercial fertilizer every two or three months; a light feeding with a nitrogenous fertilizer every month and a feeding with a complete chemical fertilizer twice a year; or "a feeding every time the grass begins to turn yellow." Although over-feeding is something to be avoided—by observing precautions on labels or, in the case of bulk organics, by using common sense—few of us ever approach an overfed lawn.

In mild winter areas, growth may slow down in winter, but the grass seems to remain responsive to a nitrogen fertilizer. In these areas a feeding will almost always liven up a mustard-colored winter lawn. Six months later, a feeding will put springtime growth back into a cool-season grass lawn that is going through the summer doldrums or even laboring under attacks by lawn moths, traffic, and weeds.

The principles of fertilizing outlined in the chapter on soils apply to lawns as well as other plants. Here is the meaning of the words on the label that refer to nitrogen:

Nitrate or nitrogenous—the form of nitrogen that is available to the plant as-is, regardless of temperatures.

Ammoniacal or ammonic—available to plants when converted by bacteria to nitrates. There is evidence of direct utilization, too. Speed of conversion depends upon soil temperatures. It's only a matter of hours in midsummer, but much, much longer when ground is cold.

Organic—describes sludge, cottonseed meal, and any others that must be broken down by bacteria. These are slower than any inorganic form.

Urea—a synthetic organic that water and the enzyme urease change immediately to inorganic ammonia. Conversion to available nitrate follows.

Urea-form or urea formaldehyde—a nitrogen fertilizer that has been specially compounded (stabilized) for slow release.

HOW MUCH TO FEED?

The package or sack of fertilizer you buy will carry instructions on how much and when to apply.

If your idea of the correct timing or correct amount does not coincide with the manufacturer's you can make your own adjustments, using the following formula: University of California recommends 1 pound of actual nitrogen per 1,000 square feet per month (when grass is growing—not during the months when ground is frozen or grass is naturally dormant). To figure pounds of "actual nitrogen," take the percentage of total nitrogen, as stated on the label, times the weight of the fertilizer. For example, a 12-pound package of fertilizer (doesn't matter whether it is liquid or dry) containing 17 per cent nitrogen will yield approximately 2 pounds of actual nitrogen, or enough to feed 2,000 square feet for a month or 1,000 square feet for two months. The figuring:

12 pounds x .17 = 2.04 pounds

MOWING THE LAWN

Obviously, you mow your grass when it begins to get shaggy. How often this might be depends on your feeding and watering schedule, the type of grass you grow, the season and the climate. Generally, during the warmer months a well-fed lawn needs a mowing at least once a week—rye grass and other fast growers may need cutting twice weekly, or even every other day.

In winter, mowing time in California may come up as seldom as every three or four weeks; in the Northwest, not at all. Don't mow grass that is wet or frozen (in fact you should stay completely off grass that is frozen).

Sometimes it is a good idea to rake the lawn before you mow it. A raking not only picks up sticks and litter, but also lifts any long shoots so they can be trimmed neatly.

Leave the Clippings

Allowing the clippings to remain on a lawn is a good way of adding organic matter to the roots and of replenishing the soil with some of the nutrients that the grass took out of it.

If you are going to leave the clippings on, clip promptly when the lawn is ready. The clippings then are short and will drop between the grass blades without being very conspicuous. If you are late in mowing, the grass that you cut will make a "hay crop," stay on top, dry, and become unsightly.

Lawn Edging

A lawn mower only levels grass. You eventually need tools of various sorts to trim it around the edges because almost all grasses spread horizontally in one way or another. An edger, with a rotating wheel that pulls grass across an upright cutting edge, works like this for trimming along walls and paved areas.

THE DICHONDRA LAWN

Dichondra is a soft, green, ground-hugging, broad-leafed plant—not a grass. In the milder parts of California and Arizona it is used quite widely as lawn.

Dichondra has some definite advantages as a turf plant (and, like grasses, some disadvantages, too). Watching it boom in popularity in California during the 1950's made us believe that someday it may be taken for granted as a turf plant wherever average winter temperatures don't drop below 25°.

Sow the seed any time between March 1 and October 15. Although dichondra germinates fastest in midsummer, people have had trouble with it then because it is difficult to keep the new seedlings moist enough. Seed sown in March, April, or May gets firmly enough established by summer to withstand the moisture loss on hot summer days.

In winter the ground is too cold to germinate the seeds. They will just sit there until spring and then begin to sprout. Meanwhile, you have to battle weeds that sprout in the cold ground.

Best Soil for Dichondra

Dichondra grows better in light, sandy loam soil because water can penetrate better, roots grow deeper, summer water-stress is less. Heavy clays or adobes should have peat moss, ground bark, or wood shavings plus nitrogen, or sand dug into the top 6 inches before dichondra is planted in it.

In March, April, or May dichondra seed needs no mulching. Just rake the seed gently to bring it into contact with the soil surface, and roll it with a light roller.

If you sow in summer, apply a covering of damp peat moss no deeper than ⅜ inch. Keep the seedbed moist, either way. At time of seeding, apply a complete fertilizer to the seedbed. Follow the label's instructions for new lawns.

What About Dichondra in Mixes?

The scheme of sowing dichondra with white Dutch clover was thought of some years ago when dichondra was priced like diamonds. Another old notion of sowing a mixture of dichondra and a grass such as perennial rye has been completely forsaken. Straight dichondra simply needs no nurse crop, not if it's sown in spring on a well-prepared soil, watered well, and fed frequently. The nurse crop turns out to be more nuisance than benefit.

An old argument for using clover with dichondra was that the clover would, in theory, come up before the dichondra and offer shade and protection. Then, in later seasons, the nitrifying nodules on the clover roots would simply supply nitrogen to the dichondra and thereby make the dichondra grow stronger.

Instead, what often happened was that you'd get more clover than dichondra—permanently.

Left unmowed, clover grows to about 6 or 7 inches, dichondra grows only about 3 inches. Frequently the clover would shade the dichondra out of existence. In addition, clover requires no nitrogen, dichondra requires it. If you skip a feeding (which is easy to do when you see the lawn green with clover), clover takes over at dichondra's expense.

Some seed companies recommend the clover-dichondra mix if you want to sow in late fall or midwinter (the latter is not a wise time to sow any kind of lawn). If you use the mix and want to keep the two plants at a balance or give the dichondra the upper hand, mow to dichondra leaf height frequently and feed regularly as described below.

Plug Planting

Starting a dichondra lawn from flats was at one time the only method used.

The criticism that "plug planting creates a lumpy surface" can often be attributed to improper techniques. Seed planting can also create a lumpy surface if your soil is not properly leveled.

By nature, dichondra makes a smooth surface, and when properly grown and cared for, it should give you an even surface.

Plug planting is practical if you desire an immediate effect or if the areas are small like those between stepping stones or on banks and slopes. Carefully insert the plug so that the top is level with the ground, and tamp it in patiently and gently. This care will make the difference between a smooth or lumpy planting.

Plugs should be no smaller than 1 inch square—preferably 2 inches square or larger. The larger the plug, the quicker the dichondra responds to transplanting. To get the strips or plugs, turn the flat over on a level surface and cut through the soil with a knife or saw. Or you can rent or buy a dichondra transplanter from your nurseryman. This instrument, which works like a big cooky cutter, will not only cut the dichondra plugs but will also make identically sized holes in your planting area.

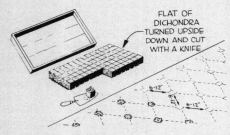

FLAT OF DICHONDRA TURNED UPSIDE DOWN AND CUT WITH A KNIFE

In placing plugs into soil, make sure that runners at the top of the plug are at soil level or just below. Then, press each plug down hard.

Frequent Mild Feedings Best

Regular watering is dichondra's first important need, including long waterings in summer to make the roots grow deep. Along with the careful watering, dichondra needs a continual supply of nutrients.

Dichondra seems to respond more noticeably than grass to the frequent-mild-feeding type of schedule. Try this: Feed with the lightest feeding recommendation on a fertilizer's label, once every 2 to 4 weeks.

LAWN DISEASES

Sometimes a lawn just begins to die, all over or in patches, and the usual ministrations—careful watering, fertilizing, spraying for lawn moth or grubs—do nothing. The slow death continues. This happens most frequently in summer or early fall although it can happen at any time of the year.

The lawn owner can deduce that if it's not bad watering practice, lack of nutrients, or insects causing his trouble, it must be a fungus. His lawn has been attacked by one or more fungus diseases.

For the record, here are descriptions of the various lawn diseases. The descriptions are presented with slight tongue in cheek because there are several that rarely if ever show the classic symptoms. Furthermore, a lawn is often hit by a combination of two or three diseases. After each disease description below you will find the fungicides which have effectively controlled it. If you aren't sure of your disease diagnosis, the sagacious choice would be one of the broad spectrum fungicides that you find listed again and again under the various diseases.

Going out, or melting out (Helminthosporium). First over-all sign, as seen from a distance, is a gradual indefinite yellowing. In infected areas, look for bright yellow leaf blades with brown spots and darkened borders. Eventually the whole leaf turns brown. Effective: phenyl mercuric acetate, captan, Phaltan, Tersan 75, zineb, Acti-Dione R2, Kromad, Tersan OM, Ortho Lawn Fungicide.

Fading out (Curvularia). General yellowing or fading of grass in patches, often surrounding green islands of healthy grass. Tips of grasses turn yellow or tan. Effective: phenyl mercuric acetate, Acti-Dione R2, Kromad, Ortho Lawn Fungicide.

Grease spot (Pythium). Infected blades turn dark and become matted together, giving a greasy appearance in streaks through the lawn. Sometimes a white, cottony mold growth shows on grass blades. Effective: captan, phygon, zineb, Acti-Dione R2, Tersan OM, Ortho Lawn Fungicide.

Copper spot (Gleocercospora). Not common. In small areas through lawn, grass blades become covered with orange to copper-colored fungus spores. Rub a white cloth on the spots and it will pick up red. Effective: Semesan, phenyl mercuric acetate, Cadminate, Kromad, Tersan OM.

Rust (Puccinia). Small reddish pustules form on leaf blades and stems. On Merion bluegrass a cloud of brown dust arises when mowed. Blades shrivel and die. Feeding to force growth seems as effective as any chemical. Effective: ferbam, maneb, phygon, Tersan 75, zineb, Acti-Dione R2, Tersan OM.

Brown patch (Rhizoctonia). Light attacks result in blackened leaf blades. In heavy attacks, blackened blades form an expanding large irregular smoke ring and the areas look almost as if they were drying out from lack of water. Blades inside the ring become light brown. Effective: Calo-Clor, Calocure, Semesan, phenyl mercuric acetate, captan, PCNB, Tersan 75, Acti-Dione R2, Kromad, Tersan OM, Ortho Lawn Fungicide.

Dollar spot (Sclerotinia). Many small (approximately 2-inch) bleached or gray-colored spots. When fungus first starts, infected areas have water-soaked appearance. Sometimes the spots merge to make large, straw-colored areas. When dew is on the grass, you can see cobwebby growth on the spots. Effective: Calo-Clor, Calocure, Semesan, phenyl mercuric acetate, Cadminate, PCNB, Acti-Dione R2, Kromad, Tersan OM, Ortho Lawn Fungicide.

Pink patch, red thread (Corticum). Active in lawns the year around. Causes yellowing discoloration of grass in spots 2 to 12 inches in diameter. Within those areas, look very closely or use a magnifying glass and you can see pinkish webbing on the lower part of the leaf blades and sometimes woven from leaf to leaf. Effective: Cadminate, Kromad.

Snow mold (Typhula). Dirty white patches appear in the lawn, varying from almost white through shades of light tan to buff. Margins to the spots are rather distinct. Dead grass can be pulled up easily. It has been found in all seasons and almost all places, but is quite common in early spring after snow melts. Effective: Calocure, Semesan, phenyl mercuric acetate, Cadminate, Tersan 75, Kromad, Tersan OM, Ortho Lawn Fungicide.

Fusarium patch or pink snow mold. Tan to dark brown patches appear in the fall, sometimes in spring, seldom in summer unless it is cool and moist. The margins on the patches are rather indefinite. Effective: phenyl mercuric acetate, Cadminate.

Timing for Preventive Application

Enough said about cures. Far better to prevent the possibility of lawn disease infection before it happens. And since most diseases come on in summer, "before it happens" means in spring—start in the month of May. Four applications at 10-day to two-week intervals should render any lawn almost completely immune to disease attack. (Red thread and fusarium patch or pink snow mold come at almost any season, so for them there cannot be any calendar-pegged time of preventive application.)

Weak lawns are vulnerable. If your lawn has had midsummer trouble before and you are applying a broad spectrum fungicide as a preventive measure, don't let the lawn suffer from lack of water. Two of the chief suspects in the midsummer plague complex—curvularia and helminthosporium—are present most of the time, and go into action on weakened grass. Poor watering and lack of fertilizer when it was needed in spring make grass weak fast in early summer.

Check water penetration. See if soil is equally moist at all levels in the top foot; it should be. A mat of thatch—tightly interwoven dead grass growth between grass and the soil—can slow entry of water into soil. Dense soil can also slow entry of water, causing most of it to run off onto the sidewalk and down the street. Get rid of thatch in fall or spring with a vertical-cutting machine, available at some rental agencies. Correct compacted soil by aerating with a plugging tool that removes cores of soil. A corer works like this.

If a spot is very hard, the corer at first will probably give you only very light penetration. Put a sprinkler on the partly treated spots and let the ground absorb the water to the run-off point, then turn off the water. A day or so later, core again. This time the corer will go in farther.

Do not use household bleach. The end decomposition product of chlorinated household bleach in soil is common salt. Thus, while it is true that the bleach will often clean up a fungus infestation, the saline soil which results will lead to even more serious problems.

Fairy Ring and Other Mushrooms

A toadstool or mushroom is the fruiting body of a type of fungus. The actual vegetative portion from which the mushroom grows is the mycelium, a filament-like underground growth. The mycelium feeds on organic matter. Sometimes, old pieces of wood, or clods of turned-under turf in the soil under the grass, can support the mycelium.

Mushrooms sometimes grow in an expanding circle, called a fairy ring. A mycelium growth is always just beneath the ring of mushrooms. Sometimes this mycelium is so dense and tough that water and air cannot get through to the grass roots, and the grass either suffers temporarily or dies completely. However, the mycelium inside the circle deteriorates as the mushroom-mycelium circle expands, and in deteriorating it supplies nutrients to the grass roots. The grass inside a fairy ring is often greener than anywhere outside.

Mercurial fungicides will check the growth of underground mycelium for a season or so. Poke holes in the lawn around the mushroom-infested area, and pour the fungicide down the holes.

112 LAWNS

TWELVE COMMONEST LAWN WEEDS

If we always grew only what we thought we sowed in a lawn, the whole business of lawn keeping would be a lot easier. The trouble is that soils generally are full of dormant weed seeds—waiting for the right conditions to make them sprout. Furthermore, it is almost impossible for a batch of lawn seeds to be 100 per cent pure. Harvesting at the seed farms brings in some foreign seeds. Blowers, sifters, and machines at the seed company plants take most of them out again; but a few get through, and you sow them with the grass seed. In addition wind, birds, and foot traffic are forever bringing new seeds to a lawn.

Regular mowing, watering, and fertilizing will discourage and choke out the "weak sisters" among weeds—mustard, wild oats, foxtail, and others. We haven't even considered those kinds of weeds here. The weeds on these pages are the Western "toughies" that either thrive under lawn care or are too tough to be crowded or mowed out.

1. COMMON PLANTAIN *(Plantago major)* and **BUCKTHORN PLANTAIN** *(P. lanceolata).* The weed in the photograph is common plantain. Buckthorn type has longer, narrower, more pointed leaves. Plantains aren't as difficult to get rid of as they are widespread and persistent, 2,4-D or 2,4,5-T is fairly sure to control them. Roots are shallow and fibrous and come up easily if you pry up or dig them out with a strong knife.

2. SHEEP SORREL, DOCKS (Rumex species). These weeds make serious trouble in lawns and garden beds. Their tenacious root systems remain in the earth and grow even after you pull the plant tops off. The weed pictured is curly dock. Its husky, brownish tap-root may go down 2 feet or more before stems show above ground. Sheep sorrel, a close relative, has arrow-shaped leaves, spreading roots. Curly dock is susceptible to 2,4-D, 2,4,5-T, or 2,4,5-TP, although there may be regrowth requiring retreatment. Sheep sorrel probably is more susceptible to mixtures containing 2,4,5-T or 2,4,5-TP. A very troublesome but sure method of control is to dig out the roots and the rootstocks that grow outward.

3. COMMON DANDELION *(Taraxacum officinale).* This old enemy needs no introduction. Reason it's such a pest is because its downy seeds blow in all directions and germinate easily. Plants grow so flat that the mower goes right over them. It is very susceptible to 2,4-D, 2,4,5-T, or 2,4,5-TP treatment. If you have only a few dandelions, try spot treating them with a swab or applicator to save trouble of spraying. They don't pull easily because leaves grow so flat, but if you can get a prying tool underneath the leaf cluster, they come up with little resistance.

4. PERENNIAL MOUSE-EAR CHICKWEED *(Cerastium vulgatum).* This is the only weed you can find in some well kept lawns. It grows in among the grass blades and isn't always obnoxious. However, it has a different color and texture. It is almost impossible to pull, but repeated use of 2,4,5-T or 2,4,5-TP will kill it. Neburon is effective. 2,4-D seems ineffective.

5. CRABGRASS *(Digitaria ischaemum* and *D. sanguinalis).* Former is smooth type (shown in photograph), latter is hairy; on both types, the seed head resembles a bird's foot. This is a bad one. Chemical controls: *In late winter or early spring,* crabgrass seeds from last year that would otherwise sprout this year can be killed with any pre-emergence crabgrass control product containing any one of these ingredients: standard lead arsenate; calcium arsenate; chlordane; new materials yet to come which are now only in the experimental stage. *In spring,* when crabgrass seedlings have 2 to 4 leaves, kill them by applying crabgrass control products containing any of the following: amine methyl arsenate,

disodium methyl arsenate, phenyl mercuric acetate, dalapon (spot-treated). Two or more applications may be needed. These controls may discolor the lawn briefly. *From midsummer into fall,* when crabgrass is in its full glory, use disodium methyl arsenate, amine methyl arsenate, or dalapon (spot-treated). Help to increase effectiveness by watering lawn before application and by following up with a second treatment 7 days later.

6. CREEPING VELVET GRASS *(Holcus mollis).* This grayish-green fuzzy-bladed grass appears in clumps that gradually enlarge. In early morning, dew held on leaf fuzz makes plants stand out. Likes drought, poor drainage, low fertility, compact soil. Control: Try changing these conditions; or dig out clumps; or spot-treat with dalapon.

7. ENGLISH DAISY *(Bellis perennis).* English daisies in a lawn are good or bad, depending on your feeling toward them. Some people plant and encourage them there for a meadow effect and, for their pink and white flowers in spring. Leaves lie under mower, but you can pull plants with a prying tool. 2,4,5-TP, or a mixture of 2,4-D and 2,4,5-T work better than 2,4-D alone.

8. WILD OR CUT-LEAFED GERANIUM *(Geranium dissectum).* This is really a pretty little weed when it flowers, but like mouse-ear chickweed it mars a perfect texture. Susceptible to 2,4-D or 2,4,5-TP combinations, and it pulls rather easily if ground is moist.

9. YELLOW OXALIS *(Oxalis corniculata).* You have real trouble if this weed is in your lawn or garden. It seems to have roots all along its stems, so that pulling is next to impossible. Several successive applications of 2,4,5-T or 2,4,5-TP will kill it. It has been discouraged by heavy applications of ammonium sulfate, removing source of shade that it needs in order to thrive, and by digging out plants early and burning them. Force lawn grasses to smother it. In dichondra lawns, use a monuron oxalis control product.

10. ANNUAL BLUEGRASS *(Poa annua).* This is a weedy cool-season grass that is encouraged by shade, heavy watering, or weakened turf (look for low-growing ragged seed-clusters and boat-shaped leaf tips). It dies in mid-summer, but only after it has broadcast its seed. In Bermuda grass country, annual bluegrass is often sown and cherished because it, like several other grasses, will give green color to an otherwise winter-brown Bermuda lawn. To control, remove the conditions it likes or use dalapon or sodium TCA in careful spot applications. Lead arsenate and calcium arsenate pre-emergence crabgrass controls will also control this weed. Pull it. Mow low and frequently to check seeding.

11. COMMON CHICKWEED *(Stellaria media).* Chickweed is an annual that usually starts with the first fall rains. It dries up in exposed places when weather warms, but continues in moist places. Pulling is easy but slow and tedious. Successive applications of 2,4,5-T or 2,4,5-TP will kill it. Neburon works, too. Try to kill the chickweed when it is young and tiny.

12. BUR CLOVER *(Medicago hispida).* Gather all the runners to the plant's central crown and pull up firmly and slowly from moist ground (immensely satisfying experience). Susceptible to 2,4,5-T or 2,4,5-TP. When weed is growing vigorously, 2,4-D will work.

LAWN INSECTS

Two classes of lawn insects do damage to lawns: those that feed on the leaf blades and other *above ground* parts; and those that feed on roots and other *below ground* parts of the grass plant. To know this difference will help make your insecticide applications effective.

Cutworms, sod webworms (lawn moth larvae), skipper larvae, and leafhoppers, feed above ground. To get them you water the lawn and then apply a

lawn insecticide, after which you leave the grass alone for a few days until the insecticide does its action.

White grubs, billbug grubs and soil mealybugs are below-ground pests. To get at them you apply the insecticide and then put on copious amounts of water to drench the material down deep where the insects are.

The treatments for underground lawn pests last much longer than those for above-ground, leaf-blade pests—for obvious reasons. The insecticide that you wash into the ground stays put, but the kind you apply to the leaves will be mowed off and washed off in just a few weeks. Furthermore, new untreated leaves will grow in just a few days in summertime.

In the east, grubs are lawn pests of more consequence than in the west. Eastern gardeners speak of "grub-proofing," meaning a deep-soaked application of lindane, chlordane, dieldrin, and aldrin that will last from 3 to 5 years. In the west, where neither the grub nor the grub-proofing operation is as well known, some lawn owners wastefully go through the grub application every year or even several times a year, when once every 3 years should be adequate.

The late-winter or early-spring chlordane application to kill crabgrass seed, will also kill grubs. In this case the material stays on the surface; directions do not call for washing it into the soil. But the percentage of active ingredient is so high that rainfall and watering will ultimately bring killing strengths of chlordane down to the level where the grubs are.

Anyone who has reason to study lawn pest control much will soon see a great difference between the *modus operandi* for killing lawn insects and that for controlling diseases.

With lawn insects prevention is hardly worthwhile unless, of course, your lawn is attacked repeatedly by the same insect. Then, you'd be only prudent to have some toxic insecticide laying in wait for him the next time. But, the need for prevention doesn't come up often.

Compared to selecting a lawn fungicide that will work, selection of an effective lawn insecticide is easy. Chlordane, lindane, DDT, dieldrin, and aldrin all work on all of the turf insects, above or below ground. Malathion and dibrom work faster on the above-surface lawn pests but shouldn't be used for the below-ground insects.

Symptoms and Controls

Here are descriptions of the damage done by the leading lawn insects:

Irregular-shaped brown-colored areas: Lawn Moths. If it is a lawn of any kind that is less than two years old, or a bent grass lawn of any age, and especially if tan moths fly over the grass at dusk, suspect lawn moth (sod-webworm). Apply almost any insecticide. Many have specific directions on the label for sod webworm control. For best results, cut and water the lawn before application. Do not water for at least 48 hours after the treatment so the chemical can dry on the grass blades and grass crowns.

Dead grass in definitely defined patches: White Grubs. Pull on the grass. If it comes up like a wet doormat, the cause is probably white grubs. You may even find some grubs underneath the sections you pull up—little U-shaped grayish white worms shaped like fat shrimps. If you aren't squeamish, you can hand-pick the worms from under each patch and know that you have dealt with them in the most direct way. Replace the mat of dead grass. It will grow back in several weeks. Chlordane, aldrin, and dieldrin are prescribed for best chemical control. If the label mentions white grubs, it will specify a rather heavy dosage. With this chemical treatment, water heavily after application. You have to get the material down to the level where the larvae are eating.

The control for grubs will also control wireworms which you never see but which bore into the underground parts of stems and feed on the roots of grass.

Orange, brown, and yellow butterflies fly over the lawn during the heat of the day: Fiery Skipper. Symptoms, other than the butterflies, are: Isolated round dead spots, 1 to 2 inches in diameter, eventually coalescing and killing large areas of the lawn. Small brownish-yellow worms may be inside the grass within these spots. Sometimes white cottony masses show in the lawn. The white, cottony masses are the cocoons of a parasite which may, by itself, check the skipper's advances. Otherwise, controls are the same as for sod webworms.

Dead spots 1 or 2 inches in diameter, with grass chewed below the mowing level: Cutworms. Do the spots contain a hole about the thickness of a pencil leading down into the roots? These are indications of cutworm, a serious pest among broadleafed plants as well as on grass and dichondra lawns. The controls for sod webworm will kill cutworms, too.

Central shoots of grass plants dead: Frit fly. The small, black frit fly has 4 generations of larvae a year. The spring and fall larvae live in young grass stems, eating and eventually killing the central shoots, causing the plant to send out side shoots. Some species of lawn grasses are very susceptible to this pest. Two or three sprays or dusts during the summer with DDT should control it.

Slugs and snails on the grass at night. Best controls are the liquid metaldehyde slug and snail sprays. Make a solution and pour it on the lawn through a sprinkling can.

Ants. The same controls prescribed above for lawn moths, fiery skippers, and cutworms will kill ants.

Gardener's Language

Every profession, every trade, almost every operation in which several people must work together acquires its own special set of words. They come into use through the need to avoid repetition of long drawn out instructions or to avoid confusion and misunderstandings. When two bricklayers talk about a *running bond* or *jack on jack*, both know exactly the pattern of bricks they are talking about. A magazine has its *tear sheets, layouts, galleys*, etc. When you join with bricklayers or magazine people you don't insist that everyone around you "stop that nonsense and talk English." When you join a trade you learn its language.

As the special gardeners' words appear in this book they are translated at least once. However, when we get into the directions on how to care for a plant we must employ the jargon of the trade to avoid endless explanations.

Here's a typical set of directions for caring for a plant. Words in italics have special meanings to the gardener:

"*Culture:* Plant in *half shade* in a soil *rich* in *humus*. Because the plant is *shallow rooted*

ABOVE. Shopping for a plant by its common name may cause both you and your nurseryman unnecessary confusion. All three of the above plants are commonly called "Dusty Miller" and yet all three are totally different in appearance and are entirely different plants.

water frequently. Apply a summer *mulch* rather than *cultivate*. *Subject to attack* by aphis and red-spider. *Prune* immediately following bloom in spring by *cutting back* to *non-flowering wood*. Easily *propagated* by either *softwood* or *hardwood* cuttings, or by seed in March-April."

All of the garden words used here are defined in the chapters on starting plants from seed, plant propagation, and garden care, but a few quick definitions here will help to show how much more you can get out of individual plant directions if you are familiar with the exact meaning of the words used:

Half shade. As shade measurements are loosely given and cannot be followed in any exact way, "half shade," "part shade," "filtered sunlight" are used interchangeably. Half shade can mean morning sun and afternoon shade, or shade except in early morning and late afternoon. In every case, the purpose of the direction is to avoid the hot overhead sun. Wherever summers are hot, the afternoon sun should be avoided if the plant requires "part shade." No one term is used throughout the book for the reason that each has slightly different connotations as to degree of shade and if read with all the other qualifications of the plant, the term takes on a more definite meaning.

116 GARDENER'S LANGUAGE

Rich in humus. The word "humus" is used to designate any vegetable material added to the soil. The long way to say the same thing: Soil should contain vegetable matter that eventually is converted to humus. The "rich" indicates that manure, leaf mold, or compost should be used rather than peat or sawdust.

Shallow-rooted. A plant is shallow-rooted if the majority of its roots are in the first 12 inches of soil.

Mulch. A covering of the soil with any material that insulates the soil—roofing paper, sawdust, rice hulls, pumice, manure, peat moss, straw, leaf mold and the like. Summer mulches to control weeds are not effective unless 3 inches thick.

Cultivate. In the home garden the term is used for all operations that keep the soil free of weeds and in a loose crumbled condition. The hoe and the hand cultivator are the tools used. In the above directions the warning against cultivation is made because the plant is surface-rooted and would lose feeder roots if the surface were chopped by a hoe.

Subject to attack. Various plants attract insects periodically throughout their growth. A plant "subject to attack" must be watched for a build up of those insects they play host for.

Cut back to non-flowering wood. (See chapter on pruning.) This simply means to cut off all branches that have finished blooming but allow all the others to remain.

Softwood-hardwood cuttings. (See chapter on propagation.)

In condensing the directions on how to use and care for plants it is necessary to use words representing a long series of operations. In reading such directions don't let the unknown word slip by. Go back to the chapter covering that phase of plant propagation or plant care and make the word your own. Actually, you learn gardening by understanding the meaning of such words as these: blocking out, damping off, dibble, drill, float, pinching back, pricking out, flats, seedlings, acid soil, adobe soil, alkaline soil, soil air, soil structure, soil texture, organic, inorganic, and on and on.

BOTANICAL NAMES vs. COMMON NAMES

Few beginners object to the words of trade dealing with garden operation, but many cry out against the use of botanical names of plants. Chances are that if you are new to gardening and garden books, one of the first questions you'll ask yourself as you turn the pages of this book is *Why can't they give plants simple English names?*

The botanical name is a recognized scientific name. It is linked with a complete description of the mature plant in the literature of botany and horticulture.

The botanical name is understood and accepted everywhere.

A legitimate botanical name on a small plant in the nursery can tell you what that plant will look like when it is mature. It says in effect: the parent of this plant fits the description of the plant so named. Let's say that the label reads *Prunus ilicifolia.* The nursery might have preferred to call it *California wild cherry.* But under that name you would be unable to find out anything definite about it. There is more than one wild cherry. But the plant *Prunus ilicifolia* is described and its measurements given in all standard reference manuals.

Correct botanical names on plants are the correct keys to all of the literature written on those plants.

Since, in most cases, when you buy a plant, you buy only a promise of another larger plant, the name must be keyed to a description of the mature plant if you are to know what you are buying.

BOTANICAL NAMES AND LABELS

The plant descriptions in this book expand for you the nurseryman's plant labels.

At the present time most of the Western nursery catalogs and the labels in the nursery follow in general names according to L. H. Bailey's *Standard Encyclopedia of Horticulture, Hortus Second,* and *Manual of Cultivated Plants.*

For that reason, plant names in this book are according to Dr. Bailey's publications.

Although these publications list a greater variety of cultivated plant material than any other one manual in the United States, they fail to include many of the new introductions exclusive to the West. For our authority on naming such plants, we have turned to experienced Western botanists.

The important fact is that this method of listing makes it possible for you to use this book as a buying guide, a reference book for plants at Western nurseries. All the names used by Western nurseries have been cataloged according to a known system, and to each name has been added the essential facts of size and habit of growth.

The surprising thing is that as you use the book you realize that the botanical system of naming makes a lot of sense. It's logical, definite, and precise. It makes order out of disorder.

PRINCIPLES OF NAMING PLANTS

The system for assigning names and classifications to plants dates back to the work of Linnæus, a great Swedish botanist and naturalist of the 18th century. He saw that the indiscriminate naming of plants then in practice could lead to nothing but chaos.

Under his system, plants that have characteristics in common are grouped together into categories, and their names relate them to the group to which they belong. They are given two-part names: a generic name that identifies the general group to which they belong; and a specific name that identifies the particular plant. The general name identifies the plant's GENUS (see chart); the specific name, its SPECIES. A third name is added for varia-

HOW PLANTS ARE CLASSIFIED AND NAMED

First the broad FAMILY
Botanists group plants into FAMILIES according to structure of leaves, flowers, fruit, seeds. Olive Family at right has 20 members.

Next class—the GENUS
Next, each group of plants within family that have common characteristics are grouped into a GENUS (pl. GENERA), e.g., OSMANTHUS.

SPECIES vary from the genus
Differences within a genus are grouped into SPECIES—the class most familiar to gardeners. These can vary widely. Within the Osmanthus Genus, are several species. They differ in shape of leaves, color of blossom, height of mature plants, time of bloom.

VARIETIES differ from species
Not all plants that are grouped in a species are exactly alike. They may differ in color or size of flower, shape or color of leaves, etc. Those that differ are called VARIETIES or SUBSPECIES. The Osmanthus variety shown differs from its species in leaf coloration.

A HYBRID resembles both parents
As a rule, species do not combine with each other, but there are exceptions known as HYBRIDS. Some species can be crossed with others or with varieties, either naturally or artificially. Example: Osmanthus hybrids combine leaf and flower characteristics of parent species.

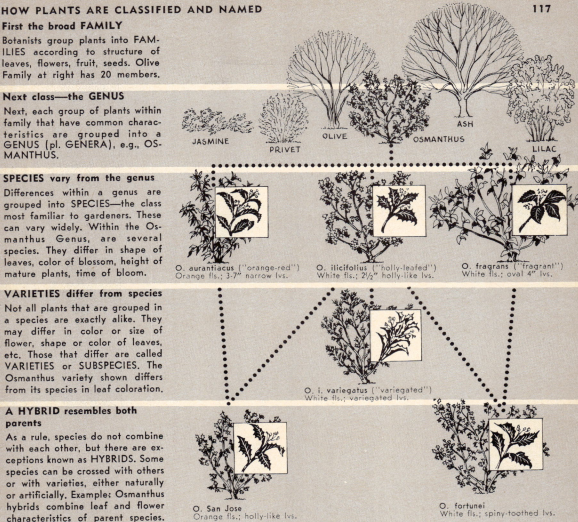

tions within a species. These variants are called VARIETIES or SUBSPECIES.

In this book, these different names are shown in different type faces. In the encyclopedic listings, for example, we follow this style:

GENUS NAME. *(Botanical synonym, if any).* COMMON NAME. Then follows a description of the plant, its culture, and uses. The individual species are shown this way:

G. species. Following standard botanical shorthand, the name of the genus is abbreviated to an initial letter. The varieties are shown in this manner:

G. s. variety. Again, initial letters are used for both genus and species.

The "botanical synonym" listed in parentheses above is an earlier name that has been officially replaced. We show it because the plant may still be marketed under its obsolete name.

GUIDE TO LATIN DESCRIPTIVE WORDS
Botanical names are written in Latin so they may be understandable to all people in all languages.

Genus names are usually classical words that have a general or indefinite meaning. Species names are usually descriptive—color, form, leaf structure; commemorative—named after the man who discovered the plant; or geographical—the locality where it grows or originated.

Let's take apart the label on a variety of the familiar Douglas fir. The tag reads *"Pseudotsuga taxifolia glauca."* Broken into its parts, this name tells this story:

Pseudo = FALSE
tsuga = HEMLOCK } FALSE HEMLOCK
taxi = YEW
folia = LEAF } LEAVES LIKE A YEW
glauca = BLUISH-GREEN

Reassembled, this name indicates that the Douglas fir closely resembles the hemlock, and it has bluish-green foliage like that of the yew tree.

The following words occur again and again in the scientific names of plants. All are descriptive adjectives used in naming species and varieties.

118 GARDENER'S LANGUAGE

COLOR OF FLOWERS OR FOLIAGE

These words indicate color of flower or foliage:

albus—white
argentatus—silvery
aureus—golden
azureus—azure, sky blue
cœruleus—dark blue
cæsius—blue gray
candidus—pure white, shiny
canus—ashy gray, hoary
carneus—flesh colored
cereus—waxy
citrinus—yellow
coccineus—scarlet
concolor—one color
croceus—yellow
cruentus—bloody
discolor—two colors, separate colors
glaucous—as though sprinkled with light powder
incanus—gray, hoary
luteus—reddish yellow
purpureus—purple
rubens, ruber—red, ruddy
rufus—ruddy

FORM OF LEAF

Several words indicate the form or character of the leaf or foliage.

In coining names for *species* the originator expressed his own opinion. If he thought the leaf looked like a holly leaf he combined the word *holly* and *foliage* and the *species* carried the name *ilicifolia*. If he wishes to make the size of the leaf denote the difference between species he called one *large* (macro) *leafed* (phylla) or *macrophylla*.

Thus we have numerous leaf descriptions that are most helpful in getting a picture of the plant.

acerifolius—maple-like leaves
aquifolius—sharp leaves
augustifolia—narrow leaves
buxifolius—leaves like boxwood
ilicifolius—holly-like leaves
laurifolius—laurel-like leaves
parvifolius—small leaves
populifolia—poplar-like leaves
salicifolius—willow-like leaves

SHAPE OF PLANTS

These words indicate form or growing habit of entire plant:

adpressus—pressing against, hugging
altus—tall
arboreus—tree like
capitatus—head like
cneorum—low, evergreen
compactus—compact, dense
confertus—crowded, pressed together
contortus—twisted
decumbens—lying down
depressus—pressed down
elegans—elegant; slender, willowy
fastigiatus—branches erect and close together
humifusus—sprawling on the ground
humilis—low, small, humble
impressus—impressed upon
nanus—dwarf
procumbens—trailing
prostratus—prostrate
pumilus—dwarfish, small
pusillus—puny, insignificant
repens—creeping
reptans—creeping
scandens—climbing

WHERE IT CAME FROM

These indicate native habitat:

australis—southern
borealis—northern
campestris—of the field or plains
insularis—of the island
littoralis—of the seashore
montanus—of the mountains
riparius—of river banks
rivalis—of brooks
rivularis—loving brooks
saxatilis—inhabiting rocks

The suffix *-ensis* (of a place) is added to place names to specify the native habitat of the place the plant was first discovered.

canadensis—of Canada
canariensis—of the Canary Islands
capensis—of the Cape of Good Hope area
chilensis—of Chile
chinensis—of China

PLANT PECULIARITIES

Some of the words that are repeatedly used are useful in setting the plant apart:

armatus—armed
baccatus—berried, berry-like
barbatus—barbed or bearded
campanulatus—bell or cup shaped
ciliaris—fringed
cordatus—heart-shaped
cornutus—horned
crassus—thick, fleshy
decurrens—running down the stem
dendron—tree
diversi—varying
edulis—edible
floridus—tree flowering
fruticosus—shrubby
fulgens—shiny
gracilis—slender, thin, small
grandi—large, showy
ifer, iferous—bearing or having. For example, *stoloniferous*, having stolons
laciniatus—fringed or with torn edges
lævigatus—smooth
lobatus—lobed
maculatus—spotted
mollis—soft, soft hairy
mucronatus—pointed
nutans—nodding, swaying
oides—like or resembling. For example: *jasminoides*, like a jasmine
obtusa—blunt or flattened
officinalis—medicinal
patens—open spreading growth
pinnatus—constructed like a feather
plenus—double, full
plumosus—feathery
præcox—precocious
pungens—piercing
radicans—rooting—especially along the stem
reticulatus—veined
retusus—notched at blunt apex
rugosus—wrinkled, rough
saccharatus—sweet, sugary
sagittalis—arrow-like
scabrous—rough feeling
scoparius—broom-like

Container Gardening

As garden living increases its demand for space, and paving or hard surfaces take over larger areas, the opportunities for exciting, more concentrated use of plant material increases. When dining, loafing, and reading move out into the garden, the relationship between plants and people becomes more intimate; close-ups are more frequent.

With raised beds, seat walls, tubs, boxes, planters big and little, you find yourself sitting alongside plants more frequently than in the walk-through garden. The raised bed backed by a fence immediately suggests a stage for plants. The tubs and boxes are "props" for changing scenes. The seat alongside a low wall is an invitation to plant miniatures so that they can be studied and admired at near eye-level—or to get close to fragrant plants. Floor-to-ceiling windows or doors opening to the terrace let the plants outside become part of the indoor design and color scheme.

Container gardening is not restricted to containers or to the garden living room. If you consider this type of gardening in its broader sense, the containment of a shrub or tree in espalier form against a wall, or the planted square in a paved terrace—also figure here.

Here are sketches for 12 different situations which illustrate some of the opportunities in container gardening:

1. Raised bed against a fence.
2. Raised bed in open.
3. Plant boxes on terrace.
4. Inset in terrace.
5. Large tub planting.
6. Tub and box grouping.
7. Seat alongside raised bed.
8. Wall for plants to spill over.
9. Plant boxes on fence or wall.
10. Hanging baskets.
11. Miniature display.
12. Indoor-outdoor planting.

ABOVE. Sand-blasted redwood box contains Echeveria pulvinata. Simple, well-designed containers of this type, made of material that weathers well, can be used in many ways on patio or terrace floor. Shallow-rooted succulents are particularly adapted to such boxes.

120 CONTAINER GARDENING

RAISED BED AGAINST A FENCE

Informal espalier against fence, with low or trailing plants in front.

Evergreen pear *(Pyrus kawakami)*, prostrate rosemary *(Rosmarinus officinalis Lockwoodii)*. Sun.

Southern magnolia *(M. grandiflora)*, star jasmine *(Trachelospermum jasminoides)*. Sun.

Fatshedera *(F. lizeii)*, Hahn's ivy *(Hedera helix Hahnii)*, partial shade.

Lodgepole pine (espaliered), kinnikinnick *(Arctostaphylos uva-ursi)*. Sun or light shade.

RAISED BED IN THE OPEN

A small tree, low shrubs or clumps of a shrubby perennial, and ground cover make a complete planting in a raised bed.

Purple leafed plum *(Prunus blireiana)*, Senecio greyii, catmint *(Nepeta mussinii)*.

Flowering crabapple *(Malus floribunda)*, India hawthorn *(Raphiolepis indica rosea)*, Iberis sempervirens.

Olive, *Sedum spectabile*, prostrate rosemary.

Fruiting quince *(Cydonia oblonga)*, Convolvulus cneorum, Cerastium tomentosum.

Dianthus Little Rubies, *Sedum spathulifolium* Cape Blanco, creeping thyme *(Thymus serpyllum)*.

LARGE TUB PLANTING

Tubs large enough for small trees or large shrubs. Ground covers soften edges of the box.

Tree wisteria, blue or white violas.

Star magnolia *(M. stellata)*, Iberis sempervirens.

Japanese maple *(Acer palmatum)*, and bronze-leafed carpet bugle *(Ajuga metallica crispa)*, interplanted with small colonies of hardy cyclamen.

Flowering peach or apricot, forget-me-nots.

TUB AND BOX GROUPING

Large tubbed plant forms background for pots of smaller plants.

Mugho pine *(Pinus mugo mughus)* in tub; azaleas (Belgian Indicas or Kurumes); cyclamen.

Heavenly bamboo *(Nandina domestica)* in tub; big blue lily turf *(Liriope muscari)*, dwarf bamboo *(Sasa pygmaea)*.

Corsican hellebore *(Helleborus lividus)* in tub; *Corydalis lutea, Campanula carpatica*.

White marguerite in tub; salmon or scarlet geraniums, white petunias.

PLANT BOXES ON TERRACE

Daphne odora, violets, lily-of-the-valley *(Convallaria majalis)*. Shade.

Santa Cruz Island buckwheat *(Eriogonum arborescens), Cerastium tomentosum*. Sun.

HANGING BASKETS

Modular boxes in multiples of one size or in mixed sizes form interesting patterns. With two or three sets of such boxes, you can have color through the year.

Spring: Cyclamen, primulas, violas; daffodils, forget-me-nots, sweet alyssum; tulips, linaria, violas. Use a tubbed flowering tree for height.

Summer and fall: *Felicia amelloides*, petunias; dwarf yellow French marigolds, ageratum Midget Blue; wishbone flower *(Torenia fournieri)*, trailing lobelia Sapphire; pink or yellow cushion chrysanthemum, lobelia Emperor William.

SEAT WALL ALONGSIDE RAISED BED

Proximity of seat to planting invites use of miniature or fragrant plants, as suggested here.

Meyer lemon, *Lantana camara*, yellow sun roses *(Helianthemum nummularium)*. Sun.

Heliotrope *(Heliotropium)*, purple and white petunias, alyssum Carpet of Snow. Sun.

White Ginger Lily *(Hedychium coronarium)*, peppermint geranium *(Pelargonium tomentosum)*. Tender; protect from frost, or set out in pots and lift before cold weather. Half shade.

Trailing, or almost trailing plants which spill over the sides of containers. Some of the best trailers are perennials which need staking in the garden.

Trailers: *Campanula isophylla, C. i. alba, C. i. mayii; C. fragilis, C. f.* Fanny Senior; *C. poscharskyana; Erigeron karvinskianus;* Hahn's ivy; *Lotus berthelotii; Pelargonium tomentosum; Saponaria ocymoides; Sedum sieboldii.*

Trail if given the chance: shrimp plant *(Beloperone guttata); Convolvulus cneorum; Iberis sem-*

pervirens; Lotus mascœnsis; Nepeta mussinii, N. hederacea variegata, oxalis, *Silene maritima.*

INSET IN TERRACE

Here is an opportunity for a pattern planting of miniature shrubs, trees, and perennials.

Shrubs and trees: Dwarf Hinoki cypress, dwarf forms of juniper, spruce, arborvitae *(Thuja).*

Perennials: Dwarf columbine, *Armeria juniperifolia, Campanula elatines garganica, C. carpatica, Dianthus neglectus, D.* Little Joe, evergreen candytuft, dwarf geranium, *Saponaria ocymoides.*

For surprises, tuck in small species bulbs.

PLANT BOXES ATTACHED TO WALL

Double fence with a plant box between: ingenious way to achieve interesting space division, add color.

Primroses *(Primula polyantha),* dwarf forget-me-nots, February Gold daffodils. Spring, partial shade in warmer sections.

Browallia speciosa, dwarf pink fibrous begonias, trailing lobelia. Summer-fall, partial shade.

Fancy leafed geranium Mrs. Cox or Miss Burdette Coutts, helianthemum Sunlite. All year, sun.

SUCCULENT DISPLAY

Easiest-to-grow conversation piece for a patio or terrace is a large concrete or terra cotta bowl, or a metal dish container planted with different succulents. Here are kinds you might use:

Small: *Sedum arachnoideum, S. guatemalense, S. spathulifolium* Cape Blanco; pebble plants (*Lithops, Pleiospilos*).

Medium: *Aloe aristata, Crassula falcata, Echeveria elegans, Kalanchoe blossfeldiana.*

Large: *Aloe arborescens, Crassula argentea, Kalanchoe beharensis, Portulacaria afra.*

INDOOR-OUTDOOR DISPLAY

With a wide overhang for frost protection, you can usually duplicate the indoor planting on the outside of the glass. In colder climates, move outdoor plants inside for winter.

Philodendron selloum, dieffenbachia, peperomia, indoors; dracaena, Rex begonias, coleus outdoors.

Epidendrum, cymbidiums, cypripediums.

Fatshedera lizeii indoors and outdoors, with pots of agapanthus (summer) and clivias (spring) for color outside.

WALL FOR PLANTS TO SPILL OVER

Use trailers that billow softly over the wall; or plants with stems which follow and mold themselves to contours.

Lotus berthelotii, Melianthus major. Sun.

Cotoneaster dammeri, sun. *Ficus pumila,* part shade.

Kinnikinnick *(Arctostaphylos uva-ursi), Ceanothus gloriosus.* Sun.

CONTAINER GARDENING

A visit to a nursery will show you that practically any plant will grow in a container. A plant that looks content and thrifty in its pot or can in a nursery row will probably do so in a container on your terrace if you give it good care. But plants that look as though they would be better off in the ground are hardly likely to be assets in tubs or boxes.

Your decision to grow a plant in a container should be based solely on whether it will perform or look better with its roots contained than it will in the ground. If you live in a cold climate or in an area with special soil or water problems, containers offer the only safe way to grow certain plants with critical soil or temperature requirements.

Bulbous Plants. With few exceptions, bulbs and tubers are good container subjects. Tuberous begonias are notoriously so. Cyclamen, hyacinths, clivia, hippeastrum, certain types of tulips, and many varieties of daffodils are on the preferred list—and if sufficient root depth is provided—some lilies, also. (For pot culture of bulbs, see chapter on bulbs.)

Annuals. Any annual whose size and growth habit can be maintained in relation to the container is a candidate. These, however, are naturally good pot plants: Lobelia, dwarf petunias, browallia, *Primula malacoides,* schizanthus, and cineraria.

Perennials. Perennials that become more compact and flower more freely in containers than with unlimited root space are: geraniums (common and Martha Washington), marguerites, francoa, trailing and chimney bell campanulas, cushion and cascade chrysanthemum, *Sedum sieboldii,* heliotrope, hellebores, and hosta (funkia).

Shrubs. *Aucuba japonica,* azaleas, bamboo in variety, bouvardia, boxwood, *Camellia japonica,* and *C. sasanqua.* Citrus (dwarf types), *Fatsia japonica,* fuchsias, gardenia, *Hibiscus rosa-sinensis,* hydrangea (lace-cap variety is especially beautiful), *Magnolia stellata,* Mugho pine, *Nandina domestica,* oleander, *Pieris japonica, P. forrestii, Pyrus kawakami* (espaliered), rhododendron (dwarf kinds especially), floribunda roses, tree peony, *Skimmia japonica.*

Succulents. *Aloe aristata, Cotyledon orbiculata, Crassula argentea, C. falcata, Echeveria elegans, E. pulvinata, Sedum sieboldii.*

Trees. *Acer palmatum,* citrus (kumquat, dwarf orange, lemon, calamondin), *Eriobotrya japonica* (espaliered), *Ficus retusa, Magnolia grandiflora* (espaliered).

Soil and Containers. The type of container and soil mixture you use depends, of course, on the plant material. When using trees and shrubs for their structural character—as in ancient Chinese container culture—both container and type of soil are deliberately chosen for the purpose of dwarfing the plant. (Here, definite distinction must be made between dwarfing or restraining growth by means of root binding or space limitation, and dwarfing by consistent root pruning. The latter method of dwarfing does not enter in here.) Ideal container plants as far as trees and shrubs are concerned are those that dwarf themselves without root pruning. If, for example, you pot dwarf junipers or pines in a gravelly soil, these plants will keep their natural dwarf form without any help from the pruning shears.

Four basic ingredients are included in most soil mixtures: compost or soil; manure; sand; and leaf mold or peat moss. Proportions can be varied to make a lean or rich mixture depending on the plant and what you want it to do—grow lush or be restrained.

A general potting mixture for most plants: 2 or 3 parts garden loam (depending on whether soil is light or heavy in texture); 1 part coarse sand; 1 part peat moss; 1 part well rotted cow manure.

124 CONTAINER GARDENING

In sections where soils are high in salinity, or where textural quality is poor, many gardeners prefer to omit or reduce the amount of soil and to add more sand and peat moss.

The U. C. Mix, highly recommended for container plants, is discussed in the chapter on soils.

Whatever type of container you use, be sure it drains freely. Large tubs and boxes should have several holes (see illustration).

For further information on container culture, see the *Sunset* book, *Gardening in Containers*.

Watering. Watering schedules vary according to type of plants, soil mixtures, containers, and climatic conditions. Safest rule is to water thoroughly when necessary and to allow the plant to take up most of the soil moisture before watering again.

Tuberous begonias and cinerarias potted in a porous soil mixture may need water every day—often twice a day in warm dry weather. Succulents, on the other hand, may not need water oftener than once a week or less.

FERTILIZING. Because of restricted root space and constant leaching of nutrients by watering, potted plants generally need feeding oftener than those in the open ground. A monthly application of balanced fertilizer during the active growing season is recommended for most flowering or fruiting plants.

For further information on container culture, see the *Sunset Book*, *The Portable Garden*.

HERE IS HOW TO POT A PLANT:

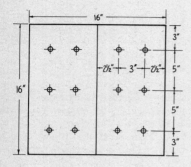

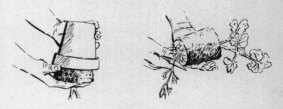

Before potting on plant into next size container, trim old overgrown roots to stimulate new ones

Place enough coarse gravel in the bottom of the container so that the dirt will neither sift through the holes nor clog them so the water won't pass through freely.

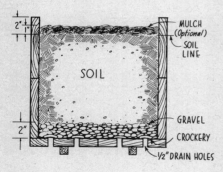

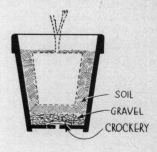

Correctly potted plant: drainage in bottom, fresh soil mix on all sides for new roots to grow into

Redwood, cedar, or other rot-resistant woods make good containers for most plants. A 16-inch square is a good size for larger plants and will last for many years.

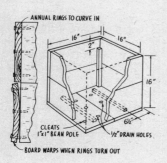

Pot firmly so that there will not be any air holes. Water thoroughly by soaking pot in basin from below

Annuals

Plants whose life cycle—from seed sprouting to seed setting—is completed in a year or less are called annuals. By common consent, gardeners have included in the annual group many perennials that give a better account of themselves when treated as annuals. Snapdragons, petunias, pansies, and violas are a few of the plants that will live over from year to year in warm winters but are replaced annually because their first season of bloom is superior to any that follow.

Annuals run on fast clockwork. With some, everything is timed to get seed produced before death by winter cold. With others the growth cycle is timed to the length of day. In almost every case you have rapid growth to work with. For quick color you look to the annuals.

Some annuals rush from seed to flower in less than two months. Transplants, by-the-dozen or in flats at your nursery are often full-budded when you buy them and ready to bloom in a week or two after planting out.

With annuals alone you can have a succession of bloom throughout the year in warm winter sections, and from before last frost in the spring to beyond first frost in the fall in the cold winter areas. But succession of bloom requires planning and close following of planting dates. Many gardeners, planning for spring, summer and winter flowers, haven't the heart to pull out and replace the spring blooming crop in time to get the summer crop under way.

The uses for annuals that have proved most satisfactory to most gardeners call for combinations of annuals, perennials, and shrubs. When a garden is not dependent upon annuals for its seasonal appearance, the bringing in of seasonal color seems to be an easy task. But when the garden is arranged so it falls apart unless every flower is in full dress, the planting and care of annuals may become a chore.

Planting Season

In the following profiles of individual flowers we have indicated the type and planting dates by

126 ANNUALS

assigning each a group number—I, II, III.

In group I are all the plants that, in warm winter sections, can be sown in late summer or fall for winter or early spring bloom.

In group II are those that can be sown in early spring for late spring or early summer bloom.

In group III are the warm weather annuals—those planted in late spring for summer or fall bloom.

Those annuals that will grow in early spring or summer or over a mild winter are so noted by assigning them to all three groups.

These group classifications allow you to plan your plantings exactly according to the weather in your zone.

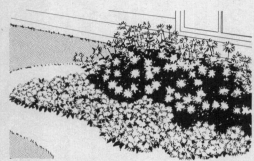

BLUE AGERATUM AS EDGING WITH FALL PERENNIALS

Zones 1-6

In respect to annuals, the climates in zones 1 to 6 vary from 70 days between frosts in high altitude areas to 285 days in oceanside gardens.

In most cases the long growing season is low in summer temperatures; the short season has high summer temperatures.

If your climate has no summer heat to speak of—as in most areas directly influenced by the ocean—the cool-weather annuals, group II, are your best bets for both spring and summer.

In the shorter growing seasons where spring changes to hot summer, the warm-weather annuals, group III, should be favored.

The shorter the season the greater the value of starting seed indoors or under glass. (See chapter on how to start plants.) Plants with a month or more of growing time behind them can be set out in the quickly warming spring of the short growing season to give bloom in a few weeks.

By observing plant growth of an assortment of annuals through one season, you can see how each plant responds to your spring, summer, and fall.

In the second year you will be able to take advantage of the extra long spring or the extra summer heat or any other peculiarity your climate provides.

Zones 7 and 11

When you move into zones 7 and 11—California's interior valleys—you almost have to forget the group I procedures. The carry-over of high summer temperatures into September prevents planting out until October. Furthermore, winter temperatures drop into the twenties often enough to make winter planting hazardous.

The spring climate also becomes critical by being of such short duration. Planting of cool weather plants, group II, should be made early enough to get them out of the way by mid-May.

Zone 8

The low desert areas of Southern California and Arizona offer another situation. Here the one practical growing season for annuals is from February to mid-May. Day temperatures are on the increase, but low night temperatures rule out all except the cool weather annuals, group II.

Where winters are definitely cold and prevent growth of annuals in any season except the stretch of spring and summer days between last and first killing frost, the gardener is concerned with groups II and III—the cool-weather annuals and the warm-weather annuals.

Planting dates in these areas are according to the seed packets. The key words on the packet are either "after last frost" or "as soon as ground is warm."

ALYSSUM AS COVER FOR FADING BULB BEDS

Zones 9, 10, 12, 13

Spring and summer planting pose no special problems. The natural urge to plant everything comes with the spring and most gardeners in the warm spring areas overdo their planting. Even though you are in an area where frosts are long past don't try to rush the season with warm weather annuals. Stay with group II until the ground has warmed and night temperatures are above 45°.

Late summer planting is the most difficult to manage. Generally throughout this area the October and November days are warm enough to convince anyone that any of the annuals would grow. Actually, the drop of night temperatures below 45° slows growth to nearly a standstill.

The whole trick of getting bloom during winter is to get an early enough start to have the plants in bud stage by the time they hit a night temperature of 45°.

PLANTING GUIDE FOR ANNUALS

WINTER OR EARLY SPRING BLOOM (MILD WINTER AREAS)
(Group I: Sow in late summer or fall)

Alyssum. SWEET ALYSSUM.
Anchusa capensis. CAPE FORGET-ME-NOT.
Antirrhinum majus. SNAPDRAGON.
Brachycome iberidifolia. SWAN RIVER DAISY.
Calendula officinalis. POT MARIGOLD.
Centaurea. BACHELOR BUTTON. CORNFLOWER.
Cineraria. FLORIST'S CINERARIA.
Clarkia. MOUNTAIN GARLAND.
Collinsia bicolor. CHINESE HOUSES.
Cynoglossum amabile. CHINESE FORGET-ME-NOT.
Delphinium ajacis. LARKSPUR.
Diascia barberae. TWINSPUR.
Dimorphotheca. CAPE MARIGOLD. AFRICAN DAISY.
Eschscholtzia californica. CALIFORNIA POPPY.
Gilia. FAIRY STARS. BIRD'S EYES.
Helichrysum bracteatum. STRAWFLOWER.
Iberis. CANDYTUFT.
Lathyrus odoratus. SWEET PEA.
Linaria maroccana. TOADFLAX. BABY SNAPDRAGON.
Linum grandiflorum rubrum. SCARLET FLAX.
Lupinus. LUPINE.
Lychnis coeli-rosa. VISCARIA. ROSE OF HEAVEN.
Malcomia maritima. VIRGINIAN STOCK.
Myosotis sylvatica. FORGET-ME-NOT.
Nemesia strumosa.
Nemophila menziesii. BABY-BLUE-EYES.
Mathiola. STOCK.
Papaver. POPPY.
Primula malacoides. FAIRY PRIMROSE.
Reseda odorata. MIGNONETTE.
Scabiosa atropurpurea. PINCUSHION FLOWER.
Viola. VIOLA. TUFTED PANSY. HEARTSEASE.

LATE SPRING OR EARLY SUMMER BLOOM
(Group II: Sow in early spring)

Abronia umbellata. PINK SAND-VERBENA.
Ageratum houstonianum. FLOSS FLOWER.
Alyssum. SWEET ALYSSUM.
Anagallis. PIMPERNEL.
Anchusa capensis. CAPE FORGET-ME-NOT.
Antirrhinum majus. SNAPDRAGON.
Arctotis. AFRICAN DAISY.
Brachycome iberidifolia. SWAN RIVER DAISY.
Browallia. AMETHYST FLOWER.
Calendula officinalis. POT MARIGOLD.
Callistephus chinensis. CHINA ASTER. ASTER.
Centaurea. BACHELOR BUTTON. CORNFLOWER.
Chrysanthemum carinatum. SUMMER CHRYSANTHEMUM.
Cineraria. FLORIST'S CINERARIA.
Clarkia. MOUNTAIN GARLAND.
Cleome spinosa. SPIDER FLOWER.
Collinsia bicolor. CHINESE HOUSES.
Convolvulus tricolor. BUSH MORNING GLORY.
Coreopsis tinctoria. ANNUAL COREOPSIS.
Cosmos bipinnatus. COSMOS.
Cynoglossum amabile. CHINESE FORGET-ME-NOT.
Delphinium ajacis. LARKSPUR.
Dianthus. PINK.
Diascia barberae. TWINSPUR.
Didiscus caerulea. BLUE LACE FLOWER.
Dimorphotheca. CAPE MARIGOLD. AFRICAN DAISY.
Eschscholtzia californica. CALIFORNIA POPPY.
Gaillardia pulchella. ANNUAL GAILLARDIA.
Gilia. FAIRY STARS. BIRD'S EYES.
Godetia. FAREWELL-TO-SPRING. SATIN FLOWER.
Gypsophila elegans. BABY'S BREATH.
Helianthus annuus. COMMON SUNFLOWER.
Helichrysum bracteatum. STRAWFLOWER.
Iberis. CANDYTUFT.
Lathyrus odoratus. SWEET PEA.
Lavatera trimestris. TREE MALLOW.
Limonium (Statice). SEA LAVENDER.
Linaria maroccana. TOADFLAX. BABY SNAPDRAGON.
Linum grandiflorum rubrum. SCARLET FLAX.
Lobelia erinus.
Lupinus. LUPINE.
Lychnis coeli-rosa. VISCARIA. ROSE OF HEAVEN.
Malcomia maritima. VIRGINIAN STOCK.
Mimulus tigrinus. MONKEY FLOWER.
Myosotis sylvatica. FORGET-ME-NOT.
Nemesia strumosa.
Nemophila menziesii. BABY-BLUE-EYES.
Mathiola. STOCK.
Nigella damascena. LOVE-IN-A-MIST.
Papaver. POPPY.
Petunia hybrida.
Phlox drummondii. ANNUAL PHLOX.
Primula malacoides. FAIRY PRIMROSE.
Reseda odorata. MIGNONETTE.
Salpiglossis sinuata. PAINTED-TONGUE.
Salvia splendens. SCARLET SAGE.
Scabiosa atropurpurea. PINCUSHION FLOWER.
Schizanthus. POOR MAN'S ORCHID. BUTTERFLY FLOWER.
Tagetes. MARIGOLD.
Torenia fournieri. WISHBONE FLOWER.
Vinca rosea. MADAGASCAR PERIWINKLE.
Viola. VIOLA. TUFTED PANSY. PANSY. HEARTSEASE.
Xeranthemum annuum. COMMON IMMORTELLE.

SUMMER OR FALL BLOOM
(Group III: Sow in late spring)

Ageratum houstonianum. FLOSS FLOWER.
Alyssum. SWEET ALYSSUM.
Amaranthus. AMARANTH.
Anagallis. PIMPERNEL.
Arctotis. AFRICAN DAISY.
Celosia. COCKSCOMB.
Centaurea. BACHELOR BUTTON. CORNFLOWER.
Convolvulus tricolor. BUSH MORNING GLORY.
Coreopsis tinctoria. ANNUAL COREOPSIS.
Dianthus. PINK.
Gaillardia pulchella. ANNUAL GAILLARDIA.
Gypsophila elegans. BABY'S BREATH.
Helianthus annuus. COMMON SUNFLOWER.
Impatiens balsamina. BALSAM.
Limonium (Statice). SEA LAVENDER.
Linum grandiflorum rubrum. SCARLET FLAX.
Lobelia erinus.
Mathiola. STOCK.
Mimulus tigrinus. MONKEY FLOWER.
Nicotiana. FLOWERING TOBACCO.
Petunia hybrida.
Phlox drummondii. ANNUAL PHLOX.
Portulaca grandiflora. ROSE MOSS.
Reseda odorata. MIGNONETTE.
Salvia splendens. SCARLET SAGE.
Tagetes. MARIGOLD.
Tithonia rotundifolia. MEXICAN SUNFLOWER.
Torenia fournieri. WISHBONE FLOWER.
Zinnia.

ABRONIA UMBELLATA. Pink Sand-Verbena. Low-spreading plant in full sun, dry soil. Finely cut foliage. Bright rosy-lilac, verbena-like flowers in summer and fall. Fragrant at night. Var. *grandiflora* has larger leaves and flowers. CULTURE: I, II. Sow in open ground in spring or fall. Thrives in poor, sandy, or shallow soils, where it often self-sows. Best along coast, although adaptable in all zones including desert. USE: Banks, seaside gardens, rock gardens.

AFRICAN DAISY. See ARCTOTIS; DIMORPHOTHECA

AGERATUM HOUSTONIANUM. Floss Flower. All zones in summer; in winter only in 12, 13. ½-2 ft. according to variety. Hairy, green leaves. Tiny, lavender-blue, white, or pink flowers crowded into compact heads resembling small tassels. Dwarf types form compact mounds so covered with flowers that you can hardly see the leaves. Taller types have a looser, more branching growth habit. CULTURE: II, III. In zones 12, 13, ageratum may be sown as late as August for fall bloom. Rich, moist soil. Appreciates light shade in warm interiors, will not take reflected heat. USE: Dwarf types for neat, even edgings. *Blue Perfection* 1 ft., and taller, blue type are invaluable fillers in the perennial border, combine well with most annuals, particularly *Phlox Drummondii*, petunias, marigolds, and zinnias.

ALYSSUM. (*Lobularia maritima*). Sweet Alyssum. 4-10 in. Foolproof, universal favorite that blooms in 6 weeks from seed. Tiny, honey-scented flowers in compact heads. *Carpet of Snow* and *Little Gem*, 4 in., pure white; *Violet Queen*, 6 in., bright violet; *Royal Carpet*, 4 in., rich purple dotted with occasional lighter flowers. CULTURE: I, II, III. Sow seed in place every few weeks for successive bloom. Reseeds freely, and may become a pest, but plants pull easily. USE: Over bulb beds, between paving stones, as a cover at the base of tubbed shrubs and trees; lowest forms for edgings.

AMARANTHUS. Amaranth. 1-5 ft. Odd plants—related to cockscomb—grown mainly for their vivid-colored foliage and spikes or clusters of rich red flowers in late summer and fall.

  A. caudatus. Love-Lies-Bleeding. 3-5 ft. Dark red flowers carried in long, slender, nodding panicles.

  A. hybridus hypochondriacus. Prince's Feather. 4-5 ft. Slender growth habit. Flowers purple, green, or red, in erect spikes. Foliage green, gold, red, or purple.

  A. tricolor. St. Joseph's Coat. 1-3 ft. Grown for brilliant foliage from which the plant derives its name. Leaves 2½-4 in. wide, blotched and streaked with red, yellow, and yellow-green.

CULTURE: III. Seed in flats, but best sown where it is to bloom in late spring. Full sun, plenty of water.

USE: Showy, but difficult to combine with other plants. Tallest types best in background, against walls, fences, or tall shrubs.

AMETHYST FLOWER. See BROWALLIA

ANAGALLIS. Pimpernel. 6-8 in. Annuals rarely seen, but easily recognized as refined relatives of the common, sprawling weed with small, bright orange flowers. Leaves arranged in spirals around square stems. Best garden form is *A. arvensis coerulea*, gentian-blue, ¾-in. flowers. CULTURE: II, III. Sow seed in place in spring. May take 3 weeks to germinate. Warm, moist, fairly rich soil. Blooms summer into winter in mild-winter sections. USE: Rock gardens, window boxes, pots. Effective with portulaca, alyssum.

ANCHUSA CAPENSIS. Cape Forget-Me-Not. 1½-2 ft. Biennial grown as an annual. Narrow, dark green, lanceolate leaves are slightly rough, but the plant in general is refined compared to the perennial anchusa *A. italica*. which is inclined to be coarse and on the weedy side. The horticultural variety *Blue Bird* delights with its intense, indigo-blue, forget-me-not-like flowers in summer. CULTURE: I, II. Grows in full sun in ordinary or slightly enriched soil, with average watering. USE: A really good blue for summer borders, particularly sharp and stimulating in combination with clean, clear yellows such as that of hunnemannia, dwarf marigold *Yellow Pigmy*, or taller African marigold *Yellow Supreme*.

ANTIRRHINUM MAJUS. Snapdragon. 6 in.-4 ft. Short-lived perennial usually treated as an annual. Typical cool-season plant, reaching its greatest perfection in spring and early summer before hot weather arrives. Unsurpassed in border and arrangements for spiky form and beautiful colors, including soft to deep shades of pink, rose, salmon, yellow, copper, maroon, crimson, and also pure white. Available in tall (3-4 ft.), intermediate (15-18 in.), and dwarf (6-9 in.) forms. The tetra strain (produced by treating regular varieties with the drug colchicine), forms stockier plants with thicker stems, heavier and darker green leaves, and larger, more ruffled flowers with thicker petals. Although fine for cutting, tetras are not as graceful garden flowers as taller snapdragons. CULTURE: I, II. Set out from flats in early fall in zones 7-13; in spring in 1-6. Give rich soil, feed regularly until growth is rapid and sturdy. If fall-planted snapdragons reach bud stage before cold weather, they will bloom through winter and spring. Rust is most serious enemy of snapdragons. Rust-resistant strains do not guarantee complete freedom from rust, because snapdragons may be subject to more than one strain of rust. One way to obtain rust-free plants is to grow them from cuttings of side-shoots taken from healthy plants. Overhead watering helps to disseminate rust spores. Rotate plantings each year. USE: Taller types in wide borders—beautiful with delphiniums, Madonna lilies, polyantha roses—also good for cutting. Dwarf forms effective in rock gardens, raised beds, and pots.

ARCTOTIS. African Daisy. 1½-2½ ft. Free-blooming, bushy, South African annual.

  A. stoechadifolia grandis. 2½ ft. Silvery-white petals, blue center; white-woolly foliage. *A. s. grandis* hybrids in apricot, yellow, terra cotta, and white, with dark centers, gray foliage.

CULTURE: II, III. Sow where plants are to bloom. Full sun, not too rich soil.

USE: Splashes of color along drives, on gentler slopes. Although flowers close at night, they are otherwise good for cutting. Partly developed buds will open in water indoors.

ASTER. See CALLISTEPHUS
BABY-BLUE-EYES. See NEMOPHILA MENZIESII
BABY'S BREATH. See GYPSOPHILA ELEGANS
BACHELOR BUTTON. See CENTUREA
BALSAM. See IMPATIENS BALSAMINA
BIRD'S EYES. See GILIA
BLANKET FLOWER. See GAILLARDIA PULCHELLA
BLUE LACE FLOWER. See DIDISCUS CAERULEA
BLUE THIMBLE FLOWER. See GILIA
BRACHYCOME IBERIDIFOLIA. Swan River Daisy. 6-12 in. Flowers, like miniature cinerarias, bloom in white, rose, blue, and dark violet in late spring or early summer.

Finely cut foliage. CULTURE: I, II. Sow seed in place in spring or fall. USE: Plant in large, broad masses; ineffective in small groups. Sow thickly over spring flowering bulbs, among snapdragons and stock, in rock gardens, under light foliaged deciduous trees.

BROWALLIA. AMETHYST FLOWER. 1-2 ft. Brilliant, blue flowers like a giant lobelia are almost always in bloom. Worth the trouble of starting from seed; nurseries rarely carry the plants.

B. americana. (*B. elata*). 2 ft., flowers blue or violet. *Sapphire*, a horticultural variety, 9-12 in., dark blue flowers with white eye, extremely floriferous, is considered the best.

B. speciosa. Bushy, to 3 ft., fully covered with bright violet-blue flowers with a white throat.

CULTURE: II. Requires warmth and constant moisture. Seed sown in spring in flats or in open ground; may take 3 weeks to germinate. Set plants in part shade in moist, rich earth. Blooms all spring and summer if started early. May be cut back and potted up over winter for greenhouse bloom.

USE: Superb in pots, in borders in warm shade.

BURNING BUSH. See KOCHIA SCOPARIA
BUTTERFLY FLOWER. See SCHIZANTHUS
CALENDULA OFFICINALIS. POT MARIGOLD. 1-2 ft. Most reliable, cool-season annual, giving bloom in winter or early spring. Usual colors of orange and yellow, also softer, pastel shades, including apricot, cream, lemon. CULTURE: I, II. Seed sown in place or in flats. Will grow in rich or poor soil with little or plenty of water. USE: Solid masses of single colors. Long-lasting cut flowers. Keep old flowers removed. Pots and boxes.

CALIFORNIA POPPY. See ESCHSCHOLTZIA CALIFORNICA
CALLIOPSIS. See COREOPSIS TINCTORIA.
CALLISTEPHUS CHINENSIS. CHINA ASTER. ASTER. 1-3 ft. Long-established favorite for cutting and also for summer gardens, although its frequent need for staking and susceptibility to various pests and diseases reduce its usefulness as a garden flower. Available in many new forms and in most colors except pure yellow. The range includes light to deep pink, rose, lavender, blue; crimson and scarlet; and white. Types include:

Giant Branching. Large, double flowers on long stems.

Crego. Full, feathery flowers. Frilled, ribbon-like petals curled and twisted.

American Beauty. Peony-like, 4-in. flowers.

Giants of California. Improved Crego. Largest of all asters.

Queen of the Market. Early. Full, double, 3-in. flowers.

Princess. Crested centers. Multiple rows of flat petals.

Sunshine. Quilled centers radiating over contrasting color of ray petals.

Pompon. Round pompons of quilled petals. Few short outer petals.

Single Rainbow. Large, single daisies in wide color range.

CULTURE: II. Temperamental. Subject to many pests and diseases, most serious of which are root aphis, aster yellows, and fusarium wilt. Overwatering produces the ideal situation for the latter two diseases, especially in heavy soil. Never plant in same location in successive years. Sudden check in growth is serious. Usually started in flats, but sowing in place in mid-spring may produce healthier plants. Choose wilt-resistant strains of seed.

USE: In rows for cutting. In the garden, blocks of single graded colors are most effective.

CANDYTUFT. See IBERIS.
CAPE FORGET-ME-NOT. See ANCHUSA CAPENSIS
CAPE MARIGOLD. See DIMORPHOTHECA
CELOSIA. COCKSCOMB. 1-3 ft. Richly colored annual that revels in heat and moisture. Best suited to warm-summer interior sections.

C. argentea. PLUME OR FEATHER COCKSCOMB. 2½-3 ft. Long spikes of silky, feathery blooms in brilliant pink, crimson, and pure gold. Foliage of same color as flower. Dwarf varieties available. *Golden Fleece*, golden yellow, excellent tall variety.

C. argentea cristata. CRESTED COCKSCOMB. 3 ft. Odd, flat flowers resembling cock's comb in vivid shades of velvety crimson, yellow, orange, and red. Foliage green or colored.

C. argentea childsii. WOOLFLOWER. 2½-3 ft. Flower heads in globular masses resembling balls of yarn. Colors: Pink, yellow, orange, crimson.

CULTURE: III. Seed sown in place in late spring germinates readily. Thinning unnecessary. Easily transplanted. Ample water, rich soil produce best plants. Thrives on extreme heat. Adapted to stiff clays and adobe.

USE: Cockscomb and woolflower are novelties, difficult to place with other plants. Plume types are more graceful, can be combined with zinnias, marigolds and chrysanthemums in harmonizing shades. Long lasting cut flowers.

CENTAUREA. Annual forms include these two old-fashioned flowers of easy culture:

C. cyanus. BACHELOR BUTTON. CORNFLOWER. 2-2½ ft. The blue form is a traditional favorite for cutting and boutonnieres. Also available, but not so desirable, in purple, rose-pink, and white. At its best in cooler weather; doesn't like summer heat.

CULTURE: I, II, III. Grows readily from seed sown either spring or fall. For cutting, sow seed in place in rows, thin to 4-6 in. apart. Overhead watering breaks down more widely spaced plants unless securely staked and tied.

USE: Definitely best as a cut flower.

C. moschata. SWEET SULTAN. 1½-2 ft. Much more stocky than *C. cyanus*. Bright green, deeply toothed leaves. Flower heads thistle-like to 2 in. Musk fragrance. Colors: Lilac, purple, white, yellow, rose. Superior cut flower.

CULTURE: II. Sow seed in place in spring or set out transplants. Add lime to acid soils.

USE: Interesting in arrangements; soft yellow especially useful.

CHINA ASTER. See CALLISTEPHUS CHINENSIS
CHINESE HOUSES. See COLLINSIA BICOLOR
CHRYSANTHEMUM CARINATUM. SUMMER CHRYSANTHEMUM. TRICOLOR CHRYSANTHEMUM. 1-3 ft. Rather ragged appearing, deeply cleft, and divided foliage. Showy, single, daisy-like flowers with bizarre markings in purple, orange, scarlet, salmon, rose, yellow, and white. In zones or ringed with multicolored bands and contrasting dark eye. Blooms all summer and fall. CULTURE: II. Sow seed in spring in flats or open. Prefers heavy soil. Pinch to induce bushiness. USE: Cut flower.

CINERARIA. (*Senecio*). FLORIST'S CINERARIA. 10 in.-2 ft. Perennial, commonly grown as an annual. In favored, shady spots, re-seeds heavily from year to year. Large, dark green leaves, velvety on the underside, on compact, bushy plants. Clusters of 3-5 in., daisy-like flowers in soft and vivid shades of pink, white, lavender, and blue, and in purple, carmine, and rose. Late winter and early spring flowering in mild regions; spring and early summer in others. *C. stellata*, STAR CINERARIA. 2 ft., open, spreading clusters of smaller flowers. Available in separate colors. Daintier and better for informal planting than larger flowered types. *Multiflora nana* strain is 10-12 in. high, good in pots, foreground of shady borders. CULTURE: I, II. Set out from flats in fall in mild climates or in spring in cold sections. Seeds are extremely fine and costly; difficult to handle except in greenhouse conditions. Set plants in semi-shade in rich, light, well-prepared soil with generous amounts of leaf mold and rotted manure added prior to planting. Keep pushing with light feedings of liquid fertilizer. Never let dry out. Overhead watering, particularly on warm days, helps to keep large leaves from wilting. Subject to serious damage from snails, leaf miner, and aphis. Although requiring special attention to reach perfection, few flowers exceed the beauty of well-grown cinerarias. USE: Shade border in protected locations, under trees. Ideal pot plants.

CLARKIA. 1-3 ft. Western natives with brittle stems, showy flowers in racemes. Closely related to godetia.

C. elegans. MOUNTAIN GARLAND. 3 ft. Very double flowers to 1 in. across in showy spires. Colors include: Orange, salmon, creamy-yellow. Var. *salmonea* (sometimes listed as *Salmon Queen*), soft salmon shades, is one of the best. There is also a scarlet variety.

C. pulchella. 1 ft. Slender, upright, reddish-stemmed plant. Lobed 4-petaled, medium-sized flowers in shades of rose, lilac, pink, or white. Sparsely foliaged, but heavy flowering. Hybrids with dainty, double flowers are choicer than the species.

CULTURE: I, II. Sow seed in fall or early spring where plants are to stand. Best in warm, sandy, not-too-moist soils. Performs best before weather gets hot.

USE: Sow thickly in rows for cut flowers, or naturalize with other wild flowers, such as gilia, godetia, collinsia.

CLEOME SPINOSA. SPIDER FLOWER. 4 ft. Loose, shrubby plants inclined to bareness at the base. Soft pink to rose-pink or white flowers with extremely long, protruding stamens and pistils. *Pink Queen* is an improved variety. *Helen Campbell*, a sport of *Pink Queen*, has large, pure white flowers in bigger heads. CULTURE: II. Sow seed in spring where flowers are to grow. Thin to 2 ft. Blooms June to frost. Self-sows readily. At its best in rather dry soil in warm situation. May get out of hand in overly moist soils. USE: Back of border, as summer hedge, or low screen. Effective in masses against a fence covered with blue morning glory.

COCKSCOMB. See CELOSIA

COLLINSIA BICOLOR. CHINESE HOUSES. 1-2 ft. Rather uncommon California native. Quaint, snapdragon-like flowers to 1 in. are held in tiers on thin, somewhat hairy, sticky stems. Upper lip of flower is white, lower one rose or violet. Blooms in spring and summer. CULTURE: I, II. Sow seed in place in spring or fall. Unlike most natives, this one likes enriched, moist soil in part shade. Self-sows in good soil. USE: Naturalizing, and for front of border. Gives an effect similar to that of linaria.

CONVOLVULUS TRICOLOR. BUSH MORNING GLORY. 1 ft. high, spreading wider. Flowers resemble small morning glories, come in intense, deep blue, pink, and red. Horticultural var. *Royal Ensign*, bright ultramarine-blue, yellow throat circled with white, is especially worthwhile. Blossoms cover the plant, remain open all day in full sun.

CULTURE: II, III. Because it does not transplant successfully, sow in place in late spring. Notch or scrape the hard-coated seeds before planting. Will grow in any soil, but is at its best in moderately rich, light soil. USE: Edgings, banks, and rock gardens.

COREOPSIS TINCTORIA. *(Calliopsis).* ANNUAL COREOPSIS. 1½-3 ft. Flowers similar to perennial coreopsis. Slender, wiry-stemmed, almost leafless, much-branched plant covered in summer with small, round buds, and velvety, daisy-like flowers in yellow, orange, maroon, bronze, and near crimson, banded with contrasting colors. Both dwarf and double varieties. Blooms profusely. CULTURE: II, III. Sow seed in place. Prefers full sun and not too much moisture. USE: Cutting. Large-scale edging in country gardens.

CORNFLOWER. See CENTAUREA

COSMOS BIPINNATUS. COSMOS. 2½-6 ft. Familiar summer and fall annual carrying single or double crimson, rose, pink, yellow, orange, and white flowers. Improved varieties with 4-6-in., single flowers. Others are fully double, or have crested and frilled centers. Early and late-flowering types. CULTURE: II. Sow seed in place or set out of flats in early spring. Re-seeds freely. Blooms July to frost. Adapted to many soils, but best in a light, not-too-rich one. Tall types damaged by heavy winds. Dwarf forms easier to manage. USE: Tall varieties useful in background or as filler among shrubs. Good cut flowers if placed in water immediately after gathered.

CYNOGLOSSUM AMABILE. CHINESE FORGET-ME-NOT. 1½-2 ft. Biennial treated as an annual. Blue or white flowers like forget-me-nots borne in loose, airy sprays throughout late spring and summer. Plants larger than ordinary forget-me-nots, have gray-green foliage. CULTURE: I, II. Sow in place or set out plants in spring in sun or partial shade. Ordinary soil; not too much fertilizer. Not adapted to hot summers in interior sections. USE: Ideal for foreground of border, along walks, under trees in filtered shade. Effective with orange-yellow Siberian wallflower. Pots and windowboxes. Fillers in mixed bouquets.

DELPHINIUM AJACIS. LARKSPUR. 3-4 ft. Cool-season annual, ranking second only to snapdragon as a cut flower, and valued for its spiky form in the garden. Double florets in pink, rose, salmon, lilac, blue, purple, carmine, and white, arranged like perennial delphinium in tall, upright spires. Finely cut foliage covers the stems from the bottom of the flower spikes to the ground. CULTURE: I, II. Sow seed in place in full sun in fall and through winter in mild-winter sections for early and late-spring bloom. For cutting, sow in rows, thin seedlings to 8-10 in. As weather warms in spring, mildew usually attacks stems and foliage. For control, see page 49. USE: In addition to cutting, larkspur is effective in drifts of single colors in borders. To hide frequently unsightly foliage, grow behind bushy plants such as godetia and scabiosa.

DIANTHUS. PINK. 12-16 in. Forerunner of modern garden pinks is the old-fashioned Chinese pink *(Dianthus chinensis)*, now less used than strains originating from it. *D. c. heddewigii*, large, single or double flowers in many colors and markings, borne singly or in loose clusters on slender, upright, 1-ft. stems, is one of the earlier hybrids.

D. heddensis. Tetraploid type, hybrid between *D. chinensis* and the variety *heddewigii*, carries single, 2-in. flowers on 16-in. stems in many shades of red, rose, and pink, also in white. It is more tolerant than either of its parents to heat and cold.

D. chinensis laciniatus. Double flowers with petals cut

and fringed. Its variety, *Gaiety*, also double, has charmingly fringed and twisted petals in bright, sparkling colors. What all of these modern hybrids lack in fragrance, they make up for in vigor, longevity, and heavy flowering.

CULTURE: II, III. Sow seeds in flats in early spring or in the open ground where plants are to grow in late spring. Almost any garden soil except one that is acid or extremely heavy. Full sun.

USE: Perky, bright edgings; attractive with gray-foliaged and white-flowered plants. Although effective in mass plantings in formal beds, they seem most in character in mixed borders with such flowers as Chinese delphinium, Chinese forget-me-not, love-in-a-mist, lobelia, sweet alyssum, and true forget-me-not.

DIASCIA BARBERAE. TWINSPUR. 1 ft. A stranger to most gardeners although it is by no means new. Related to nemesia, which it resembles in shape of flower, except that it has two prominent spurs at the back. The appealing rich salmon pink two-lipped, twin-spurred blooms are ½ in. across, appear on slender-stemmed branching plant. CULTURE: I, II. Sow seed in early spring. Plant out in fairly thick groupings in full sun in cooler climates; give some shade in warmer inland areas. Rich soil, fairly generous watering. USE: Excellent rock garden filler, low border plant. Combines beautifully with lobelia, dwarf ageratum, Chinese delphinium.

DIDISCUS CAERULEA. (*Trachymene caerulea*). BLUE LACE FLOWER. 1½-2 ft. Old, but little-known annual that needs cool culture. Thin, rangy plant resembling wild carrot in texture. Dainty, lavender-blue flowers, arranged in round heads, have protruding stamens that contribute a lacy effect. CULTURE: II. Sow seed in place in spring for bloom from summer to frost. Best in cool climates. Full sun or light shade inland. USE: Long-stemmed cut flowers with good keeping qualities.

DIMORPHOTHECA. CAPE MARIGOLD. AFRICAN DAISY. 6-12 in. Showy, sun-loving, daisy-flowered South African annuals blooming in late winter and spring in milder climates. Deserves wider use.

D. annua ringens. 1 ft. White flowers with blue ring around center. Horticultural var. *Glistening White*, has white dark-centered flowers 4 in. across on plants 6-8 in. high.

D. aurantiaca. 1 ft. Satiny, single, daisy-like flowers to 2½ in., in orange. Attractive hybrids in white, yellow, apricot, and salmon.

CULTURE: I, II. Broadcast seed in well-prepared soil and rake in lightly. Plant in full sun because flowers close in shade.

USE: Gay, free-flowering; mixed hybrids effective in large plantings. Borders, parking strips, hillsides, window boxes, and pots.

ESCHSCHOLTZIA CALIFORNICA. CALIFORNIA POPPY. 1 ft. Rich orange-colored, California wild flower. Hybrids available in single and double forms in orange, carmine and cream, cream, cherry-red, yellow, salmon, red, and pastels. Satiny-textured flowers 2-3 in. across, close at night. Silvery-green, finely cut foliage. CULTURE: I, II. Poppies ask only to be sown in place in fall or spring and nature will do the rest. Drought-tolerant, very long blooming through spring and into summer. Self-sow readily. USE: One of the best natives for naturalizing on hillsides, along drives, particularly in country gardens.

EUPHORBIA MARGINATA. SNOW-ON-THE-MOUNTAIN. 2 ft. Related to poinsettia. Grown for its unusual, variegated foliage. Light green, oval leaves, upper ones margined with white. Flowers unimportant. Rather loose rangy habit. CULTURE: II, III. Seed sown in place in late spring or under glass for transplanting when weather is warm. Do not thin. USE: Interesting and worth using for light contrast with darker or brighter-colored flowers. Effective with plume cockscomb for extremes of color contrast. Good cut flowers if stems are dipped in boiling water or held in flame for few seconds.

FAIRY STARS. See GILIA
FAREWELL-TO-SPRING. See GODETIA
FLOWERING TOBACCO. See NICOTIANA
FLOSS FLOWER. See AGERATUM
FORGET-ME-NOT. See MYOSOTIS SYLVATICA; CYNOGLOSSUM AMABILE

GAILLARDIA PULCHELLA. ANNUAL GAILLARDIA. BLANKET FLOWER. 1½ ft. Good for at least six months' bloom. Single and double, daisy-like flowers in warm shades of red, yellow, orange, maroon, and combinations of these colors. Coarse plants becoming woody as they get older. CULTURE: II, III. Sow in open in late spring or transplant from flats. Drought and heat-tolerant. Self-sows. USE: Excellent, long-lasting cut flowers.

GILIA. Western natives. 6 in. to 2 ft. Members of the phlox family.

G. capitata. QUEEN ANNE'S THIMBLE. BLUE THIMBLE FLOWER. 2 ft. Loose, bushy plants carrying dainty heads of 1 in., blue flowers on 2 ft., bare stems above sparse, finely dissected foliage. Blooms in late spring or early summer.

G. micrantha. FAIRY STARS. 6-8 in. Tiny heads of red, yellow, and white flowers. Not commonly known. Use in same way as Virginian stock for ground cover or miniature bouquets.

G. tricolor. BIRD'S EYES. 1-2 ft. Flowers more phlox-like than other species; lilac flowers have a spotted, yellowish tube marked with purple in center.

CULTURE: I, II. Seed in place preferably in fall or in early spring. Water if spring rains are meager. Taller growing in cooler climates.

USE: Fairy stars combines nicely in an edging with sweet alyssum.

GODETIA. Spring- and early-summer-blooming California native much glorified by hybridizing. 1-2½ ft. Related to, and similar in flower form to evening primrose. Cool season annual, does not like midsummer heat.

G. amoena. FAREWELL-TO-SPRING. 1-2 ft. Double flowers, borne up and down stem. Resemble, but are larger than clarkia.

G. grandiflora. SATIN FLOWER. Single, satin-textured flowers, rose-red varying to white with darker blotch in center, in clusters at top of stem. Doubles in rose and red shades. Most attractive—and superb for cutting—are the single, named varieties in salmon-orange, salmon-pink, carmine, and white.

CULTURE: II. Sow seeds in place in spring. Sun but with light shade in hot interiors. Requires moisture, but should not be overfed.

USE: Cutting; if cut when top bud is open, lower buds will continue to open over a period of several days. Single godetias especially effective in borders. Combine salmon-pink *Sybil Sherwood* with Chinese delphinium; *White Purity* with carmine-red and white *Kelvedon Glory*.

GYPSOPHILA ELEGANS. BABY'S BREATH. 1½-2 ft. Myriad small, white flowers on delicate stems. Short blooming period; make successive sowings for extended bloom. In warmer weather will bloom in less than 6 weeks. White most commonly used, but available also in rose and carmine. CULTURE: II, III. Seed sown in place from earliest spring at successive intervals for continuous cutting. If soil is acid, add lime or gypsum. USE: Good short-term substitute for perennial gypsophila. Useful as delicate textured filler in gardens and bouquets.

HEARTSEASE. See VIOLA

HELIANTHUS ANNUUS. COMMON SUNFLOWER. 7-10 ft. Vigorous, fast-growing, coarse-leafed annuals with large, daisy-like flowers in pure gold, red, bronze, or brown, sometimes in zones in contrasting colors. Doubles and named hybrids superior to the old type. Some have flowers like large chrysanthemums or dahlias. CULTURE: II, III. Large seeds sown in place in spring. Will grow with some neglect but responds to care. Requires full sun. USE: Temporary screen. Plant tall varieties in background of large borders.

HELICHRYSUM BRACTEATUM. STRAWFLOWER. Everlasting. 3 ft. Yellow, pink, orange, lavender, white, very double, daisy-like flowers useful for dried bouquets. CULTURE: I, II. Sow seed in spring or fall in full sun. Not particular about soil, stands drought and some neglect. USE: To prepare for winter arrangements: Cut before center opens and strip foliage for easier handling. Hang upside down in cool place to dry. Disbudding will increase size of flowers.

IBERIS. CANDYTUFT. 6-15 in. Cool-season annual, flowering in mild climates in winter and early spring from fall-sown seed. Seed sown in spring will bloom into summer until weather becomes hot. Clusters of white, purple, lavender, or crimson flower heads on bushy plants.

I. amara. HYACINTH-FLOWERED CANDYTUFT. 15 in. Pure white flowers arranged in 4 to 6 large, hyacinth-like trusses on each plant.

I. umbellata. GLOBE CANDYTUFT. 1 ft. Bushy plants completely covered with pink, rose, salmon, lilac, or white flowers clustered in parasol-like heads. Dwarf hybrids in same colors grow compactly to 6 in.

CULTURE: I, II. Sow seeds in place from early fall through spring for successive blooms. Not adapted to warm, dry climates. Full sun, ordinary soil, and regular watering.

USE: Hyacinth-flowered candytuft is a long-lasting substantial cut flower, grown commercially for this purpose in some areas. Globe candytuft makes charming, pastel covers for bulbs, drifts in perennial borders. The dwarf hybrids are wonderful for edgings, window boxes, and pots. Excellent bedder if solid colors are planted. Grown in pots for spring bloom.

ICELAND POPPY. See PAPAVER

IMPATIENS BALSAMINA. BALSAM. 8 in.-2½ ft. A quaint, old favorite with lots of appeal for those who like tidy, clean, rather formal-looking plants covered with very double flowers in rich colors. (Not to be confused with *I. holstii*, shade-loving, 3-ft. perennial with semi-transparent stems and slender-spurred pink, red, and purplish flowers.) Double camellia-flowered variety forms compact, symmetrical bushes to 2½ ft., with blooms strikingly like miniature camellias in soft to rose-pink, lilac, scarlet, white; others with variegations. Double-flowered dwarf hybrids grow to 8 in. CULTURE: III. Sow seed in flats in early spring and set out after frosts in full sun in rich, well-drained soil. Wants lots of moisture. USE: Precise-looking in informal beds, edgings, pots. Attractive with full edgings of lobelia, alyssum *Carpet of Snow*, or ageratum *Midget Blue*.

JASMINE TOBACCO. See NICOTIANA

KOCHIA SCOPARIA. SUMMER CYPRESS. MEXICAN FIRE BUSH. BURNING BUSH. 2-3 ft. Var. *trichophila* is the form most commonly grown and probably is the same as the variety offered in nurseries under the trade name *Childsii*. Old-time plant almost forgotten in recent years, often used as temporary hedge because of its symmetrical, oval, compact habit and rapid growth. Fine-textured foliage is bright green all summer, turning purplish-red in autumn. CULTURE: I, II. Sow seed in place in spring. Self-sows readily. Full sun, average soil conditions. USE: Good space divider. May be sheared to form a low, formal hedge.

LARKSPUR. See DELPHINIUM AJACIS

LATHYRUS ODORATUS. SWEET PEA.

Sweet peas are grown to gather by the basketful—fresh, dainty, fragrant, and long-stemmed—for use as cut flowers. Everything you do in growing them is directed to perfection of individual flower rather than to a mass of color in the garden. The difference in flowers from carefully tended vines, as opposed to carelessly tended ones, is reward enough for taking pains.

Here's how to grow perfect sweet peas.

1. Prepare for a deep root run in rich soil.

2. Prepare for loss in seed germination by sowing thickly.

3. Prepare for bird and insect attack in the first stages of growth.

4. Give vines supports to climb on before they appear to need it.

5. Never let the vines lack for water.

6. Pick flowers at least every other day and remove all seed pods.

7. Choose the type or class of sweet pea that suits your climate and the time of year you want flowers.

There are three distinct classes of sweet peas. The differences between these classes determine flower production for your area and are more important to the grower than the flowers themselves.

Early-flowering Spencers. The "early-flowering" means that unlike the summer-flowering class they ignore day length in producing blooms. In contrast, the summer-flowering type requires a 15-hour day length. The "Spencer" in the name means that the ruffled type of flower has been bred into it. Only the early-flowering class should be used for planting in the greenhouse to get Christmas bloom or for planting in the ground in August in the warm-winter sections of California.

Summer or late-flowering Spencers. This class should have a long, cool growing period and cool weather in the blooming season. Because in many sections of California, the weather is hot by the time the 15-hour day is reached, this class has not been as successful in California as in the Northwest, or in England. Plant in early spring.

Cuthbertsons. Outstanding qualities of the Cuthbertson sweet pea: its ability to grow in hot weather, vigorous growth, extra long stems, long blooming season, and heavy flowering. In California it is best planted between October and early January for spring and summer bloom; elsewhere, from February to April, or just as soon as the soil can be worked.

If soil has not been deep-worked previously, dig a trench 12-18 in. deep. Fill with 6 in. of compost and/or rotted manure; add 3-4 in. of topsoil and sow seed. Seed pack will call for sowing 1 in. apart and thinning to 3 in. later. However, a final spacing of 6-12 in. apart generally produces healthier vines and just as many flowers.

Soon after the seed germinates and grows to 2-4 in., fill in around it with soil, and continue as it grows until almost to soil level.

Trellis, strings, or wire should be in place so that the vine can find supports as soon as a tendril is formed. Don't let it wave around looking for something to climb on. It may give up the idea of being a climber.

Where climate prevents early planting or soil is too wet to work, it's a good idea to start 3 or 4 seeds in 3 in. pots or plant bands, indoors or in a protected place, and transplant when weather has settled. Set 1 ft. apart, thinning to 1 strong plant. If tendrils form before you set them out, place a small stake or twiggy branch in the pot for support.

When sowing seeds in wet ground, make a small, 2-in. deep trench and fill it with sand. Seed sown in moist sand will not be subject to rot.

Covering the seed bed with wire until the seedlings are 4-6 in. high will avoid destruction by birds. Place bait for snails before growth shows above ground.

To get large flowers, direct the energy of the plant to flower production as soon as blooming season begins. Do not allow seed pods to ripen. Pick flowers before they fade. Pinch out side shoots that form where the flower stem branches from the main stalk.

Run the rows north and south to give the vines full benefit of the sun. Keep them growing with a steady schedule of watering, letting the water soak in to full depth of the roots, 18-36 in. Give the vines air space; keep trellis or wire out from wall or fence. Best results come from free-standing supports.

LAVATERA TRIMESTRIS. TREE MALLOW. ANNUAL MALLOW. 3-4 ft. Single, satiny, hollyhock-like flowers on coarse, shrubby plant with typical mallow foliage. The variety *splendens rosea*, rosy carmine, is an improvement over the old form. *Loveliness*, pink shaded with carmine, now ranks as the best horticultural variety. CULTURE: II. Sow seeds in place in spring for bloom through summer and up until frost. Full sun, thrives in moist, fairly rich soil, but will accept poorer conditions. USE: Colorful summer hedge, filler in the back of new shrub borders.

LIMONIUM (STATICE). SEA LAVENDER. 1-1½ ft. Strawy, everlasting-type flowers in dense heads on erect stalks. Thick, dark green leaves.

Limonium bonduellii. Winged, clear, bright yellow flowers. Thick-lobed, 6-in. leaves.

L. sinuatum. Dark blue, lavender, rose, and white blooms. Leaves in basal clusters.

L. suworowii. More dwarf. Bright rose flowers in slender spikes.

CULTURE: II, III. May be started from seed sown in place in spring in full sun. Seem to thrive best along the coast. Drought-tolerant, endure neglect.

USE: Sow in rows in the cut flower garden, dry flowers for winter use. Do not place flowers in water. Effective edging and border plant in beach gardens.

LINARIA MAROCCANA. TOADFLAX. BABY SNAPDRAGON. 10-15 in. Flowers resembling tiny snapdragons in lavender, violet, pink, purple, red, yellow, chamois. Horticultural var. *Fairy Bouquet* has larger flowers, mostly in pastel shades, on a compact plant, 10 in. high. Most recent introduction is the variety *Northern Lights,* 15 in. high, profusely covered with flowers in bright red, orange, yellow, carmine, as well as bicolors and pastels. CULTURE: I, II. Sow seed thickly in place in spring or fall. Make successive sowings for a long period of bloom. Seed may take nearly 3 weeks to germinate. Thin seedlings to 1 ft. apart. Plant in sun or light shade in rich, moist soil. USE: Unusual ground cover for spring-flowering bulbs, or drift planting in borders. Sow in generous amounts; small patches are spotty and ineffective.

LINUM GRANDIFLORUM RUBRUM. SCARLET FLAX. 1-1½ ft. Five-petaled flowers in brightest scarlet are carried in profusion on erect, slender-stemmed, fine-foliaged plants. Each bloom lasts only a day, but more keep coming on. CULTURE: I, II, III. Sow seed in fall or early spring. In mild climates may be sown at any time except during hottest weather. Really at its best in cool season in full sun. Grows in ordinary soil, but excels in one that is enriched. USE: Offers a quick, easy way to get bright patches of early color in bare spots in borders. Striking with gray plants, or combined with white godetia, candytuft, or larkspur.

LOBELIA ERINUS. 4-12 in. Summer's most dependable and popular, low-growing blue flower. Compact or trailing growth habit, foliage light, medium, or dark green to correspond with light, medium, or dark blue flowers. Many horticultural varieties, including: *Crystal Palace*, deepest blue, dark red foliage; *Emperor William*, bright mid-blue, medium-green leaves; *Cambridge Blue*, light blue with light green foliage. All are compact types. Trailing or spreading varieties are: *Sapphire*, deep blue with a white eye; *Gracilis*, ultramarine blue; *Hamburgia*, light blue with white eye. CULTURE: II, III. Sow seeds from late winter (under glass) to May (for later bloom in mild climates). Wants rich, moist soil; sun in cool summer areas, otherwise in light shade. For second bloom, cut back after main flowering and feed. USE: Edgings, ground covers, pots, hanging baskets, and window boxes. Trailing varieties look graceful and soft falling over the edge of tubs or pots containing larger plants.

LOVE-IN-A-MIST. See **NIGELLA DAMASCENA**

LOVE-LIES-BLEEDING. See **AMARANTHUS**

LUPINUS. LUPINE. 1-4 ft. Familiar harbingers of spring in moist fields and grassy hills along the Pacific Coast, lupines are used comparatively little in gardens. Species listed here are definitely cool-season plants, need atmospheric and soil moisture. Blue, purple, or rose flowers, often with contrasting white or yellow, have the form characteristic of all members of the pea family. Leaves are composed of several leaflets arranged like spread fingers of a hand.

L. hartwegii. 3-4 ft. Native of Mexico, with blue, white, or rose flowers in July and August.

L. nanus. 12-15 in. California native. Rich blue, fragrant flowers with white spotted standards are among first lupines to bloom.

CULTURE: I, II. Sow seed in place in fall after inoculating it with nitrogen-fixing bacteria to encourage formation of nodules on roots and consequent increased vigor of growth. Sun in cool, coastal areas, otherwise part shade. Loose, rich soil that is moist but not wet.

USE: Broadcast alone or in combination with other wild flowers on slopes, under high-branching trees.

LYCHNIS COELI-ROSA . *(Viscaria cardinalis)*. VISCARIA. ROSE OF HEAVEN. 1 ft. Little known but valuable for its showy, single, 1-in., saucer-shaped rose, blue, lavender, and white flowers with contrasting dark eyes. Much branched habit of growth, providing many stems for cutting. CULTURE: I, II. Sow seed in place in spring or fall in sun or light shade. Best in well-fertilized, moist soils. USE: Colorful filler in borders. Cut for mixed or old-fashioned bouquet.

MALCOMIA MARITIMA. VIRGINIAN STOCK. 4-6 in. Charming miniature stock with ½-in., 4-petaled, scentless flowers in white, cream, pink, rose, crimson, and lavender.

CULTURE: I, II. Blooms in 6 weeks from seed sown in place in fall, spring, or practically any time except in hot or very cold weather. Prefers moist, moderately rich soil in full sun or in part shade in warm inland areas. USE: Delightful bulb cover, edging, or ground cover. Combine with white and purple alyssum and blue nemophila for a multi-colored carpet over bulbs or in the foreground of shrub borders. Always sown in mixed colors.

MARIGOLD. See TAGETES.

MATHIOLA. STOCK. 2-3 ft. Fragrant familiar annuals which thrive under same cool growing conditions as snapdragons, calendulas, violas, and larkspur.

M. incana, ever-popular garden and cut flower for late winter and spring. Gray-green foliage forms a basal rosette for spicily fragrant, 1-in. flowers in white, rose, pink, purple, chamois, cream, carmine-rose, and blood red. Branching types carry flowers on central and side spikes. Improved COLUMN STOCK produces a single, tall, main stalk with very large flowers; is considered best for cutting. Branching types include: NICE; GIANT PERFECTION; WINTER BLOOMING STOCK; BROMPTON (fall blooming); SUMMER or TEN WEEKS STOCK, blooms in late spring and summer; GIANT IMPERIAL, long bloom in summer.

M. bicornis. EVENING SCENTED STOCK. Undistinguished-looking plant with small, single, lavender flowers that have a delightful fragrance at night.

CULTURE: I, II. Any sudden check is serious. If possible sow in place in fall or spring according to variety. Otherwise, sow in flats, transplant before plants become flatbound. Prefer light, well-drained, fertile soils. Plant on ridges in heavier soils. Subject to stem rot if overwatered. Grow in rows for cutting. Do not cultivate or disturb roots.

USE: Mainly for cut flowers. Less desirable for bedding, although base-branching types in separate colors are quite effective.

MEXICAN FIRE BUSH. See KOCHIA SCOPARIA
MEXICAN SUNFLOWER. See TITHONIA ROTUNDIFOLIA
MIGNONETTE. See RESEDA ODORATA

MIMULUS TIGRINUS. MONKEY FLOWER. 1 ft. Short-lived perennials treated as annuals. The variety *Queen's Prize* has gloxinia-like flowers in red or yellow, strikingly spotted with maroon or brown. Toothed leaves and succulent stems are light green. Sprawling growth habit. CULTURE: II, III. Sow seed in flats in spring. Set out in rich, preferably light, moist soil in full or part shade. Blooms late spring through summer. USE: Pots and hanging baskets. With ferns, forget-me-nots, and cinerarias in shade borders. Typical waterside plant.

MONKEY FLOWER. See MIMULUS TIGRINUS
MOUNTAIN GARLAND. See CLARKIA PULCHELLA

MYOSOTIS SYLVATICA. FORGET-ME-NOT. 6-12 in. Indispensable for the exquisite blue of its tiny but profuse flowers in winter (in mild climates) and spring, and its ability to bring color into the shade. Available in various shades of clear blue, in dwarf and medium heights. CULTURE: I, II. Sow fresh seed in fall or early spring. Set out in moist, light, enriched soil in light shade or in sun where spring is cool. Blooms most of year in mild climates. Self-sows readily. Shake old plants over ground where you want new ones to grow. USE: Cover for bulb beds, particularly daffodils and tulips; carpet under spring-flowering shrubs and trees; pots and boxes.

NASTURTIUM. See TROPAEOLUM

NEMESIA STRUMOSA. 7-15 in. Small, orchid-like flowers in rich pinks, rose, orange, scarlet, blue, and yellow, marked in contrasting colors. Base-branching plants with slender stems, require fairly close planting to support each other. *Suttoni* strain has larger flowers; *Nana compacta* is dwarf. Available in separate colors of blue, scarlet, orange, red and white. CULTURE: I, II. Sow seed indoors in spring in cold climates, in fall where winters are mild. Prefers cool conditions, light shade in warmer sections. Plant in enriched soil kept moist, not wet. Keep plants growing rapidly, pinch to make them bushy. USE: Interplant with bulbs, set in broad masses in front of shrubs. Charming in window boxes and pots.

NEMOPHILA MENZIESII. BABY-BLUE-EYES. 8-12 in. A California native that blooms as freely in gardens as it does in the wild. Appealing blue, cup-shaped, 1½-in. flowers with white centers blossom on half-prostrate, half-upright stems against a background of light, green, finely divided foliage. CULTURE: I, II. Broadcast seed rather thickly in early spring or in fall in mild regions. Any soil, but must be kept moist. Light shade helps to prolong bloom. Where happy, seeds itself. USE: Charming addition to spring garden. Very informal. Wide range of uses: choice in pots or hanging baskets; wonderful for a blue carpet under tall daffodils or yellow, white, pink, or mauve tulips; trailing habit adapts it to pots and hanging baskets.

NICOTIANA. FLOWERING TOBACCO. 1½-5 ft. Mostly rapid growing, vigorous plants; some large and coarse like the true tobacco (*N. tabacum*), and others like the following, quite refined. All have night-scented flowers whose long, slender tubes are topped by 5 petals forming a slightly star-shaped, open cup. Flowers nearly close on sunny days, open at dusk. Leaves are hairy and sticky like those of petunias.

N. alata grandiflora. (*N. affinis*). JASMINE TOBACCO. (See chapter on perennials.)

N. sanderae. 3 ft. More branching growth habit, with velvety red, rose, and lavender flowers. Horticultural variety *Crimson Bedder*, deep crimson, is especially handsome.

Horticultural variety *Daylight Sensation Hybrids*. 2 ft. Recent, improved variety in scarlet, crimson, rose, maroon, mahogany, violet, yellow, coral, lilac, chartreuse, and white. Flowers remain open in full sun.

Horticultural variety *Orange Blossom*, 18 in., upright, with dainty, white, scented flowers. Good in pots.

CULTURE: II, III. Comes slowly but uniformly from tiny seed sown indoors in flats in early spring or broadcast in late spring. Prefers partial shade inland. Enriched soil, plenty of moisture. Self-sows in mild climates.

USE: Near the house and in night gardens where the fragrance can be enjoyed. Plant among evergreen shrubs. If flowers are cut in full bloom and placed in water, they will remain open.

NIGELLA DAMASCENA. LOVE-IN-A-MIST. 1½ ft. Round, high centered, double, light blue or white flowers with finely cut petals among even more finely textured, bright green foliage. Horticultural variety *Miss Jekyll*, with large, semi-double, high-centered flowers of intense sky-blue, much superior. Curious, papery-textured, horned seed pods to 1 in. long are dried for indoor decoration. CULTURE: II. Sow seed in place in early spring. Thin to 6 in. Does not transplant well. Sun, average soil and moisture. Self-sows. USE: Filler in borders where it may be sown among established plants. Effective with salmon-pink godetia *Sybil Sherwood*, snapdragons, or sweet William. Cover for tall bulbs. Cut flowers for mixed bouquets.

PAINTED-TONGUE. See SALPIGLOSSIS SINUATA

PANSY. See VIOLA

PAPAVER. POPPY. Provides riotous color in spring and early summer. Leaves, lobed or deeply cut and hairy.

P. rhoeas umbrosum. SHIRLEY POPPY. 2-3 ft. Single and double, crinkly-petaled flowers are white, pink, salmon, rose, orange, and scarlet, or bi-colored. Although individually short-lived, blooms appear in profusion through spring and into summer in cool regions.

CULTURE: I, II. Mix fine seed with sand and sow in place, as seedlings cannot be transplanted. Successive sowings from fall to spring for longer bloom. Full sun, ordinary soil, no fertilizer, and not too much water. Self-sows readily.

USE: In big masses along boundaries, among evergreen shrubs, with wild flowers.

P. nudicaule. ICELAND POPPY. 1½ ft. Perennial treated as annual. Best poppy for cutting; invaluable for color in winter and early-spring bloom in milder areas. Yellow, orange, salmon, pink, rose, white, and cream flowers on slender, wiry stems. Many excellent strains.

CULTURE: I. Sow seed in flats in summer in mild-winter sections, set out in fall for winter bloom. In other areas, set out in spring for early summer color. Light, well-drained soil; rots in heavy wet soil.

USE: Combine with violas and pansies for winter color where climate permits. Most effective closely planted. For cut flowers that last, select flowers in bud and burn tips of stems.

PETUNIA HYBRIDA. 6 in.-2 ft. Continuing improvement in color and form within this popular flower family has brought the petunia a long way since the days when it was an unimpressive, single flower on a rangy plant. There are many types and scores of varieties in colors scaling from soft pink to deepest velvety-red, silver-blue to richest purple, and in cream and pure white. In addition to the regular single *P. hybrida*, also available in improved forms, there are these horticultural varieties:

Nana compacta. 9 in. Dwarf, compact, symmetrical, covered with bloom. Edgings, pots.

Nana erecta. 12 in. Slightly higher edging; bedding.

Grandiflora. (Giant single). 1-2 ft. Flowers 4 in. or more across, smooth edged but deeply lobed.

Grandiflora superbissima. GIANT RUFFLED. 12-15 in. Flowers beautifully veined and marked, 5-7 in. across, in deep rose, burgundy, salmon, white, and pink. Often ruffled and fluted.

Doubles. Very choice, fully double-fluted or carnation-like in rose, pink, salmon, white, and deep purple. Pots or bedding. These petunias are extremely difficult to grow from seed. Buy rooted cuttings and grow these plants under glass.

CULTURE: II, III. Sow seed in late winter or early spring or set out plants after frosts. Seeds are microscopic and should be mixed with fine sand and sprinkled over surface of finely screened, moist soil-mix in seed pans or flats. Cover with glass and keep warm in greenhouse or east window. Remove glass when seeds have sprouted and transplant when large enough to handle. Prick out into flats or individually into pots or bands, set out after frosts. Propagate choice plants by means of tip cuttings under glass.

Although petunias are usually considered tough and able to stand abuse, the highly bred, double, ruffled, and fringed types need good care. Those grown in pots and other containers need careful watering and light but regular fertilizing for vigorous growth and abundant bloom. Pinch to encourage bushy growth and remove faded flowers.

PHLOX DRUMMONDII. ANNUAL PHLOX. 1-1½ ft. Large heads of 5-petaled, flat-surfaced blooms in rose, red, crimson, scarlet, white, salmon, soft pink, chamois, violet and lilac, often with contrasting eyes. Available in mixed and separate colors. Larger flowers are frilled. CULTURE: II, III. Sow seed in flats or in open in spring. Full sun, fairly rich soil and regular moisture. Keep old flowers picked. USE: One of best fillers in borders to replace spent pansies, violas, and calendulas. Broad, generous plantings also effective. Dwarf types make good edgings. Fine cut flowers.

PIMPERNEL. See ANAGALLIS

PINCUSHION FLOWER. See SCABIOSA ATROPURPUREA

POOR MAN'S ORCHID. See SCHIZANTHUS

POPPY. See PAPAVER

PORTULACA GRANDIFLORA. ROSE MOSS. 6 in., spreading to 12 in. Dazzlingly colorful, summer ground cover or low bedding plant. Succulent, reddish stems and roundish, 1-in. leaves. Flowers resemble 1-in., full-blown roses or cactus blossoms, bloom only when the sun shines and come in these iridescent colors: pink, rose, lavender, orange, red, white, and pastels. CULTURE: III. Seed mixed with fine sand and broadcast in spring when weather is warm. Transplants easily. Full sun, any soil. Although drought-tolerant, portulaca will perform better with some care. Cuttings of selected plants root readily in moist sand. Reseeds heavily. USE: Ideal for parking strips, slopes, quick colors in rock gardens, walls.

PRIMULA MALACOIDES. FAIRY PRIMROSE. 8-12 in. Dainty plants for partially shaded spots in late winter and early spring in mild climates. Easily grown if snails are kept in check. Low rosettes of soft, pale green foliage. Delicate, straight stems encircled with tiers of tiny flowers in pink, rose, white, and lavender. CULTURE: I, II. Sow seed in flats in summer, set out in fall for winter and spring bloom in mild regions. Enrich soil with leaf mold and rotted manure. Provide slight shade and ample moisture. Cannot tolerate heat, wind, or drought. USE: Cool-looking carpet under high-branching trees. Interplant with spring bulbs—daffodils, tulips, Dutch iris. Pots, window boxes, raised beds, planters.

PRINCE'S FEATHER. See AMARANTHUS

QUEEN ANNE'S THIMBLE. See GILIA

RESEDA ODORATA. MIGNONETTE. 1 ft. Sweetly fragrant, easily grown, old-fashioned annual that enjoys cool growing conditions. Small, greenish-yellow, brownish-red, or silvery-white flowers tightly arranged in 8-10 in. spikes on bushy plants. In addition to the old type, there are horticultural varieties with longer spikes in golden-yellow, coppery-red, deep red, and white. None, however, equals the original mignonette in fragrance. CULTURE: I, II, III. Successive sowings in spring or fall in enriched soil gives long bloom period. Sun in cool sections, partial shade inland. Growers often fertilize with fish emulsion in the bud stage to increase size of plant. USE: Cut flowers, herb and old-fashioned gardens, pots.

RICINUS COMMUNIS. CASTOR BEAN. CASTOR OIL PLANT. 6-15 ft. Bold shrub-like annual persisting as a perennial in mild-winter climates. Palmately lobed leaves sometimes 2-3 ft. across are extremely tropical looking. Small, white, unimpressive flowers tightly clustered in

2-ft. panicles are followed by spiny reddish pods containing three 1-in.-long marbled seeds which contain the deadly poison, ricinus. Plants are grown commercially for castor oil extracted from seeds. Many horticultural varieties, of which the red-leafed and white-veined types are most effective and popular. CULTURE: II, III. Sow in place in spring after frost. In warm-summer areas it will grow 10 ft. in a single season, and where winters are mild, will live over and become quite woody and tree-like. In sections where tops die down, cut it nearly to the ground; it will sprout from the roots. USE: Quick screen, background for big summer annuals such as tall zinnias, marigolds, and tithonias.

ROSE MOSS. See PORTULACA GRANDIFLORA

ROSE OF HEAVEN. See LYCHNIS COELI-ROSA

SALPIGLOSSIS SINUATA. PAINTED-TONGUE. 2½ ft. Flowers shaped much like petunias are richly and bizarrely colored in deep, rich tones of mahogany-red, red-orange, yellow, pink, rose, purple, and bi-colors. Marbled and penciled with gold or contrasting colors like a tapestry. Erect plant with very sticky stems and leaves. Var. *gloxiniæflora* larger and showier than the type. There is also a dwarf, more compact form. CULTURE: II. Sow seed in place in spring in full sun. Does not grow well in hot, dry climates. Blooms summer to frost. Fairly rich soil, but should not be watered too heavily. Pinch to induce branching. USE: Handsome cut flowers. In beds interplanted with annual gypsophila and an edging of dwarf yellow marigolds, and dwarf blue ageratum.

SALVIA SPLENDENS. SCARLET SAGE. 1-3 ft. Dazzling, strong scarlet concentrated in tubular flowers and colored bracts (floral leaves) blooming in terminal spikes from early summer to frost. Square stems and dark green leaves. *America, Blaze of Fire,* and *Bonfire* are more compact, earlier blooming varieties. CULTURE: II, III. Start seed in early spring and transplant after frosts. Prefers fairly rich soil and generous moisture. USE: Strong color to be used and combined with care. Best with white or gray; for example: with white petunias, verbena, zinnias, or with centaurea, artemisia, or senecio.

SATIN FLOWER. See GODETIA

SCABIOSA ATROPURPUREA. PINCUSHION FLOWER. SWEET SCABIOUS. MOURNING BRIDE. 2½-3 ft. Dense, rounded heads of closely clustered flowers with protruding white stamens resembling pins, the full head producing the effect of pincushion. Numerous blossoms on stiff, wiry stems are lavender, lavender-blue, maroon, salmon-pink, white, deep rose, deep mahogany, black-purple, and crimson. CULTURE: I, II. Sow seed in spring for summer flowering. In mild regions, sow in fall for early bloom. Thrives in sun, any soil that isn't poor. Somewhat but not entirely drought-resistant. May require staking. Keep flowers picked to prolong bloom. USE: Best for cutting. In borders in single or harmonizing, mixed colors.

SCHIZANTHUS. POOR MAN'S ORCHID. BUTTERFLY FLOWER. 1½ ft. Great quantities of small, orchid-like flowers in vari-colored, soft pink, rose, lilac, purple, and white, cover the bushy, ferny-foliaged plants. Cool-season annual, enjoying same conditions as *Primula malacoides* and cinerarias. CULTURE: I, II. Start seed indoors in flats. Be patient, as seed may take 4 weeks to germinate. Set out plants in spring in moist, loose, well-fertilized soil in part shade. Pinch to induce branching. USE: Pot plant; in borders with primroses, forget-me-not, primulas.

SEA LAVENDER. See LIMONIUM (STATICE)

SHIRLEY POPPY. See PAPAVER

SNAPDRAGON. See ANTIRRHINUM.

SNOW-ON-THE-MOUNTAIN. See EUPHORBIA MARGINATA

SPIDER FLOWER. See CLEOME SPINOSA

ST. JOSEPH'S COAT. See AMARANTHUS

STOCK. See MATHIOLA

STRAWFLOWER. See HELICHRYSUM BRACTEATUM

SWAN RIVER DAISY. See BRACHYCOME IBERIDIFOLIA

SWEET ALYSSUM. See ALYSSUM

SWEET PEA. See LATHYRUS

SWEET SULTAN. See CENTAUREA

TAGETES. MARIGOLD. ½-3 ft. Robust summer-to-fall annuals in tall, medium, and dwarf forms, all with finely divided, odoriferous foliage and flowers in warm colors. More satisfactory under somewhat cool conditions. Not a typical warm-climate annual as is zinnia, for example.

T. erecta. AFRICAN MARIGOLD. 2-3 ft. Upright plants with sturdy, branching, center stalks bear large, fully double flower heads resembling double carnations, dahlias, or chrysanthemums in lemon-yellow, golden-yellow, or orange. Some varieties have odorless foliage.

CULTURE: II, III. Heavy feeders, requiring rich soil and plenty of water. Easily grown from seed sown in place in spring or transplanted from flats. Set plants 2 in. deeper than they were in flats. Avoid overhead watering whenever possible, as stems break off readily.

T. patula. FRENCH MARIGOLD. ½-3 ft. Much-branched, compact plants and smaller flower heads in rich mahogany, yellow, or orange, and bi-colors. Some are dwarf.

CULTURE: II, III. Best grown from seed sown in place. Need less fertilizer and water than the African marigolds.

T. tenuifolia pumila. 1 ft. or less. Miniature with bright yellow, tiny, single flowers in great profusion on compact plants with fine-textured foliage. Same culture as for the French varieties.

USE: Cut flowers and bedding. Single, clear-colored marigolds, particularly the soft yellows, are useful fillers in perennial borders. Dwarf, double, French varieties such as *Yellow Pigmy, Butterball,* and *Sunkist;* and *T. tenuifolia pumila* make tidy, long-blooming edgings. Dwarf forms for edging.

TITHONIA ROTUNDIFOLIA. *(T.speciosa).* MEXICAN SUNFLOWER. 4-8 ft. Perennial grown as an annual; a 12-ft. shrub in its native Mexico and Central America. Striking, 3-in. orange-vermillion flowers resembling single dahlias carried on upright, bushy plants luxuriantly clothed with velvety, dark green, 6-in. leaves. Bloom extends from July to frost.

Horticultural var. *Torch* is a new dwarf type growing to 4 ft., with 4-5 in., fiery, orange-scarlet flowers.

Fireball, an improved form of the taller tithonia, also has 4-5 in., brilliantly colored blooms.

CULTURE: III. Sow seed in place in spring. Rapid grower in full sun in a warm, not-too-rich soil. Quite drought-resistant.

USE: Tall types belong in the background and against fences where their dazzling, orange-red flowers can be seen above other plants. Effective with blue *Salvia uliginosa* or against *Heavenly Blue* morning glory. *Torch* makes a bushy summer hedge, is a useful filler in new shrub borders.

TORENIA FOURNIERI. WISHBONE FLOWER. 1 ft. A charming, little-known but worthwhile summer and fall-blooming annual for part shade. Bushy plants are covered with small, snapdragon-like flowers of sky-blue with deep violet lips and a yellow throat. Stamens are arranged in shape of wishbone—hence the common name. CULTURE: II, III. Sow seed in spring in flats. Set out in high shade in soil enriched with leaf mold and kept uniformly moist. USE: Pots; tends to trail slightly in hanging baskets and windowboxes, where it combines beautifully with trailing lobelia. In borders, plant with fibrous begonia, lobelia, small ferns.

TREE MALLOW. See LAVATERA TRIMESTRIS
TOADFLAX. See LINARIA MAROCCANA
TROPAEOLUM. NASTURTIUM. Tender. Rapid growing perennials grown as annuals, some with tuberous roots. Grow from 1-6 ft.

T. majus. GARDEN NASTURTIUM. Climbing or trailing, to 6 ft. or more, bright green round kidney-shaped leaves on long petioles. Flowers are 5-petaled, to 2½ in. across, refreshingly fragrant, in reds and yellows with stripes and spots of darker red or brown. Var. *nanum* TOM THUMB NASTURTIUM, dwarf strain available in double, often ruffled forms, in yellows, mahogany, orange, scarlet, cherry red, shades of pink.

Var. *Burpeei.* GOLDEN GLEAM NASTURTIUM. Semi-tall or trailing with long-stemmed, golden yellow, scented large double or semi-double flowers.

Semi-tall large doubles are also available in many beautiful colors.

T. peregrinum. CANARY BIRD FLOWER. Climbing 10-15 ft. with deeply 5-lobed leaves, and 1-in. canary yellow fringed flowers with green curved spurs. Prefers part shade and moist soil.

CULTURE: II, III. Sow seed in place in full sun, or light shade in hot-summer climates. Thrive in dry, sandy, gravelly soils, although any that is well-drained will do. Fertilizer produces excess leaf growth, few flowers.

USE: Trailing and semi-trailing types will cover fences, slopes, tree stumps, rocks. Use dwarf forms for bedding, edgings, quick color in rock gardens, and in pots. Good cut flowers.

VERBENA HORTENSIS. (See p. 162)
VINCA ROSEA. MADAGASCAR PERIWINKLE. 1½ ft. Tender, heat-loving perennial often grown as annual. Showy, 5-petaled, phlox-like blooms to 1½ in. Come in pure white, white with rose eye, bright rose, and blush pink with a red eye. Laurel-like, glossy, green leaves cover the bushy plants. CULTURE: II. Blooms first season if sown early in flats under glass. Does not require a rich soil, but needs a good deal of moisture. Give it light shade in inland sections. Lives over winter in mild climates. USE: A fine, low, bushy hedge or edging; neat, attractive potted plants.

VIOLA. 6-12 in. The generic name *Viola* belongs to several important garden plants, including not only that commonly named viola, but also the pansy and the garden violet. The two former plants are considered here. For VIOLET see chapter on perennials.

V. cornuta. VIOLA. HORNED VIOLA. TUFTED PANSY. 6-8 in. Compact plants are thickly covered with small, spurred, pansy-like, self-colored flowers in blue, blue-violet, white, apricot, ruby, and yellow. Practically unfailing source of winter and spring color in mild regions, flowers spring through summer in cool sections where it lives over as a perennial. Varieties in light lavender-blue to deepest violet-blue, apricot, ruby, yellow, and white.

V. c. papilio. Large, fragrant flowers are violet with a purple center. Excellent edging viola.

V. tricolor hortensis. PANSY. HEARTSEASE. 6-12 in. This old favorite is available in new, improved strains with large flowers 2-4 in. across in white, blue, mahogany-red, rose, yellow, apricot, and purple and bi-colors.

CULTURE: I, II. Sow seed in flats in July or August or in early spring. Plant in full sun for winter and early-spring borders and in cool climates, in half shade for summer borders and in warmer areas. Both violas and pansies require maximum amount of moisture and deeply enriched soil. Incorporate into the soil liberal amounts of humus. Start feeding shortly after setting out, and continue through the growing season for maximum results. Bait for snails and treat for sowbugs. Long period of bloom if old flowers are kept picked.

USE: Invaluable edgings and fillers in perennial borders. Violas are superb accompaniments to spring bulbs, ground covers under flowering shrubs and trees. Both can be grown in pots, window boxes, and outside planters.

VIRGINIAN STOCK. See MALCOMIA MARITIMA
VISCARIA. See LYCHNIS COELI-ROSA
WISHBONE FLOWER. See TORENIA FOURNIERI
WOOLFLOWER. See CELOSIA
XERANTHEMUM ANNUUM. COMMON IMMORTELLE. 2½ ft. An everlasting flower with fluffy, double, 1½ in., daisy-like flowers in pink, lavender, white, and shades of violet-purple. Scant foliage is silvery-green. Var. *perligulosum* is very double. CULTURE: II. Sow seed in spring in place in full sun. Accepts almost any soil. USE: Cut flowers dried for winter bouquets.

ZINNIA. ½-3 ft. A typical, hot-weather annual with flowers 1 in. to 6 in. across, in almost every color except blue, with growth habit sprawling to stiffly upright.

Zinnia elegans. From this Mexican species, originally purple or lilac, have stemmed many large horticultural varieties carrying such names as *Giants of California, Giant Dahlia Flowered, Cactus Flowered, Luther Burbank Hybrids,* and others with shaggy, curled, or quilled petals. Flowers 5-6 in. across and 2 in. or more deep, are held on upright stems on strong, branching plants 3 ft. high.

A medium-height, medium-flowered variety of *Z. elegans* is the CUT-AND-COME-AGAIN, 2 ft., with flowers 2 in. across, one of the finest for cutting.

Dwarf forms: 5 in.-1½ ft. high, include *Baby* or *Pompon, Lilliput, Tom Thumb, Cupid,* and *Gracillima.* Small, very double flowers come in a complete range of zinnia colors. *Z. augustifolia haageana,* 18 in., semi-double to double, yellow flowers marked orange, dark red-brown, some tipped with contrasting colors. *Z. linearis* is a 1-ft. species with single, 1¼-in. bright orange flowers with light yellow stripes.

CULTURE: III. Grows rapidly and blooms in 45 days from seed sown in place after weather really warms up. Can also be sown in flats and transplanted. Successive sowings in mild climates will produce flowers from late spring to frost. Plant in full sun in enriched soil. Add gypsum or lime to acid soils. Irrigate by furrow method. Subject to mildew in foggy areas—also toward end of blooming season in warmer sections. Control diabrotica and snails.

USE: Tall varieties, mediums, and pompons for bedding and cut flowers. Dwarf types for edgings and large-scale ground covers.

Perennials

Commonly the word perennial is used to describe those plants that die down in winter, after storing food in their roots for regrowth of tops the following spring. Those plants that bloom year after year but escape winter damage by storing food in bulbs, tubers, and rhizomes, rather than in roots, are generally referred to as bulbs, or specifically by the type of root.

In the mild-winter sections of the West, wider use is being made of the evergreen type of perennial, those plants whose leaves are attractive the year around.

Here, too, a number of sub-shrubs similar in growth habit to the woody perennials are used interchangeably with them.

In terms of use the line dividing annuals, perennials, shrubs, herbs, tubers, bulbs, and rhizomes, is very vague and very elastic.

It is a mistake therefore to approach the use of perennials as plants to be used exclusively in a "perennial border." Too many gardeners have assumed that because they don't have a perennial border they can't use perennials.

The list of perennials is long and the plants are infinitely varied in use and adaptability. Each Western subclimate offers special opportunities for some section of the group.

In the mountain sections of the West you can grow many of the choice alpine perennials that sicken and die at sea level.

In the warm-winter areas of Southern California, a number of perennials fail in spirit and vigor because of lack of winter cold and a dormant season. But for every one crossed off the list there's another added because of winter mildness.

Let's walk through a few Western gardens and check the uses that have been made of perennials.

PERENNIALS IN PATIOS AND TERRACES

Situation: There's a large paved area with two 6 by 6-foot flower beds inset in the pavement. Needed is something fairly low growing that will stand close-up inspection every month in the year.

Solution: A planting of *Arabis albida variegata*, dianthus Beatrix, and mugho pine. Or iberis Little Cushion, veronica Blue Spire, and *Sedum spectabile*.

PERENNIALS IN NARROW BEDS NEXT TO HEDGES

Situation: Too often you find yourself with a 2 by 4-foot space between a paved area, such as a driveway or path, and a hedge. The hedge roots offer too much competition for the average plant.

Solution—in sun: A simple ground cover of santolina, helianthemum, or *Sedum amecamecanum*.

All are drought-resistant and can compete with other roots.

Solution—in shade: A combination of *Sedum spectabile* (pink), or its more vivid variety *Brilliant*, and an edging of the blue *Campanula portenschlagiana*. *Bergenia crassifolia* with *Saxifraga umbrosa* as an edging.

PERENNIALS IN NARROW BEDS

Situation: Narrow beds that are not complicated by hedge or tree roots.

Solution: Many choices for both sun and shade, but those listed below have worked well in the narrow-bed situations. Often such narrow beds are ideal places for collections of special plants. As you walk along you can examine each variety individually without stepping off the path.

Low-Sun	Low-Shade
Achillea (dwarf varieties)	Aquilegia
Alyssum saxatile	Campanula
Ceratostigma plumbaginoides	Primula
Convolvulus mauritanicus	Violet
Dianthus in variety	
Euphorbia myrsinites	
Nepeta mussinii	

Medium-Sun	Medium-Shade
Hunnemannia	Aquilegia
Iris germanica	Dicentra
Lavender	Francoa
Penstemon	Hellebore
Shasta daisy *Esther Reed*	Hosta
	Platycodon

Large-Sun	Large-Shade
Canna	*Anemone japonica*
Centaurea	Ferns
Chrysanthemum	Fuchsia
Geranium	Phlox
Salvia uliginosa	
Shasta daisy *Marconi*	

PERENNIALS NEXT TO OPEN FIELDS

Situation: You have more space than you want to take care of. The field or natural cover beyond the garden site is attractive in spring and winter but brown and dry in summer. A typical California situation.

Solution: The following list includes perennials and a shrub or two that do not require much water, that reach a screening height in midsummer, and that should be cut back in the fall.

Most of them can be used in single massed plantings. Of special merit for this purpose are: *Achillea filipendulina*, bocconia (*Macleaya cordata*), *Boltonia asteroides*, cannas, Michaelmas daisy, phlomis, *Romneya coulteri*, *Salvia leucantha*, *Salvia uliginosa*, *Solidago virgaurea*.

Mixed plantings will suggest themselves. We like these: The native gray-foliaged buckwheat (*Eriogonum giganteum*) with the clear blue sage (*Salvia uliginosa*); a mass of gray *Romneya coulteri*; and clumps of *Solidago virgaurea Golden Wings*.

In the Pacific Northwest the transition between garden and wild could well be patterned after the farmland roadsides where escapees from gardens intermingle with the natives.

PERENNIALS IN SHRUB BORDERS

Situation: The newly-planted shrub border. Needed are well-mannered perennials that fill out and complete the shrub planting and offer seasonal color.

Solution: The following perennials have foliage that combines well with the youthful shrubs.

Aquilegia hybrids
Calceolaria integrifolia
Ceratostigma willmottianum
Coreopsis grandiflora
Felicia amelloides
Geraniums
Korean hybrid chrysanthemums
Santolina chamæcyparissus
Senecio cineraria
Senecio greyii
Senecio leucostachys

Situation: A more or less mature shrubbery border with indentations and bays that not only allow the shrubs to show to better advantage, but provide space for occasional plantings in depth.

Solution: Here you have several opportunities. You can choose the long-lived perennials that resent the disturbance they usually get in a changing mixed border. Or you can devote a bay to one species whose color range is most charming when planted en masse, such as the hybrid columbine, alstrœmeria. Or you can bring together those perennials that do well in some shade and are interesting for foliage and flower.

PERENNIALS AS SUBSTITUTES FOR ANNUALS

To every gardener intent upon color in the garden every month in the year, there comes the time when the moving in and moving out of annuals seems like too much work. And so he turns to perennials.

To this annual gardener, plants are flowers that make solid sheets of color. A planting of zinnias is successful when blossom touches blossom. Petunias, marigolds, snapdragons are thought of in the same way.

The perennials he wants to find are the mass color producers. These, we think, fit his requirements:

Aster frikartii
Coreopsis
Garden border chrysanthemums
Shasta daisies
Violas

140 PERENNIALS
PERENNIAL BORDER

The classic perennial border is a very definite garden. It is a collection of perennials arranged in a harmonious pattern of color, form, and texture. It is a symphony opening in early spring in subtle muted tones that increase in volume and intensity as growth becomes fully active. The tempo quickens with the advancing season and rises to a full early summer crescendo whose overtones extend into midsummer. Then follows a movement that ebbs and flows and finally works up to a second climax in the warm full tones of Indian summer and autumn.

In each season, the dominant theme is played by certain key perennials with synchronized or overlapping periods of bloom. These perennials are usually repeated at intervals to establish a flow of uniform colors throughout the border.

Plant forms play an important part in the perennial border. Staccato notes are sounded by sword-shaped leaves of iris; by silver-blue needles of festuca; by flowering spires of lupine, veronica, kniphofia, liatris, delphinium, and cimicifuga. There is a full rounded quality in clumps of day lily, Michaelmas and Shasta daisies, cushion chrysthemums, and columbines. Filmy clouds of statice and gypsophila play the lightest and softest notes.

This symphony reaches its fullest and most exciting expression in the double border—or in like borders repeated on either side of a path. Color flows from one side of the path to the other—from one end of the border to the other—through opposing groups of the same plants. These groups, however, should not be placed directly opposite each other, but in such a way that the eye is always carried in a diagonal line from one side to the other, down the length of the border.

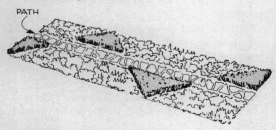

The classic perennial border, of course, is quite complicated and needs lots of space. The larger the border, the bolder the plant groupings. If you use giant delphiniums or massive verbascums or foxgloves, the border should be at least 8 to 10 feet wide and 60 feet long. A 12 by 100-foot space would be even better.

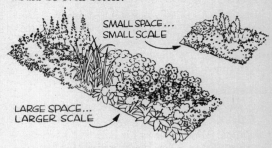

Ideally, the perennial border should be placed so that you can look down it from a main vantage point such as the terrace—not directly into it broadside. When you look down a perennial border, masses of bloom, although actually separated, appear to merge, and bare spots are not noticeable.

Although in a large border you have mixed colors, contrasts, and harmonies, it is best to work mostly with single colors in each section of the border, and to use more harmonies than contrasts. When combining flowers of different colors, remember that two colors often combine to form a third

color. Thus red and blue make purple, pink and blue make mauve. Lemon yellow and white relieve and cleanse muddy colors, grays soften harsh colors.

Use a well-balanced proportion of tall, medium-height, and low plants. While the tallest plants should be kept mostly in the background, bring them down into the middle of the border occasionally to avoid monotony. For the same reason, medium-height plants should come into the front of the border now and then.

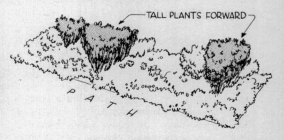

To get as long a succession of bloom as possible, group early flowering plants behind later flowering ones. For example, plant Michælmas daisies in front of Oriental poppies; nepeta in front of perennial alyssum; statice in front of sweet William.

BLOOM CALENDAR FOR PERENNIALS
(For time to sow, plant, divide, see encyclopedia.)

FOR SPRING BLOOM

Aethionema. Pink, rose.
Anemone. White, pink, bluish-purple.
Arabis. White, pink.
Arctotis. Many colors.
Aquilegia. Many colors.
Aubrieta. Lilac, rose, purple.
Begonia (fibrous). White, pink, rose, red.
Bergenia. Pink, rose, lilac.
Cheiranthus. Many colors.
Chrysanthemum frutescens (Marguerite). White, yellow.
Digitalis. White, pink, rose, purple.
Doronicum. Yellow.
Epimedium. Pink, red, yellow, white.
Helleborus. White, purple, rose, pink, red, maroon, chartreuse.
Iberis. White.
Lithospermum. Blue.
Primula. Many colors.
Saxifraga. White, pink, rose-purple, lemon yellow.
Shortia. Pink, white.
Tulbaghia. Rose-lavender.
Viola. Many colors.

FOR LATE SPRING-EARLY SUMMER BLOOM

Alyssum. Yellow.
Anchusa. Blue.
Astilbe. Rose, crimson, pink, white.
Begonia (fibrous). White, pink, rose, red.
Bellis perennis. White tipped with pink or red.
Billbergia. Blue, red.
Brunnera. Blue.
Calceolaria. Yellow to red-bronze.
Chrysanthemum frutescens (Marguerite). White, yellow.
C. maximum (Shasta Daisy). White.
Delphinium. Blue, white, pink-lavender, purple.
Dianthus. White, pink, rose, red.
Dicentra. Pink, white.
Echium. Blue-purple.
Erigeron. White, pink, lavender.
Euphorbia. Chartreuse, yellow.
Gaillardia. Yellow.
Gazania. Varied colors.
Gentiana. Blue.
Gerberia. Most colors except blue.
Geum. Yellow, orange, red.
Gypsophila. White, pink.
Heuchera. White, pink, red.
Kniphofia. Scarlet, yellow, white, cream.
Limonium. Purplish-lavender.
Linum. Blue, yellow.
Meconopsis. Blue.
Nierembergia. Blue, violet-blue.
Paeonia. White, cream, pink, rose, red.
Papaver. Many colors.
Pelargonium. Many colors.
Penstemon. Many colors.
Phlox. Pink, rose, lavender, white.
Rehmannia. Rose-pink, cream and white.
Scabiosa. Lavender, white.
Trollius. Yellow, orange.
Tulbaghia. Rosy-lavender.
Yucca. White, creamy white.

FOR SUMMER BLOOM

Achillea. White, yellow.
Althaea. White, red, rose, yellow, salmon.
Anchusa. Blue.
Anthemis. Yellow
Armeria. White, rose-pink.
Begonia (fibrous). White, pink, rose, red.
Catananche. Lavender-blue.
Centranthus. Crimson, pale red, white.
Chrysanthemum coccineum (Painted Daisy). Crimson, pink, white.
C. frutescens (Marguerite). White, yellow.
C. maximum (Shasta Daisy). White.
Coreopsis. Bright yellow.
Corydalis. Yellow
Dianthus. Many colors.
Erigeron. White, pink, lavender.
Eryngium. Lavender-blue.
Gaillardia. Yellow.
Gerberia. Many colors.
Glaucium. Orange, golden-yellow.
Gypsophila. White, pink.
Heliotropium. Purple, violet.
Hosta. White, blue, lavender.
Impatiens. Pink, violet, white.
Kniphofia. Scarlet, yellow, white, cream.
Lavandula. Lavender, purple.
Linum. Blue, yellow.
Lotus. Scarlet, yellow.
Lychnis. Scarlet, white, pink, rose.
Monarda. Pink, scarlet.
Nepeta. Lavender, lavender-blue.
Nicotiana. White, pink to dark red.
Oenothera. Rose-pink, yellow.
Onosma. Yellow.
Penstemon. Many colors.
Phlomis. Yellow.
Physostegia. White, lavender-rose, rose-pink.
Platycodon. Blue-violet, white, pink.
Polemonium. Lavender-blue.
Rehmannia. Rose-pink, cream and white.
Santolina. Yellow.
Scabiosa. Lavender to deep lavender-blue.
Silene. Reddish-purple, purple, rose.
Thalictrum. Lilac, purple, yellow.
Thermopsis. Golden-yellow.
Tulbaghia. Rose-lavender.
Verbascum. Purple, red, white, pink, rose, yellow.
Verbena. Lavender, rose-pink, white, purple.
Veronica. Violet-blue, blue.

FOR LATE SUMMER-FALL BLOOM

Acanthus. White, lilac, rose.
Aconitum. Blue, white, lilac.
Anchusa. Blue.
Anemone. White, pink, bluish-purple.
Anthemis. Yellow.
Arctotis. Many colors.
Aster. Blue, pink, lavender, purple, white, rose, dark red.
Begonia (fibrous). White, pink, rose, red.
Boltonia. White, violet, purple.
Campanula. Blue, white, pink.
Chrysanthemum frutescens (Marguerite). White, yellow.
C. maximum (Shasta Daisy). White.
C. morifolium (Florist's Chrysanthemum). Many colors.
Delphinium. Blue, white, pink-lavender, purple.
Dianthus. Many colors.
Dimorphotheca. White.
Echinops. Lavender-blue.
Erigeron. White, pink, lavender.
Ernygium. Lavender-blue.
Eupatorium. Blue, violet.
Felicia. Blue.
Francoa. White, pink.
Gaillardia. Yellow.
Gerberia. Many colors.
Gypsophila. White, pink.
Helenium. Yellow.
Helianthus. Yellow.
Helichrysum. White.
Heliopsis. Yellow.
Hunnemannia. Yellow.
Kniphofia. Scarlet, yellow, white, cream.
Linum. Blue, yellow.
Liriope. Violet.
Lythrum. Rose-pink.
Penstemon. Many colors.
Potentilla. Yellow, red.
Rehmannia. Rose-pink, cream and white.
Reinwardtia. Yellow.
Salvia. Lavender, blue, white.
Scabiosa. Lavender to deep lavender-blue.
Sedum. Pink, red.
Solidaster. Yellow.
Stokesia. Blue, purplish-blue, white.
Trachelium. Lavender-blue.
Tradescantia. Violet-blue, blue, white.
Tulbaghia. Rosy-lavender.

ACANTHUS MOLLIS. Bear's Breech. Spreading plant with basal clusters of huge notched, shining dark green leaves to 2 ft. that are said to have suggested foliage designs for Greek Corinthian columns. Rigid spikes of whitish, lilac or rose flowers with green or purplish spiny bracts rising 3 ft. above foliage; blooms in late summer. Var. *latifolius* has larger, more ornamental leaves and is hardier than the species.

Culture and Climate: Hardy zones 7-13. Prefers shade but will take sun in coastal areas. Keep leaves washed off in summer. Plants should be cut back hard each year to encourage growth of fresh new leaves. Bait for slugs and snails. Divide clumps in October-March. Plant where it can be confined. Roots travel underground, make plant difficult to eradicate.

Use: Tropical foliage and lush foreground effects. Combines beautifully with bamboo, philodendron, large leafed ferns, camellias, and azaleas.

ACHILLEA. Yarrow. Most important for flowers of circular disc form. Most useful in contrast to spire-like growers. Gray or green bitter-aromatic, usually ferny foliage. Small flowers tightly packed in broad flat-topped clusters in summer. A favorite with flower arrangers for their everlasting quality, if picked before color is lost and dried in a cool dry place.

A. ageratifolia. Greek Yarrow. Tufted silvery mound to 8 in. Silvery-gray feathery foliage. Flowers white.

Use: Fine edging plant with good all year foliage for patio beds or containers.

A. argentea. Silvery Yarrow. (See chapter on ground covers.)

A. filipendulina. Fernleaf Yarrow. Stout vigorous erect plants to 5 ft.; green divided foliage; chrome yellow flowers.

Use: Combine with delphinium for definite contrast in form and complement in color. Excellent cut flowers fresh or dried.

A. millefolium. Common Yarrow, Milfoil. Erect or spreading to 3 ft. Bright green or gray-green finely cut foliage. White flower clusters borne on long stems. Var. *rosea* has rosy-pink flowers.

A. ptarmica. Sneezewort Yarrow. Lower growing to 2 ft., narrow saw-toothed leaves and dense clusters of white flowers. Improved horticultural varieties are *Pearl* with double flowers; *Boule de Neige* (Snowball) with fuller more perfect flowers; *Perry White* with larger 1-in. flowers.

A. taggetea. Horticultural variety growing to 18 in. with gray-green divided leaves and 3-4 in., flat heads of soft lemon-yellow flowers from June to September.

use: One of the best yarrows for borders and cutting. Its soft color combines beautifully with the deep blue of *Delphinium chinensis Blue Mirror* or *Anchusa capensis Blue Bird.*

A. tomentosa. Woolly Yarrow. (See chapter on ground covers.)

Culture and Climate: Hardy all zones. Full sun, any well-drained soil. Stake taller plants. Avoid overwatering. Sow seeds in spring. Divide clumps in spring and fall. Plant from cuttings.

ACONITUM. Monkshood. Stately perennial with basal clusters of large delphinium-like leaves. Helmet or hood-shaped flowers usually in blue, white, or lilac shades in tall spikes high above the foliage. Blooms late summer and early fall. Before you plant aconitum, it is important to know that the roots and flowers contain a deadly poison.

A. napellus. Aconite Monkshood. Grows to 4 ft. Flowers deep blue, the broad helmets with long visors. Horticultural varieties are available in white, shades of blue, blue and white, flesh-colored, or pink; but are considered less satisfactory than the species.

A. fischeri. Azure Monkshood. Grows to 5 ft. Late blooming plant with mauve, blue, or white flowers.

Culture and Climate: Adapted to zones 1-6. Shade. Difficult to establish in warm dry climates. Needs moisture; should never dry out. Sow seeds in spring, or late summer and early fall, for bloom the following year. Divide clumps in early spring or late fall, or leave undivided for years. Goes completely dormant in winter.

Use: Substitute for delphinium in shade. Combines effectively with thalictrum, *Anemone japonica*, astilbe, hosta, and francoa.

AETHIONEMA. Stonecress. In or out of bloom these low growing shrublets are fine little plants with their neat small leaves and masses of pale pink or rose flowers clustered at the ends of the branches in spring. Flowers last better than the true candytuft which they resemble.

A. coridifolium. Lebanon Stonecress. Grows 4-10 in. with blue-green narrow 1-in. leaves and soft pink flowers.

A. pulchellum. Closely resembles *A. coridifolium* except it is more spreading and trailing in habit. Grows to 6 in. with rosy-pink flowers.

A. grandiflorum. Persian Stonecress. Tallest of the stonecresses, growing to 12 in. Rose-colored flowers on slightly drooping branchlets.

A. warleyense. *(A. Warley Rose).* Compact growing hybrid form, 6-8 in.; 18-in. spread; blue-green needle-like foliage; deep rose flowers in May and June. Resembles a miniature daphne and is sometimes used as a substitute for *Daphne cneorum* in places where the latter will not grow. Propagated from cuttings only.

Culture and Climate: Zones 3-13. Sun. A Mediterranean plant, very drought resistant when planted in deep soil. Sow seeds in spring. Cuttings in late fall or winter.

Use: Fine in combinations with other miniatures. Good for topping a low wall or for planting beside low rocks.

AFRICAN DAISY. See **DIMORPHOTHECA ECKLONIS; GERBERIA JAMESONII; ARCTOTIS**

AJUGA REPTANS. Carpet Bugle. (See chapter on ground covers.)

ALTHAEA ROSEA. *(A. chinensis).* Hollyhock. Stately biennial or short-lived perennial, with broad rough maple-like leaves. Wand-like stems bear spikes of large wide-open single or double flowers to 3 in. or more, in white, red, rose, yellow or salmon. Blooms early summer to September. Var. *Triumph Supreme* has double fringed flowers which bloom very early. In addition to the usual pinks, rose and white, has unusual shades of scarlet, orange and buff. It is more resistant to rust than many of the older varieties. culture and climate: Hardy all zones. Sun. New plants should be grown and set out every 2 yrs. use: Especially suited for background borders, or against walls and trellises. Group plantings are best, so try harmonizing shades of hollyhocks.

ALYSSUM SAXATILE. Basket-of-Gold, Golden-Tuft Alyssum. Low growing, spreading plant 4-12 in. with soft, gray foliage. Attractive dense masses of tiny bright golden-yellow flowers from spring into early summer. Var. *luteum Silver Gold* is a more refined plant with pale lemon-yellow flowers.

CULTURE AND CLIMATE: Hardy all zones. Sun. Shear back one half for intermittent bloom during summer. Becomes less woody if sheared after each bloom. Sow seeds in early spring or early fall. Self-sows readily in garden.

USE: One of the most useful and satisfactory plants for edgings, in borders, rock gardens and walls, ground cover for bulb beds.

ANCHUSA AZUREA *(A. italica)*. SUMMER FORGET-ME-NOT, ITALIAN BUGLOSS. Tall loose spreading plants to 4-5 ft. with large coarse hairy leaves. Blue forget-me-not flowers in large fountain-like sprays top every branch. Blooms late spring through early fall if fading flowers are picked regularly. Varieties are available in dark blue, blue with a white eye, gentian blue, and pale blue.

A. myosotidiflora. See *Brunnera macrophylla*.

CULTURE AND CLIMATE: Hardy in all zones. Prefers sun. Dies out in heavy wet clay. Rank tall growth may smother nearby perennials so give it plenty of room. Needs no fertilizer and does best in poor soils. Sow seeds in early spring (flowers first year). Divide roots in fall. Grows easily from root cuttings. Difficult to eradicate.

USE: Good companion plants for the difficult-to-harmonize orange-reds of Oriental poppies, large Shasta daisies, and yarrow.

ANEMONE. (Also see chapter on bulbs.) Herbaceous perennials with attractive white, pink, or bluish-purple flowers.

A. japonica. JAPANESE ANEMONE, WINDFLOWER. For September garden color in a shaded location this anemone is indispensable. Graceful stems 2-4 ft. high rise from a tuft of dark green soft-hairy lobed leaves, bear saucer-shaped white, or shades of silvery-pink or rose flowers with yellow stamens. The pink flowers last longer than the white. Many named varieties; Queen Charlotte is the best known semi-double pink and Whirlwind the most popular semi-double white.

CULTURE AND CLIMATE: Hardy all zones. Blooms fall at first frost. Partial shade. Will take sun if kept well watered. Slow to establish, but once started, spreads readily if left alone. Divisions or root cuttings in spring.

USE: Best planted in clumps in front of shrubbery, a vine-covered wall or even along paths where there is no small planting. Adds shimmering fall color under high branching trees. Combines nicely with camellias, azaleas, daphne, foxglove, chimney bellflower, ferns, hydrangeas, agapanthus, and fuchsias. A beautiful effect in border planting along a shaded pool.

A. pulsatilla. EUROPEAN PASQUE FLOWER. Attractive alpine plant growing in clumps 9-12 in. Fern-like foliage complements the 2½-in. bluish-purple or violet flowers with golden stamens. Blooms in April and May followed by handsome seed heads like feathery smoky-gray pom-pons. Var. *alba* has white flowers.

CULTURE AND CLIMATE: Hardy all zones. Best adapted to cool, moist climates. Sun or partial shade. Sow seeds or make divisions in spring.

USE: A few clumps in the perennial border give color at Easter time. Combines well in the rock garden with primroses, arabis, and the pink Rosina violet. Seed heads are favorites for flower arrangements.

ANTHEMIS TINCTORIA. GOLDEN MARGUERITE. Erect shrubby perennial to 2-3 ft. with angular stems. Foliage heavily scented, of finely divided light green leaves. Golden-yellow 2-in. daisy flowers borne on long leafless stems in summer and fall. Var. *Moonlight* has pale yellow flowers. Var. *Grallagh Gold*, a European introduction with the habit of Moonlight, but has deep gold flowers.

A. nobilis. CHAMOMILE. (See chapter on ground covers.)

CULTURE AND CLIMATE: Hardy all zones. Prefers full sun. Grow *A. tinctoria* from seed, named varieties from stem cuttings or divisions in fall or spring.

USE: Perennial border with delphinium, *Veronica spicata*, *Aster frikartii*.

AQUILEGIA. COLUMBINE. Erect branching plants 2 in. to 4 ft. high with clear green thin compound leaves divided into numerous roundish leaflets—foliage so attractive that even without the flowers the plant is worthwhile. Beautiful long stemmed showy flowers in rainbow hues bloom in the spring. Sepals and petals often in contrasting colors. In the varieties generally available the flower petals are long spurred, but you can also get seeds of short spurred or spurless types.

The columbine used often in hybridizing is *A. longissima*, LONGSPUR COLUMBINE. Grows to 3 ft. with gray-green foliage and delicately fragrant lemon-yellow flowers with 5-in. spurs. This species is a parent of some of the largest, longest spurred, durable flowers in unusually beautiful pastel shades.

Large-flowered, long-spurred varieties available include: *Mrs. Scott Elliott* hybrids, in mixed, mostly pastel shades; *Copper Queen*, coppery-red; *Silver Moon*, white; *Dobbie's Imperial* hybrids in brilliant colors. If you like blue, try *A. caerulea*, ROCKY MOUNTAIN COLUMBINE, with deep blue sepals and white petals. *A. chrysantha*, GOLDEN COLUMBINE, has spurs 2½ in. long; grows to 4 ft. Although the flowers of our far Western native, *A. formosa*, SITKA COLUMBINE, are not quite so large as others, they make up in brilliance—sepals and petal spurs are fiery red, the petals yellow.

Dwarf long or short spurred species of particular interest are: *A. alpina*, ALPINE COLUMBINE, grows to 12 in. with blue 2-in. flowers. *A. buergeriana*, YUKON COLUMBINE, to 12 in.; flowers 1½ in., yellow-tinged purple. *A. flabellata nana*, DWARF FAN COLUMBINE, see chapter on miniatures.

An almost spurless type is *A. clematiflora*, a hybrid of garden origin. Grows to 1½ ft. Pale pink and blue 3-in. flowers.

CULTURE AND CLIMATE: Hardy all zones. Best in partial shade; tolerates sun on coast. Cut back to ground after flowering to induce new growth. subject to leaf miner, aphis, red spider and root rot. Sow seeds in summer for flowers the following year. Self-sows and crosses in the garden. Divisions in autumn that should be replanted immediately. Best to replace plants at least every 3 years.

USE: Plant clumps in borders where ornamental foliage and later the spectacular flowers can be appreciated. With thalictrum or Japanese anemone it makes a pleasing shady bed perennial. Or combine yellow columbine with the blue of brunnera. Lilies, ferns, primroses, and campanulas are other fine companions. Also looks well under lacy leafed birches.

ARABIS. ROCKCRESS. Year-around attractive foliage; white, pink or rose-purple flowers in early spring.

A. albida. WALL ROCKCRESS. Gray-foliaged mats to 6 in. White ½-in. flowers almost obscure the plant in early spring. Var. *flore-pleno*, double white flowers; var. *variegata*, pale yellow-edged leaves and single white flowers.

CULTURE AND CLIMATE: Hardy all zones, but needs shade in hot dry areas. Sun and part shade. Drought resistant; objects to soggy soil during growing season. Cut half back after blooming for compact plants. Sow seeds in early spring or fall. Cuttings late fall and winter.

USE: Useful low growing perennials for filling out borders, pattern planting, small beds, dry wall, or edgings.

ARCTOTIS. AFRICAN DAISY. Hybrids within this genus are, deservedly, one of the most popular evergreen perennials for winter color in the mild winter sections of the West. The profusely blooming, shiny-rayed, 3-in. daisies range in color from white, through pink, lavender, yellow, and brilliant orange to purple. They grow rapidly to make a wide-spreading, 12-18 in. high, 36 in. wide plant with grayish-green, cut or lobed leaves. Blooms from late fall to early spring, many plants producing some bloom throughout the year. CULTURE AND CLIMATE: Zones 3-13. Hardy to 10°. Must have full sun for flower production. Requires plenty of room. USE: Plant in mass in broad bands along a driveway, or as a colorful, deep-carpeted ground cover.

ARMERIA MARITIMA. COMMON THRIFT. Evergreen tufted mounds spreading to 1 ft., with long, spiky, grass-like leaves. Small white to rose-pink flowers borne in tight round heads on sturdy 6-10 in. stems. Blooms profusely all summer, and intermittently throughout year. Many named varieties; *Glory of Holland* grows to 2 ft., with large 1-in. deep pink flowers from early spring through summer. Var. *Pink Perpetual* grows to 9 in., blooms profusely.

CULTURE AND CLIMATE: Hardy all zones. Adaptable but prefers full sun. Shear flowers after bloom. Sow seeds in spring and fall. Divide throughout year, preferably early spring or late fall.

USE: Dependable well-behaved plant for rock gardens, or edging walks and paths. Just the right height for a border and makes an excellent green curb. Effective massed in larger areas—as a ground cover, on banks, or under trees. Especially handsome planted in squares on a terrace pattern, in raised beds, or anywhere you want a bold pattern.

ARTEMISIA. WORMWOOD. We list here several species which are valuable for their interesting leaf pattern and silvery-gray or white aromatic foliage. Small yellowish or white flowers in loose or dense leafy clusters are of no particular ornamental value.

A. albula Silver King. Slender, spreading plant to 3½ ft., with silvery-white foliage, the lower leaves ovate, 3-5 lobed, the upper very narrow, not lobed.

A. frigida. FRINGED WORMWOOD. Dwarf compact plant to 1 ft., with white, lacy, highly ornamental foliage.

A. pontica. ROMAN WORMWOOD. Shrub-like growing to 4 ft., with feathery silver-gray foliage.

A. purshiana. CUDWEED WORMWOOD. White woolly foliaged plant to 2 ft., with ovate, or narrower, mostly undivided leaves.

A. stelleriana. BEACH WORMWOOD. DUSTY MILLER. Dense, silvery-gray plant to 2½ ft., with 1-4 in., lobed leaves. Hardier than *Senecio cineraria* (dusty miller), this artemisia is often used in its place in colder climates.

CULTURE AND CLIMATE: Hardy zones 3-13. Foliage looks rather sad in long wet winters. Full sun. Keep on dry side. Divisions in spring or fall.

USE: Excellent for the mixed border where the white or silvery leaves soften harsh reds or oranges, and blend beautifully with blues and lavenders.

A. stelleriana combines well with asters, delphiniums, larkspur, *Salvia patens,* and *Felicia amelloides;* effective in a gray planter with dwarf lavender, catmint (nepeta); or is an especially charming companion for floribunda roses such as *Vogue* and *Pinky.*

ASTER. MICHAELMAS DAISY. HARDY ASTER. Perennial asters, although not comparing in individual flower size with the annual asters, make up for this in profusion of daisy-like flowers in shades of blue, pink, lavender, purple, white, rose, or dark red, with yellow or orange centers. Their fortunate habit of flowering after such mainstays as delphinium are through blooming makes them one of the best perennials for late summer and fall color. The hundred or so named varieties vary from 6-in. mounds to 6-ft. plants and offer a wide range of selection for the rock garden, for edgings, and for the middle and back of the perennial border.

A. novae-angliae. NEW ENGLAND ASTER. From this 5-ft., hairy-leafed, purple-flowered species have been developed some excellent hybrids including: *Survivor,* large rose-pink flowers, said to be superior to *Harrington's Pink,* a long-time favorite. *Peace,* pinkish-lavender; *Plenty,* soft lavender-blue; *Prosperity,* deep rose-pink; *Winston Churchill,* ruby-crimson. All grow 3½ to 4 ft. high.

A. novi-belgi. NEW YORK ASTER. Grows to 3 ft. with smooth, 6-in. leaves and bright, blue-violet flowers. Varieties include: *Adorable,* large-flowered, deep, clear pink; *Beechwood Challenger,* darkest of the reds; *Mt. Everest,* white; and *Violetta,* deepest, richest violet-blue.

A. dumosus. BUSHY ASTER. Grows to 3 ft. with narrow, 3-in. leaves and blue or white flowers. Some excellent, lower growing hybrids have been produced. *Marjorie,* rose-pink, grows to 12 in.; *Nancy,* lavender-blue flowers; grows to 6 in. Newly introduced are the dwarf Oregon asters *Pacific Amaranth,* 12 in., amaranth red; *Pacific Horizon,* 12 in., light lavender-blue; *Purple Feather,* 15 in., purplish-violet.

A. frikartii. WONDER OF STAFA. Forms a well-shaped bush to 18 in. with gray-green leaves. Lavender-blue, 2½-in. daisies bloom from April to December and in mild winter climates continue almost all year if left unpruned.

A. alpinus. ALPINE DAISY. ROCK ASTER. Low growing to 6-10 in. with leaves mostly in a basal tuft. Violet-blue, 1½-in. daisies on long stems in early summer. Var. *alba* has white flowers.

CULTURE AND CLIMATE: Hardy all zones. Sun. Highly resistant to insects and diseases, although foliage is subject to mildew in late fall. Tall varieties should be staked. Avoid excess watering. Divide clumps each year in early spring or late fall.

USE: Taller forms are invaluable for late-season color in background of perennial border among shrubs. A grouping that delights year after year is blue Michaelmas daisies with goldenrod, with a background of bright sumac. Dwarf asters form a neat border plant for edging a shrub or flower bed, also add late season color in the rock garden. *Aster frikartii* can serve as a low summer hedge or as a middle distance stand-by in the perennial border.

ASTER, STOKES. See STOKESIA LAEVIS

ASTILBE. GOAT'S BEARD, MEADOW SWEET, FALSE SPIRAEA. Generally a 2-3 ft. plant, but with varieties that grow to 6 ft. and one that dwarfs at 6 in. Valuable for color in the shade garden from May through July. Leaves are much divided, almost fern-like. Flowers on wiry stems, are graceful, pointed plumes of rose, purple, crimson, pink, or white. Some of the named varieties are: *Deutschland,* 2 ft., creamy-white; *Fanal,* 2 ft., deep, rich garnet-red; *Peach Blossom,* 2½ ft., shell-pink; *Crispa,* 6 in., pink. (Deutschland combines beautifully with Fanal.) CULTURE AND CLIMATE: Sun or shade depending on light intensity. Best climate and soil is that of cool-summer areas of the Pacific Northwest and coastal northern California. Zones 3-6, 9-10. Seldom successful in Southern California. Needs a cool, moist soil, rich in humus. Cut back after flowering. Clumps should be divided before they get too crowded—every 4-5 years. USE: In shade, combine with fuchsias, hydrangeas, and lilies; in sun combine with peonies, delphinium, iris. Often planted at edge of pools. Grows well in pots and tubs. Superb cut flower.

AUBRIETA DELTOIDEA. COMMON AUBRIETA. Low spreading plants with gray-green leaves. Covered in early spring with tiny rose or pale to deep lilac or purple flowers. Named varieties include: *Eyrei*, rosy-lilac; *Dr. Mules*, purple; *Gloriosa*, pink; *Gurgedyke*, deep purple; *Vindictive*, rose-red; *Purple Knoll*, deep blue-violet. Blooms late winter and early spring.

CULTURE AND CLIMATE: All zones. Full sun except in hot sections where light shade is recommended. After flowering, cut back plants one-half. Sow seeds in late spring for blooms the following spring. Difficult to divide clumps; cuttings better.

USE: Rock gardens and walls; between stepping stones; ground cover; edging; cover for small bulbs.

BABY'S BREATH. See GYPSOPHILA
BASKET-OF-GOLD. See ALYSSUM SAXATILE
BEAR'S BREECH. See ACANTHUS MOLLIS
BEE BALM. See MONARDA

BEGONIA. A large and varied group of succulent-stemmed perennials, most of them adapted to outdoor planting in mild regions; elsewhere as house or conservatory plants. They may be divided into 3 groups: tuberous begonias, grown principally for their large, colorful flowers (see chapter on bulbs); the fibrous-rooted begonias or bedding begonias; and the rhizomatous types grown mainly for their handsome foliage.

Fibrous-rooted or bedding begonias:

B. semperflorens. Erect, bushy plants to 18 in., with green or reddish stems and crisped, oval, 2-4 in. leaves that vary from lettuce green to reddish-green. Flowers are white, pink, rose, or red and are almost everblooming.

Many horticultural varieties available, including the following: *Adeline*, very compact, 8-in., dwarf, with light green foliage and bright pink flowers; *Carmine*, bronzy-red foliage and bright rose flowers; *Christmas Cheer*, neat mounds of bronzy foliage to 8-10 in., with dark crimson flowers; *Ile de France*, light green foliage and pure white flowers; *Prima Donna*, light green foliage and coral-pink flowers; *Snowbank*, compact plant to 8 in., with light green foliage and pure white flowers; *Vernon*, 12-18 in., with dark foliage and blood red flowers.

B. fuchsioides. Taller growing to 2-3 ft., with erect, slender stems. Ovate, lopsided, 1½-in. leaves are tinged red when young. Scarlet, fuchsia-like flowers ½-¾ in. broad. Extensively used in greenhouses.

B. digwilliana. Reported to be a hybrid of *B. semperflorens* and *B. fuchsioides*. Tall, open-growing, erect, or nearly erect plant to 2 ft. Reddish stems with dark, rich green, elliptic, 2-4 in. leaves. Flowers rosy-scarlet, fading almost to white in deepest shade, borne in drooping clusters.

CULTURE AND CLIMATE: Zones 9, 10, 12, and 13. Prefers partial shade in protected locations. Rather difficult to grow from seed. Can obtain plants from nurseries in late spring. Divide clumps in spring and fall. Cuttings root easily. In areas subject to frost, take cuttings in fall, hold them over in winter in coldframes, then set them out in the border in the spring.

USE: Fibrous begonias are not particularly effective as single plants, but large numbers of them will make a bright, carefree bed or border, or a colorful ground cover in a shaded area. Use them in boxes or in inserts in a paved terrace. Wherever you use them, put the plants close together in masses, 6 in. apart. *B. digwilliana* is more suitable for mass plantings than edgings.

Rhizomatous begonias:

B. rex. The outstanding rhizomatous begonia usually grown indoors. Magnificently colored leaves practically unrivalled by any foliage plant for texture, form, and brilliance. Maroon, lilac, rose, light and dark green, and silvery-gray are blended in bands and mottlings to make unusual leaf displays. The shield-like leaves may be unlobed or have sharply pointed lobes; are frequently crisped or wavy-margined, often with a long, pointed tip.

Begonia specialists continue to improve this group by hybridizing the Rex with other species. Plants of some forms become enormous.

A new strain of dwarf varieties has been developed. They are compact in habit with dense foliage that makes a rich, solid mat of color. Bred into the dwarfs is a spiraled, waved, and fluted form with a wide variation in color and mottling. One variety, *Georgia Lou Fisher*, has leaves that are maroon at the ruffled edges, then banded with concentric, half-inch rings of moss green, light apple green, and iridescent lilac, with dark green at the center. The leaf is crepe-like in texture, netted with veins, and overlaid with bright red "frost." A typical plant of this variety in a 5-in. pot measures 14 in. across and 6 in. in height, the mature leaves being more than 6 in. in diameter.

There is also a miniature, small-leafed strain, identical with the giant-leafed varieties except that the plants are more compact, and have improved form and color. The dwarfs are perhaps more heavily spotted and marked than the Rex, and all have a characteristic whorl at the center of each leaf.

CULTURE AND CLIMATE: Outdoors in zones 12 and 13. Shade. Protect from wind; subject to damage from saline water. Best grown in containers from cuttings.

USE: Excellent in the shade garden in protected patios during summer. Move indoors in cold-winter climates.

BELLFLOWER. See CAMPANULA

BELLIS PERENNIS. ENGLISH DAISY. Flat or tufted rosettes of dark green leaves. Stems 3-6 in. high bear solitary, 2-in. daisies, the white rays tipped with pink or red, giving the appearance of entirely pink or red flowers. Most used garden varieties are double forms. Bloom in spring and early summer. Var. *Dresden China* is a very dainty plant with tiny, exquisite, pink button-like heads. CULTURE AND CLIMATE: Hardy all zones. Sun. Seeds and divisions. USE: Perennial border or edging plant: Combines well with dwarf forget-me-not, white cushion dianthus, *Iberis sempervirens Little Cushion*.

BERGENIA. Thick rootstocks send up clumps or colonies of large, thick leaves, dark green and glossy. Above them, thick leafless stalks bear clusters of pink, rose, or lilac flowers.

B. cordifolia. (*Saxifraga cordifolia*). HEARTLEAF BERGENIA. Rose-pink flowers in graceful nodding clusters, sometimes partially obscured by the large leaves. Flowers in early spring.

B. crassifolia. *(Saxifraga crassifolia).* WINTER BLOOMING BERGENIA. Rose, lilac, or purple flowers in dense erect clusters stand well above the leaves, blooming in January and February.

B. ligulata. *(Saxifraga ligulata).* More refined than *B. crassifolia*, with light green leaves and white flowers.

CULTURE AND CLIMATE: Zones 3-13. Partial or complete shade. Tolerates neglect but if not sheared will become leggy, overgrown, and unattractive. Best to divide clumps every two years (in fall) and discard old plants.

USE: Serves well in a shaded planting bed, on a porch or terrace, in a car port. Gives color in the garden at the time of year when any color is valuable.

BETHLEHEM SAGE. See PULMONARIA

BILLBERGIA.
These small relatives of the pineapple offer a kind of tropical eccentricity found in few other groups. Stiff leaves growing in basal clusters resemble some of the small aloes. Bracts and tubular flowers in showy spikes in spring and summer.

B. nutans. Most common species. Has long spikes of rosy-red bracts and drooping green flowers with petals edged in deep blue. Leaves are clear green, spiny, to 1½ ft. long.

B. pyramidalis. Dense 4-in. spikes of bright red bracts and red flowers with violet-tipped petals. Spiny green 3 ft. leaves.

B. sanderiana. Blue flowers with rose-red bracts in loose nodding 10-in. clusters. Leathery bronzy 1 ft. leaves dotted with white.

CULTURE AND CLIMATE: Indoor-outdoor plants except in zone 13. Require shade, very little soil and almost no feeding. Weak root systems act mainly as anchors. By October first, plant will have produced offshoots from base. Cut them off with sharp knife and set them in pots. Use light potting mixture—leaf mold, sand and compost. Can be made to grow on limbs of trees or pieces of bark, like orchids, by wrapping roots in sphagnum moss and leaf mold.

USE: Interesting in patios or indoor planters. Good cut flowers for unusual flower arrangements.

BISHOP'S HAT. See EPIMEDIUM
BLEEDING HEART. See DICENTRA

BOLTONIA.
Tall bushy perennials with flowers like miniature Michaelmas daisies.

B. asteroides. Grows to 8 ft., with narrow, 5 in. leaves. White to violet and purple flowers in ¾-in. heads. White form is particularly dainty and useful.

B. latisquama differs from *B. asteroides* in its larger, 1-in. heads of blue-violet rayed daisies.

CULTURE AND CLIMATE: Hardy all zones. Sun. Seed. Divisions in late fall or spring.

USE: In back of a perennial border, among perennials with coarser flowers, boltonia's fine-textured, airy quality compares with that of gypsophila or statice.

BRUNNERA MACROPHYLLA. *(Anchusa myosotidiflora).* FORGET-ME-NOT ANCHUSA.
Loosely branched perennial to 1½ ft. Dark green heart-shaped leaves. Each plant a bouquet of airy sprays of ¼-in., blue forget-me-not flowers in spring and summer. CULTURE AND CLIMATE: All zones. Prefers part shade. Remove dead flowers to encourage second crop. Increase by divisions. USE: To be enjoyed in a spring garden, planted under trees just inside the shade line with yellow primulas, white iberis, and yellow narcissus. Base planting for forsythia, deciduous magnolia, camellias.

BUGLOSS, ITALIAN. See ANCHUSA AZUREA

CALCEOLARIA INTEGRIFOLIA. *(C. rugosa, C. fruticohybrida).* BUSH CALCEOLARIA.
Much-branched shrubby plants to 2-3 ft., with dark green crinkly 2 in. oval leaves. Small ½-1 in. flowers, often called "ladies' purses," are pouch-like, yellow to red-bronze, held in loose, irregular clusters. Blooms in late spring.

Var. *Golden Nugget* or *Yellow Gem* is lower growing to 18-24 in., erect in full sun, spreading in shade. Takes more sun than species and has longer flowering period, April-September.

CULTURE AND CLIMATE: Zones 7-13. Does well in hot desert areas. Winter kills at 20°. Sun or partial shade. Cuttings taken in early spring or late fall.

USE: In sun, combine with verbena and felicia against a background of delphinium and day lilies. In partial shade, with English primroses and fibrous begonias. A good container plant.

CAMPANULA. BELLFLOWER.
Large group of biennials and perennials, including types that are low and tufted, trailing, or erect. Flowers are bell-like or star-shaped in shades of blue, white, or sometimes pink. Low-growing, trailing forms:

C. isophylla. ITALIAN BELLFLOWER. Roundish, 1½-in. leaves and pale blue, 1-in., starry flowers in summer and fall. Var. *alba* probably best known, has white flowers, cascades to 2 ft. Var. *mayi* is less vigorous, has soft gray leaves and lavender-blue flowers.

C. fragilis. Vine-like stems trailing to 16 in., with roundish, toothed leaves and 1½-in., pale blue stars in summer. *Fanny Senior*, soft blue flowers, is an improved variety.

USE: Favorites for window boxes, pots, and hanging baskets. Combine beautifully with trailing lobelia, hanging fuchsias, and begonias, which bloom at the same time.

Low growing dwarfs, or somewhat spreading, 6-15 in.:

C. elatines garganica. *(C. garganica).* (See chapter on miniatures.)

C. carpatica. TUSSOCK BELLFLOWER. CARPATHIAN BELLFLOWER. (See chapter on miniatures.)

C. portenschlagiana. *(C. muralis).* DALMATIAN BELLFLOWER. (See chapter on miniatures.)

USE: Qualifies as an admirable edging plant because of its tidy, compact habit and long flowering period—May to July—often giving a second bloom in early fall.

C. porscharskyana. SERBIAN BELLFLOWER. Tufted but more spreading, with starry, lavender flowers in spring and early summer.

USE: Allow to grow informally in cool rock walls and shaded rock gardens, on banks, or around a pool overhung by trees. Effective companions for fuchsias and begonias.

Upright plants, 1½-6 ft.:

C. persicifolia. PEACH LEAF BLUEBELL. Strong-growing perennial to 2 ft. Many smooth, 4-8 in., basal leaves, the quite narrow, 2-4 in. stem leaves somewhat resembling those of a peach tree. Lavender-blue, 1-1½ in. wide, open, cup-shaped flowers in May and June. Of the varieties and horticultural forms of this species available, *Telham Beauty*, the variety frequently seen, grows to 2-3 ft. and has clear lavender-blue or white flowers.

USE: Best of the bellflowers for mixed border and for cutting.

C. pyramidalis. CHIMNEY BELLFLOWER. Tallest of the genus, growing to 5-6 ft.; stems with many short, flowering branchlets. Long stalked, 2-in., almost heart-shaped leaves. Saucer-shaped, 1-in. flowers are lavender or white, bloom later than other bellflowers—August and September.

USE: Can be used in the shady border in much the same way as foxglove and windflower *(Anemone japonica)*. In fact, these three planted in the back of a border provide color in late spring, summer, and fall. With care and proper staking chimney bellflower is spectacular in large pots.

C. rotundifolia. BLUEBELL OF SCOTLAND. HAREBELL. A wildling that roams in one form or another through Europe, Asia, and North America. Simple or much-branched plants to 1½ ft., the basal, 1-in. leaves are almost round, the 3-inch stem leaves are narrow. Bright blue, 1-in., cup-shaped flowers in loose, graceful clusters in June, July.

USE: Plant them where they can run wild and ramble among bulbs and other plants that grow informally. Attractive in masses in light shade under birch trees.

C. medium. CANTERBURY BELL. Old-fashioned favorite for cutting. Stout, rather rank, leafy biennial to 2-4 ft. with dense, coarse, wavy-margined leaves, the basal leaves 6-10 in. long, the stem leaves 3-5 in. Many varieties, with flowers inflated, bell-shaped, urn-shaped, single or double, in shades of violet, blue, lavender, pink or white.

CULTURE AND CLIMATE: Hardy all zones. Most bellflowers prefer partial shade, although in cool, coastal climates they will take sun. Cutting back after first bloom will often encourage a second crop. Divide clumps in fall every 2-3 years; Telham Beauty should be divided every year. Also can be grown from seed sown in summer, or cuttings in spring.

CAMPION. See LYCHNIS

CANDYTUFT, EVERGREEN. See IBERIS SEMPERVIRENS

CANTERBURY BELL. See CAMPANULA

CAPE MARIGOLD. See DIMORPHOTHECA ECKLONIS

CARNATION. See DIANTHUS

CATANANCHE CAERULEA. CUPID'S DART. Grows to 2 ft., with narrow, hairy, nearly basal leaves. Lavender-blue, 2-in. flowers, borne on long stems, look like strawflowers and can be dried. Blooms June-August. CULTURE AND CLIMATE: All zones. Full sun. Flowers from seed first year. USE: Good for dry, hot border.

CATCHFLY. See LYCHNIS; SILENE

CATMINT, CATNIP. See NEPETA

CENTAUREA. Grown principally for their soft white velvety foliage. Because the common name, dusty miller, is applied in some nurseries to centaureas and also to *Senecio cineraria*, it's a little difficult to get the plant you want when buying by the common name. Here's how the 2 most popular dusty millers measure up.

Senecio cineraria. This is the well known, old-fashioned dusty miller. Spreading, somewhat shrubby plant to 2 ft. Gray, soft, velvety leaves are very finely dissected. Yellow, ½-in. flower heads in loose clusters in summer.

Centaurea cineraria. DUSTY MILLER. More compact and lower growing to 10-12 in., with white foliage mostly in a basal clump. Leaves coarser, strap shaped, with broad roundish lobes. Solitary, yellow, 1-in. flower heads on long stems in summer.

If you want the old-fashioned dusty miller with the finely divided leaves, ask for *Senecio cineraria*. If you want the presently very popular and more modern plant with the broad, lobed leaves, ask for *Centaurea cineraria*.

C. gymnocarpa. *(C. argentea)*. VELVET CENTAUREA. Also often called dusty miller. Somewhat resembles *C. cineraria*, but the leaves are more finely dissected, and has small, purple flowers generally hidden by leaves.

CULTURE AND CLIMATE: Zones 7-13. Full sun. Sow seeds and make cuttings in summer.

USE: An edging of silvery centaureas will key down the shouting midsummer red of annual salvia, or quiet the bright oranges and reds of zinnias, marigolds, and tithonias. Subtle and soft combined with pale pink, or lemon-yellow plants. Wonderful for the night garden, especially with white flowers.

CENTRANTHUS RUBER. *(Valeriana coccinea, V. rubra)*. RED VALERIAN, JUPITER'S BEARD. Rank invasive plant that is difficult to eradicate when established. Grows to 3 ft., with bluish-green, 4-in. leaves. Small, crimson or pale red flowers in dense terminal clusters, in summer. Var. *albus* has white flowers.

CULTURE AND CLIMATE: Hardy all zones. Sun, half-shade, burns in extreme heat. Withstands drought. Spreads by roots or self-sows. Has escaped from gardens and grows wild in many sections of the West.

USE: Best as a soil binder in difficult areas.

CERASTIUM TOMENTOSUM. SNOW-IN-SUMMER. (See chapter on ground covers.)

CERATOSTIGMA PLUMBAGINOIDES. *(Plumbago larpentiæ)*. BLUE LEADWORT. (See chapter on ground covers.)

CHEIRANTHUS CHEIRI. WALLFLOWER. Erect bushy plants to 1-2½ ft.; with narrow, bright green, 3-in. leaves. Fragrant, ½-in. flowers in rich velvety tones of yellow, orange, brown, red, and even pink, rose and burgundy, in dense clusters at the tops of the leafy stems. Blooms February-May. Many horticultural varieties are available including double-flowered forms. CULTURE AND CLIMATE: All zones. Plant in semi-shade where sun is bright; in the open otherwise. Give a high ground situation or add sand to provide best possible drainage and avoid winter waterlogging. Sow seeds in spring. Make cuttings to increase stock of special varieties. USE: Rich source of winter color. Use mixed wallflowers behind polyantha primulas to reflect their yellow-to-red coloring. Colorful accents when planted in dirt crevices of a gray stone wall. Good cut flowers.

CHILE AVENS. See GEUM CHILOENSE

CHRISTMAS ROSE. See HELLEBORUS

CHRYSANTHEMUM. A large genus containing some of the best known, most popular and useful perennials for summer borders and cutting.

C. coccineum. *(Pyrethrum roseum)*. PAINTED DAISY. PYRETHRUM. Bushy clumps to 2-3 ft. with finely divided, almost fern-like, bright green leaves. Solitary, single daisies on long stems are deep crimson to pale pink and white. Also available in double forms. Bloom in June and again in late summer if plant is sheared to the ground after first bloom.

CULTURE AND CLIMATE: Hardy all zones. Best in full sun. Remove dead blooms immediately to keep plant from going to seed. Divide clumps or sow seeds in spring. Double forms do not always come true from seed.

USE: Mainly for cutting, or for the middle of the perennial border.

C. frutescens. MARGUERITE. PARIS DAISY. Rapid growing, shrubby perennial to 3 ft., much branched, becoming woody at the base. Bright green, coarsely divided leaves. Bears a profusion of long-stemmed, solitary, 1½-2½ in., white daisies. One variety has lemon-yellow flowers. Blooms the year around in mild climates.

CULTURE AND CLIMATE: Zones 9-13. Prefers full sun and loose, dry, not too fertile soil. Grows beautifully near the coast; with more water, grows successfully inland where, however, it may frost. Flowers get smaller as plants become older. Grow new plants from cuttings every 2 or 3 years. Easily grown from cuttings; bloom in 3-4 months.

USE: Marguerites thrive equally well in the ground and in containers. Grown commercially as cut flowers.

C. mawii. MOROCCO CHRYSANTHEMUM. Half-shrubby plants to 1½ ft. Attractive, gray-green, finely cut leaves; a profusion of pink, 1½-in. daisies, tinted rose on the under side.

CULTURE AND CLIMATE: Zones 9-13. Short-lived. Same culture as *C. frutescens*. Seed, cuttings.

USE: Sunny, dry, mixed border with verbena, felicia, dusty miller.

Chrysanthemum maximum. SHASTA DAISY. Sturdy, spreading, perennial to 1-3 ft., with deep green, long, narrow-toothed leaves, and white, gold centered, 2-4 in. daisies.

Through hybridizing, first by Luther Burbank, later by others, this old-fashioned, coarse plant is hardly recognizable today. Today's varieties are results of crossing *C. maximum* with other species to develop a tri-hybrid. Subsequent horticultural varieties differ from *C. maximum* in having larger, better formed flowers that are longer blooming. They're available in single, semi-double and shaggy-double, or fringed kinds, and bloom from late spring to fall.

Some named varieties are: *Beaute Nivelloise* grows to 30 in.; one of the largest, with fringed, double flowers to 7 in. across on sturdy stems. *Chiffon* has fringed petals in 2 rows, giving a lacy, ruffled appearance. *Esther Reed* has large, pure white flowers, resembling a double pyrethrum, on strong, 2-ft. stems. Very floriferous, invaluable for border decoration or cutting purposes. *G. marconi* has large, shaggy flowers, 5-7 in. across. May-November. *Charming* has beautiful double flowers without any curled petals. Excellent for arrangements. May-October bloom. *Edgebrook Giant* is tall plant to 3½ ft. Flowers 5-7 in. across. May-October. *Alaska* has single flowers about 4 in. across. May-October. Good bushy plants.

CULTURE AND CLIMATE: Hardy all zones. Prefer full sun. Excel in enriched, deeply dug soil. Remove dead blooms to encourage new flowers. Rapid spreading habit necessitates yearly division of clumps.

Selected forms of Shasta daisy do not come true from seed and increase so rapidly from small divisions that it is not worthwhile growing them from seed.

Shasta daisies are almost completely free from attacks by insects and diseases.

USE: Combine with Oriental poppies, delphiniums, hardy asters, heleniums, rudbeckias, veronicas.

C. morifolium. FLORIST'S CHRYSANTHEMUM. See separate section, page 164.

C. parthenium. FEVERFEW. Compact, very leafy, shrub-like plants to 1-3 ft., the deeply cut leaves yellowish-green. Small, ⅗-in. white daisies with yellow centers, many in open clusters at the ends of the branches, bloom from summer well into fall.

CULTURE AND CLIMATE: Hardy all zones. Prefers sun and tolerates neglect. Divide clumps in spring or fall. Seeds. Self-sows readily and may become a nuisance.

USE: Good for uncultivated areas, as along boundaries or drives in country gardens.

CINQUEFOIL. See POTENTILLA

COLUMBINE. See AQUILEGIA

CONEFLOWER, PURPLE. See ECHINACEA PURPUREA

CORAL BELLS. See HEUCHERA SANGUINEA

COREOPSIS GRANDIFLORA. Erect, spreading to 3 ft. with smooth, narrow, 3-5 parted, dark green leaves. Large, bright yellow, 2½-in., daisy flowers on long wiry stems above the foliage, all summer. Var. *Double Sunburst* has large, semi-double, golden-yellow flowers. Var. *Mayfield Giant* is an exceptionally vigorous grower with deeper yellow flowers. CULTURE AND CLIMATE: Hardy all zones. Full sun. Drought resistant. Sow seeds in spring; divide clumps in fall and spring, or just cut to the ground—the plant will soon resprout. USE: Invaluable as a source of yellow for many months. Associate with delphinium, anchusa, *Veronica spicata*, and other blues.

CORYDALIS LUTEA. Many-stemmed, spreading plant to 15 in. tall with masses of gray-green foliage similar to columbine. Yellow, ½-in. flowers in short clusters. Blooms throughout summer. CULTURE AND CLIMATE: All zones. Partial shade. Divide clumps in spring and fall. Plants self-sow and sometimes behave like annuals. USE: Attractive alongside a pool or in rock gardens.

COWSLIP LUNGWORT. See PULMONARIA

CUDWEED EVERLASTING. See HELICHRYSUM PETIOLATUM

CUP FLOWER. See NIEREMBERGIA HIPPOMANICA

CUPID'S DART. See CATANANCHE CAERULEA

CUSHION PINK. See SILENE

DAISY, AFRICAN. See ARCTOTIS; DIMORPHOTHECA; GERBERIA JAMESONII

DAISY, ENGLISH. See BELLIS PERENNIS

DAISY, TRANSVAAL. See GERBERIA JAMESONII

DELPHINIUM. Anyone who has seen more than one garden knows the tall, stately delphinium whose color was once practically a synonym for blue. Now its colors range from white to pink-lavender through many shades of blue to almost black. Not so well known but deserving of wide use are the low-growing Chinese types and the medium types, Belladonna and Bellamosum.

Pacific Giants. Tall-growing hybrids developed in California—the undisputed leaders in the delphinium clan. They grow to 8 ft. with sturdy, dense spikes of ¾-in. flowers. Depending on the season, they bloom in late spring or early summer and again in early fall, or in mild autumns as late as November.

Grow best in full sun where summers are cool. In hot interiors either give them filtered shade or plant in fall so that first blooming period will be early and over before high summer temperatures climb high. Best treated as annuals in warm-winter sections where they tend to bloom themselves out. In these areas they are sold in flats along with the regular bedding plants.

The weight of the spikes of these giants is such that staking is always necessary.

Bellamosum—Belladonna types. Although these are less spectacular than the giants they are easier to use with other flowers. Growing to 3 ft. with many branching stems topped by rather blunt spikes of less formal and more loosely arranged flowers. Bellamosum is dark blue; Belladonna, a light silvery blue. They do not need staking.

Chinese Delphiniums. Low, bushy, rounded plant with many branched stems. Single, open, 1-in. flowers in loose, airy sprays. Three varieties are commonly available: *Azure Fairy*, the softest blue; *Blue Butterfly*, deep blue; *Blue Mirror*, also a deep blue, but unlike Blue Butterfly, the flowers have no spurs and they face upward.

CULTURE AND CLIMATE: Hardy all zones. Easily started from fresh seed available in July. Seedling will be large enough to plant out in a cold frame or protected corner by October. By March or April you will have sturdy clumps that will develop rapidly to give bloom in early summer.

One-year-old clumps from the nursery will give you more spikes per plant than you'll get from seedlings.

Soil should be rich and deep. Work into the bottom of the planting holes a cupful of lime or bone meal.

When planting be sure not to cover the crown and watch that water does not settle around it.

Bait for snails as soon as you see the first sign of green growth. If rabbits or birds are a problem, you may have to cover plants with wire screen.

As soon as plant is 6-8 in. high give it a lift with a light application of your favorite balanced fertilizer.

Cut back plants immediately after first flowering, leaving about 8-12 in. of stem. When the new growth appears, remove the old stalks completely. Give the plants another light application of a balanced fertilizer.

After the second bloom cut back again and if winters are cold mulch with straw. Because delphinium tops—particularly of the Chinese type—disappear in winter, it's wise to mark their positions.

USE: The classic combination of delphiniums and Madonna lilies is still as good as the day it was first tried. The tall types need lower companions that will give color when the delphinium first blooms. Yellow snapdragons, white *Campanula persicifolia*, tall, yellow columbine, light pink penstemon are good choices.

The medium height types, Belladonna and Bellamosum, are invaluable middle of the border blues. If you want delphiniums for cutting, these should be your first choice.

The Chinese delphinium can be used in front section of the border or in masses. They are especially nice with salmon godetia or the clear yellow hunnemannia.

DIANTHUS. PINK. Dianthus—dainty garden pinks, old-fashioned sweet William, large-flowered carnations—are synonymous with fragrance in the garden.

D. caryophyllus. CARNATION. Much branched, shrubby plants to 1-3 ft., sometimes becoming woody at the base. Narrow, blue-gray leaves. Large double, usually spicily fragrant flowers borne on long stems, bloom almost continuously from late spring to late fall. Varieties are available in solid colors—white, pink, rose, red, yellow, and salmon—as well as combinations of these colors in stripes, variegations, or edgings (picotee).

CULTURE AND CLIMATE: Hardy zones 4-13. Full sun, or light shade in warmer sections where flower colors are apt to fade. During growing season plants benefit from monthly applications of a well-balanced, commercial fertilizer. When small, pinch back at least once, and sometimes twice to produce bushy, compact plants. For large flowers, remove all but terminal bud. Stake plants to prevent sprawling or toppling. Maintain uniform moisture at all times. Cuttings in spring. Layering.

USE: Because their floppy habit and need for staking make them difficult to manage in borders, carnations are best grown as cut flowers. Grow them in pots or tubs if you can't find the right spot for them in the garden. They are also at home in the herb garden with an edging of thyme, nepeta, pinks, or sweet alyssum.

D. barbatus. SWEET WILLIAM. Vigorous, erect biennials to 1-2 ft., growing in clumps. Dark to light green, smooth, flat leaves form basal mats of foliage. Leafy stems are topped by rounded clusters of 1-in., delicately fragrant, single or double flowers, in spring and early summer. Flower colors range from purplish-maroon to white, with vivid scarlet, pink, salmon, flesh, wine-color, rose, and other shades, some with rings or eyes in the center of the flower. A dwarf form is available in mixed colors, single or double; will make compact, 12-in. mounds.

CULTURE AND CLIMATE: Hardy all zones. Prefers sun but will tolerate partial shade. Blooms the second year from seed.

The garden pinks with spicily fragrant blooms in white, rose, pink, salmon and red are typical cottage garden flowers. They are available in a number of species and horticultural forms. (Also see chapter on miniatures.)

D. plumarius. COTTAGE PINKS. GRASS PINKS. Matted, gray-green, tufted foliage. Stalks to 12-18 in. bear cinnamon-spiced, single or double flowers in many colors, with the petals attractively fringed. Bloom from June to October:

D. caesius. CHEDDAR PINK. Neat, compact mounds of blue-gray foliage topped by showy, fragrant, rose-pink flowers with toothed petals. Blooms May and June.

D. deltoides. MAIDEN PINK. Mat-forming dwarf with 1-in. leaves. Small white, cerise or crimson flowers, often marked with lighter colors, borne on forked stems 4-8 in. high, bloom in June and July, sometimes again in fall.

D. allwoodii. Hybrid resulting from a cross between the cottage pink and carnation. Compact tufts of blue-gray foliage. Bright flowers on long stems in spring and summer. Many horticultural varieties are available, the flowers with entire or fringed petals, in many colors. Many miniatures are included in this group.

D. latifolius Beatrix. Long-blooming plant to 8 in., spreading to 12 in., with bright green, fairly wide foliage. Clusters of double pink flowers bloom 9 months of the year after plants are well established.

D. noeanus. Silvery-gray tufts, with 6-in. stems carrying flaming red, single flowers from April to November.

D. Mrs. Dina Weller. Compact, to 6 in., bearing a profusion of single, lavender-pink flowers with much deeper center ring. May to June.

D. Rose Cushion. A cushion miniature, to 4 in., with masses of tiny, rose-colored pinks blooming in April to June.

D. Wallace Red. Blue-gray foliage in a 10-in. mound contrasts strikingly with crimson-red, double flowers that bloom in mild climates from April to November.

CULTURE AND CLIMATE: Full sun, and well-drained soil with lime added. Plants demand severe shearing to retain neatness, and also to encourage longer blooming. Cuttings in spring or fall for carnations and other dianthus with long or trailing stems. Layering. Divide clumps in spring or fall.

USE: Pinks—particularly the plumarius and latifolius types—are natural in mixed borders. Lower and cushion forms make fine edging or rock garden plants. Some, such as *D. neglectus* and *D. cæsius* grow easily in chinks of walls. *D. latifolius Beatrix* makes an attractive ground cover under tree roses.

DICENTRA. BLEEDING HEART. Herbaceous perennials with graceful light green much divided foliage making a lacy background for the rose-purple, pink to white heart-shaped flowers.

D. spectabilis. COMMON BLEEDING HEART. Leafy stemmed plants to 2 ft.; leaves and leaflets broadest of the bleeding hearts. Large pink to rose-pink flowers loosely arranged along one side of the flower stalks. Blooms in late spring. Var. *alba* has white flowers.

D. formosa. PACIFIC BLEEDING HEART. Native to shady woods along the Pacific coast. Stemless plants, the basal leaves finely cut, more fern-like than *D. spectabilis*. Leafless stalks 8-18 in. high bear terminal clusters of ¾-in. rose-purple, sometimes white flowers. Blooms April to June. Var. *Sweetheart* is a horticultural form developed from the rare white form of the native. Has tremendous vigor and increases rapidly. Blooms from spring to fall.

CULTURE AND CLIMATE: All zones, but short lived in mild-winter areas. Partial shade. Protect from wind. After blooming, foliage yellows and dies back. Root cuttings or clump division in early spring.

USE: Valuable in shade plantings with begonias, ferns, fuchsias, and campanulas. Good shady ground cover.

DIGITALIS PURPUREA. FOXGLOVE. A big and bold plant. Tall stems to 5-8 ft., rising from large, woolly leaves, carry at their tops 18-24 in. spikes of tubular, 3-in. flowers in white, pink, rose or purple. The inside of the flower is dotted with darker colors. Blooms in spring or later, depending upon the climate.

Color range has been extended by the introduction of new strains. You can find them in clear yellows, in salmon shades, and in pastel shades of pink, apricot, buff, rose and mauve.

CULTURE AND CLIMATE: Hardy all zones. Best in shade or partial shade, but will grow in sun in coastal areas. Grows readily from seed, and has gone wild along northwest coast.

USE: Big and bold, so give it room. Use in bays between evergreen shrubs or under high branching trees.

DIMORPHOTHECA ECKLONIS. CAPE MARIGOLD, AFRICAN DAISY. Woody based, much branched, leafy perennial to 2-3 ft. with soft green narrow leaves. Long stems bear single 3-in. daisy flowers, white rays tinged lavender or blue on reverse side surround a dark blue center. Daisies close at night or on cloudy days. Blooms early summer to first frost.

CULTURE AND CLIMATE: Zones 7-13. Full sun. Sow fresh seed. Cuttings in spring. Readily self-sows.

USE: In borders in the same manner as marguerite. Good cut flower.

DIPLACUS. MONKEY FLOWER. (See chapter on natives.)

DORONICUM. LEOPARDS BANE. Showy yellow daisy-like 2-4 in. flowers on long stems arise from dense dark green leafy mounds.

D. plantagineum. PLANTAIN LEOPARDS BANE. Grows to 5 ft., with ovate toothed leaves. Earliest blooming of the group.

D. pardalianches. Grows to 4 ft., with heart-shaped leaves. Starts blooming when *D. plantagineum* is through. Will bloom again in autumn if cut back as soon as the flowers die.

Two lower growing species are *D. caucasicum*, CAUCASIAN LEOPARDS BANE, and *D. clusii*, DOWNY LEOPARDS BANE, growing to 2 ft., with the brightest yellow flowers of all. Time of bloom depends on the region, generally very early spring.

CULTURE AND CLIMATE: All zones, but needs too much attention in all warm summer sections. Light shade. Remove faded flowers to encourage second flowering before plants die down. Divide clumps after flowering every two or three years.

USE: Best when planted in groups of 5, 6, or more in border shaded by deciduous trees. Excellent for planting with tulips. Flowers good for cutting.

DUCHESNEA INDICA. INDIAN MOCK STRAWBERRY. (See chapter on ground covers.)

DUSTY MILLER. See CENTAUREA

ECHINACEA PURPUREA. (*Rudbeckia purpurea*). PURPLE CONEFLOWER. Rather coarse bushy plants forming clumps to 4-5 ft. with 8-in. ovate leaves. Large rosy-purple flowers on long stems, with cone-shaped centers, the encircling 3-in. rays spreading or drooping. Late summer bloom. Var. *The King* has 4-in. flowers in dusty rose with dark conical centers. Var. *White Luster* is a dwarf to 3 ft. with white rays around greenish-brown cone.

CULTURE AND CLIMATE: All zones. Full sun. Drought resistant. Divide clumps in spring or fall.

USE: Striking coneflowers provide bold and unusual accent with other perennials. Long-lasting cut flowers.

ECHINOPS RITRO. SMALL GLOBETHISTLE. Rigidly branched plants to 3 ft. with whitish, very spiny, finely cut leaves. Steel blue flowers in round, 2-in. bristly balls. Blooms late summer.

CULTURE AND CLIMATE: Hardy all zones. Full sun. Needs little care. Divide clumps in spring or fall.

USE: Border, where its misty blue and unusual form combine especially well with sunflowers, such as yellow helenium, and Michaelmas daisies.

ECHIUM FASTUOSUM. PRIDE OF MADEIRA. A shrubby perennial for special places. Large, robust, 3-4 ft. clumps of hairy, gray-green, narrow leaves form rounded, irregular mounds. Spikes of blue-purple flowers stand out dramatically, well above the foliage, in May-June.

E. rubrum (often sold under the name of *E. roseum*). TOWER OF JEWELS. A biennial with tall spires of reddish-rose flowers.

CULTURE AND CLIMATE: Zones 7-13. Hardy to 15°. Sun. Likes poor, dry soil.

USE: For bold effects against walls or at the back of a wide perennial border and on slopes. Very effective with *Limonium perezii*, particularly near seacoast.

EPIMEDIUM. Low trailing plants, almost shrub-like, with leaves composed of 2 or 3 small, pointed, heart-shaped leaflets held on graceful wiry stems. Delicate clusters of small, waxy, pink, red, yellow, or white flowers that resemble a bishop's cap.

E. grandiflorum roseum. *(E. macranthum roseum, E. roseum).* BISHOP'S HAT. Foliage, bronzy-pink in spring, green in summer, bronze in fall, forms a 10-in. high ground cover above which loose clusters of pinkish flowers appear in spring.

Other species and varieties offer flowers in white, lilac, yellow, red with yellow spurs.

CULTURE AND CLIMATE: All zones. Shade and part shade. Thrive best in same growing conditions as rhododendrons. Divide clumps in spring or fall.

USE: Fine ground cover at edge of a shaded path or massed under trees.

ERIGERON. Erect or trailing plants with white, pink, or lavender, daisy-type flowers.

E. karvinskianus. *(E. mucronatus).* Graceful, trailing plant to 10-20 in., with 1-in., toothed or lobed leaves. White or pinkish, ¾-in., daisy flowers freely blooming late spring to frost. Effective in walls, hanging baskets; practical to naturalize on slopes.

E. speciosus. Lavender-pink flowers blooming in summer on branching stems to 20 in. Var. *Quakeress* has larger flower, blooms into late fall. In perennial border, combines nicely with *Scabiosa caucasica*.

CULTURE AND CLIMATE: Zones 7-13. Sun or partial shade. Will stand neglect. Cut back yearly after bloom to keep under control. Seed. Divide clumps in spring or fall every third year.

Any number of other erigerons—all excellent, free-blooming daisies—are mostly blue summer editions of Michaelmas daisies.

ERYNGIUM AMETHYSTINUM *(E. coelestinum).* AMETHYST ERYNGIUM. Erect rigid plants to 2-3 ft., with steel blue or purplish stems sparsely clothed with dark green, whitish spined, deeply cut leaves. Many-branched flower stalks, topped with ¾-in. blue balls, blooming July-August.

CULTURE AND CLIMATE: Hardy all zones. Sun. Sow seeds in spring.

USE: Striking in flower arrangements. Can be dried for winter use.

EUPATORIUM COELESTINUM. MISTFLOWER. Bushy clumps of thinly branched purple stems 1-2 ft. clothed with triangular, toothed, lightly hairy 3-in. leaves. Light blue to violet flowers appear in fluffy heads, resembling those of the tall growing ageratum. Blooms in solid masses, August and September.

CULTURE AND CLIMATE: Hardy all zones. Sun or part shade. Divide clumps in spring or fall.

USE: Where a light and airy blue-violet would be effective in border. Good cut flower.

EUPHORBIA. Erect or prostrate and spreading perennials with stiff roundish, blue-gray leaves in closely set spirals. Gives effect of a succulent, but foliage not fleshy.

E. myrsinites. MYRTLE EUPHORBIA. Prostrate and spreading at the base, then erect to 15 in. Chartreuse to yellow flowers in loose, flattish clusters top every stem in spring and summer. Combines well with succulents and gray plants.

E. wulfenii. Erect plant to 2 ft., with flat heads of chartreuse-yellow flowers in early spring. Stunning in containers.

CULTURE AND CLIMATE: All zones. Sun or part shade. Will stand neglect. Cut back after flowering. Grows easily from seed. Divide clumps in spring or fall.

FELICIA. Erect or trailing plants with bright green to blue-green foliage and daisy flowers.

F. amelloides *(Agathea coelestis).* BLUE MARGUERITE. Attractive low growing, somewhat scrubby plant to 18 in. with roundish leaves. Sky-blue, yellow-centered flowers on long stalks bloom all summer and fall, sometimes through winter.

F. aethiopica. Improved type with deeper blue flowers, better foliage and habit of growth. Grown only from cuttings.

USE: Ideal plant for the mixed border, where it is as useful as geraniums and marguerites, and where its foliage adds a green spot in winter. Use for summer blue on a bank or in a parking strip. Interplant with pink and white verbenas. Try it with yellow marguerites in a large planter or tub.

F. petiolata rosea. Subshrub with trailing branches. Deep-pink, yellow-centered flowers.

CULTURE AND CLIMATE: Zones 7-13. Sun or partial shade. Keep dead flowers removed and shear severely toward end of summer to encourage growth that will bear new crops of flowers in the fall. Sow seeds in spring. Self-sows in garden.

USE: Attractive plant for hanging baskets.

FESTUCA OVINA GLAUCA. *(F. glauca).* BLUE FESCUE. (See chapter on ground covers.)

FLAX, INDIAN YELLOW. See REINWARDTIA INDICA

FORGET-ME-NOT. See BRUNNERA MACROPHYLLA; OMPHALODES VERNA; ANCHUSA AZUREA

FOXGLOVE. See DIGITALIS PURPUREA

FRAGARIA CHILOENSIS. WILD STRAWBERRY, SAND STRAWBERRY. (See chapter on ground covers.)

FRANCOA RAMOSA. MAIDEN'S WREATH. Spreading plant with basal clumps of large crisp wavy-margined green leaves, attractive throughout the year. Small white or pinkish flowers in spikes at the ends of slender arching stems 2-3 ft. tall. White form best. Blooms from late summer through fall.

CULTURE AND CLIMATE: Hardy all zones. Prefers partial shade, but grows well in full shade. Best in sheltered position. Any soil except heavily alkaline. Wants fair share of water. Sow seeds in spring. Blooms the first year if sown early. Divide clumps in spring or late fall.

USE: A very distinctive plant in shady borders with ferns, foxgloves, primroses; in the foreground of azaleas, camellias, kalmias, and rhododendrons; or by itself in pots and tubs. A superb cut flower—particularly effective in all-white arrangement with small pompon dahlias.

FRINGE BELL. See SHORTIA SOLDANELLOIDES

GAILLARDIA ARISTATA *(G. grandiflora).* COMMON PERENNIAL GAILLARDIA. Heads larger and flatter than on the annuals (see chapter on annuals). Shaggy, rather coarse plant to 2 ft., with hairy toothed or divided 4-in. leaves. Yellow 4-in. daisy flowers on long straight stems from April to December.

Many hybrids have been developed with a wide range of flower colors. Flower rays often banded in 2 colors, the width varying. Sometimes the centers are a different color.

CULTURE AND CLIMATE: Hardy all zones. Sun, semishade in hot climates. Needs no care. Pull old leaves from clump to keep tidy. Seed sown in July through September. Increase by division.

USE: Good in mixed perennial border with anchusa,

blue delphinium, russet snapdragons, yellow geum, yellow and bronze chrysanthemums. Fine for cut flowers.

GAZANIA. The favorite garden forms are low growing clumps spreading rapidly to form a solid mass of foliage. Leaves usually long and narrow, sometimes divided, dark green above, white woolly beneath. Abundant gaudy daisy flowers variously striped, banded, blotched or spotted on backgrounds of scarlet, wine, rose, white, yellow, bronze or orange. Bloom almost all year. Flowers close at night, in shade, or on cloudy days.

G. ringens, the common orange gazania, has 1½-in. flowers, the orange rays varying to yellow, with a brown-black, white-eyed spot at the base.

G. pavonia has 3½-in. flowers, the orange-yellow rays with a white-ringed black spot at the base.

Many new gazanias are said to be hybrid descendants of this species and the dark-eyed yellow *G. splendens*. One such descendant is *Copper King*, which grows to about 1 ft. Its flowers include rich iridescent tones of yellow-orange, and brown with red-violet at the base of each ray, the base flecked with blue and buff. Blooms from October to April.

CULTURE AND CLIMATE: Zones 7-13. Full sun. Seed sown in early March. Seed packets usually contain mixed colors. Will self-sow in garden. Large mounded plants ready to give you a solid cover of flowers are available in containers at many nurseries. Increase by dividing clumps in midsummer.

USE: As colorful utility plants, they are widely used for parking strips, bank covers and pattern plantings.

GENTIANA ACAULIS. STEMLESS GENTIAN. Low-growing tufts of deep green foliage to 4 in. high. Nestled among the leaves are large, 2-in., tubular, dark blue flowers in early summer. CULTURE AND CLIMATE: Hardy all zones. Light shade. The most tolerant of a rather difficult group, and once established should not be disturbed. Seeds. USE: Few blues are more famous than the blue of the gentian. Best in cool, moist pockets in the rock garden.

GERANIUM. See PELARGONIUM

GERBERIA JAMESONII. TRANSVAAL DAISY, AFRICAN DAISY. The most richly textured and sophisticated of all daisies. Gray-green basal rosette of lobed or cut 10-in. leaves, from which rise slightly curving stems to 18 in. bearing the beautiful 4-in. slender-rayed daisies. Single or double flowers in delicate tones of yellow, white, cream, pink, coral, deep rose, pale orange, and red. Bloom May to December with heights of bloom in early summer and late fall.

CULTURE AND CLIMATE: Zones 7-13; more difficult to grow in 10-13. Sun, half shade in hot climates. Shelter from wind. Plant with crown at least ¼ in. above soil. Needs perfect drainage. Water deeply but allow soil to become almost dry between waterings. Seed in August. Divide every 3 years in early spring. Divide in February leaving 2 or 3 buds on each division.

USE: Most handsome grown alone, particularly in separate shades or mixtures of harmonizing shades.

GEUM CHILOENSE. CHILE AVENS. Evergreen perennial from which are derived most of the garden forms. Dark green hairy foliage in 15-in. basal clumps, the leaves with large terminal leaflet and many smaller lateral leaflets. Leafy flowering stems rise to 2 ft. bearing 1½-in. flowers.

Geums usually grown are semi-double, in colors of yellow, orange or red. Hybrids available in apricot and copper. Bloom starts in May and continues until midsummer. Some of the available varieties are *Mrs. Bradshaw*, the well-known bright red; *Lady Stratheden*, yellow; *Fire Opal*, orange-scarlet; *Princess Juliana*, coppery-orange.

CULTURE AND CLIMATE: All zones. Sun; thrives in part shade in hot summer areas. Seeds sown in early fall or spring produce blooming plants the first year. Division of clumps in fall.

USE: Substantial, long-blooming plant. Colorful in mixed border with blue Michaelmas daisies, lobelia, cornflower, purple sage.

GLAUCIUM FLAVUM. (*G. luteum*). YELLOW HORNED-POPPY. Grows to about 2 ft., with gray-green or whitish, dissected leaves. Brilliant orange to golden-yellow, 2-in. poppies, solitary on stiff stems, look as though they were varnished. Even though flowers last briefly, bloom usually continues from June to August. Flowers followed by slender, unusually long seed pods. CULTURE AND CLIMATE: Hardy zones 7-13. Treat as an annual in colder sections. Sun. Cutting back to new basal leaves once a year improves plant. Seed. USE: Striking with other gray plants, interesting with succulents.

GLOBE THISTLE. See ECHINOPS RITRO
GOAT'S BEARD. See ASTILBE
GOLDEN DROPS. See ONOSMA STELLULATUM TAURICUM

GYPSOPHILA. Many slender, stiffly radiating branches carry sprays of minute flowers to give the plant an airy see-through quality. It's an indispensable plant where you wish to counter the solidity of heavier plants. Useful for masking earlier-blooming perennials, particularly Oriental poppies that go dormant in midsummer.

G. paniculata. BABY'S BREATH. Diffusely branched to 3 ft.; narrow, 4-in. leaves. White flowers in May and June. Var. *Bristol Fairy* is the most desirable double white.

G. oldhamiana and **G. pacifica** are 3 ft. high with single pink flowers.

G. repens. CREEPING BABY'S BREATH. A miniature growing to 6 in., with trailing branches. Var. *bodgeri Rosy Veil*, one of the best, grows to 15 in. and has tiny pink flowers all summer long. Var. *rosea* is prostrate, with dainty, single, pink flowers, May-October. Var. *alba* has white flowers, May-October.

CULTURE AND CLIMATE: Hardy all zones. Best adapted in cool sections. Sun. All gypsophila grow easily from seed except Bristol Fairy, which must be grown from cuttings or root grafts.

USE: Good cut flowers. Dwarf forms fine for rock gardens or for spilling over sunny walls.

HELENIUM AUTUMNALE. (*H. grandiflorum*). COMMON SNEEZE-WEED. Lemon yellow to bright yellow, 2-in. daisies in August or September on tall, many-branched stems to 6 ft. with 5-in. toothed leaves.

H. a. Moerheim Beauty, an exceptionally good form, is lower growing to 2½-3 ft. Its deep, luminous, red flowers are tipped with yellow and have a small, cushiony, brown center. Blooms in early July to late August.

CULTURE AND CLIMATE: Hardy all zones. Full sun, likes heat. Cut off old flowers regularly for long bloom. Best to divide every year or two, but will stand neglect for several years.

USE: Combine with blue salvias, perennial asters, or anchusa. Good cut flowers.

HELIANTHEMUM NUMMULARIUM HYBRIDS. SUN ROSE. (See chapter on ground covers.)

HELIANTHUS. SUNFLOWER. The sunflower of the farmyard with its enormous sunny heads, is an annual (*H*.

annuus, see chapter on annuals). The smaller growing perennials, although rather coarse for the perennial border, are very enthusiastic producers of color in September-November.

H. angustifolius. SWAMP SUNFLOWER. More graceful plant to 6-7 ft., with narrow, 7-in. leaves. Yellow, 3-in. daisies with purple centers bloom in October.

H. decapetalus. (*H. multiflorus*). THINLEAF SUNFLOWER. Parent of many of the horticultural forms, many of which look like dahlias. Grows to 5 ft., with rough, ovate, 5 in. leaves. Numerous yellow, 3-in. daisies with yellow centers bloom in fall. Var. *flore-pleno* and var. *grandiflorus* have double flowers. Var. *Lodden Gold* grows to 4-7 ft. and has golden, double, 4-in. flowers, October-November.

CULTURE AND CLIMATE: Hardy all zones. Full sun. Requires staking. Cut to ground after blooming. Divide every 2 years.

USE: Country places. Cutting garden.

HELICHRYSUM PETIOLATUM (*Gnaphalium lanatum*). CUDWEED EVERLASTING. Woody-based shrubby plant to 2 ft., with rather trailing stems spreading to 4 ft. Small oval white-woolly leaves and creamy-white papery flowers, turning to beige as they age, in 2-in. clusters; in fall.

CULTURE AND CLIMATE: Zones 7-13. Sun. Needs lots of room, summer watering and good drainage. Cut back to keep tidy and to prevent woodiness. Cuttings.

USE: Ornamental white foliage interesting in bank cover. Dried flowers good in arrangements.

HELIOPSIS SCABRA INCOMPARABILIS. Closely allied to the perennial sunflowers. Grows to 3-4 ft. with rough-hairy stems and leaves. Rich golden-yellow semi-double 3-4 in. blooms top long wiry stems; bright color in July continuing until fall. Var. *Gold Greenheart*, a newer version, is yellow with a green center when opening, becoming double clear yellow when fully open.

CULTURE AND CLIMATE: All zones. Sun. Plants die to ground in winter making new growth each year. Division every 3 years is beneficial.

USE: A tailor-made perennial for interior valleys. Coarse, bold plant, best in shrubbery border, good for cutting.

HELIOTROPIUM. HELIOTROPE. Old-fashioned plants grown for the delicate, sweet fragrance of the flowers. In mild climates they become almost shrub-like to 4 ft. Rich, dark green foliage contrasts well with the ample clusters of blue-purple to dark violet flowers in summer. Var. *Black Beauty* has an abundance of stunning, deep violet-purple flowers. CLIMATE AND CULTURE: Zones 7-13. Tender. Sun. Seeds germinate in 8-10 days. Set plants into pots or cans for winter protection; move into garden as soon as frost danger is over. USE: To enjoy the delightful flower fragrance, keep them in containers on patio or terrace. When set out in the garden, combine well with purple and white petunias, white nicotiana.

HELLEBORUS. Although most often planted for its flowers which bloom at such a useful time—winter and early spring—this plant is a good low evergreen when out of bloom. Good clean foliage of 6-10 in. leaves divided fan-wise into leaflets.

H. niger. CHRISTMAS ROSE. The first to flower; grows to 1½ ft., with dark green foliage, the basal leaves divided into 7 or more leaflets. A profusion of white or purplish 2½-in. blossoms on single leafy stems bloom from December, in a mild winter, to early spring. Var. *altifolius* is a taller plant to 2½ ft. with larger, purple mottled flowers.

H. orientalis. LENTEN ROSE. Similar to *H. niger*, has branched flower stems bearing green to purple-rose flowers, and blooms later. Horticultural forms of *H. orientalis* have produced interesting variations in flower color—pink, white, rose, red, maroon or purple.

H. lividus. (*H. corsicus*). CORSICAN HELLEBORE. Interesting and distinctive among the hellebores. Vigorous grower to 3 ft.; foliage pale blue-green, the rather stiff leaves divided into 3 leaflets which are prickly edged. Large clusters of pale chartreuse flowers remain on the plant until May.

H. foetidus. Grows to 1½ ft., has deeply cut leathery leaves, but the leaflets are narrower than *H. niger*. Small 1-in. pale green, red-tipped flowers in clusters.

H. viridis. Another chartreuse-flowered species grows to 2 ft. Leaves with 7-11 leaflets. Small 1-in. pendulous blossoms.

CULTURE AND CLIMATE: Hardy all zones, but adapted to cool summer areas and slightly acid soils. Shade or light shade. Plantings should not be disturbed, so give them a permanent place in the garden. Ripe seed sown in July in open ground will germinate the following spring. Bloom best during the second or third year after planting. Can be purchased in pots or cans.

USE: Especially effective as ground cover under high branches of trees or large shrubs; with ferns, daphne, kalmia, pieris, azalea, rhododendron, camellias and early flowering bulbs. Interesting foreground with fatshedera, fatsia and acanthus. Purple-leafed ajuga goes well with hellebores as contrasting edging. Good cut flowers.

HEPATICA. LIVERLEAF. Small woodland plant for the early spring garden, often blooming in colder climates before snows melt. Leaves are 3-parted into blunt lobes (*H. americana*) or pointed lobes (*H. triloba*). Leathery, bronze-green, new leaves shield tender flower buds through winter; new leaves appear after flowering. Starlike, 1-in. flowers in white, clear blue, pink and lavender shades, on slender, hairy, 6-in. stems. Delicate fragrance on a warm day. CULTURE AND CLIMATE: Hardy all zones, but best where winters are severe. Shade. Hepaticas seed readily, but colors must be kept separated or a muddy strain will eventually replace the clear colors. USE: Plant hepaticas in drifts in shady, moist spots, either in a wild garden or among rocks where sun will not reach them. Plant a few in a shallow pan to be placed on the patio or terrace where you can watch the cycle: delicate flowers contrasted with bronzed thick leaves, then the unfolding of soft and furry new foliage. Silky, 3-sectioned seed pods are almost as delightful as the flowers that precede them.

HEUCHERA SANGUINEA. CORAL BELLS. Neat evergreen foliage tufts of round leaves with scalloped edges. Slender flowering stems 12-18 in. bear the dainty bells from April to July; height of bloom in May and June. Hybrids now available in white and from softest pink to red, with the reds of a warmer tone, and the flowers larger. Var. *Perry's White* has white flowers; var. *Rosamondii* is coral-pink.

CULTURE AND CLIMATE: Zones 3-13. Sun, half shade. Susceptible to root mealybug. Divide clumps every 2 years. New divisions in October will bloom from June to August.

USE: Rosettes of evergreen foliage especially useful in foreground of borders or along paths. Attractive with *Campanula poscharskyana* in a partially shaded location. Suitable for cutting.

HONEY BELL. See MAHERNIA VERTICILLATA

HOSTA. *(Funkia).* PLANTAIN LILY. Their real glory is in their leaves—large, heart-shaped, shining, with distinct vertical veins. Useful in many ways in shady situations.

H. plantaginea. *(Funkia grandiflora, F. subcordata).* FRAGRANT PLANTAIN LILY. Probably the most spectacular. Green, 10-in. leaves. Very fragrant, large, white, 5-in. flowers on 2½-ft. stems, in August.

H. fortunei variegata. Bluish-green, 5-in. leaves with a white margin. Blue, 1½-in. flowers on 2-ft. stems, in midsummer.

H. sieboldiana. *(Funkia glauca).* SHORT CLUSTER PLANTAIN LILY. Bluish-green, 10-15 in. leaves. Many slender, drooping, pale lilac flowers on short stems nestled in the foliage, in August.

H. undulata. WAVY LEAF PLANTAIN LILY. Stout plant. Light green, wavy margined, 6-in. leaves, striped and splashed with cream or white. Pale lavender, 2-in. flowers on stems to 2½ ft., in May-June.

H. caerulea. *(Funkia ovata).* BLUE PLANTAIN LILY. Deep green, 9-in. leaves. Lavender-blue, 2-in. flowers on stems to 3 ft., in July-August.

CULTURE AND CLIMATE: Hardy all zones. Shade. Requires lots of moisture. Spreads rapidly. Cut to ground at advent of cold weather. Very attractive to slugs and snails. Spread bait as soon as new shoots appear above the ground and continue to bait through the growing season. Divisions.

USE: Combines well with other shade-loving plants. Rich looking in pots and tubs. Foliage attractive in flower arrangements.

HUNNEMANNIA FUMARIAEFOLIA. MEXICAN TULIP POPPY. GOLDENCUP. Hardy. 24 in. Upright, bushy perennial often grown as an annual with thick, finely cut, gray-green foliage and 3-in. clear, soft yellow flowers with crinkled petals. Horticultural variety *Sunlite* has larger semi-double flowers. Blooms summer and fall.

CULTURE: Sow seeds in spring where plants are to grow. Thin to 12 in. Drought tolerant, prefers a warm, dry, sunny location with some lime in the soil. Dies out if over-watered.

USE: Showy planted in solid masses by itself; also striking with scarlet-flowered *Zauschneria californica, Anchusa capensis, Penstemon heterophyllus,* and Chinese delphinium Blue Mirror. If picked in bud, the blooms will last a week, surpassing all other poppies as cut flowers.

IBERIS SEMPERVIRENS. EVERGREEN CANDYTUFT. Low growing compact mounds to 8-12 in., spreading to 2 ft. Excellent dark green foliage, fresh looking throughout the year. Flat clusters of small snowy-white flowers from in early spring until June. Hybrids have been developed with more compact growth habit and greater profusion of bloom. Available are: *Little Cushion, Little Gem, Purity,* and *Snowflake.*

CULTURE AND CLIMATE: Zones 3-13. Best in sun, will grow in light shade. Shear back occasionally to keep it neat and encourage new bloom. Increase by cuttings.

USE: Shows to advantage when spilling over a stone wall. Excellent edging for flower or shrub border. Use along paths. Combines nicely with violas or *Alyssum saxatile.* As evergreen base for shrubs, trees, and larger perennials in containers.

IMPATIENS. SNAPWEED, TOUCH-ME-NOT. An old-fashioned perennial that is fast growing enough to be treated as an annual, sturdy enough to substitute for a shrub. Semi-transparent, red-striped stems, glossy, rich green leaves, slightly flattened, 5-petaled flowers. The name snapweed comes from the explosive quality of its ripe seed pods.

I. holstii. Makes a 3 ft. high, 3 ft. wide shrub where it is perennial. Scarlet, 1¾-in. flowers on long stalks borne toward tops of stems. Blooms in summer. Many hybrids have been developed that are more compact and have a good color range: pink, salmon-pink, red, ruby, purple, violet, and white. Var. *liegnitzia (I. nana liegnitzia)* is more compact than the type.

CULTURE AND CLIMATE: Hardy zones 9-10, 12-13. Treat as an annual in colder sections. Filtered shade. Grows rapidly from seed.

USE: Best planted in masses or in drifts. Goes well with ferns and is good texture contrast to the heavy, dark green leaves of tuberous begonias.

JACOB'S LADDER. See POLEMONIUM

JASMINE TOBACCO. See NICOTIANA

JUPITER'S BEARD. See CENTRANTHUS RUBER

LAVANDULA. LAVENDER. Can you imagine a garden without lavender somewhere about? Dried flower spikes of English and French lavenders are best for sachets. (Also see chapter on herbs.)

L. officinalis. *(L. spica, L. vera).* ENGLISH LAVENDER. To 3-6 ft., with gray, narrow, 5-in. leaves. Light lavender flower spikes in summer. Var. *Munstead,* a dwarf strain to 1 ft., is smaller in every way.

L. stoechas. SPANISH LAVENDER. Stocky plant to 18 in. or more, with narrow, ½-in., gray leaves. Rich dark purple flowers in fat little spikes, with a terminal tuft of large purple bracts. Blooms in early summer.

L. dentata. FRENCH LAVENDER. Handsome plant to 4 ft., with bright green leaves that are square-toothed along the edges. Lavender-purple flowers in short spikes. Remarkable for its ever blooming habit.

CULTURE AND CLIMATE: All zones. Full sun. Thrives in sandy or rocky soil. Go easy on water and fertilizers. Prune immediately after flowering. Start from cuttings at almost any time of the year.

USE: Use as informal hedges, or edgings; on banks, along drives and fences; and in herb and rose gardens. Natural companion for rosemary, rockrose, sun rose, nepeta, and verbena. French lavender adds a cool touch to hot dry borders.

KNIPHOFIA *(Tritoma)* **UVARIA.** POKER PLANT. TORCH LILY. Often called red hot poker. (New hybrids offer softer colors and dwarf forms.) A coarse plant, with large rather unruly dense clumps of long grass-like leaves to 3 ft. Thick flower stalks to 5 ft. bear dense spikes of scarlet or yellow flowers.

Named varieties available in both dwarf and taller forms in soft and saffron yellow, cream and pure white.

CULTURE AND CLIMATE: Hardy all zones. Sun. Cut back old flower stalks. Division. New hybrids will not stand as much neglect as old-fashioned red hot poker.

USE: Perennial border, mass planting in waste areas. Especially good use—in great drifts of yellow and red on a bluff above the ocean.

LENTEN ROSE. See HELLEBORUS

LEOPARD'S BANE. See DORONICUM

LILY TURF. See LIRIOPE MUSCARI

LIMONIUM. *(Statice).* SEA LAVENDER. Clouds of hundreds of florets, each no bigger than the head of a pin, in many-branched clusters, give the flowering portion of the plant a likeness to baby's breath. Basal clumps of large, leathery leaves are evergreen. Although delicate looking the flowers are crisp and papery and can be used in dry bouquets.

L. perezii. *(Statice perezii)*. Spectacular clusters of minute purplish-lavender florets spotted with white, on 3-ft. stems.

L. latifolium. *(Statice latifolia)*. Lower growing; flowers in more delicate filmy sprays on stems to 1½ ft.

CULTURE AND CLIMATE: Zones 9-10, 12-13. Sun and part shade. Seeds.

USE: Use its rounded, soft form as a contrast to spiky foliage of iris or to solid discs of Shasta daisies.

LINUM. FLAX. (Also see chapter on annuals.) Well-behaved. Rewarding in flower and leaf. Growing to 1½-2 ft., with fragile shallow-cupped flowers which last a day but followed on the next day by so many more flowers that you are never conscious of any loss.

L. perenne. PERENNIAL BLUE FLAX. Airy plants with soft, somewhat heather-like, blue-green 1-in. leaves. Wiry, much-branched flower stalks bearing 1-in. sky-blue flowers carried well above the foliage. Blooms in early May well into fall.

L. narbonnense. Improvement over *L. perenne* but a somewhat stouter plant with larger, 1¾-in. deeper blue flowers.

L. flavum. GOLDEN FLAX. Bright green leaves and golden-yellow 1-in. flowers on a spreading plant about 1 ft. high. Blooms April to June.

CULTURE AND CLIMATE: Hardy all zones. Sun. Seed, cuttings, divisions.

USE: Plant blue flax with yellow day lilies, yellow floribunda roses or zinnias. Or try the annual scarlet flax interplanted with the blue.

LIRIOPE MUSCARI. BIG BLUE LILY TURF. Evergreen. Fast growing. A fountain of firm, dark green, narrow, grass-like leaves to ¾ in. wide and 18 in. long. Long, dense clusters of small, violet flowers are thick among the grassy leaves. CULTURE AND CLIMATE: Zones 7-13. Sun or shade. Division is easy, although not often needed. USE: Best as a permanent border plant. Can also be grown in pots or tubs.

LITHOSPERMUM DIFFUSUM. *(L. prostratum, Lithodora diffusa)*. Evergreen. Sturdy perennial with trailing, mat-like habit and narrow dark green leaves. Slender sprays of small, wonderfully blue, ½ in. flowers, in early spring. Var. *Heavenly Blue* has small, well-polished leaves and truly gentian blue flowers. Var. *Grace Ward* has larger flowers and, if possible, a more intense blue. CULTURE AND CLIMATE: Hardy all zones. Best adapted to zones 1-6. Sun. Seeds and cuttings. USE: Plant in a stone wall or beside a step—any place where you will see it often and at close range. Growing with stemless gentian in crevices among rocks, each strengthens and reinforces the strong color of the other.

LIVERLEAF. See HEPATICA

LOTUS. Low or trailing shrubs—the two mentioned here being valued mainly for their fine foliage. Flowers have the characteristic shape of all members of the pea family to which lotus belongs.

L. berthelotii. Trailing shrub with slender, 2-3 ft. branches covered thickly with fine silvery-gray leaves—the whole effect being that of a soft, fluffy shawl. Narrow, sweet-pea-shaped, 1-in. flowers, scarlet fading to orange. Var. *atrococcineus,* dark crimson, spotted black. Blooms in June and July.

L. mascaensis. Erect and bushy, but inclined to cascade slightly and gracefully over sides of hanging containers. Narrow, silky, gray leaflets. Bright yellow flowers in late spring.

CULTURE AND CLIMATE: Zones 12, 13, probably also in 10. Tender. Sun or part shade. Trim in early spring to keep neat.

USE: Hanging baskets, pots, tops of walls. Use *L. berthelotii* as a ground cover on slopes in mild winter sections.

LUNGWORT. See PULMONARIA

LYCHNIS. CAMPION, CATCHFLY. Brilliant summer flower color.

L. chalcedonica. MALTESE CROSS. Loose, open growing, hairy perennial 2-3 ft., with ovate leaves. Scarlet 1-in. flowers in dense terminal heads. Var. *alba* has white flowers.

L. viscaria splendens flore-pleno. Compact low evergreen rosettes of grass-like foliage, the flowering stalks to 1 ft. Double, pink to rose ½-in. flowers in loose clusters in summer.

CULTURE AND CLIMATE: Hardy all zones. Sun. Seeds sown in early spring. Division every 3 years in October-December.

USE: Will drown out other colors, so use it by itself to brighten a dull corner. Gray tones it down interestingly.

LYTHRUM SALICARIA ROSEUM SUPERBUM MORDENS PINK. *(L. roseum superbum)*. Forms a 2 ft. wide clump of tall and slender stems to 3-5 ft. high. Willow-like foliage at base, rose-pink, ¾-in. flowers grow densely along the top 8-18 in. of the stem. CULTURE AND CLIMATE: Hardy all zones. Sun. Likes lots of water and will grow at edge of streams or ponds. USE: Effective when massed in groups. Valued for cut flowers in late summer and fall.

MAHERNIA VERTICILLATA. *(M. odorata)*. HONEY BELL. An evergreen sub-shrub valued for the honey-like fragrance of its bell-shaped yellow flowers; blooms in spring and sporadically throughout the rest of the year. Somewhat straggling, the woody stems spread to 3 ft. Green, finely divided, 1-in. leaves. CULTURE AND CLIMATE: Zones 7-13. Sun. Keep cutting off dead flowers or it may bloom itself to death. Grow from cuttings. USE: Plant at top of dry walls or banks over which its stems can sprawl freely.

MAIDEN'S WREATH. See FRANCOA RAMOSA

MALTESE CROSS. See LYCHNIS

MARGUERITE, BLUE. See FELICIA

MARGUERITE, GOLDEN. See ANTHEMIS TINCTORIA

MARGUERITE. See CHRYSANTHEMUM

MARIGOLD, CAPE. See DIMORPHOTHECA ECKLONIS

MATILIJA POPPY. See ROMNEYA COULTERI

MEADOW RUE. See THALICTRUM

MEADOW SWEET. See ASTILBE

MECONOPSIS BETONICIFOLIA. HIMALAYAN POPPY. A touchy but beautiful blue poppy with gold center. In spring and early summer 3-in. flowers are carried on 2-4 ft. stems above low growing, bluish-green, downy leaves. CULTURE AND CLIMATE: Hardy all zones, but restricted to gardens where soils and exposures are just right for rhododendrons. Give it light shade, perfect drainage, summer watering, and protect from wind.

MICHAELMAS DAISY. See ASTER

MONARDA. BEE BALM, WILD BERGAMOT. An old-time plant becomes a new fashion, offering spice and color to the garden. Rather robust, leafy plant to 3 ft. Foliage aromatic like mint. Twisted petals of the pink or scarlet flowers form a shaggy ring above colorful bracts. Blooms in July or August. CULTURE AND CLIMATE: Hardy all zones. Sun or part shade. Drought-resistant. Divisions in spring. USE: In large borders and in country places, with *Salvia uliginosa*, English lavender, artemisia Silver King.

MONKEY FLOWER. See DIPLACUS

MONKSHOOD. See ACONITUM

MOSS CAMPION. See SILENE

MULLEIN. See VERBASCUM

MYRTLE EUPHORBIA. See EUPHORBIA

NEPETA. Aromatic herbs with trailing or semi-spreading branches; gray or green foliage. Lavender or lavender-blue flowers in clustered whorls or spikes at the tips of the stems in summer.

N. mussinii. Trailing gray-foliaged perennial with ¾-in. leaves and lavender-blue ½-in. flowers in loose spikes.

N. Souvenir Andre Chaudron. An excellent more upright form to 1½ ft., with semi-spreading branches to 2 ft.; green foliage on wiry stems. Deep blue flowers, larger than *N. mussinii*, in loose spikes.

N. cataria. CATNIP, CATMINT. Formerly a favorite in gardens and so-named "catnip" because cats are fond of this sweet herb.

CULTURE AND CLIMATE: All zones. Sun. Shear after first bloom to encourage second flowering. Cuttings or seed.

USE: The gray foliage of *N. mussinii* is an unfailing softener along the edges of a border of mixed flowers. Lovely by itself in a dry wall of gray stone.

NICOTIANA. TOBACCO. Perennials, most often treated as annuals. Valued for their fragrance at night.

N. alata grandiflora. (*N. affinis*). JASMINE TOBACCO. Flowers, like flaring tubes, white inside and pale violet outside, are held (2-3 ft.) above a rather coarse plant, with dull green sticky leaves. Flowers of this popular species close during the heat of the day.

Hybrids and named varieties of nicotiana offer more compact forms with flowers that do not close during the day, in colors shading from pink to dark red.

CULTURE AND CLIMATE: Treat as an annual. Generally volunteers all over the shady garden.

USE: Plant near patio or terrace to enjoy evening fragrance.

NIEREMBERGIA HIPPOMANICA. DWARF CUP FLOWER. Low mounds of color from April through the summer. Var. *violacea* (*N. cœrulea*) is 4-12 in. high with bright blue, cup-shaped flowers almost smothering the foliage. Var. *Purple Robe*, an improved form of var. *violacea*, is more compact, with richer, deep violet-blue flowers.

N. rivularis. WHITE CUP FLOWER. (See chapter on ground covers.)

CULTURE AND CLIMATE: Hardy all zones. Sun. Trim back severely in fall, and if necessary, divide and replant to keep it neat and tidy. For attractive plants sow fresh seed every few years.

USE: Best used as edgings, or as a foreground plant in the perennial border.

OENOTHERA. EVENING PRIMROSE, SUNDROPS. Valued for showy flowers in tough rough places, in summer.

O. speciosa childsii. (*E. tetraptera childsii, E. rosea mexicana*). MEXICAN EVENING PRIMROSE. Trailing, slender, 10-12 in. stems, with rose-pink, 1½-in. flowers.

O. missouriensis. Prostrate, sprawling stems to 10 in. high. Soft, velvety, 5-in. leaves. Clear yellow flowers, 3-5 in. across.

O. hookeri. Western native. Biennial, to 2-6 ft. Bright yellow, 3½-in. flowers open from late afternoon to sunrise.

O. tetragona. (*O. youngii*). SUNDROPS. Perennial or biennial to 2 ft., with reddish stems and good green foliage. Bright yellow, 1½-in. flowers.

CULTURE AND CLIMATE: Sun. Spreads by underground runners and will take over a hillside, vacant lot, or roadside. Self-sows; easy from seed.

OMPHALODES VERNA. CREEPING FORGET-ME-NOT. An herbaceous plant to 8 in. Leafy runners creeping along the ground to 1 ft.; dark green, somewhat rough, oval, 1-in. leaves. Dainty, intense blue, ½-in., forget-me-not flowers with white eyes, in loose clusters. March-May. Var. *alba* has white flowers. CULTURE AND CLIMATE: Hardy all zones, but best in zones 1-6. Shade and half sun. Needs acid soil and excellent drainage. Increase with sections of rooted runners. USE: Naturalize with spring bulbs along woodland paths.

ONOSMA STELLULATUM TAURICUM. GOLDEN DROPS. Low-growing, irregular clumps to 8 in., spreading to 18 in., with rough, dull-green narrow leaves and lateral branching stems. Fragrant, long, tubular, yellow, 1½-in. flowers in one-sided clusters, curved at the tip, similar to a "fiddleneck." CULTURE AND CLIMATE: Hardy all zones, but best adapted to zones 1-6. Sun or part shade. Cut back at intervals. Cuttings. USE: In rock gardens, or include in a low planting scheme of grays and yellows.

PAEONIA. PEONIES. The genus *Pæonia* includes many perennial herbs and shrubs with tuberous or thickened root stocks. The commonly cultivated peonies are distinguished in the nursery trade as herbaceous peonies and tree peonies. Most of the herbaceous peonies are hybrids of *P. albiflora* and *P. suffruticosa*. The tree peony is *P. suffruticosa* (see chapter on shrubs).

Herbaceous Peonies

The peony is the best known indicator of the effect of warm winters on many perennials. The plant is tolerant of almost all types of soils, it will stand summer temperatures in the highest ranges, but it will not continue to bloom without a winter chilling period.

Just how much winter chilling is necessary has not been measured. It is known to perform satisfactorily where Dec., Jan., and Feb. have temperatures in the 25-35° range. This qualifies the peony for the interior valleys and high deserts of California.

A well-grown peony clump in cold-winter areas will reach a height of 3-4 ft., with an equal spread, by the first of May. Large, deep green, attractively divided leaves on many stout stems give the spectacular flowers an effective background. Flowers vary in form from single-petaled types to full rounded balls, from 1 in. across to more than 10 in.; they vary in color from white, through cream, delicate pink, deep rose, to dark burgundy red. Individual varieties have a rather short flowering span, but by choosing early, mid-season, and late varieties you can have bloom from May through June.

CULTURE: Because peonies are best when allowed to remain in one spot undisturbed for several years, the soil should be dug deeply and fertilized with well-rotted manure before planting. Plant in early fall. Do not plant deeper than 2 in. under the surface of the soil. If planted too deeply, peonies may not bloom. Don't fertilize the freshly planted divisions. Feed established clumps in the same way you do other plants in the garden.

Diseases and insect attacks are rare. The peony's worst enemy is botrytis blight. As soon as you notice withered and blackened stems or brown spotted leaves, cut them out and burn them.

To increase your supply divide clumps in early fall. Carefully lift the large fleshy root, cut off the foliage, and cut the root into sections with at least three good eyes to each section. If this is done early, the cut will callus over quickly and new rootlets will grow before spring. Remember that the peony does not need dividing and is better off in a garden position where it will not be disturbed.

PAPAVER. POPPY. Brilliant flamboyant Oriental poppies and bright or pastel-colored Iceland poppies are the two perennial species considered here.

P. orientale. ORIENTAL POPPY. Many of the forms included in this group may be hybrids of *P. orientale* and *P. bracteatum*. Strong, bold plants to 4 ft., with coarse, hairy, divided leaves. Large blossoms often 6-8 in., sometimes double, range in color from orange-scarlet through salmon and salmon-pink to an occasional white. Bloom in late spring and early summer.

CULTURE AND CLIMATE: Hardy all zones. Give full sun and a deep rich soil. Succeed best where summers are warm and moist, winters cold. Because Oriental poppies are tap-rooted, they move easily only when dormant, in August. Plants need dividing about every 3 or 4 years. Increase plants by making root cuttings at dividing time. Grown from seed you will get mostly reds.

USE: For color, no perennial can shout down the Oriental poppy. Exciting in the perennial border with tall or Belladonna and Bellamosum delphiniums in shades of blue.

P. nudicaule. ICELAND POPPY. Daintier than the Oriental poppy, with a wider color range and a longer period of bloom. Slender, wiry stalks, 1-1½ ft., with divided leaves mostly at the base. The shallow-cupped flowers to 3 in. across are slightly fragrant. Usually there is a larger proportion of light colors, yellows, whites, and softer oranges, although some strains include pink, apricot, and salmon shades. Bloom in winter if planted in early fall, otherwise in early spring.

CULTURE AND CLIMATE: Can be planted in all zones. Best treated as annuals in warm-winter climates where they bloom in 6 months from seed sown in summer or fall. Plant out in spring in cold climates where they winter-kill.

USE: For an especially exciting effect, plant cream, orange, and yellow Iceland poppies in front of snapdragons in autumn shades.

PASQUE FLOWER. See ANEMONE

PELARGONIUM. GERANIUM. Shrubs and perennials, popular and beloved the world over. Common garden plants in mild-winter regions, and just as common indoor-outdoor pot and window garden plants in areas where the ground freezes every winter. Reach perfection in the foggy coastal belt along the Pacific Coast. Tall, dwarf, and trailing species, many with foliage zoned and marked in contrasting colors. Flowers white and in many shades of pink, salmon, orange, lavender, purple, and red.

P. hortorum. COMMON GERANIUM. GARDEN GERANIUM. Stout, vigorous, succulent stemmed plants to 3 ft. or more, less in dwarf and miniature forms, becoming woody when grown in the open in mild regions. Round or kidney-shaped velvety leaves with scalloped margins, often with a broad color zone inside the edge. In fancy-leafed geraniums, leaves are strongly patterned, usually zoned, colorful and contrasting. Single or double flowers, in white and many shades of red, pink, and salmon, in roundish clusters on long stems. A great many varieties, of which these are typical and popular: Alaska, single white; Fiat Supreme, double shrimp pink; Emile Zola, single salmon; Maxime Kovalesky, orange; Alice of Vincennes, single red shading through pink to white center; Alphonse Picard, semi-double scarlet.

P. domesticum. LADY WASHINGTON PELARGONIUM. MARTHA WASHINGTON GERANIUM. Erect or somewhat spreading to 3 ft. More rangy in habit than common geranium. Leaves heart-shaped to almost kidney-shaped, dark green 2-4 in. broad, the margins crinkled, with unequal sharp teeth. Large showy flowers 2 in. or more across in loose rounded clusters, resembling and often as lovely as azaleas in white and many shades of pink, red, lavender, purple, with brilliant blotches and markings of darker colors.

P. peltatum. IVY GERANIUM. Trailing plants to 2-3 ft. or longer. The smooth, glossy, bright green leaves to 2-3 in. broad are 5-lobed like ivy. Few to several 1-in. single or double flowers in rounded clusters on long stems are white, pink, rose, red, and lavender, often blotched in contrasting colors. Widely used as a ground cover on slopes, in parking strips.

P. tomentosum. PEPPERMINT GERANIUM. Somewhat shrubby or semi-trailing plant; will climb to 5-6 ft. with support. More tender than common geranium. Gray-green 3-5 in. leaves are 5-7 lobed, covered with soft silvery fuzz, give off a peppermint scent when rubbed or crushed. White flowers with red centers are not showy. Where adapted outdoors, it is a wonderful ground cover under trees, in raised beds.

P. crispum. LEMON GERANIUM. FINGER BOWL GERANIUM. Leafy erect plant to 2 ft. Small 1-in. roundish leaves with toothed and crisped margins, exuding a lemon scent when crushed. Pink or rose flowers with darker markings are ¾-1 in. long.

P. limonium. LEMON GERANIUM. Probably derived from *P. crispum*. Has shiny deep green lemon scented leaves and purple or lilac flowers.

P. odoratissimum. NUTMEG GERANIUM. Many stemmed with slender straggling branches 12-20 in. long. Delicately nutmeg-scented, gray-green 1-2 in. scalloped leaves. Small ¼-in. white or whitish flowers.

P. quercifolium. OAKLEAF GERANIUM. Sturdy shrubby plant to 3 ft. with 2-4 in. rough, deeply lobed leaves giving off a pungent woodsy scent. Blush to rose or violet flowers with darker markings are ¾ in. long. Often planted by doors or gates in older gardens.

P. graveolens. ROSE GERANIUM. Shrubby plant to 2-3 ft., with abundant foliage of much divided and cut leaves with a strong pleasant fragrance. Leaves once used for flavoring apple jelly. Small ½-in. rose or pinkish, veined purple, flowers are not showy.

CULTURE AND CLIMATE: Zones 9, 10-13; tops, and sometimes roots, may be winter-killed in 7 and 8. Damaged at temperatures below 26°. Full sun, light shade in hot-summer climates. Will grow in practically any well drained soil, with moderate watering. Too rich soil and too much water cause them to go to leaf and to flower less profusely. Fertilize lightly when necessary. Constant grooming — pinching, removing faded flowers, cutting back older plants severely to renew growth — keeps geraniums in good form. Geraniums in pots especially need this treatment.

For potted geraniums, use a potting mixture including 3 parts garden soil, 1 part leaf mold or peat moss, and 1 part coarse sand. If soil is heavy clay, use only 2 parts and add more sand. Pot firmly in not-too-large pots, since geraniums grow best when they are slightly rootbound. In shifting into larger pots, use only the next largest size. When watering potted geraniums, do so thoroughly, but allow the soil to become moderately dry before watering again. Occasional fertilizing of potted geraniums—never oftener than once a month—is necessary to keep them in top condition. Use 1 level teaspoonful of balanced commercial fertilizer for a 5-in. pot, and water it in thoroughly.

Propagate by softwood cuttings. For good cutting material, prune established plants in summer or early fall after main blooming period, wait until resulting new growth becomes firm enough to snap off clean. (See chapter on vegetative propagation.)

USE: All types of geraniums are adapted to pot culture. Common or garden geraniums are century-old favorites for bedding, and have a happy artless way of growing against fences and along garden paths and drives. Salmon, coral, and scarlet varieties combine beautifully with grays such as dusty miller, *Senecio greyii*, *Teucrium fruticans*, santolina, and artemisia.

Martha Washington geraniums, having longer internodes and being inclined toward ranginess, are not generally as satisfactory for bedding or border planting, although often grown this way. Sinking them in the ground in pots, so that roots are confined, tends to reduce straggliness. They are handsome in pots.

Fancy leafed geraniums can be used in about the same way as the larger common geraniums in positions where smaller plants are needed. Some such as Miss Burdett Coutts, Distinction, and Mrs. Cox, are superb bedding or edging plants.

Dwarf geraniums—true dwarfs or miniatures in every way—are fascinating to look at closely in window boxes and on pot shelves.

Scented leafed types should be grown in pots or boxes placed at arm's length—for fragrance's sake—in the patio

PENSTEMON. BEARD TONGUE. Penstemon has everything it takes to make an all-around perennial: excellent form, attractive foliage, and abundant, long-blooming, colorful flowers. Although cultivated penstemons are a common garden item, there are a number of Western natives usually available only in specialty nurseries and not so well known, that deserve increased consideration.

P. gloxinioides. Often treated as an annual in cold climates. Garden hybrids forming compact bushy plant to 2-3 ft., with glossy, clean, bright green, narrow leaves on upright or slightly arching stems. Tubular flowers, in loose terminal spikes, come in almost every color and combination of colors except blue and yellow. If cut back when bloom is over in the fall, they will flower again in April and continue to September or October. Many named forms in separate shades of pink, red, and white.

CULTURE AND CLIMATE: Zones 4-13. Perennial treated as an annual in cold-winter climates. Full sun, partial shade in warm inland sections. Comparatively free of pests. Susceptible to root rot if kept too wet. To keep the plants vigorous and fresh-looking, cut old stems to the ground once a year, in between times cut flower stalks back to a strong side shoot. Easily grown from seed, although for separate colors of *P. gloxinioides*, you must propagate from tip cuttings. Clumps can be divided, but it is best to grow new plants as they are more vigorous.

USE: Penstemons in mixed colors are best combined with white flowers such as phlox or physostegia. Pink penstemon effective with *Scabiosa caucasica*, *Aster frikartii*, *Erigeron speciosus* Quakeress. Not a good cut flower.

P. heterophyllus purdyi. BLUE BEDDER PENSTEMON. A Western native long recognized as a superb garden plant. Grows 10-12 in. with early summer flowers varying from light purple to intense blue, the latter color being most admired and characteristic.

CULTURE AND CLIMATE: Zones 4-13. Best in full sun; light gravelly soil, and not too much water. Short lived in rich, moist soil. Cut back after bloom. Renew plantings every 2 or 3 years by growing a fresh crop from seed sown as soon as ripe, July-October.

USE: Dry border, slopes. Combine with hunnemannia, zauschneria, glaucium.

P. barbatus. *(Chelone barbata)*. Native to Arizona south to Mexico. Open, shrubby perennial growing to 6 ft., with narrow, bright green leaves. Long, loose, graceful spikes of 1-in., tubular, red flowers in May, June.

CULTURE AND CLIMATE: Zones 6-13. Same culture as *P. heterophyllus*.

USE: Striking with Matilija poppy, bush poppy *(Dendromecon rigida)*, and the buckwheats.

P. centranthifolius. SCARLET BUGLER. California native—Central Coast Range south to Southern California and Lower California. Loose growing, to 3 ft., of informal habit, with blue-green leaves and narrow, 1-in. scarlet, tubular flowers in early summer. Same culture as *P. heterophyllus*.

USE: Excellent drought resistant perennial for dry borders—particularly effective combined with gray plants: senecio, artemisia, centaurea.

PHLOMIS FRUTICOSA. JERUSALEM SAGE. An old-time, almost forgotten perennial. Rugged and woody, with coarse, woolly, gray-green, wrinkled leaves; grows to 4 ft. Yellow flowers arranged closely in circles around stiff stems, bloom from June to September. CULTURE AND CLIMATE: All zones. Sun. Subject to scale. Cuttings. USE: Good for poor or dry soil on slopes, along fences in country places. In character with artemisia, dusty miller, rosemary, verbascum, and the buckwheats.

PHLOX. The perennial members of this genus are roughly divided here into low-growing or rock-garden types and the tall summer phlox.

P. paniculata. SUMMER PHLOX. Long-lived and permanent perennials best adapted to warm-summer, cold-winter climates. Sturdy, erect, leafy stems to 3-5 ft. with thin, dark green, 5-in. leaves. Large dome-shaped clusters top each stem, the 1-in. flowers appearing in every shade of pink and rose—from delicate blush to deep red—and in lavender, purple, and white. Long summer-to-fall blooming period.

CULTURE AND CLIMATE: Hardy all zones. Best in light shade, because colors tend to bleach in sun. Requires rich soil and plenty of water. A summer mulch of manure, compost, or peat helps to keep roots cool. Inclines to mildew late in season if foliage is wet in evening. Remove faded flowers to prolong bloom. Divide every few years, using young shoots on the outside of the clump and discarding old, hardened centers. Seed does not reproduce the type.

USE: Where it succeeds, phlox is probably used more than any other perennial to give color at the 3-5 ft. level in late summer. Use care in arranging several varieties of phlox in a border. Salmon pinks and scarlets clash conspicuously with pinks and reds that have a blue cast. In a small garden, it is best to confine planting to single color group. In a long border, separate the groups or make the transition between colors by plantings of white varieties or one of the whites with a dark eye. Planting or rearranging phlox so that colors complement one another is easiest while the plants are in bloom. Moving at this time does not seem to set the plants back. It is also an excellent cut flower.

P. divaricata. SWEET WILLIAM PHLOX. Wiry-stemmed perennials to 12 in. with many creeping shoots. Ovate or oblong, 2-in. leaves. Fragrant, 1½-in. flowers in loose, open clusters form a solid mass of color that varies considerably in different plants. Some flowers are almost a clear pink, others range through all possible shades of lavender, even to reddish-purple. Blooms in spring.

CULTURE AND CLIMATE: Hardy all zones. Best in light shade, but it will thrive in full sun west of the Cascade Mountains. Seed. Tends to self-sow.

USE: Because it tends to spread by re-seeding, it is better adapted to naturalized areas where it can ramble without being disturbed. It is a natural companion for perennial candytuft, which also is at home in a rockery setting. Combines well with red or pink tulips, or makes pleasing alternating drifts with yellow daffodils.

P. subulata. MOSS PINK. GROUND PINK. Creeping, mat-forming perennial to 6 in., with crowded, ½-in. stiff, needle-like leaves. The ¾-in. flowers range in color from pink, rose, and scarlet to lavender-blue. Bloom in late spring and early summer. There are a number of horticultural varieties.

CULTURE AND CLIMATE: Hardy all zones. Sun. Requires a porous, not too rich soil and perfect drainage. After flowering cut back to ½ the diameter and top dress with gritty loam. Seed in spring, or by stem cuttings.

USE: Few plants do more for the rock garden or wall than this alpine-type phlox. Once established, they make spreading plants covered with bloom in early summer.

PHYSOSTEGIA VIRGINIANA. *(Dracocephalum virginianum).* FALSE DRAGON HEAD. Strong growing. Any climate. Accepts almost any soil. Important in the border for spikes of white, lavender-rose, rose-pink from June to August. Var. *Summer Snow* to 3 ft. high, 2 ft. wide, has shiny, dark green foliage and numerous stalks ending in spikes crowded with 1 in. long, funnel-shaped, glistening white flowers. Those on lower half of the 10-in. spike open first. Var. *Summer Glow*, to 4 ft. 18 in. spikes of lavender-rose flowers. Var. *Vivid* grows to 2 ft., carries rose-pink flowers in 10-in. spikes.

CULTURE AND CLIMATE: Hardy all zones. Sun or part shade. Stake after 2 ft. high unless surrounding plants hold it erect. Cut to ground after blooming. Clumps spread and take more and more space. Divide and discard every second year; select new divisions from outside of clump.

USE: Good mid- to late-summer color for border. Combine with medium-height, blue or white Michaelmas daisies, *Veronica spicata, Stokesia lævis,* and *Erigeron speciosus.*

PINK. See DIANTHUS

PLATYCODON GRANDIFLORUM. *(Campanula grandiflora).* BALLOON FLOWER. Upright to 3½ ft. high, 1½-3 ft. wide. Foliage light olive-green. New shoots look like asparagus tips. Buds, swollen and balloon-like, appear on top half of stiff stalks and open into deep blue-violet, white, or soft pink, star-like bells from June to August. Double flowers have been developed. CULTURE AND CLIMATE: Hardy all zones. Takes two or three years to become established. Because it dies down completely in winter, location of the plant should be marked to avoid digging into roots in early spring. Don't disturb; long brittle tap root and crown are easily damaged, are also favored by gophers. Let old stems die before cutting back. Full sun in cool areas; half shade in warmer sections for lush growth and to protect flowers from fading. USE: Supplies good blue or pink in late summer after many perennials have finished blooming. Similar in effect to early-flowering, peach-leaf bellflower *(Campanula persicifolia).*

POKER PLANT. See KNIPHOFIA

POLEMONIUM. Lush rosettes of finely divided, fern-like foliage, attractive as a ground cover. Clusters of bell-like flowers in summer.

P. caeruleum. JACOB'S LADDER, GREEK VALERIAN. Clusters of lavender-blue, 1-in. flowers held 1-2 ft. above the rosettes.

P. reptans Blue Pearl. A garden hybrid, much smaller and neater than Jacob's ladder, to 8 in.

CULTURE AND CLIMATE: Hardy all zones. Shade or half shade. Division.

USE: Combine with ferns, campanulas, bleeding heart, annual mimulus, and lilies.

POLYGONATUM MULTIFLORUM. EURASIAN SOLOMON'S SEAL. Leafy stems, arching to 3 ft., turn deep yellow in fall. Clusters of greenish, bell-like, ½-in. flowers in spring. CULTURE AND CLIMATE: Hardy all zones. Set out plants any time during winter dormant period. Division. USE: As an accent in damp, shady corners with ferns, bleeding heart, and plantain lilies.

POPPY, HIMALAYAN. See MECONOPSIS BETONICIFOLIA

POPPY, MATILIJA. See ROMNEYA COULTERI

POPPY, YELLOW HORNED. See GLAUCIUM FLAVUM

POTENTILLA. CINQUEFOIL. Very useful plants of interesting foliage that cheerfully flower all summer and into the fall in spite of poor soil, little water, and a hot location.

P. fruticosa. SHRUBBY CINQUEFOIL. Native to the high mountains of the West. A shrubby, many-branched, deciduous plant with shreddy red-tinted bark and dense foliage. The compound leaves, divided into 3-7 small leaflets, are gray-green above, hairy and white beneath. From June-August, bears clusters of buttercup-yellow 1-in. flowers. Rather like a single rose, each has a mound of delicate pistils and stamens in center of petals.

P. nepalensis Miss Willmott. Low growing to 10 in. and spreading to make an 18 in. wide clump. Green, fan-like leaves of 5 leaflets. Magenta-red, ½-1 in. flowers in summer.

P. cinerea. (See chapter on ground covers.)

CULTURE AND CLIMATE: Hardy all zones. Sun. Tolerant of alkaline soils and unfavorable conditions.

USE: One of the best answers to what to plant where the hose can't quite reach and nothing seems to do well.

160 PERENNIALS — Encyclopedia —

PRIDE OF MADEIRA. See **ECHIUM FASTUOSUM**

PRIMROSE, EVENING; MEXICAN EVENING. See **OENOTHERA**

PRIMULA. See page 166

PULMONARIA. LUNGWORT. Long-stalked leaves in basal tufts, and sprays of funnel-shaped flowers. Will grow in shade that discourages most flowering plants.

P. saccharata. BETHLEHEM SAGE. Grows to 1½ ft., with white-spotted, roundish leaves. Flowers whitish or reddish-violet.

P. angustifolia. COWSLIP LUNGWORT. Tufts of rough, oblong, pointed leaves to 12 in. Purple-blue flowers as early as February. Var. *cærulea* and var. *azurea* have bright blue flowers.

CULTURE AND CLIMATE: Hardy all zones. Shade or half shade. Divide every 4 years.

USE: Plant under early-flowering, deciduous trees, on shaded slopes.

REHMANNIA ANGULATA. Dark green, hairy, deeply toothed leaves form large spreading rosettes. Tubular 3-in. flowers, resembling foxgloves, hang in graceful clusters on 18-in. stems. Color is a deep rose-pink with band of scarlet on upper lip, orange dots inside lower lip. Blooms from spring to fall. Var. *tricolor* has bright purple flowers that become violet-rose with whitish throat. Var. *alba*, with several flowers on a spike, is two-toned cream and white. CULTURE AND CLIMATE: Zones 7-13. Grown in cool greenhouses in colder sections. Shade or part shade. USE: Rehmannia's color and spiky form highlight shade borders. Handsome, long lasting for indoor arrangements.

REINWARDTIA INDICA. (*R. trigyna*). INDIAN YELLOW FLAX. Grows shrub-like to 3-4 ft. Brilliant yellow, flax-like, 2-in. flowers are borne in great profusion, in late fall and early winter. Blooms do not last long, but for weeks new ones open daily. CULTURE AND CLIMATE: Zones 7-13. Hardy to 15°. In warm winters, lives over as a shrub; in cold winters is a perennial, generally killed to the ground. Sun or part shade. Pinch to make more compact. Spreads by underground roots. Increase by rooted stems. Divide in spring. USE: For winter color in perennial and shrub borders. Combine with intense winter blue of *Eranthemum nervosum*, with chartreuse of *Crotalaria agatiflora*.

ROCKCRESS. See **ARABIS**

ROCKCRESS, WALL. See **ARABIS**

ROMNEYA COULTERI. MATILIJA POPPY. (See chapter on natives.)

ROSE, CHRISTMAS; LENTEN. See **HELLEBORUS**

RUE, MEADOW. See **THALICTRUM**

SAGE. See **SALVIA**

SAGE, BETHLEHEM. See **PULMONARIA**

SAGE, JERUSALEM. See **PHLOMIS FRUTICOSA**

SALVIA. SAGE. (Also see chapter on natives.) Valued for its gray and gray-green foliage as well as for its spiky form and color in late summer and fall.

S. farinacea. MEALYCUP SAGE. Rapid growing to a 3-ft. mound, with gray-green, hairy, 4-in. leaves. Above it, rise 8-in. spikes of violet-blue, ½-in. flowers, blooming in June and well into fall. Var. *Blue Bedder* and var. *Royal Blue* are choice varieties with lavender-blue flowers on willowy stems.

S. azurea grandiflora. (*S. pitcheri*). PITCHER SAGE. Spikes of intense blue, 1-in. flowers on slender, wand-like, 4-ft. stems.

S. patens. GENTIAN SAGE. Lower growing to 2½ ft., with dull green arrow-shaped leaves. Gentian blue, 2-in. flowers in looser clusters than Pitcher sage. Differs in culture from the rest in the group. It is not as hardy and should be given part shade.

S. uliginosa. BOG SAGE. Tallest of the blue flowered sages, it grows to a substantial 6 ft.

S. leucantha. MEXICAN BUSH SAGE. Graceful, shrub-like habit of growth to 2 ft., with gray or gray-green foliage. Long slender branches end in spikes of velvety, soft, violet-purple and white flowers in summer and fall.

CULTURE AND CLIMATE: All except S. *patens* are hardy heat-loving plants able to get along with little care. Pitcher sage and S. *farinacea* are often treated as annuals, but are satisfactory perennials if divided every third year, using divisions from outside the clump. S. *uliginosa* requires staking, and cutting of underground runners if you wish to keep it from spreading. S. *leucantha* is very tolerant of drought.

USE: Pitcher sage and S. *farinacea* are especially helpful in mixed border plantings of warm-summer annuals. They take much of the heat and harshness out of the strong-colored zinnias and marigolds.

SANTOLINA CHAMAECYPARISSUS. LAVENDER COTTON. An evergreen aromatic compact plant which, if allowed to grow to its maximum height of 2 ft., becomes woody, uneven and ragged. Best treated as a clipped dwarf, and kept to 1 ft. or less. Brittle, woody stems densely clothed with rough, finely divided gray leaves. Best in the spring when growth is new. Bright yellow, buttony ¾-in. heads on unclipped plants in July-August.

S. virens. Dark green, narrow linear foliage, small soft yellow heads on a plant of similar growth habit.

CULTURE AND CLIMATE: Hardy all zones. Sun. Frequent trimming to keep neat. Cuttings. Renew every four years.

USE: Edging walks. Especially nice border for rose beds. Use to divide colors in patterned block planting of bright annuals.

SAXIFRAGA. SAXIFRAGE. A remarkably large and varied group of herbaceous and evergreen perennials which includes small encrusted, mossy, and cushion types considered by some to be the mainstay of rock gardens; a few adapted to borders (see bergenia), and one—S. *sarmentosa*—a favorite for pots and hanging baskets. Aside from the bergenias, saxifrages are comparatively little known by Western gardeners except in the Northwest where the alpine and rock garden types are well adapted and expertly grown.

The available rock garden forms can be roughly divided into 3 groups: Encrusted type, typified by the jewel-like beading of lime at the edge of the silvery, gray or bluish leaves. Mossy type, with tufts of bright green narrow leaves, or leaves divided into narrow lobes, thus resembling moss. Cushion type, forming tight mats of broader foliage.

Encrusted types:

S. aizoon. Narrow curving strap-shaped 1¼-in. leaves in dense basal silvery rosettes. Creamy-white flowers with minute purple spots carried in airy clusters. Many varieties and forms of this species with gray, silvery or bluish leaves and flowers in shades of rose-purple, bright pink, lemon yellow, or white.

S. lingulata. Basal rosettes of silvery 3-in. leaves that curve upward. Flowers are white spattered with tiny maroon dots.

S. marginata. The tiniest of the encrusted saxifrages, to 3 in., forming mats readily. Flowers are white in a light airy cluster.

CULTURE AND CLIMATE: Zones 1-6, 10. The encrusted saxifrages grow best in full sun in cool fissures and crevices of rocks and in dry walls tilted so that moisture won't gather in the crown. They prefer a sharp, limey, gritty soil, and are extremely drought resistant.

USE: Where adapted, most carefree and satisfying of sun-loving rock garden plants. Wonderful texture and pattern value.

Mossy types:

S. decipiens. Mossy green tufts of leaves cut into 3-5 narrow lobes. White flowers in spring.

CULTURE AND CLIMATE: Zones 1-6, 10. Mossy saxifrages grow well in any soil but should not be subjected to hottest sun.

USE: Smooth, fine textured evergreen carpet under trees, or in a permanent bulb bed.

Cushion types:

S. umbrosa. LONDON PRIDE. Rosettes of thick, ovate, 2½-in., shiny green leaves, to 3 in. tall and wide; airy pink flowers on wine red stems in May. Var. *primuloides*, grows to 6 in., has primrose-like leaves and rose-pink flowers.

CULTURE AND CLIMATE: Zones 1-7, 9-13. Unlike other cushion saxifrages which need a gritty soil mixture of limestone, leaf mold and light sandy loam, London Pride will get along in almost any soil.

USE: In drifts in moist shade along paths or under trees. Edging, shaded rock garden. Flowers long lasting when cut, add delicate grace to small arrangements.

S. sarmentosa. STRAWBERRY GERANIUM. Trailing to 2 ft. with runners rooting at joints. Round 4 in. leaves like geraniums are reddish below, veined with white above. Small white 1-in. flowers.

CULTURE AND CLIMATE: Zones 1-7, 9-13. Any soil. Requires partial shade and plenty of moisture.

USE: Window boxes, pots, containers, over low walls.

SCABIOSA CAUCASICA. PERENNIAL PINCUSHION FLOWER. (See chapter on annuals for other scabiosa.) Few flowers can beat these perennials for continuous production of color. Some varieties start blooming in May and where winters are mild, continue to offer a few good-sized flowers after Christmas. The name pincushion comes from the fact that the stamens protrude beyond flowers in the 2½-in. flower heads. Flowers are carried on wiry stalks above a 2½-ft. clump of medium green, finely-cut foliage. The *Isaac House* hybrids are a superior strain producing semi-double, ruffled, or fluted flowers in shades of lavender to deep lavender-blue. CULTURE AND CLIMATE: Hardy all zones. Sun. No special requirements. Division. USE: Excellent in mixed or mass plantings. Fine cut flowers.

SEA LAVENDER. See LIMONIUM

SEDUM SPECTABILE. SHOWY SEDUM. This hardy, robust succulent is invaluable for late summer and fall color and strong interesting form. Gray-blue-green leaves, stems to 15-20 in. high are grouped neatly in a round clump and topped by large, fluffy, flat clusters of small, star-shaped, pink flowers. Var. *Brilliant* has rich amaranth-red flowers. CULTURE AND CLIMATE: Zones 3-13. Grows equally well in sun or part shade, but the stems stouter and flower color brighter in sun. Easy to increase from divisions in fall or early spring. USE: Presentable all year, with new growth appearing soon after old stems have been removed. Try it with lamb's ear or catmint in foreground, blue salvia, veronica, and *Anemone japonica* in background. A solid pocket of color in the rock garden. In pots or tubs this sedum brings late summer color onto the terrace.

S. sieboldii. Dwarf, spreading trailer with blue-green, roundish leaves, and rose-pink fluffy heads in September-October. Stems and leaves have ruddy fall coloring. Excellent in pots and hanging baskets in lathhouses or other partially shaded locations.

SENECIO. See CENTAUREA

SHASTA DAISY. See CHRYSANTHEMUM

SHORTIA SOLDANELLOIDES. (*Schizocodon soldanelloides*). FRINGE BELL. A small aristocrat. In spring, dainty pink or white, nodding, 1-in. bells with fringed petals appear on stems above 6-in., round, dark green, leathery leaves. CULTURE AND CLIMATE: Hardy all zones. Full shade, part shade. USE: Good ground cover for rhododendrons and azaleas. For miniature garden where blossoms can be enjoyed at close range.

SILENE. CATCHFLY. These two low growing, wide-spreading species are among the finest silenes:

S. acaulis. CUSHION PINK, MOSS CAMPION. Cushiony rosettes of moss-like foliage spread out to form a green mat. Reddish-purple, ½-in. flowers in summer.

S. schafta. Slightly higher growing than moss campion. Small roundish leaves in rosettes with rose or purplish flowers.

CULTURE AND CLIMATE: Hardy all zones. Sun and half shade. Seeds, divisions, cuttings.

USE: Attractive in edgings of raised beds or planter boxes.

SNAPWEED. See IMPATIENS

SNEEZEWEED. See HELENIUM AUTUMNALE

SOLIDASTER LUTEUS. Soft yellow, little daisies bloom in clusters on slender stems growing to 2 ft. Valuable for its dainty texture and late yellow color. Heaviest bloom in August; continues bloom into September. CULTURE AND CLIMATE: Hardy, but not adapted to hot interiors. Sun. Floppy habit, so stake early. Division. USE: For soft yellow in perennial borders. Combine with blues of anchusa Bluebird, cynoglossum Firmament, *Penstemon heterophyllus* Blue Bedder; and lavender of *Aster frikartii*, or dwarf blue Michaelmas daisies.

SOLOMON'S SEAL. See POLYGONATUM MULTIFLORUM

SPIDERWORT. See TRADESCANTIA VIRGINIANA

STOKES ASTER. See STOKESIA LAEVIS

STOKESIA LAEVIS (*S. cyanea*). STOKES ASTER. Woolly stemmed perennial to 1½ ft., 1-ft. spread; with 8-in. dark green leathery leaves which are spiny at the base. Blue, purplish-blue, or white daisy-like flowers carried above the foliage, July to September. Var. *Blue Moon*, a superior form, has 5-6 in. sky-blue flowers on 12-18 in. stalks.

CULTURE AND CLIMATE: Hardy all zones. Sun. Summer water. Remove old flower heads. Easy to grow from seed. Self-sows in garden.

USE: Treat stokesia as a permanent member of the border. Combine it with perennial phlox, kniphofia hybrids. Cannas grown behind this plant make an attractive combination. Excellent cut flower.

162 PERENNIALS

STONECRESS. See **AETHIONEMA**

SUMMER FORGET-ME-NOT. See **ANCHUSA AZUREA**

SUNDROPS. See **OENOTHERA**

SUNFLOWER. See **HELIANTHUS**

SWEET VIOLET. See **VIOLA ODORATA**

THALICTRUM. MEADOW RUE. Airy perennials with delicate fresh green foliage resembling that of columbine. Sprays of flowers with large drooping stamens and sometimes showy sepals.

T. aquilegifolium. Grows to 3-4 ft., with gray-green foliage. White flowers with flossy tufts of long purple or pink stamens, in June or July.

T. glaucum. DUSTY MEADOW RUE. Similar to *T. aquilegifolium* but slightly taller. Fragrant pale yellow flowers in July.

T. dipterocarpum. CHINESE MEADOW RUE. Most tender of the species, and blooms later—from July to October. Grows to 4 ft., with nodding rose or lilac flowers with lemon-yellow stamens. Var. *album* has white flowers.

Two dainty dwarf species are: *T. kiusianum*, with green foliage turning purplish in fall, purple flowers; *T chelidonii*, with large showy lilac or purple flowers.

CULTURE AND CLIMATE: Hardy all zones. Sun or partial shade. Give plenty of moisture. Protect from wind. Division or seed.

USE: Gives same airiness in shade as baby's breath gives in sun. Effective combined with lilies, late iris, peonies. Pleasing contrast to sturdier perennials.

THERMOPSIS CAROLINIANA. Similar to lupine in appearance but not so stocky. Slender stem to 5 ft. Smooth, green leaves divided fan-wise into 3 leaflets. Golden-yellow, sweetpea-shaped flowers in long, narrow, 6-12 in. spikes, in June and July. CULTURE AND CLIMATE: Hardy all zones. Sun. Requires staking. Cut to ground after blooming. Seeds sown in fall or in spring over heat. Division. USE: In borders with delphinium, blue salvia, *Aster frikartii*.

THRIFT. See **ARMERIA MARITIMA**

THROATWORT, COMMON. See **TRACHELIUM CAERULEUM**

TOBACCO. See **NICOTIANA**

TORCH LILY. See **KNIPHOFIA**

TOUCH-ME-NOT. See **IMPATIENS**

TRACHELIUM CAERULEUM. COMMON THROATWORT. An interesting, little-known perennial that adds fluffy clouds of deep lavender-blue to the border in summer and early fall. Grows to 2 ft., has ovate toothed 3-in. leaves. Tiny flowers set precisely into a rounded 3-5 in. head. CULTURE AND CLIMATE: Zones 7-13. Hardy to about 20°. Sun or part shade. Seeds or cuttings. USE: In border with afternoon shade, combine with meadow rue, balloon flower, spiderwort and perennial phlox. In sun, effective with chiffon daisy, *Aster frikartii*, white physostegia.

TRADESCANTIA VIRGINIANA. COMMON SPIDERWORT. An old-fashioned perennial recently replaced by larger-flowered hybrids. Dense clusters of violet-blue, 1-in. flowers are carried on stems among grass-like foliage; July to October. Named varieties offer various shades of blue and a white form. CULTURE AND CLIMATE: Hardy all zones. Shade or sun. Sturdy and easy to grow. Give it lots of water. Division.

T. fluminensis. WANDERING JEW. (See chapter on indoor plants.)

TRANSVAAL DAISY. See **GERBERIA JAMESONII**

TROLLIUS. Perennial belonging to the buttercup family, adapted to shady, moist spots. Grows to 1-2 ft. with shiny, finely-cut, dark green leaves and double yellow and orange, globe-like flowers resembling ranunculus. Bloom in May-June to September.

Usually planted are improved forms of *T. europæus*, GLOBE FLOWER, and *T. ledebouri*, which blooms later. CULTURE AND CLIMATE: Hardy all zones. Shade or part shade. Require rich soil and lots of moisture. Subject to aphis. Seeds, from which it takes 2 to 3 years to bloom. Divisions. USE: Bright flowers of trollius are valuable for lightening shade. Are always happy in moist gardens or near a pool. Good cut flowers.

TULBAGHIA VIOLACEA. SOCIETY GARLIC. Unusually attractive clusters of rosy-lavender, star-like flowers rise to 18 in. above a clump of gray-green, narrow, 12-in. leaves that smell like onions when crushed. Blooms almost throughout year in milder climates. CULTURE AND CLIMATE: Zones 7-13. Sun. Seeds. USE: Good associate with *Trachelium cœruleum* or Munstead lavender.

VALERIAN, GREEK. See **POLEMONIUM**

VERBASCUM. MULLEIN. Stately sun-loving, summer-blooming perennials, with broad leaves closely hugging the stems. Saucer-shaped flowers in straight spikes.

V. phoeniceum. PURPLE MULLEIN. Stems with nearly smooth leaves. Purple or red flowers in a simple slender spike to 2-4 ft. The Phœniceum hybrids are probably the best strain, with flower colors available in white, pink, rose and purple.

V. olympicum. Stems and large leaves white with dense soft hairs. Bright yellow, 1-in. flowers are clustered in many-flowered 5-ft. spikes.

CULTURE AND CLIMATE: Hardy all zones. Sun. Seeds.

USE: Try coarse massive *V. olympicum* in the back of a wide perennial border or in a barrier planting with *Salvia uliginosa* or *Salvia leucantha*. Plant the Phœniceum hybrids in the middle of the border with lavender scabiosa and soft pink penstemon.

VERBENA. Carefree spreading plants that are invaluable for their bright sheets of color in summer and fall.

V. hortensis *(V. hybrida)*. GARDEN VERBENA. The most commonly grown garden species. Although perennial it is usually treated as an annual. Grows to 6-12 in. high, spreading to 12-18 in. Densely branched, with dark green or gray-green wrinkled, often dissected leaves. Phlox-like flowers in compact heads, in shades of pink, rose, red, blue, purple, mauve or white.

Some of the hybrids are more compact and bushy in habit: Var. *Snow White* has white flowers, and var. *Firelight* has vivid red flowers.

V. pulchella. (Formerly called *V. erinoides*). Low, prostrate, spreading plant, with dark green, crinkly, much-divided leaves. Small lavender flowers in dense heads. Var. *maonettii* forms neat clumps and has flowers striped rose-pink and white. Spreads rapidly, makes a solid mat in warm locations. Foliage may look shabby in cold winters.

V. rigida *(V. venosa)*. The rough, persistent, purple verbena of the old-fashioned perennial borders. Erect, prickly hairy stems to 12-24 in. Narrow, oblong, toothed leaves. Intense purple flowers in 1-3 in. spikes.

CULTURE AND CLIMATE: Hardy zones 3-13. Sun. Likes ordinary soil. *V. pulchella* needs moisture, but *V. rigida* and *V. hortensis* are drought-resistant. Cuttings, division or seed. Garden verbena will reseed itself.

USE: Use *V. pulchella* for bank covers receiving occasional watering, and in informal edgings. *V. rigida* and *V. hortensis* are valuable for covering dry banks, grown along paths or drives where watering is infrequent; striking in front of light blue *Plumbago capensis*.

VERONICA. SPEEDWELL. Handsome perennials from 4 in. to 2½ ft., valued for their tidy, rounded, foliage clumps and spiky flower clusters.

V. spicata. Erect or ascending stems to 2 ft., with ovate or oblong, 2-in., gray-green leaves. Small, violet-blue flowers in dense, long, pointed spikes are carried high above the foliage. Bloom at intervals from summer to fall.

V. longifolia. (*V. maritima*). More upright to 2½ ft. with narrower and longer, 4-in. leaves and spikes of soft lavender-blue flowers in June, July.

V. rupestris. A dwarf tufted form with dark green foliage and bright blue flowers in May.

V. Blue Spire. An exceptionally beautiful horticultural form to 2 ft. with rich, dark green, shiny leaves and dark blue flower spikes in July, August, often into September.

CULTURE AND CLIMATE: Plant veronica in full sun. Cut back after first bloom for a second though smaller crop of flowers. Seeds and division.

USE: Blue spikes combine effectively in sunny borders with pale yellow day lilies, soft pink penstemons, white Esther Reed or chiffon daisies.

VIOLA ODORATA. SWEET VIOLET. A lot of things have happened to this old-fashioned favorite in the last few years. There are doubles and singles, and colors from deepest purple to rose-pink. You can find types for ground covers, hanging baskets, or for cut flowers. Unlike its relative *Viola cornuta* (see chapter on annuals) which is generally propagated by seed, this violet is increased by divisions, offsets, and runners.

Some of the varieties that have proved themselves are:

V. o. Marie Louise. Fragrant flowers are double, two-toned: white and bluish-lavender. Strong growing type, spreading.

V. o. Royal Elk. Another strong grower with 7-in. leaves and large blue-violet flowers on 9-in. stems. Unlike many large violets, this variety is fragrant and it keeps well after it's cut.

V. o. Swanley White. Fragrant, double, white flowers. Long trailing stems make it suitable for hanging baskets, pots, window boxes.

V. o. Lady Lloyd George. Its large, double-centered flowers are lavender-mauve and exquisitely fragrant.

V. o. Charm. Small white flowers on neat clumps.

V. o. Royal Robe. Its large, deep bluish-violet flowers are shaped more like a pansy than a violet.

V. o. Rosina. Small, pink-violet flowers on a dainty plant. Excellent as a ground cover in part shade.

CULTURE AND CLIMATE: Grow in part shade; give lots of water while blooming; pick blossoms often for prolonged bloom. Shear rank growers to ground in late fall so that flowers will bloom before new leaves become large. Plant strong growers by themselves. Add compost and commercial fertilizer if plants have not been vigorous. Use bone meal rather than a high-nitrogen fertilizer, if leaves are strong and blooms are shy. Cut off runners; keep plants clean. Soggy soil encourages mold, leaf spot, and root rot.

USE: Use for close-up enjoyment in pots and boxes. Naturals as ground cover in shade. Less vigorous varieties make good edging plants along shady walk or border.

WALLFLOWER. See CHEIRANTHUS CHEIRI
WINDFLOWER. See ANEMONE
WORMWOOD. See ARTEMISIA
YARROW. See ACHILLEA

YUCCA. Bold, dramatic structural quality invites use of these plants in contemporary gardens. All are suited to warm, dry climates, need full sun.

Y. filamentosa. ADAM'S NEEDLE. Nearly stemless plant to 4-5 ft. Basal rosettes of sword-like, gray-green, 2½-ft. leaves with long, curly threads on the margins. White, waxy, bell-like flowers in large, loosely branched clusters are borne on 3-12 ft. stalks. Blooms in early summer.

Y. elephantipes. (*Y. gigantea*). Becoming tree-like, with several trunks of varying heights to 15 ft. Big, drooping, soft, 4-ft. leaves are rich dark green, and without sharp, spiny tips. Handsome large spikes of creamy-white bell-like flowers in late spring.

Y. whipplei. SPANISH BAYONET. OUR LORD'S CANDLE. Native to mountains of Southern California, south Coast Range and southern Sierra Nevada. Stemless plants with dense basal rosettes of rigid, spine-pointed, gray-green, 1-1¾ ft. leaves. Flowering stems to 6-14 ft. Drooping, bell-shaped, 1-2 in., creamy-white blossoms are borne in large branched spikes to 3-6 ft. long. Blooms in April to June. After the plant flowers and produces seed, it dies and new plants either arise from rooting stems or from the germination of seeds.

CULTURE AND CLIMATE: Zones 7-13. Indifferent as to soil, but more luxuriant in a sandy, well-drained loam. Propagated by seeds, offsets, stem cuttings, rhizome cuttings.

USE: Commanding plants whose blossoming stalks stand out handsomely on slopes, the top of walls, in wide borders, or in large tubs in patios and on terraces. They combine well with subtropicals such as banana, ginger, caladium, canna, aloe, cordyline, palm, and strelitzia.

Perennials
CHRYSANTHEMUMS

There are many reasons why growing chrysanthemums is such a fascinating hobby:

You find an amazing, wide variation in growth habits, flower forms, and colors.

Flower forms are constantly being changed. There is always something new.

The chrysanthemum plant responds to attention. You get quick action from fertilizers.

You can work with pots and containers in small space. With many chrysanthemums it's easier to produce prize-winning bloom by growing in pots.

They are most satisfactory and long lasting as cut-flowers.

TYPES OF CHRYSANTHEMUMS (See also p. 147)
To a gardener who is thinking of over-all garden effect first, and chrysanthemums second, there are many surprises in the garden-border types.

The emphasis upon garden-border types varies by climates. In California the classifications of chrysanthemums follow the flower-structure names used in the florist trade—button, pompon, spoon, spider, and others. However, in the Pacific Northwest varieties are grouped both by flower structure and by garden culture. Catalogs list Early English Sprays, Early American Sprays, and other garden-culture classification. In the class called *Sprays* are the many varieties that carry a terminal cluster, or spray, of several flowers.

The objective of chrysanthemum breeders in the Northwest is to develop a plant that doesn't need staking, is of good garden form, and that flowers profusely soon enough to escape winter rains west of the Cascades and early fall frosts east of the Cascades.

Here are the types according to flower form:

Button pompons. The smallest pompons, less than 1½ inches across.

Pompon. Blooms may be flat or nearly globular, neat and compact, with flat, fluted, or quilled petals. Disbudded pompons, about 5 inches in diameter. In this classification may be found an extremely large number of varieties in a wide range of colors covering a long period of bloom.

Singles or *Daisy.* Come in all sizes and forms. Petals may be short and rigid or long and drooping, but are arranged regularly and form a fringe. Excellent for cutting.

Spoon. Unusual tubular petals broaden at ends to form distinct spoons that are frequently of a different color from rest of petals, producing interesting contrast.

Cushion. Flowers made up of unequal tiered petals, bloom prolifically from early September until frosts. A very dwarfed, compact type. Use in pots; highly recommended for flower borders.

Anemone. One or more rows of petals with a large raised center disc or cushion; sometimes the same color as petals, at other times different. (This type becomes very large when disbudded.)

Spider. Some may have petals only, or there may be varying numbers of disc flowers at center. True spiders have curling tubular petals ending in fish-hook tips. Must be disbudded for good results.

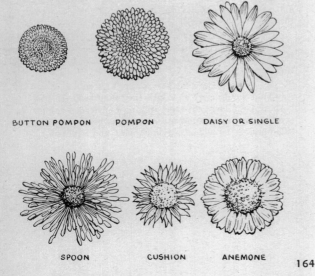
BUTTON POMPON POMPON DAISY OR SINGLE SPOON CUSHION ANEMONE

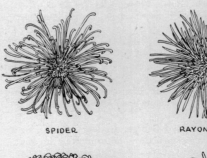
SPIDER RAYONNANTE

EXHIBITION

DECORATIVE

Rayonnante. Most flowers of this type consist of petals only. The petals are long, closed tubes except for small opening near pointed tips; radiate outward from center of flower.

Exhibition. These are divided into two types—*incurved* and *reflexed.* Petals of incurved type close in toward the center, forming a round ball type of flower. Petals of reflexed type turn back.

Decorative. One of the so-called unclassified types. Slender petals. Form of these petals varies considerably: long, narrow or broad, flat (overlapping like shingles on a roof); edges of petals rolled inward (boat-shaped); edges curled toward back of petal; rolled petals pointed strongly upward or outward from center of flower (spiky appearance); petals of some florets near center of flower are curled and twisted although outer petals are flat with tips notched (fringed appearance).

Feathery. Carnation-like with cupped or twisted and curled petals.

Cascade. Any small-flowered chrysanthemum with a limber willowy stem can be trained as a cascade, standard or espalier. (See below on how to train.)

Japanese. Petals, usually long and more or less curled, are twisted and intertwined with those of other florets, giving entire flower a shaggy appearance.

CULTURE

The culture of chrysanthemums is not exacting. In general they demand above-normal supplies of nutrients and water. When planting garden chrysanthemums with other plants, rely on small additions of fertilizers at frequent intervals.

Here's how to handle a special bed of chrysanthemums:

Soil

To prepare a planting bed: Add well-rotted manure or peat moss 2 inches deep over the bed, superphosphate, and balanced commercial fertilizer—about 1 pound of each to 100 square feet. Work these into soil 2 or 3 weeks before planting.

Planting

Chrysanthemums should receive sun at least two-thirds of the day, but shade from afternoon sun in hot climates. Do not place them close to hedges, shrubs, or trees whose roots compete for soil nutrients.

Watering

Deep watering at intervals spaced according to soil structure is the rule with chrysanthemums. (See chapter on watering.)

Lack of water causes the plants to harden and to lose the lower leaves from the stems. Excess water will have the same effect on leaves but will also cause a blackening of the foliage.

Excessive over-head watering is not recommended. If the foliage is left wet, it frequently develops yellow spots that may become dead, dry areas. Some varieties can take any amount of overhead watering, some show damage.

Fertilizing

How much nitrogen to apply in the beginning depends of course on the richness of your soil. Better to start with too little nitrogen. It's much easier to add than subtract. The plants will indicate excess nitrogen by overly lush, succulent growth; large, dark green foliage; weak stems; fewer flower buds; and dull flowers.

Make a second application when the stems show signs of becoming hard or the leaves lose their dark green color and become yellowish.

You may need a third or fourth application, but hold off fertilizers containing nitrogen at about 2 weeks before blossoming time. Nitrogen at that time delays flowering and reduces color intensity.

It is seldom necessary to make 3 or 4 applications if your soil is normally fertile.

HOW TO PRODUCE LARGE FLOWERS

Pinch out the tip of the one-stemmed rooted cutting and the growing plant will send out new shoots in the angles of several of its uppermost leaves.

Select 1-4 or more of these lateral shoots for continued growth. The first crown bud is developed at the tips of these lateral shoots.

Nip off (disbud) the first crown buds so that below them new shoots will develop on the branch or stem.

Select one or more of these branches for continued growth. Each shoot selected develops a second crown bud at its tip. Below the tip new shoots will in turn start out in leaf axils.

Pinch or rub out all these new shoots to make the second crown bud flower. But to make a terminal bud produce the flower, let at least one of the shoots below the second crown continue growing. Such a shoot produces not only one, but a cluster of flower buds at its tip—the terminal bud cluster.

From this cluster choose a particular bud for flowering—generally the center of the true terminal bud. (Often best to select more than one bud in case the bud intended for flowering is misshaped or injured. Then the injured one is removed and a second bud flowers.) Disbud the remaining ones.

HOW TO CASCADE CHRYSANTHEMUMS

You can cascade almost any variety of chrysanthemum that produces its blooms all along the stem. The smaller-flowering types with slender, pliable stems are most suitable.

Because cascades require a long growing season, cuttings usually are started in January or early February. Nurseries specializing in chrysanthemums have rooted cuttings in the spring, ready for training.

Plants purchased in 3 or 4-inch pots in the spring may be shifted directly into 6-inch pots for the first training stage. Two or three shifts will be necessary during the growing season. Repot the

166 CHRYSANTHEMUMS

plants each time before they have a chance to form a network of roots around the inside of the pot. Make the final shift to a 10 or 12-inch pot, or to a redwood or cedar box, about the middle of July.

Soil, fertilizing, and watering are the same as in chrysanthemum pot culture.

When the plant is 12 inches high, pinch out the tip to encourage side growth. Don't pinch main top leader after this, but pinch side shoots again when 3 or 4 inches long. This makes the plant bushy.

To make a trellis, bend a 9-foot length of No. 10 wire into elongated U, place single wire in center, reinforce with 2 crosspieces. Insert trellis one inch from stem, bend at 45° angle, 6 inches above pot rim.

Gently bend plant over wire. Tie main stem at intervals with raffia or paper-covered wire as plant grows along the frame. Place the pot so the wire points north. Support pot firmly to prevent tipping.

At regular intervals until September 1, pinch back all lateral side shoots at second or third leaf. This encourages many side shoots and a fuller, bushier plant.

During the growing season, gradually and gently bend wire and plant into a horizontal position. It should be in a horizontal position by the middle of September.

After the middle of September, place the pot so end of wire points south. Continue to bend (cascade) plants from horizontal to a downward position. This position should be permanent by mid-October. When the buds show color, place in high position so sprays will not touch ground.

POST-BLOOMING CARE

When the blossoms have faded and the stems look dry at the end of the flowering period, cut the stalks down to within 8 inches of the ground. Label each clump with a permanent waterproof label, so you can plant in the spring without guess-work as to flower colors.

If the soil is heavy and water is apt to stand during the winter, lift the clumps with plenty of soil adhering and set them together on top of the ground in an out-of-the-way place. Sawdust or sand may be thrown over and around the clumps. They may be left until time for spring planting.

Perennials

PRIMROSES

Name the types of primroses grown in the West and you call the roll of the lands of the Northern Hemisphere. Primroses from every climate and almost every growing condition are represented here. But even then only a few of the 600 species and countless hybrids of this genus will have been named. How many more will adapt themselves to some Western climate no one knows.

Every type of gardener can find what he is looking for in primroses. He can approach them with the serious fervor of a collector of rare gems, or with no more awe than he would a viola.

In primroses there are many collector's items and, at the same time, plenty of foolproof, easy-to-grow, hardy perennials.

Some idea of the variety in types, their possibilities in your garden, and the appeal primroses have to the hobbyist can be seen in the following brief outline of how the various primroses are being handled now.

ENGLISH PRIMROSES

These are the best adapted and most widely planted types. In every climate zone of the West some spot can be found where they will grow. In all but the desert climates they can be planted in masses for springtime color year after year.

Primula vulgaris (P. acaulis.) Bears single flowers on short stems among crisply crinkled leaves. Color range is from white through yellow, red, purple or blue.

P. VULGARIS

P. JULIÆ (WANDA)

P. juliæ hybrids. Results of crosses between the miniature Caucasian species *P. juliæ*, and species of English primroses. Extremely vigorous, free-flowering hybrids with tuft-like rosettes of leaves. Single blooms with a few rather than one to a stem, are in shades of red, yellow, blue and pure white. Var. *Wanda*, a stalkless cushion type with deep blue-violet flowers, was best known before more recent varieties became widely distributed.

Double-flowered sports of English primrose are available. Leading favorites are the rose-violet Marie Crousse, Double Lavender, Double White, Moonlight, and Burgundy Beauty.

P. polyantha. Most gardeners associate the word primrose with the polyanthus type. Flowers are carried in clusters at the top of stiff stems, 6-12 inches above rosettes of green basal leaves.

Flower show judges have definite specifications for rating polyanthas. A good primrose of this type should have a good balance between flowers and foliage. Plants should measure to 12 inches in height, with many flower clusters to a plant and many flowers to a cluster. Each individual flower within the cluster must be erect and from 1 to 2 inches across. The cluster should be full and round, and all stems should be strong and stout, holding the flowers well above the foliage. Leaves should be crisp and of a good clean green.

Both *P. vulgaris* and *P. polyantha* will develop 8 to 10 divisions every two years. Divide every other year. Lift clump, wash divisions, cut back roots to about 4 inches, and plant at once. Best time is following the blooming period, usually May, June, or September.

Cultural requirements of primroses are comparatively simple. The main thing is to work rich humus into the upper surface of the soil and to apply a 2 to 3-inch mulch of the same material after planting to keep the plants warm in winter, cool in summer, and retain moisture throughout the growing period.

You'll get better effect by planting in large drifts of single colors in mixed masses. The giant hybrids are useful as cut flowers.

The plants are not attractive when out of bloom and many gardeners pot them up, plunging them in the ground where wanted for spring color or using them in patios or on porch or terrace. If left in the border, sow or set out annuals or perennials which will mask the off-season appearance.

WARM CLIMATE PRIMROSES

Although there are no species of primula which are native to subtropical climates, there is a group of primulas from southern China which have found an important place in California gardens. The three species in this group which are generally available are *P. obconica*, *P. sinensis*, and *P. malacoides*.

All three are excellent pot plants and have long been used as such. Northwest gardeners grow these tender varieties by giving them winter protection and bringing them out in pots, placing them in the ground in the spring when the frosts are past.

P. obconica. A perennial, best treated as an annual because of its short life. Large flowers in pink and lilac pastel shades provide bloom from early spring to late fall and a scattering throughout the year. The large, somewhat furry basal leaves give a nettle-like rash to people with sensitive skin. The obconicas are now sold by the flat as bedding plants by nurseries throughout California. Need semi-shade; quite hardy, and seem to perform better in cooler sections.

P. sinensis. A relatively uncommon species somewhat like *P. obconica*, but smaller. Large flowers in compact clusters in white, red, pink, and blue shades. Grows to 8 inches. Var. *stellata:* Smaller, star-shaped flowers in looser clusters. Other hybrids available with larger flowers.

P. malacoides. FAIRY PRIMROSE. See annuals chapter.

These primulas are planted in warm winter areas in early fall for winter and early spring bloom. They are surprisingly hardy for their dainty looks and will weather winter storms without too much damage.

ALPINE TYPES

Naturally the alpine types are at their best under rock garden conditions where their long roots can penetrate the rocky surface layers into a cool, richer soil below.

In all high-elevation gardens of the West these primroses more than make up for many less hardy plant groups that can't be grown. In the sea-level sections of the Pacific Northwest gardeners who grow any of the alpines are growing these primroses successfully.

P. auricula. The typical species of the Auricula section of primroses, and from which the section received its name. Actually the group includes 25 species and varieties of alpine primroses native to the Pyrenees and mountains of southeastern Europe. However, most of the Auriculas in cultivation are hybrids between *P. auricula* and one or more other species of this section.

P. POLYANTHA

P. OBCONICA

P. SINENSIS

P. AURICULA

168 PRIMROSES

Many of these hybrids are characterized by rosettes of thick leaves, some with a mealy coating or a white margin; and strong, fleshy stems supporting clusters of flowers with heavy substance and mild fragrance. Blooms are available in yellow, cream, purple, rose, and brownish tones.

P. DENTICULATA

P. denticulata often erroneously called *P. cashmiriana*, is a Himalayan native. Flowers may vary in coloring from deep lavender-blue, pink and red tones to white and are carried in thick, round-headed clusters.

P. rosea grows at elevations of 10,000 to 12,000 feet in the Himalayas. It blooms quite early, having large rose-pink flowers in loose clusters, and distinctive, pointed, glossy leaves that are quite red when they first come out in early spring.

P. cortusoides, native to Siberia, carries handsome magenta flowers on 6-10 inch stems over a long period of bloom.

CANDELABRA TYPES (ASIATIC)

The candelabra primroses are so called because they carry their flowers in whorls, or concentric rings, on the upper portion of 2-3 ft. stems.

Most primroses are concentrated in Himalayan meadows ranging from 8,000 to 11,000 feet elevation in a comparatively small circle encompassing southwestern China, southeastern Tibet, northern India, and Burma. Because they are accustomed to the wet monsoon season from April to October, they need a great deal of moisture during the spring and summer months. These primroses will grow best in a heavy, humus-rich soil similar to that of their native habitat.

P. pulverulenta. Probably best known of candelabra primroses. The original species which has red flowers with an orange-brown eye, has been largely superseded by modern strains, such as Bartley which produces flowers in various shades of pink and salmon on stems 2 to 3 feet high.

P. bulleyana. An early summer-blooming type with striking reddish orange buds that open into chrome yellow flowers held above strong, upstanding foliage. Hybrids have produced several other new shades, including buff, apricot, and orange.

P. beesiana. A candelabra with rosy lavender to purple blooms on 2 to 3-foot stems. Blooms about the same time as *P. bulleyana*.

P. cockburniana. Smaller and daintier than most of this type, with vivid, orange-scarlet flowers in 3 to 5 whorls on 12-inch stems.

P. japonica. One of the finest primroses in its class. Large flowers, arranged in 5 whorls, are white to deep purple, and bloom through May and into June on stems 24 to 40 inches tall. This is an exception to the candelabra group, being a native of Japan instead of the Himalayan mountains. It therefore requires less moisture than the others.

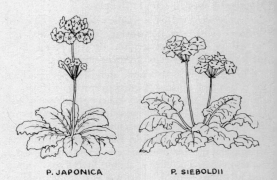

P. JAPONICA   P. SIEBOLDII

WOODLAND PRIMROSES

The primula species known as woodland primroses are Asiatic primrose types that grow in a woodland soil, spread by creeping roots, and produce dainty, light-colored flower clusters in late April, May and into the summer. After the plants set seed, they become dormant and lose their leaves. Plants need dividing only every 3 to 4 years, or when smaller flowers indicate overcrowding. Divide and replant in the spring.

The natives of Japan and southeastern Asia require less water and a less rich soil than other primroses, but thrive handsomely when treated like the others.

P. sieboldii. Numerous flower stalks rise stiffly 8 to 12 inches above the base of large, soft, crinkly leaves. Each stalk is topped by a cluster of from 4 to 8 delicate flowers, about an inch across, and opening flat like phlox blossoms. Color range runs through white, pink, to red in pastel shades. A shaded or sunny spot in the perennial border will suit this primrose well, as it becomes dormant after flowering and remains so until the following spring.

P. saxatilis. Similar to *P. sieboldii*, but more dainty and fragile in appearance. Flowers are a clear lavender-pink on stems to 12 inches. With plenty of moisture it will bloom from April to November. Use in rock garden, naturalized in the woods, or massed under fruit trees.

P. polyneura. Larger in leaf than *P. sieboldii* and blooms a little later. Flowers vary in color from pink to lavender and purple shades, and characteristically have a bright orange eye.

Bulbs

There are few things in life about which you can say, "of this I can be sure." But as a gardener holds a bulb in his hand in October, he feels very sure that spring will bring him color. A perfect flower is already formed within its sleek brown jacket. It seems fantastically simple that all he has to do to bring that flower out of hiding is to give the bulb a cool dark berth in the soil of his garden.

Because of the reliability of bulbs, you can plan for special effects with almost complete certainty that the picture, at least as far as the bulbs are concerned, will materialize.

With bulbs, you can tie the color of early flowering fruit trees or shrubs into the ground below. Consider pink scillas under a pink flowering plum, white daffodils under a white flowering peach or under white-trunked birches, yellow trumpet daffodils in front of valencia orange trees.

You can relieve monotonous stretches of low green ground covers such as ajuga or vinca with drifts of daffodils, paper white narcissus, scillas, or tulips. Obvious though it is, a mixed planting of tall red Darwin tulips and yellow trumpet daffodils will light a drab or shadowy corner better than a floodlight.

Perhaps the subtlest and most enjoyable way to use bulbs is in small colonies where you would least expect to find them.

Slip a few crocus or miniature daffodils into an irregular crack between paving stones, and scatter a few seeds of white or purple alyssum for spring flowers amid fading daffodil foliage.

Bulbs succeed where other plants fail

The delicate grace of spring flowering bulbs does not suggest planting them where garden conditions are rough-and-tough. And yet, time and time again daffodils, scillas, snowflakes, and other bulbs have succeeded where more robust looking plants have failed.

All bulbs prefer a deep cool loam but they will take what they can get and make the most of it.

BULBS IN CONTAINERS

Growing bulbs in boxes and pots has these advantages:

1. You can move the bulb foliage out of sight as soon as the blooms fade. When the potted bulbs are plunged into place in the garden, the removal after blooming releases planting space that ordinarily would be taken up by the slow ripening foliage for weeks.

2. Pots protect bulbs from gophers.

3. You can change your mind up to the last minute on where you want color if you are carrying it around by the pot or box-full.

How to plant in containers

Bulbs must have space for root development.

BLOOM CALENDAR FOR BULBS
(For planting recommendations, see encyclopedia.)

FOR WINTER-SPRING COLOR

Anemone. Blue, red, white.
Babiana. Lavender, red, lilac, blue, yellow, white.
Bletilla. Lavender, purple.
Bomarea. Red, yellow.
Calochortus. White.
Camassia. Blue, white.
Chionodoxa. White, pink, lavender, blue.
Clivia. Orange, salmon, red.
Convallaria. White.
Crocus. Yellow, orange, lavender, purple, white.
Cyclamen. White, pink, rose, red.
Daffodil. Yellow, white.
Eranthis. Yellow.
Erythronium. White, yellow, lavender.
Freesia. Rose, lavender, mauve, purple, yellow, orange, white.
Fritillaria. Red, orange, yellow, white.
Galanthus. White.
Hippeastrum. Red, orange, white.
Hyacinthus. White, pink, blue, purple, cream.
Iris. Many colors.
Lachenalia. Red, yellow.
Leucojum. White.
Leucocoryne. Pale blue.
Muscari. Blue, white.
Ornithogalum. White.
Ranunculus. Cream, white, red, yellow, orange, pink, rose.
Scilla. White, lilac, blue, pink, rose.
Sparaxis. Red, white, yellow.
Trillium. Maroon, greenish-yellow, white.
Tulip. Many colors.

FOR LATE SPRING-SUMMER COLOR

Achimenes. Pink, blue, orchid, lavender, purple.
Acidanthera. Creamy-white.
Allium. White.
Alstroemeria. Orange, yellow, salmon.
Begonia (tuberous). Yellow, orange, pink, salmon, apricot, red, white.
Bloomeria. Golden yellow.
Brodiaea. Violet-purple, yellow, white, lilac.
Dierama. Lavender-pink, purple, near-white.
Galtonia. White.
Gladiolus. Many colors.
Gloriosa. Red, yellow.
Haemanthus. Red.
Hemerocallis. Yellow, bronze, orange, pink, rose, red, bicolored.
Hymenocallis. White.
Polianthes. White.
Sinningia. Blue, purple, pink, red, white.
Tigridia. Red, rose, yellow, orange, white.
Tritonia. Orange, apricot, yellow, scarlet.
Watsonia. White, rose, red.
Zantedeschia. White, yellow, rose.

FOR LATE SUMMER-FALL COLOR

Agapanthus. Blue, white.
Amaryllis. Rose-pink, white.
Canna. Red, pink, yellow, white, apricot, orange.
Colchicum. Lavender, rosy-lilac, white.
Crocus. Yellow, orange, lavender, purple, white.
Dahlia. Many colors.
Lycoris. Red, yellow.
Nerine. Pink, rose, red, salmon, scarlet, orange.
Polianthes. White.
Schizostylis. Crimson, pink.
Sternbergia. Yellow.
Vallota. Orange-vermilion.
Zephyranthes. White, yellow, pink, rose-pink.

Bulbs must have the equivalent of the cool dark depth of soil to develop roots before top growth starts. Since you can't plant deep in a 6-inch pot and still get root space, what do you do?

You plant just beneath the container surface of the soil and in some way provide a 6-inch layer of cool darkness above the pot throughout the winter. Several methods of getting winter darkness are followed:

Sink the pots in a 12-inch deep trench and cover with earth. Place the pots in large boxes and cover with peat, sand, or sawdust.

Place the containers in a coldframe and cover with mulch.

In all methods the medium used to cover and the soil in the pots is kept damp through the time they are buried.

Sufficient root development should take place in 7-10 weeks depending upon the variety. Check by lifting a pot or two, tipping out the ball of soil to see whether roots have developed. By the time they are ready for removal, top growth may be 2-4 inches high. Until this stem growth greens up the pots should be shaded from the direct sun.

If the containers are left outdoors, the bulb growth will develop in the same time as with soil-planted bulbs. By bringing them into a greenhouse or indoors you can force bloom ahead of the normal season.

Don't be afraid to crowd bulbs in container planting.

With small bulbs, such as crocus and freesia: Place 6-8 bulbs, depending on their size, in a 5-inch pot.

With large to medium-sized bulbs, such as daffodils and tulips: 3-5 bulbs in a 7-inch pot; 6-8 bulbs in a 10-inch pot.

With very large bulbs, such as hyacinths: 1 bulb in a 4-inch pot; 3 bulbs in an 8-inch pot; 5-6 bulbs in a 10-inch pot.

— Encyclopedia —

ACHIMENES. Tuber. Tender. Closely related to gloxinia and requires same treatment. Flowers are tubular, wide open to 1-3 in. across, borne in the leaf axils. Color ranges through pink, blue, orchid, lavender and purple. Blooms profusely in summer for 8-10 weeks. CULTURE: Plant January 15 or later. Set 4-6 of the tiny tubers in a 6-in. shallow pot. If outdoors, plant in partial shade. Prefers an acid soil; equal parts of sandy loam and leaf mold make a good planting mixture. Keep soil moist while growing. When plants die down, remove and store tubers the same as you would tuberous begonias. USE: Effective in pots and hanging baskets.

ACIDANTHERA BICOLOR. Corm. Tender. Simple stems bearing 1 or 2 gladiolus-like leaves. Fragrant, long-tubular, drooping, creamy-white flowers, with conspicuous blackish-crimson spot in center, borne 4-8 on 15-in. stems.

A. murielae. (see *Gladiolus murielæ*, p. 176).
CULTURE: Sun and well-drained sandy loam. Lift and store like gladiolus corms.

USE: Cutting; in borders behind or among annuals such as petunias, phlox, ageratum.

AGAPANTHUS. Tuberous rootstock. Half hardy. Plants ranging in size from 1-ft. dwarfs to 5-ft. giants. Bold irregular masses of dark green strap-shaped leaves. Towering stems bear funnel-shaped 2-in. flowers, many in rather loose or compact umbrella-like clusters. Color ranges through almost all the blues, sometimes white.

A. africanus. *(A. umbellatus).* LILY-OF-THE-NILE. AFRICAN LILY. Most commonly planted. Blue flowers, 20-50 or more in a cluster. Free blooming, except in dense shade, for summer and fall effect. Var. *albidus* has pure white flowers. Var. *mooreanus.* Deciduous, hardier than other forms. Lower growing to 18-24 in., with compact habit. Narrow leaves are stained purple at base. Dark blue flowers, June-August. Var. *mooreanus minor,* also deciduous, is so diminutive that 3-5 plants may be grown in a 6-in. pot.

A. orientalis. A more robust species, to 4 ft., with broader, softer leaves, and 40-100 flowers in a cluster.

CULTURE: Sun except in warm inland sections, where part shade is necessary to avoid burning of leaves. Best in loamy soil, but will grow in heavy soils under poor conditions. Give liquid manure or balanced fertilizer, and a good supply of water during growing season. Forms large clumps which need dividing only every 5 or 6 years—or when flowers become scarce and smaller in size.

USE: Effective in wide borders, particularly with yellow day lily; also with *Lilium regale* or *L. formosanum (L. philippinense formosanum).* Handsome in tubs or large pots. Massive enough to plant in front of large shrubs.

ALLIUM NEAPOLITANUM. Bulb. Hardy. Grows to 1 ft.; the grass-like leaves to 1 in. wide, have strong onion odor when crushed. Flowers white, becoming papery, in few-flowered nodding clusters to 3 in. across. CULTURE: Requires no special treatment, accepting sun or shade, any soil. USE: Will naturalize readily. Good for growing under deciduous trees, on slopes, along creek banks, boundaries, or any place where they can multiply and run wild without infringing on other plants. Flowers last well when cut.

ALSTROEMERIA. Tuber. Half hardy. Leafy stems to 2-5 ft. high, topped by broad clusters of azalea-like flowers in a wide range of colors, predominantly orange and yellow, usually marked or spotted in darker colors. Blooms from May to midsummer.

A. aurantiaca. PERUVIAN LILY. INCA LILY. Best known species, growing to 3 ft., carrying orange-yellow 1½-in. flowers marked with red and brown. Blooms in June. Var. *lutea* is a clear yellow form.

A. chilensis hybrids. CHILEAN LILY. Among the most beautiful, producing large broad clusters of flowers in creamy-white, lemon-yellow, yellow-orange, pink, salmon-pink to red, sometimes with 2 or more colors combined in one flower. Grows to 4 ft.

A. haemantha. Among the hardiest and easiest of culture. Grows to 2-3 ft. Reddish-yellow flowers are spotted with purple and tipped with green.

A. ligtu. Grows to 3-5 ft. Has rather sparsely leafed stems that begin to defoliate as plants come into bloom. Flowers 2 in. long, and 2 in. across, in shades of pink, streaked with deep maroon.

A. pelegrina. LILY OF LIMA. Grows to 2 ft. Large (2 in.) flowers are lilac spotted with red-purple. Var. *alba* has white unspotted flowers.

A. pulchella. *(A. psittacina).* More tender than other species. Grows to 2-3 ft.; bearing clusters of 5 or 6 nodding dark red flowers tipped with green and spotted with mahogany.

A. violacea. Flowers in an unusual shade of violet are borne in large clusters.

CULTURE: Best in cool, moist, deep, sandy to medium-heavy loam to which well-rotted manure, leaf mold, or peat have been added. Good drainage is important. Plant tubers 6-8 in. deep, and 12 in. apart. Leave undisturbed as long as possible, relying upon fall mulching to protect in cold regions. Difficult to re-establish; little bloom until second year after transplanting. Top-dress with well-rotted manure each spring as soon as growth starts. Water heavily in April, May, and June; then taper off gradually. Best in partial shade in warm-summer climates; in sun near coast.

USE: Good for prominent position in garden. Effective in colonies or large masses, alone in a border or in front of shrubs like aucuba. Excellent cut flowers.

AMARYLLIS BELLADONNA. *(Callicore rosea).* BELLADONNA LILY. Bulb. Half hardy. Bold strap-shaped leaves in clumps, spreading 2-3 ft. in fall and winter; dormant in spring and summer. Rosy-pink, heavily scented, 3½-in. flowers are borne 6-12 on the tops of naked reddish-brown 2-3-ft. stems in August. Var. *major* has rose-pink flowers in July. Var. *minor* has smaller flowers that are deeper pink, with white centers, and bloom 2 weeks later. Var. *rosea,* the latest blooming, has white flowers edged with rose-pink, and a yellow throat. CULTURE: Will grow in almost any soil. Drought resistant. Plant bulbs so that tops are even with or a little above the soil. In mild-winter sections may be left in ground the year around. Disturb as seldom as possible. Right after bloom (early fall) is the best time for transplanting. Refuses to bloom for 4-5 years if disturbed at wrong season. USE: Plant in clumps or borders preferably behind perennials or annuals that will hide the conspicuously bare stems. Allow room so vigorous spring foliage does not smother adjacent plants. Agapanthus and amaryllis are a long-time favorite combination.

ANEMONE. WIND FLOWER. (Also see chapter on perennials.) Tuber. Hardy. Bright green, finely divided leaves, mostly in basal tufts, the flowering stems rising to 6-14 in. Showy flowers solitary. Early spring blooming.

A. apennina. Grows to 6-9 in.; sky blue flowers to 1½ in.

A. coronaria. POPPY-FLOWERED ANEMONE. The common anemone of the florists. Grows 12-14 in. Showy poppy-like flowers to 2½ in. across, in various combinations of blue, red and white. Some of the named strains are: *De Caen* grows to 12-14 in., has single flowers in mixed colors; *St. Brigid,* grows to 12 in., with double or semi-double flowers in mixed colors; *Blue Poppy* has blue single flowers; *Pure White* has large single white flowers.

CULTURE: *A. coronaria* prefers sun; *A. apennina* slight shade. Plant bulbs in October to November. In cold sections plant in early spring, or if planted in November, mulch with 6-8 in. of leaf mold or peat moss after the first hard frost. Soak bulbs an hour in water before planting. Plant 3 in. deep, 6 in. apart, in rich, light, well-drained garden loam, or start in flats of damp sand. Keep moist through blooming season.

USE: Effective in rock gardens, borders and pots. Excellent cut flowers.

BABIANA. BABOON FLOWER. Corm. Tender. Grows to 6-12 in. Several hairy plaited sword-like leaves are arranged edgewise along the stem. Showy, slender, tubular, freesia-like flowers are borne in spring in terminal spikes or clusters.

B. plicata. Grows to 6 in. or less, the leaves usually taller than the flower spikes. Fragrant lavender and cream flowers.

B. stricta. Taller growing, to 1 ft., the leaves half as tall as the flower spike. Flowers red or lilac to 1½ in. long. Var. *rubro-cyanea* has blue flowers with a bright red throat; var. *sulphurea*, pale yellow and white flowers.

CULTURE: Requires the same culture as freesias. Sun loving. Plant 3 in. deep, 3 in. apart, in October and November. May be left in ground for several years in warm climates, never in cold, heavy, wet ground. When established will take considerable neglect.

USE: Attractive edging or rock garden plants. In colder climates plant in pots.

BLETILLA STRIATA. Terrestial orchid with tuberous rhizomes. Hardy except in colder sections, where it is grown in pots indoors. Stems 10 to 15 in.; leaves bright green, 1-2 in. wide, plaited or grooved. Soft lavender to purple orchid-like flowers 1 in. long, 3-7 in a raceme that is longer than the leaves. Often bloom for 6 weeks. CULTURE: Likes same cultural conditions as tuberous begonias. Plant in partial shade under deciduous trees. When well established, rhizomes multiply readily. USE: In borders with tuberous begonias, fuchsias, lilies, bleeding heart, ferns. To grow in pots indoors, pot bulbs in November, keep in cool dark place for 2 months, move into light, warm (60°) spot for bloom in March.

BLOOMERIA CROCEA. (*B. aurea*). GOLDEN STARS. Corm. Half-hardy, will stand several degrees of frost. Native to California—south Coast Range, coastal Southern California. Closely related to and looks like brodiæa. Grows 12-18 in., with grass-like basal leaves. Slender stems carry open clusters of star-like flowers that are golden-yellow, striped with darker lines. Blooms in May and June. CULTURE: Full sun. Prefers light, warm, well-drained soil. USE: Good for naturalizing in mild climates where corms can dry off after blooming; otherwise replant in autumn. Adapted to pot culture and forcing.

BOMAREA CALDASII. (*B. caldasiana*). CLIMBING PERUVIAN LILY. Tuber. Tender. Twining herbs to 4 ft., native of woodlands, closely allied to alstrœmeria. Oblong 3-6 in. parallel-veined, spreading leaves on twisted stalks. Long-lasting red and yellow tubular 1½-in. flowers borne 6-30 in nodding clusters in spring, are followed by ornamental seed pods. CULTURE: Likes roots in shade, tops in half shade. Requires rich, fibrous soil and abundant water in growing season. Liquid manure beneficial. Cut to the ground in late fall, keeping roots as dry as possible through the winter. USE: Most effective and in character growing at the base of a tree, with support to lead twining stems to lower branches. Can also be grown on fences against walls, and in large containers on trellises.

BRODIAEA. Corm. Hardy. Mostly native to the Pacific Coast. Several basal grass-like leaves. Slender stems bear loose or compact clusters of tubular or bell-shaped flowers, May-July.

B. californica. One of the best for garden use. Stems to 1½-2 ft. bear loose clusters of 10-20 violet-purple 1½-2 in. flowers in late June and July.

B. capitata. BLUE DICKS. Many stems from 1 corm, to 2 ft. Deep violet-blue, rarely near-white, small flowers are borne in compact head-like clusters in March or April. Larger and more profuse under cultivation.

B. coronaria. HARVEST BRODIAEA. Grows to 1½ ft. Bears loose clusters of 6-15 violet-purple funnel-shaped 1¾-in. flowers in July.

B. ixioides. GOLDEN BRODIAEA. Grows to 1½ ft. Flowers, in loose clusters, are salmon-yellow, veined with dark purple, ¾ in. long, in early spring. Var. *splendens* has larger bright yellow flowers.

B. lactea. WILD HYACINTH. Grows to 1½ ft. Has white or lilac ½-in. flowers in dense clusters in spring.

B. laxa. ITHURIEL'S SPEAR. GRASS NUT. Grows to 2 ft. Bears loose clusters of 1¾-in. bluish-violet, rarely white, flowers.

CULTURE: Prefer well-drained, sandy, gritty soil, or heavier soil lightened with coarse sand or leaf mold. Never use manure. Plant September to November; 2-2½ in. deep, 2-3 in. apart. Water moderately, allow to dry off and ripen after flowering. In cold areas, force gently in pots like freesia in a greenhouse or coldframe. All brodiæas naturalize on open slopes or in sunny wild gardens if water is withheld in summer. Long-lasting cut flowers.

CALOCHORTUS. MARIPOSA LILY. GLOBE TULIP. Corm. Hardy. Western natives bearing slender, narrow leaves along the stems, and cup-shaped or globe-shaped flowers.

C. albus. FAIRY LANTERN. Slender, leafy stems to 2 ft. The white 1¼-in. flowers are like dainty, nodding lanterns. Blooms March to May.

C. amabilis. GOLDEN GLOBE TULIP. Like *C. albus*, but lower growing, to 15 in., and the flower lanterns are a rich yellow.

C. amoenus. PURPLE GLOBE TULIP. Grows to 1½ ft. and has rosy-purple lanterns. Var. *major* is a robust form to 24 in., and with many branched stems.

C. maweanus. (*C. cœruleus maweanus*). CAT'S EAR. Grows to 8 in., with white, or purple tinged 1-in. wide-open cup-like flowers, that are furry inside. Blooms in March and April.

C. venustus. MARIPOSA TULIP, BUTTERFLY TULIP. Erect branched stems to 10 in. or more. Showy cup-shaped flowers are 2-4 in. across, in white, or pale lilac, with reddish-brown spots and markings. Blooms in May and June.

CULTURE: Globe tulips and cat's ear, both woodland plants, like light shade, loose soil, leaf mold and plenty of water. Mariposa tulip, growing in open fields, blooms in the sun as long as roots are shaded; likes light, porous soil, good drainage, and must be kept dry in summer. All stand considerable cold, but not alternate freezing and thawing; mulching helps. Plant September-December in California; in cold climates plant just as freezing starts, to prevent premature root growth. Space corms 2-4 in. apart, 2½ in. deep.

USE: Globe tulips and cat's ear, while less showy than Mariposa tulip, have distinct charm and are easily grown. Well suited to rock gardens and woodlands. Plant Mariposa tulips on slopes or in open out-of-the-way sections of the garden where bulbs can dry out in summer.

CAMASSIA. CAMASS. Bulb. Hardy. Western natives with attractive narrow basal leaves that form very early and are followed in late March by long-stemmed clusters of starry blue flowers. Buds open successively from the bottom up to the top of the stalk. Flowers are mostly deep blue, the white forms less striking. CULTURE: Growing natively in wet marshy mountain meadows, camassias require plenty of water when in bloom. Otherwise need no special care. Plant bulbs 4-6 in. apart and 4 in. deep. After bloom, the camassias quietly disappear, as the foliage dries up quickly. USE: *C. leichtlinii* is the tallest (to 2 ft.) and the strongest variety for garden use. There are also dwarf forms for rock gardens.

CANNA. Rhizome. Half-hardy. Best suited to warm, inland valleys, do poorly in foggy coastal areas. Tropical perennial to 3-6 ft., with bold, handsome, glossy green or bronzy foliage, and terminal clusters of showy flowers in shades of red, pink, yellow, white, apricot and orange. Some of the flowers are 6-8 in. across, of one color, spotted, or splotched. Blooms in summer and fall.

Some of the outstanding varieties are: *Ambassador*, foliage dark bronze, giant crimson flowers; *Austria*, yellow with crimson marking in throat; *Baltimore*, immense deep pink flowers; *City of Portland*, silvery-pink flowers; *Copper Giant*, large bronze flowers suffused with rose; *Eureka*, pure white flowers; *Golden Wedding*, canary yellow flowers; *King Humbert*, glowing red flowers, bronze foliage; *Panama*, terra cotta red flowers, throat and edge of petals spotted with golden-yellow; *The President*, dazzling red flowers; *Uncle Sam*, vivid crimson flowers; *Wyoming*, deep orange flowers and bronze foliage.

CULTURE: Plant in open sunny positions in soil enriched beforehand with plenty of well-rotted manure. Water generously throughout the summer. Plant roots in March and April, about 5 in. deep and 18 in. apart, divide clumps every 3 or 4 years. In cold climates, cannas should be lifted and stored in autumn. In less severe climates the clumps may be left in the ground. Since they are evergreen in mild-winter climates, it is best to cut back the foliage in late fall to make place for new growth.

USE: Effective in bold mass plantings in backgrounds and in shrub and large perennial borders. New lower-growing forms are good tub plants.

CHIONODOXA. GLORY-OF-THE-SNOW. Bulb. Hardy; best in cold climates. Grows to 5-8 in., with narrow basal leaves and blue or white short tubular, open flowers in loose terminal spikes. Blooms in early spring.

G. luciliae. Flowers are bright blue, with a white center, to 1 in. across. Var. *alba* has white flowers; var. *rosea*, pink flowers.

G. gigantea. Like *G. luciliæ*, but larger, with soft lavender flowers.

G. sardensis. Dark blue flowers without white center.

CULTURE: Likes sun or partial shade and any reasonably good loamy garden soil, plenty of moisture and light. Plant September to October, approximately 3 in. deep. Replant about every third year.

USE: Naturalize under flowering shrubs such as forsythia, spiraea, or flowering almond. Combines well with yellow crocus, snowdrop, winter aconite, and violet.

CLIVIA. KAFIR LILY. Bulb-like. Tender. Basal clumps of long, dark green, lustrous, strap-shaped leaves. Amaryllis-like 3-in. flowers are borne 10-25 in large rounded clusters, in various shades of orange, including those with rich salmon or red tones. Blooms from December to March.

C. miniata. Hardiest species. Leaves 1½ ft. long and 2 in. wide. Flowers on 18-in. stiff stems are soft orange-yellow. Hybrids of *C. miniata* vary in color and form, some glowing orange-red, others with white or yellow throats.

C. nobilis. Has wider, less pointed leaves, and many drooping flowers that are narrower and shorter than *C. miniata*, in red and yellow, tipped green.

CULTURE: Prefers full shade, rich, heavy soil kept moist at all times. In November, when growth is slower, water less, but do not let foliage wilt. Needs occasional applications of liquid manure; otherwise may be left undisturbed for several years. Does well outdoors in warmer sections. Can be grown in pots indoors in colder areas.

USE: Clivia is particularly handsome in pots, tubs, or boxes. Foliage is more luxuriant in containers than in open ground. If you do grow it in the garden, try planting it near camellias, large ferns, the bird-of-paradise flower, or gardenias.

COLCHICUM. AUTUMN CROCUS. Corm. Hardy. Basal, rather broad leaves, are lush in spring, yellowing in June. Showy cup-like lavender, rosy-lilac, or white flowers resemble the true crocus. Blooms from August to September.

C. autumnale. Grows to 4 in., with 2-in. wide leaves. Flowers are purple or white, sometimes double to 4 in. long and 4 in. wide, blooming in autumn. Var. *album* has white flowers. Var. *majus* is more robust, with rosy-purple flowers.

C. bornmuelleri. Grows to 8 in., with 2-in. wide leaves. Flowers, rose or lilac turn purple, with a white tube, are 5 in. across. Early flowering.

C. speciosum. Taller growing to 12 in., with 4-in. wide leaves. Flowers, violet with white or pink throat, are 6 in. across. Var. *album* has large white flowers.

CULTURE: Likes partial shade, loamy soil, preferably damp or wet. Plant 2-3 in. deep as soon as dormant or immediately after blooming.

USE: Best in moist, sunny or half shaded border. If undisturbed, will colonize and increase readily. Best grouped by themselves. Good in pots. Excellent cut flower.

CONVALLARIA MAJALIS. LILY-OF-THE-VALLEY. Pips. Hardy, best in cold climates. Stems to 6-8 in. arise from 2 broad basal leaves, bear fragrant, small, bell-shaped white flowers, sometimes double or tinted pink. Blooms in early spring. CULTURE: Shade. Rich soil containing lots of humus such as leaf mold, peat or rotted logs to provide a cool, moist root run. Clumps or divisions are available in nurseries in November and December. Set clumps 1-2 ft. apart. Place single roots (pips) 4-6 in. apart, 1½ in. deep. Once planted, they should be left undisturbed for about 5 years. Top-dress yearly with rotted leaf mold, peat moss or well-rotted manure. USE: Ideal carpet planting between camellias, rhododendrons, pieris. Requires same conditions and will bloom along with many of them, and provide a cover of green leaves at other times of the year.

CROCUS. Corm. Hardy. Clean, deep green, grass-like basal foliage which disappears after the flowers have bloomed. Showy, long-tubed, cup-shaped flowers in shades of yellow, orange, lavender, purple or white. There are scores of crocus species that bloom between September and February. By careful selection you can have a practically continuous crocus show from fall to spring.

C. aerius. Lilac-lavender flowers with a yellow throat. Blooms in January.

C. biflorus. Flowers tinged with purple, the outer segments with 3 stripes of purple, the throat tinged yellow. Spring blooming.

C. chrysanthus. Sweet scented golden flowers with black-tipped anthers, blooming in February. Varieties come in white, cream, yellow and gray-blue flowers.

C. etruscus. Clear mauve flowers with yellow throat. Blooms in February.

C. imperati. Flowers lilac or white with 3 dark purple stripes on the outside segments. Blooms in very early spring.

C. korolkowii. Orange-yellow flowers with soft brown on the outer segments. Blooms in December.

C. laevigatus fontenayi. Inside of the flower cup varies from lilac to mauve with violet markings, the outside buff tinted. Blooms in December.

C. medius. Rich lavender flowers, striped violet in the throat, with startling red stigmas. Blooms in October.

C. sativus. SAFFRON CROCUS. Lilac or purple flowers with long scarlet styles which are the commercial source of saffron. Blooms in November. Especially fond of warm, sunny locations.

C. speciosus. Most showy and vigorous of the species. Large blue-violet flowers with brilliant vermilion-orange anthers. Blooms in October. Varieties of this species have 6-in. blooms in white, lilac and blue, also with bright orange anthers.

C. susianus. CLOTH OF GOLD. Brilliant orange-gold flowers, the segments with dark brown stripe down the outer side. Blooms in January.

C. tomasinianus. Although slender and delicate in form, it is quite rugged and extremely prolific when established. Flowers are silvery lavender-blue, sometimes with a dark blotch on the tip of each petal. Blooms in February.

C. zonatus. One of the finest and best-known species. Flowers are a delicate pinkish-lavender with white stamens. Blooms in September.

CULTURE: Likes sun, but will tolerate high light shade. Loose, well-drained soil. Give corms a chance to ripen in summer. If watering must continue, give them a sandy spot where moisture will drain away quickly. Plant corms 2-3 in. deep, or half again their own depth.

USE: Cluster them in pockets in the rockery or in a miniature garden, if the planting space is small and close to the house. Drift them in front of shrubbery, in light woods, or underfoot in orchards where the grass won't be clipped short until mid-May. Plant them on a steep slope or rock wall above a path where the individual beauty of each flower is brought close to the eye. Leave them undisturbed to form thick mats and use to cover the ground under permanent plantings of broad-leafed evergreens, such as rhododendrons or azaleas.

CYCLAMEN. Tuber or corm. Hardy to tender, depending on species. If you live in a mild winter section, you have a choice of two types: the large flowered florists' cyclamen, which will bloom from November to April; and the smaller, hardy cyclamen, which is available in several species whose combined blooming periods stretch from late July to early spring. In cold winter areas, depend on hardy types for outdoor bloom, and grow florists' cyclamen in pots indoors.

Attractive heart-shaped leaves, sometimes variegated, forming luxuriant basal clumps. Leaves appear either before or with the flowers. Colorful, showy flowers in white and shades of pink and rose.

C. atkinsii. Hardy. Shining, deep green leaves are lightly mottled with silver-white. Pink to pale-rose flowers on 4-6 in. stems, bloom January to March. Var. *album* has white flowers.

C. coum. Hardy. Leaves are round and glossy, deep green, without marbling or variegation. Deep crimson-rose flowers on 4-6 in. stems. Blooms February and March. Var. *album* has white flowers with a red base.

C. europaeum. Hardy. Almost evergreen. Has large rounded leaves, slightly marbled, and purple beneath. Bright crimson flowers, paling slightly toward the tip, on 5-6 in. stems, distinctly fragrant. Blooms July to September.

C. indicum. FLORISTS' CYCLAMEN. Tender to half-hardy. Many named forms of this species are available, with exceptionally large flowers in white, or shades of pink or rose, on 6-8 in. stems, from November to April. Leaves are green or sometimes variegated.

C. neapolitanum. Leaves are light green, handsomely marbled with silver and white. Flowers, pale to deep pink, with crimson center on 4-6 in. stems, from August to October. Var. *album* has white flowers.

C. repandum. Leaves are ivy-shaped, bright green and marbled silver-white. Flowers are deep pink at the tips, fading to pale carmine at the base on long stems, in April and May.

CULTURE: Cultural requirements similar to those of tuberous begonias. Best when planted in an east or northeast exposure, or in the filtered shade of high branching, deep rooted trees or tall shrubs. A rich, porous soil with plenty of leaf mold is ideal. Hardy cyclamen need a small amount of lime, while the florists' type prefers a soil slightly on the acid side. Plant cyclamen so upper half of corm or tuber protrudes above the soil level. If set too low, water is apt to settle in the crown and cause rot. Plant directly in the ground or in pots plunged rim-deep into the soil. In pots where root systems are confined, more flowers and less foliage will be produced. Can be grown from seed, generally flowering in 2 years. Also available as small plants in flats, or in 3-in. or 4-in. pots.

Cyclamen should be kept slightly on the dry side during dormancy from late June to August or September. Keep moist once growth resumes. Occasional overhead spraying is beneficial.

Although relatively pest free, are occasionally infested with cyclamen mite or thrip. Mites will crinkle and distort the foliage. Thrips cause streaks in the flowers. Control mites by spraying with aramite or a similar miticide. Control thrips with DDT sprays.

USE: Effective massed in borders or planted under tall rhododendrons, azaleas, tree ferns, Japanese maple. Combine with smaller ferns, hellebores, forget-me-nots, London pride, and pink, blue, or white primroses.

DIERAMA. FAIRY WAND. Corm. Half-hardy. Graceful plants to 4 ft., with long, slender, grass-like 2-ft. leaves. Bell-shaped flowers in nodding spikes at the ends of tall, arching stems. Blooms in spring and summer.

D. pendula. Clear, lavender-pink 1-in. bells in March or April.

D. pulcherrima. Has stiffer leaves and stems than *D. pendula*. Bright purple or almost white 1½-in. flowers in May and June.

CULTURE: Plant in full sun to form permanent clumps. Grow from divisions or obtain container-grown plants.

USE: Naturalize in clumps beside pools or in moist soil.

ERANTHIS HYEMALIS. WINTER ACONITE. Tuber. Hardy, grown in severe-winter areas, rarely successful in warmer sections. Appealing member of the buttercup family, its single yellow buttercup-like blooms, sitting on a ruff of bright green leaves above an otherwise leafless 3-in. stem. CULTURE: Flowering in earliest spring, as soon as frost is off the ground in cold climates, it enjoys coolness and moisture, and light shade under trees. Plant as soon as available, in July or August, setting tubers 3 in. deep and 4 in. apart. Grow best in a loose, leafy soil, although they accept less favorable soils. Do not disturb often. To replant, lift sections of clumps rather than divide singly. Lifting and replanting while in bloom is sometimes recommended. USE: Happiest and appears most at home naturalized in woodland-like plantings with other small bulbs, such as *Scilla sibirica* and snowdrop (galanthus).

ERYTHRONIUM. DOG-TOOTH VIOLET. Bulb. Hardy, but does best in cool climates. Spring-blooming, woodsy plant, largely native to Oregon, Washington, and California. Two basal leaves, sometimes mottled; slender stems carry small nodding white or pastel-colored flowers in February to April.

E. californicum. FAWN LILY. Grows to 1 ft. Leaves richly mottled with brown; creamy-white 1¼-in. flowers. Var. *bicolor* has fragrant white and chrome-yellow flowers.

E. grandiflorum. Grows to 2 ft. Leaves are not mottled; 2-in. flowers, bright buttercup-yellow.

E. hendersonii. Grows to 1 ft. Brown-mottled leaves; light purple, 1¼-in. flowers, maroon-centered, with strongly recurved segments.

E. revolutum. DOG-TOOTH VIOLET. Grows to 1 ft. Green leaves mottled with white; lavender-purple or white flowers in clusters of 1-4 to a stem. Var. *johnsonii* has leaves mottled with dark brown and rose-colored flowers.

E. tuolumnense. Grows to 1 ft. Has glossy, yellow-green, unmottled leaves and deep golden-yellow 1¼-in. flowers.

CULTURE: Likes cool shade, and rich, thoroughly drained, moist, fibrous soil. Plant bulbs ¾ in. deep, September to December. Best left undisturbed. A top mulch of rotted leaves, peat, spent tanbark, or coarse compost is advisable.

USE: Since erythroniums like shade, they can be grown among shrubs. Plant in colonies with bulbs spaced an inch and a half apart. Combine with native ferns, wild ginger, oxalis, trillium, and native fritillarias.

FREESIA. Bulb-like corm. Tender, hardy outdoors only where the ground does not freeze. Slender, stiff, wiry stems, 12 to 18 in. high; broad, grass-like leaves; tubular, fragrant flowers in early spring.

F. hybrida. In this horticultural group are found many hybrids and variants called colored freesias which have large flowers of rose, lavender, mauve, purple, yellow, and orange. Sweetly fragrant, although not as strongly so as the old-fashioned white.

F. refracta alba. The familiar white and exceedingly fragrant freesia, with smaller flowers than the colored hybrids. Grows to 12 in., multiplying rapidly when well established.

CULTURE: Plant bulbs from August to November—the earlier the better—in sun, in light, well-drained soil. Set bulbs 2 in. deep with points up. Divide when clumps get crowded. Easily grown from seed sown in flats in July or August, producing flowers the following spring.

USE: Plant freesias in beds where you can let them increase without concern for their untidy post-blooming period. Grow a large number especially for cutting. Plant in pots, boxes, or tubs for the terrace.

FRITILLARIA. Bulb. Hardy. Simple stemmed plants, with alternate or whorled leaves. Flowers bell-like, nodding, often unusually colored and mottled. Although several species are native in the West, not all are readily available.

F. imperialis. CROWN IMPERIAL. Old-fashioned, but now little grown. Thick, leafy stems, with strong-smelling foliage, grow to 2-3 ft. Red, orange, or yellow 2-in. bells are carried on curved stalks in clusters under a crown of leaves.

F. meleagris. CHECKERED LILY. GUINEA-HEN FLOWER. Grows to 12 in., with 1-3 nodding 3-in. bells that are checkered and veined with purple and maroon. Var. *alba* has white flowers.

CULTURE: Partial shade, deep, rich, well-drained soil. Plant bulbs 4-5 in. deep in September, for April to May bloom.

USE: Naturalizing with shade-loving natives such as erythronium, ginger, and trillium. Plant in masses because they do not bloom every year and are likely to rest after flowering, during which time they produce only a single large leaf that lies flat on the ground.

GALANTHUS. SNOWDROP. Bulb. Hardy. Best in cold climates; dies out after a year or two in mild climates. Early spring-blooming plants with 2 or 3 basal leaves and solitary white flowers, the segments green-tipped.

G. elwesii. GIANT SNOWDROP. Grows to 1 ft. or more, with gray-green 8-in. leaves to ¾ in. wide; flowers 1¼ in. long.

G. nivalis. COMMON SNOWDROP. Differs from giant snowdrop in its narrow ¼-in. wide leaves and slightly smaller flowers. Double and larger flowered forms are available.

CULTURE: Prefers cool moist locations. Cover bulbs to 1 in. Otherwise culture similar to daffodils. Leucojum (snowflake), which is taller, but has similar flowers, is often grown in preference to snowdrop in mild climates.

USE: Plant in naturalized drifts around deciduous trees, or with other low growing bulbs such as muscari, *Scilla sibirica*, and crocus.

GALTONIA CANDICANS. SUMMER HYACINTH. Bulb. Tender. Luxuriant foliage of strap-like leaves to 2½ ft., resembling amaryllis. In midsummer, 4-ft. stems carry spikes of fragrant white 1½-in. bells. CULTURE: Plant bulbs 4-5 in. deep, in full sun and a rich, light soil. Bulbs planted in February and March will bloom in July. In mild climates they make a large clump which may be left undisturbed for several years. In the north, plants should be lifted and stored in peat moss; or mulch them heavily to prevent freezing. USE: A group of summer hyacinths is most effective against a green background of shrubbery or a hedge. Also good for pots, tubs, mixed borders, and cutting.

GLADIOLUS. Corm. Tender to half-hardy. Grows to 18-24 in. Sword-shaped leaves; flowers tubular and flaring, sometimes ruffled, carried in simple or branching spikes. Blooms, depending on species and time of planting, from spring until fall.

G. colvillei. SWEET GLADIOLUS. BABY GLADIOLUS. Tender in cold-winter sections. Grows to 18 in.; flowers red, peach pink, and white, perfect miniatures of the larger gladiolus. Extremely useful for cutting.

CULTURE: Plant corms 4 in. deep in October or early November in mild-winter areas. Growth starts soon after planting, flowers appear in March or early April. In cold climates, plant in spring for early summer bloom.

G. hortulanus. GARDEN GLADIOLUS. Best known and most widely planted species, growing 3-4 ft. high. Heavy tapering spikes bear large flowers in a remarkable color range from softest pink to deepest red, from delicate lavender to deepest purple, and from light cream to glowing orange.

CULTURE: Plant at 15-day intervals from early spring to July 1 for bloom from June 1 to frost. Average size corms produce bloom in 65-100 days, smaller corms take longer. Should have full sun, away from surface rooting plants. For maximum insurance against diseases and pests, treat corms with a commercial gladiolus dust or liquid disinfectant before setting out. Planting depth varies according to type of soil and size of corms. Set corms deeper in sandy soil than in heavy soil. Deep planting produces the best blooms and provides a firm support for the heavy stalks. Recommended planting depths in average garden soil—neither very light nor very heavy—are as follows: Jumbo corms, 6 in. deep; No. 1, 2, 3, 4 sizes, 4 in. deep; cormels (small corms produced around the bottom of the large corm), ½ in. deep. If soil is poor, work in balanced commercial fertilizer, bone meal, or fish meal before planting, at the rate of 4 pounds to 100 square feet. Do not place fertilizer in direct contact with corms. Side-dress with same fertilizer when the second leaf appears on the stalk. Water thoroughly once a week. For control of thrips and mites, spray regularly after plants are 3 in. high with a contact spray containing DDT or TEPP, or a 10% DDT dust. If lower leaves show yellow streaks, indicating fusarium wilt, pull out and burn infected plants immediately. Spray the rest of the planting with a carbamate fungicide such as zineb. Botrytis, indicated by moldy brownish-gray spots on leaf, stem, or flowers, can be controlled by destruction of infected plants, and spraying with ferbam (a type of zinc carbamate).

For cut flowers, cut stalks when lower buds begin to open. If kept in water, flowers will continue to open for many days. In cutting, let at least 4 leaves remain on the plant to supply nutrients for the maturing corm.

Dig the corms when the foliage begins to yellow, but before the tops die back completely. After digging, cut tops off just above the top of the corm, and dry in the sun. When the old corm at the base of the new corm comes off easily, the new corm is ready for storing. Best way to store is in paper or string-mesh bags hung in a cool dry place. Add to each sack about ½ teaspoon of commercial bulb disinfectant or 5% DDT dust. Gladiolus requires dormancy of at least 1½ months at 40° or 2 months at 50°.

G. murielae. *(Acidanthera murielæ).* ACIDANTHERA. ABYSSINIAN SWORD LILY. Grows to 2½ ft. Foliage and flowers reminiscent both of gladiolus and ixia. Tubular 5-in. blooms are creamy-white with chocolate blotch and extremely fragrant. Culture same as for garden gladiolus.

G. primulinus. Grows to 2-4 ft. Graceful spikes carry 3-5 primrose-yellow, hooded flowers. Hybrids in colors ranging through cream, apricot, salmon, orange.

G. tristis concolor. Tender. Grows to 2 ft. Pale greenish-yellow flowers with spicy fragrance. Culture same as for *G. colvillei*.

USE: All forms of gladiolus are superb cut flowers. Smaller types are useful in lighter, dainty arrangements, the large garden gladiolus for spectacular ones. The smaller species of gladiolus are easier to use in the garden where they are most effective in groups behind solid rounded plants such as *Felicia amelloides*, or soft, fairly high edgings such as *Nepeta mussinii* or chiffon daisies.

GLORIOSA. GLORY LILY. Tuber. Greenhouse plants except in Southern California. Interesting members of the lily family that actually climb to 10 ft. on wires or trellis by means of tendrils formed at the tips of the leaves. Red or yellow lily-like flowers with reflexed or spreading segments. Bloom in July and August.

G. rothschildiana. Bears long-stalked 3-in. crimson flowers that are yellow and whitish at the base, the segments strongly reflexed and sometimes slightly wavy-margined.

G. superba. Similar to *G. rothschildiana*, but the flowers are yellow changing to red, the segments spreading or reflexed, much crisped as if twisted.

CULTURE: Plant the 4-6 in. tubers horizontally in sandy soil enriched with humus, in full sun. In the greenhouse pot up in February. Outdoors plant in ground or tubs in March. When they are up, keep them growing rapidly by feeding liquid fertilizer at 3-week intervals. Withhold water in the fall. When tops die, lift tubers and store like dahlias.

GLOXINIA. See SINNINGIA SPECIOSA

HAEMANTHUS KATHERINAE. BLOOD LILY. Bulb. Tender. Rare, showy South African plant, usually grown in pots. Nearly evergreen, to 3 ft., with broad tapering light green leaves, drooping gracefully in umbrella fashion on a short stem. Spectacular bright red flowers, in a rounded cluster 9 in. across on a separate leafless stem, open successively in summer over 2-4 weeks. CULTURE: Plant the large bulbs singly in January or February in an 8-10 in. pot, in equal parts of peat or leaf mold and loam, with enough coarse sand to make a gritty, porous mixture. Cover the lower half of the bulb with the mixture, potting firmly. For best growth haemanthus requires a night temperature of 50 to 55°. Water moderately until plants are in active growth, then increase the amount. On warm sunny days, syringe overhead and provide shade, especially during flowering. Older plants respond to feeding with liquid manure. Start withholding water when plant begins to go dormant. Yearly re-potting is not advisable, since haemanthus resents root disturbance. Increase by means of offsets taken from mother plant in early spring. USE: Handsome summer pot plant for terraces and patios.

HEMEROCALLIS. DAY LILY. Fleshy, somewhat tuberous roots; often classed as a perennial. Hardy. Deciduous and evergreen species. Large clumps of long sword-shaped leaves. Wide-open lily-like flowers are yellow, bronze, orange, pink, rose, red, and bicolored, sometimes scented, in clusters at the ends of branching stems. New varieties compete with iris in extensive range of colors and combinations of colors.

H. aurantiaca. Strong-growing, evergreen, to 3 ft. Flowers rich orange-copper, in July. Var. *major* has larger flowers to 6 in. across, and without coppery tinge.

H. flava. LEMON LILY. Grows to 3 ft. Leaves to 2 ft. Fragrant 4 in. yellow flowers in June.

H. fulva. TAWNY DAY LILY. Grows to 6 ft. Burnt orange 5 in. flowers, the segments with wavy margins. Bloom in late summer. Var. *Kwanso* has double golden-bronze flowers.

H. thunbergii. Much like *H. flava*, but bears pale yellow flowers a month later.

CULTURE: Any good garden soil. Will grow in sun or part shade, with little or lots of water, although for luxuriant growth in warm climates abundant moisture and semi-shade are necessary.

USE: Excellent standby in summer borders, where it combines with delphiniums, Michaelmas daisies, Shasta daisies, Oriental poppies. Effective near pools, streams.

HIPPEASTRUM. AMARYLLIS. Bulb. Half-hardy. Grows to 1-2 ft. Usually listed in catalogs as amaryllis.

H. advenum. OXBLOOD LILY. Grows to 1 ft. Flowers, different from the hybrid hippeastrums, are dark red, 2 in. long, 3-4 on a stem, appear in spring ahead of the narrow blue-green leaves.

CULTURE: Plant 6 in. deep in late August or early September in full sun. Not adapted to pot culture.

USE: In sunny borders with *Sternbergia lutea,* which blooms at the same time.

H. hybridum. GIANT AMARYLLIS. Name applied to many horticultural forms. Practically evergreen, broad strap-shaped leaves. Sturdy 2-ft. stems carry 2-4 large lily-like flowers in spectacular shades of orange and red, some white with stripes and blotches, also pure white.

CULTURE: Usually grown in pots, and if desired in the garden, shifted outside in summer. Pot bulbs in November-December. Set a 3-in. bulb in a 7-in. pot, larger bulbs in correspondingly larger pots. For a potting mixture, use a rich, sandy loam, with bone meal added. Never use manure. Set the bulb with 2/3's above the surface and water to settle. Keep slightly moist until growth starts, then increase watering. Keep potted bulbs in a cool, light spot, at a temperature below 50°, until roots form. Never place in a warm, sunny place during rooting period, since tops will start growing prematurely and plants will fail to flower, flower poorly, or will not flower at all. After a good root system has formed, gradually give plants more warmth, but never keep at a temperature higher than 50°.

After flowering, keep the bulb in active growth as long as possible to build up the bulb which has shrunk during the bloom period, and to encourage formation of offsets. A good way to keep hybrid amaryllis through the summer is to plunge the pots in the garden, or shift from the pot to the ground without breaking the ball.

USE: Usually grown in pots, although in warm winter climates, can be grown in the garden. When planting outdoors, cover with only 1-2 in. of soil, since they will not bloom if planted too deep.

HYACINTHUS ORIENTALIS. COMMON HYACINTH.
Bulb. Hardy. Grows to 8-18 in., with bright green, lance-shaped, fleshy, basal leaves. Rather large, fragrant, bell-shaped, flowers are borne in dense terminal spikes on stout, succulent stems. Forms are available with single or double flowers in colors ranging from white to light and dark pink, various blues and purples, and a so-called yellow, that is actually more cream than yellow. Blooms mainly in March and April, forced bulbs in pots in January. Var. *albulus*, ROMAN HYACINTH, is lower, growing to 6-8 in., with slender, narrow leaves and loose spikes of white, bluish to light blue flowers in February. CULTURE: Sun loving, but tolerates moderate shade. Plant September and October in light, enriched soil. Bone meal is satisfactory and can be added close to planting time. If soil is heavy put a handful of coarse sand at base of each bulb. Plant 5-6 in. deep and 5-6 in. apart. In sections where gophers are a problem, plant in wire baskets. To grow in pots, use light, rich soil mixture, provide good drainage; one bulb to each deep 5 in. pot. Tip of bulb should protrude above the soil in pot. Sink pots in coldframe or peat and cover with 3 in. peat until roots begin to show through drainage hole; then bring into light. If buds appear while stems are still short, put a cardboard collar around plant to draw the stems up. Bring onto terrace or in house just before buds open. USE: Usually planted in solid colors in formal beds, but can be used in drifts or informal groups in flower border. Effective in bold mass in front of shrubbery.

HYMENOCALLIS CALATHINA. BASKET FLOWER,
SPIDER LILY, SEA DAFFODIL. Bulb. Hardy except at high altitudes. Long basal, strap-shaped leaves. White fragrant flowers resemble daffodils except for the spidery collar around the bloom, are borne in clusters at the tops of 2-ft. naked stems. Blooms in June and July. CULTURE: Sun. Prefers sandy soil, lots of water. Plant bulbs in late May and be sure to lift before frosts in autumn. USE: One of the finest and most unusual summer blooming bulbs for the border.

IXIA. AFRICAN CORN LILY. Corm. Half-hardy. Grows to 12-18 in., with grass-like leaves. Flowers are cup-shaped, in terminal spikes. Colors come in combinations such as orange and amber, with a deep brown center, yellow with purple center, white with carmine blotch, brilliant crimson, light blue with a maroon eye, or a mixed strain with colors from white to deep pink. Blooms from late April to late May or early June. CULTURE: Full sun; light, perfectly drained soil. Plant corms 2 in. deep in protected spots. After blooming, should remain in ground until July, then lift and store in cold climates. Can remain in ground in mild sections, often volunteering from self-sown seed. USE: Excellent cut flowers. Because of mixed colors, not as useful in borders.

LACHENALIA PENDULA. CAPE COWSLIP, AFRICAN
HYACINTH. Bulb. Tender. Grows to 1 ft. or more, with 2 basal, 2 in. wide leaves. Pendulous 1½ in. flowers, in spikes, the outer segments yellow and red above, the inner segments red, purple-tipped. Blooms in January and February. Var. *superba* is an improved horticultural form. CULTURE: Full sun. Plant in pots of rich loam and keep in coldframe until last of November. In mild climates may be started in flats or in open ground, and later shifted to pots when in full bloom. Be sure not to let it dry out, since flowers will be inferior. USE: Rock gardens, pots.

LEUCOCORYNE IXIOIDES. GLORY OF THE SUN. Bulb.
Half-hardy. Grows to 1 ft. Distinctive Chilean native, with very narrow grass-like leaves. Extremely fragrant pale blue flowers, with white throats, are borne in clusters on wiry stems. CULTURE: Plant bulbs 3 in. deep and 5 in. apart in late September or early October. Give full sun and a well-drained, gritty soil and provide even moisture until after bloom, when bulbs should be dried off. Because bulbs tend to work downward into the soil, some prefer planting in pots or place wire mesh under the planting bed. Raised beds ideal. USE: Splendid cut flowers, often lasting about a week. Combine with other bulbs requiring same conditions, such as babiana, ixia, brodiæa, and daffodils.

LEUCOJUM. SNOWFLAKE. Bulb. Hardy. Grows to 12-18
in., with strap-shaped basal leaves. Nodding, bell-shaped white flowers, tipped with green.

L. aestivum. SUMMER SNOWFLAKE. Leaves to 18 in., flower stems sometimes higher, with 3-5 dainty drooping bells of white tipped with green.

L. vernum. SPRING SNOWFLAKE. Lower growing (to 12 in.). Most commonly planted. Flowers like large snowdrops (galanthus).

CULTURE: Plant bulbs 4 in. deep in sun or partial shade. Will grow in almost any soil, but does best in one that is rich, well drained, and light. Can be left undisturbed for several years. Equals the daffodil for ease of culture and long life.

USE: Naturalize in drifts under deciduous trees with scillas and daffodils.

LYCORIS. SPIDER LILY. Bulb. Hardy outdoors if given
winter protection. Similar to nerine, native of China and Japan. Deciduous plant to 2 ft., with narrow basal leaves which disappear before the red or yellow flowers come out in late summer or early fall. Long stamens and narrow petals produce thread-like appearance.

L. aurea. Bright yellow 3-in. flowers on 2-ft. stems in late August. Somewhat tender; protect from heavy frosts.

L. radiata. Bright rosy-red flowers with a gold sheen. Var. *alba* has white flowers. Hardy and permanent; does best in half-shaded position. Can be left undisturbed for many years.

L. sanguinea. Flowers orange-crimson, 2 in. long, in loose clusters, bloom in summer, give best color in light shade.

L. squamigera. Large, fragrant, lilac-pink flowers in summer, on 2-ft. stems. Hardier than other lycoris, can be planted in colder (not hard winter) areas if bulbs are set 6 in. deep and winter-mulched.

CULTURE: Full sun, except where noted. Same treatment as nerine.

USE: Although adapted to outside borders in warm-winter climates, are most effective in pots.

MUSCARI. GRAPE HYACINTH. Bulb. Hardy. Narrow, more or less fleshy basal leaves. Small, unusually pendulous flowers, mostly blue, in dense spikes, top the stems. Blooms February to May.

M. armeniacum. Grows to 4-9 in., the leaves exceeding the flower stalk. Many ¼ in. deep violet, white tipped, fertile flowers, sterile flowers at the tip of the spike pale blue. Var. *Heavenly Blue* has gentian blue flowers.

M. botryoides. Taller growing to 12 in., the leaves equaling the flower stalk. About 12 small ⅛-in. flowers to a spike. Var. *album* has white flowers.

M. comosum. FRINGE HYACINTH. Flowers borne on brown spotted stalks to 12-18 in., in a loose, narrow cluster, the fertile blossoms greenish-brown, the sterile ones purple-blue.

The forms commonly cultivated are: Var. *monstrosum* FEATHER HYACINTH. All sterile flowers, converted into fringy tufts of narrow violet-blue segments. Var. *plumosum (M. plumosum)* PLUME HYACINTH. Similar to var. *monstrosum*, but flower plume is more branched and reddish-purple.

CULTURE: Best in sun, but endures light shade. Easy to grow in ordinary, well-fertilized garden loam. May be left in ground for some time before lifting and dividing.

USE: Most effective when planted in masses or groups, such as under flowering fruit trees, forsythia, or deciduous magnolias. Also used as edgings or in the rock garden. The feather or plume hyacinths are effective in clumps among or in front of spring blooming shrubs such as dwarf heather, correa, and pink diosma; interplant with blue or purple violas, pansies, alyssum Violet Queen, or *Primula malacoides* to hide untidy fading foliage.

NERINE. Bulb. Tender. Native of South Africa. Grows to 3 ft., with strap-shaped basal leaves. Delicate looking, spidery, wavy-petaled flowers in shades of pink, rose, red, salmon, scarlet, and orange. All flowers have a fascinating golden sheen. Blooms in fall.

N. bowdenii. Grows to 18 in. Carries clusters of 12 or more large pink flowers, with rose-colored stripe in the center of each segment. Blooms in October.

N. curvifolia fothergillii. Grows to 12-18 in. Iridescent red flowers. Blooms late summer before foliage appears.

N. filifolia. 10-12 in. Thread-like, evergreen foliage, dark pink flowers, with narrow crinkled petals in clusters of 6-18 on wiry stems.

N. sarniensis. GUERNSEY LILY. Crimson flowers with bright red stamens protruding to give a spidery effect.

CULTURE: Sun. Plant bulbs 3 in. deep in fall—outdoors in mild climates, in pots in cold areas. Plant 3 bulbs in a 5-in. pot. Prefers a rich, sandy loam, lots of water until after bloom. Withhold water during resting period from May to August.

USE: In borders or rock gardens for striking fall bloom, or in pots for color on patio or terrace.

NYMPHAEA. WATER LILY. Rootstocks, sometimes tuberous. Perennial aquatic plants, the floating leaves and flowers spreading 2-5 ft. or more. Long stems bear at the tips large, flat, roundish or heart-shaped bright green leaves, often reddish beneath. Medium to large showy flowers, often fragrant, in colors ranging from pure white to cream, pink, yellow, blue, rose and red. Blooms as early as April (in California) to late fall.

There are numerous species and hybrids, varying in degree of adaptability to different regions. One of the hardiest is *N. odorata*, with dull green leaves, usually reddish beneath; fragrant white flowers, 3-5 in. broad. Var. *rosea* has larger pink flowers. Var. *sulphurea* has leaves blotched with brown, and light yellow 4-5 in. flowers.

CULTURE: Blooms well only in sun, but will grow in slight shade. Plant small sections of rootstock in large pots or boxes made of rot-resistant wood in soil well enriched with rotted cow manure, and a little bone meal. Containers are then submerged in pool. There should be 12-18 in. of still water above container top; lilies do not grow well in running water. After 3-4 years take up and divide. In most parts of California it is unnecessary to remove plants during winter. In very cold regions, plants are removed to tanks or tubs under glass, or to separate, covered pool. May also be taken up in boxes and stored in cellar. Do not allow to dry out. Subject to aphis, leaf miner, leaf spot.

ORNITHOGALUM. Bulb. Half-hardy. Narrow or in some species, wider basal leaves; the flowers borne in spikes or rounded clusters at the ends of leafless stems in April and May.

O. arabicum. ARABIAN STAR OF BETHLEHEM. Grows to 2 ft., the leaves 2 ft. long and 1 in. broad. Fragrant 1-in. white, star-like flowers, with a prominent black pistil, in spikes.

CULTURE: Needs sun. Plant so they get at least half a day of sunshine, in any good garden soil. Bulbs are large and should be set 6 in. deep.

USE: Scores high among spring flowering bulbs for aromatic fragrance. Flowers long lasting in the garden or when cut.

O. thyrsoides. CHINKERINCHEE. Grows to 1½ ft., the strap-like leaves 1 ft. long and 2 in. wide. White or yellow ¾-in. flowers in dense clusters. Var. *album* has white flowers; var. *aureum*, golden-yellow flowers.

CULTURE: Sunny, well-drained soil. Plant 3-4 in. deep. Bulbs are hardy when dormant, but foliage has a tendency to freeze. Withhold water in late summer in colder sections to harden.

USE: Excellent cut flowers.

O. umbellatum. STAR OF BETHLEHEM. Grows to 6-12 in., the narrow leaves to 1 ft. long and 1/3 in. wide. White 1-in. flowers, the segments striped green on the back, are borne in rounded clusters.

CULTURE: Sun or shade; any soil, provided there is adequate drainage. Plant 3-4 in. deep. Increases rapidly and may become invasive. Fairly permanent.

USE: Best for naturalizing on banks, or in grass. Combines well with the vigorous-growing *Scilla hispanica (S. campanulata)*.

POLIANTHES TUBEROSA. TUBEROSE. Tuber. Tender. Sturdy plants with long, narrow, bright green, basal leaves. Flower stems to 2-3½ ft., bear narrow spikes of heavily fragrant, pure white, funnel-shaped flowers. Blossoms appear in late spring and continue intermittently through summer, and often into fall. CULTURE: Sun. Any ordinary, enriched garden loam. Requires plenty of heat and moisture. Not tolerant of alkaline water. Plant tubers 3 in. deep. After foliage has died down in the fall, lift the tubers and store in a rather warm, dry place. Can be grown in pots and forced for early bloom. Good tubers will show green or some sign of life at the top or growing point. Others should be discarded. USE: If you find exotic, heavy fragrance oppressive, don't put tubers too close to an outdoor sitting area. Many prefer to plant them in pots. In warm climates, combine in borders with ginger, caladium, coleus, other tropical plants.

RANUNCULUS ASIATICUS. PERSIAN RANUNCULUS, TURBAN RANUNCULUS. Tuber. Half-hardy. Erect leafy plants to 12-18 in. high with bright green, finely dissected leaves. Flowers are globular, 1-4 on long stalks, blooming profusely from February to April. Many improved forms, with very double or ruffled, large camellia-like blooms in cream, white and brilliant colors—red, yellow, orange, pink, rose. CULTURE: Sun-loving, or half-shade in warm climates. Plant October through January. Do not plant too early, as warm weather often causes tubers to rot in the ground. Soak tubers 2 or 3 hours before planting, and then set them about 1 in. deep in light, loamy soil, the claws pointed down. Cover young plants with wire, as the birds have a fondness for the new foliage. Water and feed as for annuals. Lift tubers in summer and store dry. Virus infection prevalent in tubers and may carry over, causing distorted growth the following spring. Best to start with new tubers each year. USE: Among annuals or perennials in the mixed border, but choose companions carefully, as colors are very strong. Try planting some in containers. Excellent cut flowers.

SCHIZOSTYLIS COCCINEA. KAFIR LILY. Rhizome. Tender. Related to gladiolus and iris. Grows to 2 ft., with iris-like leaves to 1½ ft. Tall spikes of deep crimson flowers to 2 in. across, the tube 1 in. or more. Blooms in October to December. Var. *Mrs. Hegarty*, a more attractive form, has clear pink flowers in late October and early November. CULTURE: Likes sun, part shade in hot areas. Indifferent to soil; requires plenty of moisture. Plant in spring or fall in sheltered locations. USE: Extremely effective, long-lasting flowers.

SCILLA. SQUILL. Bulb. Hardy. Plants with narrow basal leaves, and white, lilac, blue, pink or rose flowers in terminal spikes.

S. amoena. STAR HYACINTH. Grows to 6 in. Wheel-shaped, ¾-in. flowers are blue to white, 4-6 in a cluster. Blooms in spring.

S. autumnalis. AUTUMN SQUILL. Grows to 6 in. Rose-colored flowers appear July to September.

S. hispanica. *(S. campanulata).* SPANISH BLUEBELL. Large, vigorous plant to 20 in. Bell-like, nodding 1-in. flowers, 12 or more in a spike, blooming in May and June. It can be had in named varieties in blue, white, rose, and pink, although the blues and whites are more desirable.

S. peruviana. PERUVIAN SCILLA. Grows to 1 ft. Star-shaped ½-in. bluish-purple or reddish-purple flowers, 50 or more in dense, short clusters. Blooms in early spring. Var. *alba* has white flowers.

S. sibirica. Grows to 6 in. Deep blue, nodding, ½-in. flowers, 3 or more in a spike, appearing in early spring. Best in cold-winter areas.

CULTURE: Sun or shade. Light, moderately fertilized loam and plenty of moisture during the growing season. Plant bulbs in October or November, 2-4 in. deep. Need not disturb for years.

USE: Scillas are at their best in informal drifts among shrubs or under deciduous, particularly flowering, trees. Delightful interplanted with pink and white English daisies, primroses and forget-me-nots. Can be forced in pots. Good cut flowers.

SINNINGIA SPECIOSA. *(Gloxinia speciosa).* GLOXINIA. Tuber. Tender. Grows to 6 in. Fuzzy, velvety, oblong leaves. Exotic, large, bell-shaped flowers, heavily ruffled along the edges, in gorgeous blues, purples, pinks, red, and pure white—some with dark spots, others with blotches of solid colors. Older plants may yield 100 blooms in one season. CULTURE: Tropical plants requiring greenhouse conditions—lots of light, but no direct sun. Need humidity, night temperatures not under 50°, with 63° to 65° considered ideal. Keep out of drafts and dry air. When in bloom in late spring or early summer, can be moved onto terrace. Start from seed in the same way as tuberous begonias. Seedlings come into bloom at irregular intervals, thus spreading bloom over many months. Tubers—available between December and March—can be potted 1 in. deep in pots just large enough to accommodate them. Use same potting mixture as recommended for tuberous begonias. After potting, water sparingly until the first leaves appear, increasing amounts after a strong root system has formed. Water around base of plant or from below, since water on leaves causes them to rot. Shift into larger pots when roots begin to fill their present pot. For rapid growth and large flowers, feed regularly throughout the growing and flowering period with fish emulsion at the rate of 1 tablespoon to 1 quart of water. Never apply fertilizer when plants are dry—water the plants first, then fertilize a few hours later. After flowering, gradually withhold water until the plants are completely dormant. Store bulbs in a cool, dark place at a temperature of about 50°. Keep tubers just moist enough to prevent them from shriveling. In January or February, when the plants show signs of starting into active growth, shake off the soil and repot the tubers. Gloxinias can also be propagated from leaf cuttings and offsets. For leaf cuttings, use mature leaves with a small portion of the leaf stalk attached. Insert in sand, preferably with bottom heat, and keep on the slightly dry side. After the tuber forms on the bottom of the cutting, pot it up as you would a seedling. To increase gloxinias by offsets, remove the little shoots from the side of the plant when they have 4 leaves. Offsets usually bloom earlier than leaf cuttings. USE: In pots; outdoors in mild climates.

SPARAXIS TRICOLOR. WAND FLOWER. Corm. Half-hardy. Colorful plant to 12 in., with sword-like leaves. Funnel-shaped 1-in. flowers, like small gladiolus, are carried in spikes. Colors are red with a dark center, white with a yellow center, pure yellow, and mixtures, including flowers in purple and yellow, white and purple with dark blotch. Blooms in April and May. Strains have been developed which offer larger flowers, and brighter colors, in orange, red, or yellow, with black and gold markings. CULTURE: Full sun. Thrives in poor soil, with little water. Plant in fall in mild climate; in spring in colder areas. Set corms 2 in. deep. Multiply rapidly from main bulbs and underground stems. Blooms in 18 months from seed. USE: Best as cut flowers. Separate colors effective in borders and rock gardens, mixtures less so. Use as a border, an edging. Good cut flowers.

STERNBERGIA LUTEA. Bulb. Hardy. Looks like a long-stemmed crocus. Narrow basal leaves are fresh green all winter. Bright yellow 1½-in. flowers are borne singly or in pairs on short stems in August and September. CULTURE: Sun. Will take heavy soil, but needs good drainage. Plant bulbs in midsummer, 6 in. deep. Increases rapidly. USE: In borders, where it combines effectively with blue marguerite (*Felicia amelloides*), *Aster frikartii*, or *Limonium latifolium*.

TIGRIDIA PAVONIA. TIGER FLOWER. Bulb. Tender. Grows to 1-2½ ft., with narrow grass-like leaves. Showy, triangular flowers to 6 in. across are cup-shaped, with 3 large segments in solid color and 3 small ones that are brilliantly blotched or spotted. Forms are available in bright shades of red, rose, yellow, or orange, also a white form with red markings. Blooms in July and August. Flowers last only one day, but new ones appear daily for weeks. CULTURE: Full sun in cool areas, light shade where it is hot—sun will fade the flowers. Requires moist soil enriched with humus. Plant bulbs 4 in. deep and 4-6 in. apart. Lift them in the fall or leave them in the ground. USE: Most effective when grown in clumps, in front of small evergreen shrubs such as boxwood or *Myrtus communis compacta*. Interplant with spring-blooming iris; the tigridias will take over when the iris fade. Use in the flower border in front of white phlox or Shasta daisies.

TRILLIUM. WAKE ROBIN. Bulb-like. Hardy. Solitary stalks to 1½ ft. bear 3 broad ovate leaves at the top. Flowers are solitary or clustered in the leaf axils. Bloom in early spring.

T. chloropetalum. (*T. sessile chloropetalum, T. sessile californicum*). Western native, growing to 1½ ft. Leaves to 6 in. Deep maroon, greenish-yellow, or white, 1½-3½ in. erect flowers are nestled in the leaves.

T. grandiflorum. Eastern native. Stout stems 8-18 in., the leaves 2½-6 in. Flowers on stalks, with spreading segments, have green sepals, white petals fading to rose-pink. There also are double flowered forms.

T. ovatum. Western native similar to *T. grandiflorum*, but the sepals and petals are narrower.

CULTURE: Shade or partial shade. Require moist soil, with leaf mold incorporated. Roots transplanted easily after flowering.

USE: Best in woodsy location in filtered shade under high branching trees. Effective with ferns, lilies and azaleas, near stream or pool.

TRITONIA. (*Montbretia*). Corm. Hardy. Resembles gladiolus in flower and habit. Grows to 1 ft., with narrow leaves, mostly near the base of the stem. Short tubular, flared flowers are borne on simple or branched spikes. Newer hybrids bear flowers to 4 in. across in colors of orange, apricot, chrome yellow and scarlet. Long period of bloom, July to September. *T. crocata*, often called the flame freesia (although it isn't a freesia), has 2 in. orange-red flowers, makes a stunning show in rock gardens. CULTURE: Full sun. Light, well-drained soil with plenty of humus, peat and well-rotted manure added. Set bulbs 4-6 in. deep and 6 in. apart. In most sections of the Northwest, lift and store corms in winter. USE: Ideal in foreground of shrubbery bed, where they will bring a splash of summer color into the green background. Excellent cut flowers.

VALLOTA SPECIOSA. SCARBOROUGH LILY. Bulb. Tender, but will take light frost. Leaves to 2 ft. long and 1 in. wide, appearing with the flowers. Orange-vermilion, 3 in. broad, funnel-shaped flowers in clusters at the top of 3-ft. stems. Blooms in summer and fall. CULTURE: Shade. Needs water and perfect drainage all year. Plant first in small pot with light soil. Transplant when roots crowd pot, using rich mixture of equal parts peat, cow manure and turfy loam; add a little sand and charcoal. Can remain in same pot 3-4 years. Manure or commercial fertilizer beneficial, but avoid direct contact with bulb. Do not let dormant bulb dry out completely in winter. USE: Best in pots. One of the few bulbs that has been grown successfully under eucalyptus and acacia trees.

WATSONIA. Bulb. Half-hardy. Somewhat similar to gladiolus; the stems bearing sword-like leaves. White, rose, or red, long tubular, flared flowers in terminal or branched spikes. Blooms from April to September, according to locality. CULTURE: Same as for gladiolus. USE: For mixed borders, cutting.

ZANTEDESCHIA. CALLA. Rhizome. Half-hardy. Long stalked, broad arrow-shaped or heart-shaped dark green leaves, sometimes variegated, usually in basal clumps. Inconspicuous flowers are borne on a central spike, surrounded by a large, showy bract.

Z. aethiopica. COMMON CALLA. Grows to 3 ft., the arrow-shaped leaves to 1½ ft. long and 10 in. wide. White flower bract to 10 in. long. Blooms almost continuously in mild climates. Var. *minor* is lower, growing to 1½ ft., the flower bract to 4 in. long.

CULTURE: Shade or full sun along the coast. Must have moist soil well enriched with manure. Plant rhizomes at least 6 in. deep to insure against freezing.

USE: Goes well in front of broad-leafed evergreens, which set off its strong pattern. Makes handsome large-container plant. Interesting in mass planting under trees. Excellent cut flower.

Z. elliottiana. GOLDEN CALLA. Grows to 18-24 in. Bright green, white-spotted, heart-shaped leaves, to 10 in. long and 6 in. wide. Flower bract, rich yellow, to 6 in. long. Blooms in June or July.

CULTURE: Sun along coast, part shade in warm inland areas. Any well-drained soil. Plant rhizomes 2 in. deep, 12 in. apart.

USE: Low growing, more friendly and warmer in color than the common white calla, better adapted to pots. In the garden try it with blue violas, primroses, or forget-me-nots in the foreground.

Z. rehmanii. RED CALLA, PINK CALLA. Dwarf to 12-18 in., with narrow 1-ft. leaves to 1¼ in. wide, bright green with white spots. Flower bracts to 5 in. long, rose or red or sometimes nearly white with a red margin. Blooms in May.

CULTURE: Same as the yellow calla, but should be planted only 6 in. apart.

USE: Narrow border or edging plants.

ZEPHYRANTHES. ZEPHYR LILY. Bulb. Half-hardy. Small plant with grass-like basal leaves. Showy, funnel-shaped, white, yellow, pink or rose-pink flowers, to 4 in. across, are solitary at the top of hollow stalks. Blooms in summer and fall.

Z. ajax. Horticultural hybrid with straw yellow flowers on 8-in. stems.

Z. candida. Pure white, sometimes tinged with rose, on 1-ft. stems. Vigorous, forms large clumps.

Z. grandiflora. Flowers, rose or pink, to 4 in. across.

Z. pulchella. Buttercup yellow flowers, 1 in. across.

CULTURE: Plant in sun. In native habitats, blooms after rains, terminating a dry period. In areas of heavy frost, lift and store bulbs in winter.

USE: Especially suited to pot planting.

Bulbs
TUBEROUS BEGONIAS

The tuberous begonia has always been a spectacular flower, but improvements from year to year have built it up into the "unbelievable" class. The color range of the plant is wide—yellow, orange, pink, salmon, apricot shades, about every conceivable shade of red, and white.

The double-camellia type is the largest. Flowers, from 5 to 8 inches in diameter, resemble large camellias and roses.

DOUBLE　　DOUBLE-PICOTEE　　RUFFLED

The double-camellia picotee types were developed by intercrossing the large camellia type with the small marmota type. Camellia-formed flowers are sometimes smaller, with two-toned combinations of color with contrasting edges.

The fimbriata type, often called the carnation type, is a popular bedding and pot plant. Flowers resemble large carnations and the plant is more compact than other types. Cut flowers are used in corsages.

The fimbriata plena type is double frilled; also called carnation type. This group has been greatly improved in recent years with some flowers now reaching the size of the camellia type, but with a more refined form. It is strong, makes a bushy growth, and is especially desirable for bedding and pot plants.

ROSE　　NEW TYPE　　CRESTED

Flowers of the ruffled-camellia type are as large as the regular camellia variety. This type was derived from crossing the camellia-flowered with the fimbriata type.

Other types available as seedlings include: double rosebud, single-crested, and single-frilled.

Where to plant

Tuberous begonias are show-offs. Most flowers, by comparison, seem pale and insignificant. That's why it's a good idea to use tuberous begonias all by themselves, not in mixed plantings. If you do combine them with other flowers, it's best to let the begonias dominate and simply use other plants as foils, or backgrounds.

Here are some planting suggestions and notes on begonia culture:

Begonias in shrubbery borders. Solid plantings of begonias look rich and lush against a background of evergreen shrubs such as boxwood, myrtle, camellia, euonymus, viburnum, holly, or yew.

Begonia carpets under trees. This is one of the popular ways to use tuberous begonias. Often it's a good way, too, but the trees must be high branching, must let in enough light for good flower production, and must not have invasive roots. Remember, begonias do not thrive in complete shade. Neither are they at their best under trees that drop a constant litter of leaves or twigs. Leaves of some trees, madrone and live oak, for instance, are so thick and water-repellent that they actually may cause a drought condition unless removed frequently. Invasive roots also rule out under-tree planting under some trees. However, you can overcome the problem of root competition by growing begonias in pots and sinking them in the ground.

Begonias with other flowers. Despite their highly individual character, tuberous begonias accept with grace such soft, billowy edgings as the violet-blue dwarf campanula *(C. portenschlagiana)* and starry-flowered *C. elatines garganica* and *C. porscharskyana.*

Violas make useful edgings in cooler sections where they continue to bloom during the summer months. The blue or white violas are most effective; yellows are a little strong; the apricot variety is attractive with begonias in the same tones.

Begonias with ferns. This is a natural association. Begonias and many ferns enjoy the same warm, humid conditions. Deer, lady, maidenhair and Brauns holly ferns are low to medium height types that combine beautifully with begonias. Woodwardia and sword ferns make effective, rich green backgrounds.

Begonias in wooden boxes. Many growers prefer wooden boxes to any other type of container for begonias. They find that wood holds the moisture better than clay pots. There is also a pleasing compatibility between the container and the dark, rich, leaf mold used as a growing medium. Many variations are possible with cedar and redwood boxes.

Begonias in raised beds. Begonias thrive in raised beds where soil has been specially prepared and

182 TUBEROUS BEGONIAS

drainage is excellent. They are particularly effective in redwood and brick-faced beds—the red in their leaves and stems picks up the color of the brick and wood.

All-important

Remember that begonias are one-way facing plants. If you are planting seedlings, face the plant the way the leaves are pointing. If you plant tubers directly where they'll bloom, you will have to shift the wrong-facing plants after the leaves have formed enough to determine direction.

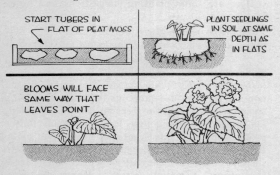

Care and feeding

Every summer, this question is asked many times: *What makes the flowers drop off my tuberous begonias before they have reached their prime?* There are three usual answers: overwatering, overfeeding, too warm weather. If you master these handicaps, more than likely you will have mastered begonia culture.

Watering. Begonias do require more water than the average garden plant. But remember there is a limit. Too much water can cause trouble. Water often enough to keep the soil always moist, but not soggy.

Good drainage is very important. One reason why the standard growing mixture consists of peat moss, leaf mold, and sand, or leaf mold, light loam, and manure, is that such mixtures allow water to pass through, and yet are absorbent enough to retain a sufficient quantity for the plant's use.

Feeding. A begonia tuber is like a potato—it has in it all the makings of a new plant. That's why there's no need to fertilize at the start. In fact, if you fertilize heavily during early stages of growth, you may find yourself with an ungainly, leggy plant. This has been done all too often by well-meaning beginners.

Usual procedure is to start feeding after the plants are well established. Some growers give the first feeding at the bud-forming stage.

Fertilizing tuberous begonias is more a matter of how much and how often than what type of fertilizer to use. You can get good results with almost any kind of fertilizer, preferably one on the acid side or with a neutral reaction. It's easy to tell by the appearance of the plant when it needs feeding: If the leaves are light green, and cupped upward, the plants will take a feeding. If the leaves are dark green, and tend to crimp downward, don't feed.

Shading. There is a popular misconception that tuberous begonias should be grown in full shade. But in coastal areas, where the summer sun isn't really hot, they do quite well with shade only during the middle of the day. Sun in the morning and late afternoon is beneficial. Most of the commercial begonia growers are in coastal areas. They grow their begonias under 50 per cent lath—which means that the plants get half the available sunlight all day. In the hot interior valleys, more shade is necessary. There, you might provide extra shade at midday, in addition to lath. Humidity should be increased in the valley, too. Twice-daily sprinkling with a fine mist spray is the usual procedure.

Morning and late afternoon sun, and regular overhead watering are just what tuberous begonias get in their native jungles in Central and South America. The jungle tops cut out most of the midday sun, but a lot of direct sunlight does get through. The plants thrive under jungle rains.

Size of blooms

There was a time when most begonias under cultivation were weak stemmed. To make a plant in bloom look presentable, you had to support the big flowers with wire topped with a hook. In the past 10 years or so, the weak-stemmed trait has been bred out of most strains. Now you rarely find one needing a stake to hold up the blooms.

What are the plant breeders trying to develop today? Size of bloom is still a major interest. A flower that looks up is another goal that has been partially reached. Doubleness of flowers is still desired, but because very double flowers are heavy, growers are developing ruffled petals that give a double effect rather than growing the true full-petaled doubles. Floriferousness is also very desirable, especially in hanging basket type *B. lloydii*.

There is some confusion regarding tubers and flower size. The characteristics inherent in a particular strain and not the size of the tuber determine the size and quality of the flower. A large tuber does not necessarily produce a large flower, but a large tuber will produce *more* flowers than a small one.

Pests

The tuberous begonia is, in general, a very healthy plant that suffers little damage from pests. Slugs and snails are probably the only pests that are a real threat to its existence. Remember to put a ring of bait all around the planting area, but not too close to the plants. The bait attracts the snails, and invites them into the planted area. You want to attract them away from the plant, not to it.

Under certain conditions, and in some areas, however, some other pests are attracted to tuberous begonias. Aphis, although found to some extent, attack only rarely. Cyclamen mite is a pest to watch if you grow tuberous begonias in a greenhouse. It is seldom found outdoors or under lath.

In Northwest gardens, the brachyrinus weevil or strawberry-root weevil has become a widespread enemy. In the fall, after you dig your tubers and before you store them, it would pay to examine them closely for weevils and weevil holes. If the weevil is inside, you will have to dig it out and charcoal dust the incision, hoping for the best. To be sure that none winter over in your tubers, dip in lindane or chlordane.

Diseases

1. *Rotting*. Stem-rot or mold causes trouble with tuberous begonias.

In soils to which manure has been added there is danger of stem-rot in newly planted seedlings. Sharp sand around the stem will generally prevent this rotting off.

Flowering plants should be kept clean of the debris of old flowers and stems. Old petals falling in the crotch of the leaves may start mold.

When you pick the flowers, leave all of the flower stem on the plant. The cut you have made will start stem-molding immediately. If you leave a long stem, the stem will fall off before the mold has had time to reach the tuber. If the main stem becomes badly molded, cut off below the infected part or remove entirely. Keep plant on the dry side until it sends up new shoots.

2. *Mildew* is the most serious disease of the tuberous begonia. A new variety of mildew appeared a few years ago and so far is not easily controlled. Dusting of sulfur before the mildew appears will prevent it, but the sulfur is unsightly and is not effective once the mildew forms. Check with your supplier of plants for latest control method. Keeping the foliage dry, at least by nightfall, will help prevent its spread.

Other varieties of tuberous begonia

Tuberous begonias are not limited to the well-known large-flowered hybrids—which are ever so colorful, but not always easy to use. Look for two less familiar types, *Begonia boliviensis* and the multiflora tuberous begonias. They are quite different, and really easy to use in the garden. They grow more like regular garden plants.

B. boliviensis grows upright. Its long, erect branches reach a height of about 3 feet. Clustered on the branches are many 5-petaled, salmon-red flowers with yellow stamens. The leaves are long and pointed. You start them and grow them just as you do the regular hybrids. Because this begonia grows tall and gives masses of a single color, it is ideal for a background planting. The plants will need staking.

The multiflora tuberous type grows lower—about the size of the large-flowered hybrids. In bloom, it is covered with little begonia-type flowers, about 1½ inches in diameter. Flowers are in 3 colors—yellow, apricot, and red. Multiflora's main advantage is lots of flowers. In a big planting you get an effect of solid color rather than splashes of many different colors.

Bulbs

DAFFODILS

Daffodils (*Narcissus*) deserve their reputation as the best spring bulb investment for the gardener. They are sure to bloom, increase in numbers year after year, and rarely fall prey to pests or diseases. Even the gopher, number-one enemy of bulbs, passes them up because of their bitter taste.

The larger nurseries and garden stores carry from 15 to 30 varieties of daffodils. A better than average bulb catalog offers 50 varieties. There are some 300 varieties listed in growers' catalogs. But to most gardeners there is but one daffodil—the King Alfred. This giant golden trumpet daffodil has long been a nine-to-one favorite in the total sales of bulbs.

However, in recent years some of the newer varieties have dropped out of the high-priced collector's item class and at a competitive price are challenging King Alfred.

But besides the spectacular and familiar trumpet daffodils, there are many other types in a wide variation of size, form and color combinations. By planting various types, a succession of bloom can be obtained to provide a continuous flow of color for more than two months each spring.

The signal that begins the daffodil season in all sections is given by the exquisite little cyclamineus hybrid, February Gold, followed by the large yellow trumpets. The procession continues with the large cupped varieties, the small cups, the pure white poeticus types, the jonquil hybrids, and winds up with the triandrus hybrids.

The following list groups the outstanding and representative varieties and hybrids of the various types of daffodils:

The following terms are used to describe the shape or form of daffodils:

- *petals, perianth, perianth segments*—the open, flat or recurved circle of petals behind the trumpet.
- *trumpet, crown, cup, eye*—the central, cup-shaped part of the flower. The size of the cup determines which of these terms is used.

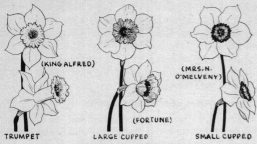

TRUMPET DAFFODILS

Characteristics: The trumpet or crown is as long as or longer than the perianth segments. All are long-stemmed, from 16 to 18 inches in height.

King Alfred. The standard, most popular daffodil. Very large, long-stemmed, and sturdy. A golden yellow.

Dawson City. A dependable variety of good form with broad, flat perianth and a long flanged trumpet. Rich golden yellow.

Diotima. One of the finest of giant yellow trumpets. Graceful flowers with a deep primrose yellow, star-shaped perianth and deeper colored trumpet.

Golden Harvest. Very large flowers, blooming earlier than King Alfred. Deep yellow with overlapping perianth and a well-shaped trumpet rolled back at the rim.

Beersheba. One of the best white trumpet daffodils. This large, beautiful flower has a flat perianth and a long slender trumpet. It is creamy-white when first opened, but becomes a pure white.

Mrs. E. H. Krelage. A bicolor, with a pale yellow trumpet when first opened, but fading to a uniform ivory white. Good form and lovely waxy texture.

LARGE-CUPPED VARIETIES

Characteristics: Slightly shorter trumpets than the trumpet daffodils, the crown being more than $1/3$ but less than equal to the length of the perianth segments. This group includes the Incomparabilis and most of the Leedsii daffodils.

These are considered to be better performers in California gardens than the King Alfred and seem better able to stand a sudden burning sun. All bloom early enough to avoid early summer heat in the warm sections of the West.

Carlton. Large, clear lemon-yellow flowers with a frilled cup. A free-blooming, vigorous grower with very long stems.

Fortune. The standard daffodil of this type, probably the most popular next to King Alfred. Famous for its uptilting bloom on 24-inch stems. The broad, flat perianth is a soft yellow, and the crown a glowing orange.

Tunis. A large flower of excellent texture. Broad creamy white petals; the large, flaring yellow crown fades to cream with the frilled edge a pale coppery gold.

Dick Wellband. Pure white overlapping petals, broad spreading cup is a bright orange-red. Excellent for cutting because the blooms are long lasting and the striking color of the cup doesn't fade.

Francisca Drake. White reflexed petals with a wide, deep cup which is golden yellow at base shading to flame at the frilled edge. A good companion for Dick Wellband.

John Evelyn. Broad, creamy white perianth; large flat cup a fine apricot-orange with a frilled edge.

Mrs. R. O. Backhouse. The "pink daffodil." A white perianth with a long, slim trumpet of shell pink with darker edges. Looks delicate but is long lasting.

SMALL-CUPPED VARIETIES

Characteristics: Smaller cups or crown than the large-cupped varieties, being not more than $1/3$ of the length of the perianth segments. This group includes the Barrii and some of the Leedsii varieties. Generally later bloom than the foregoing.

Diana Kasner. A free flowering daffodil with a cream yellow perianth and large fluted yellow cup with a red frill. Long stems. Shade lightly from late spring sun in warm areas.

Mrs. Nette O'Melveny. An unusually graceful flower on tall slender stems. A clear white perianth with a wide, soft lemon yellow cup picoteed at the edge with orange. Give it afternoon shade.

Hades. Vigorous growth and tall stems. A creamy white, flat perianth with a deep cherry-red cup, the deepest in color of all the red cupped varieties.

Hera. Broad petals of creamy white with a yellow rimmed cup. A good alternate for Mrs. Nette O'Melveny.

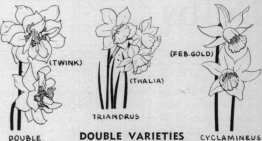

DOUBLE VARIETIES

Cheerfulness. A fragrant flower with a combination of white and creamy yellow in the double cup against a white perianth. Two to five flowers on tall stems.

Twink. Early, long-lasting blooms on tall stems. The outer petals are a soft yellow, the inner petals a clear orange.

Texas. Large double flowers of bright yellow with shorter orange petals. Tall stems.

Royal Sovereign. One of the best doubles. The flower is creamy white interspersed with shorter frilled petals of soft primrose yellow.

TRIANDRUS VARIETIES

The hybrids of *N. triandrus* have larger flowers and taller stems than the species, but have its general characteristics: narrow, rush-like foliage, pure white flowers in drooping clusters, and gently reflexed petals. The sweetly fragrant flowers appear on 12-18 inch stems.

Moonshine. Graceful, star-shaped, creamy white flowers appear in clusters of 2 to 3 to a stem. These exquisite blooms grow well in shade and naturalize easily in rock gardens.

Thalia. Delicate, fragrant flowers of pure white in clusters of 2-3 on tall stems. Excellent for cutting.

Silver Chimes. This hybrid of *N. triandrus* and polyanthus daffodils produces large clusters of 6 or more beautifully shaped white and primrose-yellow flowers on strong, slender stems. Good for forcing in pots, or naturalizing in rock gardens. Not entirely hardy in very severe climates.

CYCLAMINEUS VARIETIES

The *N. cyclamineus* varieties are distinguished by reflexed petals reminiscent of cyclamen. These very early, small, slender daffodils appear in shades of yellow.

February Gold. A very early 6-inch miniature which blooms in earliest spring. The bright yellow flowers have a recurved perianth and a straight fluted trumpet tinted with orange. One of the best for early forcing and is long lasting both in the garden and when cut.

Beryl. Graceful, drooping flowers with primrose-yellow perianths and small, globular orange cups shading to gold.

JONQUILLA VARIETIES

The jonquils and their hybrids have highly fragrant clusters of yellow flowers. The foliage is narrow and rush-like.

Golden Perfection. A hybrid of *N. jonquilla* and a yellow trumpet daffodil. The large flowers appear in clusters of 2-3 on tall stems and have broad, overlapping petals of citron-yellow with a gold cup. A long-lasting cut flower. In the garden, it is at its best in informal plantings and in pots.

Trevithian. A fragrant, free-flowering jonquil. Pale lemon-yellow perianth, with a clear yellow, shallow cup.

Lanarth. Deep, golden yellow perianth and a shallow cup of gold flushed with orange.

TAZETTA VARIETIES

Varieties of *N. tazetta* are the polyanthus or bunch-flowered narcissus. The poetaz daffodils, hybrid of *N. tazetta* and *N. poeticus*, are included in this group. The white and yellow flowers have small cups and grow in clusters. They grow very well in the shade.

Also in the Tazetta class is the paper white narcissus, which has pure white flowers and is an old favorite for naturalizing, cutting, and early forcing in pots.

Glorious. The early flowers are clustered on tall stems, and have a white perianth with an orange cup edged with red.

St. Agnes. A beautiful variety with a very flat white perianth and an orange-scarlet cup.

Geranium. Flowers appear in large clusters, with 7 to 8 flowers per stem. A pure white perianth with a flat cup of deep orange-red.

POETICUS VARIETIES

The Poet's Narcissus. Fragrant single flowers with snowy white petals and flat frilled cups edged with red.

Actaea. The largest and best of the *N. poeticus* varieties. The flowers are carried on long stems and have broad, pure white petals and a large, flat cup of yellow edged with red.

SPECIES

N. bulbocodium conspicuus. Hoop Petticoat Daffodil. An early blooming miniature whose 6-inch grasslike foliage appears in autumn ahead of the flowers. The bright yellow flowers bloom in February-March, and have a flaring trumpet like a small starched yellow petticoat on a slender pointed perianth. Requires a sandy peat soil with a fair amount of moisture while growing, but not in summer.

N. cyclamineus. Cyclamineus Daffodil. Blooms in early spring on tiny 4-6 inch stems. The bright yellow flower has unusually long tube and the narrow perianth segments are turned straight back. Same general culture as *N. bulbocodium conspicuus*. Once planted should not be disturbed for many years.

N. jonquilla simplex. True Jonquil. The small, heavily scented, and rich yellow flowers appear in graceful clusters on 12-inch stems. Narrow rush-like leaves are about the same height. Variety *flore pleno* has double-flower.

N. juncifolius. Smallest of the jonquils. The small, flat-cupped golden yellow flowers grow on 3-4 inch stems. Foliage is rush-like. An intensely fragrant miniature.

N. minimus. A small form of the trumpet daffodil, and the tiniest of all daffodils. Dainty little yellow trumpet flowers bloom in February on 3-inch high stems. Prefers peaty soil. Naturalizes well.

N. triandrus albus. ANGEL'S TEARS. A miniature with clusters of tiny, creamy white flowers with globular cups and point, reflexed perianths. The little bulbs, about the size of peas, should be planted in a mixture of leaf mold and sand and provided with the best of drainage. Protect from sun.

CULTURE

When planting for successive bloom, place early blooming varieties toward the back of the planting, let the later ones flower along the edge when there will be plenty of annuals coming on to cover the fading bulb foliage.

Daffodils, like gladiolus, enjoy facing the sun. Always place them against a background which will force them to face the path or other vantage point from which they can be seen. In the early flowering season the sun is mainly from the south, so the background—fence, wall, hedge, or shrubbery—should be to the north. The large trumpet daffodils especially need such a background.

Although most daffodils want full sun, those which bloom later in the season do better in filtered shade, particularly in Southern California.

Plant from early to late fall in deeply dug soil. Add no manure. Ordinarily there is no need to add fertilizers at the time of planting. However, where the soil really is poor, scatter enough bonemeal to cover the area and dig it in before planting.

Usually depth of planting is 2½ times the size of the bulb, but if you set daffodil bulbs deep enough to avoid damage when spading the soil and space them 8 inches apart, you will not have to replant them until they show signs of deterioration due to overcrowding. With many varieties this will not be for several years; some increase much faster than others, however, and may need dividing every 2 or 3 years.

Bulbs

DAHLIAS

For sheer volume of color from July to frost, it is hard to find a plant to match the dahlia. It will always deserve a place in the garden for that reason alone. Another virtue of dahlias is their many flower types—resembling marigolds, chrysanthemums, carnations, or zinnias.

Dahlias grow best in a bed by themselves. The large dahlias, especially, should be planted in a cutting garden where they can be given their own cultural needs. If you prefer to use dahlias with other garden plants, look to the lower-growing and smaller flower types within the following: star, collarette, cosmos, pompon, miniature, and dwarf. They are more apt to be in scale with the garden of average size than the huge 10 and 12-inch exhibition types.

Planting time

Don't plant until the soil is warm. There is no advantage in early planting, because the dahlia needs rapid growth in warm soil to manufacture its richest color and to attain maximum size. Some growers will not ship tubers until April 1. Even in the warmest sections of the West many gardeners hold off planting until late April or May. In some cases, early planting, especially if followed by heavy rains, is likely to result in rotting of the tubers. In hot summer areas dahlias planted too early will come into bloom in midsummer when the hot sun is rough on the flowers.

Soil preparation

The soil in the planting bed reserved for dahlias can be prepared in advance. Two to 3 months before planting, spade the bed deeply, then spade in manure, compost, or peat moss if needed. If preparation of soil is delayed until a short time before planting, use no manure.

Overwintering

Dahlia specialists differ on the best way to handle dahlia tubers from the time you lift them in the fall until you plant again. Any one of these methods is satisfactory:

1. Separate tubers immediately after lifting clumps in fall. Dust freshly cut surfaces with sulfur. Imbed tubers in a box of sand, or sawdust, and store them in a cool, dry place.

2. Don't separate tubers in fall. Lift clumps from the ground with dirt around roots and cover them with dry soil, sand, or sawdust. Two to 4 weeks in advance of next spring's planting, separate clumps, allow cut surfaces of tubers to dry, and place tubers in moist sand in a shady spot. Eyes will have developed into sprouts by planting time.

3. Lift clumps from the ground. Cut stalks as close to clump as possible and turn clump over so that any moisture drains out of stalk. Roots can be separated at leisure during winter when fall work is over. Each tuber must have an eye. The eye is always on the stem at or above the point

where the root or tuber joins it. If eyes have receded to such an extent that they can't be recognized, roots can be sorted later in spring when eyes start to show.

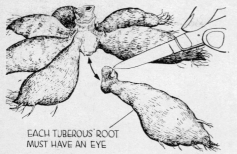

EACH TUBEROUS ROOT MUST HAVE AN EYE

Planting procedure

Dig holes 6 inches deep and 3 to 4 feet apart. Place the stake, then set the tuber flat on a 6-inch-high cushion of well pulverized soil in the bottom of the hole with the eye or bud pointing toward, and about 2 inches from, the stake. Cover the tuber with 3 inches of soil and water thoroughly. When sprouts show, begin to fill around them with soil, and continue—up to ground level—as they develop.

Another method, one which eliminates staking, is spot planting. Plant 10 dahlias in an area 4 by 5 feet. Plant 2 in each corner, 6 inches in from border, and 2 in center. This basic planting unit can be used or modified for various garden situations. Such a unit is dramatic and effective. Spottiness is avoided. Best effects with 10 dahlias of the same variety in a unit. It is a particularly useful arrangement in planting singles and collarettes whose habit of growth is slender, without much leafage at the base.

Watering schedule

Water at time of planting and not again until growth is above the ground—from 3 to 5 weeks. From this time on, frequency of watering depends on type of soil and amount of leaf. Because plants draw very little water from the soil when they are small, frequent watering will create a soggy condition in which the tuber may rot. But after leaves are in full production and buds are set, dahlias require lots of water.

Fertilizing schedule

Because the dahlia stores food one year to be used the next, it needs no additional food during its early growth. There's enough food stored to promote root growth until the leaves of the plant are in full production. Don't be lavish at any time with fertilizers high in nitrogen. Excess nitrogen forces excessive leaf growth and may cause crown rot and rotting of tubers in storage.

Cultivating

It is best to keep weeds down and soil open by mulching rather than by cultivating. Dahlias are surface feeders and cultivating disturbs surface roots. Summer mulching is especially beneficial because it keeps surface roots cool.

Pinching and disbudding

To avoid the top-heavy, ungainly appearance characteristic of large dahlias, pick out the center stalk above the top leaves when the plant has 3 sets of leaves. This will force out 6 strong side laterals and the result will be a rounded bush with bloom distributed all over the plant, rather than a tall lanky one with all the color at the top.

To produce extra-large flowers, remove all but the end (or terminal) buds on these side stalks. After all of the first-bloom flowers have been picked, cut the plant back to one joint on the main stalk, or to where 2 side branches show strong growth, to produce the second batch of large flowers.

The smaller types of dahlia need no further pruning or budding after the first pinching. However, you get the finest show pompons by cutting the plant to the ground 7 weeks before show-time.

Cut-flowers

If you want longer lasting cut-flowers, don't pick dahlias right after watering or during the heat of the day. Pick dahlias only when the flowers are fully open as the buds do not develop well after being cut.

After cutting the flowers, crush stem ends or make a long diagonal cut in the stem to give a larger surface for water absorption. Place dahlias in a deep container of water for several hours before arranging.

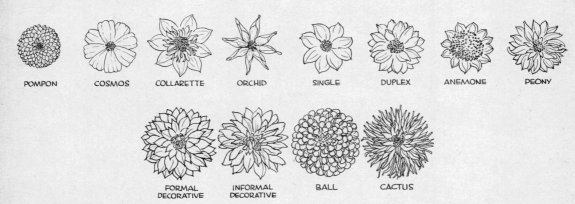

Bulbs

IRIS

The variation in the colors, shapes, and sizes of iris is so vast that few gardeners have seen them all. The basic classifications of iris are, of course, botanical. Iris separates into two main divisions: types with rhizomes or fleshy rootstocks (rhizomatous type); types with a basal bulb rather than a rhizome (bulbous type).

RHIZOMATOUS-TYPE

The main divisions of the rhizomatous type are the bearded, beardless, and crested iris. All have rhizomes or fleshy rootstocks that are lifted, divided, and replanted—usually immediately. The differences between these 3 divisions are based primarily on flower characteristics.

BEARDED IRIS

The bearded iris include all iris that have short, fuzzy hairs at the base of the drooping petals or "falls." (The upright petals are known as "standards.")

There are 3 types of bearded iris: dwarf, intermediate, and tall. Although all three have their place in the garden, the tall iris is by far the most popular.

The tall bearded iris is adaptable to a wide range of climatic conditions, is easy to grow, and is practically free from diseases. It not only gives good bloom the year after planting but for several years without replanting.

While the iris is primarily a garden flower, it also is useful for cutting. As the stems on each clump increase, a few can be cut for the house, where the unopened buds will open out in water. And its broad, gray-green foliage has a decorative value at all times of the year both in the garden and in arrangements.

Location: Sun is needed for flower production. Give bearded iris full sun in cool-summer climates; sun for half day in hot-summer areas.

If the planting site is not naturally well drained, build up beds raised 4 to 6 inches above the surrounding soil.

Overly rich soil produces lush foliage, few flowers. Don't add fertilizer unless the garden soil is unusually poor.

Planting: Planting time should be keyed to the digging and shipping time of iris growers. Washington and Oregon iris growers can ship plants from the first of July to early autumn. California growers begin a month earlier and ship until the heavy rains come. In cool-summer areas, buy early and divide old plants early. In hot-summer areas, plant and replant when the weather cools in September.

Plant single rhizomes, not clumps, one foot apart and just beneath the surface. Spread roots so that they will have a wide and deep feeding area.

Point the growing end in the direction you want the plant to spread. If you are planting the rhizomes in a group, point the growing end outward from the center. On a slope, plant so they will grow upward, not down and out of the ground. If rhizomes grow toward each other, you will in time have a traffic jam.

After-planting care: Iris accept the same amount of water given other flowers around them but will get along with less. If they are planted by themselves in a dry situation be sure they have a thorough soaking a month before flowering time.

Clumps of iris give their best bloom in the second and third years, often fair in the fourth. After that time new and old rhizomes are too crowded to get adequate food and must be divided.

Some gardeners postpone replanting at the end of the third or fourth year by digging out the old rhizomes in the center of the clump, and refilling the hole with compost. But it is best to dig up and divide the whole clump and replant in another place. Or, you can enrich the existing soil with compost or rotted manure and replant with single, fresh terminal rhizomes. In replanting, cut back foliage to about 6 inches to assist re-establishment of the rhizomes.

Trimming back leaves of established iris plants in summer does no harm. They soon produce new leaves, anyway; do not cut these. After late autumn, cut back and remove old or dried up foliage.

Provide winter protection only where the ground freezes hard. Cover with branches, hay, or leaves to prevent heaving from alternate freezes and thaws.

Pest and diseases: Bearded iris have few pests or diseases—and fewer in the West than elsewhere. Iris borer is seldom seen in California, but where it occurs, spraying with DDT before the blooming season seems to be most effective. Rhizome rot, a bacterial disease, occurs occasionally about flowering time when too much water and heat are present. Lift badly affected plants, cut out the soft parts and immerse the rhizomes a few minutes in a rose-red solution of potassium permanganate. If damage is slight, uncover the rhizome, clean out mushy areas and slowly pour the solution over the affected parts. The leaf spot that sometimes disfigures new foliage in warm humid spring weather can be reduced by spraying the plant with Bordeaux mixture from the time new growth begins until it has reached near normal height.

Iris in the garden: In or out of bloom, the bearded iris has unusual garden value. The pointed, sword-like leaves give contrasting vertical forms among plants of rounded or squat form. Their soft gray-green is never harsh or out of key with other plant colors. Use bearded iris for their color and form in drifts throughout the mixed perennial border.

Do not interplant with anything that crowds or shades the rhizomes. To produce flowers next season, the plants need sun and warmth through the summer.

ONCO-HYBRID   LOUISIANA   NATIVES

Dwarf Bearded Iris

The dwarf bearded iris (hybrids of *I. pumila* and *I. chamæiris*) are the first iris to bloom in the spring. They are exact counterparts of the regular bearded iris, except that they grow to only 3 to 12 inches in height. These dwarfs are best used in masses in rock gardens or as wide edgings for borders and walks.

Give them the same cultural treatment as the regular bearded iris.

Oncocyclus and Regelia Iris

These iris are not true bearded iris but so closely related that they are included in the group.

The Regelias are a group of iris with beautiful and often strikingly veined flowers. The 3 species of Regelias that are generally available to collectors are *I. korolkowii*, *I. stolonifera*, and *I. hoogiana*.

The Oncocyclus iris group is tender and more demanding than the regular bearded iris, but their flower heads are enormous and the colors are quite different, predominately purple, light gray, and almost black.

This group is best represented by the mourning iris (*I. susiana*), which has large, globular flowers of silvery-gray, veined with purple-black, and the so-called black Syrian iris (*I. atropurpurea*), with standards of blackish-red and falls of black, tinged with crimson. Both of these Oncocyclus species have characteristically short, unbranched stems and small foliage. They are native to a region of rainless summers and therefore are adapted to hot-summer areas. However, with proper care, they will accept average garden conditions.

The Onco hybrids are a result of crossing Oncocyclus species with those of the bearded iris. These hybrids combine the huge, orchid-like flowers of the Oncocyclus with the taller, more strongly branched, and larger foliaged characteristics of the bearded iris. Fortunately also, they are adapted to a wider range of climatic conditions than the Oncocyclus species.

A second group of Onco hybrids are the Oncogelias. These are the results of crossing Oncocyclus species with the Regelias. The variety *Luna* is probably the most beautiful of these exotic hybrids, with red-violet veins, etched on a cream background, flushed with deep pink and lilac. A rich splash of purplish-black appears in the center of each fall.

BEARDLESS IRIS

Aside from the absence of a beard, the chief characteristics of this group of iris are their graceful form, fibrous root system, and a fondness for water. All iris native to North America are beardless; others in this classification are the Siberian, Japanese, Spuria, and winter irises.

Louisiana Iris

The 3 species of iris found growing in the swamps and bayous of southeastern Louisiana are *I. fulva*, *I. foliosa*, and *I. giganticærulea*. Hybrids of these species that have been taken into cultivation have produced graceful flowers of pure white, yellows, pinks, reds, and purples, and a complete range of blues. Their climatic adaptation is surprisingly wide, tolerating cold New England winters, and growing very well in Southern California if given enough water.

Because their native situations are in bogs or along bayous they do well in any similar conditions. However, they will adapt to most gardens where soil, fertilizer, and water are sufficient for vegetables. Filtered shade is necessary in warm climates; plant in full sun in the North. Propagation is similar to that of the bearded iris.

Pacific Coast Native Iris

The 3 important Western native iris are *Iris douglasiana*, *I. tenax*, and *I. innominata*.

I. douglasiana is native to California Coast Range from Monterey County north to Oregon. It forms a large clump of foliage from which rise 1 to 2-foot stems, each carrying 2 to 3 flowers in shades of white, cream, yellow, or lavender-pink. Some gardeners consider the flowers superior to the dwarf bearded iris, but the large clump of foliage makes this native more difficult to use in the small garden.

I. tenax is found in the wooded areas of Washington and Oregon. The flowers are daintier than those of *I. douglasiana* and appear singly on a stem 12 to 20 inches long. Although lavender is the prevalent color in this species, some flowers are white, gray, blue, or purple.

I. innominata, a native of southwest Oregon, grows in low, tufted clumps with flowers of golden-yellow, striped with deeper shades, including brown. Naturalizes beautifully under trees and is particularly effective along shaded paths.

Give these iris a moist, slightly acid, peaty soil. In hot sections, a little shade; elsewhere, full sun. The plants form big clumps in a short time, and may be left undisturbed for several years. Divide clumps in the spring when new growth is just beginning, and they will re-establish themselves fairly rapidly.

SIBERIAN

JAPANESE

SPURIA

Siberian Iris

Iris sibirica grows wild in the wet meadows of central Europe. Domesticated, it is one of the daintiest members of the iris family. Butterfly-like flowers on 2 to 4-foot stems come into bloom just as the late varieties of the bearded iris are fading. The flowers of the Siberian iris are white, very pale to deep blue, and lavender.

Like the Japanese iris, this iris loves moisture, and is happiest when it is grown in clumps near a pool, stream, or lawn. If the lawn is sloping, plant it at the end to which water is likely to drain.

Lift and divide in September or October. Enrich old soil with rotted manure. Remember that the Siberian species needs acid soil. A liberal mulch of rotted manure applied in early spring left on through the summer helps keep roots cool and moist.

Japanese Iris

The exotic, richly-colored Japanese iris (*I. kœmpferi*) is not the prima donna that some gardeners would have you believe. Its cultural requirements are simple and no more demanding than those of other iris.

The flat, transparent flowers bloom in July, extending the iris season into the summer. Both double and single flower forms are available, with a color range from purple through blue, pink, and white, with veinings of the same or contrasting colors.

This iris is definitely a moisture-lover, and grows best in a slightly shaded, almost soggy place. However, it is not a bog plant and should be kept fairly dry during its resting period in the winter. The soil should be rich, warm, and on the acid side. The deep moisture required by the Japanese iris can best be had by flooding. Occasional feeding with an acid-base fertilizer will help to maintain acidity in alkaline soils. Keep lime away from this iris, as it will injure the plant.

Slight shade is necessary because the 2 to 3 foot masses of stiff, straight leaves may burn in hot sun.

Divide roots every 3 to 5 years. The best time is October and April.

Spuria Iris

The spuria iris are a group of fine, tall plants characterized by the strong, upright growth of their stiff, grass-like leaves. This group includes species from both Europe and Asia.

The 4 to 5-foot clumps produce long stems and large, rather stiff flowers. These bloom from March to June, depending on climate. The white and yellow varieties are most familiar, but brown and blue shades are also available. The rather spidery form of the flowers, not unlike those of the Dutch iris, accounts for the name "butterfly iris."

This iris is a rank grower and tends to over-run the garden. Requires large quantities of water in the spring, little or none in summer. Divide the clumps in the fall.

UNGUICULARIS

CRISTATA

DUTCH

Winter Iris

The earliest blooming iris is the winter iris, *Iris unguicularis* (*I. stylosa*), whose flowers appear in January and February, although they often bloom as early as November.

This beardless species has delicate, fragrant, bluish-lavender blooms, the falls with white veins and yellow markings at the base.

Foliage is reed-like and tall, with the flowers carried on 6 to 9-inch stems below the tops of the foliage. Cut back this evergreen foliage to a few inches above the ground in September or the flowers will be hidden.

Winter iris make excellent cut flowers, which may be picked while in bud to open after they have been put in water.

Leave lots of room for spreading, as *I. unguicularis* can be left undisturbed for many years. Divide and replant clumps either in April or September.

CRESTED IRIS

The crested iris are a small group more closely related to the bearded iris than to the beardless. The common characteristic of this group is a small crest at the base of the falls. The chief value of crested iris in the garden is its ability to thrive under much shadier conditions than other iris. In this group are the following species:

I. cristata. A native of America, this miniature iris has broad leaves and small lavender flowers with golden crests. Blooms in April. Widely adaptable, but prefers cool, damp soil, light shade, and summer moisture. Divide immediately after flowering.

I. tectorum. A native of China. Low-growing, broad, ribbed leaves about 1 foot long. The flowers are purple-blue with white crests, or pure white.

Grows well in rich soil on the acid side, requires half shade. Replant every 2 or 3 years.

I. japonica. Considered the most beautiful of the crested iris. Tall, 2-foot plants bear flowers with fringed, pale lavender petals and orange crests. They will grow in almost any soil and in part shade.

Culture and propagation is similar to that of the bearded iris.

BULBOUS-TYPE IRIS

Those iris that fall into the bulbous class all have a basal bulb in which food is stored to enable the plant to become completely dormant in the summer. The bulb can then be lifted and stored until replanting.

Bulbous iris are dainty members of the extensive iris clan. They are smaller in every way than the tall, sturdy, bearded types, and must be massed together to produce an effect in the garden. Flowers come early—in March and April in California and later as you move northward.

Dutch Iris

The Dutch iris are the modern counterparts of the old Spanish iris *(I. xiphium).* Although called Dutch because they were hybridized in Holland, actually their ancestry is Spanish and North African.

Dutch iris are especially valued for cut flowers. Blooms are available in blues, yellow, white, and combinations of these colors, and are carried on stiff 20 to 28-inch stems above the narrow, grass-like foliage. Flowering time is March and April in mild-winter areas, May and June in colder sections.

Dutch iris are not demanding as far as culture is concerned. Set the bulbs from 2 to 4 inches apart and from 3 to 4 inches deep. Time of planting varies with the climate. In most sections of California, it is safe to plant bulbs toward the latter part of September.

In colder areas early planting may produce tender spears that may be injured by hail or ice. In such areas keep the bulbs stored in warm, dry, well-ventilated rooms, and plant out quite late in the year. Protect newly planted bulbs with a mulch of straw, evergreen boughs, or similar material.

After bloom, allow foliage to ripen before digging up. Before storing or replanting, cure the bulbs outside in a warm spot protected from direct sunlight. Iris bulbs should not be kept out of the ground for more than 2 months.

When planting Dutch iris, clump the bulbs together in oval drifts, staggering them 3 or 4 deep so that the blooms will form a solid mass of color. Combined with the right plants, Dutch iris, with their butterfly-like flowers poised high on tall stems, are remarkably effective in spring borders.

When cutting Dutch iris for arrangements, be sure to leave at least 2 or 3 leaves and about six inches of stem above the top of the bulb; as with all bulbous plants, as much as possible of the food in leaves and stems should be returned to the bulbs where nutrients are stored for next year's flowers. Cut the iris just after the flowers have unfurled. The flowers will last for several days if they are not kept in too warm a room and if the water in the container is changed daily.

JUNO RETICULATA ENGLISH

English Iris

Although the species *Iris xiphioides* is known as English iris, it is a native of the Pyrenees. The large flowers have a rather loose texture, and are available in shades of blue, lavender, purple, and white. English iris bloom in May.

These iris require plenty of water and a fairly rich soil. It is necessary to lift the bulbs only every 3 or 4 years; lift and replant in late August.

The Junos

The junos are a group of bulbous iris that are identified by their fleshy, thong-like feeding roots and their distinctive foliage. The leaves are deeply channeled, set alternately on the stem; the 6 to 10 flowers are produced on short stems from the base of the leaves.

The available species of juno iris are:

I. bucharica. To 12 inches. White and yellow flowers.

I. græberiana. To 12 inches. Clear medium blue flowers with a white streak on the fall.

I. orchioides sulphurea. To 8 inches. Small, light yellow flowers with brown blotch on each fall.

I. sindjarensis. Large, light to medium blue flowers on 4-inch stems.

I. vicaria. To 12 inches. White flowers tinged with blue.

I. willmottiana alba. To 10 inches. White with yellow blotch and a touch of green on the falls.

The juno iris are not particular as to soil but should have good drainage. Bulbs may be lifted in summer after blooming and replanted in autumn, or left undisturbed for many years.

The Reticulatas

Iris reticulata, another bulbous type, is so dainty and fragrant that it should find a place in many more gardens. Blooming very early—usually in February — it bears blooms with violet-purple standards and falls edged with gold, on 8 to 10-inch stems. The netted, or veined petals, from which the name reticulata is derived, are characteristic of this species. However, its really distinguishing feature is a violet-like fragrance.

Bulbs

LILIES

Until recently, growing lilies was something of a gamble. The species planted in home gardens were the same plants that had grown wild for thousands of years in valleys, on windswept beaches, on mountainsides. Naturally, these lilies resented drastic changes in environment. A lily from northern China felt out of place in Southern California; another from the sunny Mediterranean resented transfer to the cool, moist conditions in the Northwest.

Now you can buy hybrid lilies that are about as easy to grow as any other bulb. By crossing lilies from cold climates with those from warm climates, hybridizers have produced lilies that will grow in either climate. Into these hybrids have been bred new colors, new forms, unusual resistance to diseases. Unlike foreign-grown lilies, hybrid strains are produced close to home and can be delivered soon after they are dug.

Here, in order of their blooming, are the various types of lilies now available.

Rainbow Hybrids and Golden Chalice Hybrids (June)
The lily season begins with the bright-colored Rainbow hybrids. Many upright, cup-shaped flowers grow on each stem. They run in colors from pale yellow, through tangerine and orange-red, to deep maroon-red. The Rainbows are actually a new edition of the candlestick lilies that are familiar to anyone who has gardened in the Midwest.

The Golden Chalice hybrids come from one end of the Rainbow's color range—the golden yellows—and they are vigorous and robust.

Rainbows and the Golden Chalice strain are so strong that they multiply very rapidly. If you remove scales from the main bulbs just after flowering and plant them in shallow, moist sand, they will root, grow, and produce bulblets and good plants that will flower again in two years. These lilies also increase naturally by bulb division and by means of underground bulblets that form on the stem. Plant at a 6-inch depth in order to get the bulblets and to prevent the bulb from splitting into several different crowns.

Plant these lilies in clumps of 5 or 7 bulbs in a perennial border, or among small shrubs or low growing annuals.

Lilium Martagon Album (Late June)
This is a white-flowering sport, of bulb mutation, of the wine-red or purple *L. martagon* that grows wild in large sections of eastern Europe. Dainty, waxy flowers grow symmetrically on pyramidal, 4-foot stems. This is still a rather rare lily. When well cared for, the bulbs seem to persist forever. We know of one large clump of these lilies that has been growing for more than 20 years in the same location—a garden corner sheltered by dwarf Japanese cutleaf maples. The contrast in colors between the lush green of the lily foliage, the red-maroon of the maples, and the ivory-white of the flowers is demanding, but very pleasant to look at, too. This lily is useful among almost any low, evergreen shrubs.

L. Martagon album

Plant the bulbs in the sun no deeper than 4 inches in well-drained soil.

Mid-Century Hybrids (June, July)
The Mid-Century hybrids, a large group, are the offspring of a match between the well-known tiger lily and the candlestick lily. From both parents, these hybrids inherited vigor and an unusual adaptability to new conditions. They have enormous strength, hardiness, and a tolerance to practically all soils. You can see at a glance that they inherited the rich coloring of their parents. The broad color range is from mahogany, through orange, to yellow—mostly in commanding tones. Colors may be vibrant and strong, as in the variety called *Enchantment*, which is a vivid nasturtium-red. It blazes in the sun and stands out on dark days. But there are also delicately colored varieties with a warm glow; examples are the salmon-shaded *Harlequin* and the *Pagoda* in hues of topaz to amber.

Mid-Century Hybrids

These strong-growing lilies have straight, stiff stems. They often grow extra bulbils (aerial, fleshy leaf buds or bulbs) at the base of their leaves. You can pick off the bulbils when they are about ready to drop and set them out in rows to make blooming plants within 2 years.

New Madonna Lilies, the Cascade Strain (Late June) The Cascade strain, an improved form of the ancient white Madonna lily, has increased in vigor (its stems are straight and tall) and in resistance to disease. Average performance is generally better than that of the finest, old-fashioned Madonna lilies of the past. Lily breeders are working to bring new colors to these pure white flowers.

Plant Madonna lilies earlier than the other kinds of lilies. It's a good idea to order in July or August so you can plant them by September 15. The bulbs are unusual because they are dormant only for a short time in August.

Bellingham Hybrids (July) Bellingham hybrids, the results of crosses among Pacific Coast natives, are perfectly at home in West Coast gardens. They also make beautiful, long-lasting cut flowers. Out of green whorls of foliage, thin, slender flower stems rise to a height of 5 to 7

Bellingham hybrid

feet. About 20 bell-shaped (recurved) flowers in colors that range from deep cherry-red, through orange, to palest yellow—all freckled with maroon, purple, or black—form on the stems.

A few of the Bellingham hybrids have been named. Among them, *Shuksan* (orange with maroon spots) is probably the most valuable for general garden use.

You will see Bellingham hybrids at their best in part shade where soil is cool and light. Five inches is recommended planting depth. Apply a winter mulch in colder sections.

Regal Lilies and Olympic Hybrids (July) We are now reaching the second stage of the lily season. In early July, lilies with trumpet-type flowers begin to open. First among them is the old, familiar Regal. This type, no longer the undisputed

L. centifolium Olympic Hybrid

queen of them all, can nevertheless be a beautiful flower when well grown. Without question, it is sturdy and hardy. The flowers are rather small, opening in cart-wheel fashion, with all the blooms in only one tier, as a rule.

The Olympic hybrids, the Regal lilies' possible successors, are a more graceful, trumpet type. They have a new quality that was lacking in the Regals. The Olympics' wide-flaring flowers stand in tiers around the stem, making a pyramidal flower spike with a long succession of bloom. Flower color is usually white, with the exterior greenish brown or wine red. They combine well with any color and stand out beautifully against a solid green background.

Best placement is 12 inches apart, 5 to 6 inches deep, in sun.

Fiesta Hybrids (July) This group comes on when the trumpet lilies do. Fiestas have recurved flowers borne rather close to tall stems that reach 5 feet. As with all lilies, lower flowers open first and the others follow so slowly that the plants stay in bloom over a long period. The color range runs from pure canary yellow, through deeper golden tones, to soft or intense orange; and from scarlet and warm cherry-red, through darker red, to deep maroon. The extremes in color—light yellows and dark maroons—occur only sporadically in the strain. But growers are paying special attention to these colors and will soon balance the color range. Even now, though, the colors are particularly attractive for indoor use and the stems are easy to arrange and handle.

Fiesta hybrid

This is a hardy and dependable group. They perform best in the sun. Plant 5 inches deep and 10 inches apart.

Aurelian Hybrids (July and August) This very colorful group is just now coming into wide use. It has a long history of development. Parentage was among trumpet lilies and wild lilies from Asia: *L. leucanthum centifolium* (early, tall, graceful, wide and expanded flowers with a wave in the petals); *L. sargentiæ* (later, narrow, more funnel-like blooms); *L. sulphureum* (late, ivory-yellow trumpet flowers); and *L. henryi* (orange, nodding flowers on thin, swaying stems). The crossing was always between *L. henryi* and any one of the other three.

The Aurelian hybrids, which resulted from this parentage, fall into three broad groups: (1) The Sunburst strain resembles one of its parents, the

Chinese *L. henryi*, but has larger flowers, wider and longer petals, and comes in a great variety of colors; (2) the Golden Clarion strain resembles its trumpet-lily parents but comes in colors ranging from ivory to deepest golden yellow, and from orange shading into pink, salmon, and buff hues, and (3) the Heart's Desire strain is truly midway between *L. henryi* and the trumpet lily, having large, white, bowl-shaped flowers, many with orange or golden centers.

Aurelian Hybrid

As do the Mid-Century hybrids, the Aurelian strains descend from parents that contribute strength, vigor, hardiness, tolerance, and adaptability to changed conditions. The plants grow 5 to 7 feet tall, bearing from 10 to 20 flowers, all large and all in well-balanced, pyramidal heads. Backed by evergreens or large shrubs, they make a garden picture. Part shade is best for all the Aurelian hybrids—they are inclined to fade in sun. Plant 6 inches deep and 12 inches apart.

Large Flowering Species from Japan (August and September)

The next group of lilies are late-flowering species from Japan. One, *L. speciosum*, has two excellent named varieties: *White Champion* and *Red Champion*. Another, *L. auratum*, is waxy white, bowl shaped, with a golden streak and, often, crimson spots. These lilies are favorites because of their exotic charm, their colors, and their unusual fragrance. They are easy to grow.

Plant 6 inches deep, 12 inches apart in sun or part shade.

Hybrids of these lilies from Japan are now available. The best, *Jillian Wallace*, originated in Australia but it has made impressive performances in this country. One plant carried 7 flowers at one time, each measuring more than 9 inches across. The rich, carmine-red of *L. speciosum* seems to have spilled over on the huge, golden-striped, bowl-shaped flowers of *L. auratum*. The result is an August-blooming lily, 5 to 7 feet high, with white flowers, banded and heavily spotted with crimson.

L. Formosanum (September)

With the flowering of *Jillian Wallace*, the season begins to wane. The late-flowering strain of *L. formosanum* is still to come. It's a tall-growing, white, trumpet type. This lily will flower for you until frost or until the approaching wet season cuts it down. It also comes in dwarf and medium-sized forms, in early and midseason types. It's good for full sun or part shade. Plant the small bulbs 5 to 6 inches deep.

Some Pointers on Growing Lilies

Always treat lilies as living plants—never as dormant bulbs. For good results, move and transplant them in the fall (except Madonna lilies, which should be planted in July, August, or early September). In fall most lilies are through flowering and have built up their strength for next season's growth. We have found that lilies that are shipped long distances and then kept out of the ground in warm and dry places, lose their vitality and have difficulty establishing themselves.

Lilies require good drainage; ideally the soil should be moist, porous, mellow, and rich. If you can grow healthy annuals and perennials or a good vegetable garden, you shouldn't have the slightest difficulty with lilies. They do best in a soil that is neutral, or slightly acid; but some of the adaptable new strains, such as Olympic hybrids, have thrived in parts of the West where the soil is definitely on the alkaline side. Lilies will not tolerate excess water.

One of the top enemies of lilies is bulb rot, caused by soggy soil around the bulb. Avoid soggy soil by placing lily bulbs on the *surface* of an extra-thoroughly prepared and conditioned bed, then mounding 7 inches of soil mix over them. Best mix is composed of equal parts of leaf mold, sand, and well-rotted manure. Keep the raised soil in place with a board siding or a few rocks. Water with set sprinklers turned low. No matter how long the water runs, it won't stand around the bulbs. Elevated planting makes for warmer soil, stem rooting above the bulb, and better growth.

Lilies should be grown in full sun where summer light intensities are low, with high filtered shade all day where summer light intensities are high.

Once lilies are established in a good location, they will thrive and multiply. Each year many of them will produce more bulbs and better flowers until, as with daffodils and iris, they get so crowded that the young bulbs cannot find enough nourishment. Then they begin to get smaller and stop flowering altogether. When this happens, transplant clumps in fall after the flowers are gone.

Bulbs

TULIPS

In the spring garden the tulip is the proudest flower, never mixing informally with other plants, holding itself apart as one individual, one plant, one stem, one perfect flower. However, as a group of individuals they create our most appealing spring pictures, especially when unified by a ground cover planting of early-flowering annuals.

By choosing type and varieties you can enjoy tulips from April to June. By including species tulips in your collection you spread their uses into every part of the garden.

The cold-winter climates of the West have the most complete choice of species and varieties. The tulip needs a yearly drop in temperatures to 40° in the soil or in storage in order to rebuild the flower in the bulb. Therefore, in all warm winter areas, no attempt is made to grow the very early flowering hybrids or the species.

In getting acquainted with tulips, either through catalogs or at your nursery, a little knowledge of tulip history comes in handy.

Back in the 17th Century all of Europe suddenly decided to get rich quick with tulips. A grower of the regular self-colored species discovered a freak. The "one-color" bulb produced a flower that was feathered or checked with many colors.

The break in color was produced by a disease, probably mosaic, and although the color of the "broken" tulip was reproduced in the divisions of the broken bulb, plants from the seed of broken flowers produced normal flowers.

Prices of these unusual breaks rose to fantastic heights. The bubble broke when the hundreds of thousands of new bulbs flooded the market. There were fewer people who wanted tulips to look at than people who wanted tulips to get rich with.

The names of many classes of tulips date back to Europe's tulip mania period.

The Breeders of today are the solid-colored tulips that were developed in the race to produce a superior broken tulip. They differed in two respects from the earlier tulips: colors were in the dull pastel shades, and the petals were flat at the ends.

The Cottage types were not named to suggest an inferior tulip, as cottage compared to palace, but merely because the first breeding stock of this class was found in English cottage gardens. Although there are variations in type, the identifying characteristic of the cottage tulip is the pointed petals.

The Darwin type was arrived at by selection of Breeders. The characteristic shape of the Darwins emphasizes the flat petal-ends of the Breeders.

The Broken tulips sold today are found in each type. Broken tulips from the Breeders are known as Bybloemens or Bizaares according to their markings.

The Darwin broken tulips are classed as Rembrandts.

Other classes listed in the catalogs are: Single and Double Early, Parrot, Lily-flowered hybrids, and species. Taken altogether they present a multitude of garden opportunities. Here are a few members, typical ones of each group, listed in order of their season of bloom in the garden.

EARLY TULIPS (April-flowering)

The Early tulips are more shallow in flower and shorter in stems than the later flowering groups. One of the best classes for forcing indoors. They are not satisfactory in warm-winter climate areas.

Single Early. Large single flowers on short, 10-16 inch stems. Bright colors in yellows, reds, oranges, and whites. Two favorite varieties are *Keizerskroon*, crimson-scarlet with a wide band of bright yellow, and *General De Wet*, golden orange stippled with scarlet.

Double Early. Double, peony-like flowers on 10-12 inch stems, blooming a little later than the Single Early. About the same color range. Plant in masses for most effective bloom. Typical varieties: *Boule de Neige*, snow white; *Electra*, cherry-red.

MIDSEASON TULIPS

The two types which follow the Early tulips and precede the May-flowering by 10 days or so:

Mendel. A cross of the Darwin and Cottage varieties. Outstanding varieties are *Krelage's Triumph*, crimson-red; *Orange Wonder*, red edged with orange; *Weber*, white with rose border.

Triumph. A cross of Cottage and Single Early. Large, single or full double flowers on strong straight 20-inch stems.

EARLY SINGLE

EARLY DOUBLE

CLUSIANA

KAUFMANNIANA

PRAESTANS

196 TULIPS

LATE TULIPS (May-flowering)

Breeders. Large, rounded flowers on tall stiff stems to 40 inches. Wide range of colors with orange, bronze, and purple shades predominant. Typical varieties: *Bronze Queen,* orange-red with yellow edge; *Louis XIV,* bluish-violet with tawny margin.

Cottage. This group offers the widest range of colors of any of the classes—whites, pinks, reds, and yellows. Rather open flowers with pointed petals on 18-30 inch stems. Typical varieties: *Advance,* scarlet with outside shaded rose; *Golden Harvest,* lemon yellow.

Lily-flowering. Classified as a sub-group of Cottage tulips, these are hybrids resulting from a cross of a pink Darwin tulip and *T. retroflexa.* Graceful, lily-shaped flowers with long pointed petals. Available in shades of yellow, pink, red, and white.

Darwins. Very large egg- or cup-shaped flowers with a square base on sturdy stems to 30 inches. A full range of clear colors, often with shadings of contrasting colors. Some varieties: *Clara Butt,* a famous soft, salmon-pink; *Pride of Haarlem,* an older variety, rich purplish-rose.

Double May-flowering. Large, full double, peony-like flowers on stems to 20 inches. Varieties: *Mount Tacoma,* pure white, the largest double; *Coxa,* bright red edged with white.

Parrots. These strange and exotic tulips are sports of the solid colored tulips. Their long, deeply fringed and ruffled petals have striped, feathered, or flamed markings. Brilliant colors in widely varied combinations. Typical varieties: *Fantasy,* sport of Clara Butt, salmon-pink with scarlet and green markings; *Blue Parrot,* bright blue; *Therese,* shades of bright scarlet with white base.

Broken. As explained above, these are the tulips that caused the tulip mania of the 17th Century.

Byblœmens—(broken Breeders), rose-violet markings on a white undercolor.

Bizarres—(Broken Breeders), red-brown markings on a yellow undercolor.

Rembrandts — (broken Darwins), stripes and flames of color appear on grounds of yellow, red, violet, brown, or white.

SPECIES TULIPS

The species or botanical tulips are in many ways the most interesting of all tulips. There is greater variety in size, form, and character. They also are the earliest to bloom, usually in March and early April. Most of them have stocky sturdy stems and stand up well in blustery spring weather.

Species tulips look their best when grouped thickly in pockets among rocks or among paving stones. They thrive under rock garden growing conditions—sun and good drainage.

T. acuminata (T. cornuta). To 12-18 inches. An unusual tulip with very narrow, red and yellow twisted petals.

T. chrysantha. To 6 inches. Very small flowers, cherry red outside, interior a pure, light yellow. A dainty tulip for the rock garden.

T. clusiana. LADY TULIP. To 10 inches. The small, slender, pointed flowers have cherry red outer petals and white inner petals, and resemble a vertically striped candystick. A fragrant miniature for rock gardens. Does well in warm as well as cold climates.

T. dasystemon. To 6 inches. The stems bear several small star-shaped flowers, canary yellow with white tips.

T. eichleri. To 8-10 inches. Very large, brilliant scarlet flowers with black base edged with yellow. One of the best for garden cultivation.

T. fosteriana. To 12 inches. Large, brilliant red flowers. Variety *Red Emperor:* Very early blooming; huge, startling red blossoms, often 6-8 inches across, on 16-inch stem. A beautiful tulip, but difficult to use with other flowers because of its overwhelming size and color. Other varieties available in shades of red and red-orange.

T. kaufmanniana. WATERLILY TULIP. To 6-8 inches. Early blooming. Large, lily-shaped flowers marked with red on the outside, yellow center. A beautiful tulip with many hybrids in yellows, red, and white.

T. prœstans. To 12-15 inches. A large, early blooming species with several bright orange-red flowers. *Fusilier* is an improved variety.

CULTURE

Give tulips full sun except where May temperatures are unusually high. Follow the rule of planting 2½ times as deep as the bulb is wide, except in warm winter areas where they should be planted deeper. Plant in September-October in cold winter areas but delay until November in warm winter sections. In the latter, it is a wise precaution to buy bulbs in September-October and store in refrigerator (40-45°), if you have room, or in a cool basement for about 1 month.

Gophers and field mice consider tulip bulbs a great delicacy. You'll get complete protection by planting in baskets of ¼-inch wire mesh.

Best effect when planted in groups 4-5 inches apart. Place bulbs at same depth to insure uniformity of blooming and height.

DARWIN

COTTAGE

PARROT

LILY

Vines

Gardeners in the West have been making several changes in the vine department. The significant one is in the ways they are building structure to display vines instead of using vines to display structure. Vine supports are often built into the architecture of the house. More gardeners use a fence to display a vine than plant a vine to hide a fence. More plant a vine to enhance the architecture of the house than to hide it.

The functional use of vines in building and furnishing outdoor living rooms has become most important. If you are making plans for additions or changes in garden or house take a few hours off to really look at a few mature vines. They are, of course, interesting in themselves. Each has individuality. Some vines are opaque; some are transparent. Shiny leaves reflect light; dull leaves absorb it. Some leaves let light shine through in glowing translucence. Vines have texture, large scale and small, according to leaf size. There are bold textures to use with strong architectural lines and delicate textures for slender columns and narrow trim lines. There are vines that take wind and vines that need complete protection. The manner of their climbing —by clinging, twining, scrambling, or leaning—will have much to do with their use.

Once you are acquainted with a vine you can fit it to its best use.

THE MULTIPLE USE OF VINES

Vines are valuable as interceptors of the hot Western sun. When grown directly on the wall, a vine of higher heat resistance must be chosen than if trained away from the wall, as on a trellis set 2-4 feet out from the western wall of the house. There is much to be said in favor of building any trellis out from the wall of the house. The vine itself will be healthier because of air circulation; you can get at the vine to prune it; the planting hole can be made away from the foundation of the house.

198 VINES

One solution to the problem of glass areas that receive too much sun is the vine-covered, free-

standing vertical screen. Set up as a series of baffles they can cut off most of the sun's rays without shutting out the view.

Where there is any amount of wind, a 5 or 6-foot fence is not adequate wind protection. By extending the wall of the house with a trellis, you can get the effect of an 8-10 foot wall as soon as the vine

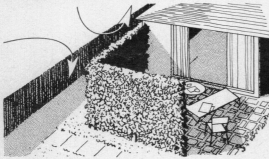

covers it, without the forbidding look of a high solid wall. The lattice for the vine will in itself break up the wind while the vine is taking over.

All of the stockade feel of board, grapestake or masonry fences can be overcome with vines. Vines, especially ivy, can be used with wire fencing to create a completely foliaged fence. Such vine fences can be built up across large front lawns, seen so commonly in older neighborhoods, to give an added area of privacy without the solid wall look that a fence gives.

Vines can be used to enrich the architecture by:
    softening a fascia line or a corner
    tracing a design on a wall
    encircling a post
    providing color against the house
    saying welcome at a doorway.

Vines trained on ropes can be used in many interesting ways. They can carry a line of color above a fence or give overhead direction to a path, or just decorate for fun.

SUPPORTS FOR VINES

Vine structures must be heavy enough to hold the weight of vine and prevent swaying and damage to the vine fabric. Wherever possible the top weight of a tall growing vine should be carried by the fascia, or an outrigger or a rafter. Don't make the mistake of thinking that a strong trunking vine is self-supporting.

As top weight piles up it is liable to topple over unless tied or fastened in some way at the top. Supports for tall growing vines, that can be fastened to an overhead when the vines reach it, may consist of a simple ladder device or a single wire or two. In this way they act as vertical guides rather than as permanent supports.

HOW VINES CLIMB

Twining. Plants twist vertically as they grow. Some twine clockwise, others counter-clockwise. Some twine closely, others loosely. Almost all twiners have too small a turn for a large post or tree. A cord or covered wire is the best support.

Some of the twiners: Actinidia, akebia, celastrus, morning glory, mandevilla, polygonum, solanum, thunbergia, star jasmine, wistaria. Both vertical and top supports are needed, as many spill over from the top. Most of them tend to become heavy eventually.

Tendrils. Vines with fingering devices that close down and fasten to a support, to themselves, or to neighboring plant material. Tendrils grow out straight until they make contact and take hold, then they contract into a spiral spring to draw the vine up to the support.

Tendrils may be formations of stem or leaf. The leaves of clematis wrap around the supports. The tendrils of gourds are like branches.

Clinging. Several of the tendril climbers have special devices for clinging to solid surfaces. The tendrils of Boston ivy and Virginia creeper are furnished with suction-cup discs. Several have hook-like tips or claws that enable them to hook into small crevices or irregularities. Campsis and Doxanthus are examples.

Root-bearing stems. English ivy, *Ficus pumila,* and climbing hydrangeas are equipped with roots along the stems that grow toward the shady inside of the vine. Reaching a wall they take hold by means of rootlets.

Weavers. The jasmines and roses climb without twining and without tendrils by weaving. New shoot growth grows toward the dark side of the vine and thus weaves through the older canes.

Scrambling—Leaning. Several shrubs with vine-like habits are in this group. They are not primarily climbers but are used and sold as such.

PLANTING AND CULTURE

The same attention should be given a vine in planting as is given a shrub or tree. Drainage, root space, adequate supplies of food are just as important to a vine as a shrub. When crowded between shrubs or among other plants, compensate for the crowding by light but frequent applications of fertilizers. Special watering attention should be given to vines planted under overhangs. You can't depend on rains to saturate the soil.

— Encyclopedia —

ACTINIDIA CHINENSIS. YANGTAO. Deciduous. Sun or partial shade. All zones. Growth to 30 ft. Leaves 5-8 in. long. Small cream colored flowers in August are followed by 2 in. round fruits; edible, flavor of gooseberry. Twining vine but sparse structure permits easy management and training to display its unusual qualities.

Leaves, medium green above, white-velvety beneath, are individually handsome in outline and venation. They space themselves in attractive, controlled growth pattern, as if each were posing for a painter of Japanese prints.

The foliage mass has subtle color appeal, with the soft, green of leaves blending into dark red stems. Velvety texture invites closer inspection.

Plant for close-up pleasure from a room of the house, as along the top of a window, or as a special treat along the guest tour of the garden. Train around a post, against a fence or trellis. Very good against a wall.

AKEBIA QUINATA. FIVELEAF AKEBIA. All zones. Deciduous, or evergreen in mild winters. Moderate growth to 15 ft. Twining. Dainty leaves, each a multiple of 5 leaflets. Its quaint, secretive blossoms, dully purple, are more in the nature of a surprise than a show.

This akebia being neither too crowded nor too thin makes for good patterning against fence or wall. The vine might be likened in design to a paisley shawl, and like a shawl, it can be flung across a fence for special interest. An example: akebia growing beside a gate on a 4 ft., pale yellow board fence. A dwarf Mugho pine, planted to shade its roots, provides the green in winter when akebia is leafless.

ALLAMANDA CATHARTICA. Evergreen shrubby climber. Sun. Very warmest spots in zone 13. Height to 10 ft., depending upon amount of pruning and pinching. Dense foliage of dark green rather thick roundish, 6-in. leaves. Flowers golden-yellow tubes, flaring to 3 in. wide, with white mark in throat; June. There are many horticultural forms, offering larger flowers, and variations in color.

AMPELOPSIS BREVIPEDUNCULATA. BLUE-BERRY CLIMBER. Deciduous. Hardy all zones. Strong rampant climber, with twining tendrils, to 20 ft. Large, handsome, 3-lobed, 5-in. leaves. Many clusters of small grapes turn from greenish-ivory to a brilliant metallic blue in late summer and fall.

Grows in full sun or shade. Give it strong support on trellis or arbor. Use for dense summer shade.

Boston ivy and Virginia creeper, formerly included in the genus *Ampelopsis* are now placed under the genus *Parthenocissus* because, unlike *Ampelopsis,* both have discs at the ends of their tendrils.

ANEMOPAEGMA CHAMBERLAYNII. *(Bignonia chamberlaynii).* GOLDEN TRUMPET VINE. Not known to be in cultivation. The plants sold under this name or *Bignonia chamberlaynii* are probably *Doxantha unguis-cati* (which see).

ANTIGONON LEPTOPUS. QUEEN'S WREATH. CORAL VINE. ROSA DE MONTANA. Evergreen. Zones 6-13. Revels in high summer heat. Once established, recovers quickly from any frost damage. Fast growing, tendril climber to 40 ft. Foliage, of 3-5 in. heart-shaped or arrow-shaped leaves, is open and airy. The small, rose-pink flowers are carried in long trailing sprays from midsummer to fall.

Give it the hottest exposure in the garden for best flowering. Water generously while in bloom; let it dry off during the rest of the year. Plant it for its summer color rather than as a screen.

ASPARAGUS. Hardy outdoors in zones 12 and 13, in protected spots of zones 9 and 10; indoors elsewhere. Ornamental half of the asparagus genus—graceful climbing and trailing relatives of the garden vegetable—are as sadly neglected a group of plants as any in horticulture. While almost everyone is familiar with the common florist forms, principally asparagus fern and smilax, few of the hundred-odd other species are planted in Western gardens. As a matter of fact, few gardeners realize there are ornamental asparagus other than the two or three in commerce.

There are many forms: Some are rampant climbers with runners 40 feet or more that range along a fence or reach up into the branches of a tree; some are delicate trailing species, some are dwarfs, ideal for potting, some are medium size, upright shrubs. Foliage varies from light to dark green and comes in all sorts of fine, ferny, or coarse textures.

Though the foliage of many ornamental asparagus species looks as delicate and perishable as maidenhair fern, it's unbelievably tough and wilt-resistant. The small leaves are actually cladodes or branchlets with many of the water-retaining characteristics of succulents and cacti. They'll hold up in dry winds which would lay almost any fern flat on the ground. The root system, like that of edible asparagus, is thick and fleshy, developed to hold and conserve moisture. While the plants like moisture and delight in liberal watering, they tolerate drought to a degree that's astonishing in a plant so lush and green.

A. plumosus. ASPARAGUS FERN. Perhaps the most popular species, some of its forms rivaling the finest ferns in beauty. Woody, climbing vine which may reach 20 ft. or more when it's happy, with fern-like fronds made up of bright green ¼-in. needle-like leaves. Bears purplish-black berries in the fall. Usually trained on a trellis, against a lathhouse wall, or over porches, a fine foliage background for fuchsias, begonias, camellias, and other shade plants. Used in quantity by florists as cut foliage because it holds up for days without wilting.

There are several varieties: Var. *compactus* and var. *nanus* are dwarf forms, suitable for potting or planting outdoors under trees with the lacy foliage of ferns and columbine. Var. *robustus,* another vine, is a very rank grower. Var. *tenuissimus* is a wiry, slender-stemmed, shrubbier form. Var. *comorensis* is a strong-growing, light green climber.

A. sprengeri. Another well known form, commonly grown in hanging baskets. Graceful, twiggy, arching stems, with slender, light green needle-like 1-in. leaves, are covered with clusters of fragrant pinkish flowers in summer. Bright red berries in winter. Drought resistance makes *A. sprengeri* an ideal container plant in dry areas where a single forgotten watering would be fatal to container-grown ferns.

A. asparagoides. SMILAX. Still found in old gardens but rarely listed by nurserymen. Tall, slender, branching vine may go to 20 ft. in warm climates. Glossy, oval, 1-in. leaves, and small ¼-in. dark purple berries. Most smilax is grown in hothouses for the florist trade, while its virtue as a garden plant is ignored.

A. falcatus. Native of tropical Asia and Africa, is one of the largest and finest members of the clan. Giant vines rapidly climbing to 50 ft. Stems are thick and woody, foliage of dark green, sickle-shaped, 3-in. leaves. Clusters of fragrant white flowers appear from time to time during summer, followed by brown berries. Trained against a broad expanse of wall or over a building, it makes a magnificent background for tropical plants.

A. virgatus. (*A. elongatus*). Differs from most other species in its shrubby habit. Stands erect, to 3-6 ft. with dark green needle-like foliage. Use it as a feathery accent in the same situation you might use one of the larger ferns.

Ornamental asparagus makes the most of almost any soil, but responds wonderfully to regular feeding with high-nitrogen fertilizers. Unlike ferns, it prefers a slightly alkaline soil.

In general, asparagus grows best in partial shade, and will survive under minimum light conditions in patio corners, under carports, and in other dark areas where many other plants would tend to pale and grow spindly. Like most shade plants, however, they'll take almost full sun in cool areas near the ocean.

When grown in pots, they tend to become rootbound quickly. This means regular potting into larger containers or dividing clumps and potting them separately. They're easy to propagate by division of clumps or, as most growers do, by seed, which comes in the fall and germinates very easily. A seedling grows into a sizeable plant in a single season.

BEAUMONTIA GRANDIFLORA. HERALD TRUMPET. EASTER LILY VINE. Evergreen. Zones 12-13. Twining climber of moderate growth to 10 ft. and as wide. Large, dark green, 8-in. oval leaves, smooth and shiny above, downy beneath, give the vine a lush tropical effect. From May until late September, carries fragrant, trumpet-shaped, 5-in. white flowers—just like Easter lilies. Blooms are produced only on wood 2 or 3 years old. Best grown on loose frame in full sun, or espaliered on a south or west wall.

BIGNONIA. Botanists have reclassified the plants formerly in this genus so that the trumpet vines you knew as *Bignonia* are now placed in other genera. Many are still sold under the old names. Since most gardeners still compare one "bignonia" to another when they make their selections we have brought them all under *Bignonia* and cross refer them to the genus under which they are described.

B. australis. See **Pandorea.**
B. buccinatorius. See **Phaedranthus.**
B. chamberlaynii. See **Anemopaegma, Doxantha.**
B. cherere. See **Phaedranthus.**
B. chinensis. See **Campsis.**
B. jasminoides. See **Pandorea.**
B. radicans. See **Campsis.**
B. speciosa. See **Clystostoma.**
B. tweediana. See **Doxantha.**
B. violacea. See **Clystostoma.**

BOUGAINVILLEA. Evergreen. Sun. Zones 12-13 and borderline in 9-11. Some Northwesterners grow the vine in containers; move it to cold greenhouse in winter. Strong-growing, twining climber to 20 ft. Leaves are alternate, medium size, medium green. Insignificant flowers are seated in the middle of 3 bracts. It is these bracts that transform an everyday green vine into a spectacle of brilliance and gaiety, dazzling in the sunshine, tinting nearby shadows with reflected light. Many forms bring many colors—coronation hues, from purple-reds to magentas, to scarlets. Height of bloom, in July.

Bougainvillea is at its best on a warm wall where there is not much color competition. Can be controlled by pruning. Responds to rich soil, heavier than normal fertilizing.

CALONYCTION ACULEATUM. MOONFLOWER. Perennial usually treated as an annual. Very fast growth to 20-30 ft. Leaves, large, 3-8 in.; heart-shaped, form a dense mass. Flowers are flaring tubes 5-6 in. across and 5-6 in. long, fragrant, lavender-pink or white; blooms from July to frost. Colored ones close during the day and open after sundown. White variety often remains open until noon. For a blue and pink or white color combination, make alternate plantings of moonflower and blue morning glory along a fence. Seeds must be soaked or notched before sowing. Let them remain in water for a day or two—until they swell to twice or 3 times the size of seeds in the packet. Support with strings, wire, trellis.

CAMPSIS. TRUMPET CREEPER. Deciduous. Vigorous climbers that cling to wood, brick, and stucco surfaces with aerial rootlets. There are 3 species available: 1 from China, 1 from central United States, and a hybrid of the two.

C. radicans. *(Bignonia radicans, Tecoma radicans).* COMMON TRUMPET CREEPER. All zones. Sun. Fast growing to 40 ft. Leaves of 9-11 leaflets, 1½-3 in. long. Flowers, deep orange-red, funnel-shaped, in clusters of 6-12, appear in August-September.

The vine is so bursting with health and beauty that it's hard to keep within bounds. Dense, strong, medium-green foliage piles up in tiers like wistaria foliage.

Use it for large-scale effects; a quick summer sun screen. Can be trained as flowering hedge; branches become self-supporting after the first year if guided and shortened.

C. grandiflora. *(C. chinensis, Bignonia chinensis).* CHINESE TRUMPET CREEPER. Zones 5-13. Not so vigorous, tall growing, or hardy as the American native, *C. radicans.*

C. tagliabuana. Hardy all zones except —20° in zone 1. All hybrids of the American and Chinese trumpet vines are grouped under this name. Var. *Mme. Galen* with salmon-red flowers is most generally available.

CARDIOSPERMUM HALICACABUM. BALLOON VINE. Perennial, generally treated as an annual. Fast growth to 5-10 ft. Leaves divided into deeply-toothed, oblong leaflets. White 1¼-in. flowers, several in a cluster. Best known for its 1-in. inflated seedpods. Train it on a trellis where the pods can be viewed from below.

The balloon vine likes heat and accepts hot, dry, desert conditions. Seeds should be planted directly in ground when soil is warm; do not transplant.

CELASTRUS SCANDENS. BITTERSWEET. Deciduous. Hardy all zones, but produces best fruit where it gets winter chilling. Twining to 20 ft. Leaves carried alternately on slender, angled branches. Prized for its crimson berries enclosed in orange pods, carried throughout the winter. Very useful for long-lasting indoor arrangements.

Vigorous, bittersweet will become tangled mass of intertwining branches unless held under control by regular pinching and pruning.

CISSUS. A group of tender, evergreen vines distinguished for their foliage. They show in many ways their close relationship to both the Virginia creeper and the true grape. Their hardiness varies somewhat by species but all except *C. hypoglauca* show frost damage at about 23°. Recovery is rapid. These species are available in California nurseries.

C. antarctica. KANGAROO TREEBINE. An extremely vigorous climber when established. Medium green foliage. Shiny leaves, 3-4 in. long and 1-1½ in. wide. A useful evergreen where foliage is wanted that doesn't call attention to itself. Sun or part shade.

C. capensis. EVERGREEN GRAPE. Rapid grower. Needs constant pruning and pinching during growing season to keep it under control. Leaf size and shape similar to the true grape. New growth reflects the colors of the hairs on surface of both leaves and stems, giving it a rosy-rust color. As leaves develop, they turn to a strong light green, burnished with copper. Used as an overhead screen, the evergreen grape is not too light for summer and not too dense for winter. Will take full sun but roots should be shaded.

C. gongylodes. Tall climbing with 3-fingered leaves that are 3-lobed. Small, reddish-brown flowers. When the season's growth stops, a tuber grows out at the end of each branch. New plants can be produced from these tubers.

C. hypoglauca. The hardiest of the group. Rapid growth to 15 ft. in 1 season. Foliage is strong in texture with silvery-bronze color tones. Highly polished, 5-fingered leaves. A multipurpose vine, in sun or shade.

C. rhombifolia. Needs all-year warmth for fast growth. Attractive leaves of 3 rhomboidal leaflets, with edges scalloped between points where the veins terminate. Bright olive-green foliage with bronzy tones from the rusty hairs above and beneath the new leaves. It is especially handsome with redwood and related colors.

C. striata. A miniature Virginia creeper with small 5-leaflet leaves nicely spaced along reddish stems. Use to make long traceries against plain surfaces, as ground cover, or to cover walls where fine texture is wanted. Sun or shade. Hardier than evergreen grape. Thrives in San Francisco Bay Area.

CLEMATIS. A genus of some 230 species, of which 8 are important to Western gardens. All except *C. armandii* are deciduous and hardy in all zones.

C. armandii. EVERGREEN CLEMATIS. Zones 4-13. Fast-growing evergreen to 20 ft. Highly valued for both bloom and foliage. Glossy, dark green leaves, 3-5 in. long, arch downward and arrange themselves along the stem in a pattern of repetitions. Glistening white, 2-in., open, star-like flowers in clusters in March-April.

Slow to start, the vine really races when established. Must be trained at weekly intervals during growing season to prevent new arms with their reaching tendrils from snarling. Select the arms that will give you the design you want and cut off everything else.

Interesting uses include training along fence tops and rails, outlining roof gables, accenting an entrance.

C. montana. ANEMONE CLEMATIS. Vigorous climber. Leaves of 3 cut-toothed leaflets. Anemone-like flowers about 2 in. across, open white, turn pink; in June. Var. *rubens,* PINK ANEMONE CLEMATIS, has reddish young growth, rose or pink flowers. Blossoms from old wood, so prune lightly.

C. jackmanii. Strong growing; will reach 20 ft. in one season after being cut back to the ground. Easily controlled, however, and can be kept at 6 ft. Has leaves divided into leaflets, the upper ones simple; 7-in.-wide, purple flowers from July on. Vine can be pruned severely as flowers are carried on new wood. Usual method is to cut back to within 2 joints of the base of the new growth made in the previous season. Cut back when the buds begin to swell in early spring.

Some of the *C. jackmanii* hybrids are: *Gypsy Queen,* deep violet, with wine-crimson in it. *Star of India,* purple, barred with red; *Mme. Andre,* deep rich crimson; *Ramona,* sky-blue flowers.

C. lanuginosa. A parent of many fine forms. Grows only to 5-6 ft. Leaves simple or with 3 entire leaflets. Flowers 6 in. across, lavender or bluish-gray in July.

C. lawsoniana. Thought to be a cross of *C. patens fortunei* and *C. lanuginosa.* Flowers 6-8 in. across, rosy-purple and dark veined.

C. l. henryi. The best known form of *C. lawsoniana.* Very large, white flowers, 7-9 in. across; July-August. Modest grower; can be used for tracery on light frame, trellis, baffle. Can be cut back; flowers borne on new wood.

C. paniculata. SWEET AUTUMN CLEMATIS. Vigorous, fast growing. Leaves of 3-5 entire or lobed leaflets. Has few equals for profusion of blooms; forms a thick blanket of fragrant, snowy-white, star-shaped, 1-in. flowers; in autumn. Since flowers are on new growth, you can control by severe cut-backs. Use as ground cover, as filler, to hide raw banks, to climb a tree.

C. patens. LILAC CLEMATIS. Less vigorous, to 12 ft. Leaves of 3-5 entire leaflets. Flowers 4-6 in. across, white to violet; in May and June. One of the parents of such important hybrids as: *Mrs. James Baker*, flowers nearly white, ribbed with dark carmine; *Duchess of Edinburgh*, double white flowers; *Nelly Moser*, mauve-pink with darker red bar; *Sophia*, flowers deep lilac-purple on edges, with light green bars.

All borne on last season's wood; hold pruning to thinning out unwanted growth and encouraging new growth to fill in.

C. tangutica. GOLDEN CLEMATIS. To 10 ft. Leaves divided into 3 or 4 pairs of toothed or lobed leaflets. Golden flowers in June and generally again in the fall. Flowers are followed by feathery fruits.

CULTURE: How to be sure of which pruning method to follow? Since there is some confusion as to the classification of the hybrids, we believe that you are safe in following this rule. Treat all late-blooming vines as needing new wood; all those blooming in June and earlier, as needing old wood.

In planting, take care that the stems are not bent or twisted in any way. Plant deep. Peg down main stem to first joint so that it is buried. Roots will form along stem. Stake at time of planting and set a circle of wire or stakes around the plant to protect brittle stems.

CLIANTHUS PUNICEUS. PARROT-BEAK. Evergreen. Zones 7-13. Moderate growth to 12 ft. The foliage of this shrub-like vine, hangs gracefully in an open pattern, made up of sprays of small light green, glistening leaflets. Flowers, rose-scarlet, sweet-pea-shaped, with 3-in. parrot-beak keels, swing downward between the leaves. June blooming.

Give it a protected warm location. If soil is heavy add sand, manure, or compost. Water generously throughout blooming season. Train as espalier or on support in open to bring out full beauty of leaf and flowers.

CLYTOSTOMA CALLISTEGIOIDES. (*Bignonia speciosa, B. violacea*). VIOLET TRUMPET VINE. Evergreen. Sun or part shade. Zones 7-13. Treat as perennial in colder climates. Strong growing; will clamber over anything. Needs support on wall. Extended shoots hang down, making the vine one to look up into. Leaves divided into 2 glossy dark green, 2-4 in. leaflets with wavy margins. Violet-lavender or pale purple trumpets 3 in. long and nearly as wide, are borne in sprays at end of shoots in April and July.

COBAEA SCANDENS. CUP-AND-SAUCER VINE. Perennial, treated as an annual. Fast growth in warm weather to 20-30 ft. Climbs by curls or twining branched tendrils, will cling to rough surfaces without support. Leaves divided into 2 or 3 pairs of oval 4-in. leaflets. Flowers bell-shaped, first greenish then violet or rosy-purple; also a white-flowered form.

Seeds hard coated, often rot before germinating when sown in usual manner outdoors. Start seeds in 4 in. pot. Notch side of seed with knife and press edgewise into soil which has been moistened. Barely cover the seed. Keep moist but not wet. Transplant to warmest, sunniest location possible when weather warms.

CONVOLVULUS MAURITANICUS. GROUND MORNING-GLORY. (See chapter on ground covers.) Perennial, evergreen in mild winters. Prostrate, twining, spreading to cover a 3-ft. area. Small oval leaves, covered with white soft hairs. Flowers, 1 in., blue with white throat, in summer.

Use in sun or part shade. Blooms more profusely and is more compact in the sun. Good effect in hanging baskets or spilling over a wall.

DISTICTIS LACTIFLORA. (*D. cinerea*). VANILLA SCENTED TRUMPET VINE. Evergreen. Sun and part shade. Zone 13. Frost damage at 24°. More restrained than most trumpet vines; can be kept in bounds without severe pruning. The leaves, with their 2-3 deep green, oblong, 2½-in. leaflets, make attractive pattern the year around. Three-inch trumpets in various shades of violet, lavender, and white, flow through the vine for almost 8 months.

D. riversi. ROYAL TRUMPET VINE. This patented hybrid with *D. lactiflora* as one parent, is larger in leaf and flower—yellow tubes, 6 in. long, face of royal purple with orange throat.

DOLICHOS. Perennial twining vines which produce a dense cover of bright green leaves divided fan-wise into 3 leaflets.

D. lablab. HYACINTH BEAN. Perennial, often grown as an annual. Fast growth to 10 ft. Leaflets very broad, ovate, to 3-6 in. Several sweet-pea-like flowers, purple to white, are carried on rigid stems, well in front of the foliage. Flowers followed by attractive velvety 1-in. long seed pods. Use for quick screen.

D. lignosus. AUSTRALIAN PEA VINE. Somewhat woody perennial. Leaves with small triangular 1½-in. leaflets. Several small white or rose-purple flowers clustered at the ends of long stalks. Often remains evergreen in mild winters. Use it to grow up frames, string with wire, to screen warm or play area through summer months. Plant seed directly in the ground, since plants are difficult to move from pots or flats. Full sun.

DOXANTHA UNGUIS-CATI. (*Bignonia tweediana*, also sometimes sold under the name of *Bignonia chamberlaynii* or *Anemopaegma chamberlaynii*). CATS-CLAW. YELLOW TRUMPET VINE. Evergreen, deciduous in cold winters. Hot sun. Zones 7-13 with preference for heat of interior valleys and desert. Fast growing and high climbing, with "claws" that will cling to almost anything. Inclined to produce leaves and flowers at end of stems. Leaves of 2 ovate, glossy green, 2-in. leaflets. Yellow trumpets that flare to 2 in. wide are borne in early spring. Prune severely after blooming to keep this rampant vine under control.

EUONYMUS FORTUNEI. WINTERCREEPER. Evergreen. Hardy all zones. Woody creepers and trailing shrubs. (See chapter on shrubs for description of species and varieties.)

As a ground cover the wintercreepers take sun or shade but have a tendency to mound up. If not given a support on which to climb the plant remains small and bushy. As a climber it covers a flat surface as an even, very orderly mat.

Probably the most hardy evergreen vine. Full sun or part shade. Easy to grow. Adapted to most soils.

FATSHEDERA LIZEI. Evergreen. Zones 7-13. Young leaves will tip burn at 20-25°; makes rapid recovery from frost injury. This shrubby vine is a hybrid between *Fatsia japonica moseri* and *Hedera helix hibernica* (Irish ivy). Fatshedera clearly shows characteristics of both parents. Dark green, highly polished, large 6-8 in. leaves with 3-5 pointed lobes, look like those of giant ivy.

Shrubby like fatsia, yet sends out long trailing stems like ivy.

No special soil requirements. Susceptible to black aphis.

Fatshedera is a challenge to a plant sculptor. Its tendency to grow vertically can be altered by persistent guidance before the stems harden. Stem elongation can be stopped by pinching out. Can be pruned or manipulated into almost any form. With favorable growing conditions, fatshedera will put on considerable weight, so don't rely on fragile or makeshift supports.

Although the vine will take considerable sun, looks best in shade. One of the few really indoor-outdoor plants—perfectly at home in the entrance and in the living room.

FICUS PUMILA. (*F. repens*). CREEPING FIG. Outdoors in zones 7-13; indoors elsewhere. Sometimes reluctant to start climbing but once it takes hold will cling adhesively to stone, cement, wood, and brick. The growing fingers of the creeping fig grow outward and upward in slow curves, embroidering as they go with small, tough, rounded leaves, delightfully varied in color from yellow-greens to deep and rust-green. As the vine ages, fruiting branches bear leaves of larger scale.

No special culture needed. In addition to wall cover, the creeping fig is often trained to cover the risers of steps or the exposed cement foundation of a house. Will not climb on hot, south and west facing walls. Does well in shade of porch. Handsome on conservatory walls.

GELSEMIUM SEMPERVIRENS. CAROLINA JESSAMINE. Evergreen. Sun. Zones 7-13. Twining, shrubby; moderate growth to 20 ft. Clean pairs of glistening warm-green 4-in. leaves hang in neat foliage patterns on long streamers. On a trellis they cascade and swing in the wind, pointing downward with lifting ends. Fragrant tubular, yellow flowers to 1-1½ in. long, appear in early spring.

Since gelsemium is of moderate growth and about half-way between dainty and strong in texture, it can be used in many ways. It can be trained as a garland along the eaves of a porch or allowed to cover a fence where it will carry skyward the many yellows in the spring garden.

GOURD. Although a number of genera and species produce ornamental gourds, the most commonly planted are the following 3 annual vines: *Cucurbita pepo ovifera*. YELLOW-FLOWERED GOURD. Produces the great majority of small ornamental gourds, in many shapes and sizes. These may be all one color or striped. *Luffa cylindrica*. DISH CLOTH GOURD, VEGETABLE SPONGE GOURD. Also has yellow flowers. Bears cylindrical gourds 1-2 ft. in length, the fibrous interior of which may be used in place of a sponge or cloth for scrubbing and cleaning. *Lagenaria siceraria* (*L. vulgaris*). WHITE-FLOWERED GOURD. Bears gourds from 3 in. to 3 ft. in length. These may be round, bottle-shaped, dumbbell-shaped, crooknecked, coiled or spoon-shaped.

All are fast growing and will reach 10-15 ft. Sow seeds when ground is warm. Start indoors if growing season is short. Gourds need all the summer heat they can get to develop fruits by frost. If planting for ornamental gourd harvest give vines wire fence support so that large gourds can be held up individually. Plant seedlings 2 ft. apart. Once the vine gets underway, it will take regular deep waterings.

Harvest gourds when vines are dry. Cut some stem with each gourd so that you can hang it up to dry. Don't rush the drying by exposing to the sun or baking. During the drying period fungi may create a mottled pattern on surface of gourd. Many persons like the pattern. If you don't, wash the gourd with a disinfectant; after a week or so when gourds are thoroughly dry, soak them overnight to loosen thin outer skin. Then scrape or brush off until surface is clean. Now, when dry, the surface of the gourd can be treated like wood. Paint or lacquer for protection; diluted clear lacquer will protect without changing appearance of gourd.

HARDENBERGIA COMPTONIANA. (*Kennedya comptoniana*). LILAC VINE. Twining evergreen. Zones 7-13. Sun or shade. Does well on north or east wall. Slow growing to 7-8 ft.

A vine of delicate beauty. Leaves divided into 3, sometimes 5, dark green oval, or narrower, 2-3 in. leaflets. Open growing, with foliage casting its shadow in patterns.

Late winter, early spring blooming is important garden event. Masses of deep blue-violet flower clusters are like miniature wistarias at close range, more like froth at a distance.

Can be trained as a bush, but at its best when helped to show its open-pattern qualities. Planted at the base of Carolina jessamine (*Gelsemium sempervirens*) it will reach into the taller grower and display its blue with the gelsemium's yellow.

H. monophylla. (*Kennedya bimaculata*). SINGLE LEAF LILAC VINE. Coarser, more shrub-like, the leaves commonly with only 1 2-4 in. leaflet.

HEDERA. IVY. (Also see chapter on ground covers.) The West uses two species of ivy with equal generosity, the English and the Algerian. The latter has only one variety, the variegated form, but English ivy offers so many variations that it's next to impossible to classify them. Here are the dimensions of the typical plant of the two species grown in the West.

H. canariensis. ALGERIAN IVY. CANARY ISLAND IVY. Hardy in zones 7-13. Climbs by aerial rootlets. More tolerant of hot sun than English ivy. Leaves 5-8 in. wide, 3-5 lobed, and more widely spaced along the stems than English ivy. Var. *variegata* has leaves edged with greenish-white.

H. helix. ENGLISH IVY. Hardy all zones. Climbs by aerial rootlets. Leaves, dark green with pale veins, on sterile shoots are broadly ovate to triangular, 3-5 lobed, 2-4 in. wide at base and as long. On fertile shoots leaves are not lobed and are more ovate.

The fertile shoots branch out from the vine when fruiting begins and stop sending out aerial rootlets. Plants developed from cuttings of the fertile shoots develop into non-climbing shrubs. This form is called var. *arborescens*.

English ivy has a prodigious capacity for sporting—producing out of a clear sky a stem with leaves completely different from those on the rest of the plant. When cuttings are made of these stems, a new variety comes into existence.

The small and miniature-leafed varieties are useful in hanging baskets and as ground covers where a more restrained, finer texture than that of the regular English ivy is wanted. Some of the small-leafed varieties are: Var. *hahnii*. Light green leaves; dense-branching growth. Refined ground cover for small areas. Var. *conglomerata*. Slow-growing dwarf. Makes a very dense hedge. Var. *minima*. Leaves ½-1 in. across with 3-5 angular leaves.

An idea of the variety in forms can be had from the names of the ivys in the trade: *Dragon Tongue, Fan, Gold Dust, Pin Oak, Needle Point*.

In garden design, ivies can become fences (see below), roofs, or archways. The whitish and yellow variegated forms are interesting against dark backgrounds or when

204 VINES

used to lighten dark corners. The many delicately cut forms are for intimate use as traceries against brick or stucco, or as trailers from above a retaining wall.

The large-leafed English ivy will take shade or sun in all but the hot interiors. Small-leafed varieties are more susceptible to sunburn. Algerian ivy is best adapted in hot summer climates. The variegated form of Algerian ivy is preferred over the English variegated for ground cover and fences wherever it is hardy. Annual trimming and cutting back necessary to keep ivy from getting bunchy.

HOYA. WAX PLANT. Evergreen. Twining planting with small aerial rootlets. Of the 100 or more species, one is grown in the West.

H. carnosa. Grown as an indoor plant except in favored spots of zone 13 where it is used as any other vine—climbing posts, tree trunks, or grown in pots on shaded terraces and porches. Stiff, succulent, and wax-like leaves are red when small, turning green as they mature. The very fragrant flowers tightly fit into almost perfect clusters of creamy velvet white. In the center of each flower is a perfect 5-pointed star with a dark pink center.

Thrives best in partial shade at a temperature of 70° or more, when it starts growth in spring. Give deep and thorough soaking and then withhold water and allow soil to partially dry out before soaking again. Add manure, leaf mold, and sand for organic matter and drainage. In cool climates allow hoya to go dormant in winter months and water infrequently, only enough to keep the leaves from shriveling.

HIBBERTIA VOLUBILIS. GUINEA GOLD VINE. Evergreen. Zone 13. Fast growth, twining, to 8-10 ft. Leaves,

JASMINE CHART

Name	Dec. Ever.	Climate	Habit	Foliage	Flowers
J. beesianum	Dec. or Semi-ever.	Zones 3-13, but only in protected spots in 3-6. Sun and part shade.	Rank, fast growing, twining vine to 30 ft.	Dark, dull green 1-in. leaves.	Very fragrant, pink or deep rose flowers.
J. dichotomum GOLD COAST JASMINE	Ever.	Zones 7-13. Sun or semi-shade.	Rapid growing vine noted for seeding itself where it's not wanted.	Thick, glossy, oblong pointed leaves to 3 in. in 2's and 3's.	Fragrant clusters of white flowers opening at night in June.
J. floridum SHOWY JASMINE	Ever.	Zones 7-13. Sun or semi-shade.	Modest half-climber of rather rambling growth, angled shoots to 3-4 ft.	Smooth leaves of 3 leaflets 1½-in. long.	Clusters of 1½-in. yellow flowers in almost continuous bloom.
J. humile ITALIAN JASMINE	Ever.	Zones 7-13. Sun or semi-shade.	Erect willowy shoots will reach to 20 ft. and arch to make a 10-ft. mound. Can be trained as shrub.	Light green leaves of 3-7 leaflets, ovate to lance-shaped 2-in. long.	Fragrant clusters of bright yellow 1-in. flowers, July-September.
J. h. revolutum (J. revolutum) and J. h. glabrum (J. wallichianum) are distinguished from the species by their talle growth and more numerous leaflets and flowers.					
J. magnificum	Ever.	Zones 7-13	Climbing shrub	Simple, opp., leathery, shiny dark green leaves.	Fragrant white (purplish in bud) pinwheels to 1 in. across in 3-flowered clusters
J. mesnyi (J. primulinum) PRIMROSE JASMINE	Ever.	Zones 3-13, but not in cold spots of 3-6. Damaged at 5°. Sun or semi-shade.	Strong growing, long, sweeping, arching branches best treated in waterfall fashion—caught firmly at desired height and then allowed to spill over.	Dark green leaves of 3 lance-shaped leaflets, 1-3 in. long.	Bright lemon-yellow, 2-in. flowers scatter themselves through green foliage fountain February-April.
J. nudiflorum WINTER JASMINE	Dec. to semi-dec.	Zones 3-13. Sun or semi-shade.	Slender, willowy branches to 10-15 ft. Use as trailer to cascade over wall or embankment.	Glossy green leaves of 3 leaflets make a flowing curtain foliage.	Yellow, 1-in. flowers before leaves expand in January-March.
J. officinale COMMON JASMINE POET'S JASMINE	Semi-ever. to dec.	Zones 3-13. Sun or semi-shade.	Twining climber to 30 ft. with slender, angled shoots. Covers trellis or pergola rapidly.	Compound leaves of 5-7 leaflets 2-in. long, with larger terminal leaflet.	Fragrant, white, 1-in. flowers all summer long.
J. o. grandiflorum (J. grandiflorum) SPANISH JASMINE	Semi-dec.	Zones 7-13. Sun.	More shrub-like than J. officinale. Grows to 15 ft.	Same as J. officinale.	Very fragrant. Larger and showier than J. officinale.
J. stephanense (J. beesianum x J. officinale)	Dec. to semi-ever.	Zones 3-13, but not in frost pockets in 3-6. Sun or semi-shade.	Vigorous climber to 20 ft., slender angled shoots.	Both simple and compound leaves with 5 leaflets, dull green above, downy beneath.	Fragrant, soft, pale pink 1-in., flowers in terminal cluster.

waxy dark green, about 3 in. long, 1 in. wide. Flowers look like 2½-in. single roses of bright clear yellow. Blooms in late summer.

Sun or semi-shade. More in scale with the small garden than cup-of-gold vine; can be used on trellises, on arches over paths and doorways, or on a support in a large container or tub.

HUMULUS JAPONICUS. JAPANESE HOP. Hardy. Grows to 20-30 ft. Rapid climbing, twining annual vine with large, luxuriant, deeply lobed leaves. Does not make true hops. Var. *variegatus* has foliage streaked and blotched with white.

Sow seeds in spring where plants are to grow. Grows in sun or partial shade preferring a light rich soil. Insect and disease resistant.

Train on trellis, arbor or fence for quick effects.

HYDRANGEA PETIOLARIS. CLIMBING HYDRANGEA. Deciduous. Hardy all zones. When established becomes a vigorous climber, clinging to wood or stone by aerial rootlets. Becomes a small, bushy shrub if not allowed to climb. Green, smooth, heart-shaped, 4-in. leaves. White flowers in showy, flat, 10-in. wide clusters in June. A worthwhile, hardy climber from both flower and landscape point of view.

IPOMOEA PURPUREA. MORNING GLORY. Half-hardy. Annual vine growing to 15 ft. Plants of twining habit, with heart-shaped 5-in. leaves. Funnel-shaped flowers to 5 in. across in white, rose, blue, purple, and red. Named varieties are available for separate color plantings: *Heavenly Blue, Scarlett O'Hara, Pearly Gates*. Flowers open only in the morning.

Sow seeds (notched to hasten germination) in spring where plants are to grow; thin to 6 in. Can be started earlier indoors in bands or small pots and set out in ground after frost. Blooms summer to frost. Self-sows, but resultant plants are of an inferior strain. Likes full sun and an unfertilized soil.

Train on trellis, arbor, or fence for quick effects. Plant several in a large pot or tub, and train on wire cylinder or stakes.

JASMINUM (See chart on left)

Jasmine is one of the first plants that comes to mind when you think of fragrance in the garden. As you can see in the opposite chart, the plant has many forms and uses.

The nurseries in zones 3-6 generally offer both *J. nudiflorum* and *J. officinale*. Most widely distributed in California are *J. mesnyi* and *J. officinale grandiflorum*.

Most jasmine give little hint of the eventual square footage when seen in the nursery gallon can. Most of them need pruning, shaping, and constant heading back.

The Spanish jasmine (*J. officinale grandiflorum*) is a vigorous grower but dainty in scale. Profuse laterals of dainty compound leaves reach into space around it, but never fill it. Tiny pinwheel blossoms are held in airy suspension. Its cloud of foliage can soften a corner, provide light overhead screening, or make a post or pillar of bloom.

All jasmine are adaptable to various soils and garden culture.

KENNEDYA BECKZIANA. Perennial herb, climbing by twining, must be given support for woody stems. A close relative of hardenbergia, but with larger, sweet-pea-shaped flowers that are red with a yellow-green blotch at the base, borne in pairs on short side stalks.

LANTANA. (See chapter on shrubs.)

LATHYRUS ODORATUS. SWEET PEA. (See annuals.)

LONICERA. HONEYSUCKLE. Climate adaptation by varieties. Shrubs and shrubby vines. (See chapter on shrubs.) A most complex genus. Here are the varieties available in the West.

L. confusa. Half evergreen. Zones 7-13. Slow to moderate growth to 8-10 ft. Ovate, 2½-in., gray-green leaves. Fragrant, 1¾-in., white flowers changing to yellow, in short clusters.

L. heckrottii. Deciduous. Zones 3-13. Viny shrub to 12-15 ft. with oval, 2-in. leaves. One of the most free flowering. Fragrant, 2-in. flowers are orange-yellow, shaded purplish-crimson on the outside, in spikes.

L. h. Gold Flame. Deciduous. Zones 3-13. Very popular in Pacific Northwest. Vigorous growth to 15 ft. Fragrant flowers, creamy-white inside, bright pink to rose outside, are borne in profusion from early spring to frost.

L. hildebrandtiana. GIANT BURMESE HONEYSUCKLE. Evergreen. Zones 9-10, 12-13. Fast growing, tall climbing. Dark, glossy green, 4-6 in. leaves in informal groupings allow glimpses of rope-like, supple stems. Long, to 7-in., tubular flowers open creamy-white and show reluctance to leave the vine, change to yellow and then a dull orange before dropping.

L. japonica chinensis. (*L. chinensis*). PURPLE JAPANESE HONEYSUCKLE. Evergreen to semi-evergreen. Hardy all zones except in coldest area of zone 1. Fast growing to 30 ft., covering more than 150 square ft. Leaves dark, green above, purplish-green beneath. Fragrant, slender, tubular, 1-in. flowers are borne in pairs, white inside, purplish outside.

L. japonica halliana. (*L. halliana*). Evergreen to semi-evergreen. Hardy all zones except coldest sections of zone 1. Deep green, oval, 3-in. leaves. White flowers changing to yellow. The most commonly planted and the most vigorous, becoming a weed unless controlled by an iron hand and sharp shears.

L. periclymenum. WOODBINE. Zones 3-13. Deciduous. Strong grower to 20 ft. Rich, lush foliage of thick, green, 3-in. leaves, whitish beneath. Fragrant, deep purplish-red flowers, fading to yellow.

L. sempervirens. TRUMPET HONEYSUCKLE. All zones except coldest areas in zone 1. Evergreen to semi-evergreen. Twining to 15 ft. if supported; a small shrub otherwise. Not fragrant, but very showy, orange-yellow and scarlet, 2-in., trumpet-like flowers in spikes.

L. tellmanniana. Deciduous. Hardy all zones to 0°. Fragrant, 2-in. flowers in clusters of 6-12, glowing yellow flushed with red in bud and at tips, appearing in June.

All honeysuckle must be watched for aphis. All will stand some shade. No special soil problems.

MANDEVILLA SUAVEOLENS. CHILEAN JASMINE. Deciduous. Sun. Zones 7-13. Fast growing to 15 ft. and more. Dark green, heart-shaped, 3-in. leaves on long sweeping stems. In mass the foliage is a perfect foil for the clusters of wide-flaring 2-in., fragrant white trumpets. Flowering is free and continuous from July to September.

Since it is deciduous, use it for large scale summer effects where leafless winter habit is no drawback. Make use of its gardenia-like perfume and plant near bedroom windows and entertainment areas.

VINES

MONSTERA DELICIOSA. *(Philodendron pertusum).* CERIMAN. MEXICAN BREADFRUIT. (See chapter on indoor plants.) Evergreen. Warmest sections of zone 13. Hardy to 28°. Indoor plant elsewhere. Vigorous growing climber, with long, hanging, cord-like, aerial roots along the stems. Heavy, deep green leaves to 2-3 ft. long and as wide, are much divided and perforated with holes. Flowers are not unlike a calla lily. A thick, central, 10-in. spike, bearing the closely set, tiny flowers is surrounded by a white, 12-in., boat-shaped bract. Central spike becomes a solid, cone-like, edible fruit, the flavor a cross between a pineapple and banana.

Filtered shade. Requires growing space and a sturdy support on which to tie its heavy, trailing stems. When planted outdoors best grown at the foot of a highbranching tree, using the trunk for support. Otherwise plant in tub, box, or large pot in rich soil. Being a rapid grower its roots will fill a container in a comparatively short time. However, can be kept in the container for several years if fed once a month with a balanced fertilizer of liquid manure. Ripe fruit is doubtful unless you provide conservatory conditions of high humidity and lots of warmth. Will flower outdoors in southern coastal sections.

In warm climates where monstera is grown outdoors, it makes a striking and exotic patio or courtyard plant. In cold areas it is seen most often in conservatories, or is grown as a greenhouse or house plant.

MUEHLENBECKIA COMPLEXA. MATTRESS VINE, WIRE VINE. Evergreen. Zones 7-13. Small-leafed, with glossy black or brown wiry stems; tremendous vigor and spread. Seldom in the market today. No doubt the toughest vine for beach planting. Will cover, pull together, and hold everything that needs a common bond. Start in pure sand, if necessary within reach of the high tide line. You might protect it with a trunk or piece of driftwood (probably deposited by the sea and too heavy to move). May be a bit slow to start, but later will make its way.

OXERA PULCHELLA. Evergreen vine or viny shrub. Zones 12-13, hardy to 27°. As a shrub it will mound up to 6 ft.; if given support can be trained to 10 ft. Leaves are leathery, very dark green, oblong to 5 in. Clusters of 2-in. waxy-white trumpets furnish spring or winter display of unusual quality. Grows best in high shade or not too hot sun. Makes a pleasant associate of *Raphiolepis umbellata ovata* and nandina.

PANDOREA. Evergreen. Sun. Zone 13 and with protection in 7-12. Woody vines or evergreen shrubs climbing by twining stems.

P. jasminoides. *(Bignonia jasminoides. Tecoma jasminoides).* JASMINE PANDOREA. Fast growing, high climbing. Beautifully modulated compound leaves, of 5-9 shining dark green ovate 2-in. leaflets, provide year-long cover from base to towering top. The over-all texture is strongly lacy. Blossoms equal the leaves in distinction—clusters of 2-in. long, frilled tubes, white with red throats. Blooming season is long—August through October—because of progressive blooming within each flower cluster. Flowers drop neatly after maturing. Var. *rosea* is a rose-colored form.

P. pandorana. *(Bignonia australis, Tecoma australis).* WONGA-WONGA VINE. Flowers are small, to ¾ in., yellow or pinkish-white, the throat spotted with violet.

PARTHENOCISSUS. Hardy deciduous vines, including the familiar Virginia creeper and Boston ivy or Japanese creeper, have been transferred to this genus because of their tendrils with disc tips. These species and varieties are available:

P. henryana *(Ampelopsis henryana).* SILVER VEIN CREEPER. Less hardy than Virginia creeper but similar in leaf form and growth habit. Foliage is more refined. Soft olive-green leaves touched with undertones of copper or brown have a subtle variegation—midrib and veins show through the almost translucent leaves like silvery threads. Use it in a somewhat shady location for close-up view, at front entrance or in the cool patio.

P. quinquefolia *(Ampelopsis quinquefolia).* VIRGINIA CREEPER. Leaves consist of 5 separate 6-in. leaflets with saw-toothed edges. Unlike the Boston ivy the Virginia creeper sends out side shoots that droop, giving the vine a less tight and monotonous surface. When used on an overhead trellis these drooping branches give the vine movement, waving in a passing breeze.

P. q. engelmannii. Foliage is denser and leaves much smaller than *P. quinquefolia*.

P. tricuspidata *(Ampelopsis tricuspidata).* BOSTON IVY, JAPANESE CREEPER. Glossy leaves are variable in shape, mostly 3-lobed and often 8 in. wide. Climbs tightly and rapidly to make a very dense and very even wall cover.

P. t. lowii. Leaves are small to 1½ in. and deeply lobed.

P. t. veitchii. SMALL-LEAVED BOSTON IVY. Small young leaves are purple. More widely distributed in Southern California than other Boston ivies. The small leafed varieties can be trained in patterns more easily than the large leafed species. Clings with tenacity to the smoothest surfaces.

These vines do not quite live up to their high reputation for fall color in the mild winter sections of the West, but it still must be counted as one of their virtues.

Both the Silver Vein creeper and Virginia creeper offer unusual opportunities for traceries and transparencies in plantings behind translucent glass or plastic screen.

PASSIFLORA. Evergreen to semi-evergreen. Vigorous fast growing, climbing by tendrils to 20-30 ft. Hardiness varies by species. The flowers interested the early Spanish missionaries in South America, home of many of the passion vines. In them they saw many symbols of the passion of the Lord. For example: the lacy fringe or crown, a halo, or by some, the crown of thorns; the five stamens, the five crucifixion wounds; the ten petal-like parts, the ten faithful apostles.

Passion vines available in Western nurseries are:

P. alato-caerulea *(P. pfordtii).* The most widely planted and one of the hardiest. Once established, it can be grown as a perennial in cold winter climates. Fragrant 3½-in. flowers are white shaded with pink and lavender; the crown a deep blue or purple. Bloom all summer long against increasingly thick foliage.

P. caerulea. BLUECROWN PASSION FLOWER. Greenish-white flowers, the crown white and marked with purple. Flowers are smaller than *P. alato-cœrulea* and leaves are 5-parted.

P. edulis. PASSION FRUIT, PURPLE GRANADILLA. Adapted only in zone 13. Extremely vigorous vine where adapted. Hardy to 28°. White flowers with a white and purple crown. Deep purple, fragrant fruits 3-in. long. Fruits used in making beverages, sherbets, and jellies.

P. incarnata. MAYPOP PASSION FLOWER. Hardy to 10°. Native of southeastern United States. Inclined to be weedy. White 2-in. flowers with purple crown. Oval, 2½-in., yellow fruits are edible.

P. jamesonii. Hardy to 25°. Rose and coral-red 4 in. flowers. A fast-growing bank cover.

P. manicata. RED PASSION FLOWER. Hardy to 25°. Medium growth to 12-15 ft. Probably the most spectacular in flower—vivid scarlet with a blue crown.

P. mollissima. SOFTLEAF PASSION FLOWER. Hardy to 25°. Rich clear rose-pink flowers.

P. racemosa. Hardy to 25°. Rosy crimson to deep scarlet 4-in. flowers with a purple and white crown hang down from the main stem in long wiry clusters. A beautiful flower and a handsome vine.

Passion vines are tolerant of many soil conditions. Plant in sun. Water with increasing generosity as the vine develops. Because of their rapid growth and heavy foliage production, these vines need ruthless cutting back usually after the second year. The increasing density of foliage, if not cut, invites insects and the inner parts of the vine become dirty. The fast-growing passion vines will quickly cover bare raw banks left in hillside excavations.

PHAEDRANTHUS BUCCINATORIUS. (*Bignonia cherere, B. buccinatorius*). BLOOD-RED TRUMPET VINE. Evergreen. Sun. Adapted to zone 13 with frost damage at 24° but sold and planted with hope in zones 7-13. Once established it's a strong, high-growing climber. Leaves of 2 ovate or oblong 3-in. leaflets. Clusters of long, 4-in. tubes stand well out from body of vine in sunset color scheme—gradations from yellow to rose-red. Colors are exciting when viewed against a blue sky; in garden a nice complement is nearby bloom of blue. Flowering, in bursts throughout the year—whenever weather warms. Plant wherever a strong growing vine is needed; effective on walls, or high trellis. Prune yearly to keep under control. Feed and water generously.

PHASEOLUS COCCINEUS. SCARLET RUNNER BEAN. Annual, fast twiner to 10 ft. Foliage and culture are same as pole bean; beans edible in green stage. The difference is in flowers. There's no brighter scarlet than found in its long flower sprays bearing from 10-20 sweet-pea-shaped flowers. Blooms all summer. Support on strings on trellis. Give deep and thorough waterings. Full sun.

PLUMBAGO CAPENSIS. CAPE PLUMBAGO. Half vine—half shrub. With support it will grow to 12 ft. and spread almost as wide. Left to itself, it will mound up to 6 ft. and sprawl out 8-10 ft. Foliage pleasantly full of oblong 1-2 in. leaves. The light blue of its flowers in phlox-like clusters, is one of summer's most welcome colors in the hotter sections of the West. Its cool and delicate color is a foil for almost anything. For example, it combines well with the magenta of the common Bougainvillea, or the bright orange of *Tecomaria capensis*.

The ability of this plant to carry such a peace-making color skyward is good reason for taking the trouble to train it as a vine. It must be tied to a support. The main stem must be encouraged by removing suckers as they appear.

POLYGONUM AUBERTII. SILVER LACE VINE. Evergreen-deciduous. In zones 1-6, it's deciduous. Zones 7-13, evergreen. Glossy heart-shaped 1½-2½ in. crinkly-edged leaves, the new leaves often bronzy red. It's a foamy mass of small creamy-white flowers from April to October except where cut back each year by frost, or desire to restrain it, or to start fresh and clean. Such cutting back delays blooming date to August.

Use it for quick overhead shade. Water by deep slow soaking during the blooming season.

QUAMOCLIT PENNATA. CYPRESS VINE. Fast growth to 10-20 ft. Slender and twining; foliage very dainty; the leaves divided into thread-like segments appearing fern-like. Small 1½-in. tubular flowers of orange, scarlet, or white, flare to shape of a star. Flowers open in early morning, when vine is planted in sun; will accept part shade and look better there. Will form tracery on a structure without hiding it. For faster germination, notch the seed with a knife or soak in warm water until it swells. Sow in spring when soil warms or sow earlier indoors in pots and transplant. Support with strings, wire, or trellis.

SCHIZOPHRAGMA HYDRANGEOIDES. JAPANESE HYDRANGEA VINE. Deciduous. Similar to, but slightly less showy than *Hydrangea petiolaris*, which see.

SOLANDRA GUTTATA. CUP-OF-GOLD VINE. Evergreen. Zone 13 and protected spots in zone 10. Woody vine to 20-25 ft., and wide spreading. Large broad leaves, 4-6 in. long, shiny above, downy beneath. Fragrant golden-yellow, brownish-purple striped, trumpet-shaped flowers 6-8 in. across. Blooms February-April.

Give it full sun. Benefits by yearly pruning. Sometimes cut back to make a rough hedge. One of the most salt-water tolerant of all vines, it can take the salt spray directly above tide line.

SOLANUM. NIGHTSHADE. Deciduous-evergreen. Zones 7-13. Worth trying as a perennial vine in 2-6. Four species are used in the West.

S. dulcamara. BITTERSWEET. NIGHTSHADE. Trailing perennial to 4-6 ft., with ovate 4-in. leaves. Small ½-in., purple or white flowers in summer followed by 1-in. red fruit which is poisonous.

S. jasminoides. POTATO VINE. Deciduous or evergreen depending on winter temperatures. Fast growth to 30 ft. Twines with many stems. Leaves are small, 1¾-in. bright green. Small flowers in clusters of 8-12, are white, tinged with blue. Foliage is merely a back-drop for the effervescent spring blooming. Individual flowerlets are fragile open cups, with a nice design in the centers. USE: Sun or part-shade for flowering, or as quick overhead filtered shade. Should be cut back severely in fall or early winter or it will gradually lose its vigor.

S. macrantherum. Woody climber having beautiful violet blooms in clusters, followed by red berries.

S. wendlandii. COSTA RICAN NIGHTSHADE. More spectacular than the common potato vine. More vigorous, higher climbing; the leaves larger and often divided. Large 6-in. clusters of 2½-in. lilac-blue flowers. Useful where a rampant overhead summer foliage mass can be used. Leaves slow to break out in the spring, so you have the advantage of the warm spring sun.

SOLLYA FUSIFORMIS. (*S. heterophylla*). AUSTRALIAN BLUEBELL CREEPER. Evergreen. Zones 9-10, 12-13. Damaged at 20°. A low climber or trailing subshrub with pale green, dainty, glossy, 1-2 in. leaves on delicate, twining stems. Masses of brilliant blue, ½-in. bells through most of the summer.

Full sun or part shade in coastal areas, part shade inland. Water generously.

Admirably adapted to pot and tub use. Place potted vine on a low wall and allow its branches to spill down. Satisfying as a ground cover on half shaded banks, alongside steps, in rock gardens, and around pools.

STEPHANOTIS FLORIBUNDA. MADAGASCAR JASMINE. Evergreen; outdoors in zone 13, indoors elsewhere. A woody climber to 10-15 ft. Glossy green, leathery, 4-in. long leaves. Fragrant white funnel-shaped 1-2 in. flowers carried in loose open clusters.

When grown indoors the plant should be rested, kept on the dry side, at about 55° temperature during the winter, and then brought into a warm room. Very susceptible to mealy bug and scale.

STREPTOSOLEN JAMESONII. Evergreen viny shrub. Adapted in zones 8a, 12-13; of limited use in 9-11. If allowed no support and not pruned it will pile up loosely to 4-6 ft. like *Plumbago capensis*. Flowing down a slope or trained against a wall it may cover 10-15 ft. Leaves are slightly ribbed, oval, 1½ in. long. Small 1-in. flowers are carried in large loose terminal clusters. Color ranges from orange through apricot to soft yellow. Blooms throughout the year. Give it warm spot and plenty of water with good drainage, of course.

TECOMARIA CAPENSIS. (*Tecoma capensis*). CAPE HONEYSUCKLE. Evergreen. Hardy zones 9-10, 12-13, grown in Palm Springs. Damaged at 22°. Vine or vertical shrub to 15-25 ft. Compound leaves are neatly composed of very dark and glistening green leaflets. Brilliant orange-red tubular 2-in. blossoms in compact clusters from October through winter.

Particularly effective espaliered against a wall. Pruning adds to stiffness unless done selectively. When left alone and given space will cascade down a bank.

Needs sun. Tolerant of many soil types.

THUNBERGIA. Climate by species. This genus includes the simple little black-eyed Susan vine, the dazzling, orange clock vine and the vigorous, blue sky flower.

T. alata. BLACK-EYED SUSAN VINE. Perennial, used as an annual. A trailing plant that would rather grow up than down; has triangular, 3-in. leaves. Flowers are small, the flared portion of the tube measuring about 1 in. wide. Flower colors are available in orange, yellow, or white, all with jet-black centers. Use in hanging baskets, windowboxes and as ground covers in small, sunny spots. Start seed indoors and plant out as soon as weather warms.

T. gibsonii. ORANGE CLOCK VINE. Zone 13. Hardy to 28°. A perennial, twining plant that can also be used as an annual; with heart-shaped, 2-3 in. leaves. Solitary, bright orange flowers, the tube flaring to 1½ in. wide, are held out from the foliage on 4-in. stalks. The structure of the flower is unusual: 2 large, green and brown bracts enclose the bud, then open slightly to allow the flower tube to break through, but always conceal the calyx.

Although useful in many ways, the strong flower color can dominate a small garden if not used with restraint. Used frequently as a ground cover where it spreads over a 6-ft. square area in no time. Cascades over retaining walls and climbs without special supports. Blooms all year where weather is warm.

T. gregorii. Similar to *T. gibsonii* in growth but flowers are larger and not so orange in color.

T. grandiflora. SKY FLOWER. Zone 13 and protected locations in 9, 10, and 12. Hardy to 26°. A very vigorous twiner, building up a profusion of lush, green foliage of 8-in., heart-shaped leaves. Slightly drooping clusters of 2-5 flaring, tubular, 2½-3 in., delicate blue flowers, with 2 large, green bracts enclosing the base. Where adapted it blooms profusely throughout fall, winter, and spring.

Too vigorous a vine to handle easily in the small garden. Removal of dead blossoms is quite a chore in itself.

TRACHELOSPERMUM JASMINOIDES. (*Rhynchospermum jasminoides*). STAR JASMINE. Evergreen. Sun or shade. Zones 7-13. Twining on slender stems to 20 ft. Leaves are sturdy, gleaming black-green, making the white of the small flowers, in clusters, whiter, reflecting sunlight in spots as bright as mirrors. Though leaves are not large, the total visual effect is definite and strong.

The famous fragrance of this vine can be extended through a long summer season by placing some plants in the sun, and others in partial shade.

Support is essential. Use heavy string or cord to lead vine in the direction you have chosen. Strong wiry stem will develop. Train on posts, baffles, walls, fences—where fragrance can be enjoyed, night lighting can pick out starry blooms; and where a well groomed appearance is needed all-year. So frequently used as a ground cover that you should be sure when buying star jasmine for a vine that you don't pick out one that has been pinched back to grow horizontally.

T. fragrans. Zones 12-13. Tall climbing vine much like *T. jasminoides*, but has larger leaves and much larger flowers that are similar to stephanotis, in late summer and fall. Requires warm wind-free exposure in light shade, ample moisture, and spring and summer applications of fertilizers high in nitrogen and phosphoric acid. Effectively used with large philodendrons, clivia hybrids, kentia and chamædorea palms.

TROPAEOLUM. NASTURTIUM. (See annuals.)

VITIS. GRAPE. (See chapter on home food garden.) When you are looking for a screen to intercept the summer sun, or for a series of large leaves on a patio wall, or for a summer cover for a cloistered walk, consider grape vines. There's a variety especially adapted to each subclimate.

WISTERIA. Deciduous. Twining woody vine, strong-growing and long-lived. Its springtime flowering is one of nature's masterpieces. Before the leaves appear, sweet-pea-shaped flowers arrange themselves in clusters in orderly and diminishing sequence from top to bottom. Individual leaves are composed of many leaflets.

W. floribunda. JAPANESE WISTARIA. Hardy all zones except colder sections of zone 1. Leaves 12-16 in. long are divided into 15-19 leaflets. Violet or violet-blue flowers in 1½-ft. clusters. This species is not generally sold by Western nurseries. The long-cluster variety is listed as var. *macrobotrys* in Southern California and var. *longissima* in northern California and the Pacific Northwest. The 3-4 ft. cluster length can't be depended upon. Most of them drop before such length is attained. Variety *rosea* has pale pink or rose-colored flowers. Variety *violaceoplena* has double, violet flowers.

W. sinensis. (*W. chinensis*). CHINESE WISTARIA. Most widely planted. Slightly fragrant, violet-blue, 1-in. flowers in 12 in. clusters. Leaves divided in 7-13 leaflets. Variety *alba* is a white-flowered form.

W. venusta. SILKY WISTARIA. Similar to Chinese wistaria except leaves are velvety. Both white and violet-flowered forms are available.

When you plant remember that the main stem will develop into a good-sized, picturesque trunk. Once the vine starts to grow the long-reaching stems extend great distances. Can be trained to one or two stems by pinching out side stems as they develop in the spring. A beautiful, romantic garden symbol when trained along eaves or roof overhang. Easily trained as a tree by tying to a stake, removing side shoots and cutting back when dormant.

Because tendency to heavy blooming seems to be inherited, the usual extreme measures of root pruning are not necessary when you buy a plant produced by a cutting from a free-blooming plant.

To promote blooming at an early age do most of your pruning by pinching the first year or so. Don't cut back heavily until the vine has developed a strong blooming habit.

Ground Covers

The term "ground cover" could be applied literally to almost any plant that grows. However, through common usage, it has come to stand for the many and varied low growing plants of spreading habit that are used primarily to hide unsightly areas of bare soil with minimum maintenance.

VALUES OF GROUND COVERS

The work in getting ground covers established is paid for many times over as the garden becomes established.

There is less weeding under shrubs and trees. Waste spaces, where other plants fail, are covered. Banks and slopes, where any cultivating invites erosion, can be held in place with hundreds of roots that prevent washing out by heavy rains.

In areas where summer temperatures are in the 90-100° range, all soils exposed to direct rays of the sun are subjected to temperatures ranging well above air temperatures. Under such conditions vegetable matter in the soil is rapidly burned up, and soil becomes lifeless. Ground covers can be used like a mulch to slow down water losses, keep roots cool, and to prevent chemical changes within the soil.

The planting distances specified in the following plant descriptions are more or less arbitrary. Closer planting is possible in most cases to get quick effect. You'll get a better cover and use less plants if you stagger the planting, in diamond shape pattern rather than row on row squares.

LAWN SUBSTITUTES, LARGE AREA

There are two types of ground covers in this class:

1. Those that are used to maintain the general appearance of a lawn and some of its usability. Examples are:

Dichondra *(Dichondra carolinensis)*; lippia *(Lippia canescens)*; creeping thyme *(Thymus serpyllum)*; woolly thyme *(T. s. lanuginosus)*.

To the gardener who is looking for something that will give him the equivalent of a well groomed lawn the year around without any maintenance except occasional watering, these covers are disappointing in some respects. But when used within their limitation, they are most valuable.

All lawn substitutes require the same careful soil preparation that is necessary with lawn grasses. Substitutes of this type also have the same weed problems as lawn grasses. In general, weeds are more difficult to control since the selective weed killers cannot be applied in the same way as to grasses. (See chapter on lawns.)

Few substitutes are as winter-hardy as grass. Dichondra shows winter damage at temperatures below 20° and cannot be used in zones 1-6. Lippia is hardy in all zones but its winter appearance is brown and shabby. The thymes are hardy and have fair winter appearance in all but the coldest areas. The problem of getting a complete cover in a short time is even more difficult to solve with substitutes than with grass.

Mowing is almost eliminated with ground covers. However, if a smooth, even texture is wanted, the lawn mower should be used at least three times

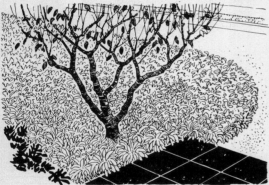

a year, when plants are in full growth. With thyme some thinning and rolling will be necessary because the "lawns" tend to crowd and hump up with age.

2. The second type of lawn substitute is that which makes no attempt to look like a lawn. Ivy and wild strawberry *(Fragaria chiloensis)* are most commonly used in this class.

The requirements call for a rather flat surface and year-long satisfactory appearance. Texture can be coarse but still neat enough for situations where it will have close inspection.

Lawn-size plantings of any of the above ground covers, dichondra and lippia excepted, require patient attention through two growing seasons. Soil between plants should not bake or harden. A mulch of peat moss will keep soil moist and cool and smother some weeds. Ivy seems to take forever to start growing and then comes on with a rush.

If ground is level wild strawberry can be kept low and compact by cutting once or twice a year with the lawn mower. Raise the blades to cut 2 inches high. Water, weed and fertilize and you'll have a smooth attractive surface.

LAWN SUBSTITUTES, SMALL AREA

Certain ground covers can stand some traffic and can be used between stepping stones, near pools, as an extension of the lawn, under trees, along a drive or path, as a foreground for shrubs. Examples are:

Chamomile *(Anthemis nobilis);* turfing daisy *(Matricaria tchihatchewii);* Irish moss *(Arenaria verna cæspitosa);* creeping thyme *(Thymus serpyllum);* woolly thyme *(T. s. lanuginosus).*

NO-TRAFFIC COVERS

The list in this class is a long one and can be expanded to include any low growing plant that is attractive when massed. We list here those that have attractive appearance throughout the year; are rather compact in growth; or are of even-spreading habit. They are especially useful in creating geometric patterns and for planting between shrubs or roses. Some are effective over bulb beds. Gray foliage plants in this group offer many opportunities for contrast when combined with green covers, and for highlighting against dark colors of house, fence, paving, or larger plants. Examples: Carpet bugle *(Ajuga reptans);* Aaron's beard *(Hypericum calycinum);* twinflower *(Linnæa borealis);* wintergreen *(Gaultheria procumbens);* sun rose *(Helianthemum);* stonecrop *(Sedum spathulifolium);* lambs ears *(Stachys lanata);* snow-in-summer *(Cerastium tomentosum);* blue fescue *(Festuca ovina glauca);* silvery yarrow *(Achillea argentea).*

COVERS OF UNEVEN TEXTURE

Ground covers of uneven texture, which need not be rigidly controlled, can be used as bank covers; among rocks; and for difficult-to-reach places. Some are especially drought and wind resistant. There is a wide selection for shade and sun. (See index for bearberry, heathers, mahonia, ceanothus not described in this chapter.) Examples are: Prostrate rosemary *(Rosmarinus officinalis prostratus);* Japanese spurge *(Pachysandra terminalis);* bearberry or kinnikinnick *(Arctostaphylos uva-ursi);* Cotoneaster dammeri *(C. humifusa);* Cotoneaster microphylla; Cotoneaster horizontalis;* heathers; Point Reyes ceanothus *(Ceanothus gloriosus);* long-leaf mahonia *(Mahonia nervosa).*

GROUND COVERS

ACAENA. SHEEP BUR. Attractive trailing perennials which form rather large loose mats close to the ground. Small rose-like leaves divided into leaflets. Although there is an acæna native to California, the species most commonly grown in gardens are from New Zealand.

A. buchananii. Densely silky, silvery-gray plant, the stems prostrate and rooting at the joints. Small ¾ in. leaves with 11-13 finely toothed leaflets.

A. microphylla. Plants smooth or sparingly silky, the pale gray-green 2 in. leaves with 7-13 deeply divided leaflets. Var. *inermis (A. inermis)* has longer leaves.

A. glauca. Like *A. microphylla* but with grayer leaves. Use in areas where a gray-green loose, fine-textured mat is wanted. Makes soft gray-green ground cover for dwarf spring flowering bulbs. Try it along a path in front of hebe and leptospermum, or under high pruned pines.

No traffic. Plant 6-12 in. apart. Sun and part shade. Adapted in zones 3-13.

ACHILLEA. YARROW. Low, sun-loving, evergreen perennial with gray or green foliage. At best in lean, sandy, dry soil. Becomes weedy and rampant in rich soil or if fertilized. Shear after bloom for compact growth.

A. argentea. SILVERY YARROW. Leaves deeply divided, silvery-gray with a silky sheen; form a tidy compact mound, 3-6 in. high, from which come airy heads of pure white flowers in spring and summer. Perfect for precise patterned areas or in raised beds. Try combination of silvery yarrow with blocks of *Sedum amecamecanum*, *Festuca ovina* var. *glauca*, and helianthemum Sunlite. Use it in drifts in open border or rock garden.

A. tomentosa. WOOLLY YARROW. Flat mat of finely cut, dark green, woolly foliage; flat heads of golden-yellow flowers on stems 6-10 in. May or June; all year if dead blooms are removed. USE: Edging; cover.

No traffic. Plant 12 in. apart. Sun. Adapted to all zones.

AJUGA. CARPET BUGLE. Creeping evergreen perennial. Small rosettes of leaves which form a thick mat that lies almost flat to the ground. Semi-prostrate stems reach a length of 3-12 in. Purple-blue, or sometimes pink, flowers in 3-6 in. stiff spikes bloom from late winter to early summer. Grows best in filtered shade with lots of moisture. Has unusual ability to thrive in sun if watered thoroughly. Accepts almost any soil.

A. reptans *(A. repens).* Widely available variety. Shiny dark green leaves; showy purple-blue flowers which may be removed by mowing if desired. Var. *alba* has light green leaves; white flowers. Var. *atropurpurea* has bronze leaves; blue flowers. Var. *multicolor* has foliage spotted and variegated with yellow, brown and red; blue flowers. Var. *variegata* has leaves splashed and edged creamy white; blue flowers.

Two other carpet bugles: *A. genevensis Rosy Spire*. Bright green leaves and pink flowers. *A. metallica crispa* (often sold as *A. reptans atropurpurea*). Dark bronze leaves with metallic quality and crisped edges; blue flowers.

Carpet bugles are fast growing. Fine for quick cover on slopes; in parking strips where there is little traffic; under trees; between stepping stones; near pools; and in decorative ground patterns with other contrasting plants. Try flat-growing ajuga next to thick-leafed yellow-green *Sedum amecamecanum*. Use as attractive low foreground for shade-loving taller ground cover sarcococca, or with hellebore, or nandina.

No traffic. Plant 6-12 in. apart for quick cover. Filtered shade best. Adapted to zones 3-13; but injured above ground by sustained cold.

ANTHEMIS. CHAMOMILE. Herbs with finely-cut, strong-scented foliage and white or yellow flowers. (See also chapter on herbs.)

A. carpatica. Grows to 6 in. Similar to turfing daisy, but has a slightly coarser leaf; white daisy blooms in late summer. Full sun or light shade; wet or dry soil.

A. nobilis. CHAMOMILE. Grows 3-6 in. high or more. Finely-cut, moss-like foliage is light bright green. Aromatic; sends out strong fragrance when stepped on. Although quite low growing when young, tends to become rangy with age; requires mowing or shearing back. Has small flowers with white rays and yellow centers held on erect stems in late summer. The chamomile most often used as ground cover is the rayless form of *A. nobilis*. White rays are absent, leaving small, round yellow centers that look like little buttons. Best in full sun.

The chamomiles may be used as lawn substitutes. For lawn effect, mow and roll a few times during the year. For pattern planting keep neat and compact by occasional clipping.

Stands traffic. Plant 12-24 in. apart. Full sun or light shade. Adapted to zones 3-13.

ARENARIA VERNA CAESPITOSA. IRISH MOSS. Compact, dense, moss-like mass of bright green foliage; tiny white flowers in summer. Needs more frequent watering than a lawn. Soil should be loose, friable, preferably with quantities of peat moss incorporated. Unless thinned, by cutting out narrow strips, will crowd itself in lumpy surface.

Best uses between stepping stones and in small half-shaded areas where a plush panel carpet can be given close attention.

Light traffic. Plant 6 in. apart. Partial shade preferred but will take sun. Adapted to zones 3-13.

ASPERULA ODORATA. SWEET WOODRUFF. Attractive, low-spreading evergreen perennial reminiscent of deep shaded woods. Slender square stems 6-8 in., encircled every inch or so by whorls of eight aromatic leaves. Clusters of tiny white flowers show above clean green foliage in spring and summer.

Although famous for its use as a perfume and a flavoring, has long been overlooked as ground cover. Crushed leaves smell as pleasant as freshly mowed hay; for centuries have been used for making May wine.

Given a shady garden location, soil rich in leaf mold, and abundant moisture, sweet woodruff will spread rapidly; may even become a pest. Dies out quickly in hot sun and dry soil. Happily located it self-sows freely from tiny seeds or can be increased by root division. Use in informal marginal areas of garden where you want woodland effect.

No traffic. Plant 18-24 in. apart. Shade. Adapted to all zones.

BACCHARIS PILULARIS. DWARF BACCHARIS, DWARF CHAPARRAL BROOM. Evergreen. Prostrate native shrub, 6-12 in. or more in height, with spread of 2-10 ft. Light green foliage effective at a distance. Has great utility. Strong deep-growing roots hold soil, sand dunes, or hillsides with ineradicable cover. Habit rather straggling in poor soils, but well formed and rounding in good soils with some deep moisture. Dense growth in sun. Once established needs little water.

No traffic. Plant 2-3 ft. apart on center. Sun. Adapted to zones 9-13.

CERASTIUM TOMENTOSUM. SNOW-IN-SUMMER. Medium textured low-spreading, silvery-gray carpet. Profuse small flowers in summer; foliage good most of the year, less gray in winter. Needs severe shearing back after blooming. Sun-loving, drought resistant, thrives with little care. With overwatering, may become rampant, untidy.

Sturdy plant with a riotous joy of living. Give it room on warm, sunny bank to run wild with purple alyssum, iris, hens and chickens, *Sedum amecamecanum*. Let it run over rock walls; put in a wide border with wild strawberry or chamomile. For subtle understatement—use it next to the deeper gray-leafed sun rose (*Helianthemum apenninum roseum*). To highlight a ground pattern, use it next to a dark green cover such as creeping thyme or dichondra. Makes stunning white carpet under white flowering oleanders or silver-variegated box elder, or on a bank between olive trees. If used as outline, walks and parking areas are easier to see at night. For sheer impact of color, use under mass planting of scarlet-red floribunda roses such as Floradora or Geranium Red.

No traffic. Plant divisions 18-24 in. apart. Sun. Adapted to zones 3-13.

CERATOSTIGMA PLUMBAGINOIDES. (*Plumbago larpentiæ*). BLUE LEADWORT. Dwarf, wiry-stemmed perennial to 1 ft., spreading by means of underground stems which seldom root, but may get out of hand occasionally. Especially desirable because of its clusters of intense, blue phlox-like flowers that appear in early fall when good blue flowers are very scarce. Autumn cold turns the bronzy-green leaves a rich red-brown. Although bedraggled for a short time in winter, fresh green leaves appear in early spring. An eye-appeal ground cover; plant it where you can enjoy its beauty in season, but forget it when out of season.

Flowers freely in considerable shade and is drought tolerant; prefers light, warm soils; will tolerate a sunny location if given enough water. Cut back after bloom or in early spring. Remove old crowns as they show signs of aging, replacing with rooted stems. Hardy, but may need winter protection in cold areas.

Try it combined with English boxwood and ajuga, or near gray hens and chickens. Interplant with *Oenothera tetragona*.

No traffic. Plant 18-24 in. apart. Best in half shade but will tolerate sun. Adapted to zones 7-13.

CONVOLVULUS MAURITANICUS. GROUND MORNING-GLORY. Gray-green prostrate perennial, woody at base. Will grow 1-2 ft. tall, spreading to 3 ft. across, usually less. Lavender-blue, 1-2 in., funnel-shaped flowers from June to November. Will tolerate heavy, clay soils if watered enough; best in light gravelly soil with very good drainage. Little watering after it has been established. Don't be afraid of this one; not invasive like its weedy cousins.

For informal, simple effects: on dry bank grouped with sun roses, snow-in-summer, *Nepeta mussinii*; pleasant trailing over a wall or rock outcropping; in a garden bed —a low-keyed foreground foil to highlight the yellow fruits and shiny green leaves of dwarf Meyer lemons.

No traffic. Plant 3 ft. apart. Likes sun. Adapted to zones 3-13.

COTONEASTER. (Also see chapter on shrubs.)

C. dammeri. (*C. humifusa*). BEARBERRY COTONEASTER. Evergreen. Flattest of the cotoneasters. Hardy, vigorous; grows in sun or shade; dry or moist soil. Handsome though uneven woody plant; neat all year and fine for close-up viewing. One of the very best of its type.

Unusually effective in manner of following surface contours, flowing around and over rocks, cascading over wall.

C. horizontalis. ROCK COTONEASTER. Not evergreen, but so heavily covered with bright red berries that leaves are not even missed in winter. Mass plantings maintain flat surface up to 3-4 ft. high. Good in any soil; sun or shade.

Good combination with low growing junipers. Heavy textured and especially good in banks and low dividers to discourage traffic.

C. microphylla. ROCKSPRAY COTONEASTER. Evergreen. Smaller leafed with darker rosy-red berries. Sends out long runners that frequently root. Will cascade over rocks or hardpan, making dense curtain of foliage. Useful in parking strips.

Discourages traffic. Plant 3-4 ft. apart. Sun or shade. Adapted to all zones.

DICHONDRA CAROLINENSIS. (*D. repens*). DICHONDRA. LAWN LEAF. Matted perennial spreading by underground runners. In full sun, the small round green leaves are about ¼ in. diameter. In shade, leaves are larger and stems longer.

Not particular as to soil; grows under acid, neutral, or alkaline conditions. Unfortunately, dichondra requires just as much weeding as grass lawn and weeding cannot be done by selective weed killer. Mowing is not a regular task but must be done whenever bunching up occurs. Does not kill Bermuda grass; over-rides it and gives greener over-all appearance in early spring. Best use is in small areas of light traffic where use of lawn mower is awkward or impossible.

Prepare soil and seed dichondra the same as a lawn. Best sown between March and August. Be sure seed is thoroughly dried and bleached; otherwise germination will be low.

Stands traffic. Grows readily from seed. Sun or shade. Adapted to zones 7-13. Winter damage at 20°.

DUCHESNEA INDICA. INDIAN MOCK STRAWBERRY. Coarse-textured, strawberry-like perennial trailer having bright green, long-stalked leaves, with 3 leaflets, on branches that root firmly along the ground. Small yellow flowers followed by conspicuous ½ in., inedible red berries which show above the foliage. As a wilder cousin of the strawberry, should be tried in the less cultivated marginal areas of big gardens. Does not make neat, dressy close-up ground cover. Has run wild in parts of the United States and is just now being recognized as good ground cover in West.

Garden picture: red-berried duchesnea carpeting shady bank under native dogwood.

No traffic. Plant 18 in. apart. Sun or shade. Adapted to zones 1-13.

FESTUCA OVINA GLAUCA. (*F. glauca*). BLUE FESCUE. Blue-gray ornamental grass that grows in distinct tufts 4-10 in. high. Has typical fine, hair-like leaves of the green fescue lawn grasses. Will not tolerate wet, poorly drained soil. Benefits from occasional cutting back. Fine textured cover for eye appeal only. Makes a delightful contrast to broad-leafed silver and gray plants as well as green ones.

A colorful parking strip with minimum care: squares of blue fescue alternated with squares of and a border of red brick. A gray shag rug under the red wistaria tree. Excellent ground cover under blue Atlas cedar, or Koster spruce.

No traffic. Plant divisions 6-12 in. apart depending on effect desired. Sun. Adapted to zones 3-13.

FRAGARIA CHILOENSIS. WILD STRAWBERRY. SAND STRAWBERRY. Low, compact, lush evergreen mat of thick glossy, dark green 3-parted leaves, with rapid spreading, rooting runners. Large, 1-in. white flowers in spring and bright red ¾-in. fruits in the fall. Grows from 6-8 in. high, but can be kept lower by mowing two or three times a year, leaving ruff 2 in. high. Mowing eliminates surface runners, increases root development and thickens growth. Not for extremely hot areas. Needs regular watering to look attractive.

Small plants set out in late fall will establish covering the following summer. Plants started at any season will produce thick cover in 6-8 months.

Not a ground cover to be walked on, though it stands some abuse. Weedy habit of growth makes it difficult to keep within a small area. Occasional cutting back is necessary. If yellow leaves appear in late summer, counteract with applications of iron sulfate.

Makes a rich, green carpet under strawberry tree; contrast its glossy leaves with feathery texture of pines, beefwood or *Acacia verticillata*. Use to bind the sand on windswept beaches; let it be a growing mulch for canyon floors. Effective used with gray plants such as: lambs ears, *Teucrium fruticans*, blue chaste tree.

Traffic. Set plants 18-24 in. apart. Sun on coast, shade or part shade inland. Adapted to zones 3-13, except hot dry areas.

GAULTHERIA. Low-growing gaultherias make high-quality ground covers in special locations. Beautiful, evergreen foliage, attractive, small, bell-like flowers and gay-colored berries give all-season attractiveness.

G. ovatifolia. OREGON WINTERGREEN. OVAL LEAF WINTERGREEN. A Western native. Forms a creeping mat to 8 in. Has thick, roundish, 1½-in., dark green leaves. Small, white or pinkish flowers in July, followed by scarlet fruits.

G. humifusa. (*G. myrsinites*). WESTERN WINTERGREEN. ALPINE WINTERGREEN. Another Western native. Tufted mat to 4 in. with oval, ¾-in. leaves, white flowers in July and scarlet fruits.

G. procumbens. CHECKERBERRY. Grows to 6 in., with creeping stems. Oval, 2-in., glossy leaves, white, nodding flowers in late summer and red berries during the winter months.

G. nummularioides. A creeper with bristly stems and round, ⅝-in. leaves. Flowers pale, pinkish-white in summer, followed by bluish-black fruits.

G. miqueliana. More woody than the other species; a miniature shrublet to 8 in., with light green, roundish leaves. White or pinkish, nodding flowers in April. White corrugated fruits in summer.

HEDERA. IVY. (See chapter on vines.) Evergreen woody vines with thick, leathery leaves. Accepts almost any soil, prefers shade, water, but will tolerate some sun and drought. Prune in spring to keep tidy and compact. Many varieties.

H. canariensis. (*H. algeriensis*). CANARY ISLANDS IVY. Large, rounded, 6-in. bright green leaves widely spaced on the stem. Likes sun and heat. Var. *variegata* has leaves edged with yellowish-white.

Excellent in raised beds, or in decorative ground patterns with other plants. More tender than *H. helix*.

H. helix. ENGLISH IVY. Dark green leaves more or less deeply lobed and quite variable in size, shape and markings. Many horticultural forms, small to large leaves, dark green to variegated, in a wide range of leaf sizes and patterns. Grows in sun or shade. Not hardy in zones 1-2.

Popular old-timer and still one of the best for a relatively fast, thorough, covering job. Use for big banks or to blanket a contained area.

H. h. Hahnii. HAHN'S IVY. Small green leafed form producing a softer effect than the species. Finer in texture and smaller in scale. A variegated form of Hahn's ivy is also available.

For small-scaled intimate garden areas; decorative ground patterns. Use near informal garden pools with dwarf maple, bleeding heart, or small ferns; under small conifers with a background of azaleas or aucuba. Lighten the ground under mature pines or other dark-foliaged trees by planting the green and white variegated form. Use it to make a green rope at the base of a raised planting bed; along a house next to a gravel path. Let it trail over shaded rocks. Good foreground for fuchsias. Use anywhere a work-free lush green carpet is wanted. To avoid trimming grass edges, use as a green border to lawn along walks, borders, drives and steps. You can push a lawn mower right into it; the few leaves clipped off every time will keep it looking neat.

No traffic. Plant 24 in. apart. Shade, some sun depending on variety. Adapted by variety.

HELIANTHEMUM NUMMULARIUM HYBRIDS. SUN ROSE. Mostly prostrate, evergreen shrublets with dense glossy green or gray-green foliage. Compact or somewhat trailing. Growing 6-8 in. high, with 3 ft. spread. Gay flowers in pink, peach, apricot, orange, yellow, white or red; single or double depending on the variety. Bloom profusely from April to June; again in fall if sheared back severely after first bloom. Each flower lasts a day, or half a day, but buds continue to open regularly over a long period of time. Somewhat slow to establish. Resent root disturbance; do not cultivate around them. Like lime.

Sun roses are especially good as a low border for lantana, citrus, or plumbago. Well suited for use on a sunny slope, as they are easy to maintain and fairly drought resistant. Try a planting of a green-leafed variety like Flame (or New Bricks, Stanford) with a gray-leafed form like *H. apenninum roseum* (soft, rose flowers), tuck in some dianthus for change of texture and frame it with a background of *Raphiolepis indica rosea* trimmed low. Use helianthemum Sunlite (bright green foliage, clear yellow flowers that hold all day) in a dry wall with *Convolvulus mauriticus*.

No traffic. Plant 2½ ft. apart. Full sun. Adapted to zones 3-13.

HELXINE SOLEIROLII. BABY'S TEARS, ANGEL TEARS. Creeping, moss-like little perennial herb with light green, tiny, round leaves, and inconspicuous white flowers. Lush and fragile-looking, it forms a dense mat 2-3 in. high. Roots readily from any piece of stem. May become a real pest.

Cool luxuriant cover for ferns and other shade plants near pools; ground mulch for fuchsias and camellias. (Tear away excess growth around plant stems occasionally.) Can be used between stepping stones but the leaves crush badly if stepped on. Best used in out-of-the-way, neglected shady spots where neat cover is wanted with minimum amount of care, as under garden potting bench.

No traffic. Plant any distance; travels fast and far. Shade. Adapted to zones 7-13.

HYPERICUM. ST. JOHNSWORT. Evergreen. Erect shrubs or prostrate and only semi-woody. Brilliant splashes of golden-yellow flowers over the cool-looking green foliage in the heat of summer. Satisfactory in sun but best in dappled shade of overhead trees.

H. calycinum. AARON'S BEARD. Spreading evergreen, or semi-deciduous in cold areas, to 1 ft., 4-in. leaves medium green in sun, yellow-green in shade. Bright yellow, 3-in. flowers with a showy center mass of stamens in July. Spreads by means of underground runners—strong and invasive in sun, but controlled in shade. Cut to ground every third year. Excellent soil binder for steep banks if watered. Otherwise requires very little care.

Plant 18 in. apart.

H. coris. Grows 6-12 in. Neat 1-in. green leaves and profuse ¾-in. yellow flowers in April-June. Fine rockery plant.

Plant 1 ft. apart.

H. moserianum. GOLD FLOWER. Evergreen. Hybrid form of bushy, arching habit to 2 ft. high. Use for massing under trees, shady banks and many places where other plants do not thrive. Useful for creating an undulating effect with lower ground covers like ajuga or pachysandra. Use next to low spreading junipers.

Plant 3-4 ft. apart.

No traffic. Plant according to species. Sun or filtered shade. Adapted to zones 3-13.

LINNAEA BOREALIS. TWINFLOWER. Dainty flat, shining, evergreen mat of tiny 1-in. leaves on vining runners. Twin pale pink bell flowers ⅓ in. long on each 4-in. stem. Fragrant. Grows best in moist peaty or woodsy soil.

Use in small, close-up areas: in shady raised beds; adjoining a terrace. Gives mass of delicate color and texture with tiny wood ferns.

No traffic. Plant 1-3 in. apart. Shade or semi-shade. Adapted to zones 1-6.

LIPPIA CANESCENS. (*L. repens*). LIPPIA. Creeping and spreading to form a flat, ground-hugging mat with very gray foliage. Lilac flowers clustered in small, dense, cushiony ½-in. heads.

Not a good all-year cover because of brown, dead look in winter. Best use in extremely hot, desert conditions. As tough in sun as ivy is in shade.

L. nodiflora. MAT GRASS. California native. White flowers; used as ground cover to resist erosion on levees of lower Sacramento and San Joaquin rivers.

Light traffic. Plant small divisions 1 ft. apart. Full sun. Adapted to all zones.

MATRICARIA TCHIHATCHEWII. TURFING DAISY. Perennial. Finely cut dark green foliage gives effect similar to fern-like moss. Makes loose mat about 2 in. high covered in spring and summer with little white daisies on wiry 6-in. stems. Thrives on poor dry soil; spreads rapidly. Water until established.

Striking in meadow-like situations. Charming artless covering in dry ground among rocks, beneath trees, or between paving stones.

Stands traffic. Plant 12 in. apart. Full sun. Adapted to all zones.

MENTHA REQUIENII. JEWEL MINT OF CORSICA. Miniature moss-like perennial creeper, growing only ½ in. high. Flat, compact, cushiony mat of delicate, tiny, round, brilliant green leaves; diminutive light purple or violet flowers in summer. When pinched, or crushed underfoot, it releases a delightful, refreshing fragrance that is more like sage than mint. Will tolerate heavy soils; prefers sandy loam. For shady, moist places.

Much slower and more choice than baby's tears (*Helxine soleirolii*) which it somewhat resembles. Can be used for same purposes; is aromatic besides, and never an invasive pest. Use *Mentha requienii* for garden fragrance; between stepping-stones on the floors of terraces or paths. Plant seeds or young plants in tiny crevices in rock garden for a green spray to pinch in passing by. Cover bare ground in front of ferns or hellebores.

Light traffic. Plant 6 in. apart. Shade. Adapted to zones 3-13.

MESEMBRYANTHEMUM. Under this common name we have grouped a number of plant groups which botanists now classify as distinct genera: *Cryophytum, Carpobrotus, Lampranthus, Oscularia*. In garden usage and in the vocabulary of most gardeners they are mesembryanthemum, or just ice plant.

Annual, or evergreen perennial, succulents with fleshy leaves on trailing or semi-erect stems. Daisy-like flowers in all colors except blue, so profuse in number and so intense in color, the effect is often blinding. Sun-loving; heat and drought tolerant; thrive on sterile soils. Will take moderate amount of moisture in the garden if soil is well drained. Perennial plants do not withstand severe frosts.

No traffic. Annuals and perennials may be grown from seed. Often self-sow. Perennials may also be grown from cuttings planted 2 ft. apart. Full sun. Adapted to zones 7-13.

Cryophytum crystallinum. (*Mesembryanthemum crystallinum*). ICE PLANT. Native along Southern California coast, Lower California, Mediterranean region, South Africa. Annual herb with fleshy, prostrate stems spreading 3-5 ft. Foliage covered with watery, glistening bubbles like little ice crystals. White to rose small flowers. Wants a warm, sunny exposure. Interesting drapery for wall or sunny bank.

Carpobrotus. Trailing perennials with stems often several feet long. Leaves 3-sided and very fleshy, bright green, sometimes tinged reddish. Flowers large and showy.

C. chilense. (*Mesembryanthemum æquilaterale*). SEA FIG. Native along the California coast. Lightly fragrant, rosy-purple flowers make a summer-long splash of vivid color that is best kept to itself.

C. edulis. (*Mesembryanthemum edule*). HOTTENTOT FIG. Native of South Africa; now naturalized on Los Angeles Co. coast. Similar to sea fig but differs in its curved leaves and pale yellow (the common form) to rose flowers.

Both species are very fast growing and fine for holding drifting sands. Good for warm hillside or steep bank to which few plants will cling. Soil binder for stabilizing soil on hillside cuts along highways or to hold dirt fills. Dead blossoms untidy. Although rather coarse, useful in seldom-watered marginal areas or dry sandy spots around country homes.

Lampranthus. Usually more bushy than prostrate perennials. But they will also cover the ground under their own power. Brilliantly colored showy flowers: bronze yellow, salmon, orange, red, purple, pink and white. Look to *L. aurantiacus, L. brownii*, and *L. roseus* for colors less dominating than other members of the group.

Oscularia deltoides. (*Mesembryanthemum deltoides*). This familiar small-leafed, rose-lavender small flowered perennial is a favorite for carefree slope cover. Will grow where you need a ladder to plant it. In late May, June, and early July it looks like a colorful velvety carpet. The rest of the year it is gray-green. One objection to this species is that it gets woody and messy underneath. To correct this, shear back heavily after bloom.

MICROMERIA CHAMISSONIS. YERBA BUENA. Native creeping perennial with minty, fragrant foliage. Round or oval small leaves and small white, lavender-tinted flowers. The plant spreads as much as 3 ft. across by means of long slender stems rooting as they go. Reroots at the tips. Vigorous in loose, leafy, moist soils in the shade.

Let it make a smooth, rippling coverlet over a shady moist piece of ground under trees; near a pool; over garden slopes; or in the rock garden where its invading habit will not become a nuisance. Place within pinching distance of a path to intrigue the passing visitor.

No traffic. Plant 2½ ft. apart. Shade. Adapted in zones 3-13.

NIEREMBERGIA RIVULARIS. WHITE CUP. Prostrate, perennial mat of closely packed green leaves only 3-6 in. high; sprinkled in summer with 2-in. creamy-white, cup-shaped flowers with yellow throats. Half sun to full shade in moist, well drained soil. Occasionally dies back in winter, but revives quickly in spring. Topdress with sifted leaf mold.

Merits wider use. White cup has an unsophisticated appeal; is simple and direct. Not persistent or sturdy; do not put next to over-vigorous neighbors that may elbow it out of the way. Ideal tumbling down sunny slopes in coastal areas, or cool hillsides in the warmer sections of the West. Spike up a plain planting of woolly thyme with a backing of white cup. Group it with broom, sun roses, prostrate cotoneaster. Plant it in a solid mass that follows or curves around a low bank.

No traffic. Plant 12 in. apart. Half sun to full shade. Adapted to all zones.

PACHYSANDRA TERMINALIS. JAPANESE SPURGE. Hardy perennial herb with clean, crisp, evergreen foliage. Rich, dark green 2-4 in. leaves arranged in fan-like clusters which make a decorative overall pattern. In heavy shade where spurge is happiest, it grows to a luxuriant 10 in.; in dappled shade, still happy, to 6 in.; in full sun, about the same height, but yellow and unattractive because of sunburn. Of trailing habit, it spreads by means of underground runners, which can become invasive. Although principally valuable as foliage plant, pachysandra offers small fluffy, fragrant spikes of white flowers as delightful summer dividend, followed by soft white berries. Give it rich soil on acid side with plenty of moisture, particularly while getting established.

Highly recommended as lawn substitute; as a marginal extension of lawn; or as panel planting to shrub border. Very handsome with *Pieris japonica*. Excellent for edging driveways and walks and for carpeting parking strips not used too intensively. Wonderful under broad-leafed evergreens, such as California live oak, and conifers; competes successfully with their roots. Good alternate material for much-used vinca and ivy for cool effect on a shady tree-covered bank.

Light traffic. Plant well rooted shoots 6-12 in. apart. Best in shade or filtered shade. Adapted to all zones.

POTENTILLA CINEREA. CINQUEFOIL. Dainty, bright green tufted creeper 2-6 in. high; leaves fern-like, divided into 5 leaflets. Butter-yellow stemless flowers in spring and summer. Perfectly hardy, adaptable alpine plant; grows in shade or in sun with plenty of moisture. Vigorous fast growing in the foggy coastal districts; slower elsewhere with a tendency to brown in winter. Very few weeds after the cover closes in tight.

Use cinquefoil as welcome change from vines, ivy, or ajuga as cover under a small tree. Put a bright green floor of it under gnarled gray olive trees or pink flowering red ironbark (*Eucalyptus sideroxylon rosea*). Combine with ajuga and day lilies in filtered shade; in sunny beds—plant with blue fescue, agapanthus, or dwarf mugho pine.

No traffic. Plant 6-10 in. apart. Sun or shade. Adapted in zones 7-13.

RANUNCULUS REPENS. CREEPING BUTTERCUP, BUTTON BUTTERCUP. Hardy, prostrate perennial to 2 ft., stems straggling, or rooting at the joints, to form a mat. Leaves 3-parted into broad lobes, making lush, shiny, dark green cover. Small 1-in. waxy yellow double flowers, like buttons, in late spring and summer. Vigorous; becomes a weed in lawns. Grows best in filtered shade; mildews in heavy shade.

Use in out-of-the-way garden spots for easy minimum-upkeep cover. Informal effects. Naturalize under birch trees with the spring flowering bulbs.

No traffic. Plant 12 in. apart. Filtered shade. Adapted in all zones.

ROSE. For a restrained rose ground cover the rose-pink Compton Creeper is one of the best.

The Mermaid, a single yellow with excellent foliage all year and almost continuous bloom, will cover a circle 10 ft. in diameter in about 3 years. Mermaid, with its strong and sharp thorns, should not be planted near a traffic lane. Banksia, the thornless yellow or white, makes a beautiful hillside cover.

Almost any strong growing climbing rose—such as Peace, Frau Karl Druschki, Tallyho, Charlotte Armstrong—can be pegged down as a ground cover. Here's how to do it. The first year, prune as usual. The second year tie the long canes at the tips to short stakes. The bending of the long canes causes new flower growth all along the pegged down stem. We've seen a Frau Karl Druschki treated this way. It covered a circular bed 12 ft. in diameter and was bearing more than 200 snow white blooms.

ROSMARINUS OFFICINALIS PROSTRATUS. DWARF ROSEMARY. Low spreading form of the familiar culinary shrub. (See herb, shrub chaps.) Spreads 4-8 ft. wide and stays under 15 in. high. Dark green narrow leaves; light blue flowers in April and May. Likes full sun; good drainage; gravelly, not too rich soil. *R. o. lockwoodii* has lighter bright green foliage and bluer flowers.

Difficult to praise this hardy dwarf shrub too highly. Use at base of sunny bank with background of helianthemum, sedum, or convolvulus. Plant along paths and steps to take advantage of aromatic fragrance of bruised leaves. Try next to velvety gray leaves of lambs ears or snow-in-summer for contrast.

No traffic. Plant 3-5 ft. apart. Full sun. Adapted to zones 4-13.

SEDUM. STONECROP. Succulent evergreen low herbs of trailing habit of growth. Will grow in poor soils, sun or shade. Drought resistant.

S. amecamecanum. MEXICAN SEDUM. Dwarf. Thick-leafed yellow-green foliage about 6 in. high; yellow star-shaped blossoms in spring and summer.

Very useful for decorative ground patterns. Gives clean cut contrast with dark green ajuga, strawberry, vinca or ivy.

S. spathulifolium. Plump, silvery rosettes to 4 in. with soft gray, small spoon-shaped fleshy leaves; tiny, upright, bright yellow flowers in late summer. Fairly slow growing, it does not become overgrown and weedy-looking but maintains itself as a low neat mat. Ideal for hot, dry locations.

Good seen close-up, as on a bank above a walk. Attractive in pattern with other stonecrops and sempervivum. Rock garden subject, with nice relationship to rock textures. Combine with heather in the filtered shade of white birches. Garden picture: red oak, hens and chickens, snow-in-summer and *Sedum spathulifolium*. Use under olive trees for subtle gray harmony.

S. s. Cape Blanco. Similar in appearance to the species, but the leaves covered with silver powder that makes them appear luminous on the darkest day.

Cape Blanco sedum is particularly attractive as a foreground cover for bright-colored gazanias, *Hebe hectori*, helianthemum, or Transvaal daisies.

S. spurium Dragon's Blood. Buds and stems are bronzy red; flowers bright carmine-red turning dark crimson. Medium green to reddish-bronze foliage is almost completely hidden with blooms during July, August and September.

Use as a ground cover under a spreading oak as a substitute for the more sombre covers like ivy or vinca. Neat appearance close-up.

Stands no traffic. Plant 9-12 in. apart. Sun or shade. Adapted in zones 3-13.

STACHYS LANATA. LAMBS EARS. Hardy herbaceous perennial with soft woolly gray leaves, growing to 18 in. and spreading twice as wide. Summer whorls of two-lipped small purple flowers in spikes. Lambs ears look sad and mushy in winter rains. Frost kills many leaves; should be cut back in spring.

Use for contrast in ground pattern; the woolly gray leaves stand out dramatically against dark foliage of wild strawberry. Also contrast with bright green needle-like foliage of *Arenaria montana*. For subtle harmony with various tones and textures of gray combine with sun roses, blue fescue, dianthus, woolly thyme, *Sedum spathulifolium*, snow-in-summer.

Stands no traffic. Plant 18 in. apart. Best in full sun. Adapted in zones 3-13.

THYMUS. THYME. Low growing, aromatic, woody plants; erect, semi-prostrate, or creeping in habit. Long-lived and very persistent. Ideal for hot, dry locations in clay, sand, or gravelly soils. Withstands neglect with cheerful fortitude. (See also chapter on herbs.)

T. serpyllum. MOTHER OF THYME, CREEPING THYME. Prostrate perennial forming flat growing, close-napped carpet of tiny dark green aromatic leaves, soft and fragrant under foot. Small purplish flowers blooming from June to September. Thrives on dry poor soils in the full heat of the burning sun. Can stand abuse, but is more luxuriant out of line of direct traffic.

T. s. albus. Completely prostrate, dark green mat, solidly covered with diminutive white flowers in summer. Clings to stone and is at home in rock gardens; tucked in crevices; spilling over small outcroppings; softening the harsh outlines of steps; blurring the sharp edges of paving stones. Simple modest plant of great charm.

T. s. argenteus. SILVER THYME. More erect; leaves variegated with silver.

T. s. coccineus. Creeping, 2-3 in., with very dark green foliage; bright carmine-red flowers. (Similar varieties: *T. s. carneus*, Purdy's and Reiter's varieties.)

T. s. lanuginosus. WOOLLY THYME. Downy, silver-gray, leaves in flat to undulating mat 2-3 in. high. Seldom blooms. Very drought resistant. Tends to look a bit ragged in winter, but never dies back completely.

Stunning with *Euphorbia myrsinites* and soft yellow Hyperion day lilies.

These thymes are good lawn substitutes in small areas. Not neat enough for big areas because of tendency to form bare spots. Ideal on steep, sunny bank, between paving stones, along paths, in parking strips along the street; sturdy creeper in the rock garden. Plant a silver garden spot with elæagnus, lavender, iris, and woolly thyme.

Try white-flowering mother of thyme with *Diosma ericoides* or white heather.

Use with these perennials: dianthus, arabis, aubrieta, *Alyssum saxatile citrinum*.

Takes traffic. Set divisions 12-15 in. apart in fall or spring. Full sun. Adapted to all zones.

TRACHELOSPERMUM JASMINOIDES. (*Rhynchospermum jasminoides*). STAR JASMINE, CONFEDERATE JASMINE. (See chapter on vines.) Slow to start and a long time developing into form, but a superior permanent ground cover in moist, cool, fertile soils.

To train as a ground cover tack it down with heavy wires bent like hair pins. Held down as it grows, it will maintain a height of 1½-2 ft., eventually spreading to 4-5 ft. Can be trimmed to make a smooth cover.

Use it to extend a lawn. Very satisfactory under trees and shrubs which require summer watering. Group in a raised bed with *Siphonosmanthus delavayi*, dwarf mugho pine, veronica Crater Lake Blue, and *Iberis sempervirens* Snowflake. Tuck in a rope of Hahn's small-leafed ivy at the base of the bed.

Stands no traffic. Plant 3-5 ft. apart depending how fast you want complete cover. Takes shade or full sun if given frequent waterings. Adapted zones 7-13 but must have shade protection in areas of extreme heat. Will tip burn in heavy sustained freeze.

VINCA. PERIWINKLE, MYRTLE. Trailing or creeping evergreen. Thrives in any or all soils within reason; gets along with little moisture if grown in shade. Does well in sun provided it has lots of water. Seems entirely immune to insects and diseases.

V. major. The commonly known periwinkle. Glossy dark green 2-in. oval leaves, lavender-blue 1-in. flowers on a trailing plant that may grow to 2 ft. high. Generally 6-12 in. where it has room to spread. Trailers reach out 10-15 ft. Sometimes used in upper story or deck window boxes to get festoon effect. Excellent as a ground or bank cover for naturalizing in out-of-the-way, neglected garden spots with poor soil; invasive pest in wrong location.

V. minor. DWARF PERIWINKLE, DWARF RUNNING MYRTLE. To 6 in., spreading to 3 ft. Like *V. major* but more dwarf, with smaller leaves and flowers. Blooms freely in early spring and again in fall. Has tendency to mound but becomes more compact when clipped annually. Var. *alba* has white flowers. Var. *alpina* has light green foliage and semi-double wine-red flowers. Needs some shade for best development. Not as vigorous as *V. minor*. Var. *bowlesii* is a superior form with broader foliage and larger, deeper blue flowers. Slow growing and more compact, it stays within bounds and requires less maintenance.

Use *V. major* for tough problems. *V. minor* and its forms are good for large areas but neat enough to stand close inspection. Tight growth habit discourages weeds.

Contrast *V. minor* with the purple leaves of flowering plum Thundercloud.

Picture: sheet of vinca's blue flowers under flowering crabapples with a background of *Sedum amecamecanum*.

Light traffic. Plant 12 in. apart. Sun or shade. Adapted all zones.

Shrubs

Gathered into this group are the woody plants varying in height from 6 inches to 15 feet. As a group they occupy a more or less permanent place in the garden.

Once upon a time the word *shrub* laid a heavy hand upon the gardener. He wasn't supposed to look upon the *shrub* as just another plant.

If a plant was called a perennial he could enjoy it for a few years and throw it away. If it was called a bulb he could use it for a season or two and then discard it without feeling that he had made a mistake in buying it in the first place. But if it was called a shrub he was expected to have and to hold and to cherish it forever.

Now it so happens that there are shrubs and shrubs. All shrubs should not be measured by their ability to occupy a permanent place in the garden.

There are shrubs that require several years to reach their peak of performance, after which they maintain their character for many years. They are the permanent shrubs. They are the forms to be used in building a garden.

But here in the West there are many shrubs that grow so rapidly they fulfill their function in a year or two after planting and in five years or less outgrow their usefulness. Many of our fast growing, broad-leafed evergreens are in this class. If we were to call these plants semi-permanent perennials, we would remove them as soon as they outgrew their usefulness rather than point them out as inferior shrubs.

The next time you look at a shrub in your garden that has outgrown the spot in which it is planted, think what you would do with it if it were called a marguerite. Although, in a mild climate, the marguerite will grow into a 4-5 foot wide shrub, most gardeners have no trouble discarding it before it reaches that size. Unlike rosemary, lavender, cotoneaster, it isn't called a shrub.

There are shrubs that serve the same purpose as perennials. Varieties of such deciduous flowering shrubs as philadelphus, deutzia, and weigela are in this class. Their value is in the flower color they provide in their season and they should not be treated as shrubs in the sense of essential materials in building the form of the garden.

There are shrubs with restrained growth habit that are transients in the garden. They are moved in for their form, foliage, or color and used as long as they retain those qualities. Some of the small heathers and brooms are best used in this way. Many other examples are discussed in the chapter on container gardening.

There are shrubs that are enjoyed as collections. Here we find camellias, rhododendrons, azaleas, and fuchsias.

In our listing and appraisal of shrubs available to Western gardeners we have carefully considered the uses of the shrub in the garden. Those which have special or limited use are so classified. Each plant is judged on 7 points: form, function, four-season performance, foliage, flowers, fruit, and fragrance.

All appraisals were necessarily influenced by the needs of the small garden. High ratings were given those plants in scale with small homes.

High ratings were earned by those plants of unusual adaptability to special or changing climatic conditions.

Form and function were rated on the plant's usefulness in solving problems in design and problems in gaining garden privacy, sun and wind control.

Using this method of scoring, we compiled a list of approximately 50 most useful shrubs for each of the subclimates of the West. Few of these most useful shrubs rate high on every one of the 7 points. All rate high on more than 3 points.

A list of the winners proves several things.

Within the list of most *useful* shrubs there's variety enough in color and flower to satisfy most demands for individuality in gardening.

The fact that many commonly available plants are on the winners' list does not detract from the quality of the list. The common shrubs listed can be made uncommon by intelligent, imaginative use.

In this list are the basic forms with which you build the all-season framework of your garden. Once this framework is built you can bring in hundreds of items of seasonal color or none. With or without the accessories of seasonal color the basic framework is attractive and satisfying.

Here are the winning shrubs as we found them. These 22 names lead to the most widely adapted and most useful shrubs for Western gardens. They do well in at least 10 out of the 13 subclimates. See the encyclopedia section for details on species and variety.

Arbutus unedo	Mahonia
Aucuba	Osmanthus
Azalea	Photinia
Berberis	Pinus mugo
Ceanothus	Pittosporum
Cotoneaster	Pyracantha
Elæagnus	Raphiolepis
Euonymus	Rosmarinus
Fatsia	Santolina
Juniperus	Sarcococca
Ligustrum	Teucrium

Add these 30 names for consideration as additions to the basic plant list, if you garden in zones 7-13. Those starred are adapted in the hottest areas:

Azara microphylla	*Cocculus
Bambusa	*Convolvulus cneorum
Carissa	Corynocarpus lævigata
*Cassia	Eugenia
*Citrus	Feijoa
Griselinia	Pittosporum
*Lagerstrœmia	*Plumbago
*Lantana	Prunus ilicifolia and P. lyonii
Leptospermum	
*Leucophyllum texanum	Psidium
Michelia fuscata	Punica granatum
Myrsine africana	Pyrus kawakami
*Myrtus communis compacta	Rhus
	Sollya fusiformis
Myrtus ugni	Tetrapanax
*Nerium	Xylosma senticosa

Add these names to the basic list of most useful shrubs where climate favors them. Check them if you garden in zones 1-6, 9-10. Those starred are sure to spread to zones 12-13.

Acer circinatum and A. palmatum	Pernettya
	Pieris
*Berberis verruculosa	Philadelphus
Calluna	Prunus laurocerasus zabeliana
Deutzia	
Erica	Rhododendron
*Gaultheria (see natives)	Skimmia
	Stranvæsia
*Garrya (see natives)	*Vaccinium ovatum
Kalmia	Viburnum

The usefulness and attractiveness of a shrub in your garden depends more upon how it is used than upon the attractiveness of the shrub as an individual plant.

A shrub that has no appeal when seen with other shrubs may create a sensation when placed against a redwood fence. A plant that entrances with its leaf form when you stand beside it may be nothing when viewed from 50 feet.

There is only one way to learn to use a plant and that is to learn to see it. A shrub has volume, form, texture, and color. Changes in light from low morning light, to high noon, to low evening light change the color and form of a shrub. Some reflect light; some absorb light; some let the light filter through. Leaf colors differ from almost white to gray; from light green to almost black-green; from blue-green to yellow-green.

Look at the color of the foliage of plants the next time you travel the Pacific Coast. The north country is blue and blue-green. The further south you travel the more yellow-green you pick up. The high mountains are in the cold blue of granite; the seashore is in the warm tones of sandstone.

There's a difference, of course, between looking at just any plant anywhere and the plant you own. All of us who grow and care for plants are inclined to see them close up and in bloom even when they are 100 feet away and out of bloom. The memory of last year's flowers covers the plant with flowers until the next year's bloom takes over.

The gardener who wants to use shrubs effectively must see them as they are from every viewpoint, rather than from what he knows them to be. When you really see shrubs you realize that the combination of flowers, foliage, and form gives the plant a definite character.

The character of the plant dictates its use.

There are places in the garden where a bold, commanding plant is needed. In another spot you need a lacy, delicate individual with see-through qualities. Near the entrance door the plants should be tailored, elegant, aristocratic.

In the following list we have grouped a few shrubs and trees by their character as seen by landscape architects. Do you see them in the same way?

Bold, assertive, dominant, individual, commanding, tropical, splashy:

Acanthus
Agave
Cortaderia selloana
Echium fastuosum
Fatsia japonica
Gunnera
Magnolia grandiflora
Melianthus major
Musa
Phormium tenax
Rhododendron
   (large leafed)
Ricinus communis
Schefflera digitata
Tetrapanax papyrifera
Yucca

Informal rather than tailored, rough rather than polished:

Arbutus unedo
Convolvulus cneorum
Elæagnus pungens
Eriogonum arborescens
Feijoa
Garrya
Hakea
Metrosideros tomentosa
Rhamnus

Arching, fountainlike, gracefully curving, arching sprays:

Azara microphylla
Cestrum elegans
Cocculus laurifolius
Cotoneaster parneyi
Crotolaria agatiflora
Deutzia gracilis
Forsythia suspensa
Hebe hulkeana
Hypericum moserianum
Jasminum humile
   revolutum
Kolkwitzia amabilis
Spiræa
Xylosma senticosa

Well groomed, neat, trim, polished, smart, tailored, elegant, aristocratic:

KURUME AZALEAS

Aucuba
Azalea
Buxus
Camellia
Carissa
Choisya ternata
Cocculus laurifolius
Corynocarpus
Gardenia
Hebe buxifolia
Ilex aquifolium
Magnolia grandiflora
Myrsine africana
Osmanthus aquifolium
Pieris
Pinus pinea
Raphiolepis umbellata
   ovata
Rhododendron (dwarf)
Sarcococca
Skimmia
Ternstrœmia
   gymnanthera
Viburnum davidii

Willowy, drooping, pendulous, weeping:

Camellia sasanqua
Leptospermum
   lævigatum
Maytenus boaria
Pittosporum
   phillyræoides
Podocarpus
Salix babylonica

PITTOSPORUM & BOX HEDGE

220 SHRUBS

Lacy, delicate, airy, open, fine textured:

Acer palmatum
  dissectum
Azalea altaclarense,
  A. mollis
Azara microphylla
Betula
Genista monosperma
Nandina domestica
Phyllostachys
Spiræa prunifolia

Indefinite, fillers:
(Deciduous plants that are without winter character and are valued mainly for their flowers. Evergreens that have the restful quality of not calling attention to themselves.)

Abelia
Abutilon
Berberis
Brunfelsia
Ceanothus
Cistus corbariensis
Correa magnifica
Dabœcia cantabrica
Daphne mezereum
Duranta stenostachys
Euonymus japonicus
Hydrangea
Lonicera
Melaleuca
Philadelphus
Ribes sanguineum
Syringa

OSMANTHUS SKIMMIA & SARCOCOCCA

Dense, opaque, no look-through quality, mass, solid block, well organized:

Buxus sempervirens
Castanopsis
  chrysophylla minor
Coprosma
Escallonia
Eugenia paniculata
  australis
Euonymus japonicus
Griselinia
Ligustrum
Myoporum
Pittosporum
Prunus laurocerasus,
  P. lusitanica,
  P. lyonii

Rangy, indeterminate, but willing to be guided:

Chænomeles lagenaria
Chionanthus præcox
Fatshedera
Fuchsia
Pyracantha
Pyrus kawakami

An important fact to keep in mind when working out the shrub pattern for your garden is that the fewer varieties you plant in any one area the better chance you have of getting a pleasing combination.

Generally speaking, repeating the same shrub emphasizes its character and good points. Also, a weak plant can be made important by massing by itself. For example, the rather ordinary abelia hasn't a strong enough outline to stand by itself, and when mixed with other shrubs it is overwhelmed. However, several together will form a soft mass of rosy tipped leaves and pale pink flowers that is just what is needed to counterbalance the bulk and harshness of a large expanse of masonry.

The principle that the most pleasing plantings are those that are held to 2 or 3 things repeated is especially true when a building is background for the planting. Then the shrubs are more closely related to the building than they are to earth, sky, and other plants. Having a number of different leaf textures, sizes, and colors simply confuses everything. It's like having a brick wall laid in four bond patterns in different color bricks.

BLOOM CALENDAR FOR SHRUBS
(For planting recommendations, see encyclopedia.)

FOR SPRING COLOR

Azalea. Pink, rose, red, orange, salmon, white, violet.
Berberis. Yellow.
Chaenomeles. Rose, red, white, pink.
Cytisus, Spartium, Genista. Yellow.

Daphne. Rosy-pink, lilac-purple.
Erica, Calluna, Daboecia. White, pink, rose, red.
Forsythia. Yellow.
Paeonia. White, pink, red, orchid, magenta.
Philadelphus. White.

Rhododendron. Pink, rose, red, white, yellow.
Spiraea. White.
Syringa. Pink, magenta, lavender, purple, white.
Viburnum. White, pink.

FOR SUMMER COLOR

Abelia. White, lavender-pink, carmine-purple.
Fuchsia. Many colors.

Hydrangea. Blue, pink, white.
Lantana. Yellow, orange, lavender-pink.

Nerium. Pink, rose, red, yellow, white.
Weigela. Red, pink.

FOR FALL AND WINTER COLOR

Camellia. Red, pink, white, variegated.
Cotoneaster. Red berries.

Erica. White, pink, rose, red.
Ilex. Red, orange berries.
Nandina. Bronzy foliage turning crimson in winter.

Photinia. Bronzy foliage, red berries.
Pyracantha. Red berries.

ABELIA. Evergreen and deciduous. Hardiness by species.

A. grandiflora. GLOSSY ABELIA. The old standby and still deservedly the most popular. Widely grown in zones 4-13. Severely cut back in 3° winter; becomes half-deciduous at 15°. A vigorous grower to 6-8 ft. high and 4 ft. wide, with graceful arching branches if not made compact by pruning. Very clean, glossy, ½-in., ovate leaves turn bronzy in the fall. Small tubular flowers, white or tinged pink, are borne in profusion from July to October. After the flowers fall, the sepals are persistent and give a purplish tinge to the ends of the branches. Attractive in flower arrangements. Var. *sherwoodii* is a dwarf form to 3 ft., with smaller flowers and leaves.

A. gaucheri. EDWARD GOUCHER ABELIA. Hybrid between *A. grandiflora* and *A. schumanii*. Hardier, lower growing and more lacy than the glossy abelia. Lilac-pink flowers June to October.

A. floribunda. MEXICAN ABELIA. About 20° is its limit. Tall growing to 8 ft. and spreading to 12 ft. Carmine-purple, 1½-in. flowers, in June and July.

A. schumanii. The deciduous species is more slender in growth habit. To 3-5 ft., with 1-in. leaves and lavender-pink flowers.

The abelias are so adaptable and used in so many situations where they must be clipped that the natural beauty of the shrub is overlooked. Even where given massed space in parks it is seldom pruned correctly. Since the flowers are borne on new wood, the shrub benefits by yearly removal of some of the old wood. The more stems that are cut to the ground in winter, the more open and arching will be the next summer's growth.

Grows and flowers best in sun but will stand some shade. Not particular as to soils. Seldom bothered by pests.

ABUTILON. FLOWERING MAPLE. CHINESE BELLFLOWER, CHINESE LANTERN. Evergreen. Zones 9-10. Rapid growing and rangy shrubs that are planted primarily for the pleasure provided by the flowers. The coarseness and ranginess can be avoided by pinching and pruning.

A. hybridum. Upright arching growth to 8-10 ft. and spreading as wide. Broad maple-like foliage. Drooping, bell-like flowers in white, yellow, pink, and red. Main blooming season from April through June.

A. megapotamicum. Vine-like growth to 10 ft. and as wide. Leaves are small, cut-leaf maple in outline. Flowers like red and yellow lanterns gaily decorate the long rangy branches from May-September. This vine-shrub is more graceful in detail than in entirety, but can be trained to an interesting pattern.

A. vitifolium. Grows quickly to 8 ft. in the open, and will reach 20 ft. when planted against a wall. Gray-green leaves. Light lavender-blue, sometimes white, flowers in May-June. Tends to become leggy and leafless at base of plant.

A. v. Vesuvius. Fast growth to 6 ft. Brilliant orange-scarlet 2-in. flowers blooming throughout the year in warm winter areas.

Abutilons enjoy the same conditions as fuchsias—moist soil and partial shade. However, they will not bloom in full shade. When planted in areas where winter temperature drops below 25°, they must have protection of a warm wall or overhanging eaves. Tip branches from the start to encourage compact growth.

Abutilon can be used as a container plant indoors in winter and out on a terrace in summer.

AFRICAN BOX. See MYRSINE AFRICANA

ALTHAEA. See HIBISCUS SYRIACUS

AMELANCHIER. SERVICE BERRY. Deciduous. All zones, but need winter cold for best performance. Shrubs and small trees valued for year-around interest. Clusters of white flowers usually before leaves unfold in spring; small fruits in summer; colorful autumn foliage; good winter form.

A. alnifolia. WESTERN SERVICE BERRY. SASKATOON SERVICE BERRY. Native to mountains of California, Oregon, Washington, British Columbia, and east to the Rocky Mountains.

Shrub-like growth to 12-15 ft. Foliage color changes from bronzy-red in spring, to light green in summer, to yellow, apricot-orange, and dull, dusty red in autumn. Pure white flowers, each with 5 strap-like petals, in April. Flowers followed by edible purple fruits. If you can beat the birds to harvesting them, use these little apple-like fruits in pies and jams. The Indians made pemmican from these berries.

A. canadensis. SHADBLOW SERVICE BERRY. Slender, tree-like form to 30 ft. Leaves in spring are tinged with pink. A graceful outline of gray branches in winter.

A. stolonifera. An upright, dense, twiggy shrub to 4 ft., spreading by underground roots to form a solid clump. Small black fruits in late summer.

A. laevis. A slender, gray-branched tree to 20 ft. New growth is purplish.

Amelanchier has not been widely used in Western gardens, but is worth trying in cool, moist, spots in partial shade. Use it against a dark background to emphasize the delicate values of flower, foliage, and winter form.

ANDROMEDA. See PIERIS

ARALIA. See FATSIA JAPONICA

ARBUTUS UNEDO. STRAWBERRY TREE. Evergreen. Zones 3-13. Damaged in severe winters in zones 3-6, but worth the risk. Remarkably good performance in both climate and soil extremes from desert to seashore. Slow to moderate growth to 8-20 ft. with equal spread. Normally has basal suckers, stem sprouts. Can be pruned, not sheared, to make an open-crowned tree. Dark green, handsome red-stemmed leaves are oblong and 2-3 in. long. Clusters of small white or greenish-white, urn-shaped flowers and red and yellow, ¾-in. round fruit, somewhat strawberry-like in its wartiness, appear at the same time in fall and winter.

Allowed to go its own way, the strawberry tree forms a rather rangy, thick shrub screen. Far more effective used that way than when sheared back for foundation planting. As a well trained, small tree, becomes more interesting with age. Excellent specimen tree on a high lawn where structure can be looked up into.

Although tolerant of various soils, it will be a healthier tree if a generous amount of peat moss is mixed into the soil. Frequent spraying for aphis is necessary.

A. menziesii. MADRONE. (See chapter on natives.)

ASTER FRUTICOSUS. SHRUB ASTER. Evergreen. Zones 7-13. One usually thinks of asters as annual or perennial herbaceous plants but here is an aster that is actually a shrub. Rounded, bushy plant to 3-4 ft. high and 3-ft. wide, with rather narrow, dark green leaves. Solitary, 1½-in., daisy flowers are lavender with yellow center, covering shrub from early April to late June.

Full sun. Grows in any well-drained, fairly dry soil. Prune after bloom to discourage its tendency toward legginess.

Shrub aster is good for hillsides or dry gardens. With wistaria and yellow Banksia rose it is lovely around Easter time.

AUCUBA. Evergreen. Hardy in zones 3-13, and unusually tolerant of soil and temperature extremes. Important shrubs to Western gardeners. Well behaved in deep shade; has all-year interest.

A. japonica. GREENLEAF AUCUBA. Moderate growth to 6-10 ft. high and 5-7 ft. wide forming an irregular, bulky, informal shrub. Clean, thickish, lush green, 7-in. leaves are ovate or oblong with margins coarsely toothed above the middle. The total foliage effect is coarse in texture. Minute, dark maroon flowers in March are followed by clusters of bright red, ¾-in. berries from October to February. Because fruit is borne on female plants only, both sexes must be planted to insure fruit crop.

Of the varieties of *A. japonica*, the best known is var. *variegata*, GOLD DUST PLANT, with green leaves speckled with yellow. Other variegated forms are: var. *crotonifolia* with green and white, croton-like leaves; and var. *fructo-alba* with silver, variegated leaves and pale pinkish-buff fruit. A new horticultural form, var. *albo-marginata*, is a slow-growing, semi-dwarf shrub with 8-in. leaves variegated dark green, light green, yellow and white.

The two green-leaf varieties are: var. *angustifolia* with long, narrow leaves and var. *nana*, a dwarf form.

Aucubas grow best in full shade. Leaves sunburn in hot summer sun and blacken when exposed to winter sun. Water generously. Adapted to heavy soil with poor drainage, lean, sandy, alkaline soils, or rich soils. Prune by cutting back to joint or node, and the plant looks untouched.

Use for those shady, dark, difficult spots where nothing seems to grow. Plant in mass behind *Skimmia japonica*. Variegated forms will lighten dark shady corners and combine with heavy ferns. Good companions: fatsia, euonymus, hydrangea. Plant in large tubs or boxes for the shady terrace.

AUSTRALIAN FUCHSIA. See CORREA

AZALEA. See p. 261

AZARA MICROPHYLLA. BOXLEAF AZARA. AROMO. Evergreen. Zones 7-13. By withholding water in late summer to harden shrub before winter cold, *Azara microphylla* is grown successfully in the Northwest as a protected wall shrub.

Slow growing when small, fast when established, to 12-18 ft., spreading 8-12 ft. Fan-like, branching habit makes it a natural for espaliering and for planting against walls. Leaves are ½-in., glossy, dark green. Flowers in February-April are inconspicuous but release a slight vanilla fragrance. Small orange berries.

Needs shade from hot sun; plenty of moisture. After flowering, the foliage may turn yellowish and old leaves fall. At that time an extra application of fertilizer will turn shrub green again. At the same time a light pruning and pinching will encourage the plant to fill out.

Azara, eurya, daboecia, ophiopogon are good companions.

BANANA SHRUB. See MICHELIA FUSCATA

BEAUTY BERRY. See CALLICARPA

BEAUTY BUSH. See KOLKWITZIA AMABILIS

BELOPERONE GUTTATA. SHRIMP PLANT. Evergreen but best treated as a perennial. Zones 12 and 13, and elsewhere as an indoor-outdoor plant. Will grow to a 3 by 4 ft. mound but can be kept much lower. Flowers are white, spotted with purple, enclosed in coppery-bronze, overlapping bracts forming compact, drooping spikes 3 in. long, lengthening to 6-7 in. if allowed to remain on plant.

If you have a liking for orange tones, the shrimp plant is worth fussing over. The plant will take sun but the bracts and foliage fade unless grown in partial shade. Plant is easy to use in a pot or tub. To make an attractively shaped plant, pinch continuously in early growth until compact mound of foliage is obtained and then let bloom. To encourage continued bushiness, cut back stems when flower bracts turn black.

Nurseries list both *B. guttata* and *B. tomentosa*. As far as we can tell the same plant is being sold under two names.

BERBERIS. BARBERRY. Deciduous and evergreen. Hardy all zones with exception of some evergreen species. There are so many work-horses in the barberry stable that it is very easy to overlook the three or four thoroughbreds there, particularly the polished and pert *B. verruculosa* and the all-season performer *B. darwinii*. Not all of the "spiny barberries" are formidable barriers.

B. buxifolia nana. (*B. dulcis nana*). DWARF BARBERRY. Evergreen to 15-18 in. high and 24 in. wide. Small, dark green leaves. Orange-yellow flowers in May, followed by dark purple fruits. Use as a traffic regulator or where yellow bloom in an evergreen is important.

B. darwinii. Evergreen. The showiest of the barberries. Fountain-like in growth habit to 4-10 ft. high and 5-7 ft. wide. Small, crisp, dark green, holly-like leaves. Clusters of orange-yellow flowers in early spring, followed by dark blue berries that last well into the winter. The flowers are so thick along each branch that it's difficult to see the foliage. Wonderful as a background to *Mahonia aquifolium*.

B. gagnepainii. BLACK BARBERRY. Evergreen. Open and rangy to 6 ft. Well protected with spines. Use in hedge row planting in the country place.

B. julianae. WINTERGREEN BARBERRY. Evergreen, or semi-deciduous. One of the hardiest barberries. Dense, upright form to 6 ft., with slightly angled branches. Spiny. Reddish fall color. Another work-horse.

B. pruinosa. HOLLYGREEN BARBERRY. Evergreen. A dense but graceful growth to 5 ft. Well-armored barrier.

B. stenophylla irwinii. Evergreen. Graceful arching growth habit to 18 in. Attractive, dark green foliage. Yellow flowers in May. Very hardy. Use as low hedge; on banks; as attractive foreground for higher shrubs.

B. thunbergii. JAPANESE BARBERRY. Deciduous. Graceful sweeping form with arching sprays to 4-6 ft. high and as wide. Small, oval, bright green leaves turn in fall to yellow, orange, and red. After leaves fall, the bead-like, scarlet berries set close to the branches are very showy.

B. t. atropurpurea differs from the species in color only. Leaves are red-purple when planted in sun, but fade in the shade. The most used barberry in Southern California. Colored foliage should be in enough volume to avoid the solitary red mound appearance.

B. verruculosa. Evergreen. A very neat, tailored shrub with informal elegance. Grows to 3 ft. high and wide, but can be held to 18 in. without becoming clubby. Perky, glossy, dark green leaves are white beneath. Interesting highlighting of occasional red leaves among the green in fall and winter. Very choice and very easy to use in spots where low-growing evergreens are suitable, on banks, in foreground of shrub border, in block planting on a terrace.

B. wilsoniae. Almost evergreen. Moderate growth to 6 ft. high and as wide but can be held to a 3-4 ft. hedge.

Sturdy, but has fine texture with light green, 1-in. leaves. Very small yellow flowers in May are followed by beautiful coral berries. A barrier hedge and handsome, too. Not so hardy as most barberry.

BOTTLE BRUSH. See CALLISTEMON MELALEUCA

BOUVARDIA. Evergreen. Outdoors in zone 13. Tried as indoor-winter, outdoor-summer plant in colder sections without success. Bouvardia are loose, often straggling shrubs noted for showy clusters of tubular flowers. The bitter truth is that the fragrant species is the most tender of the lot and has the worst appearance after the flowers are gone. The non-fragrant pink or red-flowered types are hardier and better behaved in the garden.

B. humboldtii Albatross. To 2-3 ft. high, with opposite leaves. Snow-white, heavily fragrant, 3-in. flowers.

Non-fragrant species: *B. leiantha*, leaves in whorls of 3 or 5, deep red, ½-in. flowers; *B. ternifolia (B. jacquinii)*, to 6 ft., with leaves in whorls of 3 or 4, and with 1¼-in. red flowers. Several horticultural varieties available in shades of red, coral, or pink.

Grow in tubs with mixture of peat moss, sand, and leaf mold. Feed with cottonseed meal or fish fertilizer. Prune and pinch to develop new wood.

BOXWOOD. See BUXUS

BRACHYSEMA LANCEOLATUM. SWAN RIVER PEA BUSH. Evergreen. Zones 7-13. One of the few shrubs that bloom almost all year. Low growing to 3 ft., with grayish-silver, narrow, 4-in. leaves and many bright red, sweet-pea-shaped flowers.

Because it thrives under most adverse conditions, it is a good hillside plant.

BREATH OF HEAVEN. See COLEONEMA;DIOSMA
BRIDAL WREATH. See SPIRAEA

BRUNFELSIA CALYCINA FLORIBUNDA (*B. floribunda*). YESTERDAY-TODAY-AND-TOMORROW. Evergreen, deciduous in a cold winter. Zones 7-13. Grows compactly to 5-6 ft. and spreads as wide. Its ovate-oblong, 4-in. leaves are bronzy green in early spring, dark green by summer. Earns its common name through its three-day flower color change from purple to lavender to white. Flowers are long tubes, flaring into 5 flat segments 2 in. across; appear in clusters of 2 and 3. Long season of bloom reaches peak in spring. Var. *eximia*. FADING BRAZIL RAINTREE. A 2-3 ft. shrub with a greater mass of bloom but a short season. Var. *macrantha* (*B. grandiflora*) has larger, 8-in., rich dark green leaves and deep purple flowers with a lavender-blue ring around a white eye.

Best in rich, slightly acid soil. Needs excellent drainage and generous waterings. Semi-shade seems best, but grows in full sun along the coast.

Brunfelsia is a well-mannered shrub capable of associating with camellias, daphne, and azaleas. Distinctive as a patio shrub in or out of tub. Effective when planted on outside fringe of a group of high branching trees that give light afternoon shade.

BUDDLEJA (*Buddleia*). BUTTERFLY BUSH. Evergreen-deciduous. Hardy all zones, but freezes to ground in 10° winters. Many improvements have been made in the old-time butterfly bush, but still a scraggly, informal shrub in need of drastic pruning for shaping and renewal of flowering wood. Earns its keep by flowers alone.

B. davidii. (*B. variabilis*). BUTTERFLY BUSH. SUMMER LILAC. Sage-scented shrubs to 20 ft. high and 10-15 ft. wide. 10-in. leaves, dark green above, densely white-hairy beneath. Fragrant flowers, lilac with an orange eye, are carried in 10-in. spikes from July-October. Many hybrids of the common butterfly bush are available. Var. *Isle de France*, one of the best forms, has deep purple spikes and is a compact bush, if pruned hard.

B. alternifolia. FOUNTAIN BUDDLEIA. Shrub or small tree to 12 ft. or more. Willow-like stems. Arching branchlets carry short, dense clusters of lilac flowers all along their length. Needs warm summer climate for flower production. Prune all flowering branches immediately after blooming.

B. colvilei kewensis. Showy shrub ultimately reaching to 30 ft., with silvery-green, 7-in. leaves. Flowers, rose-pink with large white eye, in massive drooping clusters to 1½ ft. long. Because flowers are borne on old wood, pruning is held to thinning out for gradual renewal.

Buddlejas like to grow, and wear themselves out doing it in any soil. Tolerant of alkaline soil and of hot summer sun. All except *B. colvilei kewensis* should be cut back almost to the ground each spring.

Because this large, vigorous plant has only seasonal value, use for quick screens and windbreaks in large places where winter appearance is not important.

BUXUS. BOXWOOD. Evergreen. Climate adaptation according to species. So rarely seen except in trimmed and controlled forms that few people know the boxwood as a shrub of soft, billowy habit, or know the taller species with dense foliage arching almost to the ground. The boxwoods used in the West are:

B. microphylla japonica (*B. japonica*). JAPANESE BOXWOOD. Used in zones 7-13. Turns bronze in 20° temperatures when exposed to morning sun. Growth is slow to medium; to 4-6 ft. if not controlled. Foliage of Japanese boxwood is lighter green than that of English boxwood, but its structure is more compact.

You can tell the difference between Japanese boxwood and English boxwood by comparing leaves. The leaf of the Japanese is slightly broader above the middle; the English leaf is slightly broader below the middle. Practically all of the boxwood sold in flats in Southern California is Japanese boxwood.

B. sempervirens. ENGLISH BOXWOOD. COMMON BOXWOOD. Zones 3-13 with some winter damage in 3-6. Preferred boxwood in 9-10, and the favorite in the Northwest. Slow growing to 15-20 ft., with an equal spread. Densely branching, with lustrous dark green leaves; easily controlled by shearing.

B. s. suffruticosa. TRUE DWARF BOXWOOD. This dwarf variety is widely used in the Northwest, less frequently in northern California, and is scarce in Southern California. It's slower growing than the species; leaves are smaller, giving it a denser form and texture. There's a silver-edged, variegated form available.

Other vareties of English boxwood are: Var. *arborescens*, TREE BOXWOOD, rapid grower to 15-20 ft., more open and loose in character than the species; var. *rotundifolia*, ROUND LEAF BOXWOOD, bluish-green, broad, oval leaves; var. *myrtifolia*, MYRTLE LEAF BOXWOOD, lower growing to 4-5 ft., with narrow leaves; var. *aureo-variegata*, GOLDEN BOXWOOD, one of the smallest forms, to 1 ft., with yellow leaves.

B. harlandii. KOREAN BOXWOOD. Considered one of the best varieties for warmer climates. Hardy to 5°. Grows more rapidly than English boxwood, to 2 ft. Remains very dense and compact in habit. Similar to Japanese boxwood except that Korean boxwood's leaves are narrower and brighter green. Although more resistant to heat and drought, should be generously watered for best results.

Boxwood is taken for granted and seldom receives any

special attention. Can be petted with mulches and fertilizers into better appearance. Subject to scale and nematodes.

CAJEPUT TREE. See CALLISTEMON; MELALEUCA

CALLIANDRA. Evergreen. Zones 10 and 13; borderline in 9 and 12. The Trinidad flame bush and the Brazilian flame bush are the most commonly distributed species and are similar in growth habit and culture.

C. tweedii. BRAZILIAN FLAME BUSH. Plants sold under the name of *C. guildingii* are *C. tweedii*. Probably the hardiest calliandra. Slow to moderate growth to 6-8 ft. with a 5-8 ft. spread. Loose and open; graceful in every way. Leaves are lacy and fernlike, divided into very short leaflets. Each branch bears terminal clusters of greenish-white flowers with 3-in. stamens of brilliant crimson, form feathery balls, powder puffs, or pompons, according to your choice of descriptive words. Blooms February to fall; all year in favored gardens.

Planted where drainage is good. On hillsides it is a natural with Matilija poppy, bush poppy, *Teucrium fruticans* and shrubby artemisias. Rabbits like the young plant, so guard with wire in native plantings. Although drought-resistant when established, flame bush needs water in the first summers. Train by thinning out branches to retain interesting zig-zag, horizontal branching.

C. inaequilatera. PINK POWDER PUFF. Use only in favored spots of zone 13; will stand 14° on a south wall. Grows to 6-8 ft. with an equal spread. However, it can be trained as an informal espalier, preferably on a south wall. Foliage is dark green with bronzy new growth. Leaves with longer, 1-2¼ in., and broader leaflets than *C. tweedii*. Flowers are a watermelon-pink; October-March. Give it regular, deep watering.

CALLICARPA. BEAUTY BERRY. Deciduous. Hardy all zones. Beauty berries are grown principally for their attractive fall fruits. The whole tone of the plant after the leaves are gone in the fall is due to the many thick clusters of violet or purple fruits. They last for quite a time if the birds don't get them early.

C. americana. FRENCH MULBERRY. AMERICAN BEAUTY BERRY. Grows to 6 ft., with 6-in. leaves, white or rusty-hairy beneath. Tiny clusters of closely set, bluish flowers in May-July.

C. japonica. JAPANESE BEAUTY BERRY. Grows to 6 ft., with 5-in. leaves. Pink or whitish flowers in August.

C. bodinieri giraldii (*C. giraldiana*). Taller growing to 10 ft., with shorter, 4-in. leaves turning purple in fall. Pink flowers.

Beauty berry likes partial shade, and plenty of water. Takes any soil, but will produce better berries in good soil. Should be pruned back severely in late fall or early spring to produce plenty of new wood for flowering.

Callicarpa, snowberry, and coral berry may be combined to make an interesting group for a spot of fall color in the garden. The branches of the callicarpa are whiplike and very graceful, so you should give it room in which to develop naturally.

CALLISTEMON and **MELALEUCA.** BOTTLE BRUSH. Evergreen. Zones 7-13 but damaged at 15°. Useful, fast-growing shrubs or small trees. Colorful flowers in dense spikes (or heads) with protruding stamens like bristles in a brush, hence bottle brush. Woody seed capsules surrounding the branch stay put and increase in number each year.

The botanical differences between callistemon and melaleuca are not obvious to the gardener and because of their similar culture and uses, the two are considered here as a single group. Arbitrary distinctions may be made—callistemon generally has longer leaves and larger flowers that are mainly red; while melaleuca flowers are white, pink or lavender, but red in only one species. Perhaps the melaleucas are a bit sturdier and tougher.

In choosing a species, remember that there are more differences than color of flower. Some of the bottle brushes are so unlike any other plant in your garden that they may appear out of place.

C. lanceolatus. (*C. citrinus*). LEMON BOTTLE BRUSH. Rounded shrub or small tree to 10-25 ft. with 6-10 ft. spread. Narrow, 3-in. leaves are rather stiff. When the new growth appears, these brushes put on quite a show by adding a few more reddish leaves every day until the entire shrub is wine-colored streaked with green. Plant's brushes are bright red in May and June and again in August.

C. rigidus. STIFF BOTTLE BRUSH. Erect, sparse, rigid shrub or small tree to 20 ft. Inclined to lose all leaves from trunks and carry an irregular 10-ft. wide top. Gray-green leaves are very narrow and 5 in. long. Redeeming feature is its production of dense red brushes in June. Seed cases very prominent. A very difficult plant to handle in the garden.

C. viminalis. WEEPING BOTTLE BRUSH. Pendulous, branched shrub or small tree. Fast growing to 20 ft. with a 15-ft. spread; 6-in. leaves are soft, light green with bronzy tips. Bright red flowers in May-July and scattered blooming throughout the year. Use in lawns as a single tree or with groups. Thrives on plenty of moisture.

C. Red Chico. FIREBALL BUSH. Rounded shrub to 8 ft., with arching branches. Brilliant, fiery red flowers from April-July.

M. armillaris (*M. alba*). DROOPING MELALEUCA. Graceful shrub or small tree to 30 ft., with dark green, needle-like leaves to ¾ in. White flowers in 2-in. spikes.

M. decussata. LILAC MELALEUCA. Shrub 15-20 ft. high; ½-in. blue-green leaves and lilac flowers in 1-in. spikes.

M. ericifolia. HEATH MELALEUCA. Shrub or small tree to 25 ft. Dark green, needle-like, 1-in. leaves reminiscent of heather. Yellowish-white flowers in 1-in. spikes.

M. hypericifolia. DOTTED MELALEUCA. Large shrub 8-10 ft. high and as wide. Narrow, dull green, 1½-in. leaves. Orange-red flowers in dense 2-3 in. spikes, May-July.

M. leucadendra. CAJEPUT TREE. Distinctive small tree to 20 ft. Shreddy, light colored bark and 4-in. leaves. Creamy-white flowers in 6-in. spikes. Needs plenty of water for best growth.

M. nesophila. PINK MELALEUCA. Neat, rounded shrub to 8 ft. Gray-green, 1-in. leaves. Pink or rose flowers in dense heads; May-July. One of the best for ocean exposure.

M. styphelioides. Tree-like shrub eventually becoming a small tree 40 ft. high. ¾-in. leaves are sometimes twisted. Creamy-white flowers in 2-in. spikes. One of the best for quick lacy growth.

Use bottle brushes (except those tabbed as needing lots of water) in dry difficult situations, for windbreaks, in seashore plantings. These shrubs can take the salt wind of the ocean.

Prune in late summer or early fall to discourage legginess and remove unsightly dead twigs. Head back selected branches. Don't shear.

CALLUNA. See *Erica*.

CAMELLIA. See p. 253

CARISSA. NATAL PLUM. Evergreen. Zones 8-13 with these reservations: Foliage is damaged at temperatures below 26°. Young plants are killed by lower temperatures. Plants which become established through a period of mild winters are able to recover from a damaging 20° freeze. Old plants can be seen throughout all southern zones—in Palm Springs, Ontario, Riverside, etc. They endure summer heat and thrive in coastal fog, in both sun and shade.

Where frosts come seldom, the carissas are as serviceable as privet, with polished leaves, and flowers almost as fragrant as those of the star jasmine. Their shiny red fruits look like plums and taste better.

C. grandiflora. A rounding shrub of loose habit, generally 5-7 ft., but occasionally to 18 ft. Leaves ovate to 3 in.; flowers white, 2 in. across, appear throughout the year. Red plums 1-2 in. long. For best fruit production, plant in groups to provide cross pollination.

Use as formal or informal hedge. Its dense habit and spines discourage traffic through it. Can be trained as an espalier.

C. g. alles. (*C. alles*). If you are interested in fruit production, this is the variety. A horticultural form developed from a chance seedling and propagated from cuttings. Has a more horizontal habit of growth, to 5 ft. Bears larger flowers and fruits. This variety must have a plant of *C. grandiflora* as a companion for fruit production.

C. g. nana compacta. Lower and denser form to 3-4 ft. There are variations in seedlings.

C. g. nana compacta tuttlei. True to type from cuttings. Small leaves, dense.

C. g. prostrata. Name applied to *C. grandiflora* seedlings which show low horizontal growth. When prostrate form is selected and propagated from cuttings, the plants will form a spreading glossy mat no deeper than a ground cover of Algerian ivy.

C. carandis. Leaves shorter and more pointed than *C. grandiflora*. Rangy growth habit, well suited to espaliering. Small pink flowers followed by small black fruits.

The carissas are almost foolproof. They accept wide variations in soils, sun, and shade. Overwatering in heavy soils must be avoided. Fruit production is best in sun with deep but widely spaced irrigations. Fruit attracts birds. The smaller varieties make excellent tub plants and could be used as indoor-outdoor plants when winters are too cold for carissa.

CARYOPTERIS. BLUEBEARD. Deciduous. Hardy all zones. Although not spectacular, these shrubs combine easily with plants of difficult colors.

C. incana (*C. mastacanthus, C. tangutica*). COMMON BLUEBEARD. BLUE SPIRAEA. Spreading, rounded shrub sometimes grown as a shrubby perennial, grows to 3-4 ft. Gray-green, 3-in. leaves, and lavender-blue, fringed, ¼-in. flowers in spikes in late summer.

C. clandonensis. BLUE MIST. A hybrid with *C. incana* as one parent. Hardier than the parent, lower growing to 2 ft., narrower leaves, powdery blue flowers from August to autumn frosts.

Sun loving, fast growing plants. Requires any good, well drained soil and moderate watering. Prune back severely in late fall or winter.

Blue flowers and silver foliage bring cool colors to shrubbery or flower border during the hottest part of the summer. Combines well with rockroses or plants with yellow or brilliant magenta flowers.

CASSIA. SENNA. Evergreen. Zones 9-10 and 11-13. Killed to the ground at 20° but recovers. Other than *C. artemisioides* the cassias are too rank and coarse for the average garden.

C. artemisioides. WORMWOOD SENNA. FEATHERY CASSIA. Attractive, light textured shrub to 3-5 ft., with feathery gray leaves and sulfur-yellow flowers. Important for its winter bloom, January-April.

Of the other species: *C. splendida*, GOLDEN WONDER SENNA, a wide, 10-ft. shrub giving a mass of golden-yellow flowers, November-January; *C. tomentosa*, WOOLLY SENNA, rank growing to 15 ft., can be trained as a small tree; *C. corymbosa*, FLOWERY SENNA, yellow blooms spring to fall, and unattractive when not in bloom; *C. nairobensis*, to 10 ft., December-April bloom with larger yellow flowers than other species.

The small growing, feathery cassia should be used where its light and airy structure would be effective. The taller cassias are used best in native or hillside plantings and combined with bottle brush, *Rhus ovata* and *R. integrifolia*.

Give cassias full sun; plant where they get good drainage. They are well adapted to both desert and coastal conditions.

CATHA EDULIS. ARABIAN KHAT. Evergreen. Zones 8a, 10-13. Shrub to 3-8 ft., best pinched back while young and kept to 5 ft. Has red stems and trunk. Oval bronzy-green shining 3-4 in. leaves, turn redder from Oct.-April where nights are cold. Tiny white flowers are not conspicuous. Is of particular value in poor soil and difficult low maintenance situations. The burnished glossy foliage of medium sized leaves is valuable in stepping down from such large leaves as those of loquat to small-scale foliage.

CERATOSTIGMA. Technically an evergreen, but should be treated as a perennial. Hardy zones 4-13; will freeze to the ground in zones 4-6. Should be cut back each winter regardless of frost. All plumbagos are important, blue flowering shrubs from June to December.

C. willmottianum. CHINESE PLUMBAGO. An airy, wiry-branched shrub to 4 ft., with dark green, 2-in. leaves. Bright blue, phlox-like, 1-in. flowers in clusters. Leaves turn yellow to red at first frost, and shrub is unsightly thereafter. Prune back 1 ft. or more to clean it up. Chinese plumbago will hold its own share of the color load in annual or perennial borders. Combine with white or yellow.

C. griffithii. BURMESE PLUMBAGO. Less airy, more moundy and denser in growth than Chinese plumbago.

C. plumbaginoides (*C. larpentiæ*). DWARF PLUMBAGO. (See chapter on ground covers.)

Ceratostigma is very tolerant of soils, watering schedules, and sun and shade.

CESTRUM. Evergreen. Zone 13 and protected gardens in 10-12. Fast growing, flowering shrubs that are inclined to be rangy and top heavy if not consistently pruned.

C. purpureum (*C. elegans*). RED CESTRUM. Hardiest of the cestrums. May be used as a shrub, as a semi-climber, or as an espalier against fence or wall. Grows to 10 ft. with arching branches, soft 4-in. leaves. Masses of 1-in., reddish-purple flowers in spring and summer; scattered bloom throughout the year. Flowers are followed by shiny, plum-red fruits.

C. parqui. WILLOW-LEAVED JESSAMINE. To 6 ft., with 6-in. willow-like leaves. Flowers, greenish-white or greenish-yellow, are powerfully fragrant at night. Berries black. Neither shrub, flowers, nor fruit are as attractive as those of other cestrums, but *C. parqui's* perfume is potent.

C. aurantiacum. ORANGE CESTRUM. A brilliant show of orange flowers, followed by white berries.

C. nocturnum. NIGHT JESSAMINE. Very tender, but comes back after freeze. Will grow in Zone 12. To 12 ft., with 4-in. leaves, creamy-white flowers and white berries. Powerfully fragrant. Reseeds itself all over the garden.

Cestrums need a warm, shady position with generous treatment in feeding and watering. They will grow weedy and rangy unless consistently nipped back for compactness and cut back severely after flowering or fruiting.

CHASTE TREE. See VITEX AGNUS-CASTUS

CHAENOMELES. FLOWERING QUINCE. Deciduous. Hardy all zones. Picturesque, practically indestructible shrubs of varying growth habit. Branches are attractive when out of leaf—strong in line with an oriental feeling. Some grow to 10 ft. and spread wider; some are compact and low growing; most are thorny; a few are thornless. Chænomeles are the first flowering shrubs to bloom each year. As early as January you can take a budded stem or two indoors, place it in water in a warm window and watch the buds break into bloom.

Many, many named varieties are offered. Difficult to tell what growth pattern you are buying. Here is a guide through a few of the names:

C. lagenaria. (Includes all flowering quince sold as *Cydonia japonica*, or *C. j. rosea*, or *C. j. rubra grandiflora*). Erect growing type to 6 ft. or more, with a greater spread. Named varieties of *Chænomeles lagenaria* are: *Afterglow*, double flowers, white in bud turning soft rose; *Appleblossom*, pink and white flowers; *Snow*, pure white, 2½ in. flowers; *Red Ruffles*. Also in this group are varieties of lower growing habit such as: *Blood Red*, restrained and compact; *Stanford Red*, graceful and spreading, almost thornless, tomato-red, 2-in. flowers.

C. cathayensis. Hybrids of great vigor growing to 5-8 ft. high, 3-4 ft. wide. Unlike others because erect branches are thickly set with short lateral shoots that set flower buds freely. Some of the Cathayensis hybrids being sold are: *Cardinal; Flamingo; Enchantress*, shell pink flowers; *Cynthia*, soft rose flowers becoming peach pink; *Fire; Mandarin*. The two low and compact forms are: *Minerva*, rose-red 2½-in. flowers; *Salmon Pink*.

C. superba. Hybrid of *C. lagenaria* and the little known, low-growing *Chænomeles japonica*. Growth is bushier and generally more spreading. Named varieties: *Texas Scarlet*, watermelon-red, 2-in. flowers; *Crimson and Gold*, dark red flowers with golden stamens; *Charming*, long, unbranched, thornless shoots, pink flowers; *Coral Beauty*, rosy coral with frilled petals.

C. sinensis. CHINESE QUINCE. Grows to 20 ft., with elliptic 3-in. leaves that turn scarlet in autumn. Pink, apple-blossom flowers in spring, followed by large, 7-in., yellow fruits that are aromatic. Fine fall foliage color in Southern California.

Flowering quince is adapted to almost any soil, even poorly drained types. Sun.

Use against a sunny rock wall, in hedges or in the cutting garden.

CHAMAECYPARIS. FALSE CYPRESS. A variable genus of coniferous evergreen shrubs and trees. Four species, 2 Pacific Northwest natives and 2 introductions from Japan, are available in a bewildering variety of form, texture, foliage color, and size.

The tall-growing forms are discussed in the chapter on trees. Here we list and compare the 3-20 ft. shrub forms.

To make it easier to see the differences, we lead off each variety with height and form.

C. lawsoniana. PORT ORFORD CEDAR. LAWSON CYPRESS. (See chapter on trees.)

To 2-5 ft.—clumpy, upright and dense: Var. *minima*, dark green foliage; var. *minima aurea*, gold foliage; var. *minima glauca*, blue-green cast to foliage. Used individually in pots, tubs.

To 3-4 ft. high and 8 ft. wide: Var. *nestoides*, BIRDS NEST CYPRESS, rounded and spreading with heavy-textured, medium-green foliage. Used in shrub border or as informal backgrounds for flower border.

To 4 ft. high and 6 ft. wide—symmetrical: Var. *forsteckiana*, slow growing, wide spreading, very thick and heavily branched. Used in mass, or as low, wide hedge.

To 6-8 ft.—tapering column: Var. *ellwoodii*, dense, compact, with lacy, silver-blue foliage of light, delicate texture. Too definite and stiff to combine with other plants.

To 6 ft.—broad pyramid: Var. *azurea*, distinguished by its bright blue foliage. Used as accent. Difficult to group.

To 6 ft.—upright, rounded: Var. *compacta*, full-branched, light-textured gray-green foliage.

To 6-8 ft.—spreading pyramid: Var. *fletcheri*, feathery, blue-gray foliage, turning even grayer in winter. Handsome against darker greens.

To 10-12 ft.—rounded, spreading: Var. *nidiformis*, BIRDS NEST CYPRESS, a big edition of var. *nestoides*, but more upright growing and with softer texture.

C. nootkatensis. NOOTKA CYPRESS. ALASKA YELLOW CEDAR. (See chapter on trees.)

To 3-5 ft.—narrow pyramid: Var. *compacta*, a miniature tree rather than a shrub. Attractive, blue-green foliage. Handsome in containers.

C. obtusa. HINOKI FALSE CYPRESS. (See chapter on trees.)

To 3 ft.—upright, rounded: Var. *nana*. Deep green foliage in flat, stratified planes. Smooth, reddish-brown bark peels in thin strips. Branching pattern makes it effective planted in mass on a slope.

To 4-6 ft.—rounded: Var. *ericoides*, fluffy gray-green foliage, turning purple-brown in winter. Used for its color change. Grows scraggly as it ages.

C. pisifera. SAWARA FALSE CYPRESS. (See chapter on trees.)

To 3 ft.—dense mound: Var. *squarrosa nana*, sea-green foliage on graceful, arching branches. Prune to keep compact.

To 3 ft.—compact mound: Var. *aurea nana*, slow growing; golden foliage. May turn a muddy color in winter if planted in full sun.

To 8 ft.—loose mound: Var. *filifera*, THREAD CYPRESS. Weeping branches with dark green, thread-like twigs. Contrasts nicely with Mugho pine. Good background for winter sweet or witch hazel. Var. *filifera aurea*. Slower growing and smaller, with golden-green new growth. A dwarf form is available.

CHAMAELAUCIUM. GERALDTON WAXFLOWER. Evergreen. Zones 7-13. Has a dainty, airy grace rarely found in evergreen shrubs. The bright green, needle-like foliage and the showy sprays of winter-blooming, waxy, pale pink or rosy flowers are cherished for flower arrangements of long lasting beauty.

C. ciliatum. Fast growth to 10-12 ft. with an 8-12 ft. spread. Blooms from January to mid-April.

C. uncinatum. Differs from *C. ciliatum* in longer leaves, often hooked at the tip.

Grows best in a sunny dry spot, preferably in a loose, gravelly soil. Go easy on the watering in summer. Don't hesitate to cut it freely for flower arrangements, since in any case it should be pruned back heavily after bloom. If it shows tendency to sprawl, tie young plants to 5 ft. stakes.

Use on banks, or grow in cutting garden. May be espaliered against walls and fences. In the garden it makes a nice showing with heather, Cassia artemisioides, rosemary, Correa pulchella, and Genista monosperma.

CHIMONANTHUS PRAECOX (*C. fragrans*, *Meratia præcox*, *Calycanthus præcox*). WINTERSWEET. Deciduous. Hardy all zones but most useful in 1-6. Tall open shrub growing slowly to 10 ft. Many slender basal stems with light green, 6-in. leaves. The pale yellow, 1-in., fragrant flowers appear before the leaves, January-February in mild winter. Var. *grandiflora* has larger leaves and flowers.

Wintersweet is valued for its color in winter-barren gardens rather than for its summer performance. Best suited for cutting material in winter bouquets. Be generous in blossom cutting, and there will be no need for pruning after flowering.

CHOISYA TERNATA. MEXICAN ORANGE. Evergreen. Zones 3-13. When established, will recover quickly from severe winter damage. Foliage damaged at 15°, but shrub lives through 5° cold spell.

Rapid growing to 6-8 ft. and spreads as wide. Lustrous, yellow-green leaves, held toward the end of the branches, are divided into fans of 3 leaflets; fans give shrub a rounded, dense mass appearance. Clusters of fragrant white flowers, somewhat like small orange blossoms, open in very early spring and bloom continuously into April, intermittently through summer.

Use in full sun in cool summer areas; in interior valleys better by far in semi-shade. One of the best uses is an informal hedge. Groups exceptionally well because it will shape itself to form a mass effect.

In pruning, rather than shear off the ends, thin out branches to force replacement wood from the interior of the shrub. Spray for mealybug and scale. Susceptible to root and crown damage in soils of slow drainage. Don't plant deeper than planted in nursery can.

With all its faults it's an attractive shrub in Western gardens.

CHORIZEMA VARIUM. BUSH FLAMEPEA. Evergreen. Zones 12-13. Hardy to 24°. Low-growing shrubs to 2 ft., with glossy, dark green, holly-like leaves on slender graceful branches. A riot of orange-red and red-purple blossoms, resembling small sweet peas, cover the plant throughout winter and spring.

Likes sun or partial shade. Prune back severely after flowering to keep in good form and foliage. Good winter color for ground cover or edging, if you can use it harmoniously. Also attractive spilling over a wall.

CISTUS. ROCKROSE. Evergreen. Zones 3-13. An impressive list of virtues can be added up for rockrose; is drought-resistant when established; prefers poor, lean soil; takes hot sun and desert conditions; will flourish in reach of salt spray and ocean winds.

C. ladaniferus maculatus. CRIMSONSPOT ROCKROSE. Compact grower to 3-5 ft. high with equal spread. Foliage a cool green above and whitish underneath. Large, 3-in., white flowers, with dark crimson spot at base of each petal, bloom from June to July.

C. laurifolius. LAUREL ROCKROSE. Rather open growth to 6-8 ft. high and 4 ft. wide. Tends to become leggy if not pruned. Dark grayish-green, 2½-in. leaves. Large white flowers in July.

C. cyprius. BROWN-EYED ROCKROSE. Graceful growth to 6 ft. high and 3-4 ft. wide. Deep green leaves, whitish below. Flowers are similar to *C. ladaniferus maculatus*.

C. hybridus (*C. corbariensis*). WHITE ROCKROSE. Spreading growth to 2-3 ft. high and 4 ft. wide, with gray-green, crinkly leaves and 2-in., white flowers with yellow centers.

C. albidus. WHITELEAF ROCKROSE. Upright open growth to 4-5 ft. White hairy foliage. Rose-lilac, 2½-in. flowers with petals blotched yellow.

C. purpureus. ORCHID ROCKROSE. Compact growth to 4 ft. high and 4 ft. wide. Dark green foliage. Reddish-purple, 3-in. flowers with red spot at base of each petal.

C. Doris Hibberson. Compact growth to 3 ft. with equal spread. Gray-green foliage, and clear pink flowers with crinkled silky petals.

The rockroses are short-lived unless fast surface drainage is provided and a pruning program carried out. They can be kept healthy and neat by removing to the base a portion of the old canes from time to time, but cannot stand cut-backs of all stems at one time.

Use on dry banks. Combine with helianthemum, dwarf ceanothus and wild buckwheat. Deer won't eat cistus.

CLERODENDRUM. GLORYBOWER. Evergreen. Climate adaptation according to species. Rapid growing, rather coarse shrubs, each stem topped with clusters of showy, tubular flowers that have long protruding stamens.

C. bungei. (*C. fœtidum*). ROSE GLORYBOWER, CASHMERE BOUQUET. Zones 3-13. A thicket of vigorous shoots to 6 ft. or more high. Large, heart-shaped, 1-ft. leaves, dark green above, rusty-hairy beneath, have an unpleasant odor when bruised. Quantities of fragrant, rosy-red, ¾-in. flowers in dense, 4-8 in. broad clusters in spring and summer.

C. trichotomum. HARLEQUIN GLORYBOWER. Zones 3-13. Tall, upright shrub to 8-10 ft., with soft, hairy, ovate, 5-in. leaves. Many flat, loose clusters of fragrant white flowers with bright red calyx in early summer. Followed in fall by steel-blue berries, contrasting attractively with the red calyces. Var. *fargesii* (*C. fargesii*). Hardier than the species, it makes a smaller bush, has smooth leaves and a green calyx that turns pink.

C. myricoides. BLUE GLORYBOWER. Not readily available. Grows to 5-6 ft. and nearly as broad, with good, glossy foliage. Clusters of blue, 1½-in. flowers appear during spring, summer, and fall.

Full sun or partial shade, well drained soil, and protection from wind. If killed to ground by frost will come up from the roots in spring. Prune severely to discourage legginess.

For best effect clerodendrons should have plants grouped in front of them because of legginess. Flowers excellent for cutting, and berries of *C. trichotomum* are useful in arrangements.

COCCULUS LAURIFOLIUS. Evergreen. Zones 7-13. Slow growing when young, moderate when established. A graceful arching shrub to 20-25 ft. and spreading as wide. Beautiful foliage—even the stems and twigs green and glossy, and the 6-in. long, oblong leaves a shining dark green.

Excellent for background foliage in shade; one of the few large shrubs that will grow in dense shade. Pest resistant and soil tolerant. Prune to keep it from becoming leggy. Foliage is useful in indoor arrangements, and is a good Southern California substitute for the salal leaves of the Northwest.

COLEONEMA and **DIOSMA.** Evergreen. Zones 7-13. Botanists have moved the old pink diosma out of the genus *Diosma* and into the genus *Coleonema*. However, for all gardening uses the two genera can still be considered together.

Diosma reevesii. Most generally offered; has the best growth habit. Round, compact shrub to 3-4 ft. high and 3 ft. wide. Dark green, needle-like leaves and myriads of starry, tiny white blossoms in summer.

D. ericoides. BREATH OF HEAVEN. Larger than *D. reevesii.*

Coleonema pulchrum (*Diosma pulchra*). PINK DIOSMA. Rounded to 2-3 ft. high, 3 ft. wide. Valued for its rosy-pink winter bloom; out of bloom appearance is rather nondescript. Good on a hillside.

All species need light soil and sun. Plant along walks where in passing you can bruise the foliage and enjoy its pleasant fragrance.

CONVOLVULUS CNEORUM. BUSH MORNING GLORY, BUSH GLORYBIND. Evergreen. Zones 7-13. A shrubby member of the morning glory vines. Rapid growing to 2-4 ft. and as wide. Compact plant if grown in full sun, looser habit in light shade. Smooth-as-silk, silvery-gray foliage. Pink buds open into white, or pinkish morning-glory flowers. Blooms from May-September.

Best in full sun, flowers tend to close up in shade. Needs light soil with perfect drainage. Avoid planting where it will get frequent watering, such as near a lawn. Susceptible to nematodes. Spray for red spider. Regarded as a delicacy by rabbits. With all its faults, it is one of the most useful in the dwarf shrub group.

Very effective when used in mass or in border with such plants as *Teucrium fruticans*, Matilija poppy, and yellow marguerites. Attractive in containers.

COPROSMA. MIRROR PLANT. Evergreen. Zones 9-10, 12-13. Must be rated near top of a list of shrubs for seashore planting.

C. baueri. Rapid growth to 10 ft. with a 6-ft. spread. Makes an open, straggly shrub if neglected or planted in the wrong place but a beautiful plant when properly cared for. You can't imagine shinier, glossier leaves. They're dark to light green, 3 in. long, ovate or oblong. Inconspicuous greenish or white flowers; small yellow or orange berries. Var. *variegata* has leaves blotched with yellowish-green.

Two prunings a year will keep it in good shape and at any height you want it. Thin and cut back in winter; pinch back new growth in spring to direct growth and thicken foliage. Where shrub receives ocean wind, no pruning will be necessary. Except in foggy areas, give it part shade; water generously.

Use as a hedge, screen, wall shrub, informal espalier.

C. kirkii. Lower growing, spreading, and much branched, with narrower leaves. Can be used as deep ground cover if pinched back. Interesting in tubs.

C. petriei. A rare creeper with miniature shiny leaves. Excellent ground cover in small areas.

CORAL TREE. See ERYTHRINA

CORONILLA GLAUCA. HONEY CORONILLA. Evergreen or semi-deciduous in cold winters. Zones 4-13. A rather light and airy shrub to 5 ft. and spreading as wide, with gray-green twigs and foliage. Leaves are divided into 5-7 roundish leaflets. Fragrant, sweet-pea-shaped, bright yellow flowers, 5-7 in a cluster, are winter blooming in the South; March-May in the North.

Not a shrub for a prominent or important place in the garden. A filler where lightness would be useful.

CORREA. AUSTRALIAN FUCHSIA. Evergreen. Zones 9-10, 12-13. There are nurserymen and gardeners who succeed with correa in the hot interior valley, but evidence of failure is frequent enough to put it on your danger list there.

C. pulchella. Best known of the correas. Low growing to 2-2½ ft., spreading 6-8 ft. Its densely set leaves are deep green above and gray green below. November-April the branches are loaded with pendulous, light-pink, bell-shaped, ¾-in. flowers.

Other species: *C. alba*, silver gray foliage, white flowers in summer; *C. harrisii*, brilliant scarlet flowers January-April; *C. magnifica*, upright to 4-5 ft., chartreuse flowers; *C. neglecta*, compact low growth less than 1 ft., orange-red flowers.

Sun or shade. We have seen correa in full sun in the Sacramento Valley and in semi-shade along the Southern California coast. They should not be given full sun and reflected heat.

Use this shrub where it can spread and don't baby it too much.

CORTADERIA SELLOANA. PAMPAS GRASS. Evergreen. Zones 10-13. Herbaceous in cold-winter areas but root-hardy throughout. Giant ornamental grass. If planted in spring from a gallon can it may achieve 8 ft. or more in height and 3 ft. or more in spread by fall. Established colonies eventually grow to 20 ft. if uncontrolled. Conspicuous white to chamois or pink plume-like 1-3 ft. flower clusters on long stalks arise from a dense mass of saw-toothed, grassy leaves, in late summer and dominate the clump for many months.

Any soil supplies foothold for the undemanding roots, which along with seedlings may become pests in a medium sized garden, but valuable in loose-fill dry slopes or mucky water-logged lands.

Cortaderia's chief attractions are its strong vertical line, its color quality, the informal coarse texture, and its cutting value, the flowers dried naturally or dipped and tinted. An interesting foil for ranch style, Mediterranean or contemporary dwellings where its owner is willing to limit its spread. Repeats the feeling of all coarse-leafed subtropicals such as wigandia, phormium, dasylirion, most palms, and many other grasses.

COTONEASTER. All evergreen species are hardy in zones 3-13, deciduous species hardy all zones. Cotoneasters are a much used and very much abused group of evergreen and deciduous shrubs. So many good ones have been planted in such bad but prominent places that many beginning gardeners associate cotoneaster with bad planting. The truth is that the group contains many of great landscape value.

Low growing species:

C. dammeri. (*C. humifusa*). BEARBERRY COTONEASTER. (See chapter on ground covers.) Evergreen. Forms a flat, dense mat of long, trailing branches that root as they spread. Rarely over 6 in. high. Glossy bright green, 1-in. leaves, white flowers, scarlet berries.

Best use: As a bank ground cover; trailer for walls; trail over edge of tubs; in steep rockeries because it follows irregularities.

C. decora (*C. conspicua decora*). NECKLACE COTONEASTER. Evergreen. Arching branches. Same growth habit as *C. horizontalis*, except taller to 3 ft. White flowers followed by clear red fruits.

Best use: In a low foundation planter box.

C. adpressa. CREEPING COTONEASTER. Deciduous. Spreading to 3 ft., with slightly arching branchlets to 1 ft. Pinkish flowers and bright red fruits.

Best use: Ground cover.

C. microphylla. ROCKSPRAY COTONEASTER. (See chapter on ground covers.) Evergreen. Spreading to 3 ft. with branchlets arching to 2 ft. Tiny ⅓-in. leaves, dark green above and gray beneath, are studded closely along the branches. Rosy-red berries follow white flowers.

Seldom uniform in growth. If not grown in poor or dry soil, it will soon form a rank tangled mass.

Best use: Alongside steps; spilling over a wall.

C. horizontalis. ROCK COTONEASTER. (See chapter on ground covers.) Semi-evergreen to deciduous. Branches grow in neat, flat fans, horizontal to the ground. Wide spreading but mounds to 3 ft. Where winters are cold, scarlet berries color the branches to such an extent that you don't realize that it's leafless.

Best use: Excellent in masses for winter color where seen from above. Informal espalier; trained on wire as narrow informal hedge.

Medium to tall species:

C. parneyi *(C. lactea)*. Evergreen. Zones 2-13. Very handsome evergreen shrub with graceful arching habit. Grows to 6 ft. with spread of 8 ft. Dark green, rather leathery, 2-in. leaves. Clusters of small pink flowers are followed by brilliant red fruits, October-December.

Probably the most satisfactory of the upright growing cotoneasters. Both foliage and fruits entitle it to admission to the garden.

C. apiculata. CRANBERRY COTONEASTER. Deciduous. More upright, rounded growth to 6 ft., with small ½-in. leaves and bright red fruit.

C. divaricata. SPREADING COTONEASTER. Deciduous. To 6 ft., with dark green, shiny, ¾-in. leaves.

C. glaucophylla. BRIGHT BEAD COTONEASTER. Semi-evergreen. Rather compact grower to 7 ft., with gray-green, 2-in. leaves and dull red fruits.

C. salicifolia. WILLOWLEAF COTONEASTER. Evergreen or partially evergreen. Rapid growth to 15 ft. with a 15-18 ft. spread. Wrinkled, willow-like leaves are dark rich green above and grayish-green beneath; white flowers in 2-in. clusters; bright red fruits.

C. pannosa. SILVERLEAF COTONEASTER. Semi-evergreen with arching branches to 10 ft. Soft, silvery-gray foliage; clusters of white flowers; coral red fruits. This species and the rather similar orange-berried *C. franchettii* have been badly abused in many ways. Forcing them into rounded or square forms or cramping them into corners destroys their natural character. All tall growing cotoneasters must be given space to develop their fountain pattern of long branches rising from the base in graceful curves. Growth should not be headed back. Prune by cutting back old wood to the ground.

CROTALARIA AGATIFLORA. CANARY BIRD BUSH. Zones 7-13. When damaged by frost, makes a quick comeback. Fast growing shrub to 6-12 ft. and spreading wider than high. Can be pruned into a 3-trunked tree. Leaves with 3 grayish-green, 3-in. leaflets. Spectacular chartreuse 1½-in. flowers in clusters, sometimes 14 in. long, bloom summer and fall.

Give it sun and any soil. Branches are brittle; prune by thinning to remove criss-cross branches and to lighten the foliage and flower load. If thinning is consistent, you'll prevent the normal unattractive periods.

The yellow-green flowers will harmonize with almost any color. Try it with red geraniums or bright colored zinnias. Makes an interesting foil for erythrina or *Echium fastuosum*. Flowers are appreciated as cut flowers and by humming birds and orioles.

CYTISUS, GENISTA and **SPARTIUM.** BROOM. Evergreen or deciduous, sometimes almost leafless the year around. Zone adaptation by species. *Cytisus, Genista,* and *Spartium* carry the common name broom, and for all practical purposes they are included together. They range in size from large spreading shrubs to diminutive shrublets adaptable to the miniature garden (see chapter on miniatures).

Tall growing brooms:

Cytisus canariensis. *(Genista canariensis)*. CANARY ISLAND BROOM. Zones 7-13. The genista of florists. Many-branched evergreen shrub to 6-8 ft., spreading to 3-4 ft. Bright green leaves divided into ½-in. oblong leaflets. Bright yellow fragrant flowers in terminal short clusters, spring and summer.

Cytisus racemosus. *(Genista racemosa,* sometimes sold in nurseries as *Genista fragrans)*. Zones 7-13. Evergreen shrub similar in appearance to *C. canariensis*, but the leaflets are larger and bright yellow flowers are borne in long loose spikes in late spring.

Cytisus scoparius. *(Genista scoparia, Spartium scoparium)*. SCOTCH BROOM. Zones 4-13, damaged at 15° but recovers quickly. A mass of green wand-like stems growing to 10 ft., spreading to 5-6 ft. Small divided leaves, the leaflets to ½ in. long, the branches often almost leafless. Rather large, showy, golden-yellow flowers, delightfully fragrant in spring and summer.

Many hybrids have been developed that show more self-restraint and offer beautiful and usually parti-colored flowers. These hybrids are generally of lower stature than the one parent *C. scoparius*. *C. burkwoodii (C. scoparius burkwoodii)*, has Venetian red flowers shaded to rose, with a touch of brilliant yellow. Var. *andreanus*, a fine old variety, has yellow flowers with deep crimson wings. *Donard Seedling* has rich pink, red and orange flowers. *Dorothy Walpole* has rose-pink flowers with velvety crimson wings. *Lord Lambourne* has scarlet and cream-colored flowers. *Pomona* has orange and apricot flowers. *San Francisco* has red flowers. *Stanford* has mainly red flowers. *St. Mary's* has pure white flowers.

Cytisus multiflorus. (Sold in nurseries as *C. albus*). WHITE SPANISH BROOM. Zones 3-13. Deciduous shrub to 10 ft., with erect grooved branchlets. Leaves usually simple, sometimes divided into 3 roundish ½-in. leaflets. Sprays of small white ½-in. flowers in May.

Genista monosperma. BRIDAL VEIL BROOM. Zones 9-10, 12-13. Grows to 20 ft. spreading to 10 ft., with slender graceful gray, almost leafless branches. Stems covered with white fragrant flowers in late winter and spring.

Spartium junceum. SPANISH BROOM. Zones 3-13. Grows to 6-8 ft. to make a dense bushy shrub of many green, almost leafless stems. Bright yellow 1-in. flowers all along the stems, bloom continuously from July to frost.

Medium to low brooms:

Cytisus praecox. WARMINSTER BROOM. Zones 3-13. Compact evergreen shrub to 3-5 ft., spreading to 3-5 ft. Clean, green, divided leaves, the leaflets to ¾ in. Many creamy-yellow, heavily fragrant flowers. Blooms in March.

Cytisus kewensis. KEW BROOM. Zones 3-13. One of the finest dwarf brooms. Deciduous shrublet to 12 in., spreading to 3-4 ft., its trailing branches covered with large creamy-white blossoms in late spring.

Genista hispanica. Zones 3-13. Gorse-like spiny shrub to 2 ft., with golden-yellow flowers in May and June.

Brooms do well in the poorest dry soil in full sun; their only requirement is good drainage. Too much summer water can damage them. Light pruning and removal of dead flowers in the summer will prolong their life as a useful flowering shrub.

Brooms are most commonly known for their spring display of brilliant flowers, also quite unique for their bright green often leafless stems, which become more predominant during the winter. The prostrate forms are useful for ground covers and will form handsome trailing masses of cascading branches. However, in the upright forms the reedy texture, unless very deftly used in the garden, is not particularly appealing for a "close-up" shrub. The flowers are borne so heavily and are generally so brilliant that they will be striking from quite a distance. The objections to the upright varieties stem largely from their rather ungainly appearance while not in bloom. But in order to take full advantage of their brilliant spring color they are perhaps best in a mass located at enough distance so they will be unnoticed the rest of the year.

DABOECIA. See *Erica*.

DAPHNE. Evergreen and deciduous. Climate adaptation according to species. Of the many species, 3 are widely grown in the West: *D. odora* is the favorite in the milder sections; *D. cneorum* and *D. mezereum* are popular in the Northwest but infrequently grown in California.

D. odora. WINTER DAPHNE. Evergreen. Hardy zones 3-13. In good health it's a very neat, handsome plant, slow growing to 3-4 ft. and spreading to 5-6 ft. Rather narrow, 3-in. leaves are glossy rich green. Flowers—pink to deep red on the outside with creamy pink throats—appear in nosegay clusters at ends of the branches in February-March.

D. o. marginata. Has yellow margins around the leaves, and is probably better known, at least in California, than the all-green species.

Other varieties of *D. odora* are: Var. *alba*, waxy white flowers; var. *Rose Queen*, larger clusters of pink flowers. Both varieties have dark green foliage.

Poor drainage is the most serious enemy of *D. odora*. Where the water table is very high in winter, winter daphnes should be planted in raised beds or on gentle slopes. Will tolerate but do not require an acid soil; should not be given heavy mulches of peat moss or sawdust. Needs the morning sun but will suffer in hot afternoon sun and reflected heat. Blossoms fail to set where summer heat is low.

Temperamental is the word for *D. odora*. You get the feeling after working with them that some want to grow and some don't. Those that want to grow can be packed in clay soil and run over with a lawn mower, and they'll keep on blooming. Those that don't want to grow will sulk while you're fussing over them and die for no reason at all.

Prune *D. odora* when in bloom or immediately after bloom. Remove laterals just below the ends of branches. You can regulate the shape of the shrub by the manner of cutting. Cutting to inside buds will encourage upright growth; cutting to outside buds will produce a more spreading habit of growth.

D. cneorum. ROSE DAPHNE, ROCK DAPHNE. Best adapted in zones 3-6. Low-growing evergreen with trailing branches spreading to 3 ft. or more and mounding to less than 1 ft. Small, dark green, 1-in. leaves, bright rosy-pink fragrant flowers in May. Will stand some sun if roots are cool. After bloom period, to prevent dieback, top dress with equal parts of peat moss and coarse sand.

D. mezereum. FEBRUARY DAPHNE. Deciduous. Adapted in zones 3-6. Upright, stiffly twigged growth to 3-4 ft. In January-February clusters of fragrant lilac-purple flowers appear along the twigs before the 3-in. leaves come out. Bright scarlet berries in summer are supposed to be poisonous.

D. Somerset. Evergreen. Zones 3-13. Grows to 3 ft. with an equal spread. Smaller in leaf and more open in form than *D. odora*. Rosy-pink flowers at ends of branches in April and May. Although successful in England, results on the Pacific Coast have been disappointing. Seldom is vigorous enough to keep going.

DAUBENTONIA TRIPETII (*Sesbania tripetii*). SCARLET WISTARIA TREE. Deciduous. Zones 7-13. Neither a wistaria nor a tree, and the color is more burnt orange than scarlet. A fast growing shrub to 8-10 ft. high and 6-8 ft. wide, with fern-like leaves. Showy, drooping clusters of yellow and orange-red, sweet-pea-shaped flowers from May through summer. The pods that follow are 4-angled or winged.

Full sun and high heat suit the wistaria tree. Annual pruning in late fall will give it new wood for flowering. Use where you can handle orange-red. Don't expect this shrub to be a permanent part of your garden.

DEUTZIA. Deciduous. Hardy all zones but not effective where winters are extremely mild. Two definitely different types are available: the strong-growing, many-stemmed, tall types; and the dainty, neat, low growing types.

D. scabra. FUZZY DEUTZIA. The old timer that was planted more for close-up view of flowers, rosy-pink on the back and white inside, than for either form or foliage of the shrub. Quickly becomes a very dense and coarse plant to 10 ft. high and as wide if not pruned severely after blooming. Head back to strong laterals; cut to the ground some of the old wood each year. Var. *plena Pride of Rochester*, the most commonly planted, bears large clusters of small, frilled, double flowers. Blooms throughout a 3-4 week period, May-June.

D. gracilis. SLENDER DEUTZIA. Many slender stems arch up from the base of the plant to 3 ft. and droop gracefully to spread 5 ft. Bright green, narrow, 2½-in. leaves give foliage a fine texture. Clusters of snowy white flowers in May.

D. lemoinei. Hybrids with *D. gracilis* as one parent. Also neat and of graceful habit. Snowy-white flowers with pinkish or purplish outside, according to variety.

The low deutzias are useful in many ways. Use in front of taller shrubs; as informal hedges; under flowering crab-apples and flowering cherries.

DIOSMA. See *Coleonema*.

DOMBEYA. Evergreen. Zone 13 and the warmest areas of 12. All are tender but come back quickly after frost damage. Admired for tropical looking, large heart-shaped leaves and hydrangea-like flowers from November to January.

D. calantha. Fast growth to 15 ft. with 10-ft. spread. Erect flower clusters are like soft pink hydrangeas.

D. cayeuxii. To 10 ft. Spectacular winter color. Has pink flowers in dense, drooping clusters. If not removed, faded brown flowers give plant an untidy look following bloom.

D. wallichii. To 30 ft. One of the parents of *D. cayeuxii* with larger heavier leaf and red flowers in dense, drooping clusters.

Dombeya has no special cultural requirements. Needs warmth and sun.

DURANTA REPENS (*D. plumieri*). SKY FLOWER. GOLDEN DEWDROP. PIGEON BERRY. Evergreen. Zones 8-13, if located where moisture can be held at even level. Fast growing shrub-tree to 15 ft. Branches somewhat vine-like and spiny with 1-4 in., glossy green, oval leaves carried in opposite pairs along the branch. Its common names describe flower and fruit. Tips of branches are loaded with small, ½-in., blue flowers, like forget-me-nots; attractive to butterflies. Yellow berries follow the bloom in August. Needs constant thinning and pruning to keep under control. Used as large shrub in El Centro, California, area with excellent results. The sky flower should rate wider use in hot summer sections of California because of its adaptability and late summer flowers.

D. stenostachya. BRAZILIAN SKY FLOWER. Not as hardy as *D. repens*. Neater and more compact; larger leaves. Reaches a height of 8 ft. Blue flowers in summer its chief asset; winter and spring appearance is without interest.

ELAEAGNUS. Evergreen or deciduous. Climate adaptation by species. Shrubs or small trees, valued for their unusually handsome foliage. Leaves have silvery or golden scales that glisten in the sun. Flowers are inconspicuous but slightly fragrant; berry-like fruits are decorative.

E. pungens. SILVERBERRY. THORNY ELAEAGNUS. Evergreen. Zones 3-13. Slow growing, variable in habit, generally sprawling from 6-15 ft. Can be kept low or trained in any fashion by pruning. Laurel-like, wavy-margined, 2-4 in. leaves are rusty or gray-green above, silvery-rusty beneath. Berries are silvery and brown when young, red when mature. Var. *fruitlandii*. FRUITLAND SILVERBERRY. Stems and leaves much more silvery and brown when young. Var. *reflexa*. Leaves very brown, scaly beneath, margins not wavy.

Among the variegated-leaf forms are: Var. *marginata*. SILVEREDGE ELAEAGNUS. Leaves margined with silver. Var. *maculata* (*E. p. aureo-maculata*). YELLOW-SPOT ELAEAGNUS. Leaves with large yellow blotch in the center. Var. *variegata*. YELLOWEDGE ELAEAGNUS. Leaves margined with yellowish-white.

Elæagnus and its variegated forms are coming into their own again. Its renewed popularity is due in part to the gardener's appreciation of leaf-color accent and contrast but mostly because he has learned to train and shape the shrub. It's the type that once was called scraggly; now it's picturesque. Can be used in tubs and boxes. Easy to train as informal wall or fence espalier. Good hedge material.

E. angustifolia. RUSSIAN OLIVE. OLEASTER. Deciduous. Hardy all zones. Rapid-growing, irregularly-shaped, spiny, large shrub or small tree, 12-20 ft. Picturesque, crooked trunk with shiny, dark brown bark, especially ornamental in winter. Silvery-gray, narrow leaves; olive-like fruits yellow and silvery, in late summer.

One of the very few completely hardy, gray-foliaged shrubs.

E. philippensis. Evergreen. Moderate to rapid growing, erect and spreading shrub to 10 ft. Silvery-gray leaves are unusually attractive in contrast with dark green foliaged plants. With guidance by pinching and shaping its interesting structural pattern can be refined and developed.

Elæagnus is not particular as to soil or water. Can take hillside treatment. Will tolerate shade but its foliage interest is dependent on sun.

ENKIANTHUS CAMPANULATUS. Deciduous. Hardy all zones but best adapted in 3-5. Slow growth to an ultimate 15 ft. with a 4 ft. spread. A quality shrub with an irregular, upright and slender branching pattern. Bluish-green, pointed, 1½-2½ in. leaves are carried in whorls at the end of the branches and give shrub a very open character. In May pendulous clusters of yellow, red-veined bells hang from below the leaves. Blooms are followed by small seed capsules that remain on the tree into winter. Leaves turn brilliant red in fall.

Requires same culture as rhododendrons and azaleas and associates well with them. Needs cool root run. Mulch with peat moss and sawdust.

While only *E. campanulatus* is obtainable at nurseries now, you can expect introduction of other species: *E. chinensis*, salmon-red flowers; *E. cernuus rubens* (*E. rubens*), deep red flowers; *E. deflexus*, yellowish-red flowers with darker veins.

ERANTHEMUM NERVOSUM. (*E. pulchellum*). Evergreen. Zones 12 and 13. Takes little frost. Shrub to 2-5 ft. Oval, 8-in., prominently veined, slightly toothed leaves add interest and distinction to the green stems, together creating a slightly open pattern. Spikes of vivid indigo blue flowers to ¾ in. across and 1 in. long arise from under veined bracts, adding color in winter and well into spring.

Requires shade, ample water, good drainage and plenty of humus. May be pruned to 2 ft. and should definitely be pinched back slightly, 2 or 3 times early in the growing season, to induce branching, density and more flowers. May also be cut to the ground after flowering in spring to stimulate new growth, overcome legginess or frost damage. Effective with lucullia, the larger-leafed Indian azaleas, or with *Senecio petasitis* and cineraria.

ERICA, HEATH. **CALLUNA,** HEATHER. **DABOECIA,** IRISH HEATH. Evergreen. These three separate genera are brought together by usage under the common name "heathers." Their use by climates depends more on soil conditions than on hardiness. Adaptability noted by species.

ERICA. Narrow, shiny green, needle-like leaves carried in whorls. Bell-like or tubular flowers. Soil requirements vary by species, but in general they need a soil that's slightly acid, peaty and friable, with perfect drainage.

The following species have small bell-like flowers:

E. carnea. Thrives in zones 3-5 and in acid soil in zones 9-10. Will get along in heavy soils, but should have no fertilizers. Stiff and straight spires form a "porcupine" bush, 8-15 in. high and 2-3 ft. wide. Tends to spread and become unsightly unless pruned annually to a clump. Carmine flowers from January through May.

Var. *Springwood White.* One of the best for winter flowering. Low growing to 6-15 in. and wide spreading to several ft. Vivid green, "fir-needle" leaves; white flowers with chocolate-colored anthers, January-May.

Var. *King George.* Sturdy spikes in a slight arc form a dense, dark bronzy-green mass, 6-10 in. high and 2-3 ft. wide. Rosy-crimson flowers from November through February.

Var. *vivellii.* Stiff, well branched stems form almost as compact a mass as King George. Foliage has more metallic sheen in winter. Blood red flowers, February-May.

Var. *Ruby Glow.* Very low growing to 4-8 in., wide spreading to 15-24 in. Sends out odd spikes that need pruning. Brilliant, ruby flowers from January-May.

E. mediterranea. Loose, upright growth to 4-7 ft. Lilac-pink flowers from January-April.

Var. *hibernica alba.* Compact growth, almost pincushion shaped, to 8-12 in. high and 18-24 in. wide. White flowers from January-May.

E. darleyensis (*E. mediterranea hybrida*). Most generally used of all heathers. Available in most nurseries. Spreading growth to 2 ft. high and 4 ft. wide. Becomes sloppy if not pruned annually. Small, rosy-purple bells range along twigs; long season of bloom, November-May. There is a white-flowered form of this variety.

E. ciliaris Dawn. A most interesting hybrid. Long curving stems have deep rose flowers at the ends. During rapid growth in spring, the new foliage changes from carmine to orange, to yellow, to green. Flowers from June-October. Prune annually to keep under control and to encourage new multi-colored foliage. Will take a rich peaty soil and more water than other species.

E. tetralix. Another species that prefers a moist peaty soil. Inclined to be stiff and formal. To 1½ ft. high and 2 ft. wide. Grayish woolly foliage; rose-colored flowers from June-October. Prune by cutting back in early spring to force compactness and prevent toppling.

E. vagans. CORNISH HEATH. Dark green, ⅜-in. leaves. Clusters of pink flowers from July-October.

Var. *Mrs. D. F. Maxwell.* One of the most popular and most abused. Likes to grow in a dense mass, to 2 ft. high and 3 ft. wide, unless controlled by shears. Cherry-pink flowers from July-October.

Var. *Lyonesse.* Taller growing to 3-4 ft.; clear white flowers, July-October.

Var. *St. Keverne.* More compact growth to 18 in., clear pink flowers in dense spikes from July-October.

E. cinerea. TWISTED HEATH. Much branched, dense bush, 2 ft. high and as wide. Spikes of rosy-purple flowers from June-September.

Var. *C. D. Eason.* Dainty, closely woven plant. Low growing to 12 in. high and 24 in. wide. Bright red flowers from June-September.

E. arborea alpina. TRUE HEATHER. Slow growing to 6 ft. with a 3 ft. spread. Clusters of white flowers, April-June. Finest texture of any ericas.

E. lusitanica (*E. codonodes*). SPANISH HEATHER. Does well in zones 12 and 13. Grows to 10 ft., with grass-green foliage. Flowers pink in bud, opening white, bloom February-March. Tolerates poor drainage and heavy soils.

E. canaliculata. Most of the plant material long cultivated and sold as *E. melanthera* or its varieties is *E. canaliculata.* One of the best for zones 12 and 13. Grows to 6 ft. Spreading branches with leaves dark green above and white underneath. Dark pink to rosy-purple flowers in fall and winter. Drought-resistant.

Var. *boscawieniana* is the usual form in cultivation. Taller growing to 18 ft., with more erect, almost columnar branches. Pale lilac flowers in fall and winter.

E. subdivaricata (*E. persoluta*). Grows to 2 ft. Var. *alba* (*E. persoluta alba*) has white flowers. Var. *rosea* (*E. persoluta rosea*) has rosy flowers.

The following species have tubular flowers:

E. doliiformis (*E. blanda*). Low growing to 1 ft. Rosy, ½-in. flowers clustered at tops of the branches.

E. cruenta. Grows to 3 ft., with 6-8 in. spikes of blood-red flowers in fall and winter.

E. hyemalis (*E. hiemalis, E. hieliana, E. hyalina*). Grows to 2-3 ft. White-tipped, pink, 1-in. flowers borne along the branchlets in winter. Var. *alba* has white flowers.

E. Felix Faure. Low compact plant with rose-pink flowers.

E. John McClaren. Low compact plant with flowers a lovely shade of pink.

CALLUNA. Seldom grown outside of zones 3-5. Small, overlapping, scale-like leaves. All give the appearance of rather soft, evergreen bushes that can and should be sheared.

C. vulgaris. SCOTCH HEATHER. This species is not outstanding, but its varieties are most useful. Some of them are:

Var. *alba.* Upright grower to 2-3 ft. high and 1-2 ft. wide. For compactness, shear in early spring. White flowers from July-September.

Var. *aurea.* Early golden foliage turns rusty red in winter. Rank and ungainly unless severely pruned.

Var. *foxii nana.* Makes a dense, rounded plant, 6 in. high and 10 in. wide. Needs no pruning.

Var. *H. E. Beale.* Grows to 2-3 ft.; has a loose habit. Soft pink, double flowers from August-September.

DABOECIA CANTABRICA. IRISH HEATH. Grows to 1½-3 ft. Leaves are wider than those of the other heather genera and are glowing green above, with gray undersides. Airy clusters of pale purple flowers from May-November. Var. *alba* is a pure white form. Suited to a rich, moist, peaty soil.

In general, heathers need a light, slightly acid soil, but some accept heavy soil and moisture. Almost all are better plants when pruning is enjoyed by the gardener. Note the pruning warning by species. How to use heathers in the garden? That's like asking how to use shrubs in the garden. You can't give a general answer that's worth much. Look to the heathers for: evergreen foliage that passes through interesting seasonal color changes, winter color, low spreading evergreen growth on banks and hillsides, year-around bloom by grouping varieties.

ERYTHRINA. CORAL TREE. Deciduous-evergreen. Zones 12-13. Commonly thorny, coarse, rapid growing shrubs or small trees. Fan-like leaves divided into 3 leaflets. Large showy clusters of 3-in. flowers.

E. cristi-galli. COCKSPUR CORAL TREE. Thorny shrub to 12-15 ft. high and as wide. Crimson flowers in late spring, again in late summer. Cut back old wood each year after flowering.

E. bidwellii. Hardiest (to 15°) of the coral trees. Short thick trunk to 12 ft. Long slender spikes of crimson flowers.

E. caffra. (*E. constantiana*). Evergreen in frostless area. Large-boled broad-crowned tree to 25 ft. and as wide, with scarlet flowers 7 months out of the year.

E. coralloides. Small tree to 20 ft., with coral-red flowers appearing before leaves.

No special culture other than good drainage. Must have full sun and warmth.

Most of the coral trees, because of their broad spread, are best for large places. Use *E. cristi-galli* as bright accent against a house or patio wall. Combine it with gray-foliaged plants such as *Teucrium fruticans*.

ESCALLONIA. Evergreen. Zones 4-13. Freezes to the ground at 10°, but sprouts from roots. Best adapted in zones 9, 10, 12, 13, but effectively used in the interior valleys.

These virtues — wind hardiness, clean appearance, glossy leaves, clusters of small white, pink, or red, urn-shaped flowers in late summer and early fall—place the escallonias among the first 10 most useful shrubs for Western gardens.

E. montevidensis. (*E. alba*). WHITE ESCALLONIA. The tallest, widest grower of all, to 25 ft. and as wide in Southern California, an 8-10 ft. shrub in the Pacific Northwest. Sometimes trained as a small tree. Fast growing, graceful and spreading, with dark green glossy 3-4 in. leaves. White flowers in terminal clusters in late summer and fall.

E. organensis. PINK ESCALLONIA. Handsome, very leafy, dense shrub to 12-15 ft. and as broad, with arching angled branches. Bronzy-green, 3 in. leaves. Pink to rose-red flowers in short, broad clusters in early summer. Tips burn in beach plantings.

E. franciscana. Rather loose growth to 10 ft. with a tendency to throw out long branches. Has chocolate brown bark; dark green ½-1 in. leaves, and rosy-pink flowers blooming throughout the summer. Often used as informal wall espalier.

E. franciscana is widely distributed as *E. rosea* by Western nurseries. The name "rosea" is often applied to various other rose-colored forms of escallonia.

E. rubra. RED ESCALLONIA. Rather erect and compact growth to 5-6 ft., with glossy dark green rounded 2 in. leaves. Red or crimson ½ in. flowers in short terminal clusters. Blooms throughout the warmer months.

The horticultural varieties of escallonia are for the most part lower growing shrubs. More slender and compact and easier to fit into the small garden. Var. *C. F. Ball*. To 3-4 ft. high, compact, with bright red flowers. Var. *Alice* is similar in growth and flowers. Var. *Apple Blossom*. To 5 ft. A sprawling plant with pinkish-white flowers. Var. *William Watson*. To 4 ft. Spindly growth unless pruned occasionally. Ruddy cerise flowers.

Escallonias will tolerate direct coastal conditions and will stand wind. Will take full sun along the coast if generously watered but prefer part shade inland. Their one bad habit—holding dry flower heads longer than they should for neat appearance—can be corrected by pruning back as soon as the flowers fade. Tall growing species will benefit by removal of one-third of old wood each year. The lower growing hybrids need pruning every third year. The newer hybrids, because of their lower stature, can be placed nearer the front of the shrubbery border; they combine well with fuchsias, hydrangeas, osmanthus, and mahonias.

EUONYMUS. A genus of evergreen and deciduous shrubs with several surprise packages. The low growing and creeping varieties of *E. fortunei* are remarkably hardy and important to all cold winter gardens. Respond to imaginative handling and can be used as vines, ground covers, spillers, leaners, or low sprawling shrubs. Gardeners in California are more familiar with *E. japonicus*, the substantial, fast growing shrub much used for its bright green, glossy foliage. With few exceptions the deciduous species, valued for fall color, are not grown by Pacific Coast nurserymen.

E. fortunei (*E. radicans acutus*). WINTER CREEPER. Evergreen. All zones. Sun or shade. Trails or climbs by rootlets to 35 ft. with a 10-ft. spread. *E. fortunei* is more important as a name than as a plant, for the varieties rather than the species proper are more valued in Western gardens.

E. f. radicans (*E. radicans*). COMMON WINTER CREEPER. Evergreen. Hardy all zones. Sun or shade. Ivy and other competitors have crowded it out of California's nursery lists, but it's a deservedly popular item in the states to the north. Neither flowers nor fruits amount to much, but its pattern of 1-in., oval leaves of good medium green every month in the year is enough.

If given no support, *E. f. radicans* is not viny. If given a concrete wall to cover, it will do the job completely, either as an even flat mat or in tracery or pattern. You can keep the plant in place on a 3-ft. fence.

E. f. vegetus (*E. radicans vegetus*). BIGLEAF WINTER CREEPER. Evergreen. Hardy all zones, but does best in zones 1-6. Highly recommended for Idaho, Utah, and eastern Washington. Hot dry conditions reduce growth. Sun or shade. Leaves, 1½-2 in., glossy, medium green. Flowers are inconspicuous but are followed in August-September with orange berries in little "hat boxes." New growth in April and May is an interesting chartreuse.

Bigleaf winter creeper is more irregular in growth habit than *E. f. radicans,* and sends out larger branches with side branches developing later. Trained as an informal espalier, *E. f. vegetus* has lots of character. Easy to train by tipping and thinning. Will grow as a vine if given support to 20 ft., or will spread slowly as a 1 ft. high ground cover. Grows slowly in first two years and then adds 4 ft. a year if not restrained.

Other varieties of *E. fortunei* are: Var. *coloratus* (*E. radicans coloratus*), PURPLE LEAF WINTER CREEPER, leaves reddish and purple in fall and winter; var. *gracilis*, leaves variegated with white, yellow, pink, or combinations of these colors (often used in hanging baskets); var. *minimus* (*E. radicans minimus*), creeping plant with small, ½-in. leaves.

E. japonicus. EVERGREEN EUONYMUS. Zones 3-13. Full sun. Upright shrub to 10-15 ft. high and 6 ft. wide. Usually held lower by pruning and shearing. Older shrubs are attractive when trained as trees with curving trunks and irregular, umbrella-shaped tops.

Popularity deserved for the bright green cleanliness of the shrub's foliage is threatened by the plant's susceptibility to mildew.

Many variegated forms are sold. There are forms having leaves with narrow white border; edged and marked with white; edged with yellow; blotched with yellow; bordered with silvery white.

Although *E. japonicus* combines with shrubs of similar upright habit (photinia and laurestinus, for example), it is a soil robber. Less vigorous shrubs shouldn't be asked to associate with it.

E. j. microphyllus (*E. pulchellus*). BOXLEAF EUONYMUS. SMALL LEAF EUONYMUS. Zones 3-13. Compact to 1-2 ft. high and half as wide. So formal looking, with its small dark green leaves, that it always ends up trimmed as a low hedge.

When used as a restrictive planting in front of camellias, lilacs, or other upright shrubs, it seems less greedy of soil space than boxwood.

The deciduous euonymus provide unusual color interest in the fall and generally give a more generous colorful show of fruits. The variety most frequently grown in the Northwest is:

E. alatus compactus. DWARF FLAME EUONYMUS. DWARF WINGED EUONYMUS. An upright mound 6 ft. high and as wide. Branches are corky winged with very unusual brown and green bark. Leaves turn rose-red in fall, and purple fruits with orange seeds put on a show at the same time.

SHRUBS — Encyclopedia —

EUPHORBIA PULCHERRIMA. *(Poinsettia pulcherrima).* POINSETTIA. Outdoors in "poinsettia belts" of zones 10 and 13; outside these mild areas it's the Christmas pot plant. As a landscape plant the poinsettia tends to grow tall and leggy to 10 ft. and more. Thinning of branches during summer will increase size of flowers, heading back at 2 months intervals encourages denser foliage and smaller blooms. Sports and hybrids of the old single red variety are available. The double red *Henriette Ecke* is the most popular.

Where adapted, the poinsettia needs no special garden care. The best soil is slightly on the acid side. When attempting to carry over a Christmas pot plant remember that poinsettias, like chrysanthemums, are short-day plants. Many gift plants have been under reduced hours of light to bring them into bloom. So follow this procedure: Locate plants near a sunny window, away from artificial light, so the indoor day will conform closely to the natural one. Water well, but provide good drainage. When leaves fall naturally in late winter, cut stems back to two "eyes," reduce watering to a minimum, and store plants in a cool place until spring. After ground warms up, pots may be plunged in a sunny spot outdoors in the garden. Chances are they'll grow much too tall for use indoors next Christmas, however. If you want florist-size plants for the holidays next year, make late-summer cuttings with four or five eyes or nodes.

EURYA EMARGINATA. Evergreen. Zones 7, 9-13. Moderate growth to 3-8 ft. Can be held back to modest height or trained as espalier. A very valuable plant where small-scale in leaf pattern is wanted. Tiny black-green leathery oblong leaves are stiffly arranged along light brown stems. Give it slightly acid soil by adding peat, leaf mold, pine needles. Needs consistent moisture. Adapts poorly to dry winds or extreme heat.

EXOCHORDA RACEMOSA *(E. grandiflora).* COMMON PEARL BUSH. Deciduous. Hardy all zones. An old, reliable flowering shrub of rather loose and open habit, with slender, branching pattern that offers good winter texture. Grows to 10-15 ft. and as broad. Soft, bluish-green, 2½ in. leaves. Large, pearly-white, 2 in. flowers in loose narrow clusters, in May.

Sun. Remove spent flowering branches immediately after bloom.

Plant singly or in groups of 3 or 6. Give it a dark background to show up the gleaming flowers. Because of its rather open appearance, should be faced with lower growing shrubs such as spiræa, deutzia, or abelia. In large mass planting combine with *Weigela florida* and *Lonicera tatarica*. In small gardens can be used as a small tree by selectively thinning the lower branches to form a high crowned plant.

FATSIA JAPONICA *(Aralia sieboldii, Aralia japonica).* Evergreen. Used in zones 4-13, but not consistently hardy in zones 4-6. It's as lush and bold as a true subtropical. Grows rapidly to 8-15 ft. with a 4-13 ft. spread. Large, glossy, dark green, deeply lobed leaves are as wide as 16 in. Clusters of small, white flowers in December are followed by small, shiny black fruits. Var. *moseri* is a compact lower growing form. Variegated-leafed forms are also obtainable.

Fatsia will take full shade and all but the hottest sun. Leaves lack luster in sun and become yellowish. Tolerant of all garden soils and of confinement in containers.

Although fatsia is widely used, it will never be commonplace when used with imagination. It is a natural choice wherever a bold leaf pattern is wanted. The structure and pattern value is lost when planted in massed groups. Often by thinning you reveal an interesting structure that will make an exciting pattern against a wall. Tub or box planting offers many opportunities of training, shaping, and dramatizing.

FEIJOA SELLOWIANA. PINEAPPLE GUAVA. Evergreen. Zones 7-13. One of the hardiest subtropical shrubs. Moderate growth to 15-18 ft., spreading to 15 ft. Can be held back to 8 ft. by annual pruning. Oval leaves, 2-3 in. long, are gray-green above, silvery white beneath. Very unusual, exotic 1-in. flowers with white fleshy petals that are purplish inside; many showy dark red stamens. May-July. Fruit edible. (See chapter on home fruit garden for information on fruit, varieties, etc.)

Takes full sun but will tolerate some shade. Use as an informal hedge or combined in a shrubbery border with *Pittosporum crassifolium*, olearias, *Senecio greyii*. Don't be afraid to thin out and clean up pineapple guava by pruning in late winter. No special cultural requirements.

FIREBALL BUSH. See CALLISTEMON, MELALEUCA

FIRETHORN. See PYRACANTHA

FORSYTHIA. GOLDEN BELLS. Deciduous. Hardy all zones, but needs winter cold to produce a spectacular burst of bloom. One of the earliest shrubs to bloom; in late February or early March in average winters, yellow bells encase each branch.

F. suspensa. WEEPING FORSYTHIA. Dense, upright-growing shrub to 8-10 ft. high and 6-8 ft. wide, with drooping, vine-like branches. Rather thin, light green, 4-in. leaves. Golden-yellow flowers in February-March. Var. *fortunei* (F. *fortunei*) is very similar to the species, but stiffer and more erect.

F. intermedia. BORDER FORSYTHIA. Grows to 10 ft., with branches arching to 20 ft. Var. *spectabilis* has very generous masses of bright yellow, 1-in. flowers.

F. viridissima. GREENSTEM FORSYTHIA. Rather stiff-looking shrub to 10 ft. high and 8 ft. wide. Deep green foliage; yellow flowers with a greenish cast. The only forsythia with fall color—purplish-red foliage.

F. Dwarf Arnold. Low growing to 2 ft. and spreading to 4 ft. Tips of arching branches root when they touch the ground.

F. Spring Glory. Branches bend under heavy load of pale yellow flowers. A good one for cuttings in January to force into indoor bloom.

Forsythias are tolerant of most soils, sun-loving, and easy to grow. Prune yearly by cutting back old wood during or after flowering. Because of its nondescript form when not in bloom, it should be planted at a distance, or specially trained against a wall in a fan shape.

FRENCH MULBERRY. See CALLICARPA

FUCHSIA. See p. 255

GARDENIA. Evergreen. Zones 7-13. Slow to moderate growth to 2-6 ft. Three forms available at California nurseries.

G. jasminoides. When it receives the soil and climate it wants, this gardenia grows luxuriantly to 6 ft. with a regular branching habit and foliage as glossy green as that of a camellia. Extremely fragrant, waxy-white, single and semi-double flowers, in summer. Disbudding necessary if corsage flowers are wanted. Varieties *Mystery* and *Veitchi* are the forms most generally sold and grown in California. *Mystery* is typical of the species. *Veitchi* has smaller flowers but more of them. Foliage, too, is smaller. A low-growing, dwarf form, 6-8 in. high and 12-14 in. wide, is available. It's catalogued as *Gardenia radicans*.

Ask 100 nurserymen about the gardenia and half will praise it and half curse it. Charting the locations of the for and against opinions, these seem to be the facts on culture and climate: It performs beautifully where days are hot and nights are warm. In temperatures of 100° and more it thrives in full sun. In cool, coastal areas the plant looks miserable. With high heat it takes water and fertilizer in generous amounts.

Soil should be acid. Foliage yellows from lack of iron and from lack of magnesium. Treat for chlorosis with applications of iron and sulfur. If the foliage does not green up, apply magnesium. Feed with a commercial fertilizer once a month, from March-September.

Where adapted and properly fed and watered, these gardenias can be used freely in mass plantings and as hedges. Where climate is sometimes right and sometimes wrong, use as a tub plant. Spray for Fuller's rose weevil if leaf damage shows up. Watch for scale.

G. thunbergia. A more open, taller growing gardenia with pointed, 6-in. long leaves and large white flowers, 3-in. across. Not quite so hardy as *G. jasminoides Mystery*. Will lose buds at 24°. More tolerant of various soils and needs less heat.

GREVILLEA. Evergreen. Adaptability by zones. (See chapter on trees for *Grevillea robusta*, the silk oak.) Of the many shrubs in this genus, only the following are available.

G. banksii. Zone 13. Moderate growth, 2-10 ft. high and as wide, rather open in growth habit. Bronze-green deeply cut leaves. Exotic red flowers in 4-in. clusters, bloom intermittently throughout the year.

Used in shore planting where reached by ocean spray. Very fussy about drainage.

G. rosmarinifolia. Zones 9-10, 12, 13. Moderate growth to 6 ft. Not a particularly conspicuous plant even when in bloom; but where adapted its narrow 1½-in. leaves like those of rosemary are attractive throughout the year. Red or white flowers in short clusters in winter.

Gardeners do not agree on the reliability of this shrub. Seems very touchy about hard water and poor drainage. Short-lived in some areas. Best used as tub plant or on dry banks.

GREWIA CAFFRA. LAVENDER STARFLOWER. Evergreen. Zones 9-10, 12-13. Rather tender to 20°. Rapid growing, rather sprawling shrub that lends itself naturally to espalier. Grows to 6-10 ft. with a 10-ft. spread. Grayish-green, oblong, finely-toothed, 3-in. leaves. Small, lavender-blue, star-like flowers with yellow centers from late spring to fall.

An easily controlled shrub for a warm, sunny wall or fence. Can be allowed to spread over rocks or along a pool. Excellent in windy, sunny exposures. Prune every year after bloom.

GRISELINIA. Evergreen. Zones 7-13 except desert areas. Upright shrubs of such good behavior in growth habit and such polished thick leathery leaves that you describe them immediately as well groomed.

G. littoralis. KUPUKA TREE. A tree in New Zealand, it seems to settle down in California to a shrub to 10 ft. and about as wide. Leaves are roundish, wedge-shaped at base, 4 in. long.

Best in full sun with plenty of water. Grown from gallon cans it will reach 8 ft. in 3 yrs. and form a dense compact screen or windbreak. Used with satisfaction along Southern California beaches.

G. lucida. Slower growing, smaller than the kupuka tree but with more open growth habit and larger leaves to 7 in. that are very unequal at base. An excellent choice as a foliage plant in a shady location.

GUNNERA CHILENSIS. Evergreen. Zones 10-13. At its best in fog belt along coast from San Francisco south. An astonishing, extremely fast-growing plant suggestive of giant rhubarb. Deeply lobed and cut leaves to 5-8 ft. in diameter, are held on fleshy, stiff-hairy stalks to 6 ft. or more long. Comparatively small, colorless flowers in spike 3 ft. high; fruit red. Seeds appear on corncob-like structure.

Successfully grown in filtered shade where soil is rich in humus, high in nitrogen, and never dries out; happy in bog conditions. Becomes deciduous either from frost or dry, warm wind. A day with very low humidity and high temperatures will wither leaves unless sprinkled copiously and often. Regardless of winter damage, plant is improved in appearance by cutting back to the base each winter.

Combines effectively in light shade with *Crinum amabile* (green winter, herbaceous summer), *Alocasia macrorhiza* (evergreen elephant ear), Clivia, rhizomatous begonias, *Bergenia ligulata*; or farther north with water-loving iris, bamboo, and coarse-needled pines.

G. manicata. Similar to *G. chilensis* but leaves are rounded, not lobed or cut.

HAKEA. Evergreen. Zones 7-13. Tough and tolerant shrubs or small trees. Especially good for seacoast.

H. laurina. SEA URCHIN. PINCUSHION TREE. Small, round-headed tree or large shrub to 30 ft. Narrow, dark green, often red-margined, 6-in. leaves. Showy, crimson and gold flowers in round clusters are accurately described by both common names. Bloom in midwinter, sometimes late fall.

H. suaveolens. SWEET HAKEA. Shrubs to 10 ft., or sometimes to 20 ft. Stiff, needle-like, deep green, 4-in., leaves branched into stiff, spiny-tipped segments. Fragrant, white flowers in fluffy clusters, bloom in fall and winter.

Will grow in poor soils if drainage is good. Requires minimum maintenance and is immune to most pests and diseases.

HEBE. Evergreen. Hardiness according to variety. Cool coastal climates preferred over hot interiors. Formerly united with *Veronica* and still sold in many nurseries as *Veronica*, but now considered separate because of hebe's shrubby, evergreen habit. More than 15 species and varieties available. Of these, the following illustrate some of the possibilities of the group.

H. buxifolia. BOXLEAF HEBE. Zones 3-13. Most widely available of all the hebes. To 3-5 ft. and spreads as wide. Leaves are much smaller than other hebes, to ⅓ in. long, and similar to that of boxwood. In May-June bears 1-in. spikes of white, tinged with lavender, flowers. Foliage, rather than flowers, is its virtue.

H. andersonii. Zones 7-13. Makes a 4-ft. mound with 4-in. oblong leaves and lilac flowers in 4-in. spikes; June-September.

H. cupressoides nana. Zones 3-13. Slow growing to 2 ft. Rounded, 1-ft., mound in 4 yrs., with light green, cypress-like foliage. If and when it blooms, the not very showy flowers are white.

H. elliptica Autumn Glory. Zones 3-13. A 2 by 2 ft. mound with deep purple flowers; late season—July-November.

Other species: *H. carnea*, CRIMSON HEBE, to 6 ft., rosy-crimson flowers; *H. hectori* (see chapter on miniatures);

H. salicifolia, WILLOWLEAF HEBE, to 6 ft., 6-in. white spikes; *H. chathamica*, to 1½ ft. and spreading to 5 ft., lavender-blue flowers in 1-in. spikes; *H. hulkeana*, to 2-3 ft. Pale lilac, long flower spikes.

The change of names has been confusing and a setback to a number of useful shrubs. The low growing types are especially useful foliage plants.

There are objections to hebes on the grounds that they soon become straggly and floppy. Gardeners, seeing this floppiness, often shear the plant, thus causing more top growth and more floppiness. Correct pruning is the secret. Cut old bloom spikes, and the branches that bear them, to the ground every year.

Likes rich soil, ample moisture. Give it sun along the coast and some shade inland. Becomes rangy in deep shade.

HIBISCUS. Both a tropical evergreen shrub and a tough, hardy perennial are included in this genus.

H. rosa-sinensis. CHINESE HIBISCUS. ROSE OF CHINA. Wants more winter warmth and humidity than it can get in California. Grows to a rather open, 8-10 ft. shrub in frost-free spots of zone 13. Rather slow to become established and when hit by frost is slow to recover. In all but favorable climates it's best treated as an expendable item and used only where its loss would not make a hole in the garden. Worthwhile coddling for its dark green, glossy, foliage. Many, many varieties offer either single or double, 6-in., broad flowers in a wide range of colors—pale yellow to amber, white and shell pink to rose, and bright vermillion.

Give hibiscus full sun, regular watering, regular feeding, and a mulch of leaf mold during the summer months.

Because of its bold-textured foliage and spectacular flowers the hibiscus is not a plant to associate freely with other shrubs or flowers. It is most effective in self-groupings, or with other evergreens that don't offer too much contrast, or in containers.

H. syriacus. *(Althæa frutex).* ROSE OF SHARON. Hardy all zones. Rather stiff, upright shrub to 5-12 ft., with single or double, hollyhock-like, 3-in. flowers in a wide color range—white, pink, red, scarlet, purplish, or bluish. These hardy shrubs die to the ground in winter and come back with a rush in spring to bloom from midsummer to frost, opening successively along the stems. The added color range beyond the bluish-purple of the older forms have given these old-timers a new lease on the gardener's affection.

Plant in sun. Don't let them dry out. Perform best in hot situations. Give them a warm corner or a patio wall.

HOLLY. See ILEX

HYDRANGEA. Deciduous. Hardy all zones. Bold in foliage and enthusiastic in growth. The hydrangea is too overpowering a shrub to be dropped anywhere in a garden. However, when massed in filtered shade of high-branching trees or planted in tubs or on a paved terrace, hydrangeas become exciting plants.

Wider selection in species and varieties has helped revive interest in them.

H. arborescens. SMOOTH HYDRANGEA. Upright, dense shrub to 10 ft., with grayish-green, ovate, 4 in. leaves. White flowers in 6 in. clusters from June to frost.

H. a. grandiflora. HILLS OF SNOW. Its rather flat-headed clusters of creamy-white flowers rate this variety far superior to the species.

H. macrophylla. *(H. hortensia, H. opuloides).* BIG-LEAF HYDRANGEA. Symmetrical shrub to 12 ft., with thick, shining, broadly ovate, 8 in. leaves. Blue, pink or white flowers in flattish or rounded, 6-8 in. clusters.

The French hybrids extend the color range to rose, carmine, red, deep blue, violet, and snow-white.

H. paniculata grandiflora. PEE-GEE HYDRANGEA. An upright shrub of coarse texture that can be trained as a small 25 ft. tree. Best when held to a 10-15 ft. shrub. Foliage of 5 in. leaves turns bronzy in fall. White flowers in large, upright, 10-15 in. long clusters slowly change to pinky-bronze as they fade.

H. petiolaris. CLIMBING HYDRANGEA. (See chapter on vines.)

H. quercifolia. OAKLEAF HYDRANGEA. A handsome, broad, rounded, 6 ft. shrub, with deeply lobed, oak-like 8 in. leaves that turn bronze or crimson in autumn. Creamy-white flowers in rather open clusters. Well worthwhile for bold foliage effect. Makes a dense, compact, 3 ft. shrub when pruned to the ground each spring. Unlike other hydrangeas, it will get along in a rather dry, sunny area.

Hydrangeas are easy to grow in a fertile, porous soil and respond to additions of leaf mold and manure, generous overhead and soil watering in the summer months. Shade them from overhead sun.

If pruned heavily in February and March, the large growing types can be maintained at 4-5 ft. Cut out stems that have bloomed, leaving those that did not flower.

Monthly applications of aluminum sulfate during the blooming period will induce pink flowers to turn blue, and keep the violet and blues from turning pink. Applications of superphosphate fertilizer may cause the same reactions.

Summer color, fresh looking foliage regardless of heat, ability to grow in shade, and easy upkeep, make hydrangeas a natural for large areas under trees. Good textural relationship with wood and masonry make them valuable in containers on shady terraces.

HYPERICUM. Evergreen and semi-evergreen shrubs and subshrubs. (See chapter on ground covers for low growing types.)

H. patulum henryi. Zones 4-13. Shrub to 4 ft., with light green, oblong 2½-in. leaves on graceful willowy branches. Brilliant, golden-yellow 2-in. flowers from July-October. Adapted to almost any soil. Best in part shade in interior valleys.

In warm areas can be used wherever a medium height yellow is needed—massed foundation, untrimmed hedges, or in groups. In cold-winter sections its often shabby winter appearance rules it out of all-year important locations. Use it as yellow complement with blue and white hydrangeas.

H. floribundum. Zones 9-10, 12-13. Shrub to 6 ft. Smaller leaves than *H. patulum* and 2-in. flowers are carried in clusters.

ILEX. HOLLY. Evergreen. Climate adaptation by species. From familiar English holly to its many obscure cousins, from foot-high, sprawling dwarfs to 50-ft. trees, from easily obtained, standard varieties to rare curiosities, there is a holly for every collector's taste. Some have leaves with sharp spines, others with smooth margins. There are types with rich, dark green foliage, others with silver and gold variegations. Berries may be red, orange, yellow, or black.

The slow-growing hollies usually need a male plant (pollenizer) to insure a crop of berries on the female plant. Grafted stock is also available; certain species are infertile.

I. aquifolium. ENGLISH HOLLY. All zones, but prefers zones 3-6. Grown everywhere with varying success depending on special soil treatment; not recommended for alkaline soils and hot interiors. Best known and is the traditional Christmas holly. Slow growing to 40 ft. Flowers in May and June followed by scarlet berries.

There are many horticultural forms, both green leafed and variegated. Some of the best known green-leafed forms are: Var. *angustifolia,* NARROWLEAF HOLLY, is a small pyramidal shrub to 4-6 ft., with narrow spiny leaves; var. *ferox,* PORCUPINE HOLLY, SCREW-LEAF HOLLY, grows to 30 ft., with twisted spiny leaves and no berries; var. *fertilis* is a heavy fruiting strain; var. *bacciflava* (var. *fructo-luteo*) has yellow fruits; var. *pendula* has a weeping habit; var. *Jan Van Tol,* DUTCH HOLLY, has spineless or almost spineless leaves.

Several of the variegated forms are: Var. *albo-marginata,* compact tree to 40 ft., leaves with silvery-white margins; var. *aurea mediopicta,* yellow leaves with green margins; var. *variegata,* leaves variegated with silver and gold.

I. cornuta. CHINESE HOLLY. Adapted to warm, dry climates. Grows and berries successfully in zones 7-13, but seldom berries or grows anywhere near full height in zones 3-6. Resembles English holly, but lower growing, usually as a shrub, to 10 ft. Leaves have fewer spines. Being self-fertile, will set berries without pollen from other plants. Fruits heavily with big, scarlet berries at Christmas time. Var. *burfordii,* BURFORD HOLLY, performs exceptionally well in zones 7-13; has leaves with no spines.

I. crenata. JAPANESE HOLLY. Zones: (See English Holly.) Shrub to 20 ft. high, with oval or oblong, wavy-toothed leaves. Flowers in May or June, followed by black berries. Var. *convexa* has nearly round leaves. Var. *helleri* is a dwarf to 6-8 in. Var. *microphylla* has small, ½ in. leaves. Var. *rotundifolia* has round, glossy leaves.

Japanese holly and its varieties have inconspicuous black berries, but are popular because of their varied habit of growth and foliage. The species is less desirable than the varieties.

I. pernyi. PERNY HOLLY. Zones: (See English Holly.) Large shrub or tree to 30 ft. Glossy, 1 in. leaves with 1-3 spines on each side; berries red. Var. *veitchii* has larger leaves with 4-5 spines on each side.

Holly prefers a rich, slightly acid loam, but will grow in almost any well drained garden soil, in sun or shade. Growth is more compact in sun and berry set is heavier.

Spray twice a year—in March or April and again in September—for mealybug and scale. Use an oil emulsion, which will loosen the black "honey-dew" coating caused by these insects at the same time it controls them. With an addition of nicotine sulfate, this spray will also be effective on leaf roller and leaf moth.

ITEA ILICIFOLIA. HOLLYLEAF SWEETSPIRE. Evergreen. Zones 7-13. Hardy to 15°. Graceful shrub to 10 ft. Glossy, dark green, 4 in., spiny-toothed leaves resemble English holly. Small, greenish-white flowers are carried on drooping, 12-in. spikes in spring.

I. yunnanensis. Stronger growing. Leaves not so holly-like as *I. ilicifolia* and white flowers in shorter, erect, 6-in. spikes. Not readily available.

Best foliage in partial shade. Any soil. Requires ample moisture in summer months.

Hollyleaf sweetspire is a superb foliage shrub that deserves to rank with holly, camellia, rhododendron, and other shrubs with exceptionally desirable foliage. For those who cannot grow English holly and desire holly foliage at Christmas, this shrub is the answer. Also useful in green backgrounds and as an unclipped, informal hedge. Grows well under high branching tree. Foliage fine for cutting and is long lasting.

JACOBINIA. Evergreen. Zone 13; greenhouse plants elsewhere. Showy tropicals with large leaves and red, orange, or yellow tubular flowers.

J. carnea. Fast growth to 4 ft., with oblong 7-in. leaves and tubular rose-purple or pink 2-in. flowers in dense clusters at the top of thickly foliaged stems. Commonest species in cultivation.

J. ghiesbreghtiana. To 5 ft., with 6-in. leaves. Orange or crimson 1½-in. flowers in loose clusters.

J. pauciflora. To 2 ft., with small oval ¾-in. leaves and small, yellow, scarlet tipped flowers.

Plant jacobinias in part shade, giving them the same treatment as you would fuchsias or hydrangeas. Inclined to become ragged if neglected. Grown as indoor potted plants in cold climates.

JASMINUM. JASMINE. (See chapter on vines.)

JUNIPERUS. JUNIPER. (Also see chapter on trees.) Evergreen. Hardy all zones. Of the some 45 species and varieties sold by Western nurserymen the majority are in the ground cover, low-shrub, and tall-shrub classes. The low and prostrate forms have great utility value as ground covers and permanently low, foundation plants, and for use in planter boxes. The medium-height junipers are of 2 types: the loose, wide-spreading forms that have many garden uses when massed as backgrounds, covers of waste spaces, evergreen dividers, etc.; the columnar or pyramidal forms in most instances must be considered as individuals for special situations. The latter, taller types are more tree-like in form, both formal and irregular. Some, like the twisted juniper, are very "picturesque" in form.

Junipers have two kinds of leaves on the branches. One type is scale-like, with tiny, triangular, closely overlapping scales that make the branches look like braided cords. The other is needle-like, with rather short, stiff needles that give the branches a finer-textured look. Some of the most commonly used junipers have both textures on one plant, and these also give a fine-textured effect.

Low-growing junipers

When you buy a low-growing prostrate or mounded form of juniper be sure you get one that will continue to be low growing. There are many plants at the nursery that are low growing in youth but quickly mound up to 4 ft. or more in your garden. The following will stay under 2 ft. in most climates or can be kept to 2 ft. by minimum pruning in any climate.

J. chinensis armstrongii. Looks like a small Pfitzer juniper. Low, arching habit to 2 ft. Has both scale-like and needle-like leaves.

J. chinensis japonica. Spreads slowly to form a broad, low mound less than 2 ft. high with stout, horizontal, main branches. Has all needle-like leaves.

J. chinensis sargentii. Similar to *J. japonica* but more rounded and finer in texture. Many needle-like leaves and many often scale-like. Good ground cover. There are also variegated forms of similar habit.

J. conferta. SHORE JUNIPER. A low, 1-2 ft., uneven and informal mat of blue-green foliage. Leaves all needle-like. Stands salt spray and submergence. A natural with stone. Not adapted in hot interiors.

J. horizontalis. *(J. prostrata).* CREEPING JUNIPER. Prostrate, creeping to form a low, 18-in., compact mat of blue-gray foliage. Var. *Bar Harbor,* considered very choice by many, has gray-green foliage. Var. *douglasii,* WAUKEGAN JUNIPER, is moderately fast growing, spreading to 20 ft. or more, and to less than 2 ft. high. Soft, metallic-blue foliage turns interesting shades of purplish-blue in fall. An excellent ground cover, handsome on steep banks, or cascaded over rocks. Best adapted in zones 1-5. Var. *plumosa,* ANDORRA JUNIPER, is spreading, slightly mounding to 15-18 in., with gray-green, feathery foliage tinged bronze in fall. Widely distributed. *J. horizontalis* and its forms have both scale-like and needle-like foliage, except var. *plumosa,* which has all needle-like foliage.

J. sabina tamariscifolia. TAMARIX JUNIPER. Wide spreading to 15 ft. or more, and less than 18 in. high, with sprays of rather fine, bright green foliage; has both needle-like and scale-like leaves. One of the most useful, small junipers. A variegated form has occasional branches dappled creamy-white.

Medium-height junipers
Upright Shrub Forms

The upright-shrub forms have unusual garden value. Unlike the definite form of pyramidal, conical, and columnar conifers, these junipers go together with ease to form borders, dividers, and mass cover. As strong-growing, spreading shrubs they should never be substituted for the columnar form or for the true, low growing types.

J. chinensis pfitzeriana. PFITZER JUNIPER. An open, spreading, fast-growing shrub to 10 ft. high and 15 ft. wide with rather fine-textured, gray-green foliage. Lower growing forms with softer texture, and forms with greenish-yellow foliage are available.

J. hetzii. Under this name Western nurserymen sell this vigorous-growing juniper. Upright, widely irregular growth to 12 ft., with strong, spreading branches and light gray foliage.

J. sabina. SAVIN JUNIPER. A dense, wide-spreading shrub, variable in height, usually under 6 ft., and spreading to 20 ft. Soft, matted, green foliage. Needle-like leaves on young plants; mostly scale-like leaves on adults. Good massed as a filler for a large area.

J. squamata meyeri. Has an irregular outline with upward-growing limbs. Gray-blue foliage, silvery beneath. Leaves all needle-like. Best used as a specimen or color accent.

J. virginiana kosteri. KOSTER JUNIPER. Graceful, wide-spreading habit to 5 ft. tall and 10-15 wide, with blue-gray foliage. Leaves mostly scale-like.

J. virginiana tripartita. FOUNTAIN RED CEDAR. Very informal, loose, upright-spreading form to 10 ft., with blue-gray foliage.

Pyramidal Shrub Forms

J. chinensis torulosa. TWISTED JUNIPER. An interesting, narrow, columnar form, to 10-15 ft., with open, twisting branches and dark green foliage of scale-like leaves. Makes an unusual accent, specimen, or tub plant. A variegated form has tips of branches splashed with creamy-white.

J. excelsa stricta. SPINY GREEK JUNIPER. Pyramidal, perfectly symmetrical, small tree. Has short, spiny, silvery-blue needles. Tends to brown in winter in cold-winter gardens.

KALMIA. Evergreen. Hardy all zones, but best adapted to zones 1-6 and 10. Grows wherever rhododendrons are successful.

K. latifolia. MOUNTAIN LAUREL. Slow growth to 8 ft. with 6-8 ft. spread. Glossy, leathery, 3-5 in. leaves. Deep pink buds and lighter pink flowers in the same cluster create an apple-blossom effect. Long season of bloom, May-June.

Kalmia needs the same treatment and attention as rhododendrons. Don't crowd kalmias. Let their companions be lower growing rhododendrons, camellias, heathers.

K. polifolia. BOG KALMIA. (See chapter on natives.)

KARO. See PITTOSPORUM

KERRIA JAPONICA. Deciduous. Hardy all zones. Valued most in zones 1-6 for winter effect of bare branches and for spring flowers.

A graceful, rather open, rounded shrub to 8 ft. with a 5-6 ft. spread. Leaves, bright green turning yellow in the fall, are somewhat triangular and irregularly toothed. March to May feature is crop of flowers that look like single golden-yellow roses. In winter kerria's bright-green naked branches form a wonderful contrast when planted in front of darker evergreen. Kerria should be silhouetted where possible, rather than hidden inside a mixed shrub border. Var. *pleniflora* has double flowers and is the more commonly planted form.

Kerria prefers part shade. Because it suckers by underground shoots, don't plant with shrubs that dislike crowding. Remove suckers with spade. Prune drastically after flowering, cutting out branches that have flowered and all dead wood.

KOHUHU. See PITTOSPORUM

KOLKWITZIA AMABILIS. BEAUTY BUSH. Deciduous. Hardy all zones, and one of the few deciduous shrubs widely used in California. Upright, gracefully arching growth to 8 ft., with an equal spread; gray-green 3-in. leaves. Clusters of small pink trumpet-like flowers bloom continuously along the branches in June, followed by conspicuous brown, bristly seed pods that remain until midwinter. Brown flaky bark of the stems gradually peels off during winter.

Beauty bush takes a few years to get set for heavy flowering. To enjoy the decorative seed pods, prune in early spring. No special soil or attention necessary. Will stand some shade but blooms best in the sun.

KUPUKA TREE. See GRISELINIA LITTORALIS

LANTANA. Evergreen or deciduous in cold weather. Zones 7-13. Hardy to 24°, but is planted in colder areas because plant repairs frost damage quickly. Viney shrubs or shrubby vines of great vigor; widely planted in warm sections as a ground cover.

L. camara. Treated as a shrub it will grow to 6 ft.; given support on a wall it will reach to 20 ft. Leaves are dark green, veiny, ovate, 1-5 in. long. Small flowers in dense, flat, 1-2 in. heads, open yellow or orange, then change to red or scarlet.

L. montevidensis. *(L. sellowiana).* TRAILING LANTANA. Probably the hardiest of the lantanas. A low, rapid grower with trailing branches to 3 ft. Small, 1-in. leaves and fragrant lavender-pink flowers in dense heads.

L. callowiana Goldrush. A new hybrid between *L. montevidensis* and *L. camara.* Graceful, low, trailing habit, deep green foliage and saffron yellow flowers.

Full sun is necessary for lantanas if you want plenty of color. Will mildew in shade. Best when not fertilized or overwatered. A yearly cutting back and thinning out in early spring helps to keep them from getting woody.

Lantanas, particularly the dwarf or trailing forms, are excellent cover for a sunny rock wall or bank. Very pleasing in containers, when controlled by pinching back. Use the gray *Teucrium fruticans* or *Senecio greyii* with lantana to soften its bright harshness.

LEPTOSPERMUM. TEA TREE. Evergreen. Zones 7-13. Apparently the only reason all leptospermums are now called tea trees is that Captain Cook treated his scurvy-plagued crew with tea made from the leaves of *L. scoparium* in New Zealand in 1773.

L. laevigatum. AUSTRALIAN TEA TREE. A distinct contribution where informality is the pattern of the garden. Although listed as a large shrub to 10-15 ft., it is more useful as a small tree to 30 ft. When allowed to spread, its branches twist into grotesque and interesting shapes quite in keeping with the gray shaggy bark. Its slender drooping branches are densely covered with very small, ½ by 1-in. gray-green leaves. As with any tree, you can encourage or restrain the natural twisting habit. White, ¾-in. flowers in late spring. Var. *reevesii* is a more compact dwarf form.

Handpick your Australian tea tree from the nursery block. Each plant is an individual, especially in the larger, 5-gallon class. When you find the right shape or pattern, you can almost let the plant dictate its use or placement. If you find a plant with a picturesque branching habit, a wall will provide an attractive background. When used to create a high screen, plant 6 ft. apart. Don't worry about young tree shape for screen use. Close planting will force a rather straight and tall growth.

Excellent screen or hedge plants right at the ocean's brim. Used for holding the shifting sand dunes in San Francisco's Golden Gate Park. Interesting use: Paul's scarlet roses and leptospermum alternating on a long wire fence. Leptospermum, planted 15 ft. apart and clipped to lie flat against the fence.

L. scoparium. BROOM TEA TREE. A large shrub to 10-18 ft. with 6-10 ft. spread. Green to reddish, pointed, ½-in. leaves and white ½-in. flowers. This species includes many varieties and forms with bright rose, pink, and carmine flowers.

Lammert's hybrids were developed from these species. The hybrids are dwarf and semi-dwarf, 2-4 ft., with double flowers in white, pink, and red. Leaves are green and in the reddish shades. The rather drab appearance of the dwarf hybrids in the nursery gives no indication of their ultimate garden beauty.

All leptospermum do best in a sandy soil and in sun. Wherever soil lacks iron, they are quick to show a yellowing of the leaves. Treat soil or plant for chlorosis. (See chapter on soils.)

LEUCOPHYLLUM TEXANUM. TEXAS RANGER. Evergreen. Zones 6-13, best 7, 8, 9, 11, and 12. Hardy to at least 10°. Rather compact, slow growing, silvery-foliaged shrub to 5-12 ft., 4-6 ft. spread. Of great value in dry, hot areas as round-headed mass of good gray. Light rose-purple, 1-in., bell-shaped flowers.

Adapts itself to fog-belt conditions especially on dry hillsides above the sea, but there it seldom blooms well. No amount of wind or heat phases leucophyllum, and apparently it thrives on alkali as long as the drainage is at least fair. In desert areas it serves as a clipped hedge. Combines beautifully with *Teucrium fruticans*, *Convolvulus cneorum*, and where the blossoms are profuse (lower desert), it is a fine foil for magenta bougainvillea and purple lantana.

LEUCOTHOE CATESBAEI. DROOPING LEUCOTHOE. Hardy all zones but best adapted to zones 3-6. Slow growing to 2-4 ft. with 2-6 ft. spread. Arching branches droop to the ground. Long, leathery, 3-6 in. leaves are a lustrous dark green, turning a beautiful bronzy-purple in fall and winter if in full sun, otherwise a bronzy-green. Drooping clusters of creamy-white, lily-of-the-valley-like flowers hang below the branches in early spring.

Best in slightly acid soil and partial shade. Prune by removing old flower heads. If growth becomes too rank, cut to ground to give shrub a fresh start. Looks unhappy when planted alone. Use in mass as a carpet or subshrub for rhododendrons, azaleas, kalmias and pieris. Often cut for decoration when in bloom.

LIGUSTRUM. PRIVET. Deciduous and evergreen. Don't rule out all privets in your garden just because you've seen too many privet hedges. There are 17 species and varieties sold by Western nurseries. Some make very serviceable small trees, others are worthy of foundation planting for dramatizing in a tub. Many gardeners who have seen privets as hedges do not realize they all have beautiful creamy-white flowers.

L. lucidum. GLOSSY PRIVET. Zones 3-13. Froze to the snow line at 10° in an extreme Northwest winter but recovered quickly. Will grow to 25-30 ft. as a small tree but can be held to 5-6 ft. Glossy, deep green, long-pointed, 4-6 in. leaves. 10-in. flower clusters in late spring and in summer.

L. japonicum. JAPANESE PRIVET. Evergreen. Zones 3-13. Shrub or small tree similar to and confused with *L. lucidum*, but Japanese privet is lower growing, to 10-12 ft. Leaves, 3-4 in. long, are smaller, shorter pointed, and more glossy than the glossy privet, whose flower clusters are also bigger and denser. Var. *rotundifolium* (*L. coriaceum*) has nearly round, 2½-in. leaves, sometimes notched at the tip. More dwarf, growing to 4-5 ft.

The privet sold as *L. texanum*, TEXAS PRIVET, is probably a form of *L. japonicum*. At least it is more like *L. japonicum* than *L. lucidum*. Grows no higher than 6-9 ft.; leaves are very glossy.

L. ovalifolium (*L. californicum*). CALIFORNIA PRIVET. Evergreen or semi-deciduous. Zones 3-13. Inexpensive hedge plant, fast growing to 15 ft. if not pruned. Dark green, oval, 2½-in. leaves. Flower clusters to 4 in. long. Leaves of var. *variegatum* are marbled with pale yellow; var. *aureo-marginatum* has leaves edged with yellow.

L. vulgare. COMMON PRIVET, ENGLISH PRIVET. Deciduous. All zones. Light green, 2½-in. leaves. Root system less greedy than in California privet. Var. *lodense* is a dwarf compact form of the English privet.

L. sinense. CHINESE PRIVET. Deciduous. Zones 3-6. Fast growing to 12 ft., with 3-in. leaves and hairy, 4-in. flower clusters.

L. henryi. Evergreen. Zones 7-13. (Not tested in 3-6.) Softer in texture than other privets. Bushy, branching shrub to 10-12 ft. but can be held back to 3-4 ft. Dark green, pointed, 2-in. leaves. Flower clusters, 5 in. long.

The privets are not particular as to soil, heat, or wind but show quick response to water and fertilizer.

One of the best uses of *L. japonicum* and *L. lucidum* is in informal high screens. You get the benefit of flowers when the shrubs go untrimmed. All of the lower growing species are satisfactory in large tubs or boxes.

LILAC. See SYRINGA

LILY-OF-THE-VALLEY SHRUB. See PIERIS

LONICERA. HONEYSUCKLE. (Also see chapter on vines.) Evergreen and deciduous. Hardy all zones. Besides the well known climbers in this genus there are a number of shrub species.

L. nitida. BOX HONEYSUCKLE. Evergreen. Shrub to 6 ft. with erect densely leafed branches. Small dark green ovate ¼-½ in. leaves. Fragrant creamy-white ½-in. flowers in June, followed by translucent blue-purple berries.

Grows rapidly in any good garden soil in sun or shade. Tendency toward untidiness but if constantly pruned makes an excellent 6-ft. hedge. It is supposed to withstand salt spray.

L. morrowii. MORROW HONEYSUCKLE. Deciduous. Grows to 6 ft., with dense mound-like habit of growth and widespreading branches. Oval 1-2 in. leaves are dark green above, grayish beneath. Small ½-in. flowers are white changing to yellow, May-June. Small berries are blood red.

L. pileata. PRIVET HONEYSUCKLE. Evergreen. Low, almost prostrate shrub with stiff horizontal branches spreading to 3 ft. Dark green 1½-in. privet-like leaves and small white fragrant flowers in May, followed by translucent violet-purple berries.

Grows well under ordinary cultural conditions. Prefers sun but can take a little shade, particularly inland. Excellent ground cover for holding banks. Combines well with creeping euonymus and low growing barberries.

L. korolkowii zabelii. Deciduous. Grows to 12 ft., with spreading branches. Smooth ovate bluish-green 1-in. leaves and small pink flowers in May and June, followed by bright red fruit.

L. tatarica. TATARIAN HONEYSUCKLE. Deciduous Upright, vigorous shrub to 6-8 ft. Forms a dense mass of thin twiggy branches, looser and more attractive in partial shade. Ovate 2-in. leaves are dark green or bluish-green. Small light or deep pink flowers in late spring and early summer followed by red fruits. Var. *alba* has pure white flowers. Var. *rosea* has flowers that are rose outside, pink inside. Var. *sibirica* has deep pink flowers.

Sun or shade. Almost any soil; disease and pest resistant. Will withstand heavy pruning. Neat appearing plant at all times.

L. fragrantissima. WINTER HONEYSUCKLE. Deciduous or partially evergreen. Grows to 8 ft. with long slender branches. Rather stiff, leathery broadly oval 1-3 in. leaves are dull dark green above, pale beneath. Very fragrant ⅝-in. creamy-white flowers in March and April. Red berries.

Can be used as a clipped hedge.

L. syringantha. LILAC HONEYSUCKLE. Deciduous. Erect twiggy shrub to 6-8 ft. with oval ½-1 in. leaves and a profusion of ½-in. pinkish or lilac fragrant flowers in spring, followed by small red berries.

LOROPETALUM CHINENSE. Evergreen. Zones 4-13. Compact shrub, of varying height, to 3 ft. in short-season climate zones; to 10 ft. or more in zone 13. Gives a great show of downy-white to cream, 1-in. flowers of great delicacy and pattern value against light green, pointed, 2-in. leaves.

Prefers light shade in most inland areas, full sun in fog belt. Wants ample water at all times. May be controlled with minimum pruning, clipped to formal specimen or hedge, or lightly thinned to low, open shrub along foundations or under windows. Combines attractively with xylosma, *Osmanthus fragrans*, skimmia, raphiolepis, nandina, mahonia species. Rare, but worth looking for.

MACKAYA BELLA. Evergreen. Zones 12-13. Tender; top blackens at 30°. Soft-textured, black-green 2½-in. leaves, with wavy, slightly toothed margins. Lavender, funnel-shaped, 2½-in. flowers in 6-in. terminal clusters bloom in late spring.

This 4-8 ft. shrub is strictly for the shade—the deeper the better—and also requires some acidity and good drainage. Frost is seldom a problem because the plant must have overhang protection from sun. In poorly drained soil, mackaya is frequently attacked by cyclamen mite and thrip. To encourage bushiness, pinch when young, and prune lightly after bloom.

One of its best uses is as an espalier with light pink *Impatiens holstii* and *Campanula poscharskyana* planted below.

MAHONIA. Evergreen. (Also see chapter on natives.) Two non-native species are well worth considering.

M. bealei. Hardy all zones. Tree-like shrub to 12 ft. Flat whorls of branches grow horizontally from an erect trunk. Grayish-green leaves of 9-15, ovate, 5-in. leaflets with stiff, spiny teeth on the margins. Clusters of yellow flowers in spring followed by bluish berries.

Handsome addition to shade garden. Fine solo performer but also good for mass use. Effective against the glass wall of a patio where one can look through its open branches into the garden. Combines well with rich browns of stonework or with the redwood tones of house or fencing.

M. lomariifolia. Zones 7-13. Hardy to 20°. When young, a single vertical stem rises to 6-8 ft., then new stems appear at the base of the plant ultimately producing a good-sized, multiple-trunked shrub to 10-12 ft., with a branch pattern all its own. Leaves of 21-29, rather narrow, thick, spiny leaflets. Clusters of yellow flowers in early spring followed by bluish berries.

At present, a rare plant in cultivation but destined to become more available because it is easy to propagate by seed or from suckers and offshoots. Grows best in half shade.

Most effective when grown alone in a doorway or patio; or in the shade garden with a carpet of *Ajuga reptans* under it.

MELALEUCA. See **CALLISTEMON; MELALEUCA**

MELIANTHUS MAJOR. HONEY BUSH. Evergreen. Zones 7-13. Has endured 25° of frost without injury. Bold-patterned foliage shrub, producing an arresting effect in full sun. Blue-gray-green leaves 1 ft. or more long made up of 9-11 toothed leaflets are unique in texture and pattern value. Exotic, twisted, 1-ft. terminal spikes of red-brown 1-in. flowers appear in late winter and early spring.

Although perhaps most effective grown as a sprawling mass, with old canes removed frequently to make room for fresh new growth, this rapid-growing ornamental usually reaches 6 ft. but may possibly achieve 12-14 ft. in height and width, within two years, especially in southern coastal areas. It is amazingly adaptable to pruning, crowding of roots, almost any soil, hot sun or considerable shade, quantities of water or dry conditions. In lower desert and southern end of the San Joaquin Valley, however, it is best in some shade. Dry, persistent leaves on lower stems become messy, requiring an occasional hand-picking.

Melianthus serves as a pot plant, in windowboxes, in lush tropical gardens, or with bold-leafed succulents in a boulder garden. Effective with *Tetrapanax papyrifera*, cyperus, or gray plants.

MICHELIA FUSCATA (*Magnolia fuscata*). BANANA SHRUB. Evergreen. Zones 9-10, 12-13. A shrub of glossy, clean foliage, eventually reaching to 15 ft. high and 8 ft. wide but regarded as a small shrub in its first 5 years. Deep green, lustrous, oblong, 3-in. leaves. Flowers resembling dwarf, 1½-in., magnolia blossoms, open in March—creamy-yellow with purple or brownish shadings. They may lightly perfume the garden for a month or more with a rich banana-like fragrance.

The banana shrub has no special cultural requirements other than protection from hot afternoon sun. Some who have grown it swear that it needs some direct sun to bring out its fragrance; others are sure that it is equally fragrant when grown in warm shade.

Use in tub or box on patio, terrace, or near outdoor living areas.

MIRROR PLANT. See **COPROSMA**

MURRAYA. ORANGE JESSAMINE. Evergreen. Zones 12-13, occasionally 10-11. May be badly damaged at 25°. Especially needs warm nights. Choice, glossy-foliaged shrubs worth the extra effort that may be required to grow them in some sections.

M. paniculata. GIANT ORANGE JESSAMINE. Usually grows to 6-10 ft. and almost as broad, with open habit and graceful, pendulous branches. Dark green, glossy leaves are divided into 3-9 ovate, 1-2 in. leaflets. Pure white, ¾-in., bell-shaped flowers have the fragrance of jasmine. Occasionally blooms in the spring and always in late summer and fall. Mature plants bear small, red fruits.

Good companion plants are *Trachelospermum jasminoides*, *Jasminum magnificum*, and all species of brunfelsia.

M. exotica. COMPACT ORANGE JESSAMINE. Although usually considered botanically the same as *M. paniculata*, it presents a different appearance when grown in the garden. Slower growing, more upright and compact, seldom exceeds 6 ft. in height and 4 ft. across. Leaves are lighter green, the leaflets smaller and stiffer. Flowers are usually less profuse.

Makes a beautiful hedge in rich, deep, perfectly drained soil.

Murraya is best in high shade or half day's sun without strong reflected heat. Requires excellent drainage, high-nitrogen fertilizer, and frequently a feeding of iron sulfate to counteract chlorosis. Recovers slowly from cold, wet winters. Wants plenty of moisture in warm season. Appears at its best from July to November.

MYRSINE AFRICANA. AFRICAN BOX. Evergreen. Zones 7-13. Leaf burns at 18°. Slow growing to 3-5 ft., slightly floppy in first 2-3 years but gathers speed once its roots are deep, and stiffens with maturity to make one of our best-dressed and most adaptable foliage plants. Elliptic very dark green, glossy ½ in. leaves are closely set along the vertical dark red stems. Flowers are inconspicuous.

Equally happy in part shade or full sun, and reasonable drainage. Generally without pests and is strongly smog resistant. Spray with water to keep leaves clean, glossy and insect free.

Fine texture and solid dark coloring supply splendid background for mixed flower borders, and is also good for low hedges. Excellent cut foliage. In the landscape it repeats the leaf texture of *Azara microphylla* and *Lonicera nitida*, and continues some of the feeling of eurya and a few of the buxus species, if unclipped.

MYRTUS. MYRTLE. Evergreen. This genus includes several of the most useful, basic evergreen shrubs for California gardens.

M. communis. TRUE MYRTLE. Zones 7-13. Rounded shrub to 5-6 ft. high and 4-5 ft. wide, with glossy, bright green, pointed, 2-in. leaves, pleasantly aromatic when bruised. White, ¾-in. flowers with many fuzzy stamens in summer, followed by bluish-black, ½-in. berries. Var. *buxifolia*, BOXLEAF MYRTLE, has smaller, elliptical leaves. Var. *microphylla* has small, overlapping leaves.

Use as an informal or formal hedge, or in a massed shrubbery border. Plant along a walk, where the aromatic foliage can be appreciated.

M. c. compacta, DWARF MYRTLE, is a slow-growing, very compact shrub with small leaves.

This low-growing plant has the rare combination of simple qualities that make plants universal favorites. It's a many-soil, many-climate plant—completely adaptable. In the nursery can, its compact structure and small, clean, shiny green leaves give it the look of a plant that would stay small forever.

Many uses: as low hedges, foundation shrubs, or combine with small conifers.

M. ugni. (*Eugenia ugni, Ugni molinæ*). CHILEAN GUAVA. Evergreen. Zones 9-10, 12-13. Scraggly when young, maturing to a compact, round-headed shrub 3-6 ft. The small, leathery, ½-in. leaves are dark green above, whitish beneath, with the margins somewhat inrolled. White, rose-tinted flowers appear in late spring or early summer and are followed by purple or reddish, small, ½-in. fruits.

Plant in sun along coast; in light shade inland. It likes a neutral or slightly acid soil. Where soils are not favorable, plant in containers with mixture of peat moss, sand, and rotted manure. Don't allow the plant to dry out in summer heat.

This tidy, restrained plant adds an elegant note to patios, courts, or terraces. It is pleasant to have close at hand in a much-passed corner, or under low windows. The flavor of the fruit is a mixture of strawberry and guava. Use the fruits fresh, or make into jelly, conserve, or jam.

NANDINA DOMESTICA. HEAVENLY BAMBOO. SACRED BAMBOO. Evergreen, semi-deciduous in cold winters. Zones 4-13. Loses leaves at 10°. Killed to ground at 5°. Not a bamboo but a member of the barberry family. Earns its common name by presenting a light and airy structure pattern of slender, unbranched, cane-like stems and fine-textured, delicate, much divided leaves.

Nandina is slow growing to 6-8 ft. (Can be held at 3 ft. indefinitely by pruning old canes to the ground.) New leaves tinged pink and bronzy-red unfold in spring; turn soft light green as they mature, then pick up purple and bronze tints in fall, and often turn a fiery crimson in winter. Display of loose, erect, 12-in. clusters of small creamy-white or pinkish flowers begins in late spring and is followed in autumn with masses of shiny red berries.

Will grow in sun or shade. Fall and winter color better when nandina is grown in sun. If you especially want winter color, buy your plants in winter when you can see their color. Apparently winter color is inherited. Need more than one plant to produce berries. Give plant rich soil and regular watering. Add iron to alkaline soils.

Nandina is one of the ten most useful shrubs in Western gardens. No other shrub can substitute for it when light and airy verticals are wanted. Effective in oriental and tropical groupings. One of few plants for narrow, restricted areas because of upright non-spreading quality. Dramatic patterns with night lighting. Can be grown in tubs and boxes and is a plant you like to be close to. Remember that nandina gains character by cutting old canes to the ground and allowing the plant to renew itself. Don't shear or cut off tops.

NEILLIA LONGIRACEMOSA. Deciduous. Hardy all zones. Graceful shrubs to 6-7 ft. with a 3-ft. spread.

Dense, handsome, bright green leaves resemble our native salmonberry, but hold on well into December. The weight of the tubular, pink flowers in 3-4 in. clusters causes branch tips to droop downward. Blooms from late April to mid-June.

Fairly new in the nursery trade. Imported from England where commonly used as a hedge or screen.

NERIUM OLEANDER. OLEANDER. Evergreen. Zones 7-13. A sturdy, tough, attractive summer-flowering shrub, invaluable in the hot, dry interiors. Moderate growth to 20 ft. high and 25 ft. wide. Normally grows as a many-stemmed, many-branched shrub, but can be trained as single multiple-trunked tree. Foliage of dark green, long, narrow, 5-8 in. leaves is attractive at all times in any weather. From May or June to October oleander is most generous with 2-3 in. flowers.

Many varieties are available, their differences being in flower only. You'll find single and double flowers in shades of white, light pink, salmon-pink, deep rose, red and light yellow.

Oleanders are not particular as to soil, but they need high light intensities for good flower production. They can take wind, heat, and heat plus reflected heat.

Careful pruning will bring better flower display and a more graceful shrub or tree. In early spring, remove old flowering wood, cutting some branches nearly to the ground. If you want to hold growth to lower height, pinch out tips or head lightly. Control the number of stems by removing suckers. Don't cut them, pull them off.

Usual use, and a good one, is as border for road or driveway. Oleanders make effective tub specimens for entrances, decks, and warm terraces. They bloom in youth and can be held to moderate size for years.

Although often seen trained to a single trunk form by staking and removing spreading and suckering growth, the multiple-trunk form should not be overlooked. By selecting a few stems and removing all others, you can build an open, graceful, small tree with all the character of a multiple-trunked olive tree. All parts of the shrub are supposed to be poisonous if eaten.

OCHNA MULTIFLORA. FUN SHRUB. Evergreen. Zones 9-10, 12-13. Damaged at 20°. Moderate growth to 4-6 ft. with 5-6 ft. spread. Dark green, leathery, oblong, 3-in. leaves are bronzy in the spring. Flowers go through 3 stages from early summer to September: first they are a spot of yellow about the size of a butter cup; then the sepals turn a vivid red; next, 5 or more green, seed-like fruits protrude from the red center, and later the seeds turn jet black. At this stage children call it the Mickey Mouse plant.

Best in partial shade and in slightly acid soil that has good drainage. Since ochna needs special soil and is a plant that makes conversation, tub or box planting is logical.

OLEANDER. See **NERIUM OLEANDER**

OSMANTHUS AND SIPHONOSMANTHUS. Evergreen. Hardy zones 3-13, but suffers in alkaline soils. Useful foliage plants in part shade. Subtle fresh fragrance something like that of hyacinths. Botanists separate *Osmanthus* and *Siphonosmanthus* on the differences in flower structure, but for ornamental purposes they can be considered together.

O. aurantiacus. ORANGE OSMANTHUS. Slow growth to 8 ft., with rather narrow, dark green, 3-7 in. leaves. Very fragrant, orange flowers in October. The hybrid, *San Jose*, is a cross between *O. aurantiacus* and *O. ilicifolius*. Glossy, holly-like foliage; orange flowers in October.

O. fortunei. Hybrid between *O. fragrans* and *O. ilicifolius*. Slow growth to 6 ft., with ovate, spiny-toothed, 4-in. leaves. White flowers in spring and summer.

O. fragrans (*Olea fragrans*). SWEET OLIVE. SWEET OSMANTHUS. Tall growing to 10 ft. (occasionally to 30 ft.), spreading to 10-12 ft. Shiny, dark green, oval, 4-in. leaves. Fragrant, white flowers hidden by the foliage in spring and early summer. May become leggy unless trained in youth by pinching.

O. ilicifolius. (*O. aquifolium, Olea aquifolium, Olea ilicifolium*). HOLLY OSMANTHUS. Slow growing, symmetrical shrub to 6-8 ft. (sometimes to 20 ft.), spreading almost as wide. Holly-like, dark green, 2½-in. leaves. Fragrant, white flowers in fall, winter or early spring. Var. *variegatus* has leaves variegated with white.

Siphonosmanthus delavayi (*Osmanthus delavayi*). DELAVAY OSMANTHUS. Slow growing, arching branched shrub to 4-6 ft. and as wide. Small, dark green, ovate 1-in. leaves with notched margins. Fragrant, small white flowers in abundance from March-May.

Osmanthus grows best in partial shade or shade, but will grow in full sun where summers are mild. Strong winds will turn the flowers brown. Needs slightly acid soil and average moisture. Prune regularly, by pinching and cutting back.

To capture its spicy flower fragrance, plant osmanthus in tubs on patio or on terrace near an entrance or under a window. The shiny cleanliness of these shrubs, their medium texture, and ability to grow in shade also make them most useful in backgrounds, where they never steal the garden show.

OSTEOMELES SCHWERINIAE. Deciduous or semi-evergreen. Hardy all zones but seems best adapted in 3-6, 9-10. Twiggy, slender branched shrub to 10 ft., with gray-green compound leaves made up of 15-31 small ⅓-in. leaflets. White, ½-in. flowers in June.

Full sun. No special garden care. Prune after flowering. Thinning improves structure. Use where fine texture is needed. Best against a wall.

PAEONIA. TREE PEONY. (See chapter on perennials for herbaceous peonies.) Deciduous. Hardy all zones, but not successful in sections without winter cold or with high summer heat. Unlike the herbaceous peonies that die to the ground each year, the tree peonies make a woody growth of picturesque, gnarled branches to 4-6 ft. Leaves are attractively cut and divided. Flowers, ranging from single to semi-double to very double, are unbelievably large, often 10-13 in. across. Colors vary from pure white through all shades of pink to deep red, into orchid and magenta.

Most of the tree peonies available are hybrids of the species *P. suffuticosa* and *P. lutea*.

P. suffruticosa. TREE PEONY. A rather open shrub with twisting branches growing very slowly to 4-6 ft. sometimes to 8 ft. Bluish-green foliage with bronze tints makes a distinctive background for huge single flowers of pale pink to clear crimson, 4-12 in. across, in May.

P. lutea. GOLDEN PEONY. Lower growing to 3-4 ft. Pale yellow flowers; less prominent because they hang down into the foliage.

More than 30 named varieties available. All are relatively expensive because they take from 4-7 years to bloom.

Tree peonies have several definite requirements. They should be shaded from the hot afternoon sun. Protection from wind by staking or lattice frame is generally necessary. Although winter hardy, they should not be planted in frost pockets, because early new growth and buds may be killed by late frosts.

The best time to plant is when shrub is dormant in late September and October. Dig a hole 3 ft. wide and 2 ft. deep. Scatter bone meal in the bottom. Mix peat moss with the soil used in filling the hole. (Northwest gardeners should mix in garden lime.) Set plant in the hole with graft 2-4 in. below ground level.

As soon as new growth starts in spring, apply a balanced commercial fertilizer at the rate of a tablespoon per plant. Keep plants moist all summer.

Don't do any pruning until just before the new growth starts in the spring. At that time part of the flower stems will have dried up and it will be easy to see the proper place for making the cut, which is just above the strong new eyes. Also remove dead flowers after they bloom in spring.

Usually most effective when planted by themselves against a background of dark green foliage. Particularly appealing when used in interlocking combinations of separate colors, rather than as single specimens.

PERNETTYA MUCRONATA. Evergreen. Hardy zones 2-13. Freezes at —11°, slow recovery. Valued for its large brilliant berries in winter. Compact, much-branched shrub to 2-3 ft. Stems of new growth are dark red. Glossy, dark green, ovate, ¾ in. leaves, some of which become red or bronzy in winter. White to pink, nodding, ¼ in., bell-like flowers bloom in late spring. Berries are about ½ in. in diameter, fleshy and soft, with a metallic sheen. Best known are forms with purple, red, or white berries; less available are forms with rose, maroon, clear pink, or black fruits. Fruit remains until knocked off by a hard rain or severe frost; in mild winters will stay on until March.

Adaptable to most garden conditions. For best performance need full sun and a light, peaty, well drained soil that is not too rich. Too much shade, water, or fertilizer gives rank, loose growth and no berries. Some plants produce heavy pollen and no berries. Put a heavy pollen producer near a berry producer and the berry set will be doubled or trebled. Spreads by underground stolons, which sometimes become invasive. Root-prune with spade to keep under control. Any awkward growth can be controlled by pruning.

Use pernettyas in sunny windowboxes and in tubs, as low plantings close to the house, as companions for heathers, or in a low border for a spring-flowering deciduous planting. They make an excellent informal low hedge. Also combine happily with azalea, skimmia, rhododendron, mahonia, daphne and pieris. Useful for table decorations.

PHILADELPHUS. Deciduous. Hardy all zones, except *P. mexicanus.* A group of shrubs highly valued for their late spring color and fragrance.

P. coronarius. SWEET MOCKORANGE. Strong growing to 8-10 ft. with fountain-like form. Light green, 3-in. leaves. Clusters of creamy-white, very fragrant 1½-in. flowers in June. The old favorite and the best of the large growing mockoranges.

P. cymosus. Hybrid with *P. lemoinei* as one parent. Moderate growth to 6-8 ft. Several horticultural forms are offered. Leaves oblong, to 4 in. Fragrant flowers are often double, 2 in. across, and carried in clusters of 3-9, in June.

P. gordonianus. (See chapter on natives.)

P. grandiflorus. BIG SCENTLESS MOCKORANGE. Fast growing to 10 ft. Ovate leaves to 5 in. White 2-in. flowers in small clusters. Best adapted to zones 1-5.

P. lemoinei. Hybrid between *P. coronarius* and a low growing, small-leafed species, *P. microphyllus.* There are many horticultural varieties in this group of hybrids. Most are dainty and graceful. All bear a profusion of 1½-in. flowers in late spring.

P. lewisii. (See chapter on natives.)

P. mexicanus. MEXICAN MOCKORANGE. Hardy to 12°. Grows to 15-20 ft. if given supports. Best when framed as an informal espalier against fence or wall. Long supple stems with 3-in. leaves, and small clusters of 1½-in. flowers.

P. virginalis. Hybrid, with the hybrid *P. lemoinei* as one parent. Grows to 6 ft. without the density of *P. coronarius* or the daintiness of *P. lemoinei.* Its value is in its flowers alone. They are snowy white, double, fragrant, 2-3 in. across, in clusters of 3-7, blooming in May-June.

Prune each year after flowering. Remove old wood that has flowered. To keep the plant youthful and within bounds, remove some of the old growth to the ground and allow the new shoots to replace it.

Give them full sun in cool summer areas; part shade where sun is hot. Adapted to most soils and have no special cultural requirements.

PHILLYREA DECORA. Evergreen. Hardy zones 3-13. Handsome shrub to 6-8 ft., with a clean, crisp appearance. For its foliage quality, rate this shrub right up with the aristocrats—camellia, skimmia, osmanthus. Glossy, 3-5 in. leaves are rich dark green above, yellowish-green beneath. Small white flowers in dense clusters appear in April and May. If you plant a male shrub with the female shrub, the latter will produce oval, bright red, ½-in. berries that ripen to purple-black in late fall.

Phillyrea does well in normal garden soil and is not particular about exposure. A rare item now, but certain to become more available in the future.

PHORMIUM TENAX. NEW ZEALAND FLAX. Evergreen. Zones 7-13. Actually a perennial but usually treated as a shrub because of its size. Grows 4-15 ft. Sword-like, stiffly vertical leaves arranged in fan pattern become dense clumps spreading to 6 ft. or more; they are best thinned at least every other year for design value. Reddish-brown stalks that tower above the leaves bear curiously shaped dark red to yellowish flowers in spring.

There are many varieties of different heights, foliage color, leaf width, and rate of growth. Some of the forms available are: the commonly planted green form with 6-8 ft. leaves; wide gray-green, 8-10 ft. leaves with red midrib; green, 6-ft. leaves with white or yellowish edge; greenish-bronze, narrow, 4-ft. leaves and dark red, 6-ft. leaves.

Any soil or exposure; tolerant of great heat, much cold, salt air and ocean spray and even poorest drainage. Can take water or survive without much water. Excellent windbreak along southern coast; or for strongly tropical feeling. Variegated and wide-leafed gray-green forms do well under eucalyptus. Flowers dry well and vie with the foliage in flower arrangements.

PHOTINIA. Evergreen and deciduous. Climate adaptability by species. Genus includes a famous California native, Toyon, and a group of shrub-trees valued and admired for foliage color.

P. serrulata. CHINESE PHOTINIA. Evergreen. Hardy to 10° and widely grown in zones 3-13. Vigorous growth to 30 ft. if not controlled by pruning. Noteworthy on several counts: In spring, copper and scarlet new growth at tips of the curving branches is backed by the mature foliage of dark lustrous green, oblong, 4-7 in. leaves. In fall, foliage becomes bronzy and carries through winter a scattering of bright crimson leaves. Small white flowers in tight, flattish, 4-7 in. heads, in May, are followed by bright red, ¼-in. berries in fall and winter.

P. s. nova. Less vigorous and lower growing than Chinese photinia. Tends to bloom at an earlier age.

P. s. nova lineata. Same habit of growth, but leaves are striped creamy-white down the center.

Chinese photinia and its varieties need a regular spray program for aphis and mildew.

P. glabra. JAPANESE PHOTINIA. Evergreen. Moderate growth to 10 ft. Just as colorful as *P. serrulata*, but smaller in all ways.

P. villosa. Deciduous. Hardy all zones. An upright spreading-branched, vigorous shrub or small tree to 15 ft. Roundish 3-in. leaves, and 2-in. clusters of small white flowers. Valued for its bright red fruits and autumn color.

Plant photinias in sun if you want good color. Easy to grow. Your main job is to keep them ever-youthful in appearance by never allowing new growth to become a long, stiff bare switch. Pruning at frequent intervals not only keeps the shrub under control but brings out the new growth that has such lovely coloring.

Use as informal hedge or tall screen. For contrast combine with any of the gray-colored shrubs.

PICEA. SPRUCE. (Also see chapter on trees.) Hardy all zones. Best adapted in 1-6. A group of forest giants and dwarfs. Considered here are the low growing forms.

P. abies procumbens. To 2 ft. high and 5 ft. across in 20 years. Low irregular growth habit with close compact branches. Upturned branch ends give it an interesting texture. New growth is light shiny green turning dark and lustrous. An excellent ground cover for small contained areas.

P. abies repens. Similar in growth habit to *P. abies procumbens*, but more symmetrical and with more horizontal effect. Use grouped on a slope, or in raised planting boxes.

P. abies maxwellii. To 2 ft. high and 4 ft. wide. A rounded dwarf form with heavy short twigs.

P. abies nidiformis. To 1½ ft. with 4 ft. spread in 20 years. Adds 1-2 in. of growth yearly. Low, rounded nest-like mass of branchlets.

P. glauca conica. Slow growing, ½-1 in. yearly, to 7 ft. in 35 years. A miniature tree of perfect conical shape. Very short and very fine needles. New foliage is bright green fading to gray-green. Handsome tub plant—a miniature Christmas tree for many years.

PIERIS. Evergreen. One of the West's most distinguished shrubs. Although hardy in all zones, requires special soil treatment in zones 7-13. Not a shrub for the deserts.

All are slow growing, well mannered, and of interest in form, leaf, or flower every month in the year.

P. japonica (*Andromeda japonica*). LILY-OF-THE-VALLEY SHRUB. Lustrous, dark green, pointed, 3-in. leaves held in graceful radial clusters give the 6-10 ft. shrub a rather open character as it matures. In youth it's a dense, highly polished specimen worth dramatizing in a tub. When new leaves appear in early spring the plant picks up tones of bronzy-pink to scarlet. In fall delicate strands of greenish-pink buds hang from the tips of branches, fatten during winter, and in very early spring open into pearly-white urn-shaped flowers.

P. floribunda (*Andromeda floribunda*). More compact and rounded, to 3-6 ft. high and 4-6 ft. wide. Longer leaves. Spikes of flowers are held upright rather than drooping. Will stand hotter, drier conditions than *P. japonica*.

P. forrestii. CHINESE PIERIS. More vigorous than *P. japonica*. Leaves wider and longer, flowers larger. Most striking feature of Chinese pieris is the flaming red of the new foliage.

P. nana (*Arcterica nana*). (See chapter on miniatures.)

Pieris' natural climate is the Pacific Northwest, but if planted in shade and in pure peat or peat and leaf mold, it thrives in Southern California. Needs same treatment as, and associates with, azaleas. Don't crowd pieris in combination with other shrubs, but give them a place of their own where they will be emphatic as a single group.

PIMELEA FERRUGINEA. ROSY RICE FLOWER. Evergreen. Zones 10 and 13. A rounded shrub to 3 ft., valued by adventuresome gardeners for the good texture of its crisp, pointed, shiny green ½-in. leaves. Foliage is suggestive of *Hebe buxifolia* and some of the myrtles but with more distinction. Long-lasting, rose-colored flowers in round clusters bloom intermittently throughout the year. Looks well with *Myrtus ugni* and *Myrsine africana*.

Unfortunately the plant is hard to find. It is difficult to grow in nurseries and is seldom permanent in any garden. May die out after 2 or more years for no apparent reason. At its best in the San Francisco Bay region.

PITTOSPORUM. Evergreen. Large shrubs or small trees, varying in hardiness, growth habit, and usefulness.

P. tobira. TOBIRA. JAPANESE PITTOSPORUM. Zones 7-13. Hardy to 15°. The most widely planted species. A spreading shrub to 6-15 ft. Can be held to 6 ft. by selective pruning of stems, but should not be sheared. Some forms are more dwarf than others, but no pittosporum should be trusted as a foundation plant. Foliage is clean looking at all times with leathery, dark green, 4-in. leaves. Clusters of creamy-white flowers with fragrance of orange blossoms are followed by brownish fruits.

P. t. variegata. Probably the most useful of all. Gray-green leaves outlined in white stand out beautifully from darker greens. Being shade tolerant, this variety can be used to lighten dark areas. Growth can be held at 5 ft. Prunings effective in indoor arrangements.

P. crassifolium. KARO. Hardy to 20°. Rather slow growth to 25 ft. with 15 ft. spread. Gray foliage; maroon-colored, ½-in. flowers in clusters. Drought-resistant. Takes seashore conditions.

P. eugenioides. TARATA. Hardy to 15°. Fast growing to 15-40 ft. with 20 ft. spread. Glossy, yellow-green, 4-in. leaves and clusters of fragrant, yellowish, ¼-in. flowers. Has a rather sickly look compared to other pittosporums.

P. heterophyllum. ROCK PITTOSPORUM. Hardy to 20°. Spreading to 5-10 ft. high, with glossy, yellow-green, rather small leaves and fragrant pale yellow flowers. Low growth makes it more useful in small garden.

P. phillyraeoides. WILLOW PITTOSPORUM. Hardy to 20°. Slow growing to a weeping-willow-like tree 20 ft. tall and 15 ft. wide. Intensely fragrant, small yellow flowers. Will take desert heat.

P. rhombifolium. QUEENSLAND PITTOSPORUM. Hardy to 20°. Slow growing to 20-40 ft. shrub or small tree. Small white flowers in spring are very fragrant. In fall and winter, clusters of large yellow berries stand out against glossy, dark green, diamond-shaped leaves.

P. tenuifolium (*P. nigricans*). TAWHIWHI. KOHUHU. Hardy to 18°. Large shrub or small tree to 15-30 ft. Light green, 2½-in. leaves with wavy margins. Dark purple, ½-in. flowers in spring.

P. undulatum. VICTORIAN BOX. Hardy to 16°. Large shrub or small round-headed tree to 20-40 ft. with a 30 ft. spread. Dark green, glossy, 6-in. leaves. Fragrant, creamy-white flowers; orange fruits rather messy when they split and drop their seeds.

In large gardens the taller growing pittosporums are very effective as high dense screens. The lower growing species are good as informal hedges or as space dividers.

PLUMBAGO CAPENSIS. CAPE PLUMBAGO. (See chapter on vines.)

POINSETTIA. See EUPHORBIA PULCHERRIMA

POLYGALA DALMAISIANA. SWEET-PEA SHRUB. Evergreen. Zones 7-13. A bushy shrub to 5 ft. with small 1-in. leaves. Valued for its continuous show of purplish-rose flowers. Difficult color to handle in most gardens. Color combines well with pale blue of *Plumbago capensis*, deeper blue of *Ceratostigma willmottianum*.

POMEGRANATE. See PUNICA GRANATUM

PRIVET. See LIGUSTRUM

PRUNUS. A very large genus that includes all of the stone fruits—almonds, apricots, cherries, peaches and plums—and many other shrubs and trees you wouldn't expect to find associated with them. Many of the species have been given special places elsewhere in the book. Those considered as shrubs are described below; those treated elsewhere are cross-referred to the part of the book where they appear.

P. amygdalus. (See chapter on fruits. See Flowering Almonds.)

P. armeniaca. (See chapter on fruits. See Flowering Apricots.)

P. blireiana. (See Flowering Plums.)

P. campanulata. CHINESE FLOWERING CHERRY. FORMOSA CHERRY. TAIWAN CHERRY. (See Flowering Cherries.)

P. caroliniana. *(Laurocerasus caroliniana).* CAROLINA LAUREL CHERRY. Evergreen. Hardy zones 7-13. Upright well branched shrub, moderate growth to 20 ft. Can be trained as a small tree. Glossy green, luxuriant foliage of 2-4 in. entire margined leaves. Small creamy-white flowers in 1-in. spikes, bloom February-April.

Not demanding of soil or culture. Use as an informal high hedge. Since it is not wide branching at base, the Carolina cherry does not steal much space from the garden.

P. cerasifera. CHERRY PLUM, MYROBALAN. (See Flowering Plums.)

P. cerasifera atropurpurea. (See Flowering Plums.)

P. cistena. DWARF REDLEAF PLUM. PURPLE SAND CHERRY. (See Flowering Plums.)

P. glandulosa. ALMOND CHERRY. (See Flowering Almonds.)

P. ilicifolia. HOLLYLEAF CHERRY. ISLAY. (See chapter on natives.)

P. jacquemontii. (See Flowering Cherries.)

P. laurocerasus *(Laurocerasus officinalis).* ENGLISH LAUREL. CHERRY LAUREL. Evergreen. Hardy zones 3-13. Fast growing shrub or tree to 20 ft. Leathery, glossy, 3-6 in. leaves give foliage a heavy effect in a trimmed hedge. Unpruned, the English laurel makes a tall wind screen or a handsome tree in a formal situation.

A dwarf form of *P. laurocerasus* is available in Northwest nurseries. More compact in growth habit; and leaves are smaller than English laurel. Can be held to a 4-ft. high and 2-ft. wide hedge with very little pruning.

P. l. zabeliana. ZABEL LAUREL. Evergreen. Hardy zones 3-13. A valuable broad-leafed shrub increasing in use as it becomes known. Moderate growth to 6 ft. with an equal spread, but can be held lower by removing the branches that grow upward. Leaves are half as wide as those of English laurel but about as long, and have the same waxy, very clean appearance. Leaves are flat on horizontal branches.

Extremely tolerant of variations in soil and exposure, the Zabel laurel can be used in many ways. As a bank cover, with its long, soft branches pegged down, it makes a flat glossy mat. Can be used as espalier. Very useful in narrow strip between house and walk where half the branches will lie flat on the ground and half will fan up the wall.

P. lusitanica *(Laurocerasus lusitanica).* PORTUGAL LAUREL. Evergreen. Hardy zones 3-13. Slower growing than English laurel and generally treated as a large shrub, but will become a 60-ft. tree where ideally adapted. Glossy dark green leaves to 5 in. long. In spring and early summer, small creamy-white flowers in 5-10 in. spikes extending beyond the leaves, are followed by long clusters of dark purple fruits.

Not particular about soil or culture. Dense branching habit makes it a useful background plant. Seems to be able to do anything the English laurel can do and with more grace. The general color and texture of the shrub harmonize well with either brick or stone.

P. lyonii *(P. ilicifolia integrifolia).* CATALINA CHERRY. (See chapter on natives.)

P. mume. JAPANESE APRICOT. (See Flowering Apricots. See Flowering Plums, *P. blireana.*)

P. naden. (See Flowering Cherries, *P. sieboldii.*)

P. persica. (See chapter on fruits. See Flowering Peaches.)

P. pissardii. (See Flowering Plums, *P. cerasifera atropurpurea.*)

P. serrulata. ORIENTAL CHERRY. (See Flowering Cherries.)

P. sieboldii. NADEN CHERRY. (See Flowering Cherries.)

P. subhirtella. HIGAN CHERRY. (See Flowering Cherries.)

P. subhirtella autumnalis. (See Flowering Cherries.)

P. subhirtella pendula. (See Flowering Cherries.)

P. triloba. FLOWERING PLUM. (See Flowering Plums.)

P. yedoensis. YOSHINO CHERRY. (See Flowering Cherries.)

PSIDIUM. GUAVA. (Also see *Feijoa*, Pineapple Guava. Evergreen. Zones 7-13. Defoliates at 15° but generally recovers. All species of guava thrive in the same climate as citrus. Among the most attractive, versatile, and useful of the subtropical plants. Not only are they highly ornamental but they produce delicious edible fruits.

P. cattleianum. STRAWBERRY GUAVA. Large, open shrub, moderate growing to 8-10 ft., or sometimes an excellent small tree to 15 ft. Glossy, dark green, bronze-tipped, 3 in. leaves. White, 1 in. flowers with many stamens, resemble those of common myrtle. Flowers followed by 1½ in. deep, claret-red fruits. Var. *lucidum* has yellow fruits.

P. guajava. LEMON GUAVA. Tender to 26°, won't take desert heat. Taller and more open in habit with larger, prominently veined, 6-in. leaves. Large, yellow, 1-3 in. fruits with musky flavor and mild acidity.

Guavas like sun. Do well in practically any type of soil, but rich, loamy soils are best. You can enjoy the fruit from September to February, if you plant one in a north exposure and another in a position facing south. The plant in the warmer exposure will start bearing first. Drastic thinning when the fruit first sets makes the remaining fruit larger and better.

Guavas make attractive informal hedges. Try strawberry guava as a division between flower and vegetable gardens. Can be kept low by continuous pinching and light pruning. The fruits may be enjoyed fresh or made into many types of desserts, each having a distinctive flavor all its own.

PUNICA GRANATUM. POMEGRANATE. Deciduous. Zones 7-13. (See chapter on Home Food Garden.) Whether you choose the fruiting tree or the dwarf flowering shrub, you'll find yourself owning a lot of decorative values. There are months when you could call them flowering shrubs, and months when they're spectacular with fruit, and weeks of colorful fall foliage.

P. g. Wonderful is the name of the commercial fruit variety. Rather than being trained as a tree, it is most often seen as a fountain-like clump, a shrub of several stems to 10-15 ft. high and spreading to 8-12 ft. Glossy bright green leaves are rather narrow and 3-in. long. Orange-red, 1½-in., bell-shaped flowers held near the ends of the branchlets. Fruits are brownish-yellow turning to a burnished red as the leaves change to saffron yellow.

Produces best in hot summers. Soil and water requirements are not specific. Left to itself, the shrub will become a thicket by suckering. Structure is most interesting when suckers are removed and the shrub held to a few trunks. Where there's space these large shrubs can be planted 12 ft. apart to make a colorful hedge screen.

P. g. nana. DWARF POMEGRANATE. A miniature of the large shrub, growing to 3 ft. It is almost evergreen in mild winters. The dwarf is bushy, compact, and well mannered. It blooms as an infant and bears fruit when no more than 12 in. tall. Its tiny fruits are dry and not edible. There are double-flowered forms and several color variations from yellow to orange. As a container plant, it can progressively move from a 6 in. pot to a 14 in. box in about 5 years.

An excellent companion plant is *Ceratostigma willmottianum*, which blooms at the same time and offers striking blue contrast. The many uses—as low hedges, along paths, in shrub groups—will suggest themselves when you see the shrub.

PYRACANTHA. FIRETHORN. Hardy zones 3-13. Not many years ago the pyracanthas were declining in popularity because of their frequent misuse. The large vigorous growers were crowded into small places and held back by butchering. Today, sold as wall espaliers they top the list of best sellers in the berried shrub class. Because pyracanthas have been variable in form and color, many seedlings have been selected and named by growers. More than 15 forms are available.

P. coccinea. The hardiest species. Grows as a rounded bush to 8-10 ft. or climbs to 20 ft. against a wall. Clusters of white flowers in March and April, followed by red berries in November.

Var. *Government Red.* One of the favorite pyracanthas in the Pacific Northwest. Red berries.

Var. *lalandii.* A vigorous grower to 20 ft., with orange berries.

P. crenato-serrata. *(P. yunnanensis).* Generally more prostrate than some in habit, rarely reaching more than 6 ft. and spreading to 10 ft. Orange to coral berries last through the winter..

Var. *graberi* produces scarlet berries in very large clusters. Adapted to espalier training.

Var. *Santa Cruz.* A very dense, prostrate form easily kept at 1½ ft. and spreading to 6 ft. and more. Large clusters of red berries. Flowers in March and April; berries October-February.

P. koidzumii. *(P. formosana).* Fast growing to 10 ft. and spreading to 8 ft. Easily held at any height. Large scarlet berries in big clusters November - February. Adapted to espalier training.

P. k. Stribling. A seedling sport, growing to 15 ft. high and 12 ft. wide in an upright pattern with pendulous branches. Clusters of red berries continuous all along the branches.

The following are horticultural varieties of unknown parentage:

Var. *Rosedale.* A patented and popular variety generally and widely sold as an espalier. A naturally upright grower.

Var. *rubra.* Somewhat similar to Rosedale.

Var. *Victory.* To 10 ft. high and 8 ft. wide with dark red berries in December.

Var. *San Jose.* Wide spreading. Same color but larger berries than *P. graberi.*

Var. *Radiance.* Very early fruiting and early maturing. Orange berries.

Var. *Walderi.* Low growing and wide spreading. Red berries.

The pyracanthas ask for no special care and tolerate neglect. Give them full sun. Prune by pinching to direct growth of plant. In cutting branches remember that berries are produced on second-year wood; cut branches that have berried back to laterals rather than cut off both new and old wood.

Espaliering can cover a wall or can be held to a trellis in a pot. The wide-spreading types are useful as hillside plants and ground covers for rough places. The tall and wide-growing forms make good hedgerows on country places.

RAPHIOLEPIS. Evergreen. Hardy 7-13; borderline in zones 4-6 but worth the chance. Top damaged; but root hardy to 5°; killed at 0°. The distribution of pink India hawthorn *(Raphiolepis indica rosea)* that began in San Jose, California, in 1938, started this genus on the road to fame.

R. indica. INDIA HAWTHORN. Neat shrub, slow growing to 5 ft. and spreading as wide. 3½-in. long, dark green leaves. Pinkish, ½-in. flowers in loose clusters in April.

R. i. rosea. PINK INDIA HAWTHORN. Slow growing to 3-5 ft. with wider spread. Variable in growth habit; generally grows outward in a sort of reclining position, but keeps its head up. Irregular in form, dense or open in structure. Its 2-3 in., shiny leaves are light bronzy in new growth in the spring, then light green to dark green. Light pink flowers in high-crowned clusters cover half the foliage of the plant from February through May; a scattering of bloom throughout the rest of the year. The flowers are followed by clusters of blue-black fruits.

Much of the popularity of *R. i. rosea* is due to its ability to serve as a foundation plant for houses with no foundation. Being slow growing it remains a low shrub for many years. As it grows old its need for early pruning becomes apparent. When you buy raphiolepis, hand pick them the way you want to use them. You will find some growing naturally flat and others more upright.

You can encourage rather flat growth by removing the central or crown branches if there are any. Height can be leveled off at any stage by cutting back the vertical branches. Likewise, you can encourage erect growth by leaving vertical branches intact and removing some side branches.

Widely adapted to soils and culture, sun and shade. Less compact and fewer flowers when grown in shade.

R. i. rubra. COATES CRIMSON RAPHIOLEPIS. Horticultural variety that's more compact than *R. i. rosea,* with light to fairly deep crimson flowers.

R. umbellata ovata. ROUNDLEAF YEDDO HAWTHORN. Possibly more hardy than *R. indica rosea*. Slow growing, compact shrub to 6-8 ft. and about as wide as high. Growth habit stiff and irregular; often one portion of the plant succeeds in outgrowing other sections, giving it an interesting irregular structure. White flowers in June.

R. delacouri. A hybrid between *R. i. rosea* and *R. u. ovata*. ¾-in. pink flowers in 4-in. clusters intermittently from March to August. A slow growing, rounded shrub; good for tubs.

RHAMNUS ALATERNUS. ITALIAN BUCKTHORN. (For other rhamnus, see chapter on natives.) Evergreen, or partially so. Zones 4-13. Upright vigorous shrub, or small tree, to 20 ft., with oval 2-in. glossy rich green leaves. Tiny yellowish flowers in clusters, followed by bluish-black fruits. Var. *argenteo-variegata* (var. *variegata*) has leaves edged with creamy-white.

Excellent fast growing clean looking shrubs for shade or sun. Tolerant of drought, heat and wind. Makes a splendid hedge, clipped column. The variegated form is nice contrast in the shrub border or to brighten a corner or dark background. Very effective trained against brown and brick colors. Ideal tub plants.

RHODODENDRON. See p. 257

RHUS TYPHINA. STAGHORN SUMAC. (For other rhus, see chapter on natives.) Deciduous. Hardy all zones. Very large, loose, open shrub to 30 ft., spreading to 20-25 ft., with interesting velvety branches curving inward like a deer's antlers. Large compound leaves of 11-31, 5-in. toothed leaflets, top the branches in rich green tufts presenting a tropical aspect in summer. In fall, leaves turn brilliantly scarlet. Tiny greenish flowers in dense terminal clusters in June and July are followed by crimson red fruits.

Survives extremes of heat and cold and will grow in clay or gravel, on dry banks, and under other adverse conditions. With careful pruning and training, it would be possible to get a 6-8 ft. clearance which would enable you to walk under it.

Because of its odd pattern, it is most effective when used alone and where it may be silhouetted against a wall or sky. It also may be planted with highbush cranberry and oakleaf hydrangea for autumn color border.

ROBINSONELLA CORDATA. Evergreen. Zones 12-13, possibly 10. Hardy to about 25°. Tree or large shrub to 20 ft. with one or more trunks. Foliage medium green, medium sized, much like smaller leafed species of dombeya, also suggestive of mallow. Dense clusters of small hibiscus-like clear blue-lilac flowers envelop entire tree like a blue cloud from February to April. Fast growing, easy culture, needing average water and drainage. Effective in lawn, shrubbery or mixed flower border with Belle of Portugal rose behind, eranthemum and cineraria beneath, and flanked by the shell pink, fragrant lucullia.

ROCKROSE. See CISTUS
ROSE. See p. 264
ROSE OF CHINA. See HIBISCUS
ROSE OF SHARON. See HIBISCUS

RONDELETIA CORDATA. Evergreen. Zones 10, 12-13, limitedly successful in zone 11. Medium to fast growing to 6-8 ft. in southern coastal area, but may grow to 15 ft., with 8 ft. spread under favorable conditions. Upright growth habit when young, becoming loose and spreading at maturity. Clean, glossy, golden-green to dark green, 5-in. opposite leaves. Small tubular soft salmon-pink flowers, with yellow throats, in 6-in. flattish clusters appear profusely in February, with peak show usually in late March, blooming often until June.

Prefers sandy loam but with adequate drainage and fertilizer will tolerate heavy adobe. Best in filtered sun but will take considerable shade. Sensitive to sudden frosts and resents reflected sun from white wall. Bothered by few pests, but is sometimes attacked by beetles and small caterpillars. Easily controlled with spray.

Combine with *Rondeletia amœna*, which is similar, but with more conspicuous ribbing on leaves, considerable bronze in new growth, and slightly later bloom. Particularly effective with *Raphiolepis umbellata ovata, R. indica rosea,* and *Xylosma senticosa.*

ROSMARINUS OFFICINALIS. COMMON ROSEMARY. Evergreen. Zones 3-13. A rugged, picturesque shrub if kept at 4 ft., but will reach 6 ft. if allowed to go its own way. Narrow, aromatic leaves are glossy, dark-green above, grayish-white beneath. Small clusters of light lavender-blue, ½-in. flowers in winter and spring. Var. *Heavenly Blue,* an improved form, grows into a roundish shrub 2-3 ft. high, with semi-trailing branches. Flowers are a truer blue than the species. Var. *alba* has white flowers. Var. *prostratus,* and var. *Lockwoodii* (see chapter on ground covers).

About the only ways you can kill rosemary are to give it too much water, poor drainage, or too rich soil. If starved, it will grow slowly and compactly. It seems to get along best in sun-drenched places rarely reached by the hose.

A favorite low hedge plant. Some plant specialists say it is touchy about being pruned, but we've seen rosemary hedges that have been clipped for many years and are almost as dense as yew. Cut back severely after bloom.

Interesting combined in the dry border with cistus, *Senecio greyii, Teucrium fruticans,* and artemisia.

SARCOCOCCA. Evergreen. Zones 3-13. Partly defoliated at 5°. Increasing in popularity because of ability to maintain orderly growth and polished appearance in complete shade. Adapts itself to hot interiors, cool coast. Three forms are available:

S. ruscifolia. Slow growth, 6 in. a year, to 4-5 ft. with a 3-4 ft. spread. Glossy, waxy, green, ovate, wavy, 2-in. leaves densely set on the branches. Fragrant small white flowers hidden in the foliage during January-March, are followed by red berries that turn blue-black when ripe.

Because of its loose growth habit, S. *ruscifolia* will form a natural espalier if planted close to a wall. Some branches fan out against the wall; forward growing branches can be removed.

S. hookeriana. Very slow growth to a more compact and wider shrub. Leaves narrower. Fruits are a glossy blue-black. Var. *humilis* will spread to 8 ft. before it reaches 1½ ft. in height.

Because of slow growth sarcococca can be treated as a low growing shrub in the many shady locations where height is not wanted. Var. *humilis* will maintain itself as a ground cover under low-branching trees. All are valuable in plantings in car-ports, breezeways, and entrance courts where there is no direct sun at any time.

All prefer slightly acid soil and plenty of moisture. Will take sun in the coolest summer areas.

SCHEFFLERA. Evergreen. Fast growing tropical foliage plants, planted outdoors in zones 12-13 where temperatures remain above 30°, and widely used as indoor plants elsewhere.

S. actinophylla. (*Brassaia actinophylla*). Fast growing to 20 ft., with horizontal tiers of glittering bright green compound leaves of 6-8 oblong 6-in. leaflets. Effectively planted very close in groups of 2-5, each at a different height.

In addition to ample moisture, rich soil and reasonable drainage, the important requirement is full light right down to the base of the plant.

S. digitata. NEW ZEALAND SCHEFFLERA. Evergreen. Adapted to zones 12-13 in colder locations than S. *actinophylla*. Compared to that species, S. *digitata* has rather lax and leaning trunk-like stems that group into clusters; its leaflets are dull rather than highly glossy.

Use as a strongly diagonal espalier against a wall in tub or open ground. When planted where it has space to grow, it becomes a many-stemmed open shrub, spreading to 10 ft. with a height of 15 ft. When conditions are to its liking, will ultimately develop from inconspicuous greenish flowers, airy panicles of tiny bright orange-yellow fruit in autumn.

SENECIO GREYII. (For other senecios, see chapter on perennials.) Zones 4-13. One of the most handsome gray plants—a spreading shrub to 4-5 ft., its stiff, slightly curving stems carrying 3½-in. leathery gray-green leaves outlined with silvery-white. Yellow daisy flowers in summer are not particularly noteworthy. Grows best in full sun in not too rich soil, with little or moderate watering. Prune yearly to keep well filled out with new growth. Combine in sunny borders with geraniums, zauschneria, cistus, rosemary, purple and red-leafed shrubs. Attractive in arrangements with flowers of all colors, particularly scarlet and orange, and lasts extremely long when cut.

SENNA. See CASSIA

SERVICE BERRY. See AMELANCHIER

SHRIMP PLANT. See BELOPERONE GUTTATA

SILVERBERRY. See ELAEAGNUS

SKIMMIA. Evergreen. Hardy except in coldest sections of zone 1. An easy-to-grow natural for zones 3-6, but needs special attention in zones 7-13. Wherever adapted, it's one of the most useful plants for shade. Slow growing, compact, rounded form with glossy, rich green, 2-5 in. leaves carefully arranged. When massed, forms a flat level surface of leaves. Clusters of very tiny white flowers are held above the foliage in April and May. Brilliant red holly-like berries in fall and through December.

S. japonica. (*S. fragrans*). Slow growth to 2-5 ft. high, 3-6 ft. wide. Both male and female plants necessary for berry production.

S. reevesiana (*S. fortunei*). Lower growing to 2 ft. Self-fertile.

S. foremannii. Hybrid between S. *japonica* and S. *reevesiana*. Self-fertile.

In the Northwest, skimmia is not particular as to soil, but should be given peat and sand in all alkali soil areas. Will thrive where azaleas grow. Leaves, yellow in sun, become darker green the deeper the shade.

Plant in shade under low windows. Use to flank entrance walks. Good in tubs and boxes in shady carports. Mass on shady banks.

SOLANUM. NIGHTSHADE. Deciduous and evergreen. Genus includes herbs, trees, shrubs, and vines. (See chapter on vines.) The shrub species planted in the West are:

S. pseudo-capsicum. JERUSALEM CHERRY. Evergreen. Grown outdoors in zone 13; popular as a house plant in colder areas. In warm and protected spots grows to 3-4 ft., with smooth, shiny, 4-in., oblong leaves; white, ½-in. flowers; followed by scarlet or yellow, ½-in. fruit. October-December. Var. *clevelandii* is a low grower to 12 in. high, with red fruit, 1 in. in diameter.

S. rantonnetii. Zone 13. Hardy to 25°. A sprawling, slender-branched, nearly evergreen vine-shrub to 6 ft., with oval, bright green, 4-in. leaves and clusters of violet, yellow-centered, 1-in. flowers, blooming most of the year. If used as a shrub, it should be pruned to keep a bushy habit of growth. Give it support when used as a vine; let it sprawl as a ground cover. Sometimes trained as a standard.

SPARTIUM. BROOM. **See CYTISUS**

SPIRAEA. BRIDAL WREATH. Deciduous. Hardy all zones. Gardeners who know spiræa only as a tall-growing, white-flowering, spreading shrub, should check upon the many varieties in the group. They vary in color, growth habit, and time of bloom. The following are the most commonly available.

S. bumalda Anthony Waterer. Blooms in June after early-flowering spiræas have finished and continues in fall. A dense, stiff, rounded bush to 2-3 ft., with rosy-red flowers in flat-topped clusters. Often used as a perennial plant in flower borders. Pot gardeners move it into the patio when in flower and plunge pot in a remote corner of garden when dormant.

S. cantoniensis. (*S. reevesiana*). REEVES SPIRAEA. Tall-growing to 5-6 ft.; late blooming, June. Bluish-green, smooth leaves and white flowers in dense, rounded clusters.

S. prunifolia plena. BRIDAL WREATH. A graceful plant growing to 6 ft. high and spreading as wide. Small, dark green leaves turn a rich red in fall. Small, double, white flowers are like small rosettes; appear in early spring.

S. thunbergii. A showy, billowy shrub to 5 ft., with very fine-textured foliage that turns to a soft reddish-brown in fall. The first to bloom in early spring. White flowers in rounded clusters.

S. vanhouttei. The most commonly planted. Upright, spreading growth to 6 ft., with long, arching branches. Showy, snow-white flowers in rounded clusters in late spring.

All spiræas are easy to grow. Plant in sun or part shade. Prune annually, cutting flowering wood to the ground as soon as flowers fade.

The tall-growing spiræas are at their best against a background of dark green, evergreen shrubs.

STACHYURUS PRAECOX. Deciduous. Zones 3-13; best adapted in zones 3-6. Very early-blooming shrub to 12 ft. Slender, spreading branches bear ovate 5½-in. leaves. Flower buds formed in autumn, remaining bare and exposed during winter. In colder sections buds are often killed by frost if not protected. Yellow, bell-shaped flowers in slender, drooping, 2-3 in. clusters appear before the leaves in early spring. Small, greenish-yellow berries with reddish cheeks in September and October.

Because it blooms at about the same time, use to supplement forsythia. Fine for background.

STAR BUSH. See TURRAEA OBTUSIFOLIA

STRANVAESIA DAVIDIANA. Evergreen. Zones 3-13. Informal, wide-spreading, robust grower to 6-20 ft. In winter holiday season valuable for cut branches. Clusters of showy red berries compete with purple and bronze,

4-in. leaves from late fall to Christmas. White flowers in 4-in. clusters put on a good spring show.

Although adaptable to many situations, stranvæsia is used mostly in zones 3-6. Must have space to grow in and not overly rich soil. Best when associated informally with vigorous-growing natives.

SYRINGA. LILAC. Deciduous. Hardy all zones, but adaptability varies by species and culture. The common lilac, one of our oldest garden plants, has gone through many years of selection and hybridization. Today the fragrant lilac ranges in color from pure white to pinks, magentas, lavenders, and deep purples. Growth habit varies from low and spreading to tall and upright.

S. chinensis. CHINESE LILAC. Not a native of China as the name implies, but a hybrid of the common and Persian lilac. Considered more graceful in growth and of finer foliage texture than the common lilac. Airy, open clusters of rose-purple flowers in great profusion in May.

S. persica. PERSIAN LILAC. Graceful, loose form to 6 ft., with arching branches and 2½-in., pointed leaves. Clusters of pale violet flowers make a billowy mass in May. Var. *laciniata* has lobed or cut leaves that appear fern-like. Blossoms are continuously distributed along the branches.

Both the Persian and Chinese lilac are better adapted to hot-summer climates than the common lilac and are commonly available in Southern California nurseries.

S. vulgaris. COMMON LILAC. Shrub or small tree to 20 ft. There are more than 90 varieties listed by wholesalers and another 100 or more are available from specialists. These few suggest the variations in color:

WHITE: *Ellen Willmott*, heavy, compact flower clusters.

PINK: *Alice Eastwood*, double flowers, claret-colored in bud, opening to a deep pink; *Marechal Foch*, single, pink blossoms in graceful sprays.

BLUE: *President Lincoln*, single, large flowers of wedgewood blue; *Blue Hyacinth*, individual flowers like those of hyacinths are very large and a bright blue; *Ami Schott*, double, light blue flowers offset with pink buds.

DEEP PURPLE-RED: *President Poincaré*, double, dark reddish-purple flowers that fade to lavender; *Volcan*, single, delicate, fluffy, purple flowers.

Lilacs need a slightly alkaline soil. Where it's acid, as in parts of the Pacific Northwest, treat with a ½-in. layer of lime, lightly cultivated into the surface of the soil beneath the dry-line of the plants.

Plant in full sun in cool-summer climates; give filtered shade where sun is hot.

Lilacs need a cold dormant season to produce full quota of bloom. Growers in warm-winter climates should force dormancy by drying off the plant after it has flowered. Water generously when in flower, but withhold water from August on.

No drastic pruning necessary with this long-lived shrub, but light pruning and pinching from the start can be used to direct and control growth.

Scale insects are often a problem. Two dormant oil sprays between December and February 15th will clean them up.

As back-of-the-flower-border shrubs, the lilacs lift up colors from low-growing annuals and perennials into the sky.

TAMARIX. TAMARISK. Deciduous. Climate adaptability by species. Remarkably adaptable plants that take kindly to salt spray along the seacoast as well as to the heat, drought, and alkaline soil of the desert.

T. aphylla. (*T. articulata*). ATHEL TREE. Grows to 30 ft., sometimes taller, with jointed branchlets that are greenish and give the tree an evergreen appearance in winter. Minute sheathing leaves are like beefwood. Pink flowers in terminal clusters appear several times a year.

T. gallica. FRENCH TAMARISK. Shrub or small tree to 12 or sometimes to 30 ft., with grayish foliage on long, arching branches. White or lavender-pink flowers in slender, 1-2 in. clusters, in summer.

T. parviflora. (usually listed as *T. africana*, which species is probably not in cultivation). Grows to 15 ft. with graceful, airy, arching branches with reddish bark. Pink flowers in 1-1½ in. spikes on the branches of the previous year, in spring.

T. pentandra. (*T. hispida æstivalis*). SALT CEDAR. Spreading, feathery shrub to 15 ft. Small, pale blue-green leaves. Tiny, pink flowers in branched clusters to 3 ft. from July until fall.

Tamarisk, although adaptable to rugged conditions, appreciates good garden conditions. Carefully prune in winter to thin out the center and prune back old flowering branches.

The Athel tree (*T. aphylla*) is a notoriously good windbreak for desert gardens. Several grouped together provide welcome shade. *T. parviflora* and *T. pentandra*, while also suitable for low windbreaks and informal hedges, may also be planted for decorative effect in shrubbery borders. They are particularly effective when pruned to form graceful, pendulous shrubs, under which bulbs, small shrubs, and flowers may be planted to advantage. The rank, sprawling habit of *T. gallica*, that makes it of little use in smaller gardens, requires the spaciousness of larger properties to be effective. Because it produces best when cut to the ground every spring, it should be used as a background plant to conceal its nakedness during the off season. It has escaped cultivation and become native in Texas, Arizona, and New Mexico.

TARATA. See PITTOSPORUM

TAWHIWHI. See PITTOSPORUM

TEA TREE. See LEPTOSPERMUM

TERNSTROEMIA GYMNANTHERA. (*T. japonica*). Evergreen. Zones 3-13. Its restrained growth and quiet elegance place it high on the list of shrubs of landscape value. Slow growing to 5-8 ft. high and as wide, and can be held back by pruning. Handsome, dark green to bronze, 2-in. leaves with red stalks. Foliage becomes quite bronze and shiny in full sun. Cream colored, slightly fragrant, ¾-in. flowers, bloom May-June.

Valued for its glossy, polished foliage and unusual adaptability to various soils and climates. Successfully grown in desert areas when given shade. Give it the same culture as its relative, the camellia.

Effective companion plants are camellia, azalea, nandina, clethra.

TETRAPANAX PAPYRIFERUM. (*Fatsia papyrifera*). RICE PAPER PLANT. Evergreen. Zones 9-13. Hardy to about 25°. In cold sections of 9 and 11 frequently freezes to the main stem or to the ground. Slender, curving, tan or taupe-gray trunk, may sprout stems from the base, or again from spreading roots to form a colony of varying heights. Foot-wide, deeply lobed leaves in clusters radiating from the tops of the stems. Leaves gray-green above, almost white beneath, increase in size with maturity. Incidental but effective are the giant clusters of creamy-white flowers on tan, furry stems, in December.

Some shade in hot inland valleys, but can be gradually acclimated to almost any exposure. Tolerates almost any soil. Long-established clumps difficult to eradicate either by freezing or drought because of deep root system that spreads by underground runners.

Shadow pattern from the large, long-stemmed leaves is an important element in garden design; especially suited to patios or against walls. If you must plant beneath them, use self-sufficient plants like *Fatsia japonica*, Acanthus, and *Melianthus major*.

TEUCRIUM. GERMANDER. Evergreen. Zones 4-13. Two species of germander are excellent choices for sunny dry locations. They are heat and drought resistant and require little attention.

T. fruticans. BUSH GERMANDER. Silver-stemmed loose shrub to 4-5 ft. Ovate 1¼-in. leaves gray-green above, silvery-white beneath—the over-all effect is silvery-gray. Lavender-blue ¾-in. flowers in spikes at the ends of the branches bloom most of the year.

Does well in hot locations, can take heavy soil, and requires little water. Thin and cut back in late winter or early spring.

Use it as an informal hedge, against a redwood screen, or in a curved mass near the end of a lawn area, but far enough from it to avoid overwatering. Bring its color out fully by planting next to reddish foliaged shrubs or trees such as phormium and purple leafed plum.

T. chamaedrys. Hardy to 0°. Low growing to 1 ft., spreading to 2 ft., with thickly set, dark green toothed ¾-in. leaves; rose or red-purple ¾-in. flowers in loose spikes in summer.

Plant in full sun in almost any well drained soil. Will rot in heavy soil. Water moderately. Cut back after flowering.

An especially good little edging plant that can substitute for boxwood. For foregrounds of evergreen plantings or as low bordering hedge in the perennial or rose garden.

THEVETIA NEREIFOLIA. YELLOW OLEANDER. Evergreen. Zones 12 and 13, best in 8a around Palm Springs, Brawley and Yuma, where there is highest light intensity, hottest sun and little frost. Grows to 4-6 ft. in one season in this area and after several frost free years may attain a height of 15-20 ft. Round-headed shrub with light open structure and arresting golden-green foliage of long narrow 6-in. leaves. Although not profuse, the fragrant yellow or apricot, 2-3 in., funnel-shaped flowers bloom almost constantly from June through November.

Most effective with parkinsonia, *Callistemon viminalis*, oleander, and many cacti. (One plant which measured 20 ft. through and as high against a south wall in hills above Phoenix, Arizona, furnished quite a sight in mid-May flanked by a pair of magnificent bronze bougainvilleas.)

THRYALLIS GLAUCA. Evergreen. Zones 8a, 12 and 13. Soft rather open shrub to 5 ft., with red stems clothed with 2-in. leaves that are dark green, strongly flecked with bronze-red shadings. Abundant many-flowered clusters of deep yellow ¾-in. flowers adorn the shrubs from summer to late fall. Well adapted to warmth, drought, and sterile soil, but also does well with average water and fertilizer if drainage is excellent. Fine foil for *Acacia pendula*; a sequence subject for *Catha edulis* and *Berberis thunbergii atropurpurea*.

THUJA. ARBORVITAE. Conifer. (Also see chapter on trees.) Hardy all zones. A dependable group of evergreen conifers ranging from trees 100 ft. or more tall to shrub forms less than a foot high. They all have scale-like leaves in flat sprays, often carried on edge. Foliage is usually yellow-green, varying to golden. Thujas are neat, contained plants—never surprising or dramatic—always compact and symmetrical, either round, oblong, or pyramidal in habit.

The dwarf and shrub forms are limited in garden use by their definite outline and positive color. They are easiest to use as a hedge. Most of them are forms of the tree species *T. orientalis* or *T. occidentalis*. The forms of *T. orientalis* tend to be more compact and symmetrical. They have, in general, fan-like, flattened sprays of foliage carried vertically, giving the plants a definite, linear look. Some varieties are susceptible to a blight and need spraying in the fall. The forms of *T. occidentalis* are generally faster growing, more spreading and open, with a looser, coarser texture than those forms of *T. orientalis*. Foliage habit not quite so vertical in effect. Generally hardier. Has a tendency to turn brown in winter.

Thujas prefer moist, rich, well-drained soil; need protection from burning winds when young, tend to "brown out" in winter. When they need trimming, they should be thinned from the inside, never sheared.

The dwarf forms and shrubs can be divided into groups by their well-defined shapes.

Small, round forms: The smallest arborvitæs are very round and globe-like. They can be used singly in rock gardens, as tub plants, or in a line as a small, formal border or divider.

T. occidentalis globosa. GLOBE ARBORVITAE. Makes a small, compact ball to 18 in. in diameter. Foliage bright green.

T. occidentalis nana. LITTLE GLOBE ARBORVITAE. A similar, dwarf form.

T. occidentalis umbraculifera. Has a rounded top. but is not completely globe-shaped.

T. occidentalis woodwardii. A larger variety, spreading to 3 ft. in diameter. Medium green foliage turning shades of brown in Northwest winters.

T. orientalis Rosedale. Grows to 4 ft. A rather irregular, globe-shaped plant. Blue-green foliage turns bronze enough to make it useful for fall color.

T. orientalis sieboldii. Another neat, low, compact, globular shrub. Bright green foliage.

Pyramidal, columnar, and rounded, upright forms: The shrubs in this group range from 5-20 ft. Pyramidal forms are easiest to use as single plants. Columnar and rounded, upright (elliptical) forms can also be used as shrub borders, hedges, or backgrounds. The smaller ones can be used in foundation plantings.

Forms with golden foliage: Arborvitæ have some of the best golden forms of any of the conifers. New growth is golden-yellow, changing slowly to green. Color is brightest in the spring but holds throughout the year. Good for winter color, year-around accent.

T. occidentalis aureo-variegata. GOLDSPOT ARBORVITAE. An upright, rounded form with golden-yellow, variegated foliage. Doesn't brown badly, takes trimming well, and makes a good hedge.

T. occidentalis lutea. GEORGE PEABODY ARBORVITAE. Pyramidal in form. New growth is light yellow-gold that holds well in winter.

T. orientalis aurea-nana. BERCKMANN'S GOLDEN ARBORVITAE. Makes a low, compact, broad, rounded pyramid that will eventually reach 5 ft. Handsome, bright golden, new foliage on slender twigs. Very slow growing An excellent garden specimen. Can be used, with care, in foundation plantings. Very good winter color.

T. orientalis beverleyensis. GOLDEN PYRAMID ARBORVITAE. Upright, pyramidal shrub of interesting open form, growing to 10 ft. Larger and looser in habit than Berckmann's golden arborvitæ. Good color. A valuable accent plant.

T. orientalis bonita. BONITA ARBORVITAE. Narrow, pyramidal, cone-shaped, to 18-20 ft. Leaves tipped with golden-yellow.

Forms with green foliage:

T. occidentalis hoveyi. HOVEY ARBORVITAE. A very hardy variety growing to 6-8 ft. Upright, rounded, with medium green foliage. Turns brown in severe winters.

T. occidentalis fastigiata. (*T. o. pyramidalis*). AMERICAN PYRAMIDAL ARBORVITAE. Narrow, compact, columnar plant, fast growing to 15-25 ft. Deep green foliage tends to brown up in winter. Planted close together makes an excellent low-maintenance hedge. Impressive alpine effect when planted in groups. Needs moist soil.

T. occidentalis robusta. WARE ARBORVITAE. Strong, fast grower to 6-8 ft. Pyramidal habit; deep green leaves.

T. occidentalis spiralis. DOUGLAS PYRAMIDAL ARBORVITAE. A stiff, pyramidal plant to 18-20 ft., with yellow-green foliage. Branching makes a spiral pattern. Interesting as an individual.

T. orientalis stricta. (*T. o. pyramidalis*). GREEN PYRAMID ARBORVITAE. Pyramidal habit; dense, deep green foliage.

TIBOUCHINA SEMIDECANDRA. (*Pleroma splendens*). PRINCESS FLOWER. Evergreen. Zones 10-13, best in zone 13; limited by frost and dry air in zone 11. Among the showiest of our subtropical shrubs to 5-15 ft. Foliage of exquisitely ribbed, velvety green 4-in. leaves that are thinly edged with red. Branch tips, buds and new growth conspicuously shaded with orange and red-bronze dense velvety hairs. Considerable red in older leaves adding autumnal touch especially in winter months. Brilliant purple 3-in. blossoms in terminal clusters appear intermittently from early May to January, at times covering entire bush. Performs best in somewhat acid soil with its roots in the shade where it is cool at all times, and its head in the sun; or on east exposure protected from strong wind. Grows rapidly, developing a somewhat leggy habit. Easily overcome by some pruning after each mass of bloom, and heavy pruning in early spring, followed by generous feeding of iron sulfate and ammonium phosphate. Strong coloring of both leaves and flowers requires careful placement in the garden. Especially pleasing with *Viburnum rhytidophyllum* and heliotrope. Equally effective with *Bougainvillea braziliensis*, *Limonium perezii* and perhaps *Plumbago capensis*.

TURRAEA OBTUSIFOLIA. STAR BUSH. Charming, slightly temperamental shrub, slow growing to an eventual 4-5 ft., with roundish 2 in. leaves. Produces quantities of pure white, 1½-in. flowers, like loosely open stars, arranged in corsage-like clusters over the entire bush. Long season of bloom, at its peak Sept.-Oct. Must have perfectly drained soil, high shade or an east exposure without much reflected heat.

Attractive planted with hebe Autumn Glory, whose blue flowers precede those of the star bush. Also delightful in front of ternstrœmia, mature specimens of nandina, or *Brunfelsia calycina floribunda*.

VERONICA. See **HEBE**

VIBURNUM. Deciduous or evergreen. Climate adaptability by species. The viburnum group is a large one, and its members vary widely in appearance, general uses, and cultural requirements. In choosing between them you are concerned with distinct differences.

There are more than 30 species and varieties available in Western nurseries. The following are the favored ones. To point up the differences we have classified them under evergreen and deciduous, fragrant and non-fragrant species.

Deciduous—fragrant flowers

Whether *V. burkwoodii* or *V. carlesii* should head this group depends on your winter climate. The former is preferred in moderately cold winter climates, and the latter is the only one widely distributed in Southern California.

V. burkwoodii. Hybrid between *V. carlesii* and *V. utile*. More successful in zones 2-6 than in 7-13. To 5-7 ft. high, 4-5 ft. wide. Dark green, glossy, ribbed, leaves, to 3½ in. long, become purplish-bronze after first frost. Almost evergreen; out of leaf for very short time. Rounded, 4-in. clusters of white flowers, pink in bud stage. Blooms as leaves unfold from February-March, depending on climate.

Early growth is quite straggly, but matures into handsome plant. Blue-black berries in fall.

V. carlesii. In cold winter gardens, this hardy parent of the more tender *V. burkwoodii* is probably the highest scoring viburnum—outstanding for fragrance, early flowering, flower color, and velvety-red, soft fall color.

V. fragrans. The earliest of all viburnums to bloom. Less hardy, larger growing that *V. carlesii*. Smaller flower cluster, more pink than white.

All 3 in the group are of similar height and form. All prefer a position where they get dappled shade of high branching trees or an eastern exposure.

Deciduous—non-fragrant flowers

A group of tall-growing shrubs in which are found the varieties bearing the large, white snowballs.

V. opulis. EUROPEAN CRANBERRY BUSH. HIGHBUSH CRANBERRY. Used mostly in zones 1-5. To 12-15 ft. high, 7-10 ft. wide. Maple-like, 3-5 lobed, 4-in. leaves are dark green turning red in autumn. Round, white, 4-in. heads of white flowers, May-June. Showy, scarlet fruits in fall.

V. o. nanum. Miniature form seldom over 2 ft. high with small, bronzy leaves and red stems. Foliage plant, rarely flowers.

V. o. roseum. (Var. *sterile*). COMMON SNOWBALL. Large, snowball-like heads of pure white, sterile flowers, no berries.

V. tomentosum. DOUBLEFILE VIBURNUM. Popular in zones 1-6. Grows to 10 ft. Ovate, 4-in. leaves. Flattish, 4-in. clusters of white flowers in May. Fruits are first red, then blue-black in fall.

V. t. sterile. (*V. t. plenum*). JAPANESE SNOWBALL. White and greenish-white sterile flowers in large round clusters, no fruits. Those who have had aphis trouble with the common snowball (*V. opulus roseum*) should give this hardy variety a trial.

V. t. mariesii. Wide spreading, horizontal branches in tiers. Flat, white flower clusters all along the branches.

The sterile forms give the best show of flowers. All tall-growing viburnums can be trained as a small tree. Give full sun or partial shade.

Evergreen—fragrant flowers

V. odoratissimum. SWEET VIBURNUM. In zones 7-13 where given protection of house or high wall and deep, moist soil. To 10-12 ft. high and 12-15 ft. wide. Handsome, dark green, varnished, ovate leaves to 6 in. long. Many turn red in the fall. Fragrant, white flowers in oblong, 4-in. clusters in late spring and early summer.

Berries, first red, then black, are very attractive in the red stage.

Slow to get going but a worthwhile addition where such a large shrub can be used.

V. rhytidophyllum. LEATHERLEAF VIBURNUM. Zones 4-13. Widely adapted. Does well in hot interiors if given semi-shade and plenty of water. A bold, handsome shrub to 6-10 ft. high with a 4-8 ft. spread. Deeply wrinkled leaves 7 in. long, dark green and shiny above, gray or white-hairy beneath. Huge, 8 in. wide, flat clusters of yellowish-white flowers in April. Berries, first red, then black.

V. suspensum. SANDANKWA VIBURNUM. Zones 7-13. To 8-10 ft. high and as wide. Bright green, glossy, ovate leaves to 4 in. Pinkish flowers in 1½-in. clusters, in June-July. Berries red, then blackish.

Foliage has hard-to-define odor. Must be sprayed for aphis at intervals. Beautiful foliage when clean.

V. tinus. LAURESTINUS VIBURNUM. Zones 3-13. The most widely distributed evergreen viburnum. To 10 ft. high and as wide. Dark green, glossy, oblong leaves, to 3 in. White or pinkish flowers in flattish, 3-in. clusters, bloom over a period of several months in fall, winter, and early spring. Berries black or deep blue.

Susceptible to mildew along coast, so needs free circulation of air around it. Give plenty of water except in late summer, as forcing it may cause lush growth liable to be damaged by cold.

V. t. lucidum. (*V. lucidum*). SHINING LAURESTINUS. Has larger leaves. Does not mildew.

V. t. robustum. A trade-name, horticultural variety widely sold in Southern California. Similar to *V. tinus lucidum*, but has coarser and rougher foliage, and less pink in flowers. Does not mildew; no special care or culture. Good background shrub or informal hedge.

V. t. strictum. To 6-10 ft. high and 3 ft. wide. Leaves somewhat more ovate than *V. tinus*. White flowers, slightly pink in bud, in 4-6 in. clusters. Late winter and early spring. Black berries. Late spring to fall.

Excellent for hot places. Can be used where a formal accent plant with interesting leaf is needed. Disease-resistant.

Evergreen—non-fragrant flowers

There is wide variety in form and climate preference in this group.

V. davidii. Very choice and useful in zones 3-5, but practically useless in mild-winter areas of California. Low growing to 2-3 ft. and as wide. Leaves very large for the size of the plant, are dark green, deeply veined, elliptical, to 5½ in., with margins slightly toothed. Small, white, comparatively insignificant flowers in 3-in. clusters. Clusters of metallic, turquoise-blue berries.

Attractive throughout the year, it is valuable as low-growing foundation plant and as foreground shrub in shrub borders.

V. japonicum. (*V. macrophyllum*). JAPANESE VIBURNUM. Widely distributed in zones 11-13; less in zones 7-10; no sale in 1-6. To 10 ft. high and as wide. Dark green, glossy, ovate leaves to 6 in. long, with margins slightly toothed above the middle of the leaf. Seldom blooms. Flowers are white, flattish, 4-in. clusters. Red berries in fall. Easy to grow but needs regular spray program to keep free of aphis and red spider.

VITEX AGNUS-CASTUS. CHASTE TREE. Deciduous. Zones 2-13. Shrub with gray twigs; leaves divided fanwise into 5-7 4-in. leaflets that are dark green above, gray beneath. Conspicuous spikes of lavender-blue flowers suggestive of lilacs, bloom in summer and early fall. Winter branch pattern has unusual value.

Plant varies in size from 8 to 12 ft. on rocky, dry, hot hillsides in its northern range, to 25 ft. along the irrigation ditches of Phoenix area, where it is a valuable shade tree. However, in rich, moist soil the bloom is much paler, scarce, and inferior in quality. Needs summer heat for abundant bloom; probably at its best in the San Joaquin and inner coastal valleys, also in desert sections of south.

Combines startlingly with *Poinciana gilliesii, Spartium junceum*, and *Daubentonia tripetii* or the lighter shades of crape myrtle. Also good with the smaller-leafed grays.

WEIGELA. Deciduous. Hardy all zones. Holds its own even in the land of the broad-leafed evergreens because it furnishes color after the color of the many spring flowering shrubs is gone.

W. florida (*W. rosea*). Fast growth to 8-10 ft. high and 6-8 ft. wide. Rather coarse and rangy with arching branches. Dark green, pointed, 4-in. leaves. Pink to red, 1-in., funnel-shaped flowers are crowded along entire length of flowering branches, in May and June.

W. f. variegata. Widely available and popular. Has rather bright cream-and-green splotched foliage.

Other species and numerous varieties are available in a variety of colors ranging from white through pale pink to deep red. Var. *Bristol Ruby* has large, ruby-red flowers in late spring with recurrent displays in midsummer and fall. Var. *Eva Rathke* is lower in growth, to 3-4 ft., with deep red flowers that appear a month later than most weigelas.

Weigela calls for no special care other than pruning, which must be done to maintain an attractive shrub. After flowering, prune the branches that have bloomed back to the unflowered laterals. Leave only one or two laterals per stem. Cut some of the oldest stumps to the ground. Thin new suckers to a few of the most vigorous.

Use as backgrounds in perennial border or as summer screens. The low-growing types can be used as colorful space dividers within the garden.

XYLOSMA SENTICOSA. Evergreen. Adapted in zones 7-13. Hardy to 10°. Thrives in desert heat. Extremely tolerant of various soils. No pests. Should be rated as one of the most useful evergreen shrubs for California-Arizona. A shrub so durable and also beautiful is more than a gardener has the right to expect. Grows in a spreading manner to 4-6 ft. with clean-cut, always attractive, lustrous, yellowish-green foliage. In spring plant is highlighted with bronzy new growth at the tips of the branches. The leaves are pointed ovals 2 in. long. Flowers not conspicuous to the eye, are slightly fragrant.

Xylosma thrives in full sun and will take shade. Can be clipped to form a hedge but will get woody. It's at its best trained informally against a wall, or cascading over a wall, or as a bank ground cover.

Shrubs

CAMELLIAS

Camellias are the most democratic of the garden aristocrats. They are ready to reward with exquisite perfection in flower and foliage any gardener in any climate on the Pacific Coast. To the collector they are a never-ending source of surprise. The commonly known *C. japonica* seems capable of producing endless variety in flower form, and though it is limited to white, red, and intermediate colors, the variations and combinations it offers in this range are extensive. Despite the great number of pinks and reds, each introduction offers something new.

The delicate beauty and much wider landscape use of *C. sasanqua* is generally overlooked by those with the spectacular beauty of *C. japonica* on their minds, but it is worthy of special attention as a valuable shrub in its own right.

CAMELLIA JAPONICA

Reading a camellia catalog is a bewildering experience. Page after page of varieties and all wonderful. A little less confusing is a shopping trip through the nursery when they are in bloom. Among the hundreds of varieties there are a few in each color class and each form class that refuse to be outmoded, no matter how many new varieties are introduced. We list some of such camellias here, not as a tight recommended list but as worthwhile representatives of the various colors and forms.

Flower forms represented in the following list and illustrated on the next page:

Semi-double: More than 9 petals, usually 14 to 20, with central stamens.

Incomplete double: Numerous petals intermixed with stamens.

Complete double: Few or no stamens, petals regularly imbricated (overlapped), incompletely imbricated, or arranged irregularly in a convex mass. Stamens are fewer or absent as the number of petals increases.

Culture

Check the places where camellias are grown—in Southern California, in the interior valleys, along the entire coastal strip, in the Willamette Valley, on the shores of Lake Washington—and you can be sure that these aristocrats of the garden are most tolerant of soils and climate. Certainly the old tree-sized specimens have long since outgrown any special soil given them when they were planted.

But the home garden cannot rely on their adaptability. Certain basic requirements should be met.

Give camellias an acid soil. If your soil is alkaline make the planting hole 2 by 2 feet and refill below and around the plant with a mixture of peat moss, oak leaves, rotted manure and topsoil. Add sulfur if topsoil or water is highly alkaline.

Provide perfect drainage. If the soil in your garden is a heavy clay, plant in a raised bed 18 inches above the clay in a mixture of organic material and loam.

Mulch with peat or compost to keep roots cool and to provide a continuous supply of organic material.

Feed with fertilizers that give an acid reaction. Make light applications before growth starts in the spring and again about 4 months later.

Keep the soil moist. Establish a schedule of watering according to your soil and weather.

Daily syringing of leaves through the summer months promotes healthier plants.

Filtered shade of high branching trees gives ideal light conditions. Lath cover is best substitute. At least protect from hot sun by planting on east or north side of the house.

RED

Adolphe Audusson

FLOWER: Extremely large, dark red, semi-double of good substance, with a cylinder of prominent, yellow stamens.

BLOOM PERIOD: Midseason.

GROWTH HABIT: Rapid, compact; small leafed, dark, glossy foliage.

COMMENTS: An outstanding red that occasionally throws beautiful variegated sports.

Blood of China (*Victor Emmanuel*)

FLOWER: Salmon-red, large, semi-double.

BLOOM PERIOD: Late.

GROWTH HABIT: Vigorous, compact.

COMMENTS: Some consider late bloom a disadvantage. New growth appears while flowers are in bloom, causing buds to drop. Not free blooming. Performance is variable.

C. M. Hovey (*Colonel Firey*)

FLOWER: Dark red, large, regularly imbricated double.

BLOOM PERIOD: Mid-late.

GROWTH HABIT: Medium, slender.

COMMENTS: Although this old-timer seems to be losing ground in the favorite column, it is still considered finest of red camellias by its supporters. Shy blooming when young. Bloom often bleaches out.

Flame

FLOWER: Very large, semi-double of deep, flame red, with prominent, yellow stamens.

254 CAMELLIAS Shrubs

BLOOM PERIOD: Midseason.

GROWTH HABIT: Fast, vigorous, upright, but not compact.

COMMENTS: One of the most beautiful reds.

Coquette *(Glen 40)*

FLOWER: Deep red, incompletely imbricated double.

BLOOM PERIOD: Midseason to late.

GROWTH HABIT: Slow, compact, upright.

COMMENTS: The flowers show an unusual undertone of orange.

Mathotiana *(Julia Drayton, Purple Emperor, Mathotiana Rubra)*

FLOWER: Carmine, very large, incompletely imbricated double. Distinct, deeper colored veins.

BLOOM PERIOD: Midseason to late.

GROWTH HABIT: Upright, with branches growing out and up; broad, blunt tipped leaves, often reflexed along margins.

COMMENTS: One of the heaviest, largest blooms. As the flower ages outer edges turn purple.

Pope Pius IX

FLOWER: Rose-red, large, regularly imbricated double.

BLOOM PERIOD: Midseason.

GROWTH HABIT: Medium fast, somewhat compact, upright.

COMMENTS: Long-lasting blooms make this one of the finest reds for corsages.

Ville de Nantes

FLOWER: Large, semi-double, dark turkey-red, sometimes spotted with white, frequently fluted, with serrated petals.

BLOOM PERIOD: Early to midseason.

GROWTH HABIT: Medium to slow, fairly compact, upright.

COMMENTS: Not a large flower, but repeatedly a camellia-show winner.

PINK

Debutante

FLOWER: Most delicate light pink, large, irregular complete double form with tightly clustered petals.

BLOOM PERIOD: Early to midseason.

GROWTH HABIT: Vigorous, upright.

COMMENTS: Shy blooming when young. Excellent for corsages.

Eleanor Hagood

FLOWER: Pale pink, medium to large, regularly imbricated double.

BLOOM PERIOD: Late.

GROWTH HABIT: Rapid, upright.

COMMENTS: Regarded as equal to *Pink Perfection* without the bud-drop habit of that old favorite.

High Hat

FLOWER: Pale pink sport of *Daikagura*, with irregular complete double flowers.

BLOOM PERIOD: Early. Buds open at different times from November through March.

GROWTH HABIT: Slow, compact; long, sharp-pointed leaves.

COMMENTS: An excellent corsage flower.

Kumasaka

FLOWER: Large rose-pink, incomplete double. Petaloids mixed with stamens.

BLOOM PERIOD: Midseason to late.

GROWTH HABIT: Rapid, compact, upright, rounded shrub.

COMMENTS: Should be in every garden. Free blooming, even as a young plant. An old-timer that we can safely recommend to every gardener.

Lady Clare *(Grandiflora rosea)*

FLOWER: Deep pink, almost red, 5-6 inch semi-double with long, yellow stamens in a central cylinder.

BLOOM PERIOD: Midseason.

GROWTH HABIT: Rapid, hardy, bushy, spreading, horizontal branching.

COMMENTS: Very free flowering. Will always be a favorite. Because of horizontal branching habit, it is excellent for espaliering.

WHITE

Alba plena

FLOWER: Perfectly formed, pure white, regularly imbricated double, 4 in. and larger, that never shows stamens.

BLOOM PERIOD: Early.

GROWTH HABIT: Slow, bushy.

COMMENTS: Regarded in California as the best white, one of the finest camellias grown. Gets into trouble because of its early blooming in the Northwest.

Finlandia *(Dearest, Nellie White)*

FLOWER: Large, semi-double, white, with fluted petals golden stamens.

BLOOM PERIOD: Early to midseason.

GROWTH HABIT: Medium. Compact foliage but branches are spaced far apart, making it an open plant.

COMMENTS: White as snow; golden stamens add to its airiness.

Purity

FLOWER: White, regularly imbricated double, sometimes showing short stamens.

BLOOM PERIOD: Late.

GROWTH HABIT: Vigorous, upright.

COMMENTS: One of the hardiest of the white camellias. An old-timer and very reliable. Late blooming is an advantage in white camellias, as rain damage can often be avoided.

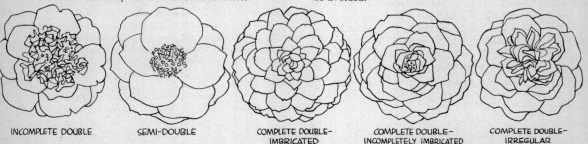

INCOMPLETE DOUBLE | SEMI-DOUBLE | COMPLETE DOUBLE-IMBRICATED | COMPLETE DOUBLE-INCOMPLETELY IMBRICATED | COMPLETE DOUBLE-IRREGULAR

RED AND WHITE

Donckelari
FLOWER: Very large semi-double of glowing red, strikingly marbled white.
BLOOM PERIOD: Midseason.
GROWTH HABIT: Slow, bushy.
COMMENTS: One of the finest of its type. Variable in amount of variegation.

Finlandia Variegated *(Margaret Jack)*
FLOWER: Variegated form of white Finlandia, large-fluted, semi-double white streaked crimson, with prominent, golden stamens.
BLOOM PERIOD: Midseason to late.
GROWTH HABIT: Medium, compact foliage, but branching habit is open.
COMMENTS: Sometimes displays exciting variegations from almost pure white to pure pink.

PINK AND WHITE

Chandleri Elegans Variegated
FLOWER: Very large, incomplete double, rose-pink and white.
BLOOM PERIOD: Early to midseason.
GROWTH HABIT: Slow, spreading.
COMMENTS: An old favorite but a must in any collection. Its habit of growth makes it easy to espalier.

Daikagura Variegated *(Kivosu)*
FLOWER: Large, irregular complete double, bright rose-pink splotched white. Small petaloids, clustered in center.
BLOOM PERIOD: Early and over long period.
GROWTH HABIT: Slow, compact.
COMMENTS: Generally flowers in fall when no camellias are out and there are still a few blooms in March. Seems to have a permanent place in the camellia Hall of Fame. Unfortunately foliage is subject to winter damage in Northwest.

Nagasaki *(Nikenjaku, Empress of Russia, Candida Elegantissima)*
FLOWER: Very large, semi-double of rose-pink marbled white to almost solid white, many stamens in full, open flower.
BLOOM PERIOD: Early to midseason.
GROWTH HABIT: Slow, spreading, liable to go out of balance.

COMMENTS: In California, begins blooming in November and continues through camellia season.

CAMELLIA SASANQUA

This willowy shrub should be compared not to *C. japonica* but to all winter-blooming vines or viny shrubs. Only then can its many virtues be seen: Has polished, dark green foliage every month of the year; restrained in growth; pliable enough to be trained as vine, espaliered, or used as ground cover.

Its growth habit varies from strong and upright to weeping, to arching in form.

Varieties offer choice of single, semi-double, and double forms in many color variations: dainty, white blossoms edged with pink, resembling apple blossoms; single, cup-shaped, white flowers with a faint blush of peach to lavender; soft pink, semi-double, boutonniere flowers.

CAMELLIA RETICULATA

A new race of reticulatas—the first to come out of China since the importation of Captain Rawes of *C. reticulata* itself into England in 1820—now is available on the Pacific Coast.

These are representative of the varieties:

Great Butterfly Wings. Semi-double, 6-inch flowers, varying from deep rose-pink to light crimson. Large, long, fluted petals rise from center of bloom at various angles like butterfly wings. Center is quite open, showing stamens in single compact group.

Shot Silk. Flowers, 4 inches across, are light pink, pin-pointed with a deeper shade. In bright sunlight these pin-points sparkle like diamond points. Fluted petals are arranged in loose, spherical balls that hang down from the branches like Japanese lanterns.

Chang's Temple. According to Chinese sources, this variety was discovered recently in the ruins of Chang's Temple. Deep pink to light red flowers variegated with white, with wavy, fluted petals. Described in Chinese literature as flowers 6-8 inches across—but has not attained these proportions in America.

Shrubs FUCHSIAS

The fuchsia is the delight of the beginner in gardening and of the specialist as well. The fuchsia likes to grow. It's dependable and demands no special diet or unusual care; it is attacked by few pests and is resistant to most diseases. At the same time it is almost instantaneously responsive to any attention bestowed upon it, especially to regular watering and feeding. It is so easily propagated by cuttings and grows so enthusiastically that there's no excuse for having anything short of a perfect plant. You can always have a stand-in ready to replace the imperfect ones.

Climate Adaptation

Fuchsias grow to perfection in a rich, moist, slightly acid soil, moist atmosphere, and filtered sunlight. They are naturals in the mild fog-cooled coastal climates.

In the interior climates—zones 7, 11, 12—they should have protection of lath or a wide spreading tree.

Overhead sprinkling, moist mulches, and wind protection will help make up for lack of moisture in the air.

In the warmer sections of zones 4 and 5, fuchsias are grown with winter protection of the roots by mulching with sawdust or peat. In the colder sections and throughout zones 1-2, they can be given complete winter protection by one of these methods:

If grown in containers, pots or boxes, cut them back before the first frost, let them dry off, and store them in basement or greenhouse. Surround the containers with sawdust or peat and keep this surrounding mulch damp through the winter.

If grown in the ground, dig them out with a good sized ball of earth and lay them on their sides in a trench. The depth of the trench will depend upon how deep the ground freezes but an 8-inch cover of sawdust or peat is generally enough insulation. In spring, after the last killing frost, you'll find the buried fuchsia sprouted and ready to grow.

Soil and Water

If you want to give them special soil, add well-rotted manure and leaf mold to the soil of your garden until it's crumbly and water drains through it rapidly. Generally, ⅓ leaf mold, ⅓ manure, and ⅓ topsoil gives the desired soil structure.

The fuchsia is shallow rooting and requires water frequently so drainage must be fast enough to carry away all excess.

A 3-inch mulch of peat or sawdust will keep roots cool and supply moist air when watered frequently.

You can't overwater fuchsias if drainage is good. Keep the soil in and around the root zone moist at all times. This may mean watering 2-3 times a week in ordinary summer weather, perhaps every day during extremely hot, dry spells.

Overhead sprinkling—as well as soil soaking—is especially important on hot or windy days.

Fuchsias in containers must be watered every day in warm summer months. Soak all the soil in the container.

Feeding

If there ever was a plant for feeding experiments, the fuchsia is it. Use any complete fertilizer, organic or inorganic, and apply as directed by the manufacturer with this exception: cut the specified amount in four parts and apply once a week after growth gets underway in the spring. If you are growing fuchsias in containers, treat half of them with one fertilizer and half with another. The fuchsia responds so quickly that you can see which fertilizer acts best with your soil in a week or two.

Pruning

You should prune fuchsias rather heavily each year after the last severe frost of your area. As fuchsias flower on new wood each year, and severe pruning forces out new wood, it follows that severe pruning will result in more flowers. Heavy pruning consists of cutting back all weak branches to the stem, and cutting back the remaining good branches to one or two pairs of dormant buds.

Fuchsias in pots need root pruning as well as above-ground pruning in order to make the bush more thrifty and to give more room for growth next year. Cut branches back to a simple framework, and prune roots proportionately. Repot in a soil mixture such as recommended above.

Training

One word of warning to those about to try their skill at training: Be sure you know the growth habit of a fuchsia before you attempt to train it. Ask your nurseryman or an experienced grower about the type you are buying.

Growing fuchsias in bush form is easy. You control the shape of the plant by regular pinching or pruning. Shortening of the main branches and pinching back of shoots produces a bushy, stocky plant. Leave the branches fairly long if you want a plant with a loose, open habit of growth.

Almost any fuchsia that produces long straight branches will make a good espalier. Such a bush may have 10 or 12 branches. All but 3 or 4 should be removed at the base.

Train the 3 or 4 remaining branches in a fan shape against a wall or lattice. All undesired growth, including the dormant buds on the trained branches, should be cut off. This will concentrate the vigor in the trained branches. When the branches have grown to the desired length, pinch off the tips to force production of sideshoots.

Pyramid fuchsias produce more flowers per plant than any other form. When the plant has made 3 or 4 sideshoots, the leader, or central stem, is pinched out and the topmost sideshoot tied to the stake. After 3 or 4 new sideshoots have formed, the above process is repeated. The lowest sideshoots are left longest to form the broad base of the pyramid; each succeeding tier of sideshoots is shortened slightly more than that below so as to taper off the pyramid.

Pinching out the leader should be followed after an interval of 5 or 6 days by the pinching back of all the sideshoots.

A single, soft, bushy plant in the center of an 8-inch pot will make a satisfactory hanging fuchsia. If you want quick results, put three small plants in a 10-inch pot. Pinch back the branches and never let seed pods develop. Flowers should be removed before they begin to fade, and before their pollen is ripe.

Don't expect a single yearly pruning to take care of the shaping of your fuchsias. Cut out superfluous branchlets and weak growth whenever they appear throughout the growing season. Dormant buds appearing in badly located positions should be removed before they begin to grow. Training throughout the growing season will produce a shapely, vigorous, floriferous plant.

Shrubs
RHODODENDRONS

The West has many exclusive advantages in gardening but none so little appreciated as its opportunity to raid the great storehouse of *new* and *different* plants called rhododendrons.

The opportunity is not for the Pacific Northwest alone. In California, wherever the gardener has created a climate for azaleas, fuchsias, tuberous begonias, and ferns, he has a climate for at least some rhododendrons.

The new rhododendrons—new only because we haven't used them yet—are not just new colors in the old familiar forms, or refinements in flower and leaf. Many of the rhododendrons being grown in the West are so unlike the commonly known types that if you would see them without a label you wouldn't identify them as rhododendrons.

In the rhododendron genus there are shrublets that grow less than a foot high and spread 3 feet and more. And there is an 80-foot giant from Burma with a 30-inch leaf. Tender species now being grown in greenhouses in the Pacific Northwest can be made to feel at home along California's coast. There are low growing shrubs with all the usefulness of daphne and with no more temperamental traits. Dozens of these *new* rhododendrons can be grown in tubs and boxes for many years and can give you interesting leaf color and pattern all year.

Why have we been slow to take hold of rhododendrons in a bold manner? One reason is the complexity of the genus; another is the erroneous belief that the so-called average gardener isn't ready for the better rhododendrons until he knows the rhododendron language.

The English horticulturists who have been collecting, studying, hybridizing, and classifying rhododendrons for a long, long time (our familiar Pink Pearl received award of merit in England in 1897) have built a classification that goes something like this: more than 800 species (wild rhododendrons) have been collected and identified. These 800-plus species are divided into 40 *series* or groups. The series are again divided into *subseries*, and there are about 40 of these. In addition to the *species* there are many thousand *hybrids* that are crosses between species or between species and hybrids or between hybrids themselves.

The advantages of this detailed family-tree classification are many. Every rhododendron has a pedigree—you can trace back the line of ancestors to its original parents. If you know the parents, you can recognize their offspring when you meet them.

We have charted below a few species with a few of their hybrids. They were chosen because each represents a different class-type of rhododendron, each has definite characteristics in leaf or flower, each passes on those characteristics to its progeny.

These are famous species. In the list of their hybrids you'll find many of today's outstanding rhododendrons. More important, through these few species you can put a seemingly complex rhododendron world into a simple order.

MOUPINENSE AND ITS HYBRIDS

In the *R. moupinense* and its hybrids we have a group of dwarf shrubs of garden value whether in or out of leaf. They are as easily fitted into a garden scheme as evergreen azaleas. The species is tender for the Northwest but much appreciated in the California January garden. The hybrids are better adapted but on the borderline in the Northwest.

R. moupinense. A spreading slow-growing shrub with small shiny, always green leaves. Azalea-like flowers, 1-1½ inches, white, sometimes pink and even deep rose. The hybrids of the species have all the virtues of the parent plus greater hardiness.

BRIC-A-BRAC. Much grace and charm. Low growing to 1½-3 feet. Flowers white with conspicuous chocolate anthers, in March.

BO-PEEP. Retains the attractive low growth habit of *R. moupinense*. Flowers cream with a yellow eye.

REPENS AND ITS HYBRIDS

The *R. repens* group introduces red trumpets on low-spreading, beautifully foliaged shrubs. Curiously the species itself is one of the most-difficult-to-grow rhododendrons. Its hybrids, on the other hand, are easily grown and all are adapted to both California and the Northwest.

R. repens. A creeping shrublet to 6 inches and eventually spreading to 30-40 inches. (*Eventually* in this case means 30-40 years if you can keep it alive that long.) Flowers trumpet-shaped, bright

258 RHODODENDRONS Shrubs

scarlet and large for the size of the plant. Very difficult to grow but noteworthy because of its hybrids.

CARMEN. Many of the virtues of *R. repens* but grows faster and blooms younger. Dark red flowers in March-April.

LITTLE JOE. A cross of *R. repens* and May Day. Bright scarlet flowers on almost prostrate branches; leaves 1½ inches long, dark green; trumpet-shaped 2-inch flowers.

ELIZABETH. Spreading with eventual height of about 5 feet, but can be held to 2½-3 feet by pruning. Clusters of light blood-red flowers in May. Considered by many growers to be one of the best semi-dwarf hybrids ever produced. Very free flowering, very easy to grow, excellent in pots or tubs.

WILLIAMSIANUM AND ITS HYBRIDS

Once you have seen the combination of green and bronzy leaves that distinguishes the *R. williamsianum* blood line, you'll recognize any member of this group whether its nodding bells are showing or not. The species can be grown in coastal California. Bow Bells does exceptionally well under California conditions. Moonstone and Bow Bells are most popular in the Northwest.

R. williamsianum. Grows in dense twiggy mass with its lower branches tight to the ground. Heart-shaped leaves of rich green with new growth in contrasting bronze. Rate of growth so slow that it is treated as a small shrub, although eventually it will reach 5 feet with a 10-foot spread. Flowers waxy, nodding 2-inch bells, pink to rose, April-May.

HUMMING BIRD. A strong resemblance to this parent, although not as compact in growth. Same bronzy new foliage. Bell-shaped flowers in a loose truss, carmine in bud, opening to a deep pink. Mid-April to mid-May. Not so easy to grow as either Moonstone or Bow Bells.

MOONSTONE. Low growing, rounded, neat and compact to 1-3 feet. Flowers, large cups, cream with faint red markings in April.

Bow BELLS. Low and compact, shell-pink, deep pink, May. Without a doubt one of the best pink semi-dwarfs.

Other distinguished progeny of *R. williamsianum* are:

A. J. IVENS. Neat habit, pale pink flowers, May.

COWSLIP. Full and neat, pinkish-white flowers, April.

GRIFFITHIANUM AND ITS HYBRIDS

Rhododendron hybridists have long prized the huge flowers of *R. griffithianum* and have used the species in developing numerous hybrids. More than any other, this group typifies rhododendrons to most people. To the grower, the one great fault of the species is its slowness in reaching blooming age —12 years.

The ever-popular Pink Pearl came about through a series of crosses intended to hold the flower beauty of the species in a hardier hybrid.

R. griffithianum. Large shrub, 15-20 feet high and as wide. Long narrow leaves, pale green above, gray beneath. Flowers, 5-6 in loose trusses, each translucent white, wide-flaring bell 5-6 inches across; edges often frilled; in May.

LODERI KING GEORGE. Shows its parentage with large trusses of pure white flowers, each floret 5½-6½ inches across; May.

Many of the Loderi group are equally desirable —Loderi Venus, and Loderi Superlative, are examples. All are pink in bud turning white as flowers open.

CORNISH CROSS. Of same type with varying tones of translucent pink on the shrub at one time. May.

Several of the Griffithianum hybrids need the most protected garden locations in the Pacific Northwest but are right at home in California. Examples: Gill's Crimson, Cornish Cross, Penjerrick. The history of the Loderi group in California indicates that they do well in coastal areas but do not like dry winds and high heat.

GRIERSONIANUM AND ITS HYBRIDS

The *R. griersonianum* introduces the two-tone leaf and the flaring bells in loose trusses. Here again the species is tender in the Northwest but the hybrids are hardy. Adaptation in California is indicated by the hybrid.

From the California hybridizer's standpoint the species has two great assets: its habit of blooming very young and its wonderful color, both of which it imparts to its progeny.

R. griersonianum. Moderate growth to 7 feet and spreading as wide as tall. Handsome long-pointed leaves are medium green above, a pale buff beneath. Well-balanced, loose trusses of flaring bells of geranium scarlet, no blue in it; in June.

MAY DAY. Lower growing to 1½-4 feet, but bright scarlet bell-shaped flowers (in May) and pointed leaves show its relationship to *R. griersonianum*. Satisfactory in California if given shade.

FABIA. Shiny, pointed, perky leaves. Flowers, bell-shaped, 6-8 in a flat truss, in orange, yellow, or salmon; in late May. Accepts California conditions.

TALLY HO. Medium height, scarlet bells in May. One of the best reds for California.

Other hybrids from this parent: Arthur Osborne, Azor, Vulcan, Bonfire.

THE MADDENII

This series offers outstanding rhododendrons in several classes: a spectacular exotic for the warmest locations on the Southern California coast; an epiphyte or two (in the Himalayan rain forests these grow in pockets of humus in the tops of trees); several fragrant species and hybrids for California; and a dwarf or two that are at home almost anywhere in the West. All have very handsome foliage. The foliage will have its characteristic lushness if grown in high shade in pure peat with an abundance of water.

R. nuttallii. Tall growing, eventually to 30 feet. Large, strongly-veined leaves. New growth is reddish purple, slowly changing to green with purplish glints. Fragrant flowers like yellow trumpets, 6 inches long and flaring as wide, hang down from a flat truss 12-14 inches across; in April-May. Very tender. Can't take much below 30°. A greenhouse plant in the Northwest, an experiment in the most favored Southern California coastal gardens. Needs filtered shade, and constant moisture.

R. dalhousiae. An epiphyte in its native habitat but grows well as a terrestial if grown in humus in filtered shade. Growing to 12-15 feet. Fragrant trumpet-like flowers are white flushed with pink; in May.

R. rhabdotum. To 12 feet. Flowers creamy yellow, striped with red; in July.

R. maddenii. Dense habit of growth, to 6-9 feet. Fragrant 2-inch trumpets, white flushed with rose; in May. Best species for all coastal areas of California.

COUNTESS OF HADDINGTON. A cross of *R. dalhousiæ* and *R. ciliatum*. Tubular, rose-white, waxy, fragrant flowers in compact trusses; in May. Excellent performance in California coastal areas.

R. ciliatum. Rather loose, interesting structure to 4 feet with 5-6 foot spread. Light-green, deeply veined leaves. Clusters of flaring, 2-inch, tubular flowers present a solid front of pale pink to white; in February-March.

RACIL. A neat shrublet with the same free flowering habit. Flowers, apple-blossom pink in April.

CILPINENSE. More compact and lower growing. Flowers, white to pink in February-March.

R. ciliatum is one of the hardiest species in the tender Maddenii series, yet its early bloom makes it safe only in California gardens. On the other hand, its hybrids—Racil and Cilpinense—are safe in the warmer areas of the Northwest.

THE EDGEWORTHII

The Edgeworthii, very similar to the Maddenii, should be given some support since they tend to trail. This characteristic is evident in the hybrid Fragrantissimum.

R. bullatum. To 8 feet. An epiphyte. Flowers saucer-shaped, 3-5 inches across, white or tinged with pink.

PRINCESS ALICE. A cross of *R. edgeworthii* and *R. ciliatum*. Fragrant. One of the hardiest in the series. Successful in Portland.

FRAGRANTISSIMUM. A cross of *R. edgeworthii* and *R. formosum*. Fragrant. Very popular in San Francisco Bay Area. Has straggly habit of growth but can be controlled by pruning.

TWO RHODODENDRON TREES

The impressive leaves of *R. sino-grande* and *R. falconeri* make these trees worth growing even if they never bloom—and they do take about 20 years to do that. They are now being grown in both California and the Northwest. Because of leaf size, they need protection from the wind. All-important requirement: deep watering.

R. sino-grande. To 20-30 feet. 30-inch leaves. Flowers 2-2½ inches in clusters of 20; white, or cream with purple blotches.

R. falconeri. To 40-50 feet. Leaves, 8-12 inches, dark green above, rust color beneath. Clusters of 20 or more 1½-2¼ inch creamy white to pale yellow flowers.

SCARCE AND PLENTIFUL

Not all rhododendrons are available at your nursery. Several of the dwarfs and exotics we have mentioned are grown by only a few specialists. To a gardener who has been touched by the spell of rhododendrons, this scarcity is part of the fun of growing them.

There are many rhododendrons available in quantity. You can see them at your nursery in the spring and you can be your own judge of quality.

BUY IN BLOOM

It's a good idea to buy in bloom. However, in choosing from a display of rhododendrons in bloom at your nursery there is some danger in *blossom blindness*. You may become so entranced with the bloom that you forget to notice how the plant grows.

In your looking, note the following. Out of the countless good varieties, we have selected those representatives of each color and class that have proved themselves and are readily available. They are classified by color, height, relative growing season, and hardiness. The symbols of the American hardiness ratings—H-1 (-25°), H-2 (-15°), H-3 (-5°), H-4 (5°), H-5 (15°)—are followed. The H-2 listings are based on too little experience to be safe and should be used as indicators for experimenters in Zone 2 and favorable locations in Zone 1.

RED-LOW: *Elizabeth*, H-4, see above; *May Day*, H-3, see above.

RED-MEDIUM: *Britannia*, H-3, late May; *Cornubia*, H-5, February; *Gill's Crimson*, H-5, April; *Jean Marie de Montague*, H-3, May; *Mars*, H-2, late May; *Unknown Warrior*, H-3, April and May; *Vulcan*, H-2, May.

RED-TALL: *Cynthia*, H-3, May; *David*, H-3, May; *Earl of Athlone*, H-4, late April; *Lady Chamberlain*, (orange-red), H-5, May.

PINK-LOW: *Bow Bells*, H-3, see above; *Racil*, H-3, see above; *Humming Bird*, H-4, see above.

PINK-MEDIUM: *Azor*, H-4, June; *Betty Wormald*, H-3, mid-May; *Naomi*, H-4, May; *Mrs. Furnival*, H-3, May.

PINK-TALL: *Alice*, H-3, May; *Mrs. G. W. Leak (Cottage Garden's Pride)*, H-4, early May; *Loderi Venus*, H-4, May; *Pink Pearl*, H-3, May.

WHITE-LOW: *Bric-A-Brac*, H-3, see above; *Cilpinense*, H-4.

WHITE-MEDIUM: *Loder's White*, H-4, early May; *Sweet Simplicity*, H-2, late May.

WHITE-TALL: *Beauty of Littleworth*, H-3, early May; *Loderi King George*, H-4, May; *White Swan*, H-3, May.

YELLOW ORANGE-LOW: *Broughtonii Aureum (Azaleadendron)*, H-3, May-June; *Dido*, H-4, early May; *Fabia*, H-4, see above; *Goldsworth's Yellow*, H-3, May; *Moonstone*, H-3, see above; *Unique*, H-3, late April.

YELLOW-MEDIUM: *Souvenir of W. C. Slocock*, H-3, early May.

BLUE LAVENDER-LOW: *Blue Diamond*, H-3, mid-April; *Blue Peter*, H-2, early May; *Blue Tit*, H-3, mid-April.

BLUE PURPLE-MEDIUM: *Fastuosum Plenum*, H-2, May; *Purple Splendour*, H-2, May.

BLUE LAVENDER-TALL: *Susan*, H-2, mid-May.

WHERE TO PLANT

The ideal rhododendron planting site in the Northwest is under trees that give a filtered light. Trees such as dogwood and deciduous oak are the best. All trees with shallow, greedy root systems—elms, poplars, locust—should be avoided. Conditions short of this ideal, and more realistic in the case of newly planted gardens, are: north and east sides of buildings, fences, large shrubs; and under lath.

The best rhododendron setting in California is likely to be the outdoor living room. Wherever climates are modified for enjoyment by human beings, a better environment for rhododendrons is created. Azaleas and rhododendrons in tubs or raised beds in or near an outdoor sitting area are most likely to get the attention to watering and the degree of sun and shade they want.

Both azaleas and rhododendrons need sunlight for flower production. The idea is to give them as much as they will take without burning leaf or blossom.

SOIL REQUIREMENTS

In the Northwest most experienced growers follow the rule of mixing top soil and humus of some kind.

General mixtures are: ½ peat, ½ soil; or ½ leaf mold, ½ soil.

In California, wherever there is any question about the suitability of soil, plant azaleas and rhododendrons in straight peat moss or a mixture of ½ peat, ½ sand. The switch to pure peat has allowed the azaleas and rhododendrons to enter areas such as California's Sacramento and San Joaquin valleys, which a few years ago were considered too hot and too dry for either plant group.

The best planting method if drainage is good: dig a hole twice the width and depth of the container and fill with peat moss. The extra depth creates a moisture-holding reservoir below the roots.

If there is any question about drainage, plant in raised beds.

Azaleas and rhododendrons should have moist, cool soil at all times. But water-logged soil smothers roots.

WATERING

Overhead watering is highly recommended. In dry summer areas, daily sprinkling overhead helps supply the air moisture these plants need. But don't neglect a weekly, slow soaking of the root area.

In all areas where salts in the water are a problem, plant azaleas where the root area can be flushed out with an occasional excessive irrigation. Regular watering that doesn't drain beyond the root area will build up a harmful salt content. If drainage is good, it's difficult to over-water rhododendrons.

FERTILIZING

Don't overdo it. Apply any "complete" acid fertilizer.

Shrubs AZALEAS

This series of the rhododendron genus provides every section of the West with a wide choice of extremely useful shrubs, both evergreen and deciduous.

In the evergreen groups, hybridists have been developing hardier and more colorful types faster than gardeners can absorb them. The various groups are so different in climate adaptation and use that each must be considered separately.

First let's look at the evergreen azaleas.

INDICAS. (BELGIAN INDICAS, BELGIAN HYBRIDS)

Least hardy of the evergreen azaleas, they find their favorite climate in zones 9, 10, and 13. However, with protection from direct sun and with moisture control they thrive in zones 7 and 12. Where winter temperatures drop below 20°, the Indicas suffer from bark splitting.

Their many uses in landscaping are similar to those of the Kurumes. (See below.) Some of the large double-flowering varieties are almost too gaudy for unrestricted garden use and show off best in a tub.

Following is a list of a few of the best Indicas, with notes on growth habit where it is not average. Flowering season is from February to April in all but the mildest winter areas where some varieties bloom in October and again in March.

Albert and Elizabeth. Double pink shading into white centers.
Avenir. Double coppery pink.
Dr. Bergman. Various shades of pink and rose-red.
Etoile de Belgique. Open growth; requires pruning; 3 in. semi-double red flowers.
Hollandia. Double orange.
Niobe. Double white with chartreuse tint.
Orchidæflora. Unusually large; fuchsia pink.
Paul Schaeme. Double salmon pink; very free flowering.
Pink Pearl. Open growth; needs control by pinching; flowers like double apple blossoms.
William Van Orange. Low growth habit; single lacquer-red, ruffled flowers.

KURUMES

The hardy varieties of the Kurumes extend the evergreen azalea range out of California and into zones 4-5.

The Kurumes generally are taller growing than the Indicas. The compact type will reach 3-5 feet in 10 years. Tall growers will reach 6-8 feet. (Type of growth by variety is listed below.) All types can be controlled by pruning. The shingled or stairway effect, typical of Japanese trained plants, is achieved by cutting back stems at various heights. Flowers of the Kurumes are smaller and simpler than those of the Indicas, but the quantity of bloom makes up for smaller size. Season of bloom is from March to May.

AZALEAS Shrubs

Varieties generally available listed in order of blooming:

Coral Bells. Low and spreading in its first few years; shell pink flowers.
Hexe. Low and dense growth; crimson-red flowers.
Hinodegiri. Low, broader than high, violet-rose, red flowers.
Sherwood Orchid. Spreading, medium height, violet flowers.
Snowflake. Dense, compact growth, white flowers.
Ward's Ruby. Upright, dark ruby-red flowers.

The Kurumes and Indicas are generally obtainable in small sizes at a low cost per plant and therefore can be used economically in mass plantings. Used by the dozen in one color or gradations of several colors, they are especially effective in low foundation plantings. When out of bloom the clean leaves give the planting a well-groomed appearance.

PERICAT HYBRIDS

The Pericats could be grouped with the Kurumes without misleading anyone. They may be a little brighter and cleaner than the Kurumes.

Two important varieties are: *Sweetheart*, spreading, 3-5 feet high, salmon-pink flowers; *Twenty Grand*, low and spreading, semi-double, violet-red flowers.

SOUTHERN INDIANS

These azaleas, that have brought azalea fame to the Deep South, are proving satisfactory in California where winter temperatures are above 20°. Varieties divide themselves into two groups. The mediums are 3-5 feet high, compact, dense, and usually late blooming. The tall varieties, above 5 feet, are fast growing, of rather open habit, and generally earlier blooming.

Medium growers: *Fielder's White*, large, single, frilled white flowers; *Brilliant*, single rose; *Glory of Sunninghill*, single orange-red.

Tall growers: *Formosa*, violet-red; *President Clay*, rose-opal; *Pride of Mobile (Elegans Superba)*, rose-pink with purple blotches.

RUTHERFORD HYBRIDS

The varieties vary in hardiness, but generally the plant will stand 10°, although the buds show damage at 23°. Growth habit is bushy, in the 2-4 foot range, and attractive all year.

Flowers vary between Kurume and Indica type. They are single, semi-double, double, and hose-in-hose. Several varieties are fragrant. Season of bloom is shorter, more concentrated, and later than that of Kurumes.

GLENN DALES

Hardy in zones 2-13, but generally available in Pacific Northwest only.

No group of azaleas has a more varied parentage than the Glenn Dales. Some are rangy and fast growing; a few are compact and slow growing. Some have large soft leaves; others have foliage as fine as any Kurume.

The majority of Glenn Dales should be considered in a quite different category from the so-called low evergreen azaleas. The Glenn Dales are a first class group of medium shrubs for use in partial shade and, in some localities, in full sun.

Flower colors usually are very clear, and flowers remain on the plant and hold their color for 2-3 weeks. When flowers do fall, they drop clean and do not get rusty looking as do blooms on the Kurumes.

The following list will give you some ideas of the color and bloom selection offered in the Glenn Dales:

Anchorite. Erect, broad, spreading to 4 ft. 2-in. rose-pink flowers, in April.
Aphrodite. Erect, with broad top to 4 ft.; 2-in., pale, rose-pink flowers, in mid-April.
Carmel. Tall, spreading to 5 ft.; 2-in. mahogany-red flowers, in early April.
Copperman. Dense growth, spreading to 4 ft.; 3-in. orange-red flowers, in mid to late May.
Fantasy. Loose growth to 4 ft.; 2-in. white flowers striped with dull red, in April.
Fashion. Erect and arching to 6 ft.; 2-in., two-toned rose flowers, in May.
Geisha. Tall, erect to 6 ft.; 2-in. white flowers striped with pink, chartreuse blotch, in mid-April.
Gorgeous. Erect and spreading to 5 ft.; 4-in., begonia-rose flowers with heavy blotch, in mid-season.
Greeting. Erect to broad, spreading to 4 ft.; 2-in., ruffled, coral-rose flowers, in mid to late April.
Janet Noyes. Compact to 3 ft.; 2½-in. rose flowers with scarlet throat, in mid-May.
Jongleur. Erect to 6 ft.; 2-in. and larger, rose flowers, in late April.
Pixie. Bushy, broad, spreading to 5 ft.; 2-in. white flowers with rays of pink, in mid-April.
Sagittarius. Dense, spreading, not over 2 ft.; 3-in. pink flowers with salmon overtone, in late May and June.
Treasure. Densely branched shrub to 6 ft.; 3-4 in. pink-flushed white flowers, in late April.

GABLE HYBRIDS

The hardiest of the evergreen azaleas. Can be planted anywhere temperatures stay above a −10°. Compared to Kurumes, the winter foliage of the Gables is sparse but it's a good evergreen for cold winters. Blooming season starts in late April and continues through May. Here are three typical varieties:

Louise Gable. Medium height; double salmon-pink flowers.
Purple Splendour. Medium height; frilled purple flowers.
Rosebud. Low growing, pearl-pink flowers resembling miniature roses.

MACRANTHAS

Hardy zones 3-13. The low-growing varieties in this group being compact, small leafed, dense, are especially attractive and valuable for use in small areas, raised beds, and planter boxes. Don't overlook these:

Flame Creeper. Single 2-in. red flowers.
Gumpo. Single 3-in. white flowers.
Rosæflora. Double 2-in. rose flowers.

DECIDUOUS AZALEAS

As more and more new deciduous azaleas become available, the need to classify the whole tribe becomes increasingly necessary. There must be some reference points if we are to avoid getting lost in a sea of unrelated names.

You can't build a clean-limbed family tree for the Exbury hybrids or the Knaphill, Ghents, or any group, but you can understand each group better if you know something about how they came about.

Here are some of the species that have been used in developing the various hybrids. All are worth knowing in their own right.

American Natives

R. arborescens. (Allegheny Mountain regions). Fast-growing to 10 ft. Flowers are variable, 1½-2¼ in. tubes, white with overtones of pink. Bloom appears in late May and June after leaves are out.

R. calendulaceum. FLAME AZALEA. (Tennessee and Kentucky). To 4-10 ft., sometimes more. Flowers, gradually opening tubes to 2½ in. long, in clusters of 5-25, in gold, orange, to flame-scarlet, in early June. A well known hybrid: *Gloria Mundi.*

R. nudiflorum. (Allegheny Mountain regions). Upright to 7-10 ft. Very similar to *R. arborescens.* Flowers, 1¾ in. wide, white to deep pink, in late May. Also varieties with orchid colored flowers.

R. occidentale. (See chapter on natives.) Westerners are exploring the possibilities of developing superior forms through selection of native variants. Flowers have a white corolla with an Indian yellow blotch. There are varieties with pale pink corollas and also with pale Indian yellow corollas. Some flowers are heavily marked with carmine rose.

R. roseum. (Northeastern U. S.). One of the best American species. To 5-7 ft. Flowers, 1¼-1¾ in., bright pink and fragrant in clusters of 5-9 in May about the time the leaves appear.

R. vaseyi. (Carolinas). Upright, irregular spreading shrub to an eventual 15 ft. Bright green 4 in. leaves turn crimson in fall. Flowers, pink, almost white in clusters of 5-8, in May before the leaves.

R. viscosum. (From Maine to South Carolina). Variable in form, according to locale or origin, from low growing to a 15-ft. shrub. White, spicily fragrant, 1-1½ in. flowers in July. Extremely sticky, often called swamp honeysuckle.

Asiatic Species

R. japonicum. (Japan). Upright to 6 ft. Flowers, 2-3 in., carried in clusters of 6-12, salmon-red, orange, orange-red, in late May. A vigorous growing shrub. Many varieties of it are worth growing in their own right. Var. *aureum* has rich yellow flowers.

R. molle. (China). Erect and stiff to about 6 ft. Flowers, 2½ in., in clusters of 6-10 on tips of twigs; yellow to golden orange, often with large greenish blotch; blooms in April before the leaves. Not so hardy as *R. japonicum.*

Evergreen—Deciduous

R. mucronatum. (China-Japan). (*R. ledifolium*). Partly evergreen. Two types of leaves as with *R. obtusum.* To an eventual 6 ft. but generally 3 ft., and spreading. Flowers, 3 in., single, white and slightly fragrant.

R. obtusum kaempferi. TORCH AZALEA. (Japan). Deciduous and evergreen. Two kinds of leaves, one in summer, one in spring. Summer leaves persist through the winter if temperatures are not too low. The forms of this series are variable in growth, hardiness, and flower size. Generally 1¾-2½ in. orange-red flowers in mid-May. Blooms much later in San Francisco.

R. poukhanense. (Korea). Deciduous, evergreen where winters are mild. Spreading to 3 ft. Single lavender-purple 2-in. flowers in April. Hardy for a semi-evergreen. Much used in development of the hardy evergreen Gable hybrids.

In a Class By Itself

R. schlippenbachii. (Korea). A densely branched spreading shrub to 6-8 ft. Leaves in whorls of 5 at tips of branches. Large single pink 2-4 in. flowers in clusters of 3-6, in April-May in cold sections, later in San Francisco. An exceptionally good species. Widely adapted.

Hybrid Classes

Mollis hybrids. Hybrids of *R. molle* and *R. japonicum.* Upright growth to 4-5 ft. Flowers 2½ in. wide in clusters of 7-13. Colors are in the yellow-orange-rose color range. Blooms mid to late May according to variety.

Well known varieties: *Anthony Koster, Koster's Brilliant Red.*

Ghent hybrids. The Belgians, Dutch, and English, in the 1830's, took the American species—*R. calendulaceum, R. nudiflorum, R. viscosum,* and others—and crossed them with each other and with *R. molle* and with *R. luteum,* a European, yellow flowered species.

Later, about 1870, they used the Western native, *R. occidentale,* in the crosses and crossed the result with the Mollis hybrids.

Some of the representative forms of this group are:

Altaclarensis—said by some to be a hybrid of *R. molle* and *R. viscosum,* a richly colored orange yellow.

Gloria Mundi—orange with deeper orange blotch

Unique—tangerine orange color

Knaphill, Exbury, and Ilam hybrids. About 1900, Anthony Waterer's Knaphill Nursery started a new breeding program, again bringing several American species into the Ghent and Mollis hybrids. *R. viscosum, R. arborescens, R. nudiflorum,* and later *R. calendulaceum* and *R. occidentale* were used in this program.

Waterer's work was carried forward at the Rothschild gardens in Exbury, England, and in the Ilam estate of the late Edgar Stead of New Zealand.

The Exbury group shows the greatest departure from the old forms. The flowers are unbelievably large, some up to 5 in., and are carried in large clusters.

However, the quality of the Knaphills and the Ilams does not suffer by comparison. Ilam No. 5, for example, bears huge trusses of ruffled, deep red, 5-in. flowers. Flowers of the Knaphills are larger and more durable than those of the old forms. Colors range from near-whites through cream, pink, rose, stronger red, to orange. Some plants have dwarf spreading habits. They bloom late midseason.

Shrubs

ROSES

The rose stands alone, head and shoulders above all other flowers in the West, across the country and in every corner of the temperate world where it can be grown. It has held first place in the hearts of gardeners since the beginning of history, ever since man first looked to the soil for something to fill the eye as well as the stomach. In all probability, roses will continue to hold first place until the last gardener lays down the last hoe.

You don't have to look for the reasons—magnificent bursts of bloom in spring and fall with many varieties also flowering throughout the summer, richness in color, beautiful flower form, fragrance, and a wonderful willingness in the plant to perform under extremes of climate and garden management so long as its few basic needs are satisfied. In the beauty of the individual bloom, the modern hybrid tea is simply unsurpassed. Whether you have one plant or a thousand, there's a special thrill, a special kind of excitement, in every perfect flower.

CLASSES OF ROSES

Today's roses are, of course, descended from ancient species roses—single-flowered, spring-blooming, brambly plants growing wild, mainly in temperate areas of the world. Because garden roses are as old as gardening, they have been tinkered with, hybridized, selected, crossed and back-crossed for centuries. The family tree of today's roses, fundamental to any botanical system of classification, is extremely complicated. Separating the various classes botanically is beyond the scope of this book.

MODERN ROSES

Here are the roses most widely planted today—the kinds you are likely to encounter at nurseries as bare-root stock in midwinter to early spring or in containers during the growing season:

Hybrid Teas

Best loved and most frequently grown of all roses, outselling all other classes combined. "Rose" in any general discussion usually refers to this class.

Intensive research in the past 25 years has resulted in enormous progress in hybrid teas; newer varieties are big-growing, vigorous, and disease-resistant, with flower buds longer and more graceful. *Charlotte Armstrong*, perhaps the most important hybrid tea yet developed in the West, has given rise to many award-winning descendants.

Most hybrid teas are of the basic *bush* form, growing from 2½ to 6 feet or more, depending on parentage, culture, pruning methods, and climate. Thick new canes "break" low on the plant, grow out and up for 3 feet or more, and terminate in a flower bud. More flower buds originate at various points below the terminal one. Bush hybrid teas are the roses of the formal garden, the cutting bed, and the glass-house for the florist trade.

Climbing habit seems to occur sooner or later in most bush varieties. It results from a common mutation or sport in which the growing tip continues to elongate to perhaps 20 feet or even more, with flowers produced from laterals along its length. Many of the most desirable bush hybrid teas are also available as climbers.

The *pillar* rose falls somewhere between the two. Perhaps it is best described as a very long-caned bush type, growing to 8 feet or more. Canes are not pliable like those of the climber but grow erect with a little support.

Tree or standard roses do not represent a distinct growth habit, but a propagation method. They are produced by budding bush varieties on specially selected tall-caned understocks. Any rose, if it isn't too vigorous, can be produced as a standard.

Floribundas and Polyanthas

These smaller-flowered, low-growing roses bear flowers in masses almost continuously from spring into fall. They carry traits of hardiness and disease-resistance from a set of ancestors entirely separate from those of the hybrid teas.

Polyanthas are old-timers in the rose garden. Flowers are less than 2 inches in diameter, and the color range is limited. Two old favorites are *Margo Koster* and *Cecile Brunner*.

Floribundas, crosses of polyanthas and hybrid teas, produce flowers that are larger than the polyanthas, borne in sprays or in clusters. In many of the varieties, flower form is identical to the hybrid teas, but the blooms are only about half the size. Unlike the more formal hybrid teas, floribundas are adaptable to a variety of garden uses. They make attractive foundation and border plants, and some varieties can even be induced to grow happily in tubs or large pots. *Vogue* and *Circus* are just two of many popular floribundas.

Grandifloras

This is a class of roses resulting from crosses between the floribundas and hybrid teas. Grandifloras combine many of the best features of both parents. Plants are vigorous, some varieties growing to 6 feet or more, with blooms that approach the hybrid teas in quality as well as size. Flowers are borne both in sprays and singly on long stems. Grandifloras carry the everblooming habits, hardiness, and disease resistance of the old polyantha types. *Queen Elizabeth* and *Carrousel*, two established favorites, are also available as climbers.

Miniature Roses

These are derived from the old China roses (*R. chinensis*), are tiny, 6-12 inch plants with very small, but often perfectly formed blooms. Novelties, suitable for containers, borders, or the rock garden.

Large-flowered Climbers

These are based on some of the same ancestors as the polyanthas. They include one of the most popular of all roses, Paul's Scarlet, a spring bloomer which repeats if pruned after first bloom.

OLD ROSES

Tea Roses

Tea roses, immediate ancestors of hybrid teas, are vigorous and everblooming, and, like their famous descendants, produce large, attractive flowers. Petal substance is inferior, however, and flower necks are weak, causing flowers to droop. Tea roses, too, are generally less hardy than hybrid teas.

Hybrid Perpetuals

These dominated the rose world from 1840 to 1890 and were crossed with the teas to become parents of the hybrid teas. They're hardier and rangier than hybrid teas, producing flowers that are large and handsome, though lacking the refinement of the open bloom and the popular long, streamlined bud form of the hybrid tea. "Perpetual" refers to their habit of blooming in fall as well as in spring. *American Beauty*, famous in the 'nineties, was a hybrid perpetual, but you'll have to go to a specialist to find it today. One hybrid perpetual you will find almost everywhere is *Frau Karl Druschki*, still considered by many the finest white rose in existence.

Other Old Types

The Noisettes (*Marechal Niel*, a yellow climber, is still considered a superb rose), the Giganteas, the moss roses, and other old-fashioned roses—bourbons, damasks, chinas, cabbage roses and others—are of great sentimental interest to collectors. Few modern roses can match the magnificent *fragrance* of the old roses. One disadvantage is the relatively short bloom period of many of the old roses.

Species Roses

Species roses and their hybrids are hardy, spring-blooming forms mainly of value in landscaping. For this reason, many of them are called shrub roses. The rugosa hybrids, *R. hugonis*, and others are vigorous, rampant forms with handsome, disease-resistant foliage, fine for hedges and backgrounds. Most of them thrive on neglect.

R. wichuraiana, a trailing species, is still planted extensively; brambly *R. multiflora* and *Red Robin* are used as living fences; *Lady Banks* and *R. bracteata's* rampant hybrid *Mermaid* are all valuable roses in the right place.

GROWING ROSES SUCCESSFULLY

Successful rose growing depends on these things:

1. Buying healthy, vigorous Grade 1 plants in varieties suited to your climate.
2. Locating and planting them properly.
3. Supplying their four basic needs: water, nutrients, proper pruning, and pest control.

CLIMATIC REQUIREMENTS

The ideal rose climate is one that gives them enough summer heat for good growth, enough humidity or thin, high cloudiness to prevent petals from burning. Winters are cool enough for dormancy, yet not so cold as to damage lower canes and roots by freezing. In such a climate, virtually any rose you find in the nursery bin will do reasonably well, and most of them will perform superbly. As your climate varies from the ideal, more care is necessary in selecting varieties.

Summer cooler than normal

Buy roses with fewer petals, flowers that open readily in cool weather. Pastel colors are best—deep tones tend to get "muddy." Look for high disease-resistance, inherent in variety. Many red and pink roses are susceptible to mildew, most whites tend to "ball up" under foggy conditions.

Plant in full sun only, using walls to trap and reflect heat, provide shelter from prevailing winds. Spray regularly for mildew, rust, or black spot; reduce watering in cool weather.

Good varieties: *Peace, President Hoover, Etoile de Hollande, Eclipse, Sutter's Gold, Saturnia,* and *Virgo* are among the many roses which thrive where summers are cool.

Summer hotter than normal

Intense summer heat often causes premature opening and "cabbaging" in flowers, burning, rapid fading. Best blooms come in spring and fall, with the exception of some varieties that thrive in summer.

Midday shade in summer gives best blooms. In the hot valleys of California, many roses are grown successfully with only morning sun. Plants located on northern exposures, at margins of trees, or similarly shaded locations, will produce better flowers under midsummer heat, but they tend to start later in spring, flower shyly, grow spindly in fall.

Mulch heavily to keep roots cool and to keep

266 ROSES Shrubs

soil from drying out and crusting.

Good varieties: *Charlotte Armstrong, Nocturne, Frau Karl Druschki, Chrysler Imperial, Tiffany*, and *Crimson Glory* are only a few of many outstanding roses for hot summer planting.

Winter colder than normal

Main consideration is hardiness; main cultural requirements, shorter pruning and hilling soil over canes for winter protection.

BUY HEALTHY PLANTS

In general, it's better to plant bare-root roses in midwinter or early spring, depending on climate. Container planting during the growing season can be successful, too, but the nurseryman has usually pruned roots of dormant stock—often rather severely—to fit into the can. Canned stock, too, has frequently been planted late, after new roots have begun to form—past the ideal planting time. If you buy canned stock, select vigorous plants growing in 3-gallon or 5-gallon cans. (Plants in 1-gallon cans have been root-pruned so severely it's best to avoid them entirely.) Container grown plants must be watered very frequently; daily watering is advisable during hot weather.

Bare-root roses purchased very late in the season may not break and develop properly unless special precautions are taken to protect the canes. Hot, dry winds will quickly desiccate buds and canes. To prevent this, mound moist soil, peat moss, or other mulch well up around the canes. After leaves begin to expand, knock down the mulching material.

Grading System

The rose you buy is graded under a standard system. Best grade is No. 1, with 3 or more strong canes starting 3 inches or less above the bud union. At least 2 canes must be 18 inches long or more. Second best is No. 1½, which must have 2 or more canes at least 15 inches long. Last is No. 2 grade, with 2 canes of 12 inches or more.

You're wisest to insist on No. 1 or 1½, either of which will develop into a good plant. With No. 2 plants, you're starting out with a handicap. Canes should be plump, fresh, and heavy. Avoid plants with shrivelled canes, indicating dryness. Mail-order plants that have dried out slightly may often be revived by burying them, top and all, in moist soil for several days.

Patents vs. non-patents

A tag on a rose plant indicating it is a patented variety has no bearing on its value. It merely reserves growing rights to the originator or licensee. Many patented roses are excellent, proven varieties (virtually all of the new hybrid teas carry patent tags). But other patented roses may be completely unsatisfactory.

The All-American symbol (A.A.R.S.), on the other hand, means a great deal. It indicates the rose has been observed for 2 seasons and found to be a superior variety in test gardens in many parts of the country under the careful supervision and rigid judging standards of the people who know roses best. In recent years, especially, many of the A.A.R.S. winners have been developed in the West and are supremely well-suited to Western conditions.

PLANT IN RIGHT LOCATION

Roses need light to bloom and heat to grow. In cool areas they should have sun all day; in warmer areas, 6 hours of sun at the very least. In the discussion of rose climates, above, you'll find suggestions for selecting and growing roses in your particular area.

Spacing of plants is important because roses suffer from poor air circulation between plants, especially in humid climates. In cool climates, roses don't reach the size they do in warmer areas and can be planted closer together—perhaps 2 feet apart on centers, in the case of floribundas. Farther south, 3 feet is minimum, even more for vigorous growers like *President Hoover*. Polyanthas may be set closer together depending on vigor of each variety.

PLANT THE ROSE PROPERLY

In mild climates, where most roses are grown in the West, the plant is set with the bud union just above soil level. Where there's snow in winter, the eastern practice of setting the bud union just below soil level is recommended.

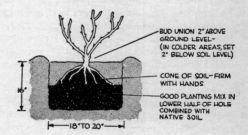

You may improve structure of soil by adding a moderate amount of peat moss or compost before planting, but don't add commercial fertilizers until the plant is well on its way. Any reasonably good soil is sufficient as a start because a good part of the plant's energy during the early weeks of the growing season comes from food already stored in stems. Toward the end of the first growing season, a light sprinkling of fertilizer on the surface of the soil around the plant, well watered in, will provide nutrients without the risk of burning tender, new roots.

WATER REGULARLY DEEPLY

The rose is a thirsty plant. Rose bushes will perform at their vigorous best only when their roots are kept well watered during the growing season. Flood irrigation is the best and simplest method of watering. It is a good idea to use one of the hose attachments that breaks the force of the stream, thereby preventing splash as well as unsightly gouges in the soil. Overhead sprinkling is popular in some hot, dry areas, but in general is much less satisfactory than the flood irrigation method. It washes off insecticidal dusts and spray residues from the foliage, and also makes plants more vulnerable to rust, mildew, and black spot. If you use the overhead method, sprinkle early in the morning on a day when foliage will be certain to dry off in two hours or less.

Whichever system you use, make certain that water gets down deep into the root zone—18-24 inches. Use the following amounts of water to soak an area 2 by 2 feet to a depth of 24 inches: 5 gallons in sandy soil, 8 gallons in loam, 13 gallons in clay. Soaking only the top few inches is not only useless but harmful, because the rose's feeder roots will struggle almost to the surface of the ground in search of moisture. Even in a properly watered rose, feeder roots are fairly near the surface (although water roots go down deep); for this reason, it is always advisable to go easy whenever it becomes necessary to cultivate around a rose. Try to just barely scratch the surface.

Water deeply—but only as often as necessary. It is better to let the soil dry out slightly and to allow the plant to draw heavily on its reservoir of water before filling it up again than to water too frequently. Frequency of watering varies by type of soil. As a rule of thumb, figure on a watering interval of 4 to 10 days if you have sandy soil, 8 to 15 days with loam, 15 to 30 days with clay. During hot, dry spells, it will be necessary to water more frequently.

FEED REGULARLY IN GROWING SEASON

For the first year, newly planted roses should be well watered but should not be fertilized. The young plants have more than enough food in the planting soil, and adding fertilizer would hamper their root development and retard growth. Once established, however, roses are hungry and respond to feeding like few other garden plants. As always, the trick is to feed regularly in small amounts, never in large applications at one time.

In mild climates, feeding begins in February after pruning; elsewhere it comes later. Application of fertilizers should be synchronized with the blooming periods of your roses so the plants will receive the food when they need it; ideal time to fertilize is when a blooming period has come to an end and new growth is just beginning for the next blooming period. One prominent rosarian has a description for these feedings which may help you to remember when it is time to fertilize: "Pat-on-the-back . . . good job . . . come-on-do-it-again."

Use a complete fertilizer. Whether you use the powdered, pelleted, or liquid form is relatively unimportant; what matters is that you follow directions carefully, apply at the proper time, and follow immediately with a deep irrigation.

In addition, a 2 or 3-inch mulch of manure is important, in order to save water, keep soil surface from baking hard, and build a healthy soil structure. On the Pacific Coast, apply manure in February or March and again in early June.

If soil or tap water tends to be alkaline (as it is in many Western areas), work a heaping tablespoonful of soil sulfur into soil around each plant, just after winter pruning. Best soil for roses is a slightly acid one, and unless you have a serious alkalinity problem, one sulfur application should hold the soil at about the proper acidity (pH) for an entire season. A pH of 6 to 7 is ideal for roses.

PRUNE PROPERLY

The following method of pruning is based on these principles:

1. Blooms are produced on new wood. Therefore you should prune roses annually to encourage strong, new, flowering wood. Otherwise blooms will grow on tiny twigs and be useless as cut flowers.

2. In the mild-winter climates of the West, it is best to prune conservatively. Cutting back to half of the previous year's growth is a good rule to follow. Canes should be a minimum height of 18 inches after pruning. Where winters are cold (below 10° F) and dormancy is complete, roses may be pruned more severely; for winter protection, mound loose soil up around the canes to a height of 10 to 12 inches.

3. The best time to prune is at the end of the dormant season. Exact date will vary by climate.

4. The healthy plant is one that is constantly renewed. Try to substitute new canes for old each year. Gardeners are more likely to fail in maintaining vigorous roses because they ignore this fact than for any other reason.

The old advice that says "be sure to remove suckers" should be amended to say "be sure the sucker you remove isn't a new cane."

The vital, normal replacement wood comes from the bud union (knobby looking section that should be just above ground surface) or slightly above. In most cases, the leaves of these new canes will be the same color as those on the bush itself. Suckers generally have lighter colored leaves and innumerable small thorns, and they always come from below the bud union.

Hybrid Tea Roses

Here's how to prune an established hybrid-tea rose bush step-by-step:

1. Remove all the obviously dead wood.

2. Remove wood that is heavily scaled, sunscalded, or covered with lesions.

3. Remove any branch that crosses through the

center of the plant or that rubs heavily on any other branch.

4. If new, large basal canes formed during the preceding growing season, remove an old cane for each new one to renew the plant. If suckers are present, cut them out completely. (If you only stub them, they will grow right back.) Remove soil to expose the point of the sucker's origin and cut it off clean at the base. Use a sharp knife, or break it off cleanly with your fingers.

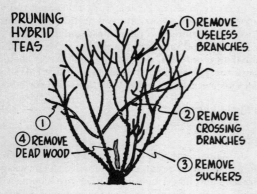

5. Stand back to see if the bush is balanced. Remove branches that make it appear lopsided.

6. Now you have a frame of clean branches. Next, look to the wood that was formed last year.

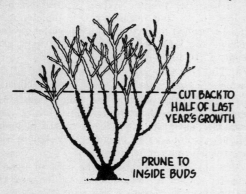

Although you can safely prune any rose according to these general rules, individual plant characteristics may call for some slight changes. Some roses throw little or no new wood from the base; allow them to establish a vigorous framework during the early years and then cut back rather lightly each season thereafter. Watch for a new cane so that old wood can be removed.

Prune unusually vigorous growers lightly. *Peace*, one of the all-time great roses, is a very strong grower that does its best when only about ⅓ of the previous year's growth is pruned.

Cutting Hybrid Teas and Grandifloras

Proper pruning throughout the year is also important. When you pick the flowers, always leave 2 or 3 good growth buds; later growth will result in a more attractive branching form if you cut to an outside-facing bud.

Remove any dead wood when you notice it. When basal canes—the important renewals—come up, treat them in either of two ways: (1) you can let them go, but they may make what growers call a "candelabra cane," with many smaller flowers that can be disbudded to make a few good-sized blooms; or (2) pinch out the tip bud, when the cane is about 10 inches high, to make several regular-blooming canes that are also capable of making replacements next winter.

Late-summer clean-up pruning consists of removing any dead wood, cutting back to 2 or 3 growth buds any bloom stems that were not previously cut, and opening up the bush if an unusual number of basal canes has been produced. Never prune heavily in summer.

Grandifloras should be pruned about the same as hybrid teas. Cut back to one-half of the previous season's growth.

Polyanthas and Floribundas

Because profusion of bloom is the object in growing these shrub-form roses, prune them rather lightly to encourage development of a multiplicity of small wood. Polyanthas and floribundas are naturally more twiggy than hybrid teas.

Tree Roses

Because it is impossible to renew the main cane, be careful to keep the permanent cane in good health. Proper staking is more important than pruning. At planting time, place the plant's supporting stake on the south side of the trunk to shade it against sunscald. In the hottest areas, it is wise to wrap the trunk with burlap. Tie the stem to the stake with coarse burlap or canvas strips. Where winds are high, cross-tie the top to the stake.

Prune to shape and cut back the branches to 12-14 inches from the trunk. Remove old wood if vigorous new shoots are produced. Always paint all cuts on the tree roses because the death of one stem eventually may be the death of one entire side of the top.

Climbing Roses

Most climbers respond to thinning and training into position, with occasional renewal of some of the older branches. Hybrid-tea climbers should not be trained on fan or other narrow, upright trellises because vertical growth becomes bare. On a fence, train them horizontally along the top and tie the tips down below the horizontal. This bending causes buds to break all along the canes. These buds produce flowering wood 2 to 3 feet long. Upright branches will bear just as bush roses do; prune them back to 2 or 3 eyes every time a bloom is cut. This same shoot will produce many blooms during the season if each bloom is cut back to 2 or 3 eyes. Original canes will become old and scaly after a number of years. Try to

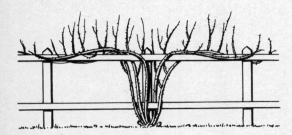

encourage the vigorous new canes that come from the base to replace the older canes. Do not retain too many basal canes. Climbers will do best with 2 or 3; never keep more than 4. If more start, retain new ones and cut off older ones at the base of the cane.

Thin out natural climbers such as *Paul's Scarlet* heavily after flowering in the spring. About all that is necessary is to remove the oldest canes from time to time and train the new canes as they are produced. Because profusion is always the desire with these roses, prune after flowering to allow maximum wood to develop for next year's flowers.

Cut back hybrid tea climbers during the dormant season, at the same time that you prune hybrid tea bush roses.

Sometimes climbers are wanted on narrow trellises or fans in spite of the fact that this is against their natural way of growth. If you insist on training a climber on an upright trellis, one way to increase flowering is to train the young shoots into "S" shapes as they mature. This creates horizontal portions of stem that will produce flowering wood.

After Dormant Pruning

Pull off all the leaves after the dormant pruning job is done. Many fungus diseases harbor over in old leaves. Rake them up and burn them.

Brush with shellac all cuts larger than the size of a lead pencil. Do not use tar paint—it will often cause dieback. If you grow roses in regions where the yellow horntail wasp is active it may be advisable to paint all cuts, regardless of size, as insurance against the introduction of the destructive wasp egg and consequent larvae into the cut cane.

Clean all crowns at ground level by flushing with a strong stream of water. Remove old manure and dirt from the crown.

CONTROL PESTS AND DISEASES

Of the pests that affect roses, aphis are far and away the most notorious and are, happily, the easiest to control. Any number of insecticides will kill them. The trick is to spray regularly during the height of the aphis season—those periods when plants are in new growth. Aphis have an astonishing capacity to reproduce and it's often necessary to spray weekly or every few days. Red spider mite will do more serious damage to a rose than any of the other insect pests, causing complete defoliation in severe cases. Other pests include thrips, various chewing insects, and borers. Most of them are controllable with multi-purpose insecticides (see page 50).

The principal disease is mildew, which occurs in humid regions or in other areas during cool, moist seasons. For control, spray with a fungicide containing copper, sulfur, dinitro capryl phenyl crotonate, or captan. Phaltan, a wettable powder, controls not only mildew but rust and black spot. You can also help prevent mildew by keeping water off rose leaves during cool, moist seasons. Irrigate instead of watering overhead. In chronically foggy areas, choose mildew-resistant roses. Reds in general are susceptible. The most resistant foliage is hard, glossy, and leathery, rather than soft and dull in finish. Many of the roses introduced since the middle 1950's have excellent resistance to mildew.

Black spot, another important disease, is characterized by black spots appearing on leaves, which then yellow and fall. It is frequently encountered in the East and Northwest, but is comparatively rare in California. For control, you can choose from several effective spray materials, including Phaltan; captan; ferbam; and sulfur in combination with maneb or zineb.

Rose leaf rust is a fungus disease that is quite prevalent in many areas of the West. Its appearance, usually in late spring, is first denoted by small bright orange spots on the undersides of the leaves. The infection spreads, particularly with warm weather, forming thick powdery masses of orange spores. A spray containing Phaltan or ferbam provides good control, or you may use a wettable sulfur spray plus 10% of maneb or zineb.

Rose varieties differ in susceptibility to rust as they do with mildew. Best cure is prevention, mainly by removing all diseased leaves on the plant and on the ground at pruning time and burning them.

Chlorosis is not a disease, but the symptoms of a nitrogen or an iron deficiency. It is usually caused by excessive alkalinity in the soil, which ties these nutrients up so they are unavailable to the plant even though they may be present in the soil. Where there is an iron deficiency leaves turn yellow, with lines of green marking the veins. A spring application of sulfur will increase soil acidity, and supplemental applications of iron sulfate —up to a cupful per plant in serious cases—or iron chelate usually turns leaves green fairly quickly. Water it in after applying.

For more information on roses, see the *Sunset* book, *How to Grow Roses*.

270 ROSES Shrubs
ENCYCLOPEDIA OF ROSES

The roses listed below are favorites everywhere, but all of them are particularly suitable to the West. Some of them are old favorites, others are newer introductions.

The American Rose Society (ARS) national ratings are compiled from reports of hundreds of rose growing members, and are subject to annual revision. A rating of 10 is a perfect rose; 9 to 10 is outstanding; 8 to 8.9 is excellent; 7 to 7.9 is good; 6 to 6.9 is fair.

All-America Rose Selections (AARS)—not to be confused with the above-mentioned ARS—are an annual selection of one or two outstanding introductions. In this list, AARS winners are indicated by an asterisk (*).

HYBRID TEAS

Name	Color	Fragrance	Disease Resistance	Height	ARS Rating	Comments
ANGEL WINGS	Yellow, white, pink	Fragrant	Resistant	4-5'	7.5	Delicate, attractive blooms on long, strong stems.
AUDIE MURPHY	Bright red	Slight fragrance	Resistant	4-5'	7.8	Beautiful, Eclipse-type buds. A Northwest favorite.
BURNABY	Creamy yellow	Delicate fragrance	Resistant	3-4'	8.1	This Canadian rose is a vigorous, profuse bloomer.
CAPISTRANO*	Deep rose-pink	Strong fragrance	Resistant	5-6'	7.4	Bushy, upright plant; good bloomer. Leathery foliage.
CHARLOTTE ARMSTRONG*	Red to dark pink	Slight fragrance	Resistant	3-4'	9.0	Strong grower; abundant blooms; an all-time great.
CHRYSLER IMPERIAL*	True red	Very fragrant	Resistant; some mildew	3-4'	8.8	A magnificent red. High-centered bud opens to a 40- to 50-petalled bloom.
CONFIDENCE	Pink blend	Very fragrant	Fair resistance	3-4'	8.3	Bloom is blend of yellow, white, peach pink.
COUNTESS VANDAL	Pink and buff	Fragrant	Mildews some in cool areas	2½-4'	7.5	Exhibition-type blooms; a fine cutting rose.
CRIMSON GLORY	Velvety crimson	Very fragrant	Mildews some in cool areas	3-4'	9.1	A long-time favorite red; vigorous; prefers warm climate.
DAINTY BESS	Dusky pink	Fragrant	Some mildew	3-4'	8.4	Most popular of the singles. Good cut flower if cut in tight bud.
DUET*	Salmon to crimson	Slight fragrance	Very resistant	3-5'	New	1961 All-America. Medium-size flower. Cuts well.
ECLIPSE	Light yellow	Fragrant	Resistant	3-4'	8.1	Exceptional, streamlined buds on long, straight stems.
ETOILE DE HOLLANDE	Deep red	Very fragrant	Some mildew	3-4'	8.1	One of the best reds; color rarely blues.
FIRST LOVE	Dawn pink	Slight fragrance	Resistant	3-4'	8.0	Blooms profusely. Outstanding for cuttings, arrangements.
GAIL BORDEN	Pink, red, apricot	Slight fragrance	Resistant	3½-5'	7.6	Large, truly glamorous flower, up to 70 petals.
GARDEN PARTY*	White, pink shadings	Fragrant	Some mildew	4-5'	New	1960 All-America. Descended from Peace and Charlotte Armstrong. Large blooms.
HELEN TRAUBEL*	Apricot pink	Mild fragrance	Resistant	4-5'	8.7	Vigorous plant. Long, tapering buds. A lovely rose.
LADY ELGIN	Orange-buff	Fragrant	Resistant	4-5'	7.6	Flower is new dark gold color. Vigorous; attractive foliage.
LOWELL THOMAS*	Yellow	Good fragrance	Resistant	3½-5'	7.7	A consistently reliable yellow.
McGREDY'S IVORY	Ivory white	Delicate fragrance	Fair resistance	3-4'	7.2	Many-petalled blooms borne freely on vigorous bush.
MISSION BELLS*	Salmon pink	Slight fragrance	Resistant	3-4'	7.9	Nearly always in bloom. Likes plenty of sun.
MOJAVE*	Tones of orange	Slight fragrance	Resistant	3-4'	7.4	Has a lovely rich color. Long stems, fine for cutting.
NEW YORKER	Rich red	Fragrant	Some mildew	3-4'	8.0	Long-time standard bearer of the medium reds.
NOCTURNE*	Dark red	Very fragrant	Mildews in cool areas	3-5'	8.1	Not good in coastal areas; needs dry heat.
PEACE*	Yellow, cerise	Delicate fragrance	Resistant	3½-5'	9.6	One of the greatest roses. Magnificent blooms. Vigorous.
PRESIDENT HOOVER	Orange, pink	Fragrant	Mildews slightly	5-6'	7.7	Tall grower; lovely, large flowers; a great favorite.
SATURNIA	Red, yellow	Very fragrant	Mildews	2½-3½'	8.1	In cool climates one of our most beautiful roses.

HYBRID TEAS (Continued)

Name	Color	Fragrance	Disease Resistance	Height	ARS Rating	Comments
SIGNORA	Orange-red	Slight fragrance	Resistant	4-5'	7.4	A fine Italian rose; handsome plant; long stems for cutting.
SNOWBIRD	White	Fragrant	Resistant	2-3'	7.1	A dependable white. Prolific bloomer; good keeper.
STERLING SILVER	Silvery lavender	Very fragrant	Resistant	3'	7.1	First of its kind in this color. A great new rose.
SUTTER'S GOLD*	Orange, yellow	Very fragrant	Resistant	4-5'	8.1	An exquisite rose; color is at its best in cool areas.
TAFFETA*	Pink, yellow, salmon	Strong fragrance	Some mildew	3-4'	7.2	Does best in warm climate. Outstanding flowers.
TANYA	Orange	Slight fragrance	Resistant	3½-4'	New	Large blooms, apricot orange to burnt orange.
TEXAS CENTENNIAL	Light red	Very fragrant	Mildews slightly	5-6'	7.8	A sport of President Hoover. Large blooms; vigorous grower.
TIFFANY*	Silvery pink, flushed gold	Very fragrant	Resistant	3-4'	8.8	A truly impressive rose, at its best in warm areas.
VIRGO	Pure white	Mild fragrance	Mildews slightly	2½'	No rating	Superb streamlined buds, wonderful for arrangements.
WHITE KNIGHT*	Pure white	Mild fragrance	Mildews slightly	3-4'	7.2	First white hybrid tea rose to win an All-America award. Long stems, fine for cutting.

GRANDIFLORAS

Name	Color	Fragrance	Disease Resistance	Height	ARS Rating	Comments
CARROUSEL	Vivid dark red	Slight fragrance	Resistant	3-4'	9.0	Flowers 3 to 4 inches in diameter, hold color well.
EL CAPITAN	Cherry red	Slight fragrance	Resistant	5'	New	Extremely free blooming. Flowers hold color well.
GOLDEN GIRL	Clear yellow	Slight fragrance	Resistant	3-4'	New	Blooms hold color best if plant is in partial shade.
MONTEZUMA	Salmon orange	Slight fragrance	Resistant	3-4'	8.5	Great cutting rose. "Blues" some in cool weather.
PINK PARFAIT*	Blend of pastel-pink	Slight fragrance	Resistant	3-4'	New	1961 All-America. Compact plant. Likes cool weather.
QUEEN ELIZABETH*	Delicate clear pink	Slight fragrance	Very resistant	5-7'	9.0	Tall, stately plant; lovely blooms. Stems nearly thornless.
ROUNDELAY	Dark red	Slight fragrance	Resistant	5'	8.0	Handsome, high-centered blooms. Vigorous plant.
STARFIRE*	Currant red	Slight fragrance	Resistant	4-6'	8.1	Blooms singly and in clusters on 6 to 12-inch stems.

FLORIBUNDAS

Name	Color	Fragrance	Disease Resistance	Height	ARS Rating	Comments
BETTY PRIOR	Carmine to shell pink	No fragrance	Resistant	4-5'	9.0	Red buds open to pink, single flowers. Vigorous.
CHINA DOLL	Pink	Slight fragrance	Resistant	15-18 in.	7.3	Compact, profuse-blooming plant, excellent for low borders.
CIRCUS*	Orange, buff, pink	No fragrance	Resistant	2½-3'	7.8	Everchanging colors; a real eye-catcher.
FASHION*	Coral pink	Slight fragrance	Mildews slightly	2½-3'	8.9	Low-spreading bush, delightful color; fades some in sun.
FIRE KING*	Brilliant vermillion	Slight fragrance	Mildews slightly	3-4'	New	1960 All-America. Long lasting double blooms.
FLORADORA*	Scarlet-orange	No fragrance	Some mildew	3-4'	8.6	Vigorous, upright. Fades some in hot weather.
FRENSHAM	Deep crimson	Slight fragrance	Some mildew	3-4'	8.6	A superb floribunda; produces masses of unfading blooms.
FUSILIER*	Iridescent vermillion	Slight fragrance	Mildews	2½-3½	7.8	Dazzling red. Makes a handsome tub plant.
GOLD CUP*	Deep yellow	Sweet fragrance	Resistant	3'	7.1	Generally regarded as a fine yellow floribunda.
HEAT WAVE	Fiery red	Slight fragrance	Resistant	4-5'	7.8	Well formed blooms; a good red for cutting.

(Continued on next page.)

FLORIBUNDAS (Continued)

Name	Color	Fragrance	Disease Resistance	Height	ARS Rating	Comments
IVORY FASHION*	Ivory white	Sweet fragrance	Resistant	2-3	8.0	High centered flowers open to reveal nest of golden stamens.
LITTLE DARLING	Yellow, pink, orange	Fragrant	Resistant	4-5'	8.4	One of the most appealing of all floribundas. Unique color.
MA PERKINS*	Light pink	Mild fragrance	Resistant	2-3'	7.9	Sturdy, compact grower. Blooms make lovely corsages, bouquets.
MARGO KOSTER	Red-orange	Slight fragrance	Resistant	2'	7.9	A long-popular polyantha. Blooms shaped like egg cups.
PINKIE*	Pink	No fragrance	Resistant	2½-3½	7.6	Baby polyantha, flowers 2 inches across. Fine for low hedges.
RED PINOCCHIO	Dark red	Slight fragrance	Resistant	2-3'	8.8	Small, perfectly formed double blooms. Hardy.
ROSENELFE	Clear pink	Slight fragrance	Resistant	3-4'	8.2	One of the best floribundas for cutting and arrangements.
SARABANDE*	Scarlet-orange	Slight fragrance	Very resistant	2½-3'	New	1960 All-America. Semi-single flowers; yellow stamens
SPARTAN*	Orange-red	Sweet fragrance	Resistant	2½-3'	8.3	Perfectly formed blooms of 35-40 petals. Vigorous plant.
VOGUE*	Cherry	Spicy	Resistant	2½-3½'	8.2	A great favorite. High-centered flowers. Ideal for massed color.

CLIMBERS AND PILLAR TYPES

Name	Color	Fragrance	Disease Resistance	Height	ARS Rating	Comments
CLG. CARROUSEL	Vivid dark red	Slight fragrance	Mildews slightly	10'	New	A grandiflora climber. Stems long enough for cutting.
CLG. CECILE BRUNNER	Light pink	Fragrant	Slight mildew	20-30'	8.5	The "Sweetheart rose." Still most popular baby rose.
CLG. ETOILE DE HOLLANDE	Deep red	Very fragrant	Resistant	15-20'	8.6	Best of the red climbers; repeats bloom freely.
CLG. MRS. SAM McGREDY	Salmon copper	Fragrant	Mildews slightly	15-20'	8.9	Generally rated best of all climbers.
CLG. PEACE	Yellow, cerise	Delicate fragrance	Resistant	15-20'	7.2	A truly impressive sight when fully matured.
CLG. PICTURE	Light pink	Slight fragrance	Mildews	8-15'	8.4	A better climber than a bush; good bloomer.
CLG. QUEEN ELIZABETH	Delicate clear pink	Mild fragrance	Very resistant	15'	New	A sport of the highly regarded grandiflora.
GLADIATOR	Rose-red	Delicate fragrance	Resistant	8-10'	8.1	Pillar type. Large blooms, continuous bloomer.
GOLDEN SHOWERS*	Yellow	Fragrant	Very resistant	8-10'	7.3	Pillar type. 4-5 inch flowers. A continuous bloomer.
HIGH NOON*	Yellow	Slight fragrance	Very resistant	8-12'	7.9	Pillar type, but in mild areas often grows to 20 feet.
PAUL'S SCARLET	Scarlet	Slight fragrance	Mildews slightly	10-15'	9.1	Profuse spring bloomer. Can repeat if cut back after flowering.

Flowering Fruits

Some gardeners could no more imagine the coming of spring without some flowering fruit trees about, than they could picture Christmas without colored lights. Certainly no plant can say "spring is here" any faster than a flowering fruit tree.

The deciduous trees and shrubs that are generally classified as flowering fruit trees are the free-flowering species of the genera *Prunus* and *Malus*. The *Prunus* genus includes the plum, peach, apricot, cherry, almond; *Malus* presents the flowering crabapple.

We have gathered them in one chapter, not because they constitute all of the flowering trees, but because they have a similar function in the garden. There is need to choose and compare. We have attempted in all cases to supply the usually missing bit of information—the size and structure of the tree. It is important, we think, to consider the character of the tree out of bloom since that is what you live with 50 weeks out of the year.

FLOWERING ALMONDS

The flowering almonds, *Prunus glandulosa*, have no resemblance to the common nut tree, *Prunus amygdalus*. The flowering almonds are hardy in all but the coldest sections of the West. They are small, much-branched spreading shrubs. The flowers, resembling light fluffy pompon chrysanthemums, are set close to the slender branches. They are single or double, pink or white depending on variety.

The flowering almonds are listed in several ways in catalogs and nurseries.

P. g. sinensis. The double pink form, growing to 6 ft., is also listed as *P. amygdalus rosea plena* and *P. amygdalus Doublepink*.

P. g. alboplena. The double white form is sometimes listed as *P. amygdalus Doublewhite*.

There are dwarf forms in pink and white that grow no higher than 3 ft. They are listed one way or another as described above, with *nana* tacked onto the name chosen.

FLOWERING APRICOTS

Most of the flowering apricots sold today are varieties of *Prunus mume*, the Japanese apricot, rather than of *Prunus armeniaca*, the orchard apricot.

Prunus mume. JAPANESE APRICOT. A round-headed, rather open tree to 30 ft. Fragrant, pink, single blossoms in late April. Fruits are like small plums and are very sour. Highly regarded as fruit delicacy by the Japanese.

P. m. alboplena. Double white flowers.

P. m. Bonita. Double crimson flowers.

P. m. Dawn. Double shell pink flowers.

P. m. Peggy Clarke. Double deep rose flowers.

P. m. Rosemary Clarke. Double white flowers with extremely long stamens and a red calyx.

The varieties are not as vigorous as the species and are generally about 20 ft. high when mature. Earlier blossoming, too—in January and early February. Annual pruning is necessary for good flowering effect. Here's how: Allow the tree to grow for one year after planting, then prune back all the shoots to 6-in. stubs, as with flowering peach. The next year, cut back half the whips (young branches without sideshoots), leaving 6-in. stubs. The other half of the whips should be cut back the following year. Continue this routine in succeeding years.

Have been grown in zones 3-5, but blossoms are often damaged. Best in zones 7-13. Good drainage is essential. Since flowers are borne on two-year wood and tree must be renewed by annual removal of half the wood, it's not a tree to be planted close up. Best in background or behind a fence.

FLOWERING CHERRIES

The cherries find their favorite climate in the Pacific Northwest zones of 1-6. In the mild-winter areas of Southern California the only species sure to blossom with full effectiveness is *Prunus campanulata*. In the coldest areas of the West many of the *P. serrulata* series are of doubtful hardiness. The following are recommended as the hardiest: *P. subhirtella*, *P. yedoensis*, *P. sieboldii*, and *P. serrulata Kwanzan*.

The double and triple naming of the flowering cherries is very confusing. In some cases the mix-up is not important to the buyer because the difference is slight, but there are important differences in form and height that should be known. In the following list we have brought together all the names used in the nursery trade and have attached them to the tree to which they belong.

P. campanulata. CHINESE FLOWERING CHERRY. FORMOSA CHERRY. TAIWAN CHERRY. A densely branched, bushy, small tree to 20 ft. Rose-colored, single, 1-in. flowers in early spring, followed by red fruit in summer. Adapted to Southern California, where it blooms weeks earlier than other cherries.

P. jacquemontii. JACQUEMONT CHERRY. Hardy all zones. A very fast growing, bushy, rounded shrub. Of interest for its burst of single pink flowers in February-March and edible, ½-in., red "cherries" in clusters in May and June.

P. serrulata. ORIENTAL CHERRY. The following varieties are sold by Western nurseries:

P. s. Amanogawa. Spire-like columnar form to 20 ft. Fragrant, light pink, semi-double, 1¾-in. flowers.

P. s. Kwanzan (var. *Seki-Numa*, var. *Yae-Kanzan*). Stiffly upright tree, giving a bronze tone to the landscape. Fast growing to 18-25 ft. Tips of the long, straight growth should be pinched out to encourage side branching. Deep pink, double, 2½-in. flowers. There's a lot of blue in the pink.

P. s. Ojochin. A vigorous grower to 25 ft. Single, large, crinkled flowers, pink in bud, pale pink or white when open.

P. s. Shirofugen (*P. s. albo rosea*). Fast-growing to 20 ft. Spreading habit; often allowed to grow shrub-like. Later flowering than most, the pink buds open into double white flowers just as the new bronzy leaves are forming.

P. s. Shirotae (var. *Mt. Fuji*, var. *Kojima*). Slow growing to 20 ft. and spreading to 40 ft. or more. Horizontal branching pattern. Fragrant, double and semi-double, white, 2½-in. flowers with ruffled petals, hang under long horizontal branches. Definitely a tree to look up into, so plant on bank, or above retaining wall, or in its youthful years in a raised bed. Not dependable in very cold winter sections. Blooms are better than many other cherries after mild winters.

P. subhirtella (var. *Higan Sakura*). HIGAN CHERRY. Slow growing to 30 ft.; dense and bushy, wide spreading with branches often to the ground. Light pink, single, 1-in. flowers in great profusion in April.

P. s. autumnalis. A small tree of spreading habit to 20-30 ft. Begins flowering after the leaves have fallen in late October or November. Scattered bloom throughout a mild winter, heavy bloom again in early spring with the opening of the new leaves. Flowers, stemless in fall but with stems in spring, are semi-double white, flushed with pink.

P. s. Beni Higan (var. *rosea*, var. *Beni Higan Zakura*). Pale pink flowers with red calyces in great profusion in early April.

P. s. pendula. WEEPING FLOWERING CHERRY. Weeping branches, slender leaves, give the tree a graceful, light and airy effect. At tulip time, April and May, pendulous branches are covered with clusters of small, light pink blossoms. *P. s. pendula plena rosea* (var. *Yae Beni-Shidare*) is the double-flowered form.

Weeping cherries aren't easy to handle. The form is not one that you can crowd. It needs to stand alone in a special spot.

P. sieboldii (*P. naden*). NADEN CHERRY. A slow growing, rather upright tree to 15-20 ft., with very light pink, semi-double, 1½-in. flowers. The first double to bloom.

P. yedoensis. YOSHINO CHERRY. Moderate growth to an eventual 50 ft. Rather broad spreading, with light and open limb structure. Clusters of single, 1-in. flowers go through interesting stages—in early spring on bare branches they are deep rose in bud, then shell pink in flower, finally fading to white as the new leaf growth crowds them off the branches. This species makes up most of the planting around the Tidal Basin in Washington, D. C.

Vars. *Akebono, Daybreak,* and *Stribling's Pink* are seemingly smaller forms, but in all other respects identical.

All cherries are shortlived in heavy, poorly drained, and shallow soil. Water deeply, but at infrequent intervals in summer while trees are young.

FLOWERING PEACHES

For flowers alone no other flowering tree can beat the peach. In the southern sections of the West where the lack of winter cold causes many of the more sophisticated flowering trees to sulk and bloom poorly, the flowering peach is by all counts the favorite.

However, unless its drawbacks are recognized, the peach is a very disappointing tree. It must be sprayed during the dormant season for peach-leaf curl. The wood that has borne flowers must be cut back each year at flowering time. Cut back to 6-inch stubs. New growth will be luxuriant by the end of the summer and covered by flowers the following spring.

Because of severe spring pruning the peach is at its best where the structure of the plant is not important—in the vegetable garden, behind evergreen shrubs, fence, or wall.

Prunus persica. PEACH. The flowering peaches are cultivated forms of this species. Some of the varieties are:

P. p. Altair. Double pink flowers in late February, juicy white-fleshed peaches in August. Prune as you would a fruit tree.

P. p. Burbank. Double pink flowers.

P. p. Helen Borchers. Clear pink, 2½-in. flowers.

P. p. Peppermint Stick. Striped, red and white flowers.

P. p. Two-Star (See peaches in chapter on Home Food Garden for details on flowering-fruiting peaches.)

Flowering peaches should be regarded as temporary trees, to be removed when too woody. Very susceptible to root and crown rot. Should not be planted where winter or summer drainage is poor.

FLOWERING PLUMS

There are more species and varieties of the deciduous flowering plums than most gardeners realize.

Prunus triloba. FLOWERING PLUM. A dainty, dwarf tree with a definite trunk and slender branches, growing to 12 ft. Flowers, like double pink roses, are set all along the previous summer's shoots. Prune when flowering or immediately following.

P. cistena. DWARF REDLEAF PLUM. PURPLE SAND CHERRY. Dwarf tree to 10 ft. Purple leaves; single white flowers in May.

P. cerasifera. CHERRY PLUM. MYROBALAN. Because this species can stand heavy wet soil, its seedlings are used as rootstocks for plums, prunes, and apricots. Although the species varies in size and vigor, its small white flowers in February give the tree a delightful white smoky appearance. Should be in any flowering tree collection where there's space for a woodland effect.

Seedlings of the purple-leafed strains of Myrobalan show great variation both in leaf color and in growth habit. Distinct differences in varieties may or may not be noticeable in the individual trees you buy. All bear reddish small plums that are edible and used for making jam.

P. c. atropurpurea (*P. pissardii, P. c. pissardii*). PURPLELEAF PLUM. Widely used for contrast in foliage color. Its Y-shaped outline of branches makes it useful for planting among large shrubs. The tree is rather awkward when planted alone. Small whitish-pink, single flowers in February or even late January.

P. c. Vesuvius. The darkest of the flowering plums. Foliage is almost black.

P. c. Hollywood. Red and green leaves. Comparatively large clusters of small, pink flowers.

P. c. Thundercloud. Dark, coppery foliage. More rounded form than purpleleaf plum.

Hybrid *P. blireiana* (*P. c. blireiana*), a cross between purpleleaf plum and *Prunus mume*. A less vigorous tree than purpleleaf plum, but of more graceful form. Reddish-bronze leaves. Double pink flowers cover the stems before the leaves appear, in February-March. Var. *Newport* is said to be improved form of *P. blireiana* with more blossoms.

Hardy all zones. The need for winter chilling is greater for *P. triloba* and *P. cistena* than for any of the *P. cerasifera* series. The apricot parentage (*P. mume*) of *P. blireiana* gives it a low chilling requirement and makes it popular in Southern California.

The flowering plums tolerate almost any soil condition. Should be in sun for good leaf color, but will take some shade. Prune flowering wood or cut branches immediately following blossom fall. If the purple foliaged plums had no flowers, they would be used just as widely for the contrasting lift they give to gray-green and dark green backgrounds.

MALUS—FLOWERING CRABAPPLE

Name	Ht. Spread (in feet)	Structure	Foliage	Flowers	Fruit
M. adstringens Hopa	Fast to 25 by 20	Vigorous, fast growing, upright branching without interlacing branch habit of typical crab.	Dense foliage, dark green with slightly brown cast.	Fragrant, single rose-red, 1½-in. April.	Orange-red, ¾-in.; excellent for jellies.
M. atrosanguinea	Mod. to 18 by 18	Upright branching with drooping tips. Open and irregular, sparse branches and foliage.	Purplish-green with more sheen than average crab.	Fragrant, crimson to rose-pink; very profuse. Late April-May	Yellow to brown, ⅓-in., hanging through winter in withered state.
M. baccata mandschurica	Mod. to 40 by 20	Vase shaped, bushy and dense.	Dense foliage.	Fragrant, white, 1-in.; earliest to bloom. April.	Bright yellow and scarlet, ½-in., in profusion.

MALUS—FLOWERING CRABAPPLE

Name	Ht. Spread (in feet)	Structure	Foliage	Flowers	Fruit
M. coronaria	Mod. to 30 by 20	Weeping, somewhat columnar but wider at mid-height. Rather variable. (**M. c. charlottae**, double-flowered form.)	Very dense foliage.	Violet scented, pale pink. May-June.	Green, 1-1½-in.; of no garden value.
M. floribunda **JAPANESE CRAB**	Slow to 20 by 30	Not vigorous, but sturdy. Irregular, angular branching. Sometimes almost horizontal.	Dense, fine-textured, dull green.	Fragrant, pink fading to white, 1½-in., single. May.	Small, ⅜-in., yellow and red; non-edible.
M. f. arnoldiana (M. arnoldiana)	20 by 30	Form with long arching branches, giving it a broad, spreading habit of growth.	Larger leaves than **M. floribunda**.	Larger and paler than **M. floribunda**. May.	Yellow and red.
M. f. scheideckeri (M. scheideckeri)	20 by 16	Upright growth habit with interesting interlacing of branches, giving it a typical "rugged" crab form.	Dark green, glossy.	Semi-double, deep pink opening to a lighter shade. May.	Uninteresting, small, yellow, ⅝-in.
M. halliana parkmanii (M. parkmanii)	Very slow to 15 by 12	Arching branch structure forming rather globe-shaped, small tree to 5 ft. in 10 yrs. (Hort. var. **Katherine** considered an outstanding improvement.)	Dark green leaves; rather sparse foliage.	Double, rose, 1¼-in., in clusters on dark, wine-red stems. May.	Dull red, ¼-in.; not ornamental.
M. hupehensis (M. theifera) **TEA CRAB**	Mod. to 15 by 20	Rigid, spreading branches at base with upright side branches.	Dense, bushy foliage.	Pink fading almost white; very profuse. April-May.	Greenish-yellow with some red; not ornamental.
M. ioensis plena **BECHTEL'S CRAB**	Mod. to 25 by 18	Vase shaped. Least desirable for form and foliage but widely planted for large flowers. (Hort. var. **Prince Georges** has more dense foliage.)	Sparse, coarse, soft green. Subject to fungus.	Large, double, pink, resembling small roses; short period of bloom. May or June.	Yellowish-brown, 1-1¼ in.; but usually practically fruitless.
M. sargentii	Slow to 10 by 20	Low, broad, and spreading. One of the best dwarf forms. Variable; some must be pruned to hold low growth habit.	Dark green, larger leaves, 3-lobed.	Pure white, 1-in., in clusters of 5-6. May.	Wine-red, ¼-⅜ in.; hang on through winter.
M. sieboldii	10 by 12	Spreading, graceful shrub form. Broader than tall. Angular, twiggy branched. One of the best. Prune to keep graceful.	Not too dense.	Pink to deep rose, ⅜-in., in clusters of 3-6. April.	Red or brownish yellow, ¼-in.
M. spectabilis albiplena	15 by 12	Spreading, interlacing branch structure eventually wider than tall, with flat top.	Glossy, medium dark green leaves.	Double, white, rose-like. April-May.	Yellowish, ¾-1 in.; very bitter.
M. s. riversii	15 by 12	Double, pink form of **M. spectabilis**. Upright habit of growth.	Large glossy leaves.	Double, rose-like, pink, in abundance. April-May.	Yellowish, ¾-1 in.; very bitter.
M. sylvestris aldenhamensis (M. purpurea aldenhamensis)	Fast to 20 by 20	Tree form like wild apple.	Unusual purple bark and leaves.	Semi-double, purplish-red. April.	Deep purple-red.
M. s. eleyi (M. purpurea eleyi)	Fast to 20 by 20	Irregular, leggy, wide as tall. Fast growing but retains pleasing graceful forms. Reddish twigs.	Dark green leaves with reddish veins and stalks; attractive foliage.	Wine-red, 1¼-in. April.	Heavy crops of purplish-red, ¾-in.
Red Silver Crab	Fast to 15 by 15	Form of **M. s. eleyi**. Much like it in habit. Irregular branch pattern, the branch tips slightly drooping.	Reddish or purplish-bronze leaves; attractive foliage.	Deep wine-red. April.	Dark purplish-red, ¾-in.
M. s. lemoinei (M. purpurea lemoinei)	Fast to 25 by 18	More columnar than **M. s. eleyi**. Rather open and delicate in appearance.	Purple leaves, or somewhat bronzy.	Dark crimson. April.	Purplish-red.
M. s. niedzwetzkyana (M. pumila niedzwetzkyana)	Fast to 25 by 18	Develops rapidly; irregular branch pattern. Red-wooded. One of the parents of all forms with red leaves.	Large purplish-green leaves.	Purple-rose, 1½-in. April.	Wine-red, 2-in.
M. zumi calocarpa	25 by 15	Upright branching, but weeping in habit.	Larger leaves, 2-4 in., 3-lobed on vigorous shoots.	Open, soft pink fades to white. May.	Small, glossy red, ½-in.

Olive

Silk tree

Monterey pine

Trees

A tree is a woody plant which, if left to its own devices, will eventually grow larger than most shrubs.

Trees have been catalogued too long as "specimens," standing alone, trained to look like a picture in a book. Actually, as you have seen many times in a forest, the habit of growth of a tree is variable to an exciting degree. Trees are not constant, invariable, structural forms. Each has its individual growth characteristics, which change when the tree grows in the open, according to its association with other trees, or according to the proportion of shade, sun, or wind. Recognizing this fact we can put trees to better use by controlling or encouraging their natural tendencies, and by placing them according to any one of their growth habits.

SHRUB OR TREE?

It is difficult to separate shrub from tree when the plant is viewed within the garden. Botanically, the classification is likewise baffling. Should shrub stop or tree start at 8, 15, or 20 feet? Golden privet is leggy, but presentable at 15 feet. *Syringa vulgaris* booms upward rapidly and decisively, yet it is a shrub. Our classification in this book has been made on the basis of use. If a plant can serve one of the purposes of a tree, in about the same growth period as a tree, it will be indexed under trees.

Many plants classified as hedge plants will become small trees if not trimmed. The privet is the best known example. On the other hand, many plants classified as forest trees can be used as hedge plants. Trees are not constant in form.

NEW WAYS TO LOOK AT TREES

When you consider how many forms these plants called trees can assume, you realize how much you miss when you limit your thoughts of them to the mental picture of the typical tree form.

Here are just a few examples:

Where you want a large bold leaf, the fig tree often works better than a vine. As with many other trees, the fig will cover the surface of fence and wall more quickly than most permanent vines.

In redwoods and many other conifers, you have hedge material that gets up into the air fast, but can be held to the size you want with no more pruning than is needed for privet.

Silk tree (Albizzia julibrissin) is street tree or a ground cover, depending upon how tree is pruned from the start. When pruned in the beginning to branch from 8-foot height, the branches will grow out laterally to make a canopy over the street. When pruned to branch near the ground, the silk tree grows low and wide.

USING TREES TO SOLVE PROBLEMS

There is one important point to keep in mind when considering the use of trees in a form other than that generally considered natural. It is generally just as much work to train and keep a tree in the so-called natural form as in the form you would like it to grow in.

If you think of trees in the broad classes of "street trees," "lawn trees," "specimens," and "wind breaks," your need for trees is extremely limited. There isn't room for many "specimen" trees in a small garden.

On the other hand, trees become very useful plants in many situations if you start your thinking with the *situation* rather than the tree.

Questions like these will lead to many tree discoveries: What can I plant on that fence that will give a good pattern of green right now? What can I use to cut down some of the hot sun on that west wall? What will shut out the view of the neighbors —next year? What should I use on the slope below us?

Following are suggestions that will lead you into the excitement of using trees to solve landscape, decoration, and functional (climate control) problems. We have grouped trees by uses in the garden. In working with our lists, note that climate adaptability is noted in very broad terms. Read the specific recommendations by climate zone in the individual tree descriptions.

Trees You Can Garden or Maintain a Lawn Under

... trees that give, or can be pruned to give, filtered sunlight; can be lived under, gardened under. Roots not too invasive.

Celtis occidentalis
Ficus retusa
Gleditsia triacanthos inermis Moraine
Koelreuteria paniculata
Pistacia chinensis
Quercus species
Sophora japonica
Tilia americana

Trees for Parking Strips

... trees that are moderate in height, high enough to walk under; slow growing, round headed or high spreading, clean and not voracious.

Aesculus carnea briotii
Cinnamomum camphora
Cratægus phænopyrum
Ficus retusa
Flowering cherry
Flowering crabapple
Ginkgo biloba
Lagerstrœmia indica
Magnolia grandiflora
Metrosideros tomentosa
Pistacia chinensis
Tristania conferta
Zelkova serrata

Flowering Trees to Look Down Upon

... trees with upright flower clusters or blossoms along top of branches. Use on low ground of slopes; below decks of hillside houses.

Aesculus carnea briotii
Albizzia julibrissin
Cornus nuttallii
Eucalyptus ficifolia
Jacaranda acutifolia
Lagerstrœmia indica
Magnolia grandiflora
Paulownia tomentosa

Flowering Trees to Look Up Into

... trees whose flowers hang down and are best seen from below. Use on slopes, place them on high ground.

Halesia carolina
Laburnum watereri
Sophora japonica
Styrax japonica

Tall Screens and Low Windbreaks

... small trees—large shrubs that can be planted a few feet apart to serve as a high fence for more privacy and better wind protection than a 6-foot hedge or fence; screens to block the winter sun.

Duranta repens
Eucalyptus globulus compacta
Eucalyptus macrandra
Libocedrus decurrens
Ligustrum japonicum
Myoporum lætum
Myrica californica
Prunus ilicifolia
Prunus laurocerasus
Prunus lusitanica
Prunus lyonii
Rhamnus alaternus
Sequoia sempervirens

Trees for Winter Form

... trees that have interesting form and picturesque branch pattern, add character to a leafless landscape.

Acer palmatum
Betula species
Cercis canadensis
Cornus nuttallii
Cydonia oblonga
Fagus sylvatica atropunicea
Ficus carica Mission
Lagerstrœmia indica
Liquidambar styraciflua
Nyssa sylvatica
Platanus racemosa
Populus alba pyramidalis
Rhus glabra
Rhus typhina

Trees for Winter Color

... trees whose colorful bark or twigs brighten a dull winter day.

Betula species
Cercidiphyllum japonicum
Cornus kousa
Cornus stolonifera
Lagerstrœmia indica
Oxydendrum arboreum
Salix babylonica aurea

Trees for Fall Color

Acer palmatum
Acer saccharum
Betula species
Cornus kousa
Cornus nuttallii
Fraxinus velutina glabra
Ginkgo biloba
Larix decidua
Liquidambar styraciflua
Liriodendron tulipifera
Nyssa sylvatica
Oxydendrum arboreum
Persimmon
Pistacia chinensis
Quercus species
Sorbus aucuparia

Small Shade Trees for Patio-Terrace

... small trees of upright, spreading habit and changing interest (they are viewed intimately). These trees represent a wide range in density of shade. All are neat.

Cercis canadensis
Cratægus phænopyrum
Ficus retusa
Halesia carolina
Harpephyllum caffrum
Hymenosporum flavum
Lagerstrœmia indica
Ligustrum japonicum
Pyrus kawakami
Schinus terebinthifolius
Tristania conferta

Trees for Containers

Acer palmatum
Flowering apricot
Flowering cherry
Lagerstrœmia indica

278 TREES

Trees for Small Places
... trees, small or slender, or light weight, that use very little garden space but are not the type to sit under.

Cercis canadensis
Chionanthus virginica
Cornus florida
Eucalyptus species
Flowering cherry
Flowering crabapple
Lagerstrœmia indica

Trees Most Tolerant of Wet Soil
... trees that will live in a lawn, or a low, wet spot in your garden.

Acer species
Alnus rhombifolia
Betula species
Liriodendron tulipifera
Nyssa sylvatica
Platanus species
Tilia species

Trees Whose Trunks Should Not Be Hidden by Shrubs
... trees with beauty in trunk form and color; trunks should be seen for complete picture.

Agonis flexuosa
Arbutus menziesii
Betula species
Cornus alba sibirica
Fagus sylvatica atropunicea
Lagerstrœmia indica
Leptospermum lævigatum
Olea europœa
Platanus racemosa

HELPFUL POINTERS

Rate of Growth
No one who knows trees likes to give a definite answer to the question "How fast will it grow?" The average rate of growth can be estimated according to the inherent qualities of the tree. Usually this rate is stated roughly as slow, moderate, and fast.

As we have used these terms, slow means 6 inches or less growth a year. Moderate means an increase in height between 1 and 2 feet a year. Fast means 3 to 6 feet a year.

But remember that this rate of growth is simply an average rate. What is true in one climate may be utter nonsense in another. In California's Sacramento Valley the gingko tree is a moderate-to-fast grower; but in the Northwest it may just sit and do nothing or add a few inches a year. The Douglas fir adds 18 inches a year in western Washington but lags along with less than 6 inches in Santa Barbara.

The oaks are regarded as slower growers and about the last choice for planting for shade. However, we know of 30-year-old oaks with 60-foot-wide spreads. Many of the oaks respond to water and fertilizer and grow rapidly. None of the usual oak-root trouble from watering seems to develop if the watering program starts when the tree is young.

The fact that a tree is slow growing in your climate is to your advantage or disadvantage depending on the use you wish to make of it. There is no sense in choosing a slow grower if your need is to blot out the heat of the Western sun. On the other hand a decorative row of liquidambars planted 8 to 10 feet apart along a driveway makes beautiful sense regardless of whether the trees are 6, 10, or 16 feet tall.

Thinning Foliage
Trees can be changed from dense shade to filtered sunlight. Many an old oak tree which has grown dense and is heavy with small branches can be made into a sunshine filter if you thin out the branches in the top around the center. Thinning out any tree to allow the sun to filter into flower beds has a most beneficial effect upon the health of the tree by giving life to leaves otherwise completely shaded.

HOW TO PLANT A TREE

Trees come in three kinds of packages. Deciduous trees may come to you in any one of three ways. Those that are available bare root are dug, sold, and planted during the dormant season—December into or through March.

Conifers or broadleafed evergreens come to you with roots in a burlap covered ball or in a can, and should be planted as soon as possible after they are dug.

Other trees in cans may be planted any time. To avoid the risk of injuring roots while trying to cut a can with makeshift tools, ask your nurseryman to cut the can for you.

Test for drainage. If there is any question of drainage due to heavy soil or hardpan, fill each planting hole with water and check the rate of drain-off.

If the water doesn't drain, follow one of the corrective methods described below.

Trees with Root Ball
To plant balled and burlapped trees and shrubs from cans:

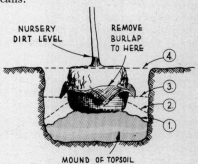

1. Dig hole 8-12 in. wider and 4-6 in. deeper than root ball.
2. Fill back with topsoil, forming a mound on which root ball will be placed.
3. With burlap still around ball, see how plant fits the hole.
4. When nursery-dirt ring around trunk is slightly above ground-level, the planting depth is right.

5. Fill in enough soil to hold root ball in place.
6. Fold back the burlap from the ball.
7. Fill ½ full with soil and tamp soil to remove air pockets.
8. Fill hole with water twice, making sure at end of soaking that water hasn't run through filled soil and left the root ball dry.
9. Fill with soil to ground level.
10. If you are planting a tree or shrub from a tin can during the summer months, watch leaves closely for signs of wilting during the first two or three weeks. It usually takes about that long for the roots to grow out of the original earth cylinder and get a good hold on the surrounding soil. Meanwhile, your plant will require water as often as it would if it were still in a container.

Bare-root Trees

For bare-root trees in good soil, dig hole large enough to allow roots to spread out naturally without cramping. Mound soil at bottom of hole, using fertile topsoil. Hold tree trunk so that planting depth will be same as planted in nursery. Dirt ring above roots shows that level. When laying out roots, watch for breaks and bruises. Remove broken roots with a smooth clean cut.

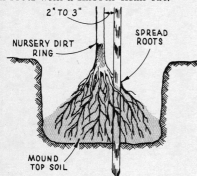

Fill and firm soil about the roots. Work the first filled soil in and around the roots. Use your fingers to work soil around and under the roots. Avoid air pockets.

Soak to settle soil when hole is ¾ full. After water drains away, fill up the hole with loose topsoil. Water again.

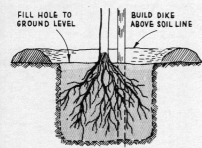

For watering basin build 6-inch high dike in a circle around tree. Make the basin a few inches wider than the planting hole so that you will be sure to have moist soil ready when the roots begin to extend themselves. Build dike above ground level so that when removed there will be no basin to hold winter rains.

Option in watering method is the 4-in. clay tile drain set vertically and either capped or filled with gravel. For best results, set 4 tiles around the tree at a distance of 2-3 inches beyond roots. Advantage of tile drain is that topsoil is dry and need for weeding and cultivating is lessened.

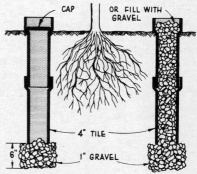

Planting in Shallow Soils

First step in planting is to correct the drainage in shallow soils underlaid with impervious hardpan. If you can, bore through the hardpan with a posthole auger. Below the hardpan you may run into gravel that will carry off excess water, and then your problem is solved. If you don't hit a gravel layer, or can't bore through the hardpan, there are other ways, namely:

1. *Tile drains above hardpan* offer another solution which works best when planting a row of trees in location where drainage ditch is possible.

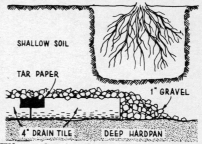

2. *When there's shallow soil and no outlet through hardpan:* Place soil above original grade and contain it in 6-foot-square raised bed 18 in. high.

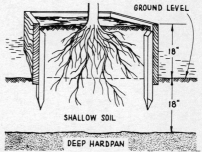

280 TREES

3. *Crack the hardpan with heavy machinery.* Another solution to the hardpan problem is to go into the entire planting area with heavy equipment and break up the hardpan to a depth of 3 feet. Subsoilers that rip deep into hardpan can be rented from some larger landscape contractors.

Planting in Heavy Clay

For successful planting in heavy clay, build uniform soil structure rather than use special mix in relatively small pocket. Instead of filling the large planting hole with a perfect soil mix, go as far as you can in improving all the area of soil the tree will occupy. The addition of pumice, sawdust, and other correctives mixed evenly and deeply into a wide area will give a better root climate than concentrated improvement in one spot.

No matter how porous the soil mixture you use in a planting hole, you won't get good drainage as long as the clay at the bottom and sides is poorly drained.

When soil and root ball have different structures. Many balled and container trees come to you from growing grounds with far different soil from that of your garden. Whether lighter or heavier, you may have trouble giving the tree the right amount of water. Check for weeks after planting to see that the root ball is neither drying up nor becoming waterlogged.

Staking Young Trees

Supporting the young trees with stakes or guy wires is good practice regardless of tree size or whether it is evergreen or deciduous. Unless newly planted balled evergreens are firmly anchored, winter winds may rock them out of the soil. Deciduous trees often suffer root damage from wind sway even though they appear normal without staking.

Use a stake that is stronger than the tree. A 2-by-2-in. stake is best. It should be long enough to reach the crown of the tree when driven deep into firm soil—2 to 3 ft.

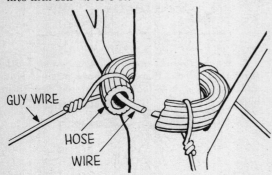

In staking trees that are balled or from containers, drive the stake outside the root ball, generally 1 ft. from trunk of tree.

Tie to stake with wire run through a piece of hose; or with sash cord, light rope, canvas strips. If 3-in. wide strips of old cotton sheeting are used, they will slowly weather and will break with a pop when the tree wants them to pop.

Use one stake for 6-7 ft. trees, 2 in. or less in diameter. Use 2 or 3 stakes for trees 2-4 in. in diameter.

For larger trees, or when stakes cannot be driven deep, guy wires will be needed. See illustration. Tree should be protected from wire damage with hose or other soft material. If wired tree is in lawn, it's a good idea to drive short lengths of pipe into the ground with top below grass level and to tie wires to stakes inserted in the pipe. This makes for easy removal of wires when lawn must be mowed.

Feeding and Mulching

Feeding should not start until tree is established—6 months or a year after planting.

1. Be sure the fertilizer is placed deep enough in the soil to discourage surface feeding.

2. If fertilizer is slow acting, apply it in the fall.

3. If quick acting, apply in spring. The point to remember is that the tree should have nutrients available when it begins its rush of new growth.

4. Avoid any fall feeding of evergreens with quick acting fertilizers.

5. Use amounts according to the fertility of your soil. Safe average dosage is 2 pounds of 5-10-10 balanced fertilizer for each inch of tree trunk's diameter. Follow fertilizer manufacturer's directions.

6. To apply: draw a line around tree a few inches beyond drip line. Draw another circle half the distance to the tree trunk. Bore holes 18 inches deep at 3 ft. intervals in the circles. Divide the total dosage for the tree into even portions for these holes; then fill holes with water.

For trees you wish to keep from sending out roots or expanding their root systems, keep the fertilizer inside the perimeter or drip line of the tree.

Mulch to avoid soil packing and weeds. Watering and normal garden traffic may pack down soil above the roots and thus shut out needed air in the soil. Prevent this by covering soil around tree with a 3-4 in. cushion of peat moss or sawdust.

TRANSPLANTING TREES

How much work is involved in transplanting a tree? Which trees can be transplanted bare root? How large a tree can I transplant? You should have the answers to these questions before you choose or plant a tree for a *"temporary"* effect or decide to do some garden rearranging.

Fortunately the fastest growing deciduous trees can withstand transplanting best. Those trees that the nursery receives bare root generally can be transplanted bare root. The exceptions are the fruit trees, which should be planted as one- or two-year-olds and not moved. Among the trees that are least bothered by transplanting are: elm, maple, ash, locust, sycamore. Such trees can be used for temporary screening and shade, and transplanted when they have outgrown their space—at 12 to 16 feet in height. Those that can be transplanted bare root but suffer are: dogwood, birch, white oak, walnut. Deciduous trees that should be planted with a ball of soil are: liquidambar, tulip tree, deciduous magnolias, Japanese maple.

Bare-root Transplanting

The only time to transplant is when the tree is dormant, leafless.

Here are step-by-step directions for transplanting a tree bare root:

Step 1. Draw a circle around the trunk with a radius of 10 inches for every inch of trunk diameter (measured 1 foot above ground). That is, the circle for a tree 1 inch in diameter would be 20 inches across; for a 4-inch tree the circle would be 6 feet in diameter.

Step 2. Dig a trench at least 18 inches deep (if your soil is that deep), cutting roots as you go.

Step 3. Comb the dirt carefully from the roots. Use a narrow-tined spading fork as a comb.

Step 4. After roots are exposed, rock the tree gently to loosen all roots not cut when the ditch was dug.

Step 5. If tree has a long tap root, undercut at a slant to get as long a root as you can.

Step 6. Lift the tree out and plant in new hole immediately or cover roots with dampened peat, sawdust, or loose soil to keep them from drying out.

Transplanting with Root Ball

In transplanting any evergreen material it is wise to do as much root cutting as possible several months in advance of transplanting. By cutting the full depth of the spade in a circle around the tree in early spring, you give the roots a chance to branch out within the ball area. By winter, when the transplanting is done, the root system within the ball will adequately support the tree. Whatever root loss you have will be below the 8-inch level and transplanting shock will be much less severe.

You can buy a commercial anti-wilt spray to slow down the transpiration of the tree during the transplanting process. It will help reduce shock of transplanting.

All evergreen trees and the difficult-to-transplant deciduous trees should be moved in this manner.

Step 1. Water soil several days in advance of digging so that it will be damp, but not so wet that it falls away from the roots. Mark a circle around the tree. The size will depend upon your estimate of root zone. It should be not less than 14 inches for a 4-foot tree. If the tree is naturally short and the trunk between 1 and 2 inches thick, the diameter of the ball should be at least 20 inches.

Step 2. Dig a trench, outside the circle, to depth in ratio to ball—10 inches for a 14-inch ball, 15 inches for a 20-inch ball, etc.

Step 3. Cut roots as you go, with pruning shears, to avoid jarring dirt loose from root ball. Use saw on large roots. Cut tree side of trench inward so bottom half of ball is 1-2 inches narrower than top.

Step 4. If soil is firm, and holding together as a ball, undercut with spade and tip ball over on a square of burlap you have placed alongside the ball. Bring burlap up around the ball, draw tight, and pin it with nails.

Step 5. If soil is light and inclined to drop away from roots, complete the burlap covering and tying in the hole.

Here's how to get burlap under root ball: Roll up half the width of the burlap. Tilt ball to one side and shove rolled-up section as far as you can under the ball. Tilt the ball back onto the flat section of burlap. The rolled-up section is now free to unroll.

— *Encyclopedia* —

ABIES. FIR. Conifer. 20-50 ft. under cultivation. Sun or partial shade. The drier and hotter the climate, the less the likelihood of success. Familiar Christmas tree form is symmetrical, pyramidal. Needle-like, often flattened leaves, dark green and shining above, sometimes silvery beneath, or gray-green. Erect cones hard to see as they are usually borne near the tree tops, and disintegrate when ripe, leaving only a spike.

A. concolor. WHITE FIR (called SILVER FIR at Christmas time). Most commonly planted. Grows 18 in. a year in zones 3-7 but to 6 in. zone 13. Effectively used as hedge. Plant associates: Douglas fir, Engelmann spruce, aspen.

A. procera. *(A. nobilis).* NOBLE FIR. Extensively cultivated in the eastern United States. Needs high elevations in California.

A. balsamea. BALSAM FIR. Dwarf habit in cultivation.

A. cephalonica. GREEK FIR. Sugary buds at tips of branches.

A. pinsapo. SPANISH FIR. Slow growing. Short, stiff needles spread uniformly around branches. Most adaptable of firs in zones 9-11, 12-13.

Equal to white fir in garden use is the DOUGLAS FIR. This is not a true fir. (See chapter on natives.)

ACACIA. Evergreen. The history of acacias in California has been one of alternating high hopes and deep despair. In 1933 more than 90 species and varieties were planted in gardens and along streets and highways. The freeze of 1937 removed all but the hardiest varieties from the Sacramento and San Joaquin valleys and other areas where tender varieties are borderline.

All varieties fell into disrepute as street trees. As gardens grew smaller, all but one or two acacias were ruled out. Their short life, shallow roots, and brittle limbs were against them as permanent trees.

Now the list of available varieties is again expanding. This time the acacias will hold their own. Experience has shown where each variety will not work. We have learned to accept their disadvantages and to use them accordingly. And we are introducing more and more shrubby species which are easier to use than large ones.

TREES

Available species are classified and analyzed in the following chart. No definite recommendation on climate adaptability is given. Since the acacia is fast growing and used as a temporary filler, losses by occasional deep freezes are not serious. All are used in zones 9-10, 12-13. The following are planted in zones 7-13: A. armata, A. cultriformis, A. decurrens, A. melanoxylon.

ACACIA

Name	Height	Spread	Foliage	Bloom	Comment
A. armata KANGAROO THORN	10-15'	10-12'	Light green. 1", wavy leaves. Armed with thorns.	Small yellow balls, Feb.-Mar.	Because blooms when young, it is often used as a pot plant in cold sections. Grown as a shrub barrier in California. Shrublike.
A. baileyana BAILEY ACACIA	20-30'	15-20'	Feathery, blue-gray.	Yellow, Jan.-Feb.	Hardiest. Most commonly planted. Use as temporary filler between slower growing trees.
A. b. purpurea PURPLE BAILEY ACACIA	20-30'	15-20'	Same, except new foliage.	Same	New foliage is purple to lavender. Cutting back is necessary for continuation of colored foliage.
A. cultriformis KNIFE ACACIA	10-15'	6-10'	Silver-gray	Yellow, Mar.	Leaves look like small paring knife blades stuck into the stems.
A. decurrens GREEN WATTLE	to 50'	30-40'	Feathery, dark green.	Yellow, Feb.-Mar.	Longer lived than A. baileyana and will take more water and wind.
A. d. dealbata SILVER WATTLE	Same	Same	Feathery, silvery-gray.	Same	Same
A. elata CEDAR WATTLE	to 90'	60-70'	Like the pepper tree.	Yellow, erratic.	The giant of the acacias. Longlived but fast growing—as much as 25' in 3 years. Slows down in heavy soils—only 25-30' in 20 years.
A. longifolia EVERBLOOMING ACACIA, SYDNEY GOLDEN WATTLE	to 20'	to 20'	Dark green. Leaves 3-6" long, with several parallel veins.	Golden in tufts along the branches in summer.	Shrub or tree. Large billowy mass to the ground if not trained. Used as dense border, soil-holding near beach. Often sold in nurseries as A. latifolia.
A. melanoxylon BLACKWOOD ACACIA	to 40'	to 20'	Dark green. Leaves 2-3" long.	Straw colored in Mar.-Apr.	A tree that should be ruled out of use except when drought resistant tree is needed in waste land.
A. pendula WEEPING ACACIA	Slow, to 25'	to 15'	Blue-gray on very long weeping branches.	Yellow, erratically in Apr.-May.	A tree difficult to use. Best in large groups of drought resistant plants. Use as a weeping specimen tree.
A. podalyriaefolia PEARL ACACIA	10-20'	8-15'	Soft gray. Leaves 2", rounded.	Pale yellow, Nov.-Mar.	Shrub, or can be trained as rounding, open-headed tree. Excellent for patio use. Damaged at 24°. Good winter color.
A. pravissima SCREWPOD ACACIA	to 20'	to 15'	Green, resembling Knife Acacia.	Large flower sprays in Mar.	Drooping branches on a small upright tree.
A. pruinosa FROSTY ACACIA	to 60'	to 40'	Light green. Fern-like new growth in copper shades.	Cream and yellow from June-Sept. Fragrant.	Dense, spreading, beautiful tree. Needs monthly water.
A. pycnantha GOLDEN ACACIA, GOLDEN WATTLE	to 25'	to 15'	Lime green, shaped like Eucalyptus.	Large yellow fragrant golden balls in great profusion in Mar.	Erect tree. Stems of new growth are golden. Older stems shade to plum red.
A. retinodes WATER WATTLE, FLORIBUNDA ACACIA	to 20'	to 20'	Yellow-green. Leaves have single midrib with feather veining.	Yellow, in comparatively small heads. Blooms most of the year near coast.	Excellent quick screen. Often sold in nurseries as A. floribunda.
A. riceana RICE ACACIA	8-20'	8-20'	Bunches of short needles on long weeping branchlets.	Yellow in Mar.	Tree; now in parks only. Worth commercial introduction. One of the few that need water.
A. saligna GOLDEN WREATH WATTLE	10-20'	15-25'	Dark green.	Yellow, Apr.	Weeping habit with showy, large flowers.
A. verticillata STAR ACACIA	to 15' Can be held to 3'	to 15'	Dark green, needle-like.	Pale yellow, April-May.	Looks more like an airy conifer than an acacia. Excellent as low hedge, in planters, in wind.

ACER. MAPLE. Deciduous or part evergreen. All zones. More widely used in cold winter sections where fall color is certain. As a group they are tolerant of various soil and water conditions.

Before considering the medium and large maples, let's take a look at the unusual species:

A. palmatum. JAPANESE MAPLE. Deciduous. Best in zones 1-6, 9, 10, 13. Needs extra protection from sun and dry wind in hot interiors. Slow growing to 20 ft. Normally many stemmed. Most airy and delicate of all. Small leaves are deeply cut and sawtoothed. All year interest: young spring growth is glowing red; summer's leaves are soft green; foliage turns scarlet in fall months; slender leafless branches in greens and reds provide winter pattern. Enjoys filtered sunlight. Lean soil best if plant is to be dwarfed. Used effectively on north and east walls, in perennial borders, in patios, sometimes trained as a small lawn tree. Seen under oaks, as background for ferns and azaleas, alongside pools. Invaluable in tub and pot garden. Used indoors next to floor-to-ceiling window. Since it is inclined to grow in planed surfaces, pruning to accentuate this growth habit is easy. You might plant so that at eye level the planed leaf structure will be visible. Prune to plane downward when given a water foreground.

Two varieties are: *A. p. atropurpureum*. RED JAPANESE MAPLE. Bronze, bronzy green, and green leaves. *A. p. dissectum*. LACELEAF JAPANESE MAPLE. Deeply dissected fern-like leaves.

A. circinatum. VINE MAPLE. (See chapter on natives.)

A. oblongum. EVERGREEN MAPLE. Zones 9-13. Partially evergreen, growing to 20 ft. with 10 ft. spread. Leaves, deep green and oblong, are quite unlike those of the American natives.

A. ginnala. AMUR MAPLE. Deciduous. Hardy all zones but can't take extreme heat. Shrub or small tree of graceful and neat growth. 6 to 20 ft. Much appreciated in zones 1 and 2 where landscape architects like it as a substitute or supplement to Japanese maple. Stands well alone or with rock or fern.

A. negundo. BOX ELDER. Deciduous. All zones. Does well in hot arid sections. Rapid growing to 75 ft. Slender, dome shaped. Use it only as a temporary tree for retaining bank, quick screens. Short lived, subject to pests and diseases; branches brittle. *A.n. californicum*. CALIFORNIA BOX ELDER. (See chapter on natives.) *A. n. variegatum*. SILVER VARIEGATED BOX ELDER. Smaller tree of very light green leaves with yellow margins. Striking, beautiful when planted in front of darker, taller trees.

Medium and large maples:

A. macrophyllum. BIGLEAF MAPLE, OREGON MAPLE. (See chapter on natives.) Interesting use: Seedlings used as ground cover in large area.

A. platanoides. NORWAY MAPLE. Deciduous, to 60 ft., but in most locations levels off at about 30 ft. with spread of about 20 ft. Dense foliage. Yellow flowers in spring. Very adaptable, tolerating many soil and climate conditions. Handsome ornamental tree for a very large garden. Once widely recommended as a street and avenue tree, but now objected to in many areas where aphis cause a honeydew drip. *A.p. schwedleri*. SCHWEDLER MAPLE. Hardy all zones but in trouble in extreme heat, extreme cold. Young leaves are bright red, turn dark red to purplish-green in summer, and then to gold in autumn. This variety is smaller and more upright than the species. Var. *schwedleri Crimson King*. Keeps its red-purplish color throughout spring and summer. Poor performance in Southwest but valuable in Northwest where reds, silvers, purples are needed during summers.

A. saccharinum. (*A. dasycarpum*). SILVER MAPLE. Deciduous. Hardy but no good in extreme heat. Subject to chlorosis in 12, 13. Leaves light green above, silvery beneath. Fast growing, eventually to 100 ft., if all conditions right. Usually 40 ft., with 40-ft. spread. Forms a rather open crown, which casts a light to medium shade. Eventually too large for the small garden but used as fast grower for quick shade. Tolerates wet soil. .

A. saccharum. SUGAR MAPLE. Deciduous. All zones— the colder the better. Usually to 40-50 ft. One of the most beautiful and symmetrical trees of the eastern forest. Soft, luminous pinkish-apricot fall color. Too large, too dense for home or street planting.

A. rubrum. RED MAPLE, SCARLET MAPLE. Deciduous. All zones except extreme heat. To 120 ft. in eastern and southern sections. Usually a 40-ft. tree with an 18-ft. spread, forming a pyramidal crown. Red flowers before leaves. Red leaves in fall. Tolerant of seacoast conditions, and of wet soil.

AESCULUS. Deciduous. All zones except in colder parts of 1 and in 7 and 8 where foliage burns in dry winds. Needs summer moisture, too.

A. carnea. RED HORSECHESTNUT. Moderate growth to 40 ft. with 30-ft. spread. Round headed with large, dark green leaves, divided fan-wise into 5 leaflets, casting dense shade. In April-May the tree wears hundreds of 8-in. plumes of soft pink-to-red flowers. *A. c. briotii* has scarlet flowers. A well-behaved flowering tree for summer shade. Favored in many communities as street tree. Free from pests. Lends itself to symmetrical plantings, rather than to irregular garden design.

A. hippocastanum. HORSECHESTNUT. Moderate growth to 60 ft. with 40-ft. spread. A bulky, dense round-to-pyramidal tree. Use for generous and dense shade in country places. Widely planted as street tree in Seattle area.

All horsechestnuts drop their leaves early in the fall. If leaflets become seared on the edges, spray for leaf blight.

A. californica. CALIFORNIA BUCKEYE. (See chapter on natives.)

AGONIS FLEXUOSA. (*Leptospermum flexuosum*). PEPPERMINT TREE, AUSTRALIAN WILLOW-MYRTLE. Evergreen. Zones 8-13. Low spreading, slow growing to 25-35 ft. Many weeping branches, eucalyptus-like foliage; small white flowers in June. Bark juniper-like color and quality. Worthwhile.

AILANTHUS ALTISSIMA. (*A. glandulosa*). TREE-OF-HEAVEN. Deciduous. All zones. Fast and rank to 50 ft. Planted a century ago in California's gold country where it now runs wild. Suckers over a wide area. A weed in mild areas of California. Has best reputation where cold winters or hot deserts hold it in check. Takes worst city conditions.

ALBIZZIA JULIBRISSIN. SILK TREE. Deciduous. Zones 2-13, especially 8, 9, 10, 11. Rather rapid growth to 40 ft. with a wider spread. However, may be headed back to give a 10-or-20-ft.-high umbrella. Pink fluffy flowers like pincushions cover ferny-leafed branches in June, July and August. Sensitive leaves close at night. Exotic looking but is tough and hardy to zero degrees. Train as canopy over terrace or patio. The beauty of the tree is worth the sweeping up of the litter of leaves, flowers and pods. Gives filtered shade. Unpruned albizzias grow in tiers and usually have several stems. Because of undulating form, the silk tree is especially beautiful when viewed from above. Stands alkali soils and lawn irrigation. It's not an easy tree to get off to a good start. Occasionally a newly set-out tree may grow slowly because its roots were cut severely during field digging or were root pruned to pot within a container. When held in a container too long, the tree may die back to within 2 ft. of the soil and branch from that point. This habit of low branching is responsible for conflicting reports on the tree's value. Those who have seen it as very low growing can't possibly picture it as a street tree; yet we have seen streets canopied with silk trees, with no branch lower than 8 ft.

A. lophantha. PLUME ALBIZZIA. Deciduous. Zones 9, 10, 12 and 13. Fast growing and short lived where best adapted. Its rapid growth and feathery foliage gives it temporary value but it becomes shabby and ungainly with age. Greenish flowers. Should not be used as a permanent ornamental tree.

ALNUS. ALDER. Deciduous. Climate adaptation varies by species.

A. cordata. ITALIAN ALDER. Zones 7-13, except 8. Fast growth to 40 ft. with 25 ft. spread. Typical alder structure: tall, straight trunk, spreading or ascending branches. Leaves like evergreen pear in texture, glossy dark green above, lighter underneath, heart-shaped. Small, ½ in. long cones hang on throughout the year.

A good lawn tree because of its short deciduous period; cleanliness; form; restless foliage in slightest breeze; ability to stand frequent watering.

A. rhombifolia. SIERRA ALDER. WHITE ALDER. (See chapter on natives.)

ANNONA CHERIMOLA. CHERIMOYA. (See chapter on evergreen fruit trees.)

ARALIA CHINENSIS. CHINESE ARALIA. Evergreen. All zones except 1 and 2. Very fast growing to 20-25 ft. Short lived. Related to the spiny DEVIL'S WALKING STICK, *A. spinosa*, but in no way as forbidding. Foliage, of compound leaves, the leaflets to 6 in. long, gives filtered shade. Attractive white flower clusters. A tree to be looked up into. Northwest planting: a clump of Chinese aralias above Altaclarensis azalea.

ARAUCARIA. Conifer. Evergreen, with flat, stiff, closely overlapping dark green leaves. Look out for the large woody cones borne 40-80 ft. up, and weighing 10-15 pounds. Four species are grown in the West. A strange group. All susceptible to golden mealy bug.

A. araucana. (*A. imbricata*). MONKEY PUZZLE TREE. All zones except extreme cold areas in Zones 1, 7, and 8. A weird curiosity. Rope-like branches closely set with sharp leaves form a strange pattern.

A. cunninghamii. AUSTRALIAN HOOP-PINE. Zones 12-13. Another sky-touching conifer. Foliage tufted at end of branches.

A. bidwillii. BUNYA-BUNYA. Zones 11-13. Moderate growth to 80 ft. Columnar. Drooping main branches.

A. excelsa. NORFOLK ISLAND PINE. Zones 12-13. Moderate growth to 100 ft. and more. Many in Santa Barbara. Prefers the coastal strip. In colder climates used as house plant and indoor Christmas tree.

ASH. See FRAXINUS
AVOCADO. See PERSEA
BANANA. See MUSA

BAUHINIA. ORCHID TREE. Evergreen. Zones 11-13.

B. variegata. PURPLE ORCHID TREE. (Botanists say that trees sold as *B. purpurea* are *B. variegata*.) Does best away from coast in warm locations without winter cold below 22°. Moderate growth to 20 ft. with an equal spread; umbrella-like form with round to flat head. Light green, two-lobed, 4 in. long leaves close up at night. Rose colored 2-3 in. flowers with purple and yellow markings look like Vanda orchids from a distance; bloom in spring; are followed by 10 in. long pods. Tree becomes leafless for a short time during the flowering period. *B. v. candida*. White flowers. Use as a small shade tree; a novelty in flowering trees.

B. galpinii. RED BAUHINIA. Evergreen or semi-deciduous. Semi-climbing habit; needs some support. Clusters of scarlet flowers from spring to fall. At its best when trained against a wall.

BEECH. See FAGUS
BEEFWOOD. See CASUARINA

BETULA. BIRCH. Deciduous. All zones except 8. Light, graceful, moderately fast to extreme of 80 ft. with 30 ft. spread. Average mature tree 30 ft. to 40 ft., spreading to half its height.

B. pendula. (Most often sold as *B. alba*). EUROPEAN WHITE BIRCH. Delicate and lacy. Upright branching with weeping side branches. Subject to tip borer.

B. p. dalecarlica. (*B. p. laciniata, B. laciniata*). CUTLEAF EUROPEAN WHITE BIRCH. CUTLEAF WEEPING BIRCH. Deeply cut leaves; both main branches and side branches are weeping. Has tendency to burn in hot sun.

B. p. fastigiata. (*B. alba pyramidalis, B. alba fastigiata.*) Upward thrusting branches. Use as high screen, as you would a small lombardy poplar.

B. p. purpurea (*B. alba atropurpurea*). PURPLE LEAF BIRCH. Similar to *B. p. dalecarlica* in leaf and structure but leaves are bronze-purple.

B. p. youngii. (*B. alba youngii*). YOUNG'S WEEPING BIRCH. Irregular drooping branches. Should be staked to make erect trunk.

B. papyrifera. CANOE BIRCH. Same growth characteristics as *B. pendula* but leaves are larger and bark is white. No black clefts in bark when tree is old.

B. nigra. RIVER BIRCH. Red-brown bark. More elm-like in growth habit.

The birches are easy trees to get along with even in the smallest garden. They can be used in lawn, border, or as a high screen.

In the Northwest, the birch is the "lady of the forest," bringing lively grace into a group of Douglas fir and cedar. In winter, the leafless branch structure, blue in hue, adds another reason for planting it. Birches and water go well together: for example, along a lakeshore, with iris. As a street tree in the colder sections of the West, its white trunk and gray blue branches are most colorful and cheerful in contrast to the dark brown of other street trees. In autumn, its rather fragile yellow can be counted on, even in mild winter sections, if the trees are hardened off in advance by withholding water late in the summer.

The natural habit of the birch, after a fire or cropping by deer, is to spring up in clumps of several trees in a circle not more than 1 ft. in diameter. These individual trunks eventually grow together as one tree. Clump planting (3 trees in one hole) is suggested as a variation on the popular planting of 3 trees, 6 ft. apart.

For a screen which is interesting as well as functional, plant your own *forest* of birches. Get 5, 9, 12, 15 or more trees—bare root when they are available and when soil conditions permit planting—and set them out in staggered forest formation, some clumped together, others spaced 4 or 5 ft. apart. Locate your grove at the property line, or at a building or fence corner, rather than in the middle of a lawn or other open space.

Birch cannot be kept on the dry side; does not do well in all day full sun in hot interiors.

BIG TREE. (See chapter on natives.)
BIRCH. See BETULA
BOTTLE TREE. See BRACHYCHITON
BOX ELDER. See ACER NEGUNDO
BRISBANE BOX. See TRISTANIA CONFERTA
BRACHYCHITON. Three quite different trees come under this general label. All are natives of the Australian desert.

B. acerifolium. (*Sterculia acerifolia*). FLAME TREE. Zones 9, 10, 12, 13. Slow-growing, deep-rooted evergreen-deciduous to 50-90 ft. with equal spread. Drops its maple-like leaves for June-July blooming, when it flames with clusters of scarlet flowers.

B. discolor. (*Sterculia discolor*). PINK FLAME TREE. Zones 9, 10, 12, 13. Same growth as red flame tree. Maple-like leaves. Large pink flowers in June and July. Young pods and flowers are covered with short brown wool. Erratic in appearance; some branches bare, others leafy.

B. populneum. (*Sterculia diversifolia*). BOTTLE TREE. Zones 8-13. Slow growing evergreen to 60 ft., and with 30-ft. spread. Leaves vary, simple and 3-lobed, but foliage gives effect of poplar. Noted for heat tolerance, seed pods, and bottle-shaped trunk. Small, white bell-shaped flowers in May and June; woody, canoe-shaped, 2-3 in. seed pods that follow, delight the pod and cone collector and arranger. The litter of pods puts the bottle tree in the messy class. Effective as screens or high, wide windbreaks. Deep shade and drought resistance rate it high in desert areas.

BROUSSONETIA PAPYRIFERA. PAPERBARK MULBERRY. Deciduous. All zones except coldest spots in zone 1. Moderate growth to 50 ft. with a low spreading head to 40 ft. Smooth gray bark. Heart-shaped, usually deeply lobed, 4-8 in., gray-green hairy leaves. Unusually tolerant of poor soils and unfavorable climate conditions. Valuable as a small shade tree where soil limits choice. Normally spreads rapidly by root suckers. Plant in a 5-ft. wide basin, 6 in. deeper than soil level, to help prevent spread of suckers.

CALLITRIS ROBUSTA. STURDY CYPRESSPINE. Conifer. Zones 7, 8, 11 and 12. Moderately fast growth ranging from 15 ft. to 70 ft., depending upon soil drainage and heat. Often multiple trunked. Short, erect branchlets are thickly covered with scale-like, black-green leaves. Good prospect for hedges and small windbreaks in Southwest dry inland areas. Rare.

CALODENDRUM CAPENSE. CAPE CHESTNUT. Evergreen. Zones 12 and 13. Even there, leaves of young trees burn badly in the "big freezes" but recovery is complete. Moderate growth to 60 ft., generally 25-40 ft. Round headed, very symmetrical. Glossy green foliage gives a rich background to a profusion of bloom in summer. Narrow-petalled flowers, rosy lilac with brown spots, in great clusters 6-12 in. across. Fairly wind-hardy and does well in coastal exposures. Disadvantage: unpredictable in blooming time and seasonal habits. May bloom June, July or December. May hold its leaves or drop them. Requires rapidly draining soil. Water deeply and infrequently. Don't keep the soil at the moist level.

CAMPHOR TREE. See CINNAMOMUM CAMPHORA
CARAGANA ARBORESCENS. SIBERIAN PEASHRUB. Deciduous. All zones. Fast-growing shrub or small tree to 20 ft. with spread of 15 ft. Compound leaf, 4-6 pairs of leaflets. Twigs angled and spiny; yellow blossoms, late spring, not showy; inclined to legginess. Nearly indestructible and valuable where cover is wanted in poor, dry land.

CAROB. See CERATONIA SILIQUA
CARROT WOOD. See CUPANIA ANACARDIOIDES
CARYA ILLINOENSIS. (*Carya pecan*). PECAN. Deciduous. Zones 8a, 11-12. Majestic handsome tree with or without nuts. Best growth in extreme summer heat. (See chapter on deciduous fruit trees.)

CASIMIROA EDULIS. WHITE SAPOTE. Evergreen. Best in avocado belts of zones 11-13, but considered hardy to 20°. Tree growing to 30-50 ft., unless upright growth is stopped by removal of terminal bud to induce lateral branching, as is practiced in commercial plantings. (See chapter on fruit trees.) Leaves divided fan-wise into 3-7 ovate, or narrower, 5-in. leathery leaflets. Compares favorably with the Brazilian pepper in form and versatility. Excellent evergreen patio tree.

CASTANEA. CHESTNUT. Deciduous. The "spreading chestnut tree." The American chestnut is disappearing because of chestnut blight. Two imports are available in the West.

C. mollissima. CHINESE CHESTNUT. All zones. Moderate growth to 60 ft., spreading to 40 ft. A handsome tree with 4-6 in. leaves. Edible nuts. Good shade tree for a country place. Too big and too many burs for the garden.

C. sativa. SPANISH CHESTNUT. Zones 8-13. Larger tree than *C. mollissima* in ideal climate. More round-headed. Rated as 30-ft. tree in California. Planted for nuts. Plant away from house as the pollen odor is very strong and disagreeable. Too dirty a tree for a garden area. Best for large country planting.

CASTANOSPERMUM AUSTRALE. MORETON BAY CHESTNUT. Evergreen. Zones 12 and 13. Moderate growth to 30 ft. with a 40-ft. spread. Leaves like walnut but glossier, larger. Flower plumes in yellows and red in July. Edible nuts. Too tender to be trusted for permanent place in garden.

CASUARINA. BEEFWOOD, SHE-OAK. Evergreen.

C. equisetifolia. HORSETAIL BEEFWOOD. Zones 6-13. Fast growth to 40-60 ft. with 20 ft. spread. Narrow, upright, with pendulous branches and very long needles (really branchlets). Tree has loose, wispy look.

C. stricta. COAST BEEFWOOD. Fast growth to 10-30 ft. Open, pine-like. May burn in gale locations.

Use in near-desert or as windbreak for ocean wind and spray. Not a pleasant garden subject but of real service in tough situations. In windbreaks, tamarix is a good companion with its clouds of pink blossoms in spring.

CATALPA. Deciduous. All zones. Noted for large heart-shaped leaves and clusters of white or pink flowers in late spring.

C. bignonioides. COMMON CATALPA, INDIAN BEAN. Smaller than *C. speciosa*, reaching 20-50 ft. according to climate and soils. Var. *nana*, UMBRELLA CATALPA, a dwarf form, is often grafted high to take advantage of spreading umbrella shape.

C. speciosa. WESTERN CATALPA. Zones 1-13. Slow to moderate growth, to 40-70 ft., with 25-ft. spread. Round-headed and very dense. Excellent for country roadsides but not recommended as garden tree.

The climate adaptability of the catalpa—at home in extreme heat, safe in extreme winter cold—rates it high in performance. Dropped flowers, leaves and 12-in. stringbean-like pods lessen its value to some gardeners. It is so distinctive in form and leaf that it doesn't mix well with other trees. Rightly called a "striking specimen," it is difficult to use in a small garden. The small umbrella catalpa should be valuable for terrace shade.

CEDRUS. CEDAR. Conifer. Zones by species. These are the true cedars. For INCENSE CEDAR see Libocedrus.

C. atlantica. ATLAS CEDAR. All zones except 1 and 2. Grows to 60-120 ft. Branches are twisted and covered with tufts or clusters of bluish-green, less than 1 in. long, needles. A rather stiff tree. Open and sparse when young. Used at doorways of public buildings after stunting by root pruning. Not as space stealing as the deodar but still too large for average lot. Must be given a 30 ft. radius. A good tree for an unused lot you don't wish to sell. Var. *argentea* has silver needles. Var. *glauca* is more spreading and open in form; has bluish-gray needles; rivals the popular blue spruce in color; slow growing.

C. deodara. DEODAR CEDAR. All zones except 1 and 2. Leaves burn to snow line in cold spots of 3-5 in unusual winters. Fast growing, 3 ft. a yr. in California; 1½ ft. a yr. in Pacific Northwest, to 80 ft. with 40-ft. spread at base. Seen throughout the West in parks, public grounds, avenues. Softer, lighter texture than other conifers; openly spaced, sweeping, graceful branches; drooping leader is characteristic. Often planted following a short stay in the house as a living Christmas tree. Unfortunately, the wide spread of this stately tree makes it a bad choice for the small lot. Dwarf form, *C.d. compacta*, is being grown.

C. libani. CEDAR OF LEBANON. All zones. Slow growing to 100 ft., less than 15 ft. in 15 years. Very variable in growth habit. Usually a narrow pyramid in youth, spreading picturesquely as it matures. Upright or spreading leading shoot (do not prune). Branches wider than tree height, often resting on ground. Majestic, with long, horizontal arms and irregular crown.

CELTIS. HACKBERRY. Deciduous. Zones by species. All elm-like in growth habit and leaf. All have staunch supporters among tree experts.

C. australis. EUROPEAN HACKBERRY. Zones 6-13. A smaller tree than *C. occidentalis*. Successful street tree in Palo Alto, California. Drought tolerant; pest resistant; long lived; in leaf 1-2 months longer than the common hackberry.

C. occidentalis. COMMON HACKBERRY. All zones. (Often grown in East and Middle West where it is rated a 120 ft. tree.) In the Northwest it is called a moderately fast grower to 40-60 ft., and in the southern deserts a fast grower to 80 ft. Average height of specimens we've seen is under 40 ft., with a 20 ft. spread. Medium-dense shade; leaves appear in April or later. Smaller size and relative resistance to pest and disease make it a good substitute for the elm. Most enthusiastic supporters are in California's Sacramento and San Joaquin Valleys. An excellent street or shade tree. Accepts adverse conditions: cold, extreme heat, wind, alkali soil. In California, not certain to grow when planted bare-root. Try to buy in cans.

C. sinensis. (*C. yunnanensis*). YUNNAN HACKBERRY. Zones 5-13. Moderately fast grower to 40 ft. in California. Partially evergreen in contrast to long dormant season of other species. Not fully tested in all climates and conditions.

CEPHALOTAXUS DRUPACEA. JAPANESE PLUM YEW. Conifer. All zones except 1, 2 and 3. Slow growth to a 6-20 ft., bush-like tree. General appearance is that of yew. Dark green needle-leaves are larger and marked with two wide gray bands beneath; green plum-like fruit. Used in Japanese gardens. Can be trimmed as hedge. Takes average garden conditions and partial shade.

CERATONIA SILIQUA. CAROB, ST. JOHNS BREAD. Evergreen. Zones 7-13, wherever olives grow. Slow growing to 40 ft. and as wide. A handsome, dense, round-headed tree. Leaves divided into 4-6 round, shiny, dark green leaflets with slightly wavy edges. Flattened, leathery, 1 ft. pods are valued for stock feed. Successful street tree in Southwest, especially in desert areas. May be grown as a many-branched shrub for windbreak. Tolerant of alkaline soils and drought. Practically pest free. Naturally a deep-rooted tree, it should be encouraged in the habit by one deep watering during the summer. Frequent irrigation will make it a shallow-rooted tree. Male trees give off strong pungent odor when in bloom; female trees offer the problem of pod pick-up.

CERCIDIPHYLLUM JAPONICUM. KATSURA TREE. Deciduous. All zones except where it can't be protected from strong hot winds, dry soil. Slow to moderate growth to 16-20 ft. with 12 ft. spread in Pacific Northwest; fast growing, 3-4 ft. a year in the Southwest. Tends to develop several stems, upright, arching. Roundish 4 in. leaves arranged horizontally in neat pairs along branches. New growth is tinted red throughout growing season. Foliage always fresh looking. Yellow and scarlet leaves in fall. Var. *magnificum* has larger leaves, faster growth. Seven-year-old specimen in Yakima, Washington, is 12 ft.

C. j. sinense. CHINESE KATSURA TREE. More upright in growth habit than *C. japonicum*, with darker foliage; deeper crimson in fall coloring. Extremely delicate looking tree with an unusual amount of character.

Use where light and dainty pattern is needed. In Japanese maple class for design quality. Stands smog

RED BIRCH   OREGON ASH   DOGWOOD   SPRUCE   SILVER FIR   RED FIR   HEMLOCK   PINE   ELDERBERRY

and water from lawn sprinklers. Can't take summer sun plus reflected heat from house wall or concrete pavement.

CERCIS. REDBUD. Deciduous. Small shrub-like trees to 25-35 ft. Natives of the West, Europe, China and East coast are grown here.

C. canadensis. EASTERN REDBUD. All zones and hardiest of the species. Round-headed, branches becoming more horizontal with age. Light green, heart-shaped leaves. Rose-magenta sweet pea-shaped flowers in clusters on brown bare branches in early spring.

C. chinensis. CHINESE REDBUD. Zones 3-11. Leaves are shiny with transparent line around edge. Rosy-purple flowers. Seems well adapted to zones 11-13.

C. occidentalis. WESTERN REDBUD. Zones 2-11. (See chapter on natives.)

C. siliquastrum. EUROPEAN REDBUD. JUDAS TREE. Zones 2-11. Flat topped tree-shrub to 25 ft. Magenta flowers.

Use redbuds as flowering trees where off-beat color will not clash. Eastern redbud often develops into tree of exceptionally strong horizontal branch pattern making it valuable when winter form is an asset.

CHAMAECYPARIS. FALSE CYPRESS. Evergreen conifers. (See chapter on shrubs for lower growing forms.) There are so many variables in the members of the genus that any general statement would be misleading. See species for climate adaptability.

C. lawsoniana. PORT ORFORD CEDAR. LAWSON CYPRESS. A native forest tree, limited in range to a narrow strip along the coast of southern Oregon from Coos Bay south to the Mad River in northern California. In the forest it's a magnificent 200-ft. tree with lacy, drooping foliage sprays and a conical crown. In cultivation it's much lower growing and is pyramidal or columnar, depending on variety. Its many forms are available throughout the Pacific Coast and are well adapted in zones 2-13, but too tender in cold sections of zone 1.

The species makes a good windbreak or high sun screen. Can be planted as close as 3 ft. apart, without becoming thin or straggly. Can be topped at 10 ft. or more.

The following varieties have the pyramidal form of the species, but vary in foliage color. All are in the 30-40 ft. range, but can be held to desired height: Var. *aurea*, compact pyramid with golden-yellow foliage the first years, then turning green; var. *albo-spica*, cream-white branch ends give it a patchy look; var. *lutea*, golden foliage; var. *Triomphe de Boskoop*, blue-green foliage.

C. l. allumii. BLUE LAWSON CYPRESS. SCARAB CYPRESS. Most popular tree variety. Compact, narrow pyramidal form with outstanding metallic-blue new foliage carried in flat, slightly twisted planes. Foliage tends to brown in center of tree. Useful as a large formal hedge to 30 ft.

C. l. erecta. GREEN COLUMN CYPRESS. Columnar form, dense foliage in bright green sprays, lower limbs almost touch the ground. Older plants tend to get bare at base. Var. *erecta aurea* is slower growing, with golden foliage. Var. *erecta glauca* has blue-green foliage.

C. l. pendula. WEEPING LAWSON CYPRESS. To 20-30 ft. Wide spreading, horizontal branches with branchlets drooping almost vertically. Gray-green foliage, too distinctive to group easily. Var. *pendula glauca* has blue-gray foliage.

C. l. stewartii. WINTERGOLDEN LAWSON CYPRESS. To 30 ft. Upright, slender, pyramidal form. Gold-tipped, green foliage retains color throughout winter.

C. l. wissellii. To 15-18 ft. Slender and upright with striking twisted foliage, dark green with hint of blue. Has interesting and dramatic texture, but it is particularly susceptible to pests and diseases.

C. nootkatensis. NOOTKA CYPRESS. ALASKA YELLOW CEDAR. Native, ranging from southeastern Alaska, British Columbia, Washington to southern Oregon. Found along streams, valleys and gulches. A mature tree, 250 years old, averages 2-3 ft. in diameter and 80 ft. high. In cultivation it's a slow growing, dense, fine-textured pyramid. The species and dwarf form are available in Pacific Northwest nurseries, but there is no general distribution in California. Considered the hardiest and best of the genus where grown in New York.

C. obtusa. (*Retinospora obtusa*). HINOKI CYPRESS. Hardy zones 2-13 and mildest sections of zone 1. Generally pyramidal in habit, and although rated as a 120-ft. tree, it is more like 40-50 ft. here in the West. Actually it is so slow growing that many gardeners treat it as a dwarf and train and shape to emphasize its irregular branching habit.

C. o. aurea. GOLDEN HINOKI CYPRESS. Slow growing to 30-40 ft. The lustrous, dark green foliage is yellow when young. Hard to combine with other foliage colors. Branchlets are flattened in horizontal planes.

C. o. crippsii. To 30 ft., but can be kept down. Pyramidal in form. Soft golden foliage, turns green in shade. Has more open habit than most chamæcyparis. With careful pruning you can give it an effective horizontal "Japanese" effect. Good pattern against the sky.

C. o. filicoides. To 15 ft. Gently curved limbs with small, drooping branches. Light green foliage has a rather loose, fern-like texture.

C. o. gracilis. To 20 ft. Graceful, upright, with slightly pendulous branches and bright green foliage. Has a weeping look.

C. pisifera. (*Retinospora pisifera*). SAWARA CYPRESS. Hardy zones 3-13. All should be regarded as small trees and not planted where eventual height of 20-30 ft. would make trouble. All must be pruned annually to encourage new growth to hide dead foliage on inner branches.

C. p. plumosa. PLUME CYPRESS. To 20-30 ft. Broad, conical, and compact with loose, blue-green foliage; new growth quite blue; very short soft needles. Var. *plumosa aurea*, GOLD PLUME CYPRESS, new growth is golden turning green.

C. p. squarrosa. MOSS CYPRESS. To 20-30 ft. Irregular, densely-branched tree with silvery, gray-green, soft feathery foliage. Var. *squarrosa veitchii* with its light, airy, blue-green foliage, is a color and texture improvement.

CHESTNUT. See CASTANEA

CHIONANTHUS. FRINGE TREE. Deciduous. All zones.

C. virginica. WHITE FRINGE TREE. Slow growth to 20 ft. Rather airy and open in character; of much grace. White flowers hang down in 6-in.-long clusters in May and June. Oval leaves, 4-6 in. long, turn yellow in the fall. Beautiful flowering tree of many uses: in shrub border its bloom gives delphiniums a white backdrop; alone on a terrace it gives light shade; will lighten somber evergreens. Mature trees in Chino, California. and in Seattle attest its wide adaptability to climates and soils.

C. retusa. CHINESE FRINGE TREE. Large, leathery leaves; in leaf longer than *C. virginica*. Flowers in white lacy clusters cover the tree in April to make it a white ball.

CINNAMOMUM CAMPHORA. CAMPHOR TREE. Evergreen. Zones: better in 9-10, 12-13, than in 7 or 11. Rather slow growing to 50 ft. with a spread of more than 100 ft. Most 20-year-olds are about 30 ft. with equal spread. Compact oval crown with light green foliage, bronze tinged in the spring. Rather heavy trunk, enlarged at base.

The camphor tree rates high as a street or avenue tree because it is strong wooded and wind resistant; needs no pruning; is adaptable to soil and water variations; and is evergreen with an interesting change of leaf color. Is not a good tree for the small garden because it is difficult to grow plants under; fallen leaves don't decompose easily; has highly competitive root system; creates dense shade.

CLADRASTIS LUTEA. YELLOW WOOD. All zones. Deciduous. Moderate growth to 30 ft. A rather open tree with round head about half as wide as tree is high. Resembles a small English walnut until it blooms. Leaves divided into 7-9 oval, shiny, bright green 4 in. leaflets turn a bright yellow in fall. Clusters of 1-in. white flowers in June. At its best when grouped with larger evergreens. Another small tree from eastern states worth attention in the West.

CLETHRA ARBOREA. LILY-OF-THE-VALLEY TREE. (See crinodendron for another lily-of-the-valley tree.) Evergreen. Zones 10 and 13. Likes best a warm, sheltered spot along the coast. Moderate growth to 20 ft. with 10 ft. spread in shrub-like form. Glossy bronzy-green 4 in. leaves. Notable for upright clusters of white, fragrant, miniature cap-shaped flowers in late summer.

Give clethra protection of high branching trees or an eastern exposure. Winters of unusual cold will damage the tree unless protected, but will come back from the roots. Needs abundant moisture and slightly acid soil. One of the best small trees.

CORNUS. DOGWOOD. Deciduous varieties hardy all zones but best adapted because of soil requirements to zones 3-6. Evergreen varieties adapted to zones 9, 10, 12, and 13; borderline in zones 3-6. Should not be planted in desert areas.

If natural requirements of the deciduous dogwoods are taken literally, this important tree group is ruled out of most of California. Likes cool, deep, leafy, somewhat acid soil and abundant water. Prefers filtered shade of high branched larger trees or the open spaces between such conifers as redwoods or pines. However, the dogwood is finding increasing acceptance in interior areas such as the Sacramento Valley, where several mature specimens of *C. florida* in both shade and full sun are to be seen.

The following chart compares the species by height, color, etc. Here are some suggestions for use in the garden.

CORNUS—DOGWOOD

VARIETY	Height - Width	Branch - Twig	Fruit - Seeds	Leaf Color	Flower-Bracts
Cornus alba WHITE DOGWOOD TARTARIAN DOGWOOD	Upright shrub to 10 ft., spreading about 7 ft.	Blood red	White and bluish white	Yellow green to red to crimson in winter	White in April-May
C. a. sibirica SIBERIAN DOGWOOD	Upright shrub to 7 ft. with 5-ft. spread	Coral red	Same	Same	Same
C. amomum SILKY DOGWOOD	Shrub-like or small tree to 14 ft. with 5-ft. spread	Purple	Blue, partly white	Hairy leaves, silky beneath	White in May
C. capitata EVERGREEN DOGWOOD	Evergreen. Shrub or small tree to 20 ft. with 8-ft. spread	Green	Scarlet berries	Slate-green to red	Cream color. May-June
C. florida	Tree to 20 ft. spreading 10 ft. at 2/3 its height	Upright gray twigs at end of branches	Deep red fading to rust	Green to red	Creamy white. Sometimes both May & Sept.
C. f. rubra PINK FLOWERING D.	Same	Same	Same	Same	Pink or rose in clusters
C. f. welchii	Same	Same	Same	Variegated	Same
C. kousa KOUSA DOGWOOD	Shrub or small tree to 15 ft. with 6-ft. spread	Gray tips to branchlets	Small red fruits in bracts	Medium green to yellow to red	Small creamy white, very open. Jun.-Jul.
C. mas CORNELIAN CHERRY DOGWOOD	Airy, twiggy shrub or finely branched tree to 10 ft. with 7-ft. spread	New twigs green-yellow. Old branches black	Scarlet inch-long. Used in jellies	Green to yellow to red	Clusters of yellow in Feb.-Mar.
C. nuttallii PACIFIC DOGWOOD WESTERN DOGWOOD	Tree to 50 ft. with 15-ft. spread	Gray twigs	Very pronounced red-orange seed buttons	Light green to yellow with touch of red	Large, greenish white to cream. May and Sept.
C. sanguinea BLOODTWIG DOGWOOD	Shrub to 10 ft. with 8-ft. spread	Notable for red twigs and branches. Spring prune for twiggy growth	Black	Green, lighter beneath	Greenish white
C. stolonifera REDTWIG DOGWOOD	Rapid growing shrub to 8-10 ft. with equal spread	Red twigs and branches. Prune back yearly, new growth is redder	White	Heavy dark green, gray underneath. Red in fall	Dull white
C. s. flaviramea YELLOWTWIG DOGWOOD	Same	Yellow twigs and branches	Same	Same	Same

C. florida. FLOWERING DOGWOOD. Has the best garden constitution, and will thrive where the more temperamental native Pacific dogwood will perish. *C. florida* is so popular in the Pacific Northwest that it is regarded as "native" by local gardeners. Always plant it free of confinement. Ideal use: group in open filtered shade with rhododendrons, azaleas, skimmia, pieris, mahonia, and ferns. Winter form is interesting when placed against a grapestake fence.

C. f. rubra. PINK FLOWERING DOGWOOD, with its red autumn color and interesting horizontal branching is spectacular when shown against white or gray background or associated with *Magnolia stellata*. Also effective when mass planted with white flowering dogwood. Garden picture: One pink flowering dogwood pruned to a flat spreading shape, occupying a back lawn area as a graceful canopy, more than 20 ft. across.

C. nuttallii. PACIFIC DOGWOOD, offers a myriad of planed surfaces when flowering, the bracts being parallel to the earth. Use with ferns and rhododendrons, fir and spruce, or with chamæcyparis. Never use alone except as dominant feature in a courtyard or patio, when it should be pruned for height.

C. stolonifera. REDTWIG DOGWOOD, is a rank-growing swamp shrub but is easily controlled in cultivation. Effective groupings: Yellowtwig and redtwig dogwoods; redtwig near red-berried holly, cotoneaster or pyracantha; redtwig with yellow stemmed willow and green stemmed leycesteria. The vari-colored whips are good substitutes for flowers in dead-of-winter gardens.

C. alba sibirica. SIBERIAN DOGWOOD, seems to look its best when planted in clumps around an artificial or natural pool, with ferns.

C. kousa. KOUSA DOGWOOD, with its June-July bloom should be planted to make the most of late bloom and the yellow-to-red fall color. Var. *chinensis* now grown in Southern California, seems to be less demanding in acid-soil requirement than *C. florida*. The variety is larger in all parts than the species.

CORYNOCARPUS LAEVIGATA. NEW ZEALAND LAUREL. Evergreen. Zones 12-13 and protected spots in 9-11. Moderate growth to 20-40 ft., making a slender shrub or small tree. Valued for its large glossy leaves, sometimes 8 in. long, resembling those of the evergreen magnolia. Within its safe climates, a worthy addition to list of favorite small trees for high evergreen backgrounds, informal hedges, and screens. Caution: Leaves burn in full sun except along the coast. Orange, 1-in. fruits are toxic.

COTINUS COGGYGRIA. (*Rhus cotinus*). SMOKE TREE. Deciduous. All zones. Moderate growth to 15 ft. A shrub-tree, creating a broad urn-shaped mass, usually as wide as high. In late summer its misty flowers, in purple, fuzzy-looking puffs, make the whole tree look like a cloud of smoke. Oval leaves turn yellow or orange-red in the fall. Useful in dry and rocky situations, as fall color accent in large shrub borders; also as background for perennial border.

C. c. purpurea. PURPLE LEAF SMOKE TREE. Richer purple when in flower; has spring through summer leaf-color change. New leaves open up deep red and slowly change to green. With new growth coming on constantly, the foliage has a purplish cast all summer. To increase fall color, starve the plant. Thin when dormant.

CRAPE MYRTLE. See LAGERSTROEMIA INDICA

CRATAEGUS. HAWTHORN. Deciduous. Hardy, but does not thrive in hot, dry areas; does not give fall color or produce berries in mild winter sections.

C. phaenopyrum. (*C. cordata.*) WASHINGTON THORN. Moderate growth to 25 ft. with 20 ft. spread. Light and open limb structure with spreading branches. Lustrous green leaves 2-3 in. long, with 3-5 sharp-pointed lobes; turn to red and orange in fall. Small white flowers in broad clusters, in May. Shiny, bright red berries hang on until Christmas-January. Branches have long thorns. More delicate in flower and fruit, more graceful in twig and branch pattern, than other hawthorns. One of the preferred street trees.

C. oxyacantha paulii. PAUL'S DOUBLE SCARLET HAWTHORN. Moderate growth to 18-25 ft. with 15-20 ft. spread. Forms a rather round dense head with twiggy growth. Many flattish clusters of red double flowers. Other varieties: var. *alba*, double white; var. *rosea*, single pink. Fruits drop early. Attacked by aphis in many areas.

C. lavallei (*C. carrierei*). CARRIERE HAWTHORN. To 25 ft. with 10 ft. spread; rather erect, slightly spreading. Dark green, apple-like foliage of leathery 3-4 in. leaves, turning bronze red in fall, remaining on tree until late winter. Noted for its clusters of large orange-to-red berries which hang on through winter.

C. Autumn Glory. Hybrid with *C. oxyacantha* as one parent. More vigorous; seems to require less winter chilling than other hawthorns; has larger berries than its parent.

All of the hawthorns should be kept on dry side to avoid rank growth.

CRINODENDRON DEPENDENS. (*Tricuspidaria dependens.*) WHITE LILY TREE, LILY-OF-THE-VALLEY TREE. (Another tree with the common name of lily-of-the-valley is clethra.) Evergreen. Zones 4-13. Like an evergreen oak in leaf and general appearance. Moderate growth to 25 ft. with spreading crown. Wears hundreds of small, white, bell-shaped flowers in June and July, followed by attractive cream and flame colored seed pods. Start training and shaping as soon as the tree takes hold. It may tend to grow shrub-like, or half the branches will turn down while the other half stick up. Place it where you can see the setting sun strike into the tree and light up the miniature bells. This is one tree that thrives on frequent watering, and will do well in a lawn. Give it a mulch of peat moss, and water twice weekly in dry weather.

CRYPTOMERIA JAPONICA ELEGANS. PLUME CEDAR. JAPANESE CEDAR. Conifer. Zones 3-6 and 9-13. Not successful in extreme summer heat or severe winters. Slow growing to 20-25 ft. in a broadbased pyramid form. Tree is more spreading than usual type of cryptomeria. A soft-textured conifer with feathery foliage, green in summer and copper colored in winter. Needs open space to be appreciated. Don't plant against wall or any flat surface. Use above rock formation or water, planting a ground cover underneath to keep grass down. Offset with bamboo and complement with birch or Irish juniper. Rates high as tree for fall color.

CUNNINGHAMIA LANCEOLATA. CHINA FIR. Conifer. Zones 4-13. Moderate growth to 30 ft. with 20 ft. spread. Looks as an oriental tree should look: heavy trunk, stout branches with drooping branchlets, sharp needles. Among the palest of needled evergreens in spring and summer; turns brown in winter. Except for pines, it's one of the few conifers that can be used with big-leaved rhododendrons, fatsias, magnolias, without losing character.

CUPANIA ANACARDIOIDES. (In nurseries often labeled incorrectly as *Blighia sapida*) CARROT WOOD. Evergreen. Zones 11-13. Moderate growth to 30 ft. with

290 TREES

CITRUS DATE PALM MAGNOLIA BANANA CEDAR FAN PALM COTTONWOOD EUCALYPTUS DRACAENA, SMOKE TREE

20-ft. spread. Leaves are made up of 6-10 leaflets each 4-in. long and leathery. Recommended years ago as street tree for the Southwest but seldom planted. For those who want something different, it's a good shade tree for a small garden.

CUPRESSUS. CYPRESS. Conifer. Hardy all zones. Rapid-growing trees, or sometimes shrubby, with aromatic foliage; tiny leaves closely hugging the branchlets, these appearing cord-like; oval woody cones, each scale often with central knob, which may be curved or not.

C. sempervirens. ITALIAN CYPRESS. MEDITERRANEAN CYPRESS. One of the oldest conifers in cultivated use. Grows to 80 ft. with erect or horizontally spreading branches; and almost smooth gray bark. Var. *stricta* (var's. *fastigiata* and *pyramidalis*). COLUMNAR ITALIAN CYPRESS. The classic cypress; erect branches form dense narrow columnar tree to 60 ft. or more.

C. arizonica. ARIZONA CYPRESS. Grows to 40 ft. high, rarely 70 ft.; short horizontal branches form a narrow pyramidal or broad open head.

C. forbesii. FORBES CYPRESS. TECATE CYPRESS. Slender branched, bushy, small tree to 20 ft.; bark smooth, shining, cherry red.

C. goveniana. GOWEN CYPRESS. Tree to 50 ft., usually a shrub in its native haunts, less than 20 ft. high; in poor soil only 1-2 ft. high and covered with cones; slender branching, forming a broad open head.

C. macrocarpa. MONTEREY CYPRESS. A beautiful tree to 40 ft. or more high, becoming irregular and picturesque when exposed to sea conditions; branches forming a broad spreading head; bark dark reddish-brown, thickly ridged.

Well known as a planted tree in many parts of the world. Has lost favor because it is subject to coryneum canker, and when attacked dies rapidly.

CYDONIA OBLONGA. COMMON QUINCE. Deciduous. Generally overlooked by planters of both flowering fruit trees and home orchard trees as well. These four virtues make the common quince worth considering as an ornamental: In spring it wears white or pale pink 2-in. flowers at tips of leafed out branches; in autumn, its yellowing foliage gives color; fruits are yellow, fragrant; its winter form can be dramatic in pattern of gnarled and twisted branches. Slow growing shrub or small tree to 10-25 ft. Tolerates wet soil. Unlike the flowering quince, chaenomeles, its branches are thornless.

CYPRESS. See CUPRESSUS

DAVIDIA INVOLUCRATA. DOVE TREE. Deciduous. All zones. Rate of growth varies by climate and garden. Reported as botanical garden item in zone 13; yet we have seen the dove tree add 3 feet of healthy growth in one year in Arcadia, California. Generally seen as a 20-30 ft. tree but will go to 50-60 ft. in zones 4 and 5.

Somewhat resembling the linden in shape, it forms a loose, open pyramid of upward curving, slender branches. Large oval leaves, bright green, strongly veined, with dense, silky hairs beneath.

In May and June develops red-anthered flowers in profusion between two large, long, paper-white bracts which hang down like fluttering wings of doves. Flowers are followed by green fruit with purple bloom.

Use it where you can enjoy the bloom, but separate it from other flowering trees, since it should not compete, but rather capitalize on its uniqueness. Varies so greatly in performance and planting that it should be on experimental basis. Mix leaf mold or peat moss into soil and mulch with leaf mold.

DAWN REDWOOD. See METASEQUOIA GLYPTOSTROBOIDES

DIOSPYROS KAKI. ORIENTAL PERSIMMON. Deciduous. Zones 7-13. Slow growing to 20-40 ft. Carefully and beautifully formed, round-headed tree. Leathery leaves, ovoid, 2-3½ in. wide, dark green turning yellow and red in the fall. Bright orange fruit ripens in November after the leaves have fallen.

A favorite of many California landscape architects for fall color. Train against a wall as an informal espalier; plant behind a wall to allow branches to spill over. A tree for edible fruit, fall color, Thanksgiving table decorations, and better than average winter interest when leafless.

Needs deep rich soil or consistent fertilizing program for fruit production. With poor soil or haphazard irrigation, tree is likely to drop immature fruits. See chapter on deciduous fruit trees.

DOGWOOD. See CORNUS
DOVE TREE. See DAVIDIA INVOLUCRATA
ELM. See ULMUS
EMPRESS TREE. See PAULOWNIA TOMENTOSA

ERIOBOTRYA JAPONICA. LOQUAT. Evergreen tropical fruit tree. Zones 7-13, except extreme hot-dry sections. Moderate growth to 15-20 ft. with 15 ft. spread. Bold, leathery, ribbed leaves 6-12 in. long; dark glossy green above, rusty hairy beneath. Small, fragrant flowers in compact clusters in fall; edible fruits are first bronze, then green, and a bright yellow-orange color when ripe in spring.

Most interesting as a bold-leafed espalier on stucco or light wood wall. Can be pruned to make a dense hedge, 6 ft. wide to 15 ft. high. (See chapter on evergreen fruit trees.)

EUCALYPTUS. It's unfortunate that most gardeners attribute the greedy habits, huge size, and messiness of the common blue gum (*E. globulus*) to all its relatives. Actually, many types of eucalyptus are modest-growing "quality" subjects, beautifully adapted to Western gardens.

Most so-called refined forms of eucalyptus are easy to care for, particularly after a year or so in the garden. Whether upright, weeping, or shrubby, they are strong

― Encyclopedia ―

in character and can be extremely effective elements in garden design.

Of the 525 or more species of eucalyptus, you're almost sure to find one to fit your landscape. Availability at nurseries is spotty, however. You may have to go to a specialist for rarer species.

The chart compares the species of greatest interest to Western gardeners. The species starred in the "comment" column are those that are worth being called flowering trees. Many others have flowers but are not noted for them.

EUCALYPTUS

VARIETY	Zones	Height	Width	Growth-Foliage-Flowers	Comments
E. caesia GUNGURRA (MALLEE)	12-13	15 ft.	8 ft.	Moderate growth, graceful, weeping tree. Silver trunk, gray-green leaves. Rosy flowers in winter.	A delicate little tree that looks best over a wall fence or bank. Blooms when 2 years old.
E. camaldulensis (E. rostrata) RED GUM	7-8a 12-13	70 ft.	30 ft.	Fast growing. Tall, open, spreading; medium green leaves. Gray bark.	Interesting spreading form.
E. citriodora LEMON SCENTED GUM	13	50-75 ft.	15-20 ft.	Moderate growth. Very slender and graceful. White to gray trunk.	Effectively used in closely planted groups as with birch.
E. cladocalyx (E. corynocalyx) SUGAR GUM	13	to 150 ft.	to 50 ft.	Fast growth. One of the big ones seen along the roadside from San Diego to Santa Barbara.	Drought resistant but not hardy in the desert. Fine near coast.
E. cornuta YATE TREE	7, 9-13	35 ft.	20 ft.	Fast growth when there's water. Round headed enough for shade. Trunk often crooked.	One of the many that do well under direct coastal conditions.
E. crucis	13	10-20 ft.	5-10 ft.	Fast growing tree or shrub. Open and spreading. Bluish gray foliage.	New growth most attractive. Prune to keep it coming. Good for cut foliage.
E. eremophila TALL SAND MALLEE	12-13	25 ft.	15 ft.	Moderate growth. A small tree suitable to home gardens.	* Clusters of yellow flowers in late winter.
E. erythrocorys ILLYARIE	12-13	15-20 ft.	7-10 ft.	Moderate growth. Open form with leaves as big as those on biggest eucalyptus. Yellow flowers.	* Scarlet buds. Large chartreuse to yellow flowers, scattered through the year.
E. erythronema RED FLOWERED MALLEE	13	15-20 ft.	6-10 ft.	Moderate growth. Tree-shrub. Slender, rounded, rather open.	* Small red flowers in February-March.
E. ficifolia RED FLOWERING GUM	13	30-50 ft.	20-40 ft.	Slow growth. More round headed, more dense, less graceful than typical eucalyptus.	* White to salmon, orange, red flowers in July and at intervals.
E. globulus BLUE GUM	9-10 12-13	to 200 ft.	20-50 ft.	The big one you see used as windbreaks.	Keep it out of the garden.
E. g. compacta DWARF BLUE GUM	Same	to 30 ft.	15 ft.	A small edition of the giant. Bushier.	A quick screen; low windbreak; or dense well shaped tree.
E. gunnii CIDER GUM	Hardy 4-13	40-75 ft.	20-40 ft.	Moderate growth. Rough brown bark. Dense, dark green foliage.	Has very small top-shaped pods carried in clusters of 5 to 12.
E. lehmannii	12-13	25 ft.	20 ft.	Moderate growth. Rounded, and spreading with foliage carried low. Tints of red throughout foliage.	Stands adverse conditions in regard to heat, soil, and water, but is not hardy in winter cold sections.
E. leucoxylon WHITE IRONBARK	7-13	50-60 ft.	12 ft.	Moderate growth. Slender with pendulous branches. Gray-green leaves, white trunk.	Tolerant of California interior soil and winter.
E. l. rosea PINK FLOWERED WHITE IRONBARK	7-13			Same	* Pink flowers, spring and summer.
E. macrocarpa DESERT MALLEE	11-13	15 ft.	15 ft.	Moderate growth. Rambling, shrubby. Large and leathery leaves, dusty white.	* At intervals, round (golf-ball) buds split to release 4 in. wide pink flowers.
E. maculata SPOTTED GUM	13	50-70 ft.	15-20 ft.	Moderate growth. A very slender, graceful tree. Smooth bark sheds in patches.	See E. citriodora may be better choice.
E. m. citriodora LEMON SCENTED GUM				See E. citriodora	
E. polyanthemos REDBOX GUM SILVER DOLLAR GUM	7-13	to 70 ft.	15 ft.	Moderate growing, open, pendulous. Light green-gray rounded or egg-shaped foliage.	Many uses. Topped to widen and provide screen. Trained rather flat against a wall. Good for cut foliage.

(Continued on next page.)

EUCALYPTUS (continued)

VARIETY	Zones	Height	Width	Growth-Foliage-Flowers	Comments
E. populifolia POPLAR GUM	12-13	to 40 ft.	to 40 ft.	Moderate growth. Round headed with large roundish shiny leaves. Foliage reminds you of the poplars.	Best used as a shade tree.
E. preissiana BELL-FRUITED MALLEE	13	to 15 ft.	6 ft.	Spindly growth; hardly a tree; stiff green leaves.	* Grown for its large yellow flowers at intervals.
E. pulverulenta SILVER MOUNTAIN GUM	7-13	20-30 ft.	7 ft.	Moderate growth—open. Silver gray, roundish leaves	Youthful leaves most attractive. Cut back for new growth.
E. robusta (E. multiflora) SWAMP MAHOGANY	7-13	60-80 ft.	20-30 ft.	Fast growth. Leathery foliage looks rugged. Limbs brittle	Takes desert heat and cold, but for fast growth needs water.
E. rudis DESERT GUM	7-13	80 ft.	20 ft.	Fast growth. Foliage copper color when young, then green blue. Brittle.	Stands heat and cold but not remarkably drought resistant. Needs irrigation in desert.
E. sideroxylon rosea RED IRONBARK	7-13	40 ft.	10 ft.	Slow to moderate growth. Slim and airy. Bluish green leaves. Bronze in winter.	* Pink masses of bloom in spring and summer.
E. tereticornis (E. umbellata) GRAY GUM, SALT GUM	7-13	50-70 ft.	20-30 ft.	Fast growth. Grayish bark which flakes off in thin layers.	Difficult to train at start. Needs staking. Will stand seashore or desert.
E. torquata CORAL GUM	13	15-20 ft.	6-8 ft.	Moderate growth. Slender. Red trunk, gray foliage.	* Profusion of rosy-coral buds in midsummer followed by delicate rose colored flowers. Blooms for weeks.
E. viminalis WHITE GUM	7-13	200 ft.	50 ft.	Fast growing to make tallest eucalyptus. Creamy white branches. Light green leaves on pendulous branchlets.	Gets along in poor soil. Tough.

ENCYCLOPEDIA OF TREES (continued)

EUGENIA. Evergreen. Zone 13. Some variation in hardiness, but probable severe damage by unusual freeze must be considered. Because easily sheared and pruned, often used as hedge. Appreciated for handsome glossy green, often bronze tinted, foliage; creamy flowers; often edible fruits.

E. cyanocarpa. BLUE LILI-PILI. Slender little tree to 10-20 ft. White ¾ in. flowers in terminal clusters followed by dark blue edible fruit.

E. edulis. *(Myrciaria edulis).* CHERRY OF THE RIO GRANDE. Small tree-like shrub to 7-8 ft. Flowers white, followed by red, later purple, fruits that resemble large Tartarian cherries. Combines especially well with guava, carissa.

E. jambos. *(Syzygium jambos).* ROSE APPLE. Willowy, sparsely clothed shrub to 8-10 ft. or eventually a broad, small tree to 30 ft. Greenish-white 3-in. flowers. Fruit, 2-in. apple, pink-flushed, rose-scented. May be eaten fresh, candied, or in preserves. Graceful habit enhanced when placed against a wall.

E. paniculata. *(E. hookeri).* Small, slender tree to 15-25 ft. or eventually 40 ft. Glossy green, bronze-tinted 3-in. long leaves. Edible, rose-purple, ¾-in. fruits. Var. *australis (E. myrtifolia.)* AUSTRALIAN BRUSH CHERRY. Remains more bushy and has smaller fruits. Use as tall screen or as narrow clipped hedge. Dwarf form, var. *Armstrong.* Compact, low and dense. May be used as informal hedge.

E. smithii. *(Acmena smithii).* LILI-PILI TREE. Slow-growing small slender tree to 10-25 ft. Bronzy-green, 3-in. leaves; small white flowers in terminal clusters, followed by drooping clusters of lavender-pink berries in winter. Needs partial shade and slightly acid soil. Rare.

E. uniflora. SURINAM CHERRY. Compact shrub or small tree to 15-25 ft. Fruits, size of small tomato, change color from green to yellow, then to orange, and finally to bright scarlet or crimson in the edible stage.

Eugenias may be planted in full sun or partial shade. Soil should have drainage to allow for frequent waterings without waterlogging.

Surinam cherry and the lili-pili tree are particularly useful as high screens as they take up little garden space.

FAGUS. BEECH. Deciduous. *F. grandifolia (F. americana),* AMERICAN BEECH, and *F. sylvatica,* EUROPEAN BEECH, are occasionally planted in parks and large gardens, and seem best adapted to the Pacific Northwest.

F. sylvatica atropunicea. *(F. s. purpurea).* PURPLE BEECH. All zones except hot interiors. More frequently planted in zones 1-5. Trunk subject to sunburn in hot summer areas. A dense pyramid with branches to the ground. Valuable because of purple foliage. Color varies in seedlings and selected forms of the variety have been given names, as black beech, red-leafed beech, copper beech. Watch for leaf color when you buy. Weeping and cutleaf varieties are available.

FICUS. FIG. Usually evergreen. Climate adaptability varies by species. The average gardener would never expect to find the commercial edible fig, the small leafed climbing fig, the banyan tree, and the potted rubber plant under one common heading. Botanically they are classed as one genus because they all bear small or large figs.

There are 11 species available in Southern California nurseries. The adaptability and use in the garden varies greatly. Just how many species of this family should be brought into the garden is hard to tell. Many more than are now in the trade have been tested and are proving satisfactory in various botanic and test gardens throughout the Southwest. Here is a short analysis of the characteristics and possibilities of the species now available.

F. benghalensis. BANYAN TREE. Native to India but you have probably seen it in Hawaii. Where adapted as in Hawaii and Florida, it grows to 100 ft. and spreads by sending down aerial roots which become secondary trunks. In arid climate of California the aerial roots are not prominent. Broad 4-8 in. leaves and paired red ½-in. figs.

Just how tender to frost is the banyan tree is hard to tell. A tree in Whittier has reached 30 ft. with a trunk diameter of 18 in.; there's another specimen in Redlands; a tree in Los Angeles was lost at 20°.

F. benjamina. WEEPING CHINESE BANYAN. More tender to frost than *F. retusa nitida*. Pendulous graceful poplar-like tree to 30 ft. with shining oval 2-5 in. leaves and figs becoming red. Generally used as a tub plant, but has been grown out-of-doors in Santa Monica. Reported successful in low desert at Palm Springs and El Centro.

F. carica. EDIBLE FIG. (See chapter on home food garden.)

F. macrophylla. MORETON BAY FIG. Best adapted to coastal Southern California. Fast growth to enormous dimensions. Specimen in Santa Barbara has a spread of more than 150 ft., with massive buttressed trunk above soil surface, also surface roots. Blunt oval 10-in. leaves are 4 in. wide, brownish underneath. Purple 1-in. figs spotted with white.

F. mysorensis. MYSORE FIG. Fast growth to a large tree. Leaves are leathery and glossy above. Bears orange-red figs in pairs. One growing in Santa Barbara is 20 ft. tall.

F. retusa. INDIAN LAUREL FIG. GLOSSY LEAF FIG. Most widely planted rubber tree. Fast growth to 50 ft. Somewhat pendulous in habit. Dense, dark green, dull glossy foliage, of roundish 2-4 in. leaves. Yellowish or reddish ⅓-in. figs. An attractive garden subject and tub plant. Use as a large shrub or screen in partial shade. Var. *nitida*. (*F. nitida*). Similar to *F. retusa* in appearance, but becomes a larger tree and its leaves are more pointed. Often sold under the name of *F. retusa*, or *F. nitida*.

F. religiosa. PEEPUL, BOTREE. A large tree in the tropics, but rather small and shrubby, and does poorly in Southern California. Leaves are roundish with a long tail-like point. Purple ½-in. figs.

F. rubiginosa. RUSTY LEAF FIG. Fast growing broad tree to 50 ft.; variable in habit—sometimes with aerial roots, but often remaining bushy; deep green oval 5-in. leaves are rusty beneath; ½-in. warty figs. Var. *australis*, the more common form, is less rusty-leafed than the species.

F. elastica. COMMON RUBBER TREE, RUBBER PLANT. Less hardy than *F. macrophylla*. Most frequently used as a pot plant; will grow rapidly outdoors but subject to frost damage. One tree in Whittier, California, is 30 ft. tall. Has leathery, 5-12 in., smooth, glossy leaves. Yellowish ½-in. figs.

F. lyrata. (*F. pandurata*). FIDDLELEAF FIG. Leaves shaped like a violin are 10-15 in. long and rough leathery texture. White dotted 2-in. figs. Usually grown indoors but when planted out in protected, part-shaded locations, will grow to 15-25 ft.

Here are a few of the species not yet available, but that may have a future place in California gardens:

F. ovata. Tree to 30 ft., with a large broad crown. Successful planting in Oxnard City Park, and Santa Barbara, California.

F. roxburghii. Beautiful shrub to 10 ft. Mahogany red new growth, and broadly ovate to orbicular leaves.

F. nekbudu (*F. utilis*). Successful plantings at the Huntington Botanic Garden, Montebello, and San Diego.

F. lacor (*F. infectoria*). Successful planting at the Huntington Botanic Garden, and Riverside.

F. watkinsiana. Large tree successfully planted at Huntington Botanic Garden and Elysian Park in Los Angeles.

FIG. See FICUS
FIR. See ABIES

FIRMIANA SIMPLEX. CHINESE PARASOL TREE. Deciduous. Zones 7-13 except desert. Small slow-growing, 15-50 ft. tree with light gray-green bark. Trunk is often without side branches to 4 or 5 ft., at which point it divides into 3 or more slender, upright and slightly spreading stems which carry deeply lobed, tropical-looking 12-in. leaves. Each stem looks as if it could be cut off and carried away as a parasol. Most interesting for fruits which are like 2 opened green pea pods. Should be used in patio or court protected from strong winds. Unusually hardy for a tree so tropical looking.

FRAXINUS. ASH. Deciduous; sometimes evergreen. Climate by species.

F. velutina. ARIZONA ASH. Zones 6-13. Native to Southern California east to Texas. Moderate growth to 40 ft.; spread varies with age; rather pyramidal in youth, more round but open-headed in maturity. Don't be surprised if you don't get much shade for several years. Leaf is made up of 3-5 willow-like leaflets, 2-4 in. long. Tolerates alkaline soil. Var. *coriacea*. MONTEBELLO ASH, LEATHERLEAF ASH. Now planted in zones 7-13 only but not tested beyond. Leaves are more leathery and less hairy, the leaflets broader than the species. Var. *glabra*, MODESTO ASH, SMOOTH ASH. Now planted in zones 3-13. The most widely distributed ash in the West; has smooth leaflets.

The Modesto and Montebello ash have earned great popularity in the warm sections of California. For years they have been heralded as pest free, soil adaptable, wind hardy, and beautiful in their summer green and fall yellow. Rumors of disease and pest trouble from one or two localities are putting question marks after these trees. Check with your park department.

F. uhdei. SHAMEL ASH. Evergreen and deciduous. Zones 7-13. Has spread rapidly throughout California since its introduction from Mexico a few years ago. Fast growth to 30 ft. with 15-20 ft. spread. Admired for bright green, glossy, 18 in. leaves which are divided into leaflets. When winters are warm, the foliage persists through the winter; leaves fall in frost areas. Inclined to grow very lanky unless cut back a few times in its youthful stage. Seedlings vary greatly in leaf, growth and hardiness. Look for selected forms.

F. pennsylvanica lanceolata. GREEN ASH. Zones 1-6. Moderate growth to 30-50 ft., to form a compact oval crown. Gray-brown bark; dense twigs. Bright green 10-12 in. leaves are divided into 5-9 rather narrow 4-6 in. smooth leaflets. Subject to leaf burn in hot, windy areas.

F. americana. WHITE ASH. Zones 1-6. Moderate growth to 60-80 ft. Straight tall trunk. Symmetrical lines. 8-15 in. leaves are divided into 5-9 ovate leaflets which are dark green above, paler beneath, turn purple in autumn. Subject to leaf burn.

F. ornus. FLOWERING ASH. All zones. Moderate growth to 30-40 ft., the 8-10 in. leaves divided into 7-11 ovate or oblong 2-3 in. leaflets, turn yellow and lavender in fall. Fragrant white flowers in dense 3-5 in. clusters in May and June.

F. oregona. OREGON ASH. Zones 1-10. Native in California north to British Columbia. Grows to 30-80 ft. Bright green 6-12 in. leaves are divided into 5-7 oblong or oval 2-5½ in. smooth leaflets.

FRINGE TREE. See CHIONANTHUS

GINKGO BILOBA. MAIDENHAIR TREE. Deciduous. Broad-leafed conifer—a living fossil—sole survivor of a Chinese family of trees. Common name comes from similarity between leaf of ginkgo and single leaflet of maidenhair fern. The tree is not fern-like; its leaves are flat, fan-shaped. Adapted to all zones, but varying in behavior by zones. Rate of growth varies by climate, and growth habit varies by tree. For example: In Hoyt Arboretum in Portland, Oregon, 37 ginkgos, each 4 ft. high, were planted in 1933. Twenty years later none had produced fruit; some showed very little growth; the largest measured 12 ft. high. Some were globular in shape, others flat crowned or pyramidal. In Palo Alto, California, a 5-ft. tree will reach 9 ft. in 5 yrs. An 8-ft. tree, bare root from nursery, will reach 12 ft. in 5 years.

In California's Sacramento Valley, gardeners call the ginkgo a moderately fast grower. There are good 40-50 ft. specimens in the old sections of California cities—Sacramento, Santa Rosa, Hollister, San Luis Obispo. Will grow to 70-80 ft. There are weeping forms (var. *pendula*) in the Los Angeles State and County Arboretum and an umbrella form in Santa Cruz.

In general the ginkgo is an open, sparse airy tree, but clean cut and aristocratic. Sometimes gawky in youth but always a picturesque character as it matures. Leathery leaves are light green in spring and summer, turning to a golden buttery-yellow in fall; hang on for weeks and make a golden carpet when they fall.

No serious pests and diseases. Does best, of course, in deep, well drained soil, but adapts itself to almost any garden condition. Used as lawn and street tree. Tolerant of city smoke and smog. Outstanding and beautiful in containers when well grown. Three ginkgos in a large box reached 5 feet when they were 10 years old.

The ginkgo is an outstanding example of need for vegetative propagation of many trees. The female tree produces flesh-covered nuts with an unpleasant odor. Only male trees should be planted. However, sex cannot be determined until seedling blooms, about 25 years from seed. To be sure of tree's sex you must find trees from cuttings or grafts. Nuts of the ginkgo are edible and sold at Oriental markets as silver nuts. On counts of long life, unusual beauty, and fall color, the ginkgo rates near the top of the list of trees for the West.

GLEDITSIA. LOCUST. Introduction of the horticultural variety, Moraine locust, described below, has brought new acceptance to the locust name. It does not have the thorns or the long tough pods of *G. triacanthos* but holds the beauty of honey locust's finely divided foliage and fall coloring.

G. triacanthos inermis Moraine. MORAINE LOCUST. Deciduous. All zones. Fast growing to 40-60 ft. with equal spread. Very open growth habit. Compound leaves, each with 20-30 leaflets, ½ by 1 in. Fall coloring is clear yellow. A tough, long lived tree in spite of its rapid growth. Accepts any soil condition; stands drought. Lets enough light through so that a lawn can be grown under it. Rates high as large tree for large garden.

GOLDENCHAIN TREE. See LABURNUM
GOLDENRAIN TREE. See KOELREUTERIA

GORDONIA ALATAMAHA. (*Franklinia alatamaha*). FRANKLINIA. Deciduous. Zones 3-6, 9, and 10. Moderate growth to 20-30 ft. Upward-curving branch pattern. Spoon-shaped leaves 4-6 in. long, bright green shiny above, paler beneath. Especially useful because of late flowering. Pure white, cup-shaped, 3-in. flowers with yellow stamens. August-September. Excellent small shrub-tree for acid soil areas. Takes on brilliant red tints in fall if tree is given plenty of moisture in early spring and dried off toward end of summer.

GREVILLEA ROBUSTA. SILK OAK. Evergreen. Zones 7-13, where temperatures stay above 15°. Fast growth in warm zones to 100 ft. with 40 ft. spread. Tall, slender; usually has main trunk dividing 10 ft. above ground in 2 or 3 secondary trunks; fern-like leaves; orange-yellow, 6-10 in. flower trusses borne in summer in 1-sided 4-in. clusters on short leafless branches.

There are treemen who will have nothing to do with the silk oak. They point out these faults: subject to frost, root rot, chlorosis, limb breakage, scant bloom. There are gardeners in Palm Springs, Santa Barbara, Fresno, Los Altos, and many other California towns who have their silk oaks and like them very much. We have seen it used as indoor-outdoor tub plant in Kent, Washington. It's an interesting tree and worthwhile where the garden is big enough for secondary trees and where heat and drought are problems. Look for narrow leaf and pyramided forms.

G. banksii. Evergreen shrub or tree to 12 ft. with deeply divided dull green leaves and dark red flowers in early spring. Too fussy about drainage for most areas.

GYMNOCLADUS DIOICA. KENTUCKY COFFEE TREE. Deciduous. All zones, except extremes in 1. Moderate growth to 50 ft. (100 ft. in Eastern United States) with equal spread; trunk often made up of several parallel branches; compound leaves 1½-3 ft. long, made up of many leaflets 1-3 in. long; clusters of greenish-white flowers in June, followed by thick 6-10 in. long pods which hang on all winter. Gets its common name from dark seeds in pod. Used as a street tree in zones 1-6, this coarse, messy, sturdy large tree of the pea family is not for small gardens. Used as background tree for interesting foliage and change of color: leaves, pink when unfolding, turn to clear yellow in fall.

HALESIA CAROLINA. (*H. tetraptera*). SNOWDROP TREE, SILVER BELL. Deciduous. Probably all zones except 1-2. Mature trees scattered from Seattle to San Diego. Moderate growth 20 to 50 ft. with 15 to 30-ft. spread, depending on climate. Seattle specimens 25 ft.

Rates high as a flowering tree in May when clusters of snowdrop-white, 1-in. flowers hang from graceful, spreading nearly leafless branches. Leaves, triangular, finely toothed, turn yellow in fall. Said to have preference for cool, deep, leafy soil and abundant water but seems to be adapting to Southern California conditions.

H. monticola. MOUNTAIN SILVER BELL. Is a larger tree, 40-60 ft., with larger leaves.

HAMAMELIS MOLLIS. CHINESE WITCH-HAZEL. Deciduous. Zones 3-6, 9 and 10. Slow-to-moderate growth to 30 ft. with 15-ft. spread, vase shape when small. Coarse, fuzzy texture; woolly, serrated leaves, 3-6 in. long turn yellow in the fall. Important feature is winter bloom and fragrance. Spidery yellow flowers cling tightly to bare branches, December-February.

Yellow flowers are effective against gray or red brick. Can be trained as wall-shrub. Valuable contribution to

Pacific Northwest gardens in lighting up winter gardens otherwise inclined to be drab. In large garden, plant along edge of woodland. Plant in mass but keep open, in order to appreciate spidery texture. No special culture required in climates where adapted.

HARPEPHYLLUM CAFFRUM. KAFIR PLUM. Evergreen. Zones: best in 13 but survives in warm sections of 9, 10, and 12, coming back from base after freeze damage. Fast growth to 30-35 ft. with 20-25 ft. spread. Round crown but easily trained to structurally interesting shade or lawn tree. Leaves are leathery, glossy, each made up of 13-15 narrow leaflets, 2½ in. long; unfold bright red and turn to dark green. Very small white flowers, followed by tart but edible dark red fruits resembling large olives.

Because of its well-groomed tropical appearance in youth, age, and in every season, and because of its fast growth, easy culture and wind hardiness, rates high as shade tree for small garden. Only drawback is its fruit drop.

HAWTHORN. See CRATAEGUS

HOHERIA. Species of this genus have been grown in San Francisco's Golden Gate Park and propagated in limited quantity in the Bay area. Are also being tried in Southern California. Importance of hoherias to the small garden is their well-behaved root system. They keep their place.

H. angustifolia. Evergreen. Small, slender, airy, thin-leafed tree to 30 ft. Small star-shaped flowers. July-August.

H. lyallii. (*H. lyallii ribifolia, Gaya lyallii*). Deciduous. Flowers like white cherry blossoms, in July.

H. populnea. Dark green leathery leaves, rather dense foliage. Tall and slender to 40 ft.

HYMENOSPORUM FLAVUM. SWEETSHADE. Evergreen. Zones 9, 10, 12, and 13, and borderline in zones 7 and 11. Slow to moderate growth; 40-50 ft. with 10-15 ft. spread. Graceful, upright, slender habit in first 10 years, open enough to make the tree look well against a wall where you can see tracery of branch pattern. Leaves, 2-6 in. long, 1-2 in. wide, like those of some of its near relative pittosporum, are crowded toward the end of the branches. Clusters of yellow flowers in early summer with pronounced orange blossom honey fragrance. Early training necessary as branches spread out in almost equal threes, creating weakness for splitting. Cut out weaker shoots and let fewer strong ones take over. No other special cultural demands. Trees along the coast have best appearance.

JACARANDA ACUTIFOLIA. JACARANDA. Evergreen. Deciduous for very short time Feb. or March. Variable. Zones 11-13 and most favorable spots, 9; fair in 8a. Moderate to fast growth to 40 ft. with 25-ft. spread, generally 25 by 15 ft. Rather open, irregular, oval head. Fern-like leaves. Features profusion of lavender-blue, 2-in., tubular flowers in 8-in. clusters; in June, but may flower from May-Sept.

This spectacular tree is at its best where not subjected to strong winds or frequent watering. Tends to become misshapen in windy locations, and straggly when forced by fertilizers and water. Must be staked first few years to make it grow straight. Gives a poor performance in heavy soils. Depending upon how you look at it: flowers falling to the ground form a colorful carpet beneath the tree; or are very messy on patio floor or lawn. Excellent choice for planting below eye level. A good tree to look down upon.

JUGLANS. WALNUT. Deciduous.

J. californica. SOUTHERN CALIFORNIA BLACK WALNUT. Native to Southern California. Tree-like shrub or small tree 15-30 ft., commonly with several stems from the ground. Leaves to 6-12 in., divided into 9-19 oblong-ovate leaflets to 2¼ in. long. Seldom cultivated.

J. hindsii. CALIFORNIA BLACK WALNUT. Native to central California, in scattered localities. Tree to 30-60 ft., with single tall trunk and broad crown. Leaves divided into 15-19 leaflets to 3-5 in. long. Used as root stock for English walnut.

J. nigra. BLACK WALNUT. Hardy all zones; used as a street tree in zones 1 and 2. Native to eastern United States. High-branched tree to 150 ft., with round crown, and deeply furrowed brown bark. Leaves divided into 15-23 ovate-oblong leaflets to 2½-5 in.

J. regia. ENGLISH WALNUT. (For varieties by zones, see chapter on home food garden.) The walnut of commerce. A fast growing, good looking tree for large gardens.

J. cinerea. BUTTERNUT. Zones 1-4. Tree to 100 ft., trunk with gray fissured bark. Leaves divided into 11-19 leaflets to 5 in. long.

Spreads of 80 ft. for black walnut and 70 ft. for English walnut are not uncommon. Leaves, if left on ground, are injurious to lawns. Husk on the nuts stains hands brown; stain can be removed with lemon juice. Unless your soil is deep don't plant walnut.

JUNIPERUS. JUNIPER. (See chapter on shrubs for lower growing forms. Also see chapter on natives.) Hardy all zones. Although there are a number of forms available none is particularly useful in the average garden. Used mostly as individuals or in windbreaks. All are pyramidal to columnar, from 20-40 ft. with dark green to gray-green foliage.

J. chinensis. CHINESE JUNIPER. Columnar to slightly spreading to 40 ft., with slender branches and gray-green foliage. Var. *aurea* is a very good, golden form to 30-40 ft. Var. *columnaris* has a narrow, pyramidal habit and blue-green foliage. Var. *foemina*, the female form, has softer foliage, and older plants produce attractive blue berries. Var. *keteleeri*, a small tree to 20 ft., has a rather open, irregular, pyramidal form. Medium green leaves on horizontal branches that turn up at the ends.

J. communis aurea. CANADIAN GOLDEN JUNIPER. Grows 30-40 ft. Has golden foliage on drooping branches, the young growth a pale golden-yellow.

J. communis hibernica. IRISH JUNIPER. Grows to 20 ft. Many stems grow vertically from the base to give a bushy, upright appearance. Branch tips and center tends to brown.

J. communis suecica. SWEDISH JUNIPER. Columnar habit to 40 ft., with drooping branchlets.

J. scopulorum. ROCKY MOUNTAIN JUNIPER. WESTERN RED CEDAR. A bushy, low-branching tree that grows to 30 ft. in cultivation. Blue-gray foliage.

J. virginiana. EASTERN RED CEDAR. Compact, pyramidal tree to 30-50 ft. Has handsome blue berries. Very hardy, makes a good windbreak for cold exposures.

KAFIR PLUM. See HARPEPHYLLUM CAFFRUM

KATSURA TREE. See CERCIDIPHYLLUM JAPONICUM

KOELREUTERIA. Two species are available: one all-climate, adaptable; one tailored to California.

K. paniculata. GOLDENRAIN TREE. Deciduous. All zones except coldest sections of 1. Slow growth to 20-30 ft. with 10-20 ft. spread. Open growth, light shade.

Leaves, 15 in. long, made up of 7 to 15 ovate leaflets. Features clusters of bright yellow flowers, 8 to 14 in. long, in late June, July. Fruit, a conical capsule, ripens in the fall. A most valuable tree where other trees suffer, in arid sections and in alkali soils. But is not long lived—40-50 years; bladder-like capsules, rather unsightly, hang on until late fall.

K. formosana. CHINESE FLAME TREE. Zones 6-13. All trees seen in California coastal area formerly called *K. bipinnata* have been identified by Rehder as *K. formosana*. Probably hardier in colder areas but early frost damage makes tree unsightly. Moderate growth to 20-40 ft. and may do 60 ft., with equal spread. In foliage and flowers similar to *K. paniculata;* leaves more compound, twice divided into leaflets instead of once. Important difference is in pods, which give this species the "flames" of orange and red in late summer and fall. Interesting in all stages of growth; adaptable; no pest troubles; no soil troubles. It's a valuable tree for California. Should be headed high and carefully shaped when used as shade tree for terrace or patio. Roots are well behaved; you can plant under it.

LABURNUM. GOLDENCHAIN TREE. Deciduous. Hardy all zones but needs winter cold. Poor performer in all mild winter zones. Three varieties are available, but the hybrid with the 10-20 in. long flower clusters sold under the name of *L. watereri* or *L. vossii* is the universal favorite.

L. watereri. *(L. vossii)*. LONGCLUSTER GOLDENCHAIN. Slow growth to 12 ft. Tree or shrub depending upon how pruned; vase-shaped; trunk and branches always slender regardless of age; light green bark, gray-green, compound leaves arranged like clover leaves. All-important feature: long (up to 20 in.) clusters of yellow flowers in late spring, very similar to wistaria. Needs protection from afternoon sun in warm sections. Lack of water causes leaves to fall very early. Pods often unsightly. Not effective without a neutral colored background and therefore not easy to place in a garden. Often used in background to bloom with lilacs or purple rhododendrons.

L. anagyroides. COMMON GOLDENCHAIN. Less spectacular blooms; grows to 20-25 ft.

L. alpinum. SCOTCH LABURNUM. To 30-35 ft. Hardier, later blooming than the common goldenchain. Flowers, fruits, and seeds are poisonous.

LAGERSTROEMIA INDICA. CRAPE MYRTLE. Deciduous. Zones 7, 8a, 11, 12, and warm, dry spots in 9. Planted along the coast, but mildews badly. Slow growing shrub-tree; 8-30 ft. As shrub, spreads wide as high; trained as a tree, becomes vase-shaped with most attractive trunk and branch pattern. Bark sheds to reveal a smooth pinkish inner bark. Rather light-textured foliage of 1 to 2-in. leaves, light green in spring, then green to dark green, and orange or yellow in fall. Crinkled crape-like flowers on spikes 6 to 8 in. long, white, pink, lavender, rose; long blooming season—July, August, September.

Needs full sun and summer warmth. Mildews in shade. Can't be sure about color unless you see it in bloom. Over-fertilizing and over-watering cut down on flower quantity. Crape myrtle rates high among all flowering shrubs and trees in favorable climates. Should always be trained to display beauty of trunk and planted where its winter branch pattern is not lost.

LAGUNARIA PATERSONII. PRIMROSE TREE. PYRAMID TREE, COW ITCH TREE. Evergreen. Zones 12 and 13. (Should be hardy wherever acacia is grown.) Moderately fast to slender 20-40 ft. Regularly spaced branches form pyramid. Its great virtue is in its 2-4 in., thick, olive-green, gray-backed leaves; very wind hardy. Hibiscus-like, pink to rose, 2-in. wide flowers in summer. Planted closely, this tree makes a serviceable hedge that's happy right along the ocean. Main drawback is the brown seed pods, which irritate the skin on contact. Pods hang on and on, but continue to spill their seeds.

LARIX DECIDUA. *(L. europæa)*. LARCH. Deciduous conifer. Best in zones 1-6. Moderate growth to 30-70 ft. Slender horizontal branches and drooping branchlets, arranged in horizontal pattern, create a pyramid. Notable as it breaks dormancy with thousands of very pale green feathery tufts. Stands away from all other conifers again in the fall when its needles turn yellow and orange before dropping. Unlike most conifers, needles of larch are soft to touch and feathery in appearance. They do not have the pitchy odor of the typical conifer needles.

L. occidentalis. WESTERN LARCH. Very similar; has sharper, stiffer needles. Does not do so well in cultivation.

Small, globular cones decorate branches against winter sky in a delightful sort of polka-dot pattern. Larch is lovely planted near water—it reflects apple green.

LAURUS NOBILIS. SWEET BAY. GRECIAN LAUREL. Evergreen. Hardy zones 7-13, and if protected 3-6, but best in 9, 10, 12, and 13. Slow growth to 12-40 ft.; normally a compact, broad-based, gradually tapering cone, but stands clipping so well that you see it in every formal shape. Typical: trained as an oval-headed standard for formal entrances. Watch for black scale. Don't overwater.

LEPTOSPERMUM LAEVIGATUM. AUSTRALIAN TEA TREE. (See chapter on shrubs.)

LEUCADENDRON ARGENTEUM. SILVER TREE. Evergreen. Zones 10, 12, and 13. Expect frost damage at 24°. Fast growing, short-lived, to 40 ft. Mature silhouette reminds of aleppo pine; tortuous, gray barked trunk; silky silvery-white leaves, 3-6 in., densely cover the branches. Needs soil that drains rapidly; open sunlight but with wind protection. Resents clay soil, manure, lime. Best in decomposed granite. Because of its cultural requirements and its dominating characters, the silver tree can't be planted just anywhere in the garden. Interesting in the infant stage, and so is excellent in tubs and boxes for 3 or 4 years.

LIBOCEDRUS DECURRENS. INCENSE CEDAR. One of the most popular, most adaptable conifers. (See chapter on natives.)

LILY-OF-THE-VALLEY TREE. See CLETHRA ARBOREA, CRINODENDRON DEPENDENS

LINDEN. See TILIA

LIQUIDAMBAR STYRACIFLUA. SWEET GUM. Deciduous. All zones, with exceptions noted below. Moderate growth to 100 ft., generally 60 ft., with 20 ft. spread of lower limbs; narrow pyramidal or columnar; upright and horizontal branching with beautiful spacing so that tree never looks crowded. Maple-shaped leaves are carefully displayed. All this, seemingly, in preparation for a fall color display in yellows and reds. An exciting tree to be around when it turns color. One of the few trees sure to **color in warm winter sections.**

Liquidambar is hardy to zero, has taken -10°. However, the rate of growth is much slower in all cold winter areas. On recommended list for near-desert areas; expect wind burn where there's a hot dry wind. Prefers non-alkaline soil. Withstands salt air. If you want dependable fall color, buy liquidambar in containers when it's in color.

Use as lawn tree, street tree; plant 6-10 ft. apart to make high screen or line a driveway.

LIRIODENDRON TULIPIFERA. TULIP TREE. Deciduous. Hardy all zones but intolerant of drought and alkali. Moderate to fast growth to 60-80 ft. with 40 ft. spread. Straight columnar trunk, with spreading branches high above ground forming pyramidal crown. Unusual light bluish-green, lyre-shaped, 4-lobed leaves, 5-6 in. long, turn yellow in early fall. Flowers like 2-in. tulips, greenish-yellow, orange at base, in late spring. Flowers last out of water like orchids. Tree does not produce flowers until 10 or 12 years old.

To do this beautiful tree real justice, give it plenty of room. Requires deep soil and summer watering; will drop its leaves in summer if dried off. Best for country places where water is no problem. In western Oregon and Washington, the tulip tree will reach 40 ft. in 15 years.

Needs consistent spraying for tulip tree scale and aphis, which causes the honeydew drip on walls or cars parked beneath. Has spreading, greedy root system.

LOCUST. See GLEDITSIA, ROBINIA

MACADAMIA TERNIFOLIA. QUEENSLAND NUT. Evergreen. Zones 12 and 13. Best performance within 20 miles of coast. Foliage lightly burned at 19°-25°. Moderate growth to 25-30 ft. with 15-20 ft. spread. Needs warm, moist soil with good drainage. Attractive vase shape. From a distance, looks much like evergreen magnolia: leaves, deep green, leathery, narrow and toothed, 6-8 in. long. A superb tree in every respect: size, form, foliage, and nuts. Macadamia nuts are now a commercial crop in Hawaii.

MACLURA POMIFERA. OSAGE ORANGE. Deciduous. Zones 6-13; 8a for quick shade tree. Fast, rank growing, spiny, to 60 ft. Inedible fruits, like large pale green oranges with bumps. Used in barrier plantings on farms; tolerates heat, drought, alkali soils.

MAGNOLIA.

The magnolia family is remarkable not only for its number of magnificent flowering trees and shrubs, but for their variety. The family includes both evergreen and deciduous trees in a number of different shapes and colors of blooms, different leaf forms and plant structures.

Magnolias are native to two areas—the eastern United States south through Mexico to northern South America, and in Asia from northern Japan south to Java and west to the Himalayas. Since the early 1900's, plant collectors and explorers have introduced many new species which are gradually being propagated and are becoming available to Western gardens.

Here in the West each subclimate has its preferred species and varieties. As supply at nurseries increases, use in the gardens becomes more varied. The hardy deciduous types are used in the coldest areas. Throughout zones 3-13 *Magnolia grandiflora*, *M. stellata*, and *M. soulangeana* are important in the home landscape. The lily tree, *M. liliflora*, is being used more even in Southern California where the evergreens are top favorites. The entire group finds ideal growing conditions in the mild weather sections of the Northwest and under central and northern California coastal conditions. The home gardener must watch in selecting size of the tree. All magnolias resent crowding and many of them eventually become large trees.

All magnolias are native to moist, rich, well drained woodland soils. The best time to plant magnolias is in the early spring, when the roots become active. The thick, fleshy roots are apt to decay if injured. It is most important that proper watering be continued on through the summer for magnolias resent drying out. Topdress with a good mulch of old leaves, compost, or well rotted manure. When watering, be sure that the water goes through this mulch and down to the roots.

Once established, magnolias will withstand considerable hardship. Probably the greatest single hazard is the gardener who surrounds them in early stages of growth with filler-in plants such as azaleas or rhododendrons. Like camellias, magnolias root on the surface as well as down deep for anchorage. Disturbing these feeder roots not only is dangerous to the health of magnolias, but can be downright fatal. Do not permit the soil to pack around the plant.

They should not be pruned unless absolutely necessary. If you must prune, the best time is right after flowering. Each wound should be immediately painted with a tree paint to prevent bleeding and exposure to insects.

MAGNOLIA

Variety	Dec. Ever.	Ht. Spread in Ft.	Age Blooms	Flowers	Use	Remarks
M. acuminata CUCUMBER TREE	Dec.	60-80 by about 25	12 yrs.	Greenish yellow after leaves appear.	Shade tree.	Very handsome leaves, 9 in. long.
M. campbellii CAMPBELL MAGNOLIA	Dec.	80 by 40	20 yrs.	Deep rose without, pale rose within	Protect from drying cold winter winds. Needs shelter of evergreens.	One of the best for leaves. New growth is quite rosy.
M. dawsoniana DAWSON MAGNOLIA	Dec.	25 by 20 Some are 35 by 30	15 yrs.	White inside, rosy-violet outside.	Allow for spread. Sunny exposure with wind protection.	Beautiful leaves, large flowers.
M. denudata YULAN MAGNOLIA	Dec.	35 by 30	7 yrs.	White and fragrant.	Plant where white blossoms can be seen against the sky.	Worthwhile for its delightful fragrance and flowers.
M. grandiflora SOUTHERN MAGNOLIA BULL BAY	Ever.	80 by 40	15 yrs.	Large, white, fragrant.	Plant as specimen. Needs protection from wind.	This magnificent tree is well known for its beautiful foliage and bloom.
M. g. lanceolata (M. g. exoniensis) DWARF SOUTHERN MAGNOLIA	Ever.	Smaller than above.	Earlier than above.	Same as above.	For the smaller garden, specimen in shrub border.	Valuable in smaller gardens.
M. kobus KOBUS MAGNOLIA	Dec.	30 by 20	18 yrs.	Creamy white.	Magnificent specimen, should be used as such.	Upright growth. Very hardy and useful as shade tree.

(Continued on next page.)

— Encyclopedia —
MAGNOLIA (continued)

Variety	Dec. Ever.	Ht. Spread in Ft.	Age Blooms	Flowers	Use	Remarks
M. liliflora LILY MAGNOLIA	Dec.	12 by 15	4 or 5 yrs.	White inside, purplish outside.	Plant in front of M. acuminata. It will throw its blossoms amongst the large leaves of M. acuminata.	Long season, blossoms from spring and on during the summer.
M. l. nigra	Dec.	12 by 15	4-5 yrs.	Pinkish within, dark purple without.	Often sold as M. liliflora.	Seems to be even hardier than M. liliflora.
M. macrophylla BIGLEAF MAGNOLIA	Dec.	50 by 30	12-15 yrs.	Creamy-white purplish at base. 10-20 across.	Give sheltered location out of frost pockets. Large leaves will not stand wind whipping.	Worthwhile planting for its long large leaves.
M. mollicomata	Dec.	50 by 30	20 yrs. Some at 10-12.	Rose tinted. Late Feb. to early Mar.	Give it room and protection for early bloom.	Similar to M. campbellii. The variety Lanarth is highly recommended.
M. salicifolia ANISE MAGNOLIA	Dec.	18 by 12	6 yrs.	Rosy-pink, Apr.	Another for the small garden.	Blooms before leaves arrive. Good against blue sky.
M. sargentiana SARGENT MAGNOLIA	Dec.	35 by 35	10-12 yrs.	Rose-purple to pale pink at tip. Blooms Mar.-Apr.	Do not crowd. Evergreens make an excellent background for Magnolias.	One of the most beautiful of all Magnolias!
M. sieboldii OYAMA MAGNOLIA	Dec.	10 by 6	5 yrs.	White, cup-shaped fragrant. Blooms May, often summer.	Use as single tree in small garden or as espalier.	Valuable for the small garden. Branches slender, downy.
M. sinensis CHINESE MAGNOLIA	Dec.	15-20 by 20-30	8-10 yrs.	White, saucer-shaped. Fragrant. May-June, later.	Short but spreading it may be used to fill quite a large corner.	Its prolonged blooming is in its favor.
M. soulangeana (M. liliflora x M. denudata) SAUCER MAGNOLIA	Dec.	16 by 45	3-5 yrs.	Varies according to variety from nearly white, to white within and shades of rose to purple without.	Suitable for small gardens because slow growing. Stands pruning.	This hybrid and its many varieties are placed in the very first rank.
M. stellata STAR MAGNOLIA	Dec.	10 by 20	3 yrs.	White star flowers.	Effective at top of a gentle slope with backing of evergreens.	Next to the M. soulangeana hybrids, most widely planted.
M. s. rosea	Dec.	10 by 15	3-4 yrs.	Blooms Apr. Flowers pink outside.	Along with the type, two of the best for smaller gardens.	Smaller than M. stellata. Beautiful flowers.
M. thompsoniana (M. tripetala x M. virginiana) THOMPSON MAGNOLIA	Dec.	12 by 10	4 yrs.	White flowers, spicy fragrance. Blooms July.	Does well in semi-shade in fact foliage seems better.	Not up to some but hardiness and glaucous foliage color, make it worthwhile.
M. veitchii (M. campbellii x M. denudata) VEITCH MAGNOLIA	Dec.	40 by 45	10 yrs.	Blush pink. Blooms Apr.	Needs room. If possible screen it from wind.	Considered one of the finest hybrids.
M. virginiana SWEET BAY MAGNOLIA	Dec.	to 50	8-10 yrs.	Creamy-white	Plant in semi-shade in cool, moist ground.	Cool fresh green leaves with white undersides. Very attractive. During mild winter some leaves persist.
M. watsonii (M. obovata x M. sieboldii) WATSON MAGNOLIA	Dec.	20 by 20	12 yrs.	Creamy-white crimson anthers. Blooms June-July.	Plant it so its perfume will be enjoyed.	Quite rare and expensive.
M. wilsonii WILSON MAGNOLIA	Dec.	25 by 25	10 yrs.	White, stamens rich red. Blooms May-June.	Have been known to flower when about 4 ft. high. Flowers are better if given some shade.	Choice. Should be grown more. Rich purple-brown twigs and narrow tapered leaves with silvery undersides, fragrant flowers.

MAIDENHAIR TREE. See **GINKGO BILOBA**

MAPLE. See **ACER**

MAYTENUS BOARIA. Mayten Tree. Evergreen. Zones 7-13, except 8. (Beautiful old maytens: Alongside Luther Burbank's house in Santa Rosa; on University of California campuses at Berkeley and Davis; on Stockton High School grounds.) Moderately fast to 20 ft. and then slow to 30-40 ft., or spreading 20-25 ft. Long, pendulous branchlets hang down from ascending branches, giving tree daintiness and grace. Habit and leaves reminiscent of small weeping willow. Valuable small evergreen for California's gardens. Use as lawn tree, alongside water, with good drainage; or as a single tree to look at and admire.

MELIA AZEDARACH UMBRACULIFORMIS. Texas Umbrella Tree. Deciduous. Zones 6 to 12, especially serviceable in 8a, 8b. Fast growing to 30 ft. and generally shaped like half a ball on a stick. Erect branches with drooping 1 to 3-ft. compound, dark green leaves. To keep umbrella shape, prune back.

Because of its fast growth into a usable shade tree in areas of extreme heat, drought, and frost, the Texas umbrella tree has its important place. But where choice of tree is less limited, the tree's weak and brittle wood, susceptibility to insects and disease, and litter of fruits and leaves, rule it out.

METASEQUOIA GLYPTOSTROBOIDES. Dawn Redwood. Deciduous conifer. Hardy all zones. Rapid growing in California; somewhat slower growing in the Pacific Northwest. Chinese relative of the coast redwood recently introduced into cultivation. It may best be described by comparing it with the native redwood. Foliage of dawn redwood is bright green, soft to the touch, will burn in hot afternoon sun in enclosed areas; turns light bronze before dropping in autumn. The light brown branches turn upward and are arranged in pairs, whereas the native redwood branches stand at right angles or are somewhat drooping and are spirally arranged. The native redwood is a much larger tree in the wild than the dawn redwood.

Grows best in soils that contain leaf mold or peat. Should have a good deal of moisture. Its loose, open habit makes it best suited for growing in groves rather than as individuals. Interesting container plant for lightly shaded terrace.

METROSIDEROS TOMENTOSA. New Zealand Christmas Tree. Evergreen. Zones 12 and 13. Slow to 30 ft. or shrub-like to 12 ft. Many branches from the ground up. Leaves glossy green, woolly beneath, vary in size, averaging about 1 in. wide by 3 in. long. Dark red flowers in dense clusters at end of branches, in June-July. Accepts, and thrives in coastal conditions. Will stand salt spray on leaves and salt water at roots.

MORUS. Mulberry. Deciduous. All zones. Fast growing, hardy, drought resistant. Shade and fruit tree. All are noteworthy for their variable leaves. Many different forms and sizes on one tree. Most important to the home gardener are the fruitless varieties.

M. alba. White Mulberry. Silkworm Mulberry. Fast growth to 20-60 ft. Round-headed tree. Small white flowers followed by white or violet fruit. Sometimes planted alongside cherry orchards to give birds a non-acid fruit more favored than cherries. *M. a. pendula* is the weeping form. Branches may be trained over a low arbor. Var. *tatarica.* Russian Mulberry. Smaller form and very hardy. Best for zone 1.

M. a. fruitless, kingan, striblingi. These are the fruitless varieties. Fast growth to 35 ft. with 20 ft. spread. Very useful and popular in all hot and arid sections. Thrives in any soil, even in thin gravels and on rocky slopes. Hardy to drought, heat, alkali, and neglect. Rapid growth creates shade quickly. However, the mulberry is not without its faults: defoliates in high wind; branches break easily.

M. nigra. Black or Persian Mulberry. Short trunk to 30 ft. Dark purple to black large fruit; grown for its fruit.

M. rubra. Red Mulberry. To 60 ft. Good fall color in frost areas.

MUSA. Banana. Evergreen. Zones 12 and 13 and warm sheltered spots in 9 and 10. Most commonly planted is the non-fruiting species, *M. ensete.*

M. ensete. Abyssinian Banana. Fast growth to 25 ft. Trunk 2 ft. thick; leaves 8 to 12 ft. long. Takes several years to come into flower; dies soon afterward. Should be planted where protected from wind, which frays the larger leaves. Best suited to positions against high wall spaces, in corners of patios, at back of wide tropical effect border. Attractive when grown with cannas, bamboo, aralia, and fatshedera. In locations where frost hits but summer is warm enough for fast growth, gardeners treat the banana as a perennial.

MYOPORUM LAETUM. Evergreen. Zones 10 and 13. Exceptionally fast growth, 6-10 ft. the first year. To 30 ft. with 20 ft. spread. Generally tends to grow as a large shrub and must be pruned into tree shape, with lower branches removed. Dense foliage of small, 1 by 3-in., dark green leaves, marked with translucent dots. Very resistant to salt air, it makes one of the quickest oceanside windbreaks. Not happy more than 10 miles from seashore. Can be clipped. Requires some side pruning to keep compact at base when used as screen or windbreak. Inclined to become topheavy when trained as a tree unless head is thinned out.

NYSSA SYLVATICA. Sour Gum. Deciduous. All zones. Slow growing to 30-50 ft. with 15-25 ft. spread; growth habit like pin oak in youth; more spreading, irregular and rugged with age. Crooked branches, twigs, and bark tinged with red, make a dramatic picture against winter sky. Beautiful dark green glossy leaves, 2 to 5 in. long, crowded at end of branchlets. Brilliant red fall color even in mild winter.

N. sinensis. Chinese Sour Gum. More spreading in growth habit; larger leaves; more yellow tones in fall. The nyssas challenge liquidambar's reputation of being the one tree sure to deliver fall color in mild winter areas. Like the liquidambar it takes lawn-frequency watering. Difficult to transplant, it should be established while quite young. Rate it high as a lawn tree and a tree for fall color.

OLEA EUROPAEA. Olive. Evergreen. Zones 7-13. Old orchards in the low foothills of the Sierra prove a hardiness to 10°: Extreme drought resistance—olive leaves have the ability to practically close up shop and stop transpiration.

Slow growth to 15-30 ft. Normally round headed and bushy, with gray-barked branches and willow-like leaves, dull green above, white and silver beneath. Older trees have gnarled, twisted trunk and branches. Tree can be trained from the start to create an open framework with interesting see-through quality. When trained or selected for open habit of growth, the olive tree is most effective, with its sculptured quality, in the large patio.

OLMEDIELLIA BETSCHELERIANA. Guatemala Holly. Evergreen. Zone 13. Shrub or small tree to 20-

25 ft. with 10 ft. spread. Handsome dark green, dense holly-like foliage. Full sun or partial shade. Can be shaped by pruning. Not particular as to soil. Makes an excellent tub plant and useful as a tall screen.

OXYDENDRUM ARBOREUM. SOURWOOD. SORREL TREE. Deciduous. At its best in zones 3-6. Very difficult, 7-13. Hardy all zones but needs acid soil. Slow growth to 15-20 ft. with 8-12 ft. spread. Eventually 50 ft. in ideal situation. Slender habit, with a slightly spreading head. Long, narrow, 5-8 in. shiny leaves, bronze tinted in early spring, rich green in summer, orange and scarlet in autumn. Creamy white, pieris-like, bell-shaped flowers in 10-in. drooping clusters, June-September. In autumn, when foliage is brilliant scarlet, branching clusters of greenish seed capsules extend outward and downward like the fingers of a hand; clusters turn light silvery gray, and hang on late into the winter.

Since the tree forms a mass of near-surface fibrous roots, avoid underplanting with anything needing cultivation. Small rhododendrons, heathers, azaleas do well in its shade. Thrives near lawns where sprinkling is frequent.

Has much to offer in seasonal interest: spring leaf color, summer flowers, fall color. Is good small shade tree for patio and terrace.

PARKINSONIA ACULEATA. JERUSALEM THORN. Deciduous. Zones 7-13, but important in desert areas. Fast at start, then slow growth to 15-30 ft., with spread wider than height. Sparse foliage made up of ⅛-in. leaflets on 6-12-in. leaf-stalks; small, ½-in. yellow flowers in slender erect clusters, in early summer.

Worthwhile in hot, dry, alkaline soil of desert areas. Will also take salt spray along coast. Pest resistant and free flowering. Flowering branches attractive in arrangements. Good tracery pattern of green stems against light wall. Ugly thorns, sparse foliage, "bird's nest" appearance with age, rule it out when competing with many kinds of trees.

PAULOWNIA TOMENTOSA. *(P. imperialis).* EMPRESS TREE. Deciduous. Zones 4-13. Fast growth to 30-40 ft., spreading in round head to 20-30 ft. Light green, large, 5-12-in., heart-shaped leaves (growth habit and leaves remind of the catalpa). Fragrant violet, dark-spotted flowers with yellow stripes inside, in 6-12-in. clusters in early spring.

Because of very large leaf and dominance of tree, it is difficult to use in the garden. Seen by itself, in bloom, it's spectacular but clashes with other flowering trees. Young growth and flower buds often hit by late frosts. Large leaves suffer in high winds. Hollow branches are brittle, easily broken.

PECAN. See CARYA ILLINOENSIS

PERSEA. AVOCADO. For varieties by zones see chapter on evergreen fruit trees.

PHELLODENDRON AMURENSE. CORK TREE. Deciduous. Hardy all zones, but needs winter cold. Moderate growth to 30-45 ft. Round head; light gray, deeply cut bark. Walnut-like compound leaves turn rich yellow in autumn. Fruits, hanging on after leaves have fallen, pea-sized, black, with turpentine odor. The cork tree, a gross feeder, needs a fertile deep soil. Valuable tree in areas of Idaho and Utah, where it will get high summer heat and low winter cold. Drought tolerant.

PICEA. SPRUCE. Conifer. Hardy all zones. A group of very definite conical or pyramidal large trees. (See chapter on shrubs for dwarf and low-growing forms.)

P. abies. NORWAY SPRUCE. To 150 ft. Stiff pyramid when young; branches grow more horizontal with age, with drooping branchlets. Takes on a rather forlorn look as it grows older. Used with varying success for trimmed hedges and windbreaks.

P. engelmannii. ENGELMANN SPRUCE. To 150 ft. Native to southwest Canada to Oregon and northern California, east to the Rocky Mountains. Dense pyramid with bluish-green needles. Resembles *P. pungens* but has softer foliage and is not as wide-spreading.

P. glauca. WHITE SPRUCE. To 60-70 ft. Conical form, dense habit when young, pendulous twigs, silver-green foliage. Var. *densata* is the native from the Black Hills of South Dakota. Very symmetrical, very slow-growing. Compact at all ages.

P. pungens. COLORADO SPRUCE. To 80-100 ft. Very stiff, regular, horizontal branches forming a broad pyramid. Silvery gray-green foliage. The most positive upright form of the evergreens. Var. *glauca* adds positive blue color to positive form. Of the several named varieties of blue spruce, var. *kosteriana* and var. *moerheimii* are best known. All of the blue spruces are so dominating that they overpower the small garden.

P. sitchensis. SITKA SPRUCE. To 100-150 ft. Native, Alaska to California. Broad pyramid when young with contrasting bright green and silvery white foliage.

All spruce prefer moist rather than arid conditions and in many areas suffer from mite damage.

PINUS. (See chapter on pines.)

PISTACIA CHINENSIS. CHINESE PISTACHE. Deciduous, zones 6-13. Has taken 5° in the desert without damage. Moderate growth to 40-60 ft. with 30-50-ft. spread; round headed, rather loose and open. Leaves, like those of native walnut, 5-6 pairs of leaflets. As leaves develop, new growth is quite reddish. Famous for its fall colors of scarlet, and crimson in areas where few trees really color. Furthermore, it holds its leaves long enough for cut branch arrangements. Performance is best where summers are long and hot. Often an unpredictable and erratic grower when young; needs staking for three or four years. Sometimes very late in leafing out in spring. Female tree bears scarlet fruit, turning purple in the fall.

P. vera. COMMON PISTACHE. Nut-bearing variety. Shorter, more spreading, less drought resistant, generally not as attractive. Harder to find.

The Chinese pistache rates high as a long-lived, pest-free tree for street or large garden. Can be trained to give a high canopy; roots not invasive.

PLATANUS. Deciduous. Hardy all zones. Listings in nursery catalogs and labels at the nursery are badly mixed up between *P. orientalis,* oriental plane, and *P. acerifolia,* London plane. Regardless of which you buy, you'll get the London plane. It is doubtful that *P. orientalis* can be found in the West. A closely related form, listed as *P. insularis,* is being made available. Very fast growing and attractive tree in first years. Expected to equal the California sycamore in size, with a similar habit of growth. So far seems resistant to sycamore blight.

P. acerifolia. LONDON PLANE TREE. (A hybrid between *P. occidentalis* and *P. orientalis.*) Fast growing to 40-80 ft. with 30-40 ft. spread. Can be stubbed, shaped, pruned to fit special uses, such as pleaching to create overhead canopy. Upper trunk and limbs, cream colored. Leaves, somewhat like those of the maple, are coarse, medium green, 3-5 lobed, 4-10 in. wide. The London plane tree is tolerant of almost any soil condition. It's tough and rugged and its sturdy framework of branches is attractive in winter. Blight, mites, and mildew call for spraying before the leaves are half grown in the spring.

P. occidentalis. AMERICAN SYCAMORE. Similar to London plane in appearance except that dark older bark falls off to expose a white bark on upper trunk and limbs and it is out of leaf longer. It is hardier than *P. acerifolia* and more resistant to insect and disease.

P. racemosa. CALIFORNIA SYCAMORE. (See chapter on natives.)

PODOCARPUS. Conifer. Zones 9-10, 12-13. Hardy to 10°. Evergreen trees or shrubs of irregular structure, graceful habit, and attractive foliage. It is versatile and easy to train, especially when young.

P. elongata. FERN PINE. Tree to 70 ft. in its native habitat, but grows to about 15 ft. in the garden and can be kept to 8 ft. in a tub. Graceful, rather pendulous branches with dark green, soft, willowy, 1-2 in. leaves.

Grown for many years as a house plant and now being planted widely as a garden and street tree in Southern California and in mild-winter sections of central California. Its supple branches can be espaliered against a wall, post, or pillar, or even trained to grow as a ground cover. Also useful as a large shrub or hedge, or when mature, as a shade tree. Combine with large ferns and other ornamental, shade-loving tropicals and subtropicals.

P. gracilior. Like *P. elongata*, except leaves are longer. Some of the plant material grown as *P. elongata* belongs here. Use as you would the fern pine.

P. macrophylla. YEW PINE. Slower growing, and with broader, lighter green, 4-in. leaves. Can be trained into a formal, columnar plant to 6-10 ft. high with an 18-in. spread. Var. *appressa*, a low form, has shorter leaves. Var. *maki* (*P. chinensis*, *P. japonica*, *P. sinensis*) is usually shrubby and has smaller leaves.

Yew pines are suitable for large pots or tubs, or to give height against patio walls.

In immature stages, the foliage of podocarpus may be burned in high winds, salt air, frosts, or excessively hot sun. But when mature, the foliage is quite tough. When well established, will get along with the minimum of watering, although a mulch over the roots is very beneficial. Plants being grown as trees should be staked firmly.

If you want matching pairs of podocarpus, be sure to obtain plants propagated from cuttings of the same type. There are several types, all of which differ in size and length of time required to attain maturity.

POINCIANA GILLIESII. (*Caesalpinia gilliesii*). BIRD-OF-PARADISE BUSH. Evergreen. Zones 12-13 and borderline in 7-11. Moderate growth to 10 ft. Shrub-like, airy, delicate form. Fern-like foliage. Bright yellow flowers with protruding bright red stamens, in profusion all summer. Because of airy habit, should be grown against green or neutral background. Use as wall shrub or even in large container. Needs light, well-drained soil for healthy growth.

POPULUS. Deciduous. All zones. Rule out as tree for city street or small garden; still valuable for country places. Best to locate, even there, where roots have no chance to invade septic tanks and drains.

P. alba. WHITE POPLAR. Fast growth to 40-60 ft. Broad and wide spreading. Differs from other poplars in leaf; many are 3 or 5-lobed, white-woolly beneath. Var. *pyramidalis* (*P. bolleana*) looks like a smaller edition of Lombardy poplar.

P. canadensis eugenei. CAROLINA POPLAR. Fast growth to 40-100 ft., with narrow pyramidal habit. Most notorious of the poplars for breaking and clogging drains.

P. candicans. BALM-OF-GILEAD POPLAR. Fast to 30-60 ft. Leaves, 4½-6 in. long, 3-4 in. wide. Does well in 8a, low desert.

P. nigra italica. LOMBARDY POPLAR. Fast to 40-90 ft. These beautiful spire-like trees and upward pointing branches are symbols of ranch and farm. Wind resistant.

P. fremontii. FREMONT COTTONWOOD. (See chapter on natives.)

P. tremuloides. QUAKING ASPEN. (See chapter on natives.)

PRUNUS. (See chapter on natives.)

PTEROCARYA STENOPTERA. CHINESE WINGNUT. Deciduous. Grown in 9, 12, and 13 and probably hardy in all except 1 and 2. Fast growth to 30-60 ft. Belongs to walnut family. Small one-seeded nuts with oblong wing hang down in foot-long clusters, follow drooping flower catkins that appear with leaves. Use where it's shallow; surface feeding roots will not bother. Valuable in areas of poor soil and in bare soil playyards. Good substitute for ailanthus.

PYRUS KAWAKAMI. EVERGREEN PEAR. Hardy. Zones 7-13, but consistent performer only where fruiting pear does well. Fast growing to 30 ft. with unusually limber trunk and limbs. Very unruly; requires constant pruning to keep attractive tree shape. This bad growth habit becomes a virtue when tree is espaliered.

QUERCUS. OAK. Deciduous and evergreen. Climate adaptation by species.

The oak tree is one of the most desirable trees for shade and protection of outdoor living areas. Many a Western home has been built around an oak tree. The decline in health of the native oaks is therefore of great concern to many people.

The greatest amount of trouble is found in Southern California. It is thought that the continued low rainfall has put a severe strain on oak trees in their natural state and a combination of many factors has brought about the decline of the trees in irrigated and cultivated garden areas. Plantings that require constant moisture should not be made beneath the trees. No planting should be done around the crown. In regrading a lot do not add soil to the root zone. Any cutting down of soil air by paving or grading should be avoided. If paving part of the area is desired, run lines of drain tile under the pavement. Spray for oak moth and mildew.

Many of the new introductions in the Western nursery trade promise to be free from disease.

The oaks most readily available in Western nurseries are the following:

Q. agrifolia. COAST LIVE OAK. (See chapter on natives.)

Q. borealis. NORTHERN RED OAK. Deciduous. Hardy all zones and adaptable to wide range of soils and climates. Fast growing tree to 50-90 ft. with large spreading branches forming a round-topped crown. Large leaves 5-8 in. long by 3-5 in. wide are deeply 3-7 lobed, turn dark red, ruddy brown or orange in the fall. Over-all texture is heavier than most oaks. New leaves and leaf stalks are deep red in spring.

Prefers fertile soil and plenty of water. Very susceptible to drought and difficult to transplant. Will not grow in pavement.

High branching habit makes it a most desirable broad avenue or boulevard tree. Its massive head gives wonderful shade. For large country places only.

Q. chrysolepis. CANYON LIVE OAK, MAUL OAK, GOLDEN-CUP OAK. (See chapter on natives.)

Q. coccinea. SCARLET OAK. Deciduous. Hardy all zones. Grows to 60-80 ft. Has a wide spreading irregular crown, with high, light and open branching pattern. Bark has a reddish cast in winter. Bright green 6-in., deeply lobed leaves turn brilliant scarlet in cold fall weather.

When planted in deep rich soil it is comparatively fast growing. Since the roots go deep, little competition is offered to nearby plantings. Withstands drought and requires relatively small growing area. Where warm fall rains are common, it does not produce the brilliant fall foliage for which it is noted. Where adapted is a beautiful street tree. Leaves and cut branches are sold by florists.

Q. garryana. OREGON OAK. (See chapter on natives.)

Q. ilex. HOLLY OAK, HOLM OAK. Evergreen. Zones 9-13. Moderate growth to about 40 ft., with round spreading head. Clean, glossy, dark green, toothed or entire, 3-in. leaves.

Stands wind and salt air of coast as well as inland conditions. Requires little maintenance and seems to be practically pest free.

Makes an excellent street tree.

Q. kelloggii. CALIFORNIA BLACK OAK. (See chapter on natives.)

Q. lobata. VALLEY OAK, WHITE OAK. (See chapter on natives.)

Q. palustris. PIN OAK. Deciduous. Hardy all zones but is at its best where there's plenty of moisture. Long-lived tree to 50-80 ft., with slender, pyramidal habit when young, becoming more open and round headed at maturity. Lower branches tend to droop almost to the ground, and if the bottom whorl is removed, the branches above will adopt the same habit. Has brownish-gray bark. Glossy dark green 5-in. leaves are deeply cut into spine-pointed lobes; turn yellow, red bronze and russet brown in fall.

Grows moderately fast in both coastal and inland areas when given plenty of water. Not tolerant of drought or alkali. Easy to transplant because of its fibrous root system. Stake during early stages to keep upright.

The characteristic twiggy growth gives it a delicate appearance not typical of most oaks. Drooping lower branches necessitate giving up ground space around tree thus eliminating it from consideration in some small gardens. Has tendency to hold its dead brown leaves through the winter.

Q. suber. CORK OAK. Evergreen. Hardy 7, 9-13 but thrives best where mean annual temperature ranges between 50° and 70°. Slow growing, spreading tree to 50 ft. Picturesque trunk with thick corky bark (yields commercial cork). Ovate 3-in. toothed leaves are shining dark green above, gray beneath.

Adaptable to many types of soil if drainage is good. Where soil is alkaline foliage is likely to turn yellow. Needs plenty of water. An excellent garden tree. Value as a street tree somewhat diminished when youngsters learn how easy it is to carve the cork bark.

Q. virginiana. LOUISIANA LIVE OAK. Evergreen. Zones 7-13. Large spreading tree to 60 ft. with oblong 5-in. entire leaves which are shining dark green above, whitish beneath.

Specimens in areas in Southern California, including high desert, indicate it's a satisfactory fast growing tree for that area.

The following are not generally available but worth trying where adaptation seems probable.

Q. alba. WHITE OAK. Deciduous. Hardy all zones. Where adapted grows to 75-90 ft. with broad open crown. Bright green 4-9 in. deeply lobed leaves, turn reddish-purple in fall. Interesting in winter with its gray bark and rugged growth habit.

Q. bicolor. SWAMP WHITE OAK. Deciduous. Hardy all zones. Narrow round-headed tree to 70 ft.; the lower branches pendulous. Toothed or shallow lobed 4-6 in. leaves, dark green above, whitish beneath, turn reddish in fall. Needs generous water supply.

Q. cerris. TURKEY OAK. Deciduous. Zones 7-13. Fast growing tree to 75 ft., spreading to 60 ft., with broad pyramidal head. Long 4-6 in. deeply lobed leaves are dark green above, lighter beneath, turn brown in fall. Deciduous period short.

Fine long-lived shade tree. Must be watered well when young otherwise very heat and drought resistant. Tolerant of alkali soils. Many attractive specimens throughout Southern California. Use as large shade tree or street tree.

Q. falcata. (*Q. rubra*). SOUTHERN RED OAK, SPANISH OAK. Deciduous. Climate adaptation is not known. Grows to 80 ft. Similar to *Q. borealis* but the tree is more upright in habit, and the leaves are more deeply cut, heavier in texture and densely hairy beneath.

Q. macrocarpa. BUR OAK, MOSSY CUP OAK. Deciduous. Adapted all zones except 8. Very rugged and individual looking oak to 60-75 ft., with a 30-ft. spread. Large 8-10 in. lobed leaves are glossy green above, white hairy beneath.

Although similar to *Q. alba* it is faster growing and will stand more adverse conditions. Tolerant of any type of soil. Quite pest resistant; will mildew if too wet.

Q. montana. CHESTNUT OAK. Deciduous. Hardy all zones. Fast growing tree to 75-80 ft., with vase-shaped habit. Bark is almost black. Yellow-green toothed 7-in. leaves resemble those of a chestnut, turn orange-red in fall. Will stand drought and rocky soil.

Q. phellos. WILLOW OAK. Deciduous. Zones 7-13. Upright tree to 60 ft., with lustrous light green willow-like 4-in. leaves.

Good lawn tree for home gardens and parks.

Q. robur. ENGLISH OAK. Deciduous. Hardy all zones. Large tree to 80 ft., with broad round-topped crown, and lobed 2-5 in. leaves. Var. *fastigiata*, UPRIGHT ENGLISH OAK, has a columnar head.

Relatively pest free. Many mature specimens throughout California. The columnar form makes a fine accent tree.

REDWOOD. (See chapter on natives.)

ROBINIA. LOCUST. Deciduous. All zones. Fast growing, medium to small trees capable of withstanding adverse conditions; in most cases too rank growing and brittle limbed for the garden.

R. pseudoacacia decaisneana. PINK FLOWERING LOCUST. IDAHO PINK LOCUST. Deciduous. All zones. Fast growth to 40-50 ft. with 20-ft. spread. Irregular upright or spreading form; often sparse and spindly. Soft green compound leaves made up of 7 to 19 leaflets. Pale pink, ¾ in. sweetpea-like, fragrant flowers in 4-8 in. clusters in May, followed by 4-in. dark brown pods which hang on all winter. To the pink locust's credit: it is tolerant of desert summer heat and of cold; will stand alkaline, dry, and poor gravelly soil. In spite of rapid growth, is fairly long-lived. These advantages have earned it endorsements as a street tree in many Western cities. In the small garden, its rank growth, greedy root system, brittle limbs, and poor winter form are objectionable. Var. *umbraculifera* has dense crown and spineless branches, and very few flowers.

R. hispida. ROSE ACACIA. Variable shrub to 7 ft. Leaves with 7-13 oval soft green leaflets. Rose or pale purple 1 in. sweetpea-shaped flowers, 3-5 in a cluster, May-June. Var. *macrophylla* has larger leaflets and flowers. Grown by Western nurserymen as a top-grafted tree. Var. *Monument*, built up in the same way, is recommended as a street tree.

SALIX. WILLOW. Deciduous. Hardy all zones. The useful and beautiful willow is found around the world—well over 100 species and varieties grow in the temperate and cold zones. In the West the willow is important in preventing soil erosion, for wind control, sun control, and, of course, for ornamental garden use.

S. babylonica. WEEPING WILLOW. Medium-sized tree to 30 ft., with long, graceful, drooping branches and narrow, 6-in., bright green leaves. Var. *aurea*, GOLDEN WEEPING WILLOW, has golden-yellow branchlets. Var. *crispa (S. annularis)*, RINGLEAF or CORKSCREW WILLOW, has darker green, curled and twisted leaves. Does not take up as much room as the species.

Special care should be taken in placing these graceful trees. One willow leaning over a pool or simply by itself anywhere is a study in form, color, and texture, whereas a dozen planted in a row or in a group merely creates a confused effect.

S. blanda. *(S. babylonica dolorosa, S. pendula).* WISCONSIN WEEPING WILLOW. A hybrid between *S. babylonica* and *S. fragilis*. Similar to *S. babylonica*, with bluish-green leaves. Use as you would the weeping willow.

S. caprea. GOAT WILLOW. PINK WILLOW. Grows to 25 ft. Broadly ovate, 4-in. leaves are green above and gray-hairy beneath. Has large, pink, woolly catkins before the leaves in very early spring. A delight for winter flower arrangements. It forces easily early in the season.

S. alba vitellina. GOLDEN WILLOW. Grows to 75 ft., with golden-yellow branches and twigs. Narrow, 4-in. leaves are whitish underneath. Var. *alba chermesina* has bright red branchlets.

One of the best willows for windbreaks. Does not spread from root suckers as do many other willows. If you plant either or both of these for their cheerful winter color, cut them to the ground each spring. The color is much brighter on new growth and the wands that grow from the base will form a shapely shrub before the summer is over.

S. discolor. PUSSY WILLOW. Shrub or small tree to 20 ft. with slender, red-brown stems. Oblong, 1½-4 in. leaves. Flower catkins on the male tree appear in advance of the leaves and are larger and showier than the velvety, female flower catkins.

S. purpurea nana. DWARF PURPLE OSIER. Grows to 3 to 4-ft. Has rather broad, 1-in., gray-blue-green leaves, and flower catkins with purple scales that give the catkins a purplish hue.

The dwarf willows make attractive low hedges.

Willows are among the easiest plants to propagate. Cuttings of dormant stems or branches up to 6 ft. long can be planted directly in the ground where trees are wanted, and will root quickly. Where there is sufficient moisture, willows grow rapidly regardless of soil and climatic conditions. They are invaluable in erosion control because their tenacious roots keep a foothold on loose, sandy banks, and thereby prevent streams from changing channels and removing topsoil.

Willows make an effective windbreak within a few years. Planted to the windward, they protect and help to establish slower growing, more permanent trees.

SAPINDUS SAPONARIA. SOAPBERRY TREE. Evergreen. Zones 11-13. Slow growth to 15-25 ft. with 10-15 ft. spread. Dense foliage of leathery compound leaves of 7-9 4-in. leaflets. White flowers in 10-in. clusters. Small glossy orange berries in autumn. Use it as you would a Catalina cherry.

SCHINUS. Evergreen.

S. molle. CALIFORNIA PEPPER TREE. Zones 7-13 but damaged at 15°. Fast growth to 25-40 ft. with spread equal to height; graceful drooping branches; bright green compound leaves with many leaflets make a finely cut foliage. Becomes a billowy mound laden with clusters of rose-colored berries in fall and winter. (Sometimes trees have nearly all male flowers, and if so, will not produce berries.)

Typifies old California; beautiful tree in the right place in acre planting. Should not be used as a street tree or where you wish to garden under or near it. Tolerant of adverse soils and drought. Those who see its worst side point out these faults: messy litter; scale; shallow roots; staking required. But beautiful lawns are grown under old California peppers in Ontario and many other California towns. Lawn must be heavily fertilized.

S. terebinthifolius. BRAZILIAN PEPPER. Zones 8-13, with some winter damage expected where temperatures drop below 20°. Moderate growth to 15-30 ft. Differs from California pepper in its stiffer, more irregular branch arrangement, darker green leaves or coarser texture with only 7 leaflets instead of many, and bright red berries. Useful tree for shade in patio and small garden. Does equally well in hot interiors and coastal California, except in gardens where there is no protection from wind storms. No special care. Takes lawn water treatment.

SCHLEFFLERA ACTINOPHYLLA. *(Brassaia actinophylla).* QUEENSLAND UMBRELLA TREE. (See chapter on shrubs.)

SILK OAK. See GREVILLEA ROBUSTA
SILK TREE. See ALBIZZIA JULIBRISSIN
SILVER TREE. See LEUCADENDRON ARGENTEUM
SMOKE TREE. See COTINUS COGGYGRIA

SNOWDROP TREE. See HALESIA CAROLINA

SOPHORA. There is a species for every Western climate. All deserve to be better known.

S. japonica. JAPANESE PAGODA TREE. CHINESE SCHOLAR TREE. Deciduous. All zones. Slow growing to 20-40 ft., with wide spreading green branches. In maturity has all the characteristics of an old oak. Dark green 6-10-in. compound leaves, made up of 7 to 17 small ovate leaflets. Long 8 to 12 in. clusters of yellowish-white sweet-pea-shaped ½ in. flowers, July-September. Var. *pendula*. Weeping form. Accepts average garden conditions and culture. Use it as a small tree for light summer shade.

S. secundiflora. MESCAL BEAN. TEXAS MOUNTAIN LAUREL. Evergreen. Zones 7 to 13. Slow growth to 40 ft. Fragrant, violet-blue 1 in. sweetpea-shaped flowers 4 in. clusters, in Feb.-April; 8-in. silver gray pods open to show red seeds. Inclined to be shrubby and needs pruning to become tree-like. Needs heat, good drainage, and lime soil.

S. tetraptera. NEW ZEALAND SOPHORA. Zones 7-13. To 40 ft., with large yellow 2 in. blossoms; 8-in., 4-winged pods. In youth looks like small edition of *S. japonica*.

SORBUS AUCUPARIA. *(Pyrus aucuparia)*. EUROPEAN MOUNTAIN ASH. Deciduous. Hardy all zones, but of little value 7-13. Needs cold winters to produce berries. Moderate to fast growth to 50 ft. but in most situations 20-30 ft. with 15-20 ft. spread. Sharply ascending branches for a round-headed, dense tree made up of gray-green, fine-textured compound leaves, 9 to 11, 1-in. leaflets. Feature: profuse clusters of white flowers followed by bright orange berries. Inedible fruit in July or early August hangs on through late fall to December. Autumn color yellow to rusty yellow. Virtues: hardiness, climate and soil adaptability, modest size. Limitations are in the messiness of leaf and fruit drop. Though messy, an ideal street tree where winter chilling requirements are met. Berries brighten overcast winter days. In the garden the tree should be backed up by evergreens, as its winter branch pattern is uninteresting. Prefers sun but accepts partial shade. European mountain ash is superior to American mountain ash *(S. americana)*, which has brittle branches and is subject to scale and borers.

SPRUCE. See PICEA

STENOCARPUS SINUATUS. FIREWHEEL TREE. Evergreen. Zone 13. Moderate growth to 25 ft. with 10-ft. spread. Slender and upright; dense shiny foliage, the 12 in. leaves sometimes cut into 1-4 lobes. Fantastic flowers radiate in pinwheel fashion at end of long bare stem; orange-red in tight bud stage, quite red when fully opened in tangled tassels. Continuous bloom from midsummer on through winter. One of the few trees from Australia that likes soil on the acid side.

STYRAX JAPONICA. JAPANESE SNOWDROP TREE. Deciduous. All except coldest sections of zone 1. Moderate growth to a slender, graceful tree of 30 ft.; often horizontal branching. Leaves wavy along margins, as are those of *Cornus florida*. Features clusters of small white, bell-like flowers hanging from every twig in June. Its fragrant flowers are similar to those of its relative halesia, but appear later.

Serves the same purpose as dogwood in use and is limited by the same cultural requirements (see *Cornus*). Careful pruning while young necessary to keep it from becoming a shrub, but will always have tendency to become shrubby, spreading. Plant on slopes, with a semicircle of juniper, yew, or chamæcyparis above, ajuga below. Rates high as a tree to look up into.

TAXUS. YEW. Evergreen conifers. Shrubs and trees. Many horticultural forms. With respect to foliage characters, the differences between the species are slight. The Japanese yew is the hardiest of the genus and a most useful, narrow-leaf evergreen in the colder sections of zone 1. In general, the yews are more formal, darker green, and more shade and moisture-tolerant than most cultivated conifers. All give a nice show of scarlet cup-shaped fruits in late summer or early fall.

T. baccata. ENGLISH YEW. Slow growing to 25-40 ft., with wide-spreading branches forming a broad, low crown. Needles are very dark green and glossy above, paler underneath.

T. b. aurea. Golden-yellow leaves, especially bright on tips and margins.

T. b. erecta. Erect and formal but less compact than var. *stricta*.

T. b. repandens. SPREADING ENGLISH YEW. Long, spreading branches form a 2-ft. high ground cover. Will cascade over a wall. Useful as low foundation plant. Will take shade.

T. b. stricta (var. *fastigiata*). IRISH YEW. A column of very dark green. Slow growing to 20 ft. Tends to spread near top and should be tied with wire. Handsome in corner of high, whitewashed, brick wall. A golden and a variegated form are available.

T. brevifolia. WESTERN, PACIFIC or OREGON YEW. Native to British Columbia, south to California and east to Montana. Loose, open growth to 50-60 ft. Young trees are leggy, unattractive and of little garden value.

T. chinensis. CHINESE YEW. To 35-40 ft. Leaves, almost 2 in. long, are 2-ranked, spraying out at right angles to the stem. Branchlets turn yellowish-green as the tree matures.

T. cuspidata. JAPANESE YEW. A tree to 50 ft. in Japan but mostly seen as a bushy shrub here. Leaves, 2-ranked, form a trough along the stem rather than spraying out horizontally. Vigorous growth, dark green foliage, tolerance of shade and moist soil make it a valuable garden plant. Its ability to stand any amount of shearing extends its use to hedges and screens. Varieties of tree-like habit with a strong central stem are available and used for their pyramidal or columnar form.

T. c. nana. DWARF JAPANESE YEW. Slow growing, 1-4 in. a year, to 3 ft. and spreading to 6 ft. or more (in 20 years). Very useful in low foundation planting.

T. media. A group of yews that appear to be hybrids of the English and Japanese species. The olive-green color of their branchlets set them apart from both the English and the Japanese. The form sold as *T. intermedia* by Northwest nurseries is probably *T. media;* a vigorous, broad-spreading shrub reaching 3 ft. in 4 years. Dark green needles are closely set on the stems. Var. *hatfieldii* is compact and cone-shaped with full dense foliage; var. *hicksii* is similar. Both resemble *T. baccata stricta* and lack the strong central stem of *T. cuspidata*.

THUJA. ARBORVITAE. Conifer. (For low-growing forms see chapter on shrubs.) Hardy all zones. The tree species are valuable as single plants, tall hedges, screens, or as strong backgrounds.

T. occidentalis. AMERICAN ARBORVITAE. Pyramidal trees to 40-60 ft. with open, horizontal branches that tend to turn up at the ends. Scale-like leaves are bright green above, yellow-green beneath, in flat sprays. Shade tolerant; needs moist soil.

T. orientalis. ORIENTAL ARBORVITAE. Bushy, pyramidal tree to 20-25 ft. Has upright or somewhat spreading branches, with sprays of bright green foliage carried on edge. Less hardy than American arborvitae. Good for vertical accent, in groups or in a line.

T. plicata. GIANT ARBORVITAE. WESTERN RED CEDAR. (See chapter on natives.)

THUJOPSIS DOLOBRATA. DEER HORN CEDAR. FALSE ARBORVITAE. Conifer. Hardy all zones but not for hot interiors. Very slow growth to 50 ft. Pyramid of spreading branches with graceful frond-like branchlets. Will grow in shade, in moist soil.

TILIA. LINDEN. BASSWOOD. Deciduous. All zones except 8. Of the 25 or more species in this genus only *T. americana* is available in quantity. However, more than a half dozen species have been planted in public parks and a number are being propagated.

T. americana. AMERICAN LINDEN. Hardy all zones but intolerant of drought. Moderate growth to 40-60 ft. with 16-25 ft. spread. Straight trunk continues into dense, compact, narrow crown. Dull dark green leaves, heart shaped, 4-6 in. long, and 3-4 in. wide. Loose clusters of yellowish-white flowers in June-July.

American linden is faster and taller growing in its native range than here in the West. Mature lindens in the East average 70-90 ft. high, some 140 ft.

Need for rich soil and ample moisture rule against the linden for streets or country places in dry summer sections. Another disadvantage in mild and short winter areas is 4-4½ month leafless period. Var. *fastigiata* PYRAMIDAL AMERICAN LINDEN, a horticultural variety, is a grafted upright branching form.

T. cordata. LITTLE LEAF LINDEN. Slow growth to 30-50 ft. with 15-30 ft. spread. Smaller in all parts than American linden. Very neat, clean, small-to-medium shade tree.

T. dasystyla. CAUCASIAN LINDEN. Slow to 30-40 ft. Like liquidambar in form. Not tested but thought to be adapted to Southern California interior.

T. euchlora. CRIMEAN LINDEN. Slow to 25-35 ft. with equal spread. Like mulberry tree in form.

T. petiolaris. WEEPING WHITE LINDEN. Looks like weeping mulberry with large heart-shaped leaves, light green above, silver-white beneath. Flashes green and silver in a light breeze.

T. tomentosa. SILVER LINDEN. Slow to moderate growth to 40-50 ft. with 20-30 ft. spread. Light green leaves, silvery beneath, turn with slight breeze. Creamy, fragrant flowers are intoxicating, sometimes toxic to bees.

TIPUANA TIPU. TIPU TREE. Evergreen. Zones 12 and 13. Has taken 18° without damage. Fast growing to 30 ft., spreading wider than high. Beautiful foliage of compound leaves (some say they look like large cassia leaves). Clusters of showy yellow sweetpea-like flowers in June-July. Requires no special gardening care. Stands heat and drought, but also tolerates lots of water.

TRISTANIA CONFERTA. BRISBANE BOX. Evergreen. Zone 13. (Mature trees in Santa Barbara; some planted in San Diego.) Moderate growth to 60 ft. Handsome trunk and limbs resembling the madrone (*Arbutus menziesii*); with smooth reddish-brown bark; glossy leathery leaves. Stands heat but can't take frost. Leaves tend to crowd to end of branches and tree should be pruned as it grows for better leaf distribution. Same cultural requirements as eucalyptus.

TULIP TREE. See LIRIODENDRON TULIPIFERA

TUPIDANTHUS CALYPTRATUS. Evergreen. Zones 12 and 13. Small tree to 20 ft., valuable for glossy golden-green tropical foliage effects in full sun or part shade.

Leaves divided fan-wise into 7-9 entire, drooping 7-in. leaflets. Inconspicuous green flowers. Although closely related to *Schefflera actinophylla*, it is more branched and open in habit, and has a greater resistance to cold. Available in small quantity in nurseries specializing in tropical plants. Effective with *Alpinia speciosa*, heliconia, hedychium, and clivia.

ULMUS. ELM. Deciduous and variable evergreen species. Hardy all zones.

U. americana. AMERICAN ELM. Deciduous. Fast growth to 100 ft. with 60-ft. spread to make a vase-shaped stately tree; ovate-oblong leaves 3-6 in. long. This great New England tree was first choice of the early street and park tree planters in the West. Today, its height, susceptibility to insects, diseases, and limb breakage rule it out as a street tree.

U. pumila. SIBERIAN ELM. Deciduous. Fast growth to 50 ft. Extremely hardy and tough. Takes all extremes in stride. More rank in growth and roots more invasive than the evergreen Chinese elm.

U. parvifolia. CHINESE ELM. EVERGREEN CHINESE ELM. Deciduous or evergreen depending upon winter temperatures and inheritance of the particular tree you buy. Very fast growth to 40-60 ft. with 50-70 ft. spread. Often reaches 30 ft. in 5 years. Be prepared for extreme variations in early growth and final form; the tree you buy may be anything from erect to weeping. Must be staked and pruned carefully for 2 or 3 years. Despite its faults, the Chinese elm is much used as a patio tree in small gardens in the mild winter sections of the West for high screens to shield western-facing glass. Some treemen single out *U. parvifolia* as the one elm for the small garden. Others claim that it has all the faults of the genus: roots invasive; must be sprayed for scale and disease; grows too large.

U. glabra camperdownii. CAMPERDOWN ELM. A weeping variety with very large roundish 4-8 in. leaves; grown and used in the Northwest as an odd specimen tree.

WALNUT. See JUGLANS

WILLOW. See SALIX

ZELKOVA SERRATA. SAWLEAF ZELKOVA. Deciduous. All zones except coldest areas of zone 1. Moderate to fast growth to 50-80 ft. Short trunk divides into numerous ascending stems with spreading slender branches to form a broad, round topped crown. Dark green ovate, 2-5 in. leaves are sharply saw-toothed, turn dark red in autumn.

The zelkova is about to gain acceptance in the top ten of lists of trees recommended for street and avenue use. It's an excellent shade tree where there's room for its 40-50 ft. spread. Old trees in California's interior valleys continue clean and handsome, withstanding drought and attack by insects and diseases. Probably better adapted to interior than coastal areas. Unfortunately nursery supply is very limited.

ZIZYPHUS JUJUBA. CHINESE JUJUBE. Deciduous. Zones 7-13, except direct coastal. Hardiest of the sub-tropical fruits. Moderate growth to 12 ft. Branch framework similar to that of American elm but in miniature. Oblong shiny bright green 1-2 in. leaves. Small, 2-in. dark brown fruits taste like sweet, but rather mealy, apples. A delicacy when candied.

From its interesting name, pronounced Joo-joob, to its character in and out of leaf, it's a very satisfactory small tree.

Western Specialties
NATIVES

Plants native to the West are listed throughout this book. You'll find them in chapters on annuals, perennials, shrubs, trees, miniatures, ground covers, container gardens, and even indoor gardens.

It's necessary, however, to deal with them in a separate chapter so that we can talk about them as Western gardeners do.

Gardeners in the West give different meanings to the word "native." A gardener in the summer-dry foothills of California with more land than he can find time or water for soon starts talking about natives. He means, of course, those native plants that are drought-resistant, evergreen, self policing, and extremely tolerant of abuse.

Another gardener may use the word most often to describe some favorite collector's item. He can prove to you that Western gardeners are overlooking great treasures by their lack of interest in natives.

There's also the sentimental gardener who finds the greatest beauty in a plant that he knows is a wild thing. He loses interest in natives that are too generally available.

Another user of natives, and a happy one, is the gardener who likes to have plants about him that he has discovered while vacationing elsewhere in the West.

The questions these gardeners ask from their individual viewpoints are: Which natives can I grow and how do I grow them? (And when these gardeners say *natives* they often are thinking only of plants which have not yet been completely tamed.)

For them we select a few that live up to one or more of these requirements:

1. They are available. If your local nurseryman doesn't have them, he can get them from a wholesale supplier.
2. They are equal or superior in quality to all other plants used for the same purpose.
3. They perform well in situations where few other plants will live.

Whether you are looking for tough and rough plants to solve a hillside problem or plants you have fallen in love with on your trip into the mountains, or plants that thrive with neglect, directions to help you in your search are given in this chapter.

Although the native range is not an accurate guage of adaptability, we list it for each native plant to indicate climate preferences. Climate adaptability for these natives is not given. Except for those that have become staple items in the nurseries, the natives listed here have not been sufficiently tested to define their climate limits. But many plants have shown adaptability far beyond anything indicated in their background.

Facts and Legend

Many apparently conflicting directions and suggestions for the care of native plants circulate among gardeners. Generally a little common sense will tell you which is fact and which is fiction.

First, it is obvious that native plants that have been sold for years along with all other plants without mention of native origin, do not need special treatment of any kind. Oregon grape, evergreen huckleberry, hollyleaf cherry, Catalina cherry, most of the conifers are in this class.

All fast-growing natives that are known for instability and short life should be planted with the expectation of losses when planting out, occasional die-outs each year, and on the average a short life. Such drawbacks are compensated for by the fast growth of those that do take hold and the ease of replacement for those that die out. The thing to guard against is planting fast-growing natives in a situation where permanent and well-behaved plants are needed.

Insects and Diseases

Natives as a class are not particularly insect- or disease-resistant. But, those natives that are propagated and sold in quantity by nurserymen are less susceptible than those that have not passed through a period of selection and/or hybridization.

The natives that get into trouble when grown in average garden conditions are those that have never had to face heavy soil and standing water. They may be native either to the mountains or to the desert but in discussions on their care, we have generally lumped them together as being drought-resistant, without reference to climate adaptability.

Plants in this so-called drought-resistant class of natives are generally extremely susceptible to root and crown rot. In their native state these plants have never had to contend with attacks by the water molds that cause those diseases and therefore have built up no immunity to them. When planted in a soil where poor drainage creates conditions favorable to growth of the water molds, the roots or the crown or both are quickly infected and the plant dies. This is why you hear warnings against overwatering natives.

Watering-Drainage

Actually if you give natives fast drainage, they can take almost any amount of water. Furthermore all newly planted shrubs or trees need regular, deep waterings until an adequate root system is established. Throughout the first 2 or 3 summers after planting, give them a soaking at least every month, more frequently if your soil is sandy.

Successful plantings of natives that are touchy about drainage have been established in gardens where drainage is poor or water run-off is slow, by grading up a natural raised bed. Plants in the mounded area get such quick run-off that water from lawn sprinklers causes no trouble.

In caring for natives by providing special drainage, don't forget that there are natives of the fog belt, the rain forest, the marsh, and the streamside, as well as the arid hills. Good drainage and moderate watering are not necessarily the same thing for all plants.

The culture of natives has been tested rather thoroughly in many Western botanic gardens.

White fir at right—refer to plan on following page for location of other major plantings here

Mountain meadow—garden size

One of the most provocative demonstrations of the possibilities of natives in landscaping can be seen in the Regional Parks Botanic Garden in Tilden Park, Berkeley, California. Here plants from California's High Sierra have been gathered and arranged to recreate a typical mountain meadow scene. The illustrations of native plantings reproduced on these pages were sketched there.

The meadow, of course, delights the eye of those who think that nature in her high-country gardens puts to shame all man-designed landscape. But this meadow and the experience with natives gained there, opens up new horizons in gardening and landscaping with natives.

According to James Roof, who planned and planted the Tilden meadow, many native mountain species will thrive in the lowlands with exactly as much water as lawn grass requires—*provided* the plants are given the fast drainage of raised beds of soil.

This being true, the conversion of a large lawn area into a small mountain meadow is merely a matter of adding elevated soil beds irregularly around the perimeter of the lawn. Such raised beds, small soil hummocks, or promontories, could be established in a new lawn at the time it is first graded.

The placement of the raised beds of soil determines the shape of the meadow. Those who like the way trees come down into a mountain meadow to almost close it in by sections, will bring two opposing, low promontories out from the sides of the

308 NATIVES

lawn, leaving a staggered gap between. When planted, these two promontories frame the view down the long axis of the meadow.

The trees and shrubs that frame the meadow call for no special treatment. The entire area, grass and plants, can be watered uniformly. The same watering that grass receives keeps the mountain plants cool, and water-cooling on hot summer days is the essential in growing mountain wildlings.

The alpine trees and shrubs suggested below for a home garden meadow have been tested for many years at low elevations.

Trees of the meadow

The effect of a small-scale forest can be created with the typical conifers of the high country—the pines, fir, cedar, and juniper. Several conifers have the look of a mature tree even in youth, and can be pruned to arrest growth at the desired height.

In California, the white fir *(Abies concolor)*, with its thick-swatched branches and straight-shafted trunks, will give the meadow an immediate alpine look. In the Northwest meadow the choice would be either noble fir or silver fir *(Abies amabilis)*.

For a miniature grove of a half-dozen trees, the lodgepole pine is most effective. (See chapter on pines.) Although it will grow at a rate of 18 inches a year when established, it can be tipped and dwarfed to any size over 3 feet.

In a sunny corner of the meadow, the blue-green, aromatic foliage of the Jeffrey pine is ideal. It's a slow grower—6 feet in 10 years—and with directive pruning can be made to assume the storm-blown and stunted form so admired in the high mountains.

Where there's space for a background, use the incense cedar *(Libocedrus decurrens)*. This native is available at nurseries throughout the West. Plant your cedars closely, about 10 feet apart, and top them at 10 feet. Remove the limbs from the lower 4 feet to expose the trunk and its distinctive, reddish-brown bark. The result will be as if the meadow were backed by a deep forest.

If you want to bring more of the alpine feel into the meadow, plant a Western juniper *(Juniperus occidentalis)*. Slow growing, it reaches 10 feet in 12 years.

Lower growing evergreens

The meadow's most basic low growing evergreens are the dwarf junipers. If possible, get the mountain junipers of your own area. You'll find low growing forms that spread 6-8 inches a year without mounding to more than 18 inches.

In the meadow illustrated here the broad-leafed evergreen shrubs are *Garrya fremontii* and *Carpenteria californica*.

Indian rhubarb planted around this pool. If you like more delicate textures, provide more shade and use such plants as Sierra coral bell, shooting star, fairy lantern, minulus

Deciduous small trees and tall shrubs

The only mountain tree recommended for location in the lawn proper is the mountain alder *(Alnus tenuifolia)*. Its clustered, small trunks say "mountain meadow" the moment you see it. You can let the grass run right up to it and mow around it.

Although not supposed to thrive in low altitudes the Quaking aspen *(Populus tremuloides)* is doing fine in Tilden Park meadow.

Redtwig dogwood *(Cornus stolonifera)* deserves to be included for its chianti-red winter stems alone. Prune to encourage fresh, new stems and hold in check the 5 foot high and 10 foot wide growth. Will grow in part shade behind the firs.

A mountain shrub that is valuable as a filler is the spice bush *(Calycanthus occidentalis)*.

Deciduous dwarf shrubs

Undoubtedly if you become interested in the mountain meadow idea you'll want to collect the plants you become familiar with on your mountain trips.

Don't overlook the dwarf willows that play such a major role in the mountain scene. There's no problem in collecting, since they root so readily from cuttings. From Washington south look for the gray-leafed type *(Salix eastwoodiæ)*. In California, the mono willow *(S. monica)* is worth looking for because of its neat, shiny green leaves, red stems and buds. These willows grow no higher than 3 feet, spread to 4 feet or more.

Annuals and perennials

Whether you collect seeds on your vacation trip or buy from a dealer in native plants, the growing of wild flowers can be full of surprises. No one can be sure how each alpine will perform when brought down to near sea level.

If you are a purist and insist that all plants in your meadow must be of the mountains, you won't lack for variety, but no native flower, bulb, or fern, whatever its native habitat, will look out of place there.

In small bays, corners, foreground, around a rock, or beside a small pool you can bring in bits of all of the wild country you have enjoyed—in the Olympics, along the Pacific shore, in Utah's Wasatch background, in all of the changing scenes from southern deserts to northern rain forests, from sea level to snow line.

Of course as you draw together plants from distinctly different environments, you must watch soil and moisture requirements.

The meadow is seldom without its moist, springy, peaty soil and that section will take care of many shade-loving plants of the low country.

Sun-loving native perennials lend themselves to color and texture arrangement just as readily as the so-called exotics. In fact many of the Western natives have been used in the perennial border so long that their native origin has been forgotten.

Playing with color combinations of natives should be carried out with a free and easy hand. If color schemes get a bit riotous the natives won't care.

The annual native plants, and perennial plants that you can treat as annuals, have wonderful possibilities. If you sow them thickly in an area that you have to weed frequently, these annuals will crowd the weeds and give you so much color you won't notice the weeds. For quick cover on a slope and for temporary erosion control they are not only practical but decorative.

— **Encyclopedia** —

ABIES. FIR. Looked at from a distance, all of the seven true firs of the Pacific slope look somewhat alike. All the branches of the crown point upward, the heads are sharply defined and spire or arrow-like. You'll have to look hard to find the cones as they are usually borne near the tree tops, and the cone disintegrates when ripe leaving only an erect spike. In maturity all except alpine fir and bristlecone fir are big trees 3 ft. and more in diameter and from 125 to more than 200 ft. tall. The three species used most extensively in cultivation are white fir, noble fir and grand fir. Here is where you will find the native species:

A. concolor. WHITE FIR. (See chapter on trees.) Mountain slopes, usually 3,000-7,000 ft. elevation, Cascade Mountains of southern Oregon; mountains of California; east to the Rocky Mountains. **A. grandis.** GRAND FIR, LOWLAND FIR. Northern California coast, north to British Columbia, extending east in Oregon and Washington to Idaho, Montana and Wyoming. **A. magnifica.** RED FIR. Usually at higher elevations than white fir. Cascade Mountains of Oregon to north Coast Range and Sierra Nevada Mountains of California. **A. procera.** *(A. nobilis).* NOBLE FIR. (See chapter on trees.) Coast Ranges and Cascade Mountains of Washington and Oregon. **A. amabilis.** SILVER FIR, CASCADES FIR. Southern Alaska, south in the Coast Ranges and Cascade Mountains of British Columbia, Washington and Oregon. **A. lasiocarpa.** ALPINE FIR. Subalpine, southeastern Alaska, British Columbia south through Washington, Oregon, east to the Rocky Mountains. **A. venusta.** BRISTLECONE FIR. Rarest fir, found only in the Santa Lucia Mountains, California.

ACER. MAPLE, BOXELDER. Deciduous. (See chapter on trees.)

A. circinatum. VINE MAPLE. Range: Coastal mountains of British Columbia, south in western Washington, Oregon, and mts. of northern California. Slender vine-like shrub or, rarely, a small tree 5-35 ft., with many stems from the base or single trunked. Maple leaves thin, 5-11 lobed, 2-6 in. and as broad; light green turning orange-scarlet or yellow in the fall; new spring foliage usually has reddish tints. Tiny reddish-purple flowers in clusters, April-May, followed by paired winged fruits which look like little red bow-ties among the green leaves.

One of the most beautiful of our Western natives for airy delicate grace, and one of the few maples that is small enough to be planted in the average garden. At all seasons of the year is clean, picturesque, and colorful.

Allow tree to grow untrimmed. In time its arching branches will make natural bowers—ideal settings for a collection of ferns and woodland wild flowers. Use under a canopy of tall conifers where its blazing fall color is brilliant contrast.

Although preeminently suited for underplanting, can be grown as interesting accent on the edge of a woodland or on the lawn; plant in clumps of 3 or more in full sun. Loses some of its vine-like characteristics in open situation. Slender pliable branches make it a tree to espalier against the north side of a wall or to grow flat against the shady side of a house. Its silvery contorted leafless branches make an interesting pattern in winter.

Likes moist rich soil; is slow growing but rather long lived. Trees growing in the open transplant more successfully than those growing in shade.

A. macrophyllum. BIGLEAF MAPLE. Range: Alaska to Southern California. Broad topped tree 30-95 ft.; large maple leaves deeply 5-lobed, 4-10 in. broad, dark or medium green turning yellow in autumn; tiny greenish-yellow flowers in drooping clusters followed by clusters of winged seeds in pairs which look rather like tawny drooping butterflies.

Affords dense shade. Although it does enliven its native situations with yellow hues in autumn, one must look to some of the exotic species for better yellow fall color. But if you already have one growing natively in your garden, you'll enjoy its shade on warm days.

A. negundo californicum. CALIFORNIA BOX ELDER. Range: Along streams in California valleys. Broad crowned small tree 20-60 ft.; leaves not typically maple-like, but divided into 3 toothed or lobed leaflets 1¼-5 in. long, yellow-green, turning yellow in autumn.

Rapid growing but rather short-lived. Good native to provide quick shade in the interior valley regions of California.

AESCULUS CALIFORNICA. CALIFORNIA BUCKEYE. Deciduous. Range: California coastal mountains and Sierra Nevada foothills. Shrub-like or small tree, often with several stems to 10-20 ft. or more high. New foliage pale apple-green; mature leaves divide fan-wise into 5, rich green, 3-6 in. leaflets. Striking sight in May when fragrant, creamy flower plumes make it a giant candelabrum. Large, pear-shaped fruits, with green covering splitting to reveal large, brown, shiny seeds, are favorites for fall flower arrangements.

Not cultivated in gardens because of size and early leaf drop. Will hold leaves if given summer water. Planted by a stream in coastal areas will retain its leaves until fall. Best for large country places.

ALNUS. ALDER. Deciduous. Four species are native on the Pacific Coast. One is available at nurseries and is being widely planted.

A. rhombifolia. SIERRA ALDER, WHITE ALDER. Range: Along stream banks from British Columbia southward to Idaho, Washington, Oregon, and California. It's the common alder of the Coast Range, the lower western slope of the Sierra Nevada and the lower mountains of Southern California.

Fast growth to 40-90 ft. A tall straight trunk with whitish or gray-brown bark. Branches are spreading or ascending and pendulous at the ends. Ovate 2-3½ in. leaves give the tree a dense attractive character.

Naturally suited to constant moisture, the alder thrives in lawn and garden situations. It has been known to grow 18 ft. in the first 2 years after planting out of a gallon can.

ARBUTUS MENZIESII. MADRONE, MADRONO. Evergreen. Range: From British Columbia southward through the Coast Ranges to Southern California. Mature height varies greatly by growing conditions—anything from 20 ft. to 100 ft. Generally forms a broad, round head almost as wide as tree is tall.

Usually the first thing you notice is the smooth reddish-brown terra cotta bark that peels off in thin flakes. Very thick and leathery, 3-6 in. leaves are shiny dark green on top, dull and pale gray-green underneath. In spring, large clusters of greenish-white, bell-shaped flowers bloom at the end of the branches. These are followed in early fall by clusters of brilliant red and orange berries that remain on the tree most of the winter.

The madrone can be adapted to garden conditions. It is too large for the small garden and in a large garden is not a tree that can be gardened under, because of constantly dropping leaves. The latter objection is of minor importance, if you plant it in the background—usually the best plan anyway, because it can be enjoyed most fully at a distance.

ARCTOSTAPHYLOS. MANZANITA. Evergreen. Large group of western shrubs with rich reddish or purplish bark, waxy bell-like flowers and fruits like little apples.

A. columbiana. HAIRY MANZANITA. Range: Low coastal mts., central California north to British Columbia. Erect, 3-10 ft., 3-8 ft. spread; branches with long white hairs; 3-in. leaves gray-green; white flowers in March and April; berries red-cheeked.

Appropriate on hillsides and informal gardens in which natives predominate. Red stems, berries, and contrasting leaves make it interesting and ornamental. Contrast its gray-green foliage with the rich dark leaves of *Ceanothus parryi* in background.

A. hookeri. HOOKER MANZANITA. Range: California, vicinity Monterey Bay. Shrubby mounds ½-3 ft., 3-4 ft. spread; shiny bright green ½-in. leaves; pinkish flowers in February to April. Neat clean green mounds make excellent cover for hot dry slopes.

A. manzanita. COMMON MANZANITA. Range: California, inner north Coast Range, Sierra Nevada foothills. Tall shrubs or tree-like, 6-22 ft., 4-10 ft. spread; crooked branching habit; clean pale green leaves to 1½ in.; white to deep pink flowers, February to April.

Grows well under high trees, even eucalyptus. Coarse and leggy in the wild; moderate pruning will control. Lives 20 years; in age becomes picturesque small tree with purplish-red crooked branches. Excellent for large plantings. Lovely in a native setting with other manzanitas and pines.

A. stanfordiana. STANFORD MANZANITA. Range: California, Lake, Mendocino, Sonoma and Napa Cos. Spreading shrub 3-7 ft., the pointed 1½-in. leaves bright glossy green. Pink flowers in profusion, March and April.

Relaxed and more graceful species of manzanita deserving of wider use. Its abundant, large, loose clusters of pink flowers combine well with blue-flowered ceanothus.

A. uva-ursi. BEAR-BERRY, KINNIKINNICK. Range: California, Marin Co., north to Alaska, thence widespread in northern altitudes, both hemispheres. Prostrate, spreading to 15 ft., bright glossy green leaves to 1-in., turning reddish in fall. Flowers white or pinkish, March-May, the little apples bright red or pink.

One of the best prostrate ground covers. Very popular for all types of ground cover uses in the Pacific Northwest. Slowness in starting causes weed problem. Mulch with peat moss or sawdust to keep down weeds and keep soil moist for root expansion. To keep soil porous, add sand each year until established. Excellent bank planting. Combines well with yew and Mugho pine on hillside, in large garden over rocks. Attractive ground cover or foreground for large native shrubs and trees.

All manzanitas are difficult to start but once established will survive under the most adverse soil conditions. Must have perfect drainage; don't like summer watering. Their rich reddish or purplish bark complements the foliage and contributes greatly to landscape value for all-year interest.

ASPEN. See POPULUS

ATRIPLEX LENTIFORMIS. SALT BUSH, QUAIL BUSH. Deciduous. Range: Alkaline soils; California deserts; San Joaquin and Salinas valleys. Densely branched, sometimes spiny shrub, 3-10 ft. high; 12 ft. spread; foliage very gray. Stands desert and interior valley conditions; for windbreaks or hedges.

A. l. breweri. *(A. breweri).* BREWER SALT BUSH. Almost evergreen. Range: California, coast; Santa Barbara south; Suisun marshes; Santa Catalina, San Clemente islands. Like salt bush in habit but never spiny. Grows equally well in sand on the beach proper and on cliffs above. Use for massing along windswept beaches or for wind-diverting hedges. Fine background for sheets of brilliant ice plant. Can be pruned formally if desired.

AZALEA, WESTERN. See RHODODENDRON OCCIDENTALE

BOX ELDER. See ACER NEGUNDO CALIFORNICUM
BUCKEYE, CALIFORNIA. See AESCULUS CALIFORNICA

CALYCANTHUS OCCIDENTALIS. SPICE BUSH. Deciduous. Range: Along streams, moist slopes; California, north Coast Ranges, Sierra Nevada foothills. Aromatic shrub, 4-12 ft. high; leaves bright green, 2-6 in. long;

flowers wine-colored, to 2 in. broad, like small water lilies. Not as handsome as the large flowered, more fragrant Florida species, *C. florida*, but useful if an all native planting is desired.

CARPENTERIA CALIFORNICA. CARPENTERIA, BUSH ANEMONE.
Evergreen. Range: California, localized in the Sierra Nevada foothills between the Kings and San Joaquin rivers in Fresno County. One of the finest of California shrubs. Evergreen, 3-7 ft. high; light colored bark and often purplish shoots; thick rather narrow leaves 2-4½ in. long, dark green above, whitish beneath; anemone-like white flowers 1½-2½ in. broad, June to August. Subject to aphis damage; growth sometimes gets out of control. Holds its own with other garden shrubs in all-year appearance of foliage plus distinctive white flowers in summer. Takes garden watering.

CASTANOPSIS CHRYSOPHYLLA MINOR. GOLDEN CHINQUAPIN.
Evergreen. Range: California, coast, San Luis Obispo Co., north to Del Norte Co.; inland to Sierra Nevada. Shrubby form of Giant Chinquapin; 3-15 ft. high. Narrow, trough-like leaves, to 3 in., glossy dark green above, very golden beneath. Fruits are like small chestnuts. There's nothing native looking about this shrub. If cared for by pruning will stand close inspection as a tub plant; looked at from above, it's green; from beneath, it's golden. Makes a dense hedge; good contrast in a planting of pines.

CEANOTHUS. WILD LILAC.
Evergreen and deciduous. It's difficult to imagine driving in the springtime through any of the foothills and mountains of California and not seeing any of the blues of the wild lilacs. Some 44 species are native to the state. They range in color from white to indigo blue and in form from carpets to trees.

Many have been cultivated. A few have shown unusual adaptability to home-garden environment. How well each species and hybrid is adapted to each Western climate is now being tested. Gardeners in the Pacific Northwest are finding that several species, especially *C. gloriosus*, will take temperatures to 10°. In the interior valleys of California, more and more plantings are being made.

From the 50 species, varieties, and hybrids available we have selected the following as outstanding for garden use.

C. arboreus. FELTLEAF CEANOTHUS. Range: Santa Rosa, Santa Cruz, and Santa Catalina Islands. Fast growth to 12-35 ft. with an 8-12 ft. spread. Rounded, 1-3 in. leaves, dark green above, white beneath. Flowers, varying from light to bright blue, bloom in very early spring.

Var. *Theodore Payne* and var. *Treasure Island* were introduced years ago and have been widely planted. Although the named varieties are not carried by many nurseries, the ceanothus sold as *C. arboreus* is almost sure to be a hybrid. Hybrids have been grown successfully in the heat of the valleys and along the coast of California.

C. cyaneus. SAN DIEGO CEANOTHUS. Range: Dry slopes in San Diego Co. Fast growth to 10 ft. or more but at its best as a 5-6 ft., dense and bushy shrub. Glossy, medium green, 1-2 in. leaves. In May and June its 10-in. flower spikes burst into violet-blue.

The species has the most exciting blue color of all the ceanothus and the worst garden habits. Try to keep the shrub under control by pruning and you'll ruin it; cultivate beneath its branches and you'll damage its touchy root system; even with the best of drainage and care, the plant will decide to die when it's about 5 years old.

The following hybrids have *C. cyaneus* as one parent and flower clusters of cyaneus blue: Var. *La Primavera*. Averages 6 ft. in height. Flowers in April. Var. *Sierra Blue*, propagated from selected seedlings of *La Primavera*, is a neat, erect form and will stand clipping. Used as hedges to 4-8 ft. high. Var. *Mountain Haze*, a dwarf companion to *Sierra Blue*, grows in the 2-4 ft. range.

C. gloriosus. POINT REYES CEANOTHUS. Range: Restricted to California coastal strip between Point Reyes and Point Arena. Low growing, dense mat, 4-24 in. high, spreading to 5 ft. Can be kept flat by pinching back upright growth. Leathery, roundish, dark green, ½-1½ in. leaves with somewhat spiny-toothed margins. Fragrant, lavender-blue flowers are borne in short-stalked, rounded clusters.

Probably the most useful ceanothus ground cover. Likes a well-drained, peaty soil and will take more water than other species. Hardy enough to be more widely planted in mild sections of zones 4-5.

C. griseus. CARMEL CEANOTHUS. Range: Coastal regions of central California and most plentiful on the Monterey Peninsula. Varies in growth habit from low spreading, or upright to 2-8 ft. tall, with deep green, glossy, ovate, 1-2 in. leaves, silvery underneath. Blue flowers in dense ¾-2 in. clusters, March-May.

Var. *horizontalis*. CARMEL CREEPER. Generally low and creeping but varies from 18-30 in. high with a 5-15 ft. spread. When planting out, space plants 8 ft. apart to prevent crowding and mounding.

C. impressus. SANTA BARBARA CEANOTHUS. Range: Restricted to northwestern Santa Barbara Co. and southern San Luis Obispo Co., California. Fast growing to 3-5 ft. high and as wide. Distinguished by its dense branching and its small, wrinkled, and furrowed, dark green, ¼-½ in. leaves. Flowers deep blue in ½-1 in. clusters, February-April.

Because of its rapid growth and intolerance of heavy pruning, *C. impressus* should be used for rather temporary effects—as you would use a large-growing, blue-flowered perennial. Tip prune the fast-growing branches to prevent legginess and use the shrub as a 4-year plant. Keep a new supply coming with seeds or cuttings. Give the seeds the hot water treatment.

Widely adaptable. Successful plantings in Sacramento Valley.

C. prostratus. SQUAW CARPET. MAHALA MAT. Range: Higher mountains of Washington, Oregon, and California, eastward into Nevada. Everyone who has seen this creeper wonders why it is not propagated and sold as a ground cover. So far it has resisted all attempts at taming. Squaw Carpet is not to be found in nurseries and only a few rock garden specialists have been able to grow it at low elevations.

Forms dense, twiggy mats 2-8 ft. across. Thick, leathery, dark green, ¼-1¼ in. leaves, usually with spiny-toothed margins. Flowers deep to light blue in small, rounded clusters, April-June. Var. *occidentalis*. Found in the higher mountains of the Coast Ranges in central California, appears to be more amenable to cultivation. It has narrower, often wavy, toothed leaves.

C. purpureus. HOLLYLEAF CEANOTHUS. Range: Restricted to a very small area northeast of Napa, California. Variable in growth from spreading to upright, 2-4 ft. high. Unusually long and rigid branches with deep green, holly-like, ½-¾ in. leaves. Purple-lavender flowers in short-stalked, rounded clusters.

This species has been more widely distributed in the past than now. It's a wonderful plant in its youth but needs constant pinching back to keep it from becoming leggy. Is short-lived, dying out for no apparent reason.

C. thyrsiflorus. BLUE BLOSSOM. Range: Coast Range from Santa Barbara north into Oregon. It is as variable as the area in which it is found. Color ranges from deep to a washed-out blue. Some bloom in March, some as late as June. It thrives best in direct coastal conditions. Erect growing to 4-20 ft., but usually 4-8 ft., with angled stems and dark green, glossy, 1-2 in. leaves. Flowers are borne in compact, 1-3 in. clusters.

Two dwarf forms of *C. thyrsiflorus* have been propagated and are available: Var. *Mary Lake* is a fast-growing and wide-spreading shrub to 2 ft. with prostrate and arching branches to 6-10 ft. Deep blue flowers in large, compound clusters; var. *Royal Blue* has same growth habit but with more intense blue flowers.

Hybrids from Europe

Of the many European hybrids, 3 are available from nurseries—mostly in the Pacific Northwest. They are winter hardy in zones 3-6; generally give inferior performance in zones 7-13.

Gloire de Versailles. Hybrid between *C. americanus* from eastern United States and *C. cœruleus* from Mexico. A fast-growing, deciduous shrub to 8-12 ft. if not pruned. Dark green, ovate, 2-3 in. leaves. Fragrant, bluish-lilac flowers are borne in loose, 4-6 in. clusters, in June and intermittently throughout the summer.

The shrub gives concentrated color when pruned severely, because flowers are borne on new wood. Often effectively treated as a wall shrub.

Marie Simon. Deciduous, upright growth to 4 ft. Stems are wine-red when young. Light pink flowers are borne in long clusters in June and July. Give it the same treatment as *Gloire de Versailles*.

A. T. Johnson. This European hybrid appears to have the California native *C. impressus* as one parent. An almost evergreen, erect grower to 5-6 ft. with indigo-blue flowers from May-July.

CEDAR, INCENSE. See LIBOCEDRUS DECURRENS

CERCIS OCCIDENTALIS. WESTERN REDBUD. Deciduous. Range: California in inner north Coast Range, Sierra Nevada foothills, Kern and San Diego counties, east to Texas. Bushy spreading plant or small tree to 8-20 ft. An all-year performer. In March or April produces splashes of magenta, sweet-pea-shaped blossoms followed by handsome, blue-green, 3-in., round leaves. In fall the entire plant turns light yellow or red. In winter it becomes an artistic form of bare branches covered with clusters of reddish-brown seed pods.

Seldom bothered by insects or pests. Prune to remove only dead and off-balance growth. Fast draining soil is essential.

Plant on dry, seldom-watered banks. *Ceanothus griseus* is a pleasant companion plant as its blue flowers complement the redbud.

CERCOCARPUS BETULOIDES. WESTERN MOUNTAIN MAHOGANY. Evergreen or sometimes partially deciduous. Range: Southwestern Oregon, California Coast Range, Sierra Nevada, Southern California east to Nevada. A graceful, arching shrub to 5-12 ft. or a small tree to 20 ft. Wedge-shaped, dark green, 1-in. leaves. Rather inconspicuous tan flowers, March to May, followed by tiny fruits with long, feathery, 3-in. tails.

Good native with attractive foliage for natural plantings. Does not resent garden water.

CHAMAECYPARIS LAWSONIANA. PORT ORFORD CEDAR. LAWSON CYPRESS. (See chapter on trees.)

CHAMAECYPARIS NOOTKATENSIS. NOOTKA CYPRESS. ALASKA YELLOW CEDAR. (See chapter on trees.)

CHILOPSIS LINEARIS. DESERT WILLOW. Deciduous. Range: Washes and stream beds of deserts of Southern California, eastward to Nevada and Arizona. Shrub or tree to 35 ft., with open light growth habit. Bare branches most of year. Long narrow 2-5 in. leaves. Crimped, trumpet-shaped, pink or whitish flowers, marked with purple or yellow, in spring and often continuing until fall; followed by long slender seed pods.

Valued for color in dry places or in any large native planting. Tree is very fast growing up to the time of flowering and then slows down. Rooted cuttings will grow 3 ft. the first year.

COMAROSTAPHYLIS DIVERSIFOLIA. (*Arctostaphylos diversifolia*). SUMMER HOLLY. Evergreen. Range: Coastal Southern California, into Lower California. Large shrub, or small tree to 6-18 ft. with gray bark and leathery leaves ¾-3½ in., dark green above, whitish beneath. Small white manzanita-like flowers, April-May; followed by clusters of red, warty berries similar to those of the madrone tree. Adaptable but grows best in half shade, with moisture. Can be trained into small tree by removing lower limbs. With its strong, definite manzanita-like character of growth, its handsome foliage, flowers and fruit, summer holly competes successfully with all garden plants of its type.

CORNUS NUTTALLII. PACIFIC DOGWOOD. WESTERN DOGWOOD. (See chapter on trees.) Range: Southern British Columbia through Washington, Oregon, and California.

C. stolonifera. REDTWIG DOGWOOD. (See chapter on trees.) Range: Alaska, south to California high mountains, east to the Rocky Mountains and the Atlantic Coast.

COTTONWOOD. See POPULUS

COWANIA MEXICANA STANSBURIANA. (*C. stansburiana*). CLIFF ROSE. Evergreen. Range: California, Mojave Desert; Nevada, Arizona, Utah; south to Mexico. Much branched shrub, 1-6 ft. with 3-5 lobed leaves, green above, whitish beneath. Flowers like small single roses, creamy, or sulfur-yellow, rarely white, April-June. The many very tiny fruits, with long plumose tails, soften shrub to a feathery haze after bloom. Valuable and interesting for hot, dry locations.

CURRANT. See RIBES

DENDROMECON RIGIDA. BUSH POPPY. Evergreen. Range: Dry chaparral; generally throughout lower elevations in California. Freely branched shrub 2-8 ft. with shreddy, yellowish-gray or white bark. Thick, veiny, gray-green leaves, 1-4 in. long; quantities of bright lemon-yellow 2 in. poppy flowers, March through June.

D. r. harfordii. (*D. harfordii*). ISLAND BUSH POPPY. Range: Islands off coast of Southern California. Large shrubs, or sometimes tree-like to 20 ft. with broader, less veiny leaves.

Although untidy in its native state, severe pruning back to 2 ft. in February or March keeps it looking neat in the garden. High on our list of shrubs for dry places. Good yellow and gray over a long season. Use with toyon, ceanothus, broom, salt bush. Plant as background shrubs where they will have room to spread.

DIPLACUS. MONKEY FLOWER. Evergreen. Small group of low shrubs with sticky foliage and highly colored trumpet-shaped flowers in profusion.

D. longiflorus. *(Mimulus longiflorus).* SOUTHERN MONKEY FLOWER. Range: California, south Coast Ranges, into Lower California. Many-branched shrub, 1-3 ft. high; with narrow, yellow-green leaves 1-3¼ in. long; flowers salmon-yellow or cream color, 1¾ to 2¼ in. long, April-July.

D. puniceus. *(Mimulus puniceus).* RED MONKEY FLOWER. Range: Dry hills, Southern California. Similar to *D. longiflorus* but growing to 5 ft. with dark green leaves and brick red or crimson flowers.

The striking diplacus hybrids available in nurseries are results of crosses of the two above species. These offer a wide range in flower colors: Cream, yellow, orange, buff, rose, salmon, pink, chamois, red, and mahogany. Combine with ceanothus, lupine and native penstemon on a hot dry bank for a blaze of color in late spring and early summer. Prune after flowering to keep trim.

DOGWOOD. See CORNUS
DOUGLAS FIR. See PSEUDOTSUGA TAXIFOLIA
ELDERBERRY. See SAMBUCUS
ERIOGONUM. Evergreen. Wind resistant shrubs, best in fog belt but will grow inland. Two species worth garden attention:

E. arborescens. SANTA CRUZ ISLAND BUCKWHEAT. Range: Santa Cruz, Santa Rosa and Anacapa islands, Southern California. Compact shrub 2-8 ft. high, with narrow gray leaves crowded on the ends of the branches, ½-1½ in. Flowers pink or rose in long stalked flat clusters, May to September.

E. giganteum. ST. CATHERINE'S LACE. Range: Santa Catalina and San Clemente islands, Southern California. Differs from *E. arborescens* in more freely branching habit, grayish-white foliage, ovate leaves 1-2½ in. long, and longer period of bloom.

Beautifully adapted to garden use, particularly to sunny slopes, stunning in combination with other drought resistant grays.

FALLUGIA PARADOXA. APACHE PLUME. Deciduous. Range: California, mountains of east San Bernardino Co.; Nevada; Arizona; Utah; to Mexico. Shrub 1-5 ft. with straw-colored branches and flaky bark. Small, ½-1 in. grayish leaves divided into 3-7 narrow lobes. Flowers like 1½-in. single white roses in April and May. Large clusters of feathery fruits that follow—greenish at first, turning pink or reddish tinged—create a soft colored, changing haze through which you can see the rigid branch pattern. Important erosion control plant in arid regions of the Southwest.

FIR. See ABIES
FRAXINUS. ASH. (See chapter on trees.)
FREMONTIA. Evergreen. Rapid growing shrubs or small trees; thick rough leaves, dark green above, whitish or rusty underneath with a felt-like covering of hairs; abundant large yellow, saucer-like flowers; seeds in large conical capsules covered with dense bristly rusty hairs.

F. californica. FREMONTIA, FLANNEL BUSH. Range: California, Sierra Nevada Mts., scattered localities in central Coast Ranges, Southern California mts. and desert slopes. Loosely branched shrub or small tree, 6-15 ft.; branchlets long and tough; roundish leaves entire or 3-lobed, ¼-1½ in.; flowers lemon-yellow, 1-1½ in. broad, May-June. Exceedingly variable shrub in amount of hairiness on branchlets and leaves, as well as size and shape of leaves. Var. *napensis (F. napensis).* NAPA FREMONTIA. Range: Napa Co., California. Differs from the species in thinner leaves and smaller flowers and capsules.

F. mexicana. SOUTHERN FREMONTIA. Range: San Diego Co., California, Lower California. Similar to *F. californica* but leaves more distinctly maple-like; the yellow flowers larger, often tinged with orange on the back; flowers during most of the growing season in cultivation, more abundantly May to July.

Fremontia prefers a slope planting with good drainage. In many valley gardens will take care of itself. Unreliable in habit, often becoming rangy and open. Shallow rooting, helped by staking when young. Will die if watered in summer. Prune as desired. Eye-appealing when in bloom. Picture: fremontia on a hilltop—a brilliant mass of yellow against a background of blue sky.

GARRYA. SILKTASSEL. Evergreen. Early flowering, with long pendulous flower clusters, like tassels, covering the plants. Male and female flowers borne on separate shrubs. Need both plants for producing the highly ornamental long clusters of purple fruits on the female plant.

G. elliptica. COAST SILKTASSEL. Range: Coast Ranges from southern Oregon to San Luis Obispo Co., California. Densely foliaged shrub to 4-8 ft.; or, rarely, a small tree to 20-30 ft. Elliptical 1½-2½ in. leaves, dark green above, gray woolly beneath, with crisped or wavy margins. Flower tassels, 1-10 in clusters, the yellowish male catkins slender and graceful, 3-8 in. long, pale green female catkins 2-3½ in., thicker and more rigid. December-February bloom; purplish fruit from June-September, often hangs on until the following year.

Rich handsome foliage, decorative flower tassels, purple fruit clusters, make this native do as much for the garden as many exotics. Does well in both sun and semi-shade; makes a beautiful open screen or informal hedge. Well adapted to seacoast conditions. Try it in combination with pines and golden chinquapin.

G. fremontii. FREMONT SILKTASSEL, BEAR BRUSH. Range: Cascade Mts. of Washington and Oregon, mts. of California. Differs from coast silktassel in lively yellow-green leaves with smooth margins; fruit buff to purple or black; stands more sun and cold. Gets rangy in dense shade; can be trimmed to keep neat. Fremont silktassel is a good neutral green in a background planting.

GAULTHERIA SHALLON. SALAL. Evergreen. Range: Common along coast, California from Santa Barbara Co., north to British Columbia. Spreading shrub 1-2 ft. in full sun, 4-10 ft. in shade. Nearly round glossy dark green leaves 1¾-4 in. White or pinkish bell-like flowers on reddish stalks in 6 in., loose clusters, March-June, with dusty black fruits reminding of large huckleberries.

In full sun in poor dry soil, salal is a mat-forming creeper about 1 ft. tall; makes excellent low bank or ground cover. In deep shade and rich humus with an abundance of moisture, salal becomes a shrub 8-10 ft. tall. In this situation, it combines well with rhododendrons, azaleas and other acid loving plants. Can be mass planted with sword or deer fern or combined with snowberry for contrast. Requires no pruning unless it has been neglected. In that case, it is advisable to cut the plant back almost to the ground in April and topdress lightly with peat or leaf mold. A favorite with florists for cut greens.

G. humifusa. WESTERN WINTERGREEN, ALPINE WINTERGREEN. (See chapter on ground covers.) Range: Rare in California, north to British Columbia, east to Colorado.

G. ovatifolia. OREGON WINTERGREEN, OVAL LEAF WINTERGREEN. (See chapter on ground covers.) Range: Scattered localities, higher mts. of northern California; north to British Columbia, east to northern Idaho..

GOOSEBERRY. See RIBES
HEMLOCK. See TSUGA

HETEROMELES ARBUTIFOLIA. (*Photinia arbutifolia*). Toyon, Christmas Berry, California Holly. Evergreen. Range: California, Sierra Nevada, Coast Ranges, mts. of Southern California. Large bushy shrub 6-10 ft., or multiple-trunked small tree 15-25 ft. Thick leathery, glossy dark green leaves 2-4 in., with bristle-pointed teeth. Small white flowers in large flattish clusters, June-July; followed by bright red berries, November-January.

Toyon improves under cultivation, and although drought tolerant, does not object to summer watering. If cut back properly to give abundance of year-old wood, will produce even more berries than in the wild; can be trimmed to form small single-trunked tree. Recommended in California for hillside erosion control.

HOLODISCUS DISCOLOR. Cream Bush, Ocean Spray. Deciduous. Range: Moist slopes, canyons; Coast Ranges, Southern California; north to British Columbia; east to Rocky Mts. Erect or spreading shrub to 3-20 ft. with gray-green leaves to 3 in., veiny and softly hairy to touch; creamy-white flowers in ample plume-like nodding clusters, May-July gradually turn to amber and are as lovely in August as in June. At its best in rich moist soil, in sun or partial shade. Prune back after flowering to retain graceful habit, and to remove unsightly seed pods.

HUCKLEBERRY. See VACCINUM

JUNIPERUS. Juniper. Conifer. Four species and one variety are native to the West.

J. communis saxatilis. (*J. sibirica*, *J. communis montana*). Mountain Juniper. Range: Rare in California at high elevation; coastal Oregon to Alaska; Cascade Mountains and across the continent. Low or almost prostrate shrub forming patches several feet in width. Dark green, shining, ¼-½ in., sharp needles. Fruit blue with a whitish bloom.

Use as you would the low, prostrate forms of the cultivated junipers. (See chapter on shrubs.)

J. californica. California Juniper. Range: California, inner Coast Ranges, southern Sierra Nevada foothills; desert slopes Southern California mountains. A shrub becoming tree-like to 15 ft. Foliage olive-green of mostly scale-like leaves. Berry becoming reddish-brown.

J. c. utahensis (*J. utahensis*). Utah Juniper. Range: Desert mountain ranges, California east into Nevada, Utah, Arizona, New Mexico, Colorado, and Wyoming. More compact and tree-like than California juniper.

J. occidentalis. Western Juniper. Range: Arid hills, high plains, and high mountains of Idaho, southeastern Washington, eastern Oregon south to Southern California. Tree to 10-25 ft. or more. Thick trunk with shreddy, smoky, reddish-brown bark and often picturesque, contorted branches. Foliage deep green to gray-green of mostly scale-like leaves. Berry bluish-black with a whitish bloom.

J. scopulorum. Rocky Mountain Juniper. Range: Coastal British Columbia; eastern Washington and Oregon, Nevada east to the Rocky Mountains. A native that has been available in nurseries for some time. Tree to 15-20 ft. with narrow, rounded crown and large, long limbs that tend to turn upward, the branchlets often somewhat drooping. Stringy bark is reddish-brown. Foliage varies from dark green to gray-green, of mostly scale-like leaves. Berries are bluish.

KALMIA POLIFOLIA. Pale Laurel, Bog Kalmia. Evergreen. Range: Borders of lakes, in meadows or swamps; moderate altitudes, Cascade Mountains of Oregon and Washington, north to Alaska, east to the Atlantic coast. Erect shrub to 2 ft., leaves glossy dark green above, whitish beneath, to 1½ in. long. Dainty flowers, 3 to 10 in rounded clusters, pale pink to rose-purple, 1 in. broad; June-August.

Var. *microphylla*. Alpine Laurel. High altitudes of California in Sierra Nevada Mountains, Siskiyou Mountains, north. Dwarf to 8 in., with shorter, narrower leaves.

KALMIOPSIS LEACHIANA. Kalmiopsis. Evergreen. Range: Mountains of Curry Co., southern Oregon. Slow growing to 1 ft., with 2 ft. spread; has many branches densely clothed with thick, dark green leaves. Flowers abundantly with flattish clusters of ½-in. rose-pink flowers in early spring. Grows naturally on rocky, dry slopes but the foliage is best when grown in light shade under good garden conditions. Use as you would low azaleas or dwarf rhododendrons.

LAUREL, CALIFORNIA. See UMBELLULARIA CALIFORNICA

LAVATERA ASSURGENTIFLORA. Tree Mallow. Evergreen. Range: California, coastal islands. Erect shrub to 3-8 ft. may become tree-like. Maple-like leaves 3-5 in. long. Rosy-lavender hollyhock flowers bloom freely almost throughout the year, heavily from April-August. Easily compacted by shears; able to stand considerable wind; often used as hedge on Southern California beaches.

LIBOCEDRUS DECURRENS. Incense Cedar. Conifer. Range: Mountains of southern Oregon, California, western Nevada and northern Lower California. Although it has limited native range, incense cedar is widely distributed by Western nurserymen. Symmetrical tree to 75-90 ft. with dense, narrow, pyramidal crown; trunk with reddish-brown bark. Rich green foliage in flat sprays. Small, yellowish-brown or reddish-brown cones which, when open, look like duck's bills.

Although slow growing at first, once established it may add 2 ft. per year to its height. Use it in deep soils on shaded slopes. In dry weather give it a thorough soaking about once a month. Do not plant near lawn sprinklers as it resents frequent watering. Because of its columnar habit it does not occupy much space.

LILAC, WILD. See CEANOTHUS

LITHOCARPUS DENSIFLORA (*Quercus densiflora, Pasania densiflora*). Tanbark Oak. Evergreen. Range: Coast Range from central Oregon to Santa Barbara, California; scattered in the Sierra Nevada.

Growing in mixed, crowded stands, the tanbark oak will reach for light and become tall to 60-90 ft. With room to spread, the tree assumes a more open squatty habit of growth, the crown sometimes extending almost to the ground.

Unlike the typical lobed leaves of many deciduous oaks, the leaves of the tanbark oak are simple, without lobes. Leathery 1½-by-4 in. leaves, pale green above, lead color beneath, are densely covered with whitish or yellowish hairs, the upper surface becoming smooth and almost glossy. Sharply toothed and strongly veined in much the same manner as a chestnut. Acorn cups have a bur-like cap. In habit of growth, however, the tanbark oak follows the oak pattern.

Thrives in rich, moist, well drained soil.

LYONOTHAMNUS FLORIBUNDUS ASPLENIFOLIUS. Catalina Ironwood. Range: Santa Catalina, San Clemente, Santa Rosa, and Santa Cruz Islands. Moderate growth to 30-60 ft. with 20-40 ft. spread, but can be held back by annual pruning. Reddish-brown bark peels off in long ribbons. Attractive grayish-green fern-like foliage. Leaves, 4-6 in. long, are made up of 3-7 deeply notched leaflets. Because the leaves keep so well when cut, they are sold by florists for arrangements. They have a fresh fragrance similar to citrus leaves. Small white blossoms in large flat 8-18 in. clusters stand out from the foliage. Blooms should be removed when faded.

Hardy to 20°, and adapted to California coastal conditions. Should not be planted in the hot interior valleys. Prune in winter to shape and control growth.

Available only at native plant nurseries, but destined to become a regular nursery item in all warm coastal areas where its wind tolerance and beauty make it valuable.

MADRONE. See ARBUTUS MENZIESII

MAHONIA. Evergreen. Versatile native shrubs well worth growing in your garden. Attractive leaves with holly-like spiny leaflets, handsome clusters of bright yellow flowers and colorful fruit, make these plants the best of the natives for year-around performance.

M. aquifolium. *(Berberis aquifolium).* OREGON GRAPE. Range: Southern British Columbia, south in western Washington, Oregon, to northern California. Erect freely branching shrub growing to 1-6 ft., or to 10 ft.; leaves 4-10 in., with 5-9 glossy green leaflets. Young growth usually ruddy, or bronzy; scattering of mature red leaves throughout the year, more pronounced in fall. Flowers March to May; berries bluish with a gray bloom. Adapts easily to any exposure; seems to accept any soil.

Few shrubs and certainly no native plant enjoys such universal popularity. Although generally thought of as a plant for sun in the North and for half shade in the South, it is also used in the shade in the Pacific Northwest; in full sun as foundation plant in California's San Joaquin Valley.

Growth habit calls for planting in mass rather than combining sparingly with other shrubs; effective in long foundation mass planting with *M. nervosa* in front, forming a lower step. Singly, makes fine tub plant with all-year interest; color in flowers and spring foliage; berries in summer; leaf color changing through the winter months.

Keep height and evenness of foliage under control by cutting to ground woody stems that occasionally extend high above the foliage. This renews the plant; keeps it low and compact.

M. pinnata. *(Berberis pinnata).* CALIFORNIA GRAPE. Range: Outer and middle Coast Ranges from southern Oregon, south to San Diego Co., California. Similar to *M. aquifolium* but with more crinkly leaves. Will stand more heat and drought.

M. nervosa. *(Berberis nervosa).* LONGLEAF MAHONIA. Range: British Columbia, south to Monterey Co., California. Low shrub ¾-2 ft., rarely to 6 ft.; leaves with many more and narrower leaflets than other species, glossy green above, the margins toothed with many bristle-like teeth. Flowers April-June; berries blue. Excellent ground cover; spreads rapidly. Is best in shade, but will grow in sun, becoming more compact. Needs little care. Fine on a cool slope, or for a low divider. Planting in wide bands gives a good low partial barrier as it does not invite foot traffic. Its strong open texture is emphasized under dark green pines.

M. nevinii. *(Berberis nevinii).* NEVIN MAHONIA. Range: Scattered localities in Los Angeles Co. Many-branched shrub 3-6, or to 10 ft.; with very gray foliage, leaves with 3 or 5 leaflets, margins with bristle-like or slender spiny teeth; flowers late March-May; followed by striking sprays of scarlet berries.

Adaptable to almost any soil, enjoys heavy watering but tolerates dryness. Best in full sun; will grow in partial shade. Choice ornamental for single or group planting, and properly pruned makes a fine hedge.

M. fremontii. *(Berberis fremontii).* DESERT MAHONIA. Range: Deserts, scattered localities in California, Arizona, Nevada, Utah, Colorado, Lower California, Mexico. Erect many stemmed shrub to 3-12 ft.; thick leaves pale gray-green or yellowish-green, the 3 or 5 leaflets with a few stout spines; flowers May-June; fruit dark blue to brown. Good for desert areas; associated with native juniper and piñon pine.

MANZANITA. See ARCTOSTAPHYLOS
MAPLE. See ACER
MATILIJA POPPY. See ROMNEYA COULTERI

MYRICA CALIFORNICA. PACIFIC WAX MYRTLE. Evergreen. Range: Coastal. California north to Washington. Large densely foliaged, slender branched shrub or small tree 10-35 ft., with rather narrow dark green glossy leaves 2-4½ in. long. Flowers not conspicuous, March and April; followed by ornamental purplish, waxy-coated berry-like fruits in fall and winter.

Very clean striking plant of upright, naturally bushy growth. Long life. Makes a fine hedge or tall screen. Combines well with other garden background shrubbery. Makes a handsome fairly symmetrical small tree. Thrives in moist soil; can be pruned as desired.

NUTMEG, CALIFORNIA. See TORREYA CALIFORNICA
OAK. See QUERCUS
OAK, TANBARK. See LITHOCARPUS DENSIFLORA

PACHISTIMA MYRSINITES. MYRTLE BOXLEAF, OREGON BOXWOOD, FALSE BOX. Evergreen. Range: Scattered localities in California; north to British Columbia; east in the Rocky Mts.; south to New Mexico. Densely branched 2-4 ft. shrub with ¾-in. shiny, leathery, leaves in closely spaced pairs on 4-angled twigs. Numerous tiny purplish or greenish flowers in the leaf axils, April to June. Natural form varies: taller and more open in shade; low and compact in sun. Has somewhat the appearance of boxwood but in the garden on a freezing winter day is a much more cheerful looking shrub. Especially valuable where boxwood is damaged by freezing. Stands shearing well.

PHILADELPHUS LEWISII. WILD MOCK ORANGE. Deciduous. Range: Thickets, especially along streams east of the Cascades in Oregon; north to British Columbia; east to Montana. Var. *californicus* occurs in the lower Sierra Nevada foothills; Trinity Co., south to Tulare Co. Var. *gordonianus* occurs in northern California, Oregon, Washington. Large shrub 4-10 ft.; leaves bright green, 3-5 veined, 1¼-3¼ in.; profusion of white flowers, ¾-1 in. broad, May-July. Although the flowers are single and smaller than in horticultural varieties, there are so many of them, and the habit of growth is so graceful, that the shrub as a whole is fully as lovely.

PICEA. SPRUCE. (See chapter on trees.)

PINUS. PINE. (See chapter on pines.)

PLATANUS RACEMOSA. CALIFORNIA SYCAMORE. Deciduous. Range: California interior valley and bordering foothills, south Coast Range, coastal Southern California. Fast growing to 50-100 ft. Main trunk often divides into spreading or leaning secondary trunk. Attractive, patchy, buff-colored bark. Branches often twisted and contorted. Yellowish-green, maple-like, 3-5 lobed leaves, 4-9 in. long. In late summer, dark brown, ball-like seed heads, 3 or 4 in a cluster, hang from the branches and remain throughout the winter.

One of California's most picturesque natives. Although subject to blight, a well-fed, deeply watered tree can be kept reasonably clean with a thorough spraying each spring. Seed heads prized for fall and winter flower arrangements.

POPULUS. Deciduous.

P. fremontii. FREMONT COTTONWOOD. Range: Central and Southern California, central Nevada, southern Utah, northern Arizona and western New Mexico. Fast growing to 40-60 ft. or more. Thick, glossy, yellow-green, 2-4 in. broad, triangular leaves become bright lemon-yellow in fall. Small, greenish-yellow flowers in long, slender catkins appear before the leaves. Because flowers on female trees are followed by masses of cottony seeds that may become a nuisance, it is best to plant male trees.

So easily grown from cuttings that you'll find it everywhere in the Southwest as a shade tree or windbreak. In winter the gray bark on the twigs appears almost white in the bright desert sun.

P. tremuloides. ASPEN. Range: Throughout the western mountains, but the farther south you go, the higher the elevation where you will find it. Fast growing to 20-60 ft. Dainty, light green, round leaves that flutter, quake, and rustle in the slightest summer breeze, turn a brilliant golden-yellow in fall.

Generally considered poorly adapted to low elevations, but successful in mountain meadow in Tilden Park, Oakland, California.

PRUNUS. There are 5 tree-like species of this genus native to the Pacific Coast. The following have been in the nursery trade so long and have been accepted so widely that they are seldom thought of as natives.

P. ilicifolia. HOLLYLEAF CHERRY, ISLAY. Evergreen. Hardy to 10°. Range: California Coast Ranges from Napa County southward to the Tehachapi Mts., and lower slopes of the mountains of Southern and Baja California. Moderate growing shrub or small tree to 10-35 ft. Dark green glossy 2-in. leaves are so suggestive of holly that wreath-makers find it an excellent substitute. New leaf growth in March and May is light green and contrasts pleasingly with the dark green of old foliage. 1-2 in. spikes of creamy-white ½-in. flowers are followed in June by ½-¾ in. "cherries" which turn red in September, then plum-colored, and finally black.

P. lyonii (*P. ilicifolia integrifolia*). CATALINA CHERRY. Evergreen. Range: Islands off the coast of Southern California. Moderate growth to 15-35 ft. with a spread of 7-15 ft. Leaves are as glossy as the hollyleaf cherry but larger to 2½-5 in. long, and entire rather than toothed. Flower spikes are longer to 2-5 in. and the fruit is usually black.

Both of the native cherries are tolerant of almost any soil condition. Prefer sun but tolerate some shade. Catalina cherry is easier to train as a tree; hollyleaf cherry will take any amount of pruning and clipping, and is easily held to a 4-ft. hedge. Best when used as an informal screen. Both are slow to get under way and need summer watering attention until established.

PSEUDOTSUGA TAXIFOLIA. (*P. douglasii*, *P. mucronata*). DOUGLAS FIR. Conifer. Range: Widespread forest tree; moist mountain slopes, California north to British Columbia, east to the Rocky Mountains. Handsome, pyramidal tree to 70-250 ft. in the forest. Dense, soft, fluffy foliage, the dark green, or sometimes bluish-green, ½-1½ in. needles spreading all around the branch. Reddish-brown, long-oval, 3-in. cones with obvious, 3-pronged bracts.

Sometimes referred to as the old-fashioned Christmas tree in contrast to the currently popular silver fir, the Douglas fir is adaptable to any soil except low, undrained swamplands. Not a happy tree in hot-summer, mild winter lowlands. It withstands wind well and considerable shade. Where adapted, its large size and wide spread make it space demanding. A beautiful sight, particularly in the spring when covered with apple-green tassels of new foliage. Can be used as a windbreak or as a soft-textured screen.

QUERCUS. OAK. Evergreen and deciduous. Whether you drive in the hills or through the valleys, particularly in California, you will see native oaks. Many home owners inherit one or two with their lot. Few gardeners plant them because they consider them slow-growing but actually when given the proper care their growth is moderately rapid.

Q. agrifolia. COAST LIVE OAK. Evergreen. Range: Common in Southern California, and throughout the Coast Range of California. Round headed, wide spreading tree to 20-70 ft. with smooth dark gray bark. Dense foliage of roundish holly-like deep green glossy 1-2 in. leaves.

Q. chrysolepis. CANYON LIVE OAK, GOLDEN CUP OAK, MAUL OAK. Evergreen. Range: Mountain slopes and canyons almost throughout California, to southern Oregon. Handsome round headed or somewhat spreading tree to 20-60 ft., with smooth whitish bark. Ovate 1-2 in. leaves are shiny medium green above, lead color or whitish beneath, the margins entire or toothed. Cups of the acorns, covered with golden fuzz, look like turbans.

Q. lobata. VALLEY OAK, CALIFORNIA WHITE OAK. Deciduous. Range: Rich soils, interior valleys, Sierra foothills and Coast Range away from the coast in California. Graceful trees to 40-125 ft. with round topped broad crown and spreading branches ending in long drooping branchlets which sometimes sweep the ground. Thick ashy gray checkered bark. Deeply lobed 3-4 in. leaves are deep green above, paler beneath.

Q. garryana. OREGON WHITE OAK. Deciduous. Range: British Columbia south to the Santa Cruz Mountains, California. Grows to 25-55 ft. with rounded crown. Bark whitish, scaly-checked. Leaves are lobed and resemble *Q. lobata* but they are more leathery, darker green and glossy above, rusty or white hairy beneath. Does not have the drooping habit of *Q. lobata*.

Q. kelloggii. CALIFORNIA BLACK OAK. Deciduous. Mountains of southwestern Oregon, California Coast Range, Sierra Nevada and Southern California. Grows to 30-80 ft., with dark, furrowed and checked bark. Handsome foliage: Unfolding new leaves are dusty rose in hue, becoming bright glossy green, and turn golden-orange in fall. Leaves, deeply lobed, the lobes ending in bristle-points, are 4-10 in. long, 2½-6 in. wide.

Watch that you do not create unnatural conditions or your oak will decline and ultimately die. Excessive irrigation, burial of the root area and trunk base with soil or paving over the root zone reduces the amount of air available to the roots thus decreasing normal activity and growth. Heavy nitrogen fertilization, severe pruning, or defoliation by insects promotes new growth which is subject to fungus attack. Any fertilization or pruning should be light and done in the late summer.

REDWOOD. See SEQUOIA

RIBES. CURRANTS, GOOSEBERRIES. Deciduous and evergreen. Have found secure place in Western gardens. Those without spines are known as currants, the ones with spines as gooseberries. Certain species of currant are host to the white pine blister rust and should not be planted where this disease can injure pines.

R. sanguineum. PINK WINTER CURRANT, BLOOD CURRANT. Deciduous. Range: California, San Luis Obispo Co.; north to British Columbia. Grows 4-12 ft. depending upon soil and exposure. Attractive 2½ in. maple-like leaves, March-June, deep pink to red flowers in great profusion, 10-15, sometimes 30 in 2-4 in. clusters. Berries blue-black, covered with whitish bloom. Var. *glutinosum*. PINK FLOWERING CURRANT. The more southern form has 15-40 deep or pale pink flowers in spreading or nodding clusters.

Hard to find more spectacular deciduous pink and red flowering shrubs.

R. viburnifolium. EVERGREEN CURRANT. Evergreen. Range: California, Santa Catalina Island; mainland, Lower California. Spreading, half trailing, rooting along the wine-red stems; dark green, glossy, 1-in. round leaves; flowers light pink to rose colored, February-April; berry red. Growth habit calls for ground cover use. Sun or half shade along the coast, part shade inland.

R. speciosum. FUCHSIA-FLOWERING GOOSEBERRY. Nearly evergreen. Range: California coast, Santa Clara Co., south to San Diego Co. Shrub 3-10 ft.; stems with stout spines, and also often bristly; green, thick 1-in. leaves resembling those of the gooseberry; deep crimson flowers, fuchsia-like, drooping, the stamens long, protruding, January-May; berry densely gummy, bristly. Use in barrier plantings.

RHAMNUS. Evergreen and deciduous.

R. californica. CALIFORNIA COFFEEBERRY. Evergreen. Range: Common, southern Oregon; California. Coast Ranges, Southern California mts.; east to Arizona. Clean shrub 4-6, or 10 ft.; leaves oblong, 1-3 in.; dark green above, paler beneath; berries green, then red, finally black when ripe. Partial shade. Extremely variable species. Size and texture of leaves seem to be related to situations in which the plant grows.

R. c. tomentella. CHAPARRAL COFFEEBERRY. Evergreen. Range: Interior chaparral areas throughout California. Leaves usually gray-green above, velvety-white and hairy, or silvery beneath. Fine soft gray for good contrast. Can stand more sun and heat than the species.

R. purshiana. CASCARA SAGRADA. Deciduous. Range: Northern California; north to British Columbia; east to Idaho. Large shrub, or small tree 6-30 ft.; leaves large, rather thin, deep green often bronzy, 2-8 in., good yellow color in fall; berries black.

R. crocea ilicifolia. HOLLYLEAF COFFEEBERRY, HOLLYLEAF REDBERRY. Evergreen. Range: California, middle and inner Coast Ranges, Southern California; Sierra Nevada foothills. Large shrub, or often tree-like, 2-15 ft.; leaves round, usually spiny and holly-like, glossy dark green above, golden or brownish beneath, ½-1¼ in.; berries bright red. Attractive clean foliage shrub with ornamental berries.

RHODODENDRON OCCIDENTALE. (*Azalea occidentalis*). WESTERN AZALEA. Deciduous. Range: California; Santa Cruz Mts., north to Humboldt and Shasta Cos.; Sierra Nevada Mts.; mts. of Southern California; southern Oregon. Grows erect to 10 ft., with equal spread, but usually smaller; thin light green leaves. Delightfully fragrant, showy, funnel-shaped flowers arranged in rather loose, or sometimes compact, rounded clusters; color varies from white to pinkish, the upper petal with obvious splash of yellow; coastal forms tend toward pink, with rosy throat, and buds often deep rosy in color. Flowers May, June, and into July. In the wild state, often grows with evergreen huckleberry, a combination that couldn't be bettered in a garden. Huckleberry's slightly reddish new growth is a perfect foil for azalea's flowers; leaves mask the bare stems of azaleas after their autumn foliage has fallen.

RHUS. SUMAC. Evergreen and deciduous. Handsome foliage, easy culture and many uses have been universally accepted; no longer popularly regarded as natives.

R. glabra. SMOOTH SUMAC. Deciduous. Range: Eastern Oregon, Washington, north to British Columbia, and eastward. Tall graceful shrub to about 10 ft. Leaves divided into 11-23 lance-shaped toothed leaflets, deep green above, whitish beneath, turning scarlet in autumn. Small, greenish flowers in dense clusters, June-July, followed by bright red sticky fruits.

Likes sunny dry spots. Excellent bank cover. Popular in the Northwest for its wonderful blaze of fall color. Can be used for hardy garden fill-in. Combines well with such exotics as highbush cranberry and oakleaf hydrangea to make a striking autumn border.

R. integrifolia. LEMONADE BERRY. Evergreen. Range: California, generally coastal, Santa Barbara Co. south to San Diego Co.; Lower California. Shrub, 3-10 ft.; rarely, tree-like and up to 30 ft. Leathery leaves ovate or nearly round, dark green, 1-2½ in. White or pinkish flowers in dense clusters, February-March; sometimes January-July. Fruit flat, reddish and gummy.

R. ovata. SUGAR BUSH, SUGAR SUMAC. Evergreen. Range: California, away from immediate coast, Santa Barbara to San Diego; east to desert slopes Southern California mts.; Arizona; Lower California. Erect or spreading shrub 2½-10 ft., the leathery glossy leaves ovate to nearly round, 1½-3 in., commonly trough-like. White or pinkish flowers in dense clusters, March-May; reddish, velvety fruit coated with a sugary secretion.

Among finest as individuals or background plants, and in various combinations; attractive throughout year. Stand drought or garden conditions as in lawns. Like sun and poor, sandy or clay soils; tolerate wind and salt spray. Make good ground or bank cover if kept 3 to 4 ft. high. Adaptable to trimming; excellent dense foliaged hedges. Try espaliered against wall.

ROMNEYA COULTERI. MATILIJA POPPY. Semi-deciduous. Range: California coastal mountains, Santa Barbara Co., south to San Diego Co.; Mexico. Rapid growing, shrubby, almost ungainly, perennial 3-8 ft.; many gray-green foliaged stems from a woody base; crowned with soft, large 5-in., crepe-papery, snowy-white flowers with golden centers, May-August. Var. *trichocalyx* is considered a more desirable plant than the species. Slightly hardier, more compact; blooms a little earlier.

Plants slow to start from seed; even suckers cut from established plants slow to take hold. For best results, buy plants in gallon containers. Be careful where you plant this poppy; increases rapidly in size by sending out sturdy root suckers. For better appearance and flowers, cut back plants in fall to within few inches of ground. Larger plants can be divided and moved in early winter. Although they don't require much water, a deep watering every 10-15 days during the blooming season will prolong flower production.

Don't crowd with other plants or confine in narrow borders. Use on hot sunny hillsides, along drives and roads, where they thrive with little attention and spread naturally.

SALAL. See GAULTHERIA SHALLON

SALT BUSH. See ATRIPLEX LENTIFORMIS

SALVIA. SAGE. Evergreen or semi-deciduous. Aromatic, shrubby plants well adapted to hot, dry hillsides.

S. leucophylla. PURPLE SAGE. Semi-deciduous. Range: Coastal mountains of Southern California. Shrub to 2-6 ft. with many white stems, and gray foliage of crinkly, 1-3 in. leaves. Will drop leaves in dry season. Light purple, ½-in. flowers in 3 to 5, whorled clusters. May to June.

S. clevelandii. FRAGRANT SAGE. Range: San Diego County, California. Fast growth to 4 ft.; penetrating and persistent sage fragrance. Roundish, very gray, 1-in. leaves. Blue flowers usually in solitary heads surrounded by white-woolly bracts. May-August.

S. mellifera. BLACK SAGE. Range: South Coast Range and mountains of Southern California. Compact shrub to 2-5 ft., with crinkly, dark green, 1-3 in. leaves. Many pale blue or lilac, ½-in. flowers in compact, whorled clusters top the stems. April-June.

S. brandegei. ROLLEDLEAF SAGE. Range: Santa Rosa Island, California. Like *S. mellifera* but has narrower and shorter leaves.

Attractive in foliage and flower, heat and drought-resistant, the native sages serve well as bank covers and erosion-control plants.

SAMBUCUS. ELDERBERRY. Deciduous. Generally considered wild rampant shrubs. Good uses for elderberries in many Western gardens.

S. caerulea. (*S. glauca*). BLUE ELDERBERRY. Range: California north to British Columbia, east to Rocky Mts., Mexico. Shrub 4-10 ft., often becoming small tree up to 30 ft. Leaves 5-8 in., divided into 5-9 rather firm, toothed leaflets 1-6 in. long. Small white or creamy-white flowers in flat-topped clusters 2-8 in. broad, April-August, followed by clusters of blue to nearly black ¼-in. berries, usually covered with a whitish bloom.

Quite variable in size, shape and hairiness of leaflets. Some forms occurring at higher elevations in the mountains have foliage which feels velvety to the touch. Berries edible and often used in jams and jellies.

Although the blue elderberry is the more drought-resistant of the two species mentioned here, it needs water and partial shade in Utah and other sections with hot dry summers. Low berry production is often due to insufficient water.

S. racemosa. RED ELDERBERRY. Range: California mountains from 6,000 to 11,000 ft. elevation, north to British Columbia, east to Atlantic Coast. Europe. Bushy shrub 2-6 ft.; leaves 3-6 in., divided into 5 or 7 smooth, sharply toothed leaflets. Small creamy-white flowers in dome-shaped clusters to 2½ in. broad, May-July, followed by bright red berries.

S. r. callicarpa. COAST RED ELDERBERRY. Range: Along coast, northern California north to Washington. Large shrub 8 ft., or sometimes a small tree to 20 ft. Similar to the species but the leaves are hairy beneath and the flower clusters are broader—2-5 in.

Fruits of the red elderberries are reputed to be somewhat poisonous to humans. As these plants are not drought-resistant, they must have a moist location. High mountain form grows in full sun; coastal form should have partial shade.

All elderberries are fast growers. If cut or burned back to within a few feet of the ground, they will stump-sprout readily. To keep them from becoming dense and cluttered, thin out excess twiggy growth in fall.

Use elderberries in the same way as spiræa or other large deciduous shrubs. In large gardens, they make effective screens or windbreaks. To grow them as shrubs, prune drastically every year. You can combine them with spiræa, ninebark, carpenteria, and calycanthus. If you grow blue elderberry as a tree, underplant with heuchera, wild bleeding heart, oxalis, and other low-growing native plants that like filtered sun. Some gardeners think the blue elderberry the equal of a hydrangea in the garden.

SEQUOIA. Conifer. These two famous tourist trees of California have unusual values as garden subjects in many climates of the West.

S. sempervirens. COAST REDWOOD, REDWOOD. Range: from southern Curry County, Oregon, to Salmon Creek in southern Monterey County, California. The native range is not entirely what is thought of as a fog belt. Air temperatures range from 15°-100°; the annual rainfall from 20-80 in. It is not surprising, therefore, to find redwoods in Northwest, Southern California, and interior valley gardens.

Although the mature redwoods grow from 100-340 ft. high with trunks 3-16 ft. in diameter, the ultimate height of the cultivated tree is more nearly 50-60 ft. Under favorable conditions, a redwood will grow fast and high, with only a slight taper to the trunk, at the rate of 3-5 ft. a year. Under marginal conditions, growth will be slow—1-3 ft. a year, and the trunk will develop a sharp taper.

When there's space, a natural redwood grove is the logical planting but the trees can be topped to make a long-lived, beautiful hedge.

S. gigantea. BIG TREE, GIANT SEQUOIA. Range: west slope of the Sierra Nevada from Placer County to Tulare County, occurring in disconnected "groves," 32 in number. The century-old trees are from 100-325 ft. tall, with massive trunks 5-30 ft.

As a home garden tree it is a perfectly shaped, dense, pyramidal tree, of less rapid growth than the coast redwood. Also the big tree, with its dense gray-green foliage of awl-shaped leaves, looks quite different from the coast redwood with its dark green sprays of 2-ranked, needle-like leaves. Because the big tree holds its wide spreading lower branches through the many years of its youth, the big tree is too big for small gardens.

SPIRAEA DOUGLASII. WESTERN SPIRAEA, DOUGLAS SPIRAEA. Deciduous. Range: Mountains of northern California; north to British Columbia; east to the western Rocky Mts. Many ascending stems growing to 4-8 ft.; 1½-3 in. leaves are dark green, white-velvety beneath. Each stem is topped by dense steepled 8-in. clusters of small flowers soft pink to deep rose in July and August. Responds well to cultivation. Best when treated as herbaceous perennial, cutting flowering stems to the ground in the fall. Provides attractive contrast in form when planted with pink or blue hydrangeas; helps them carry the burden of midsummer color in gardens dependent on shrubs for flowers.

SUMAC. See RHUS
SYCAMORE. See PLATANUS
SYMPHORICARPOS. WAXBERRY, SNOWBERRY. Deciduous. Low shrubs often spreading by suckers, with small clusters of tiny pink, or white-tinged pink, bell-like flowers and attractive large waxy white berries which persist after leaf fall. Hard to control because of suckers.

S. albus. COMMON SNOWBERRY. Range: California mts., usually below 2,000 ft. elev., north to British Columbia, east to New England states. Erect or spreading shrub 2-6 ft., with roundish dull green leaves, ¾-2 in. (on sterile shoots in shade to 4 in.), entire margined or often lobed on the same branch; flowering May-June.

Use as shade plants in wild garden or wooded area. Somewhat brushy; must be pruned back to keep it from becoming leggy. As light filter or underbrush, berries are rather showy in deep green Northwest fir groves or with dogwood and madrone. For red and white combination, try with red-berried huckleberry. Because of suckering habit, useful for holding soil on steep banks.

S. mollis. CREEPING SNOWBERRY, SPREADING SNOWBERRY. Range: California, north to British Columbia. Similar to *S. albus*, but usually less than 18 in. high; leaves smaller, usually velvety-hairy; flowering April-June.

Good woodland ground cover if you don't mind the lack of leaves in winter; waxy white berries cheerful.

TANBARK OAK. See LITHOCARPUS DENSIFLORA

THUJA PLICATA. GIANT ARBORVITAE. WESTERN RED CEDAR. Conifer. Range: Coastal northern California, Oregon north to Alaska, inland to Montana. Large pyramidal tree 80-190 ft., with slender drooping branchlets. Tiny closely set scale-like leaves form flat graceful lacy sprays. Has small ½-in. cinnamon-brown cones.

Often used as a lawn tree or a giant hedge. Too shallow rooted for a windbreak.

TORREYA CALIFORNICA. (*Tumion californica*). CALIFORNIA NUTMEG. Conifer. Range: California, scattered localities, Santa Cruz Mts.; North Coast Ranges; Sierra Nevada Mts. Tree with wide, open pyramidal crown, becoming dome-like with age; 15-50 ft. high, trunk 1-3 ft. in diam.; branches horizontal, slender, somewhat drooping at the tips; flat leaves rigid, sharp-pointed, 1¼-2½ in. long, dark glossy green above, yellowish-green beneath, in flat sprays; fruit plum-like, pale yellowish-green with irregular dull purple areas or streaks; seed inside resembling the nutmeg of commerce.

TOYON. See HETEROMELES ARBUTIFOLIA

TSUGA. HEMLOCK. Conifer. Two species are native to the West, 1 coastal and 1 in the high mountains.

T. heterophylla. WESTERN HEMLOCK. Range: Along the coast from Alaska to northern California, inland to southern British Columbia, northern Idaho and Montana, and into the Cascades in Oregon and Washington. Handsome tree with narrow, pyramidal crown growing to 125-160 ft. in its native range. Drooping branchlets and fine-textured, deep green to yellowish-green foliage give the tree an almost fern-like appearance. Short needles in flat sprays. Small, 1-in. cones droop gracefully from the ends of the branches.

T. mertensiana. MOUNTAIN HEMLOCK. Range: Pacific coast mountains of Alaska, south through the high Sierra Nevada of California and to northern Idaho and Montana. Grows to 50-90 ft. Less fern-like in texture than Western hemlock; foliage blue-green, the needles spreading all around the stem, giving the branches a rather plump appearance. Cones are 1½-3 in. long.

Best for large gardens. Make beautiful hedges and screens when closely planted. Can be clipped or allowed to grow naturally. Both remain a good shade of green throughout the year, especially when they receive some watering in dry seasons.

UMBELLULARIA CALIFORNICA. CALIFORNIA LAUREL. CALIFORNIA BAY. OREGON MYRTLE. Evergreen. Range: Southwestern Oregon and California from sea-level to 4,000-ft. elevation. Commonly a tree to 20-75 ft.; in gardens usually a large shrub. If allowed to grow naturally it makes a symmetrical mound of deep green, 20-25 ft. high and equally as broad. Lustrous, deep green, 3-5 in. leaves are aromatic when crushed. Small, yellowish flowers in clusters in early summer, followed by plum-like, 1-in. fruits, which are greenish to purplish.

Shade tolerant. Provides a good evergreen background where something larger than a shrub is required. The dried leaves are used as seasoning in foods.

VACCINIUM. Evergreen and deciduous. Excellent ornamental shrubs with waxy bell-like flowers and colorful edible fruits.

V. ovatum. EVERGREEN HUCKLEBERRY. Evergreen. Range: California, Coast Ranges, Santa Barbara Co., north to British Columbia. Erect shrub 2-8 ft.; leathery, dark green, lustrous leaves ovate, ½-1¼ in., with toothed margins, the new spring foliage bronzy; flowers white or pinkish, April-May; berries black, with a whitish bloom.

Foliage assumes aristocratic character when displayed in appropriate setting. Acid loving and grows best in partial shade. Good foreground plant for rhododendrons. It may take a year to establish; once established will grow slowly to a height of 2 or 3 ft. in sun, 8 to 10 ft. in shaded woodlands.

Plant in a shrub border or as drifts on a slope. Makes a neat trimmed hedge which can be kept low, the bronzy new foliage colorful in spring. Try it in a rustic redwood container on patio or terrace. Grows naturally with redwood, salal, and Monterey or Bishop pines. Popular for cut greens.

V. parvifolium. RED HUCKLEBERRY. Deciduous. Range: California, scattered localities in Sierra Nevada Mts., north Coast Ranges, north to Alaska. Grows 4-12 ft., rarely to 18 ft., with green angled branches. Thin, oval entire margined leaves ½-¾ in., light green turning color in fall. Flowers greenish or whitish, May-June; berries clear bright red.

WASHINGTONIA FILIFERA. CALIFORNIA FAN PALM. Range: Borders of California-Arizona desert south to Mexico. To 30-60 ft. or more, the long trunk topped by a globe-like crown of leaves. Each leaf is 3-5 ft. wide, and divided into a large number of folded segments that have noticeable, thread-like fibers along the edges. Flat, woody leaf stalks 3 ft. long, with sharp hooks along the edges. As the trees grow taller and new leaves form, the old leaves bend downward and become dry. Result is a skirt of old leaves completely enclosing the trunk. May extend to the ground if not trimmed. Dense clusters of small, white flowers appear in May and June, are not showy.

Drought-tolerant. Freezes easily. Trim old leaves as they are apt to be a fire hazard. Fibrous roots sometimes break the sidewalks.

Fan palm is a familiar sight almost throughout California, where it has been planted as a street tree or singly in lawns and parks.

ZAUSCHNERIA. Evergreen. Low, prostrate perennials sometimes becoming small, sprawling shrubs.

Z. californica. CALIFORNIA FUCHSIA. Range: Coast Ranges of California. Grows to ½-2½ ft. with 2-ft. spread. Gray-green, ½-in. leaves and masses of scarlet, fuchsia-like flowers in August and September.

Z. latifolia. Range: Coastal mountains of southern Oregon, mountains of northern California, Sierra Nevada, and mountains of Southern California. Differs from *Z. californica* in its larger leaves and slightly shorter flowers. Var. *etteri*, the commonly planted form, is very prostrate and has handsome, silvery-gray foliage.

Sun. Remarkably drought-resistant and will spread even in hard-baked soils. Pinch back to prevent irregular growth and to encourage branching and bloom. Will reseed itself.

Very colorful plants for dry rock gardens, banks, or spilling over dry walls.

Western Specialties
PINES

The West is pine country. Of the some 100 pine species in the world there are 20 native to the Pacific West and another 20 to nearby Mexico. Some 30 species of pine are available in Western nurseries. Because of the wide variation in growth habit, some one pine can be a good solution to almost any garden problem.

For example, most gardens throughout the West know the extremely useful Mugho pine. It's a tub plant in one garden, the key figure in a garden picture in another. California gardeners know the Monterey pine as a screen and hedge plant and as a countryside forest cover. All gardeners have seen the pines in native stands and judged them for their garden value.

But not until you have seen some of the forest pines in their youthful stages—a 10-25 year period—can you know how interesting and useful pines can be.

In the following brief tree profiles we have compared youth and age for all the pines sold by Western nurserymen. You'll discover some ugly duckling stories, straight and in reverse, in these comparisons.

We have tagged each name of a species with the letter (H) or (W). The pines of the world divide themselves into *"hard"* and *"white"* in several ways. The difference is greater than the difference between azaleas and rhododendrons. In intergrafting it is simple to make a union between *hard* and *hard*, or *white* and *white*, but almost all attempts at intergrafting between *hard* and *white* have failed.

You can see in the tree profiles that most of the *hard* species have very similar characteristics. They are the rugged characters, the coarser, more picturesque to some. The *white* pines are more symmetrical and more graceful, with a few exceptions. The *hard* pines are more often good container plants, slower of growth, more likely to assume a "mature" look when young.

PRUNING

Many young gangly pines can be made full and bushy by the simple process of shearing or topping them—as you would a hedge—into the shape you want. Many growers of pines for Christmas trees follow this method.

— Encyclopedia —

ALEPPO PINE. *P. halepensis.* (H). Zones 7-13.
Mature tree: Open round-topped head, with short branches. Grows to 30-60 ft. high. Some call it odd looking, slovenly, and untidy; some call it picturesque.

Foxtail pine

Bristlecone pine

ALL OF THESE PINES ARE 10 YEARS OLD

Scotch pine

Himalayan pine

Canary Island pine

Jeffrey pine

Youngster: Slow to start, it reaches a rather sparse-foliaged, spindly 8 ft. in 10 years. Its great virtue is its ability to thrive in arid conditions.

AUSTRIAN PINE. BLACK PINE. *P. nigra.* (H). All zones.

Mature tree: Slow growing, sometimes spreading as wide as high. May reach 75 ft. but generally less than 40. Dark green, coarse foliage. Rather uniform crown. A good, steady, sturdy tree.

Youngster: A 3-ft., spindly sapling at 5 years; reaches 7 ft. at 10 years but isn't much of a pine then.

COULTER PINE. *P. coulteri.* (H). Zones 7-13. Not hardy below 10°.

Mature tree: Moderate to fast growth to 30-80 ft. Has rather shapely, open growth with lower branches spreading widely. Somewhat coarse for the small garden; use for erosion control or screens where branching to the ground would be an advantage.

Youngster: Not attractive in early youth. Coarse foliage. Grows about 1 ft. a year from seed. After 10 to 12 years becomes more symmetrical.

BISHOP PINE. *P. muricata.* (H). Zones 7-13.

Mature tree: Fast growing to 40-75 ft. with dense, rounded, shapely crown. Makes a sturdy, beautiful windbreak on California's Mendocino coast.

Youngster: Early growth habits are about the same as for Monterey pine: 4 ft. in 5 years, 8 ft. in 10 years, 15 ft. in 15 years. Use for windbreaks, reforestation, in a country place, or shape single tree to suit your fancy.

BRISTLECONE PINE. *P. aristata.* (W). Hardy all zones.

Mature tree: Growth habit varying by exposure. At its best, 20-60 ft. with short, stout branches. Very slow growing; long lived.

Youngster: From seed to 1 ft. in 5 years; reaches 3 ft. in 10 years. Very beautiful, symmetrical, narrow-crowned tree. Has that mature, pine-tree look right from the first year.

CANARY ISLAND PINE. *P. canariensis.* (H). Zones 7-13. The most tender pine; damaged at 15-18°.

Mature tree: Fast growing, pyramidal and upright to 60-80 ft. Foliage blue-green in youth, darker green when older; denser than that of Monterey pine. As it naturally clears itself of its lower branches, can be used as shade tree over lawns.

Youngster: At 5 years it's a 4 ft., sparsely branched tree; doubles its height in the next 5 years to become a beautiful, graceful, long-needled pine. The hardy substitute for the Canary Island pine for Northwest plantings would be Ponderosa pine.

CLUSTER PINE. FRENCH TURPENTINE PINE. *P. pinaster.* (H). Zone 13.

Mature tree: Grows to 40-100 ft.; pyramidal, spreading, dense growth. Used to reclaim sand dunes in southern France and in San Francisco's Golden Gate Park. Stands sandy soils and salt spray where few other trees will grow.

Youngster: Reaches 7 ft. in 10 years from seed. Coarse foliage, not attractive in youth. Once under way it grows rapidly, adding 10 in. a year.

DIGGER PINE. *P. sabiniana.* (H). Zones 7-13.

Mature tree: Strange tree of the dry California foothills; food tree of the Digger Indians. Grows to 40-50 ft. with main trunk divided into secondary trunks. Open crown, sparse foliage of long, gray-green needles gives the tree a see-through quality.

Youngster: Starts life as a spindly seedling; at 5 years reaches 3 ft. with only a few branches. In the next 5 years it develops into a very beautiful, 8-10 ft., slender tree with gray, lacy foliage; deserves more attention.

FOXTAIL PINE. *P. balfouriana.* (W). Hardy all zones.

Mature tree: To 20-50 ft., with spreading, stout lower

Japanese black pine

Single leaf pine

Limber pine

ALL OF THESE PINES ARE 10 YEARS OLD

Lodgepole, shore pines

Jelecote pine

Monterey pine

branches and irregular upper branches. Needles in tufts at ends of twigs suggesting foxtails.

Youngster: Has the same good looks and rate of growth as the bristlecone pine, but differs in that it needs partial shade for the first 5 years. In a few years, becomes closely conical and symmetrical. Needles glossy green.

HIMALAYAN PINE. *P. excelsa. (P. nepalensis).* (W). All zones.

Mature tree: Slow growing to 60-100 ft., has a broad and open pyramidal form. Wide-spreading branches carry long, drooping, blue-green needles in clusters; very attractive, white pine.

Youngster: From seed to 5 years grows only 1-2 ft. high; at 10 years is 3-6 ft. and has gained some of the attraction of an older tree.

ITALIAN STONE PINE. *P. pinea.* (H). Zones 7-13.

Mature tree: Reaches 40-80 ft.; has thick trunk with a high canopy of many branches. Fits well in a Mediterranean type setting.

Youngster: A spindly, 4-ft. tree at 5 years; a not very attractive 5-7 ft. tree at 10 years, but beauty becomes evident with age. Becomes too large for small garden. Tolerant of heat and drought but will not suffer if generously watered.

JAPANESE BLACK PINE. *P. thunbergii.* (H). All zones.

There is little botanical difference between this pine and the Austrian pine. Has fewer, larger cone scales in comparison with *P. nigra.*

In cultivation it is slower growing than Austrian pine; reaches 4 ft. in 10 years. Much used by Japanese in dwarf-tree training.

JAPANESE RED PINE. *P. densiflora.* (H). All zones.

Mature tree: Similar in appearance to Scotch pine and can be used in the same way. A good subject for dwarfing; has a tendency to form 2 or more trunks at ground level. Reddish bark.

JEFFREY PINE. *P. jeffreyi.* (H). Hardy all zones but is high-altitude pine that doesn't seem to like warmer lowlands or any situation where watering is frequent.

Mature tree: Similar to Ponderosa pine, but is slower in growth and more bluish in foliage. Jeffrey pine is not a garden tree. Best use would be in groves in a country woodland.

Youngster: Reaches 3 ft. in 5 years; 7-8 ft. in 10 years. Not attractive as tub or container plant.

JELECOTE PINE. *P. patula.* (H). Zones 7-13. May be damaged at 18°.

Mature tree: Unusual and graceful pine, growing to 40-80 ft. Fairly regular in shape but not as compact as many other pines; has a lacy appearance and allows a good deal of light to filter through.

Youngster: One of fastest growing pines in the world; will reach 10-12 ft. in 10 years from seed. Beautiful, non-symmetrical tree with yellow-green, silky needles. A pleasant pine to have around in large garden.

KNOBCONE PINE. *P. attenuata.* (H). All zones.

Mature tree: To 30-80 ft. Twisted trunk, disorderly branches, rough, coarse effect.

Youngster: Reaches a spindly, 6 ft. in 5 years; 10-ft. tree at 10 years. Should not be planted for decorative purposes unless you carefully pick your tree. Valuable for planting on dry slopes, in unfavorable soils.

LODGEPOLE PINE. *P. murrayana (P. contorta latifolia),* and **SHORE PINE,** *P. contorta.* (H). Hardy all zones, but not at home in dry areas. The common name of lodgepole pine has been applied to both of these pines and many assume their slight differences in appearance are due to environment. Actually, they are different trees. The tree available through nurseries is generally shore pine.

Mature tree: Contorted specimens get that way from coastal winds. In protected open stands it's a thin barked, slender tree with a pyramidal crown.

Youngster: Is attractive as a 2-ft., dark green seedling. At 10 years of age, 8-10 ft. tree, very symmetrical, narrow-crowned, becoming more attractive every year. Will stand dwarfing well. A very desirable tree, the best for the small garden.

LIMBER PINE. *P. flexilis.* (W). All zones.

Mature tree: Slow growth to 20-30 ft. Thick trunk, open round top, many limber branches. Handsome tree at any age.

Youngster: A 5-year-old is 1 ft. high; a 10-year-old is 5 ft. In youth it's more stiffly horizontal in appearance.

MONTEREY PINE. *P. radiata.* (H). Zones 7-13.

Mature tree: One of the fastest growing pines, to 60-100 ft. Will develop its own individual shape according to severity and direction of wind. Normally a shapely pyramidal tree when young but develops a round, flattish crown as it gets older. Foliage dark green.

Youngster: Although slender and spindly in its first years, it becomes a well-branched tree in 6-7 years. As 10-year-old (5 years after being replanted from a nursery container), may reach 15 ft. Excellent for windbreaks, screens, large hedges, small forests, or country places.

MUGHO PINE. *P. mugo mughus.* (H). Hardy all zones.

One of the favorite and most planted pines. From infancy on, Mugho pine is always a shrubby, symmetrical little pine that usually grows no higher than 4 ft., although it may become very spreading. Has good, dark green foliage. If you want to keep it really small, pinch back the new, soft green shoots about an inch in spring. One of the best pines for containers.

PONDEROSA PINE. *P. ponderosa.* (H). Hardy all zones but not for interior valleys or desert.

Mature tree: The all important, Western lumber tree. Recognized from a speeding automobile by its plates or alligator-hide bark. (These plates do not develop until tree is 80 years old.) A stately tree with loosely arranged branches and long, tufty, deep yellow-green needles.

Youngster: In its first 5 years from seed, reaches 3 ft. In the next 5 years in California, grows 1 ft. a year; in the Northwest, up to 30 in. a year. Increases in beauty every year. Has a straight trunk and coarse branches. Excellent choice for country places where ground not too dry.

SANTA CRUZ ISLAND PINE. *P. remorata.* (H). Zones 7-13.

Similar in growth habit to the Bishop pine, but because it's a much smaller tree, can serve as a substitute for either Bishop or Monterey pine. Branches very brittle.

SCOTCH PINE. *P. sylvestris.* (H). All zones.

Mature tree: Native to Europe and eastward to western Asia, Scotch pine is most ancient of pines. Many varieties and many forms available through selection. May be any height from 20-120 ft. Branches spreading and drooping, creating an irregular, round top in maturity. Bark on older trees has an attractive orange cast.

Youngster: An attractive small tree throughout its first 10 years, when it reaches a height of 4 ft. At this stage of growth it resembles the Mugho pine.

SINGLE LEAF PINE. *P. monophylla.* (W). All zones.

Mature tree: In the eastern Sierra Nevada and San Bernardino mountains it is a small, round-headed tree to 10-25 ft. Has short trunk that is rarely straight, often divided. Seeds sold as pine nuts.

Youngster: Very slow growing to slender, 2-ft. seedling in 5 years; a 5-ft., symmetrical, narrow-crowned tree in 15 years.

Similar in performance (under cultivation) are the nut pine *(P. edulis)* and four leaf pine *(P. parryana).* Both lack the narrow crown of the single leaf pine and are more irregular in growth habit. Both look like dwarf pine trees. They should be used in containers.

SUGAR PINE. *P. lambertiana.* (W). Hardy all zones, but temperamental; difficult to grow.

Mature tree: The world's tallest pine, mature trees growing to 200 ft. or more.

Youngster: Slow growing from seed, amounts to nothing first 5 years; then adds 1 ft. a year to become an 8-10 ft., very symmetrical tree at 10 years. Dark green foliage and whorls of uniform branches. Beauty increases with age and at 25-30 ft. it is a very desirable specimen tree.

TABLE MOUNTAIN PINE. *P. pungens.* (H). All zones.

Mature tree: A scrub pine.

Youngster: Slow growing to 3-5 ft. in 10 years from seed. Attractive in a large container. Will create a heavy, dense screen.

TORREY PINE. *P. torreyana.* (H). Zones 7-13.

Mature tree: Gets an irregular, picturesque habit of growth in the ocean winds on California's south coast near San Diego and Del Mar.

Youngster: Grows rapidly from seed to produce a rank, open-foliaged, 8-ft. tree in 5 years. At 10 years grows to 16 ft. or higher; a curio, with awkward branches and sparse, gray-green foliage.

WESTERN WHITE PINE. *P. monticola.* (W). All zones.

In cultivation, has much the same character as a diminutive sugar pine. Foliage is blue-green; growth slow and uniform. Difficult to grow but worth the effort.

Western Specialties
BAMBOO

Although bamboo is not native to the West, some 70 species and varieties of these woody grasses have been grown here.

Bamboos are divided into two types by their method of growth:

Clump bamboos. This type remains confined to a limited area. The underground stem or rhizome has little or no horizontal growth. Though the clump expands its radius of growth, it does so slowly and more in proportion to the expansion of a tree trunk than to other bamboos. In general the clump types tend to be less hardy than the running type.

Running bamboos. The rhizome runs horizontally underground for varying distances before giving rise to a new culm or vertical stem. This type will in time produce extended thickets and, depending on the species, could cover acres of land if not controlled.

In size and habit, the bamboos present a tremendous range. The smallest, *Sasa pygmæa*, is only 10 inches tall, with culms the diameter of a match stick and closely enough spaced to serve well as a ground cover. From this dwarf bamboo, they range up to 50 and 80 feet tall, and up to 4 inches in diameter (giant timber bamboo) and to 8 inches in diameter (Moso bamboo).

CULTURE AND USE

The following chart summarizes some of the uses by types. Note that the range in uses is even greater than range in size.

The fact that the giant timber bamboos will form a grove with culms wide enough apart to serve as a sheltered playground for children is a surprise to those who picture bamboo always in dense thickets.

Also surprising to many is the growth habit of the hedge bamboos. These clump bamboos are easily contained and respond very well to trimming and clipping.

Many of the bamboos are made to order for sun control of the glass-walled house. (See chart.)

Here are a few guides for selecting, planting, and culture of bamboos:

A newly propagated bamboo requires 2 or 3 years before it shows its characteristic growth habit. For example, the giant timber bamboo may remain a 6-8 ft. shoot for a year or more while a mature specimen will push up new culms at the rate of several feet each day.

The rule of never buying a pot-bound plant may be disregarded in selecting bamboo. The more crowded it is in the container, the more rapid the growth when planted out.

The characteristics of certain bamboos are intensified by root confinement in containers. The Fernleaf variety of *Bambusa multiplex* will show a reduction in leaf size and an increase in number of leaves when the plants are confined in pots. Likewise, the shortened and curiously enlarged internodes of the culms and branches of buddha's belly bamboo are intensified through pot or tub culture.

Running and clump types grow equally well when roots are confined. The spreading habit of the running type can be controlled by planter boxes of redwood or cedar, either above ground or at soil level.

Plantings in larger areas can be confined by thin underground walls of 18 in. wide strips of galvanized gutter sheeting or poured concrete to depth of 3 ft. below grade.

Newly planted bamboos, like any other plant, need a good soaking at least once a week until they are established. They are really not the moisture lovers for which they have the reputation, but will tolerate much water if soil is well-drained.

Planting from containers may be done at any time of the year. Plantings of rhizomes and plant divisions are most successful when made in early fall or spring.

Bamboo may be pruned or thinned to any particular liking. Runners and new shoots are easily removed in the young, rapid-growing stage. Keep older culms cut out from the base in order to eliminate unsightly dead culms and to prevent a dense tangled mass from forming.

Hardiness of each species is noted in the chart. But many gardeners who grow bamboo in containers need pay no attention to the frost tolerance ratings and can grow even the most tender black bamboo as a perennial, protecting the roots in winter.

Because almost all bamboos constantly drop a few leaves, plant them where the accumulating mulch can add to the general atmosphere of the garden, or else be prepared to rake leaves regularly. Incidentally, there's nothing better than bamboo leaf mulch for preventing weed growth. The decaying leaves definitely inhibit most herbaceous growth but have no bad effect on shrubs or trees after the formation of brown bark. Bamboo leaves have been used successfully as a mulch in rose gardens.

Most bamboos shed too many leaves and sheaths to be anything but a nuisance at the edge of pools. The least troublesome for that purpose are *Pseudosasa japonica* and *Sasa palmata*.

In the chart that follows we have held, with two exceptions, to the bamboos that are available. However, availability is not general, and considerable searching will be necessary before you find some of the types.

SELECTED BAMBOOS FOR WESTERN GARDENS

Species	Growth Type Height	Approx. Hardiness	Description	Use and Comments
Bambusa multiplex HEDGE BAMBOO	Clump 15-35'	16°	Entire plant green throughout. Many branches at nodes. Considerable branching develops successively within a year from crowded basal nodes of earlier branches.	Use in hedges, screens, and as tubbed specimens. Responds well to trimming.
Bambusa multiplex Alphonse Karr GOLDEN STRIPED HEDGE BAMBOO	Clump 10-35'	20°	New culms and branches bright pinkish-yellow changing to golden yellow with longitudinal green stripes of differing widths irregularly spaced on internodes. Fresh culm sheaths yellowish with green stripes.	Use in hedges, screens, and as tubbed specimens.
Bambusa multiplex Stripestem Fernleaf STRIPESTEM FERNLEAF BAMBOO	Clump 6-9'	20°	Slender, yellowish culms with irregular green stripes on internodes. Foliage may be fern-like with many (10-20) small leaves on a twig. The "Fernleaf" character is intensified by pot-bound conditions and through underfeeding.	Masses of small foliage, when planted in a dense hedge, form a perfect screen. Can be clipped as low hedge. Improved by dwarfing in pots.
B. multiplex Chinese Goddess CHINESE GODDESS BAMBOO	Clump 4-6'	20°	Extremely open, arching habit. Similar to *B. m. Fernleaf*. Much finer in scale, more delicate and lacy in effect.	Particularly good in pots and boxes for silhouette and pattern effects.
Bambusa textilis TEXTILE BAMBOO	Clump 40'	17°	Culms very erect and straight with nodding tips. Free of branches to a greater proportional height than any other bamboos.	A tall, narrow accent of very neat appearing, trim lines. Culms are thin-walled and are used for weaving mats, hats, window shades, and baskets. A new import from China now being grown in test plots and botanical institutions in the West.

SELECTED BAMBOOS FOR WESTERN GARDENS

Species	Growth Type Height	Approx. Hardiness	Description	Use and Comments
Bambusa tuldoides PUNTING POLE BAMBOO	Clump 20-50'	20°	Noticeable ascending curve in basal portion of culm. Nodes very inconspicuous.	For tall accents and screen plantings. The long, slender, thick-walled culms make useful poles. An important economic bamboo of southern China.
Bambusa ventricosa BUDDAH'S BELLY BAMBOO	Clump 40'	20°	Internodes of some culms and many branches are shortened and curiously enlarged, giving rise to the name "Buddah's Belly Bambo."	The curious culm character makes it an interesting subject for tub culture. Although grown in several bamboo collections, it is not in nursery trade as yet.
Phyllostachys aurea GOLDEN BAMBOO	Running 15'	20°	Some culms show a shortening and irregular distortion of lower internodes. No two ever seem to produce the same effect.	Use as screen plantings near windows and keep thinned. Serves well in planters, as a potted subject, and for erosion control. One of the most widely grown of running bamboos. Drought-resistant where established.
Phyllostachys aureosulcata YELLOW GROOVE BAMBOO	Running 30'	15°	Culms in first year show a yellow, grooved area at internodes that fades out as they get older. Culms feel rough when fingers are moved upward over surface.	Use as a screen planting along walls or fences. Those interested in growing their own fishing poles will find this species an excellent source.
Phyllostachys bambusoides GIANT TIMBER BAMBOO	Running to 50'	15°	Culms are large, up to 4 in. in diameter. Leaves slightly wavy.	Use as screen and background where space is ample to hold its size gracefully. This species produces good timber because of large size and durability of culms.
Phyllostachys nigra BLACK BAMBOO	Running 10-20'	28°	Culms gradually turn black.	Use in screen plantings near windows; in pots and planters. Grows best in partial shade on sheltered south and west side of house. A somewhat more hardy form, **P. nigra punctata** shows some yellow spotting on otherwise brownish-black culm.
Phyllostachys sulphurea SULFUR BAMBOO	Running 25'	5°	Clear sulfur-yellow culms, except for 1 or 2 slender, green stripes on rounded part of internodes and irregular green ring immediately below node.	Attractive for screen planting. The yellow culms add much to beauty of this species. Not often seen in Western gardens but deserves wide use because of its color and hardiness.
Pseudosasa japonica METAKE	Running 6-10'	7°	Dark green leaves. Culms have a single, long, upright branch growing from each of a number of upper nodes.	Comparatively clean, it's a good choice for tubs and pots on terrace or at edge of pools. Although a running type, it spreads relatively slowly. Very drought-resistant and tolerates most any situation.
Sasa humilis LOW BAMBOO	Clump 3-4'	20°	Similar to **S. pygmaea** but much taller.	Deep ground cover, low hedge, pot or box subject.
Sasa palmata PALMATE BAMBOO	Running 5'	5°	Very large leaves seem to spread out on ends of branches as extended fingers.	Excellent where a natural, trim neatness is required. For pool edges, borders, and for pot culture. One of the hardiest bamboos.
Sasa pygmaea DWARF BAMBOO	Running 10"	20°	One of the smallest of all bamboos, very free running.	Use as ground cover or in border if confined by curbs and walls. Seems to do best in filtered shade where sun is hot.
Sinocalamus beecheyanus BEECHEY BAMBOO	Clump 35'	20°	Robust culms frequently elliptical in cross section and forming an open clump.	Use as a broadly spreading accent where there's space and background for its 35 ft. A source of edible shoots in southern China and around Canton.
Sinocalamus oldhami GIANT BAMBOO (Commonly known in the trade as **Dendrocalamus latifolius**.)	Clump 50'	20°	Culms, 2½-3 in. in diameter, form dense clumps, erect with dark green foliage to base of plant.	Tall accent as single specimens, or for tall, dense, background screens. One of the best and most commonly grown large clump bamboos. Quite drought-resistant when established.

Western Specialties

PALMS

Palms are available for many uses: Tall ones to march down a long driveway into country places; to make a grove around a swimming pool; to complete a tropical planting; for indoor planters; for protected patios. The following list classifies all palms and palm-like plants available at Western nurseries by size, growth habit, and climate adaptability.

Palms with feather-type leaves:

Archontophoenix cunninghamiana. (*Loroma amethystina*). KING PALM. (28°) Occasionally bears name of *Seaforthia elegans* or *Ptychosperma elegans*. Moderate growth to 30-50 ft. with 10-15 ft. spread. One of the most beautiful and majestic palms for relatively frost-free areas. Clean habit, narrow stature.

A. alexandrae. Similar to above except for enlargement of trunk toward base.

Arecastrum romanzoffianum. (*Cocos plumosa*—nurseries still sell it under this name). QUEEN PALM. (18°). Moderate growth to 35-50 ft. with 10-15 ft. spread. Graceful, narrow crown of arching leaves, 8-15 ft. long, with distinct bend of leaflets near midway point. Most commonly seen where palms are grown but seldom at its best because few gardeners give it enough water.

Butia capitata. (sold in the trade as *Cocos australis* or *Arecastrum australe*). PINDO PALM. (18°). Slow to 10-20 ft. with 10-15 ft. spread. Normally arching gray-green leaves form neat head ½-⅔ of its height. One of the most rugged and versatile palms. Tolerates abundant heat and dry situations.

Caryota mitis. (*C. sobolifera*). TUFTED FISH TAIL PALM. (32°). Slow to 25 ft. with 18-ft. spread. Multiple ringed trunks. Indoors only. Dislikes dry wind and cold.

C. urens. WINE PALM. Single trunk. Dark green, 12-20 ft. leaves.

Chamaedorea elegans. (also listed as *Neanthe bella*). (28°). Slow to 2-8 ft. with 7-ft. spread. Single stems. Dark green leaves to 3 ft., with 30-40 segments. Indoors or outside with some shade. Will stand neglect.

C. graminifolia. (30°). Slow to 5 by 5 ft. Delicate, graceful, open habit. Ideal tub or planter palm.

C. tepejilote. (30°). Moderate growth to 10 ft. with 8-ft. spread. Ringed single trunk with swollen joints. Graceful and strong in pattern. Indoors or outside.

C. wendlandiana. (30°). Same growth habits as *C. tepejilote* except its 4-ft. long, strong, ascending leaves have more and narrower segments.

Chrysalidocarpus lutescens. (*Areca lutescens*). MADAGASCAR PALM. (32°). Slow to 10-25 ft. with 20-ft. spread. Many erect stems forming a clump. Leaves with 40-60 pairs of segments. Indoors, except in summer.

Howea belmoreana. (*Kentia belmoreana*). (28°). Very slow to 30 ft. with 15-ft. spread. Slender trunk with strongly arching dark green fronds to 6-7 ft. Formal looking. Indoors-outdoors. Part shade.

H. forsteriana. (*Kentia forsteriana*). PARADISE PALM. (28°). Upright to horizontal dark green fronds. Tolerant of poor soil, shade, drafty areaways. Burns in strong sun. One of the finest pot subjects.

Jubaea spectabilis. (*J. chilensis*). CHILEAN WINE PALM. (25°). Slow to 60 ft. Massive, thick trunked; feather duster head. Not ornamental until mature. Collector's item.

Phoenix canariensis. CANARY ISLAND DATE PALM. (18°). To 60 ft. with 30-50 ft. spread. An enormous palm for large properties only.

P. dactylifera. DATE PALM. (22°). To 75 ft. Desert heat is required to ripen dates but the palm grows throughout California where winter temperatures are above 22°. Worthwhile.

P. reclinata. SENEGAL DATE PALM. (24°). To 15-25 ft. Leaning or reclining trunks. Resembles tender coconut palm of tropical islands.

P. roebelenii. PIGMY DATE PALM. (30°). Slow to 4-8 ft. with 3-6 ft. spread. Dainty, graceful, with short slender trunk. Lacy, arching fronds. Valuable tub plant for patio in summer, indoors in winter.

P. rupicola. DROOPING PALM. (20-24°). To 15-20 ft. and as wide. Better suited to home garden use than its sister *P. canariensis*. Scarce.

Ptychosperma elegans. (*Seaforthia elegans*). (28°). To 20 ft. Slender, single trunk, relatively few bright green leaves, with 20 or more pairs of segments. Very scarce.

Palms with fan-type leaves:

Chamaerops humilis. (24-26°). To 10-20 ft. with 25-ft. spread. Several rather stalky, up-curving trunks from common base. Closely related to windmill palm. Thrives under lawn conditions. Accepts large containers. Popular in southwest.

Erythea armata. (*Glaucothea armata*). MEXICAN BLUE PALM. (20°). Slow to 15-30 ft. with 10-12 ft. spread. Compact crown of silvery-blue, erect, stiff, fan leaves. Long, graceful, creamy flower sprays arise from center of crown and sweep to the ground. Recommended for relatively dry, hot places.

E. edulis. GUADELUPE PALM. (16°). Differs from Mexican blue palm in its light green leaves and less conspicuous flowers. Large clusters of blue-black fruit. Stands intense summer sun. Probably most tolerant of winter cold of any palm.

Livistona australis. FOUNTAIN PALM. (20°). Moderate to 30-60 ft. One of the most graceful of fan palms. Best in mild, humid situation.

L. chinensis. CHINESE FAN PALM. (25°). Moderate to 20-30 ft. Eventually develops stout trunk but appears stemless for years and can be used as large-leafed ground cover under other palms. Good in pots. Burns in the hot sun.

Raphis excelsa. (*R. flabelliformis*). LADY PALM, BAMBOO PALM. (25°). Slow to 5-12 ft. with 3-7 ft. spread. Shrubby clumps of straight bamboo-like stems that bear a fibrous network of leaf sheaths. Good in tubs indoors and out. Prefers partial shade and lots of water.

R. humilis. RATTAN PALM. (25°). Slow to 18 ft. Taller, more slender stems than *R. excelsa*. Very effective used against walls.

Trachycarpus fortunei. *(T. excelsus. Chamærops excelsa).* WINDMILL PALM. (18°). Slow to moderate growth to 15-30 ft. Neat and compact. Matting of dense fibrous "hair" covers trunk which is smaller at the base than higher up. Widely adaptable. Stands wind.

Washingtonia filifera. CALIFORNIA FAN PALM. (See chapter on natives.)

W. robusta. MEXICAN FAN PALM. To 60-80 ft. with 10-15 ft. spread. Old leaves form uneven shag petticoat on trunk, or are sometimes lacking. Larger gardens, streets, avenues.

Palm-like plants:

Cordyline australis. *(Dracæna australis).* (15°). To 20-30 ft. Small tree, ultimately branching. Stiff sword-like leaves to 3 ft. Fragrant, white, yucca-like flowers.

C. banksii. (24°). To 8 ft. with 6-ft. spread. Sword-shaped 3-5 ft. leaves, 2½ in. wide. Difficult to grow and generally short lived.

C. indivisa. *(Dracæna indivisa).* (26°). To 25 ft. with 15-ft. spread. 6 ft. long, 6 in. wide leaves. Only for the warmest areas.

C. stricta. *(C. congesta).* (26°). To 15 ft. with 10-ft. spread. Branches when mature, but may be kept narrow and upright. Good indoors and out. Give part or complete shade.

Dracaena draco. DRAGON TREE. (25°). Slow to 20 ft. with 20-ft. spread. Stout-trunked tree of strong structural value, with rounded or flat crown.

Western Specialties
SUCCULENTS

Succulents are in a class by themselves, more like miscellaneous objects of art than the usual garden plants. Most of them are easy to grow, and you can use them with an abandon that is seldom appropriate with other garden subjects.

Because most succulents are natives of warm areas with little rainfall, they have thick fleshy leaves, stems, or roots that actually act as water reservoirs. This water storage adaptation has resulted in a group of tough, drought-resistant, sun loving plants of almost every conceivable shape and texture.

Unlike most other plants, they do not blend into frothy masses of greenery. Some resemble carved pieces of white granite or brightly colored coral. Others look like perfectly formed flower blossoms made of green wax, or covered with spun glass.

You'll be happy to discover the living arrangements that you can produce with succulents. Indoors, you can arrange a small dish of them as a miniature tropical jungle for a child's room, or as a center-piece for a dining table. Outside, plant them in boxes or raised planters; let them spill out of crevices in rock walls or hug stones and driftwood within a rock garden; or use them as marble-like silhouettes against a wall or beside an entrance.

Succulents' major requirement is good drain-

SEMPERVIVUM   GRAPTOPETALUM

age. Water that is allowed to stand in planting soil often causes the roots and lower stems to rot. Because of the tremendous number of succulent plants, and because of differences in their individual requirements, it is almost impossible to give a hard and fast rule regarding the amount of water they need. Generally, though, water them once a week if soil is light and porous, and every two weeks if soil is heavy and retains moisture.

Don't worry about soil—most any type will do, so long as water drains from it well. However, if you have heavy, poorly drained soil, work coarse sand and screened leaf mold into the beds. To keep down weeds, and prevent the earth from hardening or forming a crust, put gravel on the soil surface.

For pot and dish planting, use a soil mixture containing equal parts of coarse sand, screened leaf mold, and light garden soil. To insure good drainage, place a layer of gravel in the bottom of the container. If the container doesn't have drain holes, you can keep the soil sweet by sprinkling a light layer (about ¼ inch) of crushed charcoal over the gravel before soil is added.

Succulents are found in the pineapple, lily, amaryllis, agave, carpetweed, stonecrop, spurge, cactus, milkweed, and sunflower families. Here is

SEDUM   ECHEVERIA

328 SUCCULENTS Western Specialties

a list of some of those most commonly grown in the West:

Aeonium. Stems bear rosettes of leaves at top. Much-branched *A. arboreum* grows to 3 ft. Spoon-shaped green leaves with fine hairs on edges. Yellow flowers in dense, erect, conical cluster. *A. canariense* is one of largest aeoniums. Short, thick stems terminate in rosette, often exceeding 20 in. diameter, of spoon-shaped, velvety leaves. White or yellow flowers.

Agave. The best known representative of the agave family, the century plant *(A. americana)*, is too large for the ordinary garden and the spines on the leaf margins are wicked. Yellowish green flowers produced on stalks up to 40 ft. high when the plant is 10 years old or more; suckers arise from the base after flowering as the plant dies. A lower growing agave, *A. attenuata*, grows to 5 ft. Its leaves are unarmed to 2½ ft. long and 10 in. wide. Flowers are greenish yellow in spikes to 10 ft.

Aloe. Members of the lily family. Of the nearly 200 species of aloe, the most commonly known and cultivated is *A. arborescens*. From a rosette of pointed 2-ft. leaves arise 6-to-10-ft. stems carrying dense narrow clusters of brilliant orange-red flowers in winter. *A. aristata*, a dwarf species excellent for pot planting, has myriad, 3-4 inch leaves no thicker or wider than shoestrings. *A. variegata* has strong design quality, a foot-high triangular rosette of erect triangular leaves. Because leaves are a rich dark green heavily marbled and margined with white, the plant is popularly called the partridge-breast or tiger aloe. Scarlet flowers on 10-inch stems.

Carpobrotus. Members of the ice plant family. (See page 214 of the chapter on ground covers.)

Ceropegia. Related to stapelia. Range from vines to shrubby forms. *C. woodii* is a popular trailing vine with variegated heart-shaped leaves and curious purple balloon-like flowers.

Cotyledon. Large, bell-shaped, pendant flowers in loose clusters. *C. orbiculata* grows to 3 ft. Oval-shaped leaves are pale gray to whitish, with reddish edges. Red flowers in summer.

Crassula. A very large family from South Africa. *C. arborescens* grows to 6 ft., has rounded oval leaves to 3 in. long. Clusters of rose red flowers. *C. argentea* reaches 9 ft.; oval leaves are dark green, with some red edging. Pink flowers January to April. *C. falcata* grows to 3 ft., has scythe-shaped gray-green leaves, scarlet blooms in September.

Echeveria. Handsome plants, with leaves sometimes forming spiral rosettes. Smooth species like sun; hairy forms like some shade. *E. derenbergii* forms tiny, smooth rosettes, the leaves tipped red; flowers reddish yellow. *E. elegans* has small white rosettes, pinkish flowers in spring. *E. pulverulenta (Dudleya pulverulenta)* has rosettes on short stems, red flowers. *E. pulvinata* has soft green plush leaves margined red, blooms with large crimson bells in midwinter. *E. setosa* is a very pretty plant, with numerous thick green leaves covered with short white hairs; yellow-tipped red flowers.

Euphorbia. A very large group of succulents; most contain a thick white milky juice called latex. Flowers usually small, not striking; flower bracts, however, are often very colorful. Seeds of some species explode from capsules when ripe, often scattering some distance. *E. splendens*, the "Crown of Thorns," comes in many forms; it is a very dense bush, to 3 ft. high. Stems have many spines, generally long and pointed. Flower bracts bright red.

Faucaria. Small rosettes with toothed leaves, often called tiger jaws, and large yellow blossoms in fall. A small species is *F. bosscheana*, with fleshy leaves bearing two or three large teeth on the edges toward the tip.

Graptopetalum. Leaves in rosettes on reclining stems. *G. paraguayense*, thick leaves, keel-shaped beneath, look as though they were sculptured from marble. Elegant in containers, at edge of walls over which it can trail.

Haworthia. Choice small rosettes, interestingly marked leaves. *H. fasciata*, an excellent pot plant, has white zebra stripes banding the fat, pointed leaves.

Kalanchoe. Very beautiful flowers. *K. beharensis* is woody plant, to 10 ft., arresting in form—rosettes of large arrow-shaped leaves, silvery beneath, hairy and rust colored above. Flowers woolly, yellowish green to white, violet inside. *K. blossfeldiana*, with its large clusters of fine red bloom, is generally treated as an annual because plants lose their beauty after flowering.

Kleinia. A member of the sunflower family. Fleshy stems and leaves. *K. repens* is a stiff plant with finger-like leaves colored a striking blue-green.

Lithops. Among the best known of the "pebble plants," natives of South Africa. Generally shaped like inverted cone; top is shaped like a stone with fissure across the center, from which comes flower and new growth. Best grown indoors. Must be rested from June to August. *L. bella* is brownish yellow, 1 inch in diameter, produces white flowers in early fall.

Mesembryanthemum. The ever popular trailing or low shrubby plants used throughout the Southwest as ground covers. Numerous varieties and colors. (See page 214 of chapter on ground covers.)

Pleiospilos. These gray-green split "rocks" so closely resemble the native stones among which they grow that they are difficult to find except when in flower. Need bright sunshine. Blooms are stemless or short-stalked, single or sometimes several, yellow or red. *P. nelii*, a great curiosity, is almost unbelievably rock-like in appearance; it has golden yellow flowers and is very easy to grow.

Portulacaria. One well known species of this succulent shrub is *P. afra*, which grows to 3 ft., with round fleshy leaves, clusters of small pink flowers.

Sedum. Excellent for rock planting, low edgings, and ground covers. *S. guatemalense* has procumbent stems, rooting at joints, carrying cylindrical dark green leaves, reddish on the upper one-third. Fine for containers, or as ground cover. *S. morganianum*, the donkey tail sedum, makes a wonderful hanging basket plant. (More species of sedum are described on pages 161 and 215.)

Sempervivum. Commonly called houseleek. Among the best known succulents. Easy to grow. Generally stemless rosettes. *S. arachnoideum* has tiny rosettes covered with white cobweb-like hairs. *S. calcareum* has blue-green, red-tipped leaves, pink flowers. *S. tectorum*, known as "hen-and-chickens," has hundreds of forms and hybrids, smooth leaves with reddish tip, pink to red flowers.

Senecio. Similar to kleinia, but leaves are in rosettes. *S. cinerascens (Kleinia tomentosa)* has stiff stems and leaves entirely covered with a snowy felt. *S. scaposus*, long cylindrical leaves covered with soft white felt, yellow flowers. *S. stapeliiformis*, fleshy angled stems, small rough leaves reminiscent of some stapelias.

Yucca. (See page 163 of the chapter on perennials.)

Western Specialties
MINIATURES

This short chapter is dedicated to these gardeners: Those who are interested in rock garden plants but have no rocks; those who would like to concentrate an acre of gardening in a 6-by-6-foot space; those who are attracted to beautiful little things. The miniature is not to be confused with the dwarf. The miniatures are small scale models of larger plants. You can arrange miniature trees, miniature shrublets and miniature flowers in a raised bed 4 by 4 feet square and duplicate a 40-by-40-foot normal garden.

These are but a few of the hundreds of miniature species and varieties in the plant world.

CONIFERS

CHAMAECYPARIS. Many dwarf forms are available. Here are two good ones:

C. pisifera pygmaea. (Sometimes sold as *C. pisifera squarrosa pygmœa*). Compact rounded dwarf, growing slowly to 15 in. high; lacy drooping sprays of grayish-green sharp pointed leaves.

C. obtusa nana. DWARF HINOKI CYPRESS. One of the slowest growing and most dwarf and compact conifers. Attractive, dark green foliage. Ultimate height 15 in.

CRYPTOMERIA JAPONICA NANA. Bushy dwarf, 1½ to 2 ft. high, 2½ ft. wide; twisted branches clothed with sharp, dark green, needle-like leaves, which are also twisted or curved. Likes a moderate climate, neither below zero in winter nor above 80° in summer.

JUNIPERUS. JUNIPER. Many are called dwarf which are low growing prostrate shrubs. A true dwarf is:

J. communis compressa. DWARF JUNIPER. Slender spire-like dwarf tree to 18 in., with 12-in. spread; branchlets have short, crowded, gray-green, awl-shaped, prickly leaves.

PICEA. SPRUCE. These dwarfs become very appealing pets. Greatest need is for a cool location:

P. abies procumbens. (*P. excelsa procumbens*). Very slow-growing, rounded plant, 1½ ft. high and 3 ft. wide; stiff branches radiate from the center; dark green foliage.

P. a. nidiformis. (*P. excelsa nidiformis*). Rounded compact form eventually to 2-2½ ft. high, 3½-4 ft. wide. Bright green shiny needles.

P. glauca conica. (*P. albertiana conica*). Slender, conical tree eventually reaching 3-3½ ft., with base spread of only 1 ft. Needs moist soil, part shade.

THUJA. ARBORVITAE. The following are very slow growing:

T. occidentalis globosa. TOM THUMB ARBORVITAE. A rounded shrub rarely more than 2-3 ft. high, and 2 ft. wide; bright green foliage.

T. orientalis nana. BERCKMANN'S ARBORVITAE. Globe-shaped, very compact formal dwarf to 3 ft. high, and 2 ft. wide; with bright golden foliage.

SHRUBLETS

BROOM. Includes **Cytisus** and **Genista**.

C. decumbens. PROSTRATE BROOM. Prostrate creeping plant to 8 in. high, with 20-24 in. spread; minute soft green leaves; yellow flowers in May and June.

Genista pilosa. Very slow growing, prostrate, to 1½ in. high, 8 in. wide, with intricately branched gray-green twigs; minute, round, hairy leaves; yellow flowers in short clusters in June and July.

G. sagittalis. Tangle-matted, prostrate to 2 in. high, 14 in. wide, with three-sided trailing branches; round, hairy, dark green leaves; flowers in June and July.

G. silvestris pungens. (*G. dalmatica, Cytisus dalmaticus*). Very spiny, gorse-like mound to 4 in. high, and 6 in. wide, with thin branches and tiny medium green leaves; golden-yellow flowers in terminal clusters, in June and July.

G. villarsii. Slow twiggy irregular growth to 1 in. high, 6 in. wide, with green or gray-green stems and very tiny leaves; small yellow flowers in June and July.

CARMICHAELIA ENYSII. Unusual leafless broom-like miniature growing slowly to 3-5 in. high, spreading to 4 in. Forms tangle of very flat pale green branches with small violet colored flowers in early summer. These interesting little wiry entanglements are best planted where they may be viewed closely. Can be grown in containers if drainage is provided. Prefers full sun; will tolerate some shade and may bear a few tiny leaves.

CHIOGENES HISPIDULA. CREEPING SNOWBERRY. Neat carpet-like leafy evergreen to 1½ in. high, with small round leaves to ½ in. long, the small bell-like flowers white or greenish-white in May and June followed by white berry-like fruits in August. Same requirements as heathers and azaleas. Resents being pushed around.

COTONEASTER TOM THUMB. Flat growing, slightly humpy, spreading to 8 in., in 3 yrs. Minute, ¼-in. leaves color even more brilliantly than the larger cotoneasters as winter nears; finally turn to yellow or red before they fall and expose the gracefully curved branches.

HEATHER. Includes **Calluna** and **Erica**.

Calluna vulgaris foxii nana. Moss-like heather 3-4 in. high, 12 in. wide; purple flowers in July.

Calluna vulgaris nana (*C. v. pygmœa*). Bright green rounded tufts to 4 in. high, 12 in. wide; clusters of lavender-pink flowers in August.

Erica vagans nana. To 6 in. high, 18 in. across; ivory-white flowers in August-September.

PIERIS NANA. (*Arcterica nana*). Evergreen miniature to 3 in., spreading to 6 in., forming a dense neat mat. Leaves are minute, elliptical, usually in whorls of 3, dark green and somewhat glossy turning slightly bronzy in winter. Clusters of white, bell-shaped, faintly vanilla-scented flowers, blooming in April. Choice plant for container planting in the patio or in rock garden where it may be viewed close-up and enjoyed throughout the year.

VACCINIUM VITIS-IDAEA. LINGONBERRY. Hardy evergreen, slowly growing to 1 ft. high, increasing and spreading by runners to 3 ft.; leaves dark green, lustrous above, paler beneath; nodding bell-shaped flowers white or pink, appearing in May, followed by edible red berries. Var. *minus*, MOUNTAIN CRANBERRY, is even more dwarfed

330 MINIATURES Western Specialties

than the species; leaves smaller, and the flowers rose-pink or reddish. Needs moist peaty soil, with lots of water. Takes sunny position if soil is kept moist.

PERENNIALS

AJUGA METALLICA CRISPA. (See chapter on ground covers). Smaller in all parts than common bugle flower ground cover. Crinkly-leafed with flowers in tiny blue spires just 2-3 in. high, like many-storied elfin towers. Adaptable to sun, shade, dry or moist soil.

ANDROSACE PRIMULOIDES. Series of soft rosettes that seem to be tied to each other by threadlike stems. Clusters of small pink flowers on 5-in. stems. Cool, perfectly drained limestone scree with underground irrigation suits this and other androsaces perfectly.

AQUILEGIA. COLUMBINE.

A. flabellata nana. DWARF FAN COLUMBINE. Grows to 6-8 in.; gray-blue foliage; sky blue flowers with white centers, the incurved spurs tend to emphasize its dwarf pudgy appearance. Var. *nana-alba* is perhaps better known than the blue form.

A. jonesii. JONES COLUMBINE. Stemless plant with tiny ½-in. blue or purple flowers with ⅓-in. spurs, on stems 2 in. high. Plant in partial shade in rich soil.

ARMERIA JUNIPERIFOLIA. (*A. cæspitosa*). Compact little cushions to 6 in. high; rather stiff sharp-pointed leaves; pink flowers in dense heads on inch-long stems in May and June. Excellent horticultural forms; white, clear pink, rose, red.

CAMPANULA. BELLFLOWER. Low growing alpine forms of the campanula offer small scale bells on low tufted mats in all the varieties of their taller relatives.

C. portenschlagiana (*C. muralis*) carries its violet blue, flared bells on deep green tufted mats 4-7 in. high.

C. elatines garganica (*C. garganica*) wears open stars of a much lighter violet on short stems above a tight mound.

C. carpatica, TUSSOCK BELLFLOWER, covers its compact leafy tussocks with white or lavender-blue, shallow-cupped, star-shaped flowers.

Will adapt to average soil conditions preferring, of course, well drained gritty soil. Will take sun and part shade. Blooming season is from late spring to early fall. All of the above thrive in confined quarters of rock wall or in containers. (See also chapter on perennials.)

DIANTHUS. PINK. Small forms of dianthus come in a wide assortment; small dense tufts of light green or gray-green foliage of very narrow leaves; spicily fragrant flowers in jewel-tone shades of white, rose, pink, and red, blooming from spring until fall.

D. neglectus. Example of most minute type. Green foliage forms grassy tuft only few inches in diameter. Single flowers of cherry rose with buff reverse, rise above the foliage, about 3 in., in May-June, sometimes in fall.

D. Little Joe is somewhat larger; silvery-gray tufts are compact 6 by 6 in. Flaming red single flowers will bloom from April to November if spent flowers are cut off.

D. Tiny Rubies. Tufts of gray foliage to 3 in., spreading to 4 in., with small double ruby-red sweet-scented flowers blooming in May-June.

All alpine dianthus are subject to stem rot in heavy soils; require poor, gritty soil. As plant spreads, in 2-3 years the old growth in the center of mat dies out. To keep fresh, use ⅓ of plant each year for new divisions.

DOUGLASIA VITALIANA. Gray-green tight little rosettes, 1 in. high, spreading 6 in. Tubular flowers of bright yellow in April-May. Seems to enjoy a cool spot on the north side of a rock. Soil should not be allowed to dry out.

DRABA OLYMPICA. Forms a mossy tuft 2-4 in. high and 4 in. wide. Golden-yellow flowers in compact clusters are carried just above the foliage. Spring-blooming. Will take the same treatment as dianthus.

DRYAS SUENDERMANNII. Diminutive member of the rose family. Forms a carpet by laying its branches along the ground and trimming them with tiny oak-like leaves. Nodding white single flowers in May-July are followed by unusual seeds with silver feathery tails which are actually more decorative than the flowers. Adaptable to average soils. Takes sun.

IBERIS SEMPERVIRENS. EVERGREEN CANDYTUFT. The cleanest, whitest of whites of spring. They are completely satisfactory as evergreens and as flowering plants. Of the dwarf varieties one of the choicest is *I. s. pygmæa* (*I. pygmæa*). It is semi-trailing, not over 1 in. high, spreading to 15 in. and more; flat heads of pure white flowers in early spring. These candytufts are not particular as to soil or treatment. (See also chapter on perennials.)

IRIS. Dwarf iris of the bearded type is a common sight in April; but not so well known are the dainty little species. These are representative and choice samples from a long list: *Iris cristata, I. lacustris,* and *I. gracilipes.*

Iris cristata becomes an unusual ground cover when planted beneath *Rhododendron molle.* White form equals the violet in beauty. Both are golden crested and grow 6 in. high. Plant in filtered shade.

GERANIUM.

Elf. Seldom more than a few inches high. Leaves dark gray-green with wide yellow border, zoned with irregular splashes of scarlet; small scarlet single flowers.

Fairyland. Very slow growing bush, never more than few inches high. Leaves dark grayish-green with a wide pale ivory border, zoned with irregular splashes of rose-red; single flowers of light scarlet.

Pigmy. Densely branched, spreading, seldom more than 6 in., miniature, light green, zoned leaves; profusion of red double flowers.

Ruffles. Slow growing bushlet never more than a few inches high; leaves dark olive-green to blackish-green with a darker zone; flowers semi-double, salmon.

Sprite. In several years will grow to 8-10 in.; leaves dark grayish-green with wide ivory-white border which in winter becomes coral colored; flowers single, salmon-coral.

PRIMULA in variety. There are several dwarf species in this group. Most of the *P. juliæ* hybrids are real miniatures and there are many named color varieties.

P. juliae and hybrids grow in low spreading mats to 4 in. high. Flowers ½ to 1 in. across are borne in stemless clusters. Colors are gay, intense, often with contrasting "eyes." Bloom March to April.

P. rosea grandiflora. One of the brightest flowered of the miniature primroses. Grows to 8 in. high. No hint of orange or yellow clouds its brilliant pink ¾-in. flowers. Seeds itself extravagantly when completely happy. Usually a moist spot with a bit of shade.

P. frondosa. Lovely dwarf, rosy-lavender flowers, 4 in. tall in early spring. (See also chapter on perennials.)

RAMONDA PYRENAICA. Flat rosettes of dark green, deeply toothed leaves and inch-wide clustered flowers, lilac-blue with a golden eye; in spring.

SAPONARIA OCYMOIDES. Trailing, not over 1 in. high with myriads of pink flowers in April-May.

Home Food Garden
VEGETABLES

The experts justify home vegetable gardening in terms of yields-per-square-foot, family food budgets, in vitamins and minerals—sound arguments all. Over and above this is the point they usually fail to mention, and which, to us, seems even more important: *Growing vegetables is fun.* Working with the good earth and extracting its bounty satisfies an instinct that goes back a long, long way. Beyond its economic and nutritional values, there's a rare vitamin in the home harvest that feeds the spirit of the gardener who hauls it to the kitchen.

Vegetables are exceedingly easy to grow, but if you are to get maximum results, you must understand one basic elemental fact: *The minute a vegetable plant stops growing, it's in trouble.* Unlike flowers, vegetables seldom fully recover if growth is checked. Keeping them growing fast, forcing them through to maturity, is the key to the full basket at harvest time.

A sharp cleavage in growing-heat requirements separates "warm-season" from "cool-season" vegetables and determines which of each are best adapted to your local climate. Therefore, temperature is the most important single consideration in deciding which vegetables you can grow well and what time of year you must plant them.

WARM-SEASON CROPS

The summer or warm-season vegetables require both soil warmth to germinate and long days and high temperatures (or short days and early heat), both day and night, to form and ripen fruit. In all except sweet potatoes, the *fruit* is the object of the harvest, rather than the *leaves, roots,* or *stems.*

The standard seed packet phrase, "sow when all danger of frost is past," only half explains the temperature factor. Two elements are involved. One is simple tenderness to frost and danger to young plants should a late frost occur. The other has nothing to do with frost. It is the basic need of warm-weather vegetables for *adequate growing heat* to keep them moving along without check and to ripen their crops. To cite an example: In some very cool coastal areas there are no frosts at all, yet many warm-weather crops simply cannot be grown because there just isn't enough available growing heat during the summer to mature them. In California's Imperial Valley, on the other hand, there are frosts, but soil heat is high enough in winter to support out-of-season agriculture.

Planting time for warm-weather vegetables depends, of course, on your climate, but it should always be not only "after danger of frost is past," but when the soil has lost its winter clamminess and begins to warm up.

Here are some common warm-season vegetables, arranged very roughly from lowest to highest in heat requirements: snap beans; summer squash; tomatoes; cucumbers; winter squash and pumpkins; corn; okra; cantaloupes; eggplant; peppers; lima beans; Crenshaw, casaba, and Persian melons; sweet potatoes; watermelons. Differences between adjacent crops are minor or nil, but the difference between the top and bottom of the list is very substantial.

Early varieties require less heat, late varieties more heat to mature. Number of days from seed to maturity, usually specified in the catalog or on the seed packet, is an important clue to the cool-climate gardener who wants to grow warm-season crops. Figures are based on ideal growing conditions. As available heat in his own garden falls below the ideal, the number of days required to mature the crop increases.

If there's more than enough total heat available, early varieties should be planted only at the very beginning of the season, so they're almost ready for harvest before really hot weather sets in.

COOL-SEASON CROPS

The cool-season vegetables make steady growth at average temperatures 10 or 15° below those necessary for warm-season crops—almost the difference between summer and winter in some Western areas. In addition, many of them—cabbage, for example—are frost hardy.

But the most obvious and important difference between warm and cool crops is this: we are able to grow and harvest winter vegetables during the cool months of the year mainly because we're not interested in the products of hot weather—their fruit or seeds. (Peas, the sole exception, are a fruiting crop with a definite temperature ceiling that limits them to the cool side of the calendar.)

The fleshy root of a carrot, for example, is only a by-product of its main function, which is, after exposure to coolness, to form flowers and seed in summer like other biennial plants. However, we harvest carrots and other root crops midway in their development. Likewise *leaves* of chard, lettuce, and cabbage; *stems* of rhubarb and asparagus, *immature flowers* of cauliflower, broccoli, and artichoke. In every case we harvest the plant before its main function in life is fulfilled.

332 VEGETABLES Home Food Garden

Aside from the perennial vegetables—artichokes, asparagus, and rhubarb, which are grown from divisions or crowns planted in midwinter or spring—success or failure with cool-weather vegetables depends to a large extent on how well you schedule plantings to bring them up to size in the kind of weather that makes for vegetative growth, rather than for flowering. In general, the object is to plant very early in spring so the crop matures before summer heat settles down, or in late summer so it comes in during the cool days of fall.

Local Climates and Cool Crops

The relationship between the local climate and the growing of cool-weather crops is crucial in very hot climates, where the narrow, cool segment of the year must be used to greatest advantage; in cooler climates the relationship is less crucial. In the Salinas "salad bowl," for example, head lettuce can be planted over a seven or eight-month period, since plants spend most of their growing time making leaves. In that cool area, lettuce heads well over a long season, though plantings that mature in a very hot spell are somewhat lower in quality. In the warm sections of the Southwest, on the other hand, hot weather from June on puts an end to leaf-making and throws plants into flower and seed production. In short, they "bolt." For this reason, head lettuce is usually grown as a fall crop—seeded in late summer for fall harvest, seeded in October for harvest in winter and early spring.

The cabbage schedule in the Sacramento Valley is a fairly standard pattern for growing cool-weather crops in "one-season" climates where winters are too sharp for fall planting. There, transplants are set out in January and February for spring harvest; later plantings are made in July for harvest in late fall. July heat is used to speed young plants on their way.

WHAT TO PLANT?

The seed catalog is a great tool for dreaming, but the experienced gardener puts a check rein on his imagination. Here are a few points to consider in deciding what to plant:

1. Choose vegetables you like

Select varieties that your family likes, especially kinds that are markedly better when harvested fresh from the garden. New peas and string beans, sweet corn, fresh green asparagus are all much tastier if the time from harvest to table is measured in hours instead of days. Vine-ripened tomatoes from the home garden are a new delight to one accustomed to the commercial green-picked product. It's much wiser to grow a few kinds of vegetables you're especially fond of than to develop a miniature Agricultural Experiment Station.

2. Consider maintenance time

Some vegetables are extremely easy to grow, others demand more care. If you like chard, for example, there is absolutely no excuse for not having it. It grows easily from seed, 4 plants take the space you would allow a rose bush, it looks good even in the ornamental part of the garden. Rhubarb and artichoke, both perennials, also have ornamental values, and will bear for several seasons from a single planting. Asparagus takes more space, but a single 50-foot row, planted only once, will give you something to look forward to every spring for 10 years or more, and maintenance is negligible.

3. Select varieties carefully

According to the catalog, they're all good, but they aren't—in all climates. *Improved Long Green* may be a top cucumber in one area and succumb to mildew in another where one of the mildew-resistant hybrids would thrive. Earliness or lateness can be important. Plant research is producing improved vegetable varieties each year, and you're missing a bet if you don't take advantage of it. Because the picture is constantly changing, we are not recommending varieties here, but your county agent or farm advisor can give you sound suggestions.

4. Use space well

Root crops and lettuce provide the biggest yields in the smallest space. Pole beans are worth the trouble: they produce far heavier crops per square foot than bush varieties. Staked tomatoes earn their keep more than sprawling plants; a few cucumbers trained upward—carefully tied with soft cloth strips to a fence—occupy only a fraction of the space they'd require on the ground.

5. Consider length of harvest period

Vegetables that can be harvested over a long period are better for home gardens than those that come in all at once, if you're going to eat them fresh. You can afford to plant a big carrot crop because you can harvest carrots for months. Turnips, on the other hand, get woody if left in the ground too long, and plantings should be smaller. In this respect, broccoli is better than cabbage. You can continue to harvest the small heads of sprouting broccoli for many weeks, while cabbage should be picked at maturity.

6. Plant for use

You'll make home vegetable gardening pay handsomely if you use *all* of the crop, instead of letting part of it die on the vine, tossing it on the compost heap, or giving it away. You'll only need a small plot to provide fresh produce through the summer. With a larger plot, you'd better have plans for the surplus.

PRE-PLANTING PRIMER: FOUR "MUSTS"

If you keep the basic requirements of all vegetables in mind—sun, water, and fertile soil—common sense will guide you in choosing the right spot for them and preparing it for planting. Consider these points:

1. Because vegetables need full sun, the plot should be far enough from trees or structures to avoid shade. Tree roots, too, compete with vegetables for water and nutrients. If one end of the plot gets more sun than the other, plant fruiting crops there, leaf and root crops where shade creeps in part of the day.

2. A level site is better than a sloping one, since water goes down into the soil instead of running off. If your garden is on a slope, you'll need contour furrows or, on steep slopes, terraces to hold water where it belongs.

3. Because vegetables are fast growing and hungry, they need nutrients in quantity. Root crops do best in light soil where tubers and roots can expand. Manure is still one of the best soil conditioners for vegetables. In many areas, it's possible to buy dairy manure at lower cost by the yard, apply a 4-inch layer on the soil in fall, and let winter rains work it in. By spading time in spring, texture is just right for planting. Or, you can work in manure at planting time, if it's well rotted. The perfect soil for vegetables is a loose, friable loam. Soil building techniques, discussed in detail in the chapter on soils, apply to vegetables as well as to ornamentals, but vegetables are, if anything, more demanding.

4. Soil should be thoroughly moist 2 or 3 feet down at planting time—not *after* you plant seed, but *before*. In dry areas this means diking up sections of the garden-to-be, raising 8-inch ridges in squares 6 feet or more each way, then flooding them, allowing water to sink down, and flooding again. Soil should then be allowed to dry slightly until it's workable, especially if it's high in clay. If it balls up when you squeeze a handful, it's too wet; if it crumbles, it's right. Water stored in the soil when you plant should be sufficient to germinate most kinds of seed—an important point, since sprinkling afterwards to make up for moisture deficiencies often washes out new seed or forms a hard crust over it.

PLANTING SYSTEMS

When your plot has been pre-soaked, spaded, and leveled, you're ready to plant. Here, briefly, are the principal ways of sowing. The basic thinking behind any planting pattern is to make it easy to get water into the root zone without waste and to make cultivation and weed control less work. The system that does these best for you is the one to use.

Flat Planting

Flat planting is perfectly sound practice unless flooding from rains is a hazard. Soil doesn't dry out as readily as it does under the double-row system. Low ridges are raised with the hoe before watering if you irrigate, but most home gardeners who plant on the flat use sprinklers.

Furrow Planting

The single row and furrow pattern is simply a 6-inch V-shaped ditch made with the hoe. Seed is

sown along one shoulder, just below the top. Virtually all crops, small or large, can be grown this way. As plants develop, furrows are moved outward so water reaches the ranging roots.

Double-Row Planting

Commercial truck farmers raise most small vegetables in double rows, planted a few inches from the furrow edge. While this is the classic system and makes irrigation and cultivation simplest for the commercial grower, it's hard to see its advantages

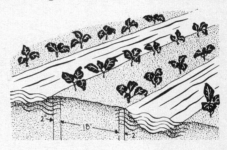

for the home gardener. Of course, high double-row planting makes for better drainage in areas where rains are heavy, and if your garden is very long and narrow, with different crops strung out like beads on a string, you can irrigate it very simply with the double row system. There are disadvantages, however. In light, sandy soils, furrows fill in after a couple of irrigations and water doesn't go where you want it to go. This means regular work with the hoe. In hot climates, plants set high dry out much faster than they would on the flat.

Hill Planting

Hill planting does not mean making mounds, but rather grouping seeds so 3 or 4 plants grow in a cluster a foot or more in diameter, either on the flat or along a furrow. The theory is that roots range out from a central point and get more foraging room in the soil. Big crops—squash, corn, and pole beans—are sometimes planted this way.

Mound Planting

Squash and melons require lots of water, yet often suffer if it covers their crowns, so they're usually grown like this. Corn and tomatoes, too, can be grown this way.

SOWING SEED

Standard practice is to plant seed at a depth equal to about 4 times its diameter. For small row crops like root vegetables and lettuce, an easy method is to take a board with regular edges—a 1 by 1 or 1 by 2—and make a drill on the prepared surface of the flat bed, shoulder of the furrow, or 2 inches from the edge of the double row bed, then drop seed into the drill, letting it trickle slowly from the paper packet. One seed per half inch of drill is enough, except for carrots. Carrots are slow and spotty in germinating, and it's best to be generous in sowing them to prevent gaps in the row. When plants are well on their way, of course, you'll thin seedlings for proper spacing.

Larger vegetables like the cole crops (cabbage family) can be sown an inch apart. They germinate very well, and, with all of them, seedlings take well to transplanting and can be used to fill in gaps in the row.

With beans, corn, squash, and other vining crops, use a trowel to plant seed about an inch deep. Again, to play safe, plant about double the quantity you need, then thin later to proper spacing.

After planting, soil should be well firmed over seed with the back of a rake or the sole of your shoe. This is important. Loose soil dries out quickly and dry soil means gaps in the row.

If weather turns unusually hot after planting in the spring, and in most planting in midsummer and fall, soil around seeds can get dangerously dry regardless of thorough pre-soaking. With small, shallow-planted seed especially, you'll have to take steps to conserve moisture. A light mulch of moist peat moss can make the difference between success and failure. Green lawn clippings, spread thin over the newly planted bed, work wonders with hard-to-germinate seed such as carrots. A newspaper or burlap cover works well, too. Inspect regularly, remove it when seedlings appear. Remember, too, that covers of any sort are havens for sowbugs, earwigs, and other pests that are as eager for seedlings to sprout as you are. Before putting the cover on, dust the row lightly with insecticide.

PLANTING TO HARVEST

Once seedlings appear, your job is to keep them moving fast.

Water regularly and deeply, soaking soil at least 2 feet down. In an average loam, it takes about an inch of overhead sprinkling to wet a foot of soil. You'll get a rough idea how deep water is penetrating by setting a can out in various areas covered by sprinklers.

Thin seedlings to proper distances when they are 2 or 3 inches high. For recommended spacings, see below.

Keep down weeds by hoeing regularly. Experienced home vegetable gardeners often use wheel hoes or power equipment. If so, they space crop rows to fit the equipment, making cultivation easy.

Fertilize. If your soil is fairly fertile to begin with, and if you've spaded in a generous dressing of manure, fertilizing should not be necessary, at least with the first crop. Commercial growers, however, have learned that fertilizing with side dressings of high-nitrogen inorganic materials like ammonium sulfate pays off in heavier yields, particularly in cole, leaf, and fruiting crops. These methods are followed depending on the soil's fertility. Bands of fertilizer, 2 inches below and 2 inches on either side of the seed row at planting; or in a shallow furrow a few inches from the row when the crop is about a third grown; or both.

VEGETABLES: CLASSES AND KINDS

Here is a brief survey of common garden vegetables by classes and kinds. Pests and diseases affecting vegetables are fully covered in an earlier chapter of this book. The *Sunset Vegetable Garden Book*, a companion volume, deals with vegetables in complete detail, including tested recipes for cooking and combining your garden favorites.

Perennials

Kinds: Artichoke, asparagus, rhubarb. All cool-season crops.

How planted: Suckers of artichoke, crowns of asparagus and crown divisions of rhubarb are planted in midwinter. Since they are perennials, special care should be given to enriching soil before planting. Artichoke suckers are planted about 6 inches deep, with tops above ground, rhubarb crowns set at about soil level, and asparagus spaced along a prepared trench (see below).

Spacing: Artichokes: plants 4 feet apart, rows 5 feet apart. Rhubarb: plant 3 feet apart, rows 4 feet apart. Asparagus: crowns 18 inches apart in the trench.

Comments: All three of these are "luxury" vegetables. They're perennial, which means one planting will bear for many years. Artichokes and rhubarb may be grown as part of the ornamental garden for decorative use as well as for the crop. A long, narrow strip at the back of a lot is worth planting to asparagus even if ordinary vegetable gardening doesn't appeal to you.

Root Crops

Kinds: Beets, carrots, onions, parsnips, white potatoes, sweet potatoes, radishes, rutabagas, turnips. All cool-season crops except sweet potatoes.

How planted: Radishes in rows 18 inches apart, plants thinned to 1-inch spacings. Beets, carrots, turnips in rows 2 feet apart, plants thinned to 2-inch spacings. Onions, parsnips, rutabagas in rows 2 feet apart, plants thinned to 3-inch spacings. White potatoes: make furrows 3 inches deep, put pieces of seed potato in bottom 12 inches apart, cover and firm. (Seed pieces should be allowed to heal for 2 days before planting.) Hill 3 more inches of soil over base of plants when two-thirds grown.

Sweet potatoes: Unlike others in group, this is a warm-season crop that demands high summer heat. Sprouts from roots are used, planted in rows 3 feet apart with 12-inch spacings.

Comments: Root vegetables, except potatoes, return highest poundage per square foot of all. Carrots are slow to germinate (see above), but are most practical because of long harvest season. Hold radish sowings to small quantities. They must be harvested and used promptly or they get punky and go to seed. Turnips and beets, too, don't keep long in the ground. Potatoes, white or sweet, are only for the gardener with unlimited space.

Cole Crops

Kinds: Broccoli, Brussels sprouts, cabbage, cauliflower, all cool-season crops.

How planted: Furrow planting best, with rows 3 feet apart. With all except broccoli, space plants 18 inches to 2 feet apart in row. Broccoli has been found to yield heavier crops per square foot when plants were spaced about 9 inches apart in row; however, wider spacing (15-18") may encourage more side shoots and a longer harvest. Cole vegetables transplant well. You can buy young plants if you don't wish to bother with seed, but seeding is almost foolproof.

Comments: Cole crops are heavy feeders, benefit from side dressings during growing season. Brussels sprouts are best held to areas near coast, demanding cool, humid climate. Best all-around member of cole group for home gardens is broccoli, with a long harvest period.

Leaf Crops

Kinds: Chard, endive, lettuce, spinach, all cool-season crops.

How planted: Chard in rows 30 inches apart, 12-inch spacing. Lettuce in rows 2 feet apart, 10-inch spacing. Spinach in rows 18 inches apart, 3-inch spacing.

Comments: Red-stemmed chard is stronger tasting, more decorative, and fits the flower border better than other chard. In warm climates, plant leaf lettuce rather than heading varieties if crop will mature in warm weather. Keep lettuce sowings small, make successive plantings to avoid waste. Spinach produces a year-around crop in cool coastal areas, but bolts in the heat.

Vine Crops

Kinds: Cantaloupes, cucumbers, late melons, pumpkins, squash, watermelons, all warm-season crops.

How planted: Furrows, hills. Cantaloupe, pumpkins, and winter squash in rows 6 feet apart, with 4 feet between hills containing 3 plants each. Cucumbers in rows 4 feet apart with 2 feet between hills of 3 plants each. Watermelons in rows 6 feet apart with 5 feet between hills of 3 plants each.

Comments: Cucumbers can be trained onto a fence or trellis, if you're careful in tying their brittle stems. In marginal heat areas, stick with cantaloupes. They require less heat to mature than other melons. Vine crops are very heavy feeders, benefit from one or even two side dressings of high-nitrogen fertilizer during growing season.

Beans and Peas

Kinds: String beans, lima beans, peas available in both bush and pole (climbing) types. Beans are a warm-season crop, peas a cool-season crop.

How planted: In furrows, with poles or trellises for climbing types. String and lima beans planted in rows 30 inches apart. Bush string beans spaced 3 inches apart in the row, bush limas 6 inches. Pole varieties in hills of 3 plants, 2 feet apart. Bush peas in rows 3 feet apart, climbing varieties 4 feet, plants 2 inches apart in the row in either case. Beans climb on single poles, strings or whatever you can invent. Peas require trellis, netting, or chicken wire.

Comments: Beans are among the best of all crops for the home garden. Pole varieties outproduce bush varieties by a considerable margin. Lima beans require a long, warm season with some humidity. Peas demand cool, humid weather: the fog belt is ideal. In marginal climates, try bush peas rather than climbing types, and plant them to mature during the cool half of the year.

Tomato, Eggplant, Pepper

Kinds: Variety is all important in tomatoes. Contact your nurseryman for recommendations. Tomatoes, eggplant, and pepper are all warm-season crops.

How planted: Furrow planting best, in rows 3 feet apart for eggplant, pepper, and early tomatoes, 4 feet apart for late tomatoes with plants 3 feet apart in the row. Unless you're going in for quantity, it's simplest to buy nursery transplants. Eggplant and pepper are self-supporting, tomatoes sprawl. You can let them sprawl, risk rotting and insect damage from fruit lying on ground; or you can stake them, pinching vine back to a single leader, tying it to the stake with soft cloth as it grows. Some gardeners devise frames to hold vines, others let vines come up through chicken wire, held off ground on a frame, and sprawl on top. In general, you'll harvest more perfect tomatoes if you devise a way to keep fruit off the ground. Caution: foliage is necessary to shade fruit, keep it from sunburning, so don't be too energetic in your pinching back.

Comments: Tomatoes are probably the number-one home garden vegetables. Night temperatures are all important to fruit set. Below 50°, nothing much happens; but fruits begin to form when night temperatures rise toward 60°. Fruit set can be increased with hormone sprays, available at nurseries. The experts recommend 2 side dressings of complete commercial fertilizer twice during the growing season.

Corn

How planted: Furrow planting best, in rows 3 feet apart with 15-inch spacing in the row. *Plant in blocks, not long lines,* to make pollination easy. As plants grow, pull furrows out so a wide area of the root zone gets water. Corn, of course, is a warm-season crop.

Comments: See discussion of early and late varieties above. Corn takes space, but it's worth it. Certain insecticides work wonders in control of its nemesis—corn ear worm (see control chart in pest and disease chapter).

Home Food Garden
SMALL FRUITS

What gardener has not imagined himself walking out in the garden before breakfast and filling a bowl with dew-laden red raspberries or plump melting strawberries? And how many forego that pleasure when they hear of the trials and tribulations between the roots of those plants at the nursery and the bowls of fruit?

How much space is needed for berries? Will they become a tangled mess? Isn't training and pruning too much of a job for the average gardener? Aren't most berries too much trouble for what you get out of them?

Berries are worth the effort if you:

1. Plant varieties that are suited to your climate and soil.
2. Provide space in the sun—you'll need at least the equivalent of an 8 by 20-foot bed.
3. Follow a few simple procedures.

To help you judge whether berries are for you, here are the essential statistics on each berry.

BLACKBERRIES

Although all of the following varieties are blackberries and receive the same gardening treatment, they are generally grouped in two classes:

Boysen, Logan, Young, and *Nectar* are generally regarded in the loganberry or boysenberry class; *Cory thornless, Cascade, Olallie, Himalaya* in the blackberry class.

1. Boysenberry class

Of all the types of bramble fruits, the Boysenberry (and its 3 similar relatives) is most adaptable as to climates and soils, most productive per square foot of garden space and the most variable in use—fresh, canned, frozen, pies, juice.

Boysen: Reddish, about 1¼ in. long, 1 in. thick. Carries a "dusty bloom"—not shiny.

Logan: Light reddish, about 1¼ in. long, ¾ in. thick. Smaller in diameter than Boysen. Lighter color when ripe. Fine hairs dull its color.

Young: Similar in shape to Boysen, but the berries are shiny. Bears 10 days earlier than Boysen, but not as heavily.

Nectar: In all respects similar to Boysen. Horticulturists claim that it is not a separate variety.

2. Blackberry Class

Cory Thornless: Round, jet black, very sweet, large berries. It leads in sales in California but is not recommended for the Northwest. The developers of Cascade and Olallie regard it as an inferior berry.

Cascade: A USDA-Oregon State College introduction. Anyone who has tasted the wild blackberries of western Washington and Oregon and north coastal California will rate this as best on all counts. The berry is shaped like the loganberry, but is ¾ its size. Ripens a very dark red, almost black, but cooks red. Seeds are much smaller than loganberry. Very juicy, very tender, and will not stand handling and shipping. It's not a commercial berry, but generally available at nurseries throughout the Pacific Coast.

Olallie: Another USDA-Oregon introduction. Seems slightly sweeter and less tart than Cascade. Now being widely planted commercially throughout California. This Oregon berry appears to be better adapted to California conditions than to its homeland. It's practically unknown in Washington. Roots are so soft, dormant nursery plants are difficult to keep in good condition for any length of time between digging and planting.

Thornless: Thornless blackberries, loganberries and youngberries have great sales appeal. However, there is no guarantee that the plants will continue to be thornless.

The thornless berry cane is a *chimera*—a sport or mutation that is capable of passing on either of two sets of hereditary factors. The outer skin of the shoots transmits the thornless characteristics; the inner cells carry the thorny characteristics. To many gardeners the advantage of thornlessness far outweighs the trouble of removing thorny canes that may appear occasionally.

Culture

SOIL: Blackberries cannot stand water-saturated or saline soils. They are naturally deep rooted. If the water table is high in the spring or if a hardpan holds water at less than 3 feet, you probably shouldn't plant blackberries.

PRUNING: You must renew blackberry growth 100 per cent each year. That's the basic principle of all methods of blackberry pruning and training. Here we describe three different pruning and training methods that follow that principle but differ according to plant spacing and the training device that you use.

If you want to grow your blackberries as unsupported bushes, tip new canes at a height of between 2 and 3 feet. Laterals will start growth immediately; head them back in early spring, leaving about a foot of growth which will be the bearing wood.

To fan the canes out and tie them to a trellis, allow the new shoots to reach 5 or 6 feet before heading. Head the laterals the same as in the first method.

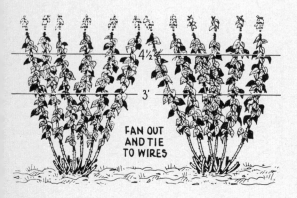

FAN OUT AND TIE TO WIRES

Home Food Garden SMALL FRUITS 337

As another possibility, you can use a trellis but not head the selected shoots. After post-harvest pruning of old canes, drape the new canes over or weave them through the wires of the trellis. The laterals may or may not be headed with this system.

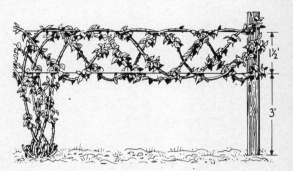

In California the long growing season encourages laterals of some newer varieties to develop side shoots, especially if the laterals are pinched or headed early in the season. In this case fruiting buds will be carried on these secondary shoots. Head back the secondary shoots and thin them out in winter or spring.

TRELLISES, TRAINING DEVICES: As you can see, a trellis or frame of some sort is essential if you want to keep your blackberries under control. You can train the canes on a fence, but unless the vines are on the south side of an east-west fence, the structure itself will cut out some necessary light and heat. Also, there may be neighbors on the other side of the fence to consider.

Commercial blackberry growers in the West generally use 12 or 13-gauge wire stretched between husky end posts (4 by 4-inch) with lighter supporting posts (2 by 2-inch) spaced along the wires between every second or third plant. Standard height—for ease of picking, pruning, and training—is 4½ feet to top wires and 3 feet or less to the lower wires.

The success of blackberry planting in home gardens is entirely dependent upon this rigid control. Once you let them take over a fence and go unpruned for a season you're lost and your neighbor is no longer a friend.

Keep space clear around the trellis and cut or pull up wide-spreading suckers as they appear.

WATER: Irrigate frequently when vines are in full leaf.

FERTILIZER: Although tests show that foliage growth is affected by applications of nitrogen only, home gardeners with average soils should use a mixed commercial fertilizer. One low in nitrogen and high in phosphorous will not cause overly vigorous growth of suckers. Best results from spring and summer feedings with commercial fertilizer will be had if a 2 inch mulch of manure is added previously—in February or March.

338 SMALL FRUITS Home Food Garden

Don't fertilize at planting time. Give light applications at time growth starts, in midspring for new canes, in midsummer for next year's buds.

WHERE TO PLANT: Cane berries need full sun in order to bear sweet berries to their full potential. Choose a spot that is in full sun at least from March to November.

HOW TO PLANT: Set plants 4-8 feet apart in a row. Three plants will give enough for canning, freezing, and fresh use.

INSECTS AND DISEASES: As far as home gardeners are concerned, the blackberry mite is the worst pest on these plants. This pest makes berries stay partly or wholly red, hard, and sour. The eggs begin to hatch in February and the mites enter the opening buds shortly thereafter. This is the best time to control them. Spray with lime-sulfur some time between late February and the end of March. Spray again in May.

Spray for red-spider—which mottles foliage—in late June.

BLUEBERRY

The commercial blueberries of the Pacific Coast are improved varieties of the highbush native blueberry of the Atlantic Coast.

Blueberries need an acid soil, moisture, and a moderately cool summer. Areas around Washington's Puget Sound are ideal, with their long spring and warm days of July and August.

The home gardener in zones 3-5 will have little trouble growing blueberries. If you have found it necessary to add peat moss or sawdust to the soil for rhododendrons or azaleas, you should do the same for blueberries. Treat them as the shallow rooted plants they are and give them a thick 4-6 inch mulch of peat moss or sawdust and keep the soil moist through the summer. Feed them with a complete commercial fertilizer in April and June, and again in July if needed. If sawdust mulch is used, increase quantity of fertilizer. The nitrogen in the fertilizer mix should be sulfate of ammonia because of its acid reaction.

Choice of variety will depend upon your taste and where you expect to plant it. Two varieties should be planted for better pollination. Varieties vary in growth habit and size. Most are upright growers to 6 feet and more; a few are rather sprawling and under 5 feet. If planted as a hedge they can be spaced 3 feet apart. In sizeable plantings they are spaced 4-5 feet apart in rows 6-8 feet apart.

Plants produce a few berries in their third year and increase production each year to their maximum yield at 8-10 years. A mature plant should yield more than 10 pints.

You can buy 1, 2, or 3-year-old plants.

Varieties rating high in flavor, ornamental value, fall coloring, and growth habit are:

Atlantic. Late season; sprawling habit. Light blue large berry, good fresh, canned, and frozen.

Stanley. Early mid-season; upright habit. Large berries at beginning of season, then smaller. Aromatic, spicy flavor. Adapted to all uses.

Concord. Midseason; large berry of rather tart flavor until fully ripe. Attractive growth habit, upright to spreading.

Weymouth. Earliest; large dark blue berries. Grows to about 5 ft. These varieties are widely grown.

Dixi. Largest of all berries. Large vigorous shrub of little landscape value.

Jersey. Late season; large berry of milder flavor, grows vigorously to become a large shrub.

Rancocas. Early midseason. Upright vigorous grower requiring careful pruning. Those who like mild, sweet berries call its flavor good; those who judge it against the spiciness of Stanley wonder why this old-timer stays in the bestseller list.

CURRANT

Growing currants is no trouble if your summer climate is cool and humid. The cool-summer areas of zone 1, 3-5, the cool valleys of 9, and zone 10 are currant climates. Depending on vigor and variety, the currant will grow to 3-5 feet and spread as wide. They do best in rather cool shady spots and will grow on the north side of a fence or under high-branching trees. *Red Lake,* a late variety, is the preferred California variety and is widely planted in the Northwest. *Perfection* and *Wilder* are good midseason varieties.

Currants bear fruit near the base of 1-year wood and on the spurs of older wood with the best fruit on 2- and 3-year wood. Aim your pruning so that at the end of the 3rd year you have 3-4 canes each of 1-year, 2-year, and 3-year wood. (See chapter on pruning.)

In some areas of the West it is illegal to plant currants or gooseberries as they might act as hosts for the white-pine blister rust. If your nurseryman doesn't know, check with your county agent.

GOOSEBERRIES

Gooseberries follow the same climate pattern as currants and need the same culture. *Oregon champion* is the preferred variety on the West Coast. *Poorman* is excellent and widely planted in zone 1. *Oregon Champion* is thornless and will grow to 3-5 feet depending on climate and treatment.

GRAPES

To grow grapes successfully in a California garden, you have to break a few orthodox planting rules and you need to know which varieties grow best in your climate. Many home gardeners mistakenly plant grape vines in the way that is recommended for trees, roses, and shrubs.

In planting grape vines, bury roots and stem below ground with only the top one or two inches of the stem above ground. Usually this calls for a hole about 16 inches deep. After filling the hole and tamping the soil firmly, mound two or three inches of loose soil over the top of the stub. Don't worry, the shoots will force their way out through the soil. Anyway, this mound settles slowly and soon sinks below the top of the vine.

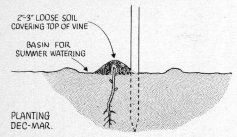

PLANTING DEC.-MAR.

To avoid planting failures, you must regard the whole vine as a root; don't let it dry out before or after planting.

Don't Shade the Grape

Don't expect a grape vine to be healthy or bear good fruit without a full quota of sunshine. In a small garden the vine should get a southern exposure. It is a good idea to train it against a wall or fence that will give it extra heat.

Do not plant near trees or buildings that will shade the vine—even partially—during the afternoon. Most vines in partially shaded locations will be miserable specimens because of the powdery, grayish mildew that will cover them and destroy flower clusters and developing fruit. Mildew is impossible to control in shady locations.

Pruning

Home vineyardists approach the job of pruning with many fears. Perhaps these simple directions will reassure you.

The first summer after planting, allow all the new shoots to sprawl over the ground. This is the vine's only year of uncontrolled freedom. The one purpose at this time is to develop as many leaves as possible to manufacture food and enlarge the root system.

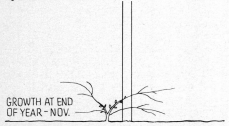

GROWTH AT END OF YEAR — NOV.

The following winter, remove all top growth except the strongest cane. If, by chance, the strongest, longest cane has reached the height at which you want branches to form or slightly beyond that point, tie it up and cut it back into strong wood (little-finger diameter) just above the branching place.

If the strong cane isn't long enough, cut it back to a stub of one or two buds. In the following spring, select one vigorous shoot that is growing upright and tie it loosely with string to the support on which you are training the vine.

This shoot will form the permanent trunk. On a trellis or arbor, you may want the trunk to branch at six or eight feet. Your selected main trunk may reach this height the following winter. If it does, and the shoot is about a foot above the level at which you want permanent side arms to form, cut off the tip of the shoot. This forces side buds to produce new branches at the desired level.

(In California this cutting of the tip is done in the second summer of growth and the lateral growth is directed to side shoots by pinching back all other shoots. Such summer training should not be attempted in the Northwest.)

The following spring, let two strong upper shoots develop, one on each side.

Train the new side shoots out laterally. New upright shoots will develop on the side arms in the spring of the third year, and will produce blossom clusters, like this:

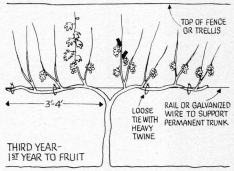

THIRD YEAR — 1ST YEAR TO FRUIT

Prune to leave two-bud spurs spaced along the cordon at about 10-inch intervals. Tie up only the shoots that are well placed and spaced along the side arms. Rub off other shoots on side arms and trunks when they are small. A good general rule is to leave one blossom cluster per shoot.

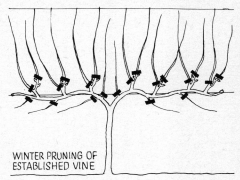

WINTER PRUNING OF ESTABLISHED VINE

In subsequent winters, cut back shoots that have borne fruit—to the basal buds. Continue to remove excess growth.

The above severe cut-back is often modified when pruning Thompson Seedless and American type grapes. These are pruned to canes from 2-5 feet long instead of spurs. The old cane that has borne a crop is removed, and a new one left in its place. Usually 3 to 4 canes are left per vine.

SMALL FRUITS   Home Food Garden

Grapes by Climates

There is only one way to avoid the disappointment of sour grapes at harvest time—choose the varieties which will be sweet. But, unfortunately, the sweet varieties you buy in fruit markets may not taste sweet when you grow them.

If you live in a table grape producing area, you know you have nothing to worry about. But outside of those limits you must choose carefully.

The broad assumption that the hardy American-type grapes are for the cold winter sections of the West and the European-type grapes are for all of California is adequate for the commercial grower of grapes but rules out many experiences in the home garden. In many cool summer sections of California, the American-type grapes such as Seneca and Diamond may be ever so much more enjoyable than any European variety. By the same token the gardener in the warm summer spots in the Northwest should consider for experiment the early-ripening varieties of the European grapes.

Following are the varieties that grow in the different Western climates:

ZONE 1
For the short but warm growing season, choose from these hardy early varieties: *Campbell Early*, *Fredonia*, *Moore Early*, *Seneca*.

ZONE 2
Here because of great heat accumulations, any of American varieties can be grown. European varieties will succeed in the warmest sections if you are willing to go to the trouble of winter protection, spreading the vines on the ground and covering them with soil.

American grapes grown in the Northwest, in order of ripening are: *Campbell Early*, *Portland*, *Fredonia*, *Ontario*, *Seneca*, *Moore Early*, *Diamond*, *Worden*, *Concord*, *Delaware*, *Niagara*, *Urbana*, *Keuka*, *Agawam*, and *Sheridan*.

ZONE 3
Best results here will be with the early varieties: *Campbell Early (Island Belle)*, *Fredonia*, *Seneca*.

ZONE 4
Stay with the early varieties in all but the warmest locations. Probable but not sure to develop their characteristic sweetness are: *Concord*, *Delaware*, *Diamond*.

ZONE 5
Both early and late American varieties ripen satisfactorily here. Given a warm south exposure with some reflective heat, the *Golden Muscat* is successful.

ZONE 6
In addition to the regular American varieties, *Pearl of Casaba* and *Golden Muscat* are sure to ripen; the European variety, *Black Monukka* is worth a trial.

ZONE 7
This is table grape country. You can choose by taste preference.

ZONE 8
Take your pick.

ZONE 9
Most localities do not have enough heat to ripen midseason and late varieties. Choose from *Cardinal*, *Black Monukka*, *Black Muscat*, *Malaga*. Popular *Thompson Seedless* may fail to ripen satisfactorily some years. Excellent substitutes for *Thompson Seedless* are the seedless varieties, *Perlette* and *Delight*. Of the two, *Perlette* requires slightly less heat. *Delight* is first choice where sun and heat are adequate.

ZONE 10
For sure ripening, avoid European varieties. Choose white varieties of the American grape: *Golden Muscat*, *Seneca*, and *Diamond*.

ZONES 11 AND 12
Here in areas of high total heat you can choose from the entire list.

ZONE 13
Under coastal influence only the early European varieties should be planted as in Zone 9. Here again the *Perlette* and *Delight* are recommended for those who like *Thompson Seedless*.

RASPBERRIES

This most delicate of berry fruits needs a slowly warming, lingering springtime in order to reach perfection. They are, therefore, well adapted to western Washington, western Oregon, and the ocean-cooled valleys of central and northern California. The quick-arriving summers of California's interior valleys cut the crop short.

The variety selection is wide; more than 10 varieties are grown and are available to the home gardener. Some are outstanding for winter hardiness, some for flavor, some for resistance to disease. Here's how they line up:

Cuthbert. This variety has the "original" raspberry flavor—the just-right blend of sugar and acid that the raspberry taster expects to find. All raspberry flavors are compared to it. It is being crowded out by types with improved hardiness and vigor.

New Washington. This is the variety that saved the berry industry in western Washington, an introduction by the Western Washington Experiment Station at Puyallup, made when no raspberry of quality and high production seemed able to withstand the mosaic virus. Large, round, firm, bright red to dark red berry—excellent flavor when frozen in syrup. Available wherever raspberries are grown.

Willamette. Developed by George Waldo, USDA, Corvallis, Oregon. Large, firm, dark red, medium-acid berry.

Lloyd George. Rated with top three in the Northwest, but susceptible to root rot in soils of all kinds.

Newburgh. Greatest virtues: wide adaptability and hardiness.

Latham. Minnesota introduction. Late flowering (after frosts), adapted to short season, cold winter areas.

Indian Summer. One of the so-called everbearing types. Bears a second crop in the fall at the tips of the maturing shoots. Large, dark red, and rather soft.

Ranere. *(St. Regis)*. Another second-crop, fall-bearing variety. Small bright red berries of fair quality.

New varieties. *Golden West*, the Western Washington Experiment Station's new yellow raspberry, is being watched with interest. *Canby*, the newest introduction by George Waldo, is a thornless, mosaic resistant variety that equals Cuthbert in quality.

Fall-Bearing; Everbearing

The fall-bearing varieties are worthwhile in areas where late spring frosts normally kill the fruit of Newburgh and Latham.

In mild winter areas, such as California coast, many growers get a second crop on all varieties by cutting back to 4½ feet immediately after harvest and giving them an extra feeding of fertilizer.

Blackcap raspberries. None of the blackcap raspberries do well in California. The varieties available in the Northwest are: *Munger, Cumberland,* and *Morrison.* There is not much difference in varieties; none developed very far beyond the wild state. Blackcaps have a flavor all their own, but they have many big hard seeds.

They should not be planted near red raspberries because of the virus they transmit.

Culture

TRAINING AND PRUNING: A workable trellis for raspberries consists of 2 posts, 2 cross arms 18 inches long on each post, and wires stretched from the end of the cross arms. Lower wire and cross arm should be 2 feet above ground, top wires, about 3 feet up, as diagrammed.

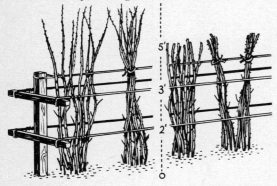

At planting time cut the 1-2 foot cane back to about 8 inches. This young cane serves mainly as a marker; new shoots arise from its base.

In spring, just before growth starts, cut out small and weak canes and cut back the remaining canes to 5 feet. Tie them to the trellis wires with a fairly heavy string to prevent wind whipping.

In July, as soon as the crop is harvested, take out the old canes that have fruited. By winter there are usually from 6 to 12 smooth, healthy canes ranging from 6-12 feet tall in each hill. To protect against whipping wind, bind the canes together and tie to one of the top wires.

Thin out these canes to about 8, if the vines are vigorous, less if growth is lagging, then cut back to 5 feet. Some varieties produce quite a few laterals on side branches, particularly during the second year. Generally, these should be cut back to 2 or 3 buds.

Divide the remaining canes in each hill equally and tie them to the top wire. Spreading them makes room for the new shoots to grow.

FERTILIZING AND PEST CONTROL: Same as blackberries.

STRAWBERRIES

You have probably noticed when reading about plants, that some are treated very seriously while others get a most casual treatment. The most serious, almost frightening, treatments are reserved for the plants with commercial importance.

The strawberry is a good example. In agricultural reports on this plant, every variety, every step in planting, and every possible pest and disease is analyzed, measured, weighed, and discussed at length. Since they are made for the benefit of the commercial grower and because they involve the expenditure of thousands of dollars, such reports must be painstaking and serious.

The trouble with these reports is that they make the growing of the plant sound so intricate and so likely to fail that the beginning gardener often backs away from growing it.

The strawberry does have a few exacting requirements and if you want a crop of berries you must meet them. But they are no more difficult to meet than those of snapdragons or stock.

Realize too that loss or failure with a few strawberry plants is not too serious in time and money. Strawberries aren't fruit trees; they are nothing more than inexpensive perennial plants and should be so regarded.

The first step is to choose the varieties that will grow in your climate and soil. Presumably every variety you find at your nursery will do that. But you can't count on that entirely because soils vary in one locality and furthermore the nurseryman must satisfy desires for something new. However, his best sellers are generally those adapted to your climate.

The only need for a guide to varieties is to show what has been done to adapt the plant to various growing conditions. If you are wise, you will plant more than one variety anyway and let your taste and climate weed out the better from the best.

Varieties Available

All areas have strawberry disease problems and locally introduced varieties are bred to meet them.

Marshall. *(Banner).* Other varieties of Marshall type which might as well be called Marshalls, include: *Oregon, New Oregon,* and *Oregon Plum.* The Marshall type strawberry is still the yardstick for flavor measurement. When new varieties are introduced, their flavor is called excellent if it approaches that of the Marshall. Unfortunately, it is susceptible to virus disease and not too vigorous. Recommended for virus-free areas of the Northwest only.

Northwest. Western Washington Experiment Station introduction in 1950. Rated but slightly inferior to Marshall in flavor. Resistant to virus yellows, but susceptible to root rot. Yields heavier than Marshall. Excellent for freezing and canning.

Brightmore. USDA-Oregon State introduction in 1942. Resistant to yellows, but needs well-drained soil. Fair flavor. Cans and freezes well. Berry size falls off after mid-season picking.

Corvallis. USDA-Oregon State introduction and another resistant variety. Later bearing and hardier than Brightmore.

Narcissa. Early bearing. Liked by those who prefer sweet berries. Judged against Marshall, it's insipid.

Dorsett. Mid-season variety. Grown mostly in central and eastern Washington.

Red Heart. Mid-season. Dark red flesh. Sometimes tastes a little stale when thoroughly ripe. Beautiful when canned or frozen.

Shasta. University of California introduction. Plants are vigorous and moderately resistant to virus yellow. Especially well-adapted to California's central and northern coastal areas. Fruit is produced the last week in April and then fairly continuously through the summer with peak of production in September.

Lassen. University of California introduction. Large plant and heavy producer. Resistant to yellows and mites, and moderately to alkali soil.

Donner. University of California introduction. Nearly equal to the Marshall in dessert quality. Main crop in spring.

Rockhill. Everbearing. Long regarded as the quality standard of its class—highest in aroma. Plants produce few if any runners. Propagated by crown division. Best when reset annually.

Gem. Excellent preserving berry. Medium size, bright red, tart flavor. Produces large number of runners.

Red Rich. Everbearing reported to have better flavor than Rockhill; red all the way through. Climatic adaptation not yet proven.

Twentieth Century, Utah Everbearer. Berries as large and attractive as those of Rockhill. Plant forms runners. Resistant to virus yellows.

Strawberry Climates

The climates for strawberries fall into five classifications:

1. The severe winter, high altitude climate with very late frosts.
2. The severe winter with longer growing season.
3. The mildly cold winter, long spring, cool to warm summers.
4. The cool winter, hot summer.
5. The mild winter, warm summer.

FOR CLIMATE NO. 1. The everbearing, *Twentieth Century*, *Gem*, and *Rockhill* are best bets. Severe frosts during blossoming time get only a portion of their crop, but ruin the entire year's crop of the one-crop varieties.

CLIMATE NO. 2. Mid-season and late bearing one-crop varieties—such as *Dorsett* and *Northwest*—are worth trying in addition to the everbearing.

CLIMATE NO. 3. Here we have the ideal strawberry climate for full production. You find it in western Washington, Oregon, and coastal or near-coastal northern California.

CLIMATE NO. 4. Central Valley regions of California are best satisfied with an early season variety or one with a chance of a fall crop. The everbearing varieties produce nothing in midsummer. The *Shasta* does well with its early and late crop.

CLIMATE NO. 5. The *Klondike* has been the standard bearer in Southern California for years. Its resistance to virus is in its favor but susceptibility to alkali soils has seriously limited its use.

Of the Donner-Shasta-Lassen series the latecomer to Southern California, *Lassen*, has shown remarkable adaptability. It outproduces *Shasta*, its nearest competitor, by 50 per cent, and yields twice as much as the old *Klondike*. *Donner*, with its better flavor, shows a low yield in saline soils.

Culture

HOW AND WHEN TO PLANT: In mild winter areas, fall planting is recommended. With early fall planting a fair crop can be expected the following spring. However, new plants are hard to find at that time.

Spring planting should be done as early as the soil can be worked.

The commercial grower follows one of several planting plans according to his soil, water and personal preference. In the hill or flat bed system the plants are usually set 18-24 inches apart in rows 3 feet apart. This flat bed system is used where no irrigation is required or the plants are sprinkler irrigated.

The raised bed with furrows between is used in California with gravity irrigation. The usual bed is 18-24 inches wide and 2 rows of plants are set in the bed.

Some growers follow the matted row system in which the plants cover the raised bed, often forming dense mats.

In each case the common method is to use the plants initially set out as mother plants and guide the runners to fill in with daughter plants 6-10 inches apart.

The home gardener need not follow any pattern. If he can find a sunny spot for 10 plants here and 5 plants there in flower garden or vegetable garden or in boxes on the patio, he can harvest strawberries.

For jams, canning, and freezing as well as fresh use, the average family can use the production of about 70 plants. If production is light due to season, variety, or culture, 70 plants will give you about 36-40 baskets, full production as many as 140-150 baskets. If planted in one place the 70 plants would need about 12 by 24 feet in space.

The home gardener will get quicker returns and more berries if he starts with the number of plants he needs and forgets all about filling in with runners. By keeping runners cut off you keep the plant busy at the one job of producing berries.

SETTING OUT PLANTS: One of the common mistakes made in planting is getting the crown of the plant too high or too low. The plant should be set so the top of the roots is just a hair below the soil surface.

To keep the roots from sticking out of the soil after watering and as the plant grows, leave the center of the bed slightly higher at planting time so that soil can be hoed to the plants when needed.

PINCH OFF BLOSSOMS? Some berry growers prevent the plant from setting fruit the first season after planting by pinching out blossoms as they appear. Stronger plants will develop if all their energy is devoted to leaf and root building.

Should home gardeners, anxious to have fruit as soon as they can, follow this practice?

If you plant in the fall, pinch off all buds as they form—in the fall. Let the spring blossoms alone.

If you plant in the spring, remove the blossoms from the weak plants only. If leaf formation is vigorous, a plant can take care of itself and berries too.

The everbearing variety Rockhill is an exception. Its first blossoms always should be removed. Let it alone as soon as its vigor is apparent.

Generally, if the runner type plants are so slow in leaf production that they will be stunted by berry production, they need an application of quick acting fertilizer.

How to feed: Go beyond the average garden practice in preparing soil for strawberries. Spade in plenty of rotted manure, about twice as much as you would like to pay for.

Time your feeding with commercial fertilizer, after the plants start to grow, with the appearance of the leaves. Pale-colored foliage indicates a need for nitrogen; dark-green foliage, an adequate supply. Don't overdo it. Too much leaf growth cuts down berry production.

About the maximum any soil will need is 4 pounds of a 10-10-10 balance of nitrogen, phosphorous, and potash to 100 square feet in a year. Better to apply in doses of one pound to 100 square feet and see what happens.

How to water: As with all plants, watering schedules will be timed to soil and weather.

Remember that the strawberry plant is relatively shallow rooted. You must maintain moisture in the first 12 inches of soil. In warm weather an irrigation every three days may be necessary. At the same time, a water-soaked soil surface is harmful to the berries, causing rot.

If you are watering a flat bed by sprinklers, irrigate in the morning so that soil surface will dry before night.

If you are watering raised beds by ditches or furrows, let the water slowly fill the ditches and penetrate laterally without flooding the surface of the soil.

The furrow method of irrigation will build up concentrations of salts in the soil, if salinity is a water or soil problem in your area. In such cases, beds will have to be leached out by flooding every 2 or 3 years. In localities where salinity is a continuous problem, flat-bed planting with overhead irrigation will keep the salts leached out, provided that drainage is good.

Home Food Garden
DECIDUOUS FRUITS

If you enjoy being exceedingly thorough, you can have the time of your life deciding about fruit trees—which to plant, where to plant, and how much care each will require.

The most thorough and carefully documented information on fruit trees is written for the commercial orchardist. It will help you if your principal interest is the production of marketable fruit.

But such information, written for the orchardist, often misleads the home gardener who has multiple requirements for fruit trees. Let's look at the standard set of rules established by commercial orchard experience, and then look at some of the ways the home gardener cheerfully, and successfully, breaks them.

PLANTING DISTANCES
The orchardist advises: For fruit production, trees should not be crowded.

This planting advice is valuable when you are planting an orchard on an acre or more. Each tree must get its full quota of sun. There should be no competition for root space or shading out of smaller trees.

The home gardener realizes that planting distances in orchards need not apply literally in the home garden. Of course, you can't have productive fruit trees in a closely planted thicket, but you can plant them in rows, against fences, on walls.

You can crowd them, too, if you give them sunlight by placement and pruning. Espaliers, cordon training, and other methods of crowded planting have been followed for centuries.

PRUNING AND TRAINING
In a small garden the home gardener can prune trees to be flat against a fence of wire or wood, or against a wall. Trees can be spaced as close as 8 feet. Whether the trees are trained in a pattern or allowed to grow 3 feet thick makes no difference. All fruit trees will stand this treatment but the easiest to handle from the pruning standpoint are those that do not need a yearly renewal of *new* wood for fruiting.

SPRAY PROGRAM
The orchardist follows a different spray program for every type of tree. Some trees receive as many as 9 applications in the course of a year.

The home gardener can follow a simple over-all program, and accept occasional damage and a worm or two.

Here's a minimum spray program for mixed fruit tree plantings: In December or January, or after pruning, apply a dormant spray such as oil and lime sulfur to apples, pears, peaches, plums—all fruits except those noted below—for control of scale insects and other overwintering insects or insect eggs. Use a copper spray with oil on apricots. Use lime sulfur on peaches for control of peach leaf curl in late winter before buds break.

To be sure of harvesting splendid, clean fruit, spray each of your fruit trees thoroughly in spring when two-thirds of the flower petals have fallen. Use a three-way mixture such as DDT, malathion, and captan (gets insects, mites, and diseases, respectively). Apples especially need the DDT to kill codling moth larvae (apple worms). Stone fruits especially need the captan to ward off brown rot (a definite need if it rains during bloom). Orchardists follow the petal-fall spraying with as many as 7 or 8 subsequent sprayings at 10-day to two-week intervals. A diligent home fruit grower might apply 2 or 3 such follow-up sprays.

THINNING FRUIT

The orchardist thins fruit at the earliest possible moment to obtain the largest possible quota of normal size fruit. Sometimes fruit thinning is done by blossom thinning with special sprays.

The home gardener can be more drastic in thinning. The one chance for the home gardener to get bigger and better fruit than he can buy is in the thinning process. The home gardener can cut down on total volume to get individual size.

SELECTION OF VARIETIES

The orchardist must select fruit varieties that can be handled, crated, shipped.

The home gardener can select, for example, tender fleshed, yet easily bruised peaches, and thus get fruits not available in fruit markets. He also has the great advantage of being able to wait until fruit is fully ripe before picking.

The orchardist selects varieties suited to his climate.

The home gardener, here, would be wise to follow orchard practice. Too often, instead, he selects by his *fruit-stand* preference. This taste preference method of selection doesn't work in many sections of the West. Your favorite fruit-stand peach may not taste like your favorite when grown in your own garden. The tree that bears your favorite apple may refuse to fruit there at all. The importance of choosing varieties to suit your climate cannot be overstressed.

ALMOND

The home gardener must choose almond trees with care. Two trees must be planted for pollination. Early blooming varieties should not be planted in late-frost areas. Cool weather is unkind to almonds; the nuts mold and otherwise prove inferior. Fortunately, the almond tree, with or without nuts, is an attractive, picturesquely branched tree, to 15-20 feet, with 30-foot spread.

Most of crop is borne on short spurs that are fruitful for about 5 years. Very little pruning is necessary until the tree has been bearing for 5 years. Then, some of the smaller branches up to 1½ inches in diameter should be removed to stimulate replacement wood.

Varieties and Climates

Jordanolo. Early blooming, excellent tree. Use in California coastal valleys. Pollenizers: *Nonpareil, Ne Plus Ultra.*

Nonpareil. Paper thin shell; best all-around variety. Pollenizers: any other variety.

Ne Plus Ultra. Others preferred, but widely adapted and used as pollenizer for *Nonpareil, Jordanolo,* or *Mission.*

Mission. (Texas). Outstanding for late blooming. Use in colder spots. Meats have a slight "bitter almond" taste which some enjoy; heavy regular production. Tree smaller than other varieties. This is the variety to experiment with in warm dry spots of Pacific Northwest. As a pollenizer, use *Nonpareil.*

APPLE

Long-lived tree of garden value for shade and design interest but slow growing and slow to come into bearing. Varieties grafted on dwarf and semi-dwarf rootstock speed up time of production. See below.

Varieties must be chosen with eye to pollination and climate. Where winters are mild, varieties of low-chilling requirement must be selected.

Varieties and Climates

ZONES 11, 12, 13 AND 8

Varieties developed for Southern California coastal mild winters are *Valmore* and *Beverly Hills.* Lack quality of standard varieties but do produce fruit. Varieties *Winter Banana* and *White Pearmain* have lowest chilling requirements of the standards. *Delicious, Jonathan, Winesap,* and *Rome Beauty* can be grown in high desert and mountains of Southern California.

ZONES 7, 9, 10

Interior valleys of central California should pass up many of the fruit-market favorites. Many sunburn or coarsen because of fast ripening. Recommended for the Sacramento and San Joaquin valleys: *Yellow Transparent, Early McIntosh, Lodi, Golden Delicious, Jonathan.*

In the higher foothill areas, add: *Delicious, Grimes Golden, Spitzenberg, Winesap, McIntosh, Rome Beauty.* As you near the coast, the variety list narrows to make these the best producers: *Yellow Transparent, Gravenstein, Golden Delicious, Jonathan, Winter Banana, White Pearmain, Yellow Newtown.*

ZONES 1-6

In Zone 1 the short growing season prevents the standard Delicious variety and its red sports from developing good finish and color. Gravenstein trees are damaged by severe winters. Recommended: *McIntosh, Jonathan, Rome, Wealthy, Lodi, Duchess, Cortland, Golden Delicious.*

In Zone 2 all varieties do well.

Zones 3 and 4 are limited in choice to apples requiring less sunlight: *Lodi, Gravenstein, Wealthy, Milton, King, Golden Delicious.*

In Zone 5 the choice widens to include all in Zone 4

plus such as: *Winesap, Stayman, Yellow Newtown,* and *Rome Beauty.*

Zone 6 has almost unlimited choice.

APRICOT

The climate pattern of the apricot is in reverse to that of the peach. While peaches do best with high summer heat, the ideal apricot climate is in the intermountain valleys of the central coast of California.

In the Northwest the summer-cool western area makes brown rot and blight almost impossible to control. Wenatchee, Yakima and The Dalles are the best apricot climates in the Northwest.

Varieties and Climates

Moorpark and *Hemskirke*. Excellent flavor, high chilling requirement, often shy bearing.

Perfection. Widely adapted, low chilling requirements, needs a pollenizer.

Reeves. Southern California coastal to low desert.

Royal Blenheim. Standard variety throughout California.

Tilton. Needs more winter cold than Royal Blenheim.

Wenatchee. Standard variety in Washington, mediocre performance in California.

Yakimene. Northwest only, high chilling requirement, seldom blooms or fruits in California.

CRABAPPLES

The varieties grown for their fruit are: *Florence, Hyslop, Transcendant* in the yellow, red-blushed class; *Montreal Beauty*, green and red; *Whitney*, yellow striped with red. Many of the flowering crabapples bear enough fruit for home supplies of jellies. See chapter on flowering trees.

FIGS

This picturesque gray-barked, fruiting subtropical is in the no-trouble class of fruit trees. Very little pruning and spraying are necessary. Left to its own devices it will reach great heights but it can be kept at ten feet or lower by annual pruning. Figs can be grown in tubs.

The *Mission* and the *Brown Turkey* have a tendency to grow shrublike with many low-spreading branches. If you are training it to become a tree follow the regular procedure of cutting back at planting and selecting scaffold branches at first winter pruning. But do not head back these primary scaffold branches. Other than directing growth no further pruning is necessary. The tree produces new wood without pruning.

When espaliering or growing flat against a fence you take advantage of the shrub-like growth and train as you please. To produce fruit when espaliered, the *Brown Turkey* must be cut back severely each year.

Varieties and Climates

In the low deserts only, you find *Beall* and the fine flavored *Black San Pedro*. In all other areas of California, the *Brown Turkey* and *Mission* are the most widely planted varieties. *Brown Turkey* is the favorite in Southern California while the *Mission* is especially well adapted to the warm valleys of northern California. In cooler summer areas the choice is *White Genoa;* along the coast the variety *King* is best. The *Kadota*, the yellow fig much used for canning, is at its best in the heat of the San Joaquin Valley.

In the Pacific Northwest, figs are borderline even in the warmest areas. The variety *Lattarula*, a fast grower, will come back after being frozen to the ground in February and will bear a crop in September.

FILBERT

This decorative small tree finds its favorite climate in Oregon's Portland-Willamette Valley area. While it bears well in the foothills of northern California, it does poorly in other areas of the state.

More than one variety must be planted for pollination. Varieties commonly planted are: *Barcelona, Du Chilly, White Aveline*. The variety *Royal* produces the largest nut of all the commercial varieties but is a shy bearer. Makes a small tree of impressive structure and ornamental quality. Catkins hang long and full; very showy in the winter months.

NECTARINES

Theoretically the nectarines should follow the peach into every area, but the varieties now being sold do not produce fruit in zones 3, 4 and 5. Oregon State College recommends *Garden State* and *Fuzzless Berta* as the most promising for Willamette Valley conditions.

Varieties and Climates

Gold Mine. Southern California coast and interior valleys. *Gower.* High desert and mountains of Southern California. *Mabel* or *Philp*. New introductions for northern California by the University of California, high chilling requirement. *Pioneer.* All California, light chilling requirement. *Silver Lode.* All California, light chilling requirement. *Freedom,* large, yellow-fleshed freestone.

PEACH

The performance of peaches illustrates vividly the importance of selecting varieties by climates. Winter chilling and summer heat requirements differ by variety. Here are some of the preferred varieties starting with the mildest winters and working up. Ripening dates vary by the locality and the season. All lists are in order of ripening with ripening date given for the average of the zone. Peaches with white flesh are so noted, all others are yellow fleshed.

Varieties and Climates

Zone 13

Four Star: Flowering-fruiting, white flesh, mid-June. *Ventura:* Excellent quality, late June. *Redwing:* Good show of flowers, white flesh, late June. *Three Star:* Flowering-fruiting, early August. *Bonita:* Early August. *Hermosa:* White flesh, early August. *Altair:* Flowering-fruiting, white flesh, mid-August.

Zone 12

Four Star. Ventura. Three Star. Bonita. Hermosa. Altair.

Zone 11

Robin: Mild, low acid, sweet, white flesh, early June. *Four Star. Meadow Lark:* More typical of peach flavor, late

June. *Ventura. Redwing. July Elberta:* Excellent quality, early July. *Three Star. Flamingo:* Semi-dwarf, excellent flavor, early August. *Bonita. Hermosa. Golden Blush:* Early August. *Merrill Nectaheath:* Clingstone (the old Heath flavor in a better peach), mid-August. *Altair.*

Zone 10
Wherever coastal influences are direct and summers cool, standard varieties seldom ripen with their full flavor quota. *Elberta* and *J. H. Hale* are apt to be bitter. For these areas, varieties developed for Southern California are worth trying: *Three Star, Redwing, Golden Blush.*

Zones 9 and 7
Blazing Gold: Early in June when peaches are scarce, these are wonderful. *Gold Dust:* similar to *Blazing Gold,* but a week later. *Redhaven:* Outstanding peach of the season, late June. *Merrill Delicious:* Good flavor and good for freezing, late June. *Nectar:* Large, attractive white peach, bruises easily, early July. *July Elberta:* Prolific quality peach, thin well for size, early July. *Strawberry Free:* White flesh, excellent flavor, mid-July. *Elberta:* The accepted standard, early August. *Fay Elberta:* Early August. *J. H. Hale:* Self-unfruitful, must be another variety in the neighborhood, early August. *Flamingo. Three Star. Merrill Nectaheath. Rio Oso Gem:* Excellent, mid-August.

Zone 8
Low desert: None. High desert: *Meadow Lark. Ventura. July Elberta. Fay Elberta. Flamingo. Bonita.*

Zone 6
In this famous fruit growing area you can almost choose to suit your taste.

Zone 5
Mayflower: Earliness is its one virtue; white flesh, early June. *Starking Delicious:* Like an early version of *July Elberta. Dixired:* Perhaps best early peach, mid-July. *Dixigem:* Flesh is non-browning, good freezer, late July. *Redhaven:* Top rating peach everywhere, late July. *Golden Jubilee:* Good canner, early August. *Nectar. Triogem:* Superior for canning and freezing, mid-August. *Halehaven:* Needs thinning for best size, mid-August. *Rochester (Pacific Gold):* Long ripening period, mid-August. *July Elberta. Goldeneast:* Stands holding well, late August. *Veteran:* Rated above average in canning and freezing, late August. *Early Elberta:* Late August. *Elberta:* Early September. *J. H. Hale:* Early September.

Zones 3 and 4
Ripening seasons are later than in Zone 5 by 2 weeks to a month. Very few varieties completely satisfactory. Best are: *Redhaven. Halehaven. Rochester. July Elberta. Veteran.*

Zone 2
In this great fruit belt you have your choice of the standards.

Zone 1
In the warmer, lower elevations these peaches are grown: *Early Elberta, July Elberta, Elberta, J. H. Hale,* and *Halehaven.*

PEAR
The pear is an excellent choice as a garden tree; easy to train and very tolerant of wet soil where it is adapted. It's a very poor choice in Southern California and in the interior valleys of northern California where fire blight and codling moth are too much for the gardener.

The pear is a noble fruit in Washington, Oregon, and coastal valleys of California. The summer pear, *Bartlett,* is adaptable to all sections. Winter standby in central Washington for eating fresh is *d'Anjou,* and for baking, *Bose. Comice,* an excellent fresh winter pear, performs best in Hood River, Medford, and California.

PECAN
There's no question about the beauty of the pecan tree, but it has some definite requirements: it needs space to grow in; becomes a 40 foot high, 50 foot wide tree. It must have deep soil, 6-10 feet. It needs the heat of a long California interior summer. If you live in the cooler sections of the interior or in a warm coastal valley, look for the University of California variety *Humble.*

Varieties and Climates
Mahan, low desert, hot interiors, has the largest nut but tree is brittle and requires more care. *Select,* slightly less heat requirement. *Delight,* well filled nut of excellent quality; less heat needed. *Humble,* less heat; try in hot coastal valleys.

PERSIMMON
It's hard to find a more beautiful, more adaptable, less troublesome tree than the Oriental persimmon. It adapts itself to all of California's climates except desert and mountain. The tree itself is hardy to 0°, but dormant fruit buds and smaller twigs may be injured at temperatures below 20°. Fruits ripen in all but north coastal areas. The tree is generally free of insects and diseases. Little or no pruning required. (Tends to bear fruit toward the ends of branches unless thinned enough to produce fruiting shoots in center of tree.)

The variety *Hachiya* is favored for shape and color of the fruit, and for tree form. Its fruits stay puckery until a frost softens them or time turns them ripe. They do not lose their astringency until almost mush. Fruits of the variety *Fuyu* are smaller and flattened like a tomato, and you can eat them when crisp. Although judged superior in fruit quality, *Fuyu* is not much of a tree compared to the ornamental *Hachiya.*

Frequently *Hachiya* has such an excessive fruit drop that few fruits are left on the tree in October. You can reduce fruit drop by avoiding shocks from watering or feeding. Soak the root area at regular 3-4 week intervals during the growing season. Fertilize with a slow acting organic such as manure in late fall rather than giving it a shot in the arm in spring or summer.

Although its natural habit is somewhat drooping, *Hachiya* can become a suitable shade tree if you remove the lower branches.

If you start training when trees are young, persimmons also make interesting espaliers.

PLUMS — PRUNES
In general both the European and Japanese plums are adapted to all Western climates. The European plums can be grown in colder areas than the Japanese plums because they are distinctly later blooming.

In the technical terms of fruit classification "Any plum that can be dried whole without removing the pit and without fermenting is a prune." So far as the Northwest home gardener is concerned, the Italian and Imperial prunes are plums to eat fresh or to can. The Italian prune is the hardiest of all varieties. In the Northwest the variety Stanley is considered an early edition of the Italian. The French prune is the California commercial dried prune.

Many of the plums need cross pollination. See pollination, p. 350.

Varieties and Climates

Japanese varieties generally recommended in zones 2-13: *Beauty:* Earliest standard shipping variety. *Santa Rosa:* Standard of all. *Satsuma:* Old favorite for jams and jellies, and a beautiful ornamental tree.

Japanese varieties specifically recommended: Zones 11-13: *Climax, Mariposa.* Zones 7-9: *Formosa, Wickson, Duarte, Howard Miracle, Kelsey.* Zones 2-6: *Peach Plum, Shiro, Duarte, Burbank, Howard Miracle.*

European varieties recommended all zones: *Imperial, Green Gage, Stanley, Italian Prune, French Prune, President, Damson,* or *Blue Damson.*

POMEGRANATE

Pomegranate can be trained as a shrub or small tree 6-10 feet high. Generally left to spread as a clump 10 feet wide and high. With very little pruning a row of pomegranates can be maintained as a shrubby screen or informal hedge. Red flowers of waxy substance are showy along with the young fruits in July. Needs heat of warm California valleys for fruit production; don't expect fruit in direct coastal areas.

The tree has unusually high alkali tolerance. In areas so high in sodium that virtually no fruit trees will grow, pomegranate lives a normal fruitful life.

The only variety is *Wonderful.*

QUINCE

Highly ornamental tree in spring-flowering and in its picturesque winter form. Very tolerant of soils and climate. Although completely hardy in the coldest winters, warm winters are no handicap; can be grown in Southern California.

Natural habit of the quince is shrubby and bushy; needs early training to direct it into a tree form. Interesting and characteristic zig-zag look of the quince is caused by development of lateral shoots each year.

Fruit is borne at tips of shoots; so after tree begins to bear, restrict your pruning to thinning out and some heading back to laterals only enough to stimulate new growth.

SOUR CHERRY

Attractive garden-size tree about ⅔ as large as the sweet cherry. Unlike the sweet cherry, does not need pollenizer. Trees bear early and are hardier than sweet cherries.

While the sweet cherry grows stiffly upright, the sour cherry grows in a spreading and irregular fashion. You can prune to increase the irregularity if your first demand is for an ornamental tree or you can remove any pendulous laterals and force a more regular upright pattern.

Montmorency is favorite in Northwest, needs colder winters than found in Southern California. There, *Early Richmond* and *English Morello* produce satisfactory crops.

SWEET CHERRY

Not a tree for the small garden. When it finds deep, well-drained soil, reaches 30 feet high and spreads an equal distance. Dies young where soil is shallow or poorly drained. Regardless of the variety you want, you must plant another cherry for pollination. With all its limitations, the traditional background of the tree is such that it is almost essential for the country place.

Varieties and Climates

Need for winter chilling rules it out of Southern California's mild winter areas. No climate in the West suits the cherry better than Oregon's Willamette Valley.

Black cherry varieties: *Black Tartarian* is early; *Bing* mid-season; and *Lambert* late. The light cherry, *Royal Ann,* matures with *Bing. Tartarian* is a pollenizer for all other varieties.

The *Van* cherry is similar to *Bing* but more resistant to cracking. *Van* is also a good pollenizer for *Bing* and *Lambert.* Varieties *Early Duke* and *Late Duke* are neither sweet nor sour.

WALNUT

Walnuts take up more space than the average home gardener can afford to give them. However, if you are looking for a very large shade tree with a nut bonus, the walnut is to be considered almost anywhere in the West where soil is deep.

The walnut tree *after it attains the look of a tree* is one of the few food producing trees that can be left to its own natural devices. However, seeing it through its early gangling stages is a trial. In the second year after planting, the branches will be growing every which way. The only way to handle this situation is to walk up to it, when it is dormant, and cut until you have a frame that looks as a tree should. And you repeat the process the following year.

Varieties and Climates

Concord. Best variety in coastal valleys, but fills poorly in hot districts. Not hardy in Pacific Northwest.

Franquette. Very late bloom. Many strains offered. Adapted to northern California interior; higher elevations, western Oregon. Variety *Carpathian,* grown in eastern Oregon, is a desirable strain of English walnut; able to take —20° winters. However, it leafs out early and is often nipped by late frosts.

Hartley. An excellent nut; good performer in most northern California districts.

Mayette. Another late blooming variety, safe where frosts are late.

Payne. Adapted generally to northern and Southern California; early bloom; subject to blight and sunburn.

Wasson. Early blooming variety for coastal districts of central California.

PRUNING

Because each fruit tree has its own characteristics, the growth cycle of each type must be known before it can be pruned correctly.

Remember, all fruits described here are borne on one-year-old wood. Growth produced in the spring and summer of one year will bear fruit the next year.

The thing that makes for different pruning techniques is *how* the fruit is borne on this year-old wood, and *how much* bearing wood is produced.

Peaches, nectarines

Look at the peach and nectarine. A young "adolescent" tree, one which will bear fruit for the first time this summer, looks like this in the winter.

Winter

Buds are spaced along the newest branches usually in groups of three small leaf buds flanked by two fruit buds. These buds and the branches they grow on were formed last summer.

In six months each center bud will have developed into either a leaf or a new shoot. The flanking buds will have blossomed and developed into fruit. And new branches will have grown from the buds at the tips of these branches.

Next summer

If the same portion of the branch is examined next winter, it will be found to be budless. This year's growth will be carrying the fruit buds.

Next winter
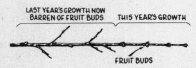

And in the following summer, the process will have repeated itself.

Following summer
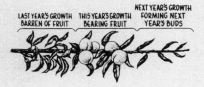

This bearing habit is peculiar only to peaches and nectarines. On no other fruit is each year's bearing portion stretched over so much new wood. This being the case, heavy annual pruning is necessary on peaches and nectarines for the following purposes: (1) to force out long new growth; (2) to keep the ever-widening bearing area close to the center of the tree.

Apricots

Again taking a maturing tree as a starting point, trace the bearing habit of the apricot. In the winter, the new growth looks about like that of the peach, with fruit buds borne beside leaf buds along the new wood.

Winter

The first summer some of these fruit buds will develop into fruit which will be borne along the branch, just as on the peach. Some of the vegetative buds will grow into short twigs.

Next summer
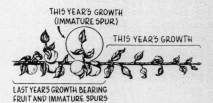

The difference between peach and apricot growth habits becomes noticeable the second winter when, after the leaves fall off, fruit spurs can be seen. A fruit spur is a short stocky shoot, seldom more than three inches long, with fruit and leaf buds packed fairly close along it. Spurs develop from vegetative buds. (On the peach, these buds grow into shoots.) In the second winter the picture looks like this.

Next winter
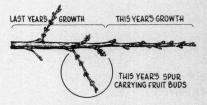

Fruit buds along this year's spurs and also those along new growth will produce fruit the following summer. It can be seen that over a long period of time most of the fruit comes to be borne on spurs because there is so much more of the old growth than new growth.

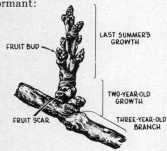

Following summer

Although it is true that once a section of wood has borne fruit it never will bear again, the fact isn't so important with the apricot as with the peach. The spurs put on only a little growth each year, and each successive year's growth bears fruit. Spurs on three-year-old wood might look like this when dormant:

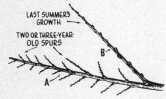

Apricot spurs are comparatively short-lived, rarely producing fruit for longer than four years, so regular pruning is essential to replace them continuously. Old branches are replaced by new.

In pruning, new branch B is allowed to grow in order that it might eventually replace older branch A, on which most of the fruit spurs are nearly through bearing.

A year later, spurs have developed on branch B. They are now carrying fruit buds and will bear fruit for the first time the following summer. By cutting out branch A, you are removing a nonproductive member and diverting growth into branch B, which will replace it.

Plums

Plum trees have about the same growth habit as the apricot, with the exception that spurs usually bear a little longer.

Cherry

The bearing habit of sweet cherries is radically different from that of peaches and nectarines. Where peach trees bear fruit on shoots which go nearly barren the next year, cherries grow from the same spurs for as long as 10 to 12 years. These spurs grow very slowly, putting on a short annual terminal growth and even shorter lateral growths, the latter being only little cushions upon which flower buds are formed. But, be it ever so stubby and insignificant, the wood on which berries are borne is one year old.

Because of the longevity of the cherry fruit spurs, there is practically no need for renewal of fruiting branches. As a matter of fact, cherries require less pruning than any other deciduous fruit tree.

Apples and pears

Apples and pears grow mostly from the ends of spurs. Although the buds may open into clusters of many blossoms, usually only one or two of them will set fruit.

Apple spurs often go through this growing and fruit setting process over a period as long as 20 years.

GRAFTING MANY VARIETIES ON ONE FRUIT TREE

As more orchard land is subdivided into residential property, more new home owners find themselves owners of one or more full-bearing fruit trees. Generally all the neighbors have the same variety and when harvest time comes there's too much fruit.

One solution to this oversupply that has suggested itself to many gardeners in such situations is grafting other varieties or fruits onto the trees they have inherited.

The business of grafting or budding new varieties into the tops of old trees is called topworking. It is common practice in commercial orchards when the existing variety has been outmoded. In both orchards and gardens, seedling trees are often worked over to established varieties.

Grafts on mature trees will come into production more quickly than those on newly planted small trees. Peaches and plums will bear the second year; apricots, the third year; apples and pears, the third or fourth year depending on variety.

The proper time for top-working is just in advance of blossoming or when the tree breaks dormancy. According to variety of fruit the time will be from mid-January to April.

Generally scions are collected when trees are fully dormant, in late fall or early winter, and stored in wet moss in a refrigerator at about 34° until time for grafting in January, February, or March.

Scions are twigs of one-year-old wood about ⅜ to ½ inch in diameter. You can usually buy scion wood from the nursery as soon as the new fruit trees are in. Such scions from small trees may not be as firm as those selected from mature trees but they are generally satisfactory.

Which variety can be grafted on which tree? How far can you go in mixing various fruits on one tree?

If you have a peach tree...

Apricot on peach? All varieties are satisfactory.

Almond on peach? All varieties are satisfactory.

Japanese plum on peach? All varieties except Climax, which fails occasionally.

European plum on peach? Most varieties, but to be safe avoid Burton, Diamond, Grand Duke, Green Gage, Jefferson, Robe de Sergeant, Sugar, and Yellow Egg.

If you have an apricot tree...

You can't put quite as many different kinds of fruit on an apricot tree as on a peach tree.

Peach on apricot? All varieties will make a satisfactory union but some are inclined to overgrow. You will have to thin fruit regularly to reduce strain at the graft.

Plum and prune on apricot? Some are easily broken at the union. These varieties (including Japanese plum, European plum, and prunes) are usually satisfactory: Burbank, Burton, Formosa, French, Giant, Golden Drop, Grand Duke, Hungarian, Imperial, President, Santa Rosa, Tragedy, Sugar, Wickson, Yellow Egg.

Almond on apricot? Not satisfactory because of weak unions.

If you have an almond tree...

Peach on almond? The wood union is usually strong but the bark union is rough. These varieties have been top-worked satisfactorily: Early Crawford, Heath Cling, J. H. Hale, Mayflower, Redhaven.

Nectarine on almond? Performance about the same as that of peach varieties. Quetta and Stanwick are not very vigorous on almond.

Plums and prunes on almond? Behavior varies and experience is limited. University of California at Davis top-worked 48 almond trees with 53 varieties of plums and prunes. These were successful: Anita, Beauty, Climax, Elephant Heart, Gaviota, Italian prune, Jefferson, Kelsey, Pond, Robe de Sergeant, Sharkey, Sugar, and Yellow Egg.

Apricot on almond? Not satisfactory; makes a very weak union.

If you have a plum tree...

Apricot on plum? Reasonably satisfactory.

Peach on plum? Not satisfactory; although many varieties of plums do well when grafted onto a peach tree, the reverse combination does not work.

Almond on plum? Not generally satisfactory, although plum on almond is successful.

If you have an apple or a pear tree...

Apples on apples and pears on pears are the only completely satisfactory combinations. However, you can go the limit on the number of varieties. We have seen 12 apple varieties on one tree.

POLLINATION

There have been enough exceptions and qualifications in pollination requirements to cause some home orchardists to ignore all warnings and go ahead and plant any variety and trust to luck.

The two exceptions might be with the cherry and the almond. The warning of self-unfruitfulness with these fruits has been repeated so often for so many years that few people will plant only one tree. That the second tree must be chosen with care is not so well known. For example you can plant three cherry trees—Royal Ann, Bing, and Lambert—and still have a pollination problem, and no cherries. Match any one of them with Black Tartarian and production is assured.

Almond is another clear-cut example. There will be no nuts unless it is cross-pollinated.

To avoid waiting 2-6 years to find out whether the tree you plant will bear fruit you can do one of two things:

1. Plant varieties known to be fruitful.
2. Provide pollenizer where needed.

Varieties that must have a pollinator. (Listed with the recommended pollinator.)

Any cherry with *Black Tartarian*.

Any almond (*Nonpareil* will take care of all except itself and *IXL*.)

Pear: *Winter Nellis* (any other pear).

Japanese Plums: *Mariposa* with *Santa Rosa*; *Satsuma* with *Wickson* or *Santa Rosa*; *Duarte* and *Burbank* with *Santa Rosa*, *Wickson* or *Elephant Heart*; *Elephant Heart* with *Santa Rosa* (fair) or *Wickson* (fair); *Wickson* with *Satsuma* or *Santa Rosa*.

European Plums: *President* with any other plum.

Apples: *Gravenstein, McIntosh, Delicious, Stayman Winesap, Thompkins King, White Pearmain, Winesap, Winter Banana, Yellow Bellflower, Northern Spy*.

There is one joker in the above list. Many apples can produce crops of parthenocarpic (seedless) fruit without benefit of cross-pollination. This ability varies by climate and variety. Unless you know that the apple variety in the above list will produce crops in your area, don't trust it.

Peach: *J. H. Hale* with any other peach.

These you can plant and expect to get fruit.

Any pear except *Winter Nellis*.

Any apricot except *Riland, Perfection*, and *Reeves*.

Any peach except *J. H. Hale*.

These plums: *Italian, Green Gage, Methley, Beauty, Santa Rosa.*

These apples: Self-fruitful—*Yellow Transparent, Grimes, Yellow Newtown, Rome Beauty;* partially self-fruitful — *Red Astrachan, Golden Delicious, Jonathan.*

Note: These are worthless as pollinators because they produce infertile pollen—*Gravenstein, Stayman Winesap,* and *Winesap.*

If you happen to have neighbors with fruit trees, some of the pollination problems may be solved. In a neighborhood of gardens where bees are at work, the home fruit gardener can depend on the bees working a greater distance than they do in an orchard. You can expect the bees to carry a distance of 200 feet or more when working through gardens. Of course if there are fruit trees in the neighborhood not bearing fruit, you'll have to find out the variety and match it up for cross-pollination with the variety you buy.

What to do if the tree you planted years ago does not bear fruit?

1. You can buy pollen and cross-pollinate by hand. There are several firms that make a business of collecting, curing, and distributing fruit pollens for artificial pollination.

2. Gathering pollen from a tree that's known to be a pollenizer and transferring it to another tree is not the simple process of cutting a spray of blossoms and shaking it over and inside the tree you want to pollinate. Blossoms are gathered at full bloom stage. The anthers are removed by rubbing the flowers over a No. 8-mesh hardware cloth. Then the pollen is cured by holding the anthers in shallow trays at room temperature for two days or more. The pollen is applied to the stigma of the flowers one to three days after the flower opens. Use a small brush, a piece of cork, the eraser on a pencil, or the bare finger.

3. You can graft on a pollinator variety. As with all top-working, the added portion may grow at a faster rate than the old tree and thus call for control by pruning.

Home Food Garden
EVERGREEN FRUITS

In the areas where avocados are grown commercially, gardeners have a long list of evergreen fruiting shrubs and trees to choose from. In addition to the well known varieties of citrus, feijoas, cherimoyas, guavas, loquats, and sapotes can be regarded as fruiting plants.

Gardeners outside the natural citrus areas grow many of these fruiting shrubs or trees as ornamentals first, and enjoy whatever fruit they produce as an unexpected dividend.

The fruit dividend on many ornamentals can be greater if the shrub or tree is chosen by named varieties.

In this chapter, in addition to discussing the well known evergreen fruits, we consider the fruit of several plants listed in the chapters on ornamental shrubs and trees.

AVOCADO (*Persea americana*)

Avocados are extremely temperamental. Some varieties are sensitive to cool weather during flowering. All suffer from strong winds, sudden hot spells. Apparently what satisfies a variety in one location, fails to satisfy it in another area. In fact the only safe rule in choosing a variety seems to be: find out what variety is producing in your neighborhood and plant that variety.

In case that answer doesn't satisfy you, or there are no avocado plantings around you, here are a few pointers.

Two races of avocados are grown in California—Mexican and Guatemalan. (The widely planted *Fuerte* is thought to be a hybrid of the two.) The Guatemalan varieties find their ideal climate in spots protected from direct ocean breezes yet cushioned by the ocean's influence—in zones 12-13. The Mexican variety—smaller and less attractive fruits—are hardier and can be found in zones 9-10. Although the tree is hardy to 20-24°, the flowers are borne in winter and temperatures much below freezing destroy the crop.

All avocados bear crops in cycles, producing a heavy crop one year and a light one the next. This alternate bearing habit is more extreme in some varieties than others.

Here are the peculiarities of the leading varieties:

Anaheim. Guatemalan. Consistent bearer. Large green fruits, June-September. Tree is small and upright in growth habit. Best for landscape use. Very tender to frost.

Haas. Guatemalan. Alternate bearing. Small black fruits, May-October. Probably the best fruit of all the avocados. Large tree spreading to 30 ft.

Nabal. Guatemalan. Very temperamental, huge tree, producing excellent fruit in very limited areas. Large green fruits, June-September.

Fuerte. Hybrid. Alternate bearing. Large, dull green fruit, November-June. Shows bud and blossom damage at 27°. Extremely large tree.

Zutano. Mexican. Upright grower. Pear-shaped fruits, Fuerte size, of good quality. Bears in 2-3 years. Hardy to 20-24°, fruit at 25°.

Duke. Mexican. Small green fruit, September-November. It is as wood-hardy as the orange, but flowers winter killed at 26°.

Mexicola. Mexican. Small black fruits, August-October. Fruits too small for commercial market; but good flavor and hardiness make this variety the best bet for coldest sections.

The following Guatemalan varieties are being planted for excellent quality of fruit in frost free areas: *Carlsbad*, *Dickinson*, and *Lyon*.

CULTURE: The all-important factor in growing avocado is good drainage, at all seasons. A high water table in the winter rainy season is often fatal even in well-drained soils. Watering should be done with drainage requirement in mind, since roots are in the top 3 ft. of soil. Irrigate to that depth, but hold off next watering until tree shows signs of wilting in the cool part of the day. Water thoroughly but as infrequently as possible.

CHERIMOYA (*Annona cherimola*)

This exotic is the type of plant that frustrates gardeners in subtropical California. The frost-free areas along the coast can't grow it because of lack of heat; the interior valleys, even where nearly frost-free, can't grow it because it scorches in the hot sun. The cherimoya therefore is reserved for the warm, protected spots in Southern California that are tempered by the ocean but not cooled by it.

Several new varieties are being tested in hopes of finding one of wider tolerances. You can choose from these: *Booth*, *Bays*, *Chaffey*, *McPherson*, and *Ryerson*. Tests have not been widespread enough to suggest which variety is more dependable.

The tree has a number of unusual characteristics. It grows rapidly in its first 3-4 years, then slows down to make a 15-foot tree with a 20-foot spread. The annual pruning necessary to produce new wood will keep it at that size. The tree begins to bear fruit at 3-4 years of age.

Light green, velvety leaves are 4-10 inches long and arranged alternately in 2 ranks along the stem.

The cherimoya goes against all normal procedure and drops practically all of its leaves for a very short period in late spring when trees about it are in full rush of leaf production. Thick, fleshy, 1-inch, fragrant flowers begin opening about the time of leaf fall and continue forming for 3-4 months. The flowers must be hand pollinated to produce a fruit crop and you can space your harvest by pollinating a few flowers throughout the long period of bloom.

Large fruits, ½-1½ pounds each, are exotic looking. The skin of most varieties looks like it is made up of overlapping leaves. The creamy-white flesh contains black seeds about the size of large beans.

The flavor and texture of the flesh is entirely dependent upon the right combination of heat at the right time. When properly ripened the flesh is buttery, almost custard-like, with a flavor blend of sweet and acid that suggests pineapples and nectarines.

CITRUS

Heat requirements of citrus have been carefully studied and tabulated. Their requirements, like those for grapes, are expressed in degree days but the base figure is 55° rather than the 45° for grapes. (See climate chapter.) *Example:* Supposing average mean daily temperature for March in your area is 56.6°. Deduct the vital 55° at which growth begins, leaving 1.6° as a "remainder." Multiply by 31, the number of days in March, and you get 49.6° accumulated heat for the month. Adding the months together produces the total heat index for your area.

Here are optimum heat indexes for several commercial citrus varieties in cool-to-hot order:

Lime, lemon ....1900°
Valencia orange ....2700°
Washington navel ....3300°
Grapefruit ....5500°

At best these are very rough estimates and do not take all heat variables into account. Yet they do provide a surprisingly accurate rule-of-thumb in deciding which kind of citrus can be grown commercially in what area.

Here's what this means to the home gardener, who differs from the commercial grower in that he is concerned only with a cube of climate measuring 8 ft. in each direction: He can tinker with raised beds and wind screens, with reflected heat and warm south or west walls, to raise growing heat far above the level of his local climate.

A gardener in Santa Barbara, for example, lives in a lemon climate. With some minor changes (perhaps a simple windbreak) he can raise an 8 ft. square of his garden into a Valencia orange climate. By planting in a raised bed, espaliering his tree against a white south wall of his house in front of a concrete patio slab, he might even boost himself out of the lemon climate clear up into the grapefruit class.

A gardener in Oakland, on the other hand, will have to work hard for lemons, still harder for Valencia oranges. Navels and grapefruit of good fruit quality will probably be completely out of reach unless he's particularly ingenious at trapping additional heat.

Watering

While adequate heat is basic to good fruit production, proper watering is vital to the health of the citrus tree itself. *More garden citrus fails from overwatering than from any other cause.*

In considering citrus for the garden, you have to face up to one all-important fact: Citrus does not thrive on the watering schedule suitable for most garden ornamentals. There are two reasons for this:

1. Citrus roots demand abundant oxygen, and are highly sensitive to concentrations of carbon dioxide characteristic of chronically wet soil. This means intermittent watering is a must, with a dry period between waterings of two weeks or more, depending on weather and locality. Cool-climate gardeners may stretch intervals between irrigations to a month. In hot climates, irrigations may be required more frequently. The tree tells you when to water: when leaves just reach the wilting point, give a thorough, deep soaking.

2. Citrus roots need heat to grow. Wet soil is cold; dry soil is warm. Constant moisture keeps soil temperatures too low for good root growth.

You can solve the watering problem in the following ways:

1. Grow citrus in a bed by themselves. Mature trees, clothed to the ground with handsome foliage, need little support from low growing companion plants.

If you wish to use companion plants, choose ones with the same watering requirements as citrus. There are many plants with colors that harmonize with yellow-and-green citrus colors, with contrasting forms and textures, and with varying heights.

2. Grow dwarfs in containers. They'll live happily in their own cube of soil for many years as striking patio plants and you can water to suit needs of each individual plant. They will not develop tree size and quantity of fruit like the trees planted in the ground, of course.

Above all, *never plant citrus in a lawn or in areas reached by lawn sprinkling.*

Frost Protection

Types of citrus vary in their cold tolerance. Here's how they rank, in tender-to-hardy order:

1. Mexican lime; 2. lemon; 3. grapefruit; 4. orange; 5. mandarin orange; and 6. kumquat.

Of these classes, limes alone rigidly demand subtropical climates. Attempt them only where frost seldom strikes or where you can protect them.

The condition of the tree at the time of the frost is all-important. Late spring frosts are murderous, striking while trees are in a flush of growth. Temperatures of duration or repetition below 32° can produce serious defoliation and even death. On the other hand, in midwinter, when growth is hard and trees are dormant, most citrus can withstand surprisingly low temperatures without injury.

Gardeners in cold areas should make every attempt to keep trees dormant until well past time of late frosts by withholding fertilizer, and limiting irrigation to the absolute minimum.

What About Shade?

Because of the rigid heat requirements of citrus, it is commonly assumed they demand full sun. However, the *natural habitat of citrus is in shade.*

In shade or filtered sun, foliage will be at its best—lush, green, and uncurled. One of the most successful grapefruit plantings is in Indio, California, where trees are grown in shade of taller date trees.

But remember the critical heat factor. If you're in a marginal area, near the lower limits of the heat requirements of the citrus variety you are trying to grow, you will have to *plant in full sun to provide adequate heat.*

ORANGES

Washington navel. Winter ripening California orange. Blooms in spring, sets fruits and ripens, ready for picking in 12 months or less, before tree blooms again. In warm sections of northern California (e.g. Oroville), the Washington navel ripens in time for Christmas. Navels, for optimum flavor, require more growing heat than Valencias.

Valencia. Summer ripening California juice orange. Matures from April to October. Fruit that sets from April bloom is not ripe until the following summer. Normally, new flowers develop on the tree along with the maturing fruit in the spring.

Summer navel. Ripens April-August. Although fruit may be somewhat inferior to Washington navel, it stores well on the tree. Leaves, probably the largest that grow on any of the commercial citrus, have a lush tropical look. Bark almost black, with a jade-green splotching. Good variety in the valley areas.

Robertson navel. Produces heavy crops of good quality fruit similar to that of Washington navel; ripens about two weeks earlier (November-May).

Torocco red juice orange. Imported from Italy. A novelty here but a choice fruit type in Europe, where its dark red juice with rich grape-like flavor is prized above that of all other varieties. Red color varies according to climate; best in hot interior valleys. Fruit with most color produced inside or on the shady side of the tree.

Shamoudi orange. Popular in the Middle East where it is classified as the highest quality orange. It has not been grown commercially here, mainly because the early navel plantings proved so successful. Like the navel, the Shamoudi matures in midwinter (December-April). Should interest the experimental gardener who wants something unusual. On dwarf rootstock it is ideal in size, shape, and foliage.

LEMONS

Eureka. Common lemon in commercial groves, along with Villa Franca and Lisbon, all much alike in fruit. Blooms and ripens throughout the year; heaviest production in spring.

Meyer. Entirely different lemon from the commercial Eureka, producing a rounder, thinner skinned, more orange-colored fruit with a tangy aroma and a high juice content many gardeners like. One of the best bets for cool climates. Bears its largest proportion of fruit in the spring. Not inherently dwarf, growing 12 ft. or more in height and 15 or more ft. in width on its own roots. If grown on dwarf rootstock, however, it is about 8 ft. high and wide at maturity.

Ponderosa. Strictly a novelty. Bears exceptionally large, thick-skinned lemons often more than 2 pounds each. Although fruit may look pithy at first glance, it is really quite juicy and mildly flavored. Very thorny; ripens in winter.

LIMES

Bearss. Stabilized seedless strain which bears larger and less variable fruits than the more common Mexican lime. Both are true limes with a distinct lime flavor, as opposed to the Rangpur lime, which is not a lime at all but is a kin to the mandarin orange. Bearss lime trees are tender and should be grown, without special care, only in areas with little or no frost. Produces good fruit in cool regions. Bears some fruit during most of the year, but heaviest production comes between winter and late spring.

GRAPEFRUIT

Marsh seedless. Commercial California grapefruit. For first-class fruit, give it the growing heat it needs to mature properly. Fruit ripens in desert areas December-May; in other sections, May-August or later. Marsh grapefruit is slow to ripen, even in desert areas; takes 18 months or more to ripen on the tree. Storing fruit on tree improves sugar content.

Novelties.

Standard commercial varieties are all products of long years of selection, while many of the novelties are hybrids created by crossing one variety with another.

Sampson tangelo. Cross between a grapefruit and the Dancy tangerine. More like the grapefruit in skin color. The juice flavor also shows its grapefruit parentage. Among the most handsome and decorative of all citrus. Thin skinned and extremely juicy, which means it is a poor shipper, doesn't keep well, and is, therefore, not grown commercially. Ripens February-May.

Minneola tangelo. Hybrid of the grapefruit and the tangerine; not as handsome a tree as the Sampson; fruit superior in taste. Ripens February-May. The Minneola is different from the Sampson in that it favors the tangerine side of its parentage. Fruit color is the most brilliant orange, with juice flavor like a superior tangerine; juice can be diluted considerably and still taste like the pure product.

Dancy tangerine. Common commercial tangerine and a familiar Christmas time fruit everywhere. Although fairly resistant to cold, it is at its best in hot climates. Produces good fruit in coastal areas near Ventura, California.

Dweet tangor. Produces juicy, egg-shaped fruits about the size of a Valencia orange. A hybrid of the Mediterranean sweet orange and the Dancy tangerine, it tastes something like a tangerine. Most of the fruit is carried at the ends of the branches, making it susceptible to burn and scorch in extremely hot or windy areas and to frost in cooler sections. Ripens March-May.

MANDARIN ORANGES

Probably best type of citrus for gardeners in areas too cool to ripen other oranges properly.

King mandarin. Has long been grown in southeast Asia, though not in California. Fruits large, as mandarins go. Bumpy, irregular skin is easy to peel; when well grown, the fruit is of top-notch quality. It ripens later (March-May) and has more exacting climatic demands than other mandarins.

Owari Satsuma. Perhaps the most tolerant of varying climates. Fruits are good commercial quality, although small in size. Bears regularly (October-January) in cool areas at the very limits of the citrus range. Ripe fruit colorful, tasty in winter, decorative in landscaping. Inclined to be pendulous and wider than high in shape. Excellent slow growing dwarf.

Kinnow mandarin. One of the varieties developed by Dr. Herbert Frost of the Citrus Experiment Station in Riverside, California; cross of King with the willow leaf mandarin. In flavor one of the best, but has a tight skin and is quite seedy. Tends to produce fruit in alternate seasons. Kinnow mandarins mature from January-May; since the tree stores fruit, leave it on the tree until November if you like.

Kara mandarin. Also developed by Dr. Frost at Riverside: is a hybrid of Owari Satsuma and King. Tree has beautiful dark green foliage and high quality fruit somewhat larger and looser-skinned than Kinnows. Fruit does not keep on the tree; ripens February-May. Kara is one of the best.

KUMQUAT

A decorative novelty. Does not belong to the genus *Citrus*, but to the closely related genus *Fortunella*. Tree size varies according to the type of rootstock used; trees may grow anywhere from 5 ft. to more than 25 ft. high. Dwarf kumquats grow approximately 8 ft. high. The tiny orange-colored fruits are borne in abundance. Eat them fresh—skin and all—or use them to make marmalade. Fruit not considered top quality, but hardiness of tree makes it a good choice. Stands temperatures lower than both the sweet and mandarin orange; bears most of the year, with heaviest production from October-January. Doesn't fruit well in coastal climates.

Eustis limequat. Hybrid of kumquat with Mexican lime. Fruit resembles the kumquat; flavor suggests the lime. Tree is small leafed, rapid growing, open in form; somewhat inferior in appearance to most citrus varieties, but is more resistant to cold than the lime. Bears throughout the year, but heaviest production comes in late fall and winter. Produces good fruit in coastal areas near Santa Barbara and Ventura, California.

FEIJOA SELLOWIANA. PINEAPPLE GUAVA. Evergreen. Zones 7-13. (See chapter on shrubs.) Attractive, ornamental, large shrub or small tree. Blossom and fruiting times vary by climate: Flowers in May in Southern California, in June in northern coastal California; fruits 4-5½ months after flowers open in the South, 5-7 months in cool sections of northern California. Fruit is pear shaped, dull green, varying in size from 1-3 in. long.

The tree seems to enjoy the heat of the valleys, but the fruit of trees grown along the coast has a richer, sprightlier flavor.

Varieties usually available are Coolidge, Superba, and Choiceana. If planting only one variety, choose Coolidge, as the other two require cross-pollination. Combination of any two will do.

No special cultural requirements.

GUAVA. (See *Psidium* in chapter on shrubs.)

The tropical guava is available in named varieties, but they are not distinctly superior to good seedlings. Size of fruit varies from 1-4 in. in length and may be oblong, round, or pear-shaped. Fruit has sweet but sprightly flavor. Flesh may be pink, yellow, or white. Unless controlled by pruning, the shrub or bush will grow to 18 ft. where adapted.

The strawberry guava has no named varieties; it comes nearly true from seed. Slower growing and better mannered than the tropical (lemon) guava, it generally finds a prominent place in the ornamental section of the garden.

LITCHI NUT (*Litchi chinensis*)

A very handsome, round-topped tree, slow growing to 20 ft. or more. Compound leaves of 3-9 leaflets are coppery when young, bright green in maturity. The trees need cool, foggy winters and tropical summers, and are as hardy as Guatemalan avocados. Many are growing well in San Diego Co. in especially favorable locations. High humidity is essential to prevent fruits from cracking open. Unless cold-resistant varieties are brought in, there are few places for the litchi nut in California, except as an ornamental.

U. S. Department of Agriculture is testing more than 75 varieties in the United States and Hawaii. Most of them are now fruiting in Hawaii.

LOQUAT (*Eriobotrya japonica*)

Yellow-to-orange fruits, somewhat pear shaped and about the size of a small egg, are produced in terminal clusters beginning, by variety, in March. Good fruit production cannot be expected where light intensities are high, as the fruits are exposed to the sun. Flowers and buds are destroyed by winter frosts that are not damaging to the tree. Best growth and production in areas under some ocean influence.

Most generally planted varieties are:

Advance. Large pear-shaped fruits with deep yellow skin and white flesh. Bears March-June. Will tolerate warm inland areas.

Champagne. Yellow skin with white flesh, rather tart and very juicy. Will tolerate warm inland areas.

Gold Nugget. Orange-colored skin and flesh. Best adapted to coastal areas.

MACADAMIA NUT *(Macadamia ternifolia)*

Nuts don't fill out as well and do not have the oil content of those grown in Hawaii. Needs a warm climate, but not adapted to the hot inland valleys. Areas near coast with winter temperatures above 27° are preferred.

Trees come into bearing in 7 years. Nuts should be allowed to drop from the tree—which they do over a long season. Dry the nuts in the sun after removing hulls and again after they have cracked.

MANGO *(Mangifera indica)*

A tropical that will exist in the frost-free areas, but that is about all.

OLIVES

All varieties of olives tend to produce heavy crops one year, followed by one or more very light crops. There is not much you can do about it, for thinning does not seem to help. Since the tree is very ornamental, not at all root-greedy, requires no pruning, and little spraying, it earns a place in California food gardens. Trees in the hot interiors produce best fruit and heaviest crops.

Varieties:

Mission. A taller tree than other varieties. Medium sized fruit in November.

Manzanillo. Fruit slightly larger and earlier than Mission. Good for pickling.

Ascolano. Fruit large with small pit, and tender.

Sevillano. The largest olives but with lower oil content.

Size of all varieties can be increased by thinning to 2-3 olives to 1 ft. of branch.

PAPAYA *(Carica papaya)*

A true tropical, successfully grown in Hawaii, the papaya seldom produces flavorful fruits even when grown in the warmest, frost-free sections around San Diego. The one factor in favor of experimenting with papaya is its speed in bearing fruit. It bears in a little more than a year from seed.

WHITE SAPOTE *(Casimiroa edulis)*

Rate this tree and its fruits near the top of the list of subtropical fruiting-ornamentals. Strong-growing evergreen to 20 feet high and as wide. Luxuriant foliage. Leaves are divided fanwise into 3-7 ovate or narrow oval 5-inch leaflets. Fruit looks like a 3-4 inch round green apple but the soft cream-colored pulp has a peach flavor.

Adapted to the same areas as lemons. Will lose leaves when subjected to several light frosts, without damage to the tree.

These varieties are being grown: *Pike*, large 4-inch fruits of good quality in fall; *Wilson*, slender tree, 3-inch fruits in August-January; *Suebelle*, large spreading tree, 3-inch, pear-shaped fruits.

Home Food Garden

HERBS

The growing of herbs is delightful gardening, with many facets of appeal. Herbs have an intriguing historic background. Their products are useful to the gourmet-gardener. Their fragrance gives enjoyment. Many are ornamental.

Herbs include all the plants that at some time in their long history were useful for seasoning, medicine, and fragrance, and for household uses such as dyes.

The traditional herb garden is formal in design, patterned after sixteenth and seventeenth century gardens that were planted within squares and rectangles. The beauty of this formal type of garden depends on the choice and arrangements of plants and a careful pruning for a trim effect.

The informal herb garden has endless placement possibilities: a hillside, a rock garden, a border planting. While not as trim in appearance in this setting, plants have the opportunity of full growth.

Most herbs can be grown from seed but more and more nurseries now stock perennial plants and annuals in season. Seeds should be thinly sown, usually where they are to be grown as they do not transplant well, and covered lightly with a sifting of soil. Press firmly with a board; keep moist. Thin to allow room for size of mature plants.

It is a fallacy that herbs thrive on neglect. They merely survive. They grow easily in average soil (preferably alkaline). Break up the soil thoroughly so that it is friable (not hard or water logged); work in well-rotted manure before planting. Give them the same amount of water that you give the annuals in your garden; do not allow them to become completely dried out. If they have been watered but still do not grow, fertilize them with either organic or chemical fertilizer. Most of them like sun but with a few exceptions grow well in coastal foggy areas. They attract few pests. For good appearance they need occasional pruning. When to prune will depend upon your particular climate and the severity of the winter. During the summer they can always be trimmed if they look untidy or are growing out of bounds.

Young leaves of culinary herbs can be cut when needed. Leaves to be dried and stored should be cut just as the plants come into bloom, when their oils are strongest, either as leaves or in branches. Dry in single layers in suit boxes, in a warm but sun-free place, turning occasionally until chip-dry. Strip leaves and store in closed containers. Seed crop is harvested when color changes to brown or gray and seeds appear to be drying.

Listed are some herbs and their uses. Medicinal uses are not included.

— Encyclopedia —

ALLIUM SATIVUM. GARLIC. Perennial. To 1 ft. CULTURE: Start from seed, or plant bulbs base downward to depth of 1-2 in. Harvest when tops begin to turn yellow. USE: Bulbs used as flavoring.

ALLIUM SCHOENOPRASUM. CHIVE. Perennial. To 1 ft. Compact; grass-like foliage; lavender flowers which should be removed to keep fresh leaves coming on. CULTURE: Start from seed or division of bulb clumps. Divide clumps every 2-3 yrs. to prevent overcrowding. Does well in ordinary soil; needs ample moisture, slight shade in hottest sections. USE: Fresh leaves valuable as seasoning; mild onion flavor. Can be grown in pot indoors.

ANETHUM GRAVEOLENS. DILL. Annual. 3-4 ft. Lacy leaves and flower heads; slender habit. CULTURE: Sow where plants are to remain; thin to 18 in. apart. Does not transplant easily. USE: Fresh leaves used in salad; on lamb chops; in pickling and in vinegars. Seeds used as flavoring.

ANISE. See Pimpinella anisum.

ANTHEMIS NOBILIS. CHAMOMILE. (See chapter on perennials.)

ANTHRISCUS CEREFOLIUM. CHERVIL. Annual. To 2 ft. Resembles parsley in leaf and root. Fine-cut, fern-like foliage; white flowers. CULTURE: Start from seed; sometimes difficult to grow; needs partial shade, ample moisture; often reseeds itself when once established. USE: Leaves used fresh or dried as flavoring; fresh leaves used as garnish and wherever parsley is indicated; mild parsley-like flavor.

ARTEMISIA ABSINTHIUM. WORMWOOD. Perennial. To 4 ft. Gray, silky, pungent, much-cut leaves. Some of the many artemisias: the low mound of *A. schmidtiana nana*; *A. stelleriana*; *A. abrotanum*; tall *A. arborescens*. CULTURE: All grow from seed, cuttings, root division; like sun and not too much water; need trimming. USE: Some have pungent fragrance in leaves; gray leaves give valuable accents in the garden.

ARTEMISIA DRACUNCULUS. TARRAGON. Perennial. To 1 ft. Loose-growing plant; smooth, narrow green leaves. CULTURE: Difficult to establish. Start from divisions or cuttings; true tarragon cannot be seeded. Dies down completely in winter. Once established will live for years and need root division. USE: Leaves either fresh or dry, used sparingly, are flavorful in salads and with egg and cheese dishes; popular in vinegar.

BASIL. See Ocimum Basilicum.

BORAGO OFFICINALIS. BORAGE. Annual. To 3 ft. Husky branched growth with bristly leaves; star-like blue nodding flowers. CULTURE: Start from seed where they are to be grown. USE: Is worthwhile for the lovely blooms which can be floated on cold drinks. Very young leaves have slight cucumber taste.

BURNET. See Sanguisorba minor.

CARUM CARVI. CARAWAY. Biennial. 1-2 ft. Carrot-like leaves; white flowers. Loose, open habit. CULTURE: Start from seed in well drained soil. Will flower early in second season; seeds mature by midsummer. USE: Dried seeds used as flavoring in pickles, vegetables, cookies.

CHERVIL. See Anthriscus cerefolium.

CHIVE. See Allium schoenoprasum.

CHRYSANTHEMUM BALSAMITA. COSTMARY. Perennial. To 3 ft. Loose and spreading in habit; sometimes weedy looking. Gray-green leaf with serrated edge often called "Bible" leaf; very fragrant of lemon and mint; small, yellow, button-like flowers. CULTURE: Start from seed or root divisions. Best in dry, sunny location. USE: Fresh or dried leaves used sparingly as seasoning especially with eggs. Old time use as book-mark in family Bible.

CORIANDRUM SATIVUM. CORIANDER. Annual. 12-15 in. Slender habit; delicate, feathery leaves; small pink umbels of flowers. CULTURE: Start from seed. Grows quickly; often self-sows. USE: Dried seeds used as flavoring.

COSTMARY. See Chrysanthemum balsamita.

COTULA CORONOPIFOLIA. BRASS BUTTONS. Perennial. Appearance, fragrance, culture and uses so similar to those of chamomile that they are often confused; distinguished by yellow button-like flower. More easily obtained than chamomile in West.

DILL. See Anethum graveolens.

FOENICULUM VULGARE. FENNEL. Perennial. 3-5 ft. Loose and erect; finely cut foliage. CULTURE: Start from seed where it is to be grown. Thin to 2 in. apart. Does best in light, well-drained soil. Variety *dulce* is smaller. USE: Young leaves and seeds taste slightly like licorice; used in salads and with fish. Stems may be eaten raw or cooked like celery.

GARLIC. See Allium sativum.

HYSSOPUS OFFICINALIS. HYSSOP. Perennial. 18-24 in. Small, orderly plant; bright blue, pink or white flowers. CULTURE: Start from seeds, cuttings, divisions. Needs sun. USE: Ornamental; may be used in perennial border or as hedge plant for herb garden if trimmed. Not edible.

LAVANDULA OFFICINALIS. ENGLISH LAVENDER. (See chapter on perennials.)

LEMON BALM. See Melissa officinalis.

LEVISTICUM OFFICINALE. LOVAGE. Perennial. 24-36 in. Tall, sturdy; yellow-green foliage; greenish-white flowers. CULTURE: Start from seed or divisions of roots. Thrives in moist, rich soil. USE: Decorative; fresh or dried leaves used as flavoring. Flavor similar to celery but stronger.

LIPPIA CITRIODORA. LEMON VERBENA. Perennial. Shrub growing from 3 ft. to 12 ft. depending on climate. Great favorite for delightful fragrance of leaves; unimportant white flowers. CULTURE: Possible to grow from cuttings; plants available at nurseries; in severe climates should be wintered in basement but elsewhere needs severe pruning in autumn. USE: For delightful fragrance; in potpourri; leaves in cool drinks.

LOVAGE. See Levisticum officinale.

MAJORANA HORTENSIS. (*Origanum majorana*). MARJORAM. SWEET MAJORAM. Perennial treated as annual in cold areas. To 2 ft. Upright growth with grayish-green leaves; white flowers in knotted clusters. One of the confused group of marjorams on which research for classification is now being done. Leaves vary, from grayish to yellow-green; some have spreading roots; flowers are white, lavender, pinkish-red and magenta. Oregano belongs in this classification but the plants so labeled are not the same in all nurseries. MEXICAN OREGANO is *Coleus amboinicus*. CULTURE: All grow easily from seed, cuttings or root division. USE: Regardless of confusion, all are attractive, fragrant, useful; popular as seasoning in salads, casserole dishes, and rich meats.

MELISSA OFFICINALIS. LEMON BALM. Perennial. To 2 ft. Fragrant green lemon-scented leaves; unimportant white flowers; roots inclined to spread but can be controlled; branches can be cut almost continually. CULTURE: Starts easily from seed or cuttings; new plants can be started from root or branch cutting if plant becomes woody. USE: Delightful lemon fragrance. Keeps well in arrangements. Leaves used in cold drinks.

MENTHA. MINT. Perennial. 18-24 in. Two species, *M. spicata* COMMON SPEARMINT, and *M. piperita* PEPPERMINT, are most often used as flavoring agents. CULTURE: Start from surface or underground runners. No special care necessary. Rampant grower, tends to run wild in small areas if not restrained by boards or tire sunk in ground, or grown in pots. USE: Fresh and dried leaves as flavoring, especially for lamb; as garnish; in cold drinks.

OCIMUM BASILICUM. BASIL. SWEET BASIL. Annual. To 2 in. Very fragrant; several other varieties available. CULTURE: Grows easily from seed; rapid grower. Requires full sun. USE: One of the best-liked herbs, either fresh or dried in salads; with tomatoes, cheese and eggs.

ORIGANUM. See Majorana hortensis.

PARSLEY. See Petroselinum crispum.

PETROSELINUM CRISPUM. PARSLEY. Biennial often grown as annual. 2-10 in. Compact plant; dark green, tightly curled leaf. CULTURE: Soak seeds in warm water for 24 hrs. before planting to speed germination. Sow 10-12 in. apart where it is to be grown; will be useful longer if not allowed to bloom. USE: Good edging or border plant for herb and vegetable gardens. Fresh leaves used as garnish and for flavor.

PIMPINELLA ANISUM. ANISE. Annual. To 2 ft. Delicate foliage and habit; tiny white flowers. CULTURE: Start from seed where they are to be grown as they do not transplant easily. USE: A few fresh leaves add flavor to salad; seeds are popular in cookies and confections.

ROSMARINUS OFFICINALIS. ROSEMARY. Perennial. 2-5 ft. depending on climate. One of the best-loved fragrant herbs; leaves like small pine needles; pale blue flower. There are now two varieties of prostrate rosemary that fall over walls; smaller leaf. (See chapter on ground covers.) CULTURE: Difficult to grow from seed; from cuttings, slow for a year; available at nurseries. In areas of severe winters, leave in ground. In mild areas they require trimming. USES: Ornamental; keeps well in arrangements; favorite seasoning herb, used sparingly.

SALVIA OFFICINALIS. SAGE. Perennial. 18 in. to 2 ft. Shrubby plant; oblong, gray leaves; spikes of violet-blue. CULTURE: Start from seed, cuttings, divisions of roots. Needs well drained soil, moderate water. USE: Decorative plant for rock garden or wall. Fresh or dried leaves used as flavoring, especially for poultry.

SANGUISORBA MINOR. BURNET. Perennial. 8-12 in. Fern-like leaves grow in rosettes close to ground; flowers whitish-pink, borne on long stems. CULTURE: Start from seed or divisions of roots; produces better plants if divided each year. Self-seeds prolifically if flowers are not cut. USE: Young leaves have a distinct cucumber flavor very useful in salads and in vinegar making.

SATUREJA HORTENSIS. SUMMER SAVORY. Annual. To 18 in. Loose open habit; narrow green leaves; pinkish white flowers. CULTURE: Sow seeds where plants are to grow; thin to 18 in. apart. USE: Fresh or dried leaves as flavoring in meats, fish, soup and vegetables.

SATUREJA MONTANA. WINTER SAVORY. Perennial. To 15 in. Low, spreading shrub. Stiff, oblong, narrow green leaves, whitish-pink flowers. CULTURE: Start from seed, cuttings, divisions, 16-18 in. apart in rows. Slow to germinate. USE: Very decorative plant; good for border or edging; well adapted to rock garden. Fresh or dried leaves used as savory in flavoring.

TARRAGON. See Artemisia dracunculus.

THYMUS VULGARIS. THYME. Perennial. To 8 in. Spreading habit; small leaf; lavender flowers. (See also chapter on ground covers.) CULTURE: Start from seed, cuttings or nursery plants about 1 ft. apart. Cuttings root quickly. One of many forms of thyme; some spreading, some erect; green, yellow or gray foliage; small lavender, white, or red blooms; many available in nurseries. USE: All are decorative, adapting themselves as ground covers, to rock gardens or walls; if trimmed, erect plants make neat borders; leaves fresh or dried are favorite seasoning in many foods.

WORMWOOD. See Artemisia absinthium.

Indoor Gardening

Here in the West in the last ten years a complete revolution has taken place in indoor gardening. We have made an almost complete change over from *gardening* indoors to indoor *designing* with plants.

The trend in use of indoor plants is linked directly to the change from small windows to large expanses, even walls, of glass. But it has come about not so much from the recognition that additional light provides a wider scope for indoor gardening as from the discovery that plants are structural forms as well as colorful or beautiful plants. The architect and interior designer has demonstrated the design value of indoor plants.

Indoor plants are no longer talked about in terms of color alone but are appraised for their form and texture. They are used in "well-balanced compositions, not restless conglomerations"; they are "bold" and "cast dramatic shadows" or "repeat outdoor forms."

Demonstrations in design value of indoor plants is not limited to the modern glass house. Today, in old and new houses alike, the dish garden, the portable planter, and all of the various containers of the florist shop and the nursery have become designs with foliage plants.

The indoor gardener interested primarily in color, or just the pleasure of watching plants grow, has actually gained by the increased interest in foliage plants. The suppliers of indoor plants, encouraged by increasing sales, have made available a wider selection of all types of plants. The list of indoor plants in this chapter is proof that no matter what type of indoor garden you go in for, there's a wide selection of color, forms, and textures.

INDOOR CULTURE

An outdoor plant can make adjustment to take care of faulty gardening. Roots spread out through the top layers of the soil when the lower layers become waterlogged or they go deeper when the surface layers dry out.

Plants grown indoors are completely at your mercy. Their roots have no place to go. They must get along with the condition of the soil within the container and with the food they find there.

WATERING

Success in growing plants indoors is more dependent on how well you control the moisture supply than on any other factor. This is especially true when plants are grown in dish gardens and other containers without provision for drainage. Drainage within such containers is provided by a layer of charcoal on the bottom and a layer of peat moss, sphagnum moss, or pumice. There are preparations on the market that combine drainage material and soil mixture. These bottom layers act as a sponge to supply both air and water. If more water is added than the sponge layers will hold, the air is crowded out.

The gardener who gets along well with indoor plants develops a watering sense. Knowing when the plant has nearly exhausted the water in the sponge, he pours in just enough water to fill the sponge and no more. Until you develop such a sympathy for the relationship between soil and plant, do this: Let the plant work in moist, but not saturated, soil; using the soil beneath the surface as an indicator, withhold water until it is no longer moist. Your schedule will probably go something like this: Most small containers, on the average of twice a week; large containers, every week or every 2 weeks, depending on plant growth.

LIGHT

A position near a north window furnishes just the right amount of diffused, natural light for plants native to shaded jungles, as are most house plants.

Very few foliage plants can tolerate direct sunlight, especially when it is magnified through clear glass. For that reason, avoid placing even those which can take more light, directly behind or below unshaded windows that face the midday sun.

Variegated foliage plants always need more light than do solid green varieties. Leaf cells in the white spots contain little or no chlorophyll and hence are not capable of carrying on photosynthesis or food manufacturing.

It is a common misconception that foliage plants benefit from an occasional outing in the garden. On the contrary, the shock of moving back and forth between two environments is often more than plants can stand.

NOURISHMENT

If the original potting mixture is rich in nutrients, the plant won't need any fertilizer until the roots have nearly filled the container. If the soil is sandy and weak in nutrients (although it shouldn't be, if you have used the right potting mixture), plants may require a feeding shortly after planting. A feeding schedule depends, too, on the size of the container and the number and type of plants contained.

A rule of the thumb that's safe is to use a dilute liquid fertilizer for watering once a month.

HOW TO KEEP PLANTS CLEAN

House dust is another foreign factor with which indoor plants must contend. Leaves covered with a film of dust cannot carry on transpiration in the normal manner. To keep them free of dust, clean the leaves top and bottom, with a damp cloth or sponge, once or twice a month.

To make the leaves shine, rub the surface with skimmed or non-fat milk or a mild soap and water solution. Commercial leaf polishes also are available. To avoid burning the foliage, be sure to water the plants several hours before you apply these preparations. Don't use oil of any kind on the leaves.

Routine washing will also keep the plants clean of insects such as mealy bug, thrips, and red spiders. (For control, see chapter on pests and diseases.)

SOIL

(See chapter on container gardening.)

— Encyclopedia —

AGLAEONEMA. Evergreen. Dark green leaves, often having attractive variegations.

A. commutatum. Grows to 2 ft. Narrow, 6-in. leaves with silver-gray markings.

A. roebelenii. Robust growth; thick stems. Very wide, oval, leathery, 10-in. leaves are mottled with gray.

A. simplex. CHINESE EVERGREEN. Low-growing, erect plant to 3 ft., with thick stems. Broad, oblong, 6-8 in. leaves with pointed tips are shiny and slightly wavy.

Thrives in poor light. Needs rich, fibrous loam. Takes abundant or little moisture. Stem or tip cuttings.

Suitable for places away from light—in dish gardens or on mantels.

AMOMUM CARDAMON. CARDAMON AMOMUM. Evergreen perennial that spreads by creeping rootstocks. On stems, to 12 in. or more, rising from bushy clumps are narrow, light green, leathery, 10-in. leaves.

Give north light. Needs warmth. Requires rich soil and abundant moisture. Likes being root-bound, so feed once a month with fish emulsion. Divide in spring, when plant gets too large for container. Cut back when rangy; new growth will appear.

Use wherever thick mass of foliage is wanted. Attractive in window boxes.

ANTHURIUM. Evergreen. Valued for its very showy, tropical-looking blooms and dark green, leathery, arrow-shaped leaves.

A. andraeanum. Long, strong center stems have aerial roots. Dark green leaves to 1 ft. or more. Yellow calla-like spikes, below which are shiny, heart-shaped, spreading, 6-in. bracts colored in shades of red, rose, pink, and white. Blooms long lasting; appear almost all year.

Give north light. Needs high temperatures. Requires a special soil mixture of: 2 parts shredded osmunda, 1 part rough leaf mold, 1 part rough manure, 1 part coarse sand. Repot every 3 years. Before aerial roots show well above pot, wrap stem with osmunda. When roots show through osmunda, cut and sink in pot. Requires moisture at all times. Feed every month with ¼ to ½ oz. ammonium sulfate to 1 gal. of water.

A. scherzerianum. Slow-growing, compact plant to 2 ft. Unlike *A. andræanum*, forms crown close to soil surface. Dark green, rather narrow, 12-in. leaves. Yellow flower spikes are spirally coiled, the 3-in. bracts bright red.

Give north light. Requires high temperatures. Prefers a rough, fibrous, chunky soil mixture of: 2 parts soil, 1 part leaf mold, ½ part sand, 1 part manure. Needs abundant moisture. Feed with ammonium sulfate every month. Division of crowns.

Use anthuriums for spectacular color. At home with tropical furnishings; on lanais.

ASPLENIUM NIDUS. (*Asplenium nidus-avis*). BIRDS-NEST-FERN. Evergreen fern with wavy, erect, lush, light green blade-like fronds, wavy along the margins, radiating from an open center. In seedling stage fronds are arching.

Give north light. Light soil. Requires moisture, but less water in winter.

Mainly when ferns are small, are used in fern dish gardens or planted with azaleas in containers. Large plants are effective by themselves.

AUCUBA JAPONICA. (See chapter on shrubs.) One of the few, commonly planted, outdoor shrubs that will take indoor conditions over a long period of time. The forms more often used as house plants are: Var. *variegata*, GOLD DUST PLANT, and var. *crotonifolia*.

Give north light. Thrives in well-drained acid soil. Needs moisture.

Use young plants for contrast against green foliage in planters. Combine in containers with small ferns. For dark corners, or as single plants in cold hallways. Mass in indoor window boxes.

CHAMAEDOREA ELEGANS (also listed as *Neanthe bella*). Evergreen. Small, slender, upright palm, slow growing to 2-8 ft. Graceful fronds divided into very narrow, rich green leaflets. (Also see chapter on palms.)

Give north light. Requires warm temperatures to 60-65°. Prefers well-drained soil. Constant moisture.

Combine with ferns in dish gardens. Use single plant for contrast against heavier foliage in built-in window boxes.

CISSUS. (See chapter on vines.) The two species commonly planted indoors are: *C. antarctica*, KANGAROO IVY, and *C. rhombifolia*, GRAPE IVY.

Give north light. Grows where cool. Needs well-drained soil and moisture.

Train as upright plant on walls having little light; as trailing plant in wall-bracket containers.

COLEUS BLUMEI. Erect-growing perennial to 3 ft. Soft-textured, 4-in. leaves with scalloped edges are colored in yellows, reds, greens, whites, and purples. Spikes of light blue flowers.

Likes sun; will stand direct light. Needs warmth. Thrives in well-drained soil. Moisture. Cut back and feed; pinch back to keep compact. Seeds. Cuttings.

Use where you can enjoy its highly colorful foliage. In sunny indoor windowboxes, in pots.

DIEFFENBACHIA. Evergreen. Erect, shrubby, large-leafed plants, with thick stems. Leaves usually spotted, marbled, or variegated in several shades of light and dark greens.

D. amoena. 3 ft. high, with broad, leathery, dark green, 18-in. leaves, with white, slanting stripes on either side of midrib.

D. picta. Wide, oval, rich green leaves to 10 in. or more, spotted with greenish-white. Var. *Rudolph Roehrs*, the best form, has chartreuse green leaves blotched with ivory and edged in green.

Give north light. Best in high temperatures, *D. amœna* requires less heat than other dieffenbachias. Water sparingly.

D. amœna is suitable for a large room where a medium-height plant would be in scale. Use *D. picta* as a single plant for showy effect—attractive in green-toned rooms (particularly *Rudolph Roehrs*), and against dark woodwork.

DIZYGOTHECA VEITCHII. (*Aralia veitchii*). Leaves divided fan-wise into 9-11 narrow, 5-6 in., wavy-margined leaflets that are dark, shiny green above, reddish-brown beneath.

Give north light. Needs warm temperatures. Soil mixture of equal parts sand and leaf mold. Requires ample moisture. Subject to pests in dry atmosphere. Propagated by hardwood cuttings.

When small, combine in dish gardens with fittonias or other plants needing warmth and moisture. As a single plant, makes a lacy pattern against a wall.

DRACAENA. Small tree or shrub with long, strap-like leaves attached to main stem in a thick circular fashion.

D. fragrans massangeana. (*D. massangeana*). Light green, somewhat arched, 3-ft. leaves with yellow stripe down center are closely set.

D. sanderiana. Slow growing, rather tall, slender plant. Gray-green, 9-in. leaves with white band are sparse and mostly upright.

D. deremensis warneckii. (*D. warneckii*). Most decorative of all the dracænas. Erect, green leaves, striped white and gray.

Give dracæna north light. Requires warmth, good drainage, and constant moisture. Feed with ammonium sulfate once every 6 weeks.

Use as single plant, or mass together in indoor window box. Young plants may be used in larger terrariums to give needed height to lower growing plants. Group 3 in a container against a dark wall.

FATSIA JAPONICA. (*Aralia japonica, Aralia sieboldii*). (See chapter on shrubs.)

Give north light. Thrives in cold temperatures. In rich heavy soil. Feed every 4 weeks.

Use in dish gardens with ferns when in seedling stage. Later, in large containers, will take the cold drafts of an entrance hall. Makes a bold pattern against walls.

FICUS. FIG.

F. diversifolia. MISTLETOE FIG. Has small, 2-in. leaves.

Has same cultural requirements as *F. retusa*.

May be grown to give effect of tall, slender tree in a home.

F. elastica. RUBBER PLANT. Commonly a tree, but in its youth is used as a pot or tub plant. Thick, glossy, deep green, 5-12 in. leaves. (Also see chapter on trees.)

F. e. belgica. (*F. e. rubra*). Rich, dark green leaves are broader and shorter than those of the common rubber plant and have bronze tone. New leaves when unfolding are reddish with distinct red rib, turning to metallic bronze.

F. e. variegata. (*F. e. doescheri*). Leaves are longer and narrower than those of *F. e. belgica* and are variegated with yellow and green.

Give the rubber plants north light. Take warm to cool temperatures. Need moisture. Don't overpot.

When small, place single plant on a table. Use 3 in a container against a screen that faces light, or plant singly in indoor window box. Stunning for modern decor.

F. lyrata. *(F. pandurata).* (See chapter on trees.)

Place in north window close to light. Needs moderately warm temperatures. Water thoroughly. If roots dry out, bottom leaves will drop. Don't overpot or overwater.

Attractive in living rooms with modern decor. Put small plants on side tables near full light or in indoor window boxes. Three tall plants in a container for a corner make a bold and stunning effect.

F. retusa. *(F. nitida).* (See chapter on trees.)

Likes any location. Takes cool or warm temperatures. Requires well-drained soil and moisture. Keep root-bound to form a miniature tree.

Use in pairs as miniature trees on mantelpiece, in indoor window box, or on bookshelf. Good where small pattern is wanted. Place against light walls in hallways.

FITTONIA VERSCHAFFELTII. Low, creeping, evergreen plant with handsome foliage. Dark green, oval, 4-in. leaves are veined with red. Var. *argyroneura* has leaves veined with white.

Give north light. Requires even warm temperature and humidity. Prefers light soil consisting mostly of leaf mold. Cuttings.

Use mainly in terrariums that retain even temperatures and humidity.

HEDERA. Ivy. (See chapters on ground covers and vines.)

Give intense north light or filtered sun. Thrives in cold temperatures. Likes well-drained soil and abundant moisture. Fertilize with fish emulsion every 4 weeks.

Best used in cool locations—on wall brackets, mantels, trellis, and in indoor window boxes. In large planters, trailing over edge of container in front of other plants.

HOYA CARNOSA. Wax Flower. (See chapter on vines.) Var. *variegata* has dark green leaves, white margins diffused with pink.

Place in south window where it can receive morning or afternoon sun. Needs warm temperature. Takes a heavy well-drained soil. In spring and summer give abundant moisture and feed with fish emulsion every 2 weeks. Likes to be root-bound.

Suitable for training on wire over sunny windows.

MARANTA LEUCONEURA KERCHOVEANA. *(M. kerchoveana).* A perennial valued for its foliage. Low-growing, spreading plant to 1 ft. Light green, roundish, 7-in. leaves are beautifully marked with chocolate brown spots when new; turn to rich, velvet, emerald-green. Leaves rise upward at night.

Give north light. Requires temperatures to 60° or above. Needs light soil, good drainage, and abundant water. Feed with fish emulsion every 2 weeks. When leaves become small and crowded, cut back in January; when new leaves appear, be sure to feed. Cuttings.

Use young plants in dish gardens, a single plant in a low container; or combine with other foliage, such as peperomia and philodendron, in indoor window boxes or entrance halls.

MONSTERA DELICIOSA. *(Philodendron pertusum).* Splitleaf Philodendron. (See chapter on vines. For indoor culture, see *Philodendron.*)

Use limited to large room or entryway. Stunning when allowed to trail up a post in planter or indoor bed that's large enough at base for mixed planting of anthuriums, dieffenbachias, marantas, and peperomias.

NEPHROLEPIS. Evergreen. Ferns with long, narrow, finely-divided leaves.

N. exaltata bostoniensis. Boston Fern. Erect or drooping, light green fronds to 2-3 ft. Has many forms. One of the best is var. *Trevillian* with erect feathery fronds.

Give north light. Thrives in a cool place. Takes well-drained, fibrous soil. Feed every 4 weeks with fish emulsion.

Best used in group arrangements. Mass in window-boxes or in cool entrance halls.

PEPEROMIA. Evergreen, usually succulent, often prostrate or semi-climbing plants. Leaves sometimes marked or variegated.

P. microphylla. Baby Tears Peperomia. Semi-climbing plant with small, light green, fleshy leaves.

P. obtusifolia. Upright or semi-climbing plant with thick stems. Dark green, fleshy, round, 4-in. leaves. Var. *variegata* has leaves variegated with yellow.

P. rotundifolia. *(P. nummularifolia,* sometimes sold in nurseries as *P. minima).* Tiny, dark green, round, ¼-in. leaves, often reddish underneath, in circles at each stem joint.

P. sandersii. Watermelon Plant. Compact, low-growing, stemless plant. Round, 5-in., gray-striped leaves on long red stalks.

Give peperomia north light. Takes cool or warm temperatures; *P. sandersii* needs warmth. Likes well-drained, light soil. Water moderately; *P. sandersii* should be given less water than others. Stem, crown, or leaf cuttings. Leaf submerged one-half in 2-in. pot of ½ leaf mold, ½ sand.

Young plants are good in planters. In dish gardens on edges of container or combined with other plants needing infrequent watering. Attractive as single plants, either upright or hanging, in large containers *(P. rotundifolia* rarely used as single plant).

PHILODENDRON. The best known and most adaptable house plant because of its tough, durable character. Natural habitat is the tropical jungle.

Trailing or climbing vines, except for a few non-vining types such as *P. wendlandii* and *P. selloum.* Leathery, lobed leaves come in many shades of green and in various shapes, occasionally variegated or mottled. Flowers, shaped somewhat like callas, usually greenish-white, appear only on mature plants and are not particularly conspicuous.

Cultural treatment of most philodendrons influences leaf size and length of internodes and leaf stalks. For example, when *P. radiatum* and *P. hastatum* are grown in larger containers with ample root space and sufficient light, their leaves tend to grow large; when rootbound and given insufficient light, leaves of these plants are smaller.

Plant each philodendron where size and shape of leaves and habit of growth can be used to best advantage. Grow small vining types of philodendrons in small containers with or without support—on a window sill or mantel. Let trailing or climbing forms vine around a room—over a doorway or mantel, or along a wall or ceiling but don't let it take over the room! Small philodendrons or some larger types when young are attractive in dish gardens. Non-vining types are excellent at an entrance way, in a doorway, or on lanais for bold dramatic effect. Train vining types on "totem poles" made of sphagnum moss or fern roots or on bamboo poles for a formal effect; twine over driftwood for something more informal.

P. oxycardium. *(P. cordatum).* Most common species. A very rugged, trailing or climbing vine, with small, heart-shaped 5-in., dark green leaves.

Achieve a tailored effect by training it on sphagnum pole so that fastened stems go up and down and not around pole. One of the best and easiest to manage.

P. radiatum. *(P. dubium).* Slow-growing climber. Dark green, arrow-shaped, 9-in. leaves irregularly divided by deep cuts on either side of midrib. A smaller edition of *P. selloum,* one of the largest leafed philodendrons, and it vines more readily.

May be used instead of *P. selloum* in small places where unusual leaf pattern and slow growth are wanted.

P. erubescens. A climber with greenish-red stems turning gray with age. The 9-in. leaves, dark green edged with copper above, reddish-blush beneath, are arrow-shaped like those of *P. hastatum*.

Use plant where reddish tones are desired—for instance, to match redwood walls. Suitable for high walls as specimen plant.

P. friedrichstahllii. Trailing or upright growth. Dark green, oblong, heart-shaped, 5-in. leaves have perforations, like Swiss cheese, within their entire margins.

Use as a small trailer.

P. hastatum. A climber. Glossy, dark jade-green, 12-in. leaves, shaped like large arrowheads, produce a clean-cut outline.

Plant singly as a tall, thin plant; for a graceful cascade, place 3 plants as trailers in a 10-in. pot on a high shelf. Good on totem poles in pots.

P. imbe. A climber. Large, long, 12-in. leaves, rich green above, rusty-colored beneath, grow close together and at right angles from stems. Red-spotted leaf stalks.

Place where underside of leaves can be seen. Use it for its attractive leaf and compact growth habit.

P. laciniatum. A climber. Dark green, 8-in. leaves with an irregularly slashed outline somewhat similar to *P. panduræforme*—except basal lobes are pointed rather than rounded. Retains leaves with age.

P. panduraeforme. A climber. Large, fiddle-shaped, dark green, 10-in. leaves are sparsely arranged; no two leaves alike. Retains lower foliage with age.

Exotic foliage makes it unsurpassed for interior decoration.

P. selloum. Largest leafed of philodendrons used as house plants. Fairly slow grower. Climber when mature, does not vine when young. Dark green leaves to 3 ft. are deeply cut. Has long aerial roots. More cold-resistant than most, hardy to 25°; used outdoors in frost-free areas.

Place where there is room for its impressive jungle-like appearance.

P. sodiroi. Usually upright growth, but can be used like *P. oxycardium* as a trailer. Olive-green, heart-shaped leaves mottled with silver-gray give plant a sheen. Upright in a 6-in. pot, leaves are 8 in. long; trailing in a 3-in. pot, 3 in. long.

More attractive when small, so keep in small containers. For contrast against green-foliaged plants or in combination with gray-foliaged plants, such as *Aglæonema rœbelenii.*

P. wendlandii. Compact type. Thick, large, green, spatular, 15-in. leaves, on 2-in., flat, wide leaf stalks, radiate from thick central stem. Does not vine. Resembles mature plant of bird's nest fern. Tolerant of extremes in temperature and humidity.

Use as single plant where plenty of space is provided for circular arrangement of leaves.

Philodendrons take even temperatures, best at 60°. Give full north light or indirect sunlight. Become leggy and lanky with insufficient light; variegated types require more light than green types. Prefers well-drained soil. Keep moist, but let surface of soil dry slightly between waterings. Overwatering will cause roots to rot off. Vining types don't always need support. When well established, feed every 4 weeks with any of the liquid or instantly soluble, dry fertilizers recommended for house plants. Stem cuttings or seeds. Most common pests are mealybug, aphis, and scale.

PHOENIX ROEBELENII. PYGMY DATE PALM. (See section on palms.) Its young growth is prized for indoor planting.

Give filtered sunlight or north light. Can stand cool or warm temperatures. Needs heavy soil. Thrives with constant moisture. Prefers being root-bound.

Use small plants in dish gardens. Picturesque as a single plant in a bronze container. Combine in indoor window box with similar arching plants that like water.

POLYSTICHUM TSUS-SIMENSE. *(Aspidium tsus-simense).* Evergreen. One of the small holly ferns. Vigorously spreading plant, with dainty, finely-divided, dark green, 2-ft. fronds.

Requires a cool, shaded place. Divisions.

Attractive in terrariums or with other small ferns in a fern dish on a low table; in dish gardens and for fern baskets.

SAINTPAULIA IONANTHA. AFRICAN VIOLET. Evergreen. Fuzzy, heart-shaped leaves with entire margins, grow in rosettes. Pale lavender flowers in branching clusters of 3 or more. Hybrids have plain or scalloped leaves, and purple, pink, white, or variegated flowers.

Best in an east window with roof overhang or suffused morning sun. Keep where temperatures average 60-70°, or they will not grow their best nor bloom profusely.

In preparing a potting mix, four basic ingredients are important: garden soil, a soil conditioner (sand, vermiculite, pumice), acid humus (peat moss or leaf mold), a slow-acting fertilizer (manure, bonemeal). Proportions used will vary with local soils and the grower. One soil mixture that has proved successful contains 3 parts leaf mold, 1 part loam, and ½ part sand.

Water plants from top or below, but in either case avoid watering crown or leaves. Using water at room-temperature or slightly warmer, wet soil thoroughly, let potting mixture dry out to the touch before watering again. Don't let water stand in pot saucers for more than 2 hours after watering the plants. If plant is well established, feed — only when soil is moist — with a slightly acid fertilizer once every 2-4 weeks. Most common pests are aphis, mites, and mealybug. Seeds and leaf cuttings.

Universally popular for window gardens.

SANSEVIERIA. Perennial plants capable of thriving in very little light.

S. hahnii. Low-growing, compact clumps of dark green leaves, mottled gray when young.

Engleman, 240
mites, 196
Norway, 187
pruning, 190-192, 282
Spurges, 13, 420
Squash, 342, 350, 356-**358**, 362,
back of chapter divider 14
borer, 357, **358**, **378**, 383
bug, **377**
pests and diseases, 357, **358**
Stapelia, 420
Star magnolia, 158, 235, 239
Starter solutions, **429**
Statice, Russian, **85**
Stem borers, **384**
Stem rots, 389
Stewarts disease, 353
Storage of
garden equipment, **262-265**
root crops, **364**
Strawberries, 342, 371, **373**, **374**,
back of chapter divider 15
propagation, **431**
varieties, **374**
Strawberry tree, 167
Street trees, **240**, **241**
Succulents, **420**
Sugar maple, **240**
Sulfate of ammonia, 368
Sulfur, 81, 84, 109, 113, 144, 146,
170, 193, 332, 358, 381, 383,
385, 388, 390, 392
Sumac, 282, 342
fragrant, 273
Sundrop, 78, **104**
Sunflower, 380, 436
Sunrose, 255
Sunscald, 230
Superphosphate, 126, 351
Swamp azalea, 171
Sweet alyssum, 77, 86, **87**, back
of chapter divider 18
Sweet bouvardia, 212
Sweet clover, 342, 343
Sweet corn, **331**, 350, **353**, 362,
429, back of chapter divider 14
dusting seeds, **422**
Sweet flag, 223
Sweet potatoes, 342, 363
Sweet rockets, 88
Sweet violet, back of chapter
divider 19
Sweetautumn clematis, 104, **105**,
200, 212
Sweetbay magnolia, 235
Sweetgum, 240
Sweetpeas, **83**, 84, **202**, 436,
back of chapter divider 18
Sweetshrub, 166
Sweetwilliams, **76**, **77**, 88
Swiss chard, 349, 350, 363, back
of chapter divider 14
Sydney-wattle, 179

T

Table, garden, **309**

Tables, listing of
bulbs
planting depth, back of
chapter divider 3
for rock gardens, back of
chapter divider 10
crops
long-harvest, 350
short-season, 350
disease control, 388-391
ferns, 246
fertilizers, 337
fruits
bramble, pruning of, 371
maturity dates, back of
chapter divider 15
small, spacing and yields, 371
germination, annual flowers,
back of chapter divider 18
germination-maturity table,
vegetable, back of chapter
divider 14
groundcovers, 72
lawn weeds, 64
lilies, 125
perennials, other dependable,
104
pest control, 380-383
pH ranges for specific plants,
342
plant foods, types, 333
plants for cutting, 436, **437**
pool plants, 223
pruning, **284-285**
shrubs for rock gardens, back
of chapter divider 10
spray dilution, 465
trees, flowering, 239
vegetable
planting, 349
harvesting, 362
vines, 200, 201, **202**
wall plantings, 255
weights and measures, 465
wildflowers, 244, 245
Tamarisk, 157, 282, 342, 437
Tanbark, 290
Tarnished plant bug, **144**, **385**
TEPP, 379, 384
Terrace, **32**, **34**, **35**, 42, 43
fireplaces, **36**, **41**, 320-324
privacy on, 46, 47
seats on, **303-306**
on slopes, **52**, 273, **274**
for special uses, **44**, **45**
surfacing, **310-319**
Terrariums, **418**, 419
Teucrium, 77, back of chapter
divider 10
Texas root rot, 389, 391
Texas-Southwest, 451-454
iris for, 93
shrub favorites, 166, **179**, **180**,
181
vine favorites, 212
Thermopsis, 77, 78
Thiram, 389, 392
Thorns, 162, **179**, 235, 239

Thornless honey locust, 239, 240,
241
Thrifts, dwarf, 255
Thrips, 107, 144, **145**, 170, 380,
382
Thunberg lespedeza, back of
chapter divider 19
Thunbergia, 201
Thyme, red, 255, 342
Tigridias, 144, 436, back of
chapter divider 3
Timothy, 59
Toadstools, 70
Tobacco, jasmine-flowered, 77,
85, **415**, back of chapter divider
18
Tobacco stems, 277
Tomato hornworm, **375**, 382
Tomatoes, 342, 346, 349, 350, **351**,
429, back of chapter divider 14
care, **351**, 360
Tools, garden, 54, 61, **62**, 70, 71,
260, **261**
maintenance, **268-271**, **288**
storage, **262-265**
Top-dressing, 71, back of chapter
divider 20
Torch azalea, 154
Torenia, 255
Toxaphene, 383
Trailers, see roses
Tree peonies, **97**
Tree roses, see roses
Trees, 17, **36-41**, 227-243
care of, **232**, **233**, **283-286**
pest, disease control, **384**, 385
pruning, **230**, 243, **280-285**
young trees, **230**, 243, **284**
evergreens, see evergreens
flowering, 16, **235-239**
fruit, see fruit trees
planting, **242**, 243
shade
planning for, back of
chapter divider 9
replacements for elms, **241**
shapes, back of chapter
divider 9
for special areas, **240**
street, **240**, 241
uses for, **229**, **231**, **234**
Trellis, **45**, 200, **208**, 248, 293,
326, back of chapter divider 7
Trillium, 245, back of chapter
divider 19
Tritoma, 114, 436
Trollius, **257**
Trumpet honeysuckle, back of
chapter divider 7
Trumpetcreeper, Chinese, back
of chapter divider 7
Trumpetvine, 200, **205**, 208, **211**
Tuberose, 114, back of chapter
divider 3
Tuberous begonia, 116, **117**,
130, **417**, back of chapter
divider 3
Tulip, 78, 126-**129**, 342, **395**,

479

Index Tu to Zo

405, 436
  lady, 124
  planting, 126, **128**, back of chapter divider 3
  waterlily, 124, back of chapter divider 10
Turnip, 349, 350, 362, 363, **364**, 428, back of chapter divider 14
Twig blight, 385
2,4-D, 57, 59, 66
  injury, 386, **387**

U

Umbrella palm, back of chapter divider 8

V

Vanhoutte spiraea, 158
Vegetables, 345-364
  diseases, 360, 390, 391
  freezing, 363
  garden plan, **36**, **346**, **348**, 349
  germination-maturity table, back of chapter divider 14
  harvesting, 362
  long-harvest crops, 350
  pests on, 360, 382, 383
  planting table, 349
  plantings, 347, **361**
  rotation of, 343
  salad crops, 354, **355**
  short-season crops, 350
  storage, root crops, **364**
  summer care, 359, 360
  varieties for freezing, 363
  vine crops, **356-358**
Veltheimia, **397**
Velvet bean, 343
Velvetplant, **401**
Verbena, 22, 77, 81, 244, 255 **258**, 342, 436, back of chapter divider 18
Veronicas, creeping, 255
Vermiculite, 277, **422**
Verticullium wilt, 388
Vetch, 343
Viburnum, doublefile, **159**
Vinca, 72, 201, 342
Vine crops, **356-358**
Vines, **199-212**
  annual, **202**
  climbers, showy, **205**
  climbing, methods of, **206**, **207**
  danger signs in, 206, **207**
  maintenance, **210**, **211**, 281
  for permanent plantings, back of chapter divider 7
  pests and diseases of, **384**, 385
  regional favorites, 212
  for special uses, 200, 201, 273
  supports, **211**, **247**, **248**, **290**, **326**
Violas, 86, **305**
Violet, 342

African, see African-violets
  Canada, 244
  birdsfoot, 342
  blue, 245
  dogtooth, *Erythronium*, 245, 418
  horned, back of chapter divider 19
  sweet, back of chapter divider 19
Virginia bluebell, 245, **422**
Virginia creeper, 200, 201, 206, 273, back of chapter divider 7
Viscaria, Tom Thumb, 255
Volutella wilt, 173

W

Wahoo, western, 165
Wake-robin, back of chapter divider 19
Walks, 22, 23, **26-29**, **69**
  concrete, **311**, **312**
  exposed aggregate, **313**
  flagstone, **318**, **319**
  wooden blocks, **314**, **315**
Wallflowers, Siberian, 255
Walls, **249-255**
  planning, **250**, **252**, **253**, 258
  planting, **25**, **251**, **254**, 255, 258, back of chapter divider 9
  retaining, **273**, **274**, back of chapter divider 10
Walnut, black, back of chapter divider 9
Wandering-Jew, 418
Washington thorn, 235, 239
Water cress, 223
Water garden, back of chapter divider 8
Water oak, 240
Water plants, see pools, garden
Watering
  aids in, **261**, **276**
  borders, 75
  evergreens, 193
  lawns, 56, 62
  vegetables, 360
Waterlilies, **222**, 436, back of chapter divider 8
Waterlily tulip, 124, back of chapter divider 10
Watermelon, 342, **356-358**, back of chapter divider 14
Watsonias, 114
Waukegan juniper, 72, 187
Weather vanes, **307**
Weeds, lawn, 59, **64-66**
Weevils, 170
Weigela, 157
Western azalea, 171
Western redcedar, 187
Western wahoo, 165
Whip grafting, **434**
White azalea, 171
White clover, 59, 343
White fir, 187, 240

White flies, 170, 380
White fringetree, 158, 239
White grubs, 67, **378**
White pine, 192
Wildflowers, 244, 245, 342
Willows, 231, 282, back of chapter dividers 9, 10
Wilt, 173, 390
Windbreaks, 177, **195**, 279
Window gardens, **395**, **404**, **405**, back of chapter divider 17
Winged euonymus, 13, 162, 239
Winter aconite, back of chapter dividers 10, 19
Winter burn, on evergreens, 195
Winter garden under lights, **417**
Winter honeysuckle, back of chapter divider 19
Wintercreeper, 16, 72, 200, 201, back of chapter divider 7
Winterhazel, griffith, 166
Wireworms, 394
Wisteria, 200, **205**, 211, 248, 342, back of chapter divider 7
Witchhazel, 239, back of chapter divider 19
Wood preservatives, back of chapter divider 12
Wooden blocks, **291**, **314**, **315**
Wooly-bear caterpillars, 380
Worm, cabbage, **376**

Y

Yarrow, 255
Yaupon, 166, **179**
Yeddo-hawthorn, 166
Yellow flag, 223
Yellow jasmine, 212
Yellow sorrel, 64
Yellow-twigged dogwood, 273
Yellow-wood, back of chapter divider 9
Yellows, 386, 388, 390
Yew, 13, 185, 187, 188, **189**, 190, **197**, **274**, 342, back of chapter divider 6
  American, 197
  Japanese, **186**, 188, 197, back of chapter divider 10
  pruning, **177**, 190, 191, 282
Yucca, 342, **437**

Z

Zabel honeysuckle, 162
Zinc, 340
  naphthenate, back of chapter divider 12
  oxide, 285
Zinnias, 74, 77, 81, 83, 86, 342, 436, back of chapter divider 18
Ziram, 388, 390, 392
Zone map of frost dates, **466**
Zoysia, 60

S. trifasciata laurentii. (*S. laurentii*). Slow-growing plant. Erect, thick, 2½-ft., spear-like leaves, light green marked with gray when young, becoming dark green, striped with golden-yellow. A compact, darker green form is now available.

Sansevierias are easy plants to care for. Take any exposure, can stand cold to warm temperatures, like any soil. Water well but infrequently. Propagate by divisions, or by leaf cuttings to 3 in. long placed in sand.

Use sansevieria in dish gardens combined with plants that like the same watering conditions. Single plants are good for places away from light—dark hallway entrances, mantel pieces, tables, indoor window boxes. The tall and low-growing sansevieria make an effective combination. *S. hahnii* will grow satisfactorily in small container for long time.

SCINDAPSUS AUREUS WILCOXII. (*Pothos wilcoxii*). Climbing plants with thick stems. Green, 1½-ft. leaves, variegated yellow.

A horticultural variety has green leaves variegated with white.

Give north light. Need warm temperatures—65-70° at night. Keep on dry side. Feed every 4 weeks as for philodendrons. Cuttings.

Used best as trailer in dish gardens, on wall brackets, for window boxes.

SAXIFRAGA SARMENTOSA. STRAWBERRY GERANIUM. (See chapter on perennials.)

Thrives in any situation. Can stand cold.

Use in dish gardens, hanging baskets, wall brackets; as edging on window boxes.

SYNGONIUM PODOPHYLLUM. Evergreen. Dwarf climbers. Soft, arrow-shaped, 6-in., dull green leaves, sometimes lobed. Var. *albolineatum* has emerald green leaves marked with silver on midrib and veins. Var. *Ruth Fraser* has silvery leaves with green border. Var. *Trileaf Wonder* has green leaves covered with a whitish powder. Var. *California Silver Wonder* is like *Ruth Fraser*, but has narrower leaves without green border.

Give north light. Takes high or low temperatures, but grows rapidly in high temperatures. Needs well-drained, fibrous soil and ample moisture.

Combine with other plants in dish gardens when small. Train on poles or pyramids for formal effect. Also may be used like *Philodendron oxycardium* as a trailer. Plant 3 in a 4-in. pot and pinch back to make bushy.

TOLMIEA MENZIESII. A Northwest native perennial to 2 ft. Basal, heart-shaped, fresh green leaves produce new plantlets at tips of leaf stalks.

Takes all exposures. Needs moisture and light soil.

Excellent plant for those who are easily discouraged with house plants. Use in dish gardens with other hardy plants. As single plant on window sills, tables, or wherever a fresh green is wanted.

TRADESCANTIA FLUMINENSIS. WANDERING JEW. Evergreen. Prostrate or trailing perennial with succulent stems. Dark green, ovate, 2½-in. leaves and small white flowers.

Withstands intense light and cold. Prefers light soil.

Grows outside in shade in wild areas as ground cover. Use indoors as trailer in dish gardens, edging for indoor window boxes, or in wall-bracket containers. Grows easily in water.

ZEBRINA PENDULA. (*Tradescantia zebrina*). WANDERING JEW. Like *Tradescantia fluminensis*, with which it is often confused, but differs in that the leaves are striped white above, and reddish-purple beneath.

Has same cultural requirements and use as *Tradescantia fluminensis*.

ORCHIDS

The climate of your living room is not an orchid climate. But a few orchids can be grown there with just a little more attention than you must give any common house plant. Such room-tolerant orchids are discussed in the following list. Look out when you use them that they don't lure you into the hobby of orchid growing.

Orchid growing is an adventure into the upper realms of gardening. It's a search for flawless beauty. It's a hobby you never master, but becomes your master long before the first orchid blooms.

CATTLEYA. Epiphytic. Most popular of the orchids. Commonly sold as corsage flowers by florists. Have stiff shiny leathery green leaves.

C. gaskelliana. Rose-purple flower has throat striped with yellow. Blooms in late summer.

C. harrisoniana. Rose-lilac flower with yellow-orange throat. Blooms late fall.

C. labiata. Rose-lilac flower with crimson-purple lip and yellow throat. Blooms in September and October.

C. mossiae. Light rose-colored flower has crimson-rose lip, often suffused with white, and yellow throat. Blooms in April continuing through June.

C. trianaei. Delicate rose to lavender flower with darker purple-crimson lip; golden throat. Blooms in December and January—providing corsage material through the holidays.

Expose cattleyas to a south or southeast window. Shade them in summer at sunniest time of day. Require temperatures to 60-65° at night; temperatures during day need not be controlled.

Most cattleyas are repotted every 2 years; for home use it's more desirable to produce a single plant than to divide when repotting. This can be accomplished by simply potting it into a larger pot each time. Osmunda is the universal potting medium for cattleyas. Water cattleyas approximately once a week or when the pots become light in weight.

Place plants on shallow water-proof trays filled with 2 in. of pebbles. This will catch the excess water and provide necessary humidity. Pebbles should be kept moist with an inch of water in tray. Evaporation of water is very rapid.

CYPRIPEDIUM. LADY SLIPPERS. Terrestrial. Some grow in wooded areas along Pacific Coast.

C. callosum. Mottled green leaves. Pale green 4 in. flower flushed and striped with dark rose-purple has warty and hairy margins; lip shaded with brownish-purple. Generally blooms in February and March, but has an indefinite flowering period.

C. insigne. Green leaves. Yellowish-green 4-in. flower spotted with brown, has lip shaded with brownish-purple. Blooms from October to January.

C. i. sanderae. Plain green leaves. Flower is greenish-yellow except for white-tipped top sepal. Blooms in fall and winter.

C. maudiae. Mottled green leaves. White flower striped with green has yellow-green lip. Blooms late summer or early fall.

Best exposure for cypripediums is north window. Needs cooler night temperatures—58°—than cattleyas. Pot in osmunda as for cattleyas, only looser, and generally use smaller pots. Or grow in soil mixture of: 3 parts fibrous loam, 1 part osmunda, 1 part sphagnum. Water approximately twice a week; should never dry out. Use same equipment as for cattleyas to maintain humidity around plants.

EPIDENDRUM. Epiphytic. Long slender thickened stems resembling a reed. Clusters of miniature cattleya-type flowers on long stems in shades of yellow, orange, lavender, rose.

Epidendrum hybrids are sold by self-describing names such as: Tangerine, Lavender, Coral Rose, Coral Red, Dusty Rose, Rose, Pink, Fuchsia Rose, Orange, Yellow Gold.

Exposure and night temperatures are the same as for cattleyas. Potting medium same as for cattleyas only looser. Can also grow in soil mixture of: 3 parts leaf mold, 1 part peat. Repot when stems become crowded in pot. Will bloom in a 3 in. pot. Feed every 4 weeks with orchid fertilizer.

ODONTOGLOSSUM. Epiphytic. Dark green leaves usually borne in pairs at top of flattened oval-shaped pseudobulb (thickened stem).

O. crispum. White flowers tinged rose and spotted with red, on arching stems. Blooms all year around, but mostly in spring.

O. grande. Arching stems carry 3-7 large yellow flowers striped with brown. Blooms in fall.

Odontoglossums like north exposure; light but not strong sunlight. Thrive in cool temperatures to 50-60°. Grow in firmly packed osmunda fiber. Water only enough to keep bulbs from shriveling in winter from the time they cease flowering until growth starts in spring.

ONCIDIUM. Epiphytic. Yellow-green leaves borne on top of short oval pseudobulb. Resemble odontoglossum in flower.

O. schillerianum. Long branched stems support many tiny yellow flowers striped with brown. Blooms in summer.

O. tigrinum. Large yellow flowers heavily spotted with brown. Blooms autumn and winter.

O. t. splendidum. Large yellow flowers striped with brown are strung on long arching stems to 2 ft. or more. Blooms late spring.

Oncidiums require considerable light and good air circulation. Thrive in cool and warm temperatures to 50-65°. Grow in loosely packed osmunda.

INDOOR-OUTDOOR PLANTS

ALOCASIA MACRORHIZA. ALOCASIA. Evergreen. Zone 13. Winter damage at 29° but will grow anew from ground if frost is not severe. A dome-shaped, center-of-interest plant to 5 ft. with a 4-ft. spread. Large, clear green, arrow-shaped 2-ft. leaves. Inconspicuous flowers borne on a central spike surrounded by a greenish-white bract, resembling a calla lily. Seeds are formed on the central spike much like corn on a cob.

A. odora is very similar, not quite so hardy. Flowers are fragrant.

Plant in filtered sunlight in sheltered, wind-protected patios or court. Needs peaty soil, plenty of water, light but frequent feedings.

ALPINIA. Zone adaptation by species. Many-stemmed, leafy plants with ginger-like rhizomes. Exotic flowers like white shells, tipped with red, burnt orange and purple, in pendant clusters at the ends of arching canes.

A. speciosa. (*A. nutans*). SHELL FLOWER, PORCELAIN GINGER. Evergreen in zones 8a, 10, 12, and 13. Dies down in winter in zones 7, 8, and 11. Root-hardy to about 15°, the most cold tolerant of all gingers. Tropical herb to 8 ft. Considerably slower-growing than hedychium but more substantial, even sometimes becoming woody. Distinguished from all other California-grown gingers by its decidedly reddish leaf sheaths, the entire stem becoming maroon at maturity. Has long, narrow, green, veiny leaves. Must be established at least 2 years to bloom. Flowers usually lack fragrance in California.

Prefers plenty of water and a little shade. Almost any soil and a wind-free exposure. Valuable plant for shady spots in the lower desert. Effective combined with bananas, *Strelitzia nicolai*, various phormium varieties, grasses, and floppy-leafed water-tolerant succulents.

A. sanderae. Zone 13 and occasionally zone 12. Herbaceous perennial to 4-5 ft., but usually smaller, with narrow green leaves striped with pure white. Rarely blooms out-of-doors. Usually treated only as a conservatory plant, with strong overhead light, little direct sun, rich moist soil and high humidity.

A. purpurata. DWARF GINGER. Evergreen. Zones 10-13. Tropical perennial to 2 ft., used particularly for dense short foliage as foreground plant for other gingers, or with bamboos and wide-bladed grasses. Rarely blooms on the West Coast. Requires a bit more shade than other gingers and may be planted appropriately under them. Needs thinning out and some cutting back toward spring. Also effective with bamburanta.

CALADIUM BICOLOR. FANCY-LEAFED CALADIUM. Successful only in completely frost-free areas of zones 12 and 13; but better to grow in a glasshouse. Tropical tuber-forming herb that occasionally grows to 4 ft., but is usually lower. Large arrow- or heart-shaped leaves on long stalks are conspicuously variegated in shades of red, rose, pink, white, silver, bronze and green.

Treat tubers in the same way as tuberous begonias (see tuberous begonias). Although difficult to grow outdoors in California because of its need for warm shade, or a combination of sun and moisture, caladiums are occasionally grown in open ground by adventuresome gardeners. When grown under glass the potted plants may be moved to a warm, windless, shaded patio for warm-weather displays with other tropicals.

COLOCASIA ESCULENTA. (*Caladium esculentum*). TARO, ELEPHANT EARS. Evergreen only in zone 13, usually dies down in winter in zones 8a, 10-12, but tubers may be left in the ground. In zones 1-9 where the ground freezes, it is best grown in containers, or the tubers lifted and stored. Tropical fast-growing herb to 6 ft. or more. Mammoth heart-shaped gray-green leaves on long stalks add a lush effect to any tropical planting within one season. Requires lots of water, some fertilizer; prefers a light mulch, and thrives equally well in sun or shade.

HEDYCHIUM. GINGER LILY. Zones 10-13. Tropical evergreen or herbaceous perennials with handsome canna-like foliage and richly fragrant flowers in dense spikes.

H. gardnerianum. KAHILI GINGER. Grows to 8 ft., the fleshy stalks with 2-ranked 1½-ft. leaves. Clear yellow flowers in terminal 1½-ft. spikes bloom from July to October. Valuable for tropical effects and great fragrance. Combines well with other gingers, bananas, grasses, bamburanta, *Tibouchina semidecandra*.

H. coronarium. WHITE GINGER LILY. Like *H. gardnerianum* except the leaves are longer and narrower and the flowers are white, appearing sparingly in late summer. Usually unattractive in California. If given the heat it needs to flower well, the foliage will burn. Blossoms are effective cut and wonderfully sweet.

H. flavum. CREAM GINGER LILY. Usually evergreen, the tallest and latest flowering of the gingers grown in California. At its best in late October, with pale yellow to buff blooms in oblong spikes. Leaves are similar to *H. coronarium* but less ragged and more attractive.

Gingers like ample moisture, light shade (full sun directly along the coast), and a soil high in humus. Sharp frost kills them to the ground, but new stalks appear in early spring. Old canes should be removed to ground when through blooming to stimulate fresh new growth.

STRELITZIA. BIRD OF PARADISE. Evergreen. Zones 8a (Palm Springs), 10-13; of questionable value in zone 11. Tropical plants of extremely individual character, with their banana-like leaves and flowers that are startlingly like tropical birds.

S. nicolai. GIANT BIRD OF PARADISE. Tree-like clumping, many-stalked perennial to 30 ft., suggests a clump of flat-sided banana plants. Gray-green, leathery, 2-ranked, 5-ft. leaves surmount the narrow trunks. White flowers, with a blue tongue, appear intermittently on established specimens. Effective associated with *Chamærops humilis*, tall fan palms, faced with *Strelitzia reginæ*, in a ground cover of *Festuca ovina glauca*.

S. reginae. BIRD OF PARADISE. Evergreen trunkless perennial to 5 ft. with gray-green 1½-ft. leaves. Spectacular orange, blue and white flowers on long stiff stems bloom intermittently throughout the year, but best in the cool season. Highly prized for its long-lasting flowers, either cut or in the garden.

The long-lived strelitzias should have full sun in coastal areas, light shade inland. Require a rich well-fertilized soil. Benefits from occasional applications of acid-base fertilizer or iron sulfate. Divide infrequently since large clumps bloom best.

Ferns

Satisfy the simple needs of ferns and they are among the most adaptable of garden plants. Members of this decorative group range in size from dwarfs a few inches high to magnificent giants to 70 feet.

In general, of course, ferns luxuriate in a deep, loose, well aerated soil rich in humus. A good planting mix consists of equal parts of leaf mold (don't sift; use in the condition it comes from the woods with small twigs, half decayed wood, and leaves); peat moss; and loam.

— *Encyclopedia* —

Tree ferns:

The large tree ferns have adapted themselves beautifully to California coastal gardens. Although in their native jungle some grow to 80 ft. and have trunks a foot in diameter, the average height of the species imported into gardens is about 8-18 ft., and spreading to 10 ft. Graceful green, up-curving fronds radiate from a brown fibrous trunk giving the tree ferns a resemblance to the smaller palms. The two most commonly planted are:

Alsophila australis. AUSTRALIAN TREE FERN. Fast growing to 18 ft. Requires half shade, or sun near coast in wind protected areas. Effective when grown singly against canyon walls, over water, or under high branching trees. Good in tubs.

Dicksonia antarctica. TASMANIAN TREE FERN. Hardiest of the tree ferns, and best for small gardens because it is lower growing, to 10 ft. Will take sun on coast. Good in tubs.

Ferns native to Pacific Coast:

Polystichum munitum. WESTERN SWORD FERN. A clumping type with narrow 3½-ft. fronds. Hardy, requiring protection only from scorching sun and drying winds. Good for naturalizing on hillsides or under trees.

Woodwardia fimbriata. (*W. radicans, W. chamissoi*). GIANT CHAIN FERN. Large coarse fern with 5-ft. fronds. Will stand considerable sun and wind and even thrives on neglect. A good background plant for low growing shrubs on north or east side of house.

Blechnum spicant. (*Struthiopteris spicant, Lomaria spicant*). DEER FERN. Has narrow, leathery, evergreen fronds to 3½ ft. Likes deep shade and moisture. Its yellowish-green fronds contrast effectively with the rich green foliage of dwarf hydrangeas and fuchsias.

Adiantum pedatum. AMERICAN MAIDENHAIR, FIVE FINGER FERN. Has soft feathery foliage to 1 ft. or more on shiny, black, wiry stems. Moisture loving. Attractive massed beside a naturalistic pool.

Athyrium filix-foemina. LADY FERN. Deciduous fern with delicate lacy fronds in dense tufts often to 3-4 ft. Effective with azaleas and dogwood.

Two ferns that don't look like ferns:

Phyllitis scolopendrium. (*Scolopendrium vulgare*). HARTS TONGUE. A rare eastern native, has glossy uncut ribbon-like fronds. Useful where you want a bold outline or silhouette.

Platycerium bifurcatum. (*P. alcicorne*). STAGHORN FERN. An epiphyte with 2 kinds of fronds: the sterile are wavy margined; the fertile, forked into segments like antlers. Best when grown on a vertical support such as nailed to a board or tree trunk.

There are many horticultural forms among the ferns, developed by crossing wild species, or by propagation under cultivation. Many have fronds adorned with various types of crests and tassels; still others have ruffled, curled, crossed or congested segments. For example, there are about 16 forms of lady fern. The wood ferns (*Dryopteris*) offer many of the best crested, congested, or otherwise varied forms.

Three popular house ferns are described in the chapter on indoor plants.

Zone Calendars

ZONE 1: INTERMOUNTAIN

November—December—January—February

Between November and March the gardener in cold-winter climates adjusts his schedule to the degree of cold he expects and the type of material in his garden.

Where temperatures are extremely low: hill soil up around roses to a depth of 10-12 inches. In late November canes of young grape vines and climbing roses should be laid on the ground and covered lightly with soil. Spread a thick mulch of sawdust, peat, straw at the base of shrubs. Hope for a snow mulch before temperatures drop.

Make the garden shipshape in advance of storms. Prop tree branches to prevent breaking under weight of snow and ice. Tie branches of shrubs and trees that may be whipped by the wind.

Avoid winter sunscald that damages south and southwest sides of trunks of young fruit and shade trees by placing tree guards around trunks.

PEST AND DISEASE CONTROL: An early (December) and late (February) clean-up dormant spray will cut down fungus spores, insect eggs, and other overwintering pest forms. Give peach trees a thorough spray-washing to control peach leaf curl.

March

PLANT: When ground can be worked and severe frosts are past, plant deciduous trees, shrubs, fruit trees, and roses. Lift and divide perennials. Sow: Seeds of tender annuals and cabbage, broccoli, cauliflower indoors. PRUNE: Where winters are likely to cause some bud damage, it's wise to delay pruning until buds show color so that you can determine amount of pruning necessary. If evergreen material has been frozen hold off on pruning dead looking branches until plant is in active growth. PEST AND DISEASE CONTROL: If you have neglected winter clean-up spraying, apply now on all dormant material.

April

PLANT AND SOW: Last frost dates are still ahead of you so hold off on planting tender annuals. Harden off seedlings in flats by giving them air and sunlight during the day. Start seeds of summer annuals in pots or flats. Plant deciduous shrubs and trees. Plant summer bulbs—gladiolus, ranunculus, and anemones can stand light frosts. PRUNE: Hedges and evergreens. Repair winter damage to trees. Paint wounds. Prune roses late this month. Shear evergreen groundcovers to get a clean matted look. PEST AND DISEASE CONTROL: Time an all-purpose spray application with the first leaves in the spring to clean the garden of insects and diseases before you see any damage. GENERAL CARE: Remove or work in winter mulch as soon as heavy frosts are past. Get all planting beds ready for May annuals.

May

PLANT AND SOW: Seeds of annuals and vegetables, transplants of annuals and perennials, summer bulbs. All the food and color of the next six months can be sown or put in its place now. Vegetables: carrots, cucumbers, muskmelon, sweet peppers, summer squash, corn, tomatoes, watermelon. PEST AND DISEASE CONTROL: Spray or dust roses. Apples and pears need spray for codling moth when two-thirds of petals have fallen; gladiolus for thrips as soon as shoots are 3 inches high. Spread snail and slug bait generously. GENERAL CARE: Check the fertilizer needs of all shrubs, trees, and vines. The vigor of such plants in the coming summer months depends largely on the nutrients available now.

June

PLANT AND SOW: Seeds of late cabbage, cauliflower, broccoli, kale, and celery to provide plants to set out in July for late fall use and winter storage. Keep up succession of corn, beans and radishes. Plant muskmelons, watermelons, squash and cucumbers. Sow seeds of flowers for August and September cutting. Plant summer and fall flowering bulbs. Set out tip cuttings of chrysanthemums. PRUNE: Conifers to shape them and make them more dense. Cut back older stems of flowering shrubs to force new flowering stems. Thin tops to allow sunlight to reach younger growth. PEST AND DISEASE CONTROL: Spray gladiolus for thrips. GENERAL CARE: Any or all plants lagging in growth or lacking good green color should have second application of fertilizer. Give lawns a dressing of a balanced commercial fertilizer. Mulch ground around strawberries with hay, straw, leaves, or sawdust to prevent rot and retain moisture. Lift spring flowering bulbs only when foliage is yellow. To prolong bloom of annuals and perennials remove dead flowers and keep seed pods from forming.

July

PLANT: Divide and replant overgrown clumps of iris, lily-of-the-valley, violets, primroses. Sow: Seeds of biennials and perennials for next year's bloom. PRUNE: Cut back chrysanthemums scheduled for October flowering. Shear back early flowering perennials. Cut back summer-flowering deciduous shrubs. PEST AND DISEASE CONTROL: Combination sprays or dusts will catch increasing populations of aphis, diabrotica, leafhopper, red-spider. GENERAL CARE: The all-important job this month is watering. Check chapter on watering. Keep the compost pile working. Don't let it dry out.

August

PLANT: Madonna lilies, fall and winter bulbs. Lift and divide iris, Oriental poppy, foxglove, and Shasta daisies. PRUNE: Remove canes of polyantha roses that have flowered. Cut canes of raspberries and blackberries to the ground after they have fruited. SPRAY: For chewing insects. GENERAL CARE: Continue regular watering schedule. Prepare new lawn site for September planting. Fertilize lawns, roses, chrysanthemums. Hold off fertilizing evergreens that should go into the winter in a hardened condition.

September

PLANT: Order spring flowering bulbs for planting later this month. Pot up a few for forcing into bloom during the holidays. Plant new lawns. Divide and replant perennials. GENERAL CARE: Clean up every foot of the garden as you harvest fruit and flowers. Add leaves and all clean vegetative material to the compost pile. Lift and store gladiolus. Pick green tomatoes and store them before frost hits the vines.

October

PLANT: Daffodil and tulip bulbs. Check chapter on each to get succession of bloom. Take cuttings of the tender geraniums and fuchsias and place them in a cutting box in a warm basement window. GENERAL CARE: Lift and store dahlias. Keep after the fall cleanup. Add leaves to the compost pile. In planning protection against frost remember that young plants need more attention than old ones. If you divided perennials last month and some of the divisions are small and shallow rooted, better protect them with a mulch.

ZONE 2: COLUMBIA BASIN

January
PLANT: Order tuberous begonias for starting indoors later this month or February. GENERAL CARE: Avoid winter sunscald that damages south and southwest sides of trunks of young fruit and shade trees by placing tree guards around trunks. Protect evergreens from sun.

February
PLANT AND SOW: Sow seeds indoors of summer annuals and these vegetables: broccoli, cabbage, head lettuce. PEST AND DISEASE CONTROL: Better go over all leafless shrubs and trees with a dormant spray.

March
PLANT AND SOW: Sow seeds of hardy annuals as soon as the ground can be worked. Vegetables: beets, broccoli, cabbage, carrots, lettuce, onions, peas, spinach. Also these perennials: asparagus, rhubarb. Plant deciduous trees, shrubs, fruit trees, roses, and grapes, as soon as possible. Plant gladiolus every 10 days for succession of bloom. PRUNE: After last heavy frost, fruit trees and summer-blooming shrubs. Prune spring-flowering shrubs when they are in bloom. Prune roses the last of the month or the first of April.

April
PLANT AND SOW SEEDS: Plant out transplants of annuals and perennials. Sow vegetables of every type. First the cool weather crops: beets, broccoli, carrots, chard, lettuce, potatoes, spinach, squash. As soon as ground warms and night temperatures rise: tomatoes, muskmelon, watermelon. PRUNE: Cut dead wood out of deciduous trees and paint wounds. Trim hedges. PEST AND DISEASE CONTROL: Spray or dust roses. Prevent build-up of insect populations with an overall dust or spray throughout the garden. GENERAL CARE: Fertilize as new growth starts.

May
PLANT AND SOW SEED: Hot weather vegetables: beans, cucumbers, peppers, corn. Transplants of annuals and perennials. Sow seeds of perennials in flats for bloom next year. Plant out tuberous begonias started indoors in February. PRUNE: Deciduous shrubs after bloom. PEST AND DISEASE CONTROL: Spray and dust for aphis, mildew, sod webworm, gladiolus for thrips. FERTILIZE: Roses, lawns, shrubs that have flowered. GENERAL CARE: Stake tall-growing perennials *before* they need it. Pinch back chrysanthemums, dahlias, and nearly all annuals.

June
PLANT AND SOW SEED: These vegetables for late summer and fall harvest: green beans, cabbage, carrots, leaf lettuce. Sow seed of annuals for late bloom. PRUNE: Deciduous shrubs after bloom. PEST AND DISEASE CONTROL: Spray or dust for aphis and red-spider. GENERAL CARE: Apply summer mulch. Give lawn a light feeding.

July
PLANT AND SOW SEED: Sow seeds of perennials and biennials for bloom next year. PEST AND DISEASE CONTROL: Spray or dust for aphis, diabrotica, caterpillars, red-spider. GENERAL CARE: Watering and fertilizing are the important jobs of the month.

August
PRUNE: Cut back canes of boysenberries, loganberries, and raspberries to the ground after they have fruited. FERTILIZE: Chrysanthemums up to the time buds show color. Continue feeding the lawn. GENERAL CARE: See chapter on watering; it's the important job this month.

September
PLANT AND SOW SEEDS: New lawns can go in this month. Plant small winter flowering bulbs—crocus, snowdrops, grape hyacinths, and scillas. Spring flowering bulbs should be planted later this month. Sow a cover crop of winter rye in beds that are to be left open for the winter. Build up the compost pile as you clean up the garden.

October
PLANT: Finish planting of spring bulbs. GENERAL CARE: Cleanup and more cleanup is the order of the month. All finished crops and dead leaves go onto the compost pile. Tidy up perennial borders in advance of bulb planting. Water evergreens thoroughly so that they enter winter with their leaves filled with water.

November
GENERAL CARE: Starting sometime in November after the tulips are in, you can enjoy the quiet time in the garden. Securing the garden for winter is just another way of preparing for spring. The mulching of evergreens with peat or sawdust, and the mulching of open ground with manure will result in a more fertile, more workable soil next spring.

December
PRUNING: December pruning should amount to no more than mild shaping to make trees and shrubs ready for winter. The best time to prune, if there is any danger of winter damage, is in March when growth starts and you can see the extent of damage. PEST AND DISEASE CONTROL: Spray leafless plants with a strong dormant spray. Cover every inch thoroughly. *Washing* describes the process better than *spraying*. GENERAL CARE: Check tree stakes and wires. Wrap tall, slender conifers with cord or fish net. Tie vines.

ZONE 3: COOL PUGET

January
PLANT: If you find a bargain in spring flowering bulbs, plant them. Flowers will not be as large or stems as long the first spring, but most will recover by the following year. Don't be afraid to sow seeds of perennials in flats outdoors. Choose those that often self-sow or need refrigeration for good germination, such as violet, pansy, viola, delphinium, lupine. PEST AND DISEASE CONTROL: When a few days of clear weather are forecast, give all deciduous shrubs and trees a thorough spraying—drench with a dormant spray. GENERAL CARE: Mulch any bare ground with a thick blanket of manure. Rain and frosts will work much of it into the soil and by spring you can put the plot in planting shape with little effort.

February
PLANT AND SOW: Late this month sow seeds of sweet peas. Sow seeds of these vegetables indoors: lettuce, cabbage, cauliflower, and broccoli. PRUNE: If there has been any winter damage, delay any pruning until next month when you can see the extent of the injury. PEST AND DISEASE CONTROL: Spray for blackberry mite when leaf buds open late this month or in March. Spray boysenberries with lime-sulfur for spur blight. Fruiting and flowering peaches must be sprayed to prevent peach leaf curl.

March
PLANT AND SOW: Seeds of hardy annuals that resent transplanting should be sown in place as soon as the soil can be prepared. They include clarkia, calendula, coreopsis, candytuft, godetia. Toward the end of the month plant out seedlings of lettuce, cabbage, cauliflower. Set out gladiolus corms for early bloom. Divide and replant perennials. Plant deciduous trees, shrubs, fruit trees, roses as soon as soil can be worked. PRUNE: Last chance to prune fruit trees. After last frost is best date for rose pruning. FERTILIZE: Lawns, pansies, primroses, roses.

April
PLANT AND SOW: All planting picks up speed as the weather warms. Vegetables: spinach, peas, turnips, beets, carrots, chard, chives, cress, parsley. The soil is too cold

for warm-weather crops—corn, beans, cucumbers. Start seeds of tomatoes in flats or pots. Shop your nursery for transplants of new annuals. PRUNE: Spring flowering shrubs while in bloom or as blooms fade. PEST AND DISEASE CONTROL: Bait for slugs and keep on baiting. If root weevil is bad in your garden, treat the soil before planting (see Pest Control Chart, p. 50). Cover the entire garden with an all-purpose spray or dust. FERTILIZE: Azaleas, camellias, rhododendrons before new growth begins. If the lawn hasn't been fertilized this year make a light application now and follow with the second in about 6 weeks.

May
PLANT: If April weather kept you out of the garden you will have to telescope two months in one. Nursery transplants of annuals and perennials will give you quick color. Plant these vegetables: beans, cucumbers, corn, lettuce, squash. PEST AND DISEASE CONTROL: Spray or dust for aphis. Bait for slugs. Spray for leaf-miner on holly and lilac. GENERAL CARE: Wait until bulb foliage is yellow before removing. Thin, cultivate, fertilize vegetables.

June
PLANT AND SOW: Sow perennials now for bloom next year. Sow seeds of vegetables for late summer and fall harvest. PRUNE: Spring flowering shrubs immediately after flowering. Brooms and heathers will look better with a little clipping. PEST AND DISEASE CONTROL: Keep up your dust or spray program in the rose garden. Check chapter on roses. GENERAL CARE: A mulch to keep the weeds down will save work in vegetable garden and perennial border.

July
PLANT AND SOW: Divide and replant bearded iris. Continue to sow seeds of perennials. PRUNE: Deciduous shrubs that have flowered. Shear back groundcovers that are setting seeds. Cut off suckers that are growing from below the graft on roses and other grafted plants. Cut back chrysanthemums. PEST AND DISEASE CONTROL: Warmer days bring out new insects. Watch for damage from thrips, diabrotica, leaf hopper, and red-spider. GENERAL CARE: Fertilize the lawn. Continue feeding chrysanthemums. Dig and store bulbs whose foliage has died.

August
PLANT AND SOW: Plant in pots for Christmas bloom—freesias, crocus, Chinese lily, and paper white narcissus. Sow seeds of schizanthus for bloom indoors. Plant Madonna lilies as soon as they are available. PEST AND DISEASE CONTROL: Now is the time to catch scale insects while they are in the migratory stage. Control red-spider and thrips. GENERAL CARE: Keep adding to the compost pile. Toward the end of the month, taper off on watering rhododendrons. They should meet the first frosts with hardened wood rather than lush growth. Another light feeding of chrysanthemums is in order. Mulch of 3 inches of sawdust will protect roots of rhododendrons, azaleas, camellias.

September
PLANT: Hardy evergreens can go in this month. Plant spring-flowering bulbs as soon as they are available. Divide and replant deep-rooted, husky perennials. GENERAL CARE: Move flowering chrysanthemums into a protected spot. Pick tomatoes as they ripen; pinch out new growth to hasten ripening of those on the vines. Start general garden cleanup.

October
PLANT: Continue bulb planting. Pot up a few daffodils and tulips for forcing into winter bloom indoors. PEST AND DISEASE CONTROL: The more thorough the garden cleanup the fewer will be the over-wintering insects. GENERAL CARE: Lift and store dahlias, gladiolus. Top dress cleaned beds with peat moss, sawdust.

November
GENERAL CARE: Getting ready for winter is wise whether the winter is to be mild or unusually cold. Heavy mulches that protect roots and stems will be valuable additions to the soil next spring regardless of their need this winter.

December
PLANT: Add to your collection of indoor plants. The Christmas rose (*Helleborus niger*) deserves a prominent place in the garden this month. PEST AND DISEASE CONTROL: Spray all leafless plants with a strong dormant spray. GENERAL CARE: Inspect winter-stored bulbs for sprouting or rotting—signs that storage is too warm and moist. Make hardwood cuttings. Check potted bulbs to see if they are full of roots.

ZONE 4: PUGET SOUND

January
PLANT: A break in the weather may give you a chance to plant or transplant deciduous trees and shrubs this month—if soil is workable or if dry soil is available to fill in around roots. PRUNE: Fruit trees, grapes, summer and fall-blooming deciduous shrubs. Hold off rose pruning until end of dormant season. PEST AND DISEASE CONTROL: Spray deciduous shrubs and trees. Be prepared to spray again if rain comes immediately after application. GENERAL CARE: Drain off low spots filled with water. Tie branches of trees that are being whipped around by wind—strips of cotton sheeting make practical winter ties for this purpose.

February
PLANT: Bare-root shrubs and trees, fruit trees. SOW: Seeds of summer annuals indoors; start seeds of vegetables that can be transplanted in greenhouse or heated frame. PRUNE: Cut back summer- and fall-blooming shrubs to old wood if this was not done after blooming last year. If possible, finish pruning fruit trees this month. Do not prune spring-flowering shrubs. PEST AND DISEASE CONTROL: Dormant spraying of roses and other deciduous material before growth starts. GENERAL CARE: Clean, rake, and remove dead branches or foliage.

March
PLANT: This month is the deadline for planting deciduous material. Lift, divide, and replant fall-blooming perennials. Cabbage, lettuce, onions, spinach, and Swiss chard can be planted now. SOW: Seeds of tender annuals and perennials indoors, hardy annuals and perennials outdoors as soon as ground can be worked. PRUNE: Grapes; roses in mid-March. Forsythia and spirea can be pruned while in bloom. Last chance to prune fruit trees. PEST AND DISEASE CONTROL: You can still use dormant sprays at winter strength, but confine the spray to dormant shrubs and trees. Bait for slugs. FERTILIZE: Violets, pansies, primroses, bulb beds.

April
PLANT: Started annuals and perennials, summer-flowering bulbs, vegetables. SOW: Seeds of summer annuals in pots or flats. Vegetables: beets, carrots, lettuce, potatoes. PRUNE: Evergreen ground covers except those that may bloom before July such as *Vinca minor*. Cut dead wood out of deciduous trees. Evergreens pruned last July or August may need some trimming now. PEST AND DISEASE CONTROL: Spray or dust roses. Spray apples and pears to control codling moth when two-thirds of petals have fallen; gladiolus for thrips as soon as shoots are 3 inches high. Spread slug bait generously. FERTILIZE: Start fertilizing azaleas, camellias, rhododendrons now before new growth begins. Fertilize roses as soon as they show signs of strong new growth.

May
PLANT: Nursery-started annuals and perennials, vegetables. **Sow:** Seeds of biennials, perennials (in separate seed bed for transplanting in the fall), annuals, these vegetables: beans, beets, carrots, cucumbers, summer squash, corn. **PEST AND DISEASE CONTROL:** Spray for aphis. Spray holly and lilac for leaf miner. If rhododendron leaves look lacy and chewed, spray for mature strawberry root weevils. **GENERAL CARE:** Stake and tie tall-growing plants and straying vines. Do not trim off bulb foliage until it becomes yellow and begins to die down. Thin spring-sown seedlings. Pinch back chrysanthemums, dahlias, nearly all annuals except for non-branching flowers like poppies and lupine.

June
PLANT: Vegetables for late summer and fall harvest. **Sow:** Seeds of annuals for late bloom. Sow biennials and perennials. **PRUNE:** Spring-flowering shrubs immediately after flowering. **PEST AND DISEASE CONTROL:** Keep up a weekly prevention program with bait, spray, or dust. **GENERAL CARE:** Apply summer mulch of sawdust, peat, or the like on flower beds, or in the vegetable garden to keep down weeds, hold moisture in the soil. Start chrysanthemum cut-back program.

July
Sow: Seeds of perennials and biennials for bloom next year. **PRUNE:** Old wood from deciduous shrubs that have flowered. Cut summer-blooming perennials close to the ground after flowering, but leave some foliage at base of plant. Cut off suckers that may have arisen below graft on grafted plants. **PEST AND DISEASE CONTROL:** Most persistent July pests are aphis, earwigs, diabrotica, leafhopper, root weevils, and red-spider. **FERTILIZE:** Summer-flowering deciduous shrubs that have already bloomed. **GENERAL CARE:** Pay particular attention to watering. (See chapter on watering.) Pick faded flowers off plants to encourage continued bloom.

August
PLANT: Lift and divide perennials that have already flowered. Plant Madonna lilies, fall and winter bulbs. **Sow:** Seeds of biennials. **PRUNE:** Cut canes of boysenberries, loganberries, and raspberries to the ground after they have fruited; carefully lift new canes onto wires. **FERTILIZE:** Chrysanthemums (up to the time buds show color), fuchsias, dahlias, and other flowers that are developing now. **GENERAL CARE:** Water heavily and thoroughly at regular intervals. Harvest leaf herbs.

September
PLANT: Spring bulbs late this month. Plant balled and burlapped evergreens. Divide and replant spring-flowering perennials. **GENERAL CARE:** Lift and store gladiolus bulbs. Repair old lawns. Prepare winter potting soil—sift a good rich mixture of loam and compost, add peat and sand if soil is excessively heavy or very sandy, store in dry place for use when usual sources are frozen or mudded in. Start fall garden cleanup; remove spent annuals; cut off old stalks of perennials; clean up leaves, grasses, weeds; pull and store stakes; burn prunings and diseased plants.

October
PLANT: Evergreens after first rains have thoroughly moistened the soil; transplant trees and shrubs; move roses if desired. **Sow:** Seeds of hardy spring annuals. **PEST AND DISEASE CONTROL:** Follow cleanup operation with multipurpose insecticide-fungicide. Put out bait for slugs and destroy eggs whenever they turn up. **GENERAL CARE:** Continue garden cleanup. Keep the compost pile working. Top dress newly cleaned garden beds—use peat moss, leaf mold, sawdust, or other clean attractive organic material. Lift and store dahlias.

November
PLANT: It's not too late to plant spring flowering bulbs. Deciduous shrubs and trees can be moved if dormancy is complete. **GENERAL CARE:** Getting ready for a mild or a severe winter is the problem of the month. A sawdust mulch over rhododendron and azalea beds is beneficial in either case. Mulch lily beds with leaf mold. All open beds to be used for annuals or vegetables will benefit by a mulch of manure, fresh or rotted. It keeps the soil from packing and adds needed humus when spaded in spring.

December
PRUNE: Broken limbs or branches that cross, rub, or grow inward to block air circulation in center of a tree. December pruning should be a process of mild shaping to make trees and shrubs ready for winter. Heading back and removing large limbs is best postponed until danger of freezing is past. **PEST AND DISEASE CONTROL:** Spray leafless plants now with winter-strength dormant spray. **GENERAL CARE:** Check stored bulbs for shriveling (too warm and dry storage), sprouting or rotting (too warm and moist storage). Make hardwood cuttings. Check staking—be sure ropes or wires are not cutting into trees or shrubs. As guards against wind damage, wrap tall slender conifers with cord or fish net, tie vines, shorten shrubs which have developed long, whippy branches which might lash around in a wind.

ZONE 5: WILLAMETTE

January
Sow: Seeds of delphiniums and tuberous begonias indoors. **PRUNE:** Fruit trees, grapes, summer and fall blooming deciduous shrubs. Hold off rose pruning until end of dormant season. **PEST AND DISEASE CONTROL:** Dormant spray clean-up of deciduous shrubs and trees should be thorough; apply spray with force and in such quantities that the bark is washed. Be prepared to spray again if rain comes immediately after application. **GENERAL CARE:** Check the garden for water run-off. Drain off low spots filled with water.

February
PLANT: Bare-root shrubs and trees, fruit trees. **Sow:** Seeds of summer annuals indoors; start seeds of vegetables that can be transplanted in greenhouse or heated frame. **PRUNE:** Cut back summer and fall-blooming shrubs to old wood if this was not done after blooming last year. If possible, finish pruning fruit trees this month. Do not prune spring-flowering shrubs. **PEST AND DISEASE CONTROL:** Dormant spraying of roses and other deciduous material before growth starts. **GENERAL CARE:** If ground has not been mulched previously, add 3-4 inches of manure to areas to be planted in March or April.

March
PLANT: Rework the perennial border. Lift, divide, and replant. Cabbage, lettuce, onions, spinach, and Swiss chard can be planted now. **Sow:** Seeds of tender annuals and perennials indoors, hardy annuals and perennials outdoors as soon as ground can be worked. **PRUNE:** Grapes; roses in mid-March. Forsythia and spirea can be pruned while in bloom. Last chance to prune fruit trees. Trim hedges of privet and laurel. **PEST AND DISEASE CONTROL:** Spray holly for scale not later than March 15. Bait for slugs. **FERTILIZE:** Violets, pansies, primroses, bulb beds. All trees will benefit from a feeding now.

April
PLANT: Started annuals and perennials, summer-flowering bulbs, vegetables. **Sow:** Seeds of summer annuals in pots or flats. Vegetables: beets, carrots, lettuce, potatoes. **PRUNE:** Shear evergreen groundcovers to promote an even fresh growth. **PEST AND DISEASE CONTROL:** Spray or dust roses; spray gladiolus for thrips as soon as shoots are 3 inches high. Spread slug bait generously. **FERTILIZE:** Start fertilizing azaleas, camellias, rhododendrons now before new growth begins. Fertilize roses as soon as they show signs of strong new growth. **GENERAL CARE:** Give

the lawn a working over. Aerate and apply top dressing of peat and commercial fertilizer.

May
PLANT: Shop the nurseries for transplants, new annuals, and perennials. Sow: Seeds of biennials, perennials (in separate seed bed for transplanting in the fall), annuals, vegetables. Wait until nights are warm and soil warms up to sow corn, beans, cucumbers, squash, and set out tomatoes. Continue sowing beets, carrots, lettuce. PEST AND DISEASE CONTROL: Spray for aphis. Watch for leaf miner on holly and lilac leaves. If rhododendron leaves look lacy and chewed, spray for mature strawberry root weevils. FERTILIZE: Spring flowering evergreens immediately after flowering. GENERAL CARE: Do not trim off bulb foliage until it becomes yellow and begins to die down. Thin spring-sown seedlings. Pinch back chrysanthemums, dahlias, nearly all annuals except for non-branching flowers like poppies and lupine.

June
PLANT: Vegetables for late summer and fall harvest. Sow: Seeds of annuals for late bloom. Sow biennials and perennials for bloom next year. PRUNE: Spring-flowering shrubs immediately after flowering. Clip heathers as they complete their bloom. Snap out spent rhododendron flower heads. PEST AND DISEASE CONTROL: Keep up a weekly prevention program with bait, spray, or dust. GENERAL CARE: Apply summer mulch of sawdust, peat, or the like on flower beds, or in the vegetable garden to keep down weeds, hold moisture in the soil. Start chrysanthemum cut-back program.

July
Sow: Seeds of perennials and biennials for bloom next year. PRUNE: Wood that has flowered from deciduous shrubs that have flowered. Cut back chrysanthemums. PEST AND DISEASE CONTROL: Most persistent July pests are aphis, earwigs, diabrotica, leafhopper, root weevils, and red-spider. FERTILIZE: Summer flowering deciduous shrubs that have already bloomed. Hold off fertilizer from tender evergreen shrubs. GENERAL CARE: Pay particular attention to watering. (See chapter on watering.) Pick faded flowers off plants for continuous bloom.

August
PLANT: Lift and divide perennials that have already flowered. Plant Madonna lilies, fall and winter bulbs. Sow: Seeds of pansy, violas, forget-me-nots, wallflowers. In favorable garden sites sow seeds of spinach, onions, turnips, kohlrabi. PRUNE: Cut canes of boysenberries, loganberries, and raspberries to the ground after they have fruited. FERTILIZE: Chrysanthemums (up to the time buds show color), fuchsias, dahlias, and other flowers that are developing now. GENERAL CARE: Deep watering, to the full depth of roots, is the secret of healthy August growth.

September
PLANT: Daffodils, hyacinths, and other spring bulbs which need a long growing season late this month. (See bulb chapter on forcing bulbs for December.) Set out new peony plants. Plant new lawns now while the soil is still warm. PEST AND DISEASE CONTROL: Check garden carefully for slugs which may have escaped bait. Burn all diseased material. GENERAL CARE: Lift and store gladiolus bulbs. Prepare winter potting soil—sift a good rich mixture of loam and compost, add peat and sand if soil is excessively heavy or very sandy, store in dry place for use when usual sources are frozen or mudded in. Start fall garden cleanup. Begin moving house plants indoors in easy stages.

October
PLANT: Evergreens, especially rhododendrons, after first rains have thoroughly moistened the soil; transplant trees and shrubs. Plant tulip bulbs and anemones late this month. Divide perennials. Sow: Seeds of hardy spring annuals. PEST AND DISEASE CONTROL: Follow cleanup operation with multipurpose insecticide-fungicide. GENERAL CARE: Continue garden cleanup and top dress cleaned beds with peat moss, leaf mold, sawdust, or other clean attractive organic material. Lift and store dahlias.

November
PLANT: It's not too late to plant some spring flowering bulbs. Deciduous shrubs and trees can be moved if dormancy is complete. GENERAL CARE: Protect or store, and take cuttings of geraniums, fuchsias, and other tender plants in case of early frost. A thick sawdust, peat, or compost mulch applied at this time serves two purposes: protection if winter is unusually severe, addition of humus to the soil. See chapter on indoor plants for container planting suggestions.

December
PRUNE: December pruning should be a process of mild shaping to make trees and shrubs ready for winter. Heading back and removing large limbs is best postponed until danger of freezing is past. Paint wounds. PEST AND DISEASE CONTROL: Spray leafless plants now with winter-strength dormant spray. GENERAL CARE: Check stored bulbs for shriveling (too warm and dry storage), sprouting or rotting (too warm and moist storage). Make hardwood cuttings. Check staking—be sure ropes or wires are not cutting into trees or shrubs. As guards against wind damage: wrap tall slender conifers with cord or fish net, tie vines, shorten shrubs which have developed long, whippy branches which might lash around in a wind. See chapter on indoor plants for planting suggestions.

ZONE 6: SISKIYOU-SIERRA FOOTHILLS

January
PRUNE: Better wait out January to see how severe the winter cold will be. If a freeze comes, delay pruning until growth starts and you can appraise the winter's damage. PEST AND DISEASE CONTROL: Spray all leafless shrubs and trees with a dormant clean-up spray. GENERAL CARE: Spread a manure mulch on beds marked for spring planting. When heavy rains come, check for poor surface drainage.

February
Sow SEED: Broccoli, cabbage, cauliflower and head lettuce in hotbed or in containers indoors. PEST AND DISEASE CONTROL: Spray dormant shrubs and trees. PRUNE: Finish pruning jobs this month, except roses which should be pruned in mid-March. Do not prune spring-flowering shrubs.

March
PLANT: Last call for planting deciduous shrubs and trees. Sow SEEDS: Indoors of annuals to be planted out next month. PRUNE: Roses late this month. PEST AND DISEASE CONTROL: Thorough clean-up of rose garden is in order. (See chapter on roses.) GENERAL CARE: Spring is an extra short season here, so get everything ready to go into full speed next month.

April
You can't find a busier month in the gardener's calendar. PLANT AND SOW SEEDS: Set out plants of broccoli, cabbage, cauliflower and lettuce. Plant early potatoes. Sow seeds of chard, beets, carrots, lettuce. Divide and replant fall blooming perennials. PEST AND DISEASE CONTROL: Watch for cutworm and slug injury. Spray or dust for aphis, flea beetles, cabbage worms. GENERAL CARE: By the end of April it should be warm enough to sow seeds of many of the warm weather vegetables. Get the soil ready now and work in compost, manure, fertilizer.

May
PLANT AND SOW SEEDS: The warm days ahead will ma-

ture any of the warm weather annuals or vegetables you may choose. Plant tomatoes, peppers, eggplants, corn, melons, squash, beans, cucumbers. Nurseries offer transplants that will bring quick color. PEST AND DISEASE CONTROL: Spray or dust for flea beetles, worms, aphis. Bait, dust, and spray for earwigs. GENERAL CARE: Now, when growth is rapid, is the time for fertilizing.

June
PLANT AND SOW SEEDS: Continue vegetable plantings for late summer and fall harvest. Sow biennials and perennials for next year's bloom. PRUNE: Spring-flowering shrubs after they have bloomed. PEST AND DISEASE CONTROL: This is the month when a regular program with a combination spray or dust really pays off.

July
PLANT AND SOW SEEDS: While the garden is at its high peak of bloom watch for ways to prolong the color. Bring in nursery-grown transplants to fill vacant places. GENERAL CARE: Cut back plants that are setting seed. Pick faded flowers to encourage continued bloom.

August
PLANT AND SOW SEEDS: Take a chance on a fall vegetable crop. Sow seeds of lettuce, spinach, turnips, carrots, and beets. Set out transplants of broccoli and cabbage. PRUNE: Boysenberries, loganberries, and raspberries.

September
PLANT: And transplant peonies. Divide and replant iris. It's a good month for lawn making. Divide and replant spring-flowering perennials. GENERAL CARE: Start the fall clean-up. Get ready for bulb planting next month. Keep the compost pile working.

October
PLANT: Spring-flowering bulbs. Lift and store dahlias, cannas, tuberous begonias, fuchsia, gladiolus. GENERAL CARE: Continue garden clean-up. Apply winter mulch of peat or sawdust.

November
PLANT: Last call for bulbs—still time to plant tulips, daffodils, bulbous iris, lilies. PRUNE: Get trees ready for winter—brace and stake. Evergreens heavy with foliage should be thinned to let wind through. GENERAL CARE: Mulch and top dress. Get vines ready for winter. Clean-up.

December
PRUNE: December pruning should be a process of mild shaping to make trees and shrubs ready for winter. Heading back and removing large limbs is best postponed until danger of freezing is past. PEST AND DISEASE CONTROL: Spray leafless plants now with winter-strength dormant spray. GENERAL CARE: Check stored bulbs for shriveling. Make hardwood cuttings. Check staking—be sure ropes or wires are not cutting into trees or shrubs.

ZONE 7: CENTRAL VALLEY
January
PLANT AND SOW SEED: Plant bare-root fruit trees, deciduous flowering shrubs, roses, berry vines. Sow seeds under glass of ageratum, petunia, cynoglossum, pinks, lobelia. Sow these in open ground: clarkia, godetia, linaria, Virginian stock. Make your selection of camellias while they are in bloom. PRUNE: Late this month is a good time to prune roses. All fruit trees should be pruned by now. PEST AND DISEASE CONTROL: Use a dormant oil spray on roses and deciduous ornamentals. Spray peaches and nectarines for leaf curl. GENERAL CARE: When the rains come watch for standing water. Dig temporary ditches to improve drainage if needed.

February
PLANT AND SOW SEED: When choosing deciduous fruit trees this month, don't overlook the persimmon and the pomegranate. Both are highly ornamental and both appreciate the heat of the Valley. All bare-root material should be planted before new growth starts. Plant perennial vegetables — artichoke, rhubarb, and asparagus. Plant gladiolus for bloom in June. Start seeds of spring and early summer annuals so that you can get transplants in the ground as soon as soil begins to warm up. PRUNE: Cut back heather after blooming. Prune fuchsia. PEST AND DISEASE CONTROL: Don't forget the dormant spray; spray peaches and nectarines for peach leaf curl.

March
PLANT AND SOW SEED: All cool weather annuals and vegetables should be underway so that they will mature before the hot weather hits them. Last call for lettuce, chard, beets, carrots. Muskmelons and corn can be sown late this month. Best month to start new lawns. Start cuttings of chrysanthemums. FERTILIZE: Almost everything — lawns, roses, vegetables, annuals, evergreen shrubs and trees. PEST AND DISEASE CONTROL: With warm weather and new growth come the aphis. Better use a combination spray and clean up the entire garden to prevent build-up of other insect populations.

April
PLANT AND SOW SEED: The increasing warmth, both day and night, makes possible seed sowing of all warm-weather annuals and vegetables. Don't overlook: verbena, cosmos, zinnia, petunia, portulaca, sunflower, tithonia. Late this month sow seeds of stringbeans, lima beans, melons. Plant rooted cuttings of grape vines. Choose azaleas in bloom. Plant dahlia and canna tubers. FERTILIZE: Camellias and azaleas before new growth gets underway. PEST AND DISEASE CONTROL: Spray or dust for aphis, mildew, codling moth on apples and pears. GENERAL CARE: Keeping pace with the weeds is the all-important job. Treat the lawn for crab grass.

May
PLANT AND SOW SEED: Nurseries now are busy supplying gardeners who want color immediately. Both annuals and perennials of every kind are available. Sow seeds of all warm-weather vegetables. Set out tomato transplants and sow a few tomato seeds. Plants from seed will come along fast. New iris will be available this month. FERTILIZE: If lawn, or camellias, or chrysanthemums are not the deep rich green they should be, give them a light application of fertilizer. PEST AND DISEASE CONTROL: Control aphis, young grasshoppers, and mildew with dusts or sprays. GENERAL CARE: Check your watering habits with root depths of plants. See chapter on watering.

June
NOTE: While it's good common sense to get all planting done before the hot weather sets in, you *can* start from scratch in June or July and still get a presentable garden before the season is over. So much of the nursery material is now sold in containers that every month is a planting month. All planting must be handled with care. Provide some temporary shade and watch the plants' watering needs.

July
Sow: Last crop of warm-weather vegetables for late harvest. Start seeds of fall vegetables—cabbages, cauliflower, broccoli—in a protected place for transplanting outdoors next month. PEST AND DISEASE CONTROL: Spray or dust for diabrotica, leafhopper, red-spider. GENERAL CARE: Watering is the secret of unchecked growth in vegetables and annuals. Camellias and azaleas must not dry out. They are surface-rooted and must be watered frequently.

August
PLANT AND SOW SEED: With protection from the sun and close attention to watering, you can sow seed of calendula, stock, and violas for transplanting in a month to 6 weeks. December bloom is possible with September warmth to speed growth. Set out transplants of cabbage,

broccoli and cauliflower for early winter harvest. PRUNE: Remove canes of berry vines that have borne fruit and lift up new vines and train them to the trellis. GENERAL CARE: If petunias are getting lanky cut them back severely and they'll come on again to bloom in September and October. Water deeply to replenish the soil reservoir to the full depth of the roots, and sprinkle the soil surface during hot spells to keep down soil temperatures. Wash down camellia foliage every day. Give the lawn another feeding to carry through the hot weather.

September
PLANT AND SOW SEED: You can look ahead to about 60 days of active growing weather before cold nights bring growth to a standstill. There may be enough warmth left in the year to carry through crops of beets, lettuce, spinach, turnips. Divide and replant iris. Plan ahead for winter color in evergreen shrubs, especially berried shrubs. FERTILIZE: Continue feeding chrysanthemums until buds show color. A final cut-back of petunias and an extra feeding will bring out a good late show of bloom. GENERAL CARE: Plan for bulb planting next month. Stake chrysanthemums.

October
PLANT AND SOW SEED: Regardless of the warm days, it's too late for successful plantings of winter flowers and vegetables. It's the best month for planting spring-flowering bulbs. All of the hardy evergreens can be transplanted now. PRUNE: Shape and brace trees against fall and winter winds but otherwise delay pruning until dormancy is complete. Prune oleander after blooming. GENERAL CARE: Give the lawn a generous feeding to carry it through the winter. Clean up all debris and fatten up the compost.

November
PLANT: Continue planting spring bulbs of grape hyacinth, daffodil, scilla, sparaxis, ixia, freesia, and tulips. Choose trees for fall color while they are in color. PEST AND DISEASE CONTROL: A spraying this month will help control many overwintering insects and spores that cause plant diseases. GENERAL CARE: Anchor all young trees securely either by stakes or wires. Cut back perennials that have bloomed. Lift and store tuberous begonias, gloxinias, canna, dahlias, gladiolus.

December
GENERAL CARE: Clean up with dormant spray, with pruning shears, with spade work before the rains. Heavy mulches of manure over the vegetable beds will add to the fertility of the soil and make spring soil preparation an easier job.

ZONE 8-A: LOW DESERT
January
PLANT AND SOW SEEDS: Following the short bite of low winter temperatures, the gardener enters a race to plant and sow almost everything. January is the month to plant berries, deciduous fruit trees, deciduous shade trees. January is midseason for many of the cool-weather annuals. Plants of cabbage and cauliflower can be set out now. Sow seeds of beets, carrots, lettuce. PEST AND DISEASE CONTROL: As in any other climate, the dormant season is the time for a clean-up dormant spray.

February
PLANT: Citrus and other evergreen material. Set out eggplant, pepper, tomato in the warmest areas. Plant gladiolus. Sow: Seeds of fast growing annuals—calendula, candytuft, nasturtium, Virginian stocks. PRUNE: Fruit trees, grapes, roses.

March
PLANT AND SOW SEED: These vegetables: beans, corn, cucumbers, melons, squash. These annuals: celosia, cosmos, portulaca, tithonia, verbena, zinnia. PEST AND DISEASE CONTROL: Watch for aphis, migratory scale on citrus.

April
PLANT: Shrubs and trees from containers, nursery plants that will either bloom quickly or live through the summer. FERTILIZE: Roses, lawns.

May
PLANT: Last call for shrubs and trees from containers. Sow: Seed of warm-weather vegetables for succession of harvests. FERTILIZE: Everything. GENERAL CARE: Practice deep watering.

June—July—August
FERTILIZE: Lightly but regularly. GENERAL CARE: Deep soaking. Regular dusting or spraying. Mulch to conserve water and keep roots cool.

September
PLANT: As the weather cools or where lath protection from sun is available, winter flower and vegetable gardens can be planted now. Quick maturing annuals will be best.

October
PLANT: Spring-flowering bulbs. Start new lawns and renovate Bermuda lawns. Continue sowing seeds of overwintering annuals.

November—December
PLANT: Bulbs, nursery transplants, berried shrubs. GENERAL CARE: Clean-up.

ZONE 8-B: HIGH DESERT
January
PLANT: Bare-root material. GENERAL CARE: Clean up in every way possible—by removing all debris that may hide insects and by a thorough, drenching, dormant clean-up spray.

February
PRUNE: Deciduous trees. Wait until next month for pruning roses. Prune spring-flowering shrubs after bloom.

March
PLANT: Almost everything in the shrub, tree, vine classes. Sow seeds in hotbeds or indoors: broccoli, cabbage, onions, tomatoes. Sow seeds in ground: spinach, turnips, lettuce. PEST AND DISEASE CONTROL: Spray and dust as warming weather brings out new insect populations. Fertilize as the rush of new growth gets under way.

April
PLANT AND SOW: Set out transplants of broccoli, cabbage, onions, tomatoes. Sow in hotbeds or indoors: eggplant, peppers. Sow in ground: pole beans, beets, carrots, chard, potatoes.

May
PLANT AND SOW: The warm days ahead will mature any of the warm-weather annuals or vegetables you may choose. Sow beans, beets, cantaloupe, carrots, chard, corn, cucumber, onions, peanuts, potatoes, squash, watermelons. Transplant from containers: eggplant, onions, peppers, sweet potatoes, tomatoes. PEST AND DISEASE CONTROL: Spray and dust for aphis. FERTILIZE: Continue feeding lawn and roses.

June
PLANT AND SOW: Continue vegetable plantings for late summer and fall harvest. Sow biennials and perennials for next year's bloom. PRUNE: Spring-flowering shrubs after they have bloomed.

July
GENERAL CARE: Watch for ways to prolong color in the flower garden. Bring in nursery grown transplants to fill vacant places. Cut back plants that are setting seed.

August
GENERAL CARE: Thorough watering and mulching to conserve water and keep roots cool is the order of the month. PRUNE: Boysenberries, loganberries, raspberries.

September
GENERAL CARE: Plant and transplant peonies. Divide and replant spring-flowering perennials. Divide and re-

plant iris. It's a good month for lawn making.

October
PLANT: Spring-flowering bulbs. Lift and store dahlias, gladiolus. GENERAL CARE: Clean-up. Keep the compost pile working.

November
PLANT: Last call for bulbs—tulips, daffodils, bulbous iris, lilies. PRUNE: Get trees ready for winter. Brace and stake. Prune and tie vines. GENERAL CARE: Apply winter mulch.

December
PRUNE: Confine pruning to mild shaping and thinning to make trees and shrubs ready for winter. Heading back and removing large limbs is best postponed until after frosts. PEST AND DISEASE CONTROL: Spray leafless plants now with winter-strength dormant spray.

ZONE 9: COASTAL VALLEYS

January
PLANT: Deciduous shrubs and trees; evergreens; berries; small fruits; roses. Select flowering quince and camellias now while they are in bloom. *Primula malacoides* and *P. polyantha* planted now will give some bloom in February and March. PRUNE: Deciduous fruit trees; roses; grapes; flowering fruit trees after bloom; ivy. PEST CONTROL: Spray deciduous trees and shrubs with strong dormant spray. Try not to let winter oil touch plants in leaf; if it does, wash off at once. Eradicate wild oats and grassy weeds now, while they are young.

February
PLANT: Roots or divisions of perennial vegetables; seedling plants of some vegetables; nursery-started annuals. Complete bare-root planting. Sow: Summer annuals in flats under shelters; hardier vegetables in open ground; tender vegetables under protection. PRUNE: Fruit trees and grape vines before buds begin to open; hybrid tea roses by middle or end of month; fuchsias back to two-thirds after frosts are over. PEST CONTROL: Complete dormant spraying of roses and other deciduous material before growth starts. Spray fruit trees; peaches for leaf curl (before buds open).

March
PLANT: Perennials; summer-flowering bulbs; nursery-started annuals; vegetables. Sow: summer annuals in pots or flats; vegetables and some cool weather annuals in open ground. Start lawns. PRUNE: Flowering shrubs after bloom; fuchsias when danger of frost is past; pyracantha; cotoneaster. PEST CONTROL: Spray for aphis; blackberry vines for mites. Start covering roses regularly with good general-purpose spray or dust. Burn tents of tent caterpillars.

April
PLANT: Started annuals; summer-flowering bulbs; vegetables; shrubs or trees from containers. Sow: summer annuals; vegetables. Make lawns. PRUNE: Flowering shrubs after bloom. PEST CONTROL: Spray roses for aphis; gladiolus for thrips; apple and pear trees for codling moth when two-thirds of petals have fallen. Control mildew with dust or multipurpose spray containing mildew fungicide. FERTILIZE: Camellias, azaleas, roses. GENERAL CARE: Keep ahead of weeds. Start deep summer watering of lawns, shrubs, trees. Pinch back annuals and perennials that need it.

May
PLANT: Hot weather vegetables; nursery-started annuals; tender bulbs; shrubs and trees from containers. Sow: Summer annuals, perennials (in flats so they are easy to water and protect from heat), vegetables. Make lawns. PRUNE: Deciduous shrubs after flowering. PEST CONTROL: Spray or dust for aphis, grasshoppers, mildew. FERTILIZE: Feed lawns with balanced commercial fertilizer once every month or six weeks. GENERAL CARE: Control weeds. Regular deep watering is usually necessary by first of May. Nip off faded blossoms of spring bulbs before they form seed pods; apply fertilizer around plants while foliage is still green; do not trim off foliage until it becomes yellow and begins to die down.

June
PLANT: Hot weather annuals from nursery flats; trees and shrubs from containers, but water carefully. Sow: Perennials; biennials; late summer annuals; vegetables. PRUNE: Climbing roses which bloom once a year after flowering. Finish pruning spring-flowering shrubs. PEST CONTROL: Aphis continue as most common pest. Red spiders are prevalent on roses, phlox, azaleas, camellias. FERTILIZE: Continue feeding lawns once every month or six weeks if necessary (see chapter on lawns). GENERAL CARE: Stake plants that need support. Water regularly. Pinch back new annuals. Make softwood cuttings.

July
PLANT: Heat-loving annuals from nursery; shrubs and trees from containers, but water carefully. Sow: perennials; winter and spring-flowering annuals in flats (July sowing of any plant means added care because of heat); fall vegetables now in flats; some summer vegetables still in open ground. PEST CONTROL: For aphis, diabrotica, caterpillars, ants, earwigs, lawn moth (sod webworms). FERTILIZE: Fast-growing annuals and perennials; new lawns. Feed fuchias lightly but regularly during flowering period. GENERAL CARE: Lift and divide spring-blooming bulbs if necessary. Scatter light mulch around shallow-rooted plants after watering to check evaporation. Water potted fuchsias daily.

August
PLANT: Fall and winter bulbs; Madonna lilies; trees and shrubs from containers, if you water well. Sow: Perennials and winter annuals in flats; winter vegetable crops. Divide and replant perennials. PRUNE: Boysenberries, loganberries, raspberries after they have fruited. PEST CONTROL: Spray or dust for mildew, aphis, caterpillars, thrips, scale. FERTILIZE: Dahlias, fuchsias, chrysanthemums (up to time buds show color); late-blooming gladiolus. GENERAL CARE: Watering is the number one job for August.

September
PLANT: Started perennials; winter vegetable crops; trees and shrubs from containers, but water well; spring-blooming bulbs late this month. Sow: Perennials, hardy annuals. Begin fall lawn plantings after September 15. FERTILIZE: Roses at least once during month. GENERAL CARE: Stake and tie fall-blooming perennials, climbing roses, vines. Lift and store gladiolus bulbs when leaves turn yellow or brown. Start fall garden clean-up: clean out dead and dying annuals; gather up fallen leaves; remove withered iris, leaves; clean up and destroy fallen fruits.

October
PLANT: Spring-blooming bulbs; lilies; perennials and biennials from nursery; started perennial seedlings; shrubs and trees from containers, except tender items. Sow: Hardy annuals. Divide perennials if needed. Last month to start new lawns. PEST CONTROL: For ants, aphis, slugs, snails. GENERAL CARE: Continue garden clean-up. Trim off spent blossoms. Cut down plants that need it, such as helenium, goldenrod, gaillardia, early chrysanthemums. Remove excess perennials and unwanted annuals. Lift and store summer bulbs if foliage has turned yellow.

November
PLANT: Perennials, spring bulbs, hardy shrubs and trees. Sow: Hardy annuals. Divide spring and early summer blooming perennials. GENERAL CARE: Cut back Japanese

anemones, hardy asters, phlox, early blooming chrysanthemums. Lift and store bulbs, corms, tubers. Stake and tie all plants that will need support during coming wind and rain. Mix potting or seeding soil in fall while ingredients are dry; store away in protected place for use in early spring.

December

PLANT: Hardy evergreens; spring bulbs; roses if available; deciduous trees; shrubs late this month. Transplant large trees and shrubs if necessary. Divide overgrown perennials or set out new perennials that haven't gone dormant. Wait a little longer before dividing plants that are subject to rot, such as delphinium. PRUNE: Deciduous fruit trees after leaves have fallen. Clean up, shape, and control growth of ornamentals by removing dead branches and thinning over-crowded centers. PEST CONTROL: Spray leafless plants now with strong dormant spray. GENERAL CARE: Prepare soil with 3-inch dressing of manure so pelting winter rains will not beat it into pavement hardness. Make hardwood cuttings.

ZONE 10: BAY AREA—NORTH COASTAL

January

PLANT: Deciduous shrubs and trees; evergreens; berries; small fruits; roses; early spring vegetables. Select flowering quince and camellias now while they are in bloom. Sow: Seeds of annuals under shelter. PRUNE: Deciduous fruit trees; and roses; ivy if it needs it. PEST CONTROL: Spray deciduous trees and shrubs with strong dormant spray.

February

PLANT: Roots or divisions of perennial vegetables; seedling plants of some vegetables; nursery-started annuals. Start such summer bulbs as tuberous begonias, gloxinias, streptocarpus under shelter. Complete bare-root planting. Sow: Summer annuals in flats, hardier vegetables in open ground, tender vegetables under protection. PRUNE: Fruit trees before leaf and flower buds begin to open; hybrid tea roses by middle or end of month; fuchsias back two-thirds after frosts are over. PEST CONTROL: Be sure to do dormant spraying of roses and other deciduous material before growth starts. Spray fruit trees; peaches for leaf curl (before buds open).

March

PLANT: Perennials; summer-flowering bulbs; annuals from nursery flats; vegetables. Sow: Summer annuals in pots or flats; vegetables and some cool weather annuals in open ground. Lawn making season starts now and continues through summer months until heavy rains become a threat in late fall. PRUNE: Flowering shrubs after bloom; fuchsias if you didn't do it last month; pyracantha; cotoneaster. PEST CONTROL: Spray for aphis. Spray for mites on blackberry vines. Start covering roses regularly with good general-purpose spray or dust.

April

PLANT: Started annuals; summer-flowering bulbs; vegetables; shrubs or trees from containers. Sow: Summer annuals; vegetables. Make lawns. PRUNE: Flowering shrubs that have already bloomed. PEST CONTROL: Spray roses for aphis; gladiolus for thrips; apple and pear trees for codling moth when two-thirds of petals have fallen. Control mildew with dust or spray containing a mildew fungicide. FERTILIZE: Camellias, azaleas, roses.

May

PLANT: Summer vegetable crops; nursery-started annuals; summer bulbs; shrubs or trees from containers. Sow: Summer annuals and perennials (in flats so they are easy to water and care for); vegetables. PRUNE: Deciduous shrubs after flowering. PEST CONTROL: Control aphis, mildew; slugs, snails. Hose off leaves to get rid of white froth caused by spittle bug. FERTILIZE: Feed lawns once every month or six weeks.

June

PLANT: Summer annuals from nursery flats; trees or shrubs from containers. Sow: Perennials and biennials; vegetables. PRUNE: Climbing roses which bloom once a year (after flowering). Finish pruning spring-flowering shrubs. PEST CONTROL: Aphis continue to be the most common pest. FERTILIZE: Lawns if necessary (see chapter on lawns). Pinch back new annuals to make them bushy and more flower-laden. Make softwood cuttings.

July

PLANT: Annuals from the nursery; trees and shrubs from containers if watered carefully. Sow: Perennials; winter and spring-flowering annuals in flats for bloom next year; fall vegetables in flats; and still some summer vegetables, in open ground. PEST CONTROL: Control aphis, diabrotica, caterpillars, ants, earwigs. Watch for signs of lawn moth (sod webworms). FERTILIZE: Fast-growing annuals; perennials; new lawns. Feed fuchsias lightly but regularly during flowering period.

August

PLANT: Fall and winter bulbs; Madonna lilies; trees and shrubs from containers if watered well. Sow: Perennials and winter annuals in flats; winter vegetable crops. Divide and replant perennials. PRUNE: Boysenberries; loganberries; raspberries after they have fruited. PEST CONTROL: For mildew, aphis, caterpillars, thrips, scale. FERTILIZE: Dahlias; fuchsias; chrysanthemums (up to time buds show color); late-blooming gladiolus.

September

PLANT: Winter vegetable crops; spring-blooming bulbs late this month unless days and nights are very hot; trees and shrubs from containers, except tender items. FERTILIZE: Roses at least once during the month. GENERAL CARE: Stake and tie fall-blooming perennials, climbing roses, vines. Lift and store gladiolus bulbs when leaves begin to turn yellow or brown. Start fall garden clean-up; clean out dead and dying annuals; gather up fallen leaves; remove withered leaves on iris; clean up and destroy fallen fruits.

October

PLANT: Spring-blooming bulbs; lilies; perennials and biennials from nursery; native shrubs and trees, and any others except tender specimens. Sow: Hardy annuals. Last month to start new lawns before heavy rains become a threat toward end of November. Divide perennials if needed. PEST CONTROL: Keep after ants, aphis. Use poison bait for slugs, snails. GENERAL CARE: Continue garden clean-up.

November

PLANT: Perennials, spring bulbs, hardy shrubs and trees. Divide spring and early summer-blooming perennials. Sow: Hardy annuals. GENERAL CARE: Cut peonies to ground after foliage withers. Cut back Japanese anemones, hardy asters, early blooming chrysanthemums. Lift and store bulbs, corms, tubers. Stake and tie all plants that will need support during coming wind and rain. Mix potting or seeding soil in fall while ingredients are dry; store it away in a protected place for use in early spring.

December

PLANT: Evergreens; spring bulbs; roses if available; deciduous trees and shrubs late this month. Transplant large trees and shrubs if necessary. Set out new perennials that haven't gone dormant. Divide overgrown perennials but wait until rains subside before dividing plants that are subject to rot, such as delphinium. PRUNE: Deciduous fruit trees after leaves have fallen. Clean up, shape, and control growth of ornamentals by removing dead branches and thinning overcrowded centers. PEST CONTROL: Spray leafless plants with strong dormant spray.

ZONE 11: SOUTHERN INTERIOR VALLEYS

January
PLANT: Deciduous shrubs and trees; berries; small fruits; roses; some summer-blooming bulbs. Transplant dormant roses, deciduous trees and shrubs. PRUNE: Fruit trees; grapes. PEST CONTROL: Spray fruit trees, other deciduous material with strong dormant spray; sycamores, with blight-preventive spray.

February
PLANT: All bare-root material; summer-flowering bulbs. PRUNE: Fruit trees and grape vines before buds begin to open; roses. PEST CONTROL: Spray for mites; peach leaf curl, mildew. Give sycamores second spraying for blight. FERTILIZE: Beds marked for vegetables; summer annuals; evergreen shrubs and trees. Feed winter-blooming flowers with quick-acting food.

March
PLANT: Perennials; summer bulbs. Last time to plant gladiolus for bloom in late June. Sow: Early summer annuals in flats under cover. Root-tip cuttings of new dahlia growth under glass. PEST CONTROL: Spray and dust for aphis, thrips, diabrotica, peach leaf curl, and brown rot. FERTILIZE: Lawns (see chapter on lawns for a choice of year-around lawn feeding schedules; deciduous trees and shrubs as they begin to show new growth. Wait until next month to feed camellias and azaleas. Feed bulb beds lightly. GENERAL CARE: For roses, uncover crowns; repair basins; apply manure mulch; when growth starts, give commercial feeding.

April
PLANT: Warm weather vegetables; broadleaf evergreens; nursery-started annuals and perennials. Sow: Vegetables; summer annuals in open ground except in coldest areas. Try dwarf dahlias from seed sown in flats (buy high quality mix). Make lawns. PRUNE: Flowering shrubs after bloom. PEST CONTROL: Spray roses, citrus, artichokes, and other aphis-susceptible plants; azaleas and young gladiolus for thrips; apples and pears for codling moth when two-thirds of petals have fallen. FERTILIZE: Azaleas and camellias before new growth begins; roses, lawns; dichondra to prevent seed setting. Give all shade plants and roses a treatment of iron sulfate to produce quick green; gardenias take double amount. GENERAL CARE: Control weeds. Begin regular deep watering. Make softwood cuttings.

May
PLANT: Hot weather vegetable crops; tender trees and shrubs; ornamentals; shrubs and trees from containers. Sow: Summer annuals in open ground. PRUNE: Deciduous shrubs after flowering. PEST CONTROL: Spray for aphis, mildew, thrips, chewing insects. Sprinkle snail bait around newly set out plants. GENERAL CARE: Combat lawn moth and crab-grass by regularly feeding turf grasses with balanced fertilizer to build up their strength; crab-grass eradicators are effective on young seedlings if repeatedly applied. Control weeds. Regular watering of lawns usually essential by first of May. Get watering equipment in shape for summer.

June
PLANT: Nursery-started annuals for quick summer bloom; sow seed for late summer and fall bloom. Plant trees and shrubs from containers. Sow: Perennials and biennials under protection; fast-growing hot weather vegetable crops. PEST CONTROL: Use good multipurpose spray or dust systematically. Aphis, red spider, thrips, diabrotica must be checked. Bait for slugs, snails. FERTILIZE: Fast-growing plants. GENERAL CARE: Protect surface roots of shrubs and border plants with thick blanket of rotted manure, compost, or straw. Stake tall flowers. Start dividing bearded iris. Cut back and pinch young border annuals. Disbud dahlias for show-size flowers.

July
PLANT: Heat-tolerant annuals, but water diligently. Early hot-weather vegetable crops can still go in; trees and shrubs from containers, with great care. Sow: Perennials for next year; winter and spring-flowering annuals in flats. PEST CONTROL: Spray or dust for red spider, thrips, chewing insects. FERTILIZE: Rapid growers need heavy feeding; slow growers, light feeding. GENERAL CARE: Give chrysanthemums last cutting back to foot or so; provide adequate supports. Cut back Shasta daisies. Prepare sweet pea trench for August planting.

August
PLANT: Sweet peas but protect from sun; trees and shrubs from containers, watered well. Sow: Perennials and winter annuals in flats under lath; winter and spring vegetables. PRUNE: Boysenberries, loganberries, raspberries after they have fruited. PEST CONTROL: Pests reach an all-time high in some places. Rather than use specific sprays or dusts, you may find it easier to rely on one good multipurpose spray or dust.

September
PLANT: Fall and winter-blooming annuals from flats, keeping well watered and protected from sun; winter vegetables; trees and shrubs from containers, if watered well; spring-blooming bulbs. Sow: Spring annuals. Divide large clumps of spring-blooming perennials. PEST CONTROL: Important pests to look for in September are red spider, aphis, scale, ants, sowbugs. Rust and mildew are most prevalent diseases. GENERAL CARE: Stake and tie fall-blooming perennials, climbing roses, vines. Renovate roses: thin lightly; remove dead wood or spent flowers; repair basins; mulch; keep well watered.

October
PLANT: Nursery-started early spring annuals; perennials; spring bulbs; winter vegetables; native shrubs and trees; ornamentals. Best month to start new lawns. Sow: Root crops; lettuce; spinach; onions. PEST CONTROL: Follow clean-up operation with thorough coverage of multipurpose spray or dust. GENERAL CARE: Continue garden clean-up. Mix compost or well-rotted manure into beds marked for replanting.

November
PLANT: Hardy evergreens; shrubs; trees; berried shrubs; cabbage crops; spring-flowering bulbs; nursery transplant of annuals; perennials. Sow: Hardy annuals. PEST CONTROL: For snails, slugs, aphis. FERTILIZE: Give final "booster shot" feeding to lawn grasses; feed bulb beds. GENERAL CARE: Continue clean-up activities.

December
PLANT: Hardy evergreens; spring bulbs (December is late for planting many bulbs, but tulips, hyacinths, ranunculas, anemones can still be planted); bare-root shrubs and trees. PRUNE: Deciduous fruits after leaves have fallen. Clean up, shape, control growth of ornamentals by removing dead branches and thinning overcrowded centers. Wait until spring to prune tender plants.

ZONE 12: SOUTHERN CALIFORNIA INNER COASTAL VALLEYS

January
PLANT: Deciduous shrubs and trees; evergreens; berries; small fruits; roses; nursery-started annuals and perennials; some summer-blooming bulbs; nursery-started cool weather vegetables late in month. Sow: Spring and summer annuals and warm weather vegetables under shelter.

PRUNE: Fruit trees; grape vines and roses late in month; ivy. PEST CONTROL: Spray fruit trees; other deciduous material; native sycamores. FERTILIZE: Young transplants; bearded iris. GENERAL CARE: Mulch bulb beds. Clean out crowns of roses and rebuild basins. Protect tender plants from frost.

February

PLANT: All bare-root material; summer bulbs; subtropicals; cool weather annuals late in month. Sow: Hot weather annuals. Divide dahlia tubers. PRUNE: Fruit trees and grape vines before buds begin to open; fuchsias when frosts are over. PEST CONTROL: Spray for mites on berries; peach leaf curl; mildew. FERTILIZE: Beds marked for vegetables; summer annuals; evergreen shrubs and trees; fruit trees as buds begin to swell; trees and lawns when weather warms up.

March

PLANT: Perennials; subtropicals; summer bulbs; root, cole and leaf vegetables; nursery-started annuals. Sow: Vegetables; summer annuals in open ground. Divide perennials. Start new lawns. Take cuttings of chrysanthemums. PEST CONTROL: Spray for aphis, migratory scale, peach leaf curl, brown rot, mildew. FERTILIZE: Lawns (see chapter on lawns for choice of year-around lawn feeding schedules); deciduous trees; roses; shrubs as they begin to show new growth.

April

PLANT: Warm weather vegetables; subtropicals; nursery-started annuals; perennials. Sow: Summer annuals; lawns. Make cuttings of chrysanthemums; root-tip cuttings of dahlias under glass. PRUNE: Flowering shrubs after bloom. PEST CONTROL: Spray roses; citrus; artichokes; other aphis-susceptible plants. Spray for thrips, mildew. FERTILIZE: Azaleas, camellias, roses, lawns. GENERAL CARE: Make softwood cuttings. Keep ahead of weeds. Begin regular deep watering. Uncover camellia crowns and replace mulch if necessary. Stake hybrid delphinium.

May

PLANT: Hot weather vegetables; tender trees and shrubs; any trees and shrubs from containers; avocados, or other subtropical fruits and ornamentals. Sow: Summer annuals. PRUNE: Deciduous shrubs after flowering. Thin branches of evergreen trees and shrubs. PEST CONTROL: Keep after aphis, chewing insects. Sprinkle snail bait around newly-set-out plants. FERTILIZE: Lawn grasses, roses. GENERAL CARE: Control weeds. Disbud roses. Water lawns deeply.

June

PLANT: Nursery-started annuals; trees or shrubs from containers. Sow: Perennials; biennials under protection; fast-growing hot weather vegetables; fall annuals. Separate leucocoryne bulbs; replant at once in pots of rich soil and plunge in ground. Divide bearded iris. PRUNE: Deciduous shrubs after bloom. PEST CONTROL: Use multipurpose spray or dust systematically. Control aphis, mildew. FERTILIZE: Any shrubs set out this season; fast-growing plants. GENERAL CARE: Protect surface roots of shrubs; border plants with thick blanket of rotted manure; compost; or straw. Stake tall plants. Pinch back young border annuals. Disbud dahlias for show-size flowers. Cut bloomed-out delphinium stalks back to top of foliage; feed lightly to force second bloom.

July

PLANT: Early hot weather vegetable crops; early tomatoes in mild areas; trees and shrubs from containers if watered carefully. Sow: Perennials; winter and spring-flowering annuals in flats; heat-tolerant annuals in open ground. Finish dividing bearded iris. PEST CONTROL: For red spider, aphis, diabrotica, Fuller's rose beetle, grasshoppers. FERTILIZE: Rapid growers need heavy feeding; slow growers, light feeding; feed lawns. GENERAL CARE: Make last cutting back on chrysanthemums; stake if not already done. Cut back delphinium and Shasta daisies after peak flowering and as soon as growth starts from base. Prepare bed for sweet peas to be planted in August. Fill in weak spots in lawns or dichondra with mulch of leaf mold and manure.

August

PLANT: Trees and shrubs from containers, but water well; end-of-summer bedding plants still available at nurseries. Sweet peas, last half of month; shade bed and young plants until 3-6 in. high. Sow: Perennials and winter annuals in flats; winter and spring vegetables. Divide and replant perennials that have bloomed. PRUNE: Boysenberries; loganberries; raspberries after fruiting. PEST CONTROL: Pests reach an all-time high now in some places. Rather than use specific sprays or dusts, you may find it easier to rely on one good multipurpose spray or dust. FERTILIZE: Fast-growing plants. GENERAL CARE: Watering is number one job for August. Light mulch applied after heavy watering will help to retain moisture. Keep up heavy watering of roses. Dig crab grass before it seeds.

September

PLANT: Fall and winter-blooming annuals; spring bulbs; winter vegetables; trees and shrubs. Last month to plant iris from nurseries for spring bloom. Sow: Winter and spring annuals. Start new lawns. PEST CONTROL: Important pests to look for in September are red spider, aphis, brown scale, ants, sowbugs, earwigs. Mildew is most prevalent disease. FERTILIZE: Sweet peas; roses. GENERAL CARE: Continue regular watering. Mulch tender surface roots. Stake and tie fall-blooming perennials, climbing roses, vines. Flush crowns, remulch roses. Thin and support sweet peas. Clean out dead leaves on old iris; get name plates renewed before winter rains.

October

PLANT: Nursery-started spring annuals; perennials; spring bulbs; winter vegetables; native shrubs and trees; ornamentals. Sow: Root crops; lettuce; spinach; onions. Divide perennials if needed. Start new lawns; seed Bermuda lawns with highland bentgrass or perennial ryegrass. PRUNE: Bush berries. PEST CONTROL: Follow clean-up operations with multipurpose spray or dust. FERTILIZE: Old lawns; sweet peas. GENERAL CARE: Continue garden clean-up. Mix compost or well rotted manure into beds marked for replanting.

November

PLANT: Spring bulbs; nursery-started annuals and perennials; hardy evergreen shrubs and trees; berried shrubs; cabbage crops. Sow: Hardy annuals. PEST CONTROL: For snails, slugs, aphis. Spray sweet peas with fungicide from base up. FERTILIZE: Bulb beds. Give final "booster shot" feeding to lawns. GENERAL CARE: Continue clean-up: Save leaves for composting. Don't throw diseased plants in compost heap.

December

PLANT: Hardy evergreens; spring bulbs (December is late for planting many bulbs, but tulips, hyacinths, ranunculas, anemones can still be planted); hardy nursery-started bedding plants; bare-root shrubs and trees late this month. PRUNE: Deciduous fruits after leaves have fallen. Clean up, shape, control growth of ornamentals by removing dead branches and thinning overcrowded centers.

ZONE 13: SOUTHERN CALIFORNIA COASTAL

January

PLANT: Deciduous shrubs and trees; evergreens; berries;

small fruits; roses; nursery-started annuals and perennials; some summer-blooming bulbs such as gladiolus; nursery-started cool weather vegetables. Sow: Spring and summer annuals; tuberous begonias and gloxinias under glass; warm weather vegetables in lathhouses or coldframes. Prune: Fruit trees; grapes; ivy if it needs it; roses when plump red growth buds are evident. Pest Control: Spray fruit trees and other deciduous plants with strong dormant spray; California sycamores for blight prevention. Watch for slugs, snails. Fertilize: Bearded iris.

February
Plant: All bare-root material—deciduous shrubs, roses, ornamental and fruit trees; bush berries; grapes; rhubarb; artichokes; summer bulbs; tropicals and subtropicals; cool weather annuals. Prune: Fruit trees and grape vines before buds begin to open; roses if not done last month; fuchsias back two-thirds. Pest Control: Spray for mites on berries, peach leaf curl, mildew; spray roses and ground around them with good fungicide. Fertilize: Beds marked for vegetables; summer annuals; evergreens. Feed shrubs and other plants as soon as new growth starts; trees and lawns when weather warms up.

March
Plant: Perennials; subtropicals; summer bulbs; warm weather vegetables; annuals from nursery flats. Sow: Vegetables; summer annuals; lawns. Make cuttings of chrysanthemums. Pest Control: Spray for aphis, migratory scale, peach leaf curl, brown rot, mildew, thrips. Fertilize: Lawns (see chapter on lawns for choice of year-around lawn feeding schedules); deciduous trees; roses; shrubs as they begin to show new growth; camellias; azaleas; bulb beds; dichondra.

April
Plant: Warm weather vegetables; tropicals and subtropicals; nursery-started annuals and perennials. Sow: Summer annuals; lawns. Prune: Flowering shrubs after bloom. Pest Control: Spray roses, citrus, artichokes, other aphis-susceptible plants. Spray azaleas and young gladiolus for thrips; apples and pears for codling moth when two-thirds of petals have fallen. Fertilize: Azaleas; camellias; roses; lawns. General Care: Control weeds. Begin regular deep watering.

May
Plant: Hot weather vegetables; tender trees and shrubs; any shrubs and trees from containers; avocados and other subtropical fruits and ornamentals. Sow: Summer annuals. Prune: Deciduous shrubs after flowering. Thin branches of evergreen trees and shrubs. Pest Control: Control aphis; mildew. Watch for chewed leaves, especially on tender young camellias and other shrubs (see pest control chart). Sprinkle snail bait around newly set out plant. Fertilize: Lawn grasses. General Care: Control weeds; crab-grass (crab-grass eradicators are effective if applied when grass is in seedling stage). Deep watering of lawns is usually essential by first of May.

June
Plant: Nursery-started annuals; trees and shrubs from containers. Sow: Perennials, biennials, fast-growing hot weather vegetables; fall annuals. Prune: Deciduous flowering shrubs after bloom. Pest Control: Use multipurpose spray or dust systematically. Control aphis, thrips. Bait for snails, slugs. Fertilize: Fast-growing plants. General Care: Protect surface roots of shrubs, border plants, with thick blanket of rotted manure, compost, or straw. Stake tall flowers. Cut back and pinch young border annuals; disbud dahlias for show-size flowers; cut delphinium stalks back to top of foliage after bloom and give light feeding to force second crop of blossoms. Do not allow roses to go dry.

July
Plant: Early hot weather vegetable crops; early tomatoes in mild areas; trees and shrubs from containers if watered carefully. Sow: Perennials; winter and spring-flowering annuals in flats; hot weather annuals in open ground, provided you water diligently. Pest Control: For red spider; aphis; thrips; chewing insects such as diabrotica, Fuller's rose beetle, grasshoppers. Fertilize: Rapid growers need heavy feeding; slow growers, light feeding. Feed lawns. General Care: Cut back chrysanthemums to about a foot so they will not be leggy and sprawling by bloom time. Prepare trench for sweet peas to be planted next month.

August
Plant: End-of-summer bedding plants that are still available; trees or shrubs from containers. Sow: Perennials; winter annuals in flats; vegetables for winter and spring harvest; sweet peas by August 25. Divide and replant perennials that have bloomed. Prune: Boysenberries; loganberries; raspberries. Pest Control: By August pests reach an all-time high in some places. Rather than use specific sprays or dusts, you may find it easier to rely on one good multi-purpose spray or dust. Fertilize: Fast-growing plants. General Care: Watering is the number one job for August. Light mulch applied after heavy watering will help to retain moisture.

September
Plant: Fall and winter-blooming annuals; winter vegetables, trees and shrubs; subtropicals. Sow: Spring annuals. Prune: Roses lightly and clean out dead flowers; dead and crossed branches; suckers. Pest Control: Important pests to look for this month include red spider, aphis, brown scale, ants, sowbugs, earwigs. Mildew is most prevalent disease. General Care: Continue regular watering. Mulch tender surface roots. Divide large clumps of spring-blooming perennials. Stake and tie fall-blooming perennials, climbing roses, vines. Clean up vegetable garden after crop has been harvested.

October
Plant: Nursery-started early spring annuals; perennials; spring bulbs; winter ornamentals; native shrubs and trees; ornamentals. Sow: Root crops, lettuce, spinach, onions. Divide perennials if needed. Start new lawns; seed Bermuda lawns with highland bentgrass or perennial ryegrass. Prune: Bush berries after fruiting. Pest Control: Follow clean-up operations with thorough coverage of multipurpose spray or dust. Fertilize: Sweet peas. General Care: Continue garden clean-up. Mix compost or well rotted manure into beds marked for replanting. Provide support for sweet peas.

November
Plant: Spring-flowering bulbs; nursery-started annuals and perennials; hardy evergreen shrubs and trees; berried shrubs; cabbage crops. Sow: Hardy annuals. Pest Control: For snails, slugs, aphis. Fertilize: Give final "booster shot" feeding to lawn grasses. Feed bulb beds. General Care: Continue clean-up activities.

December
Plant: Hardy evergreens; spring bulbs (December is late for planting many bulbs, but tulips, hyacinths, ranunculas, anemones can still be planted); bare-root shrubs and trees late this month. Prune: Deciduous fruits after leaves have fallen. Clean up, shape, control growth of ornamentals by removing dead branches and thinning overcrowded centers. Fertilize: Bearded iris. General Care: Prepare soil with 3-inch dressing of manure so pelting winter rains will not beat it into pavement hardness. Check drainage furrows; regrade beds if necessary; check run-off from roof valleys to make sure water does not collect around shrubs. Prepare frost protection cover for tender subtropicals.

Index

A

Aaron's beard, 214
Abelia, 221
Abies, 281, 309
Abronia umbellata, 128
Abutilon, 221
Abysinnian sword lily, 176
Acacia, 281; chart, 282
  rose, 303
Acaena, 211
Acanthus mollis, 142
Acer, 283, 309
Achillea, 142, 211
Achimenes, 170
Acid soil, 30
Acidanthera, 170, 176
Aconite, winter, 174
Aconitum, 142
Actinidia chinensis, 199
Adiantum, 365
Adobe soil, 26, 29
Aeonium, 328
Aesculus, 283
  californica, 310
Aethionema, 142
African box, 241
African corn lily, 177
African daisy, 128, 144, 150, 152
African lily, 171
African violet, 362
Agapanthus, 170
Agave, 328
Ageratum houstonianum, 128
Aglaeonema, 359
Agonis flexuosa, 283
Ailanthus altissima, 283
Ajuga
  metallica crispa, 330
  reptans, 211
Akebia quinata, 199
Albizzia, 283, 284
Alder, 284, 310
Aleppo pine, 320
Aldrin, 51
Algerian ivy, 203
Alkaline soil, 29
Allamanda cathartica, 199
Allium, 356
  neapolitanum, 171
Almond, 344
  flowering, 273
Alnus, 284, 310
Alocasia macrorhiza, 364
Aloe, 328
Alpine wintergreen, 213
Alpinia, 364
Alsophila australis, 365
Alstroemeria, 171
Althaea rosea, 142
Alyssum, 128
  saxatile, 142
Amaranthus, 128
Amaryllis, 176
  belladonna, 171
Amelanchier, 221
Amomum cardamon, 359
Ampelopsis, 199
Anagallis, 128
Anchusa
  azurea, 143
  capensis, 128
Anchusa, Forget-me-not, 146
Androsace primuloides, 330
Anemone, 143, 171
Anemopaegma
  chamberlaynii, 199
Anethum graveolens, 356
Angel tears, 213
Anise, 357
Annona cherimola, 352
Annuals, 125-137
  in containers, 123
  starting, 81
  time to plant, 127
Anthemis, 211
  tinctoria, 143
Anther, 12
Anthriscus cerefolium, 356
Anthurium, 359
Antigonon leptopus, 199
Antirrhinum majus, 128
Apache plume, 313
Aphis, 44, 50
Apple, 344
Apricot
  flowering, 273
  fruiting, 345
  pruning, 348
Aquilegia, 143, 330
Arabian khat, 225
Arabis, 143
Aralia, 284, 360
Araucaria, 284
Arborvitae, 250, 304, 329
  giant, 319
Arbutus
  menziesii, 310
  unedo, 221
Archontophoenix, 326
Arctostaphylos, 310
Arctotis, 128, 144
Arecastrum romanzoffianum, 326
Arenaria verna caespitosa, 211
Armeria
  juniperifolia, 330
  maritima, 144
Aromo, 222
Arsenates, 51
Artemisia, 144, 356
Artichoke, 334
Ash, 293
  mountain, 304
Asparagus
  vegetable, 334
  vine, 199
Aspen, 316
Asperula odorata, 211
Aspidium tsus-simense, 362
Asplenium nidus, 360
Aster, 144
  fruticosus, 221
  Stokes, 161
Astilbe, 144
Athel tree, 249
Athyrium, 365
Atriplex lentiformis, 310
Aubrieta deltoidea, 145
Aucuba, 222
  japonica, 360
Aurelian lilies, 193
Australian
  bluebell creeper, 207
  fuchsia, 228
  hoop-pine, 284
  pea vine, 202
  tea tree, 239
  tree fern, 365
  willow-myrtle, 283
Austrian pine, 321
Autumn crocus, 173
Avocado, 351
Azalea, 261-263
  western, 317
Azara microphylla, 222

B

Babiana, 171
Baboon flower, 171
Baby blue-eyes, 134
Baby's breath, 131, 152
Baby's tears, 213
Baby tears peperomia, 361
Baccharis pilularis, 211
Bachelor button, 129
Baits, 51
Balloon flower, 159
Balloon vine, 201
Balsam, 132
Balsam fir, 281
Bamboo, 323-325
  heavenly, 241
  sacred, 241
Bamboo palm, 326
Bambusa, 324-325
Banana, 299
Banana shrub, 240
Banyan tree, 293
Barberry, 222
Basil, 357
Basining, 37
Basket flower, 177
Basket-of-gold, 142
Basswood, 305
Bauhinia, 284
Bay
  California, 319
  sweet, 296
Bay Area climate, 23
Beans, 335
Bear-berry, 310
Bearberry cotoneaster, 212
Beard tongue, 158
Bear's breech, 142
Beaumontia grandiflora, 200
Beauty bush, 238
  berry, 224
Bee balm, 156
Beech, 292
Beefwood, 285
Beetles, 44, 49
Beets, 335
Begonia
  fibrous, 145
  tuberous, 181-183
Belladonna lily, 171
Bellflower, 146, 330
Bellingham hybrid lily, 193
Bellis perennis, 145
Beloperone guttata, 222
Bent grasses, 103
Berberis, 222
Bergamot, wild, 156
Bergenia, 145
Bermuda grass, 104
  planting, 107
Berries, 336-343
  blackberry, 336
  blueberry, 338
  boysenberry, 336
  currant, 338
  gooseberry, 338
  raspberry, 340-341
  strawberry, 341-343
Berry, service, 221
Bethlehem sage, 160
Betula, 284
Biennials
  Althaea rosea, 142
  Anchusa capensis, 128
  Campanula medium, 147
  Cynoglossum amabile, 130
  Dianthus barbatus, 149
  Digitalis purpurea, 150
  Glaucium flavum, 152
  Mathiola incana, 134
  Oenothera hookeri, 156
Bignonia, 200
Big tree, 318
Billbergia, 146
Birch, 284
Birds, control, of, 90
Bird of paradise, 365
Bird-of-paradise bush, 301
Bird's-eye, 131
Birds-nest-fern, 360
Bishop pine, 321
Bishop's hat, 150
Bittersweet, 201
Black bamboo, 325
Black-eyed susan vine, 208
Black pine, 321, 322
Blackberries, 336
Blanket flower, 131
Blechnum spicant, 365
Bleeding heart, 150
Bletilla striata, 172
Blocking-out, 88
Blood lily, 176
Bloomeria crocea, 172
Bluebeard, 225
Blueberries, 338
Blue-berry climber, 199
Blue blossom, 312
Blue dicks, 172
Blue fescue, 212
Blue grasses, 103
Blue lace flower, 131
Blue leadwort, 212
Blue palm, Mexican, 326
Bog kalmia, 314
Boltonia, 146
Bomarea caldasii, 172
Borage, 356
Borers, 47
Boston ivy, 206
Botanical names, 116
Bottle brush, 224
Bottle tree, 285
Botree, 293
Bougainvillea, 200
Bouvardia, 223
Box, 223
  African, 241
  false, 315
  Victorian, 245
Box elder, 283, 309
Boxwood, 223
Boysenberry, 336
Brachychiton, 285
Brachycome iberidifolia, 128
Brachysema lanceolatum, 223
Brass buttons, 356
Breadfruit, Mexican, 206
Breath of heaven, 228
Bridal wreath, 248
Brisbane box, 305
Bristlecone pine, 321
Broccoli, 335
Brodiaea, 172
Broom, 229, 329
Broussonetia papyrifera, 285
Browallia, 129
Brown patch, 111
Brunfelsia calycina floribunda, 223
Brunnera macrophylla, 146
Brussels sprouts, 335
Buckeye, Calif., 310
Buckthorn, Italian, 247
Buckwheat, Santa Cruz, 313
Budding, 99
Buddleja, 223
Buds
  growing, 10
  lateral, 60
  selection, 58
  terminal, 10, 60
Bugloss, Italian, 143
Bulbs, 169-196
  in containers, 123
Bunya-bunya, 284
Burmese honeysuckle, 205
Burnet, 357
Burning bush, 132
Bush poppy, 312
Bush morning glory, 130
Butia capitata, 326
Buttercup
  button, 215
  creeping, 215
Butterfly bush, 223
Butterfly flower, 136
Butterfly tulip, 172
Butternut, 295
Buxus, 223

C

Cabbage, 335
Cajeput tree, 224
Caladium, 364
Calceolaria integrifolia, 146
Calendar
  annual planting, 127
  bulb, bloom, 170
  general, 61
  perennial bloom, 141
  pest control, 43
  zone, 366
Calendula officinalis, 129
California fan palm, 327
California poppy, 131
Calla, 180
Calliandra, 224

INDEX

Callicarpa, 224
Callistemon, 224
Callistephus chinensis, 129
Callitris robusta, 285
Calluna, 231, 232, 329
Calochortus, 172
Calodendrum capense, 285
Calonyction aculeatum, 200
Calycanthus occidentalis, 310
Camass, 172
Camassia, 172
Cambium, 11
Camellia, 253-255
  japonica, 253
  reticulata, 255
  sasanqua, 255
Campanula, 146, 330
Camphor tree, 288
Campion, 155
Campsis, 201
Canary bird bush, 229
Canary Island date palm, 326
Canary Island ivy, 203
Canary Island pine, 321
Candytuft, 132, 154, 330
Canna, 172
Cantaloupes, 335
Canterbury bells, 147
Canvas
  for garden use, 66
  frost protection, 71
Cape chestnut, 285
Cape cowslip, 177
Cape forget-me-not, 128
Cape honeysuckle, 208
Cape marigold, 131, 150
Cape plumbago, 207
Caragana arborescens, 285
Caraway, 356
Cardamon amomum, 359
Cardiospermum
  halicacabum, 201
Carica papaya, 355
Carissa, 225
Carmichaelia enysii, 329
Carnation, 149
Carob tree, 286
Carolina jessamine, 203
Carpenteria californica, 311
Carpet bugle, 211
Carpobrotus, 214
Carrots, 335
Carrot wood, 289
Carum carvi, 356
Carya illinoensis, 285
Caryopteris, 225
Caryota, 326
Cascara sagrada, 317
Cashmere bouquet, 227
Casimiroa edulis, 285, 355
Cassia, 225
Castanea, 285
Castanopsis chrysophylla
  minor, 311
Castanospermum australe, 285
Castor bean, 135
Casuarina, 285
Catalina cherry, 316
Catalpa, 285
Catananche caerulea, 147
Catchfly, 155, 161
Cats-claw trumpet vine, 202
Caterpillars, 47
Catha edulis, 225
Catnip, 156
Cattleya, 363
Cauliflower, 335
Ceanothus, 311
  hybrids, 312
Cedar, 286
  Alaska yellow, 226
  Atlas, 286
  deer horn, 305
  deodar, 286
  incense, 296, 314
  Japanese, 289
  of Lebanon, 286
  plume, 289
  Port Orford, 226, 287
  red, 295
  salt, 249

Cedar (continued)
  western red, 319
Cedrus, 286
Celastrus scandens, 201
Celosia, 129
Celtis, 286
Centaurea, 129, 147
Central valley climate, 21
Centranthus ruber, 147
Cephalotaxus drupacea, 286
Cerastium tomentosum, 211
Ceratonia siliqua, 286
Ceratostigma, 225
  plumbaginoides, 212
Cercidiphyllum japonicum, 286
Cercis, 287
  occidentalis, 312
Cercocarpus betuloides, 312
Ceriman, 206
Ceropegia, 328
Cestrum, 225
Chaenomeles, 226
Chamaecyparis, 226, 287, 329
Chamaedorea, 326, 360
Chamaelaucium, 226
Chamaerops humilis, 326
Chamomile, 211
Chards, 335
Chart
  pest control, 50-51
  pruning, 57
  weed killers, 67, 68, 69
Chaste tree, 252
Checkerberry, 213
Checkered lily, 175
Cheiranthus cheiri, 147
Chemicals
  insecticides, 51
  weed killers, 66-69
Cherimoya, 352
Cherry
  Australian brush, 292
  Carolina laurel, 245
  Catalina, 316
  flowering, 273
  hollyleaf, 316
  sour, 347
  Surinam, 292
  sweet, 347
Cherry of the Rio Grande, 292
Chervil, 356
Chestnut, 285
Chickweed, 113
Chilean jasmine, 205
Chilean lily, 171
Chilean wine palm, 326
Chilopsis linearis, 312
Chimonanthus praecox, 227
China aster, 129
Chinese bellflower, 221
Chinese evergreen, 359
Chinese houses, 130
Chinese lantern, 221
Chinkerinchee, 178
Chinquapin, golden, 311
Chiogenes hispidula, 329
Chionanthus, 287
Chionodoxa, 173
Chive, 356
Chlordane, 51
Chlorosis
  leaf symptoms, 49
  symptoms, cure, 31
Choisya ternata, 227
Chorizema varium, 227
Christmas berry, 314
Christmas rose, 153
Christmas tree, New
  Zealand, 299
Chrysalidocarpus lutescens, 326
Chrysanthemum, 147, 164-166
  balsamita, 356
  carinatum, 129
Cineraria, 129
Cinnamomum camphora, 288
Cinquefoil, 159, 215
Cissus, 201, 360
Cistus, 227
Citrus, 352
Cladrastis lutea, 288
Clarkia, 130

Classification of plants, 117
Clay soil, 28, 30
Clematis, 201
Cleome spinosa, 130
Clerodendrum, 227
Clethra arborea, 288
Clianthus puniceus, 202
Cliff rose, 312
Climate, 14-25
  frost control, 70
  growing season map, 17
  heat accumulation, 16
  light intensity, 16
  summer temperature, 15
  winter chilling, 15
  zones, 18-25
Clivia, 173
Cloth of gold, 174
Clover
  bur, 113
  lawn clover, 103
Cluster pine, 321
Clytostoma callistegioides, 202
Coast valley climate, 23
Cobaea scandens, 202
Cocculus laurifolius, 227
Cockscomb, 129
Coffeeberry, 317
Coffee tree, Kentucky, 294
Colchicum, 173
Coldframes, 99
  heated, 100
Coleonema, 228
Coleus blumei, 360
Collinsia bicolor, 130
Colocasia esculenta, 364
Columbia basin climate, 19
Columbine, 143, 330
Comarostaphylis diversifolia, 312
Compost
  bin, 74
  how to make, 73
  humus source, 29
  maintenance, 73
  nutrient source, 28
Coneflower, 150
Confederate jasmine, 216
Conifers
  pruning chart, 57
Container gardening, 119
  containers, 123
  how to use plants, 119
  plant boxes, 124
  raised beds, 77
  soil needs, 123
  U.C. Mix, 31
Convallaria majalis, 173
Convolvulus
  cneorum, 228
  mauritanicus, 202, 212
  tricolor, 130
Cool-season grasses, 102
Copper spot, 110
Coprosma, 228
Coral bells, 153
Coral tree, 232
Coral vine, 199
Cordyline, 327
Coreopsis
  grandiflora, 148
  tinctoria, 130
Coriander, 356
Cork tree, 300
Corn, 336
  earworm, 46
Cornflower, 129
Cornus, 288, 312
Coronilla glauca, 228
Correa, 228
Cortaderia selloana, 228
Cortex, 11
Corydalis lutea, 148
Corynocarpus laevigata, 289
Cosmos bipinnatus, 130
Costmary, 356
Cotinus coggygria, 289
Cotoneaster, 212, 228, 329
Cottage tulip, 195
Cottonwood, 316
Cotula, 356

Cotyledon, 328
Coulter pine, 321
Cow itch tree, 296
Cowania mexicana
  stansburiana, 312
Cowslip lungwort, 160
Crabapple, 345
  flowering, 274
Crabgrass, 112
Cranberry bush
  European, 251
Crape myrtle, 296
Crataegus, 289
Crassula, 328
Cream bush, 314
Crinodendron dependens, 289
Crocus, 173
Crotalaria agatiflora, 229
Crown imperial, 175
Cryophytum crystallinum, 214
Cryptomeria japonica
  elegans, 289
  nana, 329
Cucumbers, 335
Cucumber beetle, 44
Cucumber, tree, 297
Cucurbita pepo ovifera, 203
Cudweed everlasting, 153
Cultivators, 65
Cunninghamia lanceolata, 289
Cup-and-saucer vine, 202
Cupania anacardioides, 289
Cupid's dart, 147
Cup-of-gold vine, 207
Cupressus, 290
Curly leaf, 49
Currant, 338
  flowering, 316
Cut-and-come-again, 137
Cuttings
  hardwood, 96
  potting, 97
  softwood, 95
  starting plants from, 95
Cutworms, 114
Cyclamen, 174
Cydonia oblonga, 290
Cynoglossum amabile, 130
Cypress
  Arizona, 290
  birds nest, 226
  false, 226, 287
  Forbes, 290
  Hinoki, 287
    dwarf, 329
  false, 226
  Italian, 290
  Lawson, 226, 287
  Monterey, 290
  moss, 287
  Nootka, 226, 287
  sawara, 287
    false, 226
  summer, 132
  Tecate, 290
Cypresspine, 285
Cypress vine, 207
Cypripedium, 363
Cytisus, 229, 329

D

Daboecia, 231, 232
Daffodils, 183-186
Dahlias, 186-187
Daisy
  African, 128, 131, 144, 150, 152
  English, 113, 145
  Michaelmas, 144
  Paris, 148
  Shasta, 148
  Swan river, 128
  turfing, 214
Damping-off,
  preventing, 83
Dandelion, 112
Daphne, 230
Darwin tulips, 195
Date palm, 326
Daubentonia tripetii, 230
Davidia involucrata, 290

INDEX

Dawn redwood, 299
Day lily, 176
DDD, 51
DDT, 51
Deciduous fruit trees, 343-351
   grafting, 349
   pruning, 343-349
Deer fern, 364
Deer horn cedar, 305
Delphinium, 148
   ajacis, 130
Dendromecon rigida, 312
Deodar cedar, 286
Desert climate, 22
Deutzia, 230
Dewdrop, golden, 231
Diabrotica beetle, 44
Dianthus, 130, 149, 330
Diascia barberae, 131
Dibble, 88
Dicentra, 150
Dichondra carolinensis, 212
   lawn substitute, 109
Dicksonia, 365
Didiscus caerulea, 131
Dieffenbachia, 360
Dieldrin, 51
Dierama, 174
Digger pine, 321
Digitalis purpurea, 150
Dill, 356
Dimorphotheca, 131
   ecklonis, 150
Diosma, 228
Diospyros kaki, 290
Diplacus, 312
Diseases
   of lawns, 110
   of plants, 52
Disinfecting seed, 85
Distictis lactiflora, 202
Dividing plants, 93
Dizygotheca veitchii, 360
Dog-tooth violet, 174
Dogwood, 288, 312
Dolichos, 202
Dollar spot, 111
Dombeya, 230
Donkey tail sedum, 328
Doronicum, 150
Douglas fir, 316
Douglasia vitaliana, 330
Dove tree, 290
Doxantha unguis-cati, 202
Draba olympica, 330
Dracaena, 360
   draco, 327
Dragon tree, 327
Drainage
   correcting, 75
   defined, 86
   flats, pots, 84
Drooping palm, 326
Dryas suendermannii, 330
Duchesnea indica, 212
Duranta repens, 231
Dusty miller, 147
Dwarf bamboo, 325

E

Earwig, 44
Easter lily vine, 200
Echeveria, 327, 328
Echinacea purpurea, 150
Echinops ritro, 150
Echium fastuosum, 150
Eggplant, 335
Elaeagnus, 231
Elderberry, 318
Elephant ears, 364
Elm, 305
Empress tree, 300
Endive, 335
Engineering, garden, 75
English ivy, 203
Enkianthus campanulatus, 231
Epidendrum, 364
Epimedium, 150
Eranthemum nervosum, 231
Eranthis hyemalis, 174

Erica, 231, 329
Erigeron, 151
Eriobotrya japonica, 290, 354
Eriogonum, 313
Eryngium amethystinum, 151
Erythea, 326
Erythrina, 232
Erythronium, 174
Escallonia, 232
Eschscholtzia californica, 131
Eucalyptus, 290
Eugenia, 292
Euonymus, 233
   fortunei, 202
Eupatorium coelestinum, 151
Euphorbia
   marginata, 131
   myrsinites, 151
   pulcherrima, 234
   splendens, 328
   wulfenii, 151
Eurya emarginata, 234
Evergreen fruit trees, 351-355
Evergreen pear, 301
Evergreens
   pruning, 57, 59
Exochorda racemosa, 234

F

Fading out, 110
Fagus, 292
Fairy primrose, 135
Fairy ring, 111
Fairy stars, 131
Fairy wand, 174
Fall care, 63
Fallugia paradoxa, 313
Fan palm, 319, 326
   California 319
   Chinese, 326
   Mexican, 327
Farewell-to-spring, 131
Fatshedera lizei, 202
Fatsia japonica, 234, 360
Faucaria, 328
Fawn lily, 175
Feather hyacinth, 178
Feijoa sellowiana, 234, 354
Felicia, 151
Fennel, 356
Fern, asparagus, 200
Fern pine, 301
Fernleaf bamboo,
   stripestem, 324
Ferns, 365
Fertilizer
   container plants, 124
   for lawns, 108
   for trees, 280
   function of, 28
Fescue grasses
   fine, 103
   coarse, 103
Festuca ovina glauca, 212
Ficus, 203, 292, 360
Fiesta hybrid lilies, 193
Fig, 292, 345, 360
   creeping, 203
Filament, 12
Filbert, 345
Fill, 76
Fir, 281, 309
   China, 289
   Douglas, 316
Fireball bush, 224
Firebush, Mexican, 132
Firethorn, 246
Firewheel tree, 304
Firmiana simplex, 293
Fish tail palm, 319
Fittonia verschaeffeltii, 361
Flame bush, Brazilian, 224
Flame tree, 285
   Chinese, 296
Flamepea, bush, 227
Flannel bush, 313
Flats, for starting seeds, 82
Flax, 155
   Indian yellow, 160

Flax (continued)
   New Zealand, 243
   scarlet, 133
Flea beetle, 49
Flies, 50
Floribunda roses, 264, 271
Floss flower, 128
Flowering fruit trees, 272
Flowering maple, 221
Flowering quince, 226
Flowering tobacco, 134
Flowers
   parts and functions, 12
Foeniculum vulgare, 356
Forget-me-not, 134
   cape, 128
   creeping, 156
   summer, 143
Forget-me-not Anchusa, 146
Formosa cherry, 273
Forsythia, 234
Fountain palm, 326
Foxglove, 150
Foxtail pine, 321
Fragaria chiloensis, 213
Francoa ramosa, 151
Franklinia, 294
Fraxinus, 293
Freesia, 175
Fremontia, 313
Fringe bell, 161
Fringe tree, 287
Fritillaria, 175
Frost control, 70
   winter chilling, 15
Frosted plants, 72
Fruit
   how formed, 13
Fruit trees
   deciduous, 343-351
   evergreen, 351-355
   flowering, 272
   pollinating, 350
   pruning, 348-349
Fuchsia, 255
   Australian, 228
   California, 319
Fullers rose beetle, 44
Fun shrub, 242
Fusarium patch, 111

G

Gaillardia
   aristata, 151
   pulchella, 131
Galanthus, 175
Galtonia, 175
Gardenia, 234
Garlic, 356
   society, 162
Garrya, 313
Gaultheria, 213
   shallon, 313
Gazania, 152
Gelsemium sempervirens, 203
Genista, 229, 329
Gentiana acaulis, 152
Genus, defined, 116
Geraldton waxflower, 226
Geranium, 157, 330
   cut-leaf, 113
   Martha Washington, 157
   strawberry, 363
   wild, 113
Gerberia jamesonii, 152
Germander, 250
Geum chiloense, 152
Giant bamboo, 325
Gilia, 131
Ginger, 364
Ginger lily, 364
Ginkgo biloba, 294
Gladiolus, 175
Glaucium flavum, 152
Gleditsia, 294
Globethistle, 150
Globe tulip, 172
Gloriosa, 176
Glorybower, 227
Glory lily, 176

Glory-of-the-snow, 173
Glory of the sun, 177
Gloxinia, 179
Goat's beard, 144
Godetia, 131
Going out (lawn disease), 110
Gold flower, 214
Golden bamboo, 325
Golden bells, 234
Goldenchain tree, 296
Goldencup, 154
Golden drops, 156
Goldenrain tree, 295
Golden stars, 172
Gooseberry, 316, 338
Gophers, 53
Gordonia alatamaha, 294
Gourd, 203
Grafting, 349
   principles, 98
Grand cycle of growth, 57
Grandiflora roses, 264, 271
Grapes, 338-340
Grape, 208
   evergreen, 201
   California, 315
   Oregon, 315
Grapefruit, 353
Grape hyacinth, 178
Graptopetalum, 327, 328
Grass types, 102-105
Grasshopper, 46
Grass nut, 172
Grease spot, 110
Greek valerian, 159
Grevillea, 235
   robusta, 294
Grewia caffra, 235
Griselinia, 235
Ground covers, 209-216
Ground morning-glory, 212
Guadelupe palm, 326
Guava, 245, 354
   Chilean, 241
   pineapple, 234, 354
Guernsey lily, 178
Guinea gold vine, 204
Guinea-hen flower, 175
Gum, 291-292
   sour, 299
   sweet, 296
Gunnera chilensis, 235
Gymnocladus dioica, 294
Gypsophila, 152
   elegans, 131

H

Hackberry, 286
Haemanthus katherinae, 176
Hakea, 235
Halesia carolina, 294
Hamamelis mollis, 294
Hardenbergia comptoniana, 203
Harpephyllum caffrum, 295
Harts tongue, 365
Haworthia, 328
Hawthorn, 289
   India, 246
Header boards, 77
"Heading," 60
Heat accumulation
   definition, 16
Heath, 231, 232
Heather, 231, 232, 329
Heavenly bamboo, 241
Hebe, 235
Hedera, 203, 213, 361
Hedge bamboo, 324
Hedychium, 364
Helenium autumnale, 152
Helianthemum, 213
Helianthus, 152
   annuus, 132
   bracteatum, 132
   petiolatum, 153
Helichrysum, 132, 153
Heliopsis scabra
   incomparabilis, 153
Heliotropium, 153

INDEX 381

Helleborus, 153
Helxine soleirolii, 213
Hemerocallis, 176
Hemlock, 319
Hen-and-chickens
  (Sempervivum tectorum), 328
Hepatica, 153
Heptachlor, 51
Herald trumpet vine, 200
Herbicides, 66-69
Herbs, 355-357
Heteromeles arbutifolia, 314
Heuchera sanguinea, 153
Hibbertia volubilis, 204
Hibiscus, 236
High desert climate, 22
Hills of snow, 236
Himalayan pine, 322
Hippeastrum, 176
Hoes
  kinds of, 65
Hoheria, 295
Holly, 236
  California, 314
  Guatemala, 299
  summer, 312
Hollyhock, 142
Hollyleaf coffeeberry, 317
Hollyleaf cherry, 316
Holodiscus discolor, 314
Home food garden, 331-357
Honey bell, 155
Honey bush, 240
Honeysuckle, 205, 239
  cape, 208
Hop, Japanese, 205
Horsechestnut, 283
Hosta, 154
Hottentot fig, 214
Housefly, 50
Houseleek, 327, 328
House plants, 358-365
Howea, 326
Hoya, 204
  carnosa, 361
Huckleberry, 319
Humulus, 205
Humus
  deficiency, 28
  peat moss, 29
Hunnemannia, 154
Hyacinth, 177
  feather, 178
  fringe, 178
  grape, 178
  plume, 178
  star, 179
  summer, 175
  wild, 172
Hyacinth bean, 202
Hyacinth-flowered candytuft, 132
Hyacinthus orientalis, 177
Hybrid, defined, 117
Hybrid tea roses, 264, 270
Hydrangea, 236
  petiolaris, 205
Hydrangea vine, 207
Hymenocallis calathina, 177
Hymenosporum flavum, 295
Hypericum, 213, 236
Hyssopus, 356

I

Iberis, 132
  sempervirens, 154, 330
Iceland poppy, 135
Ice plant, 214
Ilex, 236
Immortelle, 137
Impatiens
  balsamina, 132
  holstii, 154
Inca lily, 171
Incense cedar, 314
India hawthorn, 246
Indian mock strawberry, 212
Indoor gardening, 358-365
Insecticides
  chart of, 50-51

Insecticides (continued)
  chemical ingredients, 51
  dusters, 52
  how to use, 41
  sprayers, 52
  toxicity, 41, 42
Insects
  control chart, 50-51
  control program, 40
  friendly, 43
Intermountain climate, 18
Ipomoea, 205
Iris, 188-191, 330
Irish moss, 211
Ironwood, Catalina, 314
Irrigation, 37
Islay, 316
Itea ilicifolia, 237
Ithuriel's spear, 172
Ivy, 203, 206, 213, 361
Ixia, 177

J

Jacaranda acutifolia, 295
Jacob's ladder, 159
Jacobinia, 237
Jacquemont cherry, 273
Japanese creeper, 206
Japanese hop, 205
Japanese spurge, 215
Jasmine, 204-205
  Chilean, 205
  Madagascar, 207
  star, 208, 214
Jasmine tobacco, 156
Jasminum, 204, 205
Jeffrey pine, 322
Jelecote pine, 322
Jerusalem sage, 158
Jerusalem thorn, 300
Jessamine
  Carolina, 203
  night, 226
  orange, 241
  willow-leaved, 225
Jetting tool, 80
Jewel mint of Corsica, 214
Jubaea spectabilis, 326
Juglans, 295
Jujube, Chinese, 305
Juniperus, 295, 314, 329
  shrub forms, 237
Jupiter's beard, 147

K

Kafir lily, 173, 179
Kafir plum, 295
Kahili ginger, 364
Kalanchoe, 328
Kalmia, 238
  polifolia, 314
Kalmiopsis leachiana, 314
Kangaroo treebine, 201
Karo, 244
Katsura tree, 286
Kennedya beckziana, 205
Kentucky bluegrass, 103
Kerria japonica, 238
Khat, Arabian, 225
King palm, 326
Kinnikinnick, 310
Kleinia, 328
Kniphofia, 154
Knobcone pine, 322
Kochia scoparia, 132
Koelreuteria, 295
Kohuhu, 244
Kolkwitzia, 238
Kousa dogwood, 289
Kumquat, 354
Kupuka tree, 235

L

Laburnum, 296
Lace flower, 131
Lachenalia pendula, 177
Lady fern, 365
Lady palm, 326

Lady slippers, 363
Lagenaria siceraria, 203
Lagerstroemia indica, 296
Lagunaria patersonii, 296
Lambs ears, 216
Lampranthus, 214
Lantana, 238
Larch, 296
Larix decidua, 296
Larkspur, 130
Lathyrus odoratus, 132
Latin nomenclature, 118
Laurel
  alpine, 314
  California, 319
  cherry, 245
  English, 245
  Grecian, 296
  mountain, 238
  New Zealand, 289
  pale, 314
  Portugal, 245
  Texas mountain, 304
  Zabel, 245
Laurestinus, shining, 252
Laurus nobilis, 296
Lavandula, 154
Lavatera
  assurgentiflora, 314
  trimestris, 133
Lavender, 154
  sea, 133, 154
Lavender cotton, 160
Lawn moth, 45, 114
Lawns, 102-114
  Bermuda grass, 104
  diseases, 110
  grass types, 102, 105
  ground covers for, 209
  insect pests, 113
  installation, 105
  maintenance, 108
  mowing, 108
  weeds, 112
Layering, 94
Leadwort, 212
Leaf
  chlorosis of, 49
  curled, 49
  cuttings, 98
  functions of, 11
  miner, 48
  yellowed, 49
Leafhopper, 45
Leaf roller, 48
Leaf tier, 48
Lemon, 353
Lemon balm, 357
Lemon lily, 176
Lemon verbena, 356
Lenten rose, 153
Lenticel, 11
Leopard's bane, 150
Leptospermum, 239
Lettuce, 335
Leucadendron argenteum, 296
Leucocoryne ixioides, 177
Leucojum, 177
Leucophyllum texanum, 239
Leucothoe catesbaei, 239
Levisticum officinale, 356
Libocedrus decurrens, 296, 314
Light intensity, 16
Ligustrum, 239
Lilac, 249
  summer, 223
  vine, 203
  wild, 311
Lili-pili, 292
Lily, 192-194
  African, 171
  African corn, 177
  belladonna, 171
  blood, 176
  checkered, 175
  Chilean, 171
  climbing Peruvian, 172
  day, 176
  fawn, 175

Lily (continued)
  glory, 176
  Guernsey, 178
  Inca, 171
  Kafir, 173, 179
  lemon, 176
  of Lima, 171
  Mariposa, 172
  of the Nile, 171
  oxblood, 176
  Peruvian, 171
  Scarborough, 180
  spider, 177
  tawny day, 176
  of the valley, 173
  water, 178
  zephyr, 180
Lily-of-the-valley shrub, 244
  tree, 288, 289
Lima beans, 335
Limber pine, 322
Lime, in soil, 30
Limes, 353
Limonium, 133, 154
Linaria maroccana, 133
Lindane, 51
Linden, 305
Lingonberry, 329
Linnaea borealis, 214
Linum, 155
  grandiflorum, 133
Lippia, 214, 356
Liquidambar styraciflua, 296
Liriodendron tulipifera, 297
Liriope muscari, 155
Litchi nut, 354
Lithocarpus densiflora, 314
Lithops, 328
Lithospermum diffusum, 155
Liverleaf, 153
Livistona, 326
Lobelia erinus, 133
Locust, 294, 302
Lodgepole pine, 322
Lonicera, 205, 239
Loquat, 290, 354
Loropetalum chinense, 240
Lotus, 155
Lovage, 356
Love-in-a-mist, 134
Love-lies-bleeding, 128
Low bamboo, 325
Low desert climate, 22
Luffa cylindrica, 203
Lungwort, 160
Lupine, 133
Lychnis, 155
  coeli-rosa, 133
Lycoris, 177
Lyonothamnus, 314
Lythrum salicaria, 155

M

Macadamia nut, 355
Macadamia ternifolia, 297
Mackaya bella, 240
Maclura pomifera, 297
Madagascar jasmine, 207
Madagascar palm, 326
Madagascar periwinkle, 137
Madonna lily, 193
Madrone, 310
Magnolia, 297
Mahala mat, 311
Mahernia verticillata, 155
Mahogany
  mountain, 312
  swamp, 292
Mahonia, 240, 315
Maidenhair tree, 294
Maiden's wreath, 151
Majorana hortensis, 356
Malathion, 51
Malcomia maritima, 133
Mallee, 291
Mallow tree, 133, 314
Maltese cross, 155
Malus, 274
Mandarin oranges, 354
Mandevilla suaveolens, 205

382 INDEX

Mangifera indica, 355
Mango, 355
Manure, 28, 29
Manzanita, 310
Maple, 283, 309
 flowering, 221
 Japanese, 283
Maranta leuconeura
 kerchoveana, 361
Marguerite, 148
 blue, 151
 golden, 143
Marigold, 136
 cape, 131, 150
 pot, 129
Mariposa lily, 172
Mariposa tulip, 172
Marjoram, 356
Mathiola, 134
Mattress vine, 206
Mayten tree, 299
Maytenus boaria, 299
Meadow rue, 162
Meadow sweet, 144
Mealybug, 45
Meconopsis betonicifolia, 155
Melaleuca, 224
Melia azedarach, 299
Melianthus major, 240
Melissa officinalis, 357
Melons, 335
Mentha, 357
 requienii, 214
Mescal bean, 304
Mesembryanthemum, 214
Metasequoia glyptostroboides, 299
Methoxychlor, 51
Methyl bromide, 54
Metrosideros tomentosa, 299
Mexican blue palm, 326
Mexican fan palm, 327
Mexican fire bush, 132
Mexican orange, 227
Mexican sedum, 215
Mexican sunflower, 136
Mexican tulip poppy, 154
Meyer lemon, 353
Michelia fuscata, 240
Micromeria chamissonis, 215
Mignonette, 135
Mildew, 48
Mimulus tigrinus, 134
Mineral oil, 51
Miniatures, 329, 330
Mint, 357
Mirror plant, 228
Mistflower, 151
Mistletoe fig, 360
Mites, 48, 50
Mockorange, 243
 wild, 315
Moles, 54
Monarda, 156
Monkey flower, 134, 312
Monkey puzzle tree, 284
Monkshood, 142
Monstera deliciosa, 206, 361
Montbretia, 180
Monterey cypress, 290
Monterey pine, 322
Moonflower, 200
Moreton Bay chestnut, 285
Moreton Bay fig, 293
Morning glory, 205
 bush, 130, 228
 ground, 202, 212
Morus, 299
Mosquitoes, 50
Moss campion, 161
Mountain garland, 130
Mourning bride, 136
Mouse-ear chickweed, 112
Muehlenbeckia complexa, 206
Mugho pine, 322
Mulberry, 299
 French, 224
 paperbark, 285
Mulching, 72
Mullein, 162

Murraya, 241
Musa, 299
Muscari, 178
Myoporum laetum, 299
Myosotis, 134
Myrica californica, 315
Myrsine africana, 241
Myrtle, 241, 216
 crape, 296
 Oregon, 319
 wax, 315
Myrtle Boxleaf, 315
Myrtle euphorbia, 151
Myrtus, 241

N

Naming plants, 116
Nandina domestica, 241
Narcissus, 183-186
Nasturtium, 137
Natal plum, 225
Natives, 306-319
 garden use, 306
Neanthe bella, 360
Nectarines, 345
Neillia longiracemosa, 241
Nematode, 46
Nemesia strumosa, 134
Nemophila menziesii, 134
Nepeta, 156
Nephrolepis, 361
Nerine, 178
Nerium oleander, 242
New Zealand
 Christmas tree, 299
 flax, 243
Nicotiana, 134, 156
Nierembergia
 hippomanica, 156
 rivularis, 215
Nigella damascena, 134
Nightshade, 207, 248
Nitrogen-fixing bacteria, 85
Nomenclature, 115
Nutmeg, 319
Nutrient deficiency
 chlorosis, 31
Nutrient elements in soil, 27
Nymphaea, 178
Nyssa sylvatica, 299

O

Oak, 301
 black, 316
 cork, 302
 live, 301, 316
 pin, 302
 silk, 294
 tanbark, 314
 white, 302, 316
Ocean spray bush, 314
Ochna multiflora, 242
Ocimum basilicum, 357
Odontoglossum, 364
Oenothera, 156
Oil, mineral, 51
Olea europaea, 299
Oleander, 242
 yellow, 250
Oleaster, 231
Olive, 299, 355
 Russian, 231
 sweet, 242
Olmediellia betscheleriana, 299
Olympic hybrid lilies, 193
Omphalodes verna, 156
Oncidium, 364
Onions, 335
Onosma stellulatum
 tauricum, 156
Orange, 353-354
 Mexican, 227
 mock, 243, 315
Orange clock vine, 208
Orchid, 363
Orchid tree, 284
Oregon
 boxwood, 315

Oregon (continued)
 grape, 315
 myrtle, 319
 wintergreen, 213
Origanum majorana, 356
Ornithogalum, 178
Osage orange, 297
Oscularia deltoides, 214
Osier, dwarf, 303
Osmanthus, 117, 242
Osteomeles schweriniae, 242
Oval leaf wintergreen, 213
Oxalis, yellow, 113
Oxblood lily, 176
Oxera pulchella, 206
Oxydendrum arboreum, 300

P

Pachistima myrsinites, 315
Pachysandra terminalis, 215
Paeonia, 156, 242
Pagoda tree, 304
Painted tongue, 136
Palm, 326-327
 fan, 319, 326
 pigmy date, 326, 362
Palm-like plants, 327
Pampas grass, 228
Pandorea, 206
Pansy, 137
Papaver, 135, 157
Papaya, 355
Paperbark mulberry, 285
Paradise palm, 326
Parasol tree, 293
Parkinsonia aculeata, 300
Parrot-beak vine, 202
Parsley, 357
Parsnips, 335
Parthenocissus, 206
Pasque flower, 143
Passiflora, 206
Passion flower, 206
Paulownia tomentosa, 300
Peach, 345
 flowering, 274
Pear, 346
 evergreen, 301
Pearl bush, 234
Peas, 335
Peat moss, 29
Pecan, 285, 346
Peepul, 293
Pelargonium, 157
 Lady Washington, 157
Penstemon, 158
Peony, 156
 tree, 242
Peperomia, 361
Pepper, 335
Pepper tree, 303
Peppermint, 357
Peppermint tree, 283
Perennials, 138-168
 in containers, 123
 starting, 81
Periwinkle, 216
Pernettya mucronata, 243
Persimmon, 290, 346
Peruvian lily, 171
 climbing, 172
Pests
 birds, 90
 control calendar, 43
 control chart, 50-51
 control program, 40
 gophers, 53
 insects, 44-50
 lawn, 113
 moles, 54
 of native plants, 307
 weeds, 66-69, 112, 113
Petroselinum crispum, 357
Petunia hybrida, 135
Phaedranthus buccinatorius, 207
Phaseolus coccineus, 207
Phellodendron amurense, 300
Philadelphus, 243
 lewisii, 315

Phillyrea decora, 243
Philodendron, 361-362
Phlomis fruticosa, 158
Phlox, 158
 drummondii, 135
Phoenix, 326
 roebelenii, 362
Phormium tenax, 243
Photinia, 243
Photosynthesis, 9, 12
Phyllitis, 365
Phyllostachys, 325
Physostegia virginiana, 159
Picea, 300, 329
 shrub forms, 244
Pieris, 244
 nana, 329
Pigeon berry, 231
Pigmy date palm, 326, 362
Pillbug, 47
Pimelea ferruginea, 244
Pimpernel, 128
Pimpinella anisum, 357
Pinching, 55
Pincushion flower, 136, 161
Pincushion tree, 235
Pindo palm, 326
Pine, 320-323
 fern, 301
 yew, 301
Pineapple guava, 234, 354
Pink, 130, 149, 330
Pink patch, 111
Pink powder puff, 224
Pink snow mold, 111
Pinus, 320-323
Pistache, 300
Pistacia chinensis, 300
Pittosporum, 244
Plane tree, London, 300
Plant names, 118
Plantain, 112
Plantain lily, 154
Platanus, 300, 315
Platycerium, 365
Platycodon grandiflorum, 159
Pleiospilos, 328
Plum, 346
 flowering, 274
 Kafir, 295
 natal, 225
Plumbago, 225
 capensis, 207
Plume hyacinth, 178
Podocarpus, 301
Poinciana gilliesii, 301
Poinsettia, 234
Poison oak control, 68
Poker plant, 154
Polemonium, 159
Polianthes tuberosa, 178
Pollen, 12
Pollination
 fruit trees, 350
Polygala dalmaisiana, 245
Polygonatum multiflorum, 159
Polygonum aubertii, 207
Polystichum, 362, 365
Pomegranate, 246, 347
Ponderosa pine, 322
Poor man's orchid, 136
Poplar, 301, 316
Poppy, 157
 bush, 312
 California, 131
 Himalayan, 155
 Iceland, 135, 157
 Matilija, 317
 Mexican tulip, 154
 Oriental, 157
 Shirley, 135
 yellow horned, 152
Populus, 301, 316
Porcelain ginger, 364
Portulaca grandiflora, 135
Portulacaria, 328
Potatoes, 335
Potato vine, 207
Potentilla, 159
 cinerea, 215

INDEX

thos wilcoxii, 363
-marigold, 129
tting Plants, 124
cking out, 87
de of Madeira, 150
mrose, 166-168, 329
vening, 156
airy, 135
mrose tree, 296
mula, 166-168, 330
alacoides, 135
nce's feather, 128
cess flower, 251
et, 239
et honeysuckle, 240
pagation, 93
nes, 346
ning, 55
hart, 57
uts, 60
eciduous fruit trees, 343, 348-349
vergreens, 59
rapes, 339
inching, 56
rimer, 60
ses, 267
ason, 57
ed control, 56
rubs, 55
rminology, 60
ols, 60
ees, 55
us, 245, 272
ampanulata, 273
rasifera, 274
stena, 274
andulosa, 273
cifolia, 316
onii, 316
ume, 273
rsica, 274
loba, 274
dosasa japonica, 325
dotsuga taxifolia, 316
ium, 245
ocarya stenoptera, 301
hosperma elegans, 326
et Sound climates, 19, 20
onaria, 160
pkins, 335
ca granatum, 246
y willow, 303
cantha, 246
mid tree, 296
thrum, 51
s kawakami, 301

Q

il bush, 310
moclit pennata, 207
en Ann's thimble, 131
en palm, 326
nsland nut, 297
n's wreath vine, 199
cus, 301
tive species, 316
ce, 290, 347
inese, 226
wering, 226

R

shes, 335
d beds, 77
anting ideas, 120
aining walls, 79
s, 65
onda pyrenaica, 330
nculus
aticus, 179
ens, 215
iolepis, 246
is, 326
berries, 340-341
n palm, 326
ud, 287, 312
ine, Japanese, 322
spider, 48
hread, 111

Redtop grass, 103
Redwood, 318
 dawn, 299
Regal lily, 193
Rehmannia angulata, 160
Reinwardtia indica, 160
Reseda odorata, 135
Retaining walls, 79
Rhamnus, 317
 alaternus, 247
Rhizomes
 dividing, 93
Rhododendron, 257-261
 occidentale, 317
Rhubarb, 334
Rhus, 317
 typhina, 247
Ribes, 316
Rice flower, rosy, 244
Rice paper plant, 249
Ricinus communis, 135
Robinia, 302
Robinsonella cordata, 247
Rock cotoneaster, 212
Rockcress, 143
Rockrose, 227
Rockspray cotoneaster, 212
Romneya coulteri, 317
Rondeletia cordata, 247
Root
 -knot nematodes, 46
 weevils, 44
Roots
 cuttings, 98
 functions of, 10
 water needs, 34
Rosa de Montana, 199
Rose, 215, 264-272
 Christmas, 153
 cliff, 312
 climbing, 264, 272
 floribunda, 264, 271
 hybrid tea, 264, 270
 lenten, 153
 old, 265
 pests, diseases, 269
 polyantha, 264
 pruning of, 267
Rose acacia, 303
Rose apple, 292
Rosemary, 215, 247, 357
Rose moss, 135
Rose of China, 236
Rose-of-heaven, 133
Rose of Sharon, 236
Rosmarinus officinalis, 215, 247, 357
Rotenone, 51
Rubber plant, 293, 360
Rue, meadow, 162
Rust (on lawns), 110
Rutabagas, 335
Rye grasses, 103

S

Sage, 160, 317, 357
 Bethlehem, 160
 Jerusalem, 158
 scarlet, 136
St. Augustine grass, 104
St. Catherine's lace, 313
St. John's bread, 286
St. Johnswort, 213
St. Joseph's coat, 128
Saintpaulia ionantha, 362
Salal, 313
Saline soil, 30
Salix, 303
Salpiglossis sinuata, 136
Salt
 bush, 310
 cedar, 249
Salvia, 136, 160, 317, 357
Sambucus, 318
Sand-verbena, pink, 128
Sanguisorba minor, 357
Sansevieria, 362
Santa Cruz Island pine, 322
Santolina chamaecyparissus, 160

Sapindus saponaria, 303
Saponaria ocymoides, 330
Sapote, white, 285
Sarcococca, 247
Sasa, 325
Satin flower, 131
Satureja, 357
Savory, 357
Sawdust, 29
Saxifraga, 160
 sarmentosa, 363
Scabiosa
 atropurpurea, 136
 caucasica, 161
Scarborough lily, 180
Scarlet flax, 133
Scarlet runner bean, 207
Scarlet sage, 136
Scale, 45
Schefflera, 248
Schinus, 303
Schizanthus, 136
Schizophragma
 hydrangeoides, 207
Schizostylis coccinea, 179
Scilla, 179
Scindapsus aureus wilcoxii, 363
Scolopendrium, 364
Scotch broom, 229
Scotch heather, 232
Scotch pine, 322
Sea daffodil, 177
Sea fig, 214
Sea lavender, 133, 154
Sea urchin, 235
Sedum, 161, 215, 327, 328
Seed
 control by pruning, 56
 disinfecting, 85
 doll, 83
 germination, 10
 how formed, 8
 sowing in flats, 82
 sowing in open, 90
 vegetables, 334
Sempervivum, 327, 328
Senecio, 147, 248, 328
Senegal date palm, 326
Senna, 225
Sequoia, 318
Service berry, 221
Shade
 defined, 115
Shasta daisy, 148
Sheep bur, 211
Sheep sorrel, 112
Shell flower, 364
She-oak, 285
Shirley poppy, 135
Shore pine, 322
Shortia soldanelloides, 161
Shovel, 65
Shrimp plant, 222
Shrubs, 217-272
 in containers, 123
 pruning, 55-57
Siberian peashrub, 285
Silene, 161
Silk oak, 294
Silk tree, 283
Silktassel, 313
Silver bell tree, 294
Silverberry, 231
Silver lace vine, 207
Silver tree, 296
Silver vein creeper, 206
Silvery yarrow, 211
Single leaf pine, 323
Sinningia speciosa, 179
Sinocalamus, 325
Siphonosmanthus, 242
Siskiyou-Sierra foothill climate, 21
Skimmia, 248
Sky flower, 208, 231
Slugs, 46
Small fruits, 336-343
Smilax, 200
Smoke tree, 289
Snails, 46

Snapdragon, 128, 133
Snapweed, 154
Sneeze-weed, 152
Snowball bush, 251
Snowberry, 318
 creeping, 319, 329
Snowdrop, 175
Snowdrop tree, 294, 304
Snowflake, 177
Snow-in-summer, 211
Snow mold, 111
Snow-on-the-mountain, 131
Soapberry tree, 303
Society garlic, 162
Sodium in soil, 30
Sod webworm, 114
Soil
 acid, 30
 adobe, 26, 29
 alkaline, 29
 conditioners, 29
 cuts and fills, 79
 fill, 76
 for lawns, 105
 grading, 77
 heavy, 29
 humus deficiency, 28
 nutrient deficiency, 28
 nutrient elements, 27
 retaining walls, 79
 salinity, 30
 shallow, 30
 sodium excess, 30
 structure, 26
 U.C. Mix, artificial soil, 31
Solandra guttata, 207
Solanum, 207, 248
Solidaster luteus, 161
Sollya fusiformis, 207
Solomon's seal, 159
Sophora, 304
Sorbus aucuparia, 304
Sorrel, 300
Sour cherry, 347
Sour gum, 299
Sourwood, 300
Southern Calif. climates, 24-25
Sowbug, 47
Sowing seeds, 85
Spanish fir, 281
Sparaxis tricolor, 179
Spartium, 229
Spearmint, 357
Species, defined, 116
Speedwell, 163
Spice bush, 310
Spider flower, 130
Spider lily, 177
Spiderwort, 162
Spinach, 335
Spiraea, 248
 blue, 225
 douglasii, 318
Spittlebug, 47
Splitleaf philodendron, 361
Spraying
 deciduous fruit trees, 343-344
Spring care, 61
Sprinkling, 39
Spruce, 300, 329
 shrub forms, 244
Squash, 335
Squaw carpet, 311
Squill, 179
Stachys lanata, 216
Stachyurus praecox, 248
Staghorn fern, 365
Staghorn sumac, 247
Staking trees, 280
Stamen, 12
Star of Bethlehem, 178
Star bush, 251
Star cineraria, 130
Starflower, 235
Star hyacinth, 179
Star jasmine, 208, 216
Starting plants, 81-101
 annuals, 81, 127
 budding, 99

INDEX

Starting plants (continued)
  coldframes, 99
  cuttings, 95
  by division, 93
  layering, 94
  leaf cuttings, 98
  perennials, 81
  root cuttings, 98
  seeds in flats, 82
  seeds in open, 90
  transplanting, 88
  vegetables, 331-334
  vegetatively, 93
Stems
  functions of, 11
  parts of, 11
Stenocarpus sinuatus, 304
Stephanotis floribunda, 207
Sterilization
  seed compost, 84
Sternbergia lutea, 180
Stigma, 12
Stock, 134
  Virginian, 133
Stokes aster, 161
Stokesia laevis, 161
Stonecress, 142
Stonecrop, 215, 327
Stone pine, Italian, 322
Stranvaesia davidiana, 248
Strawberry, 341-343
  Indian mock, 212
  sand, 213
  wild, 213
Strawberry geranium, 161, 363
Strawberry tree, 221
Strawflower, 132
Strelitzia, 365
Streptosolen jamesonii, 208
String beans, 335
Styrax japonica, 304
Subtropical grasses, 104
Succulents, 327, 328
  in containers, 122, 123
Sugar pine, 323
Sumac, 317
  staghorn, 247
Summer care, 62
Summer chrysanthemum, 129
Summer cypress, 132
Summer holly, 312
Summer pruning, 57
Summer savory, 357
Sundrops, 156
Sunflower, 132, 152
Sun rose, 213
Swan river daisy, 128
Swan river pea bush, 223
Sweet alyssum, 128
Sweet basil, 357
Sweet cherry, 347
Sweet pea, 132
Sweet-pea shrubs, 245
Sweet potatoes, 335
Sweetshade, 295
Sweetspire, hollyleaf, 237
Sweet sultan, 129
Sweet violet, 163
Sweet William, 149
Sweet woodruff, 211
Sword fern, 365
Sycamore
  American, 301
  California, 315
Symphoricarpos, 318
Syngonium podophyllum, 363
Syringa, 249

T

Table mountain pine, 323
Tagetes, 136
Tamarix, 249
Tanbark oak, 314
Tangelo, 354
Tangerine, 354
Tangor, 354
Tarata, 244
Taro, 364
Tarragon, 356
Tasmanian tree fern, 365
Tawhiwhi, 244
Taxus, 304
Tea tree, 239
Tecomaria capensis, 208
Temperature
  frost control, 70
  heat accumulation, 16
  high-low maps, 16
  summer, 15
Tent caterpillars, 46
Ternstroemia gymnanthera, 249
Tetrapanax papyriferum, 249
Teucrium, 250
Texas ranger, 239
Thalictrum, 162
Thermopsis caroliniana, 162
Thevetia nereifolia, 250
"Thinning," 60
Thrift, 144
Thrips, 49
Throatwort, 162
Thryallis glauca, 250
Thuja, 250, 304, 319, 329
Thujopsis dolobrata, 305
Thunbergia, 208
Thyme, 216, 357
Thymus, 216, 357
Tibouchina semidecandra, 251
Tiger flower, 180
Tigridia pavonia, 180
Tilia, 305
Timber bamboo, giant, 325
Tipuana tipu, 305
Tipu tree, 305
Tithonia rotundifolia, 136
Toadflax, 133
Tobacco, 156
  flowering, 134
  jasmine, 156
Tobira, 244
Tolmiea menziesii, 363
Tomato, 335
Tools
  canvas, 66
  care of, 66
  cultivators, 65
  hoe, 64, 65
  plank, 66
  pruning, 60
  rake, 65
  shovel vs. spade, 64
  shovels, 65
Torch lily, 154
Torenia fournieri, 137
Torrey pine, 323
Torreya californica, 319
Touch-me-not, 154
Toyon, 314
Trachelium caeruleum, 162
Trachelospermum
  jasminoides, 208, 216
Trachycarpus fortunei, 327
Tradescantia, 162, 363
Transpiration, 9
Transplanting, 88
  pricking out, 87
Transvaal daisy, 152
Tree mallow, 133, 314
Tree-of-heaven, 283
Trees, 276-305
  balled
    planting, 278
    transplanting, 281
  bareroot
    in containers, 123
    planting, 279
    transplanting, 281
  deciduous fruit, 343-351
  fruit, 348
  growth rate, 278
  planting, 278
  pruning, 55
  or shrub? 276
  staking, 280
  thinning, 278
  transplanting, 280
  uses for, 276
Trillium, 180
Tristania conferta, 305
Tritoma, 154
Tritonia, 180
Trollius, 162
Tropaeolum, 137
Trumpet creeper, 201
Trumpet vine
  blood-red, 207
  golden, 199
  vanilla-scented, 202
  violet, 202
  yellow, 202
Tsuga, 319
Tuberose, 178
Tuberous begonia, 181-183
Tufted fish tail palm, 326
Tulbaghia violacea, 162
Tulip, 195-196
  butterfly, 172
  globe, 172
  Mariposa, 172
Tulip tree, 297
Tupidanthus calyptratus, 305
Turfing daisy, 214
Turnip, 335
Turpentine pine, 321
Turraea obtusifolia, 251
Tussock bellflower, 330
Twinflower, 214
Twinspur, 131

U

U.C. Mix, 31
Ulmus, 305
Umbellularia californica, 319
Umbrella tree, Texas, 299

V

Vaccinium, 319, 329
Valerian, Greek, 159
Vallota, 180
Variety, defined, 116
Vegetables, 331-336
  classes and kinds, 334
  cole crops, 335
  how to plant, 332
  leaf crops, 335
  perennials, 334
  planting systems, 333
  root crops, 335
  sowing seed, 334
  vine crops, 335
  what to plant, 332
Vegetative propagation, 93
Velvet grass, 113
Verbascum, 162
Verbena, 162
  lemon, 356
  sand, 128
Veronica, 162, 235
Viburnum, 251
Vinca, 137, 216
Vine maple, 309
Vines, 197-208
Viola, 137
  odorata, 163
Violet, sweet, 163
Virginia creeper, 206
Virginian stock, 133
Viscaria, 133
Vitex agnus-castus, 252
Vitis, 208, 338-340

W

Wake robin, 180
Wallflower, 147
Walnut, 295, 347
Wand flower, 179
Wandering Jew, 363
Washington thorn, 289
Washingtonia, 319, 327
Water, drainage and
  runoff problems, 75
Watering
  basins, 37
  container plants, 124
  hard water, 30
  interval, 37
  lawns, 108
  methods, 37
  native plants, 307
Watering (continued)
  overhead, 39
  principles of, 33
  run-off, 35
  seed flat, 85
  softened water, 31, 40
Water lily, 178
Watermelon, 335
Watermelon plant, 361
Watsonia, 180
Waxberry, 318
Wax flower, 361
Waxflower, Geraldton, 226
Wax plant, 204, 361
Weed killers, 66-69
Weeds, lawn, 112, 113
Weigela, 252
Western wintergreen, 213
White cup, 215
White fir, 281, 309
Whiteflies, 45
White grubs, 114
White lily tree, 289
White pine, western, 323
White potatoes, 335
White Sapote, 355
Wild hyacinth, 172
Willamette climate, 20
Willow, 303
  desert, 312
Windflower, 143, 171
Windmill palm, 327
Wine palm, 326
Wingnut, Chinese, 301
Winter
  garden chores, 63
  pruning, 57
Winter aconite, 174
Wintercreeper, 202, 233
Wintergreen, 213, 313
Winter savory, 357
Wintersweet, 227
Wire vine, 206
Wireworm, 47
Wishbone-flower, 137
Wisteria tree, 230
Wisteria, 208
Witch-hazel, 294
Wonga-wonga vine, 206
Woodbine, 205
Woodruff, 211
Woodwardia, 365
Woolly yarrow, 211
Worms
  corn earworm, 46
  wireworm, 47
Wormwood, 144, 356
Wormwood senna, 225

X

Xeranthemum annuum, 137
Xylem, 11
Xylosma senticosa, 252

Y

Yangtao, 199
Yarrow 142, 211
Yate tree, 291
Yellowjackets, 50
Yellow wood, 288
Yerba buena, 215
Yesterday-today-and-
  tomorrow, 223
Yew, 304
Yucca, 163

Z

Zantedeschia, 180
Zauschneria, 319
Zebrina, 363
Zelkova serrata, 305
Zephyr lily, 180
Zephyranthes, 180
Zinnia, 137
Zizyphus jujuba, 305
Zone calendars, 366
Zoysia grasses, 104